Part 4

Analysis and Management of Common Stocks

In Part 3 we considered the basic valuation principles and practices applied to all securities and how this was applied to the global asset allocation decision. In Part 4, we apply these same valuation principles and practices to the analysis and management of common stocks. The objective is to be in position to make the critical risk–return decision at the market-industry-company stock level.

You will recall from Chapter 11 that successful investment requires several steps, beginning with a valuation of the aggregate economy and market and the examination of various industries and concluding with the analysis of individual companies and their securities. Globalization of the capital markets has definitely complicated this process wherein it is now necessary to consider markets on a worldwide basis followed by the analysis of *world* industries that involve numerous, complex foreign companies.

In Chapter 12, we begin the three-step, top-down approach and discuss how to analyze the aggregate stock market using the two general valuation approaches introduced in Chapter 11— the present value of cash flow models and the relative valuation ratios. In Chapter 13, we again demonstrate these two approaches to the valuation of an industry.

Chapter 14 on company analysis begins with a discussion of the difference between a company and its stock. In many instances, the common stock of a very fine company (possibly a true growth company) may not be a good investment, which is why we emphasize that company analysis and stock selection are two separate but dependent activities. Once again, the analysis procedure is built on the two valuation approaches employed for the market and alternative industries. We also consider other techniques, such as economic value added (EVA), that provide insights regarding the economic success of a firm and its management. The overall goal of this procedure is to select one of the best companies in a superior industry during a favorable market environment.

It was noted in Chapter 11 that it is not feasible to use the standard dividend discount model to value the stock of true growth companies. Therefore, in Chapter 14 we discuss several valuation models that have been specifically developed for the analysis and valuation of growth companies.

Throughout this section, we refer back to the semistrong efficient market hypothesis. Recall that, although many studies support this hypothesis, there is a growing literature dealing with anomalies related to this hypothesis. Therefore, in this section we provide a consistent and justifiable valuation process that can be used to find

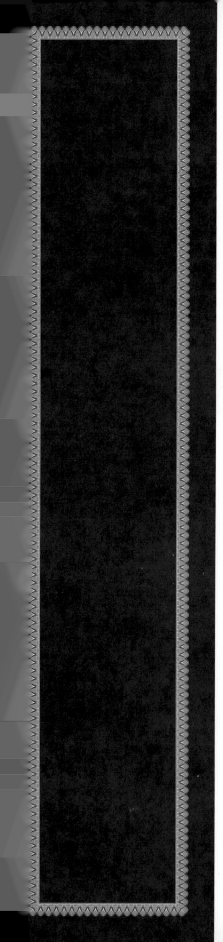

undervalued securities. You should never forget that the output of alternative valuation models is only as good as the estimated inputs and *the superior analyst is the one who provides the best estimates of the required rate of return on a security based upon its risk and the expected growth rate of future cash flows.*

Chapter 15 deals with technical analysis, an alternative or supplement to the fundamental approach discussed in the prior chapters. Rather than estimating value based on fundamental variables, the technical analyst believes that it is possible to project future stock price movements based on past stock price changes or other stock market data. Various techniques used by technical analysts for U.S. and world markets are discussed and demonstrated.

Chapter 16 deals with equity portfolio management strategies. We begin with a general discussion of passive versus active management styles. This is followed by a specific discussion of indexing, including the selection of an appropriate benchmark index, and the various methods of index portfolio investing used in practice. The concept of *tracking error* is introduced as a means of assessing how well an investor has replicated the benchmark portfolio.

The overview of active equity portfolio management strategies includes a discussion of how one constructs a portfolio that reflects the client's risk–return objectives and constraints from three different perspectives: fundamental analysis (e.g., asset class and sector rotation, stock under and overvaluation), technical analysis (e.g., overreaction, price momentum), and anomaly and attribute analysis (e.g., earnings momentum, firm size). In this discussion, we pay special attention to the conceptual and practical differences between forming portfolios based on both value-oriented and growth-oriented investment styles. Notably, all of these approaches should consider global opportunities.

We conclude Chapter 16 with a discussion of how the equity portfolio management decision fits into the investor's overall asset allocation strategy. After discussing the integrated approach to asset allocation, we also examine strategic, tactical, and insured allocation strategies. Finally, we present the basic intuition for how investors can use *derivative instruments* (such as futures and option contracts) to alter the risk and return characteristics of their equity portfolios.

Chapter 12

Macroanalysis and Microvaluation of the Stock Market

After you read this chapter, you should be able to answer the following questions:

- What are the expected and the empirical relationships between economic activity and security markets?
- What is the macroeconomic approach to estimating future market returns?
- What are the major macroeconomic techniques used to project the securities market?
- What is the leading economic indicator approach? What are its uses and shortcomings?
- What are the expected and the empirical relationships between the growth of the money supply and stock prices?
- What is meant by excess liquidity, and how is it measured?
- What is the effect of monetary policy on stock prices in the United States and around the world?
- What are the expected and the empirical relationships between inflation, interest rates, and bond prices?
- What are the expected and the empirical relationships between inflation and stock prices?
- How do the basic valuation variables differ among countries?
- What factors should be considered when analyzing the outlook for a foreign economy and its stock and bond market?
- What is the asset allocation procedure for a global portfolio?
- For a world asset allocation, what is meant by normal weighting, underweighting, and overweighting?
- How do we apply the dividend discount model (DDM) to the valuation of the aggregate stock market?
- What would be the prevailing value of the market as represented by the S&P Industrials Index based upon the reduced form DDM?
- What would be the prevailing value of the aggregate stock market based upon the present value of free cash flow to equity (FCFE) model?

- What two components are involved in the two-part valuation procedure?
- Given the two components in the valuation procedure, which is more volatile?
- What steps are involved in estimating the earnings per share for an aggregate market series?
- What variables affect the aggregate operating profit margin and how do they affect it?
- What variables determine the level and changes in the market earnings multiplier?
- What has happened to the values for the other relative valuation ratios—that is, the *P/BV, P/CF,* and *P/S* ratios?
- What additional factors must be considered when you apply this microanalysis approach to the valuation of stock markets around the world?

THE COMPONENTS OF MARKET ANALYSIS

In Chapter 11 we introduced the top-down, three-step market-industry-company investment process. This chapter is concerned with the market analysis portion of this process. In turn, this market analysis has two components that need to be considered: (1) the macroanalysis of the relationship between the aggregate securities markets and overall economic activity, and (2) the specific microvaluation of the stock market employing the valuation approaches introduced in Chapter 11.

The macroanalysis is in response to the belief that *security markets reflect what is expected to go on in the economy,* because the value of an investment is determined by its expected cash flows and its expected required rate of return (i.e., its discount rate). Clearly, both of these valuation factors are influenced by the aggregate economic environment. The objective is to consider what specific variables and economic series should be considered when attempting to project future market movements. This macroeconomy and market analysis provides important insights for our subsequent industry and company analysis.

The microanalysis builds on these macroinsights by deriving a specific valuation for the market using the approaches discussed. The result is a specific value for a market indicator series, so we can employ the decision rule wherein this intrinsic value is compared to the current market value and the investor can make an appropriate decision regarding the aggregate market. In this case, since we are considering the aggregate U.S. stock market, the decision is how to weight the U.S. stock market in a global asset portfolio—that is, underweight, market weight, or overweight the U.S. stock market depending on whether it is overvalued, properly valued, or undervalued.

MACROMARKET ANALYSIS

Fluctuations in security markets are related to changes in expectations for the aggregate economy. The prices of government and investment-grade corporate bonds are determined by the level of interest rates, which is influenced by overall economic activity and Federal Reserve policy. Aggregate stock prices reflect investor expectations about corporate performance in terms of earnings, cash flows, and the required rate of return by investors. All of these expectations are heavily impacted by the economic outlook.

Given the significant expected relationship between security markets and the economy, this section has four subsections: (1) documentation of the relationship between the economy and stock prices, (2) presentation of several economic series that provide specific insights related to the stock market; (3) specific discussion of the macroeconomic impact of inflation and interest rates on security prices, and (4) brief consideration of what additional factors should be analyzed when dealing with world security markets.

Economic Activity and Security Markets

In its monitoring of business cycles, the National Bureau of Economic Research (NBER) has examined the relationship of alternative economic series to the behavior of the entire economy and has classified numerous economic series into three groups: leading, coincident, and lagging indicator series. Further, extensive analysis of the relationship between the economy and the stock market has shown that stock prices are one of the better leading indicator series.

The evidence by Moore and Cullity (1988) and Siegel (1991) not only has indicated a strong relationship between stock prices and the economy but also has shown that stock prices consistently turn *before* the economy does. The data in Exhibit 12.1 document this relationship, beginning in the 1950s.

There are two possible reasons why stock prices lead the economy. One is that stock prices reflect *expectations* of earnings, dividends, and interest rates. As investors attempt to estimate these future variables, their stock price decisions reflect expectations for *future* economic activity, not past or current activity. A second possible reason is that the stock market reacts to various leading indicator series, the most important being corporate earnings, corporate profit margins, interest rates, and changes in the growth rate of the money supply. Because these series tend to lead the economy, when investors adjust stock prices to reflect expectations for these leading economic series, it makes stock prices a leading series as well.

Because stock prices lead the aggregate economy, our macroeconomic approach to market analysis concentrates on economic series that lead the economy by more than stock prices do. First, we discuss cyclical indicator approaches developed by various research groups. Next, we consider the money supply, as well as other measures of monetary liquidity and policy. Finally, we discuss the research related to a number of economic series expected to affect security returns (e.g., production, inflation, and risk premiums).

Exhibit 12.1	Timing Relationships between Stock Market and Business Cycle Peaks and Troughs

Stock Market Declines Associated with a Subsequent Recession

STOCK MARKET CYCLES[a]				BUSINESS CYCLES				LEAD OF STOCK MARKET OVER BUSINESS CYCLE	
Peak		Trough		Peak		Trough		Peak	Trough
Jan.	1953	Sep.	1953	Jul.	1953	May.	1954	6.0	8.0
Aug.	1956	Oct.	1957	Aug.	1957	Apr.	1958	11.0	6.0
Aug.	1959	Oct.	1960	Apr.	1960	Feb.	1961	8.0	4.0
Nov.	1968	May	1970	Dec.	1969	Nov.	1970	12.0	6.0
Jan.	1973	Oct.	1974	Nov.	1973	Mar.	1975	10.0	5.0
Feb.	1980	Aug.	1982	Jan.	1980	Nov.	1982	(1.0)	3.0
							Average	7.7	5.3

[a]Defined as market declines of approximately 15 percent or more.

Source: Jason Benderly and Edward McKelvey. "The Pocket Chartbook," *Economic Research*, Goldman, Sachs & Co., December 1987. Reprinted by permission of Goldman, Sachs & Co.

Economic Series and Stock Prices

As noted, because research has documented that peaks and troughs in stock prices tend to occur prior to peaks and troughs in the economy, our consideration of relevant economic series concentrates on two broad categories of economic series that likewise lead the economy and should provide some insights regarding the future trend of stocks. The first are sets of economic series suggested by the National Bureau of Economic Research. The second are alternative monetary series influenced by the Federal Reserve.

The Cyclical Indicator Approach

The cyclical indicator approach to monitoring and forecasting the economy is built on the belief that the aggregate economy experiences periods of expansion and contraction that can be identified by the movements in economic activity reflected in specific economic series.

Cyclical Indicator Categories   The NBER examined the behavior of hundreds of economic time series in relation to past business cycles and grouped various economic series into three major categories based on their relationship to the business cycle.

The first category, **leading indicators** of the business cycle, includes economic series that usually reach peaks or troughs before corresponding peaks or troughs in aggregate economic activity. The group currently includes the 10 series shown in Exhibit 12.2. Included are common stock prices, which have a median lead of four months at peaks and troughs and the money supply in constant (1992) dollars, which has a median lead of five months at peaks and four months at troughs.

The second category, **coincident indicators**, includes four economic time series that have peaks and troughs that roughly coincide with the peaks and troughs in the business cycle. As one might expect, many of these economic time series are used to define the different phases of the cycle.

The third category, **lagging indicators**, includes seven series that experience their peaks and troughs after those of the aggregate economy. A listing of the coincident and lagging series also appears in Exhibit 12.2.

A final category, *selected series,* includes economic series that are expected to influence aggregate economic activity but do not fall neatly into one of the three main groups. This includes such series as U.S. balance of payments and federal surplus or deficit.

Composite Series and Ratio of Series   In addition to the individual economic series in each category, a composite time series combines these economic series—for example, the *composite leading indicator index.* This composite leading indicator series is widely reported in the press each month as an indicator of the current and future state of the economy. There also are composite coincident and lagging indicator series.

Some analysts have used a *ratio* of these composite series, contending that the ratio of the composite coincident series divided by the composite lagging series acts like a leading series, in some instances even leading the composite leading series. The rationale for expecting this leading relationship for the ratio is that the coincident series should turn before the lagging series, and the ratio of the two series will be quite sensitive to such changes. As a result, this ratio series is expected to lead both of the individual composite series, especially at turning points.

Although movements for this ratio series are generally parallel to those of the leading series, its real value comes when it diverges from the composite leading indicator series because this divergence signals a change in the normal relationship between the indicator series. For example, if the leading indicator series has been rising for a period of time, you would expect both the coincident and lagging series also to be rising, but the coincident series

Exhibit 12.2	**Economic Series Included in the Conference Board Indicators**

Leading Index

1. Average weekly hours of manufacturing workers
2. Average weekly initial claims for unemployment insurance
3. Real value of manufacturers' new orders for consumer goods and materials
4. Index of consumer expectations
5. Index of 500 common stock prices
6. Manufacturers' new orders, nondefense capital goods in 1992 dollars
7. Index of new private housing starts authorized by local building permits
8. Vendor performance (the percentage of companies receiving delivery later than the industry average)
9. Real money supply, M2
10. Interest rate spread, ten-year Treasury bonds less federal funds rate

Coincident Index

1. Number of employees on nonagricultural payrolls
2. Personal income less transfer payments, expressed in 1992 dollars
3. Index of industrial production
4. Manufacturing and trade sales, expressed in 1992 dollars

Lagging Index

1. Average duration of unemployment
2. Ratio of manufacturing and trade inventories to sales
3. Percentage change in the labor cost per unit of output in manufacturing
4. Average prime rate charged by banks
5. Commercial and industrial loans outstanding
6. Ratio of consumer installment credit outstanding to personal income
7. Change in the consumer price index (inflation rate) for services

should be rising faster than the lagging series, so the ratio of the coincident to the lagging series should likewise be rising. In contrast, assume the composite leading indicator series is rising but the ratio of coincident to lagging series is flattening out or declining. This change in trend in the ratio series could occur because the coincident series is not rising as fast as the lagging indicator series or because the coincident series has turned down. Either scenario would indicate a possible end to an economic expansion or at least a less-robust expansion.

An example of such a divergence appears in Exhibit 12.3. The pattern indicates that between mid-1995 and early 1999, the two series were very consistent, as one would expect. Starting in 1999, there was a clear divergence wherein the leading indicator series experienced a clear slowdown and flattening, while the ratio series continued to rise until early 2000, when it began a decline. Also, the ratio series resumed its increase in early 2001 while the leading series did not start increasing until the end of 2001, and then it experienced a flat period during 2002. The point is, in both cases, the divergence between the series indicated a change in direction for the economy.

Analytical Measures of Performance   Certain analytical measures have been suggested for examining behavior within an economic series.

| Exhibit 12.3 | Indicator Series Performance |

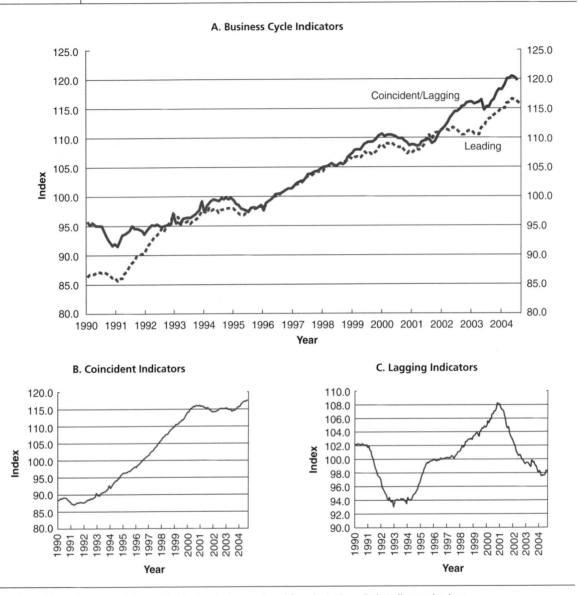

Source: Created by authors using data provided by the Conference Board from its *Business Cycle Indicators* database.

Diffusion Indexes   As the name implies, **diffusion indexes** indicate how pervasive a given movement is in a series. Diffusion index values are measured by computing the percentage of reporting units in a series that indicate a given result. For example, if 100 companies consti-tute the sample reporting new orders for equipment, the diffusion index for this series would indicate what proportion of the 100 companies was reporting higher orders during an expan-sion. In addition to knowing that aggregate new orders are increasing, it is helpful to know whether 55 percent or 95 percent of the companies in the sample are reporting higher orders. This information on the pervasiveness of the increase in new orders would help you project the future length and strength of an expansion.

You also would want to know the prevailing *trend* for a diffusion index. The diffusion index for a series almost always reaches its peak or trough before the peak or trough in the corresponding aggregate series. Therefore, you can use the diffusion index for a series to predict the behavior of the series itself.

Besides diffusion indexes for individual series, a diffusion index that shows the percentage of the 10 leading indicators rising or falling is used as an indicator of the future state of the economy.

Rates of Change   Knowing whether a series is increasing is useful, but knowing that a 7 percent increase one month followed a 10 percent increase the previous month indicates the series is growing but at a declining rate. Similar to the diffusion index, the rate of change values for a series reaches peaks or troughs prior to the peak or trough in the aggregate series.

Comparison with Previous Cycles   A set of tables and charts shows the movements of individual series during the current business cycle and compares these movements to previous cycles for the same economic series. This comparison reveals whether a given series is moving slower or faster than during prior cycles. This information can be useful because, typically, movements in the initial months of an expansion or contraction indicate their ultimate length and strength.

Limitations of the Cyclical Indicator Approach   The Conference Board acknowledges the following limitations that are also discussed in Koenis and Emery (1991):

False Signals   This is when a series that is moving in one direction suddenly reverses and nullifies a prior signal or hesitates, which is difficult to interpret. High variability in a series causes this problem.

Currency of the Data and Revisions   Some data series take time to be reported, but a bigger problem are revisions in data especially if the revision changes the direction implied by the original data.

Economic Sectors Not Represented   Examples include the service sector, import-exports, many international series.

Other Leading Indicator Series   The Center for International Business Conditions Research (CIBCR) at the Columbia Graduate School of Business has developed several additional leading indicator series.

Long-Leading Index   The *Long-Leading Index* is intended to provide earlier signals of major turning points in the economy. It includes the following series: (1) Dow Jones bond prices; (2) the ratio of price to unit labor cost in manufacturing; (3) M2 money supply in real dollars; and (4) new housing building permits.

Leading Employment Index   The CIBCR's *Leading Employment Index* is meant to forecast changes in U.S. employment. It includes the following series:

1. Average workweek in manufacturing
2. Overtime hours in manufacturing
3. Percentage layoff rate (inverted)
4. Voluntary/involuntary part-time employment
5. Percentage short duration unemployment rate (inverted)
6. Initial claims for unemployment insurance (inverted)

Leading Inflation Index   The CIBCR *Leading Inflation Index* that is intended to forecast U.S. inflation includes five variables:

1. The percentage employed of the working-age population
2. The growth rate of total U.S. debt

3. The growth rate of industrial material prices
4. The growth rate of import prices
5. The percentage of businesspeople anticipating an increase in their selling prices

International Leading Indicator Series   The CIBCR also has developed a set of composite leading indicators for eight other major industrial countries: Canada, Germany, France, the United Kingdom, Italy, Japan, Australia, and Taiwan (Republic of China). The series are comparable in data and analysis to the leading series for the United States.

Surveys of Sentiment and Expectations   Consumer expectations are considered relevant as the economy approaches cyclical turning points. Two surveys of consumer expectations are reported monthly. The University of Michigan Consumer Sentiment Index and the Conference Board Consumer Confidence Index both query a sample of households on their expectations. Although the two indexes sometimes deviate from month to month, over longer time periods they track each other fairly closely. Both indexes act as a leading indicator of the economy.

Other surveys of business expectations focus on firms' capital spending or inventory investment plans. The intent is to indicate how the business community feels about the economy and the outlook for their spending plans. The problem with survey data is that individuals' and firms' reported plans may not come to fruition. Just because a survey reports that manufacturing firms expect to increase capital spending by a certain percentage does not mean they will actually do so.

Economic statistics released by the government are another source of helpful information about current economic trends. Every Monday, *The Wall Street Journal* publishes a short commentary, "Tracking the Economy." The feature reports statistics that will be released during the coming week (for example, housing starts, agricultural production, GDP), their previous values, and their consensus forecasts. As implied by our discussion of efficient markets, investors react to economic surprises wherein the actual results deviate from the consensus forecasts (expectations).

Monetary Variables, the Economy, and Stock Prices

Many academic and professional observers hypothesize a close relationship between stock prices and various monetary variables that are influenced by monetary policy. The best-known monetary variable is the *money supply*. You will recall from your economics course that the money supply can be measured in several ways as described by Walter (1989). The government publishes numerous measures of the money supply, but M1 and M2 are the best known. The Federal Reserve controls the money supply through various tools, the most useful of which is open market operations.

Money Supply and the Economy

In their classic work on the monetary history of the United States, Friedman and Schwartz (1963) thoroughly documented the relationship between changes in the growth rate of the money supply and subsequent changes in the economy. Specifically, they demonstrated that declines in the rate of growth of the money supply have preceded business contractions, while increases in the growth rate of the money supply have consistently preceded economic expansions.

Friedman (1969) suggests a transmission mechanism through which changes in the growth rate of the money supply affect the aggregate economy. He hypothesizes that, to implement planned changes in monetary policy, the Federal Reserve engages in open market operations, buying or selling Treasury bonds to adjust bank reserves and, eventually, the money supply. Because the Fed deals in government bonds, the initial liquidity impact when the Fed buys bonds affects the government bond market, creating excess liquidity for those who sold bonds to the Fed. The result is an increase in bond prices and lower interest rates. Rising government bond prices subsequently filter down to corporate bonds, and this change in liquidity eventually affects common stocks and then the real goods market. There is the opposite effect if the Fed sells bonds to reduce bank reserves and the money supply. The impact of money supply growth on stock prices is really part of the transmission process whereby money supply affects the aggregate economy. This liquidity transmission scenario implies that the effect of a change in monetary policy initially appears in financial markets (bonds and stocks) and only later in the aggregate economy.

Financial Conditions Index   In contrast to a specific monetary series (such as money supply or the monetary base) or an individual price series (like the federal funds rate or the discount rate), Dudley and Hatzius (2000), from Goldman Sachs created a composite financial condition series (the Goldman Sachs Financial Conditions Index— GSFCI). The GSFCI is a combination of four variables that are expected to reflect the monetary policy environment. The four variables (with weights) are:

1. Real three-month LIBOR (.35)
2. Real A-rated corporate bond yield (.55)
3. Real Goldman Sachs Trade-Weighted Dollar Index (.05)
4. The equity market capitalization/GDP ratio (.05)

It is contended that this series is superior to any one series because it also considers other relevant factors such as the strength of the dollar and the growing importance of the stock market in the economy. The empirical analysis of its relationship to the economy is strong—a one-point *increase* in the GSFCI is followed (with a three-quarter lag) by about a one-percentage-point *decrease* in the growth rate of real GDP. The point is, an increase in the GSFCI reflects a tightening of the monetary environment which is signaled by an increase in interest rate—i.e., there is a heavy weighting of interest rates—the two interest rate variables constitute 90 percent of the index.

Money Supply and Stock Prices

Numerous studies have tested the relationship suggested by this transmission mechanism. Specifically, do changes in the growth rate of the money supply precede changes in stock prices? The results of these studies have tended to change over time. The initial studies by Sprinkel (1971), Keran (1971), and Homa and Jaffe (1971) generally indicated a strong *leading* relationship between money supply changes and stock prices which implies that changes in the growth rate of the money supply could serve as a leading indicator of stock price changes.

Subsequent studies by Cooper (1974) and Rozeff (1974) questioned these findings because they found a relationship between the money supply and stock prices, but they found that changes in the growth rate of the money supply consistently *lagged* stock returns by about one to three months.

Studies by Davidson and Froyer (1982) and Hafer (1985) examined the relationship of stock returns to anticipated and unanticipated money supply growth. The results indicated that money changes affect stock prices but stock prices adjust very quickly to unexpected changes in money supply growth, which implies that it is necessary to *forecast unanticipated changes* in money supply growth.

Following more than a decade of limited research on this topic, several recent studies by Jensen, Johnson, and Mercer (JJM) (1996, 1997, 1998, 2000) showed that the results of several earlier studies that examined the relationship between some economic variables and stock returns or some company variables and stock returns can be significantly affected by the prevailing monetary environment. Specifically, JJM showed that the business conditions proxies suggested by Fama and French (1989) (i.e., the term spread, dividend yield, and default spread) have a different effect on stock returns depending on the prevailing monetary policy, where monetary policy is indicated by discount rate changes (i.e., declining discount rates imply an easy monetary policy, while rising discount rates imply a restrictive policy). The JJM studies also show that the relationship between stock price returns and both size and the price-to-book value ratio that was found in studies by Fama and French (1995), and Fairfield (1994) only holds during periods of easy monetary policy. A subsequent study by Thorbecke (1997) that examined how stock returns respond to monetary policy shocks indicated that expansionary monetary policy increases ex-post stock returns. Patelis (1997) examined whether shifts in monetary policy affect the predictability of excess stock returns and found that monetary policy variables were significant predictors of future stock returns along with dividend yield.

Inflation, Interest Rates, and Security Prices

Because this chapter is concerned with the macroeconomic analysis of security markets, we should examine the macroeconomic impact of inflation and interest rates. We have noted throughout the book the critical role of expected inflation and nominal interest rates in determining the required rate of return used to derive the value of all investments. We would expect these variables that are very important in microeconomic valuation to also affect changes in the aggregate markets.

Inflation and Interest Rates   Exhibit 12.4 contains a plot of long-term interest rates and the year-to-year percentage change in the consumer price index (CPI, a measure of inflation). This

Exhibit 12.4	**Time-Series Plot of Promised Yield on Moody's Corporate Bonds and Inflation: Monthly 1982–2004**

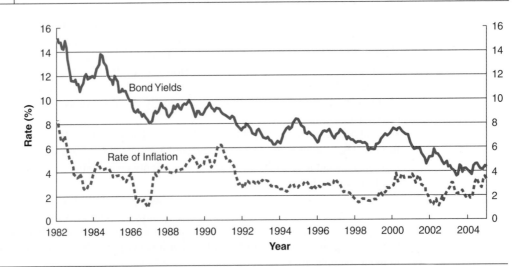

Exhibit 12.5 | **Spread between the Yield of Moody's Corporate Bonds and Inflation: Monthly 1982–2004**

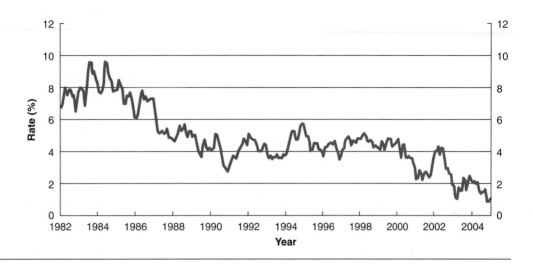

graph demonstrates the strong relationship between inflation and interest rates. We contended in our earlier discussion that when investors anticipated an increase in the rate of inflation, they would increase their required rates of return by a similar amount to derive constant real rates of return. The time-series graph of the promised yield of corporate bonds and the annual rate of inflation in Exhibit 12.4 confirms the expected relationship overall. If the relationship was perfect and investors were accurate in their *predictions* of future inflation, the difference between the interest rate and the inflation rate (the spread between them) would be fairly constant, reflecting the real return on corporate bonds. As shown, the spread between these two curves changes over time.

Exhibit 12.5 plots this spread between bond interest rates and inflation. Although the two curves generally move together, during 1983–1985, the real rates of return on these high quality bonds were in the 8 to 10 percent range, which clearly exceeds what most investors would expect on very low risk bonds.

This change in spread does not mean that there is not a relationship between inflation and interest rates; it only shows that *investors are not very good at predicting inflation.* Recall that the theoretical relationship is between *expected* inflation and interest rates, which is in contrast to these data that reflect actual inflation. Apparently, investors overestimated the rate of inflation during 1980–1983 when inflation declined rapidly, so they underpaid for bonds and experienced abnormally high real rates of return.

Interest Rates and Bond Prices   The relationship between interest rates and bond prices is clearly negative because the only variable that changes in the valuation model is the discount factor. Specifically, the expected cash flows from a straight noncallable bond would not change, so an increase in interest rates will cause a decline in bond prices and a decline in interest rates will boost bond prices. For example, if you own a 10-year bond with a coupon of 10 percent, when interest rates increase from 10 percent to 12 percent, the price of this bond will decline from $1,000 (par) to $885. In contrast, if rates decline from 10 percent to 8 percent, the price of the bond will increase from $1,000 to $1,136.

The size of the price change will depend on the characteristics of the bond. As will be discussed in Chapter 19, a longer-term bond will experience a larger price change for a change in interest rates. Therefore, we can anticipate a negative relationship between inflation and the rates of return on bonds because inflation generally has a direct effect on interest rates; and, in turn, interest rates have an inverse effect on bond prices and rates of return. One example of empirical verification for this negative relationship is provided in Exhibit 3.10, which shows a correlation of -0.11 between inflation and rates of return on long-term investment-grade bonds.

Inflation, Interest Rates, and Stock Prices   The relationship between inflation, interest rates, and stock prices is not direct and consistent. The reason is that the cash flows from stocks can change along with inflation and interest rates, and we cannot be certain whether this change in cash flows will augment or offset the change in interest rates. To demonstrate this, consider the following potential scenarios following an increase in the rate of inflation and the effect on stock prices based on the DDM.

1. *The positive scenario.* Interest rates rise due to an increase in the rate of inflation, and corporate earnings likewise experience an increase in growth because firms are able to increase prices in line with cost increases. In this case, stock prices might be fairly stable because the negative effect of an increase in the required rate of return (k) is partially or wholly offset by the increase in the growth rate of earnings and dividends (g), which means that the returns on stock increase in line with the rate of inflation.
2. *Mild negative scenario.* Interest rates increase due to inflation, but expected cash flows change very little or not at all because firms are not able to increase prices in response to higher costs. This would cause a decline in stock prices similar to what happens with a bond. The required rate of return (k) would increase, but the growth rate of dividends (g) would be constant. As a result, the k–g spread discussed in Chapter 11, would widen and stock prices would decline.
3. *Very negative scenario.* Interest rates increase due to inflation, while cash flows decline because the inflation that caused the rise in interest rates has a negative impact on earnings. For example, during 1981 to 1982, interest rates increased and remained high during a period of economic decline, which caused sales and earnings to decline. Alternatively, one can envision a period of inflation wherein the costs of production increase, but many firms are not able to increase prices, which causes a decline in profit margins. The impact of this set of events can be disastrous. Given this scenario, stock prices will experience a significant decline because k will increase as g declines, causing a large increase in the k–g spread.

In contrast to these scenarios, you can envision a comparable set of scenarios when inflation and interest rates decline. The relationship between inflation, interest rates, and stock prices is not as direct or consistent as the relationship between interest rates and bond prices. The point is, the effect of interest rate changes on stock prices will depend on what caused the change in interest rates and the effect of this event on the expected cash flows on common stock.

Notably, the actual relationship between inflation, interest rates, and stock prices is an empirical question and *the effect varies over time.* Therefore, although there has generally been a significant *negative* relationship between inflation, interest rates, and the returns on stock, as shown in Chapter 3 (Exhibit 3.10), this is not always true as shown by Reilly (1975), Jaffee and Mandelker (1976), and Fama (1981). In addition, even when it is true for the overall market, certain industries may have earnings, cash flows, and dividends that react positively to inflation and interest rate changes. In such an instance, their stock prices would be positively correlated with inflation and interest rates as demonstrated by Reilly, Wright, and Johnson (2005).

Analysis of World Security Markets

Although we have focused on the U.S. market to demonstrate the macroeconomic approach to forecasting movements in the securities markets, you must also consider a similar analysis for numerous foreign markets, including those in Japan, Canada, the United Kingdom, and Germany. While it is not feasible to consider the full macroanalysis, the following discussion considers some of the variables and economic series and some differences that will cause the macromarket analysis to imply a different outlook for alternative countries compared to the United States.

Leading economic series are available for virtually all the developed countries, and the empirical relationships to the economy are quite similar to those of the United States.

Real GDP growth is typically consistent with what is implied by the leading series. Notably, the growth rate outlook will vary between countries by at least 4 percent ranging from about one percent to over 5 percent (e.g., China). Recall that these estimates of real GDP growth will impact both the country's real rate of interest and the growth of its sales and earning cash flows.

The monetary environment of a country will clearly differ from the United States because the monetary authority in each country will be responsive to the economic outlook for *its* country, which is typically different from that of the United States.

The inflation outlook will depend on the monetary environment—that is, the ease or tightness of monetary policy. It also will be impacted by the economic environment and the point on the business cycle (recession or expansion). Again, there will be a wide range for the expected rate of inflation among countries, and the impact of these different inflation rates on security values will be as described earlier for the United States.

Similar to the United States, if you have a good understanding of the outlook for each of these critical macroeconomic variables, you will also have a view on the outlook for the bond and stock market for the country and be in a better position to derive a microestimate of the future value for the country's financial markets.

MICROVALUATION ANALYSIS

In this section, building on the microanalysis of the economy and the implications of this for the stock market, we estimate specific values for an aggregate stock market series using the various valuation models presented in Chapter 11. Therefore, this section has four subsections in which the four sets of valuation techniques are employed: (1) the dividend discount model (DDM), (2) the free cash flow to equity model, (3) the earnings multiplier technique, and (4) the other relative valuation ratios. Note that the first two subsections consider two of the present value of cash flow approaches presented in Chapter 11, while the last two subsections employ the four relative valution ratios from Chapter 11. Notably, we do not demonstrate the operating free cash flow model because of space constraints and the difficulty of estimating debt for the S&P industrials. Also, we do not use the other relative valuation ratios to derive a specific value of the market; rather, we discuss the trends for these ratios during the past 12 years to help you become familiar with them so that you can use these relative valuation ratios in subsequent industry and company stock analysis. Specifically, you will want to compare the relative valuation ratios for an industry or company to the relative valuation ratios for the market. We finish the chapter with a discussion of unique factors that should be considered when applying these valuation techniques to foreign markets.

Applying the DDM Valuation Model to the Market

In Chapter 11, we employed the dividend discount model (DDM), which estimated the value of the stock (V_j) assuming a constant growth rate of dividends for an infinite period.

12.1
$$V_j = \frac{D_0(1 + g)}{(1 + k)} + \frac{D_0(1 + g)^2}{(1 + k)^2} + \cdots + \frac{D_0(1 + g)^n}{(1 + k)^n}$$

where:

V_j = the value of stock j
D_0 = the dividend payment in the current period
g = the constant growth rate of dividends
k = the required rate of return on stock j
n = the number of periods, which is assumed to be infinite

This model, which has been used extensively for the fundamental analysis of common stock, can also be used to value a stock market series. In the appendix to Chapter 11, it was shown that this model can be simplified to the following reduced form expression:

12.2
$$V_j = P_j = \frac{D_1}{k - g}$$

where:

P_j = the price of stock j
D_1 = dividend in Period 1, which is equal to: $D_0(1 + g)$
k = the required rate of return for stock j
g = the constant growth rate of dividends

This model suggests that the parameters to be estimated are (1) the required rate of return *(k)* and (2) the expected growth rate of dividends *(g)*. After estimating g, it is simple to estimate D_1 because it is equal to the current dividend (D_0) times $(1 + g)$.

Market Valuation Using the Reduced Form DDM   In this section we will apply the model to the valuation of the S&P Industrials Index as of mid-2005. As noted, the critical estimates are the prevailing k and g for the U.S. equity market. The estimate of D_1 is the current D_0 for the latest 52-week period times $(1 + g)$. As of mid-2005, the recent trailing 52-week dividend estimate in *Barron's* was $21.40.

As discussed previously, the estimate of k is a function of the nominal risk-free rate *(NRFR)* plus a market risk premium. Because both of these components are subject to interpretation, we will consider a range of values.

The Nominal Risk-Free Rate   The alternatives for the *NRFR* are based upon the theoretical specifications that it should be a zero-coupon, default-free asset with a time to maturity that approximates the investor's holding period. The point is, such an asset would provide the asset's promised return (i.e., its yield to maturity) because there is no default risk, no reinvestment risk because it is a zero-coupon security, and no price risk because the asset matures at the end of the holding period. The range of suggested maturities goes from a three-month T-bill to an intermediate government bond (e.g., a 10-year Treasury bill), to the long-term government bond (e.g., a 30-year Treasury bill). As of mid-2005, these yields were:

3-month Treasury bill:	2.80%
10-year Treasury note:	4.50%
30-year Treasury bond:	4.80%

The Equity Risk Premium   The attitude toward the estimation of the equity risk premium has undergone significant changes during the 1990s. The initial empirical estimate of an equity risk premium was provided by the pioneering work of Ibbotson and Sinquefield (1982) in their monograph for the Financial Analysts Research Foundation. They estimated the risk premium on common stock as the arithmetic mean of the difference in the annual rate of return from stocks minus the return on Treasury bills. Although the original estimate was for 1926–1981, this estimated risk premium has been updated annually in a yearbook provided by Ibbotson Associates (annual). For example, the equity risk premium as of 2005 for 1926–2004 was 9.2 percent using the arithmetic mean of the annual values and 7.6 percent using the geometric mean of the annual values. The geometric mean is appropriate for long-run asset class comparisons, whereas the arithmetic mean is what you would use to estimate the premium for a given year (e.g., the *expected* performance next year). Because our application is to the long-term DDM model, the geometric mean value would probably be more appropriate, which implies using the 7.6 percent risk premium value.

An additional adjustment is suggested to reflect the belief that the typical investment horizon is longer than that implied by the T-bill rate. Assuming that most investors consider the intermediate time frame (5–10 years) a more appropriate investment horizon, the risk premium should be computed as the stock return less the return on intermediate government bonds. Given the typical upward-sloping yield curve, it is not surprising that this measure of the risk premium is about 1 percent less than the T-bill premium—that is, the arithmetic mean of the annual risk premiums relative to intermediate government bonds was 8.3 percent from 1926–2004 and the geometric mean of the annual risk premiums was 6.7 percent. In recent years, Ibbotson Associates has also provided a long-horizon risk premium estimate that employs the long-term government bond return. The arithmetic average for this series was 7.9 percent and the geometric average was 6.3 percent. Therefore, the long-term historical risk premium to use should be about *6.5 percent.*

Several authors have contended that there are problems with this estimate in a dynamic real-world environment. The major criticism articulated by Rozeff (1984) is that it is *too long term* and assumes that the *market risk premium is almost a constant value.* Given that we are dealing with an average value that encompasses almost 79 years, this technique will not reflect any changes over time. There are ways to adjust for this constant value problem, and there are other estimation approaches that have been suggested.

The first suggestion to adjust for the constant value is to use a constant period moving average for the Ibbotson-Sinquefield technique—for example, instead of using a single mean value for the total period since 1926, employ a 20-year moving average of the series. This would reflect any trends in the series over time. The authors computed such a series employing a moving average and using the intermediate bond return as the risk-free asset. The time-series plots clearly demonstrated that the risk premium series was not stable since the 20-year moving average values varied from about 1 percent to 16 percent. Notably, given the computation of the risk premium, it increases during years when the market does well and declines during poor performing periods. This is clearly counterintuitive to expectations.

The paper by Rozeff (1984) discusses the equity risk premium concept similar to the presentation in this book. This is followed by a review of alternative measures of the risk premium, including the Ibbotson-Sinquefield series, an estimate using the CAPM, and a brief consideration of the default risk premium (referred to as the credit risk series).

The credit risk premium concept has been referred to on several occasions in this book when discussing changes in the capital market risk premium. The notion is that changes in the absolute or percentage spread between the yield on BBB and AAA bonds indicate a change in the required rate of return by investors for accepting credit risk. Further, this change in the credit risk premium implies a change in the slope of the security market line (SML). The percent yield spread is considered a preferable measure because it adjusts for the level of yields. An advantage of the credit risk measure is that it is based on current market results and reflects prevailing investor attitudes. For a recent plot of this credit yield spread, see Exhibit 1.9, which indicates a very volatile series with peaks in 1976 and 2003.

An alternative estimate of the equity risk premium is suggested by Reichenstein and Rich (1993). They employ the Value Line forecast of dividends and capital gains. This estimated total market return less the short-term government bond yield is shown to provide better and more consistent results than an earnings price value or dividend yield, although it provides consistently biased results that can be adjusted.

A comparison used by Woolridge (1995) to justify a change in the equity risk premium is the relative volatility of stocks versus bonds. Woolridge argues that the risk premium for equity has declined from the 6 percent estimate based on the Ibbotson-Sinquefield data to about 2.5 percent because of the *increase* in bond market volatility relative to stock volatility.[1] Specifically, the equity risk premium spread has declined, not because stocks have become less volatile but because bonds have become more volatile. Thus, the difference in risk between the two asset classes is less than before, so the risk premium spread has declined. A study by Claus and Thomas (2001) derives an estimate of the equity risk premium from the discount rate that equates market valuations with prevailing expectations of future flows. Their results indicate a risk premium between 1985 and 1998 of 3 percent or less.

In summary, if you use the current intermediate government bond rate as your estimate of the minimal *NRFR*, these studies indicate that the equity risk premium should be somewhere between 2.5 percent and 6.0 percent, depending on the current environment. In turn, you can derive an indicator of the current environment by examining the prevailing credit risk spread, or the relative volatility of bonds versus stocks.

Once you have estimated the required rate of return for the current period, you must determine whether the expected rate of inflation or the risk premium on common stock will change during your investment horizon.

The Current Estimate of Risk Premium and k   Based upon the prior discussion, the total range for the equity risk premium is from about 2.5 percent (suggested by Woolridge [1995]) to about 6.0 percent (the long-run geometric average of the historical returns according to the Ibbotson data). For purposes of applying these results, we will employ three alternative risk premiums: 2, 4, and 6 percent. If we combine these risk premiums with the prior nominal risk-free rates for government bonds, we derive the following matrix of required rates of return *(k)* for the S&P Industrials Index:

	RISK PREMIUMS		
Nominal *RFR*	0.02	0.04	0.06
0.028	0.048	0.068	0.088
0.045	0.065	0.085	0.105
0.048	0.068	0.088	0.108

[1]For an analysis of relative volatility of bonds versus stocks that is consistent with the Woolridge contention, see Reilly, Wright, and Chan (2000).

The matrix indicates a range of *k* from 0.048 (4.8 percent) to 0.108 (10.8 percent). The low required rate of return assumes investors have a very short-run horizon and a very small risk premium, while the high required return implies a long-run horizon and the use of the long-run historical risk premium.

For purposes of our subsequent estimate, we will use the diagonal values from this matrix: 0.048, 0.085, 0.108 which are equal to: 4.8, 8.5 and 10.8 percent.

The Dividend Growth Rate   The earnings multiple that is applied to next year's earnings must take into account the expected growth rate *(g)* for common dividends.[2] There is a positive relationship between the earnings multiplier and the growth rate of earnings and dividends—the higher the expected growth rate, the higher the multiple.[3] When estimating *g*, you should consider the current expected rate of growth and estimate any *changes* in the growth rate. Such changes in expectations indicate a change in the relationship between *k* and *g* and will have a profound effect on the earnings multiplier.

As discussed in Chapters 10 and 11, a firm's growth rate is equal to (1) the proportion of earnings retained and reinvested by the firm—that is, its retention rate *(b)*—times (2) the rate of return earned on investments *(ROE)*. An increase in either or both of these variables causes an increase in the expected growth rate *(g)* and an increase in the earnings multiplier. Therefore, the growth rate can be stated as:

12.3
$$g = f(b, ROE)$$

where:

$$g = \text{RR} \times \text{ROE}$$

  g = expected growth rate
  b = the expected retention rate equal to $1 - D/E$
  ROE = the expected return on equity investments

Therefore, to estimate the growth rate, you need to estimate changes in the retention rate *(b)* and the return on equity *(ROE)*. The plot in Exhibit 12.6 shows that the retention rate was relatively high. Because the valuation model is a long-run model, you should estimate only relatively permanent changes, although short-run changes can affect expectations. Specifically, you should recognize that the annual retention rate, which has been quite volatile (between 45 and 60 percent), is heavily impacted by annual earnings changes (as will be discussed in the dividend payout section).

The second variable that affects *g* is changes in the return on equity *(ROE)*.

As discussed in Chapter 10, the *ROE* can be broken down using the three-component DuPont analysis as follows:

12.4
$$ROE = \frac{\text{Net Income}}{\text{Equity}} = \frac{\text{Net Income}}{\text{Sales}} \times \frac{\text{Sales}}{\text{Total Assets}} \times \frac{\text{Total Assets}}{\text{Equity}}$$

$$= \frac{\text{Net Profit}}{\text{Margin}} \times \frac{\text{Total Asset}}{\text{Turnover}} \times \frac{\text{Financial}}{\text{Leverage}}$$

This equation shows that the *ROE* increases if either the total asset turnover or the profit margin increases. In addition, you can increase *ROE* by increasing financial leverage. Because the S&P Industrials series includes the required historical information only since 1992, we examine this three-component breakdown of *ROE* for this 12-year period.

---

[2]You know that the *g* in the valuation model is the expected growth rate for dividends. In our discussion, we assume a relatively constant dividend-payout ratio (dividend/earnings), so the growth of dividends is dependent on the growth in earnings.
[3]A paper that specifically examines this relationship is Fairfield (1994).

Exhibit 12.6	Time-Series Plot of the S&P Industrials Index Retention Rate

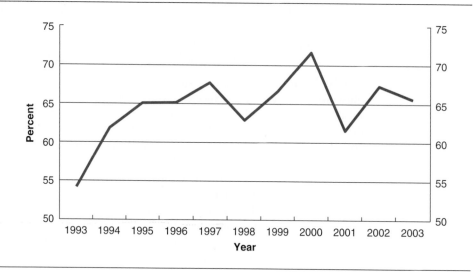

Exhibit 12.7	S&P Industrials Index Return on Equity and Return on Assets

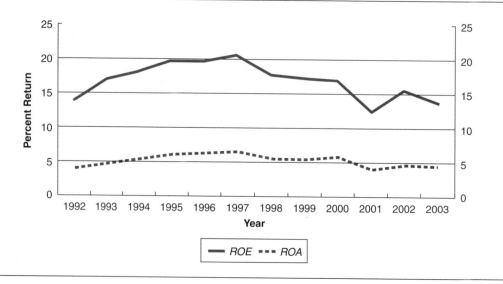

As shown in Exhibit 12.7, the *ROE* for the S&P Industrials series during the period 1993–2003 experienced a peak in 1997 followed by an overall decline, with the lowest value during the recession in 2001. An analysis of the three components of *ROE* indicates what contributed to the changes over time. First, the profit margin (Exhibit 12.8) was a major factor explaining the peak in 1997 and the low point in 2001. The second component, total asset turnover (Exhibit 12.9) increased to a peak in 1996 but then declined consistently to a low point in 2003. Combining these two variables (*PM* and *TATO*) equals return on total assets (*ROTA*) (Exhibit 12.7) that has been virtually flat for the period—it was just below 5 percent in 1993 and in 2003. Therefore, the major

Exhibit 12.8	S&P Industrials Index Net Profit Margin

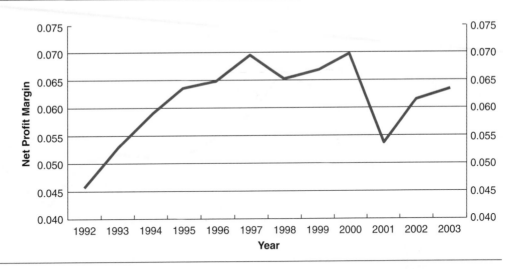

Exhibit 12.9	S&P Industrials Index Total Asset Turnover Ratio

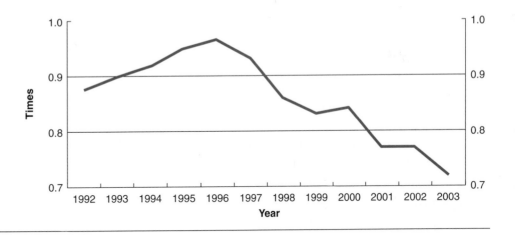

variable that contributed to the overall decline in *ROE* was the financial leverage ratio (total assets/equity) (Exhibit 12.10) that declined from about 3.60 to 3.00 in 2003.

The point is, an investor needs to estimate the long-term outlook for *ROE*, which in turn requires a long-term estimate for each of the three component ratios. Once that is established, multiply this long-term estimate of *ROE* by your estimate of *b*, the retention rate, to calculate an estimate of the long-term growth rate (*g*) of U.S. Industrial firms. For example, if you estimate that the *long-run* retention rate of firms will be 55 percent and their *ROE* will be about 14 percent, this means you would expect the long-run growth rate to be about 7.7 percent, as follows:

$$g = b \times ROE$$
$$= 0.55 \times 0.14$$
$$= 0.077 = 7.7\%$$

Exhibit 12.10 | **S&P Industrials Index Total Assets/Equity Ratio**

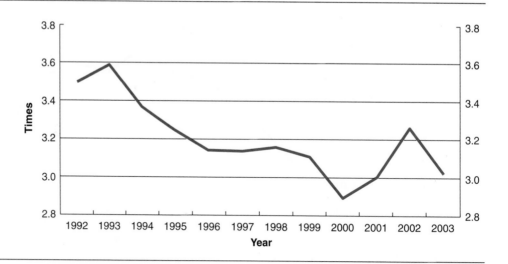

Combining the Estimates   If we combine the several estimates, they are as follows:

$$D_0 = \$21.40$$
$$k = 0.048 \text{ or } 0.085 \text{ or } 0.108$$
$$g = 0.077$$
$$D_1 = \$21.40\ (1 + g) = \$21.40\ (1.077) = \$23.05$$

Using these inputs for the reduced form DDM indicates the following three estimates of market value:

1. $\dfrac{23.05}{0.048 - 0.077} = \dfrac{23.05}{-0.029} = \text{Meaningless } (g > k)$

2. $\dfrac{23.05}{0.085 - 0.077} = \dfrac{23.05}{0.008} = 2,881$

3. $\dfrac{23.05}{0.108 - 0.077} = \dfrac{23.05}{0.031} = 744$

As noted, the first estimate is meaningless since the growth rate exceeds the required return k. The second estimate that has a $(k-g)$ spread of only 0.008 indicates a valuation of 2,881 which exceeds the current market price (late May 2005) of 1,342. Finally, the third estimate that has a $(k-g)$ spread of over 0.03 indicates a value of 744, which is substantially below the market price of 1,342. Assuming the dividend value of $23.05 is reasonable, one needs to consider what $k-g$ spread is necessary to justify the prevailing market value. Consider the following values:

$$\frac{23.05}{0.016} = 1,441$$

$$\frac{23.05}{0.017} = 1,356$$

$$\frac{23.05}{0.018} = 1,280$$

It appears that the current market value implies (requires) a k–g spread very close to 1.7 percent, which means either a k below 0.095 or an expected growth rate above 0.077. Since the 7.7 percent long-run growth rate appears fairly aggressive (optimistic), the most likely adjustment would be a k approaching 0.094. A more conservative growth estimate would mean a lower required k.

Market Valuation Using the Free Cash Flow to Equity (FCFE) Model

As indicated earlier, we will derive an estimate using this FCFE model under two scenarios: (1) a constant growth rate from the present and then (2) a two-stage growth rate assumption.

The Constant Growth FCFE Model To begin, the FCFE is defined (measured) as follows:[4]

> *Net Income*
> + Depreciation expense
> − Capital expenditures
> − Δ in working capital
> − Principal debt repayments
> + New debt issues

This technique attempts to determine the free cash flow that is available to the stockholders after payments to all other capital suppliers and after providing for the continued growth of the firm. The FCFE data for the S&P Industrials Index for the period 1994–2003 are contained in Exhibit 12.11.

Although there was overall growth in the series for the period 1994–2003 of about 9 percent, there was also substantial variation from a low point in 1994 to a peak of 58.67 in 2000, followed by three much lower values in 2001–2003. A major cause of the latter results were the large working capital additions. Preliminary indications for 2004 point toward strong earn-

| Exhibit 12.11 | Components of Free Cash Flow to Equity for the S&P Industrials Index: 1993–2003 |

Year	Net Income	Depreciation Expense	Capital Expenditures	Working Capital	Changes in Working Capital	Principal Repayment	New Debt Issued	Total FCFE
1993	33.63	31.39	42.85	64.43	N/A	6.99		N/A
1994	39.39	32.61	45.83	86.37	21.94		3.64	7.87
1995	45.55	35.62	51.85	92.70	6.33		13.1	36.09
1996	47.89	36.88	56.75	89.60	−3.1	2.85		28.27
1997	51.64	38.07	60.37	78.63	−10.97		6.83	47.14
1998	48.24	40.39	61.34	71.71	−6.92		14.14	48.35
1999	53.57	42.16	61.45	76.87	5.16		19.27	48.39
2000	58.68	43.84	62.19	59.91	−16.96		1.38	58.67
2001	42.62	46.40	62.19	83.28	23.37		34.24	37.70
2002	48.72	36.75	48.23	104.39	21.11		17.54	33.67
2003	50.77	43.50	44.82	124.45	20.06		4.35	33.74

N/A: data not available.

Source: Adapted from data in *Financial Analyst's Handbook* (New York: Standard & Poor's, 2004).

---

[4]For further discussion and detail, see Damodaran (1994).

ings, reasonable capital expenditures and working capital increases, and a "best" estimate for FCFE of about 45.00. Therefore, for the constant growth version of the model, we will use the growth estimate used in the DDM as follows:

$$g = 0.077$$
$$k = 0.085; 0.108$$
$$FCFE_0 = \$45.00 \text{ (estimate for 2004)}$$
$$FCFE_1 = (\$45.00)(1.077) = \$48.47 \text{ (estimate for 2005)}$$

Equity Values:

$$\frac{48.47}{0.085 - 0.077} = \frac{48.47}{0.008} = 6,049$$

$$\frac{48.47}{0.108 - 0.077} = \frac{48.47}{0.031} = 1,564$$

In contrast to the DDM results, this model indicates that the market at its current price of about 1,342 is undervalued even if one assumes a cost of equity of 10.8 percent. Recall that this 10.8 percent k is based on a long-term bond rate of 4.80 percent and an equity risk premium of 6.00 percent.

Alternatively, if we assume a lower perpetual growth rate of 7.0 percent, the values decline as follows:

$$\frac{48.47}{0.085 - 0.070} = \frac{48.47}{0.015} = 3,231$$

$$\frac{48.47}{0.108 - 0.070} = \frac{48.47}{0.037} = 1,310$$

Finally, if we assume 6.0 percent perpetual growth, the values are:

$$\frac{48.47}{0.085 - 0.060} = \frac{48.47}{0.025} = 1,939$$

$$\frac{48.47}{0.108 - 0.060} = \frac{48.47}{0.048} = 1,010$$

Needless to say, the valuations and the investment decisions given the current market value of 1,342 are very sensitive to the estimate of k and g and the resulting spread.

The Two-Stage Growth FCFE Model   As noted above, if one considers the total period 1994–2003, the average annual percentage growth is about 9 percent. To demonstrate this model, we assumed the following above-average growth rates during the next five years (the first stage) followed by a second stage of constant growth at 6 percent.

2005—9%

2006—8%

2007—7.5%

2008—7.0%

2009—6.5%

2010 onward—6.0%

Assuming a k of 8.5 percent and a FCFE of $45.00 in 2004, the computations are as follows:

		DISCOUNT FACTORS	
Year	FCFE	at 0.085	Present Value
2005	49.05	0.922	45.22
2006	52.97	0.850	45.02
2007	56.95	0.783	44.59
2008	60.93	0.722	43.99
2009	64.89	0.665	43.15
Continuing Value[a]	2,752	0.665	1,830.00
		Total *PV*	$2,052

$$^a\ \frac{68.79}{0.085-0.06} = \frac{68.79}{0.025} = 2,752$$

As can be seen, this set of assumptions indicates an intrinsic value of 2,052 which exceeds the current market price of the market (1,342), which implies the following: (1) the market is undervalued at this time, and (2) investors who acquire a diversified portfolio of U.S. stocks at these prices should derive a long-run annual rate of return in excess of 8.5 percent. It is also possible to arrive at this market return estimate using the k estimate from the DDM as follows:

12.5
$$k = \frac{D}{p} + g$$

Combining the current dividend yield of about 1.6 percent and the expected long-run g of 7.7 percent implies a return of 9.3 percent. Notably, this estimated return is higher than what is expected by Emmons (1999) who derives expected earnings growth based on the growth of nominal GDP of about 6 percent plus a dividend yield of 1.3 percent to arrive at a return estimate of about 7 percent (he stipulates a range of 5 to 7 percent).

The next section will discuss and demonstrate the four alternative relative valuation ratios as follows: (1) the price/earnings ratio (*P/E*), (2) the price/book value ratio (*P/BV*), (3) the price/cash flow ratio (*P/CF*), and (4) the price/sales ratio (*P/S*). We begin with the *P/E* ratio because it is the most well known and because it can be derived from the DDM. Also this model can be used to derive a specific market value.

VALUATION USING THE EARNINGS MULTIPLIER APPROACH

Two-Part Valuation Procedure

We use the earnings multiplier version of the dividend discount model to value the stock market because it is a theoretically correct model of value assuming a constant growth rate of dividends for an infinite time period. The point is, these are reasonable assumptions for the aggregate stock market.[5] Also, this valuation technique is consistently used in practice.

---

[5]Recall that these assumptions may be unrealistic for many stocks, especially for stocks of growth companies. We consider these problems for growth companies and discuss alternative growth company valuation models that consider such conditions in Chapter 14.

Recall that k and g are independent variables because k depends heavily on risk, whereas g is a function of the retention rate and the *ROE*. Therefore, this spread between k and g can and does change over time. The following equations imply an estimate of this spread at a point in time equal to the prevailing dividend yield:

$$P_j = \frac{D_1}{k - g}$$
$$P_j/D_1 = 1/k - g$$
$$D_1/P_j = k - g$$

Although the dividend yield gives an estimate of the size of the prevailing spread, it does not indicate the values for the two individual components (k and g) or what caused the *change* in the spread. More important, it says nothing about what the spread *should* be, which is the critical value that must be determined based upon estimating values for k and g.

Importance of Both Components of Value

The ultimate objective of this microanalysis is to estimate the intrinsic market value for a major stock market series, such as the S&P Industrials Index. This estimation process has two equally important steps:

1. Estimating the future earnings per share for the stock market series
2. Estimating the appropriate earnings multiplier for the stock market series based on long-run estimates of k and g.[6]

Some analysts have concentrated on estimating the earnings for a market series with little consideration of changes in the earnings multiplier for the series. An investor who considers only the earnings for the series and ignores the earnings multiplier (i.e., the *P/E* ratio), assumes that the earnings multiplier will be relatively constant over time. If this were correct, stock prices would generally move in line with earnings. The fallacy of this assumption is obvious when one examines data for the two components during the period from 1992–2003, as shown in Exhibit 12.12.

The year-end stock price is the closing value for the S&P Industrials Index on the last trading day of the year. The next column is the percentage change in price for the year. The earnings figure is the earnings per share during the year for the S&P Industrials Index, and the next column shows the percentage change from the prior year. The fifth column is the historical earnings multiplier at the end of the year, which is equal to the year-end value for the S&P Industrials Index divided by the *historical* earnings for that year. As an example, at the end of 1992, the S&P Industrials Index was equal to 507.46 and the earnings per share for the firms that made up the series were 28.03 for the 12 months ending 12/31/92. This implies an earnings multiplier of 18.10 (507.46/28.03). Although this may not be the ideal measure of the multiplier, it is consistent in its measurement and shows the changes in the relationship between stock prices and earnings over time. An alternative measure is the *forward* multiplier using *next* year's earnings (i.e., stock price as of 12/31/92 versus earnings for the 12 months ending 12/31/93). This forward *P/E* series earnings multiple t + 1 likewise experiences substantial annual changes and is the multiple we will be estimating. Typically, it is smaller and a less volatile multiple because it considers future earnings that are generally higher.

---

[6]Our emphasis will be on *estimating future values* for EPS, as well as estimating a *forward* earnings multiple using estimates of k and g. We will show the relevant variables and provide a procedural framework, but the final estimate depends on the ability of the analyst.

Exhibit 12.12 | Annual Changes in Stock Prices, Corporate Earnings, and the Earnings Multiplier for S&P Industrials Index: 1992–2003

Year	Year-End Stock Price	% Change	Earnings Per Share	% Change	Year-End Earnings Multiple	% Change	Earnings Multiple (t + 1)	% Change
1992	507.46		28.03		18.10		15.09	
1993	540.19	6.06%	33.63	16.65%	16.06	−12.71%	13.71	−10.03%
1994	547.51	1.34%	39.39	14.62%	13.90	−15.56%	12.02	−14.09%
1995	721.19	24.08%	45.55	13.52%	15.83	12.21%	15.06	20.18%
1996	869.97	17.10%	47.89	4.89%	18.17	12.84%	16.85	10.61%
1997	1,121.38	22.42%	51.64	7.26%	21.72	16.34%	23.25	27.53%
1998	1,479.16	24.19%	48.24	−7.05%	30.66	29.18%	27.61	15.81%
1999	1,841.92	19.69%	53.57	9.95%	34.38	10.82%	31.39	12.03%
2000	1,527.86	−20.56%	58.68	8.71%	26.04	−32.06%	35.85	12.44%
2001	1,333.94	−14.54%	42.62	−37.68%	31.30	16.81%	27.38	−30.93%
2002	1,005.99	−32.60%	48.72	12.52%	20.65	−51.58%	19.81	−38.18%
2003	1,271.07	20.85%	50.77	4.04%	25.04	17.52%	N/A	N/A
With Signs								
Mean		6.19		4.31	23.07	0.35	22.29	0.54
Std. Dev.		20.24		15.37		24.96		22.45
Coefficient of Var.		3.27		3.57		71.68		41.80
Without Signs								
Mean		18.49		12.44		15.54		19.18
Std. Dev.		8.69		9.30		18.91		9.78
Coefficient of Var.		0.47		0.75		1.22		0.51

Exhibit 12.13	Year-End Earnings Multiple for the S&P Industrials Index Based on Forward Earnings: 1992–2003

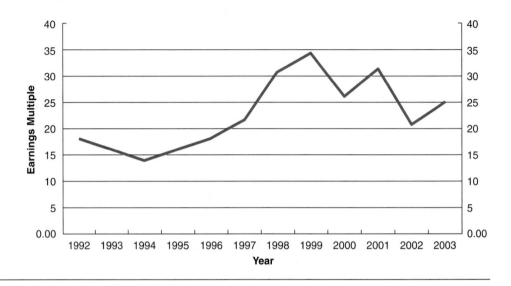

There have been numerous striking examples where annual stock price movements for the S&P Industrials Index were opposite to earnings changes during the same year as follows:

- 1998 profits *decreased* by 7 percent; stock prices *increased* over 24 percent.
- 2000 profits *increased* almost 9 percent; stock prices *declined* over 20 percent.
- 2002 profits *increased* over 12 percent; stock prices *declined* over 32 percent.

During each of these years, the major influences on stock price movements came from changes in the forward earnings multiplier. The greater volatility of the multiplier series compared to the earnings per share series can be seen from the summary figures at the bottom of Exhibit 12.12 and from the graph of the forward earnings multiplier in Exhibit 12.13. The standard deviation of annual changes for the forward earnings multiplier series is much larger than the standard deviation of earnings changes (22.45 vs. 15.37). The same is true for the relative volatility measures of the coefficient of variability. Also, the mean annual percentage change of the forward multiplier series without signs has a larger mean annual percent change value (19.18 vs. 12.44). Therefore, these figures show that, of the two estimates required for market valuation, *the forward earnings multiplier is the more volatile component.*

The point of this discussion is not to reduce the importance of the earnings estimate but to note that the estimation of the intrinsic market value requires two separate estimates and *both* are important and necessary. Therefore, we initially consider a procedure for estimating aggregate earnings followed by the procedure for estimating the forward market earnings multiplier.

ESTIMATING EXPECTED EARNINGS PER SHARE

The estimate of expected earnings per share for the market series will consider the outlook for the aggregate economy and for the corporate sector. This requires the following steps:

1. Estimate sales per share for a stock market series, such as the S&P Industrials Index. This estimate of sales involves a prior estimate of gross domestic product (GDP) because of the

relationship between the sales of major industrial firms and this measure of aggregate economic activity. Therefore, prior to estimating sales per share, we will consider sources for an estimate of GDP.

2. Estimate the operating profit margin for the series, which equals operating profit divided by sales. Given the data available from Standard and Poor's, we will define operating profit as earnings before interest, taxes, and depreciation (EBITDA).
3. Estimate depreciation per share for the next year.
4. Estimate interest expense per share for the next year.
5. Estimate the corporate tax rate for the next year.

These steps will lead to an estimate of net earnings per share that will be combined with an estimate of the forward earnings multiplier to arrive at an estimate of the current intrinsic value for the stock market series.

Estimating Gross Domestic Product

GDP is a measure of aggregate economic output or activity. Therefore, one would expect aggregate corporate sales to be related to GDP. We begin our estimate of sales for a stock market series with a prediction of nominal GDP from one of several banks or financial service firms that regularly publish such estimates. Using this estimate of nominal GDP, we can estimate corporate sales based on the historical relationship between S&P Industrials Index sales per share and aggregate economic activity (GDP).[7]

Estimating Sales per Share for a Market Series

As noted, we will use a sales figure for an existing stock market series—the S&P Industrials Index.[8] The plot in Exhibit 12.14 shows the relationship between the annual percentage

Exhibit 12.14	Scatterplot of Annual Percentage Changes in S&P Industrials Index Sales and GDP

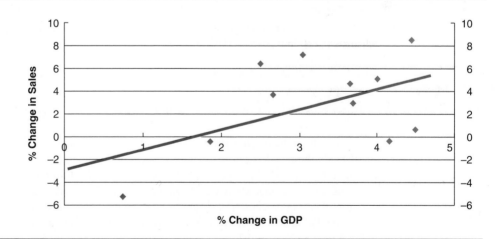

[7]This would include projections by Standard & Poor's appearing late in the year in the *Outlook;* and projections by several of the large investment firms, such as Goldman, Sachs, & Company ("The Pocket Chartroom") or Merrill Lynch, as well as by banks. *The Wall Street Journal* publishes a survey of over 50 economists every 6 months that includes estimates of various interest rates, GDP and inflation.

[8]Sales per share figures are available from 1992 in Standard & Poor's *Analyst's Handbook* (New York: Standard & Poor's Corporation). Because the composite series include numerous companies of different sizes, all data are on a per-share basis. The book is updated annually.

| Exhibit 12.15 | Nominal GDP, Final Sales of Domestic Product, and S&P Industrial Index Sales per Share: 1993–2003 |

Year	Nominal GDP (Billions of Dollars)	% Change	Final Sales to Domestic Purchasers (Billions of Dollars)	% Change	S&P Industrial Index (Dollar Value of Sales per Share)	% Change
1993	6,657.4	5.1	6,689.3	5.1	639.77	3.6
1994	7,072.2	6.2	7,098.4	6.1	672.04	5.0
1995	7,397.7	4.6	7,433.4	4.7	715.38	6.4
1996	7,816.9	5.7	7,851.9	5.6	736.65	3.0
1997	8,304.3	6.2	8,337.3	6.2	741.52	0.7
1998	8,747.0	5.3	8,768.3	5.2	738.82	−0.4
1999	9,268.4	6.0	9,302.2	6.1	801.29	8.5
2000	9,817.0	5.9	9,855.9	6.0	838.78	4.7
2001	10,128.0	3.2	10,135.9	2.8	794.48	−5.3
2002	10,487.0	3.5	10,502.3	3.6	790.86	−0.5
2003	11,004.0	4.9	11,059.2	5.3	847.38	7.1
Average		5.1		5.2		3.0

Source: *Economic Report of the President, 2005* (Washington, DC: U.S. Government Printing Office, 2005) and *Analyst's Handbook* (New York: Standard & Poor's, 2004).

changes in GDP and S&P Industrials Index sales per share contained in Exhibit 12.15. Generally, there is a strong relationship between the two series whereby a large proportion of the percentage changes in S&P Industrials Index sales per share can be explained by percentage changes in nominal GDP. The relationship is not stronger because (1) the S&P Industrials Index sales series is more volatile than the GDP series and (2) the GDP series never experienced a decline. The equation for the least-squares regression line relating annual percentage changes (% Δ) in the two series for the period 1992–2003 is

$$\% \ \Delta \ \text{S\&P Industrials Index Sales}_t = -2.66 + 1.76 \ (\% \ \Delta \ \text{in Nominal GDP}_t)$$
$$(0.90)(1.55)$$
$$\text{Adj. } R^2 = 0.41$$

These results indicate that about 41 percent of the variance in percentage changes in S&P Industrials Index sales can be explained by percentage changes in the nominal GDP. Thus, given an estimate of the expected percentage change in nominal GDP for next year, we can estimate the percentage change in sales for the S&P Industrials Index series and therefore the amount of sales per share. For example, assume the consensus estimate by economists is that nominal GDP next year will increase by approximately 6 percent (a 3.5 percent increase in real GDP plus 2.5 percent inflation). This estimate, combined with the regression results, would imply the following estimated increase in S&P Industrials Index sales:

$$\% \ \Delta \ \text{S\&P Industrials Index Sales} = -0.027 + 1.76 \ (0.06)$$
$$= 0.079$$
$$= 7.9\%$$

Given the significant uncertainty in the economy during early 2005, we will use a conservative 7 percent sales increase. Notably, this is referred to as a *point estimate of sales* because it is based on a point estimate of GDP. Although we know there is actually a *distribution* of estimates for GDP, we have used the mean value, or expected value, as our point estimate. In actual practice, you would probably consider several estimates and assign probabilities to each of them.

Alternative Estimates of Corporate Net Profits

Once sales per share for the market series have been estimated, the difficult estimate is the profit margin. Three alternative procedures are possible depending on the desired level of aggregation.

The first is a direct estimate of the *net* profit margin based on recent trends. As shown in Exhibit 12.16, the net profit margin series is quite volatile because of changes in depreciation, interest, and the tax rate over time. As such, it is the most difficult series to estimate.

The second procedure would attempt to estimate the *net before tax* (NBT) profit margin. Once the NBT margin is derived, a separate estimate of the tax rate is obtained based on recent tax rates and current government tax pronouncements.

The third method estimates an *operating* profit margin, defined as earnings before interest, taxes, and depreciation (EBITDA), as a percentage of sales. Because this measure of operating earnings as a percentage of sales is not influenced by changes in depreciation allowances, interest expense, or tax rates, it should be a more stable series compared to either the net profit margin or net before tax margin series. Our analysis begins with estimating this operating profit margin series.

After we estimate this operating profit margin, we will multiply it by the sales estimate to derive a dollar estimate of operating earnings (EBITDA). Subsequently, we will derive separate estimates of depreciation and interest expenses, which are subtracted from the EBITDA to arrive at earnings before taxes *(EBT.)* Finally, we estimate the expected tax rate *(T)* and multiply *EBT* times $(1 - T)$ to get our estimate of net income. The following sections discuss the details of estimating earnings per share beginning with the operating profit margin.

Estimating Aggregate Operating Profit Margin

Finkel and Tuttle (1971) hypothesized that the following four variables affected the aggregate profit margin:

1. Capacity utilization rate
2. Unit labor costs
3. Rate of inflation
4. Foreign competition

Capacity Utilization Rate   One would expect a positive relationship between the capacity utilization rate and the profit margin because if production increases as a proportion of total capacity, there is a decrease in per-unit fixed production costs and fixed financial costs. The relationship may not be completely linear at very high rates of capacity utilization because operating diseconomies are introduced as firms are forced to use marginal labor and/or older plant and equipment to reach the higher capacity. The figures in Exhibit 12.17 indicate that capacity utilization ranged from a peak of almost 83 percent in 1994 and 1997 to a trough of about 73 percent in 2003 following the recent recession of 2001–2002.

Unit Labor Cost   The change in unit labor cost is a compound effect of two individual factors: (1) changes in wages per hour and (2) changes in worker productivity. Wage costs per hour

Exhibit 12.16 | S&P Industrials Index Sales per Share and Components of Operating Profit Margin: 1992–2003

Year	Sales per Share	EBITDA[a]		DEPRECIATION		INTEREST		INCOME TAX		NET INCOME	
		Per Share	% of Sales	Per Share	% of Sales	Per Share	% of Sales	Per Share	Tax Rate	Per Share	% of Sales
1992	617.41	85.72	13.88%	28.80	4.66%	15.38	2.49%	13.51	32.52%	28.03	4.54%
1993	639.77	94.02	14.70%	31.39	4.91%	14.74	2.30%	14.26	29.78%	33.63	5.26%
1994	672.04	106.91	15.91%	32.61	4.85%	14.56	2.17%	20.35	34.06%	39.39	5.86%
1995	715.38	119.18	16.66%	35.62	4.98%	15.25	2.13%	22.76	33.32%	45.55	6.37%
1996	736.65	124.27	16.87%	36.90	5.01%	14.17	1.92%	25.33	34.59%	47.89	6.50%
1997	741.52	128.18	17.29%	38.10	5.13%	13.46	1.82%	25.01	32.63%	51.64	6.96%
1998	738.82	125.93	17.04%	40.40	5.47%	14.21	1.92%	23.09	32.37%	48.24	6.53%
1999	801.29	139.85	17.45%	42.20	5.26%	14.97	1.87%	29.15	35.24%	53.57	6.69%
2000	838.78	151.98	18.12%	43.80	5.23%	16.59	1.98%	32.87	35.90%	58.68	7.00%
2001	794.48	122.68	15.44%	46.40	5.84%	15.96	2.01%	17.70	29.34%	42.62	5.36%
2002	790.86	121.61	15.38%	36.80	4.65%	15.18	1.92%	20.96	30.08%	48.72	6.16%
2003	847.38	136.60	16.12%	43.50	5.13%	15.00	1.77%	27.33	34.99%	50.77	5.99%

[a]This is used as an estimate of operating earnings.

Source: Adapted from data in *Financial Analyst's Handbook* (New York: Standard & Poor's, 2004).

| **Exhibit 12.17** | **Variables that Affect the Aggregate Profit Margin: Capacity Utilization Rate, Percentage Change in Compensation, Productivity, Unit Labor Cost, and Consumer Price Index: 1992–2003** |

Year	UTILIZATION RATE (MFG.) Percent	COMPENSATION/ WORK HOURS % Change	OUTPUT/ WORK HOURS % Change	UNIT LABOR COSTS % Change	RATE OF INFLATION Percent
1992	79.4	5.3	4.0	1.2	2.9
1993	80.3	2.2	0.4	1.6	2.7
1994	82.6	2.1	1.2	0.5	2.7
1995	82.7	2.1	0.5	1.6	2.5
1996	81.1	3.1	2.7	0.7	3.3
1997	82.6	3.0	1.6	1.4	1.7
1998	82.0	5.4	2.7	3.2	1.6
1999	81.4	4.4	2.8	1.8	2.7
2000	81.1	6.5	2.8	4.2	3.4
2001	75.4	4.5	2.5	1.5	1.6
2002	73.9	3.6	4.4	−1.1	2.4
2003	73.4	4.2	4.4	−0.4	1.9

Source: *Economic Report of the President, 2005* (Washington, DC: U.S. Government Printing Office, 2005).

typically increase every year by varying amounts depending on the economic environment. As shown in Exhibit 12.17, the annual percentage increase in compensation per hour varied from 2.1 percent to 6.5 percent. If workers did not become more productive, this increase in per-hour wage costs would be the increase in per-unit labor cost. Fortunately, because of advances in technology and greater mechanization, the worker units of output per hour (the measure of labor productivity) have increased over time—our labor force has become *more productive.* If wages per hour increase by 5 percent and labor productivity increases by 5 percent, there would be no increase in unit labor costs because the workers would offset wage increases by producing more. Therefore, the increase in *per-unit labor cost* is a function of the percentage change in hourly wages minus the increase in productivity during the period. The actual relationship typically is not this exact due to measurement problems, but it is quite close as indicated by the data in Exhibit 12.17. For example, during 1996, productivity increased by 2.7 percent which was almost as much as hourly compensation that rose by 3.1 percent so there was a very small change in unit labor cost. In contrast, during 2001, wage rates increased by 4.5 percent, productivity increased by only 2.5 percent because of the recession, and, therefore, unit labor costs increased by 1.5 percent. Because unit labor is the major variable cost of a firm, one would expect a *negative* relationship between the operating profit margin and percentage changes in unit labor cost—that is, a small (below-average) change in unit labor cost, similar to what we experienced during the mid-1990s (1994–1996 and 2002–2003), should correspond to an above-average operating profit margin.

Rate of Inflation   The precise effect of inflation on the aggregate profit margin is unresolved. Finkel and Tuttle hypothesized a positive relationship between inflation and the profit margin. They contended that a higher level of inflation increases the ability of firms to pass higher costs on to the consumer and thereby raise their profit margin. Second, assuming the classic demand-pull inflation, the increase in prices would indicate an increase in general economic activity, which typically is accompanied by higher margins.

In contrast, many observers doubt that most businesses can consistently increase prices in line with rising costs. Assuming a 5 percent rate of inflation that impacts costs, the question is whether all firms can *completely* pass these cost increases along to their customers. If a firm increases prices at the same rate as cost increases, there will be a *constant* profit margin, *not* an increase. Only if a firm can raise prices by *more than* cost increases can it increase its margin. Many firms are not able to raise prices in line with increased costs because of the elasticity of demand for their products[9] which will cause the profit margin to decline. Given the alternative scenarios, it is contended that virtually no firms will be able to increase their profit margins and not that many will hold them constant. Thus one would expect the aggregate profit margin to decline when there is an increase in the rate of inflation.

Given the contrasting expectations, one needs to consider the empirical evidence to determine the relationship between inflation and the operating profit margin.

Foreign Competition   Finkel and Tuttle (1971) contend that export markets are more competitive than domestic markets, so export sales are made at a lower margin. This implies that lower exports by U.S. firms would increase profit margins. In contrast, Gray (1976) believed that only exports between independent firms should be considered and they should be examined relative to total output exported. Further, he felt that imports could have an important negative impact on the operating profit margin because they influence the selling price of all competing domestic products. Therefore, there is a divergence of expectations regarding the ultimate effect of foreign trade on the operating profit margin, so it is likewise an empirical question.

Our analysis of the annual data for the period 1977 to 2002 confirmed that the relationship between the operating profit margin and the capacity utilization rate was always significant and positive, whereas the relationship between the unit labor cost and the operating profit margin was always negative and significant. Alternatively, the rate of inflation and foreign trade variables were never significant in the multiple regression. Finally, the simple correlation between the profit margin and inflation was consistently *negative.*

Therefore, when estimating the operating profit margin, you should concentrate on the capacity utilization rate for the economy and the rate of change in unit labor cost. As an example, consider what will happen at two extremes of the business cycle. Coming out of a recession, capacity utilization will be increasing and unit labor costs will rise very slowly due to increased labor productivity, so there should be a strong increase in the operating profit margin.

In contrast, at the peak of the business cycle, firms will be operating at full capacity, so there will be declines in capacity utilization. Also due to inflation, there will be large wage increases and small increases in labor productivity that will cause large increases in unit labor cost. As a result, there should be a major decline in the operating profit margin at the peak of a business cycle.

How do you use this information to estimate an operating profit margin? The most important estimate is *the direction of the change from current levels.* The size of the estimated change will depend on where the economy is in the business cycle and the direction and size of the expected changes in capacity utilization and unit labor cost.

After estimating the operating profit margin, you can calculate the dollar value of EBITDA by applying this operating profit margin estimate to the estimated sales-per-share figure. The next step is to estimate depreciation per share. Exhibit 12.16 contains data on the operating earnings components.

---

[9]An extreme example of this inability is regulated industries that may not be able to raise prices at all until after lengthy hearings before regulatory agencies. Even then, the increase in rates may not match the cost increase.

Estimating Depreciation Expense

As shown in Exhibit 12.18, the depreciation expense per share series has declined only once since 1992 (in 2002). This is not surprising, because depreciation expense is an estimate of the fixed-cost expense related to the total fixed assets that naturally increases over time. Therefore, the relevant question is *not* whether depreciation expense will increase or decrease but by *how much it will increase.*

There are two suggestions for estimating depreciation expense. First, you can use time-series analysis, which involves using the recent trend as a guide to the future increase. Because a column in Exhibit 12.16 shows depreciation as a percent of sales, you might consider this an estimating approach—this would be a *mistake.* Depreciation is clearly a *fixed* expense, which means that it should not vary with sales. As shown in Exhibit 12.16, depreciation as a percentage of sales has varied from 4.65 percent to 5.84 percent, which is consistent with its fixed nature.

Second, you can estimate depreciation expense by estimating property, plant, and equipment *(PPE)* and then apply an historical depreciation rate to the *PPE* account. This technique requires two steps. First, estimate the *PPE* account based on the relationship between sales and *PPE*—that is, the expected *PPE* turnover. The historical *PPE* turnover series in Exhibit 12.19 was quite stable between 2.60 and 2.90 prior to increases in 1999 and 2000 (see Exhibit 12.20). Therefore, given your estimate for sales you can derive an estimate of *PPE.* The second estimate is the ratio of depreciation to *PPE,* which is in Exhibit 12.19 and plotted in Exhibit 12.21. As shown, this ratio has increased over time from about 11 percent to almost 15 percent in 2003. This trend probably is the result of the increase in technology that has tended to reduce the useful life for productive machinery, which implies a higher annual depreciation rate. Therefore, you can estimate depreciation expense from an estimate of *PPE* and the ratio of depreciation to *PPE.*

After you have estimated the depreciation expense, you subtract it from the operating profit estimate to get an estimate of EBIT.

Exhibit 12.18	**Time-Series Plot of Depreciation Expense for the S&P Industrials Index**

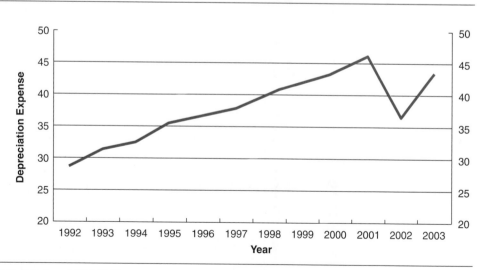

Source: Data from Exhibit 12.16.

Exhibit 12.19 Inputs Required to Estimate Depreciation Expense and Interest Expense for the S&P Industrials Index

Year	Deprec. Expense	Net PPE	Sales/ Net PPE	Deprec. Exp. Net PPE	Interest Expense	Total Asset Turnover	L-T Debt	L-T Debt T. Assets	Int. Exp. L-T Debt	L-T Govt. Bond Yield
1992	28.8	263.51	2.34	10.93	15.38	0.88	147.18	0.21	10.45	7.67
1993	31.4	254.15	2.52	12.35	14.74	0.90	139.70	0.20	10.55	6.59
1994	32.6	258.97	2.60	12.59	14.56	0.92	143.34	0.20	10.16	7.37
1995	35.6	268.66	2.66	13.26	15.25	0.95	156.44	0.21	9.75	6.88
1996	36.9	266.78	2.76	13.82	14.17	0.97	153.59	0.20	9.23	6.71
1997	38.1	271.97	2.73	14.00	13.46	0.93	160.42	0.20	8.39	6.61
1998	40.4	275.22	2.68	14.68	14.21	0.86	174.56	0.20	8.14	5.58
1999	42.2	286.26	2.80	14.73	14.97	0.83	193.83	0.20	7.72	5.87
2000	43.8	282.90	2.96	15.50	16.59	0.84	195.21	0.20	8.50	5.94
2001	46.4	287.36	2.76	16.15	15.96	0.77	229.45	0.22	6.96	5.49
2002	36.8	279.62	2.83	13.14	15.18	0.77	246.99	0.24	6.15	5.43
2003	43.5	292.06	2.90	14.89	15.40	0.76	251.34	0.23	6.13	4.30

Source: Adapted from data in *Financial Analyst's Handbook* (New York: Standard & Poor's, 2004). Reprinted with permission.

Exhibit 12.20	Time-Series Plot of the Ratio of Sales to *PPE* (*PPE* Turnover) for the S&P Industrials Index

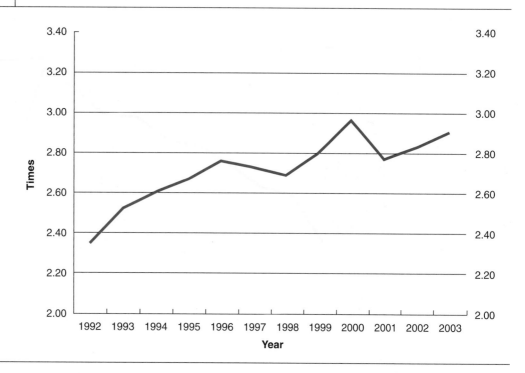

Estimating Interest Expense

The estimate of interest expense should be based on an estimate of debt outstanding (will it grow and by how much?) and the level of interest rates (do you expect interest rates to increase or decline in the future?).

The point is, to estimate interest expense you need to estimate both of these components (the amount of debt outstanding and the average interest rate on this debt) and determine the joint effect. The basic data is listed in Exhibit 12.19, while the time-series plot of debt outstanding shows a fairly constant increase in Exhibit 12.22. Finally, a time-series plot of the average interest rate on debt in Exhibit 12.23 shows a decline, but you should not assume this will continue based on the economic environment and Federal Reserve actions in 2004–2005.

An estimate of debt outstanding requires two estimates: (1) the amount of total assets for the firm based upon the firm's expected total asset turnover and (2) the expected capital structure based upon the average total debt to total asset ratio. Both of these ratios are included in Exhibit 12.19.

Similar to depreciation, interest expense is a fixed expense that is impacted by corporate financing decisions and the cost of debt (i.e., interest rates). Therefore, interest expense as a percent of sales should *not* be used when estimating interest expense.

After you have estimated the interest expense figure (time-series plot in Exhibit 12.24) this value is subtracted from the EBIT per share value to estimate EBT.

Estimating the Tax Rate

This is the final step in estimating the earnings per share for the S&P Industrials Index series. As shown in Exhibit 12.16, the average tax rate during the 12-year period was about 33 percent, which is also consistent with the tendency to move between 32 and 35 percent.

Exhibit 12.21	Time-Series Plot of the Ratio of Depreciation Expenses to *PPE* Account for the S&P Industrials Index

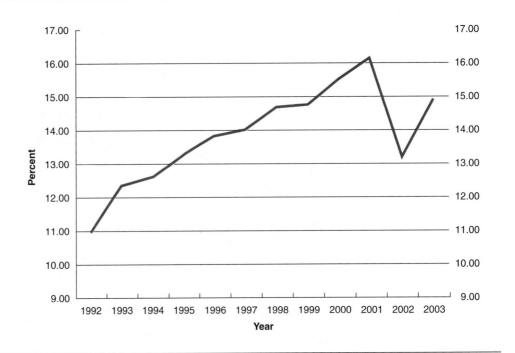

Exhibit 12.22	Time-Series Plot of Debt Outstanding for the S&P Industrials Index

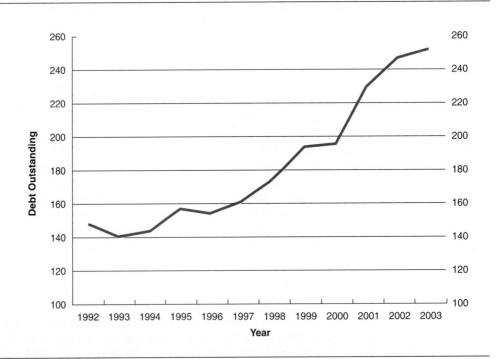

Exhibit 12.23	Time-Series Plot of Interest Rate on Debt Outstanding for the S&P Industrials Index

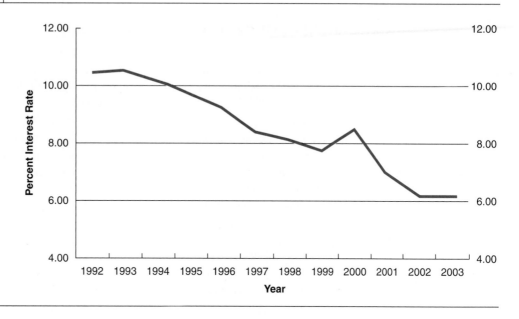

Exhibit 12.24	Time-Series Plot of Interest Expense for the S&P Industrials Index

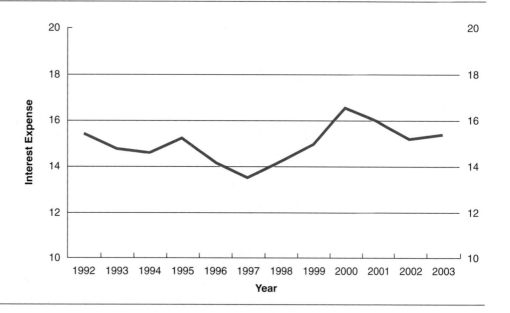

Estimating the future tax rate is difficult because it depends on political action. You must evaluate the current tax rate and recent tax legislation that affects business firms (e.g., tax credits). Once you have estimated the tax rate *(T)*, you multiply one minus this tax rate $(1 - T)$ times the EBT per share figure to derive an estimate of the net income per share for the S&P Industrials Index series.

In the next section, we demonstrate this procedure by estimating earnings per share for 2005.

Calculating Earnings per Share: An Example

The following demonstration for estimating earnings per share emphasizes the procedure rather than the actual numbers. An analyst engaged in this exercise would provide a very long, detailed analysis. In this example, we estimate earnings per share for the S&P Industrials Index during 2005 using 2004 data (most of which is estimated).

Step 1   Nominal GDP for 2005 is based on an estimate for 2004 of approximately $11,728 billion. In 2004, the economy was in the third year of an expansion following the recession in 2001. The current question is, how strong will 2005 be? Recent data have indicated that overall growth in 2005 will not be as strong as 2004 when nominal GDP grew by about 6.6 percent. Current expectations for 2005 are for real GDP to increase by 3.5 percent and for inflation to be 2.5 percent resulting in a nominal increase of 6.0 percent to $12,430 billion.

Step 2   Corporate sales have had a strong relationship with nominal GDP as shown in Exhibit 12.14. During 2004, when nominal GDP increased by about 6.6 percent, S&P sales were at an estimated $923 per share, about a 9.0 percent increase from 2003. In 2005, with GDP rising about 6.0 percent, there is an expectation of reasonable growth, but not as strong as 2004. Specifically, the consensus is that S&P industrial sales should increase by about 7.0 percent to $988 per share.

Step 3   The operating profit margin experienced an increase in 1999 and a new peak of 18.12 percent in 2000, prior to a decline to the 15.0 percent to 17.0 percent range during and following the recession in 2001. We estimate an increase in the margin during 2004 to about 17.0 percent. In 2005, we expect continued recovery in capacity utilization from the low point of 73.0 percent in the fourth quarter of 2004, which is a positive factor. In contrast, unit labor cost will experience an increase of about 2.0 percent in 2004, followed by a larger increase in 2005 because of stable wage increases but much lower productivity gains during this point in the expansion. This will have a clear negative effect on the margin. The result of these two factors should be a decrease in the operating profit margin to about 16.0 percent, which implies an operating profit for 2005 of $158 (0.16 × $988).

Step 4   The depreciation expense during 2004 was approximately $46 per share. As noted, we estimate sales in 2005 at $988 and the *PPE* turnover has been increasing steadily to almost three times. We expect some stability in this value, so we will use 3.00 as the *PPE* turnover, which implies *PPE* of $329. The depreciation/*PPE* ratio (percent) has increased steadily except in 2002 to about 15.2 percent in 2004. We assume a small increase to 15.5 percent in 2005, which implies depreciation expense for 2005 of $51 (0.155 × $329). Thus, the estimated EBIT is $107 ($158 − $51).

Step 5   Interest expense has experienced relatively small increases the last several years even though there were increases in debt outstanding, but these debt increases were partially offset by lower interest rates. In 2005, the sales estimate of $988 and a total asset turnover of 0.75 indicates total assets of $1,317. The long-term debt financing of assets has increased to 23.0 percent which implies long-term debt of $303. As noted, the rate of interest on debt declined in both 2003 and 2004 to about 6.0 percent, but this has been reversed in 2005, so we estimate an interest rate of 7.0 percent which implies that interest expense in 2005 will be about $21(.07 × $303). Therefore, EBT is estimated to be $86 ($107 − $21).

Step 6   The tax rate suggested by our earlier analysis was 33.0 percent. Using this rate for 2005 we get net income for 2005 of $57.62 ($86 × 0.67). For simplicity, we will round this to an EPS estimate of $58.

Sales	$988.00
EBITDA	158.00 (0.16)
Depreciation Expense	51.00
EBIT	107.00
Interest Expense	21.00
EBT	86.00
Taxes	28.38 (0.33)
Net Income (EPS)	$ 57.62

ESTIMATING THE STOCK MARKET EARNINGS MULTIPLIER

Given our estimate of earnings per share, the next step is to estimate an earnings multiplier. A combination of the earnings per share estimate times the estimated forward earnings multiplier provides an estimate of the intrinsic value for the stock market series. Similar to the investment decision rule with the cash flow valuations, if the intrinsic value based on the forward *P/E* ratio and estimated EPS is greater than the current market price, we should overweight U.S. common stocks; if the value is below the market price we should underweight U.S. common stocks.

Our prior discussion related to Exhibit 12.12 indicated that the earnings multiplier (i.e., *P/E* ratio) over time has been more volatile than the earnings per share series because the multiplier is very sensitive to changes in the spread between *k* and *g*. We will examine each of the variables in the *P/E* ratio equation to determine what determines the value for them and why they change. Given this understanding, we can demonstrate how an investor would estimate a value for the earnings multiplier.

Determinants of the Earnings Multiplier

Recall the variables that influence the earnings multiplier or the *P/E* ratio based on the dividend discount model:

12.6
$$P/E = \frac{D_1/E_1}{k - g}$$

where:

D_1 = dividends expected in Period 1, which is equal to $D_0 (1 + g)$
E_1 = earnings expected in Period 1
D_1/E_1 = the dividend-payout ratio expected in Period 1
k = the required rate of return on the stock
g = the expected growth rate of dividends for the stock

Therefore, the major variables that affect the earnings multiplier for common stocks in a country are

- The composite dividend-payout ratio for common stocks in a country
- The required rate of return on common stock in the country being analyzed
- The expected growth rate of dividends for the stocks in the country being analyzed

Because this equation is derived from the dividend discount model, it assumes constant growth for an infinite period. Also, the required rate of return is the long-term estimate. Therefore, the k and g projections are *long-term estimates*. Thus, although these variables can be impacted by near-term events, they should not experience major changes on a year-to-year basis.

It is easier to discuss the dividend-payout ratio after we have considered both k and g. Therefore, the order of discussion will be

- Estimating k, the required rate of return
- Estimating g, the growth rate of dividends
- Estimating D_1/E_1, the dividend-payout ratio

Estimating the Required Rate of Return (k)

The multiplier equation indicates that the earnings multiplier is inversely related to the required rate of return; the higher an investor's required rate of return, the less he or she will pay for a future earnings stream. Our prior discussions indicated that the required rate of return (k) is determined by (1) the economy's risk-free rate *(RFR)*; (2) the expected rate of inflation during the period of investment *(I)*; and (3) the risk premium for the specific investment.

Earlier in the chapter, we derived a range of estimates of k as follows:

NRFR	Risk Premium	Estimated k	Description
0.028	0.02	0.048	Short-term *RFR* and small risk premium
0.045	0.04	0.085	Intermediate *RFR* and midrange risk premium
0.048	0.06	0.108	Long-term *RFR* and historical risk premium

Estimating the Growth Rate of Dividends (g)

Earlier in the chapter, we discussed the estimated growth rate of earnings and dividends in connection with the present value of cash flow models. You will recall from Equation 12.4 that

$$g = b \times ROE$$

After a discussion of the pattern of dividend payouts over the business cycle, it was suggested that an appropriate long-run retention rate *(b)* was 55 percent.

We estimated a long-run *ROE* based upon an analysis of the three components of the DuPont analysis, which showed an overall increase in the *ROE* for the S&P Industrials Index over the past 20 years as a result of recent strong profit margins combined with a decline in the total asset turnover that was offset by an increase in financial leverage. Long run, we estimated an *ROE* of 14 percent. The combined result was

$$g = 0.55 \times 0.14$$
$$= 0.077 = 7.7\%$$

Given these estimates of k, g, and dividend payout (1 minus the retention rate of 0.55), the following section discusses the estimation of the earnings multiples.

Estimating the Dividend-Payout Ratio (D_1/E_1)

Based on the *P/E* equation, there is a positive relationship between the dividend-payout ratio and the *P/E* ratio. Therefore, if the $k - g$ spread is constant and this dividend-payout ratio increases, there will be an increase in the earnings multiplier. Recall that the dividend-payout ratio is equal to one minus the earnings retention rate *(b)*. Therefore, if the dividend-payout *increases,* there will be a *decline* in the earnings retention rate *(b),* which will cause a *decline* in the growth rate *(g)*. Thus, there is a partial offset between changes in the dividend-payout rate and the expected growth rate *(g)*.

In the discussion of the growth rate, we indicated that the retention rate was high in the 1970s, declined in the early 1980s, and has increased again since 1993. This increase in the retention rate implies that the payout ratio has declined recently.

Dividend Payout Rate—Active or Residual Decision?   When examining or attempting to estimate the dividend payout for the aggregate market or an individual firm, it is important to consider whether the dividend payout rate is (1) an *active* decision of management (and the board of directors) or (2) a *residual* outcome because the active decision is the dividend payment. Obviously, if the dividend payout rate is the active decision, the dividend payment would vary over time in line with earnings. In contrast, if the dividend payment is the active decision, this implies that the dividend payout rate is a residual decision. In this latter case, the dividend payments then would be reasonably stable and show fairly steady increases while the dividend-payout ratio would be very volatile because it would be dictated by the earnings. That is, the dividend payout rate would increase dramatically during periods of low earnings and decline significantly during periods of abnormally high earnings growth.

The time-series plots in Exhibits 12.25 and 12.26 support the residual payout theory because they show fairly constant changes in dividend payments (Exhibit 12.25) but high volatility for the dividend-payout ratio in Exhibit 12.26. Specifically, the dividend payout declined during the economic expansion of 1993–2000, experienced a small increase during the 2001 recession and declined during the economic recovery in 2002–2003. This discussion implies that the annual dividend payout is inversely related to earnings changes. Put another way, there is a positive relationship between the earnings retention rate and earnings changes. Therefore, when

Exhibit 12.25 | **Earnings per Share and Dividends per Share for S&P Industrials Index**

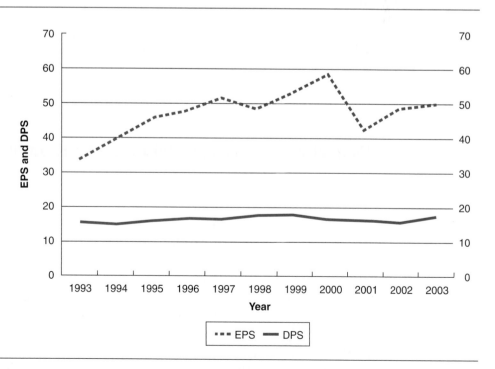

Exhibit 12.26	Time-Series Plot for S&P Industrial Index Payout Ratio

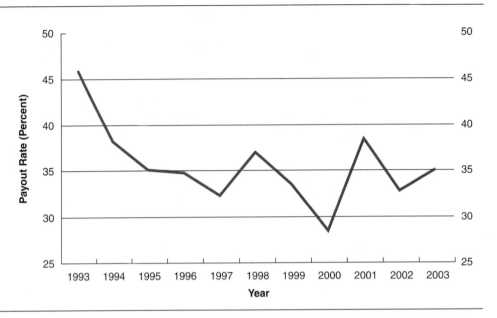

estimating the dividend-payout ratio, it is necessary to estimate the dividend payment using time-series analysis and then relate this estimated dividend to the earnings estimate. Because of its volatility, it is important *not* to emphasize annual dividend payout changes but use a *long-run perspective* regarding the dividend-payout ratio over the business cycle.

Beyond the *cyclical* pattern of the payout ratio, you should consider the *secular* trend, which appears to be declining. Specifically, there is a tendency for corporations to increase their retention rate for the following reasons. First, given the strong *ROE* over the past decade (generally between 15 and 20 percent), one could argue that corporations have more profitable investment opportunities, which justifies lower dividend payouts. Second, corporations are using an alternative way to pay dividends—that is, they are repurchasing stock, which is a more tax-efficient way to reward the stockholder. The result of repurchases is fewer shares, higher earnings per share, and higher valuation, which is not taxed like dividends to the shareholder.

Estimating an Earnings Multiplier: An Example

There are two ways to estimate the earnings multiplier. The first approach begins with the current earnings multiplier and estimates the direction and amount of change based on estimated changes in the three major components.

The second approach estimates a specific value for the earnings multiplier based on specific estimates for the three components in the *P/E* ratio equation. This approach typically involves deriving several estimates based on optimistic or pessimistic scenarios.

The Direction of Change Approach   Begin with the current earnings multiplier and estimate the direction and extent of change for the dividend payout and the variables that influence *k* and *g*. The direction of the change is more important than its size.

The variables that must be estimated are

1. Changes in the dividend-payout ratio
2. Changes in the real *RFR*
3. Changes in the rate of inflation   } Changes in *k*
4. Changes in the risk premium for common stock
5. Changes in the earnings retention rate   } Changes in *g*
6. Changes in the return on equity *(ROE)*

The dividend-payout ratio is expected to be relatively stable in the near term following lower payout values because of the strong earnings growth. In contrast, the earnings growth in 2005 is expected to be close to the long-term average, so the payout should not change.

Given the three variables that affect the required rate of return on common stocks (*k*), there will probably be a small decline in the real *RFR* in 2005 because there will be a small decline in the real growth rate. The rate of inflation was relatively low during 2004 (2.7 percent) and is expected to be similar in 2005. Finally, the equity risk premium is expected to be fairly stable in 2005 after a decrease during 2003 and especially during 2004. Therefore, given the trends in the three components, overall one would expect almost no change in *k* during 2005.

The last two factors in the earnings multiplier estimate relate to the growth rate. As discussed, we expect a stable payout rate, which implies a stable long-run retention rate. The outlook is for a small decline in the aggregate *ROE* during 2005. First, the profit margin in 2005 is expected to decline slightly relative to the strong margin during 2004. Second there should be virtually no change in the total asset turnover at this time in the economic recovery. Finally, we envision a small decline in the financial leverage ratio during 2005 as firms continue to reduce their financial leverage. The result of a small decline in the profit margin, no change in asset turnover, and a decline in financial leverage should be a small decrease in the *ROE* during 2005. Therefore, with a small decrease in the retention rate and a small decline in *ROE*, you would estimate a small decline in the expected growth rate.[10] In summary, we expect

• Stability in the payout ratio
• No change in the required rate of return
• A small decline in the growth rate

Overall, this would imply a very small decline in the earnings multiplier. The forward earnings multiplier early in 2005 is about 18 times. This discussion would indicate that the multiplier would be in the 17–18 times range during 2005.

Specific Estimate Approach   This approach derives specific estimates for the earnings multiplier based on a range of estimates for the three variables: dividend payout (*D/E*), required rate of return *(k)*, and growth *(g)*. As indicated earlier, the retention rate has fluctuated between 45 and 65 percent during the past 10 years. Therefore, a reasonable dividend-payout ratio (*D/E*) would be 45 percent.

The required return *(k)* can be estimated using the interest rate on government bonds plus an estimate of the risk premium for common stocks. An appropriate risk premium could range from 2 percent to 6 percent, depending on the government security used to estimate a nominal risk-free rate. The 6 percent is based on the long-term geometric average risk premium as indicated by the Ibbotson-Sinquefield studies for the period 1926 to 2004, using T-bills as the

---

[10]This is the most reasonable scenario given the economic environment. At the same time, there have been changes in the value of common equity caused by asset write-offs and share repurchases. Both of these events can cause a significant decline in the equity account but have little impact on operating earnings. As a result, there has been a higher *ROE* simply because of a lower equity value.

risk-free investment. Notably, during the recent period (1977 to 2004), the risk premium has been in the range of 2.5 to 5.5 percent. As noted earlier, in early 2005, the rate on T-bills was about 2.80 percent, the rate on 10-year government bonds was about 4.50 percent, and the rate on long-term bonds was 4.80 percent. Notably, these interest rates are at the low end of the range for the past 20 years, and most observers expect a small increase during the year. If there is an adjustment to reflect this, you could conceive of the following possibilities:

		Expected at Year End 2005
A. 10-year government bonds		5.0%
Historical risk premium		6.0
	Estimated k	11.0%
B. 10-year government bonds		5.0%
Low-risk premium		2.0
	Estimated k	7.0%
C. 10-year government bonds		5.0%
Medium-risk premium		4.0
	Estimated k	9.0%

Therefore, the required return (k) could be in the range of 7 to about 11 percent.

The estimate of growth should be based on the current and expected return on equity *(ROE)* and the rate of retention. The graph in Exhibit 12.7 shows that the *ROE* for the S&P Industrials Index was in the 14 to 20 percent range during the period 1992–2003, but it has been trading down since 1997 and ended at the low point. Assuming that 2005 is midway in an economic expansion that officially started in early 2002, a range of 12 to 15 percent for the *ROE* seems appropriate. As indicated earlier, the retention rate has been between 45 and 60 percent. Therefore, a conservative estimate of the growth rate would combine the 45 percent retention rate and an *ROE* of 12 percent: $0.45 \times 0.12 = 0.054$. An optimistic growth rate estimate would combine the 60 percent retention rate and a 15 percent *ROE*: $0.60 \times 0.15 = 0.09$. To summarize,

Dividend/earnings	0.40–0.55
Government securities	0.028–0.048
Equity risk premium	0.020–0.060
Required return (k)	0.07–0.11
ROE	0.12–0.15
Sustainable growth	0.06–0.08

By combining the more optimistic figures (with a positive $k - g$ spread), we can derive a reasonably generous estimate. Using the pessimistic estimates, we can derive a fairly conservative estimate. The dividend-payout (*D/E*) figure should be consistent with the retention rate.

High Estimate: $D/E = 0.45$
$k = 0.09$
$g = 0.07 \ (0.50 \times 0.14)$

$$P/E = \frac{0.45}{0.090 - 0.07} = \frac{0.45}{0.02} = 22.5 \text{ times}$$

$$\text{Low Estimate: } D/E = 0.60$$
$$k = 0.11$$
$$g = 0.06$$

$$P/E = \frac{0.60}{0.110 - 0.06} = \frac{0.60}{0.05} = 12 \text{ times}$$

Therefore, these data imply a range of earnings multipliers from about 12 times to about 23 times with a midrange of about 18 times. The midrange is consistent with the expectation of a *P/E* ratio range of 17–18 derived from the direction of change approach.

Calculating an Estimate of the Value for the Market Series

Previously, we estimated the earnings per share for Standard and Poor's Industrials Index of $58. Clearly, it would have been possible to derive additional earnings estimates.

In our work with the *P/E*, we developed several estimates for the price/earnings multiplier that varied from about 12 to 22.5. At this point, we can combine these estimates of an earnings per share of $58 and the several earnings multipliers and calculate the following estimates of intrinsic value for Standard & Poor's Industrials Index series:

$$12.0 \times \$58 = 696$$
$$15.0 \times \$58 = 870$$
$$18.0 \times \$58 = 1{,}044$$
$$21.0 \times \$58 = 1{,}218$$
$$24.0 \times \$58 = 1{,}392$$

You would compare these several intrinsic value estimates to the current price of the market, which is about 1,342—that is, only one of your estimates signals a buy. Alternatively, the current market is selling for a *P/E* of 23.1 (1,342/58), which is very close to the high *P/E* estimate.

This example is intended to help you understand the estimation procedure. The estimation of values for *D/E, k,* and *g* was not as extensive as the process used by professional analysts. In addition, we used a point estimate for earnings per share rather than a range of estimates (pessimistic, optimistic, most likely), which would have been preferable. Our discussion has provided the skeleton of the process that includes the theoretical background that forms the foundation for the fundamental analysis of stocks. It is important to understand *the relevant variables and how they relate to the critical estimates of earnings per share and the earnings multiplier.* Notably, the two critical estimates that are necessary for both the present value of cash flow models and the earnings multiplier approach are *k* and *g*—that is, the required rate of return discount rate and the expected growth rate of earnings, cash flow, and dividends.

Using Other Relative Valuation Ratios

In addition to the *P/E* ratio, several other ratios are used by investors as indicators of relative value. Specifically, when doing an industry and company stock analysis, analysts compare these valuation ratios to similar ratios for the aggregate market, other industries, and other stocks in an industry. Therefore, it is important to become familiar with the computation and historical movements for these ratios. The specific relative valuation ratios considered are

- the price-to-book-value ratio (*P/BV*)
- the price-to-cash-flow ratio (*P/CF*)
- the price-to-sales ratio (*P/S*)

Calculation of Relative Valuation Ratios   The calculation of each of these ratios is generally straightforward with some differences in the measurement of the valuation variable (i.e., BV, CF, or S). Again, it is necessary to decide whether one uses historical data or forward values—that is, do you compare current price to the *historical* valuation variable (e.g., cash flow for the prior year) or the *future expected* variable (e.g., the expected cash flow for the industry or company). As before, the authors prefer forward valuation ratios.

When computing the *price-to-book-value (P/BV) ratio* for current valuation purposes, it is equal to the current stock price divided by the equity book value per share of the entity. When computing any of the relative valuation ratios for historical exposition purposes, we use the average price each year, which is equal to the average of the high and low prices for the year. As noted, it is necessary to determine whether you want to use historical book value (i.e., compare the average stock price for Year t to the book value at the end of Year t) or use future book value (i.e., average stock price for Year t to *estimated* book value for Year $t + 1$). Similar to the P/E ratio, when you compute a future ratio, the ratio will generally be lower and less volatile. Both sets of P/BV ratios are contained in Exhibit 12.27 and plotted in Exhibit 12.28. The future ratios are computed using *actual* values for Period $t + 1$ except for the last year (2003) that would have required 2004 values that were not available.

The *price-to-cash-flow (P/CF) ratio* is equal to the average stock price for Year t divided by either the historical or the estimated cash flow per share for the entity. Similar to most analysts, we use EBITDA for demonstration purposes, even though we contend that it is a very imperfect measure of cash flow. Again, we use actual EBITDA in Period $t + 1$ for the future ratio except for the final year when the data were not available. The data are in Exhibit 12.27 and the two series are plotted in Exhibit 12.29.

The *price-to-sales (P/S) ratio* is equal to the average stock price for Year t divided by net sales per share during Year t or an estimate of sales per share for Year $t + 1$. Again, for the future P/S ratio, we use actual sales per share during Period $t + 1$ except for the final year. The results are in Exhibit 12.27, and the two series are plotted in Exhibit 12.30.

As shown in the alternative time-series plots, all the ratios (using the $t + 1$ values) have experienced overall increases during the 12-year period as follows:

Relative Valuation Ratio	Approximate Beginning Value (1992)	Approximate Ending Value (2003)
Price/Earnings	14.58	22.00
Price/Book Value	2.56	3.00
Price/Cash Flow	5.22	7.90
Price/Sales	0.77	1.25

To understand these higher valuation ratios, it is necessary to consider what factors drive the particular valuation ratio and whether these factors have changed over time. In the case of the P/E ratio, we know from DDM that the relevant variables are k and g for the economic unit. Therefore, when attempting to explain why the P/E ratio has gone from about 15 times to 22 times, you would consider what has happened to these two variables. Without going into detail, we know that k has declined over time due to lower inflation and some evidence that the market risk premium has declined. In addition, the aggregate ROE has been fairly stable so the expected growth rate has been constant. In summary, the $k - g$ spread has declined so a higher P/E is justified. How much higher it should be is subject to estimation and debate. Subsequently, we will discuss the relevant factors for the other ratios.

Exhibit 12.27 Relative Valuation Ratios for the S&P Industrials Index

Year	Price/Book Value		Price/Cash Flow (EBITDA)		Price/Sales		Price/Earnings	
	t	$t+1$	t	$t+1$	t	$t+1$	t	$t+1$
1992	2.44	2.56	5.72	5.22	0.79	0.77	17.49	14.58
1993	2.71	2.47	5.53	4.87	0.81	0.77	15.47	13.21
1994	2.54	2.36	5.02	4.50	0.80	0.75	13.62	11.78
1995	2.81	2.68	5.36	5.14	0.89	0.87	14.03	13.34
1996	3.33	3.21	6.40	6.20	1.08	1.07	16.60	15.40
1997	4.06	3.80	7.85	7.99	1.36	1.36	19.48	20.86
1998	4.86	4.26	10.21	9.19	1.74	1.60	26.65	24.00
1999	5.47	4.89	11.81	10.87	2.06	1.97	30.83	28.15
2000	5.02	4.86	11.14	13.80	2.02	2.13	28.85	39.72
2001	3.91	4.39	11.11	11.21	1.72	1.72	31.99	27.98
2002	3.65	3.11	9.32	8.29	1.43	1.34	23.26	22.70
2003	3.02		8.03		1.29		21.98	

| Exhibit 12.28 | Time-Series Plot of the Price-to-Book-Value Ratio for the S&P Industrials Index |

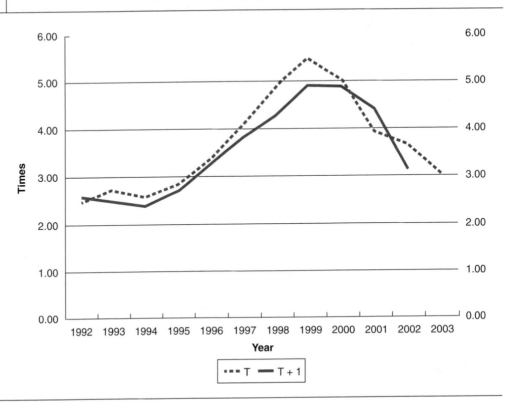

The plots also show considerable consistency between the time series using historical data for Time t and future expected data for Time $t + 1$. Given the similarity, the authors have a definite preference for using the *future* valuation variables. The point is, we know that when investors buy a stock, they are actually buying future earnings, cash flows, book values, or sales. Therefore, we will always refer to *future P/E* ratios that relate price to *expected* earnings. Although it is not always easy to obtain estimates for these alternative valuation variables beyond earnings, it is important to think in these terms if you want to use these ratios for valuation. The point is, similar to valuation using the *P/E* ratio, you can estimate the valuation variable (i.e., *BV, CF,* or Sales per share) and then apply an appropriate *future* multiple to the valuation variable to derive an estimate of intrinsic value.

MICROVALUATION OF WORLD MARKETS

Similar to our discussion at the end of the macroeconomic analysis of the market, we need to briefly consider some of the unique factors when deriving a microvaluation for markets outside the United States.

It is crucial to keep three important factors in mind. First, the basic valuation model and concepts apply globally. Specifically, value is still based on the discounted value of future cash flows whether you are in New York, London, Moscow, or Beijing. Also, the ultimate decision is still based on the relationship between estimated intrinsic value and the market price.

| Exhibit 12.29 | Time-Series Plot of the Price-to-Cash-Flow Ratio for the S&P Industrials Index |

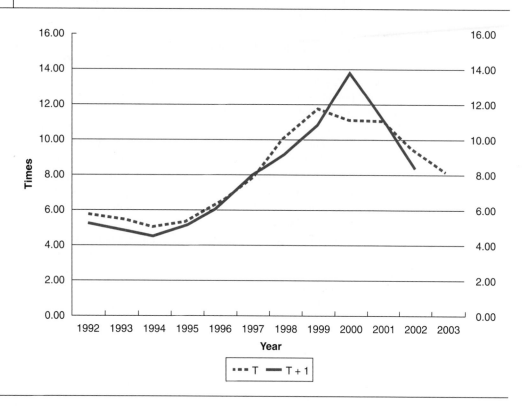

| Exhibit 12.30 | Time-Series Plot of the Price-to-Sales Ratio for the S&P Industrials Index |

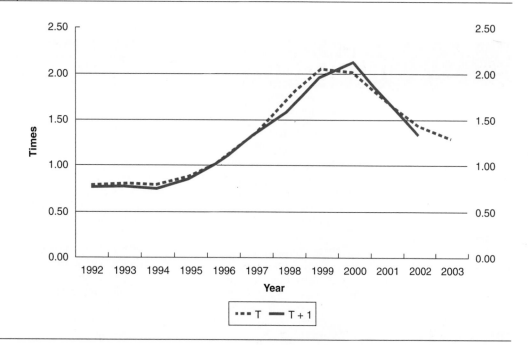

Second, while the models and concepts are the same, the input values can and will vary dramatically across countries, which means that values will differ and opportunities will differ—for example, when stocks appear overpriced in the United States they may be undervalued in Japan or Australia.

Third, the valuation of nondomestic markets will almost certainly be more onerous because of several additional variables or constraints that must be considered. The most obvious is the currency, because you must estimate a value in the local currency but you also must estimate potential changes in the value of the foreign currency relative to the U.S. dollar. The difficulty of estimating these changes or attempting to hedge this currency risk (if it is possible) becomes an added risk factor discussed in Chapter 1—exchange rate risk.

While we are considering additional risks, it is necessary to consider country or political risk, which can be very significant in many countries. This risk generally *cannot* be hedged away.

The problem is that investors in U.S. stocks generally do not think about this as a concern, even during elections. The only change in this has been terrorist risk since the 9/11 event, and this is also present around the world. The point is, country risk must be evaluated and estimated when investing outside the United States.

As a result of the two added risk factors (exchange rate risk and country risk), the required rate of return on these securities will generally be higher than for domestic stock. Notably, these added risks can be offset by higher growth expectations, such as in China and India. As always, it is the analyst who does the best estimates of these critical valuation variables (k and g) who will be the superior analyst.

Another added burden relates to different accounting conventions in alternative countries that means the analyst must understand how they account for various items and how this impacts cash flows, etc. The good news on this item is the constant movement toward international accounting standards that should substantially reduce this problem—when the international standards become resolved and are widely adopted.

In summary, as money management becomes more global and industry analysis considers global constituents, it will be a necessary part of your life to evaluate stock markets around the globe and keep these added factors in mind.

The Internet   *Investments Online*

The Internet contains a great many sources for economic and financial market information. Many banks, research firms, investment banks, stock brokerages, and government agencies feature data, analysis, or commentaries on their Web sites. Here are a few of the many web resources you may wish to examine:

http://www.morganstanley.com The home page of Morgan Stanley includes the Global Economic Forum. The Forum is a compilation of reports filed by 15 economists located around the world and is updated daily. Prior reports are available in an archive. This site features daily updates of the MSCI indexes of international markets and links to Morgan Stanley Equity Research pages.

http://www.globalinsight.com This firm, formed by the combination of DRI and WEFA, has a home page featuring a number of links to resources. Items of interest include a feature that gives a weekly analysis of international and U.S. economic news as well as current economic data.

http://www.yardeni.com Edward Yardeni is associated with Oak Associates. His home page contains links to market information, country information (including emerging markets), a weekly economic briefing, and studies of longer-term trends affecting the economy and financial markets. His site features a number of pull-down slides which provide links to Federal Reserve and U.S. Treasury information, as well as information about demographics, consumers, and marketing.

http://www.whitehouse.gov/fsbr/esbr.html This is the Economics Statistics Briefing Room of the White House Web site. It includes links to data produced by a number of federal agencies.

http://www.federalreserve.gov The home page of the Board of Governors of the Federal Reserve System. This site features data and information on a number of Fed-related activities, including research, money supply trends, Board actions, consumer information, and reports to Congress. The site includes links to each of the 12 regional Federal Reserve Banks and to a number of foreign central banks. The Philadelphia Fed's site includes access to the Livingston Surveys and Surveys of Professional Forecasters; both provide professional economists' judgments about future economic trends. The URL is **http://www.phil.frb.org/econ/forecast/index.html**

Other sites of interest include:

http://www.worldbank.org Home page of the World Bank features data and articles.

http://www.bankamerica.com From the Web site of the Bank of America, type "economic indicators" in the site's search function. Pages feature U.S. and global economic reviews, outlooks, and investment strategies.

http://www.spglobal.com/index.html is a Standard & Poor's site for their index services; it contains current headlines, weekly features, and information on the S&P stock indexes.

http://www.bis.org/cbanks.htm has links to over 100 of the world's central banks.

http://www.nabe.com The National Association of Business Economists home page includes links to a number of economic information-related sites and data sources. Links include a number of sources of international data, from both U.S. and overseas statistical agencies. The site contains helpful industry information, too, with links to the *U.S. Industrial Outlook*, Federal Trade Commission, and a number of industry trade association sites.

http://www.conference-board.org is the Web site of The Conference Board, publishers of the Index Leading Economic Indicators and many other U.S. and non-U.S.-based economic indicators.

U.S. Government Sources

It should come as no surprise that the main source of information on the U.S. economy is the federal government, which issues a variety of publications on the topic.

- *Federal Reserve Bulletin* (**http://www.federalreserve.gov/pubs/bulletin**) is a monthly publication issued by the Board of Governors of the Federal Reserve System. It is the primary source for almost all monetary data. In addition, it contains figures on financial markets, including interest rates and some stock-market statistics; data for corporate finance, including profits, assets, and liabilities of corporations; extensive nonfinancial statistics on output, the labor force, and the GNP; and a major section on international finance.

- *Survey of Current Business* (**http://www.bea.doc.gov/bea/pubs.htm**) is a monthly publication issued by the U.S. Department of Commerce that gives details on national income and production figures. It is probably the best source for current, detailed information on all segments of the gross domestic product (GDP) and national income. It also contains industrial production data for numerous segments of the economy.

- The Bureau of Labor Statistics (**http://www.stats.bls.gov**) provide data on various measures of inflation, unemployment, and productivity.

- Congressional Budget Office (**http://www.cbo.gov**), conducts a number of economic studies on behalf of the U.S. Congress. Its Web site contains much economic data. The President's Council of Economic Advisors (**http://www.whitehouse.gov/cea/**) contains policy analyses done at the president's request.

- Economic Indicators (**http://www.gpoaccess.gov/indicators/ browse.html**) is a monthly publication prepared for the Joint Economic Committee by the Council of Economic Advisers. It contains monthly and annual data on output, income, spending, employment, production, prices, money and credit, federal finance, and international economies.

- The Quarterly Financial Report (QFR) (**http://www.census.gov/csd/qfr**) is prepared by the Federal Trade Commission and contains aggregate statistics on the financial position of U.S. corporations. Based on an extensive quarterly sample survey, the QFR presents estimated statements of income and retained earnings, balance sheets, and related financial and operating ratios for all manufacturing corporations. The publication also includes data on mining and trade corporations. The statistical data are classified by industry and, within the manufacturing group, by size.

- Each January, the President of the United States prepares the *Economic Report of the President* (**http://www.access.gpo.gov/eop**), which he transmits to the Congress. The report indicates what has transpired during the past year and discusses the current environment and what the president considers the major economic problems to face the country during the coming year. An appendix contains statistical tables relating to income, employment, and production. The tables typically provide annual data from the 1940s and in some instances from 1929.
- *Statistical Abstract of the United States* (**http://www.census.gov/statab/www/**), published annually since 1878, is the standard summary of statistics on the social, political, and economic organization of the United States. Prepared by the Bureau of the Census, it is designed to serve as a convenient statistical reference and as a guide to other statistical publications and sources.

Publications of Federal Reserve Banks

The Federal Reserve System, whose URL is **http://www.federalreservebanks.org**, is divided into 12 Federal Reserve districts; each of the Federal Reserve district banks has a research department that issues periodic reports. A notable source of analysis and data is the St. Louis Federal Reserve Bank (**http://www.stlouisfed.org/**), which publishes statistical releases that contain extensive national and international data (**http://research.stlouisfed.org/ fred2/**). The Philadelphia Fed's site includes access to the *Livingston Surveys* and *Surveys of Professional Forecasters;* both provide professional economists' judgments about future economic trends. The Philadelphia Fed's URL is (**http://www.phil.frb.org/econ/index.html**).

Non-U.S. Economic Data

In addition to data on the U.S. economy, data on other countries in which you might consider investing are also important to acquire. Some of the available sources follow.

- The Economic Intelligence Unit (**http://www.eiu.com**) publishes separate quarterly reviews and

an annual supplement covering the economic and business conditions and outlook for many countries. For each country the reviews consider the economy, trade and finance, trends in investment and consumer spending, along with comments on its political environment. Tables contain data on economic activity and foreign trade.

- The Organization for Economic Cooperation and Development, or OECD (**http://www.oecd.org**), publishes semiannual surveys showing recent trends and policies and assessing short-term prospects for each country. An annual volume, *Historical Statistics*, contains annual percent change data for the most recent 20 years.
- *The Economist* (**http://www.economist.com**) prepares country reports that contain extensive economic and demographic statistics on more than 60 countries around the world. Of greater importance is a detailed discussion that critically analyzes the current economic and political environment in the country and considers the future outlook. You may subscribe to reports for a selected list of countries or for all of them. The reports are updated twice yearly.
- *United Nations Statistical Yearbook* (**http://un.org/depts/unsd/sd_economic.htm**) is a basic reference book that contains extensive economic statistics on all UN countries (population, construction, industrial production, and so on). United Nations Yearbook of International Trade Statistics, (**http://www.un.org**) is an annual report on import statistics over a four-year period for each of 166 countries. The commodity figures for each country are given by commodity code. *United Nations Yearbook of National Accounts Statistics* is a comprehensive source of national account data that contains detailed statistics for countries on domestic product and consumption expenditures, national income, and disposable income for a 12-year period.
- *International Financial Statistics*, a monthly publication (with a yearbook issue) of the International Monetary Fund (**http://www.imf.org**), is an essential source of current financial statistics such as exchange rates, fund position, international liquidity, money and banking statistics, interest rates (including LIBOR), prices, and production.
- *International Monetary Fund Balance of Payments Yearbook* (**http://www.imf.org**) is a two-part publication. The first part contains detailed balance-of-payments figures for more than 110 countries, and the second part contains world totals for balance-of-payments components and aggregates.

SUMMARY

In earlier chapters, we emphasized the importance of analyzing the aggregate markets before beginning any industry or company analysis. You must assess the economic and security market outlooks and their implications regarding the bond, stock, and cash components of your portfolio. Then you proceed to consider the best industry or company.

- Two techniques are used to make the market decision: (1) the macroeconomic technique, which is based on the relationship between the aggregate economy and the stock market; (2) the microeconomic technique, which determines future market values by applying the two valuation approaches discussed in Chapter 11 to the aggregate stock market.
- The economy and the stock market have a strong, consistent relationship, but the stock market generally turns before the economy does. Therefore, the best macroeconomic projection techniques use economic series that likewise lead the economy, and possibly the stock market. The Conference Board leading indicator series (which includes stock prices) is one possibility.
- The money supply has been suggested as a predictor of aggregate market behavior based on its relationship to the economy. Some early studies indicated a strong relationship between the money supply and stock prices and suggested that money supply changes turned before stock prices. Subsequent studies confirmed the link between money supply and stock prices, but indicated that stock prices turn with or before money supply changes. The most recent results show that monetary policy has an important impact on security market returns and also affects how stocks relate to other variables.

- Our microanalysis of the U.S. equity market considered both approaches to equity analysis—the present value of cash flow techniques and the relative valuation ratio techniques. The cash flow techniques provided a range of estimates, most of which indicated that the market was fully valued, which implies that the rates of return on common stock in the near term will be lower than the long-run historical returns.
- We considered four relative valuation ratios, including the earnings multiple (P/E) approach where we discussed a two-step approach that included estimating EPS and the P/E ratio based on the DDM. As a result, we generated a specific intrinsic market value. The other three ratios (P/BV; P/CF; and P/S) were defined and explained in anticipation of using them during industry and company analysis where the relative valuation technique compares an industry to the market and relates a company to both its industry and the aggregate market. The goal is to evaluate the relative value position of an industry or a stock. This initial analysis of the valuation ratios was intended to demonstrate the computations involved and show the increase in all the ratios. Subsequent analysis will consider what variables drive these relative valuation ratios and evaluate whether these variables have changed in a way that justifies current values.
- Finally, although we applied both sets of valuation techniques to the stock market in the United States, we know it is necessary to do a similar analysis for non-U.S. markets.

Following this aggregate market analysis, the next step is industry analysis, which is considered in the following chapter.

SUGGESTED READINGS

Baker, H. Kent, ed. *Improving the Investment Decision Process—Better Use of Economic Inputs in Security Analysis and Portfolio Management.* Charlottesville, VA: AIMR, 1992.

Copeland, Tom, Tim Koller, and Jack Murrin. *Valuation,* 3rd ed. New York: Wiley, 2001.

Damodaran, Aswath. *Investment Valuation.* New York: Wiley, 1996.

Diermeier, Jeffrey J. "Capital Market Expectations: The Macro Factors." In *Managing Investment Portfolios: A Dynamic Process,* 2nd ed., eds. John L. Maginn and Donald L. Tuttle. Boston: Warren Gorham and Lamont, 1990.

Fama, Eugene F., and Kenneth French. "Business Conditions and Expected Returns on Stocks and Bonds." *Journal of Financial Economics* 25, no. 1 (November 1989).

Finnerty, John D., and Dean Leistikow. "The Behavior of Equity and Debt Risk Premiums." *Journal of Portfolio Management* 19, no. 4 (Summer 1993).

Shackalford, Aaron L., ed. *Economic Analysis for Investment Professionals.* Charlottesville, VA: AIMR, 1997.

Solnik, Bruno. *Predictable Time-Varying Components of International Asset Returns.* Charlottesville, VA: AIMR, 1993.

QUESTIONS

1. Why would you expect a relationship between economic activity and stock price movements?
2. At a lunch with some business associates, you discuss the reason for the relationship between the economy and the stock market. One of your associates contends that she has heard that stock prices typically turn before the economy does. How would you explain this phenomenon?
3. Explain the following statements: (a) There is a strong, consistent relationship between money supply changes and stock prices. (b) Money supply changes cannot be used to predict stock price movements.
4. You are informed of the following estimates: nominal money supply is expected to grow at a rate of 7 percent, and GDP is estimated to grow at 4 percent. Explain what you think will happen to stock prices during this period and the reason for your expectation.
5. The current rate of inflation is 3 percent, and long-term Treasury bonds are yielding 7 percent. You estimate that the rate of inflation will increase to 6 percent. What do you expect to happen to long-term bond yields? Compute the effect of this change in inflation on the price of a 15-year, 10 percent coupon bond with a current yield to maturity of 8 percent.
6. Some observers contend that it is harder to estimate the effect of a change in interest rates on common stocks than on bonds. Discuss this contention.
7. An investor is convinced that the stock market will experience a substantial increase next year because corporate earnings are expected to rise by at least 12 percent. Do you agree or disagree? Why or why not?
8. Find at least three sources of historical information on nominal and real GDP. Find two sources of an annual estimate of nominal GDP.
9. To arrive at an estimate of the *net profit margin*, why would you spend time estimating the operating profit margin and work down?
10. You are convinced that capacity utilization next year will decline from 82 percent to about 79 percent. Explain what effect this change will have on the operating profit margin.
11. You see an estimate that hourly wage rates will increase by 6 percent next year. How does this affect your estimate of the operating profit margin? What other information do you need to determine the effect of this wage rate increase and why do you need it?
12. It is estimated that, next year, hourly wage rates will increase by 7 percent and productivity will increase by 5 percent. What would you expect to happen to unit labor cost? Discuss how this unit labor cost estimate would influence your estimate of the operating profit margin.
13. Assume that each of the following changes is independent (i.e., except for this change, all other factors remain unchanged). In each case, indicate what will happen to the earnings multiplier and explain why.
   a. The return on equity increases.
   b. The aggregate debt–equity ratio declines.
   c. Overall productivity of capital increases.
   d. The dividend-payout ratio declines.

PROBLEMS

1. Prepare a table showing the percentage change for each of the last 10 years in (a) the Consumer Price Index (all items), (b) nominal GDP, (c) real GDP (in constant dollars), and (d) the GDP deflator. Discuss how much of nominal growth was due to *real* growth and how much was due to inflation.

2. *CFA Examination Level I*
There has been considerable growth in recent years in the use of economic analysis in investment management. Further significant expansion may lie ahead as financial analysts develop greater skills

in economic analysis and these analyses are integrated more into the investment decision-making process. The following questions address the use of economic analysis in the investment decision-making process:

a. (1) Differentiate among leading, lagging, and coincident indicators of economic activity, and give an example of each.

(2) Indicate whether the leading indicators are one of the best tools for achieving above-average investment results. Briefly justify your conclusion.

b. Interest rate projections are used in investment management for a variety of purposes. Identify three significant reasons why interest rate forecasts may be important in reaching investment conclusions.

c. Assume you are a fundamental research analyst following the automobile industry for a large brokerage firm. Identify and briefly explain the relevance of three major economic time series, economic indicators, or economic data items that would be significant to automotive industry and company research.

 3. *CFA Examination Level III*

A U.S. pension plan hired two offshore firms to manage the non-U.S. equity portion of its total portfolio. Each firm was free to own stocks in any country market included in Capital International's Europe, Australia, and Far East Index (EAFE) and free to use any form of dollar and/or nondollar cash or bonds as an equity substitute or reserve. After three years had elapsed, the records of the managers and the EAFE Index were as shown:

SUMMARY: CONTRIBUTIONS TO RETURN

	Currency	Country Selection	Stock Selection	Cash/Bond Allocation	Total Return Recorded
Manager A	(9.0%)	19.7%	3.1%	0.6%	14.4%
Manager B	(7.4)	14.2	6.0	2.8	15.6
Composite of A&B	(8.2)	16.9	4.5	1.7	15.0
EAFE Index	(12.9)	19.9	—	—	7.0

You are a member of the plan sponsor's pension committee, which will soon meet with the plan's consultant to review manager performance. In preparation for this meeting, you go through the following analysis:

a. Briefly describe the strengths and weaknesses of each manager, relative to the EAFE Index data.

b. Briefly explain the meaning of the data in the Currency column.

4. You are told that nominal GDP will increase by about 10 percent next year. Using Exhibit 12.15 and the regression equation, what increase would you expect in corporate sales? How would this estimate change if you gave more weight to the recent observations?

5. Currently, the dividend-payout ratio (*D/E*) for the aggregate market is 60 percent, the required return (*k*) is 11 percent, and the expected growth rate for dividends (*g*) is 5 percent.

a. Compute the current earnings multiplier.

b. You expect the *D/E* ratio to decline to 50 percent, but you assume there will be no other changes. What will be the *P/E*?

c. Starting with the initial conditions, you expect the dividend-payout ratio to be constant, the rate of inflation to increase by 3 percent, and the growth rate to increase by 2 percent. Compute the expected *P/E*.

d. Starting with the initial conditions, you expect the dividend-payout ratio to be constant, the rate of inflation to decline by 3 percent, and the growth rate to decline by 1 percent. Compute the expected *P/E*.

6. As an analyst for Charlotte, Chelle, and Denise, you are forecasting the market *P/E* ratio using the dividend discount model. Because the economy has been expanding for 9 years, you expect the dividend-payout ratio will be at its low of 40 percent and that long-term government bond rates will

rise to 7 percent. Because investors are becoming less risk averse, the equity risk premium will decline to 3 percent. As a result, investors will require a 10 percent return, and the return on equity will be 12 percent.
   a. What is the expected growth rate?
   b. What is your expectation of the market *P/E* ratio?
   c. What will be the value for the market index if the expectation is for earnings per share of $63.00?
7. You are given the following estimated per share data related to the S&P Industrials Index for the year 2007:

Sales	$1,020.00
Depreciation	45.00
Interest expense	18.00

You are also informed that the estimated operating profit margin is 0.152 and the tax rate is 32 percent.
   a. Compute the estimated EPS for 2007.
   b. Assume that a member of the research committee for your firm feels that it is important to consider a range of operating profit margin (OPM) estimates. Therefore, you are asked to derive both optimistic and pessimistic EPS estimates using 0.149 and 0.155 for the OPM and holding everything else constant.
8. Given the three EPS estimates in Problem 7, you are also given the following estimates related to the market earnings multiple:

	Pessimistic	Consensus	Optimistic
D/E	0.65	0.55	0.45
Nominal *RFR*	0.10	0.09	0.08
Risk premium	0.05	0.04	0.03
ROE	0.10	0.13	0.16

   a. Based on the three EPS and *P/E* estimates, compute the high, low, and consensus intrinsic market value for the S&P Industrials Index in 2007.
   b. Assuming that the S&P Industrials Index at the beginning of the year was priced at 1,600, compute your estimated rate of return under the three scenarios from Part a. Assuming your required rate of return is equal to the consensus, how would you weight the S&P Industrials Index in your global portfolio?
9. You are analyzing the U.S. equity market based upon the S&P Industrials Index and using the present value of free cash flow to equity technique. Your inputs are as follows:

Beginning FCFE: $40.00	
k = 0.09	
Growth Rate:	
Year 1–3:	9%
4–6:	8%
7 and beyond	7%

   a. Assuming that the current value for the S&P Industrials Index is 1,600, would you underweight, overweight, or market weight the U.S. equity market?
   b. Assume that there is a 1 percent increase in the rate of inflation—what would be the market's value and how would you weight the U.S. market? State your assumptions.

Chapter 13

Industry Analysis*

After you read this chapter, you should be able to answer the following questions:

- Is there a difference between the returns for alternative industries during specific time periods? What is the implication of these results?
- Is there consistency in the returns for individual industries over time? What do these results imply regarding industry analysis?
- Is the performance for firms within an industry consistent? What is the implication of these results for industry and company analysis?
- Is there a difference in risk among industries? What are the implications of these results for industry analysis?
- What happens to risk for individual industries over time? What does this imply for industry analysis?
- What are the stages in the industrial life cycle and how does the stage in an industry's life cycle affect the sales estimate for an industry?
- What are the five basic competitive forces that determine the intensity of competition in an industry and, thus, its rate of return on capital?
- How does an analyst determine the value of an industry using the DDM assuming constant growth or two-stage growth?
- How does an analyst determine the value of an industry using the free cash flow to equity (FCFE) model assuming constant growth or two-stage growth?
- What are the steps involved in estimating earnings per share for an industry?
- How does the procedure for estimating the operating profit margin differ for the aggregate market versus an industry?
- What is involved in a macroanalysis of the industry earnings multiplier?
- What are the steps in the microanalysis of an industry earnings multiplier?
- How do you determine if an industry's estimated multiplier is relatively high or low?
- How do analysts compare relative valuation ratios such as P/BV, P/CF, and P/S to comparable market ratios?

*The authors acknowledge input to the discussions on "The Business Cycle and Industry Sectors" and "Structural Economic Changes" provided by Professor Edgar Norton of Illinois State University.

- How do industries differ in terms of what dictates their return on assets?
- What are some of the unique factors that must be considered in global industry analysis?

When asked about his or her job, a securities analyst typically will reply that he or she is an oil analyst, a retail analyst, or a computer analyst. A widely read trade publication, *The Institutional Investor*, selects an All-American analyst team each year based on industry groups. Investment managers talk about being in or out of the metals, the autos, or the utilities. This constant reference to industry groups is because most professional investors are extremely conscious of differences among alternative industries and organize their analyses and portfolio decisions according to industry groups.

We acknowledge the importance of industry analysis as a component of the three-step fundamental analysis procedure initiated in Chapter 11. Industry analysis is the second step as we progress toward selecting specific firms and stocks for our investment portfolio. In Chapter 12, we did a macroanalysis and valuation of the stock market to decide whether the expected rate of return from investing in common stocks was equal to or greater than our required rate of return—that is, should we overweight, market weight, or underweight stocks? In this chapter, we analyze different industries to determine if the intrinsic value of an industry is equal to or greater than its market price. Based on this relationship, we decide how to weight the industry in our stock portfolio. In Chapter 14, we analyze the individual companies and stocks within alternative industries.

In the first section, we discuss the results of several studies that will help us identify the benefits and uses of industry analysis. Following that, we present and demonstrate the two approaches for valuing industries. Another section raises questions that are unique to industry analysis: we consider the impact of the competitive environment within an industry on potential industry returns. We conclude the chapter with a discussion of global industry analysis, because many industries transcend U.S. borders and compete on a worldwide basis.

WHY DO INDUSTRY ANALYSIS?

Investment practitioners perform industry analysis because they believe it helps them isolate investment opportunities that have favorable return-risk characteristics. We likewise have recommended it as part of our three-step, top-down investment analysis approach. What exactly do we learn from an industry analysis? Can we spot trends in industries that make them good investments? Are there unique patterns in the rates of return and risk measures over time in different industries? In this section, we survey the results of studies that addressed the following set of questions designed to pinpoint the benefits and limitations of industry analysis:

- Is there a difference between the returns for alternative industries during specific time periods?
- Will an industry that performs well in one period continue to perform well in the future? That is, can we use past relationships between the market and an individual industry to predict future trends for the industry?
- Is the performance of firms within an industry consistent over time?

Several studies also considered questions related to risk:

- Is there a difference in the risk for alternative industries?
- Does the risk for individual industries vary, or does it remain relatively constant over time?

Based on the results of these studies, we come to some general conclusions about the value of industry analysis. In addition, this assessment helps us interpret the results of our subsequent industry valuation.

Cross-Sectional Industry Performance

To find out if the rates of return among different industries varied during a given period (e.g., during the year 2005), researchers compared the performance of alternative industries during a specific time period. Similar performance during specific time periods for different industries would indicate that industry analysis is not necessary. For example, assume that during 2005, the aggregate stock market experienced a rate of return of 10 percent and the returns for *all* industries were bunched between 9 percent and 11 percent. If this similarity in performance persisted over time, you might question whether it was worthwhile to do industry analysis to find an industry that would return 11 percent when random selection would provide a return of about 10 percent (the average return).

Studies of the annual performance by numerous industries found that different industries have consistently shown *wide dispersion in their rates of return* (e.g., a typical range of rates of return during a year will be from minus 40 percent to plus 50 percent). A specific example is the year 2004. As shown in Exhibit 13.1, although the aggregate stock market experienced a total return of almost 11 percent (the S&P 500), the industry performance ranged from 97.15 percent (general mining) to −21.65 percent (semiconductors). These results imply that *industry analysis is important and necessary* to uncover these substantial performance differences—that is, it helps identify both unprofitable and profitable opportunities.

Exhibit 13.1	How the Dow Jones U.S. Industry Groups Fared during 2004

BEST PERFORMERS		WORST PERFORMERS	
% Change 12/31/2003 to 12/31/2004		% Change 12/31/2003 to 12/31/2004	
General mining	97.15	Semiconductors	−21.65
Consumer electronics	73.82	Aluminum	−16.82
Steel	66.21	Automobiles	−16.08
Internet	60.82	Pharmaceuticals	−10.20
Coal	57.65	Gold mining	−8.46
Hotels	44.86	Elect. components and equip.	−7.86
Trucking	44.40	Airlines	−6.61
Mobile telecommunications	43.84	Soft drinks	−5.11
Tires	40.59	Media agencies	−0.91
Oil exploration and production	40.45	Broadcasting and enter.	0.75
Transportation services	39.89	Publishing	1.24
Marine transportation	37.25	Brewers	1.29
Home construction	35.79	Food retailers and whole.	1.40
Oil equip. and services	34.51	Full line insurance	1.75
Real estate holding dev.	33.00	Waste and disposal serv.	1.78
Recreational products	33.00	Paper	2.75
Bldg. materials and fixtures	32.28	Auto parts	3.32
Gambling	31.74	Telecommunications equip.	3.58
Health care providers	30.60	Drug retailers	3.88
Footwear	30.53	Investment services	6.94

Source: *The Wall Street Journal,* 2 January 2005.

Industry Performance over Time

Another group of researchers questioned whether individual industries that perform well in one time period would continue to perform well in subsequent time periods, or at least outperform the aggregate market in the later time period. In this case, investigators found *almost no association* in individual industry performance year to year or over sequential rising or falling markets.

These time-series studies imply that past performance alone does *not* help project future industry performance. The results do *not*, however, negate the usefulness of industry analysis. They simply confirm that variables that affect industry performance change over time and each year it is necessary to estimate the current intrinsic value for individual industries on the basis of future estimates of the relevant variables and compare this to the market price.

Performance of the Companies within an Industry

Other studies were designed to determine whether there is consistency in the performance of companies *within* an industry. If all the firms within an industry performed consistently during a specified time period, investors would not need company analysis. In such a case, industry analysis alone would be enough because once you selected a profitable industry, you would know that all the stocks in that industry would do well.

These studies typically have found *wide dispersion* in the performance among companies in most industries. Studies by Meyers (1973) and Livingston (1977) have also shown evidence of an industry effect in specific industries, such as oil or autos, but most stocks showed a small industry effect that has been declining over time.

Implication of Dispersion within Industries   Some observers have contended that industry analysis is useless because all firms in an industry do not move together. Obviously, consistent firm performance in an industry would be ideal, as noted, because you would not need to do company analysis. For industries that have a strong, consistent industry influence, such as oil, gold, steel, autos, and railroads, company analysis is less critical than industry analsis.

Most analysts do not expect a strong industry influence, which means that a thorough *company* analysis is still necessary. Even for industries that do not have a strong industry influence, industry analysis is valuable because it is much easier to select a superior company from a good industry than to find a good company in a poor industry. By selecting the best stocks within a strong industry, you avoid the risk that your analysis and selection of a good company will be offset by poor industry performance.

Differences in Industry Risk

Although a number of studies have focused on industry rates of return, few studies have examined industry risk measures. The studies on industry risk investigated two questions: (1) Does risk differ among industries during a given time period? (2) Are industry risk measures stable over time? The study results regarding the dispersion of risk found *a wide range of risk* among different industries at a point in time, and the differences in industry risk typically widened during rising and falling markets. The results on the analysis of risk stability were positive— an analysis of the risk measures for individual industries over time indicated that they were *reasonably stable over time.*

These findings indicate that although risk measures for different industries showed substantial dispersion during a period of time, individual industries' risk measures are stable over time. This means that the analysis of industry risk is necessary, but this anaysis of risk is useful when estimating the future risk for an industry.

Summary of Research on Industry Analysis

The conclusions of the studies dealing with industry analysis are:

- During any time period, the returns for different industries vary within a wide range, which means that industry analysis is an important part of the investment process.
- The rates of return for individual industries vary over time, so we cannot simply extrapolate past industry performance into the future.
- The rates of return of firms within industries also vary, so analysis of individual companies in an industry is a necessary follow-up to industry analysis.
- During any time period, different industries' risk levels vary within wide ranges, so we must examine and estimate the risk factors for alternative industries.
- Risk measures for different industries remain fairly constant over time, so the historical risk analysis is useful when estimating future risk.

Industry Analysis Process

An important question is, How should you structure your industry analysis? In our previous analysis of the economy and the aggregate equity market for the United States or any other country, we contended that it is necessary to examine the macroeconomy for two related reasons. First, although the security markets tend to move ahead of the aggregate economy, it is recognized that the markets are driven by what happens in the economy—that is, security markets reflect the strength or weakness of the economy. Second, most of the variables that determine value for the security markets are macrovariables such as interest rates, GDP, and corporate earnings. Therefore, our analysis of the aggregate equity market contained two components—one dealing with macrovariables such as leading indicators and monetary policy and a second being microanalysis of specific variables that affect valuation.

The point is, the industry analysis process is similar—first is a *macroanalysis* of the industry to determine how this industry relates to the business cycle and what economic variables drive this industry. This part of the process will make the second component easier and better. The second component is a microvaluation of the industry using the several valuation techniques introduced earlier. As noted, macroanalysis of the industry will make the estimation of the valuation inputs of a discount rate and expected growth for earnings and cash flows relatively easy.

The specific macroanalysis topics are:

1. The business cycle and industry sectors
2. Structural economic changes and alternative industries
3. Evaluating an industry's life cycle
4. Analysis of the competitive environment in an industry

THE BUSINESS CYCLE AND INDUSTRY SECTORS

Economic trends can and do affect industry performance. By identifying and monitoring key assumptions and variables, we can monitor the economy and gauge the implications of new information on our economic outlook and industry analysis. Recall that in order to beat the market on a risk-adjusted basis, we must have forecasts that differ from the market consensus *and* we must be correct more often than not.

Exhibit 13.2	**The Stock Market and the Business Cycle**

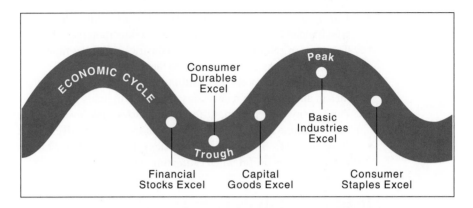

Economic trends can take two basic forms: **cyclical changes** that arise from the ups and downs of the business cycle, and **structural changes** that occur when the economy is undergoing a major change in how it functions. For example, excess labor or capital may exist in some sectors whereas shortages of labor and capital exist elsewhere. The "downsizing" of corporate America during the 1990s, transitions from socialist to market economies in Eastern Europe, and the transition in the United States from a manufacturing to a service economy are all examples of structural change.[1] Industry analysts must examine structural economic changes for the implications they hold for the industry under review.

Most observers believe that industry performance is related to the stage of the business cycle. What makes industry analysis challenging is that every business cycle is different and those who look only at history miss the evolving trends that will determine future market performance.

Switching from one industry group to another over the course of a business cycle is known as a *rotation strategy*. When trying to determine which industry groups will benefit from the next stage of the business cycle, investors need to identify and monitor key variables related to economic trends and industry characteristics.

Exhibit 13.2 presents a stylized graphic of which industry groups typically perform well in the different stages of the business cycle. Toward the end of a recession, financial stocks rise in value because investors anticipate that banks' earnings will rise as both the economy and loan demand recover. Brokerage houses become attractive investments because their sales and earnings are expected to rise as investors trade securities, businesses sell debt and equity, and there is an increase in mergers during the economic recovery. These industry selections assume that when the recession ends there will be an increase in loan demand, housing construction, and security offerings.

Once the economy begins its recovery, consumer durable firms that produce expensive consumer items, such as cars, personal computers, refrigerators, lawn tractors, and snow blowers, become attractive investments because a reviving economy will increase consumer confidence

---

[1]An excellent discussion of structural changes in the U.S. economy and the implications of these changes for the business cycle, the stock market, and some specific industries is contained in Dudley and McKelvey (1997).

and personal income. Once businesses recognize the economy is recovering, they begin to think about modernizing, renovating, or purchasing new equipment to satisfy rising demand and reduce costs. Thus, capital goods industries such as heavy equipment manufacturers, machine tool makers, and airplane manufacturers become attractive.

Cyclical industries whose sales rise and fall along with general economic activity are attractive investments during the early stages of an economic recovery because of their high degree of operating leverage, which means that they benefit greatly from the sales increases during an economic expansion.[2] Industries with high financial leverage likewise benefit from rising sales volume.[3]

Traditionally, toward the business cycle peak, the rate of inflation increases as demand starts to outstrip supply. Basic materials industries such as oil, metals, and timber, which transform raw materials into finished products, become investor favorites. Because inflation has little influence on the cost of extracting these products and they can increase prices, these industries experience higher profit margins.

During a recession, some industries do better than others. Consumer staples, such as pharmaceuticals, food, and beverages, outperform other sectors during a recession because, although overall spending may decline, people still spend money on necessities so these "defensive" industries generally maintain their values. Similarly, if a weak domestic economy causes a weak currency, industries with large export components to growing economies may benefit because their goods become more cost competitive in overseas markets.

We have identified certain industries that typically make attractive investments over the course of the business cycle. Remember, investors should not invest based upon the current economic environment because the efficient market has already incorporated current economic news into security prices. Rather, it is necessary to *forecast* important economic variables and invest accordingly. The following subsections consider how changes in several important economic variables may affect different industries.

Inflation

As noted in several chapters, higher inflation is generally negative for the stock market, because it causes higher market interest rates, it increases uncertainty about future prices and costs, and it harms firms that cannot pass through their cost increases. Although these adverse effects are true for most industries, some industries benefit from inflation. Natural resource industries benefit *if* their production costs do not rise with inflation, because their output will likely sell at higher prices. Industries that have high operating leverage may benefit because many of their costs are fixed in nominal (current dollar) terms whereas revenues increase with inflation. Industries with high financial leverage may also gain, because their debts are repaid in cheaper dollars.

Interest Rates

Financial institutions, including banks, are typically adversely impacted by higher rates because they find it difficult to pass on these higher rates to customers (i.e., lagged adjustment). High interest rates clearly harm the housing and the construction industry, but they

---

[2]As discussed in Chapter 1, operating leverage arises from the existence of fixed costs in a firm's operating structure. Industries with large fixed expenses will have high degrees of operating leverage. This means a small percentage change in sales can result in a large percentage change in operating income.

[3]As noted in Chapter 10, financial leverage arises from fixed financial costs (that is, interest expense) in a firm's capital structure. Industries that have extensive debt financing (such as banks or utilities) will have net income that is sensitive to small changes in operating income.

might benefit industries that supply the do-it-yourselfer. High interest rates also benefit retirees whose income is dependent on interest income.

International Economics

Both domestic and overseas events may cause the value of the U.S. dollar to fluctuate. A weaker U.S. dollar helps U.S. industries because their exports become comparatively cheaper in overseas markets while the goods of foreign competitors become more expensive in the United States. A stronger dollar has an opposite effect. Economic growth in world regions or specific countries benefits industries that have a large presence in those areas. The creation of free trade zones, such as the European Community and the North American Free Trade Zone, assist industries that produce goods and services that previously faced quotas or tariffs in partner countries.

Consumer Sentiment

Because it comprises about two-thirds of GDP, consumption spending has a large impact on the economy. Optimistic consumers are more willing to spend and borrow money for expensive goods, such as houses, cars, new clothes, and furniture. Therefore, the performance of consumer cyclical industries will be affected by changes in consumer sentiment and by consumers' willingness and ability to borrow and spend money.

STRUCTURAL ECONOMIC CHANGES AND ALTERNATIVE INDUSTRIES

Influences other than the economy are part of the business environment. Demographics, changes in technology, and political and regulatory environments also can have a significant effect on the cash flow and risk prospects of different industries.

Demographics

In the past 50 years, the United States has had a baby boom and a baby bust and is now enjoying a baby boomlet as members of the baby-boom generation (those born between the end of World War II and the early 1960s) have children. The influx of the baby boom and the "graying of the baby boom" have had a large impact on U.S. consumption, from advertising strategies to house construction to concerns over social security and health care. The study of demographics includes much more than population growth and age distributions. Demographics also includes the geographical distribution of people, the changing ethnic mix in a society, and changes in income distribution. Wall Street industry analysts carefully study demographic trends and attempt to project their effect on different industries and firms.

During the period from 1990 to 2005, the fastest-growing age groups in the United States were those in their 40s and 50s, teens, and those over 70; among the declining groups were those between ages 18 and 24. As of the early 2000s, more than one in eight Americans are 65 years of age or older. The changing age profile of Americans has implications for resource availability, namely, a possible shortage of entry-level workers leading to an increase in labor costs and difficulty in finding qualified persons to replace the retiring baby boomers. The aging U.S. population also affects U.S. savings patterns, as people in the 40 to 60 age bracket usually save more than younger people. This is good for the financial services industry, which offers assistance to those who want to invest their savings. Alternatively, fewer younger workers and more "saving seniors" may have a negative impact on some industries, such as the retailing industry.

Lifestyles

Lifestyles deal with how people live, work, form households, consume, enjoy leisure, and educate themselves. Consumer behavior is affected by trends and fads. The rise and fall of designer jeans, chinos, and other styles in clothes illustrate the sensitivity of some markets to changes in consumer tastes. The increase in divorce rates, dual-career families, population shifts away from cities, and computer-based education and entertainment have influenced numerous industries, including housing, restaurants, automobiles, convenience and catalog shopping, services, and home entertainment. From an international perspective, some U.S.-brand goods—from blue jeans to movies—have a high demand overseas. They are perceived to be more in style and perhaps higher quality than items produced domestically. Sales in several industries have benefited from this exercise of consumer choice overseas.

Technology

Trends in technology can affect numerous industry factors including the product or service and how it is produced and delivered. There are literally dozens of examples of changes that have taken or are taking place due to technological innovations. For example, demand has fallen for carburetors on cars because of electronic fuel-injection technology. The engineering process has changed because of the advent of computer-aided design and computer-aided manufacturing. Perpetual improvement of designs in the semiconductor and microprocessor industry has made that industry a difficult one to evaluate. Innovations in process technology allowed steel minimills to grow at the expense of large steel producers. Advances in technology allow some plant sites and buildings to generate their own electricity, bypassing their need for power from the local electric utility. Trucks have reduced railroads' market share in the long-distance carrier industry. The information superhighway is becoming a reality and encouraging linkages between telecommunications and cable television systems. Changes in technology have spurred capital spending in technological equipment as a way for firms to gain competitive advantages. The future effect of the Internet is astronomical.

The retailing industry is a user of new technology. Some forecasters envision relationship merchandising, in which customer databases will allow closer links between retail stores and customer needs. Rather than doing market research to focus on aggregate consumer trends, specialized retailers can offer products that particular consumer segments desire in preferred locations. Technology may allow retailers to become more organizationally decentralized and geographically diversified.

Major retailers use bar-code scanning, which speeds the checkout process and allows the firm to track inventory and customer preferences. Use of customer credit cards allows firms to track customer purchases and send customized sales announcements. Electronic data interchange (EDI) allows the retailer to electronically communicate with suppliers to order new inventory and pay accounts payable. Electronic funds transfer allows retailers to move funds quickly and easily between local banks and headquarters.

Politics and Regulations

Because political change reflects social values, today's social trend may be tomorrow's law, regulation, or tax. The industry analyst needs to project and assess political changes relevant to the industry under study.

Some regulations and laws are based on economic reasoning. Due to utilities' positions as natural monopolies, their rates must be reviewed and approved by a regulatory body.[4] Some regulation involves social ends. For example, the Food and Drug Administration protects consumers by reviewing new drugs. Public and worker safety concerns spurred creation of the Consumer Product Safety Commission, the Environmental Protection Agency, and OSHA. Notably, heavy regulation of an industry can result in increasing a firm's costs but also restricting entry into the industry.

Regulatory changes have affected numerous industries. A recent example is the numerous regulations and inspections following the September 11, 2001, attacks. Changing regulations and technology are bringing participants in the financial services industry—banking, insurance, investment banking, and investment services—together.

Regulations and laws affect international commerce. International tax laws, tariffs, quotas, embargoes, and other trade barriers affect different industries and global commerce in various ways.

An interesting example is how the retail industry is affected by numerous regulatory factors. First is the minimum-wage law, which impacts many retail employees. A second factor is employer-paid health insurance, which would dramatically affect the labor costs of labor-intensive service industries, such as retailing. Third, because goods must first be delivered to the stores, regulations that affect the cost of shipping by airplane, ship, or truck will affect retailers' costs. Finally, trends toward the reduction of tariffs and quotas will allow retailers to offer imported goods at lower prices (e.g., Wal-Mart), which will expand their international production (outsourcing).

EVALUATING THE INDUSTRY LIFE CYCLE

An insightful analysis when predicting industry sales and trends in profitability is to view the industry over time and divide its development into stages similar to those that humans progress through: birth, adolescence, adulthood, middle age, old age. The number of stages in this **industry life cycle analysis** can vary based on how much detail you want. A five-stage model would include

1. Pioneering development
2. Rapid accelerating growth
3. Mature growth
4. Stabilization and market maturity
5. Deceleration of growth and decline

Exhibit 13.3 shows the growth path of sales during each stage. The vertical scale in logs reflects *rates* of growth, whereas the arithmetic horizontal scale has different widths representing different, unequal time periods. To estimate industry sales, you must predict the length of time for each stage. This requires answers to such questions as: How long will an industry grow at an accelerating rate (Stage 2)? How long will it be in a mature growth phase (Stage 3) before its sales growth stabilizes (Stage 4) and then declines (Stage 5)?

Besides being useful when estimating sales, this analysis of an industry's life cycle also can provide some insights into profit margins and earnings growth, although these profit measures do not necessarily parallel the sales growth. The profit margin series typically peaks

---

[4]Technology can change natural monopolies. We mentioned earlier how some firms are generating their own electrical power. Another example is that, currently, numerous states are allowing electric utilities to compete for customers.

Exhibit 13.3 | **Life Cycle of an Industry**

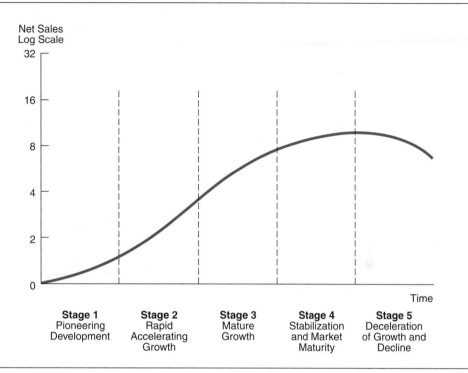

very early in the total cycle and then levels off and declines as competition is attracted by the early success of the industry.

The following is a brief description of how these stages affect sales growth and profits:

1. *Pioneering development.* During this start-up stage, the industry experiences modest sales growth and very small or negative profit margins and profits. The market for the industry's product or service during this time period is small, and the firms involved incur major development costs.

2. *Rapid accelerating growth.* During this rapid growth stage, a market develops for the product or service and demand becomes substantial. The limited number of firms in the industry face little competition, and individual firms can experience substantial backlogs. The profit margins are very high. The industry builds its productive capacity as sales grow at an increasing rate as the industry attempts to meet excess demand. High sales growth and high profit margins that increase as firms become more efficient cause industry and firm profits to explode. During this phase, profits can grow at over 100 percent a year as a result of the low earnings base and the rapid growth of sales and net profit margins.

3. *Mature growth.* The success in Stage 2 has satisfied most of the demand for the industry goods or service. Thus, future sales growth may be above normal but it no longer accelerates. For example, if the overall economy is growing at 8 percent, sales for this industry might grow at an above normal rate of 15 percent to 20 percent a year. Also, the rapid growth of sales and the high profit margins attract competitors to the industry, which causes an increase in supply and lower prices, which means that the profit margins begin to decline to normal levels.

4. *Stabilization and market maturity.* During this stage, which is probably the longest phase, the industry growth rate declines to the growth rate of the aggregate economy or its industry segment. During this stage, investors can estimate growth easily because sales correlate highly with an economic series. Although sales grow in line with the economy, profit growth varies by industry because the competitive structure varies by industry, and by individual firms within the industry because the ability to control costs differs among companies. Competition produces tight profit margins, and the rates of return on capital (e.g., return on assets, return on equity) eventually become equal to or slightly below the competitive level.

5. *Deceleration of growth and decline.* At this stage of maturity, the industry's sales growth declines because of shifts in demand or growth of substitutes. Profit margins continue to be squeezed, and some firms experience low profits or even losses. Firms that remain profitable may show very low rates of return on capital. Finally, investors begin thinking about alternative uses for the capital tied up in this industry.

Although these are general descriptions of the alternative life cycle stages, they should help you identify the stage your industry is in, which should help you estimate its potential sales growth. Obviously, everyone is looking for an industry in the early phases of Stage 2 and hopes to avoid industries in Stage 4 or Stage 5. Comparing the sales and earnings growth of an industry to similar growth in the economy should help you identify the industry's stage within the industrial life cycle.

ANALYSIS OF INDUSTRY COMPETITION

Similar to the sales forecast that can be enhanced by the analysis of the industrial life cycle, an industry earnings forecast should be preceded by the analyses of the competitive structure for the industry. Specifically, a critical factor affecting the profit potential of an industry is the intensity of competition in the industry, as Porter (1980a, b, 1985) has discussed.

Competition and Expected Industry Returns

Porter's concept of **competitive strategy** is described as the search by a firm for a favorable competitive position in an industry. To create a profitable competitive strategy, a firm must first examine the basic competitive structure of its industry because the potential profitability of a firm is heavily influenced by the profitability of its industry. After determining the competitive structure of the industry, you examine the factors that determine the relative competitive position of a firm within its industry. In this section, we consider the competitive forces that determine the competitive structure of the industry. In the next chapter, our discussion of company analysis will cover the factors that determine the relative competitive position of a firm within its industry.

Basic Competitive Forces Porter believes that the **competitive environment** of an industry (the intensity of competition among the firms in that industry) determines the ability of the firms to sustain above-average rates of return on invested capital. As shown in Exhibit 13.4, he suggests that five competitive forces determine the intensity of competition and that the relative effect of each of these five factors can vary dramatically among industries.

1. *Rivalry among the existing competitors.* For each industry analyzed, you must judge if the rivalry among firms is currently intense and growing, or if it is polite and stable. Rivalry

Exhibit 13.4 | **Force Driving Industry Competition**

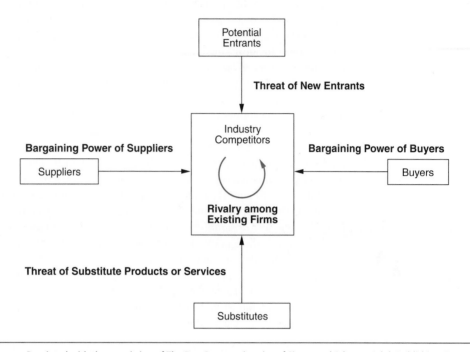

Source: Reprinted with the permission of The Free Press, an imprint of Simon and Schuster Adult Publishing Group, from *Competitive Strategy: Techniques for Analyzing Industries and Competitors* by Michael E. Porter. Copyright © 1980, 1998 by The Free Press.

increases when many firms of relatively equal size compete in an industry. When estimating the number and size of firms, be sure to include foreign competitors. Further, *slow growth* causes competitors to fight for market share and increases competition. *High fixed costs* stimulate the desire to sell at the full capacity, which can lead to price cutting and greater competition. Finally, look for *exit barriers,* such as specialized facilities or labor agreements. These can keep firms in the industry despite *below-average* or negative rates of return.

2. *Threat of new entrants.* Although an industry may have few competitors, you must determine the likelihood of firms entering the industry and increasing competition. *High barriers to entry,* such as low current prices relative to costs, keep the threat of new entrants low. Other barriers to entry include the need to invest large financial resources to compete and the availability of capital. Also, substantial economies of scale give a current industry member an advantage over a new firm. Further, entrants might be discouraged if success in the industry requires extensive distribution channels that are hard to build because of exclusive distribution contracts. Similarly, high costs of switching products or brands, such as those required to change a computer or telephone system, keep competition low. Finally, government policy can restrict entry by imposing licensing requirements or limiting access to materials (lumber, coal). Without some of these barriers, it might be very easy for competitors to enter an industry, increasing the competition and driving down potential rates of return.

3. *Threat of substitute products.* Substitute products limit the profit potential of an industry because they limit the prices firms in an industry can charge. Although almost everything

has a substitute, you must determine how close the substitute is in price and function to the product in your industry. As an example, the threat of substitute glass containers hurts the metal container industry. Glass containers kept declining in price, forcing metal container prices and profits down. In the food industry, consumers constantly substitute between beef, pork, chicken, and fish. The more commoditylike the product, the greater the competition and the lower the profit margins.

4. *Bargaining power of buyers.* Buyers can influence the profitability of an industry because they can bid down prices or demand higher quality or more services by bargaining among competitors. Buyers become powerful when they purchase a large volume relative to the sales of a supplier (e.g., Wal-Mart, Home Depot). The most vulnerable firm is a one-customer firm that supplies a single large manufacturer, as is common for auto parts manufacturers or software developers. Buyers will be more conscious of the costs of items that represent a significant percentage of the firm's total costs. This consciousness increases if the buying firm is feeling cost pressure from its customers. Also, buyers who know a lot about the costs of supplying an industry will bargain more intensely—for example, when the buying firm supplies some of its own needs and buys from the outside.

5. *Bargaining power of suppliers.* Suppliers can alter future industry returns if they increase prices or reduce the quality of the product or the services they provide. The suppliers are more powerful if they are few and if they are more concentrated than the industry to which they sell and if they supply critical inputs to several industries for which few, if any, substitutes exist. In this instance, the suppliers are free to change prices and services they supply to the firms in an industry. When analyzing supplier bargaining power, be sure to consider labor's power within each industry.

An investor needs to analyze these competitive forces to determine the intensity of the competition in an industry and assess the effect of this competition on the industry's long-run profit potential. You should examine each of these factors and develop a relative competitive profile for each industry. You need to update this analysis of an industry's competitive environment over time, because an industry's competitive structure can and will change over time.

ESTIMATING INDUSTRY RATES OF RETURN

At this point, we have determined that industry analysis helps an investor select profitable investment opportunities and we have completed a thorough macroanalysis of the industry. Our next question is, How do we go about valuing an industry? Again, we consider the two equity valuation approaches introduced in Chapter 11—the present value of cash flows and the relative valuation ratios. Beginning with the present value of cash flow models, we demonstrate the DDM with the two-stage growth assumption and then assume constant growth for the retailing industry. Following this, we consider the present value of free cash flow (FCF) model. Subsequently, we will analyze the alternative relative valuation techniques with the price/earnings ratio and analysis of the *P/BV, P/CF,* and *P/S* ratios compared to the relative valuation ratios for the market presented in Chapter 12.

Although our investment decision is always the same, the form of the comparison depends on which valuation approach is being used. In the case of the present value of cash flow techniques, we derive a present value for the industry using our required rate of return for the industry—that is, we compare the present value of the specified cash flow versus the prevailing value of the index. If our estimated present value exceeds the prevailing index value, we should overweight the industry. Alternatively, if the *PV* of cash flows is less than the market price of the industry index, it implies that the industry is overvalued (i.e., the industry will not provide our required rate of return if acquired at the prevailing market price) and we should underweight this industry in our portfolio.

Similarly, if we use the two-step *P/E* ratio approach, we compute a current intrinsic value for the industry and compare it to the current market price. If this estimated intrinsic value exceeds the prevailing market price for the industry, you should overweight the industry; if the intrinsic value is below the market price, you should underweight the industry.

To demonstrate industry analysis, we use Standard and Poor's retailing index to represent industrywide data. This retailing index (hereinafter referred to as the RET industry) contains about 30 individual companies from several retailing sectors including two drug stores. Therefore, it should be reasonably familiar to most observers, and it is consistent with the subsequent company analysis of Walgreens.

Valuation Using the Reduced Form DDM

Recall that the reduced form DDM is

13.1
$$P_i = \frac{D_1}{k - g}$$

where:

P_i = the price of Industry *i* at Time *t*
D_1 = expected dividend for Industry *i* in Period 1 equal to $D_0 (1 + g)$
k = the required rate of return on the equity for Industry *i*
g = the expected long-run growth rate of earnings and dividend for Industry *i*

As always, *the two major estimates for any valuation model are k and g.* We will discuss each of these at this point in the chapter with the understanding that we will also use these estimates subsequently when applying the two-step, price/earnings ratio technique for valuation.

Estimating the Required Rate of Return *(k)*   Because the required rate of return *(k)* on all investments is influenced by the risk-free rate and the expected inflation rate, the differentiating factor in this case is the risk premium for the retailing industry versus the market. In turn, we discussed the risk premium in terms of fundamental factors, including business risk *(BR),* financial risk *(FR),* liquidity risk *(LR),* exchange rate risk *(ERR),* and country (political) risk *(CR).* Alternatively, you can estimate the risk premium based on the CAPM, which implies that the risk premium is a function of the systematic risk (beta) of the asset. Therefore, to derive an estimate of the industry's risk premium, you should examine the *BR, FR, LR, ERR,* and *CR* for the industry and compare these industry risk factors to those of the aggregate market. Alternatively, you can compute the systematic risk (beta) for the industry and compare this to the market beta of 1.0. Prior to calculating a beta for the industry, we briefly discuss the fundamental risk factors for the industry.

Business risk is a function of relative sales volatility and operating leverage. As we will see when we examine the sales and earnings for the industry, the annual percentage changes in retailing sales were less volatile than aggregate sales as represented by PCE. Also, the OPM (operating profit margin) for retail stores was less volatile than the S&P Industrials Index OPM. Therefore, because both sales and the OPM for the retailing industry have been less volatile than the market, operating profits are substantially less volatile. This implies that the business risk for the retailing industry is *below average.*

The *financial risk* for this industry is difficult to judge because of widespread use of building leases in the industry that are not included on the balance sheet. As a result, the reported data on debt to total capital or interest coverage ratios indicate that the *FR* for this industry is substantially below the market. Assuming substantial use of long-term lease contracts, when these are capitalized, the retailing industry probably has financial risk *about equal* to the market. While the data is not available to capitalize leases for the industry, we did demonstrate how to do this for a company in Chapter 10, and this is considered in the company analysis in Chapter 14.

To evaluate the market *liquidity risk* for an industry, it is necessary to estimate the liquidity risk for all the firms in the industry and derive a composite view. The fact is, there is substantial variation in market liquidity among the firms in this industry. Firms such as Walgreens and Wal-Mart are fairly liquid, whereas small specialty retail chains are relatively illiquid. A conservative view is that the composite retailing industry probably has *above-average* liquidity risk.

Exchange rate risk (ERR) is the uncertainty of earnings due to changes in exchange rates faced by firms in this industry that sell outside the United States. The amount of *ERR* is determined by what proportion of sales is non-U.S., how these sales are distributed among countries, and the exchange rate volatility for these countries. This risk could range from an industry with very limited international sales (e.g., a service industry that is not involved overseas) to an industry that is clearly worldwide (e.g., the chemical or pharmaceutical industry). For a truly global industry, you need to examine the distribution of sales among specific countries because we know that the exchange rate risk varies among countries based on the volatility of exchange rates with the U.S. dollar. The *ERR* for the retailing industry would be relatively *low* because sales and earnings for the majority of retailing firms are mainly attributable to activity within the United States.

The existence of *country risk (CR)* is likewise a function of the proportion of foreign sales, the specific foreign countries involved, and the stability of the political/economic system in these countries. As noted, there is very little *CR* in the United Kingdom and Japan, but there can be substantial *CR* in China, Russia, or South Africa. Again, for the retailing industry, country risk would be relatively low because of limited foreign sales.

In summary, for the retailing industry, business risk is definitely below average, financial risk is at best equal to the market, liquidity risk is above average, and exchange rate risk and country risk are fairly low. The consensus is that the overall fundamental risk for the RET industry should be lower than for the aggregate market.

The *systematic risk* for the retailing (RET) industry is computed using the market model as follows:

13.2 $$\% \, \Delta \, RET_t = \alpha_i + \beta_i \, (\% \, \Delta \, S\&P \, 500_t)$$

where:

$\% \, \Delta \, RET_t$ = the percentage price change in the retailing (RET) index during month t
α_i = the regression intercept for the RET industry
β_i = the systematic risk measure for the RET industry equal to $Cov_{i,m}/\sigma_m^2$

To derive an estimate for the RET industry, the model specified was run with monthly data for the five-year period 2000 to 2004. The results for this regression are as follows:

$\alpha_t = 0.003$	$R^2 = 0.62$
$\beta_t = 0.82$	$DW = 1.83$
t-value = 7.40	$F = 68.37$

The systematic risk ($\beta = 0.82$) for the RET industry is clearly below unity, indicating a low-risk industry (i.e., risk less than the market). These results are quite consistent with the prior analysis of fundamental risk factors *(BR, FR, LR, ERR, CR)*.

Translating this systematic risk into a required rate of return estimate *(k)* calls for using the security market line model as follows:

13.3
$$k_i = RFR + \beta_i (R_m - RFR)$$

Recall that in Chapter 12 we derived three estimates for the required market rate of return based on alternative risk premiums (0.048 −0.085−0.108). For our purposes here, it seems like the midpoint is reasonable—that is, a nominal *RFR* of 0.045 and an R_m of 0.085. This, combined with a beta for the industry at 0.82, indicates the following:

$$k = 0.045 + 0.82 \, (0.085 - 0.045)$$
$$= 0.045 + 0.82 \, (0.04)$$
$$= 0.045 + 0.0328$$
$$= 0.0778 = 7.78\%$$

For ease of computation, we will use a *k* of 8.0% A microestimate of fundamental risk below average and a risk estimate using the CAPM likewise below average implies an industry earnings multiple *above* the market multiple, all other factors being equal.

Estimating the Expected Growth Rate *(g)* Recall that earnings and dividend growth are determined by the retention rate and the return on equity.

$$g = f \, (\text{Retention Rate and Return on Equity})$$

We have consistently broken down return on equity into the following three components:

$$\frac{\text{Net Profit}}{\text{Equity}} = \frac{\text{Net Income}}{\text{Sales}} \times \frac{\text{Sales}}{\text{Total Assets}} \times \frac{\text{Total Assets}}{\text{Equity}}$$

$$= \frac{\text{Profit}}{\text{Margin}} \times \frac{\text{Total Asset}}{\text{Turnover}} \times \frac{\text{Financial}}{\text{Leverage}}$$

Therefore, we need to examine each of these variables in Exhibit 13.5 to determine if they imply a difference in the expected growth rate for RET as compared to the aggregate market (S&P Industrials Index).

Earnings Retention Rate The retention rate data in Exhibit 13.5 indicate that the RET industry has a higher retention rate (79 percent versus 67 percent). This means that the RET industry would have a potentially *higher* growth rate, all else being the same (i.e., equal *ROE*).

Return on Equity Because the return on equity is a function of the net profit margin, total asset turnover, and a measure of financial leverage, these three variables are examined individually.

Historically, the net profit margin for the S&P Industrials Index series has been consistently higher than the margin for the RET industry. This is not surprising because retail firms typically have lower profit margins but higher turnover.

As noted, one would normally expect the total asset turnover *(TAT)* for a retail firm to be higher than the average industrial company. This expectation was confirmed because, as shown in Exhibit 13.6, the average *TAT* for the S&P Industrials Index was 0.86 versus 1.73 for the RET industry. Beyond the overall difference, the spread between the two series increased over the period. This change occurred because the *TAT* for the S&P Industrials Index series declined

Exhibit 13.5 | Earnings Multiplier for the S&P Industrials Index and the Retail Industry, and Influential Variables: 1993–2003

Year	EARNINGS MULTIPLIER (t+1)		RETENTION RATE		NET PROFIT MARGIN		TOTAL ASSET TURNOVER		RETURN ON TOTAL ASSETS		TOTAL ASSETS/ EQUITY		RETURN ON EQUITY	
	S&P Ind	Retail	S&P Ind	Retail	S&P Ind	Retail	S&P Ind	Retail	S&P Ind	Retail	S&P Ind	Retail	S&P Ind	Retail
1993	13.21	20.85	62.80	71.19	5.40	3.19	0.87	1.30	3.27	4.14	3.13	3.54	14.82	14.66
1994	11.78	23.48	66.97	72.42	6.03	3.14	0.89	1.40	4.91	4.40	3.42	3.47	18.41	15.30
1995	13.34	18.45	69.35	66.60	6.45	2.43	0.94	1.70	5.19	4.14	3.21	2.82	19.39	11.70
1996	15.40	17.66	67.47	78.26	6.58	2.87	0.95	1.77	5.62	5.06	3.32	2.81	20.84	14.27
1997	20.86	15.85	67.62	78.97	6.88	3.01	0.95	1.80	5.33	5.40	3.24	2.71	21.09	14.63
1998	24.00	21.65	64.18	82.98	6.43	3.45	0.88	1.94	4.90	6.69	3.27	2.66	18.37	17.84
1999	28.15	35.32	67.52	84.07	6.60	3.61	0.84	1.92	5.22	6.92	3.29	2.59	18.34	17.99
2000	39.72	32.53	71.73	82.31	6.90	2.86	0.86	1.96	5.45	5.61	3.41	2.57	20.15	14.42
2001	27.98	22.86	62.81	81.19	5.25	2.57	0.79	1.92	1.79	4.92	3.24	2.60	13.38	12.81
2002	22.70	16.18	66.79	86.22	6.23	3.71	0.76	1.84	1.92	6.82	3.17	2.49	15.06	16.99
2003	NA	NA	66.06	85.23	5.99	5.02	0.76	1.45	4.29	7.28	3.38	2.27	15.46	16.55
Mean	21.71	22.48	66.66	79.04	6.25	3.26	0.88	1.73	4.35	5.58	3.28	2.78	17.76	15.20

Source: *Analyst's Handbook* (New York: Standard & Poor's, 2004). Reprinted with permission.

Exhibit 13.6	Time-Series Plot of Total Asset Turnover for Retailing: 1993–2003

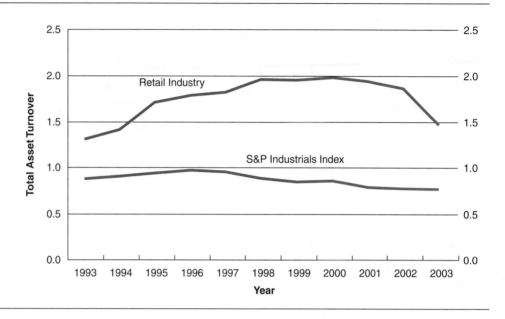

steadily over the period while the *TAT* for the RET industry experienced an overall increase, as shown in Exhibits 13.5 and 13.6. Multiplying these two ratios indicates the industry's return on total assets *(ROTA).*[5]

$$\frac{\text{Net Income}}{\text{Sales}} \times \frac{\text{Sales}}{\text{Total Assets}} = \frac{\text{Net Income}}{\text{Total Assets}}$$

When we do this for the two series, the results in Exhibit 13.5 indicate that the return on total assets *(ROTA)* for the S&P Industrials Index series went from 3.27 percent in 1993 to 4.29 percent in 2003 and averaged 4.35 percent, whereas the *ROTA* for the RET industry went from 4.14 percent to 7.28 percent and averaged 5.58 percent. Clearly, the industry *ROTA* results were superior on average.

The final component is the financial leverage multiplier (total assets/equity). As shown in Exhibit 13.5 and Exhibit 13.7, the leverage multiplier for the S&P Industrials Index experienced a small increase to 3.38, whereas the leverage multiplier for the RET industry declined, it went from 3.54 to 2.27. Although the higher financial leverage multiplier implies greater financial risk for the S&P Industrials Index series, recall that the RET industry financial leverage is understated because the leases are not capitalized.

This brings us to the final value of *ROE,* which is the product of the three ratios. The data in Exhibit 13.5 and the plot in Exhibit 13.8 indicate that the *ROE* for the RET industry was consistently lower than the market until the last two years. The average annual *ROE* was 15.20 percent for the RET industry versus 17.76 percent for the S&P Industrials Index series.

---

[5]The reader is encouraged to read Appendix 13B to this chapter, which contains a discussion of an article by Selling and Stickney (1989), wherein they analyze the components of *ROA* and relate this to an industry's economics and its strategy.

Exhibit 13.7	Time-Series Plot of Financial Leverage for Retailing: 1993–2003

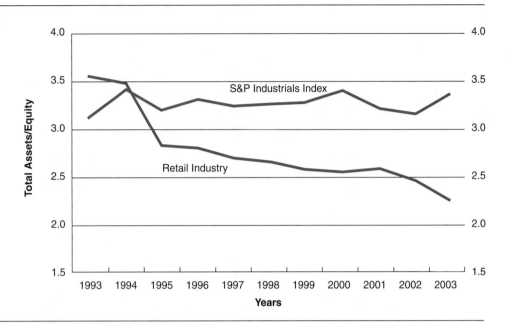

Exhibit 13.8	Time-Series Plot of Return on Equity for the S&P Industrials Index and the Retail Industry: 1993–2003

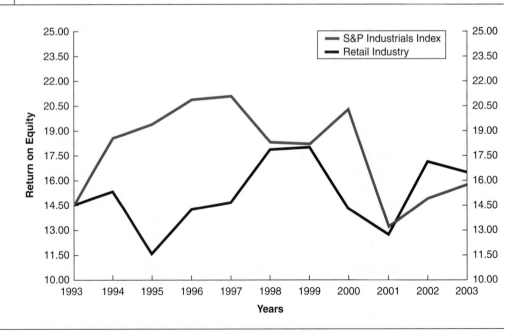

Source: *Analyst's Handbook* (New York: Standard & Poor's, 2004). Reprinted with permission.

These average percentages are quite consistent with what would be derived from multiplying the averages of the components from Exhibit 13.5 as follows:

ROE ESTIMATE BASED ON TOTAL PERIOD AVERAGES (1993–2003)								
	Profit Margin		Total Asset Turnover		Total Assets/ Equity		ROE	
S&P Industrials Index	6.25	×	0.86	×	3.28	=	17.63	
RET Industry	3.26	×	1.73	×	2.78	=	15.68	

Although examining the historical trends and the averages for each of the components is important, you should not forget that expectations of *future* performance will determine the *ROE* value for the industry. In the current case, this analysis of expectations is very important because of the positive change in relative *ROE* during the last two years (2002, 2003). As an analyst, it is necessary to determine whether the change during this period is a permanent change in the relative performance of this industry versus the market. In this case, you should be encouraged because of the strong performance of the RET industry during 2002–2003. Specifically, if you use the results for the recent five-year period (1999–2003), the *ROE* results are:

ROE ESTIMATE BASED ON RECENT FIVE-YEAR AVERAGES (1999–2003)								
	Profit Margin		Total Asset Turnover		Total Assets/ Equity		ROE	
S&P Industrials Index	6.19	×	0.80	×	3.30	=	16.34	
RET Industry	3.55	×	1.82	×	2.50	=	16.15	

Notably, using the recent results, the *ROE* results are virtually the same. Combining these recent *ROE* results with alternative retention rates provides interesting growth estimates:

GROWTH ESTIMATES BASED ON RECENT ROE WITH HISTORICAL AND RECENT RETENTION RATES						
	Recent* ROE	Historical** RR	Estimated g	Recent* ROE	Recent* RR	Estimated g
S&P Industrials Index	16.34	0.67	10.95	16.34	0.67	10.95
RET Industry	16.15	0.79	12.76	16.15	0.84	13.57

* Recent five-year average.
** Total period average.

The point is, using full-period retention results indicates a higher *g* for the RET industry. Similarly, using the retention rates for the recent five-year period indicates an even higher *g* for the industry. Given the increase in *g* for the industry when we consider the recent results, it is probably appropriate to use a growth estimate for the RET industry that is above the long-run historical estimate—that is, we will assume a near-term growth rate of 13 percent. Obviously, the best estimate of *g* would be based on an *estimate* of the three components of *ROE* for the *future* five years.

Combining the Estimates   At this point, we have the following estimates:

$$k = 0.080$$
$$g = 0.130$$
$$D_0 = \$3.10 \text{ (Estimated 2004 Dividends)}$$
$$D_1 = \$3.10 \times 1.13 = \$3.50 \text{ (Estimated Dividend for 2005)}$$

Because of the inequality between k and g (this g is above k and above the long-run market norm of about 7 percent and probably cannot be sustained), we need to evaluate this industry using the temporary growth company model discussed in Chapter 12. We will assume the following growth pattern:

2005–2007	0.130
2008–2010	0.110
2011–2013	0.090
2014–onward	0.070

Using these estimates of k and this growth pattern, the computation of value for the industry using the DDM is contained in Exhibit 13.9.

These computations imply a value of $490.48 compared to a price for the industry index of about $465.00 in mid-2005. Therefore, according to this valuation model and these k and g estimates, this industry is about 5 percent undervalued at this time. As will be shown, a fairly small change in the $k - g$ spread can have a large effect on the estimated value.

If we assumed a constant growth rate of 7 percent from the beginning and a D_1 of $3.96 the value would be as follows:

$$P = \frac{3.96}{(0.080 - 0.070)} = \frac{3.96}{0.010} = 396.00$$

Exhibit 13.9 | **Dividend Discount Calculations**

Year	Estimated Dividend	Discount Factor @ 8.0%	Present Value of Dividend
2005	3.50	—	—
2006	3.96	.9259	3.67
2007	4.47	.8573	3.83
2008	4.97	.7938	3.95
2009	5.51	.7350	4.05
2010	6.12	.6806	4.17
2011	6.67	.6302	4.20
2012	7.27	.5835	4.24
2013	7.92	.5402	4.28
Continuing Value[a]	848.00	.5402	$458.09
		Total Value	$490.48

[a]Constant Growth Rate = 7%

Continuing Value: $\dfrac{D_1}{k - g} = \dfrac{\$7.92(1.07)}{0.080 - 0.070} = \dfrac{\$8.48}{0.010} = \$848.00$

While this valuation implies the industry is overvalued, it is clearly a low estimate of value since it assumes the base growth rate of 7 percent from the beginning. The point is, the industry is undervalued assuming strong growth in the next few years, but overvalued if one estimates only market growth. Clearly, the valuation is heavily dependent on the growth estimate.

Industry Valuation Using the Free Cash Flow to Equity (FCFE) Model

Similar to the presentation in Chapter 11, we initially define the FCFE series and present the series for the recent 11-year period, including an estimate for 2004 in Exhibit 13.10. Given these data, we will consider the historical growth rates for the components and for the final FCFE series as inputs to estimating future growth for the valuation models. You will recall that FCFE is defined (measured) as follows:

Net Income
+ Depreciation expense
− Capital expenditures
− Δ in working capital
− Principal debt repayments
+ New debt issues

As noted, the FCFE data inputs and final annual value of FCFE for the RET industry for the period 1993–2004 is contained in Exhibit 13.10 along with 5-year and 10-year growth rates of the components. Using this data, we derive an estimate using the FCFE model under two scenarios: (1) a constant growth rate from the present, and (2) a two-stage growth rate assumption.

The Constant Growth Rate FCFE Model   We know that the constant growth rate model requires that the growth rate (g) be lower than the required rate of return (k), which we have specified as 8.00 percent. In the current case, this is difficult because the 10-year growth rate exceeds this. Still, in order to use the model, we assume a 10 percent growth in 2005 and 7 percent long-run growth in subsequent years. The result is as follows:

$$g = 0.07 \text{ (Long-Run Growth Beginning in 2006)}$$
$$k = 0.080$$
$$\text{FCFE (2004)} = \$9.71$$
$$\text{FCFE (2005)} = \$9.71 (1.10) = \$10.68 = \text{FCFE}_0$$

$$V = \frac{\text{FCFE}_1}{k - g}$$
$$= \frac{10.68 (1.07)}{0.080 - 0.070} = \frac{11.43}{0.01}$$
$$= 1{,}143$$

This $1,143 value exceeds the industry price of about $465 that prevailed in mid-2005. This implies that the industry is undervalued and should be overweighted in the portfolio. Notably, even if the long-run growth rate was only 6 percent, the estimated value would be $571 which would also imply undervaluation.

The Two-Stage Growth FCFE Model   As before, we assume a period of above-average growth for several years followed by a second period of constant growth at 7 percent. The period of above-average growth will be as follows based on an estimated initial 10 percent growth rate of FCFE, which is lower than what was used for dividends because the FCFE

Exhibit 13.10 | **Components of Free Cash Flow to Equity for the Retail Industry**

Year	Net Income	Depreciation Expense	Capital Expenditures	Working Capital	Change in Working Capital	Principal Repayment	New Debt Issues	Total FCFE
1993	5.45	2.76	7.37	23.18	23.18	-	-	-22.34
1994	6.20	3.05	8.51	25.52	2.34	0.69	1.42	-1.60
1995	5.06	3.77	8.93	30.50	4.98	-0.21	7.62	-5.08
1996	6.67	4.27	8.28	29.54	-0.96	0.37	-0.01	3.62
1997	7.56	4.80	9.06	29.99	0.45	-0.75	1.92	2.85
1998	9.52	5.24	10.51	28.02	-1.97	-1.75	0.11	6.22
1999	10.92	6.01	12.93	24.67	-3.35	1.76	1.50	7.35
2000	9.44	6.52	15.60	23.24	-1.43	1.86	0.84	1.79
2001	9.04	7.25	15.76	33.66	10.42	-2.46	6.55	-9.89
2002	13.21	7.00	14.23	33.21	-0.45	2.11	1.42	6.43
2003	19.29	9.11	15.70	51.11	17.90	0.77	2.80	-5.20
2004E	20.00	9.60	16.50	54.00	2.89	1.50	2.00	9.71
5-Year Growth Rate*	17.81%	12.21%	9.06%	NM	NM	NM	NM	NM
10-Year Growth Rate*	15.55%	13.00%	8.39%	NM	NM	NM	NM	NM

* The growth rates do not include the 2004 estimates.
E = estimate
NM = not meaningful

series has been fairly erratic over the past 11 years including several years when the FCFE was negative.

2005	10%
2006	10%
2007	9%
2008	9%
2009	8%
2010	8%
2011–onward	7%

Assuming a k of 8.0 percent and an FCFE of $9.71 in 2004, $10.68 in 2005, and $11.75 in 2006, the value for the industry is as shown in Exhibit 13.11. These results are very encouraging for the industry because the computed value of $1,241 is substantially above the recent market price of about $465. This apparent undervaluation would indicate that the industry should be overweighted in the portfolio.

Notably, the alternative present value of cash flow models have generated a fairly wide range of intrinsic values as follows:

Model	Computed Value
Constant growth DDM	$490
Two-stage growth DDM	$396
Constant growth FCFE	$1,143
Two-stage growth FCFE	$1,241

Because of this wide range of estimated values compared to the recent market price of $465, one indicates overvaluation and three indicate undervaluation, it is clear that a critical variable is the $k - g$ spread.

Exhibit 13.11	**Computation of RET Industry Value Using the FCFE Model and Two-Stage Growth**

Year	FCFE	Discount Factor @ 0.080	Present Value
2006	11.75	.9259	10.88
2007	12.81	.8573	10.98
2008	13.96	.7938	11.08
2009	15.07	.7350	11.08
2010	16.28	.6806	11.08
Continuing Value[a]	1,742	.6806	1,185.61
		Total Present Value	$1,240.71

[a] $\dfrac{16.28\ (1.07)}{0.080 - 0.070} = \dfrac{17.42}{0.01} = 1,742$

INDUSTRY ANALYSIS USING THE RELATIVE VALUATION APPROACH

This section contains a discussion and demonstration of the relative valuation ratio techniques: (1) price/earnings ratios (*P/E*), (2) the price to book value ratios (*P/BV*), (3) price to cash flow ratios (*P/CF*), and (4) price to sales ratios (*P/S*). Again, we will begin with the detailed demonstration of the *P/E* ratio approach, which provides a specific valuation and an estimated rate of return for the industry based upon its intrinsic value that equals an estimate of future earnings per share and an industry multiple.

The analysis of the other relative valuation ratios is also more meaningful because we can compare the industry valuation ratios to the market valuation ratios while considering what factors affect the specific valuation ratios.

The Earnings Multiple Technique

You will recall that the earnings multiple technique is a two-step process that involves (1) a detailed estimation of future earnings per share, and (2) an estimate of an appropriate earnings multiplier (*P/E* ratio) based on a consideration of *P/E* determinants derived from the DDM.

Estimating Earnings per Share   To estimate earnings per share, you must start by estimating sales per share. The first part of this section describes three techniques that provide help and insights for the sales estimate. Next, we derive an estimate of earnings per share, which implies a net profit margin for the industry. As in Chapter 12 where we estimated earnings per share for a stock market series, we begin with the operating profit margin, which leads to an estimate of operating profits. Then we subtract estimates of depreciation expense and interest expense and apply a tax rate to arrive at an estimate of earnings per share.

Forecasting Sales per Share   Assuming an analyst has completed the macroanalysis of the industry that included (1) considering how the industry is impacted by the business cycle, (2) what structural changes have occurred within the industry, and (3) where the industry is in its life cycle, the analyst would have a strong start regarding a sales estimate for the industry. At this point, we would make suggestions regarding two minor estimation techniques (time series and input-output analysis) and one major technique that should be considered for almost all industries (a specific analysis of the industry-economy relationship).

Time-Series Analysis   A simple time-series plot of the sales for an industry versus time can be very informative regarding the pattern and the rate of growth for industry sales. Analyzing this series along with designations of business cycle periods (expansions and recessions) and notations regarding major events will provide further insights. Finally, for many industries, it is possible to extrapolate the time series to derive an estimate of sales. For industries that have experienced consistent growth, this can be a very useful estimate, especially if it is a new industry that has not developed a history with the economy. If the sales growth has been at a constant rate, you should do the time-series plot on semi-log paper where the constant growth shows as a straight line.

Input-Output Analysis   Input-output analysis is another way to gain insights regarding the outlook for an industry by separating industries that supply the input for a specific industry from those that get its output. In other words, we want to identify an industry's suppliers and customers. This will help us identify (1) the future demand from customers and (2) the ability of suppliers to provide the goods and services required by the industry. The goal is to determine the long-run sales outlook for the industry's suppliers and its major customers. To extend this analysis to global industries, we must include worldwide suppliers and customers.

Industry-Economy Relationships The most rigorous and useful analysis involves comparing sales for an industry with one or several aggregate economic series that are related to the goods and services produced by the industry. The specific question is, What economic variables influence the demand for this industry? Notably, you should be thinking of numerous factors that will have an impact on industry sales, *how* these economic variables will impact demand, and how the factors might interact. In the following example, we will demonstrate this industry-economy technique for the retailing industry (RET).

Demonstrating a Sales Forecast The RET industry includes retailers of basic necessities, including pharmaceuticals and medical supplies and nonmedical products, such as food, and clothing. Therefore, we want a series that (1) reflects broad consumption expenditures and (2) gives weight to food and clothing. The economic series we consider are personal consumption expenditures (PCE) and PCE food, clothing, and shoes. Exhibit 13.12 contains the aggregate and per-capita values for the two series.

A casual analysis of these time series indicates that although personal consumption expenditures (PCE) have experienced reasonably steady growth of about 5.7 percent a year during this period, PCE food and clothes has grown at a slower rate of about 4 percent. As a result, as shown in the exhibit's last column, food and clothes as a percentage of all PCE has declined from 20.6 percent in 1993 to only 17.7 percent in 2003. Obviously, as an analyst, you would be pleased because even though sales of food and clothing have grown slower than over-all PCE, retailing sales have grown faster than both of them at about 8.5 percent.

The scatterplot in Exhibit 13.13 indicates a strong linear relationship between retail sales per share and sales of food, clothing, and shoes. Although not shown, there also is a good relationship with PCE. Therefore, if you can accurately estimate changes in these economic series, you should be able to estimate expected sales for RET.

As the industry being analyzed becomes more specialized, you need a more individual-ized economic series that reflects the demand for the industry's product. The selection of an appropriate economic series is one place where an analyst can demonstrate knowledge and innovation. There also can be instances where industry sales are dependent on several compo-nents of the economy, in which case you should probably consider a multivariate model that would include two or more economic series. For example, if you were dealing with the tire industry, you might want to consider new-car production, new-truck production, and a series that would reflect the replacement tire demand.

You also should consider *per-capita* personal consumption expenditures. Although aggre-gate PCE increases each year, there also is an increase in the aggregate population, so the increase in PCE per capita (the average PCE for each adult and child) will be less than the increase in the aggregate series. As an example, during 2003, aggregate PCE increased about 5.2 percent, but per-capita PCE increased only 4.2 percent. Finally, an analysis of the relation-ship between changes in an economic variable and changes in industry sales will indicate how the two series move together and would be sensitive to any changes in the relationship. Using annual percentage changes provides the following regression model:

13.4 $\% \, \Delta \text{ Industry Sales} = \alpha_i + \beta_i \, (\% \, \Delta \text{ in Economic Series})$

The size of the β_i coefficient should indicate how closely the two series move together. As-suming the intercept (α_i) is close to zero, a slope (β_i) value of 1.00 would indicate relatively equal percentages of change (e.g., this would indicate that a 10 percent increase in PCE typi-cally is associated with a 10 percent increase in industry sales). A β_i of less than unity would imply that industry sales are not as volatile annually as the economy is. This analysis and the levels relationship reflected in Exhibit 13.13 would help you find an economic series that closely reflects the demand for the industry's products; it also would indicate the form of the relationship.

Exhibit 13.12 | **S&P Retail Sales and Various Economic Series: 1993–2003**

Year	Retail Sales ($/Share)	Personal Consumption Expenditures ($ Billions)	PCE Food, Clothes, and Shoes ($ Billions)	PER CAPITA Personal Consumption Expenditures (Dollars)	PER CAPITA PCE Food, Clothes, and Shoes (Dollars)	Food, Clothing, and Shoes as a Percentage of PCE
1993	170.86	4,477.90	921.80	17,204.00	3,541.91	20.59
1994	197.21	4,743.30	958.70	18,004.00	3,639.21	20.21
1995	208.11	4,975.80	982.60	18,665.00	3,686.27	19.75
1996	232.78	5,256.80	1,018.90	19,490.00	3,778.36	19.39
1997	251.33	5,547.40	1,054.30	20,323.00	3,863.15	19.01
1998	276.12	5,879.50	1,100.70	21,291.00	3,986.38	18.72
1999	302.62	6,282.50	1,159.40	22,491.00	4,151.17	18.46
2000	329.76	6,739.40	1,222.90	23,862.00	4,330.57	18.15
2001	352.27	7,055.00	1,265.60	24,723.00	4,435.71	17.94
2002	355.62	7,376.10	1,307.90	25,592.00	4,538.09	17.73
2003	383.89	7,760.90	1,371.70	26,663.00	4,712.95	17.68
Mean Annual Growth	8.49%	5.66%	4.06%	4.48%	2.90%	−1.51%

Source: *Analyst's Handbook* (New York: Standard & Poor's, 2004); and *Economic Report of the President* (Washington, DC: U.S. Government Printing Office, 2003).

Exhibit 13.13 | **Scatter Plot of Retail Sales per Share and PCE—Food, Clothing, and Shoes: 1993–2003**

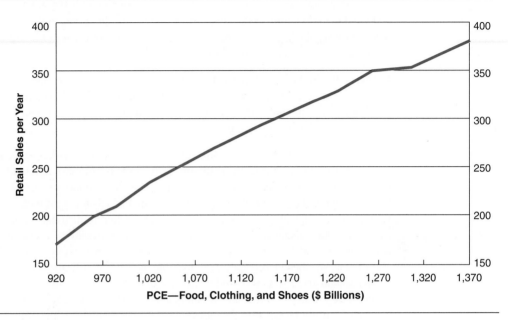

Source: *Financial Analyst's Handbook* (New York: Standard & Poor's, 2004); and *Economic Report of the President* (Washington, DC: U.S. Government Printing Office, 2003).

As indicated, there was a good relationship between retailing sales and PCE—Food, Clothing, and Shoes. The specific relationship as indicated by the regression was:

13.5   % Δ Retail Stores Sales = 4.40   +   0.55 (%Δ PCE − Food, Clothing, and Shoes)
                    (t values)   (2.17)   (1.92)
                    $r^2 = 0.34$

Given the results for this regression, the specific sales forecast begins with an estimate of aggregate PCE growth for the years in question (i.e., 2004 and 2005). Because of the importance of PCE as a component of the economy, several estimates are available. The next step is to estimate the proportion of PCE spent on food, clothing, and shoes. As noted, this proportion has declined from 20.6 percent to 17.7 percent. You apply this proportion estimate to the PCE estimate and derive an estimate of the percent change in PCE—Food, Clothing, and Shoes that is used in the regression model to derive a sales estimate for Retail Store Sales.

To demonstrate this process, we examined several economic sources which indicated that nominal PCE increased by 6.1 percent in 2004 (to $8,231 billion) and the projection was for an increase in 2005 of 5.6 percent to $8,694 billion. Regarding the percent of PCE spent on food, clothing, and shoes, we expect this proportion to continue to decline to 17.55 percent in 2004 and 17.40 in 2005. This implies values for PCE—Food, Clothing, and Shoes of $1,444.5 billion in 2004 and $1,512.8 billion in 2005, which implies growth of 5.3 percent in 2004 and 4.7 percent in 2005. Using these percentages in the Equation 13.5 regression provides retail stores sales growth estimates of 7.3 percent for 2004 ($411.91) and 7.0 percent for 2005 ($440.74). These sales growth rates are somewhat conservative relative to the long-run results for this industry.

Forecasting Earnings per Share   After the sales forecast, it is necessary to estimate the industry's profitability based on an analysis of the industry income statement. An analyst should also benefit from the prior macroanalysis that considered where the industry is in its life cycle, which impacts its profitability. How does this industry relate to the business cycle and what does this imply regarding profit margins at this point in the cycle? Most important, what did you conclude regarding the competitive environment in the industry and what does this mean for pricing and profitability of sales?

Industry Profit Margin Forecast   Similar to the aggregate market, the net profit margin is the most volatile and the hardest margin to estimate directly. Alternatively, it is suggested that you begin with the operating profit margin (EBITDA/Sales) and then estimate depreciation expense, interest expense, and the tax rate.

The Industry's Operating Profit Margin   Recall that in the market analysis, we analyzed the factors that should influence the economy's operating profit margin, including capacity utilization, unit labor cost, inflation, and net exports. The most important variables were capacity utilization and unit labor cost. We cannot do such an analysis for most industries because the relevant variables typically are not available for individual industries. As an alternative, we can assume that movements in these industry profit margin variables are related to movements in similar economic variables. For example, when an increase in capacity utilization for the aggregate economy exists, there is probably a comparable increase in utilization for the auto industry or the chemical industry. The same could be true for unit labor cost. If there is a stable relationship between these variables for the industry and the economy, you would expect a relationship to exist between the profit margins for the industry and the economy. Although it is not necessary that the relationship be completely linear, it is important for the relationship (whatever it is) to be generally stable.

The operating profit margin (*OPM*) for the S&P Industrials Index and the retail (RET) index is presented in Exhibit 13.14. The time-series plot in Exhibit 13.15 indicates that the S&P Industrials Index *OPM* experienced a steady increase from 1993 through 2000, followed by a strong decline during the recession year 2001. The margin was flat in 2002 and had a small recovery in 2003. The *RET OPM* likewise experienced a fairly steady increase that peaked in 1999, followed by small declines in 2000 and 2001, a clear recovery in 2002 and a record high in 2003. The analysis of the relationship between the *OPM* for the market and industry using regression analysis was not useful, so it is not discussed. These results indicate that the best estimate for the RET industry can be derived from the *OPM* time-series plot using what we know about the changing competitive environment and profit trends in the retail business. It is a matter of judgment for each specific industry whether you use regression analysis and/or the time-series analysis. The point is, any such mathematical analysis should be considered a supplement to the economic analysis of the competitive environment for the industry.

Either regression analysis or time-series techniques can be useful tools, but *neither technique should be applied mechanically.* You should be aware of any unique factors affecting the specific industry, such as price wars, contract negotiations, building plans, or foreign competition. An analysis of these unique events is critical when estimating the final gross profit margin or when estimating a range of industry profit margins (optimistic, pessimistic, most likely).

Beyond this discussion, which is primarily concerned with an estimate of the near-term *OPM,* it also is important to consider the long-term profitability of the industry based on the competitive structure of the industry as discussed previously.

Industry Depreciation   The next step is estimating industry depreciation, which typically is easier because the series generally is increasing; typically the only question is by how much. As shown in Exhibit 13.14, the depreciation series for RET increased every year since 1993. The time-series plots in Exhibit 13.16 relate depreciation for the S&P Industrials Index and the

Exhibit 13.14 Profit Margins and Component Expenses for the S&P Industrials Index and the Retail Industry

YEAR	EBITDA ($)		EBITDA MARGIN (%)		DEPRECIATION EXPENSE ($)		INTEREST EXPENSE ($)		TAX RATE (%)		NET PROFIT MARGIN (%)	
	S&P Ind	Retail	S&P Ind	Retail	S&P Ind	Retail	S&P Ind	Retail	S&P Ind	Retail	S&P Ind	Retail
1993	94.02	10.87	14.70	6.36	31.39	2.76	14.74	2.43	29.78	33.29	5.40	3.19
1994	106.91	13.11	15.91	6.65	32.61	3.05	14.56	1.90	34.06	35.62	6.03	3.14
1995	119.18	14.11	16.66	6.78	35.62	3.77	15.25	2.81	33.32	39.26	6.45	2.43
1996	124.27	16.85	16.87	7.24	36.90	4.27	14.17	3.01	34.59	37.84	6.58	2.87
1997	128.18	18.65	17.29	7.42	38.10	4.80	13.46	2.60	32.63	38.18	6.88	3.01
1998	125.93	21.58	17.04	7.82	40.40	5.24	14.21	2.99	32.37	36.36	6.43	3.45
1999	139.85	25.45	17.45	8.41	42.20	6.01	14.97	2.76	35.24	38.27	6.60	3.61
2000	151.98	25.46	18.12	7.72	43.80	6.52	16.59	3.09	35.90	39.45	6.90	2.86
2001	122.68	26.77	15.44	7.60	46.40	7.25	15.96	3.18	29.34	40.88	5.25	2.57
2002	121.61	29.53	15.38	8.30	36.80	7.00	15.18	2.72	30.08	36.91	6.23	3.71
2003	136.6	40.07	16.12	10.44	43.50	9.11	15.00	3.33	34.99	36.82	5.99	5.02

Source: *Analyst's Handbook* (New York: Standard & Poor's, 2004). Reprinted with permission.

Exhibit 13.15	**Time-Series Plot of the Operating Profit Margins for the S&P Industrials Index and the Retail Stores Industry: 1993–2003**

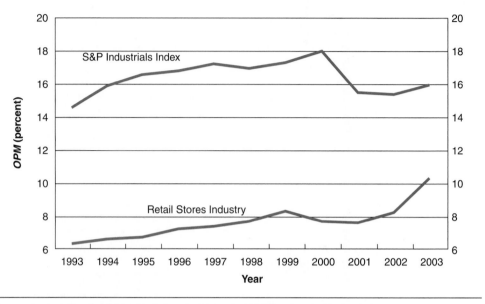

Source: *Analyst's Handbook* (New York: Standard & Poor's, 2004). Reprinted with permission.

Exhibit 13.16	**Time-Series Plot of Depreciation Expense for the S&P Industrials Index and the Retail Stores Industry: 1993–2003**

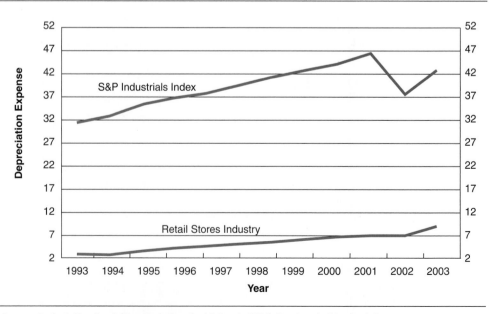

Source: *Analyst's Handbook* (New York: Standard & Poor's, 2004). Reprinted with permission.

RET industry. To estimate depreciation expense, one can consider the two techniques used in the market analysis chapter (i.e., the time-series analysis and the specific estimate technique using the depreciation expense/*PPE* ratio) or an industry-market relationship.

An analysis of the graph, as well as regression analysis of levels and annual percentage changes, indicates that the relationship between this industry and the market is not good enough to use for an estimate. Although the depreciation expense series increased at a fairly steady rate before 2002, the erratic changes in 2002, 2003 call into question the use of time-series estimates.

Exhibit 13.17 contains the components needed to derive a specific depreciation expense estimate similar to what we did for the S&P Industrials Index using the following four steps:

1. Calculate the annual *PPE* turnover for the RET industry.
2. Based upon your sales estimate and your expected *PPE* turnover ratio, estimate the expected *PPE* for next year.
3. Estimate the annual depreciation expense as a percent of *PPE* for the RET industry.
4. Estimate depreciation expense as follows:

$$(\text{Estimated } PPE) \times \text{Estimated} \left(\frac{\text{Depreciation Expense}}{PPE} \right) \text{Ratio}$$

For example, the *PPE* turnover has consistently declined since 1998. A conservative estimate would be a *PPE* turnover of 3.60. This turnover value combined with a per share sales estimate for 2005 of $441.00 implies a *PPE* estimate of $122.50. In turn, the depreciation expense/*PPE* ratio has been in the 9 percent range with the recent five-year average equal to 8.98. Therefore, we will use 9.0 percent. Applying this estimated percent to the *PPE* estimate of $122.50 implies a depreciation expense estimate of $11.02 ($122.50 × 0.09).

Subtracting an estimate of depreciation expense from the operating profit figure indicates the industry's net income before interest and taxes (EBIT).

Industry Interest Expense   An industry's interest expense will be a function of its financial leverage and interest rates. As shown in Exhibit 13.18, interest expense for the RET industry always has been relatively low when compared to the S&P Industrials Index and did not increase at the same rate during the 1980s. Therefore, looking for a relationship between the two interest expense series would not be fruitful. Your estimate for the future should be based on two separate estimates: (1) changes in the amount of debt outstanding for this industry during the year, and (2) an estimate of the level of interest rates (will they increase or decline?).

Estimating Interest Expense   The historical data needed to derive a specific estimate of interest expense are also in Exhibit 13.19. Recall the following steps used in Chapter 12:

1. Calculate the annual total asset turnover *(TAT)* for the RET industry.
2. Use your 2005 sales estimate and an estimate of *TAT* to estimate total assets next year.
3. Based on historical trends, estimate the long-term (interest-bearing) debt as a percentage of total assets ratio for the RET industry.
4. Use your estimate of total assets and the ratio of long-term debt as a percentage of total assets to estimate long-term debt for the next year.
5. Calculate the annual interest cost as a percentage of long-term debt and analyze the trend of this series.
6. Estimate next year's interest cost of debt for this industry based upon your prior estimate of market yields.
7. Estimate interest expense based on the following:

$$(\text{Estimated Interest Cost of Debt}) \times (\text{Estimated Long-Term Debt})$$

Exhibit 13.17 | **Components for Deriving Specific Estimates for Depreciation Expense and Interest Expense for the Retail Industry**

Year	Net Sales	Net PPE	PPE Turnover	Depreciation Expense	Depr. Exp./PPE	Total Assets	Total Asset Turnover	L-T Debt	L-T Debt/ Total Assets	Interest Expense	Interest Exp. L-T. Debt
1993	170.86	34.34	4.98	2.76	8.04	131.72	1.30	23.59	17.91	2.43	10.30
1994	197.21	38.40	5.14	3.05	7.94	140.71	1.40	25.01	17.77	1.90	7.60
1995	208.11	46.40	4.49	3.77	8.13	122.07	1.70	32.63	26.73	2.81	8.61
1996	232.78	50.66	4.59	4.27	8.43	131.46	1.77	32.62	24.81	3.01	9.23
1997	251.33	54.83	4.58	4.80	8.75	139.75	1.80	34.54	24.72	2.60	7.53
1998	276.12	57.03	4.84	5.24	9.19	141.99	1.94	34.65	24.40	2.99	8.63
1999	302.62	65.12	4.65	6.01	9.23	157.36	1.92	36.15	22.97	2.76	7.63
2000	329.76	72.87	4.53	6.52	8.95	168.00	1.96	36.99	22.02	3.09	8.35
2001	352.27	79.78	4.42	7.25	9.09	183.22	1.92	43.54	23.76	3.18	7.30
2002	355.62	80.82	4.40	7.00	8.66	193.45	1.84	44.96	23.24	2.72	6.05
2003	383.89	101.39	3.79	9.11	8.99	264.83	1.45	47.76	18.03	3.33	6.97

Source: *Analyst's Handbook* (New York: Standard & Poor's, 2004). Reprinted with permission.

Exhibit 13.18	Time-Series Plot of Interest Expense for the S&P Industrials Index and the Retail Stores Industry: 1993–2003

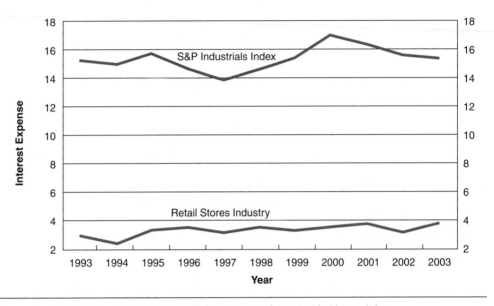

Source: *Analyst's Handbook* (New York: Standard & Poor's, 2004). Reprinted with permission.

Exhibit 13.19	Time-Series Plot of Tax Rates for the S&P Industrials Index and the Retail Stores Industry: 1993–2003

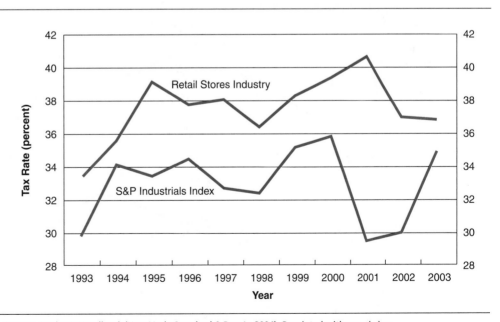

Source: *Analyst's Handbook* (New York: Standard & Poor's, 2004). Reprinted with permission.

For example, our sales estimate of $441.00 and a *TAT* that has averaged about 1.70 over the recent years including a decline in 2003 imply total assets of $259.00 next year. Long-term, interest-bearing debt has averaged about 22–23 percent of total assets for the RET industry except for 2003. If we adjust this to 20 percent for 2005, the estimate for debt is about $52.00 (.20×$259). In turn, interest expense as a percentage of long-term debt during the recent period has averaged about 7.00 percent for this industry. Based on the expectation of a small increase in market interest rates during 2005, we would estimate this interest rate to be 7.20 percent in 2005. This interest rate estimate combined with our long-term debt estimate of $52.00 implies interest expense of $3.74 (0.072 × $52.00).

Industry Tax Rate   As you might expect, tax rates differ between industries. An extreme example would be the oil industry where heavy depletion allowances cause lower taxes. In some instances, however, you can assume that tax law changes have similar impacts on all industries. To see if this is valid, you need to examine the relationship of tax rates over time for your industry and the aggregate market to determine if you can use regression analysis in your estimation process. Alternatively, a time-series plot could provide a useful estimate.

As shown in Exhibit 13.19, except for 2001, the RET tax rate has been about 38 percent. Therefore, the time-series plot is fairly informative, although you still need to consider pending national legislation and unique industry tax factors. Once you have estimated the tax rate, you multiply the *EBT* per share value by (1 − tax rate) to get your estimate of earnings per share *(EPS).*

In addition to estimating *EPS,* you also should examine the industry's net profit margin as a check on your *EPS* estimate. A time-series plot of the net profit margin series for the industry and the S&P Industrials Index is contained in Exhibit 13.20. Two important characteristics are notable. There was one significant difference between the two series. First, the S&P

Exhibit 13.20	**Time-Series Plot of Net Profit Margin for the S&P Industrials Index and the Retail Stores Industry: 1993–2003**

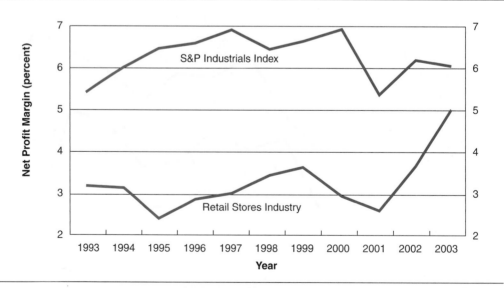

Industrials Index net profit margin series is much more volatile than that for RET. Second, although both profit margin series declined during the 2001 recession, the S&P Industrials Index recovered in 2002 but declined in 2003. While the RET margin experienced a nice recovery in 2002 and an increase to a record level in 2003, the result is a significant decline in the margin difference.

An Industry Earnings Estimate Example   Now that we have described how to estimate each variable in the equation, to help you understand the procedure, the following is an estimate of earnings per share for the RET industry using the economic forecasts from Chapter 12 and the relationship between the RET industry and the market. Our results are not as exact as those of a practicing analyst who would use this example as an *initial* estimate that would be modified based on his or her industry knowledge, current events, and expectations of unique factors.

The regressions and the plots in Exhibit 13.13 indicated that the best relationship was between RET sales and PCE Food, Clothing, and Shoes. Earlier in the chapter, we demonstrated that using that relationship along with estimates of PCE and PCE—Food, Clothing, and Shoes as a percent of PCE we derived an RET sales estimate of $441.00 per share.

As noted earlier in connection with the analysis of Exhibit 13.15, the OPM for the RET industry recovered from the recession in 2002 and then experienced a record performance in 2003 with a 10.44 percent margin. While we can envision that the industry can maintain this level of profit, we do not think it can get much higher under current conditions. Thus, we estimate an *OPM* during 2005 of 10.50 percent, which implies operating profits of $46.31 ($0.1050 \times 441.00).

Earlier we derived a specific estimate for industry depreciation expense of $11.02 for 2005. Therefore, earnings before interest and taxes would be $35.29 ($46.31 − $11.02).

Given the flat yields during 2004 and the small increase in rates envisioned during 2005, our prior specific estimate of interest expense was $3.74 in 2005. Thus, *EBT* would be $31.55 ($35.29 − $3.74).

The tax rate for the RET industry has been consistently higher than the aggregate during the last seven years. The aggregate tax rate was expected to be relatively stable in 2004 and 2005. Therefore, a rate of about 38 percent seems appropriate for the RET industry. This implies taxes of $11.99 ($31.55 \times 0.38$) and net income (earnings per share) of $19.56 ($31.55 − $11.99). This indicates a net profit margin for the RET industry of 4.44 percent ($19.56/$441.00), which is below the record margin in 2003, but higher than all prior years.

Given an estimate of the industry's net income per share (for simplicity, we will round off the *EPS* estimate to $20 per share), your next step is to estimate the earnings multiplier for this industry. Together, the earnings per share and the earnings multiplier provide an estimate of the intrinsic value for the industry index.

Estimating an Industry Earnings Multiplier   This section discusses how to estimate an industry earnings multiplier using two alternative techniques: macroanalysis and microanalysis. In macroanalysis, you examine the relationship between the multiplier for the industry and the market. In microanalysis, you estimate the industry earnings multiplier by examining the specific variables that influence it: (1) the dividend-payout ratio, (2) the required rate of return for the industry *(k),* and (3) the expected growth rate of earnings and dividends for the industry *(g).*

Macroanalysis of an Industry Multiplier: Why a Relationship?   Given that this subsection considers the relationship between the earnings multiplier (*P/E* ratio) for an industry to the *P/E* for the aggregate market, a natural question is, Why do we *expect* a relationship? The reasons are based on the variables that influence the multiplier—the required rate of return, the expected growth rate of earnings and dividends, and the dividend-payout ratio. Specifically, as you know, the required rate of return *(k)* is a function of the nominal risk-free rate plus a risk premium. The fact is, the nominal risk-free rate is the same for all investment assets and is the major reason for changes in *k*. Also, though the level of the risk premium may differ between the market and an industry, any *changes* in the risk premium are probably related.

Although the rate of growth *(g)* for an industry may differ from that of the market, and this difference in *g* is a major reason for the difference in the level of the *P/E* ratio, *changes* in the growth expectations for many industries will be related to changes in *g* for the market and for other industries because they are driven by macroeconomic growth factors that affect the overall market and most industries. Therefore, since the major factor causing a change in the *P/E* ratio for the aggregate market and alternative industries is a change in the *k − g* spread and these two variables have several components that move together, it is not unreasonable to look for an overall (macro) relationship between changes in an industry's *P/E* and the market *P/E* ratio.

An examination of the relationship between the *P/E* ratios for 71 S&P industries and the S&P Industrials Index by Reilly and Zeller (1974) during four partially overlapping 21-year periods indicated a significant positive relationship between percentage changes in *P/E* ratios for most industries examined. Notably, because there was a difference in the significance of the relationship between alternative industries and the market, it is necessary to evaluate the quality of the relationship between the *P/E* ratios for a specific industry and the market before using this technique.

The results in Exhibit 13.5 and Exhibit 13.21 for the RET industry during the period 1993 to 2003 indicate a relatively close relationship between the market and the RET industry. The *P/Es* for the market and RET industry have generally moved together, but the relationship between them has changed four times, with the market *P/E* larger since 1999. Given the recent

Exhibit 13.21	**Time-Series Plot of Annual Average Future Earnings Multipliers for the S&P Industrials Index and the Retail Stores Industry: 1993–2003**

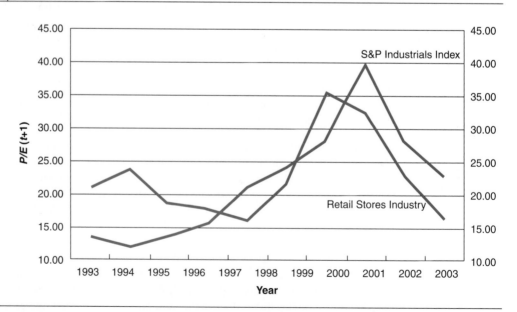

Source: *Analyst's Handbook* (New York: Standard & Poor's, 2004). Reprinted with permission.

differences in *P/E* ratios a crucial question that the analyst must consider is, Why is the RET multiplier smaller and will this differential continue?

Microanalysis of an Industry Multiplier In Chapter 12, we estimated the specific future earnings multiplier for the stock market series by estimating a range of values for the three variables (i.e., dividend payout k, and g) that determine the multiplier and derived a range of *P/E* ratio estimates. This approach provided several multiplier estimates that were used with our EPS estimate to compute a range of estimated intrinsic values for the market index.

Our microanalysis of the industry multiplier could use the same approach. Although this is reasonable, it would not take advantage of the prior work on the stock market multiplier. Because the variables that affect the stock market multiplier and the industry multiplier are similar we can compare the two sets of variables.

Therefore, in our microanalysis, we estimate the three variables that determine the industry earnings multiplier and compare them to the comparable values for the market *P/E*. This allows us to determine whether the industry earnings multiplier *should* be above, below, or equal to the market multiplier. Once we feel confident about this relationship, it is easier to derive a specific estimate for the industry *P/E* ratio. First, we need to recall the long-run relationship between the industry and market *P/E* ratios.

Industry Multiplier versus the Market Multiplier Recall from Exhibit 13.5 and Exhibit 13.21 that the *P/E* ratios for the RET industry and the market generally moved together but the relationship changed four times between 1993 and 2003. Notably, the market *P/E* has consistently been larger than the RET industry *P/E* since 1999. A comparative analysis of the factors that determine the earnings multiplier should help us determine if it is appropriate for the RET industry multiple to be smaller than the market multiple.

Comparing Dividend-Payout Ratios We can discuss the dividend-payout ratio directly or in terms of the retention rate because the retention rate is one minus the dividend-payout ratio. Analyzing the data in Exhibit 13.5 indicates that the retention rates of retail stores have consistently been higher than the retention rates for the market (79 percent versus 67 percent). This indicates a higher dividend payout for the S&P Industrials Index, and this variable alone implies a higher multiplier for the S&P Industrials Index, holding all other variables constant.

Estimating the Required Rate of Return Recall that we estimated the required rate of return *(k)* earlier in the chapter in connection with the present value of cash flow valuation models. The final estimate indicated a beta of 0.82 for the RET industry, which was generally consistent with the fundamental risk characteristics of the industry. In turn, this beta in the prevailing SML implied a k of 8.00 percent. This 8.00 percent compares to the k for the aggregate stock market derived in Chapter 12 of 8.50 percent, which implies that all else the same, the industry *P/E* should be higher than the market *P/E*.

Estimating the Expected Growth Rate (g) You will recall that we likewise estimated a growth rate for the industry early in this chapter in connection with the present value of cash flow models. Using the relationship

$$g = \text{Retention Rate } (b) \times \text{Return on Equity } (ROE)$$
$$= (b) \times (ROE)$$

we estimated a g of over 12 percent based on long-run historical results, and a g of about 13 percent using the results for the recent five-year period 1999–2003.

This 13 percent growth rate estimate compares to the growth rates for the S&P Industrials Index of between 10 and 11 percent (using the long-run retention rate or the recent five-year retention rate). Notably, the growth rates implied for both the industry (13 percent) and the market (10–11 percent) appear too high for any long-term period—that is, we typically use continuing growth rates of 6–7 percent. Therefore, while we would not use the higher growth rates for long-run estimates, the comparison appears valid for our purposes here—the industry has a higher g than the market. This implies that based on the growth factor, the industry multiple would be higher than the market multiple.

In summary, a comparison of the dividend-payout ratios indicates that the market P/E ratio should be higher; the required rate of return comparison indicates that the industry multiple should be higher; while the growth rate comparison favors the industry multiple. The consensus tends to favor a higher industry multiple. Earlier it was discussed that the forward market multiple is currently about 18 times. This implies an industry multiplier in the low 20s.

Industry Estimated Value and Rate of Return   At this point, we have an estimate of the industry earnings per share ($20.00) and an estimate for an industry earnings multiple in the low 20s based on a comparison of the industry and market components. It is not possible to derive a specific estimate using the DDM formula because the k and g for the industry are roughly equal—that is, both k and g are about 8.50 percent. Because the multiple estimate is necessarily not specific, it seems appropriate to consider an optimistic and a pessimistic estimate, with the initial estimate of intrinsic value as follows:

Optimistic Multiple:	24 × $20.00 = $480
Expected Multiple:	22 × $20.00 = $440
Pessimistic Multiple:	20 × $20.00 = $400

Given a current market price for the industry index of about $465, these results indicate that the industry is slightly overpriced based upon general expectations and the pessimistic estimate, but it is slightly underpriced if one favors the optimistic multiple.

OTHER RELATIVE VALUATION RATIOS

Similar to the market analysis, we need to consider the other three relative valuation ratios (*P/BV; P/CF;* and *P/S*) and compare their performance over time relative to similar ratios for the aggregate stock market as represented by the S&P Industrials Index.

Again, the calculations will employ the average annual price and *future* book value, cash flow, and sales. The input data derived for the industry and the S&P Industrials Index (from Chapter 12) with 10-year growth rates for each of these variables are contained in Exhibit 13.22. An important point to note for the subsequent comparison is that the compound growth rate for every RET industry variable is higher than the growth rate for the same market variable,

Exhibit 13.23 contains the four relative valuation ratios for the RET industry and for the S&P Industrials Index along with the ratio of the annual industry valuation ratio divided by the market valuation ratio. The idea is to determine for each valuation ratio the long-run relationship between the industry and the market, including any changes in this relationship. Subsequently, the goal is to explain the overall relationship and consider any changes that

Exhibit 13.22 | Inputs for Relative Valuation Ratios: The Retail Stores Industry and the S&P Industrials Index: 1993–2003

Year	RETAIL STORES INDUSTRY						S&P INDUSTRIALS INDEX					
	Mean Price	EPS	Cash Flow P/S	Book Value P/S	Net Sales P/S	Dividend P/S	Mean Price	EPS	Cash Flow P/S	Book Value P/S	Net Sales P/S	Dividend P/S
1993	115.94	4.97	8.21	37.18	170.86	1.57	523.83	21.96	58.00	191.82	639.77	12.51
1994	109.67	5.56	9.26	40.53	197.21	1.71	543.85	33.12	72.39	210.98	672.04	13.01
1995	108.85	4.67	8.84	43.25	208.11	1.69	634.35	36.01	79.27	227.12	715.38	13.96
1996	117.46	5.90	10.94	46.75	232.78	1.45	795.58	41.15	82.89	238.76	736.65	15.58
1997	152.50	6.65	12.36	51.66	251.33	1.59	995.68	42.13	83.73	247.83	741.52	16.72
1998	230.78	9.62	14.76	53.34	276.12	1.62	1,300.27	38.37	87.38	264.63	738.82	17.28
1999	335.22	10.66	16.93	60.72	302.62	1.74	1,660.54	50.25	97.73	302.08	801.29	17.40
2000	320.07	9.49	15.97	65.48	329.76	1.67	1,684.89	53.85	105.09	337.51	838.78	16.59
2001	301.48	9.84	16.29	70.54	352.27	1.70	1,430.90	19.82	68.58	348.38	794.48	15.85
2002	309.90	13.19	20.21	77.76	355.62	1.82	1,169.97	22.57	61.59	310.61	790.86	16.18
2003	317.61	19.15	28.40	116.53	383.89	2.85	1,138.53	47.12	90.88	363.74	847.38	17.23
10-yr G	10.5%	14.3%	13.0%	12.7%	8.5%	6.4%	8.1%	8.0%	4.5%	6.7%	2.9%	3.1%

Source: *Analyst's Handbook* (New York: Standard & Poor's, 2004). Reprinted with permission.

Exhibit 13.23 | Relative Valuation Ratios for the Retailing Industry Versus S&P Industrials: 1993–2002

Year	PRICE EARNINGS (t + 1)			PRICE CASH FLOW (t + 1)			PRICE BOOK VALUE (t + 1)			PRICE SALES (t + 1)		
	Retail	S&P Ind	Ratio Ind/Mkt	Retail	S&P Ind	Ratio Ind/Mkt	Retail	S&P Ind	Ratio Ind/Mkt	Retail	S&P Ind	Ratio Ind/Mkt
1993	20.85	13.21	1.58	12.52	4.87	2.57	2.86	2.47	1.16	0.59	0.77	0.76
1994	23.48	11.78	1.99	12.41	4.50	2.76	2.54	2.36	1.07	0.53	0.75	0.70
1995	18.45	13.34	1.38	9.95	5.14	1.94	2.33	2.68	0.87	0.47	0.87	0.54
1996	17.66	15.40	1.15	9.50	6.20	1.53	2.27	3.21	0.71	0.47	1.07	0.44
1997	15.85	20.86	0.76	10.33	7.99	1.29	2.86	3.80	0.75	0.55	1.36	0.41
1998	21.65	24.00	0.90	13.63	9.19	1.48	3.80	4.26	0.89	0.76	1.60	0.48
1999	35.32	28.15	1.25	20.99	10.87	1.93	5.12	4.89	1.05	1.02	1.97	0.52
2000	32.53	39.72	0.82	19.65	13.80	1.42	4.54	4.86	0.93	0.91	2.13	0.43
2001	22.86	27.98	0.82	14.92	11.21	1.33	3.88	4.39	0.88	0.85	1.72	0.49
2002	16.18	22.70	0.71	10.91	8.29	1.32	2.66	3.11	0.86	0.81	1.34	0.60

Source: *Analyst's Handbook* (New York: Standard & Poor's, 2004). Reprinted with permission.

| Exhibit 13.24 | **Time-Series Plot of Price/Book Value Ratios for the S&P Industrials Index and the Retail Stores Industry: 1993–2002** |

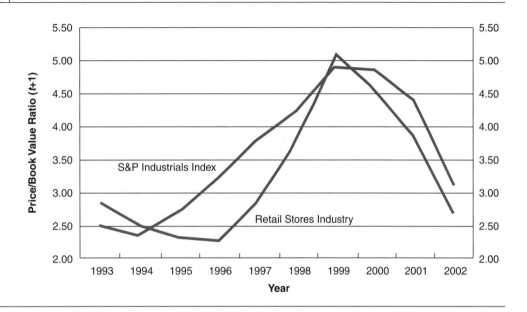

have occurred and whether these changes can be explained based upon the factors that should affect the particular relative valuation ratio. The comparative *P/E* ratios will not be discussed again.

The Price/Book Value Ratio

The time-series plot in Exhibit 13.24 shows the overall increase in the price/book value ratio experienced by both the aggregate stock market and the RET industry to a peak of almost five times in 1999 followed by declines in 2000, 2001, and 2002. Notably, the relationship between the industry and the market has been quite consistent with the market *P/BV* ratio almost always larger than the RET industry ratio.

The reason for this relationship is difficult to explain because the *P/BV* ratio should reflect the ability of the market, an industry, or a company to earn a return on equity capital that exceeds its cost of equity. In turn, this return on equity capital is the *ROE,* and we know from our earlier analysis that during the last decade, the *ROE* for the market and the RET industry has been very similar while the cost of equity for the industry is lower (*B*=0.82), so there is a larger return spread for the industry that should lead to a higher *P/BV* ratio.

The Price/Cash Flow Ratio

As shown in Exhibit 13.23 and Exhibit 13.25, the *P/CF* ratio increased for both the market and the RET industry and the industry ratio has consistently been larger. The reason for the difference in the *P/CF* ratios is akin to the *P/E* ratio—that is, a difference in the growth rate of *CF*

Exhibit 13.25	**Time-Series Plot of Price/Cash Flow Ratios for the S&P Industrials Index and the Retail Stores Industry: 1993–2002**

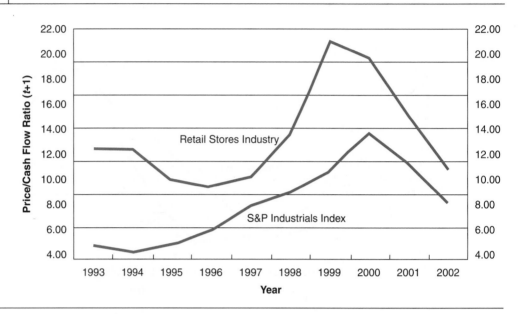

Source: *Analyst's Handbook* (New York: Standard & Poor's, 2004). Reprinted with permission.

per share and the risk (volatility) of the *CF* series over time. As shown in Exhibit 13.22, the growth rate of the industry *CF* has been consistently higher than the growth of the market *CF* (i.e., 13 percent versus about 5 percent) and the industry *CF* series has also been more consistent in its growth. An important question is whether the industry *P/CF* ratio should be about 30 percent higher than the *P/CF* ratio for the market—that is, does the difference in consistent growth of *CF* justify the fairly large difference in the *P/CF* ratios?

The Price/Sales Ratio

As shown in Exhibit 13.23 and Exhibit 13.26, the *P/S* ratio for the market has always been higher and typically by a large amount (1.4 versus 0.8 at the end of the period). In terms of what should affect the *P/S* ratio, one can think of three factors: (1) sales growth rate, (2) the uncertainty (risk) of sales growth, and (3) the profitability of sales (i.e., the net profit margin). Because the industry experienced a *higher* rate of growth for sales during the 10-year period, it is not the rate of growth. Both have likewise experienced less volatility in sales growth. In contrast, the profit margin *(PM)* has always been higher for the market, but the difference declined in 2002 and 2003. Thus, the difference is questionable.

Exhibit 13.27 is a summary of the four industry-market ratios for each of the valuation ratios. In general, the results indicate that investors' assessment of this industry relative to the market has declined during this time period, as shown by the fact that all the industry-market relative ratios declined during this period. Only the price/CF ratio for the industry is above the market. Given the higher growth rates for these variables, this could indicate a valuation opportunity.

| Exhibit 13.26 | Time-Series Plot of Price/Sales Ratios for the S&P Industrials Index and the Retail Stores Industry: 1993–2002 |

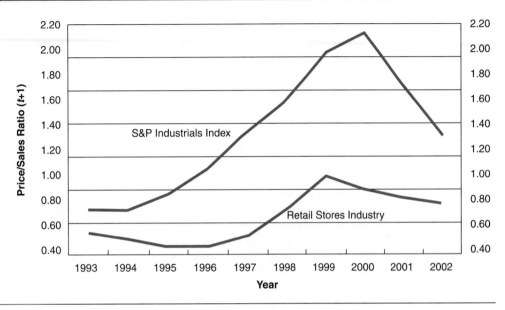

Source: *Analyst's Handbook* (New York: Standard & Poor's, 2004). Reprinted with permission.

| Exhibit 13.27 | Time-Series Plot of the Industry-Market Relative Ratios of Valuation Ratios for the S&P Industrials Index and the Retail Stores Industry: 1993–2002 |

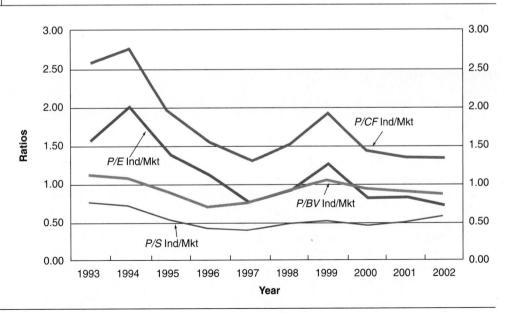

Source: *Analyst's Handbook* (New York: Standard & Poor's, 2004). Reprinted with permission.

GLOBAL INDUSTRY ANALYSIS

Because so many firms are active in foreign markets and because the proportion of foreign sales is growing for so many firms, it is necessary to consider the effects of foreign firms on industry returns. To see why this is so, consider the auto industry. Besides Ford and General Motors, the auto industry for a global investor includes numerous firms from Japan, Germany, Italy, and Korea, among others. Thus, we must extend the analysis described earlier to include global factors.

While space does not permit a complete example, the following major factors need to be analyzed in this context:

• The macroenvironment in the major producing and consuming countries for this industry. This will impact demand from these countries.

• An overall analysis of the significant global companies in the industry, the products they produce, and how successful they are in terms of the DuPont three-component analysis.

• As part of the company analysis, what are the accounting differences by country and how do these differences impact the relative valuation ratios? Because of the accounting differences, it is typically not possible to directly compare such ratios across countries but only examine them over time within a country. This problem should be reduced as the use of international accounting standards grows.

• What is the effect of currency exchange rate trends for the major countries? Significant changes can affect the demand for U.S. chemicals from specific countries and also costs assuming U.S. firms receive inputs from foreign firms.

This global industry analysis is growing in importance as documented in a study by Cavaglia, Brightman, and Aked (2000), which documents that, historically, research showed that country factors dominated industry factors in terms of explaining equity returns. The Cavaglia et al. (2000) study presented evidence that industry factors have been growing in importance and currently dominate country factors. In summary, it is important to carry out industry analysis on a global scale.

The Internet Investments Online

The Web can help researchers find information about an industry, but many industry analyses and studies are available online only to registered and paying clients of research firms, investment banks, and brokerage houses. You probably will not find up-to-date Porter analyses free on the Internet, at least not for a wide variety of industries. Web searches for industry information can focus on exploring Web sites of competitors in the industry. You may find trade group Web sites through key word searches using terms and phrases relevant to the industry you wish to study.

Because this chapter focuses on the retail industry and our company analysis is a retail drugstore chain, a little investigation brought forth the sites described below; many more exist for your perusal.

http://www.lf.com The home page for Lebhar-Friedman, Inc., a publisher and provider of information about retailers.

http://www.nacds.org This page is sponsored by the National Association of Chain Drug Stores. It contains data relevant to chain drugstores. It offers news and links to related sites.

http://www.healthcaredistribution.org This is a site of the Healthcare Distribution Management Association. This page features links to managed-care issues, public policy issues, information for pharmacies, consumers, the press, manufacturers, analysts, and investors. Contains links to a number of related Web sites.

http://Retailindustry.about.com A part of the about.com Web site, this site contains a number of links to other Web sites that deal with the retail industry and the analysis of the retail industry.

http://www.valuationresources.com This site contains links to industry information sources and economic information sources. Industry report information is segmented by SIC code.

SUMMARY

- Several studies have examined industry performance and risk. They have found wide dispersion in the performance of alternative industries during specified time periods, implying that industry analysis can help identify superior investments. They also showed inconsistent industry performance over time, implying that looking at only past performance of an industry has little value in projecting future performance. Also, the performance by firms within industries typically is not very consistent, so you must analyze individual companies in an industry following the industry analysis.

- The analysis of industry risk indicated wide dispersion in the measures of risk for different industries but a fair amount of consistency in the risk measure over time for individual industries. These results imply that risk analysis and measurement are useful and necessary. The good news

is that past risk measures may be of some value when estimating future risk.

- We discussed and demonstrated both approaches to the valuation of the RET industry. The present value of cash flow models indicated a fairly wide range of values.

- The four relative valuation ratio techniques also provided a range of results, including the two-step earnings multiple technique where the multiple results surrounded the current market price. All of the relative valuation ratios declined over time relative to the market.

- Industry analysis needs to be carried out on a global scale and must evaluate the effects not only of world supply, demand, and cost components for an industry but also different valuation levels due to accounting conventions and, finally, the impact of exchange rates on the total industry and the firms within it.

SUGGESTED READINGS

Aber, John. "Industry Effects and Multivariate Stock Price Behavior." *Journal of Financial and Quantitative Analysis* 11, no. 5 (November 1976).

Fruhan, William E., Jr. *Financial Strategy.* Homewood, IL: Irwin, 1979.

Goodman, D. A., and John W. Peavy, III. "Industry Relative Price-Earnings Ratios as Indicators of Investment Returns." *Financial Analysts Journal* 39, no. 2 (March–April 1983): 60–66.

Porter, Michael E. "How to Conduct an Industry Analysis." In *The Financial Analysts Handbook,* 2d ed., ed. Sumner N. Levine. Homewood, IL: Dow Jones–Irwin, 1988.

The following are proceedings from industry analysis seminars sponsored by the Association for Investment Management and Research (AIMR):

Balog, James (ed.). *The Health Care Industry.* Charlottesville, VA: AIMR, 1993.

Bhatia, Sanjiv, ed. *The Consumer Staples Industry.* Charlottesville, VA: AIMR, 1995.

Bhatia, Sanjiv, ed. *The Media Industry.* Charlottesville, VA: AIMR, 1996.

Petrie, Thomas, A. ed. *The Oil and Gas Industries.* Charlottesville, VA: AIMR, 1993.

Shasta, Theodore, ed. *The Automotive Industry.* Charlottesville, VA: AIMR, 1994.

QUESTIONS

1. Briefly describe the results of studies that examined the performance of alternative industries during specific time periods and discuss their implications for industry analysis.
2. Briefly describe the results of the studies that examined industry performance over time. Do these results complicate or simplify industry analysis?
3. Assume all the firms in a particular industry have consistently experienced similar rates of return. Discuss what this implies regarding the importance of industry and company analysis for this industry.
4. Discuss the contention that differences in the performance of various firms within an industry limit the usefulness of industry analysis.
5. Several studies have examined the difference in risk for alternative industries during a specified time period. Describe the results of these studies and discuss their implications for industry analysis.
6. What were the results when industry risk was examined during successive time periods? Discuss the implication of these results for industry analysis.
7. Assume the industry you are analyzing is in the fourth stage of the industrial life cycle. How would you react if your industry-economic analysis predicted that sales per share for this industry would increase by 20 percent? Discuss your reasoning.
8. Discuss at what stage in the industrial life cycle you would like to discover an industry. Justify your decision.
9. Give an example of an industry in Stage 2 of the industrial life cycle. Discuss your reasoning for putting the industry in Stage 2 and any evidence that caused you to select this stage for the industry.
10. Discuss an example of input-output analysis to predict the sales for the auto industry. Discuss how you would use input-output analysis to predict the costs of production for the auto industry.
11. Discuss the impact of the threat of substitute products on the steel industry's profitability.
12. Discuss the two variables that must be considered whether you are using the present value of cash flow approach or the relative valuation ratio approach to valuation. Why are these variables relevant for either valuation approach?
13. List the three variables that are relevant when attempting to determine whether the earnings multiple (*P/E* ratio) for an industry should be higher, equal to, or lower than the market multiple.
14. Discuss when you would use the two-stage growth FCFE model rather than the constant growth model.
15. You are examining the *P/CF* ratio for an industry compared to the market and find that the industry ratio has always been at a discount to the market—for example, the industry-market ratio of ratios is about 0.80. Discuss the variable(s) you would examine to explain this difference or to justify an increase in the industry-market ratio.

16. *CFA Examination Level II*

    Elizabeth Coronado, CFA, is analyzing Nelson Motors, Inc., one of the largest and most profitable automobile manufacturers in North America. Since the early 1990s, the fastest growing and most profitable product segment for Nelson has been its sport utility vehicles (SUV) line shown in the following exhibit.

    Coronado believes that applying the product life cycle model to Nelson's SUV product line will yield additional analytical insights into the company's recent rapid earnings growth.

    a. Identify the current product life cycle stage for the Raven, Hawk, and Eagle. Justify your choice of product life cycle stage by citing evidence from the following exhibit. [6 minutes]

       Because of the high expectations associated with the Eagle, Nelson Motors' current *P/E* is above its five-year historic range and above the auto industry *P/E*. An auto analyst states that "Nelson Motors has the best of both worlds:

       • increasing SUV profitability and
       • declining expected future earnings volatility."

NELSON MOTORS ANNUAL SUV PRODUCTION AND FINANCIAL DATA											
	1990	1991	1992	1993	1994	1995	1996	1997	1998	1999E	2000E
SUV Units Sold in Thousands											
Raven	5	10	35	70	90	100	110	112	110	105	90
Hawk	—	—	—	—	3	10	20	45	63	68	69
Eagle	—	—	—	—	—	—	—	5	32	70	110
Profit per Vehicle in $ Thousands											
Raven	9	10	9	8	8	7	7	6	5	4	3
Hawk	—	—	—	—	6	7	8	7	7	8	7
Eagle	—	—	—	—	—	—	—	10	10	11	12
Profit per SUV Model in $ Millions											
Raven	45	100	315	560	720	700	770	672	550	420	270
Hawk	—	—	—	—	18	70	160	315	441	544	483
Eagle	—	—	—	—	—	—	—	50	320	770	1,320
Total SUV Division profit in $ millions	45	100	315	560	738	770	930	1,037	1,311	1,734	2,073
Total Nelson Motors profit in $ millions	1,125	1,250	1,575	1,600	1,994	1,974	2,214	2,357	2,960	3,470	3,989
SUV Division profit % of Nelson Motors profit	4%	8%	20%	35%	37%	39%	42%	44%	44%	50%	52%
Year over year % change in total SUV profit	—	122%	215%	78%	32%	4%	21%	12%	26%	32%	20%
Model percent of SUV Division Profit											
Raven	100%	100%	100%	100%	98%	91%	83%	65%	42%	24%	13%
Hawk	—	—	—	—	2%	9%	17%	30%	34%	31%	23%
Eagle	—	—	—	—	—	—	—	5%	24%	44%	64%

b. Evaluate *each* statement, using the data presented in the exhibit (6 minutes).

PROBLEMS

1. Select three industries from the S&P *Analysts Handbook* with different demand factors. For each industry, indicate what economic series you would use to predict the growth for the industry. Discuss why the economic series selected is relevant for this industry.
2. Prepare a scatterplot for one of the industries in Problem 1 of industry sales per share and observations from the economic series you suggested for this industry. Do this for the most recent 10 years using information available in the *Analysts Handbook*. Based on the results of the scatterplot, discuss whether the economic series was closely related to this industry's sales.
3. Based on an analysis of the results in Problem 2, discuss the stage of your industry in its life cycle.

4. Evaluate your industry in terms of the five factors that determine an industry's intensity of competition. Based on this analysis, what are your expectations about the industry's profitability in the short run (1 or 2 years) and the long run (5–10 years)?

5. Using the S&P *Analysts Handbook,* plot the latest 10-year history of the operating profit margin for the S&P Industrials Index versus the S&P industry of your choice. Is there a positive, negative, or zero correlation?

6. Using the S&P *Analysts Handbook,* calculate the means for the following variables of the S&P Industrials Index and the industry of your choice during the last 10 years:
   a. Price/earnings multiplier
   b. Retention rate
   c. Return on equity
   d. Equity turnover
   e. Net profit margin
   Briefly comment on how your industry and the S&P Industrials Index differ for each of the variables.

7. Prepare a table listing the variables that influence the earnings multiplier for your chosen industry and the S&P Industrials Index series for the most recent 10 years.
   a. Do the average dividend-payout ratios for your industry and the S&P Industrials Index differ? How should the dividend payout influence the difference between the multipliers?
   b. Based on the fundamental factors, would you expect the risk for this industry to differ from that for the market? In what direction, and why? Calculate the industry beta using monthly data for five years. Based on the fundamental factors and the computed systematic risk, how does this industry's risk compare to the market? What effect will this difference in risk have on the industry multiplier relative to the market multiplier?
   c. Analyze and discuss the different components of growth (retention rate, total asset turnover, total assets/equity, and profit margin) for your chosen industry and the S&P Industrials Index during the most recent 10 years. Based on this analysis, how would you expect the growth rate for your industry to compare with the growth rate for the S&P Industrials Index? How would this difference in expected growth affect the multiplier?

8. *CFA Examination Level II*
   As a securities analyst, you have been asked to review a valuation of a closely held business—Wigwam Autoparts Heaven, Inc. (WAH), prepared by the Red Rocks Group (RRG). You are to give an opinion on the valuation and to support your opinion by analyzing each part of the valuation. WAH's sole business is automotive parts retailing.
   The RRG valuation includes a section called "Analysis of the Retail Autoparts Industry," based completely on the data in Table 1 and the following additional information.
   • WAH and its principal competitors each operated over 150 stores at year end 1994.
   • The average number of stores operated per company engaged in the retail auto parts industry is 5.3.
   • The major customer base for auto parts sold in retail stores consists of young owners of old vehicles. These owners do their own automotive maintenance out of economic necessity.
   a. One of RRG's conclusions is that the retail autoparts industry as a whole is in the stabilization stage of the industry life cycle. Discuss *three* relevant items of data from Table 1 that support this conclusion. [9 minutes]
   b. Another RRG conclusion is that WAH and its principal competitors are in the growth stage of their life cycle.
      Cite *three* relevant items of data from Table 13.1 that support this conclusion.
      Explain how WAH and its principal competitors can be in a growth stage while their industry as a whole is in the stabilization stage. [11 minutes]

9. You know the following about your industry (I) and the market (M):

ROE_I:	12%	ROE_M:	16%
RR_I:	0.60	RR_M:	0.55
$Beta_I$:	1.05	$Beta_M$:	1.00

Discuss what difference you would expect in the *P/E*s, and explain why you expect this difference.

Table 13.1 | Selected Retail Autoparts Industry Data

	1994	1993	1992	1991	1990	1989	1988	1987	1986	1985
Population 18–29 years old (percentage change)	−1.8%	−2.0%	−2.1%	−1.4%	−0.8%	−0.9%	−1.1%	−0.9%	−0.7%	−0.3%
Number of households with income more than $35,000 (percentage change)	6.0%	4.0%	8.0%	4.5%	2.7%	3.1%	1.6%	3.6%	4.2%	2.2%
Number of households with income less than $35,000 (percentage (change)	3.0%	−1.0%	4.9%	2.3%	−1.4%	2.5%	1.4%	−1.3%	0.6%	0.1%
Number of cars 5–15 years old (percentage change)	0.9%	−1.3%	−6.0%	1.9%	3.3%	2.4%	−2.3%	−2.2%	−8.0%	1.6%
Automotive aftermarket industry retail sales (percentage change)	5.7%	1.9%	3.1%	3.7%	4.3%	2.6%	1.3%	0.2%	3.7%	2.4%
Consumer expenditures on automotive parts and accessories (percentage change)	2.4%	1.8%	2.1%	6.5%	3.6%	9.2%	1.3%	6.2%	6.7%	6.5%
Sales growth of retail auto parts companies with 100 or more stores	17.0%	16.0%	16.5%	14.0%	15.5%	16.8%	12.0%	15.7%	19.0%	16.0%
Market share of retail auto parts companies with 100 or more stores	19.0%	18.5%	18.3%	18.1%	17.0%	17.2%	17.0%	16.9%	15.0%	14.0%
Average operating margin of retail auto parts companies with 100 or more stores	12.0%	11.8%	11.2%	11.5%	10.6%	10.6%	10.0%	10.4%	9.8%	9.0%
Average operating margin of all retail auto parts companies	5.5%	5.7%	5.6%	5.8%	6.0%	6.5%	7.0%	7.2%	7.1%	7.2%

A. Preparing an Industry Analysis: What Is an Industry?[6]

Identifying a company's industry can be difficult in today's business world. Although airlines, railroads, and utilities may be easy to categorize, what about manufacturing companies with three different divisions, none of which is dominant? Perhaps the best way to test whether a company fits into an industry grouping is to compare the operating results for the company and an industry. For our purposes, an industry is a group of companies with similar demand, supply, and operating characteristics.

The following is a set of guidelines for preparing an industry appraisal, including the topics to consider and some specific items to include.

Characteristics to Study

1. Price history reveals valuable long-term relationships.
   a. Price/earnings ratios
   b. Common stock yields
   c. Price/book value ratios
   d. Price/cash flow ratios
   e. Price/sales ratios
2. Operating data show comparisons of
   a. Return on total investment *(ROI)*
   b. Return on equity *(ROE)*
   c. Sales growth
   d. Trends in operating profit margin
   e. Evaluation of stage in industrial life cycle
   f. Book value per-share growth
   g. Earnings-per-share growth
   h. Profit margin trends (gross, operating, and net)
   i. Evaluation of exchange rate risk from foreign sales
3. Comparative results of alternative industries show
   a. Effects of business cycles on each industry group
   b. Secular trends affecting results
   c. Industry growth compared to other industries
   d. Regulatory changes
   e. Importance of overseas operations

Factors in Industry Analysis

Markets for Products
1. Trends in the markets for the industry's major products: historical and projected
2. Industry growth relative to GDP or other relevant economic series; possible changes from past trends
3. Shares of market for major products among domestic and global producers; changes in market shares in recent years; outlook for market share
4. Effect of imports on industry markets; share of market taken by imports; price and margin changes caused by imports; outlook for imports
5. Effect of exports on their markets; trends in export prices and units exported; outlook for exports
6. Expectations for the exchange rates in major non-U.S. countries; historical volatility of exchange rates; outlook for the level and volatility of exchange rates

Financial Performance
1. Capitalization ratios; ability to raise new capital; earnings retention rate; financial leverage
2. Ratio of fixed assets to capital invested; depreciation policies; capital turnover

[6]Reprinted and adapted with permission of Stanley D. Ryals, CFA; Investment Council, Inc.: La Crescenta, CA 91214.

3. Return on total capital; return on equity capital; components of *ROE*
4. Return on foreign investments; need for foreign capital

Operations
1. Degrees of integration; cost advantages of integration; major supply contracts
2. Operating rates as a percentage of capacity; backlogs; new-order trends
3. Trends of industry consolidation
4. Trends in industry competition
5. New-product development; research and development expenditures in dollars and as a percentage of sales
6. Diversification; comparability of product lines

Management
1. Management depth and ability to develop from within; organizational structure
2. Board of directors: internal versus external members; compensation package
3. Flexibility to deal with product demand changes; ability to identify and eliminate losing operations
4. Record and outlook regarding labor relations
5. Dividend policy and historical progression

Sources of Industry Information

1. Independent industry journals
2. Industry and trade associations
3. Government reports and statistics
4. Independent research organizations
5. Brokerage house research
6. Financial publishers (S&P; Moody's; Value Line)

B. Insights on Analyzing Industry *ROA*s

Insights on Industry ROAs

Beyond the normal analysis of *ROA* as a component of *ROE* (*ROA* times Total Assets/Equity equals *ROE*), an article by Selling and Stickney provides some interesting insights for industry analysis based upon an analysis of the two components of the *ROA* ratio (profit margin and total asset turnover) and what these two components signal regarding the industry strategy.[7] Given the two components of the *ROA*, it is possible to graph each of these values as shown in Exhibit 13C.1 and determine what each component contributed to the *ROA* at the point of intersection. As shown, it is possible to draw a constant *ROA* curve, which demonstrates that it is possible to achieve an 8 percent (or 4 percent) *ROA* with numerous combinations of profit margin and asset turnover. The particular combination of profit margin and asset turnover is generally dictated by the nature of the industry and the strategy employed by management. For example, many industries necessarily require large capital inputs for equipment (e.g., steel, auto, heavy machinery manufacturers). Therefore, the asset turnover is necessarily low, which means the profit margin must be higher. The firms in such an industry are typically in the upper left segment of the graph (Segment *a*), and improvements of *ROA* in these industries are derived by increasing profit margins because it is difficult to increase asset turnover. In contrast, industries that have commodity-type products (e.g., retail food, paper, industrial chemicals) generally have low profit margins and succeed based upon high asset turnover. These industries are generally in the lower right segment of the graph (Segment *c*) and attempt to improve their *ROA* by increasing their asset turnover rather than the profit margin (i.e., they are constrained by price competition). Industries in the middle segment *(b)* are in a more balanced position and can attempt to improve the *ROA* by increasing *either* the profit margin or the asset turnover.

---

[7]Thomas Selling and Clyde P. Stickney, "The Effects of Business Environment and Strategy on a Firm's Rate of Return on Assets," *Financial Analysts Journal* 45, no. 1 (January–February 1989): 43–52.

It is very important for an analyst to understand the nature of the industry and what contributes to the industry's *ROA* as well as what this implies about the constraints and opportunities facing the firms in the industry.

| **Exhibit 13C.1** | *ROA*—The Trade-Off of Profit Margin and Asset Turnover |

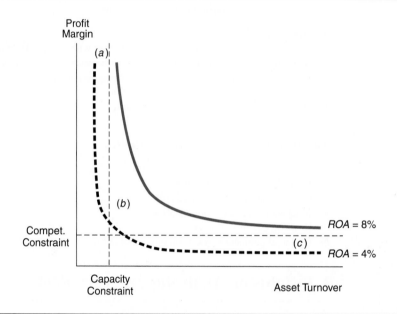

Chapter 14

Company Analysis and Stock Valuation*

After you read this chapter, you should be able to answer the following questions:

- Why is it important to differentiate between company analysis and stock valuation?
- What is the difference between a true growth company and a growth stock?
- How do we apply the two valuation approaches and the several valuation techniques to Walgreens?
- What techniques are useful when estimating the inputs to alternative valuation models?
- What techniques are useful when estimating company sales?
- How do we estimate the profit margins and earnings per share for a company?
- What factors are considered when estimating the earnings multiplier for a firm?
- What two specific competitive strategies can a firm use to cope with the competitive environment in its industry?
- In addition to the earnings multiplier, what are some other relative valuation ratios?
- How do we apply the several present value of cash flow models to the valuation of a company?
- What value-added measures are available to evaluate the performance of a firm?
- How do we compute economic value added (EVA), market value added (MVA), and the franchise value for a firm?
- What is the relationship between these value-added measures and changes in the market value of firms?
- When should we consider selling a stock?
- What is the relationship between positive EVA and a growth company?
- Why is it inappropriate to use the standard dividend discount model (DDM) to value a true growth company?
- What is the difference between no growth, simple growth, and dynamic growth?
- What is the growth duration model and what information does it provide?

*The authors acknowledge comments and suggestions on this chapter by Professor Edgar Norton of Illinois State University.

- How can we use the growth duration model to estimate the *P/E* for a growth company?
- What additional factors should be considered when analyzing a company on a global basis?

At this point, you have made two decisions about your investment in equity markets. First, after analyzing the economy and stock markets for several countries, you have decided what percent of your portfolio should be invested in common stocks. Second, after analyzing various industries, you have identified those that appear to offer above-average risk-adjusted performance over your investment horizon. The final questions in the fundamental analysis procedure are (1) which are the best companies within these desirable industries? and (2) are their stocks underpriced? Specifically, is the intrinsic value of the stock above its market value, or is the expected rate of return on the stock equal to or greater than its required rate of return?

This chapter begins with a discussion of the difference between company analysis and stock valuation. Company analysis should occur in the context of the prevailing economic and industry conditions. We discuss some competitive strategies that can help firms maximize returns in an industry's competitive environment. We demonstrate cash flow models and relative valuation ratios that can be used to determine a stock's intrinsic value and identify undervalued stocks. We also review factors that will help you determine when to sell a stock that you currently own and discuss the pressures and influences that affect professional stock analysts. We conclude with a discussion of important factors to consider when analyzing foreign stocks.

COMPANY ANALYSIS VERSUS THE VALUATION OF STOCK

This chapter is titled "Company Analysis and Stock Valuation" to convey the idea that the common stocks of good companies are not necessarily good investments. The point is, after analyzing a company and deriving an understanding of its strengths and risks, you need to compute the fundamental intrinsic value of the firm's stock and compare the intrinsic value of a stock to its market value to determine if the company's stock should be purchased. The stock of a wonderful firm with superior management and strong performance measured by sales and earnings growth can be priced so high that the intrinsic value of the stock is below its current market price and should not be acquired. In contrast, the stock of a company with less success based on its sales and earnings growth may have a stock market price that is below its intrinsic value. In this case, although the company is not as good, its stock could be the better investment.

The classic confusion in this regard concerns growth companies versus growth stocks. The stock of a growth company is not necessarily a growth stock. Recognition of this difference is absolutely essential for successful investing.

Growth Companies and Growth Stocks

Observers have historically defined growth companies as those that consistently experience above-average increases in sales and earnings. This definition has some limitations because many firms could qualify due to certain accounting procedures, mergers, or other external events.

In contrast, financial theorists such as Salomon (1963) and Miller and Modigliani (1961) define a **growth company** as a firm with the management ability and the opportunities to make investments that yield rates of return greater than the firm's required rate of return. This required rate of return is the firm's weighted average cost of capital (WACC). As an example, a growth company might be able to acquire capital at an average cost of 10 percent and yet have the management ability and the opportunity to invest those funds at rates of return of 15 to 20 percent. As a result of these superior investment opportunities, the firm's sales and earnings grow faster than those of similar risk firms and the overall economy. In addition, a growth company that has above-average investment opportunities should, and typically does, retain a large portion of its earnings to fund these superior investment projects (i.e., they have low dividend-payout ratios).

Growth stocks are *not* necessarily shares in growth companies. A **growth stock** is a stock with a higher rate of return than other stocks in the market with similar risk characteristics. The stock achieves this superior risk-adjusted rate of return because at some point in time the market undervalued it compared to other stocks. Although the stock market adjusts stock prices relatively quickly and accurately to reflect new information, available information is not always perfect or complete. Therefore, imperfect or incomplete information may cause a given stock to be undervalued or overvalued at a point in time.[1]

If the stock is undervalued, its price should eventually increase to reflect its true fundamental value when the correct information becomes available. During this period of price adjustment, the stock's realized return will exceed the required return for a stock with its risk, and, during this period of adjustment, it will be considered a growth stock. Growth stocks are not necessarily limited to growth companies. A future growth stock can be the stock of any type of company; the stock need only be undervalued by the market.

The fact is, if investors recognize a growth company and discount its future earnings stream properly, the current market price of the growth company's stock will reflect its future earnings stream. Those who acquire the stock of a growth company at this correct market price will receive a rate of return consistent with the risk of the stock, even when the superior earnings growth is attained. In many instances, overeager investors tend to overestimate the expected growth rate of earnings and cash flows for the growth company and, therefore, inflate the price of a growth company's stock. Investors who pay the inflated stock price will earn a rate of return below the risk-adjusted required rate of return, despite the fact that the growth company experiences above-average growth of sales and earnings. Several studies, including those by Solt and Statman (1989), Shefrin and Statman (1995), and Clayman (1987), have examined the stock price performance for samples of growth companies and found that their stocks performed poorly—that is, the stocks of growth companies have generally *not* been growth stocks.

Defensive Companies and Stocks

Defensive companies are those whose future earnings are likely to withstand an economic downturn. One would expect them to have relatively low business risk and not excessive financial risk. Typical examples are public utilities or grocery chains—firms that supply basic consumer necessities.

There are two closely related concepts of a **defensive stock**. First, a defensive stock's rate of return is not expected to decline during an overall market decline, or decline less than the overall market. Second, our CAPM discussion indicated that an asset's relevant risk is its covariance with the market portfolio of risky assets—that is, an asset's systematic risk. A stock with low or negative systematic risk (a small positive or negative beta) may be considered

---

[1] An analyst is more likely to find such stocks outside the top tier of companies that are scrutinized by numerous analysts; in other words, look for neglected stocks.

a defensive stock according to this theory because its returns are unlikely to be harmed significantly in a bear market.

Cyclical Companies and Stocks

A **cyclical company's** sales and earnings will be heavily influenced by aggregate business activity. Examples would be firms in the steel, auto, or heavy machinery industries. Such companies will do well during economic expansions and poorly during economic contractions. This volatile earnings pattern is typically a function of the firm's business risk (both sales volatility and operating leverage) and can be compounded by financial risk.

A **cyclical stock** will experience changes in its rates of return greater than changes in overall market rates of return. In terms of the CAPM, these would be stocks that have high betas. The stock of a cyclical company, however, is not necessarily cyclical. A cyclical stock is the stock of any company that has returns that are more volatile than the overall market—that is, high-beta stocks that have high correlation with the aggregate market and greater volatility.

Speculative Companies and Stocks

A **speculative company** is one whose assets involve great risk but that also has a possibility of great gain. A good example of a speculative firm is one involved in oil exploration.

A **speculative stock** possesses a high probability of low or negative rates of return and a low probability of normal or high rates of return. Specifically, a speculative stock is one that is overpriced, leading to a high probability that during the future period when the market adjusts the stock price to its true value, it will experience either low or possibly negative rates of return. Such an expectation might be the case for an excellent growth company whose stock is selling at an extremely high price/earnings ratio—that is, it is substantially overvalued.

Value versus Growth Investing

Some analysts also divide stocks into growth stocks and value stocks. As we have discussed, growth stocks are companies that will have positive earnings surprises and above-average risk-adjusted rates of return because the stocks are undervalued. If the analyst does a good job in identifying such companies, investors in these stocks will reap the benefits of seeing their stock prices rise after other investors identify their earnings growth potential. **Value stocks** are those that appear to be undervalued for reasons other than earnings growth potential. Value stocks are usually identified by analysts as having low price-earning or price-book value ratios. Notably, in these comparisons between growth and value stocks, the specification of a growth stock is *not* consistent with our preceding discussion. In these discussions, a growth stock is generally specified as a stock of a company that is experiencing rapid growth of sales and earnings (e.g., Intel and Microsoft). As a result of this company performance, the stock typically has a high *P/E* and price-book-value ratio. Unfortunately, the specification does not consider the critical comparison between intrinsic value and market price. Therefore, these specifications will not be used in subsequent discussions of valuation.

The major point of this section is that you must initially examine a company to determine its characteristics and use this information to derive an estimate of the intrinsic value of its stock. When you compare this intrinsic value of the stock to its current market price you decide whether you should acquire it—that is, will it be a growth stock that provides a rate of return equal to or greater than what is consistent with its risk?

ECONOMIC, INDUSTRY, AND STRUCTURAL LINKS TO COMPANY ANALYSIS

The analysis of companies and their stocks is the final step in the top-down approach to investing. Rather than selecting stocks on the basis of company-specific factors (as with bottom-up analysis), top-down analysts review the current state and future outlook for domestic and international sectors of the economy. On the basis of this macroeconomic analysis, they identify industries that are expected to offer attractive returns in the expected future environment. Following this macroanalysis, we value the firms in the selected industries. Our analysis concentrates on the two significant determinants of a stock's intrinsic value: (1) growth of the firm's expected earnings and cash flows and (2) its risk and the appropriate discount rate.

Economic and Industry Influences

If economic trends are favorable for an industry, the company analysis should focus on firms in that industry that are well positioned to benefit from the economic trends. Research analysts should become familiar with the cash flow and risk attributes of the firms they are studying. In times of economic or industry growth, the most attractive candidates may be the firms in the industry with high levels of operating and financial leverage. A modest percentage increase in revenue can be magnified into a much larger percentage rise in earnings and cash flow for the highly leveraged firm. The point is, firms in an industry will have varying sensitivities to economic variables, such as economic growth, interest rates, input costs, and exchange rates. Because each firm is different, an investor must determine the best candidates for purchase under expected economic conditions.

Structural Influences

In addition to economic variables, other factors, such as social trends, technology, and political and regulatory influences, can have a major effect on some firms in an industry. Some firms in the industry can try to take advantage of demographic changes or shifts in consumer tastes and lifestyles, or invest in technology to lower costs and better serve their customers. Such firms may be able to grow and succeed despite unfavorable industry or economic conditions. For example, Wal-Mart became the nation's leading retailer because it benefited from several smart management decisions. The geographic location of many of its stores allowed it to benefit from rising regional population and lower labor costs. Its competitive strategy, which emphasized everyday low prices, was appealing to consumers who had become concerned about the price and value of purchases. Finally, its technologically advanced inventory and ordering systems and the logistics of its distribution system gave Wal-Mart a clear competitive (cost) advantage.

During the initial stage of an industry's life cycle, the original firms in the industry can refine their technologies and move down the learning curve. Subsequent followers may benefit from these initial actions and can learn from the leaders' mistakes and take the market lead away from them. Investors need to be aware of such strategies so they can evaluate companies and their stocks accordingly.

Political and regulatory events can create opportunities in an industry even during weak economic periods. Deregulation in trucking, airlines, and the financial services industries in the 1980s led to the creation of new companies and innovative strategies. As a result, sharp price declines following bad industry news may be a good buying opportunity for astute investors. Some stocks in an industry may deserve lower prices following some political or regulatory events; but, if the market also punishes the stock prices of good companies with smaller exposures to the bad news, then an alert analyst will identify buying opportunities of underpriced stocks within an industry.

The bottom line is that, although the economy plays a major role in determining overall market trends and industry groups display sensitivity to economic variables, other structural changes may counterbalance the economic effects, or company management may be able to minimize the impact of economic or industry events on a company. Analysts who are familiar with industry trends and company strategies can issue well-reasoned buy-and-sell recommendations irrespective of the economic forecast.

COMPANY ANALYSIS

This section groups various analysis components for discussion. The first subsection continues the Porter discussion of an industry's competitive environment. The basic SWOT analysis is intended to articulate a firm's strengths, weaknesses, opportunities, and threats. These two analyses should provide a complete understanding of a firm's overall *strategic* approach. Given this background, we review and demonstrate the two valuation approaches: (1) the present value of cash flows, and (2) relative valuation ratio techniques. Following this, we discuss the significance of site visits to companies, how to prepare for an interview with management, and suggestions on when an investor should consider selling an asset. This is followed by a discussion of unique considerations regarding evaluation of international companies and their stocks. The final section of the chapter discusses the unique features of true growth companies and presents and demonstrates several models that can be used to value growth companies.

Firm Competitive Strategies

In describing competition within industries, we discussed the five competitive forces that could affect the competitive structure and profit potential of an industry. After you have determined the competitive structure of an industry, you should attempt to identify the specific competitive strategy employed by each firm in the industry.

A company's competitive strategy can either be *defensive* or *offensive*. A **defensive competitive strategy** involves positioning the firm to deflect the effect of the competitive forces in the industry. Examples may include investing in fixed assets and technology to lower production costs or creating a strong brand image with increased advertising expenditures.

An **offensive competitive strategy** is one in which the firm attempts to use its strengths to affect the competitive forces in the industry. For example, Wal-Mart used its buying power to obtain price concessions from its suppliers. This cost advantage, coupled with a superior delivery system to its stores, allowed Wal-Mart to grow against larger competitors and eventually become the leading U.S. retailer.

As an investor, you must understand the alternative competitive strategies available, determine each firm's strategy, judge whether the firm's strategy is reasonable for its industry, and, finally, evaluate how successful the firm is in implementing its strategy.

In the following sections, we discuss analyzing a firm's competitive position and strategy. The analyst must decide whether the firm's management is correctly positioning the firm to take advantage of industry and economic conditions. The analyst's opinion about management's decisions should ultimately be reflected in, and be the basis for the analyst's estimates of the firm's growth of cash flow and earnings.

Porter (1980a, 1985) suggests two major competitive strategies: low-cost leadership and differentiation. These two competitive strategies dictate how a firm has decided to cope with the five competitive conditions that define an industry's environment. The strategies available and the ways of implementing them differ within each industry.

Low-Cost Strategy   The firm that pursues the low-cost strategy is determined to become *the* low-cost producer and, hence, the cost leader in its industry. Cost advantages vary by industry and might include economies of scale, proprietary technology, or preferential access to raw materials. In order to benefit from cost leadership, the firm must command prices near the industry average, which means that it must differentiate itself about as well as other firms. If the firm discounts price too much, it could erode the superior rates of return available because of its low cost. During the past decade, Wal-Mart was considered a low-cost source. The firm achieved this by volume purchasing of merchandise and lower-cost operations. As a result, the firm charged less but still enjoyed higher profit margins and returns on capital than many of its competitors.

Differentiation Strategy   With the differentiation strategy, a firm seeks to identify itself as unique in its industry in an area that is important to buyers. Again, the possibilities for differentiation vary widely by industry. A company can attempt to differentiate itself based on its distribution system (selling in stores, by mail order, or door-to-door) or some unique marketing approach. A firm employing the differentiation strategy will enjoy above-average rates of return only if the price premium attributable to its differentiation exceeds the extra cost of being unique. Therefore, when you analyze a firm using this strategy, you must determine whether the differentiating factor is truly unique, whether it is sustainable, its cost, and if the price premium derived from the uniqueness is greater than its cost (is the firm experiencing above-average rates of return?).

Focusing a Strategy

Whichever strategy it selects, a firm must determine where it will focus this strategy. Specifically, a firm must select segments in the industry and tailor its strategy to serve these specific groups. For example, a low-cost strategy would typically exploit cost advantages for certain segments of the industry, such as being the low-cost producer for the expensive segment of the market. Similarly, a differentiation focus would target the special needs of buyers in specific segments. For example, in the athletic shoe market, companies have attempted to develop shoes for unique sport segments, such as tennis, basketball, aerobics, or walkers and hikers, rather than offering only shoes for runners. Firms thought that participants in these activities needed shoes with characteristics different from those desired by joggers. Equally important, they believed that these athletes would be willing to pay a premium for these special shoes. Again, you must ascertain if special possibilities exist, if they are being served by another firm, and if they can be priced to generate abnormal returns to the firm. Exhibit 14.1 details some of Porter's ideas for the skills, resources, and company organizational requirements needed to successfully develop a cost leadership or a differentiation strategy.

Next, you must determine which strategy the firm is pursuing and its success. Also, can the strategy be sustained? Further, you should evaluate a firm's competitive strategy over time, because strategies need to change as an industry evolves; different strategies work during different phases of an industry's life cycle. For example, differentiation strategies may work for firms in an industry during the early growth stages. Subsequently, when the industry is in the mature stage, firms may try to lower their costs.

Through the analysis process, the analyst identifies what the company does well, what it doesn't do well, and where the firm is vulnerable to the five competitive forces. Some call this

Exhibit 14.1	Skills, Resources, and Organizational Requirements Needed to Successfully Apply Cost Leadership and Differentiation Strategies

Generic Strategy	Commonly Required Skills and Resources	Common Organizational Requirements
Overall cost leadership	Sustained capital investment and access to capital Process engineering skills Intense supervision of labor Products designed for ease in manufacture Low-cost distribution system	Tight cost control Frequent, detailed control reports Structured organization and responsibilities Incentives based on meeting strict quantitative targets
Differentiation	Strong marketing abilities Product engineering Creative flair Strong capability in basic research Corporate reputation for quality or technological leadership Long tradition in the industry or unique combination of skills drawn from other businesses Strong cooperation from channels	Strong coordination among functions in R&D, product development, and marketing Subjective measurement and incentives instead of quantitative measures Amenities to attract highly skilled labor, scientists, or creative people

Source: Adapted from *Competitive Strategy: Techniques for Analyzing Industries and Competitors* by Michael E. Porter.

process developing a company's "story." This evaluation enables the analyst to determine the outlook and risks facing the firm. In summary, understanding the industry's competitive forces and the firm's strategy for dealing with them is the key to understanding how a company makes money and deriving an accurate estimate of the firm's long-run cash flows and its risks.

Another framework for examining and understanding a firm's competitive position and its strategy is the following SWOT analysis.

SWOT Analysis

SWOT analysis involves an examination of a firm's *s*trengths, *w*eaknesses, *o*pportunities, and *t*hreats. It should help you evaluate a firm's strategies to exploit its competitive advantages or defend against its weaknesses. Strengths and weaknesses involve identifying the firm's *internal* abilities or lack thereof. Opportunities and threats include *external* situations, such as competitive forces, discovery and development of new technologies, government regulations, and domestic and international economic trends.

The *strengths* of a company give the firm a comparative advantage in the marketplace. Perceived strengths can include good customer service, high-quality products, strong brand image, customer loyalty, innovative R&D, market leadership, or strong financial resources. To remain strengths, they must continue to be developed, maintained, and defended through prudent capital investment policies.

Weaknesses result when competitors have potentially exploitable advantages over the firm. Once weaknesses are identified, the firm can select strategies to mitigate or correct the weaknesses. For example, a firm that is only a domestic producer in a global market can make investments that will allow it to export or produce its product overseas. Another example would be a firm with poor financial resources that would form joint ventures with financially stronger firms.

Opportunities, or environmental factors that favor the firm, can include a growing market for the firm's products (domestic and international), shrinking competition, favorable exchange rate shifts, or identification of a new market or product segment.

Threats are environmental factors that can hinder the firm in achieving its goals. Examples would include a slowing domestic economy (or sluggish overseas economies for exporters), additional government regulation, an increase in industry competition, threats of entry, buyers or suppliers seeking to increase their bargaining power, or new technology that can obsolete the industry's product. By recognizing and understanding opportunities and threats, an investor can make informed decisions about how the firm can exploit opportunities and mitigate threats.

Some Lessons from Lynch

Peter Lynch (1989, 1993), the former portfolio manager of Fidelity Investments' highly successful Magellan Fund, looks for the following attributes when he analyzes firms.

Favorable Attributes of Firms   The following attributes of firms may result in favorable stock market performance:

1. The firm's product is not faddish; it is one that consumers will continue to purchase over time.
2. The company has a sustainable comparative competitive advantage over its rivals.
3. The firm's industry or product has market stability. Therefore, it has little need to innovate or create product improvements or fear that it may lose a technological advantage. Market stability means less potential for entry.
4. The firm can benefit from cost reductions (for example, a computer manufacturer that uses technology provided by suppliers to deliver a faster and less-expensive product).
5. The firm buys back its shares or management purchases shares which indicates that its insiders are putting their money into the firm.

Tenets of Warren Buffett

The following tenets are from Robert Hagstrom (2001). The parenthetical comments are based on discussions in the book and Berkshire Hathaway annual report letters.

Business Tenets
- Is the business simple and understandable?
  (This makes it easier to estimate future cash flows with a high degree of confidence.)
- Does the business have a consistent operating history?
  (Again, cash flow estimates can be made with more confidence.)
- Does the business have favorable long-term prospects?
  (Does the business have a franchise product or service that is needed or desired, has no close substitute, and is not regulated? This implies that the firm has pricing flexibility.)

Management Tenets
- Is management rational?
  (Is the allocation of capital to projects that provide returns above the cost of capital? If not, does management pay capital to stockholders through dividends or the repurchase of stock?)
- Is management candid with its shareholders?
  (Does management tell owners everything you would want to know?)

- Does management resist the institutional imperative?
  (Does management not attempt to imitate the behavior of other managers?)

Financial Tenets
- Focus on return on equity, not earnings per share.
  (Look for strong *ROE* with little or no debt.)
- Calculate owner earnings.
  (Owner earnings are basically equal to free cash flow after capital expenditures.)
- Look for a company with relatively high profit margins for its industry.
- Make sure the company has created at least one dollar of market value for every dollar retained.

Market Tenets
- What is the intrinsic value of the business?
  (Value is equal to future free cash flows discounted at a government bond rate. Using this low discount rate is considered appropriate because Warren Buffett is very confident of his cash flow estimates due to extensive analysis, and this confidence implies low risk.)
- Can the business be purchased at a significant discount to its fundamental intrinsic value?

The point is to make use of research on the competitive forces in an industry, a firm's responses to those forces, SWOT analysis, Lynch's suggestions, and Buffett's tenets.

ESTIMATING INTRINSIC VALUE

Now that the analysis of the economy, structural forces, the industry, the company, and its competitors is completed, it is time to estimate the intrinsic value of the firm's common stock. If the intrinsic value estimate exceeds the stock's current market price, the stock should be purchased. In contrast, if the current market price exceeds our intrinsic value estimate, we should avoid the stock.

As noted in Chapter 11, analysts use two general approaches to valuation and the following techniques.

Present Value of Cash Flows (PVCF)
1. Present value of dividends (DDM)
2. Present value of free cash flow to equity (FCFE)
3. Present value of free operating cash flow to the firm (FCFF)

Relative Valuation Techniques
1. Price/earnings ratio (*P/E*)
2. Price/cash flow ratio (*P/CF*)
3. Price/book value ratio (*P/BV*)
4. Price/sales ratio (*P/S*)

This section contains a brief presentation for each of these techniques as applied to Walgreens, the largest retail drugstore (RDS) chain in the United States. It operates 4,582 drugstores in 44 states and Puerto Rico. Its pharmacy operation generates 63.2 percent of sales.

Although we limit our demonstration to Walgreens (whose ticker symbol is WAG), your complete company analysis would cover all the firms in the RDS industry to determine which stocks should perform the best. The objective is to estimate the expected return and risk for all the individual firms in the industry over your investment horizon. The initial presentation considers the present value of cash flow (PVCF) models. Exhibit 14.2 contains historical data for Walgreens related to variables required for the PVCF models.

Exhibit 14.2 | **Walgreen Co.'s Input Data for Alternative Present Value of Cash Flow Models (Dollars in Millions, except per Share Data)**

Year	Dividend per Share	Net Income	Depreciation Expense	Capital Spending	Change in Working Capital	Principal Repayment	New Debt Issued	FCFE	EBIT	Tax Rate	FCFF	100%– Tax Rate	Time
1983	0.02	70	25	−71	−15	−3	0	6	147	45	19.9	55	1
1984	0.03	85	29	−68	−56	−3	0	−13	181	45	4.6	55	2
1985	0.03	94	34	−97	−61	−3	20	−33	209	46	−11.1	54	3
1986	0.03	103	44	−156	−72	−5	92	−86	229	45	−58.1	55	4
1987	0.04	104	54	−122	−118	−4	5	−86	243	46	−54.8	54	5
1988	0.04	129	59	−114	49	−4	31	119	263	38	157.1	62	6
1989	0.05	154	64	−121	−97	−4	0	−4	301	37	35.6	63	7
1990	0.05	175	70	−192	−69	−4	0	−20	344	38	22.3	62	8
1991	0.06	195	84	−202	−129	−24	0	−76	381	38	−10.8	62	9
1992	0.07	221	92	−145	−32	−6	0	130	429	37	185.3	63	10
1993	0.08	245	105	−185	−28	−112	0	25	483	39	186.6	61	11
1994	0.09	282	118	−290	−58	−6	0	46	550	38	111.0	62	12
1995	0.10	321	132	−310	−104	−7	0	32	629	39	101.7	61	13
1996	0.11	372	147	−364	−116	0	2	39	725	39	109.3	61	14
1997	0.12	436	164	−485	34	−1	0	148	842	39	226.6	61	15
1998	0.13	511	189	−641	−143	0	0	−84	878	39	−59.4	61	16
1999	0.13	624	210	−696	−206	0	0	−68	1028	39	−64.9	61	17
2000	0.14	777	230	−1119	−140	0	0	−252	1264	39	−258.0	61	18
2001	0.14	886	269	−1237	−569	0	0	−651	1426	38	−652.9	62	19
2002	0.15	1019	307	−934	−830	0	0	−438	1637	38	−442.5	62	20
2003	0.16	1176	346	−795	−726	0	0	1	1889	38	−3.8	62	21
2004	0.18	1360	403	−940	−748	0	0	75	2176	38	64.1	62	22

Source: Information calculated using publicly available data of Walgreen Co. Reprinted with the permission of Walgreen Co.

Present Value of Dividends

As noted in Chapter 11, determining the present value of all future dividends is a difficult task. Therefore, analysts apply simplifying assumptions when employing the dividend discount models. The typical assumption is that the stock's dividends will grow at a constant rate over time. Although unrealistic for fast-growing or cyclical firms, this assumption may be appropriate for some mature firms. More complex DDMs exist for more complicated growth forecasts including two-stage growth models (a period of fast growth followed by a period of constant growth) and three-stage growth models (a period of fast growth followed by a period of diminishing growth rates followed by a period of constant growth).[2]

We initially discuss the constant growth DDM which implies that when dividends grow at a constant rate, a stock's price should equal next year's dividend, D_1, divided by investors' required rate of return on the stock (k) minus the dividend growth rate (g):

14.1
$$\text{Intrinsic Value} = D_1 / (k - g)$$

With constant dividend growth, next year's dividend (D_1) should equal the current dividend, D_0, increased by the constant dividend growth rate: $D_1 = D_0 (1 + g)$. Because the current dividend is known, to estimate intrinsic value we need only estimate the dividend growth rate and investors' required rate of return.

Growth Rate Estimates   If the stock has had fairly constant dividend growth over the past 5 to 10 years, one estimate of the constant growth rate is to use the actual growth of dividends over this period. The average compound rate of growth is found by computing

14.2
$$\text{Average Dividend Growth Rate} = \sqrt[n]{\frac{D_n}{D_0}} - 1$$

In the case of Walgreens, the 1983 dividend (D_0) was $0.02 a share and the 2004 dividend (D_{21}) was $0.18 a share. The average dividend growth rate was

$$\sqrt[21]{\frac{\$0.18}{0.02}} - 1 = \sqrt[21]{9.00} - 1 = 0.1103$$

or 11.03 percent. Clearly, it is inappropriate to blindly plug historical growth rates into our formulas because if we do, we've wasted our time analyzing economic, structural, industry, and company influences. Our analysis may have indicated that growth is expected to increase or decrease due to such factors as changes in government programs, demographic shifts, or changes in product mix. The historical growth rate may need to be raised or lowered to incorporate our findings.

In Chapter 10, we learned other ways to estimate future growth. The sustainable growth rate

14.3
$$g = RR \times ROE$$

assumes the firm will maintain a constant debt-equity ratio as it finances asset growth. As we know from Chapter 10, *ROE* is the product of the net profit margin, total asset turnover, and the financial leverage multiplier. Thus, a firm's future growth rate and its components of *ROE*

---

[2]These were discussed in Chapter 11.

can be compared to those of its competitors, its industry, and the market. For Walgreens, the sustainable growth rate calculation using 2004 data is[3]

$$g = RR \times ROE = 0.86 \times .176$$
$$= 0.1514 = 15.14\%$$

The dividend growth rate will be influenced by the age of the industry life cycle, structural changes, and economic trends. Economic-industry-firm analysis provides valuable information regarding future trends in dividend growth. Information derived about management's plans to expand the firm, diversify into new areas, or change dividend policy can provide useful information about the firm's dividend policy. Averaging the historical growth rate of dividends (11.03 percent) and the implied sustainable growth estimate of 15.14 percent indicates a value of 13.08 percent. Although we feel that a firm's *ROE* is the critical growth factor and give this estimate more weight, we will use a conservative 13 percent for Walgreen Co.'s estimated *g* (this is also close to the firm's earning's growth rate).

Required Rate of Return Estimate   We know an investor's required rate of return has two basic components: the nominal risk-free interest rate and a risk premium. If the market is efficient, over time the return earned by investors should compensate them for the risk of the investment.

Notably, we must estimate *future* risk premiums to determine the stock's current intrinsic value. Estimates of the nominal risk-free interest rate are available from the initial analysis of the economy during the top-down approach. The risk premium of the firm must rely on other information including evaluation of the financial statements and capital market relationships.

In Chapter 10, we examined ratios that measure business risk, financial risk, liquidity risk, exchange rate risk, and country risk. These measures can be compared against the firm's major competitors, its industry, and the overall market. This fundamental comparison should indicate if the firm deserves a higher or lower risk premium than the overall market, other firms in the industry, or the firm's historical risk premium. Accounting-based risk measures use historical data, whereas investment analysis requires an estimate of the future, including any information uncovered during the top-down process that would lead to higher or lower risk estimates.

For a market-based risk estimate, the firm's characteristic line is estimated by regressing market returns on the stock's returns. The slope of this regression line is the stock's measure of systematic risk. Estimates of the economy's risk-free rate, the future long-run market return, and an estimate of the stock's beta help estimate next year's required rate of return:

14.4 $$E(R_{stock}) = E(RFR) + \beta_{stock}\,[E(R_{market}) - E(RFR)]$$

Again, this estimate of beta begins with historical market information. Because beta is affected by changes in a firm's business and financial risks, as well as other influences, an investor should increase or lower the historical beta estimate based on his or her analysis of the firm's *future* risk characteristics.

To demonstrate the estimate of the required rate of return equation for Walgreens, we make several assumptions regarding components of the security market line (SML). First, the prevailing nominal risk-free rate *(RFR)* is estimated at about 4.5 percent—the current yield to maturity for the intermediate-term (10 year) government bond. The expected equity market rate of return (R_M) depends on the expected market risk premium on stocks. As noted

---

[3]This sustainable growth rate value differs from the one in Chapter 10 because this calculation uses year-end values for *ROE*, whereas in Chapter 10, the equity value is an average of the beginning and ending values.

earlier, this is a very controversial topic wherein the estimates range from a high of about 8 percent to a low of about 3 percent. The authors reject both of these extreme values and will use a 4.0 percent risk premium (0.040) as discussed in Chapter 12. The final estimate is the firm's systematic risk value (beta), based upon the following regression model (the characteristic line):

14.5
$$R_{WAG} = \alpha + \beta_{WAG} R_M$$

where:

R_{WAG} = monthly rate of return for Walgreens
α = constant term
β_{WAG} = beta coefficient for Walgreens
equal to $\dfrac{Cov_{W,M}}{\sigma_M^2}$
R_M = monthly rates of return for a market proxy—typically the S&P 500 Index

When this regression was run using monthly rates of return during the five-year period 2000–2004 (60 observations), the beta coefficient was estimated at 0.90.

Reflecting the discussion in Chapter 12, we put together the *RFR* of 0.045 and the market risk premium of 0.040, which implies an expected market return (R_M) of 0.085. This, combined with the Walgreen Co.'s beta of 0.90, indicates the following expected rate of return for Walgreens:

$$
\begin{aligned}
E(R) &= RFR + \beta_i(R_M - RFR) \\
&= 0.045 + 0.90\,(0.085 - 0.045) \\
&= 0.045 + 0.90\,(0.04) \\
&= 0.045 + 0.036 \\
&= 0.081 = 8.1\%
\end{aligned}
$$

We will round this to 8 percent.

Present Value of Dividends Model (DDM)

At this point, the analyst would face a problem: the intent was to use the basic DDM, which assumed a constant growth rate for an infinite period. You will recall that the model also required that $k > g$ (the required rate of return is larger than the expected growth rate), which is not true in this case because $k = 8$ percent and $g = 13$ percent (as computed earlier). Therefore, the analyst must employ a two- or three-stage growth model. Because of the fairly large difference between the current growth rate of 13 percent and the long-run constant growth rate of 7 percent, it seems reasonable to use a three-stage growth model, which includes a gradual transition period. We assume that the growth periods are as follows:

$g_1 = 7$ years (growing at 13 percent a year)
$g_2 = 6$ years (during this period it is assumed that the growth rate declines 1 percent per year for 6 years)
$g_3 = $ constant perpetual growth of 7 percent

Therefore, beginning with 2005 when dividends were expected to be $0.21, the future dividend payments will be as follows (the growth rates are in parentheses):

	HIGH-GROWTH PERIOD					DECLINING-GROWTH PERIOD			
Year	Gr. Rate	Div.	8% PV Factor	PV	Year	Gr. Rate	Div.	8% PV Factor	PV
2006	(13%)	0.24	0.855	0.20	2013	(12%)	0.55	.500	0.28
2007	(13%)	0.27	0.794	0.21	2014	(11%)	0.61	.463	0.28
2008	(13%)	0.30	0.735	0.22	2015	(10%)	0.68	.429	0.29
2009	(13%)	0.34	0.680	0.23	2016	(9%)	0.74	.397	0.29
2010	(13%)	0.39	0.629	0.24	2017	(8%)	0.80	.368	0.29
2011	(13%)	0.44	0.585	0.26	2018	(7%)	0.85	.340	0.29
2012	(13%)	0.49	0.341	0.27					
		Sum		$1.64				Sum	1.72

Constant Growth Period:

$$P_{2018} = \frac{0.85(1.07)}{0.08 - 0.07} = \frac{0.91}{0.08 - 0.07} = \frac{0.91}{0.01} = \$91.00 \times 0.340 = \$30.94$$

The total value of the stock is the sum of the three present-value streams discounted at 8 percent:

1. Present value of high-growth period dividends	$1.64
2. Present value of declining-growth period dividends	1.72
3. Present value of constant-growth period dividends	30.94
Total present value of dividends	**$34.30**

The estimated value based on the DDM ($34.30) is substantially lower than the market price in mid-2005 of about $42.00. This estimated value also implies a *P/E* ratio based on expected earnings in 2005 of about $1.50 per share (that is, about 22.9 times earnings) compared to the prevailing market *P/E* of about 18 times 2005 earnings. In a subsequent section on relative valuation techniques, we compare Walgreen Co.'s *P/E* ratio to that of its industry and the market.

Present Value of Free Cash Flow to Equity

As noted in Chapter 11, this technique resembles a present value of earnings concept except that it considers the capital expenditures required to maintain and grow the firm and the change in working capital required for a growing firm (that is, an increase in accounts receivable and inventory). The specific definition of free cash flow to equity (FCFE) is:

Net Income + Depreciation Expense − Capital
Expenditures − Δ in Working Capital − Principal
Debt Repayments + New Debt Issues

This technique attempts to determine the free cash flow that is available to the stockholders after payments to all other capital suppliers and after providing for the continued growth of the firm. As noted in Chapter 11, given the current FCFE values, the alternative forms of the model are similar to those available for the DDM, which in turn depends on the firm's growth prospects. Specifically, if the firm is in its mature, constant-growth phase, it is possible to use a model similar to the reduced form DDM:

14.6
$$\text{Value} = \frac{FCFE_1}{k - g_{FCFE}}$$

where:

FCFE = the expected free cash flow to equity in Period 1
k = the required rate of return on equity for the firm
g_{FCFE} = the expected constant growth rate of free cash flow to equity for the firm

We already know from the prior dividend model that the firm's net income has grown at a rate (about 13 percent) that exceeds the required rate of return. In the case of FCFE, it is necessary to consider the effect of capital expenditures relative to depreciation and changes in working capital as well as debt repayments and new debt issues. The historical data in Exhibit 14.2 shows a growth rate that exceeded 20 percent during some periods since 1983, in contrast to the negative values in 1998–2002. The reason for the dramatic change is evident—it is the very heavy capital expenditures and the significant negative working capital items. The firm has reduced the growth rate of stores—from a net increase (new stores minus closings) of about 475 stores per year. Based on discussions with management, it appears that this slowdown in growth is due to the prevailing shortage of pharmacists. While Walgreens will continue adding stores, the slower rate of growth and a reduction in the growth of inventory will allow the firm to build on the positive cash flows in 2004. Specifically, it is estimated that in 2005 the FCFE will be about $220 million and the FCFF (free cash flow to the firm) will be about $260 million. Such volatility makes it appropriate to use the conservative 13 percent growth rate going forward after 2005. Therefore, the following example again uses a three-stage growth model with characteristics similar to the dividend growth model.

g_1 = 13 percent for the six years after 2005
g_2 = a constantly declining growth rate to 7 percent over six years
k = 8 percent cost of equity

The specific estimates of annual FCFE, beginning with the actual estimated value of $220 million in 2005, are as follows:

	HIGH-GROWTH PERIOD				DECLINING-GROWTH PERIOD		
Year	Growth	$ Million	PV @ 8%	Year	Growth	$ Million	PV @ 8%
2005	—	220	204	2012	(12%)	513	277
2006	(13%)	249	213	2013	(11%)	569	285
2007	(13%)	281	223	2014	(10%)	626	290
2008	(13%)	317	233	2015	(9%)	683	293
2009	(13%)	359	244	2016	(8%)	737	293
2010	(13%)	405	255	2017	(7%)	789	290
2011	(13%)	458	267				
		Total	$1,640			Total	$1,728

$$\text{Constant Growth Period Value} = \frac{789(1.07)}{0.08 - 0.07} = \frac{844}{0.01} = \$84,400$$

PV @ 8% = $31,034

The total value of the stock is the sum of the three present-value streams discounted at 8 percent:

	$ Million
1. Present value of high-growth cash flows	1,640
2. Present value of declining-growth cash flows	1,728
3. Present value of constant-growth cash flows	31,034
Total present value of FCFE	34,402

The outstanding shares in 2004 were approximately 1,032 million. Therefore, the per share value, based on the present value of FCFE is $33.34 ($34,402/1,032). Again, this estimated value is lower than the prevailing market price of about $42.00. This estimated value implies a *P/E* ratio of about 22.2 times estimated 2005 earnings of $1.50 per share.

Present Value of Operating Free Cash Flow

This is also referred to as *free cash flow to the firm* (FCFF) by Damodaran (1994) and *the entity DCF model* by Copeland, Koller, and Murrin (2001). The object is to determine a value for the total firm and subtract the value of the firm's debt obligations to arrive at a value for the firm's equity. Notably, in this valuation technique, we discount the firm's operating free cash flow to the firm (FCFF) at the firm's weighted average cost of capital (WACC) rather than its cost of equity.

Operating free cash flow or *free cash flow to the firm* is equal to

$$\text{EBIT} (1 - \text{Tax Rate}) + \text{Depreciation Expense}$$
$$- \text{Capital Expenditures} - \Delta \text{ in Working Capital}$$
$$- \Delta \text{ in other assets}$$

This is the cash flow generated by a company's operations and available to all who have provided capital to the firm—both equity and debt. As noted, because it is the cash flow available to *all capital suppliers,* it is discounted at the firm's WACC.

Again, the alternative specifications of this operating FCF model are similar to the DDM—that is, the specification depends upon the firm's growth prospects. Assuming an expectation of constant growth, you can use the reduced form model:

14.7
$$\text{Firm Value} = \frac{\text{FCFF}_1}{\text{WACC} - g_\text{FCFF}} \text{ or } \frac{\text{OFCF}_1}{\text{WACC} - g_\text{OFCF}}$$

where:

FCFF_1 = the free cash flow for the firm in Period 1
OFCF_1 = the firm's operating free cash flow in Period 1
WACC = the firm's weighted average cost of capital
g_FCFF = the constant infinite growth rate of free cash flow for the firm
g_OFCF = the constant infinite growth rate of operating free cash flow

As noted in Exhibit 14.3, the compound annual growth rate for operating free cash flow (free cash flow to the firm) during the 21-year period was very low and was negative between 1998 and 2003. It became positive in 2004, and it is estimated it will be $260 million in 2005. An alternative measure of long-run growth is the growth implied by the equation:

14.8
$$g = (RR)(ROIC)$$

where:

RR = the average retention rate
$ROIC$ = EBIT (1 − Tax Rate)/Total Capital

For Walgreens, the recent retention rate is about 82 percent and

$$ROIC = \frac{\text{EBIT}(1 - \text{Tax Rate})}{\text{Total Capital}} = \frac{2,176 \times (0.62)}{(7,985 + 9,264)/2} = \frac{1,349}{8,624} = 0.1564$$
$$= 15.64\%$$

Exhibit 14.3 | Inputs for Relative Valuation Technique: Walgreens, Retail Drugstore Industry, and S&P Industrials Index: 1993–2003

Year	WALGREENS					RETAIL DRUGSTORE INDUSTRY					S&P INDUSTRIALS INDEX				
	Mean Price	EPS	CF per Share	BV per Share	Sales per Share	Mean Price	EPS	CF per Share	BV per Share	Sales per Share	Mean Price	EPS	CF per Share	BV per Share	Sales per Share
1993	4.96	0.23	0.44	1.40	8.37	91.00	4.45	21.34	36.84	186.63	520.21	21.96	58.00	191.82	622.12
1994	5.06	0.29	0.50	1.60	9.32	91.27	4.55	22.41	38.68	202.90	536.52	33.12	72.39	210.98	653.75
1995	6.64	0.33	0.57	1.82	10.49	120.77	5.76	26.88	42.76	233.78	638.97	26.01	79.27	227.12	706.13
1996	9.10	0.38	0.65	2.08	11.85	158.78	9.06	17.05	44.27	265.93	795.01	41.15	82.89	238.76	727.40
1997	13.22	0.44	0.61	2.40	13.57	231.01	5.12	17.19	60.87	308.29	1006.12	42.13	83.73	247.83	750.71
1998	22.50	0.54	0.73	2.86	15.43	368.62	7.85	20.94	68.07	343.11	1285.73	38.37	87.38	264.63	750.48
1999	28.31	0.62	0.83	3.47	17.83	403.33	10.59	18.58	61.88	396.21	1651.82	50.25	97.73	302.08	812.00
2000	33.91	0.76	1.00	4.19	21.05	385.22	9.38	13.80	69.34	385.86	1692.85	53.85	105.09	337.51	853.86
2001	37.08	0.86	0.71	5.11	24.15	416.50	9.71	18.35	72.68	369.64	1363.30	19.82	68.58	348.38	811.04
2002	35.25	0.99	1.47	6.08	27.98	348.15	12.96	20.69	85.74	400.23	1133.05	22.57	61.59	310.61	781.65
2003	31.63	1.14	1.47	7.02	31.72	335.69	21.12	23.36	98.79	635.62	1097.27	47.12	90.88	363.74	847.38

Therefore,

$$g = (0.82)(0.1564)$$
$$= 0.1282 = 12.82\%$$

We will round this and begin with a growth estimate for OFCF/FCFF of 13 percent.

Calculation of WACC   We calculate the discount rate (i.e., the firm's WACC) using the following formula:

14.9 $$\text{WACC} = W_E k + W_D i$$

where:

W_E = the proportion of equity in total capital
k = the after-tax cost of equity (from the SML)
W_D = the proportion of debt in total capital[4]
i = the after-tax cost of debt[5]

Recall from corporate finance courses that there are differences of opinion regarding how one should estimate the debt and equity weights—that is, using proportions based upon relative book values or based on relative market value weights. Without getting into the reasons for each choice, it is important to recognize that the use of market value weights will almost always result in a higher WACC because it will imply more equity financing since most firms have a *P/BV* ratio greater than one (for Walgreens the *P/BV* ratio is currently in excess of 5.0). To demonstrate this, we compute a WACC using both weightings. The cost of debt and cost of equity will be the same for both sets.

WACC Using Book Value Weights

k_e = 0.080 (from prior SML calculation)

k_d = 0.043 (current interest rate of 7% and recent tax rate of 38% for WAG)
        $0.07 \times (1 - 0.38) = 0.043$

W_d = 0.30 (including leases)

W_e = 0.70

$$\text{WACC} = (W_d \times k_d) + (W_e \times k_e)$$
$$= (0.30 \times 0.043) + (0.70 \times 0.080)$$
$$= 0.013 + 0.056 = 0.069 = 6.90\%$$

WACC Using Market Value Weights

k_e = 0.080 W_e = 0.90

k_d = 0.043 W_d = 0.10

$$\text{WACC} = (W_d \times k_d) + (W_e \times k_e)$$
$$= (0.10 \times 0.043) + (0.90 \times 0.080)$$
$$= 0.0043 + 0.072 = 0.0763 = 7.63\%$$

---

[4]The proportions of debt and equity capital used in the WACC estimate will be computed using both book value weights that consider the value of capitalized lease payments as debt, and market value weights.
[5]For this estimate, we use the prevailing interest rate on corporate A-rated bonds (7 percent), and Walgreen Co.'s (ticker symbol WAG) recent tax rate of 38 percent.

Therefore, we have a range of 6.90 percent to 7.63 percent and an average of 7.27 percent. We will use a WACC of 7 percent in the demonstration.

Again, because the expected growth rate of operating free cash flow (13 percent) is greater than the firm's WACC, we cannot use the reduced form model that assumes constant growth at this relatively high rate for an infinite period. Therefore, the following demonstration will employ the three-stage growth model with growth duration assumptions similar to the prior examples.

Given these inputs for recent growth and the firm's WACC, the growth estimates for a three-stage growth model are

g_1 = 13 percent for five years
g_2 = a constantly declining rate to 6 percent over seven years.[6]

The specific estimates for future OFCF (or FCFF) are as follows, beginning from the 2005 value of $260 million.

	HIGH-GROWTH PERIOD				DECLINING-GROWTH PERIOD		
Year	Growth Rate	FCFF	PV @ 7%	Year	Growth Rate	FCFF	PV @ 7%
2005	—	260	243	2011	(12%)	537	334
2006	(13%)	294	257	2012	(11%)	596	347
2007	(13%)	332	271	2013	(10%)	655	356
2008	(13%)	375	286	2014	(9%)	714	363
2009	(13%)	424	302	2015	(8%)	771	366
2010	(13%)	479	319	2016	(7%)	825	366
				2017	(6%)	874	363
		Total	$1,678			Total	$2,496

$$\text{Constant Growth Period Value} = \frac{874(1.06)}{0.07 - 0.06} = \frac{926}{0.07 - 0.06} = \$92,600$$

$$\text{PV @ 7\%} = \$38,426$$

Thus, the total value of the firm is:

	$ Million
1. Present value of high-growth cash flows	$1,678
2. Present value of declining-growth cash flows	2,496
3. Present value of constant-growth cash flows	38,426
Total present value of operating FCF (FCFF)	$42,600

Recall that the value of equity is the total value of the firm (PV of OFCF) minus the current market value of debt, which is the present value of debt payments at the firm's cost of debt (0.07). The values are as follows:

[6]This 6 percent long-run growth rate assumption implies that we do not believe that FCFF can grow as long at 13 percent and as fast in the long run as FCFE. Given a beginning growth rate of 13 percent for only five years and a long-run rate of 6 percent means that the growth rate will decline by 0.01 per year as shown in the following example.

Total present value of operating FCF	$ 42,600
Minus: Value of debt[7]	12,681
Value of equity	$ 29,909
Number of common shares	1,032 million
Value of equity per share	$ 28.98

Again, this estimated value compares to the recent market value of about $42.00. The $28.98 value implies a *P/E* of about 19 times estimated 2005 earnings of $1.50 per share.

To summarize, the valuations derived from the present value of cash flow techniques are as follows:

Present value of dividends	$34.30
Present value of FCFE	$33.34
Present value of OFCF	$28.98
(or the PV of FCFF)	

All of these prices must be compared to the prevailing market price of $42.00 to determine the investment decision.

Relative Valuation Ratio Techniques

In this section, we present the data required to compute the several relative valuation ratios and demonstrate the use of these relative valuation ratio techniques for Walgreens compared to the RDS industry and the S&P Industrials Index.

Exhibit 14.3 contains the basic data required to compute the relative valuation ratios, and Exhibit 14.4 contains the four sets of relative valuation ratios for Walgreens, its industry, and the aggregate market. This exhibit also contains a comparison of the company ratios to similar ratios for the company's industry and the market. Such a comparison helps the analyst determine changes in the relative valuation ratios over time and consider if the current valuation ratio for the company (Walgreens) is reasonable based on the financial characteristics of the firm versus its industry and the market. To aid in the analysis, four graphs contain the time series of the relative valuation ratios for the company, its industry, and the market. Four additional graphs show the relationship between the relative valuation ratios: for the company compared to its industry and for the company compared to the stock market. We begin with the *P/E* ratio approach where we derive an intrinsic value for the stock based upon an estimate of future EPS and an earnings multiple (*P/E*) for the stock that reflects future expectations.

ESTIMATING COMPANY EARNINGS PER SHARE

An estimate of the earnings per share for the company is a function of the sales forecast and the estimated profit margin. The sales forecast includes an analysis of the relationship of company sales to various relevant economic series and to the RDS industry series. These comparisons tell us how the company is performing relative to the economy and to its closest competition.

---

[7]This long-term debt value from Chapter 10 includes the present value of minimum lease payments discounted at the firm's cost of debt (7 percent).

Exhibit 14.4 | Relative Valuation Variables: Walgreens, Retail Drugstore Industry, and S&P Industrials Index: 1993–2003

PRICE/EARNINGS RATIO

Year	Walgreens	Retail Drug	Ratio Co/Ind.	S&P Ind.	Ratio Co/Mkt
1993	22.02	20.45	1.08	23.69	0.93
1994	17.75	20.06	0.88	16.20	1.10
1995	20.42	20.97	0.97	24.57	0.83
1996	24.25	17.53	1.38	19.32	1.26
1997	30.03	45.12	0.67	23.88	1.26
1998	41.66	46.96	0.89	33.51	1.24
1999	45.65	38.09	1.20	32.87	1.39
2000	44.81	41.07	1.09	31.44	1.43
2001	43.12	42.89	1.01	68.78	0.63
2002	35.61	26.86	1.33	50.20	0.71
2003	27.75	15.89	1.75	23.29	1.19
Mean	32.10	30.53	1.11	31.61	1.09

PRICE/CASH FLOW RATIO

Year	Walgreens	Retail Drug	Ratio Co/Ind.	S&P Ind.	Ratio Co/Mkt
1993	11.27	4.26	2.64	8.97	1.26
1994	10.12	4.07	2.48	7.41	1.37
1995	11.65	4.49	2.59	8.06	1.45
1996	14.00	9.31	1.50	9.59	1.46
1997	21.67	13.44	1.61	12.02	1.80
1998	30.82	17.60	1.75	14.71	2.09
1999	34.11	21.71	1.57	16.90	2.02
2000	33.91	27.91	1.21	16.11	2.11
2001	52.23	22.70	2.30	19.88	2.63
2002	24.03	16.83	1.43	18.40	1.31
2003	21.55	14.37	1.50	12.07	1.79
Mean	24.12	14.25	1.87	13.10	1.75

PRICE/BOOK VALUE RATIO

Year	Walgreens	Retail Drug	Ratio Co/Ind.	S&P Ind.	Ratio Co/Mkt
1993	3.54	2.47	1.43	2.71	1.31
1994	3.16	2.36	1.34	2.54	1.24
1995	3.65	2.82	1.29	2.81	1.30
1996	4.38	3.59	1.22	3.33	1.31
1997	5.51	3.80	1.45	4.06	1.36
1998	7.87	5.42	1.45	4.86	1.62
1999	8.16	6.52	1.25	5.47	1.49
2000	8.09	5.56	1.46	5.02	1.61
2001	7.26	5.73	1.27	3.91	1.85
2002	5.80	4.06	1.43	3.65	1.59
2003	4.51	3.40	1.33	3.02	1.49
Mean	5.63	4.16	1.36	3.76	1.47

PRICE/SALES RATIO

Year	Walgreens	Retail Drug	Ratio Co/Ind.	S&P Ind.	Ratio Co/Mkt
1993	0.59	0.49	1.22	0.84	0.71
1994	0.54	0.45	1.21	0.82	0.66
1995	0.63	0.52	1.23	0.90	0.70
1996	0.77	0.60	1.29	1.09	0.70
1997	0.97	0.75	1.30	1.34	0.73
1998	1.46	1.07	1.36	1.71	0.85
1999	1.59	1.02	1.56	2.03	0.78
2000	1.61	1.00	1.61	1.98	0.81
2001	1.54	1.13	1.36	1.68	0.91
2002	1.26	0.87	1.45	1.45	0.87
2003	1.00	0.53	1.89	1.29	0.77
Mean	1.09	0.77	1.41	1.38	0.77

Exhibit 14.5 | **Walgreens, S&P Retail Drugstore Sales, and Various Economic Series: 1993–2003**

Year	Sales Walgreen Co. ($ Millions)	Retail Drugstores (Sales/Share)	Personal Consumption Expenditures (PCE) ($ Billions)	PCE Medical Care ($ Billions)	Medical Care as a Percentage of PCE
1993	8,295	186.63	4,454.7	700.6	15.73%
1994	9,235	202.90	4,716.4	737.3	15.63%
1995	10,395	233.78	4,969.0	780.7	15.71%
1996	11,778	265.93	5,237.5	814.4	15.55%
1997	13,363	308.29	5,529.3	854.6	15.46%
1998	15,307	343.11	5,856.0	899.0	15.35%
1999	17,839	396.21	6,250.2	939.9	15.04%
2000	21,207	385.86	6,728.4	1,026.8	15.26%
2001	24,623	369.64	7,055.0	1,113.8	15.79%
2002	28,681	400.23	7,385.3	1,210.3	16.39%
2003	32,505	635.62	7,760.9	1,301.1	16.76%
CGR	13.22	11.78	5.18	5.79	0.58

CGR = compound annual growth rate

Source: *Financial Analyst's Handbook* (New York: Standard & Poor's, 2004) and *Economic Report of the President* (Washington, DC: U.S. Government Printing Office, 2005).

Company Sales Forecast

Besides providing background on the company, these relationships can help us develop specific sales forecasts for Walgreens.

Exhibit 14.5 contains data on sales for Walgreens from its annual report, sales per share for the RDS industry, and several personal consumption expenditure (PCE) series for the period 1993 to 2003.

To examine the relationship of Walgreen Co.'s sales to the economy, we considered several alternative series. The series that had the strongest relationship was personal consumption expenditure for medicine (PCE medical care).[8] The scatterplot of Walgreen Co.'s sales and the PCE medical care expenditures contained in Exhibit 14.6 indicates a strong linear relationship, including the fact that Walgreen Co.'s sales grew faster than PCE medical care (i.e., 13.22 percent versus 5.79 percent). As a result, Walgreen Co.'s sales have gone from about 1.2 percent of PCE medical care to 2.50 percent.

We also compared Walgreen Co.'s sales and sales per share for the RDS industry. Unfortunately, it did not reflect as strong a relationship and is not used subsequently.

The figures in the last column of Exhibit 14.5 indicate that during this period, the proportion of PCE allocated to medical care went from 15.7 percent in 1993 to 16.8 percent in 2003. The increasing proportion of PCE spent on medical care is a function of the growing

---

[8] The relationship between Walgreen Co.'s sales and total PCE or per capital PCE was significant but not as strong as PCE medical care.

| Exhibit 14.6 | **Scatterplot of Walgreen Co.'s Sales and PCE Medical Care: 1993–2003** |

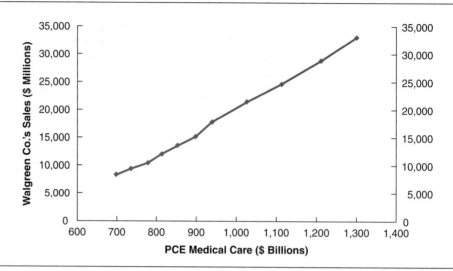

proportion of the population over 65 and the rising cost of medical care. Because Walgreen Co.'s sales are growing faster than medical expenditures, these increases should continue to be beneficial for Walgreens because over 62 percent of its sales are prescriptions. Notably, these increases in medical care expenditures continued during the economic recession in 2001−2002.

As shown in Exhibit 14.7, the internal sales growth for Walgreens going back to 1977, resulted from an increase in the number of stores (from 626 in 1977 to 4,582 in 2004) and an increase in the annual sales per store because of the upgrading of stores. The net increase in stores includes numerous new, large stores and the closing of many smaller stores. As a result, the average size of stores has increased. More important, the firm has continued to increase its sales per thousand square feet at almost 4.4 percent a year. This is a critical statistic in the retailing industry, and the fact that Walgreens has been able to experience consistent growth in this metric is significant evidence of strong management.

Sample Estimate of Walgreen Co.'s Sales   The foregoing analysis indicates that you should use the Walgreens–PCE medical care graph. To estimate PCE medical care, you should initially project total PCE and then determine how much would be included in the medical care component. As noted in Chapter 13 in connection with the industry analysis, economists were forecasting an increase in PCE of 3.6 percent during 2005, which implied a 2005 estimate of $8,694 billion. In addition, it was estimated that the percentage of PCE spent on medical care in 2005 would be almost 17.0 percent. This implies an estimate for PCE medical care of $1,475 billion, which is about a 6.5 percent increase from 2004. Based on the graph in Exhibit 14.6, which shows the historical relationship between PCE medical care and Walgreen co.'s sales, this would imply a 14 percent increase in Walgreen Co.'s sales to about $42.75 billion ($37.508 billion × 1.14).

Because Walgreens provides data on square footage and the number of stores, it allows us to compute an alternative sales estimate using the company data in Exhibit 14.7 to support the prior estimate. If we assume an increase in store area during 2005 of about 4.1 million square feet (which is less than in most years), the firm's total sales area would be about 55 million square feet. As noted, sales per square foot have likewise increased. Assuming a conservative increase to $750 of sales per thousand square feet implies a sales forecast of about $41.25 billion for 2005, a 10 percent increase over 2004 sales of $37.51 billion.

Exhibit 14.7 | **Sales, Number of Stores, and Sales Area for Walgreens: 1977–2004**

Year	Sales Walgreens ($ Millions)	Number of Stores	Annual Sales per Store ($ Millions)	Store Area (000 Sq. Ft.)	Area per Store (000 Sq.Ft.)	Avg. Sales per Thousand Sq. Ft.
1977	1,223.2	626	1.95	5,188	8.29	235.77
1978	1,192.9	641	1.86	5,390	8.41	221.32
1979	1,334.5	688	1.94	5,851	8.50	228.08
1980	1,530.7	739	2.07	6,305	8.53	242.78
1981	1,743.5	821	2.12	7,209	8.78	241.85
1982	2,039.5	883	2.31	7,815	8.85	260.97
1983	2,360.6	941	2.51	8,402	8.93	280.96
1984	2,744.6	1,002	2.74	9,002	8.98	304.89
1985	3,161.9	1,095	2.89	10,010	9.14	315.87
1986	3,660.6	1,273	2.88	11,895	9.34	307.74
1987	4,281.6	1,356	3.16	12,844	9.47	333.35
1988	4,883.5	1,416	3.45	13,549	9.57	360.43
1989	5,380.1	1,484	3.63	14,272	9.62	376.97
1990	6,047.5	1,564	3.87	15,105	9.66	400.36
1991	6,733.0	1,646	4.09	15,877	9.65	424.08
1992	7,475.0	1,736	4.31	16,811	9.68	444.65
1993	8,294.8	1,836	4.52	17,950	9.78	462.11
1994	9,235.0	1,968	4.69	19,342	9.83	477.46
1995	10,395.1	2,085	4.99	20,731	9.94	501.43
1996	11,778.4	2,193	5.37	22,124	10.09	532.38
1997	13,363.0	2,358	5.67	23,935	10.15	558.30
1998	15,307.0	2,549	6.01	26,024	10.21	588.19
1999	17,838.8	2,821	6.32	29,230	10.36	610.29
2000	21,206.9	3,165	6.70	33,684	10.64	629.58
2001	24,623.0	3,520	7.00	38,226	10.86	644.14
2002	28,681.1	3,883	7.39	42,672	10.99	672.13
2003	32,505.4	4,227	7.69	46,734	11.06	695.54
2004	37,508.2	4,582	8.19	50,927	11.11	736.51
Average annual rate of growth (%)	13.59%	7.69%	5.50%	8.88%	1.09%	4.36%

Source: Information calculated using publicly available data of Walgreen Co. Reprinted with the permission of Walgreen Co.

Another internal estimate is made possible by using the number of stores and sales per store. Walgreens is expected to open 450 stores during 2005. Assuming that it closes 85 stores as expected, this would be a net addition of 365 stores, resulting in 4,947 stores at the end of 2005. Assuming sales per store likewise continue to increase from $8.19 million to $8.50 million implies an estimate of $42.00 billion (4,947 × $8.50 million), an increase of 12 percent over 2004.

Given the three estimates, the preference is for the mid-range estimate of 12 percent, which is somewhat conservative, because we are in the fourth year of the economic expansion and recent increases have been in the 13–15 percent range. This implies a final sales forecast for 2005 of $42 billion.

Estimating the Company Profit Margin

The next step in projecting earnings per share is to estimate the firm's net profit margin, which should include three considerations: (1) identification and evaluation of the firm's specific competitive strategy—that is, either low-cost or differentiation; (2) the firm's internal performance, including general company trends and consideration of any problems that might affect its future performance; and (3) the firm's relationship with its industry, which should indicate whether the company's past performance is attributable to its industry or if it is unique to the firm. These examinations should help us understand the firm's past performance but should also provide the background to make a meaningful estimate for the future. In this analysis, we do not consider the company-economy relationship because the significant economywide profit factors are reflected in the industry results. Since we have already discussed these strategies in general, we concentrate on how they affect Walgreens.

WALGREEN CO.'S COMPETITIVE STRATEGIES

Over the years, has Walgreens pursued a low-cost strategy or has the firm attempted to differentiate itself from its competitors in some unique way? Based on its annual reports, Walgreens has pursued both strategies with different segments of its business. The firm's size and buying power allow it to be a cost leader for some of its nonprescription products, such as liquor, ice cream, candy, and soft drinks. These items are advertised heavily to attract customer traffic and to build consumer loyalty. At the same time, Walgreens has attempted to build a very strong franchise in the medical prescription business based on differentiation in service. Computer technology in the prescription area makes it possible for the firm to distinguish itself by providing outstanding service to its prescription customers. Specifically, the firm refers to itself as the nation's prescription druggist based on the number of prescriptions it fills and a nationwide computer system that allows customers to have their prescriptions filled at any of the 4,582 Walgreen Co.'s drugstores in the country. This service leadership in the growing medical field is a major goal.

The Internal Performance

Profit margin figures for Walgreens and the RDS industry are in Exhibit 14.8. The profit margins for Walgreens increased overall from 2.96 percent to 3.62 percent. In contrast, the margins for the RDS industry experienced an overall decline. Overall, Walgreens experienced a positive trend in its operating and net profit margins over the past 10 years. To predict future values, you need to determine the reason for the overall decline in the industry profit margin and, more important, what factors have contributed to Walgreen Co.'s strong positive performance.

Industry Factors   Industry profit margins have declined over the past two decades due to price discounting by aggressive regional drug chains.[9] The discussion in Chapter 13 suggested this as one of the competitive structure conditions that affect long-run profitability. Industry

---

[9]For a more complete discussion, see "Retailing—Drug Stores" in *Standard & Poor's Industry Surveys* (New York: Standard & Poor's, 2004).

Exhibit 14.8	Profit Margins and Component Expenses for Walgreens and the Retail Drugstore Industry: 1993–2003

	WALGREEN CO.			RETAIL DRUGSTORES		
Year	Operating Margin (%)	NBT Margin (%)	Net Profit Margin (%)	Operating Margin (%)	NBT Margin (%)	Net Profit Margin (%)
1993	4.90	4.82	2.96	29.96	4.55	2.78
1994	4.93	4.96	3.05	30.04	3.80	2.33
1995	5.00	5.04	3.09	31.41	4.65	2.84
1996	5.13	5.15	3.16	15.49	5.37	3.28
1997	5.30	5.33	3.84	13.29	3.54	2.02
1998	5.46	5.49	3.34	14.54	4.42	2.61
1999	5.69	5.69	3.43	10.70	3.97	2.27
2000	5.77	5.77	3.48	7.70	3.16	0.96
2001	5.68	5.67	3.48	9.60	4.42	2.69
2002	5.66	5.71	3.55	9.04	5.33	3.31
2003	5.69	5.81	3.62	6.64	3.85	2.39

analysts have observed, however, that price cutting has subsided, and they foresee relative price stability following a period of consolidation in which CVS has acquired several of the smaller, less profitable chains. In addition, drugstores have tended toward a more profitable product mix featuring high-profit-margin items, such as cosmetics, which has had a positive influence on profit margins.

Company Performance   The Walgreen Co.'s profit margin has shown consistent improvement, and a major reason has been the change in corporate structure and sales mix. The outlook for profit margins is good because the firm has developed a strong position in the pharmacy business and has invested in service (including mail-order prescriptions) and inventory-control technology that will help the firm experience strong margins on this business. The firm also has emphasized high-profit-margin items, such as greeting cards, photofinishing, and cosmetics.

Specific estimates for Walgreen Co.'s future margins typically would begin with an analysis of the firm's relationship with drugstore industry margins using time-series plots, such as those in Exhibit 14.9.[10] This time-series plot for the period 1993–2003 showed good results for Walgreens versus its industry. You should consider any unique factors that would influence this long-run relationship, such as price wars or an abnormal number of store openings or closings by the firm.

Following the analysis of the company-industry profit margin relationship, you should analyze the firm's common-size income statement. Exhibit 14.10 shows a common-size income statement for Walgreens during the period 2001–2004. An analysis of the main items of interest—cost of goods sold and SG&A expense—was encouraging. The cost-of-sales percentage declined slightly (less than 1 percent) while there was a partially offsetting increase in the

---

[10]Both the operating margin and the net before tax margin were analyzed; the results indicated that the net profit margins yielded the best relationships. The long-run relationship cannot be very good because over the total period the industry margin was declining while Walgreens experienced fairly steady increases as shown in Exhibits 14.8 and 14.9.

Exhibit 14.9	**Time-Series Plot of Net Profit Margin for Walgreens and the Retail Drugstore Industry: 1993–2003**

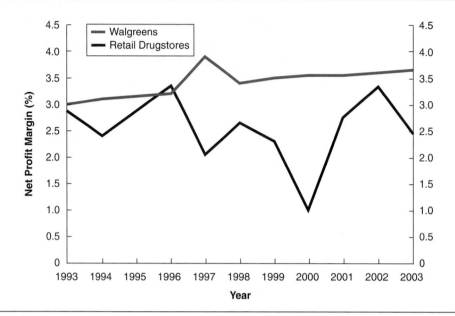

percentage of SG&A expense. As a result, the operating profit margin experienced a minimal increase from 5.68 percent to 5.71 percent. Finally, the tax rate was stable at 38 percent.

Net Profit Margin Estimate   The overall industry outlook is encouraging because of stable prices, an increase in mechanization within the industry, and the inclusion of more high-profit-margin items. Because of Walgreen Co.'s strong performance relative to its industry profit margin and a small increase in its margin as shown in Exhibit 14.10, it is estimated that the firm will show a slight increase to 3.66 in 2005.

Computing Earnings per Share   This margin estimate, combined with the prior sales estimate of $42 billion, indicates net income of $1,537 million. Assuming about 1,030 million common shares outstanding, earnings should be about $1.50 per share for 2005, which is an increase of almost 14 percent over the earnings of $1.32 per share in 2004. To find the value of Walgreen Co. stock, our next step is to estimate its earnings multiplier.

Importance of Quarterly Estimates

Once we have derived an estimate of next year's sales and net earnings, it is essential that we also derive an estimate of each of the quarterly results for two important reasons. First, this is a way to confirm our annual estimate—that is, do the quarterly estimates required to arrive at the annual estimate seem reasonable? If not, we need to reevaluate the annual forecast. Second, unless we have quarterly forecasts that confirm our annual forecast, we will not be in a position to determine whether the subsequent *actual* results are a positive surprise, negative surprise, or no surprise. Further, if the actual results are a surprise relative to our estimate, we will want to understand the reason for the surprise—for example, did we under- or overestimate sales growth and/or was it due to differences in the profit margin from our estimates? This

Exhibit 14.10	Walgreen Co. and Subsidiaries Consolidated Statement of Income (Dollars in Millions, Except per Share Data): Years Ended August 31, 2001, 2002, 2003, and 2004

	2004		2003		2002		2001	
Net sales	37,508	100.00%	32,505	100.00%	28,681	100.00%	24,623	100.00%
Cost of sales	27,310	72.81%	23,706	72.93%	21,076	73.48%	18,049	73.30%
Gross profit	10,198	27.19%	8,799	27.07%	7,605	26.52%	6,574	26.70%
Selling, occupancy, and administrative expense	8,055	21.48%	6,951	21.38%	5,981	20.85%	5,176	21.02%
Operating profit (EBIT)	2,143	5.71%	1,848	5.69%	1,624	5.66%	1,398	5.68%
Interest income	17	0.05%	11	0.03%	7	0.02%	5	0.02%
Interest expense	—	0.00%	—	0.00%	—	0.00%	(3)	−0.01%
Other Income	16	0.04%	30	0.09%	6	0.02%	22	0.09%
Operating income before income taxes	2,176	5.80%	1,889	5.81%	1,637	5.71%	1,422	5.78%
Provision for income taxes	816	2.18%	713	2.19%	618	2.15%	537	2.18%
Reported net income	1,360	3.63%	1,176	3.62%	1,019	3.55%	885	3.60%
Reported net income available for common shares	1,360	3.63%	1,176	3.62%	1,019	3.55%	885	3.60%

Source: These statements were created by the authors based upon financial statements supplied by Walgreen Co.'s

understanding is needed for an estimated *earnings revision* that reflects the new information from the company—we would probably revise each of our future quarterly estimates to arrive at a new annual estimate.

ESTIMATING COMPANY EARNINGS MULTIPLIERS

As in our analysis of industry multipliers in Chapter 13, we use two approaches to estimate a company multiplier. First, we estimate the *P/E* ratio from the relationships between Walgreens, its industry, and the market. This is the macroanalysis. Second, we estimate a multiplier based on its three components: the dividend-payout ratio, the required rate of return, and the rate of growth. We then resolve the estimates derived from each approach and settle on one estimate.

Macroanalysis of the Earnings Multiplier

Exhibit 14.11 shows the mean earnings multiple for the company, the RDS industry, and the aggregate market for the period 1993–2003. Notably, all these earnings multipliers are computed using future earnings. The Walgreen Co.'s multiplier has generally followed the industry multiplier with a company/industry ratio between 1.00 and 1.15. The Walgreen Co.'s earnings multiplier has been consistently higher than the market multiplier except during 2001–2002.

| Exhibit 14.11 | Time-Series Plot of Mean Price/Earning Ratios for Walgreens, the Retail Drugstore Industry, and the S&P Industrials Index: 1993–2003 |

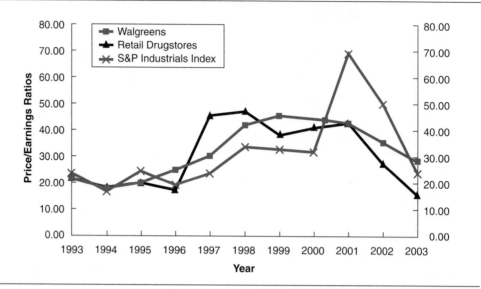

This pattern raises the question: Is the higher value for the Walgreens *P/E* relative to both its industry and the market justified? The microanalyses should provide some insights regarding this question.

Microanalysis of the Earnings Multiplier

This historical data for the relevant series are contained in Exhibit 14.12.[11] The relevant question is, Why has the earnings multiplier for Walgreens been generally higher than the market and industry earnings multiplier? As before, we are looking for estimates of *D/E, k,* and *g* to find an earnings multiplier. We will use the historical data in Exhibit 14.12 to determine patterns for the data and to develop future projections.

Comparing Dividend-Payout Ratios   The dividend-payout ratio for Walgreens typically has been lower than its industry in recent years. The Walgreens-market comparison shows that Walgreens almost always had a lower payout, which by itself would imply a lower *P/E* ratio for Walgreens than for its industry and the market.

Estimating the Required Rate of Return   To find Walgreen Co.'s required rate of return *(k),* we need to analyze the firm's fundamental risk characteristics (BR, FR, LR, ERR, and CR) and also derive an estimate based on the SML and a measure of Walgreen Co.'s systematic risk (i.e., its beta).

Walgreens should have relatively low business risk due to its stable sales growth compared to its industry and the aggregate economy. As noted in Chapter 10, for a growth company like Walgreens it is necessary to adjust for both the growth and size factor by measuring variability around the growth trend and relating this volatility to the mean as in Exhibit 14.13. As shown in the appendix in Chapter 10, after adjusting for size and trend, the results indicated that Walgreen Co.'s sales and EBIT experienced very stable growth, which indicates lower business risk.

---

[11]Although some prior tables included data through 2003 using estimates for specific ratios, it is not possible to do this for all the variables in Exhibit 14.12 as of mid-2005.

Exhibit 14.12 | Variables that Influence the Earnings Multiplier for Walgreens, the Retail Drugstore Industry, and the S&P Industrials: 1993–2004

Year	WALGREENS						RETAIL DRUGSTORES						S&P INDUSTRIALS					
	D/E	NPM	TAT	ROA	TAE	ROE	D/E	NPM	TAT	ROA	TAE	ROE	D/E	NPM	TAT	ROA	TAE	ROE
1993	33.52	2.67	3.27	8.73	1.84	16.08	35.71	2.78	2.73	7.59	1.85	14.06	45.79	5.26	0.90	3.27	3.59	16.97
1994	29.82	3.05	3.17	9.67	1.85	17.92	41.53	2.33	2.68	6.25	1.95	12.21	38.11	5.86	0.92	4.91	3.37	18.14
1995	30.77	3.09	3.20	9.87	1.81	19.10	32.98	2.84	2.61	7.41	2.10	15.53	35.02	6.37	0.95	5.19	3.25	19.63
1996	28.95	3.16	3.24	10.24	1.78	19.40	39.61	3.28	2.75	8.90	2.18	19.68	34.75	6.50	0.97	5.62	3.14	19.72
1997	26.97	3.26	3.18	10.36	1.77	19.80	40.85	2.02	2.19	4.34	2.24	9.88	32.24	6.96	0.93	5.33	3.14	20.40
1998	24.27	3.51	3.12	10.95	1.72	19.60	29.91	2.61	2.21	5.71	2.21	12.78	37.04	6.53	0.86	4.90	3.16	17.77
1999	20.97	3.50	3.02	10.57	1.70	17.91	31.00	2.27	2.10	4.69	2.85	13.58	33.36	6.69	0.83	5.22	3.11	17.31
2000	18.18	3.66	2.99	10.94	1.68	18.35	54.29	0.96	3.04	2.75	1.83	5.34	28.32	7.00	0.84	5.45	2.89	17.06
2001	16.09	3.60	2.79	10.03	1.70	17.01	19.37	2.69	2.70	7.20	1.83	13.35	38.36	5.36	0.77	4.13	3.64	15.05
2002	15.15	3.55	3.07	10.32	1.59	16.36	14.31	3.31	2.69	8.84	1.73	15.38	32.64	6.16	0.77	4.74	3.26	15.50
2003	14.04	3.62	3.02	10.31	1.59	16.34	13.00	2.39	3.78	8.98	1.69	15.29	31.51	5.89	0.76	4.29	3.02	13.57
2004	13.01	3.63	3.00	10.20	1.62	16.52	N/A	N/A	N/A	N/A	N/A	N/A	N/A	N/A	N/A	N/A	N/A	N/A
Mean	22.65	3.36	3.09	10.18	1.72	17.87	32.05	2.50	2.68	6.61	2.04	13.37	32.35	6.23	0.86	4.82	3.23	17.37

D/E = Dividend payout, equal to dividends/earnings.
NPM = Net profit margin, equal to net income/sales.
TAT = Total asset turnover, equal to sales/total assets.
ROA = Return on assets.

TAE = Leverage ratio, equal to total assets/equity.
ROE = Return on equity, equal to net income/equity.
N/A = Data not available.

Source: Adapted from data in *Financial Analyst's Handbook* (New York: Standard & Poor's, 2004).

| **Time-Series Plot of Walgreeen Co.'s Sales Used in Calculation of Sales Volatility for Walgreens from Arithmetic Mean, from Linear Growth Curve, and from Compound Growth Curve**

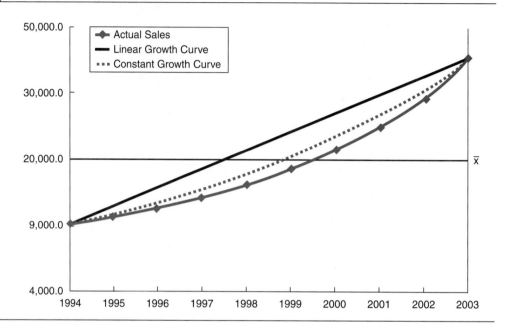

Several financial risk variables for Walgreens, its industry, and the aggregate market are shown in Exhibit 14.14. Notably, these do not consider fairly large leases of stores. Without considering these financial leases, these financial risk ratios indicate that Walgreens has comparable financial risk to its industry and substantially lower financial risk than the aggregate stock market. In contrast, as shown in Chapter 10, when the leases are considered as they should be, the firm's financial risk is equal to, or somewhat higher than the market.

The firm's liquidity risk is quite low compared to its industry and the average firm in the market. Indicators of market liquidity are (1) the number of stockholders, (2) the number and market value of shares outstanding, (3) the number of shares traded, and (4) institutional interest in the stock. As of January 1, 2005, Walgreens had 30,000 holders of common stock—a relatively large number. At mid-2005, there were over one billion common shares outstanding with a market value of over $35 billion. Clearly, Walgreens would qualify as an investment for institutions that require firms with large market value. Walgreen Co.'s stock has an annual trading turnover of 75 percent, which is below average. Financial institutions own about 460 million shares of Walgreens, which is about 45 percent of the outstanding shares. Therefore, Walgreen Co.'s large number of stockholders, very large market capitalization, fairly active trading of its stock, and strong institutional interest indicate that Walgreens has very little liquidity risk.

The exchange rate risk for companies depends on what proportion of sales and earnings are generated outside the United States and the volatility of the exchange rates in the specific countries. Walgreens has very little exchange rate risk or country risk because the firm has virtually no non-U.S. sales.

In summary, Walgreens has below-average business risk, financial risk higher than the market when we consider leases, low liquidity risk, and virtually no exchange rate and country risk. This implies that—based on fundamental factors—the overall risk for Walgreens should be lower than the market.

Exhibit 14.14 | **Financial Risk Ratios for Walgreens, the Retail Drugstore Industry, and the S&P Industrials: 1993–2003**

Year	WALGREENS*				RETAIL DRUGSTORES				S&P INDUSTRIALS			
	Total Assets/ Equity	Interest Coverage	Cash Flow/ Long-Term Debt	Cash Flow/ Total Debt	Total Assets/ Equity	Interest Coverage	Cash Flow/ Long-Term Debt	Cash Flow/ Total Debt	Total Assets/ Equity	Interest Coverage	Cash Flow/ Long-Term Debt	Cash Flow/ Total Debt
1993	1.84	6.92	0.162	0.110	1.85	22.22	2.307	0.740	3.59	4.25	0.412	0.164
1994	1.85	6.53	0.150	0.108	1.95	16.73	1.952	0.661	3.37	5.10	0.424	0.192
1995	1.94	6.46	0.128	0.092	2.10	14.59	1.741	0.614	3.25	5.48	0.431	0.196
1996	1.90	6.43	0.133	0.096	2.18	14.11	0.897	0.346	3.14	6.17	0.452	0.205
1997	1.91	6.62	0.189	0.133	2.24	7.73	0.700	0.235	3.14	6.69	0.440	0.195
1998	1.72	6.38	0.130	0.096	2.21	9.71	0.796	0.275	3.16	6.02	0.422	0.191
1999	1.70	6.14	0.118	0.087	2.85	6.54	0.351	0.165	3.11	6.53	0.417	0.191
2000	1.68	5.91	0.144	0.107	1.83	4.92	2.150	0.261	2.89	6.52	0.444	0.199
2001	1.68	5.75	0.092	0.066	1.83	25.37	2.480	0.320	3.64	4.78	0.252	0.123
2002	1.59	5.69	0.166	0.125	1.73	50.58	2.203	0.365	3.26	5.59	0.213	0.109
2003	1.62	5.26	0.131	0.100	1.69	60.73	3.054	0.375	3.02	6.21	0.302	0.154

*All Walgreen Co.'s ratios are computed with leases capitalized and include consideration of implied interest on this lease debt

Source: Adapted from data in *Financial Analyst's Handbook* (New York: Standard & Poor's, 2004).

Analysts should also consider market-determined risk (beta) based on the CAPM. As noted in connection with the cash flow models, the stock's beta derived from five years of monthly data relative to the S&P Industrials for the period 2000–2004 indicated a beta of 0.90.

These results are consistent with those derived from an analysis of the fundamental factors—both indicate that Walgreen Co.'s risk is below the aggregate market. This means that the required rate of return *(k)* for Walgreen Co.'s stock estimated earlier using the CAPM is reasonable—that is, 8 percent. By itself, this lower *k* would suggest an earnings multiplier above the market multiplier.

Estimating the Expected Growth Rate   Recall that the expected growth rate *(g)* is determined by the firm's retention rate and its expected return on equity *(ROE)*. We have already noted Walgreen Co.'s low dividend payout compared to the industry and the aggregate market, which implies a higher retention rate.

As discussed using the DuPont model, a firm's *ROE* can be estimated in terms of the three ratios: (1) net profit margin (NPM), (2) total asset turnover (TAT), and (3) the financial leverage multiplier. We also know that NPM × TAT = Return on Assets *(ROA)*. It is important to examine the relative impact of these two ratios and to compare the *ROA* of alternative firms as a measure of operating performance—that is, profitability and asset efficiency. Walgreens has experienced a small decline in TAT, but this has been offset by an increase in NPM, causing the firm's *ROA* to be relatively stable and substantially above its industry and the market.

Finally, the firm's *ROE* equals the *ROA* times the financial leverage multiplier (total assets/equity). Notably, since 1993, Walgreens has reduced its leverage multiplier from 1.84 to 1.62 while the industry and market have experienced similar declines.

As a result, the *ROE*s are similar but the financial risk is different—that is, Walgreens has a higher *ROE* but equal financial risk relative to the industry and lower risk compared to the market using the ratios in Exhibit 14.14.

Using the results for the last three years (2001–2003), the *ROE*s would be approximately as follows:

	NPM	TAT	ROA	Total Assets/ Equity	ROE
Walgreens	3.59	2.96	10.63	1.63	17.33
Retail drugstores	2.80	3.06	8.57	1.75	15.00
S&P Industrials	5.80	0.77	4.47	3.31	14.80

The foregoing is meant to highlight the difference among the three units based on recent history. An analyst would need to *estimate* future components and derive an expected *ROE* that reflects the firm's expected *future* performance.

The demonstration can be extended by combining the average annual *ROE*s derived in the preceding table and the average of recent retention rates from Exhibit 14.15 to derive expected growth rates:

	Retention Rate	ROE	Expected Growth Rate
Walgreens	0.85	17.33	0.1473
Retail drugstores	0.84	15.00	0.1260
S&P Industrials	0.77	14.80	0.1140

Exhibit 14.15	Expected Growth Rate Components for Walgreens, the Retail Drugstore Industry, and the S&P Industrials: 1993–2003

	WALGREENS			RETAIL DRUGSTORES			S&P INDUSTRIALS		
Year	Retention Rate	*ROE*	Expected Growth Rate	Retention Rate	*ROE*	Expected Growth Rate	Retention Rate	*ROE*	Expected Growth Rate
1993	0.66	16.08	10.69	0.64	14.06	9.04	0.68	16.97	11.51
1994	0.70	17.92	12.58	0.58	12.21	7.14	0.75	18.14	13.58
1995	0.69	19.10	13.22	0.67	15.53	10.41	0.77	19.63	15.04
1996	0.71	19.40	13.78	0.61	19.68	11.98	0.77	19.72	15.24
1997	0.73	19.80	14.46	0.60	9.88	5.92	0.78	20.40	15.97
1998	0.76	19.60	14.84	0.70	12.78	9.00	0.75	17.77	13.32
1999	0.79	17.91	14.16	0.69	13.58	9.43	0.78	17.31	13.57
2000	0.82	18.35	15.01	0.49	5.34	2.60	0.82	17.06	13.96
2001	0.84	17.01	14.29	0.81	13.35	10.79	0.73	15.05	10.97
2002	0.85	16.36	13.91	0.86	15.38	13.20	0.77	15.50	11.96
2003	0.86	16.34	14.05	0.87	15.29	13.31	0.80	13.57	10.79

Source: Adapted from data in *Financial Analyst's Handbook* (New York: Standard & Poor's, 2004).

Taken alone, these higher expected growth rates for Walgreens would indicate that it should definitely have a higher multiple than its industry and the market.

Computing the Earnings Multiplier Comparing our estimates of *D/E*, *k*, and *g* to comparable values for the industry and the market, we find that the Walgreen Co.'s earnings multiplier based on the microanalysis should be greater than the multiplier for its industry and the market. Specifically, the dividend-payout ratio points toward a lower multiplier for Walgreens, whereas both the lower risk analysis and the higher expected growth rate would indicate a multiplier for Walgreens above that of its industry and the market.

The macroanalysis indicated that the Walgreen Co.'s multiplier typically has been above its industry and the market, and the microanalysis supported this relationship. Assuming a market multiple of about 18 and a retail drugstore multiplier of about 20 times, the multiplier for Walgreens should be between 22 and 26, with a tendency toward the upper end of the range and beyond (22–24–26 times). Alternatively, if we inserted some earlier estimated values for *D/E*, *k*, and *g* into the *P/E* ratio formula, we would not be able to derive an estimated multiplier for Walgreens because *g* is greater than *k*. As noted in Chapter 11, because Walgreens is a true growth company, we cannot use the standard DDM formula to estimate a specific multiple. We would need to estimate a value based on the direction of change and the macroanalysis estimates of 22–24–26 times.

Estimate of the Future Value for Walgreens Earlier, we estimated 2005 earnings per share for Walgreens of about $1.50 per share. Assuming multipliers of 22–24–26 implies the following estimated future values:

$$22 \times \$1.50 = \$33.00$$
$$24 \times \$1.50 = \$36.00$$
$$26 \times \$1.50 = \$39.00$$

Making the Investment Decision

In our prior discussions of valuation, we set forth the following investment decision rule: compute the estimated intrinsic value for an investment using your required rate of return as the discount rate. If this intrinsic value is equal to or greater than the current market price of the investment, buy it. If the estimated intrinsic value is less than the market price, do not buy it, and if you own it, sell it.

Therefore, the required comparisons are the estimated values derived using the present value of cash flow models and the values estimated using the earnings multiple model to the current market price of Walgreens of about $42.00 a share. The following is a summary of these estimated values. Recall that we could not calculate constant-growth models because Walgreens has consistently experienced growth rates above its required rates of return (it is a true growth company).

Present Value of Cash Flow Models	
Three-stage DDM	$34.30
Three-stage FCFE	$33.34
Three-stage FCFF (OFCF)	$28.98
Earnings Multiple Models	
22 times estimated earnings	$33.00
24 times estimated earnings	$36.00
26 times estimated earnings	$39.00

Because none of the computed values is equal to or larger than the current market price of $42.00, you would not recommend a purchase of the stock although Walgreens is clearly an outstanding firm. Stated in terms of our earlier discussion, Walgreens is obviously a true growth company, but based on the valuations the firm's stock is not expected to be a growth stock at its current price.

ADDITIONAL MEASURES OF RELATIVE VALUE

The best-known measure of relative value for common stock is the price/earnings ratio. Analysts have also begun to calculate three additional measures of relative value for common stocks—the price/book value ratio, the price/cash flow ratio, and the price/sales ratio, which were discussed in Chapter 11.

Price/Book Value (*P/BV*) Ratio

The price-to-book-value ratio (*P/BV*) has gained prominence because of the studies by Fama and French (1992); Rosenberg, Reid, and Lanstein (1985); and Fairfield (1994). Book value is a reasonable measure of value for firms that have consistent accounting practice (for example, firms in the same industry) and can apply to firms with negative earnings or cash flows. You should not attempt to use this ratio to compare firms with different levels of hard assets—for example, a heavy industrial firm and a service firm.

Exhibit 14.16	Time-Series Plot of Mean Price/Book Value Ratios for Walgreens, the Retail Drugstore Industry, and S&P Industrials: 1993–2003

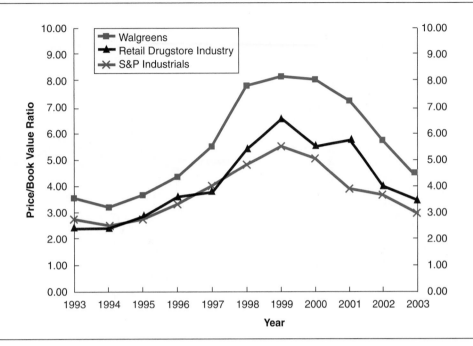

The annual *P/BV* ratios for Walgreens, its industry, and the market are in Exhibit 14.4, along with the ratio of the company *P/BV* ratio relative to its industry and relative to the market ratio. In this instance, the major variable that should cause a difference in the *P/BV* ratio is the firm's return on investment *(ROI)* relative to its cost of capital (its WACC). Assuming that most firms in an industry have comparable WACCs, the major differential should be the firm's *ROI* because the larger the *ROI*-WACC difference, the greater the justified *P/BV* ratio. We will consider this in the subsequent section on EVA.

As shown in Exhibit 14.16, the *P/BV* ratios for the company, industry, and market components have increased from about 2.5–3.5 to a peak of 5–8 and ended at 3.0–4.5. As shown in Exhibit 14.17, which contains a plot of relative valuation ratios, Walgreens has experienced a smaller increase in its *P/BV* ratio than its industry as indicated by its company/industry ratio that has gone from about 1.43 to 1.33. In contrast, the company-to-market ratio for Walgreens has increased from about 1.30 to about 1.50 at the end of the period. This latter trend is consistent with expectations because the *ROE* for Walgreens has consistently been greater than for the S&P Industrials.

Price/Cash Flow (*P/CF*) Ratio

As noted in Chapter 10, the price/cash flow ratio has grown in prominence and use because many observers contend that a firm's cash flow is less subject to manipulation than its earnings per share and because cash flows are widely used in the present value of cash flow models discussed earlier. An important question is, which of the several cash flow specifications should an analyst employ? In this analysis, we use the EBITDA cash flow measure equal to net

Exhibit 14.17	Time-Series Plot of Relative Price/Book Value Ratios for Walgreens/Industry and Walgreens/Market: 1993–2003

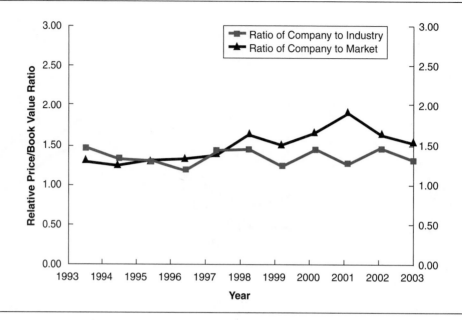

income plus interest, depreciation, and taxes because this cash flow measure can be derived for both the RDS industry and the market. Although it is certainly legitimate to have a preference for one of the other cash flow measures discussed, a demonstration using this measure should provide a valid comparison for learning purposes.

The time-series graph of the *P/CF* ratios in Exhibit 14.18 shows a general increase for Walgreens and its industry from about 10 times in 1993 to about 20 for WAG. The industry went from 5 to 15, the market *P/CF* ratio went from 9 times to 11 times. Notably, not only did the absolute value of the ratios increase, the graphs in Exhibit 14.19 show that Walgreen Co.'s *P/CF* ratios relative to its industry experienced a significant decline from a ratio of 2.64 in 1993 to a ratio of 1.50 in 2003. The company-to-market comparison experienced its low ratio of 1.26 in 1993 and experienced a rapid increase and decrease to an ending ratio of 1.79. This indicates an overall increase in the *P/CF* ratio and an increase since 1993 in the *P/CF* ratio relative to the overall market. The question becomes, what has happened to the firm's growth rate of cash flow and the risk of these cash flows that would justify this overall increase in the *P/CF* ratio relative to the market, in contrast to a decline relative to its industry?

Price/Sales (*P/S*) Ratio

The price-to-sales ratio (*P/S*) has had a long but generally neglected existence followed by a recent reawakening. Phillip Fisher (1958), in his classic book, suggested this ratio as a valuable tool when considering investments, including growth stocks. Subsequently, his son Kenneth Fisher (1984) used the ratio as a major stock selection variable in his book. In the late 1990s, *P/S* was suggested as a valuable tool by Leibowitz (1997), and this ratio was espoused by O'Shaughnessy (1997), in his book that compared several stock selection techniques.

Exhibit 14.18	Time-Series Plot of Price/Cash Flow Ratios for Walgreens, the Retail Drugstore Industry, and S&P Industrials: 1993–2003

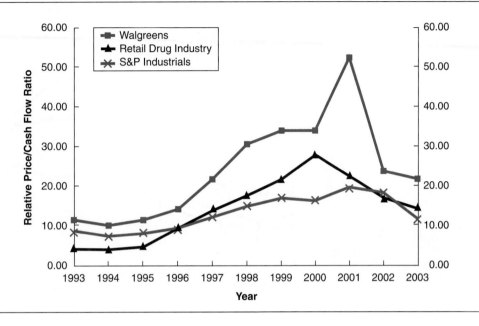

Exhibit 14.19	Time-Series Plot of Relative Price/Cash Flow Ratios for Walgreens/Industry and Walgreens/Market: 1993–2003

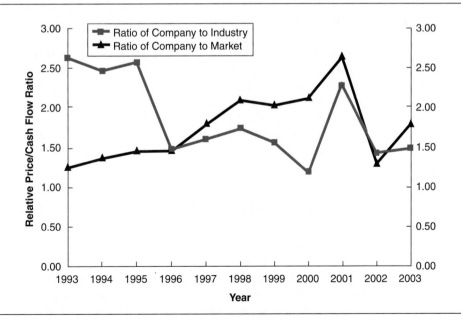

Exhibit 14.20 | **Time-Series Plot of Price/Sales Ratios for Walgreens, the Retail Drugstore Industry, and S&P Industrials: 1993–2003**

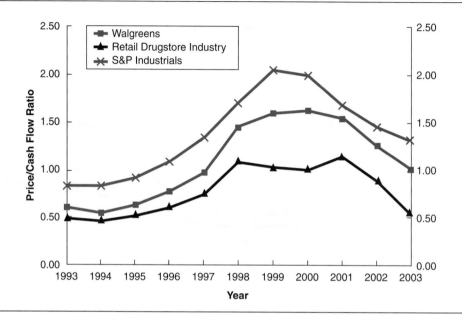

Leibowitz makes the point that sales growth drives the growth of all subsequent earnings and cash flow. Those who are concerned with accounting manipulation point out that sales is one of the purest numbers available. Notably, this ratio is equal to the *P/E* ratio times the net profit margin (earnings/sales), which implies that it is heavily influenced by the profit margin of the entity being analyzed in addition to sales growth and sales volatility (risk).

As shown in Exhibit 14.4 and Exhibit 14.20, the *P/S* ratio for Walgreens has experienced a significant overall increase from 0.59 to 1.00, compared to almost no overall increase by its industry (0.49 to 0.53) and a healthy increase by the market (from 0.84 to 1.29). This substantial relative performance by Walgreens is reflected in Exhibit 14.21, which shows the plot of relative ratios wherein the company-to-industry ratio increased notably from 1.22 to 1.89 while the company-to-market ratio went from 0.71 to 0.77. As before, the analyst must ask whether the growth of sales, the risk related to the sales growth, and the profit margin of Walgreens can justify a much higher *P/S* ratio than its industry. The positive news is that Walgreen Co.'s sales have experienced strong consistent growth relative to its industry and Walgreens has also experienced an increase in its profit margin.

Summary of Relative Valuation Ratios

Notably, the four individual, relative valuation variables increased across the board—all four relative valuation ratios increased during the 11-year period for the firm, its industry, and the aggregate stock market. The widespread increases suggest changes in some aggregate economic variables, such as economic growth and risk factors. Interestingly, Dudley and McKelvey (1997) from Goldman, Sachs, & Co. argued that the U.S. economy has experienced several significant changes that have changed the nature and length of our economic expansions and contractions.

| **Exhibit 14.21** | **Time-Series Plot of Relative Price/Sales Ratios for Walgreens/Industry and Walgreens/Market: 1993–2003** |

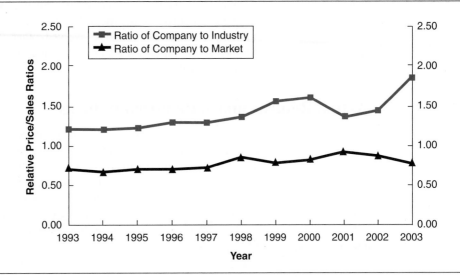

In addition to these overall increases, Walgreens experienced a larger increase than its industry in terms of its *P/E* ratio, and its *P/S* ratio, while lagging in terms of its *P/CF* ratio. Compared to the market, all the firm's relative valuation ratios increased more than the market. An investor who wants to use these ratios to determine relative value or to make an investment decision needs to explain the differences by analyzing the basic valuation factors that affect the ratios.

The following section considers some techniques used to analyze and derive values for growth companies.

ANALYSIS OF GROWTH COMPANIES

Investment literature contains numerous accounts of the rapid growth of such companies as Wal-Mart, Cisco Systems, Intel, Pfizer, and Microsoft, along with stories about investors who became wealthy because of the timely acquisition of these stocks. These very high rates of return indicate that the early and proper valuation of true growth companies can be extremely rewarding. At the same time, for every successful Wal-Mart or Microsoft, numerous firms did not survive. In addition, there are many instances where the stock price of a true growth company overcompensated for the firm's expected growth, and subsequent returns on the company's stock were below expectations. As noted in Solt and Statman (1989), the common stock of a growth company is *not* always a growth stock.

You are familiar with the DDM assumptions—that is, that dividends are expected to grow at a *constant rate* for an *infinite time period*. As explained in Chapter 11, although these assumptions are reasonable when evaluating the aggregate market and some large industries, they can be very tenuous when analyzing individual securities. *These assumptions are extremely questionable for a growth company.*

Growth Company Defined

Recall that a growth company has the opportunities and ability to invest capital in projects that generate rates of return greater than the firm's cost of capital. Such a condition is considered to be *temporary* because, in a competitive economy, if the rates of return for a given industry exceed the rates of return expected based on the risk involved, other companies will enter the industry, increase the supply, and eventually drive prices down until the rates of return earned on capital invested are consistent with the risk involved.

Actual Returns above Required Returns

The notion of a firm consistently earning rates of return above its required rate of return needs elaboration. Firms are engaged in business ventures that offer opportunities for investment of corporate capital, and these investments entail some risk. Investors determine their required return for owning a firm based on the risk of its investments compared to the risk of other firms. This required rate of return is referred to as the firm's *cost of equity*. In a state of equilibrium, the rates of return earned on risky investments by the firm should equal the rates of return required by investors. Rates of return above those required for the risk involved are referred to as *pure profits* or *excess profits*.

Excess profits are possible only in a noncompetitive environment. Assume that a medical equipment firm is able to earn 20 percent on its capital, while investors require only 15 percent from the firm because of its risk. The extra 5 percent is defined as pure profit, and numerous companies would enter the medical equipment field to enjoy these excess profits. These competitors would increase the supply of equipment and reduce the price that producers could charge for the equipment until the marginal returns equaled the required return due to risk.

Because many firms have derived excess profits for a number of years, these excess returns are probably not due to a temporary disequilibrium but rather because of some noncompetitive factors that exist, such as patents or copyrights that provide monopoly rights to a process or a manuscript for a specified period. During this period of protection from competition, the firm can derive above-normal returns. Also, a firm could possess strategies, discussed by Porter, that provide added profits (e.g., a unique marketing technique or other organizational characteristics). Finally, there may be significant barriers to entry, such as capital requirements.

In a purely competitive economy, true growth companies would not exist because competition would not allow continuing excess return investments. The fact is, our economy is not perfectly competitive (although this typically is the best model to use) because there are a number of frictions that restrict competition. Therefore, it is possible for *temporary* true growth companies to exist in our economy. The question is, How long can these growth companies earn these excess profits?

Growth Companies and Growth Stocks

Recall that a growth stock is expected to experience above-average risk-adjusted rates of return during some future period. This means that any undervalued stock can be a growth stock, regardless of the type of company. Alternatively, the stock of a growth company that is substantially overvalued could be a speculative stock because the probability of below-normal returns on the stock would be very high even if the company fulfilled expectations.

In this section, we discuss models that are meant to help you evaluate the unique earnings stream of a growth company. As a result, you should derive a better estimate of the firm's value and be able to judge whether the stock of a growth company is (1) a growth stock, (2) a properly valued stock, or (3) a speculative overvalued stock.

Alternative Growth Models[12]

In this section, we consider the full range of growth models, from no growth and negative growth to dynamic true growth. Knowledge of the full range will help you understand the life cycle of true growth companies. We assume the company is an all-equity firm to simplify the computations.

No-Growth Firm

The no-growth firm is a mythical company that is established with a specified portfolio of investments that generate a constant stream of earnings *(E)* equal to *r* times the value of assets. Earnings are calculated after allowing for depreciation expense used to maintain the assets at their original value. Therefore,

14.10 $$E = r \times \text{Assets}$$

It also is assumed that all earnings of the firm are paid out in dividends; if *b* is the rate of retention, $b = 0$. Hence,

14.11 $$E = r \times \text{Assets} = \text{Dividends}$$

Under these assumptions, the value of the firm is the discounted value of the perpetual stream of earnings *(E)*. The discount rate (the required rate of return) is specified as *k*. In this case, it is assumed that $r = k$. The firm's rate of return on assets equals its required rate of return. Therefore, the value of the firm is

14.12 $$V = \frac{E}{k} = \frac{(1-b)E}{k}$$

In the no-growth case, the earnings stream never changes because the asset base never changes, and the rate of return *(r)* on the assets never changes. Therefore, the value of the firm never changes, and investors continue to receive *k* on their investment.

14.13 $$k = E/V$$

Long-Run Growth Models

Long-run models differ from the no-growth models because *they assume some of the earnings are reinvested.* In all cases, it is postulated that the market value *(V)* of an all-equity firm is the capitalized value of three component forms of returns discounted at the rate *k*.

- E = the level of (constant) net earnings expected from existing assets, without further net investments.

---

[12]The discussion in this section draws heavily from Salomon (1963), and Miller and Modigliani (1961).

- G = the growth component that equals the present value of capital gains expected from reinvested funds. The return on reinvested funds is equal to r, which equals mk (m is the relative rate of return operator). If m is equal to 1, then $r = k$. If m is greater than 1, the projects that generate these returns are considered true growth investments ($r > k$). If m is less than 1, the investments are generating returns (r) below the cost of capital ($r < k$).
- R = the reinvestment of net earnings (E) and is equal to bE, where b is a percent of retention between zero (no reinvestment) and unity (total reinvestment; no dividends).

Simple Growth Model   This model assumes the firm has growth investment opportunities that provide rates of return equal to r, where r is greater than k (m is above 1). Further, it is assumed that the firm can invest R dollars a year at these rates and that $R = bE$; R is a *constant dollar amount* because E is the constant earnings at the beginning of the period.

The value of G, the capital gain component, is computed as follows: the first investment of bE dollars yields a stream of earnings equal to bEr dollars, and this is repeated every year. Each of these earnings streams has a present value, as of the year it begins, of bEr/k, which is the present value of a constant perpetual stream discounted at a rate consistent with the risk involved. Assuming the firm does this every year, it has a series of investments, each of which has a present value of bEr/k. The present value of all these series is $(bEr/k)/k$, which equals bEr/k^2. But because $r = mk$, this becomes

$$14.14 \qquad \frac{bEmk}{k^2} = \frac{bEm}{k} \text{ (Gross Present Value of Growth Investments)}$$

To derive these flows, the firm must invest bE dollars each year. The present value of these annual investments is equal to bE/k. Therefore, the *net* present value of growth investments is equal to

$$14.15 \qquad \frac{bEm}{k} - \frac{bE}{k} \text{ (Net Present Value of Growth Investments)}$$

The important variable is the value of m, which indicates the relationship of r to k. Combining this growth component with the capitalized value of the constant earnings stream indicates that the value of the firm is

$$14.16 \qquad V = \frac{E}{k} + \left[\frac{bEm}{k} - \frac{bE}{k} \right]$$

This equation indicates that the value of the firm is equal to the capitalized value of the constant earnings stream plus a growth component equal to the *net* present value of reinvestment in growth projects. By combining the first and third terms in Equation 14.16, it becomes

$$14.17 \qquad V = \frac{E(1 - b)}{k} + \frac{bEm}{k}$$

Because $E(1 - b)$ is the dividend (D), this model becomes

$$14.18 \qquad V = \frac{D}{k} + \frac{bEm}{k} \qquad \text{(Present Value of Constant Dividend plus Present Value of Growth Investments)}$$

It can be stated as earnings only by rearranging Equation 14.16:

$$14.19 \qquad V = \frac{E}{k} + \frac{bE(m - 1)}{k} \qquad \text{(Present Value of Constant Earnings plus the Present Value of Excess Earnings Growth Investments)}$$

Expansion Model The expansion model assumes a firm retains earnings to reinvest but receives a rate of return on its investments that is equal to its cost of capital ($m = 1$, so $r = k$). The effect of such a change can be seen in Equation 14.15, where the net present value of growth investments would be zero. Therefore, Equation 14.16 would become

14.20
$$V = \frac{E}{k}$$

Equation 14.17 would become

14.21
$$V = \frac{E(1 - b)}{k} + \frac{bE}{k} = \frac{E}{k}$$

Equation 14.18 is still valid, but the present value of the growth investment component would be smaller because m would be equal to 1. Finally, the last term in Equation 14.19 would disappear.

This discussion indicates that simply because a firm retains earnings and reinvests them, it is not necessarily beneficial to the stockholder *unless the reinvestment rate is above the required rate* ($r > k$). Otherwise, the investor in a tax-free world would be as well off with all earnings paid out in dividends. Either way, your return is k.

Negative Growth Model The negative growth model applies to a firm that retains earnings ($b > 0$) and reinvests these funds in projects that generate rates of return *below* the firm's cost of capital ($r < k$ or $m < 1$). The impact of this on the value of the firm can be seen from Equation 14.15, which indicates that with $m < 1$, the net present value of the growth investments would be *negative*. Therefore, the value of the firm in Equation 14.16 would be *less* than the value of a no-growth firm or an expansion firm. This also can be seen by examining the effect of $m < 1$ in Equation 14.19. The firm is withholding funds from the investor and investing them in projects that generate returns less than those available from comparable risk investments.

Such poor performance may be difficult to uncover because the firm's asset base will grow since it is retaining earnings and acquiring assets. Notably, the earnings of the firm will increase if it earns *any* positive rate of return on the new assets. The important point is, *the earnings will not grow by as much as they should,* so the value of the firm will decline over time when investors discount the cash flows from this reinvestment stream at the firm's cost of capital.

What Determines the Capital Gain Component? These equations highlight the factors that influence the capital gain component. Beginning with Equation 14.14, all the equations suggest that the gross present value of the growth investments is equal to

$$bEm/k$$

Therefore, three factors influence the size of this capital gain term. The first is b, the percentage of earnings retained for reinvestment. The greater the proportion of earnings retained, the larger the capital gain component. The second factor is m, which is critical because it indicates the relationship between the firm's rate of return on investments and the firm's required rate of return (i.e., its cost of capital). A value of 1 indicates the firm is earning only its required return. A firm with an m greater than 1 is a true growth company. The important question is, how much greater than k is the return? The final factor is the time period for the superior investments. How long can the firm make these superior return investments? This critical time factor often is overlooked because we have assumed an infinite horizon to simplify the computations. However,

Exhibit 14.22 | **Summary of Company Descriptions**

	Retention	Return on Investments
No-growth company	$b = 0$	$r = k$
Long-run growth (assumes reinvestment)		
Negative growth	$b > 0$	$r < k$
Expansion	$b > 0$	$r = k$
Simple long-run growth	$b > 0$ (constant $)	$r > k$
Dynamic long-run growth	$b > 0$ (constant %)	$r > k$

when analyzing growth companies, this time estimate is clearly a major consideration. In summary, the three factors that influence the capital gain component are

1. The amount of capital invested in growth investments *(b)*
2. The relative rate of return earned on the funds retained *(m)*
3. The time period for these growth investments

Dynamic True Growth Model A dynamic true growth model applies to a firm that invests a constant *percentage of current* earnings in projects that generate rates of return above the firm's required rate $(r > k, m > 1)$. In contrast to the simple growth model where the firm invests a *constant* dollar amount each year, in this model the amount invested is *growing* each year as earnings increase. As a result, the firm's earnings and dividends will grow at a *constant rate* that is equal to *br* (the percentage of earnings retained times the return on investments). In the current model, this would equal *bmk,* where *m* is greater than 1. Given these assumptions, the dynamic growth model for an infinite time period is the dividend discount model derived in the appendix to Chapter 11:

14.22
$$V = \frac{D_1}{k - g}$$

Applying this model to a true growth company means that earnings and dividends are growing at a constant rate and *the firm is investing larger and larger dollar amounts in projects that generate returns greater than* k. Moreover, the DDM model implicitly assumes that the firm can continue to do this for *an infinite time period.* If the growth rate *(g)* is greater than *k,* the model blows up and indicates that the firm should have an infinite value. Durand (1957) considered this possibility and concluded that, although many firms had current growth rates above the normal required rates of return, very few of their stocks were selling for infinite values. He explained this by contending that investors expected the reinvestment rate to decline or they felt that the investment opportunities would not be available for an infinite time period. Exhibit 14.22 contains a summary of the alternative company characteristics.

The Real World

Because these models are simplified to allow us to develop a range of alternatives, several of them are extremely unrealistic. In the real world, companies generally would combine these models. Unfortunately, most firms have made some investments where $r < k$, and many firms invest in projects that generate returns about equal to their cost of capital. Finally, most firms invest in *some* projects that provide rates of return above the firm's cost of capital ($r > k$). The crucial questions are (1) how much is invested in these true growth projects? and (2) how long do these true growth opportunities last?

Given this understanding of growth companies and what creates their value, the rest of the chapter considers various models that help you understand how to identify a true growth company and estimate specific values for these growth companies. We begin with models that are intended to identify growth companies in terms of providing excess economic value, which some contend is due to franchise value. Subsequently, we consider several models that are intended to provide a valuation of these companies by concentrating on how long the superior growth can continue and, alternatively, the extent and length of the superior growth. This final model has some similarities to the three-stage cash flow models.

MEASURES OF VALUE ADDED[13]

In addition to the DDM, which feeds into the *P/E* ratio valuation technique and the supplementary *P/BV* and *P/CF*, ratios, there has been growing interest in a set of performance measures referred to as "value added" measures. Notably, these value-added measures of performance are directly related to the capital budgeting techniques used in corporation finance. Specifically, they consider *economic profit,* which is analogous to the net present value (NPV) technique used in corporate capital budgeting. These value-added measures examine management performance based on the ability of managers to add value to the firm. They are also being used by security analysts as possible indicators of future equity returns, based on the logic that superior management performance should be reflected in a company's stock returns. In the subsequent discussion, we concentrate on three measures of value added: **economic value added (EVA)** and **market value added (MVA)**, pioneered by Stern and Stewart, and discussed in Stewart (1991), and the **franchise factor** developed by Leibowitz and Kogelman (1994).

Economic Value Added (EVA)[14]

As noted, EVA is closely related to the net present value (NPV) technique wherein you evaluate the expected performance of an investment by discounting its future cash flows at the firm's weighted average cost of capital (WACC) and compare this sum of discounted future cash flows to the cost of the project. If the discounted cash flows are greater than its cost, the project is expected to generate a positive NPV, which implies that it will add to the value of the firm and, therefore, it should be undertaken. In the case of EVA, you evaluate the annual performance of management by comparing the firm's net operating profit less adjusted taxes (NOPLAT) to the firm's total cost of capital in dollar terms, including the cost of equity. In this analysis, if the firm's NOPLAT during a specific year exceeds its dollar cost of capital, it has a positive EVA for the year and has added value for its stockholders. In contrast, if the EVA is negative, the firm has not earned enough during the year to cover its total cost of capital and the value of the firm has declined. Notably, NOPLAT indicates what the firm has earned for all capital suppliers and the dollar cost of capital is what all the capital

---

[13]This section benefited from Peterson and Peterson (1996).
[14]EVA is a registered trademark of Stern, Stewart, & Co.

suppliers required—including the firm's equity holders. The following summarizes the major calculations:[15]

$EVA =$

    (A) Adjusted Operating Profits before Taxes

    Minus (B) Cash Operating Taxes

    Equals (C) Net Operating Profits Less Adjusted Taxes (NOPLAT)

    Minus (D) The Dollar Cost of Capital

    Equals (E) Economic Value Added (EVA)

In turn, these items are calculated as follows:

Operating Profit (After Depreciation and Amortization)

Add:	Implied Interest on Operating Leases
Add:	An Increase in the LIFO Reserve
Add:	Goodwill Amortization
Equals:	*(A) Adjusted Operating Profits before Taxes*

Income Tax Expense

Add:	Decrease in Deferred Taxes
Add:	Tax Benefit from Interest Expenses
Add:	Tax Benefit from Interest on Leases
Less:	Taxes on Nonoperating Income
Equals:	*(B) Cash Operating Taxes*

(A) minus (B) equals: (C) Net Operating Profits Less Adjusted Taxes (NOPLAT)

Capital =

	Net Working Capital (current assets less non-interest-bearing liabilities)
Add:	LIFO Reserve
Add:	Net Plant, Property, and Equipment
Add:	Other Assets
Add:	Goodwill
Add:	Accumulated Goodwill Amortized
Add:	Present Value of Operating Leases
Equals:	*Capital*

---

[15]For a detailed discussion, see Stewart (1991), or Peterson and Peterson (1996). For summary discussions, see Jones (1995).

Weighted Average Cost of Capital (WACC) =

(Book Value of Debt/Total Book Value) × (the Market Cost of Debt)
(1 − Tax Rate)

(Book Value of Equity/Total Book Value) × (Cost of Equity)

(Cost of equity is based on the CAPM using the prevailing 10-year Treasury bond as the *RFR,* a calculated beta, and a market risk premium between 3 and 6 percent.)

(D)   Dollar Cost of Capital = Capital × WACC

(E)   Economic Value Added (EVA) =

(C)   Net Operating Profits Less Adjusted Taxes (NOPLAT)

Minus (D) Dollar Cost of Capital

EVA Return on Capital   The preceding calculations provide a positive or negative dollar value, which indicates whether the firm earned an excess above its cost of capital during the year analyzed. There are two problems with this annual dollar value for EVA. First, how does one judge over time if the firm is prospering relative to its past performance? Although you would want the absolute EVA to grow over time, the question is whether the rate of growth of EVA is adequate for the additional capital provided. Second, how does one compare alternative firms of different sizes? Both of these concerns can be met by calculating an *EVA return on capital* equal to

$$\text{EVA Return on Capital} = \text{EVA/Capital}$$

You would want this EVA rate of return on capital for a firm to remain constant over time, or, ideally, to grow. Using this ratio you can compare firms of different sizes and determine which firm has the largest *economic profit per dollar of capital.*

An Alternative Measure of EVA   An alternative but equal way to measure and think about EVA is to compare directly the firm's return on capital employed to the firm's average cost of capital (i.e., its WACC). As noted previously, it is this difference in the actual rate of return earned compared to the firm's required rate of return that identifies a company as a true growth company. Another way to measure EVA is to multiply this EVA spread (return on capital minus WACC) by the amount of capital employed. The appeal of this EVA spread approach is that it concentrates on the factors that create a growth company. Also, it helps the management and analysts recognize that true growth can be created by either (1) increasing the firm's return on capital, or (2) reducing its cost of capital.

Market Value Added (MVA)

In contrast to EVA, which generally is an evaluation of internal performance, MVA is a measure of external performance—how the market has evaluated the firm's performance in terms of the market value of debt and market value of equity compared to the capital invested in the firm.

$$\text{Market Value Added (MVA)} = (\text{Market Value of Firm}) - \text{Capital}$$
$$- \text{Market Value of Debt}$$
$$- \text{Market Value of Equity}$$

Again, to properly analyze this performance, it is necessary to look for positive changes over time—that is, the percent change each year. Subsequently, you need to compare these annual changes in MVA with those for the aggregate stock and bond markets, because these market values can be impacted by interest rate changes and general economic conditions.

Relationships between EVA and MVA

Although EVA is used primarily for evaluating management performance, it also is being used by external analysts to evaluate management with the belief that superior internal performance should be reflected in a company's stock performance. Several studies have attempted to determine the relationship between the two variables (EVA and MVA), and the results have not been encouraging. Although the stock of firms with positive EVAs has tended to outperform the stocks of negative EVA firms, the differences are typically insignificant and the relationship does not occur every year. This poor relationship may be due to the timing of the analysis (how fast EVA is reflected in stocks) or because the market values (MVAs) are affected by factors other than EVA—for example, MVA can be impacted by market interest rates and by changes in *future* expectations for a firm not considered by EVA. The point is, EVA does an outstanding job of evaluating management's *past* performance in terms of adding value. While one would certainly hope that superior past performance will continue, there is nothing certain about this relationship.

The Franchise Factor

The franchise factor concept is similar to EVA since it recognizes that, to add value to a firm, it is necessary to invest in projects that provide excess NPV—that is, the firm must generate rates of return above its WACC. This technique is directly related to the valuation approach we have been using since the franchise value approach breaks a firm's observed *P/E* ratio down into two components: (1) the *P/E* that is based on the company's ongoing business (its base *P/E*), plus (2) a franchise *P/E* that the market assigns to *the expected value of new and profitable business opportunities.* This can be visualized as:

14.23 $$\text{Franchise } P/E = \text{Observed } P/E - \text{Base } P/E$$

The base *P/E* is the reciprocal of the market discount rate k (it is $1/k$). For example, if the stock's market discount rate is 8 percent, the base *P/E* would be about 12.5 times.

What determines the franchise *P/E?* Not surprising, it is a function of the relative rate of return on new business opportunities compared to the firm's cost of equity (the franchise factor) and the size of the superior return opportunities (the growth factor).

14.24 $$\text{Incremental Franchise } P/E = \text{Franchise Factor} \times \text{Growth Factor}$$
$$= \frac{R - k}{rk} \times G$$

where:

R = the expected return on the new opportunities
k = the current cost of equity
r = the current *ROE* on investment
G = the present value of the new growth projects relative to the current value of the firm

The critical factors determining the franchise *P/E* are the difference between R and k and the size of these growth opportunities relative to the firm's current size (i.e., G).[16]

---

[16]For further detail and examples of the application, see Leibowitz and Kogelman (1994).

Growth Duration Model

The purpose of the growth duration model is to help you *evaluate* the high *P/E* ratio for the stock of a growth company by relating its *P/E* ratio to the firm's *rate* of growth and *duration* of growth. As discussed previously, a stock's *P/E* ratio is a function of (1) the firm's expected rate of growth of earnings per share, (2) the stock's required rate of return, and (3) the firm's dividend-payout ratio. Assuming equal risk and no significant difference in the payout ratio for different firms, the principal variable affecting differences in the earnings multiple for two firms *is the difference in expected growth.* It has been noted earlier that the growth estimate must consider both the *rate* of growth and how long this growth rate can be sustained—that is, the *duration* of expected growth. As noted earlier, no company can grow indefinitely at a rate substantially above normal. For example, Wal-Mart cannot continue to grow at 20 percent a year for an extended period, or it will eventually become the entire economy. In fact, Wal-Mart or any similar growth firm will eventually run out of excess profit investment projects. Recall that continued growth at a constant rate requires that larger amounts of money be invested in high-return projects because it requires that you invest a constant percentage of current earnings. Eventually, competition will encroach on these high-return investments and the firm's growth rate will decline to a rate consistent with the rate for the overall economy. Therefore, a reasonable and accurate estimate of the implied duration of a firm's high-growth period becomes significant.

Computation of Growth Duration   The growth duration concept was suggested by Holt (1962), who showed that if you assume equal risk between a given security and a market security, such as the S&P Industrials (i.e., a beta close to one), you can concentrate on the differential expected growth rates for the market and the growth firm as a factor causing the alternative *P/E* ratios. This allows you to compute the market's *implied growth duration* for the growth firm.

If $E'(0)$ is the firm's current earnings, then $E'(t)$ is earnings in Period t according to the expression

14.25 $$E'(t) = E(0)(1 + G)'$$

where G is the expected annual percentage growth rate for earnings. To adjust for dividend payments, it was assumed that all such payments are used to purchase further shares of the stock. This means the number of shares (N) will grow at the dividend rate (D). Therefore

14.26 $$N(t) = N(0)(1 + D)^t$$

To derive the total earnings for a firm, $E(t)$, the growth rate in per-share earnings and the growth rate in shares are combined as follows:

14.27 $$E(t) = E'(t)N(t) = E'(0)[(1 + G)(1 + D)]^t$$

Because G and D are small, this expression can be approximated by

14.28 $$E(t) \simeq E'(0)(1 + G + D)^t$$

Assuming the growth stock (g) and the nongrowth stock (a) have similar risk and payout, the market should value the two stocks in direct proportion to their earnings in year T (i.e., they will have the same *P/E* ratio), where T is the time when the growth company will begin to grow at the same rate as the market (i.e., the non-growth stock). Put another way, T is the number of years the growth stock is expected to grow at the high rate. In other words, *current prices should be in direct proportion to the expected future earnings ratio that will prevail in year T.* This relationship can be stated

14.29
$$\left(\frac{P_g(0)}{P_a(0)}\right) \approx \left(\frac{E_g(0)(1 + G_g + D_g)^T}{E_a(0)(1 + G_a + D_a)^T}\right)$$

or

14.30
$$\left(\frac{P_g(0)/E_g(0)}{P_a(0)/E_a(0)}\right) \approx \left(\frac{1 + G_g + D_g}{1 + G_a + D_a}\right)^T$$

As a result, the *P/E ratios of the two stocks are in direct proportion to the ratio of composite growth rates raised to the Tth power.* You can solve for T by taking the log of both sides as follows:

14.31
$$\ln\left(\frac{P_g(0)/E_g(0)}{P_a(0)/E_a(0)}\right) \approx T\ln\left(\frac{1 + G_g + D_g}{1 + G_a + D_a}\right)$$

The growth duration model answers the question: How long must the earnings of the growth stock grow at this expected high rate, relative to the nongrowth stock, to justify its prevailing above-average *P/E* ratio? You must then determine whether this *implied* growth duration estimate is reasonable in terms of the company's potential.

   Consider the following example. The stock of Walgreens is selling for $42 a share with expected per-share earnings of $1.50 (its future earnings multiple is 28.0 times). The expected EPS growth rate for Walgreens is estimated to be 13 percent a year, and its dividend yield has been 1 percent and is expected to remain at this level. In contrast, the S&P Industrials Index has a future *P/E* ratio of about 18, an average dividend yield of 2 percent, and an expected growth rate of 6 percent. Therefore, the comparison is as follows:

	S&P Industrials	Walgreens
P/E ratio	18.00	28.00
Expected growth rate	0.06	0.13
Dividend yield	0.02	0.01

Inserting these values into Equation 14.31 yields the following:

$$\ln\left(\frac{28.00}{18.00}\right) = T\ln\left(\frac{1 + 0.13 + 0.01}{1 + 0.06 + 0.02}\right)$$

$$\ln(1.56) = T\ln\left(\frac{1.14}{1.08}\right)$$

$$\ln(1.56) = T\ln(1.055)$$

$$T = \ln(1.56)/\ln(1.055) \text{ (log base 10)}$$

$$= 0.1931/0.02325$$

$$= 8.31\,\text{Years}$$

These results indicate the market is implicitly assuming that Walgreens can continue to grow at this composite rate (14 percent) for about 8 more years, after which it is assumed Walgreens will grow at the same total rate (8 percent) as the aggregate market (i.e., the S&P Industrials). You must now ask, can this superior growth rate be sustained by Walgreens for at least this period? If the implied growth duration is greater than you believe is reasonable, you would advise against buying Walgreens stock. If the implied duration is below your expectations, you would recommend buying the stock.

Intraindustry Analysis   Besides comparing a company to a market series, you can directly compare two firms. For an intercompany analysis, you should compare firms in the same industry because the equal risk assumptions of this model are probably more reasonable.

Consider the following example from the computer software industry:

	Company A	Company B
P/E ratios	31.00	25.00
Expected annual growth rate	0.1700	0.1200
Dividend yield	0.0100	0.0150
Growth rate plus dividend yield	0.1800	0.1350
Estimate of *T*[a]		5.53 years

[a]Readers should check to see that they get the same answer.

These results imply that the market expects Company A to grow at an annual total rate of 18 percent for about 5.5 years, after which it will grow at Company B's rate of 13.5 percent. If you believe the implied duration for growth at 18 percent is too long, you will prefer Company B; if you believe it is reasonable or low, you will recommend Company A.

An Alternative Use of *T*   Instead of solving for *T* and then deciding whether the figure derived is reasonable, you can use this formulation to compute a reasonable *P/E* ratio for a security relative to the aggregate market (or another stock) if the implicit assumptions are reasonable for the stock involved. Again, using Walgreens as an example, you estimate its expected composite growth to be 14 percent a year compared to the expected total market growth of 8 percent. Further, you believe that Walgreens can continue to grow at this above-normal rate for about five years. Using Equation 14.31, this becomes

$$
\begin{aligned}
\ln(X) &= 5 \times \ln\frac{1.14}{1.08} \\
&= 5 \times \ln(1.055) \\
&= 5 \times (0.02325) \\
&= 0.11625
\end{aligned}
$$

To determine what the *P/E* ratio should be given these assumptions, you must derive the antilog of 0.11625, which is approximately 1.3069. Therefore, assuming the market multiple is 18, the earnings multiple for Walgreens should be about 1.3069 times the market *P/E* ratio, or about 24.

Alternatively, if you estimate that Walgreens can maintain a lower growth rate of .12 for a long time period of 10 years, you would derive the antilog for 1.5794 (10 × 0.01579). The answer is 1.4386, which implies a *P/E* ratio of about 26 times for Walgreen Co.'s stock. Notably, both of these estimates are below the current forward *P/E* for Walgreens of 28 times.

Factors to Consider   When using the growth duration technique, remember the following factors: First, the technique assumes equal risk, which may be acceptable when comparing two large, well-established firms in the same industry (e.g., Merck and Pfizer) to each other. It is also reasonable for a large conglomerate, like General Electric, with a beta close to one. In the case of Walgreens, which has a beta of about 0.90, the result is conservative, meaning that the duration would be lower than the estimated 8 years. It is probably *not* a valid assumption when comparing a small firm with a beta of 1.50 to the aggregate market. In this case, the duration generated would be an underestimate of what should be required.

Second, which growth estimate should be used? We prefer to use the *expected* rate of growth based on the factors that affect g (i.e., the retention rate and the components of *ROE*).

Third, the growth duration technique assumes that stocks with higher *P/E* ratios have the higher growth rates. However, there are cases in which the stock with the higher *P/E* ratio does not have a higher expected growth rate or the stock with a higher expected growth rate has a lower *P/E* ratio. Either of the cases generates a useless negative growth duration value. Inconsistency between the expected growth and the *P/E* ratio could be attributed to one of four factors:

1. A major difference in the risk involved.
2. Inaccurate growth rate estimates. You may want to reexamine your growth rate estimate for the firm with the higher *P/E* ratio, that is, could it be higher or should the growth estimate for the low *P/E* stock be lower?
3. The stock with a low *P/E* ratio relative to its expected growth rate is undervalued. (Before you accept this possibility, consider the first two factors.)
4. The stock with a high *P/E* and a low expected growth rate is overvalued. (Before this is accepted, consider both its risk and your estimated growth rate.)

The growth duration concept is valid, *given the assumptions made,* and can help you evaluate growth investments. It is not universally valid, though, because its answers are only as good as the data inputs (expected growth rates) and the applicability of the assumptions. The answer must be evaluated based on the analyst's knowledge.

The technique probably is most useful for helping spot overvalued growth companies with very high multiples. In such a case, the technique will highlight that the company must continue to grow at some very high rate for an extended period of time to justify its high *P/E* ratio (e.g., 15 to 20 years). Also, it can help you decide between two growth companies in the same industry by comparing each to the market, the industry, or directly to each other. Such a comparison has provided interesting insights wherein the new firms in an industry were growing faster than the large competitor but their *P/E* ratios were *substantially* higher and implied that these new firms had to maintain this large growth rate superiority for over *10 years* to justify the much higher *P/E* ratio.

SITE VISITS AND THE ART OF THE INTERVIEW

Brokerage house analysts and portfolio managers have access to persons that the typical small investor does not. Analysts frequently have contact with corporate personnel by telephone (conference calls), at formal presentations, or during plant site visits. Though insider trading laws restrict the analyst's ability to obtain material nonpublic information, these visits facilitate dialog between the corporation and the investor community. The analyst can gather information about the firm's plans and strategies, which helps the analyst understand the firm's prospects as an investment.

Interviewing is an art. The analyst wants information about the firm, and top management wants to put the firm in the best light possible. Thus, the analyst must be prepared to focus the interview on management's plans, strategies, and concerns. Analysts try to gauge the sensitivity of the firm's revenues, costs, and earnings to different scenarios by asking "what if" questions.

Analysts have frequent telephone contact with the firm's investor relations (IR) department regarding company pronouncements. The chief financial officer and chief executive officer of the firm also meet with security analysts and discuss the firm's planning process and major issues confronting the industry.

The analyst should talk with people other than top managers. Talking with middle managers or factory workers during a plant tour, visiting stores, and talking with customers provide insights beyond those of management. The firm's major customers can provide information regarding product quality and customer satisfaction. The firm's suppliers can furnish information about rising or falling supply orders and the timeliness of payments. Finally, an outstanding source of information is the firm's competitors who will be happy to point out the firm's weaknesses or possible problems. They may even be willing to admit which firm is its toughest competitor.

The idea was always that analysts were able to create a mosaic regarding future expectations for the firm from numerous sources (including the company) and transmit this information to the market by sending research reports to brokerage clients and portfolio managers of pensions and mutual funds. This traditional way of doing research was changed by the SEC in 2000 when they issued the Fair Disclosure (FD) guidelines that required all disclosure of "material information" to be made public to all interested parties at the same time. The intent was to level the playing field by ensuring that professional analysts did not have a competitive advantage over nonprofessional investors. The result of this law is that many firms will not agree to interviews with analysts and will only provide information during large public presentations over the Internet.

The long-run impact of this FD requirement is not clear in terms of how firms will relate to the professional analyst community. One benefit is that analysts will spend more time with information sources beyond the firm such as trade shows, customers, suppliers, and competitors to build the mosaic.

WHEN TO SELL

Our analysis has focused on determining if a stock should be purchased. In fact, when we make a purchase, a subsequent question gains prominence: When should the stock be sold? Many times holding on to a stock too long leads to a return below expectations or less than what was available earlier. When stocks decline in value immediately following a portfolio manager's purchase, is this a further buying opportunity, or does the decline indicate that the stock analysis was incorrect?

The answer to the question of when to sell a stock is contained in the research that convinced the analyst to purchase the stock in the first place. The analyst should have identified the key assumptions and variables driving the expectations for the stock. Analysis of the stock doesn't end when intrinsic value is computed and the research report is written. Once the key value drivers are identified, the analyst must continually monitor and update his or her knowledge base about the firm. Notably, if the key value drivers appear to have weakened or there is a major change in management, it is time to reevaluate, and possibly sell, the stock.

The stock should also be closely evaluated when the current price approaches the intrinsic value estimate. When the stock becomes fairly priced (the undervaluation has been corrected), it may be time to sell it and reinvest the funds in other underpriced stocks. In short, if the "story" for buying the stock still appears to be true, continue to hold it if it has not become fully priced (i.e., market price equal to intrinsic value). If the "story" changes, it may be time to sell the stock. If you know why you bought the stock, you'll be able to recognize when to sell it.

INFLUENCES ON ANALYSTS

Stock analysts and portfolio managers are, for the most part, highly trained individuals who possess expertise in financial analysis and background in their industry. A computer hardware analyst knows as much about industry trends and new product offerings as any industry insider. A pharmaceutical analyst is able to independently determine the market potential of drugs undergoing testing and the FDA approval process. So why don't more brokerage house customers and portfolio managers who receive the analysts' expert advice achieve investment success? The following subsections discuss several factors that make it difficult to "beat the market."

Efficient Markets

As noted in Chapter 6, the efficient market is difficult to outsmart, especially if you are considering actively traded and frequently analyzed companies. Information about the economy, a firm's industry, and the firm itself is reviewed by numerous bright analysts, investors, and portfolio managers. Because of the market's ability to review and absorb information, stock prices generally approximate fair market value. Investors look for situations where stocks may not be fairly valued. Notably, because there are numerous bright, hardworking analysts, it is difficult to successfully, frequently, and consistently find undervalued shares. Put another way, in most instances, the value estimated for a stock will be very close to its market price, which indicates that it is properly valued. The analyst's best place to seek attractive stocks is not among well known companies and actively traded stocks, because they are analyzed by dozens of Wall Street analysts. Stocks with smaller market capitalizations, those not covered by many analysts, or those whose shares are mainly held by individual investors may be the best places to search for inefficiencies. Smaller capitalization stocks sometimes are too small for time-constrained analysts or too small for purchase by institutional investors.[17] The price of stocks not researched by many analysts ("neglected stocks") may not reflect all relevant information.[18]

Paralysis of Analysis

Analysts spend most of their time in a relentless search for one more contact or one more piece of information that will ensure the correct stock recommendation. Analysts need to develop a systematic approach for gathering, monitoring, and reviewing relevant information about economic trends, industry competitive forces, and company strategy. Analysts must evaluate the information as a whole to discern patterns that indicate the intrinsic value of the stock rather than searching for one more piece of information.

---

[17]According to SEC regulations, mutual funds cannot own more than 10 percent of a firm's shares. For some large funds, this constraint will make the resulting investment too small to have any significant impact on fund returns, so analysts do not bother to consider such stocks for purchase.

[18]Information on the number of analysts covering a stock is available from research firms, such as IBES and Zacks.

Because markets are generally efficient, the consensus view about the firm is already reflected in its stock price. As noted previously, to earn above-average returns, there are two requirements; (1) the analyst must have expectations that differ from the consensus, *and* (2) the analyst must be correct. Thus, the analyst should concentrate on identifying what is wrong with the market consensus (i.e., why do you differ from the consensus?), or what surprises may upset the market consensus—that is, work at *estimating earning surprises.*

Analyst Conflicts of Interest

A potential conflict can arise if communication occurs between a firm's investment banking and equity research division. If the investment bankers assist a firm in a stock or bond offering, it will be difficult for an analyst to issue a negative evaluation of the company. Advisory fees have been lost because of a negative stock recommendation. Despite attempts to ensure the independence of stock analysts, firm politics may get in the way.

The analyst is in frequent contact with the top officers of the company he or she analyzes. Although there are guidelines about receiving gifts and favors, it is sometimes difficult to separate personal friendship and impersonal corporate relationships. Corporate officials may try to convince the analyst that his or her pessimistic report is in error or suggest that it glosses over recent positive developments. To mitigate these problems, an analyst should call the company's investor relations department immediately *after* changing a recommendation to explain his or her perspective. The analyst needs to maintain independence and be objective in his or her analysis.

GLOBAL COMPANY AND STOCK ANALYSIS

As indicated on numerous occasions, a major goal of this text is to demonstrate investment technique that can be applied globally to markets, industries, and companies around the world. This chapter has been heavily concerned with presenting and demonstrating these techniques to U.S. firms. While space constraints do not allow a full demonstration to international firms, it is important to point out some of the major factors and constraints that analysts and portfolio managers need to acknowledge and adjust for when investing globally.

Availability of Data

In the United States, we suffer from information (data) overload, which is a blessing and a curse since we have more information than anywhere else in the world (which is good), but, as a result, there is a lot of information to digest and analyze. When you start analyzing international markets, industries, and stocks and cannot get the necessary data for valuation, you come to appreciate what is available in the United States. Beyond the limited amount of information, there is also the problem of timeliness (how long before you get the data?) and the reliability. (Can you believe and depend upon the data published in some countries and by some global industries?)

Differential Accounting Conventions

Even when the financial data for an industry and a firm are timely and reliable, it is necessary to recognize that the accounting rules and practices differ dramatically around the world. Not only are the financial statements very different in general presentation, but the accounting practices differ related to sales and expense recognition. The fact is, identical transactions in different countries can generate significant differences in income and cash flow. As a result, stocks in different countries will have very different *P/E* and *P/CF* ratios, not because investors differ in valuation but because the accounting numbers used are not the same. Notably, it is because of these accounting problems that many investors advocate using the price-to-sales ratio in valuations across countries since sales revenue is the least contaminated accounting figure. The good news in this regard is the movement toward the use of global accounting standards. For an overview of this transition, see Sandagaran (2001).

Currency Differences (Exchange Rate Risk)

It is widely recognized that a significant factor that must be considered by global investors is currency risk caused by changes in exchange rates among countries. While these changes can work for or against you, the point is that it creates a major uncertainty that must be considered in your evaluation of the company and its stock.

Political (Country) Risk

Again, in the United States, we are blessed with the most stable political and economic environment in the world. Therefore, by definition, every other country will have greater political/country risk, which in some cases (e.g., Russia, Indonesia, North Korea) can be substantial. Therefore, it is necessary to acknowledge this factor and estimate its effect on the cost of equity for firms in these countries.

Transaction Costs

Higher transaction costs result from less-liquid markets—where it takes longer to trade and there is more price volatility connected to a trade—or from a trade that costs more (e.g., higher commissions). Again, these costs vary dramatically among countries.

Valuation Differences

The point is, these individual differences among countries combine to cause a clear differential in the stock valuation for an international stock. Specifically, the earnings or cash flow numbers will differ and the required rate of return (the discount rate) for a non-U.S. stock will differ substantially because the nominal rate is different and there are additional risks that must be added such as exchange rate risk, political risk, and higher liquidity costs.

Summary

In summary, when investing globally, the *valuation process* is the same around the world, and the investment decision in terms of the ultimate comparison of intrinsic value and price is similar—the difference is in the *practice* of valuation that requires attention to these additional factors that must be considered by the global investor when valuing an international stock. Therefore, everything you have learned is relevant, but it must be applied differently (i.e., the inputs differ), depending on the country.

The **Internet** Investments Online

Many helpful sites have been reviewed in prior chapters, for example, examining individual firm sites and the SEC's EDGAR database for firm-specific information. Investment bank and brokerage house sites may also prove valuable, though they may expect payment for access to their published research on different firms. Still, many sites exist that allow users to examine free information and investing tips:

http://www.better-investing.org/ The home page for the National Association of Investment Clubs offers company information and investing ideas in addition to resources for those interested in setting up their own investment club.

http://www.fool.com This is the home page for the Motley Fool; despite its name, it is a well-known and popular site for investors to visit. It is chock full of data, articles, educational resources, news, and investing ideas.

http://www.cfonews.com Corporate Financials Online provides links to news about selected publicly traded firms.

http://www.zacks.com This is the Web site for Zacks Investment Research. When the user types in a ticker symbol, Zacks provides links to a company profile, financials, analysts' current stock ratings, consensus earnings estimates, and the number of analysts recommending strong buy, moderate buy, hold, moderate sell, and strong sell. Links allow the user to order brokerage reports.

http://moneycentral.msn.com/investor/home.asp offers stock screens, price charts, and links to earnings estimates and analyst reports.

http://www.iaschicago.org/ The home page of the Investment Analysts Society of Chicago includes many financial web links and sources of market and company information.

http://www.valueline.com This site was mentioned in an earlier chapter. The Value Line Investment Survey is a favorite source of information for many investors.

SUMMARY

- This chapter demonstrates how to complete the fundamental analysis process by analyzing a company and deciding whether you should buy its stock. This requires a separate analysis of a company and its stock. A wonderful company can have an overpriced stock, or a mediocre firm can have an underpriced stock.
- Although the chapter is mainly concerned with discussing and demonstrating several alternative valuation techniques, the initial section contained a discussion of the strategic alternatives available to firms in response to different competitive pressures in their industries. The alternative corporate strategies include low-cost leadership or differentiation which if properly implemented, should help the company attain above-average rates of return. In addition, we discussed SWOT analysis, which helps an analyst assess a firm's strengths and weaknesses as well as its external opportunities and threats. This strategic analysis of the firm's goals, objectives, and strategy should put you in a position to properly estimate the intrinsic value of the stock.

- When estimating a stock's intrinsic value, we can follow one or both of two approaches (the present value of cash flow, or the analysis of relative valuation ratios). We reviewed how to estimate the major inputs to the techniques and demonstrated results when these techniques are applied to Walgreens.
- We derived several estimated values for Walgreens based on the present value of cash flow techniques and applied the relative valuation ratios beginning with *P/E* ratios and the other relative valuation ratios, including the price/book value ratio, the price/cash flow ratio, and the price/sales ratio, and compared these relative valuation ratios for the company to comparable ratios for both the retail drugstore industry and the aggregate market.
- The investment decision is based on the critical comparisons of a stock's intrinsic value to the prevailing market price. If the stock's intrinsic value exceeds the market price, we would buy the stock. If the intrinsic value is less than the market price, we would not buy it and would sell it

if we owned it. The estimation of the intrinsic value can be done by using the techniques demonstrated in this chapter.

- Because of the difficulty in estimating the intrinsic value of growth firms, we considered alternative specifications for growth companies and several techniques that provide insights on the valuation of these firms. These techniques include economic value added, the franchise factor models, and a growth duration model that emphasizes the importance of estimating how long superior growth is expected to last. These models help the analyst concentrate attention on the relevant factors that determine true growth, which determines the intrinsic value of these growth companies. The critical question is, is the stock of the growth company going to be a growth stock?

- We concluded the chapter with a discussion of several unique considerations an analyst must consider when analyzing and valuing global industries or firms. The importance of different accounting conventions and the impact of exchange rate differences were highlighted.

SUGGESTED READINGS

Copeland, Tom, Tim Koller, and Jack Murrin. *Valuation: Measuring and Managing the Value of Companies,* 3rd ed. New York: Wiley, 2000.

Damodaran, Aswath. *Damodaran on Valuation.* New York: Wiley, 1994.

Hackel, Kenneth S., and Joshua Livnat. *Cash Flow and Security Analysis,* 2nd ed. Burr Ridge, IL: Irwin Professional Publishing, 1996.

Jaffe, Jeffery, Donald Keim, and Randolph Westerfield. "Earnings Yields, Market Values, Stock Returns." *Journal of Finance* 44, no. 1 (March 1989).

Palepu, Krishna, Paul Healy, and Victor Bernard. *Business Analysis and Valuation,* 3rd ed. Cincinnati, OH: South-Western Publishing, 2004.

Squires, Jan R., ed. *Equity Research and Valuation Techniques.* Charlottesville, VA: AIMR, 1998.

Squires, Jan R., ed. *Practical Issues in Equity Analysis.* Charlottesville, VA: AIMR, 2000.

Stowe, John D., Thomas Robinson, Jerald Pinto, and Dennis McLeavey. *Analysis of Equity Investments: Valuation.* Charlottesville, VA: AIMR, 2002.

QUESTIONS

1. Give an example of a growth company and discuss why you identify it as such. Based on its *P/E,* do you think it is a growth stock? Explain.

2. Give an example of a cyclical stock and discuss why you have designated it as such. Is it issued by a cyclical company?

3. A biotechnology firm is growing at a compound rate of over 21 percent a year. (Its *ROE* is over 30 percent, and it retains about 70 percent of its earnings.) The stock of this company is priced at about 65 times next year's earnings. Discuss whether you consider this a growth company and/or a growth stock.

4. Select a company outside the retail drugstore industry and indicate what economic series you would use for a sales projection. Discuss why this is a relevant series.

5. Select a company outside the retail drugstore industry and indicate what industry series you would use in an industry analysis. (Use one of the industry groups designated by Standard & Poor's.) Discuss why this industry series is appropriate. Were there other possible alternatives?

6. Select a company outside the retail drugstore industry and, based on reading its annual report and other public information, discuss what you perceive to be its competitive strategy (i.e., low-cost producer or differentiation).

7. Discuss a company that is known to be a low-cost producer in its industry and consider why it is a cost leader. Do the same for a firm known for differentiating.

8. Under what conditions would you use a two- or three-stage cash flow model rather than the constant-growth model?

9. What is the rationale for using the price/book value ratio as a measure of relative value?

10. What would you look for to justify a price/book value ratio of 3.0? What would you expect to be the characteristics of a firm with a *P/BV* ratio of 0.6?

11. Why has the price/cash flow ratio become a popular measure of relative value during the recent past? What factors would help explain a difference in this ratio for two firms?

12. Assume that you uncover two stocks with substantially different price/sales ratios (e.g., 0.5 versus 2.5). Discuss the factors that might explain the difference.

13. Specify the major components for the calculation of economic value added and describe what a positive EVA signifies.

14. Discuss why you would want to use EVA return on capital rather than absolute EVA to compare two companies or to evaluate a firm's performance over time.

15. Differentiate between EVA and MVA and discuss the relatively weak relationship between these two measures of performance. Is this relationship surprising to you? Explain.

16. Discuss the two factors that determine the franchise value of a firm. Assuming a firm has a base cost of equity of 11 percent and does not have a franchise value, what will be its *P/E*?

17. You are told that a company retains 80 percent of its earnings, and its earnings are growing at a rate of about 8 percent a year versus an average growth rate of 6 percent for all firms. Discuss whether you would consider this a growth company.

18. It is contended by some that in a completely competitive economy, there would never be a true growth company. Discuss the reasoning behind this contention.

19. Why is it not feasible to use the dividend discount model in the valuation of true growth companies?

20. Discuss the major assumptions of the growth duration model. Why could these assumptions present a problem?

21. You are told that a growth company has a *P/E* ratio of 13 times and a growth rate of 15 percent compared to the aggregate market, which has a growth rate of 8 percent and a *P/E* ratio of 16 times. What does this comparison imply regarding the growth company? What else do you need to know to properly compare the growth company to the aggregate market?

22. Given the alternative companies described in the chapter (negative growth, simple growth, dynamic growth), indicate what your label would be for Walgreens. Justify your label.

23. Indicate and justify a growth label for General Motors.

24. *CFA Examination Level I*
Using book value to measure profitability and to value a company's stock has limitations. Discuss *five* such limitations from an accounting perspective. Be specific. [10 minutes]

25. *CFA Examination Level II*
On your visit to Litchfield Chemical Corp. (LCC), you learned that the board of directors has periodically debated the company's dividend-payout policy.

    a. Briefly discuss *two* arguments *for* and *two* arguments *against* a high dividend-payout policy. [8 minutes]
       A director of LCC said that the use of dividend discount models by investors is "proof" that "the higher the dividend, the higher the stock price."

    b. Using a constant-growth dividend discount model as a basis of reference, evaluate the director's statement. [8 minutes]

    c. Explain how an increase in dividend payout would affect *each* of the following (holding all other factors constant):
       (1) Internal (implied, normalized, or sustainable) growth rate; and
       (2) Growth in book value. [8 minutes]

26. *CFA Examination Level II*
The Soft Corporation (SC) is planning to acquire a slower-growth competitor, which will materially increase SC's sales volume. The company to be acquired has pretax margins that are approximately the same as those of SC. SC plans to issue $300 million in long-term debt to finance the entire cost of the acquisition.

    a. Discuss how SC's potential acquisition might *decrease* its valuation based on a constant-growth dividend discount model. Be sure to comment on *each* of the three factors in such a model. [9 minutes]

b. Discuss *two* reasons why SC's potential acquisition might *increase* the P/E multiple investors are willing to pay for SC. [4 minutes]

 27. *CFA Examination Level II*

A generalized model for the value of any asset is the present value of the expected cash flows:

$$Value = \sum_{t=1}^{N} \frac{CF_t}{(1 + k)^t}$$

where:

N = life of the asset
CF_t = cash flow in Period t
k = appropriate discount rate

Both stock and bond valuation models use a discounted cash flow approach, which includes the estimation of three factors (N, CF_t, k).

Explain why *each* of these *three* factors is generally more difficult to estimate for common stocks than for traditional corporate bonds. [12 minutes]

PROBLEMS

1. Select two stocks in an industry of your choice, and perform a common-size income statement analysis over a two-year period.
   a. Discuss which firm is more cost-effective.
   b. Discuss the relative year-to-year changes in gross profit margin, operating profit margin, and net profit margin for each company.
2. Select a company outside the retail drugstore industry, and examine its operating profit margin relative to the operating margin for its industry during the most recent 10-year period. Discuss the annual results in terms of levels and percentage changes.
3. Given Hitech's beta of 1.75 and a risk-free rate of 7 percent, what is the expected rate of return, assuming
   a. a 15 percent market return?
   b. a 10 percent market return?
4. Select three companies from any industry except retail drugstores.
   a. Compute their P/E ratios using last year's average price [(high plus low)/2] and earnings.
   b. Compute their growth rate of earnings over the last five years.
   c. Look up the most recent beta reported in Value Line.
   d. Discuss the relationships between P/E, growth, and risk.
5. What is the implied growth duration of Kayleigh Industries given the following:

	S&P Industrials	Kayleigh Industries
P/E ratios	16	24
Expected growth	0.06	0.14
Dividend yield	0.04	0.02

6. Lauren Industries has an 18 percent annual growth rate compared to the market rate of 8 percent. If the market multiple is 18, determine P/E ratios for Lauren Industries, assuming its beta is 1.0 and you feel it can maintain its superior growth rate for
   a. the next 10 years.
   b. the next 5 years.

7. You are given the following information about two computer software firms and the S&P Industrials:

	Company A	Company B	S&P Industrials
P/E ratio	30.0	27.0	18.0
Expected annual growth rate	0.18	0.15	0.07
Dividend yield	0.00	0.01	0.02

  a. Compute the growth duration of each company stock relative to the S&P Industrials.
  b. Compute the growth duration of Company A relative to Company B.
  c. Given these growth durations, what determines your investment decision?

8. *CFA Examination Level II*
The value of an asset is the present value of the expected returns from the asset during the holding period. An investment will provide a stream of returns during this period, and it is necessary to discount this stream of returns at an appropriate rate to determine the asset's present value. A dividend valuation model such as the following is frequently used:

$$P_i = \frac{D_1}{(k_i - g_i)}$$

where:

P_i = the current price of Common Stock i
D_1 = the expected dividend in Period 1
k_i = the required rate of return on Stock i
g_i = the expected constant growth rate of dividends for Stock i

  a. *Identify* the three factors that must be estimated for any valuation model, and *explain* why these estimates are more difficult to derive for common stocks than for bonds. [9 minutes]
  b. *Explain* the principal problem involved in using a dividend valuation model to value
    (1) companies whose operations are closely correlated with economic cycles.
    (2) companies that are of giant size and are maturing.
    (3) companies that are of small size and are growing rapidly.
    Assume that all companies pay dividends. [6 minutes]

9. *CFA Examination Level I*
Your client is considering the purchase of $100,000 in common stock, which pays no dividends and will appreciate in market value by 10 percent per year. At the same time, the client is considering an opportunity to invest $100,000 in a lease obligation that will provide the annual year-end cash flows listed in Table 14.1 on the following page. Assume that each investment will be sold at the end of three years and that you are given no additional information.
    Calculate the present value of each of the two investments assuming a 10 percent discount rate, and state which one will provide the higher return over the three-year period. Use the data in Table 14.1, and show your calculations. [10 minutes]

10. *CFA Examination Level I*
The constant-growth dividend discount model can be used both for the valuation of companies and for the estimation of the long-term total return of a stock.

Assume:	
$20 = Price of a Stock Today	
8% = Expected Growth Rate of Dividends	
$0.60 = Annual Dividend One Year Forward	

  a. Using *only* the preceding data, compute the expected long-term total return on the stock using the constant-growth dividend discount model. Show calculations.
  b. Briefly discuss *three* disadvantages of the constant-growth dividend discount model in its application to investment analysis.
  c. Identify *three* alternative methods to the dividend discount model for the valuation of companies. [10 minutes]

Table 14.1	**Annual Cash Flow from Lease**

End of Year				
1	$ -0-			
2 Lease receipts	15,000			
3 Lease receipts	25,000			
4 Sale proceeds	$100,000			

		Present Value of $1		
Period	6%	8%	10%	12%
1	0.943	0.926	0.909	0.893
2	0.890	0.857	0.826	0.797
3	0.840	0.794	0.751	0.712
4	0.792	0.735	0.683	0.636
5	0.747	0.681	0.621	0.567

11. *CFA Examination Level II*
An analyst expects a risk-free return of 4.5 percent, a market return of 14.5 percent, and the returns for Stocks A and B that are shown in Table 14.2.
a. Show on a graph
(1) where Stocks A and B would plot on the security market line (SML) if they were fairly valued using the capital asset pricing model (CAPM).
(2) where Stocks A and B actually plot on the same graph according to the returns estimated by the analyst and shown in Table 14.2 [6 minutes]
b. State whether Stock A and Stock B are undervalued or overvalued if the analyst uses the SML for strategic investment decisions. [4 minutes]

Table 14.2	**Stock Information**

Stock	Beta	Analyst's Estimated Return
A	1.2	16%
B	0.8	14%

12. *CFA Examination Level II*
Scott Kelly is reviewing MasterToy's financial statements in order to estimate its sustainable growth rate. Using the information presented in Table 14.3,
a. (1) identify and calculate the *three* components of the DuPont formula.
(2) calculate the *ROE* for 1999, using the three components of the DuPont formula.
(3) calculate the sustainable-growth rate for 1999. [13 minutes]
b. Kelly has calculated actual and sustainable growth for each of the past four years and finds in each year that its calculated sustainable-growth rate substantially exceeds its actual growth rate. Cite *two* courses of action (other than ignoring the problem) that Kelly should encourage MasterToy to take, assuming the calculated sustainable-growth rate continues to exceed the actual growth rate. [6 minutes]

Table 14.3	**MasterToy, Inc.: Actual 1998 and Estimated 1999 Financial Statements for Fiscal Year Ending December 31 ($ Millions, Except per-Share Data)**

	1998	1999e	Change (%)
Income Statement			
Revenue	$4,750	$5,140	7.6
Cost of goods sold	$2,400	$2,540	
Selling, general, and administrative	1,400	1,550	
Depreciation	180	210	
Goodwill amortization	10	10	
Operating income	$ 760	$ 830	8.4
Interest expense	20	25	
Income before taxes	$ 740	$ 805	
Income taxes	265	2 295	
Net income	$ 475	$ 510	
Earnings per share	$ 1.79	$ 1.96	8.6
Average shares outstanding (millions)	265	260	
Balance Sheet			
Cash	$ 400	$400	
Accounts receivable	$ 680	$700	
Inventories	$ 570	$600	
Net property, plant, and equipment	$ 800	$870	
Intangibles	$ 500	$530	
Total assets	$2,950	$3,100	
Current liabilities	$ 550	$ 600	
Long-term debt	$ 300	$ 300	
Total liabilities	$ 850	$ 900	
Stockholders' equity	$2,100	$2,200	
Total liabilities and equity	$2,950	$3,100	
Book value per share	$ 7.92	$ 8.46	
Annual dividend per share	$ 0.55	$ 0.60	

Note: Questions 13 through 17 relate to Telluride and its subsidiaries.

13. *CFA Examination Level II*

The management of Telluride, an international diversified conglomerate based in the United States, believes that the recent strong performance of its wholly owned medical supply subsidiary, Sundanci, has gone unnoticed. In order to realize Sundanci's full value, Telluride has announced that it will divest Sundanci in a tax-free spin-off.

Sue Carroll, CFA, is Director of Research at Kesson and Associates. In developing an investment recommendation for Sundanci, Carroll has directed four of her analysts to determine a valuation of Sundanci using various valuation disciplines. To assist her analysts, Carroll has gathered the information shown in Table 14.4 and Table 14.5.

Prior to determining Sundanci's valuation, Carroll analyzes Sundanci's return on equity *(ROE)* and sustainable growth.

a. (1) Calculate the *three* components of *ROE* in the DuPont formula for the year 2000.
   (2) Calculate *ROE* for the year 2000.
   (3) Calculate the sustainable-growth rate. Show your work. [12 minutes]

Table 14.4	**Sundanci Actual 1999 and 2000 Financial Statements for Fiscal Years Ending May 31 ($ Million, Except per-Share Data)**		
		1999	2000
	Income Statement		
	Revenue	$474	$598
	Depreciation	20	23
	Other operating costs	368	460
	Income before taxes	86	115
	Taxes	26	35
	Net income	60	80
	Dividends	18	24
	Earnings per share	$0.714	$0.952
	Dividend per share	$0.214	$0.286
	Common shares outstanding (millions)	84.0	84.0
	Balance Sheet		
	Current assets	$201	$326
	Net property, plant and equipment	474	489
	Total assets	675	815
	Current liabilities	57	141
	Long-term debt	0	0
	Total liabilities	57	141
	Shareholders' equity	618	674
	Total liabilities and equity	675	815
	Capital expenditures	34	38

Table 14.5	**Selected Financial Information for Sundanci**	
	Required rate of return on equity	14%
	Growth rate of industry	13%
	Industry *P/E* ratio	26

Carroll learns that Sundanci's Board of Directors is considering the following policy changes that will affect Sundanci's sustainable-growth rate:
- Director A proposes an increase in the quarterly dividend to $0.15 per share.
- Director B proposes a bond issue of $25 million, the proceeds of which would be used to increase production capacity.
- Director C proposes a 2-for-1 stock split.
- b. Indicate the effect of *each* of these proposals on Sundanci's sustainable rate of growth, given that other factors remain unchanged. Identify which component of the sustainable-growth model, if any, is directly affected by *each* proposal. [9 minutes]

> **Note: Answer Question 13b using the following template.**

TEMPLATE FOR QUESTION 13b

Proposal	Effect on Sustainable-Growth Rate (circle one)	Component Directly Affected (If Any)
Increase in quarterly dividend	Increase Decrease No effect	
Bond issue	Increase Decrease No effect	
Stock split	Increase Decrease No effect	

14. *CFA Examination Level II*

    Helen Morgan, CFA, has been asked by Carroll to determine the potential valuation for Sundanci, Inc., using the dividend discount model. Morgan anticipates that Sundanci's earnings and dividends will grow at 32 percent for two years and 13 percent thereafter.

    Calculate the current value of a share of Sundanci stock using a two-stage dividend discount model and the data from Tables 14.4 and 14.5. Show your work. [8 minutes]

15. *CFA Examination Level II*

    Abbey Naylor, CFA, has been directed by Carroll to determine the value of Sundanci's stock using the free cash flow to equity model. Naylor believes that Sundanci's FCFE will grow at 27 percent for two years and 13 percent thereafter. Capital expenditures, depreciation, and working capital are all expected to increase proportionately with FCFE.

    a. Calculate the amount of FCFE per share for the year 2000, using the data from Table 14.4. Show your work. [6 minutes]

    b. Calculate the current value of a share of Sundanci stock based on the two-stage FCFE model. Show your work. [8 minutes]

    c. (1) Describe *one* limitation of the two-stage DDM model that is addressed by using the two-stage FCFE model.

       (2) Describe *one* limitation of the two-stage DDM model that is *not* addressed by using the two-stage FCFE model. [6 minutes]

16. *CFA Examination Level II*

    Christie Johnson, CFA, has been assigned by Carroll to analyze Sundanci using the constant-growth dividend price/earnings (*P/E*) ratio model. Johnson assumes that Sundanci's earnings and dividends will grow at a constant rate of 13 percent.

    a. Calculate the *P/E* ratio based on information in Tables 14.4 and 14.5 and on Johnson's assumptions for Sundanci. Show your work. [4 minutes]

    b. Identify, within the context of the constant-growth dividend model, how *each* of the fundamental factors shown in the following template would affect the *P/E* ratio. [4 minutes]

       Note: A change in a fundamental factor is assumed to happen in isolation, and interactive effects between factors are ignored. Every other element of the firm is unchanged.

> Note: Answer Question 16b using the following template.

TEMPLATE FOR QUESTION 16b	
Fundamental Factor	**Effect on *P/E* Ratio (circle one)**
The riskiness (beta) of Sundanci increases substantially.	Increase Decrease May increase or decrease
The estimated growth rate of Sundanci's earnings and dividends increases.	Increase Decrease May increase or decrease
The dividend-payout ratio of Sundanci increases.	Increase Decrease May increase or decrease
The market risk premium increases.	Increase Decrease May increase or decrease

    c. Explain why an increase in the dividend-payout ratio may not have the effect that the constant-growth dividend *P/E* ratio model suggests. [4 minutes]

17. *CFA Examination Level II*

One week after the spin-off of Sundanci, Carroll asks analyst Jim Martin to use economic value added and market value added to measure the performance of Sundanci. In addition to the information provided in Tables 14.4 and 14.5, Martin uses the following information in his analysis:
- Adjusted net operating profit after tax is $100 million.
- Total adjusted capital is $700 million.
- Closing stock price is $26.
    a. Calculate the following for Sundanci. Show your work. [6 minutes]
       (1) EVA for fiscal 2000
       (2) MVA as of fiscal year-end 2000
    b. Discuss the *two* primary differences in calculating economic profit (as used in EVA) versus accounting profit. [6 minutes]

18. *CFA Examination Level II*

Peninsular has another client who has inquired about the valuation method best suited for comparison of companies in an industry that has the following characteristics:
- Principal competitors within the industry are located in the United States, France, Japan, and Brazil.
- The industry is currently operating at a cyclical low, with many firms reporting losses.
- The industry is subjected to rapid technological change.

Jones recommends that the client consider the following valuation ratios:
    1. Price to earnings
    2. Price to book value
    3. Price to sales
    a. Determine which *one* of the three valuation ratios is most appropriate for comparing companies in this industry. Support your answer with *two* reasons that make that ratio superior to *either* of the other two ratios. [5 minutes]

The client also has expressed interest in economic value added as a measure of company performance. Jones asks his assistant to prepare a presentation about EVA for the client. The assistant's presentation includes the following statements:
    1. EVA is a measure of a firm's excess shareholder value generated over a long period of time.
    2. In calculating EVA, the cost of capital is the weighted average of the after-tax yield on long-term bonds with similar risk and the cost of equity as calculated by the capital asset pricing model.

3. EVA provides a consistent measure of performance across firms.

b. Determine whether *each* of the statements is correct or incorrect and, if *incorrect,* explain why. [6 minutes]

Note: Explanations cannot repeat the statement in negative form but must indicate what is needed to make the statement correct.

> Note: Answer Question 18b in the following template.

TEMPLATE FOR QUESTION 18b

Statement	Determine Whether Correct or Incorrect (circle one)	If Incorrect, Explain Why
1. EVA is a measure of a firm's excess shareholder value generated over a long period of time.	Correct Incorrect	
2. In calculating EVA, the cost of capital is the weighted average of the after-tax yield on long-term bonds with similar risk and the cost of equity as calculated by the capital asset pricing model.	Correct Incorrect	
3. EVA provides a consistent measure of performance across firms.	Correct Incorrect	

THOMSON ONE | Business School Edition

1. Identify two firms in an industry, one of which seems to follow a "cost leadership" strategy and one of which tries to be a "differentiator." How do their common-size financial statements differ? Examine their trends in *ROE* using DuPont analysis. Comment on the differences and/or similarities you find.
2. Update the analysis of Walgreens in this chapter by computing the following:
   a. average compound dividend growth rate from 1993 until the most recent year
   b. sustainable growth rate
   c. expected returns, based on Thomson One: Business School Edition's beta estimate and estimates you obtain of the current risk-free rate (the 10-year Treasury bond yield) and a market risk premium of 3 percent, 5 percent, 7 percent.
   d. present value of dividends, using the growth assumptions in the chapter. Compare your estimated value to the current market price of WAG and indicate if you would buy the stock.
3. Estimate Walgreen Co.'s free cash flow to equity and its operating free cash flow for the most recent year.
4. Using peer analysis, compare Walgreen Co.'s relative valuation ratios with those of its peers (click on the "peers" tab, then click on "overviews" and "valuation comparison").
5. Compute the current growth duration for WAG using the growth rate from Question 2b and assuming a divident yield of 1 percent. For the market assume a *P/E* of 18 times, growth of 6 percent and dividend yield of 2 percent.

Chapter 15

Technical Analysis*

After you read this chapter, you should be able to answer the following questions:

- How does technical analysis differ from fundamental analysis?
- What are the underlying assumptions of technical analysis?
- What major assumption causes a difference between technical analysis and the efficient market hypothesis?
- What are the major advantages of technical analysis?
- What are the major challenges to technical analysis?
- What is the logic for the major contrary-opinion rules used by technicians?
- What rules are used by technicians who want to "follow the smart money"?
- What is the breadth of market measures, and what are they intended to indicate?
- What are the three types of price movements postulated in the Dow Theory, and how are they used?
- Why is trading volume important and how do technicians use it?
- What are support and resistance levels and how are they used?
- How do technicians use moving-average lines to detect changes in trends?
- What is the rationale behind relative-strength line?
- How are bar charts different from point-and-figure charts?
- What are some uses of technical analysis in foreign security markets?
- How is technical analysis used when analyzing bonds?

The market reacted yesterday to the report of a large increase in the short interest on the NYSE.

Although the market declined today, it was not considered bearish because of the light volume.

The market declined today after three days of increases due to profit taking by investors.

These and similar statements appear daily in the financial news. All of them have as their rationale one of numerous technical trading rules. *Technical analysts,* or *technicians,* develop technical trading rules from observations of past price movements of the stock market and

*Richard T. McCabe, Chief Market Analyst at Merrill Lynch Capital Markets, provided helpful comments and material for this chapter.

individual stocks. The philosophy behind technical analysis is in sharp contrast to the efficient market hypothesis that we studied, which contends that past performance has no influence on future performance or market values. It also differs from what we learned about fundamental analysis, which involves making investment decisions based on the examination of the economy, an industry, and company variables that lead to an estimate of intrinsic value for an investment, which is then compared to its prevailing market price. In contrast to the efficient market hypothesis or fundamental analysis, **technical analysis** involves the examination of past market data such as prices and the volume of trading, which leads to an estimate of future price trends and, therefore, an investment decision. Whereas fundamental analysts use economic data that are usually separate from the stock or bond market, the technical analyst uses data *from the market itself* because the market is its own best predictor. Therefore, technical analysis is an alternative method of making the investment decision and answering the questions: What securities should an investor buy or sell? When should these investments be made?

Technical analysts see no need to study the multitude of economic, industry, and company variables to arrive at an estimate of future value because they believe that past price movements will signal future price movements. Technicians also believe that a change in the price trend may predict a forthcoming change in the fundamental variables such as earnings and risk before the change is perceived by most fundamental analysis. Are technicians correct? Many investors using these techniques claim to have experienced superior rates of return on many investments. In addition, many newsletter writers base their recommendations on technical analysis. Finally, even the major investment firms that employ many fundamental analysts also employ technical analysts to provide investment advice. Numerous investment professionals and individual investors believe in and use technical trading rules to make their investment decisions. Therefore, whether a fan of technical analysis or an advocate of the efficient market hypothesis, investors should still have an understanding of the basic philosophy and reasoning behind technical approaches. Thus, we begin this chapter with an examination of the basic philosophy underlying technical analysis. Subsequently, we consider the advantages and potential problems with the technical approach. Finally, we present alternative technical trading rules applicable to both the U.S. and foreign securities markets.

UNDERLYING ASSUMPTIONS OF TECHNICAL ANALYSIS

Technical analysts base trading decisions on examinations of prior price and volume data to determine past market trends from which they predict future behavior for the market as a whole and for individual securities. Several assumptions summarized in Levy (1966) lead to this view of price movements. Certain aspects of these assumptions are controversial, leading fundamental analysts and advocates of efficient markets to question their validity. We have italicized those aspects in our list.

1. The market value of any good or service is determined solely by the interaction of supply and demand.
2. Supply and demand are governed by numerous rational and irrational factors. Included in these factors are those economic variables relied on by the fundamental analyst as well as opinions, moods, and guesses. The market weighs all these factors continually and automatically.

| Exhibit 15.1 | **Technicians' View of Price Adjustment to New Information** |

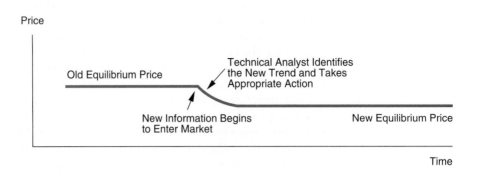

3. Disregarding minor fluctuations, *the prices for individual securities and the overall value of the market tend to move in trends, which persist for appreciable lengths of time.*
4. Prevailing trends change in reaction to shifts in supply and demand relationships. These shifts, no matter why they occur, *can be detected sooner or later in the action of the market itself.*

The first two assumptions are almost universally accepted by technicians and nontechnicians alike. Almost anyone who has had a basic course in economics would agree that, at any point in time, the price of a security (or any good or service) is determined by the interaction of supply and demand. In addition, most observers would acknowledge that supply and demand are governed by many variables. The only difference in opinion might concern the influence of the irrational factors. Certainly, everyone would agree that the market continually weighs all these factors.

In contrast, there is a significant difference of opinion regarding the assumption about the *speed of adjustment* of stock prices to changes in supply and demand. Technical analysts expect stock prices to move in trends that persist for long periods because they believe that new information does *not* come to the market at one point in time but rather enters the market *over a period of time.* This pattern of information access occurs because of different sources of information or because certain investors receive the information or perceive fundamental changes earlier than others. As various groups—ranging from insiders to well-informed professionals to the average investor—receive the information and buy or sell a security accordingly, its price moves gradually toward the new equilibrium. Therefore, technicians do not expect the price adjustment to be as abrupt as fundamental analysts and efficient market supporters do; rather, they expect a *gradual price adjustment* to reflect the gradual flow of information.

Exhibit 15.1 shows this process wherein new information causes a decrease in the equilibrium price for a security but the price adjustment is not rapid. It occurs as a trend that persists until the stock reaches its new equilibrium. Technical analysts look for the beginning of a movement from one equilibrium value to a new equilibrium value but do not attempt to predict the new equilibrium value. They look for the start of a change so that they can get on the bandwagon early and benefit from the move to the new equilibrium price by buying if the trend is up or selling if the trend is down. Obviously, if there is a rapid adjustment of prices to the new information (as expected by those who espouse an efficient market), the ride on the bandwagon would be so short that investors could not benefit.

ADVANTAGES OF TECHNICAL ANALYSIS

Although technicians understand the logic of fundamental analysis, they see several benefits in their approach. Most technical analysts admit that a fundamental analyst with good information, good analytical ability, and a keen sense of information's impact on the market should achieve above-average returns. However, this statement requires qualification. According to technical analysts, it is important to recognize that the fundamental analysts can experience superior returns *only* if they obtain new information before other investors and process it *correctly* and *quickly.* Technical analysts do not believe the majority of investors can consistently get new information before other investors and consistently process it correctly and quickly.

In addition, technical analysts claim that a major advantage of their method is that *it is not heavily dependent on financial accounting statements*—the major source of information about the past performance of a firm or industry. As we know from Chapters 13 and 14, the fundamental analyst evaluates such statements to help project future return and risk characteristics for industries and individual securities. The technician contends that there are several major problems with accounting statements:

1. They lack a great deal of information needed by security analysts, such as information related to sales, earnings, and capital utilized by product line and customers.
2. According to GAAP (Generally Accepted Accounting Principles), corporations may choose among several procedures for reporting expenses, assets, or liabilities. Notably, these alternative procedures can produce vastly different values for expenses, income, return on assets, and return on equity, depending on whether the firm is conservative or aggressive. As a result, an investor can have trouble comparing the statements of two firms within the same industry, much less firms across industries.
3. Many psychological factors and other nonquantifiable variables do not appear in financial statements. Examples include employee training and loyalty, customer goodwill, and general investor attitude toward an industry. Investor attitudes could be important when investors become concerned about the risk from restrictions or taxes on products such as tobacco or alcohol or when firms do business in countries that have significant political risk.

Therefore, because technicians are suspicious of financial statements, they consider it advantageous not to depend on them. As we will show, most of the data used by technicians, such as security prices, volume of trading, and other trading information, are derived from the stock market itself.

Also, a fundamental analyst must process new information correctly and *quickly* to derive a new intrinsic value for the stock or bond before the other investors can. Technicians, on the other hand, only need to quickly recognize a movement to a new equilibrium value *for whatever reason*—that is, they do not need to know about a specific event and determine the effect of the event on the value of the firm and its stock.

Finally, assume a fundamental analyst determines that a given security is under- or overvalued a long time before other investors. He or she still must determine when to make the purchase or sale. Ideally, the highest rate of return would come from making the transaction just before the change in market value occurs. For example, assume that based on your analysis in February, you expect a firm to report substantially higher earnings in June. Although you could buy the stock in February, you would be better off waiting until about May to buy the stock so your funds would not be tied up for an extra three months, but you may be reticent to wait that long. Because most technicians do not invest until the move to the new equilibrium is under way, they contend that they are more likely than a fundamental analyst to experience ideal timing.

CHALLENGES TO TECHNICAL ANALYSIS

Those who doubt the value of technical analysis for investment decisions question the usefulness of this technique in two areas. First, they challenge some of its basic assumptions. Second, they challenge some specific technical trading rules and their long-run usefulness. In this section we consider these challenges.

Challenges to Technical Analysis Assumptions

The major challenge to technical analysis is based on the results of empirical tests of the efficient market hypothesis (EMH). As discussed in Chapter 6, for technical trading rules to generate superior risk-adjusted returns after taking account of transaction costs, the market would have to be slow to adjust prices to the arrival of new information; that is, it would have to be inefficient. This is referred to as the weak-form efficient market hypothesis. The two sets of tests of the weak-form EMH are (1) the statistical analysis of prices to determine if prices moved in trends or were a random walk, and (2) the analysis of specific trading rules to determine if their use could beat a buy-and-hold policy after considering transactions costs and risk. Almost all the studies testing the weak-form EMH using statistical analysis have found that prices do not move in trends based on statistical tests of auto-correlation and runs. These results support the EMH.

Regarding the analysis of specific trading rules, as discussed in Chapter 6, numerous technical trading rules exist that have not been or cannot be tested. Still, the vast majority of the results for the trading rules that have been tested support the EMH.

Challenges to Technical Trading Rules

An obvious challenge to technical analysis is that the past price patterns or relationships between specific market variables and stock prices may not be repeated. As a result, a technique that previously worked might miss subsequent market turns. This possibility leads most technicians to follow several trading rules and to seek a consensus of all of them to predict the future market pattern.

Other critics contend that many price patterns become self-fulfilling prophecies. For example, assume that many analysts expect a stock selling at $40 a share to go to $50 or more if it should rise above its current pattern and break through its channel at $45. As soon as it reaches $45, enough technicians will buy to cause the price to rise to $50, exactly as predicted. In fact, some technicians may place a limit order to buy the stock at such a breakout point. Under such conditions, the increase will probably be only temporary and the price will return to its true equilibrium.

Another problem with technical analysis is that the success of a particular trading rule will encourage many investors to adopt it. It is contended that this popularity and the resulting competition will eventually neutralize the technique. If numerous investors focus on a specific technical trading rule, some of them will attempt to anticipate the price pattern and either ruin the expected historical price pattern or eliminate profits for most traders by causing the price to change faster than expected. For example, suppose it becomes known that technicians who employ short-selling data have been enjoying high rates of return. Based on this knowledge, other technicians will likely start using these data and thus accelerate the stock price pattern following changes in short selling. As a result, this profitable trading rule may no longer be profitable after the first few investors react.

Further, as we will see when we examine specific trading rules, *they all require a great deal of subjective judgment.* Two technical analysts looking at the same price pattern may arrive at widely different interpretations of what has happened and, therefore, will come to different investment decisions. This implies that the use of various techniques is neither completely mechanical nor obvious. Finally, as we will discuss in connection with several trading rules, *the standard values that signal investment decisions can change over time.* Therefore, in some instances technical analysts adjust the specified values that trigger investment decisions to conform to the new environment. In other cases, trading rules have been abandoned because they no longer work.

TECHNICAL TRADING RULES AND INDICATORS

To illustrate the specific technical trading rules, Exhibit 15.2 shows a typical stock price cycle that could be an example for the overall stock market or for an individual stock. The graph shows a peak and trough, along with a rising trend channel, a flat trend channel, a declining trend channel, and indications of when a technical analyst would ideally want to trade.

The graph begins with the end of a declining (bear) market that finishes in a **trough,** followed by an upward trend that breaks through the **declining trend channel**. Confirmation that the declining trend has reversed would be a buy signal. The technical analyst would buy stocks that showed this pattern.

The analyst would then expect the development of a **rising trend channel**. As long as the stock price stayed in this rising channel, the technician would hold the stock(s). Ideally, they want to sell at the **peak** of the cycle, but they cannot identify a peak until after the trend changes.

If the stock (or the market) begins trading in a flat pattern, it will necessarily break out of its rising trend channel. At this point, some technical analysts would sell, but most would hold to see if the stock experiences a period of consolidation and then breaks out of the **flat trend channel**

Exhibit 15.2	**Typical Stock-Market Cycle**

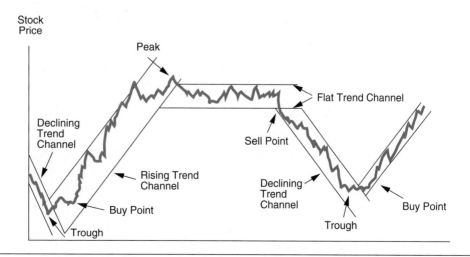

on the upside and begins rising again. Alternatively, if the stock were to break out of the channel on the downside, the technician would take this as a sell signal and would expect a declining trend channel. The next buy signal would come after the trough when the price breaks out of the declining channel and establishes a rising trend. We will consider strategies to detect these changes in trend and the importance of volume in this analysis shortly.

There are numerous technical trading rules and a range of interpretations for each of them. Almost all technical analysts watch many alternative rules and decide on a buy or sell decision based on a *consensus* of the signals because complete agreement of all the rules is rare. In the following discussion of several well-known techniques, we have divided the rules into four groups based on the attitudes of technical analysts. The first group includes trading rules used by analysts who like to trade against the crowd using contrary-opinion signals. The second group attempts to emulate astute investors, that is, the smart money. The third group includes popular technical indicators that are not easily classified. Finally, the fourth group includes pure price and volume techniques, including the famous Dow Theory.

Contrary-Opinion Rules

Many technical analysts rely on technical trading rules that assume that the majority of investors are wrong as the market approaches peaks and troughs. Therefore, these technicians try to determine when the majority of investors is either strongly bullish or bearish and then trade in the opposite direction.

Mutual Fund Cash Positions   Mutual funds hold some part of their portfolio in cash for one of several reasons. One is that they need cash to liquidate shares submitted by fundholders. Another is that new investments in the mutual fund may not have been invested. Third, the portfolio manager might be bearish on the market and want to increase the fund's defensive cash position.

Mutual funds' ratios of cash as a percentage of the total assets in their portfolios (the *cash ratio* or *liquid asset ratio*) are reported in the press, including monthly figures in *Barron's*.[1] This percentage of cash has varied in recent years from a low point of about 4 percent to a high point near 11 percent, although there appears to be a declining trend to the series.

Contrary-opinion technicians believe that mutual funds usually are wrong at peaks and troughs. Thus, they expect mutual funds to have a high percentage of cash near a market trough—the time when they should be fully invested to take advantage of the impending market rise. At the market peak, these technicians expect mutual funds to be almost fully invested with a low percentage of cash when they should be selling stocks and realizing gains. Therefore, contrary-opinion technicians watch for the mutual fund cash position to approach one of the extremes and act contrary to the mutual funds. Specifically, they would tend to buy when the cash ratio approaches 11 percent and to sell when the cash ratio approaches 4 percent.

An alternative rationale is that a high cash position is a bullish indicator because of potential buying power. Irrespective of the reason for a large cash balance, these technicians believe the cash funds held will eventually be invested and will cause stock prices to increase. Alternatively, a low cash ratio would mean that the institutions have bought heavily and are left with little potential buying power.

Credit Balances in Brokerage Accounts   Credit balances result when investors sell stocks and leave the proceeds with their brokers, expecting to reinvest them shortly. The amounts are reported by the SEC and the NYSE in *Barron's*. Because technical analysts view these credit balances as potential purchasing power, a decline in these balances is considered bearish

---

[1]*Barron's* is a prime source for numerous technical indicators. For a readable discussion of relevant data and their use, see Martin E. Zweig (1987).

Exhibit 15.3 | **Time-Series Plot of Dow Jones Industrial Average and the Bullish and Bearish Advisory Services**

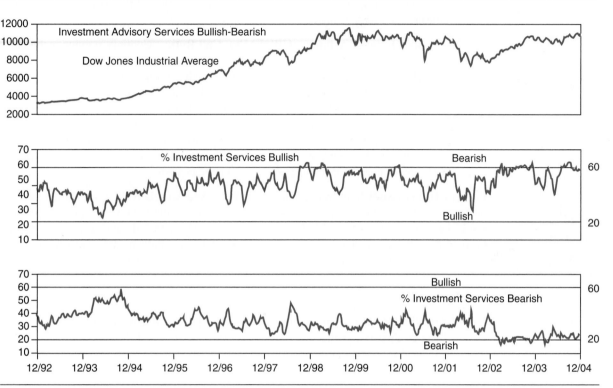

Source: Investors Intelligence Chartcraft. Reprinted with permission.

because it indicates lower purchasing power as the market approaches a peak. Alternatively, a buildup of credit balances indicates an increase in buying power and is a bullish signal.

Investment Advisory Opinions Many technicians believe that if a large proportion of investment advisory services are bearish, this signals the approach of a market trough and the onset of a bull market. Because most advisory services tend to be trend followers, the number of bears usually is greatest when market bottoms are approaching. This trading rule is specified in terms of the percent of advisory services that are bearish/bullish given the number of services expressing an opinion.[2] A 60 percent bearish or 20 percent bullish reading indicates a major market bottom (a bullish indicator), while a 60 percent bullish or 20 percent bearish reading suggests a major market top (a bearish signal). Exhibit 15.3 shows a time-series plot of the DJIA and both the bearish sentiment index and the bullish sentiment index. As of mid-2005, both indexes are near the bearish boundary values.

OTC versus NYSE Volume This ratio of trading volume is considered a measure of speculative activity. Speculative trading typically peaks at market peaks. Notably, the interpretation of the ratio has changed—that is, the decision rules have changed. Specifically, during the mid-1990s, the decision rule was in terms of specific percentages—112 percent was considered heavy speculative trading and an overbought market while 87 percent was considered low

---

[2]This ratio is compiled by Investors Intelligence, Larchmont, NY 10538. Richard McCabe at Merrill Lynch uses this series as one of his "Investor Sentiment Indicators."

speculative trading and an oversold market. The problem was that the percentages kept increasing because of faster growth in OTC trading volume and dominance of the OTC market by a few large-cap stocks. It was subsequently decided to detect excess speculative activity by using the *direction* of the volume ratio as a guide. For example, if this ratio is increasing, it would indicate a bearish speculative environment.

Chicago Board Options Exchange (CBOE) Put–Call Ratio   Contrary-opinion technicians use put options, which give the holder the right to sell stock at a specified price for a given time period, as signals of a bearish attitude. A higher put–call ratio indicates a pervasive bearish attitude for investors, which technicians consider a bullish indicator.

This ratio fluctuates between 0.60 and 0.40 and has typically been substantially less than 1 because investors tend to be bullish and avoid selling short or buying puts. The current decision rule states that a put–call ratio above 0.60—that is, sixty puts are traded for every one hundred calls—indicates that investors are generally bearish, so it is considered bullish, while a relatively low put–call ratio of 0.40 or less is considered bearish.

Futures Traders Bullish on Stock-Index Futures   Another relatively new contrary-opinion measure is the percentage of speculators in stock-index futures who are bullish regarding stocks based on a survey of individual futures traders. These technicians would consider it a bearish sign when more than 70 percent of the speculators are bullish, and a bullish sign when this ratio declines to 30 percent or lower. The plot in Exhibit 15.4 shows that as of mid-2005

Exhibit 15.4	Time-Series Plot of Dow Jones Industrial Average and the Market Vane Percentage of Futures Traders Bullish and Bearish on Stock-Index Futures

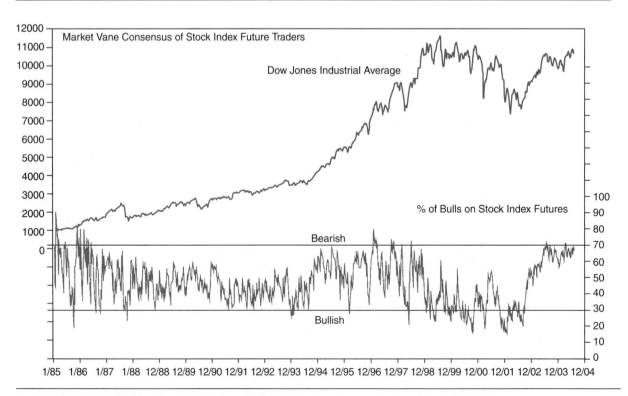

Source: Data Courtesy of Market Vane, http://www.marketvane.net.

this indicator was slightly less than 70 percent, so it is officially neutral but toward a bearish zone.

As we have shown, contrary-opinion technicians have several measures of how the majority of investors are investing that prompt them to take the opposite action. They generally employ several of these series to provide a consensus regarding investors' attitudes.

Follow the Smart Money

Some technical analysts have created a set of indicators and corresponding rules that they believe indicate the behavior of smart, sophisticated investors. We discuss three such indicators in this section.

Confidence Index   Published by *Barron's,* the Confidence Index is the ratio of *Barron's* average yield on 10 top-grade corporate bonds to the yield on the Dow Jones average of forty bonds.[3] This index measures the difference in yield spread between high-grade bonds and a large cross section of bonds. Because the yields on high-grade bonds always should be lower than those on a large cross section of bonds, this ratio should approach 100 as the spread between the two sets of bonds gets smaller.

Technicians believe the ratio is a bullish indicator because, during periods of high confidence, investors are willing to invest in lower-quality bonds for the added yield, which causes a decrease in the average yield for the large cross section of bonds relative to the yield on high-grade bonds. Therefore, this ratio of yields—the Confidence Index—will increase. In contrast, when investors are pessimistic, they avoid investing in low-quality bonds, which increases the yield spread between high-grade and average bonds, which in turn causes the Confidence Index to decline.

Unfortunately, this interpretation assumes that changes in the yield spread are caused almost exclusively by changes in investor demand for different quality bonds. In fact, the yield differences have frequently changed because of changes in the supply of bonds. For example, a large issue of high-grade AT&T bonds could cause a temporary increase in yields on all high-grade bonds, which would reduce the yield spread, and increase the Confidence Index without any change in investors' attitudes. Such a change can generate a false signal of a change in confidence.

T-Bill–Eurodollar Yield Spread   A popular measure of investor attitude or confidence on a global basis is the spread between T-bill yields and Eurodollar rates. It is reasoned that, at times of international crisis, this spread widens as the smart money flows to safe-haven U.S. T-bills, which causes a decline in this ratio. It is contended that the stock market typically experiences a trough shortly thereafter.

Debit Balances in Brokerage Accounts (Margin Debt)   Debit balances in brokerage accounts represent borrowing (margin debt) by knowledgeable investors from their brokers. Hence, these balances indicate the attitude of sophisticated investors who engage in margin transactions. Therefore, an increase in debit balances implies buying by these sophisticated investors and is considered a bullish sign, while a decline in debit balances would indicate selling and would be a bearish indicator.

Monthly data on margin debt is reported in *Barron's.* Unfortunately, this index does not include borrowing by investors from other sources such as banks. Also, because it is an absolute value, technicians would look for changes in the trend of borrowing—that is, increases are bullish, declines are bearish.

---

[3]Historical data for this index are contained in the *Dow Jones Investor's Handbook,* Princeton, NJ (Dow Jones Books, annual). Current figures appear in *Barron's.*

Momentum Indicators

In addition to contrary-opinion and smart money signals, several indicators of overall market momentum are used to make aggregate market decisions.

Breadth of Market   Breadth of market measures the number of issues that have increased each day and the number of issues that have declined. It helps explain the cause of a change of direction in a composite market index such as the S&P 500 Index. As we discussed in Chapter 5, most stock-market indexes are heavily influenced by the stocks of large firms because they are value weighted. Therefore, a stock-market index can experience an increase while the majority of the individual issues do not, which means that most stocks are not participating in the rising market. Such a divergence can be detected by examining the advance–decline figures for all stocks on the exchange, along with the overall market index.

The advance–decline index is typically a cumulative index of net advances or net declines. Specifically, each day major newspapers publish figures on the number of issues on the NYSE that advanced, declined, or were unchanged. The figures for a five-day sample, as would be reported in *Barron's,* are shown in Exhibit 15.5. These figures, along with changes in the DJIA at the bottom of the table, indicate a strong market advance because the DJIA was increasing and the net advance figure was strong, indicating that the market increase was broadly based. Even the results on Day 3, when the market declined 15 points, were encouraging since it was a small overall decline and the individual stock issues were split just about 50–50, which points toward a fairly even environment.

Stocks above Their 200-Day Moving Average   Technicians often compute moving averages of an index to determine its general trend. To examine individual stocks, the 200-day **moving average** of prices has been fairly popular. From these moving-average indexes for numerous stocks, Media General Financial Services calculates how many stocks currently are trading above their 200-day moving-average index, and this is used as an indicator of general investor sentiment. The market is considered to be *overbought* and subject to a negative correction when more than 80 percent of the stocks are trading above their 200-day moving average. In contrast, if less than 20 percent of the stocks are selling above their 200-day moving average, the market is considered to be *oversold,* which means investors should expect a positive correction. As shown in Exhibit 15.6, as of mid-2005 the percent of stocks selling above their

Exhibit 15.5	**Daily Advances and Declines on the New York Stock Exchange**				
Day	1	2	3	4	5
Issues traded	3,608	3,641	3,659	3,651	3,612
Advances	2,310	2,350	1,558	2,261	2,325
Declines	909	912	1,649	933	894
Unchanged	389	379	452	457	393
Net advances (advances minus declines)	+1,401	+1,438	−91	+1,328	+1,431
Cumulative net advances	+1,401	+2,839	+2,748	+4,076	+5,507
Changes in DJIA	+40.47	+95.75	−15.25	+108.42	+140.63

Sources: New York Stock Exchange and *Barron's.*

| Exhibit 15.6 | Percentage of NYSE Common Stocks Trading above Their 200-Day Moving Average Price |

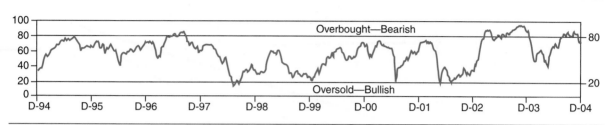

Source: Richard T. McCabe and Walter G. Murphy, Analysts, Merrill Lynch, "Where the Indicators Stand," May 3, 2005. Reprinted by permission. Copyright © 2005 Merrill Lynch, Pierce, Fenner & Smith Incorporated.

200-day moving average has been above 80 percent, which indicates an overbought, bearish signal, but recently went below the 80 percent line.

Stock Price and Volume Techniques

In the introduction to this chapter, we examined a hypothetical stock price chart that demonstrated market peaks and troughs along with rising and declining trend channels and breakouts from channels that signal new price trends or reversals of the price trends. While price patterns alone are important, most technical trading rules consider both stock price and corresponding volume movements.

Dow Theory   Any discussion of technical analysis using price and volume data should begin with a consideration of the Dow Theory because it was among the earliest work on this topic and remains the basis for many technical indicators.[4] Dow described stock prices as moving in trends analogous to the movement of water. He postulated three types of price movements over time: (1) major trends that are like tides in the ocean, (2) intermediate trends that resemble waves, and (3) short-run movements that are like ripples. Followers of the Dow Theory attempt to detect the direction of the major price trend (tide), recognizing that intermediate movements (waves) may occasionally move in the opposite direction. They recognize that a major market advance does not go straight up, but rather includes small price declines as some investors decide to take profits.

Exhibit 15.7 shows the typical bullish pattern. The technician would look for every recovery to reach a new peak above the prior peak, and this price rise should be accompanied by heavy trading volume. Alternatively, each profit-taking reversal that follows an increase to a new peak should have a trough above the prior trough, with relatively light trading volume during the profit-taking reversals. When this pattern of price and volume movements changes, the major trend may be entering a period of consolidation (a flat trend) or a major reversal.

Importance of Volume   As noted, technicians watch volume changes along with price movements as an indicator of changes in supply and demand. A price movement in one direction means that the net effect on price is in that direction, but the price change alone does not

---

[4]A study that discusses and provides support for the Dow Theory is David A. Glickstein and Rolf E. Wubbels (1983).

Exhibit 15.7 | **Sample Bullish Price Pattern**

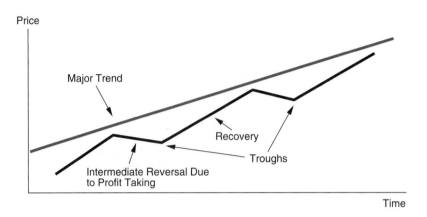

indicate the breadth of the excess demand or supply. Therefore, the technician looks for a price increase on heavy volume relative to the stock's normal trading volume as an indication of bullish activity. Conversely, a price decline with heavy volume is considered bearish. A generally bullish pattern would be when price increases are accompanied by heavy volume and small price reversals occur with light trading volume.

Technicians also use a ratio of upside–downside volume as an indicator of short-term momentum for the aggregate stock market. Each day the stock exchanges announce the volume of trading in stocks that experienced an increase divided by the volume of trading in stocks that declined. These data are reported daily in *The Wall Street Journal* and weekly in *Barron's*. This ratio is used as an indicator of market momentum. Specifically, technicians believe that an upside-downside volume value of 1.75 or more indicates an overbought position that is bearish. Alternatively, a value of 0.75 and lower supposedly reflects an oversold position and is considered bullish.

Support and Resistance Levels A **support level** is the price range at which the technician would expect a substantial increase in the demand for a stock. Generally, a support level will develop after a stock has enjoyed a meaningful price increase and the stock experiences profit taking. Technicians reason that at some price below the recent peak other investors who did not buy during the first price increase (waiting for a small reversal) will get into the stock. When the price reaches this support price, demand surges and price and volume begin to increase again.

A **resistance level** is the price range at which the technician would expect an increase in the supply of stock and a price reversal. A resistance level develops after a significant decline from a higher price level. After the decline, the stock begins to recover, but the prior decline in price leads some investors who acquired the stock at a higher price to look for an opportunity to sell it near their breakeven points. Therefore, the supply of stock owned by these nervous investors is *overhanging* the market. When the price rebounds to the target price set by these investors, this overhanging supply of stock comes to the market and there is a price decline on heavy volume. It is also possible to envision a rising trend of support and resistance levels for a stock. For example, the rising support prices would be a set of higher prices where investors over time would see the price increase and would take the opportunity to buy when there is profit taking. In this latter case, there would be a succession of higher support levels over time.

Exhibit 15.8	**Daily Stock Prices and Volume for Gillette with Indications of Support and Resistance Levels**

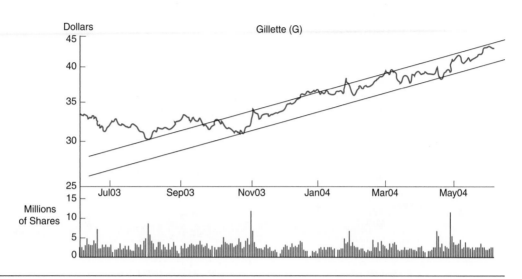

Source: Yahoo! Inc., http://finance.yahoo.com/. Reproduced with permission of Yahoo! Inc. © 2005 by Yahoo! Inc. YAHOO! and the YAHOO! logo are trademarks of Yahoo! Inc.

Exhibit 15.8 contains the daily stock prices for Gillette (G), with support and resistance lines. The graphs show a rising pattern since Gillette has experienced strong price increases during this period. At present, the resistance level is at about $44 and is rising, while the support level is about $40 and is also rising. The bullish technician would look for future prices to rise in line with this channel. If prices fell significantly below the support line on strong volume, it would be considered a bearish signal, while an increase above the $44 resistance price would be bullish.

Moving-Average Lines   Earlier, we discussed how technicians use a moving average of past stock prices as an indicator of the long-run trend and how they examine current prices relative to this trend for signals of a change. We also noted that a 200-day moving average is a relatively popular measure for individual stocks and the aggregate market. In this discussion, we add a 50-day moving-average price line (short-term trend) and consider large volume.

Exhibit 15.9 is a daily stock price chart from Yahoo! Inc. for Pfizer, Inc. (PFE) for the year ending June 4, 2004. It also contains 50-day and 200-day moving-average (MA) lines. As noted, MA lines are meant to reflect the overall trend for the price series with the shorter MA line (the 50-day versus 200-day) reflecting shorter trends. Two comparisons involving the MA lines are considered important. The first comparison is the specific prices to the shorter-run 50-day MA line. If the overall price trend of a stock or the market has been down, the moving-average price line generally would lie above current prices. If prices reverse and break through the moving-average line *from below* accompanied by heavy trading volume, most technicians would consider this a *positive* change and speculate that this breakthrough could signal a reversal of the declining trend. In contrast, if the price of a stock had been rising, the moving-average line would also be rising, but it would be below current prices. If current prices declined and broke through the moving-average line *from above* accompanied by heavy trading volume, this would be considered a bearish pattern that would possibly signal a reversal of the long-run rising trend.

| Exhibit 15.9 | **Daily Stock Prices for Pfizer, Inc. with 50-Day and 200-Day Moving-Average Lines** |

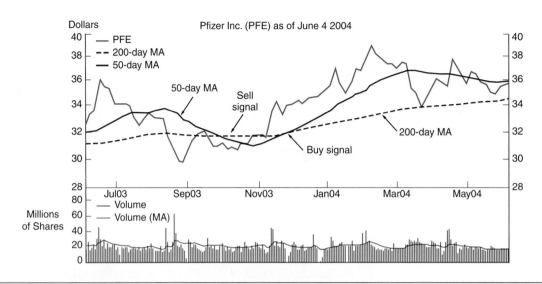

The second comparison is between the 50- and 200-day MA lines. Specifically, when these two lines cross, it signals a change in the overall trend. Specifically, if the 50-day MA line crosses the 200-day MA line from below on good volume, this would be a bullish indicator (buy signal) because it confirms a reversal in trend from negative to positive. In contrast, when the 50-day line crosses the 200-day line from above, it confirms a change to a negative trend and would be a sell signal. As shown in Exhibit 15.9, in the case of Pfizer (PFE) there was a bearish crossing in late September 2003, but it was reversed in December 2003 when there was a bullish crossing. Following this bullish crossing, the 50-day line has been consistently above the 200-day line as prices reached a peak of about $38 and were at about $36 at the end of the period. There is a cautionary signal to this chart, since the price line has broken through the 50-day line from above several times and is slightly below this MA line at the end of the graph.

Overall, for a *bullish* trend the 50-day MA line should be above the 200-day MA line, as it has been for Pfizer since December 2003. Notably, if this positive gap between the 50-day and 200-day lines gets too large (which happens with a fast run-up in price), a technician might consider this an indication that the stock is temporarily overbought, which is bearish in the short run. A *bearish* trend is when the 50-day MA line is always below the 200-day MA line. Still, if the gap gets large on the downside, it might be considered a signal of an oversold stock, which is bullish for the short run.

Relative Strength   Technicians believe that once a trend begins, it will continue until some major event causes a change in direction. They believe this is also true of *relative* performance. If an individual stock or an industry group is outperforming the market, technicians believe it will continue to do so.

Therefore, technicians compute weekly or monthly **relative-strength (RS) ratios** for individual stocks and industry groups. The RS ratio is equal to the price of a stock or an industry index divided by the value for some stock-market index such as the S&P 500. If this ratio increases over time, it shows that the stock or industry is outperforming the overall stock market, and a technician would expect this superior performance to continue. Relative-strength ratios work during declining as well as rising markets. In a declining market, if a stock's price declines less than the market does, the stock's relative-strength ratio will continue to rise. Technicians believe that if this ratio is stable or increases during a bear market, the stock should do well during the subsequent bull market.

Merrill Lynch publishes relative-strength charts for industry groups. Exhibit 15.10 describes how to read the charts. Further, some technicians construct graphs of stocks relative to the stock's industry index in addition to the comparison relative to the market.

Exhibit 15.10	**How to Read Industry Group Charts**

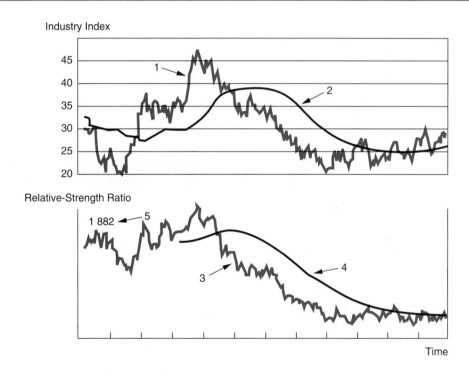

The industry group charts in this report display the following elements:

1. A line chart of the weekly close of the Standard & Poor's Industry Group Index for the past nine and one-half years, with the index range indicated to the left.
2. A line of the seventy-five-week moving average of the Standard & Poor's Industry Group Index.
3. A relative-strength line of the Standard & Poor's Industry Group Index compared with the New York Stock Exchange Composite Index.
4. A seventy-five-week moving average of relative strength.
5. A volatility reading that measures the maximum amount by which the index has outperformed (or underperformed) the NYSE Composite Index during the time period displayed.

Exhibit 15.11	A Typical Bar Chart

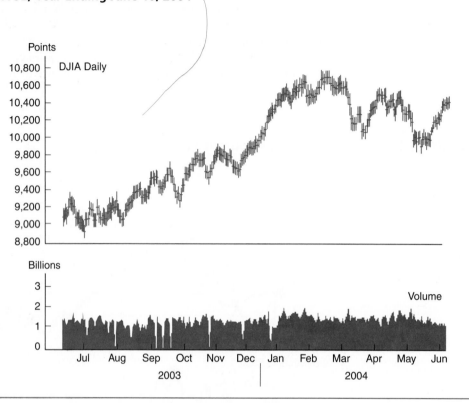

Daily High, Low, and Close for Dow Jones Industrial Average and Volume on the NYSE, Year Ending June 10, 2004

Sources: Dow Jones & Co., New York Stock Exchange, and *Big Charts* (http://www.BigCharts.com).

Bar Charting   Technicians use charts that show daily, weekly, or monthly time series of stock prices. For a given interval, the technical analyst plots the high and low prices and connects the two points vertically to form a bar. Typically, he or she will also draw a small horizontal line across this vertical bar to indicate the closing price. Finally, almost all bar charts include the volume of trading at the bottom of the chart so that the technical analyst can relate the price and volume movements. A typical bar chart in Exhibit 15.11 shows data for the DJIA from *The Wall Street Journal* along with volume figures for the NYSE.

Multiple-Indicator Charts   Thus far we have presented charts that deal with only one trading technique such as moving-average lines or relative-strength rules. In the real world, it is fairly typical for technical charts to contain several indicators that can be used together like the two MA lines (50- and 200-day) and the RS line, because they can provide added support to the analysis. Technicians include as many price and volume indicators as are reasonable on one chart and then, based on the performance of *several* technical indicators, try to arrive at a consensus about the future movement for the stock.

Exhibit 15.12	**Sample Point-and-Figure Chart**

```
50  │ │ │ │ │ │ │ │
48  │ │ │ │ │ │ │ │
46  │ │X│ │ │ │ │ │
44  │ │X│ │ │ │ │ │
42  X│X│X│ │ │ │ │ │
40  X│X│X│ │ │ │ │ │
38  │X│X│ │ │ │ │ │
36  │X│X│ │ │ │ │ │
34  │X│X│ │ │ │ │ │
32  │ │ │ │ │ │ │ │
30  │ │ │ │ │ │ │ │
```

Point-and-Figure Charts   Another graph that is popular with technicians is the point-and-figure chart. Unlike the bar chart, which typically includes all ending prices and volumes to show a trend, the point-and-figure chart includes only significant price changes, regardless of their timing. The technician determines what price interval to record as significant (one point, two points, and so on) and when to note price reversals.

To demonstrate how a technical analyst would use such a chart, suppose we want to chart a volatile stock that is currently selling for $40 a share. Because of its volatility, we believe that anything less than a two-point price change is not significant. Also, we consider anything less than a four-point reversal, meaning a movement in the opposite direction, quite minor. Therefore, we would set up a chart similar to the one in Exhibit 15.12, but our new chart would start at 40; it would also progress in two-point increments. If the stock moved to $42, we would place an *X* in the box above 40 and do nothing else until the stock rose to $44 or dropped to $38 (a four-point reversal from its high of $42). If it dropped to $38, we would move a column to the right, which indicates a reversal in direction, and begin again at 38 (fill in boxes at 42 and 40). If the stock price dropped to $34, we would enter an *X* at 36 and another at 34. If the stock then rose to $38 (another four-point reversal), we would move to the next column and begin at 38, going up (fill in 34 and 36). If the stock then went to $46, we would fill in more *X*s as shown and wait for further increases or a reversal.

Depending on how fast the prices rise and fall, this process might take anywhere from two to six months. Given these figures, the technician would attempt to determine trends just as with the bar chart. As always, the technician would look for breakouts to either higher or lower price levels. A long horizontal movement with many reversals but no major trends up or down would be considered a *period of consolidation* wherein the stock is moving from buyers to sellers and back again with no strong consensus about its direction. Once the stock breaks out and moves up or down after a period of consolidation, technical analysts anticipate a major move because previous trading set the stage for it. In other words, the longer the period of consolidation, the larger the subsequent move when there is finally a breakout.

Point-and-figure charts provide a compact record of movements because they only consider significant price changes for the stock being analyzed. Therefore, some technicians contend they are easier to work with and give more vivid pictures of price movements.

TECHNICAL ANALYSIS OF FOREIGN MARKETS

Our discussion thus far has concentrated on U.S. markets, but analysts have discovered that these techniques apply to foreign markets as well. Merrill Lynch, for instance, prepares separate technical analysis publications for individual countries such as Japan, Germany, and the United Kingdom as well as a summary of all world markets. The examples that follow show that when analyzing non-U.S. markets, many techniques are limited to price and volume data rather than the more detailed U.S. market information. The reason is that the detailed information available on the U.S. market through the SEC, the stock exchanges, the Nasdaq system, and various investment services is not always available for other countries.

Foreign Stock-Market Indexes

Exhibit 15.13 contains the daily time-series plot for the Japanese Nikkei Index. This chart shows the generally declining trend by the Japanese stock market during the period from May 2000 to April 2003, followed by rising stock prices through May 2004 and generally flat performance into May 2005. In the written analysis, the market analyst at Merrill Lynch estimated support and resistance levels for the Japanese Stock Exchange index and commented on the medium-term outlook for this market. Merrill Lynch publishes similar charts for 10 other countries and compares the countries and ranks them by stock and currency performance.

Exhibit 15.13	**Graph and Summary Comments on the Japanese Stock Market**

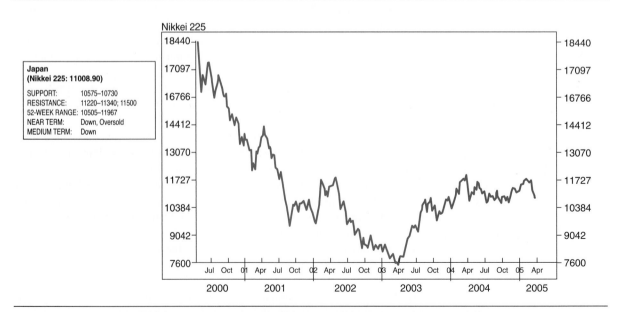

Source: Merrill Lynch, "The Global Technician," May 23, 2005. Reprinted by permission. Copyright © 2005 Merrill Lynch, Pierce, Fenner & Smith Incorporated.

Technical Analysis of Foreign Exchange Rates

On numerous occasions, we have discussed the importance of changes in foreign exchange rates on the rates of return on foreign securities. Because of the importance of these relationships, bond-and-stock traders in world markets examine the time-series data of various currencies such as the British pound and the Euro. They also analyze the spread between currencies, such as the difference between the Japanese yen and the British pound. Finally, they would typically examine the time series for the U.S. dollar trade-weighted exchange rate that experienced significant weakness during 2003–2005.

TECHNICAL ANALYSIS OF BOND MARKETS

Thus far, we have emphasized the use of technical analysis in stock markets. These techniques can also be applied to the bond market. The theory and rationale for technical analysis of bonds is the same as for stocks, and many of the same trading rules are used. A major difference is that it was generally not possible to consider the volume of trading of bonds because most bonds are traded OTC, where volume was not reported until 2004.

Exhibit 15.14 demonstrates the use of technical analysis techniques applied to bond-yield series. Specifically, the graph contains a time-series plot of world bond yields based on a seven-country composite. As shown, yields declined steadily until a trough in June 2003, followed by

Exhibit 15.14 | **Time-Series Plot of Global Bond Yields (Seven-Country Composite)**

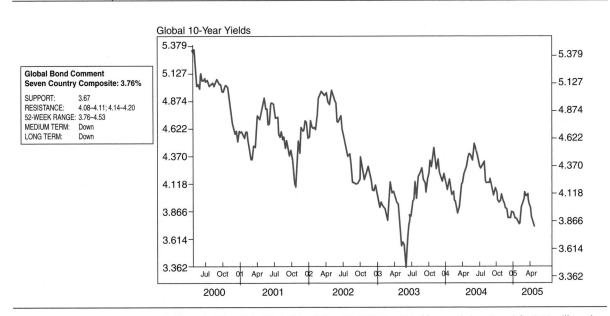

Source: Merrill Lynch, "The Global Technician," May 23, 2005. Reprinted by permission. Copyright © Merrill Lynch, Pierce, Fenner & Smith Incorporated.

a sharp recovery and a roller-coaster pattern between late 2003 and mid-2005. Notably, the outlook by the analyst is for lower yields medium and longer term. Such a technical graph provides important insights to a global bond-portfolio manager interested in adjusting his or her bond portfolio.

The Internet   Investments Online

By its nature, technical analysis uses charts and graphs, and many Web sites offer them for use by investors and analysts; some are free, but some of the sites for more sophisticated users require payment for access. Here are several interesting sites:

http://www.mta.org/ The home page of the Market Technicians Association, a professional group of chartists whose goal is to enhance technical analysis and educate investors about its role. The group sponsors the Chartered Market Technician (CMT) designation. This site features news groups, investment links, training and education sources, a journal, and a variety of technical analysis charts. Its "members" tab includes links to Web sites of its members' firms.

http://www.bigcharts.marketwatch.com/ This site offers free intraday and historical charts and price quotes. Its database includes stocks, mutual funds, and indexes. Users can learn which stocks have the largest percentage gain (loss) in price and volume and which stocks are hitting new 52-week highs (lows). Other features include momentum charts, stocks with the largest short interest, and a variety of other items of interest to technicians.

http://stockcharts.com/ This site offers a variety of charting options, including point-and-figure charts. It offers a "chart school," which offers summaries of different charting techniques and uses.

SUMMARY

- Numerous investors believe in and use the principles of technical analysis. The fact is, the large investment houses provide extensive support for technical analysis, and a large proportion of the discussion related to securities markets in the media is based on a technical view of the market.
- Their answers to two main questions separate technical analysts and efficient market advocates. First, in the information dissemination process does everybody get the information at about the same time? Second, how quickly do investors adjust security prices to reflect new information? Technical analysts believe that news takes time to travel from the insider and expert to the individual investor. They also believe that price adjustments are not

instantaneous. As a result, they contend that security prices move in trends that persist and, therefore, they can use past price trends and volume information along with other market indicators to determine future price trends.

- Technical trading rules fall into four general categories: contrary-opinion rules, follow-the-smart-money tactics, momentum indicators, and stock price and volume techniques. These techniques and trading rules can be applied to both domestic and foreign markets. They can also be used to analyze currency exchange rates and determine the prevailing sentiment in the bond market.
- Most technicians employ several indicators and attempt to derive a consensus to guide their decision to buy, sell, or do nothing.[5]

[5]An analysis using numerous indicators is the study by Jerome Baesel, George Shows, and Edward Thorp (1982).

SUGGESTED READINGS

Benning, Carl J. "Prediction Skills of Real-World Market Timers." *Journal of Portfolio Management* 23, no. 2 (Winter 1997).

Brown, David P., and Robert H. Jennings. "On Technical Analysis." *Review of Financial Studies* 2, no. 4 (October 1989).

Colby, Robert W., and Thomas A. Mayers. *The Encyclopedia of Technical Market Indicators.* Homewood, IL: Dow Jones–Irwin, 1988.

DeMark, Thomas R. *The New Science of Technical Analysis.* New York: Wiley, 1994.

Edwards, R. D., and John Magee, Jr. *Technical Analysis of Stock Trends,* 6th ed. Boston: New York Institute of Finance, 1992.

Jagadeesh, Narasimhan. "Evidence of Predictable Behavior of Security Returns." *Journal of Finance* 45, no. 3 (July 1990).

Lo, Andrew W., and A. Craig MacKinley. *A Non-Random Walk Down Wall Street.* Princeton, NJ: Princeton University Press, 1999.

Meyers, Thomas A. *The Technical Analysis Course.* Chicago: Probus, 1989.

Pring, Martin J. *Technical Analysis Explained,* 3rd ed. New York: McGraw-Hill, 1991.

Shaw, Alan R. "Market Timing and Technical Analysis." In *The Financial Analysts Handbook,* 2nd ed., ed. Sumner N. Levine. Homewood, IL: Dow Jones–Irwin, 1988.

Zweig, Martin E. *Winning on Wall Street.* New York: Warner Books, 1986.

QUESTIONS

1. Technical analysts believe that one can use past price changes to predict future price changes. How do they justify this belief?
2. Technicians contend that stock prices move in trends that persist for long periods of time. What do technicians believe happens in the real world to cause these trends?
3. Briefly discuss the problems related to fundamental analysis that are considered advantages for technical analysis.
4. Discuss some disadvantages of technical analysis.
5. If the mutual fund cash position were to increase close to 10 percent, would a technician consider this cash position bullish or bearish? Give two reasons why the technical analyst would think this way.
6. Assume a significant decline in credit balances at brokerage firms. Discuss why a technician would consider this bearish.
7. If the bearish sentiment index of advisory service opinions were to increase to 61 percent, discuss why a technician would consider this bullish or bearish.
8. Discuss why an increase in debit balances is considered bullish or bearish.
9. Describe the Dow Theory and its three components. Which component is most important? What is the reason for an intermediate reversal?
10. Describe a bearish price and volume pattern, and discuss why it is considered bearish.
11. Discuss the logic behind the breadth of market index. How is it used to identify a peak in stock prices?
12. During a 10-day trading period, the cumulative net advance index goes from 1,572 to 1,053. During this same period of time, the DJIA goes from 11,200 to 12,100. As a technician, discuss what this set of events would mean to you.
13. Explain the reasoning behind a support level and a resistance level.
14. What is the purpose of computing a moving-average line for a stock? Describe a bullish pattern using a 50-day moving-average line and the stock volume of trading. Discuss why this pattern is considered bullish.
15. Assuming a stock price and volume chart that also contains a 50-day and a 200-day MA line, describe a bearish pattern with the two MA lines and discuss why it is bearish.
16. Explain how you would construct a relative-strength ratio for an individual stock or an industry group. What would it mean to say a stock experienced good relative strength during a bear market?
17. Discuss why most technicians follow several technical rules and attempt to derive a consensus.

PROBLEMS

1. Select a stock on the NYSE and construct a daily high, low, and close bar chart for it that includes its volume of trading for 10 trading days.
2. Compute the relative-strength ratio for the stock in Problem 1 relative to the S&P 500 index. Prepare a table that includes all the data and indicates the computations as follows:

Closing Price		Relative-Strength Ratio	
Day	Stock	S&P 500	Stock Price/S&P 500

3. Plot the relative-strength ratio computed in Problem 2 on your bar chart. Discuss whether the stock's relative strength is bullish or bearish.
4. Currently, Charlotte Art Importers is selling at $23 per share. Although you are somewhat dubious about technical analysis, you want to know how technicians who use point-and-figure charts would view this stock. You decide to note one-point movements and three-point reversals. You gather the following historical price information:

Date	Price	Date	Price	Date	Price
4/1	$23\frac{1}{2}$	4/18	33	5/3	27
4/4	$28\frac{1}{2}$	4/19	$35\frac{3}{8}$	5/4	$26\frac{1}{2}$
4/5	28	4/20	37	5/5	28
4/6	28	4/21	$38\frac{1}{2}$	5/6	$28\frac{1}{4}$
4/7	$29\frac{3}{4}$	4/22	36	5/9	$28\frac{1}{8}$
4/8	$30\frac{1}{2}$	4/25	35	5/10	$28\frac{1}{4}$
4/11	$30\frac{1}{2}$	4/26	$34\frac{1}{4}$	5/11	$29\frac{1}{8}$
4/12	$32\frac{1}{8}$	4/27	$33\frac{1}{8}$	5/12	$30\frac{1}{4}$
4/13	32	4/28	$32\frac{7}{8}$	5/13	$29\frac{7}{8}$

Plot the point-and-figure chart, using Xs for uptrends and Os for downtrends. How would a technician evaluate these movements? Discuss why you would expect a technician to buy, sell, or hold the stock based on this chart.

5. Assume the following daily closings for the Dow Jones Industrial Average:

Day	DJIA	Day	DJIA
1	12,010	7	12,220
2	12,100	8	12,130
3	12,165	9	12,250
4	12,080	10	12,315
5	12,070	11	12,240
6	12,150	12	12,310

a. Calculate a four-day moving average for Days 4 through 12.
b. Assume that the index on Day 13 closes at 12,300. Would this signal a buy or sell decision?

6. The cumulative advance–decline line reported in *Barron's* at the end of the month is 21,240. During the first week of the following month, the daily report for the *Exchange* is as follows:

Day	1	2	3	4	5
Issues traded	3,544	3,533	3,540	3,531	3,521
Advances	1,737	1,579	1,759	1,217	1,326
Declines	1,289	1,484	1,240	1,716	1,519
Unchanged	518	470	541	598	596

a. Compute the daily net advance–decline line for each of the five days.
b. Compute the cumulative advance–decline line for each day and the final value at the end of the week.

THOMSON ONE | Business School Edition

1. Examine the recent (past six months) price charts for Walgreens, Intel, and Merck (or any three firms of your choosing). What channels, buy/sell points, and patterns do you see in them?
2. What does the daily price and volume chart of the Dow Jones Industrial and S&P 500 for the past year imply for future price trends in the overall market?
3. For a stock of your choice, obtain daily price data for the past three years and download it into a spreadsheet. Compute and graph 5-day and 10-day moving averages of the price data along with the daily price data. How successful were the signals generated by the moving average lines?
4. What does the daily relative strength measure indicate for trends in Walgreen Co.'s stock?
5. Using daily data for the most recent two months, construct a point-and-figure chart for Walgreens.

Chapter 16

Equity Portfolio Management Strategies

After you read this chapter, you should be able to answer the following questions:

- What are the two generic equity portfolio management styles?
- What are three techniques for constructing a passive index portfolio?
- How does the goal of a passive equity portfolio manager differ from the goal of an active manager?
- What is a portfolio's tracking error and how is it useful in the construction of a passive equity investment?
- What is the difference between an index mutual fund and an exchange-traded fund?
- What are the three themes that active equity portfolio managers can use?
- What stock characteristics differentiate value-oriented and growth-oriented investment styles?
- What is style analysis and what does it indicate about a manager's investment performance?
- What techniques are used by active managers in an attempt to outperform their benchmark?
- What are the differences between the integrated, strategic, tactical, and insured approaches to asset allocation?

Recent chapters have reviewed how to analyze industries and companies, how to estimate a stock's intrinsic value, and how technical analysis can assist in stockpicking. Some equity portfolios are constructed one stock at a time. Research staffs analyze the economy, industries, and companies; evaluate firms' strategies and competitive advantages; and recommend individual stocks for purchase or for sale.

Other equity portfolios are constructed using computer-intensive, rather than analyst-intensive, methods. Computers analyze relationships between stocks and market sectors to identify undervalued stocks. Quantitative screens and factor models are used to construct portfolios of stocks with such attributes as low *P/E* ratios, low price/book ratios, small capitalization, or high dividend yield; those neglected by analysts; or stocks whose returns are strongly correlated with economic variables, such as interest rates. Computer programs detect trading patterns and place buy-and-sell orders depending on past price movements. Computers also examine pricing relationships between the stock, options, and futures markets and place orders across these markets to arbitrage small price differences.

Managers of equity portfolios do not need to focus on the security selection process to produce superior investment returns. They can also increase an investor's wealth through their asset allocation decisions. For example, a manager acting as a market timer might split his funds into two index portfolios—one containing stocks and the other containing bonds—and then shift the allocation between these portfolios depending on which asset class he believes will perform the best during the coming period. The benefit of this strategy, which is formally known as *tactical* asset allocation, comes from correctly predicting broad market movements rather than trends for individual companies. Similarly, *insured* asset allocation is an attempt to limit investment losses by shifting funds between an existing equity portfolio and a risk-free security depending on changing market conditions.

PASSIVE VERSUS ACTIVE MANAGEMENT

Equity portfolio management styles fall into either a passive or an active category. Unlike the immunization of bond portfolios, no real middle ground exists between active and passive equity management strategies. Some argue that "hybrid" active/passive equity portfolio management styles exist (e.g., enhanced indexing), but such styles really are variations of active management philosophies. Similar to traditional active management, hybrid-style managers invest to find undervalued sectors or securities. The following discussion reviews the traditional meaning of the terms *passive* and *active* portfolio management.

Passive equity portfolio management is a long-term buy-and-hold strategy. Usually, stocks are purchased so the portfolio's returns will track those of an index over time. Because of the goal of tracking an index, this approach to investing is generally referred to as *indexing*. Occasional rebalancing is needed as dividends must be reinvested and because stocks merge or drop out of the target index and other stocks are added. Notably, the purpose of an indexed portfolio is not to "beat" the target index but to match its performance. A manager of an equity index portfolio is judged on how well he or she tracks the target index—that is, minimizes the deviation between portfolio and index returns similar to the bond index portfolio manager.

Active equity portfolio management is an attempt by the manager to outperform, on a risk-adjusted basis, a passive benchmark portfolio. A *benchmark portfolio* is a passive portfolio whose average characteristics (including such factors as beta, dividend yield, industry weighting, and firm size) match the risk-return objectives of the client.

When deciding whether to follow an active or a passive strategy (or some combination of the two), an investor must assess the trade-off between the low-cost but less-exciting alternative of indexing versus the higher-cost but potentially more lucrative alternative of active management. Not surprisingly, Sorensen, Miller, and Samak (1998) have noted that the critical factor in this evaluation is the stockpicking skill of the portfolio manager. Using pension fund performance data from the 1985–1997 period, they showed that the optimal allocation to indexing declines as managerial skill increases. However, they also conclude that some indexing is appropriate for funds in most risk objective classes. This position is supported by Alford, Jones, and Winkelmann (2003), who argue that a disciplined approach to active management—which they term *structured* portfolio management—is likely to be most effective for investors.

As an indication of the tendency for investors to select active or passive portfolio managers, Exhibit 16.1 reports the amount of money in the U.S. equity and fixed-income markets using these approaches for two recent years. The data are compiled from a survey of more than 2,500 professional managers on behalf of their clients. The main conclusion is that while active management strategies control the largest percentage of investor wealth, passively managed investment products are growing in importance at a more rapid pace. From the data it is also clear that both active and passive funds play a prominent role with investors.

Exhibit 16.1	Active and Passive Investment in the U.S. Equity and Fixed-Income Markets

Strategy	1995 (Billions)	1994 (Billions)	% Change
Active equity	$1,945.10	$1,338.01	45.4
Indexed equity	275.22	135.54	103.1
Active fixed income	1,677.45	1,370.63	22.4
Indexed fixed income	82.73	32.69	153.3

Source: Based on data from Nelson Investment Management Network.

AN OVERVIEW OF PASSIVE EQUITY PORTFOLIO MANAGEMENT STRATEGIES

Passive equity portfolio management attempts to design a portfolio to replicate the performance of a specific index. The key word here is *replicate*. As discussed in Chapter 2, the portfolio manager who earns higher returns by violating the client's policy statement should be fired; a passive manager who isn't really passive should likewise be dismissed. A passive manager earns his or her fee by constructing a portfolio that closely tracks the performance of a specified equity index (referred to as the *benchmark index*) that meets the client's needs and objectives. If the manager attempts to outperform the index selected, he or she violates the passive premise of the portfolio.

In Chapter 6, we presented several reasons for investing in a passive equity portfolio. Strong evidence indicates that the stock market is fairly efficient. For many active managers, the costs of actively managing a portfolio (1 to 2 percent of the portfolio's assets) are difficult to overcome. As we saw earlier, the S&P 500 index typically outperforms most equity mutual funds on an annual basis. Note that, although the S&P 500 is the most popular index to track, a client can choose from among dozens of different indexes.

Chapter 5 contained a summary description of many different market indexes. Domestic U.S. equity indexes include the S&P 500, Industrials, and 100; the Major Market index; the Nasdaq composite index; and the Wilshire 5000. *The Wall Street Journal* publishes the daily values of indexes for the organized exchanges, the OTC market, and various industry groups. Indexes exist for small capitalization stocks (Russell 2000); for value- or growth-oriented stocks (Russell Growth index and the Russell Value index); and for numerous world regions (such as the EAFE index); as well as for smaller regions, individual countries, and types of countries (emerging markets). Fernholz, Garvy, and Hannon (1998), as well as Khorana, Nelling, and Trester (1998), have noted that as passive investing has grown in popularity, money managers have created an index fund for virtually every broad market category.

The goal of a passive portfolio is to match the returns to the index as closely as possible; but, because of cash inflows and outflows and company mergers and bankruptcies, securities must be bought and sold, which means that there inevitably will be differences between portfolio and benchmark returns over time. In addition, even though index funds generally attempt to minimize turnover and the resultant transactions fees, they necessarily have to do some rebalancing, which means that the long-run return performance of index funds will lag the benchmark index. Certainly, substantial or prolonged deviations of the portfolio's returns from the index's returns would be a cause for concern.

Index Portfolio Construction Techniques

There are three basic techniques for constructing a passive index portfolio: full replication, sampling, and quadratic optimization or programming. The most obvious technique is **full replication**, wherein all the securities in the index are purchased in proportion to their weights in the index. This technique helps ensure close tracking, but it may be suboptimal for two reasons. First, the need to buy many securities will increase transaction costs that will detract from performance. Second, the reinvestment of dividends will also result in high commissions when many firms pay small dividends at different times in the year.

The second technique, **sampling**, addresses the problem of numerous stock issues. Statistical theory teaches us that we don't need to ask everyone in the United States for his or her opinion to determine who may win an election. Thus, opinion pollsters query only a small sample of the population to gauge public sentiment. Similarly, with sampling, a portfolio manager would only need to buy a representative sample of stocks that comprise the benchmark index. Stocks with larger index weights are purchased according to their weight in the index; smaller issues are purchased so their aggregate characteristics (e.g., beta, industry distribution, and dividend yield) approximate the underlying benchmark. With fewer stocks to purchase, larger positions can be taken in the issues acquired, which should lead to proportionately lower commissions. Further, the reinvestment of dividend cash flows will be less problematic because fewer securities need to be purchased to rebalance the portfolio. The disadvantage of sampling is that portfolio returns will almost certainly not track the returns for the benchmark index as closely as with full replication.

Rather than obtaining a sample based on industry or security characteristics, **quadratic optimization** or programming techniques can be used to construct a passive portfolio. With quadratic programming, historical information on price changes and correlations between securities are input to a computer program that determines the composition of a portfolio that will minimize return deviations from the benchmark. A problem with this technique is that it relies on *historical* price changes and correlations, and, if these factors change over time, the portfolio may experience very large differences from the benchmark.

Some passive portfolios are not based on a published index. Sometimes customized passive portfolios, called **completeness funds**, are constructed to complement active portfolios that do not cover the entire market. For example, a large pension fund may allocate some of its holdings to active managers expected to outperform the market. Many times, these active portfolios are overweighted in certain market sectors or stock types. In this case, the pension fund sponsor may want the remaining funds to be invested passively to "fill the holes" left vacant by the active managers. The performance of the completeness fund will be compared to a customized benchmark that incorporates the characteristics of the stocks not covered by the active managers.

For example, suppose a pension fund hires three active managers to invest part of the fund's money. One manager emphasizes small-capitalization U.S. stocks, the second invests only in Pacific Rim countries, and the third invests in U.S. stocks with low *P/E* ratios. To ensure adequate diversification, the pension fund may want to passively invest the remaining assets in a completeness fund that will have a customized benchmark that includes large- and mid-capitalization U.S. stocks, U.S. stocks with normal to high *P/E* ratios, and international stocks outside the Pacific Rim.

Still other passive portfolios and benchmarks exist for investors with certain unique needs and preferences. Some investors may want their funds to be invested only in stocks that pay dividends or in a company that produces a product or service that the investor deems socially responsible. Mossavar-Rahmani (1988) and Dialynas (2001) show that benchmarks can be produced that reflect these desired attributes, and passive portfolios can be constructed to track the performance of the customized benchmark over time so investors' special needs can be satisfied.

Tracking Error and Index Portfolio Construction

If the goal of forming a passive portfolio is to replicate the essence of a particular equity index, the success of constructing such an investment fund lies not in the absolute returns it produces but, rather, in how closely its returns match those of the benchmark (e.g., the Standard & Poor's 500 index). That is, the goal of the passive manager should be to minimize the portfolio's return volatility relative to the benchmark. Said differently, the manager should try to minimize **tracking error**.

Tracking error can be defined as the extent to which return fluctuations in the managed portfolio are *not correlated* with return fluctuations in the benchmark. A flexible and straightforward way of measuring tracking error can be developed as follows. Recalling the notation from Chapter 7, let

w_i = investment weight of Asset i in the managed portfolio
R_{it} = return to Asset i in Period t
R_{bt} = return to the benchmark portfolio in Period t

With these definitions, we can define the Period t return to managed portfolio as

$$R_{pt} = \sum_{i=1}^{N} w_i R_{it}$$

where:

N = number of assets in the managed portfolio

With these definitions, we can then specify the Period t *return differential* between the managed portfolio and the benchmark as

16.1
$$\Delta_t = \sum_{i=1}^{N} w_i R_{it} - R_{bt} = R_{pt} - R_{bt}$$

Notice that, given the returns to the N assets in the managed portfolio and the benchmark, Δ is a function of the investment weights that the manager selects and that not all of the assets in the benchmark need be included in the managed portfolio (i.e., $w = 0$ for some assets).

For a sample of T return observations, the variance of Δ can be calculated as follows:

16.2
$$\sigma_\Delta^2 = \frac{\sum_{t=1}^{T} (\Delta_t - \overline{\Delta})^2}{(T-1)}$$

Finally, the standard deviation of the return differential is

$$\sigma_\Delta = \sqrt{\sigma_\Delta^2} = \text{periodic tracking error}$$

so that *annualized tracking error (TE)* can be calculated as

16.3
$$TE = \sigma_\Delta \sqrt{P}$$

where P is the number of return periods in a year (e.g., $P = 12$ for monthly returns, $P = 252$ for daily returns).

Suppose an investor has formed a portfolio designed to track a particular benchmark. Over the last eight quarters, the returns to this portfolio, as well as the index returns and the return difference between the two, were:

Period	Manager	Index	Difference (Δ)
1	2.3%	2.7%	−0.4%
2	−3.6	−4.6	1.0
3	11.2	10.1	1.1
4	1.2	2.2	−1.0
5	1.5	0.4	1.1
6	3.2	2.8	0.5
7	8.9	8.1	0.8
8	−0.8	0.6	−1.6

The periodic average and standard deviation of the manager's return differential (i.e., delta) relative to the benchmark are

The periodic average and standard deviation of the manager's return differential (i.e., "delta") relative to the benchmark are

$$\text{Average } \Delta = [-0.4 + 1.0 + \cdots + 0.8 - 1.6] \div 8 = 0.2\%$$

$$\sigma_\Delta = \sqrt{(-0.4 - 0.2)^2 + (1.0 - 0.2)^2 + \cdots + (1.6 - 0.2)^2} \div \sqrt{(8 - 1)} = 1.0\%$$

Thus, the manager's annualized tracking error for this two-year period is 2.0 percent (= 1.0 percent × $\sqrt{4}$).

Generally speaking, there is an inverse relationship between a passive portfolio's tracking error relative to its index and the time and expense necessary to create and maintain the portfolio. For example, full replication of the S&P 500 would have virtually no tracking error but would necessitate positions in 500 different stocks and require frequent rebalancing. As smaller samples are used to replicate the S&P index's return performance, the expense of forming the managed portfolio would decline but the potential tracking error is likely to increase. Thus, the art of being a manager of a passive equity portfolio lies in balancing the costs (larger tracking error) and the benefits (easier management, lower trading commissions) of using smaller samples. Exhibit 16.2 estimates the tracking error that occurs from such sampling.

Alford, Jones, and Winkelmann (2003) have also shown that tracking error can be a useful way to categorize a fund's investment style. In particular, they argue that money managers can be classified using the following chart with regard to the tracking errors of their portfolios compared to the relevant benchmark:

Investment Style	Tracking Error Range
Passive	Less than 1.0% (0.5% or lower is normal)
Structured	Between 1.0% and 3.0%
Active	Over 3.0% (5.0% to 15.0% is normal)

Source: Andrew Alford, Robert Jones, Kurt Winkelmann, *A Spectrum Approach to Active Risk Budgeting, Journal of Portfolio Management* 30, no. 1 (September 2003): 49–60.

Exhibit 16.2	**Expected Tracking Error between the S&P 500 Index and Portfolios Comprised of Samples of Fewer than 500 Stocks**

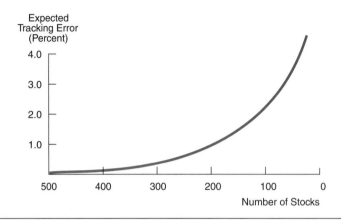

They also document that structured portfolio managers, which can be viewed as active managers with the tightest controls on the permissible level of their tracking errors, tend to produce superior risk-adjusted returns to those active managers whose investment mandates allow them to stray farther from their indexes.

Methods of Index Portfolio Investing

Although investors can construct their own passive investment portfolios that mimic a particular equity index, there are at least two prepackaged ways of accomplishing this goal that are typically more convenient and less expensive for the small investor. These are (1) buying shares in an *index mutual fund* or (2) buying shares in an *exchange-traded fund* (ETF).

Index Funds   As we discuss in Chapter 24, mutual funds represent established security portfolios managed by professional investment companies (e.g., Fidelity, Vanguard, Putnam, AIM) in which investors can participate. The investment company is responsible for deciding how the fund is managed. For an indexed portfolio, the fund manager will typically attempt to replicate the composition of the particular index exactly, meaning that he or she will buy the exact securities comprising the index in their exact weights and then alter those positions anytime the composition of the index itself is changed. Since changes to most equity indexes occur infrequently, index funds tend to generate low trading and management expense ratios. A prominent example of an index fund is Vanguard's 500 Index Fund (VFINX), which is designed to mimic the S&P 500 index. Exhibit 16.3 provides a descriptive overview of this fund and indicates that its historical return performance is virtually indistinguishable from that of the benchmark.

The advantage of index mutual funds is that they provide an inexpensive way for investors to acquire a diversified portfolio that emphasizes the desired market or industry within the context of a traditional money management product. As with any mutual fund, the disadvantages are that investors can only liquidate their positions at the end of the trading day (i.e., no intraday trading), usually cannot short sell, and may have unwanted tax repercussions if the fund has an unforeseen need to sell a portion of its holdings, thereby realizing capital gains.

Exchange-Traded Funds   ETFs are a more recent development in the world of indexed investment products than index mutual funds. Essentially, ETFs are depository receipts that give investors a pro rata claim on the capital gains and cash flows of the securities that are held in

| Exhibit 16.3 | Details of the Vanguard 500 Index Trust Mutual Fund |

A. Description

```
VANGUARD 500 INDEX FUND-INV          Objective - Index Fund-Large Cap
Vanguard 500 Index Fund is an open-end fund incorporated in the USA.  The Fund's
objective is to track the performance of the Standard & Poor's 500 Index, which
is dominated by the stocks of large U.S. companies.  The Fund attempts to
replicate the target index by investing substantially all of its assets in the
stocks that make up the Index.
```

Bloomberg Classification Data		Current / Operational Data		
Asset Class	Equity	1)GP NAV	$	107.99
Style	Index Fund	Assets(mil) 12/31/04	$	106579
Market Cap Focus	Large-cap	Inception Date	8/31/76	

Geographic Focus	U.S.

Performance/Percentile Ranking		
as of 1/28/05	Return	Rank in Obj.
3)TRA 1 Month	-3.38	64
YTD	-3.27	63
1 Year	5.48	88
2004	10.74	90
5 Year	-1.53	87

B. Historical Returns

Current	Return			Percentile
as of	Fund 1/28/05	SPX 1/28/05	Difference	Ranking in Objective
3)TRA 1 Week	.32	.32	.00	56
1 Month	-3.38	-3.37	-.02	64
3 Month	4.31	4.34	-.03	81
4)COMPYTD	-3.27	-3.26	-.01	63
1 Year	5.48	5.61	-.13	88
3 Year	2.76	2.87	-.11	87
9)HRH 5 Year	-1.53	-1.45	-.08	87
Historical	Fund	SPX	Difference	Ranking in Objective
2004	10.74	10.88	-.14	90
2003	28.50	28.68	-.18	85
2002	-22.15	-22.10	-.05	84
2001	-12.02	-11.89	-.14	89
2000	-9.06	-9.11	.05	87
1999	21.07	21.04	.03	90
1998	28.61	28.58	.04	79
1997	33.21	33.36	-.15	87
1996	22.86	22.96	-.10	93
1995	37.44	37.58	-.14	90

deposit by the financial institution that issued the certificates. That is, a portfolio of securities is placed on deposit at a financial institution or into a unit trust, which then issues a single type of certificate representing ownership of the underlying portfolio. In that way, ETFs are similar to the American depository receipts (ADRs) described in Chapter 3.

There are several notable example of ETFs, including (1) Standard & Poor's 500 Depository Receipts (SPDRs or "spider" as they are sometimes called), which are based on a basket of all the securities held in that index; (2) iShares, which recreate indexed positions in several global developed and emerging equity markets, including countries such as Australia, Mexico, Malaysia, the United Kingdom, France, Germany, Japan, and China; and (3) sector ETFs, which invest in baskets of stocks from specific industry sectors, including consumer services, industrial, technology, financial services, energy, utilities, and cyclicals/transportation. Exhibit 16.4

Exhibit 16.4	Details of the SPDR Exchange-Traded Fund

A. Description

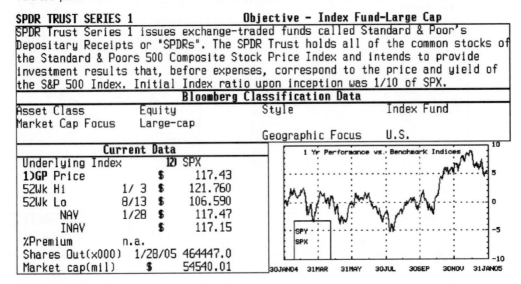

SPDR TRUST SERIES 1   **Objective - Index Fund-Large Cap**

SPDR Trust Series 1 issues exchange-traded funds called Standard & Poor's Depositary Receipts or "SPDRs". The SPDR Trust holds all of the common stocks of the Standard & Poors 500 Composite Stock Price Index and intends to provide investment results that, before expenses, correspond to the price and yield of the S&P 500 Index. Initial Index ratio upon inception was 1/10 of SPX.

Bloomberg Classification Data

Asset Class	Equity	Style	Index Fund
Market Cap Focus	Large-cap		
		Geographic Focus	U.S.

Current Data

Underlying Index		12) SPX	
1)GP Price		$	117.43
52Wk Hi	1/ 3	$	121.760
52Wk Lo	8/13	$	106.590
NAV	1/28	$	117.47
INAV		$	117.15
%Premium	n.a.		
Shares Out(x000)	1/28/05	464447.0	
Market cap(mil)	$	54540.01	

B. Historical Returns

Current	Return			Percentile
as of	Fund 1/28/05	SPX 1/28/05	Difference	Ranking in Objective
3)TRA 1 Week	.56	.32	.24	75
1 Month	-3.10	-3.37	.27	74
3 Month	4.52	4.34	.18	48
4)COMPYTD	-2.85	-3.26	.41	74
1 Year	5.57	5.61	-.04	54
3 Year	2.76	2.87	-.12	44
9)HRH 5 Year	-1.42	-1.45	.02	28
Historical	**Fund**	**SPX**	**Difference**	**Ranking in Objective**
2004	10.70	10.88	-.17	43
2003	28.18	28.68	-.51	33
2002	-21.59	-22.10	.51	62
2001	-11.75	-11.89	.13	60
2000	-9.73	-9.11	-.62	42
1999	20.39	21.04	-.66	54
1998	28.28	28.58	-.30	n.a.
1997	33.48	33.36	.12	n.a.
1996	22.55	22.96	-.41	n.a.
1995	38.05	37.58	.47	n.a.

shows descriptive and return data for the SPDR Trust certificates. Notice once again how closely the returns to these shares track the overall index.

A significant advantage of ETFs over index mutual funds is that they can be bought and sold (and short sold) like common stock through an organized exchange or in an over-the-counter market. Further, they are backed by a sponsoring organization (e.g., for SPDRs, the sponsor is PDR Services LLC, a limited liability company whose sole member is the American Stock Exchange where SPDR shares trade) who can alter the composition of the underlying portfolio to reflect changes in the composition of the index. Other advantages relative to index funds include no payment of a management fee, the ability for continuous trading while markets are open, and the ability to time capital gain tax realizations. ETF disadvantages include the brokerage commission and the inability to reinvest dividends except on a quarterly basis.

AN OVERVIEW OF ACTIVE EQUITY PORTFOLIO MANAGEMENT STRATEGIES

The goal of active equity management is to earn a portfolio return that exceeds the return of a passive benchmark portfolio, net of transaction costs, on a risk-adjusted basis. The job of an active equity manager is not easy. If transaction costs and fees total 1.5 percent of the portfolio's assets annually, the portfolio has to earn a return 1.5 percentage points above the passive benchmark just to keep pace with it. Further, if the manager's strategy involves overweighting specific market sectors in anticipation of price increases, the risk of the active portfolio may well exceed that of the passive benchmark, so the active portfolio's return will have to exceed the benchmark by an even wider margin to compensate for its higher risk.

That the job of the active equity portfolio manager is challenging is amply indicated by Exhibit 16.5, which shows the percentage of U.S.-domiciled mutual funds that were able to produce annual returns in excess of the S&P 500 index over a period of about a quarter century. Notice that for the majority of this period, the average fund manager was not able to outperform the broad index; the percentage of active funds whose return exceeded that of the index was less than 50 percent in 64 of the 96 quarters represented in the sample. However, the display also indicates that the percentage of active managers beating the market was never zero and occasionally rises as high as 70 percent, which is impressive given that there were more than 5,600 domestic equity funds by the end of 2003. Indeed, evidence provided by Brown and Goetzmann (1995) and Chen, Jegadeesh, and Wermers (2000) show that fund managers possess significant stockpicking skills that can translate into superior and persistent investment returns.

Exhibit 16.6 provides a broad overview of the different strategies that investment managers might adopt in forming their portfolios, as well as the investment philosophy that underlies each strategy. Notice, first of all, that the passive strategies we just considered are based (at least implicitly) on the notion that capital markets are efficient and so equity portfolios should be invested to mimic broad indexes and not traded actively. The realm of active management, however, is one in which managers are effectively betting against markets being perfectly efficient. For convenience, Exhibit 16.6 characterizes these bets as falling into three general categories: (1) fundamental, (2) technical, and (3) market anomalies and security attributes.

| Exhibit 16.5 | Performance of Active Mutual Funds vs S&P 500: January 1980–December 2003 |

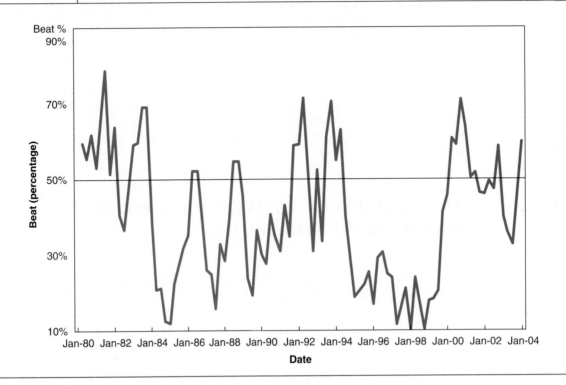

| Exhibit 16.6 | Equity Portfolio Investment Philosophies and Strategies |

Passive Management Strategies

1. EFFICIENT MARKETS HYPOTHESIS

Buy and hold

Indexing

Active Management Strategies

2. FUNDAMENTAL ANALYSIS

"Top down" (e.g., asset class rotation, sector rotation)
"Bottom up" (e.g., stock undervaluation/overvaluation)

3. TECHNICAL ANALYSIS

Contrarian (e.g., overreaction)

Continuation (e.g., price momentum)

4. ANOMALIES AND ATTRIBUTES

Calendar effects (e.g., weekend, January)

Security characteristics (e.g., *P/E, P/B,* earnings momentum, firm size)

Investment style (e.g., value, growth)

Fundamental Strategies

As we saw in Chapter 11, the three-step investment process begins at the top with an analysis of broad country and asset class allocations and progresses down through sector allocation decisions to the bottom level where individual securities are selected. The alternative to this top-down approach to investing was a bottom-up process that simply emphasized the selection of securities without any initial market or sector analysis. In similar fashion, active equity management based on fundamental analysis can start from either direction, depending on what exactly the manager thinks is mispriced relative to his or her valuation models. Generally, active managers use three generic themes in an attempt to add value to their portfolios relative to the benchmark. First, they can try to time the equity market by shifting funds into and out of stocks, bonds, and T-bills depending on broad market forecasts and estimated risk premiums. Second, they can shift funds among different equity sectors and industries (e.g., financial stocks, technology stocks, consumer cyclicals, durable goods) or among investment styles (e.g., large capitalization, small capitalization, value, growth) to catch the next hot concept before the rest of the market does. Third, equity managers can do stockpicking, looking at individual issues in an attempt to find undervalued stocks—that is, to buy low and sell high.

An asset class rotation strategy is one that shifts funds in and out of the stock market depending on the manager's perception of how the stock market is valued compared to the various alternative asset classes. Formally, such a strategy is called **tactical asset allocation** and will be described in more detail later in the chapter. Alternatively, a **sector rotation strategy** involves positioning the portfolio to take advantage of the market's next move. Often, this means emphasizing or overweighting (relative to the benchmark portfolio) certain economic sectors or industries in response to the next expected phase of the business cycle. Exhibit 16.7 contains suggestions on how sector rotators may position their portfolios to take advantage of stock market trends during the economic cycle.

In general, asset and sector rotation strategies can be extremely profitable but also very risky for a manager to follow. This is shown in Exhibit 16.8, which lists the annual returns in each of several asset and sector classes from 1985 to 2004. The chart documents the tremendous volatility that existed during this period. For instance, bonds, which comprised the best-performing asset class in 2002, made up the worst class in the following year.

| Exhibit 16.7 | The Stock Market and the Business Cycle |

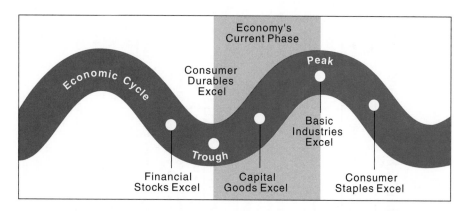

Exhibit 16.8 | Asset and Sector Class Return Performance: 1985–2004

1985	1986	1987	1988	1989	1990	1991	1992	1993	1994	1995	1996	1997	1998	1999	2000	2001	2002	2003	2004
F 56.14%	F 69.46%	F 24.64%	SV 29.47%	LG 36.40%	B 8.96%	SG 51.18%	SV 29.15%	F 32.57%	F 7.78%	LG 38.13%	LG 23.97%	LG 36.52%	LG 42.16%	SG 43.09%	SV 22.83%	SV 14.02%	B 10.25%	SG 48.54%	SV 22.25%
LG 33.31%	LV 21.67%	LG 6.50%	F 28.26%	L 31.69%	LG 0.20%	S 46.05%	S 18.42%	SV 23.86%	LG 3.14%	L 37.58%	L 22.96%	L 33.36%	L 28.58%	LG 28.25%	B 11.63%	B 8.44%	SV −11.43%	S 47.25%	F 20.25%
L 31.73%	L 18.67%	L 5.25%	S 24.89%	LV 26.13%	L −3.11%	SV 41.70%	LV 10.52%	S 18.89%	L 1.32%	LV 36.99%	LV 22.00%	SV 31.78%	F 20.00%	F 26.96%	LV 6.08%	S 2.49%	F −15.66%	SV 46.03%	S 18.33%
S 31.04%	B 15.30%	LV 3.68%	LV 21.67%	SG 20.16%	LV −6.85%	LG 38.37%	SG 7.77%	LV 18.61%	LV −0.64%	SG 31.04%	SV 21.37%	LV 29.98%	LV 14.69%	LV 21.26%	S −3.02%	SG −9.23%	S −20.48%	F 39.17%	LV 15.71%
SV 31.01%	LG 14.50%	B 2.75%	SG 20.38%	S 16.25%	SG −17.42%	L 30.47%	L 7.62%	SG 13.37%	SV −1.55%	S 28.44%	S 16.53%	S 22.36%	B 8.70%	L 21.04%	L −9.11%	LV −11.71%	LV −20.85%	LV 31.79%	SG 14.31%
SG 30.97%	SV 7.41%	SV −7.12%	L 16.61%	B 14.53%	S −19.50%	LV 22.56%	B 7.40%	L 10.08%	S −1.81%	SV 25.75%	SG 11.32%	SG 12.93%	SG 1.23%	S 12.72%	F −13.96%	L −11.88%	L −22.09%	L 28.67%	L 10.88%
LV 29.68%	S 5.69%	S −8.76%	LG 11.95%	SV 12.43%	SV −21.77%	B 16.00%	LG 5.06%	B 9.75%	SG −2.44%	B 18.46%	F 6.05%	B 9.64%	S −2.25%	B −0.82%	LG −22.08%	LG −12.73%	LG −23.59%	LG 25.66%	LG 6.13%
B 22.13%	SG 3.59%	SG −10.48%	B 7.89%	F 10.53%	F −23.45%	F 12.14%	F −12.18%	LG 1.68%	B −2.92%	F 11.21%	B 3.64%	F 1.78%	SV −6.46%	SV −1.48%	SG −22.43%	F −21.21%	SG −30.26%	B 4.10%	B 4.34%

Legend:
- **L** = Large Stocks — (Standard & Poor's 500 Index)
- **LG** = Large Growth Stocks — (S&P 500/BARRA Growth Index)
- **LV** = Large Value Stocks — (S&P 500/BARRA Value Index)
- **S** = Small Stocks — (Russell 2000 Index)
- **SG** = Small Growth Stocks — (Russell 2000 Growth Index)
- **SV** = Small Value Stocks — (Russell 2000 Value Index)
- **F** = Foreign Stocks — (MSC EAFE Index)
- **B** = Bonds — (Lehman Brothers Aggregate Bond Index)

Source: Prepared by authors using data from Standard & Poor's.

Conversely, large-cap growth stocks were the single best place to invest funds for six years (i.e., 1994–1999), but this period was bracketed by years when this sector performed quite poorly. The message from this display is clear: while there are impressive gains to be made by correctly timing the hottest (or the coldest) market sectors, a manager must be right substantially more than he or she is wrong. Because this is an extremely difficult thing to do consistently, many investors choose to interpret Exhibit 16.8 as ultimately extolling the virtue of asset and sector class diversification.

Finally, a fundamental stock-picker operating on a pure bottom-up basis will form a portfolio of equities that can be purchased at a substantial discount to what his or her valuation model indicates they are worth. As we discussed in Chapter 14, these valuation models might be based on absolute judgments about the future of the company (i.e., discounted cash flow) or relative assessments of how attractive the stock is compared with shares in otherwise similar firms that might be acquired (i.e., relative price multiples). In either case, it is usually true that the active manager will find stockpicking to be a more reliable, although less profitable, way to add value to a client than through market timing.

Technical Strategies

In Chapter 15, we discussed the role that technical analysis plays in the stock evaluation process. As we saw, assessing past stock price trends in an effort to surmise what information they imply about future price movements was one of the primary tools of this analytical approach. Active managers can form equity portfolios on the basis of past stock price trends by assuming that one of two things will happen: (1) past stock price trends will continue in the same direction, or (2) they will reverse themselves.

A **contrarian** investment strategy is based on the belief that the best time to buy (sell) a stock is when the majority of other investors are the most bearish (bullish) about it. In this way, the contrarian investor will attempt to always purchase the stock when it is near its lowest price and sell it (or even short sell it) when it nears its peak. Implicit in this approach is the belief that stock returns are *mean reverting,* indicating that, over time, stocks will be priced so as to produce returns consistent with their risk-adjusted expected (i.e., mean) returns. DeBondt and Thaler (1985) demonstrated the potential benefits of forming active portfolios based on this notion. Specifically, they showed that investing on an *overreaction hypothesis* could provide consistently superior returns. Exhibit 16.9 illustrates a summary of their experiment in which they measured returns to a portfolio of stocks that had had the worst market performance over the prior three years (i.e., losers) and a portfolio of stocks with the best past performance (i.e., winners). If investors overreacted to either bad news or good news about companies, as DeBondt and Thaler contended, we should see subsequent abnormal returns move in the opposite direction. The cumulative abnormal returns (CARs) shown in the display appear to support this notion, although the evidence is stronger for losers than for winners.

At the other extreme, active portfolios can also be formed on the assumptions that recent trends in past prices will continue. A **price momentum** strategy, as it is more commonly called, assumes that stocks that have been hot will stay hot, while cold stocks will also remain so. Although there may well be sound economic reasons for these trends to continue (e.g., company revenues and earnings that continue to grow faster than expected), it may also simply be the case that investors periodically *underreact* to the arrival of new information. Thus, a pure price momentum strategy focuses just on the trend of past prices alone and makes purchase and sale decisions accordingly. Chan, Jegadeesh, and Lakonishok (1999) investigated the profitability of this approach. They divided all of the stocks traded in U.S. markets over the period 1994–1998 into 10 different portfolios based on their past six-month price movements and calculated returns over the following year. Panel A of Exhibit 16.10 shows these

Exhibit 16.9 | **Abnormal Returns to a Market Overreaction Investment Strategy**

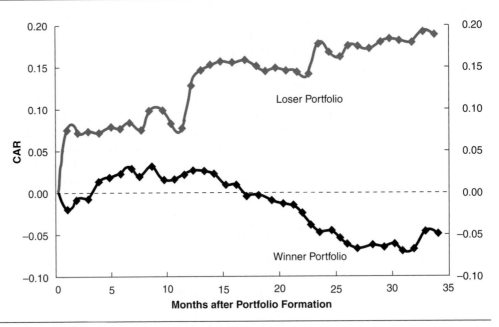

Source: Werner F. M. DeBondt and Richard Thaler, "Does the Stock Market Overreact?" *Journal of Finance* 40, no. 3 (July 1985): 793–805. Reprinted with permission of Blackwell Publishing.

annualized returns for each of the portfolios, from the one with the most positive past price trend (#10) to the worst price trend (#1). The data appear to justify the price momentum strategy in that the portfolios with the highest (lowest) level of price momentum generated the highest (lowest) subsequent returns. Also, the last column of the display shows that a momentum-based hedge fund that is long in the best-trend portfolio and short in the worst-trend one would also have been quite profitable.

Anomalies and Attributes

The price momentum strategies just discussed could either be based on pure price trend analysis or supported by the underlying economic fundamentals of the company. An **earnings momentum** strategy is a somewhat more formal active portfolio approach that purchases and holds stocks that have accelerating earnings and sells (or short sells) stocks with disappointing earnings. The notion behind this strategy is that, ultimately, a company's share price will follow the direction of its earnings, which is one bottom-line measure of the firm's economic success. In judging the degree of momentum in a firm's earnings, it is often the case in practice that investors will compare the company's actual EPS to some level of what was expected. Two types of expected earnings are used most frequently: (1) those generated by a statistical model and (2) the consensus forecast of professional stock analysts. Panel B of Exhibit 16.10 shows that, over the 1994–1998 period, earnings momentum strategies were generally successful as well, although surprisingly not to the same degree as price momentum strategies.

In our examination of market efficiency in Chapter 6, we saw several anomalies that suggested a role for active equity management. Two of these—the weekend effect and the January

Exhibit 16.10 | **Profitability of Momentum Strategies: 1994–1998**

	1 (Low)	2	3	4	5	6	7	8	9	10 (High)	10–1 (PPS)
A. Classification Based on Prior Six-Month Return											
1994	−12.00	−6.10	.0.40	2.10	0.50	−0.90	−1.80	3.10	−4.50	−6.40	5.60
1995	35.70	27.40	32.30	35.00	32.30	32.20	30.30	36.70	35.30	42.10	6.40
1996	11.90	15.60	17.90	20.20	27.90	22.50	22.00	21.90	20.40	15.30	3.40
1997	7.20	05.70	14.80	20.80	26.60	32.80	35.60	37.30	37.50	23.80	16.60
1998	−2.30	−4.40	−7.00	−3.30	−0.40	0.00	04.50	0.10	−0.80	04.40	6.70
1994–98 average	8.10	7.64	11.68	14.96	17.38	17.32	18.12	19.82	17.58	15.84	7.74
B. Classification Based on Standardized Unexpected Earnings											
1994	−2.30	−2.40	−6.80	−1.00	−4.60	−1.20	−0.10	−3.30	0.90	−2.00	0.30
1995	36.70	25.40	27.80	31.00	33.40	27.50	36.10	36.90	38.60	40.60	3.90
1996	16.30	17.90	19.20	16.30	21.90	19.60	23.10	22.70	24.70	18.40	2.10
1997	25.50	21.70	23.50	22.80	24.10	24.50	25.20	28.40	29.60	28.10	2.60
1998	−3.20	−5.20	−1.30	04.40	−0.60	5.00	−0.10	−0.60	0.00	−6.20	−3.00
1994–98 average	14.60	11.48	12.48	14.70	14.84	15.08	16.84	16.82	18.76	15.78	1.18

effect—involved investing during particular times of the year. While conceptually viable, the limitations inherent in these anomalies do not produce particularly effective portfolio strategies. That is, managers investing in stocks only in January are not likely to be able to justify their annual fees, while the number of transactions implied by the weekend effect (i.e., buy every Monday, sell every Friday) generally makes for a cost-ineffective portfolio. Remember, however, that whether or not these calendar-related anomalies produce successful active portfolios, they still are useful rules for trades that an investor plans to make anyway.

A more promising approach to active anomaly investing involves forming portfolios based on various characteristics of the companies themselves. Two such characteristics we have seen to matter in the stock market are the total capitalization of the firm's outstanding equity (i.e., firm size) and the financial position of the firm, as indicated by its various financial ratios (e.g., *P/E, P/BV*). The studies we saw in Chapter 6 came to two general conclusions about these firm characteristics. First, over time, firms with smaller market capitalizations produce bigger risk-adjusted returns than those with large market capitalizations. Second, over time, firms with lower *P/E* and *P/BV* ratios produce bigger risk-adjusted returns than those with higher levels of those ratios. In fact, we saw in Chapter 9 that low and high levels of these ratios are used in practice to define value and growth stocks, respectively.

To see another reason why these firm-specific attributes may be important to active investors, recognize that the term *sector* considered earlier in the context of rotation strategies also can be defined by different stock attributes. Thus, because the market seems to favor some attributes more than others over time, sector rotation may involve overweighting stocks with certain characteristics, such as small- or large-capitalization stocks, high or low *P/E* stocks, or stocks classified more generally as value or growth stocks. For example, Panel A of Exhibit 16.11 shows the difference in returns to portfolios invested in small- and large-cap stocks on a monthly basis from 1991–2004. The graph shows the large-cap portfolio return minus the small-cap return, so any net return above the horizontal axis indicates a period when the former outperformed the latter. Notice in particular the sizable firm size rotation and spread in returns that occurred in this period; in given months, both large- and small-cap stocks outperformed the other by over 30 percent. An important point to keep in mind, however, is that small-cap stocks are almost always riskier than large-cap stocks. This is shown in Panel B of Exhibit 16.11, which reports the difference in the standard deviations of the large- and small-cap portfolios.

Similar analysis reveals the potential benefits of forming active global portfolios around financial ratios. For the period spanning 1975–1995, Fama and French (1998) divided the stocks in 13 world markets using several different ratios, including *P/E* and *P/BV*. They formed portfolios of stocks based on the highest and lowest 30 percent of each ratio and measured returns and standard deviations over the entire 20-year period. Exhibit 16.12 summarizes their findings. For each country and each ratio, the display reports the average annual return differential between the lowest-ratio portfolio and the highest-ratio portfolio, as well as difference in standard deviation for those two portfolios. Two facts are clear from these results. First, over time, portfolios with the lowest *P/E* and *P/BV* ratios produced the highest returns everywhere in the world except Italy. Second, those low-ratio portfolios also tended to be more volatile, although this finding was far less uniform across countries. As we will see shortly, these results are important for understanding the differences between the value and growth investment styles.

Miscellaneous Issues

Regardless of which broad philosophical approach they adopt, an important issue for active managers and their clients to resolve is the selection of an appropriate benchmark (sometimes called a "normal" portfolio). The benchmark should incorporate the average qualities of the

| Exhibit 16.11 | Performance Large- and Small-Cap Portfolios: 1991–2004 |

Panel A. Rotation of Large-Cap and Small-Cap Returns

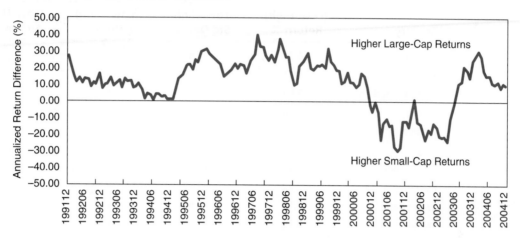

Panel B. Rotation of Large-Cap and Small-Cap Standard Deviations

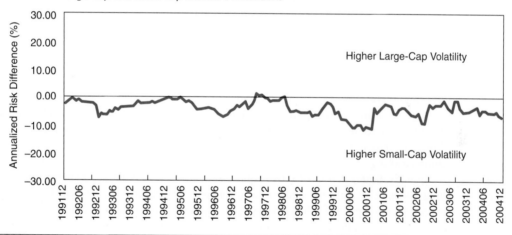

Source: Fidelity Management and Research. Data based on relative rolling 12-month returns to Russell 1000 and Russell 2000 indices.

portfolio strategy of the client. Thus, an active portfolio manager who invests mainly in small-capitalization stocks with low *P/E* ratios because the client specified this strategy should not have his or her performance compared to a broad market index, such as the S&P 500. Similarly, a global equity manager will not want to have his or her performance compared to a portfolio of stocks drawn from a single country, or even a single region in the world.

Active managers must overcome two difficulties relative to the benchmark. First, an actively managed portfolio will almost always have higher transaction costs. Second, active portfolios can often also have higher risk than the passive benchmark. One key to success is for active managers to *be consistent* in their area of expertise. Market gyrations occur, and

Exhibit 16.12 | **Performance of Ratio-Based Stock Portfolios: 1975–1995**

Country	P/E RATIO		P/BV RATIO	
	(Low–High) Return %	(Low–High) Std Dev %	(Low–High) Return %	(Low–High) Std Dev %
United States	6.71	2.87	6.79	1.13
Japan	7.47	−1.52	9.85	−2.75
United Kingdom	2.65	5.32	4.62	2.09
France	6.98	4.70	7.64	5.72
Germany	0.55	−10.20	2.75	−2.40
Italy	−5.37	−12.32	−5.99	−15.12
The Netherlands	5.11	0.59	2.30	12.06
Belgium	2.22	2.59	4.39	0.99
Switzerland	1.54	2.63	3.49	1.43
Sweden	8.19	17.67	8.02	12.05
Australia	9.67	−0.70	12.32	3.71
Hong Kong	4.99	4.02	7.16	8.47
Singapore	2.09	−5.13	9.67	9.18

Source: Eugene F. Fama and Kenneth R. French, "Value versus Growth: The International Evidence," *Journal of Finance* 53, no.6 (December 1998): 1975–1999. Reprinted with permission of Blackwell Publishing.

investment styles go in and out of favor. Successful long-term investing requires that you maintain your investment philosophy and composure while others are deviating from theirs. Another key to success is to *minimize the trading activity* of the portfolio. Attempts to time price movements over short horizons will result in lower profits because of growing commissions.

Finally, notice that most active equity strategies are inherently quantitative in nature. This suggests that computer-assisted portfolio formation procedures can be quite useful. In fact, the existence of computer databases has encouraged the use of computer screening and other quantitatively based methods of evaluating stocks. These screening methods search for portfolios of stocks with certain characteristics rather than examining individual stocks to determine whether they are underpriced. The simplest computer screens identify groups of stocks based on a set of attributes. Screens also are used to narrow the list of thousands of stocks to a manageable few that can then be evaluated using more traditional analytical means. Indeed, some managers let the computers do all the work. For example, Swales and Yoon (1992) describe *neural networks,* which are computer programs that attempt to imitate the thinking patterns of the human brain. They use vast databases and artificial intelligence capabilities to find cause-and-effect patterns in stock returns. The computer attempts to discover undervalued securities by identifying abnormal risk-adjusted return patterns and learning what stock attributes drive the market.

More complicated quantitative strategies are available that are comparable in some ways to sector rotation. Factor models, similar to those based on the APT, can identify stocks whose earnings or prices are sensitive to economic variables, such as exchange rates, inflation, interest rates, or consumer sentiment. With this information, portfolios can be tilted by trading those stocks most sensitive to the analyst's economic forecast. For example, Roll and Ross (1995) explain that a manager can try to improve the portfolio's relative performance in a recession by purchasing stocks that are *least* sensitive to the analyst's pessimistic forecast.

Some quantitatively oriented portfolio managers use what is called a "long-short" approach to investing. In the long-short approach, stocks are passed through a number of screens and assigned a rank. Stocks at the top of the ranking are purchased; stocks at the bottom are sold short. Such a strategy can be neutral on the overall market, since the value and systematic risk exposure of the long position can approximate that of the short position. The performance of the top-ranked stocks is expected to exceed that of the lower-ranked stocks, regardless of whether the overall stock market rises, falls, or trades in a narrow range.

How do managers know that these quantitative models have the potential to offer above-average risk-adjusted returns? The answer is that they hope the future will be similar to the past because these quantitative strategies have been **backtested**. This involves using computers to examine the composition and returns of portfolios based on historical data to determine if the strategy would have worked successfully in the past. The risk of testing an investment strategy in this way is that relationships that existed in the past are not guaranteed to hold in the future.

VALUE VERSUS GROWTH INVESTING: A CLOSER LOOK

One of the most important developments in active equity management during the last several years has been the creation of portfolio strategies based on value- and growth-oriented investment styles. Indeed, it is now common for money management firms to define themselves as "value stock managers" or "growth stock managers" when selling their services to clients. Exhibit 16.13

Exhibit 16.13 | **Number of Growth and Value Mutual Funds: 1991–2003**

	2003	2000	1995	1991
Growth-Oriented Funds				
Large-cap	1,245	651	174	117
Mid-cap	784	415	106	79
Small-cap	672	383	77	42
Total	2,701	1,449	357	238
Annual % increase (1991–2003)	22.4%			
Value-Oriented Funds				
Large-cap	946	615	211	133
Mid-cap	301	212	69	60
Small-cap	270	193	47	25
Total	1,517	1,020	327	218
Annual % increase (1991–2003)	17.6%			

Source: Adapted from Table 1 in Keith C. Brown and W.V. Harlow, "Staying the Course: Performance Persistence and the Role of Investment Style Consistency in Professional Asset Management," Working Paper, May 29, 2004.

indicates how pervasive these styles have become. Using the classifications of Morningstar, Inc., a leading provider of investment analysis in the mutual fund industry, the number of available growth- and value-oriented funds grew dramatically, particularly during the last decade of the reporting period. The chart shows that the available number of growth fund products expanded by more than 20 percent per year over this period, with large-cap portfolios being the most prevalent. Value fund availability did not increase quite as much but still expanded by almost 18 percent annually.

The distinction between value and growth investing can be best appreciated by considering the thought process of a representative manager for each style.[1] In Chapter 11, we saw that the price-earnings ratio for any company can be expressed as:

16.4 $$P/E \text{ Ratio } = \frac{(\text{Current Price per Share})}{(\text{Earnings per Share})}$$

where the earnings per share *(EPS)* measure can be based on either current or future (i.e., forecasted) firm performance. In broad terms, value and growth managers will focus on different aspects of this equation when deciding whether a stock should be added to an existing portfolio. Specifically, a growth-oriented investor will

- focus on the *EPS* component (i.e., the denominator) of the *P/E* ratio and its economic determinants;
- look for companies that he or she expects to exhibit rapid *EPS* growth in the future; and
- often implicitly assume that the *P/E* ratio will remain constant over the near term, meaning that the stock price will rise as forecasted earnings growth is realized.

On the other hand, a value-oriented investor will

- focus on the price component (i.e., the numerator) of the *P/E* ratio; he or she must be convinced that the price of the stock is "cheap" by some means of comparison;
- not care a great deal about current earnings or the fundamental drivers of earnings growth; and
- often implicitly assume that the *P/E* ratio is below its natural level and that the market will soon "correct" this situation by increasing the stock price with little or no change in earnings.

In summary, a growth investor focuses on the current and future economic "story" of a company, with less regard to share valuation. The value investor, on the other hand, focuses on share price in anticipation of a market correction and, possibly, improving company fundamentals.

The conceptual difference between value and growth investing may be reasonably straightforward, but classifying individual stocks into the appropriate style is not always simple in practice. Since detailed company valuations are time-consuming to produce, most analysts rely on more easily obtained financial indicators—such as *P/E* and *P/B* ratios, dividend yields, and *EPS* growth rates—to define both an individual equity holding as well as the style benchmark portfolio. Exhibit 16.14 shows one approach along these lines for classifying firms according to style and market capitalization. Notice that value stocks are defined as those that are relatively cheap (e.g., low *P/B*, high yield) and with modest growth opportunities (e.g., regulated firms) while growth stocks tend to be more expensive, reflecting their superior earnings potential (e.g., technology firms).

---

[1]This motivation is based on an excellent overview of value, and growth-oriented investment styles that can be found in Christopherson and Williams (1995).

Exhibit 16.14 | Characteristics of Growth and Value Stocks

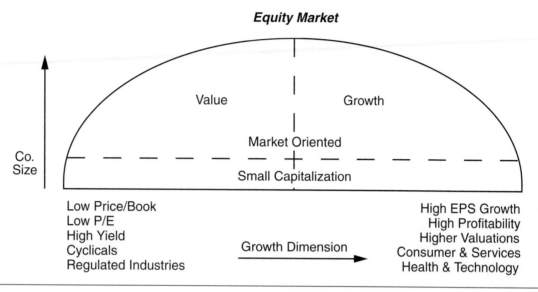

Equity Market

Value   Growth

Market Oriented

Co. Size

Small Capitalization

Low Price/Book
Low P/E
High Yield
Cyclicals
Regulated Industries

Growth Dimension →

High EPS Growth
High Profitability
Higher Valuations
Consumer & Services
Health & Technology

Source: Copyright Frank Russell Company. Reprinted with permission from Frank Russell Company, Tacoma, WA.

To get a better feel for the types of stock portfolios these two investment styles might produce, Exhibit 16.15 lists representative samples of the top holdings for the Harbor Capital Appreciation (HACAX) growth-oriented mutual fund and the T. Rowe Price Value (TRVLX) mutual fund as of December 31, 2004. Both of these funds emphasize large-cap companies but, as the chart shows, they differ in their investment approach in other important ways. Notably, HACAX's biggest holdings include technology (MSFT, DELL) and Internet (YHOO, EBAY) firms while TRVLX invests more on the industrial (HON, IP) and financial (JPM, BAC) side. On average, the stocks in the HACAX portfolio tend to have higher *P/E* and *P/BK* ratios and greater future growth potential than those in TRVLX. Also, the HACAX fund appears to hold riskier (i.e., higher beta) stocks as well as ones that pay lower dividends. Interestingly, both portfolios hold General Electric and JPMorgan Chase among their top holdings, which underscores the room for investor judgment involved in classifying stocks along the value-growth dimension.

Although investors appear to pay somewhat more attention to growth-oriented strategies, research has shown that a value approach to portfolio management tends to provide superior returns. In particular, Capaul, Rowley, and Sharpe (1993) studied the performance of value and growth portfolios (defined by relative *P/B* ratios) in six countries: the United States, the United Kingdom, Japan, France, Germany, and Switzerland. Over a 10-year period ending in June 1992, they demonstrated that global value stocks outperformed global growth stocks by an average of 3.3 percent per year. Further, value stocks outperformed growth stocks in each of the six countries considered separately. More recent evidence provided by Chan and Lakonishok (2004) supports this conclusion. Exhibit 16.16, which shows the cumulative performance of a large-cap growth index (Russell 1000 Growth) and a large-cap value index (Russell 1000 Value), indicates that this performance advantage persisted in the U.S. market through the end of 2004. This is all the more notable for the fact that much of this period was a particularly good time for the large-cap growth investment style.

Exhibit 16.15	**Top Stock Holdings of Growth and Value Mutual Funds**

A. Harbor Capital Appreciation Fund (HACAX)

Company	Ticker	Market Cap ($ Bil)	P/E	P/BV	Est. Growth EPS (%)	Div. Yld. (%)	Beta
General Electric	GE	383.7	22.77	3.47	10.75	2.43	1.05
Microsoft	MSFT	277.4	19.92	5.87	10.97	1.25	1.09
Yahoo!	YHOO	46.2	92.16	6.51	31.36	0.00	1.50
eBay	EBAY	55.8	68.55	8.25	31.30	0.00	1.19
Schlumberger	SLB	45.2	37.24	7.38	17.10	1.10	0.74
JPMorgan Chase	JPM	131.6	12.29	1.25	10.84	3.68	1.28
Dell	DELL	100.1	31.25	15.45	19.42	0.00	0.97
American Express	AXP	68.6	20.11	4.29	12.71	0.87	1.20
American Intl. Group	AIG	173.9	15.38	2.20	14.51	0.75	1.30
Starbucks	SBUX	21.7	52.79	7.82	20.86	0.00	0.88
	Average:	*130.4*	*37.25*	*6.25*	*17.98*	*1.01*	*1.12*

B. T. Rowe Price Value Fund (TRVLX)

Company	Ticker	Market Cap ($ Bil)	P/E	P/BV	Est. Growth EPS (%)	Div. Yld. (%)	Beta
General Electric	GE	383.7	22.77	3.47	10.75	2.43	1.05
JPMorgan Chase	JPM	131.6	12.29	1.25	10.84	3.68	1.28
Liberty Media	L	28.6	na	1.25	17.50	0.00	1.05
Bank of America	BAC	186.8	11.89	1.88	9.34	3.91	0.73
Coca-Cola	KO	105.4	21.24	6.61	8.67	2.56	0.76
Union Pacific	UNP	17.3	23.10	1.36	10.00	1.81	0.84
Honeywell	HON	32.8	20.98	2.92	11.49	2.14	1.36
International Paper	IP	18.9	27.14	2.30	4.67	2.57	1.00
Time Warner	TWX	81.1	22.71	1.34	12.68	0.00	0.79
DuPont de Nemours	DD	53.7	22.64	4.81	9.83	2.60	1.07
	Average:	*104.0*	*20.53*	*2.72*	*10.58*	*2.17*	*0.99*

It is tempting to conclude that value is unambiguously superior to growth as an investment style. However, it is important to note that, although value investing produces higher average returns than growth investing, this does not occur with much consistency from one investment period to another. In fact, Panel A of Exhibit 16.17 shows that there are significant differences in the value-growth return spread (based on the rolling annual performance of the Russell 1000 Value and Growth indexes) over time. During this analysis, the spread ranged from almost 40 percent in favor of value investing to more than 20 percent to the advantage of the growth style. Conversely, Panel B of the exhibit illustrates that the spread between value and growth

| Exhibit 16.16 | **Russell 1000 Growth and Value Index Cumulative Performance: January 1991–December 2004** |

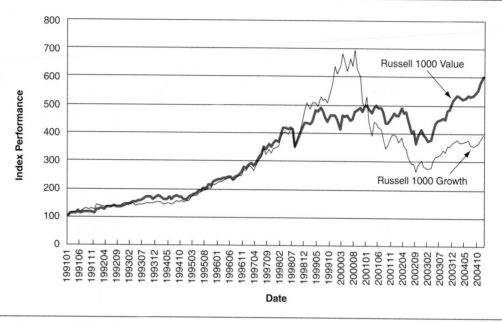

Note: January 1991 = 100
Source: Frank Russell Company.

return standard deviations, while itself volatile, is consistently negative, meaning that the growth strategy is consistently riskier than the value approach.

AN OVERVIEW OF STYLE ANALYSIS

As we have seen, there are many approaches to managing a portfolio of equity securities. The different styles that have evolved over the years include forming portfolios around stock characteristics, such as market capitalization, leverage, industry sector, relative valuation, and growth potential. Returns-based **style analysis** is an attempt to explain the variability in the observed returns to a security portfolio in terms of the movements in the returns to a series of benchmark portfolios designed to capture the essence of a particular security characteristic. Effectively, style analysis determines the combination of long positions in a collection of passive indexes that best mimics the past performance of a security portfolio.

The process of returns-based style analysis involves using the past returns to a manager's portfolio along with those to a series of indexes representing different investment styles in an effort to determine the relationship between the fund and those specific styles. Generally speaking, the more highly correlated a fund's returns are with a given style index, the greater the weighting that style is given in the statistical assessment. The goals of the analysis are to better understand the underlying influences responsible for the portfolio's performance and to properly classify the manager's strategy when comparing his or her investment prowess with that of other managers. Thus, regardless of whatever investment objective a manager might profess to follow, style analysis allows the portfolio to speak for itself.

Exhibit 16.17	Performance of Value and Growth Portfolios: 1991–2004

Panel A. Rotation of Value and Growth Returns

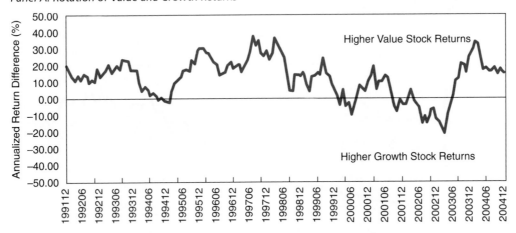

Panel B. Rotation of Value and Growth Standard Deviations

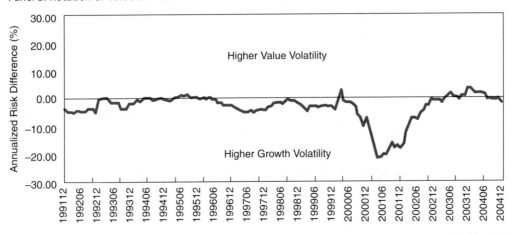

Source: Fidelity Management and Research. Data based on relative rolling 12-month returns to Russell 1000 Value and Growth indices.

Exhibit 16.18 shows a simple **style grid** that could be used to classify a manager's performance along two dimensions: firm size (large cap, mid cap, small cap) and relative value (value, blend, growth) characteristics. An investor whose portfolio produced returns best mimicked by the returns to indexes representing a small-cap value style (such as Manager A) would be plotted in the lower left quadrant of the grid. These grids are also useful in establishing the implicit investment style for any of the popular stock market indicators described in Chapter 5. For example, Exhibit 16.19 shows the style plot points for the S&P 500, S&P Midcap, Wilshire 5000, Nasdaq Composite, Russell 3000 (R3), Russell 2000 (R2), and Russell 1000 (R1), among others.[2] One interesting result in this display is that the S&P 500 can be characterized as a large-

---
[2]Exhibit 16.19 also plots the investment style for various subsets of the Russell indexes. For example, R1V and R1G are, respectively, the value and growth halves of the Russell 1000. They are created by ranking the 1,000 companies in the index by their price-to-book ratios and assigning those with the lowest (highest) ratios to the value (growth) subindex.

Exhibit 16.18 | **A Style Analysis Grid**

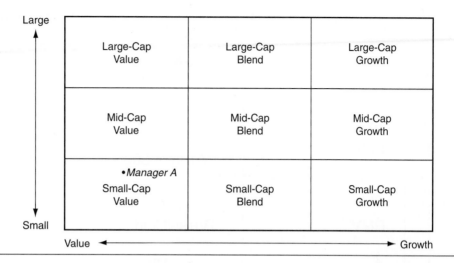

cap, blend (i.e., between value and growth) fund. As such, it may not be the appropriate performance benchmark for someone managing a mid-cap, growth-oriented portfolio.

Formally, style analysis relies on the *constrained least squares* procedure, with the returns to the manager's portfolio designated as the dependent variable and the returns to the style index portfolios as the independent variables. In practice, there are often three constraints employed: (1) no intercept term is specified, (2) the coefficients must sum to one, and (3) all the coefficients must be non-negative. As developed by Sharpe (1992), returns-based style analysis is simply an application of an asset class factor model:

16.5 $$R_{pt} = [b_{p1} F_{1t} + b_{p2} F_{2t} + \ldots + b_{pn} F_{nt}] + e_{pt}$$

where:

R_{pt} = the *t*th period return to the portfolio of Manager *p*
F_{jt} = the *t*th period return to the *j*th style factor
b_{pj} = the sensitivity of Portfolio *p* to Style Factor *j*
e_{pt} = the portion of the return variability in Portfolio *p* not explained by variability in the set of factors

As with any regression equation, the coefficient of determination can be defined as

16.6 $$R^2 = 1 - [\sigma^2 (e_p)/\sigma^2 (R_p)]$$

Because of the way the factor model is designed, R^2 can be interpreted as the percentage of Manager *p*'s return variability due to the portfolio's *style,* with $(1 - R^2)$ due to his or her *selection* skills.

The benchmark portfolios that are selected as style analysis factors should be consistent with the manager's pronounced style. This suggests that a different set of indexes might be

Exhibit 16.19 | **Investment Style of Popular Stock Market Indicators**

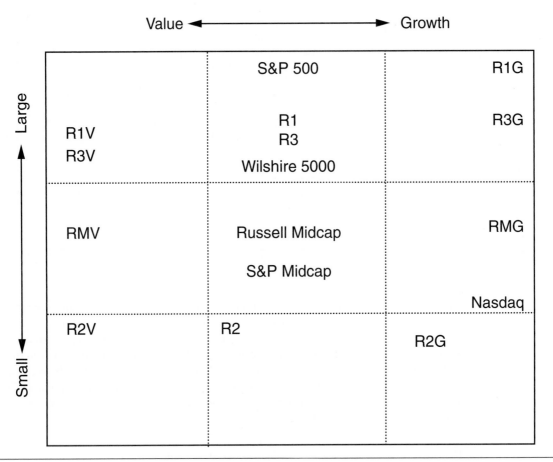

Source: Based on Fidelity Management and Research Company data.

specified for a domestic equity fund than for an international bond fund. Also, an effective benchmark portfolio should be easy to measure, available as a realistic investment alternative to an actively managed portfolio, and as uncorrelated as possible with the other style indexes. Within these broad guidelines, there are a virtually unlimited number of different benchmarks that could be used in practice. Three popular approaches are:

- *Sharpe:* Uses portfolios of T-bills, intermediate-term government bonds, long-term government bonds, corporate bonds, mortgage-related securities, large-capitalization value stocks, large-capitalization growth stocks, medium-capitalization stocks, small-capitalization stocks, non-U.S. bonds, European stocks, and Japanese stocks.

- *BARRA:* Uses portfolios formed around 13 different security characteristics, including variability in markets, past firm success, firm size, trading activity, growth orientation, earnings-to-price ratio, book-to-price ratio, earnings variability, financial leverage, foreign income, labor intensity, yield, and low capitalization (see Chapter 9).

- *Ibbotson Associates:* In its simplest style model, uses portfolios formed around five different characteristics: cash (i.e., T-bills), large-capitalization growth, small-capitalization growth, large-capitalization value, and small-capitalization value (see Cummisford and Lummer, 1996).

To illustrate how this process can be implemented, Sharpe measured the investment styles of two large institutional equity portfolios—Vanguard Trustee's U.S. Fund and Fidelity Magellan Fund—over a five-year interval. Both portfolios performed well during the period, generating respective average annual returns of 15.5 percent and 20.6 percent. However, Exhibit 16.20 shows that the managers of these portfolios followed very different styles. The

Exhibit 16.20	**Style Analysis for Two Mutual Funds**

A. Vanguard Trustee's U.S. Fund

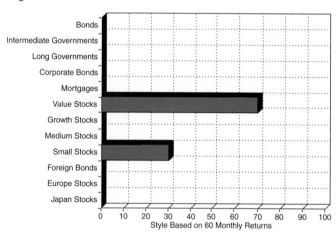
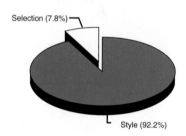

B. Fidelity Magellan Fund

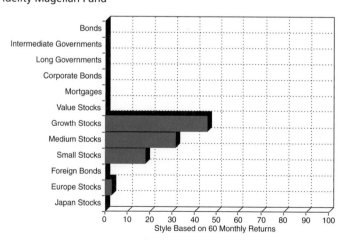
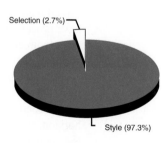

Source: William F. Sharpe, "Asset Allocation: Management Style and Performance Measurement," *Journal of Portfolio Management* 18, no. 2 (Winter 1992): 7–19.

bar charts indicate the extent to which each portfolio's returns were correlated with the underlying style factors. Accordingly, the Trustees' Fund is best thought of as being a small-cap value fund over this period while the Magellan Fund was a small-to-mid-cap growth portfolio with some global exposure. Also, security selection accounted for a relatively small amount of Magellan's return variability (2.7 percent) but was more of a consideration (7.8 percent) in the Trustees' portfolio.

Finally, style analysis can also be used to determine whether a manager is able to maintain a consistent investment style over time. This can be accomplished by reestimating the optimal combination of mimicking style indexes as additional performance data become available and then overlaying the plot points on the same grid. Exhibit 16.21 shows the connected sequence of plot points—or "snail trails" as they are sometimes called—for four different mutual funds managed by a leading investment company. Two of these funds (I and II) have well-defined style mandates and have been able to achieve relatively stable investment policies. The other two—III and IV—have exhibited considerable *style drift,* which in both cases is consistent with their flexible investment missions. Of course, an investor needs to be cautious about a manager whose portfolio exhibits unintentional style drift.

ASSET ALLOCATION STRATEGIES

An equity portfolio does not stand in isolation; rather, it is part of an investor's overall investment portfolio. Many times the equity portfolio is part of a balanced portfolio that contains holdings in various long- and short-term debt securities (such as bonds and Treasury bills) in addition to equities.

In such situations, the portfolio manager must consider more than just the composition of the equity or the bond component of the portfolio. The manager also must determine the appropriate mix of asset categories in the entire portfolio. There are four general strategies for determining the asset mix of a portfolio: the integrated, strategic, tactical, and insured asset allocation methods.

Integrated Asset Allocation

The integrated asset allocation strategy separately examines (1) capital market conditions and (2) the investor's objectives and constraints. These factors are then combined to establish the portfolio asset mix that offers the best opportunity for meeting the investor's needs given the capital market forecast. The actual returns from the portfolio are then used as inputs to an iterative process in which changes over time in the investor's objectives and constraints are noted along with changes in capital market expectations. The optimal portfolio is then revised based on this update of investor needs and capital market expectations.

This integrated approach to portfolio formation is illustrated in Exhibit 16.22. As described by Sharpe (1987, 1990), there are three key steps to integrated asset allocation. First, both capital market conditions and investor-specific objectives and constraints (e.g., risk tolerance, investment horizon, tax status) are summarized before the asset mix is determined. The processes by which the capital market and investor-specific data are summarized are shown in boxes C2 and I2, respectively, with the outcomes of those processes in boxes C3 and I3. An example of C3 might be the Markowitz efficient frontier containing portfolios of optimal risk–expected return combinations; the end product of I3 might be captured in an investment policy statement.

The second step in the integrated asset allocation process is to combine the information from the first step in order to select the single best portfolio for the investor in question. This is

Exhibit 16.21 | **Mutual Fund Styles over Time**

A. Style Consistency

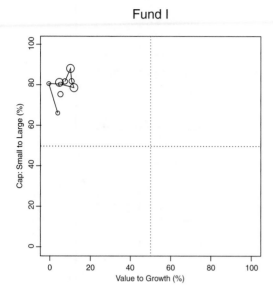

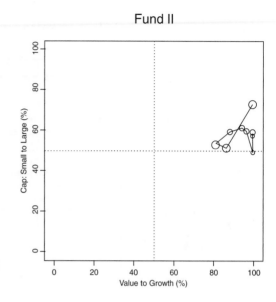

B. Style Flexibility

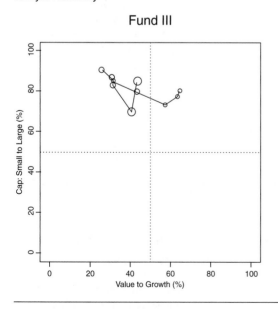

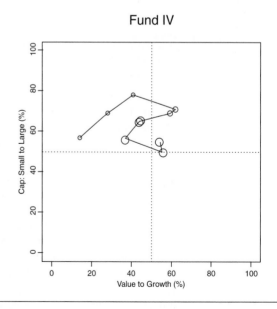

Exhibit 16.22 | **Integrated Asset Allocation**

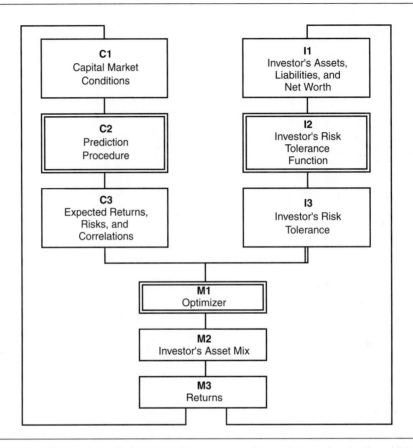

captured by the optimizer box in M1, with the resulting asset mix being shown in M2. One simple way of seeing how M1 might work would be to calculate the *expected utility (EU)* of each prospective asset mix using the following formula:

16.7
$$EU_{pk} = ER_p - \left(\frac{\sigma_p^2}{RT_k}\right) = ER_p - (\text{Risk Penalty})$$

where ER_p and σ_p^2 are the expected return and variance for Portfolio p (which come from C3) and RT_k is the risk-tolerance factor for Investor k (which comes from I3). The risk-tolerance factor is an estimate intended to capture the essence of an investor's attitude toward risk bearing. Notice that the higher this number, the more risk tolerant the investor is and, hence, the less Portfolio p has its expected return "penalized" by its risk level. The optimal asset mix for any particular investor is then the one that generates the highest level of expected utility.

As an example of the first two stages of the integrated asset allocation process, Panel A of Exhibit 16.23 shows the expected returns and variances for three different potential asset

Exhibit 16.23 | **Optimal Portfolio Selection: An Example**

A. Prospective Efficient Portfolios (C3)

Portfolio	ASSET MIX		ER	$\sigma2$
	Stock	Bond		
A	20%	80%	7%	7%
B	50	50	8	13
C	80	20	9	20

B. Risk-Tolerance Factors (I3)

Investor	RT	
1	5	(i.e., *less* tolerant)
2	40	(i.e., *more* tolerant)

C. Expected Utility Results (M2)

	A	B	C
Investor #1 *EU:*	**5.6**	5.4	5.0
Investor #2 *EU:*	6.8	7.8	**8.5**

mixes (C3), while Panel B lists risk-tolerance factors for two investors (I3). Panel C shows the result of the expected utility calculations that combine this information (M2). For instance, the expected utility generated by Portfolio A for Investor 1 is 5.6 (= 7 − 7/5), which is the largest value of the three potential allocations and therefore his optimal asset mix. Conversely, Investor 2 is more tolerant of risk and finds that Portfolio 3, which generates an expected utility level of 8.5 (= 9 − 20/40), is her optimal allocation. Notice that the risk-tolerance factor effectively deflates the risk penalty, allowing more risk-tolerant investors to pursue more volatile portfolios with higher expected returns.

The third stage of the integrated portfolio process occurs after enough time has passed that the optimal portfolio's actual performance can be compared with the manager's original expectations. This evaluation process is represented by Box M3 in Exhibit 16.22. Following this assessment, the manager can then make adjustments to the portfolio by including any new information into the optimization process. Adjustments to the initial asset mix can result from either a fundamental change in capital market conditions (e.g., increased inflation) or a change in the investor's circumstances (e.g., increased risk tolerance). It is this feedback loop that makes portfolio management a *dynamic* process.

Strategic Asset Allocation

Strategic asset allocation is used to determine the long-term policy asset weights in a portfolio. Typically, long-term average asset returns, risk, and covariances are used as estimates of future capital market results. Efficient frontiers are generated using this historical return information, and the investor decides which asset mix is appropriate for his or her needs during the planning horizon. This results in a *constant-mix* asset allocation with periodic rebalancing to adjust the portfolio to the specified asset weights.

One way to think of the strategic allocation process is as being equivalent to the integrated asset allocation process shown in Exhibit 16.22 but without the feedback loops. That is, as just described, the manager will determine the long-term asset allocation that is best suited for a particular investor by optimizing information from both the capital market and that investor. However, once this asset mix is established, the manager does not constantly attempt to adjust the allocation according to temporary changes in market and investor circumstances. Thus, as Ezra (1998) points out, the strategic allocation should define the basic nature of the trade-off between opportunity and safety that confronts the investor.

As an example of strategic asset allocation, Exhibit 16.24 shows the asset mixes for both large (Panel A) and small-to-midsize (Panel B) defined-benefit pension plans. The display lists average allocations for corporate, union, and public sector plans as of both 1997 and 2001. There are several interesting things to note. First, regardless of type, large plans appear to invest more heavily in equities than do smaller plans. Second, regardless of size, corporate and public funds invest more heavily in equities than do union funds, which allocate far more of their capital to fixed-income and cash equivalent securities. (Generally speaking, portfolios tilted more toward stocks than bonds and cash are considered to be riskier.) Third, no fund takes a particularly big position in foreign securities, although union plans make by far the smallest global allocations. Finally, consistent with the idea of a strategic allocation as a long-term view, these asset mixes remained relatively stable over the two years in question.

Tactical Asset Allocation

Unlike an investor's strategic allocation, which is set with a long-term focus and modified infrequently, a tactical approach to asset allocation constantly adjusts the asset class mix in the portfolio in an attempt to take advantage of changing market conditions. With tactical asset allocation, these adjustments are driven solely by perceived changes in the relative values of the various asset classes; the investor's risk tolerance and investment constraints are assumed to be constant over time. In Exhibit 16.22, it is equivalent to an integrated approach to asset allocation that removes the feedback loop involving investor-specific information (i.e., I2).

Tactical asset allocation is frequently based on the premise of *mean reversion,* which, as we have seen, holds that whatever a security's return has been in the recent past, it will eventually revert to its long-term average (mean) value. This assessment is usually done on a comparative basis. For instance, suppose that the ratio of stock and bond returns is normally 1.2, reflecting the greater degree of risk in the equity market. Then, if in the most recent investment period, stock returns were double those of bond returns, the tactical investor might determine that bonds were now undervalued relative to stock and most likely to be the best-performing asset class in the coming period. Accordingly, he should then overweight the fixed-income component of his portfolio, shifting, say, from a 60–40 percent initial mix of stocks and bonds to a 50–50 percent split.

For the preceding description, notice that tactical asset allocation is an inherently *contrarian* method of investing. That is, the investor adopting this approach will always be buying the asset class that is currently out of favor—on a relative basis, at least—and selling the asset class with the highest market value. In the preceding example, this was the case when the investor underweighted his stock allocation after stock prices rose substantially compared to bond prices. DuBois (1992) notes that how frequently the investor chooses to adjust the asset class mix in the portfolio will depend on several factors, such as the general level of volatility in the capital markets, the relative size of the equity and fixed-income risk premiums, and changes in the fundamental macroeconomic environment.

| Exhibit 16.24 | Strategic Asset Allocations for Defined-Benefit Pension Plans |

A. Sponsors of over $100 Million

Asset Class	CORPORATE		UNION		PUBLIC	
	2001	1997	2001	1997	2001	1997
Cash/Equivalents	4.1%	4.7%	5.5%	5.9%	2.2%	2.7%
U.S. Equity	45.4	46.9	37.9	35.1	45.8	43.8
International Equity	6.1	6.8	0.8	1.0	8.7	7.6
U.S. Fixed Income	28.2	30.0	41.1	42.0	34.6	35.4
International Fixed Income	0.6	0.8	0.1	0.3	1.3	1.7
U.S. Balanced Accounts	2.1	2.3	2.0	2.5	1.6	3.4
International Balanced Accounts	0.1	0.2	n/a	n/a	n/a	n/a
Equity Real Estate	1.1	1.5	2.0	2.0	2.3	2.3
Mortgages	0.2	0.2	1.5	2.4	0.2	0.6
Company's Own Stock	0.8	0.9	0.2	0.2	n/a	n/a
Convertibles	0.1	0.1	n/a	n/a	0.1	n/a
GICs/BICs	0.8	1.2	0.5	1.3	0.4	0.6
Venture Capital	0.5	0.3	n/a	0.1	0.9	0.5
General Insurance Account	1.8	2.0	3.1	3.6	0.1	0.1
Other	7.0	1.9	5.0	3.6	1.1	1.1

B. Sponsors of $10 Million to $100 Million

Asset Class	CORPORATE		UNION		PUBLIC	
	2001	1997	2001	1997	2001	1997
Cash/Equivalents	8.7%	9.1%	5.9%	7.5%	5.0%	6.1%
U.S. Equity	35.0	36.2	38.3	29.1	40.4	38.3
International Equity	0.5	2.4	0.1	0.3	2.4	2.5
U.S. Fixed Income	24.6	30.6	37.9	44.5	43.6	45.5
International Fixed Income	0.2	0.5	n/a	0.1	0.6	0.2
U.S. Balanced Accounts	0.6	2.9	0.2	0.6	3.1	3.5
International Balanced Accounts	n/a	0.1	n/a	n/a	0.0	n/a
Equity Real Estate	0.2	0.3	0.5	0.8	0.7	0.9
Mortgages	0.1	0.3	0.4	0.6	n/a	0.1
Company's Own Stock	0.4	0.6	n/a	0.1	n/a	n/a
Convertibles	n/a	0.2	n/a	0.1	n/a	n/a
GICs/BICs	0.1	2.1	0.1	1.7	1.0	1.1
Venture Capital	0.2	0.2	0.1	n/a	n/a	0.3
General Insurance Account	7.2	10.1	4.5	9.4	0.2	0.3
Other	9.3	4.3	7.5	5.0	1.3	1.2

Source: Nelson MarketPlace, Thomson Financial.

Insured Asset Allocation

Insured asset allocation likewise results in continual adjustments in the portfolio allocation. Insured asset allocation assumes that expected market returns and risks are constant over time, while the investor's objectives and constraints change as his or her wealth position changes. For example, rising portfolio values increase the investor's wealth and consequently his or her ability to handle risk, which means the investor can increase his or her exposure to risky assets. Declines in the portfolio's value lower the investor's wealth, consequently decreasing his or her ability to handle risk, which means the portfolio's exposure to risky assets must decline. Often, insured asset allocation involves only two assets, such as common stocks and T-bills. As stock prices rise, the asset allocation increases the stock component. As stock prices fall, the stock component of the mix falls while the T-bill component increases. This is opposite of what would happen under tactical asset allocation. Insured asset allocation is like the integrated approach without the feedback loop on the capital market side (i.e., C2 in Exhibit 16.22). It is sometimes called a *constant proportion* strategy because of the shifts that occur as wealth changes.

Selecting an Active Allocation Method

Which asset allocation strategy is used depends on the perceptions of the variability in the client's objectives and constraints and the perceived relationship between past and future capital market conditions. If you believe that capital market conditions are relatively constant over time, you might use insured asset allocation. If you believe that the client's goals, risk preferences, and constraints are constant, you likewise might use tactical asset allocation. Integrated asset allocation assumes that both the investor's needs and capital market conditions are variable and therefore must be constantly monitored. Under these conditions, the portfolio mix must be updated constantly to reflect current changes in these parameters.

The Internet   *Investments Online*

Equity-portfolio management is the "how-to"—it combines what we know of stock selection and portfolio theory with the practice of constructing, monitoring, and updating equity portfolios to meet the needs of individual or institutional clients. Several professional money managers describe their services on the Internet, and here's a sampling of some of them:

http://www.russell.com The home page of Frank Russell and Company contains descriptions of Russell's many services. Of special interest to us here are the links to Russell's indexes, including its various style indexes, for the United States and several other countries.

http://www.panagora.com The Web site of PanAgora Asset Management contains their investment philosophy, performance data and characteristics of their investment funds, and research papers on investment management topics authored by their staff.

http://www.firstquadrant.com First Quadrant is a leader in the application of quantitative investment techniques to equity portfolio management. The product section of this site features a description of its quantitative perspective of style management. Other sections allow users to order copies of research monographs and published articles by First Quadrant personnel.

http://www.wilshire.com Wilshire Associates, Inc., offers indexes, consulting, and other services to investors. This home page offers links to information about its indexes (the Wilshire 5000 is a widely used benchmark to represent the total equity market in the United States). The site offers a description of each Wilshire index, including such helpful information as the fundamental characteristics of each index and downloadable data.

http://www.rallc.com Research Affiliates, LLC is an investment advisory firm to money managers. They are compensated on the basis of the success of their strategies for their clients.

SUMMARY

- Passive equity portfolios attempt to track the returns of an established benchmark, such as the S&P 500, or some other benchmark that meets the investor's needs. Active portfolios attempt to add value relative to their benchmark by market timing and/or by seeking to buy undervalued stocks. Index mutual funds and exchange-traded funds are popular ways for small investors to make passive investments.

- Tracking error, which is defined as the standard deviation of the difference between the returns to a managed fund and a benchmark, is a convenient way to categorize various management styles. Portfolios with tracking errors of less than 1 percent are generally considered to be passive, while active equity strategies often have tracking errors in excess of 5 percent.

- There are several methods for constructing and managing a passive portfolio, including full replication of a benchmark or sampling. Also, several active management strategies exist, including sector rotation, the use of factor models, quantitative screens, and linear programming methods. Value- and growth-oriented strategies have become particularly popular in recent years, and style analysis helps the investor determine the exact investment style the manager is using.

- Since equity portfolios typically are used with other assets in an investor's overall portfolio, we reviewed several common asset allocation strategies, including integrated asset allocation, strategic asset allocation, tactical asset allocation, and insured asset allocation. The basic difference between these strategies is whether they rely on current market expectations or long-run projections, and whether the investor's objectives and constraints remain constant over the planning horizon or change with market conditions.

SUGGESTED READINGS

Ammann, Manuel, and Heinz Zimmermann. "Tracking Error and Tactical Asset Allocation." *Financial Analysts Journal* 57, no. 2 (March/April 2001): 32–43.

Bernstein, Richard. *Style Investing: Unique Insight into Equity Management.* New York: Wiley, 1995.

Burns, Terrence E. *Asset Allocation in a Changing World.* Charlottesville, VA: AIMR, 1998.

Dreman, David M. *Contrarian Investment Strategies: The Next Generation.* New York: Simon & Schuster, 1998.

Hopkins, Peter J. B., and C. Hayes Miller. *Country, Sector, and Company Factors in Global Equity Portfolios.* Charlottesville, VA: Research Foundation of AIMR, 2001.

QUESTIONS

1. Why have passive portfolio management strategies increased in use over time?
2. What is meant by an indexing portfolio strategy and what is the justification for this strategy? How might it differ from another passive portfolio?
3. Briefly describe four techniques considered active equity portfolio management strategies.
4. Describe several techniques for constructing a passive portfolio.
5. Discuss three strategies active managers can use to add value to their portfolios.

6. How do trading costs and market efficiencies affect the active manager? How may an active manager try to overcome these obstacles to success?

7. Discuss how the four asset allocation strategies differ from one another.

8. *CFA Examination Level III*
   Recent empirical research has suggested that holding portfolios of stocks classified as value (low price/book ratio) as opposed to growth (high price/book ratio) stocks in both U.S. and international markets has resulted in enhanced risk-adjusted returns. Critique the efficient market hypothesis in light of these findings.

9. Describe the difference between a price momentum strategy and an earnings momentum strategy. Under what conditions would you expect the two approaches to produce similar portfolios?

10. What are the trade-offs involved when constructing a portfolio using a full replication versus a sampling method?

11. Because of inflationary expectations, you expect natural resource stocks, such as mining companies and oil firms, to perform well over the next three to six months. As an active portfolio manager, describe the various methods available to take advantage of this forecast.

PROBLEMS

1. You have a portfolio with a market value of $50 million and a beta (measured against the S&P 500) of 1.2. If the market rises 10 percent, what value would you expect your portfolio to have?

2. Given the monthly returns that follow, how well did the passive portfolio track the S&P 500 benchmark? Find the R^2, alpha, and beta of the portfolio. Compute the average return differential with and without sign.

Month	Portfolio Return	S&P 500 Return
January	5.0%	5.2%
February	−2.3	−3.0
March	−1.8	−1.6
April	2.2	1.9
May	0.4	0.1
June	−0.8	−0.5
July	0.0	0.2
August	1.5	1.6
September	−0.3	−0.1
October	−3.7	−4.0
November	2.4	2.0
December	0.3	0.2

3. Using the data on asset returns from Chapter 3 (Exhibit 3.8), what percentage of the equity risk premium is consumed by trading costs of 1.5 percent? Assuming a normal distribution of returns, what is the probability that an active manager can earn a return that will overcome these trading costs?

4. *CFA Examination Level III*
   Global Advisers Company (GAC) is a SEC-registered investment counseling firm solely involved in managing international securities portfolios. After much research on the developing economy and capital markets of the country of Otunia, GAC has decided to include an investment in the Otunia stock market in its Emerging Market Commingled Fund. However, GAC has not yet decided whether to invest actively or by indexing. Your opinion on the active versus indexing decision has been solicited. A summary of the research findings follows.

Otunia's economy is fairly well diversified across agricultural and natural resources, manufacturing (both consumer and durable goods), and a growing finance sector. Transaction costs in securities markets are relatively large in Otunia because of high commissions and government "stamp taxes" on securities trades. Accounting standards and disclosure regulations are quite detailed, resulting in wide public availability of reliable information about companies' financial performance.

Capital flows into and out of Otunia and foreign ownership of Otunia securities are strictly regulated by an agency of the national government. The settlement procedures under these ownership rules often cause long delays in settling trades made by nonresidents. Senior finance officials in the government are working to deregulate capital flows and foreign ownership, but GAC's political consultant believes that isolationist sentiment may prevent much real progress in the short run.

a. Briefly discuss four aspects of the Otunia environment that favor investing actively and four aspects that favor indexing.

b. Recommend whether GAC should invest in Otunia actively or by indexing and justify your recommendation based on the factors identified in Part a.

 5. *CFA Examination Level III*
Betty Black's investment club wants to buy the stock of either NewSoft Inc. or Capital Corp. In this connection, Black has prepared the following table. You have been asked to help her interpret the data, based on your forecast for a healthy economy and a strong market over the next 12 months.

	NewSoft Inc.	Capital Corp.	S&P 500 Index
Current price	$30	$32	n/a
Industry	Computer Software	Capital Goods	n/a
P/E ratio (current)	25×	14×	16×
P/E ratio (5-yr avg)	27×	16×	16×
P/B ratio (current)	10×	3×	3×
P/B ratio (5-yr avg)	12×	4×	2×
Beta	1.5	1.1	1.0
Dividend yield	0.3%	2.7%	2.8%

NewSoft's shares have higher price/earnings (*P/E*) and price/book (*P/B*) ratios than those of Capital Corp. Identify and briefly discuss three reasons why the disparity in ratios may not indicate that NewSoft's shares are overvalued relative to the shares of Capital Corp. Answer the question in terms of the two ratios, and assume that there have been no extraordinary events affecting either company.

6. As the chief investment officer for a money management firm specializing in taxable individual investors, you are trying to establish a strategic asset allocation for two different clients. You have established that Ms. A has a risk-tolerance factor of 8 while Mr. B's risk-tolerance factor is 27. The characteristics for four model portfolios follow:

	ASSET MIX			
Portfolio	Stock	Bond	ER	σ^2
1	5%	95%	8%	5%
2	25	75	9	10
3	70	30	10	16
4	90	10	11	25

a. Calculate the expected utility of each prospective portfolio for each of the two clients.

b. Which portfolio represents the optimal strategic allocation for Ms. A? Which portfolio is optimal for Mr. B? Explain why there is a difference in these two outcomes.

c. For Ms. A, what level of risk tolerance would leave her indifferent between having Portfolio 1 or Portfolio 2 as her strategic allocation? Demonstrate.

7. *CFA Examination Level II*
   Briefly discuss whether active asset allocation among countries could consistently outperform a world market index. Include a discussion of the implications of *integration versus segmentation* of international financial markets as it pertains to portfolio diversification, but ignore the issue of stock selection.

8. Consider the annual returns produced by two different active equity portfolio managers (A and B) as well as those to the stock index with which they are both compared:

Period	Manager A	Manager B	Index
1	12.8%	13.9%	11.8%
2	−2.1	−4.2	−2.2
3	15.6	13.5	18.9
4	0.8	2.9	−0.5
5	−7.9	−5.9	−3.9
6	23.2	26.3	21.7
7	−10.4	−11.2	−13.2
8	5.6	5.5	5.3
9	2.3	4.2	2.4
10	19.0	18.8	19.7

   a. Did either manager outperform the index, based on the average annual return differential that he or she produced relative to the benchmark? Demonstrate.

   b. Calculate the tracking error for each manager relative to the index. Which manager did a better job of limiting his or her client's unsystematic risk exposure? Explain.

THOMSON ONE | Business School Edition

1. Consider four different stock market indexes representing different equity investment styles:
   Large-cap, Value: Russell 1000-Value (FRUS1VA)
   Large-cap, Growth: Russell 1000-Growth (FRUS1GR)
   Small-cap, Value: Russell 2000-Value (FRUS2VA)
   Small-cap, Growth: Russell 2000-Growth (FRUS2GR).
   Which of these investment styles would have been the most profitable to invest in over the following periods: (a) the past three months, (b) the past year, and (c) the past five years? [Hint: You can calculate the growth of a one dollar investment in all four strategies by taking the ratio of the beginning and ending index values for each of the respective investment periods.] Which strategy appears to have been the riskiest? Why?

2. Using the same companies represented in Panels A and B of Exhibit 16.15, update the financial information using the most recent data available. Given your analysis, would all of the various firms shown in the exhibit still qualify to be included in the same portfolio? In particular, should JPM now be classified as a value stock or a growth stock? (Note: Use the longest-term EPS growth forecast available in constructing your display.)

3. Use the "Search for Companies" function to create your own portfolio according to a specific investment style mandate (e.g., large-cap growth, high return momentum, industry-specific) of your own choosing. Once you have established this portfolio, use the "Save Set" command to name and save the identity of the portfolio companies you have selected. Analyze your portfolio's recent valuation, financial, and performance characteristics by accessing the various summary reports available under the "Portfolios" tab. [Note: You should experiment with the various search commands available in the company search menu in order to get acquainted with the multitude of portfolios that you can form as well as the scope of the financial reports that can be created for those portfolios.]

Part 5

Analysis and Management of Bonds

For most investors, bonds receive limited attention and very little respect. This is surprising when one considers that the total market value of the bond market in the United States and in most other countries is substantially larger than the market value of the stock market. For example, by the end of 2004, the U.S. market value of all publicly issued bonds was more than $18 trillion, while the market value of all stocks was about $16 trillion. On a global basis, the values are about $36 trillion for bonds versus $33 trillion for stocks. Beyond the size factor, bonds have a reputation for low, unexciting rates of return. Although this may have been true 40 or 50 years ago, it certainly has not been true during the past 15 to 20 years. Specifically, the average annual compound rate of return on government/corporate bonds for the period 1980–2004 was slightly over 10 percent versus about 14 percent for common stocks. These rates of return along with corresponding standard deviations (7 percent for bonds versus 17 percent for stocks) and the relatively low correlation between stocks and bonds (about 0.25) indicate that there are substantial opportunities in bonds for individual and institutional investors to enhance their risk–return performance.

The chapters in this section are intended to provide (1) a basic understanding of bonds and the bond markets around the world, (2) background on analyzing returns and risks in the bond market, (3) insights regarding the valuation of bonds, including numerous new fixed-income securities with very unusual cash flow characteristics, and (4) an understanding of either active or passive bond portfolio management.

Chapter 17 describes the global bond market in terms of country participation and the makeup of the bond market in major countries. Also, we examine characteristics of bonds in alternative categories, such as government, corporate, and municipal. We also discuss the many new corporate bond instruments developed in the United States, such as asset-backed securities, zero coupon bonds, high-yield bonds, and inflation protection securities. While the use of these securities globally has generally been limited to the large developed markets, it is certain that they will eventually be used around the world. Finally, we consider sources of price information needed by bond investors.

Chapter 18 is concerned with the analysis and valuation of bonds. This includes a detailed discussion of how one values a bond using a single discount rate or using spot rates. We also evaluate alternative rate of return measures for bonds. Subsequently, we consider what factors affect yields on bonds and what characteristics influence the volatility of bond returns including the very important concept of bond duration, which is a measure of bond price volatility that is important in active and passive bond portfolio management. We also consider bond convexity and the impact it has on bond price volatility. Notably, these concepts are examined for option-free securities as well as for how they apply to a growing set of securities with embedded options.

Chapter 19 considers how to use the background provided in Chapter 17 and Chapter 18 to create and manage a bond portfolio. We consider three major categories of portfolio strategies in detail. The first is passive portfolio management strategies, which include either a simple buy-and-hold strategy or indexing to one of the major benchmarks. The second category includes active management strategies that can involve one of five alternatives: interest rate anticipation, valuation analysis, credit analysis, yield spread analysis, or bond swaps. The third category includes matched funding strategies, which include constructing dedicated portfolios, constructing classical or contingent immunization portfolios, or horizon matching.

The fact that three fairly long chapters are devoted to the study of bonds attests to the importance of the topic and the extensive research done in this area. During the past 20 years, there have been more developments related to the valuation and portfolio management of bonds than of stocks. This growth of the fixed-income sector does not detract from the importance of equities but certainly enhances the significance of fixed-income securities. Finally, readers should keep in mind that this growth in size, sophistication, and specialization of the bond market implies numerous and varied career opportunities in the bond area, including trading these securities, valuation, credit analysis, and domestic and global portfolio management.

Chapter 17

Bond Fundamentals

After you read this chapter, you should be able to answer the following questions:

- What are some of the basic features of bonds that affect their risk, return, and value?
- What is the current country structure of the world bond market and how has the makeup of the global bond market changed in recent years?
- What are the major components of the world bond market and the international bond market?
- How does the makeup of the bond market differ in major countries?
- What are bond ratings and what is their purpose? What is the difference between investment-grade bonds and high-yield (junk) bonds?
- What are the characteristics of bonds in the major bond categories, such as governments (including TIPS), agencies, municipalities, and corporates?
- What are the important characteristics of corporate bond issues developed in the United States during the past decade, such as mortgage-backed securities, other asset-backed securities, zero coupon and deep discount bonds, high-yield bonds, and structured notes?
- How do you read the quotes available for the alternative bond categories (e.g., governments, municipalities, corporates)?

The global bond market is large and diverse and represents an important investment opportunity. This chapter is concerned with publicly issued, long-term, nonconvertible debt obligations of public and private issuers in the United States and major global markets. In later chapters, we consider preferred stock and convertible bonds. An understanding of bonds is helpful in an efficient market because the existence of U.S. and foreign bonds increases the universe of investments available for the creation of a diversified portfolio.

In this chapter, we review some basic features of bonds and examine the structure of the world bond market. The bulk of the chapter involves an in-depth discussion of the major fixed-income investments. The chapter ends with a brief review of the price information sources for bond investors.

BASIC FEATURES OF A BOND

Public bonds are long-term, fixed-obligation debt securities packaged in convenient, affordable denominations for sale to individuals and financial institutions. They differ from other debt, such as individual mortgages and privately placed debt obligations, because they are sold to the public rather than channeled directly to a single lender. Bond issues are considered fixed-income securities because they impose fixed financial obligations on the issuers. Specifically, the issuer agrees to

1. Pay a fixed amount of *interest periodically* to the holder of record
2. Repay a fixed amount of *principal* at the date of maturity

Normally, interest on bonds is paid every six months, although some bond issues pay in intervals as short as a month or as long as a year. The principal is due at maturity; this *par value* of the issue is rarely less than $1,000. A bond has a specified term to maturity, which defines the life of the issue. The public debt market typically is divided into three time segments based on an issue's original maturity:

1. Short-term issues with maturities of one year or less. The market for these instruments is commonly known as the **money market**.
2. Intermediate-term issues with maturities in excess of 1 year but less than 10 years. These instruments are known as **notes**.
3. Long-term obligations with maturities in excess of 10 years, called *bonds.*

The lives of debt obligations change constantly as the issues progress toward maturity. Thus, issues that have been outstanding in the secondary market for any period of time eventually move from long-term to intermediate to short-term. This change in maturity is important because a major determinant of the price volatility of bonds is the remaining life (maturity) of the issue.

Bond Characteristics

A bond can be characterized based on (1) its intrinsic features, (2) its type, (3) its indenture provisions, or (4) the features that affect its cash flows and/or its maturity.

Intrinsic Features   The coupon, maturity, principal value, and the type of ownership are important intrinsic features of a bond. The **coupon** of a bond indicates the income that the bond investor will receive over the life (or holding period) of the issue. This is known as *interest income, coupon income,* or *nominal yield.*

The **term to maturity** specifies the date or the number of years before a bond matures (or expires). There are two different types of maturity. The most common is a **term bond**, which has a single maturity date. Alternatively, a **serial obligation bond** issue has a series of maturity dates, perhaps 20 or 25. Each maturity, although a subset of the total issue, is really a small bond issue with generally a different coupon. Municipalities issue most serial bonds.

The **principal**, or **par value**, of an issue represents the original value of the obligation. This is generally stated in $1,000 increments from $1,000 to $25,000 or more. Principal value is *not* the same as the bond's market value. The market prices of many issues rise above or fall below their principal values because of differences between their coupons and the prevailing market rate of interest. If the market interest rate is above the coupon rate, the bond will sell at a discount to par. If the market rate is below the bond's coupon, it will sell at a premium above par. If the coupon is comparable to the prevailing market interest rate, the market value of the bond will be close to its original principal value.

Finally, bonds differ in terms of ownership. With a **bearer bond**, the holder, or bearer, is the owner, so the issuer keeps no record of ownership. Interest from a bearer bond is obtained by clipping coupons attached to the bonds and sending them to the issuer for payment. In contrast, the issuers of **registered bonds** maintain records of owners and pay the interest directly to them.

Types of Issues   In contrast to common stock, companies can have many different bond issues outstanding at the same time. Bonds can have different types of collateral and be either senior, unsecured, or subordinated (junior) securities. **Secured (senior) bonds** are backed by a legal claim on some specified property of the issuer in the case of default. For example, mortgage bonds are secured by real estate assets; equipment trust certificates, which are used by railroads and airlines, provide a senior claim on the firm's equipment.

Unsecured bonds (debentures) are backed only by the promise of the issuer to pay interest and principal on a timely basis. As such, they are secured by the general credit of the issuer. **Subordinate (junior) debentures** possess a claim on income and assets that is subordinated to other debentures. Income issues are the most junior type because interest on them is paid only if it is earned. Although income bonds are unusual in the corporate sector, they are very popular municipal issues, where they are referred to as **revenue bonds**. Finally, **refunding issues** provide funds to prematurely retire another issue.

The type of issue has only a marginal effect on comparative yield because it is the credibility of the issuer that determines bond quality. A study of corporate bond price behavior by Hickman (1958) found that whether the issuer pledged collateral did not become important until the bond issue approached default. The collateral and security characteristics of a bond influence yield differentials only when these factors affect the bond's quality ratings.

Indenture Provisions   The *indenture* is the contract between the issuer and the bondholder specifying the issuer's legal requirements. A trustee (usually a bank) acting on behalf of the bondholders ensures that all the indenture provisions are met, including the timely payment of interest and principal. All the factors that dictate a bond's features, its type, and its maturity are set forth in the indenture.

Features Affecting a Bond's Maturity   Investors should be aware of the three alternative call option features that can affect the life (maturity) of a bond. One extreme is a *freely callable* provision that allows the issuer to retire the bond at any time with a typical notification period of 30 to 60 days. The other extreme is a *noncallable* provision wherein the issuer cannot retire the bond prior to its maturity.[1] Intermediate between these is a *deferred call* provision, which means the issue cannot be called for a certain period of time after the date of issue (e.g., 5 to 10 years). At the end of the deferred call period, the issue becomes freely callable. Callable bonds have a **call premium**, which is the amount above maturity value that the issuer must pay to the bondholder for prematurely retiring the bond.

A *nonrefunding provision* prohibits a call and premature retirement of an issue from the proceeds of a lower-coupon refunding bond. This is meant to protect the bondholder from a typical refunding, but it is not foolproof. An issue with a nonrefunding provision can be called and retired prior to maturity using other sources of funds, such as excess cash from operations, the sale of assets, or proceeds from a sale of common stock. This occurred on several occasions during the 1980s and 1990s when many issuers retired nonrefundable high-coupon issues early because they could get the cash from one of these other sources and felt that this was a good financing decision.

---

[1]The main issuer of noncallable bonds between 1985 and 2005 was the U.S. Treasury. Corporate long-term bonds typically have contained some form of call provision, except during periods of relatively low interest rates (e.g., 1994–2001) when the probability of exercising the option was very low. We discuss this notion in more detail in Chapter 18 in connection with the analysis of embedded options.

Another important indenture provision that can affect a bond's maturity is the **sinking fund**, which specifies that a bond must be paid off systematically over its life rather than only at maturity. There are numerous sinking-fund arrangements, and the bondholder should recognize this as a feature that can change the stated maturity of a bond. The size of the sinking fund can be a percentage of a given issue or a percentage of the total debt outstanding, or it can be a fixed or variable sum stated on a dollar or percentage basis. Similar to a call feature, sinking fund payments may commence at the end of the first year or may be deferred for 5 or 10 years from date of the issue. The amount of the issue that must be repaid before maturity from a sinking fund can range from a nominal sum to 100 percent. Like a call, the sinking-fund feature typically carries a nominal premium but is generally smaller than the straight call premium (e.g., 1 percent). For example, a bond issue with a 20-year maturity might have a sinking fund that requires that 5 percent of the issue be retired every year beginning in year 10. By year 20, half of the issue has been retired and the rest is paid off at maturity. Sinking-fund provisions have a small effect on comparative yields at the time of issue but have little subsequent impact on price behavior.

A sinking-fund provision is an obligation and must be carried out regardless of market conditions. Although a sinking fund allows the issuer to call bonds on a random basis, most bonds are retired for sinking-fund purposes through direct negotiations with institutional holders. Essentially, the trustee negotiates with an institution to buy back the necessary amount of bonds at a price slightly above the current market price.

Rates of Return on Bonds

The rate of return on a bond is computed in the same way as the rate of return on stock or any asset. It is determined by the beginning and ending price and the cash flows during the holding period. The major difference between stocks and bonds is that the interim cash flow on bonds (i.e., the interest) is contractual and accrues over time as discussed subsequently, whereas the dividends on stock may vary. Therefore, the holding period return (HPR) for a bond will be

17.1
$$\text{HPR}_{i,t} = \frac{P_{i,t+1} + Int_{i,t}}{P_{i,t}}$$

where:

$\text{HPR}_{i,t}$ = the holding period return for bond i during Period t
$P_{i,t+1}$ = the market price of bond i at the end of Period t
$P_{i,t}$ = the market price of bond i at the beginning of Period t
$Int_{i,t}$ = the interest paid or accrued on bond i during Period t. Because the interest payment is contractual, it accrues over time and if a bond owner sells the bond between interest payments, the sale price includes accrued interest[2]

The holding period yield (HPY) is:

17.2
$$\text{HPY} = \text{HPR} - 1$$

Note that the only contractual factor is the amount of interest payments. The beginning and ending bond prices are determined by market forces, as discussed in Chapter 11. Notably, the ending price is determined by market forces unless the bond is held to maturity, in which case the investor will receive the par value. These price variations in bonds mean that investors in

---

[2]The concept of accrued interest will be discussed further in Chapter 18 when we consider the valuation of bonds.

bonds can experience capital gains or losses. Interest rate volatility has increased substantially since the 1960s, and this has caused large price fluctuations in bonds.[3] As a result, capital gains or losses have become a major component of the rates of return on bonds.

THE GLOBAL BOND MARKET STRUCTURE[4]

The market for fixed-income securities is substantially larger than the listed equity exchanges (NYSE, TSE, LSE) because corporations tend to issue bonds rather than common stock. Federal Reserve figures indicate that in the United States during 2004, 20 percent of all new security issues were equity, which included preferred as well as common stock. Corporations issue less common or preferred stock because firms derive most of their equity financing from internally generated funds (i.e., retained earnings). Also, although the equity market is strictly corporations, the bond market in most countries has four noncorporate sectors: the pure government sector (e.g., the Treasury in the United States), government agencies (e.g., FNMA), state and local government bonds (municipals), and international bonds (e.g., Yankees and Eurobonds in the United States).

The size of the global bond market and the distribution among countries can be gleaned from Exhibit 17.1, which lists the dollar value of debt outstanding and the percentage distribution

Exhibit 17.1	Total Face Value and Percentage of Total for Index-Qualifying Fixed Income Securities by Year (USD terms in millions)

Currency	2004	Percent	2003	Percent	2002	Percent
US Dollars	10,615,955	42.77%	10,181,215	43.73%	9,712,596	44.86%
Euro	7,526,638	30.32%	7,071,654	30.37%	6,520,821	30.12%
Japanese Yen	3,992,936	16.09%	3,645,001	15.65%	3,283,443	15.16%
Pound Sterling	1,132,734	4.56%	994,104	4.27%	877,950	4.05%
Canadian Dollar	541,192	2.18%	500,263	2.15%	470,166	2.17%
Indian Rupee	154,546	0.62%	146,524	0.63%	127,511	0.59%
Australian Dollar	143,120	0.58%	127,661	0.55%	117,588	0.54%
Swedish Krone	111,616	0.45%	106,711	0.46%	97,348	0.45%
Korean Won	110,370	0.44%	69,408	0.30%	46,400	0.21%
Danish Krone	84,643	0.34%	86,314	0.37%	90,448	0.42%
Taiwanese Dollar	81,020	0.33%	71,387	0.31%	64,611	0.30%
Swiss Franc	79,663	0.32%	68,680	0.29%	58,550	0.27%
All Other	247,119	0.99%	215,201	0.92%	184,589	0.85%
Total	**24,821,550**	**100.00%**	**23,284,123**	**100.00%**	**21,652,020**	**100.00%**
Annual Growth Rate		*6.60%*		*7.54%*		*10.36%*

Source: Adapted from data in Phil Galdi, "Growth Trends in the World Bond Markets," Merrill Lynch, January 28, 2005.

[3]The analysis of bond price volatility is discussed in detail in Chapter 18.
[4]For a further discussion of global bond markets, see Steward (2005), "International Bond Markets and Instruments"; Steward, Lynch, and Fabozzi (2005), "International Bond Investing and Portfolio Management"; and Malvey (2005), "Global Credit Bond Portfolio Management," all in *The Handbook of Fixed-Income Securities*, 7th ed., ed. Frank J. Fabozzi (New York: McGraw-Hill, 2005).

for the major currencies for the years 2002–2004. There has been consistent overall growth, at the rate of 6 to 10 percent a year. Also, the currency trends are significant. Specifically, the U.S. dollar market went from 45 percent of the total world bond market in 2002 to about 43 percent in 2004. A significant change in 1999 was the creation of the Eurozone sector, which includes a large part of Europe (i.e., Germany, Italy, France) with the significant exception of the United Kingdom. Notably, this Euro currency sector has held at about 30 percent over the three-year period.

Participating Issuers

In the Merrill Lynch report, there are five different categories of bonds for each currency: (1) Sovereign bonds (e.g., the U.S. Treasury), (2) Quasi and Foreign Governments (including agency bonds), (3) Securitized and collateralized bonds from governments or corporations, (4) Directly issued corporate bonds, and (5) High-yield and/or emerging market bonds. The division of bonds among these five categories for three large currency markets and the Eurozone during 2004 is contained in Exhibit 17.2.

Sovereigns   The market for government securities is the largest sector in Japan. It involves a variety of debt instruments issued to meet the growing needs of this government. It is generally a stable component for other currencies.

Quasi Governments (agencies) and Foreign Governments   Agency issues have become a major segment in the U.S. dollar and pound sterling market (over 12 percent) but are a smaller proportion in other countries (e.g., about 8 percent in Japan). These agencies represent political subdivisions of the government, although the securities are *not* typically direct obligations of the government. The U.S. agency market has two types of issuers: government-sponsored enterprises and federal agencies. The proceeds of agency bond issues are used to finance many legislative programs. Foreign government are issues from a country but not in its own currency (Japanese government issue in dollars and sold in U.S.).

Securitized/Collateralized Issues   These can be either government agencies or corporate issues that are backed by cash flow securities such as mortgages or car loans. Collateralized securities can include several different issues and structured cash flows. As shown in Exhibit 17.2, this has become a major sector in the U.S. and fairly strong in the Eurozone countries.

Corporations   The major nongovernmental issuer of debt is the corporate sector. The importance of this sector differs dramatically among countries. It is a slow growth factor in the United States; a smaller sector in Japan and in the Euro currency coutries and a significant part of pound sterling bonds.

The market for corporate bonds is commonly subdivided into several segments: industrials, public utilities, transportation, and financial issues. The specific makeup varies between countries.[5]

High Yield/Emerging Market   This section includes both high-yield bonds (noninvestment grade) from corporations in developed countries, and both government and corporate issues from emerging market countries such as China and India where the bonds can be either investment grade or high yield (noninvestment grade). Notably, the only currency where this sector is

---

[5]This sector of the bond market is described in more detail later in this chapter. It is possible to distinguish another sector that exists in the United States but not in other countries—institutional bonds. These are corporate bonds issued by a variety of *private, nonprofit institutions,* such as schools, hospitals, and churches. They are not broken out because they are only a minute part of the U.S. market and do not exist elsewhere.

| Exhibit 17.2 | Makeup of Bonds Outstanding by Currency: 31-December-2004 (USD terms in millions) |

	2004	
	Total Value	Percent of Total
A. U.S. Dollars		
Sovereign	3,657,702	34.5
Quasi & Foreign Govt	1,338,726	12.6
Securitized/Collateralized	2,930,919	27.6
Corporate	1,937,052	18.2
High Yield/Emerging Mkt.	751,555	7.1
Total	10,615,955	100.0
B. Euros		
Sovereign	4,820,940	64.1
Quasi & Foreign Govt	594,973	7.9
Securitized/Collateralized	924,098	12.3
Corporate	1,088,349	14.5
High Yield/Emerging Mkt.	98,278	1.3
Total	7,526,638	100.0
C. Japanese Yen		
Sovereign	3,249,865	81.4
Quasi & Foreign Govt	297,666	7.5
Securitized/Collateralized	3,598	0.1
Corporate	441,807	11.1
High Yield/Emerging Mkt.	0	0.0
Total	3,992,936	100.0
D. Pound Sterling		
Sovereign	568,551	50.2
Quasi & Foreign Govt	144,675	12.8
Securitized/Collateralized	67,618	6.0
Corporate	339,153	29.9
High Yield/Emerging Mkt.	12,737	1.1
Total	1,132,734	100.0

Source: Adapted from data in Phil Galdi, "Growth Trends in the World Bond Markets," Merrill Lynch, January 28, 2005.

significant is U.S. dollars where it constitutes over 7 percent. The other currencies have nominal amounts but these sectors are expected to grow.

Participating Investors

Numerous individual and institutional investors with diverse investment objectives participate in the bond market. Individual investors are a minor portion because of the market's complexity and the high minimum denominations of most issues. Institutional investors typically account for 90 to 95 percent of the trading, although different segments of the market are more institutionalized than others. For example, institutions are involved heavily in the agency market, but they are less active in the corporate sector.

A variety of institutions invest in the bond market. Life insurance companies invest in corporate bonds and, to a lesser extent, in Treasury and agency securities. Commercial banks invest in municipal bonds and government and agency issues. Property and liability insurance companies concentrate on municipal bonds and Treasuries. Private and government pension funds are heavily committed to corporates and invest in Treasuries and agencies. Finally, fixed-income mutual funds have grown substantially in size and their demand spans the full spectrum of the market as they develop bond funds that meet the needs of a variety of investors. As we will discuss in Chapter 24, municipal bond funds and corporate bond funds (including high-yield bonds) have experienced significant growth.

Alternative institutions tend to favor different sectors of the bond market based on two factors: (1) the tax code applicable to the institution and (2) the nature of the institution's liability structure. For example, because commercial banks are subject to normal taxation and have fairly short-term liability structures, they favor short- to intermediate-term municipals. Pension funds are virtually tax-free institutions with long-term commitments, so they prefer high-yielding, long-term government or corporate bonds. Such institutional investment preferences can affect the short-run supply and demand of loanable funds and impact interest rate changes.

Bond Ratings

Agency ratings are an integral part of the bond market because most corporate and municipal bonds are rated by one or more of the rating agencies. The exceptions are very small issues and bonds from certain industries, such as bank issues. These are known as *nonrated bonds*. There are three major rating agencies: (1) Fitch Investors Service, (2) Moody's, and (3) Standard and Poor's.

Bond ratings provide the fundamental analysis for thousands of issues. The rating agencies analyze the issuing organization and the specific issue to determine the probability of default and inform the market of their analyses through their ratings.[6]

The primary question in bond credit analysis is whether the firm can service its debt in a timely manner over the life of a given issue. Consequently, the rating agencies consider expectations over the life of the issue, along with the historical and current financial position of the company. We consider default estimation further when we discuss high-yield (junk) bonds.

Studies by authors such as Belkaoui (1980) and Gentry, Whitford and Newbold (1988) have examined the relationship between bond ratings and issue quality as indicated by financial variables. The results clearly demonstrated that bond ratings were positively related to profitability, size, and cash flow coverage, and they were inversely related to financial leverage and earnings instability.

---

[6]For a detailed listing of rating classes and a listing of factors considered in assigning ratings, see "Bond Ratings" in Levine (1988a). For a study that examines the value of two bond ratings, see Hsueh and Kidwell (1988). An analysis of the bond-rating industry is contained in Cantor and Packer (1995).

The original ratings assigned to bonds have an impact on their marketability and effective interest rate. Generally, the three agencies' ratings agree. When they do not, the issue is said to have a *split rating*.[7] Seasoned issues are regularly reviewed to ensure that the assigned rating is still valid. If not, revisions are made either upward or downward. Revisions are usually done in increments of one rating grade. The ratings are based on both the company and the issue. After an evaluation of the creditworthiness of the total company is completed, a company rating is assigned to the firm's most senior unsecured issue. All junior bonds receive lower ratings based on indenture specifications. Also, an issue could receive a higher rating than justified because of credit-enhancement devices, such as the attachment of bank letters of credit, surety, or indemnification bonds from insurance companies.

The agencies assign letter ratings depicting what they view as the risk of default of an obligation. The letter ratings range from AAA (Aaa) to D. Exhibit 17.3 describes the various ratings assigned by the major services. Except for slight variations in designations, the meaning and interpretation are basically the same. The agencies modify the ratings with + and – signs for Fitch and S&P or with numbers (1-2-3) for Moody's. As an example, an A+ (A1) bond is at the top of the A-rated group, while A– (A3) is at the bottom of the A category.

The top four ratings—AAA (or Aaa), AA (or Aa), A, and BBB (or Baa)—are generally considered to be *investment-grade securities*. The next level of securities is known as *speculative bonds* and includes the BB- and B-rated obligations. The C categories are generally either income obligations or revenue bonds, many of which are trading flat. (Flat bonds are in arrears on their interest payments.) In the case of D-rated obligations, the issues are in outright default, and the ratings indicate the bonds' relative salvage values.[8]

ALTERNATIVE BOND ISSUES

We have described the basic features available for all bonds and the overall structure of the global bond market in terms of the issuers of bonds and investors in bonds. In this section, we provide a detailed discussion of the bonds available from the major issuers of bonds. The presentation is longer than you would expect because when we discuss each issuing unit, such as governments, municipalities, or corporations, we briefly consider the bonds available in several world financial centers, such as Japan, the United Kingdom, and the several major countries in the Eurozone.

Domestic Government Bonds

United States As shown in Exhibit 17.2, a significant percent of the U.S. dollar fixed-income market is U.S. Treasury obligations. The U.S. government, backed by the full faith and credit of the U.S. Treasury, issues Treasury bills (T-bills), which mature in less than one year, and two forms of long-term obligations: government notes, which have maturities of 10 years or less, and Treasury bonds, with maturities of 10 to 30 years. Current Treasury obligations come in denominations of $1,000 and $10,000. The interest income from the U.S. government securities is subject to federal income tax but exempt from state and local levies. These bonds are popular because of their high credit quality, substantial liquidity, and noncallable feature.

---

[7]Split ratings are discussed in Billingsley, Lamy, Marr, and Thompson (1985); Ederington (1985); and Liu and Moore (1987).

[8]Bonds rated below investment grade are also referred to as "high-yield bonds" or "junk" bonds. These high-yield bonds are discussed in the subsequent section on corporate bonds.

| Exhibit 17.3 | Description of Bond Ratings |

	Fitch	Moody's	Standard & Poor's	Definition
High grade	AAA	Aaa	AAA	The highest rating assigned to a debt instrument, indicating an extremely strong capacity to pay principal and interest. Bonds in this category are often referred to as *gilt edge securities*.
	AA	Aa	AA	High-quality bonds by all standards with a strong capacity to pay principal and interest. These bonds are rated lower primarily because the margins of protection are less strong than those for Aaa and AAA bonds.
Medium grade	A	A	A	These bonds possess many favorable investment attributes, but elements may suggest a susceptibility to impairment given adverse economic changes.
	BBB	Baa	BBB	Bonds that are regarded as having adequate capacity to pay principal and interest, but certain protective elements may be lacking in the event of adverse economic conditions that could lead to a weakened capacity for payment.
Speculative	BB	Ba	BB	These bonds are considered to have only moderate protection of principal and interest payments during both good and bad times.
	B	B	B	Bonds that generally lack characteristics of other desirable investments. Assurance of interest and principal payments over any long period of time may be small.
Default	CCC	Caa	CCC	Poor-quality issues that may be in default or in danger of default.
	CC	Ca	CC	Highly speculative issues that are often in default or possess other marked shortcomings.
	C			The lowest-rated class of bonds. These issues can be regarded as extremely poor in investment quality.
		C	C	Rating given to income bonds on which no interest is being paid.
	DDD, DD, D		D	Issues in default with principal or interest payments in arrears. Such bonds are extremely speculative and should be valued only on the basis of their value in liquidation or reorganization.

Sources: *Bond Guide* (New York: Standard & Poor's, monthly); *Bond Record* (New York: Moody's Investors Services, Inc., monthly); *Rating Register* (New York: Fitch Investors Service, Inc., monthly).

Short-term T-bills differ from notes and bonds because they are sold at a discount from par to provide the desired yield. The return is the difference between the purchase price and the par at maturity. In contrast, government notes and bonds carry semiannual coupons that specify the nominal yield of the obligations.

Government notes and bonds have unusual call features. First, the period specified for the deferred call feature on Treasury issues is very long and is generally measured relative to the maturity date rather than from date of issue. They generally cannot be called until five years prior to their maturity date. Notably, *all* U.S. Treasury issues since 1989 have been noncallable.

Treasury Inflation-Protected Securities (TIPS)[9]   The Treasury began issuing these inflation-indexed bonds in January 1997 to appeal to investors who wanted or needed a *real* default-free rate of return. To ensure the investors will receive the promised yield in real terms, the bond principal and interest payments are indexed to the *Consumer Price Index for All Urban Consumers (CPI-U)* published by the Bureau of Labor Statistics. Because inflation is generally not known until several months after the fact, the index value used has a three-month lag built in—for example, for a bond issued on June 30, 2005, the beginning base index value used would be the CPI value as of March 30, 2005. Following the issuance of a TIPS bond, its principal value is adjusted every six months to reflect the inflation since the base period. In turn, the interest payment is computed based on this adjusted principal—that is, the interest payments equal the original coupon times the adjusted principal. The example in Exhibit 17.4 demonstrates how the principal and interest payments are computed. As shown in this example, both the interest payments and the principal payments are adjusted over time to reflect the prevailing inflation, thereby ensuring that the investor receives a *real* rate of return on these bonds of 3.50 percent.

Notably, these bonds can also be used to derive the prevailing market estimate of the expected rate of inflation during the remaining maturity of the TIPS bond. For example, if we assume that when the bond is issued on July 15, 2003, it sells at par for a YTM of 3.50 percent, while a nominal Treasury note of equal maturity is sold at a YTM of 5.75 percent. This differential implies that investors expect an average annual rate of inflation of 2.25 percent during this five-year period. If, a year later, the spread increased to 2.45 percent, it would indicate that investors expect a further increase in the inflation rate during the next four years.

Japan[10]   The second-largest country government bond market in the world is Japan's. It is controlled by the Japanese government and the Bank of Japan (Japanese Central Bank). Japanese government bonds (JGBs) are an attractive investment vehicle for those favoring the Japanese yen because their quality is equal to that of U.S. Treasury securities (they are guaranteed by the government of Japan) and they are very liquid. There are three maturity segments: medium-term (2, 3, or 4 years), long-term (10 years), and super-long (private placements for 15 and 20 years). Bonds are issued in both registered and bearer form, although registered bonds can be converted to bearer bonds.

Medium-term bonds are issued monthly through a competitive auction system similar to that of U.S. Treasury bonds. Long-term bonds are authorized by the Ministry of Finance and issued monthly by the Bank of Japan through an underwriting syndicate consisting of major financial institutions. Most super-long bonds are sold through private placement to a few financial institutions. Very liquid federal government bonds account for over 50 percent of the Japanese bonds outstanding and over 80 percent of total bond trading volume in Japan.

At least 50 percent of the trading in Japanese government bonds will be in the so-called *benchmark issue* of the time. The benchmark issue is selected from 10-year coupon bonds. (As of mid-2005, the benchmark issue was a 1.30 percent coupon bond maturing in 2015.) The designation of a benchmark issue is intended to assist smaller financial institutions in their trading of government bonds by ensuring these institutions that they would have a liquid market in this particular security. Compared to the benchmark issue, the comparable most active U.S. bond within a class accounts for only about 10 percent of the volume.

---

[9]This section draws heavily from excellent articles by Shen (1998); Roll (2004); and Kothari and Shanken (2004).
[10]For additional discussion, see Viner (1988), Elton and Gruber (1990), and Fabozzi (1990a).

Exhibit 17.4 | **Principal and Interest Payment for a Treasury Inflation Protected Security (TIPS)**

Par Value—$1,000
Issued on July 15, 2003
Maturity on July 15, 2008
Coupon—3.50%
Original CPI Value—185.00

Date	Index Value[a]	Rate of Inflation	Accrued Principal	Interest Payment[b]
7/15/03	185.00	—	$1,000.00	—
1/15/04	187.78	0.015	1,015.00	$17.76
7/15/04	190.59	0.015	1,030.22	18.03
1/15/05	193.83	0.017	1,047.74	18.34
7/15/05	197.51	0.019	1,067.65	18.68
1/15/06	201.46	0.020	1,089.00	19.06
7/15/06	205.49	0.020	1,110.78	19.44
1/15/07	209.19	0.018	1,130.77	19.79
7/15/07	212.96	0.018	1,151.13	20.14
1/15/08	217.22	0.020	1,174.15	20.55
7/15/08	222.65	0.025	1,203.50	21.06

[a]The CPI index value is for the period three months prior to the date.
[b]Semiannual interest payment equals 0.0175 (accrued principal).

The yield on this benchmark bond is typically about 30 basis points below other comparable Japanese government bonds, reflecting its superior marketability. The benchmark issue changes when a designated issue matures or because of a decision by the Bank of Japan.

United Kingdom[11]   The U.K. pound sterling government bond market is made up of jobbers and brokers who act as principals or agents with negotiated commission structures. In addition, there are 27 primary dealers similar to the U.S. Treasury market.

Maturities in this market range from short gilts (maturities of less than 5 years) to medium gilts (5 to 15 years) to long gilts (15 years and longer). Government bonds either have a fixed redemption date or a range of dates with redemption at the option of the government after giving appropriate notice. Government bonds are normally registered, although bearer delivery is available.

Gilts are issued through the Bank of England (the British central bank) using the tender method, whereby prospective purchasers tender offering prices at which they hope to be allotted bonds. The price cannot be less than the minimum tender price stated in the prospectus. If the issue is oversubscribed, allotments are made first to those submitting the highest tenders and continue until a price is reached where only a partial allotment is required to fully subscribe the issue. All successful allottees pay the lowest allotment prices.

These issues are extremely liquid and are highly rated because they are guaranteed by the British government. All gilts are quoted and traded on the London Stock Exchange and pay interest semiannually.

[11]For further discussion, see European Bond Commission (1989).

Eurozone[12]   The combined value of the Euro sovereign bond market is actually larger in U.S. dollar terms than the Japanese market because it includes several relatively significant markets including Germany, which was the third largest by itself, as well as France and Italy among others. Because the Eurozone includes numerous countries that were previously economically independent, the issuing process for alternative countries differs dramatically except that all of the bonds are denominated in Euros. It is likely that over time the issuing process will become more uniform, but there will always be differences.

Government Agency Issues

In addition to pure government bonds, the federal government in each country can establish agencies that have the authority to issue their own bonds. The size and importance of these agencies differ among countries. They are a large and growing sector of the U.S. bond market, a much smaller component of the bond markets in Japan and Germany, and nonexistent in the United Kingdom.

United States   Agency securities are obligations issued by the U.S. government through either a government agency or a government-sponsored corporation. Six government-sponsored enterprises and over two dozen federal agencies issue these bonds. Exhibit 17.5 lists selected characteristics of the more popular government-sponsored and federal agency obligations.[13]

Agency issues usually pay interest semiannually, and the minimum denominations vary between $1,000 and $10,000. These obligations are not direct Treasury issues, yet they carry the full faith and credit of the U.S. government. Moreover, some of the issues are subject to state and local income tax, whereas others are exempt.[14]

One agency issue offers particularly attractive investment opportunities: GNMA ("Ginnie Mae") pass-through certificates, which are obligations of the Government National Mortgage Association.[15] These bonds represent an undivided interest in a pool of federally insured mortgages. The bondholders receive monthly payments from Ginnie Mae that include both principal and interest because the agency "passes through" mortgage payments made by the original borrower (the mortgagee) to Ginnie Mae.

The coupons on these pass-through securities are related to the interest charged on the pool of mortgages. The portion of the cash flow that represents the repayment of the principal is tax-free, but the interest income is subject to federal, state, and local taxes. The issues have minimum denominations of $25,000 with maturities of 25 to 30 years but an average life of only 12 years because, as mortgages in the pool are paid off, payments and prepayments are passed through to the investor. Therefore, unlike most bond issues, the monthly payment is not fixed because of the prepayment schedule that can vary dramatically over time when interest rates change.

As we will note in Chapter 18 in connection with the valuation of bonds with embedded options, mortgages generally have a call option whereby the homeowner has the option to prepay the mortgage. There are prepayments on these securities for two reasons: (1) because homeowners pay off their mortgages when they sell their homes and (2) because owners

---

[12]For additional information on the Eurobond market, see Molinas and Bales (2004).
[13]We will no longer distinguish between federal agency and government-sponsored obligations; instead, the term *agency* shall apply to either type of issue.
[14]Federal National Mortgage Association (Fannie Mae) debentures, for example, are subject to state and local income tax, whereas the interest income from Federal Home Loan Bank bonds is exempt. In fact, a few issues are exempt from federal income tax as well (e.g., public housing bonds).
[15]For a further discussion of mortgage-backed securities, see Davidson and Ching (2005); Crawford (2005); and McElravey (2005), all in *The Handbook of Fixed-Income Securities,* 7th ed., ed. Frank J. Fabozzi (New York: McGraw-Hill, 2005).

Exhibit 17.5 | Agency Issues: Selected Characteristics

Type of Security	Minimum Denomination	Form	Life of Issue	Tax Status	How Interest is Earned
Government Sponsored					
Federal farm credit banks	50,000	Book Entry	5 to 365 days	FT SE LE	Discount actual, 360-day year
Consolidated systemwide notes	5,000	Book Entry	6 and 9 months	FT SE LE	Interest payable at maturity, 360-day year
Consolidated systemwide bonds	1,000	Book Entry	13 months to 15 years	FT SE LE	Semiannual interest
Federal Home Loan Bank					
Consolidated discount notes	100,000	Book Entry	30 to 360 days	FT SE LE	Discount actual, 360-day year
Consolidated bonds	10,000	Book Entry	1 to 20 years	FT SE LE	Semiannual interest, 360-day year
Federal Home Loan Mortgage					
Corporation debentures	10,000	Book Entry	18 to 30 years	FT ST LT	Semiannual interest, 360-day year
Participation certificates	100,000	Registered	30 years	FT ST LT	Monthly interest and principal payments
Federal National Mortgage Association discount notes	50,000	Registered	30 to 360 days	FT ST LT	Discount actual, 360-day year
Debentures	10,000	Book Entry	1 to 30 years	FT ST LT	Semiannual interest, 360-day year
Government National Mortgage Association					
Mortgage-backed bonds	25,000	Registered	1 to 25 years	FT ST LT	Semiannual interest, 360-day year
Modified pass-throughs	25,000	Registered	12 to 40 years	FT ST LT	Monthly interest and principal payments
Student Loan Marketing Association discount note	100,000	Registered	Out to 1 year	FT SE LE	Discount actual, 360-day year

(continued)

Exhibit 17.5	Agency Issues: Selected Characteristics (continued)

Type of Security	Minimum Denomination	Form	Life of Issue	Tax Status	How Interest is Earned
Notes	10,000	Registered	3 to 10 years	FT SE LE	Semiannual interest, 360-day year
Floating rate notes	10,000	Registered	6 months to 10 years	FT SE LE	Interest rate adjusted weekly to an increment over the average auction rate of 91-day Treasury bills and payable quarterly
Tennessee Valley Authority (TVA)	1,000	Registered	5 to 25 years	FT SE LE	Semiannual interest, 360-day year
U.S. Postal Service	10,000	Registered	25 years	FT SE LE	Semiannual interest, 360-day year

FT - Federal Taxable; SE - State Exempt; ST - State Taxable; LE - Local Exempt; LT - Local Taxable.

Source: Adapted from partially available and government supplied information provided to Merrill Lynch Government Securities and other authorized government securities brokers and dealers.

refinance their homes when mortgage interest rates decline as they did in 2001–2004. Therefore, a major disadvantage of GNMA issues is that their *maturities are very uncertain* (i.e., they have *high prepayment risk*).

Japan The agencies in Japan, referred to as *government associate organizations,* account for about 7 percent of the total Japanese yen bond market. This agency market includes public debt, but almost twice as much is privately placed with major financial institutions. Public agency debt is issued like government debt.

United Kingdom As shown in Exhibit 17.2, about 13 percent of the pound sterling market is agency and foreign government debt.

Eurozone As shown in Exhibit 17.2, agency bonds and foreign government bonds are less than 8 percent of the Euro bonds outstanding.

Municipal Bonds

Municipal bonds are issued by states, counties, cities, and other political subdivisions. Again, the size of the municipal bond market (referred to as *local authority* in the United Kingdom) varies substantially among countries. It is about 9 percent of the total U.S. market, compared to less than 3 percent in Japan, nonexistent in the United Kingdom, and not specifically identified in the Eurozone data. Therefore, it is not broken out as a category in Exhibit 17.2. Because of the size and popularity of this market in the United States, we will discuss only the U.S. municipal bond market.

Municipalities in the United States issue two distinct types of bonds: general obligation bonds and revenue issues. **General obligation bonds (GOs)** are essentially backed by the full faith and credit of the issuer and its entire taxing power. Revenue bonds, in turn, are serviced by the income generated from specific revenue-producing projects of the municipality, such as bridges, toll roads, hospitals, municipal coliseums, and waterworks. Revenue bonds generally provide higher returns than GOs because of their higher default risk. Should a municipality fail to generate sufficient income from a project designated to service a revenue bond, it has no legal debt service obligation until the income becomes sufficient.

GO municipal bonds tend to be issued on a serial basis so that the issuer's cash flow requirements will be steady over the life of the obligation. Therefore, the principal portion of the total debt service requirement generally begins at a fairly low level and builds up over the life of the obligation. In contrast, most municipal revenue bonds are term issues, so the principal value is not due until the final maturity date.[16]

The most important feature of municipal obligations is that the interest payments are exempt from federal income tax and from taxes in the locality and state in which the obligation was issued. This means that their attractiveness varies with the investor's tax bracket.

You can convert the tax-free yield of a municipal to an equivalent taxable yield (ETY) using the following equation:

17.3
$$ETY = \frac{i}{1 - t}$$

where:

ETY = equivalent taxable yield
i = coupon rate of the municipal obligations
t = marginal tax rate of the investor

An investor in the 35 percent marginal tax bracket would find that a 5 percent yield on a municipal bond selling close to its par value is equivalent to a 7.69 percent fully taxable yield according to the following calculation:

$$ETY = \frac{0.05}{(1 - 0.35)} = 0.0769$$

Because the tax-free yield is the major benefit of municipal bonds, an investor's marginal tax rate is a primary concern in evaluating them. As a rough rule of thumb, using the tax rates expected in 2006, an investor must be in the 28 to 30 percent tax bracket before the lower yields available in municipal bonds are competitive with those from fully taxable bonds. However, although the interest payment on municipals is tax-free, any capital gains are not (which is why the ETY formula is correct only for a bond selling close to its par value).

Municipal Bond Insurance   A significant feature of the U.S. municipal bond market is *municipal bond insurance,* which provides that an insurance company will guarantee to make principal and interest payments in the event that the issuer of the bonds defaults. The insurance is placed on the bond at date of issue and is *irrevocable* over the life of the issue. The issuer purchases the insurance for the benefit of the investor, and the municipality benefits from lower interest costs due to lower default risk, which causes an increase in the rating on the bond and increased marketability. Those who would benefit from the insurance are small government units that are not widely known and bonds with a complex capital structure.

---

[16]For a more detailed discussion of the municipal bond market, see Feldstein, Fabozzi, Grant, and Kennedy (2005). For discussion of the credit analysis of these bonds, see Feldstein and Grant (2005).

As of 2005, approximately 40 percent of all new municipal bond issues were insured. There are six private bond insurance firms: The Municipal Bond Investors Assurance (MBIA), American Municipal Bond Assurance Corporation (AMBAC), the Financial Security Assurance (FSA), the Financial Guaranty Insurance Company (FGIC), Capital Guaranty Insurance Company (CGIC), and Connie Lee Insurance Company. These firms will insure either general obligation or revenue bonds. To qualify for private bond insurance, the issue must initially carry an S&P rating of BBB or better. Currently, the rating agencies will give an AAA (Aaa) rating to bonds insured by these firms because all the insurance firms have AAA ratings. Issues with these private guarantees have enjoyed a more active secondary market and lower required yields.[17]

Corporate Bonds

Again, the importance of corporate bonds varies across countries. The absolute dollar value of corporate bonds in the United States is substantial and has grown overall and as a percentage of U.S. long-term capital. At the same time, corporate debt as a percentage of total U.S. debt has stabilized at about 30 percent because of the faster growth of agency debt. The pure corporate sector in Japan is small and declining and the ex-bank corporate sector in the Eurozone has grown to be over 14 percent. The proportion of corporate debt in the United Kingdom has increased to almost 30 percent.

U.S. Corporate Bond Market   Utilities dominate the U.S. corporate bond market. Other important segments include industrials, rail and transportation issues, and financial issues. This market is very diverse and includes debentures, first-mortgage issues, convertible obligations, bonds with warrants, subordinated debentures, income bonds (similar to municipal revenue bonds), collateral trust bonds backed by financial assets, equipment trust certificates, and asset-backed securities (ABS) including mortgage-backed bonds.

If we ignore convertible bonds and bonds with warrants, the preceding list of obligations varies by the type of collateral behind the bond. Most bonds have semiannual interest payments, sinking funds, and a single maturity date. Maturities range from 25 to 40 years, with public utilities generally on the longer end and industrials preferring the 25- to 30-year range. Most corporate bonds provide for deferred calls after 5 to 10 years. The deferment period varies directly with the level of the interest rates. Specifically, during periods of higher interest rates, bond issues typically will carry a 7- to 10-year deferment, while during periods of lower interest rates, the deferment periods decline.

On the other hand, corporate notes—with maturities of five to seven years—are generally noncallable. Notes become popular when interest rates are high because issuing firms prefer to avoid long-term obligations during such periods. In contrast, during periods of low interest rates, such as 1997 and 2001–2004, most corporate issues did not include a call provision because corporations did not believe that they would be able to exercise the call option and did not want to pay the required higher yield.

Generally, the average yields for industrial bonds will be the lowest of the three major sectors, followed by utility returns. The difference in yield between utilities and industrials occurs because utilities have the largest supply of bonds, so yields on their bonds must be higher to increase the demand for these bonds.[18]

---

[17]For a discussion of municipal bond insurance, see Feldstein, Fabozzi, Grant, and Kennedy (2005) and Kidwell, Sorenson, and Wachowicz (1987).
[18]For a further discussion, see Fabozzi, Mann, and Wilson (2005).

Mortgage Bonds   The issuer of a mortgage bond has granted to the bondholder a first mortgage lien on some piece of property or possibly all the firm's property. Such a lien provides greater security to the bondholder and a lower interest rate for the issuing firm.

Equipment Trust Certificates   Equipment trust certificates are issued by railroads (the biggest issuers), airlines, and other transportation firms with the proceeds used to purchase equipment (freight cars, railroad engines, and airplanes), which serves as the collateral for the debt. Maturities range from 1 to about 15 years. The fairly short maturities reflect the nature of the collateral, which is subject to substantial wear and tear and tends to deteriorate rapidly.

Equipment trust certificates are appealing to investors because of their attractive yields, low default record, and fairly liquid secondary market.

Collateral Trust Bonds   As an alternative to pledging fixed assets or property, a borrower can pledge financial assets, such as stocks, bonds, or notes, as collateral. These bonds are termed *collateral trust bonds*. These pledged assets are held by a trustee for the benefit of the bondholder.

Collateralized Mortgage Obligations (CMOs)[19]   Earlier we discussed mortgage bonds backed by pools of mortgages. You will recall that the pass-through monthly payments are necessarily both interest and principal and that the bondholder is subject to early retirement if the mortgagees prepay because the house is sold or the mortgage refinanced. Therefore, when you acquire the typical mortgage pass-through bonds, you would be uncertain about the size and timing of the payments.

Collateralized mortgage obligations (CMOs) were developed in the early 1980s to offset some of the problems with the traditional mortgage pass-throughs. The main innovation of the CMO instrument is the segmentation of irregular mortgage cash flows to create short-term, medium-, and long-term securities. Specifically, CMO investors own bonds that are serviced with the cash flows from mortgages; but, rather than the straight pass-through arrangement, the CMO substitutes a *sequential distribution process* that creates a series of bonds with varying maturities to appeal to a wider range of investors.

The prioritized distribution process is as follows:

- Several classes of bonds (these are referred to as *tranches*) are issued against a pool of mortgages, which are the collateral. For example, assume a CMO issue with four classes (tranches) of bonds. In such a case, the first three (e.g., Classes A, B, C) would pay interest at their stated rates beginning at their issue date and the fourth class would be an accrual bond (referred to as a *Z bond*).
- The cash flows received from the underlying mortgages are applied first to pay the interest on the bonds and then to retire these bonds.
- The classes of bonds are retired sequentially. All principal payments are directed first to the shortest-maturity class A bonds until they are completely retired. Then all principal payments are directed to the next shortest-maturity bonds (i.e., the class B bonds). The process continues until all the classes have been paid off.
- During the early periods, the accrual bonds (the class Z bonds) pay no interest, but the interest accrues as additional principal, and the cash flow from the mortgages that collateralize these bonds is used to pay interest on and retire the bonds in the other classes. Subsequently, all remaining cash flows are used to pay off the accrued interest, pay any current interest, and then to retire the Z bonds.

---

[19]For a detailed discussion, see Crawford (2005).

This prioritized sequential pattern means that the A-class bonds are fairly short term and each subsequent class is a little longer term until the Z-class bond, which is a long-term bond. It also functions like a zero coupon or PIK bond for the initial years.

Besides creating bonds that pay interest in a more normal pattern (quarterly or semiannually) and that have more predictable maturities, these bonds are considered very high quality securities (AAA) because of the structure and quality of the collateral. To obtain an AAA rating, CMOs are structured to ensure that the underlying mortgages will always generate enough cash to support the bonds issued, even under the most conservative prepayment and reinvestment rates. In fact, most CMOs are overcollateralized.

Further, the credit risk of the collateral is minimal because most are backed by mortgages guaranteed by a federal agency (GNMA, FNMA) or by the FHLMC. Those mortgages that are not backed by agencies carry private insurance for principal and interest and mortgage insurance. Notably, even with this AAA rating, the yield on these CMOs typically has been higher than the yields on AA industrials. This premium yield has, of course, contributed to their popularity and growth.

Asset-Backed Securities (ABSs)   A rapidly expanding segment of the securities market is that of *asset-backed securities,* which involve *securitizing debt.* This is an important concept because it substantially increases the liquidity of these individual debt instruments, whether they be individual mortgages, car loans, or credit card debt. This general class of securities was introduced in 1983. Since then, more than $700 billion in asset-backed securities have been issued. Beyond the mortgage securities, this market is dominated by securities backed by automobile loans and credit card receivables.

Certificates for Automobile Receivables (CARs)   As discussed by Roever (2005), CARs are securities collateralized by loans made to individuals to finance the purchase of cars. Auto loans are self-amortizing, with monthly payments and relatively short maturities (i.e., two to five years). These auto loans can either be direct loans from a lending institution or indirect loans that are originated by an auto dealer and sold to the ultimate lender. CARs typically have monthly or quarterly fixed interest and principal payments, and expected weighted average lives of one to three years with specified maturities of three to five years. The expected actual life of the instrument typically is shorter than the specified maturity because of early payoffs when cars are sold or traded in. The cash flows of CARs are comparable to short-term corporate debt. They provide a significant yield premium over General Motors Acceptance Corporation (GMAC) commercial paper, which is the most liquid short-term corporate alternative. The popularity of these collateralized securities makes them important not only by themselves but also as an indication of the potential for issuing additional collateralized securities backed by other assets and/or other debt instruments.

Credit Card Receivables   Since 1992, the fastest-growing segment of the ABS market has been securities supported by credit card loans. As described by McElravey (2005), credit card receivables are considered to be a revolving credit ABS, in contrast to auto loan receivables that are referred to as an installment contract ABS—because of the nature of the loan. Specifically, whereas the mortgaged-backed and auto loan securities amortize principal, the principal payments from credit card receivables are not paid to the investor but are retained by the trustee to reinvest in additional receivables. This allows the issuer to specify a maturity for the security that is consistent with the needs of the issuer and the demands of the investors.

When buying a credit card ABS, the indenture specifies (1) the intended maturity for the security; (2) the "lockout period" during which no principal will be paid; and (3) the structure for repaying the principal, which can be accomplished through a single-bullet payment, such as a bond, or distributed monthly with the interest payment over a specified amortization period. For example, a 5-year credit card ABS could have a lockout period of 4 years followed by a 12-month amortization of the principal.

Beyond this standard arrangement, revolving credit securities are protected by early amortization events that can force early repayment if specific payout events occur that are detrimental to the investor (e.g., if there is an increase in the loss rate or if the issuer goes into bankruptcy or receivership). Although this early amortization feature protects the investor from credit problems, it causes an early payment that may not be desirable for the investor.

Variable-Rate Notes   Introduced in the United States in the mid-1970s, **variable-rate notes** became popular during periods of high interest rates. As discussed by Fabozzi and Mann (2005), the typical variable-rate note possesses two unique features:

1. After the first 6 to 18 months of the issue's life, during which a minimum rate is often guaranteed, the coupon rate floats, so that every six months it changes to follow some standard. Usually it is pegged 1 percent above a stipulated short-term rate. For example, the rate might be the preceding three weeks' average 90-day T-bill rate.
2. After the first year or two, the notes are redeemable at par, at the *holder's* option, usually at six-month intervals.

Such notes represent a long-term commitment on the part of the borrower yet provide the lender with all the characteristics of a short-term obligation. They typically are available to investors in minimum denominations of $1,000. However, although the six-month redemption feature provides liquidity, the variable rates can cause these issues to experience wide swings in semiannual coupons.

Zero Coupon and Deep Discount Bonds   The typical corporate bond has a coupon and maturity. In turn, the value of the bond is the present value of the stream of cash flows (interest and principal) discounted at the required yield to maturity (YTM). Alternatively, some bonds do not have any coupons or have coupons that are below the market rate at the time of issue. Such securities are referred to as *zero coupon* or *minicoupon bonds* or *original-issue discount (OID) bonds*. A zero coupon discount bond promises to pay a stipulated principal amount at a future maturity date, but it does not promise to make any interim interest payments. Therefore, the price of the bond is the present value of the principal payment at the maturity date using the required discount rate for this bond. The return on the bond is the difference between what the investor pays for the bond at the time of purchase and the principal payment at maturity.

Consider a zero coupon, $10,000 par value bond with a 20-year maturity. If the required rate of return on bonds of equal maturity and quality is 8 percent and we assume semiannual discounting, the initial selling price for this bond would be $2,082.89 because the present-value factor at 8 percent compounded semiannually for 20 years is 0.208289. From the time of purchase to the point of maturity, the investor would not receive any cash flow from the firm. Notably, the investor must pay taxes, however, on the implied interest on the bond, although no cash is received. Because an investor subject to taxes would experience severe negative cash flows during the life of these bonds, they are primarily of interest to investment accounts not subject to taxes, such as pensions, IRAs, or Keogh accounts.[20]

A modified form of zero coupon bond is the OID bond where the coupon is set substantially below the prevailing market rate, for example, a 5 percent coupon on a bond when market rates are 12 percent. As a result, the bond is issued at a deep discount from par value. Again,

---

[20]These bonds will be discussed further in Chapter 18 in the section on volatility and duration and in Chapter 19 when we consider immunization.

taxes must be paid on the implied 12 percent return rather than the nominal 5 percent, so the cash flow disadvantage of zero coupon bonds, though lessened, remains.

High-Yield Bonds   A segment of the corporate bond market that has grown in size, importance, and controversy is **high-yield bonds**, also referred to as *speculative-grade bonds* and *junk bonds*. These are corporate bonds that have been assigned a bond rating as noninvestment grade, that is, they have a rating below BBB or Baa. The title of speculative-grade bonds is probably the most objective because bonds that are not rated investment grade are speculative grade. The designation of *high-yield bonds* was by Drexel Burnham Lambert (DBL) as an indication of the returns available for these bonds relative to Treasury bonds and investment-grade corporate bonds. The *junk bond* designation is obviously somewhat derogatory and refers to the low credit quality of the issues.

Brief History of the High-Yield Bond Market   Based on a specification that bonds rated below BBB make up the high-yield market, this segment has existed as long as there have been rating agencies. Prior to 1980, most of the high-yield bonds were referred to as *fallen angels,* which means they were bonds that were originally issued as investment-grade securities, but because of changes in the firm over time, the bonds were downgraded into the high-yield sector (BB and below).

The market changed in the early 1980s when DBL began aggressively underwriting high-yield bonds for two groups of clients: (1) small firms that did not have the financial strength to receive an investment-grade rating by the rating agencies, and (2) large and small firms that issued high-yield bonds in connection with leveraged buyouts (LBOs). As a result, the high-yield bond market went from a residual market that included fallen angels to a new-issue market where bonds were underwritten and issued with below-investment-grade ratings.

As a result, the high-yield bond market exploded in size and activity beginning in 1983. As shown in Exhibit 17.6, there were a limited number of new high-yield issues in the late 1970s, and they were not very large issues. Beginning in 1983, more large issues became common (the average size of an issue currently is over $250 million), and high-yield issues became a significant percentage of the total new-issue bond market (typically between 15 and 20 percent). As of 2005, the total outstanding high-yield debt constituted about 20 percent of outstanding corporate debt in the United States.[21]

An important point bears repeating: Although the high-yield debt market has existed for many years, its real emergence as a major component of the U.S. capital market did not occur until 1983. This is relevant when considering the liquidity and default experience for these securities.

Distribution of High-Yield Bond Ratings   Exhibit 17.7 contains the distribution of ratings for all the bonds contained in the Lehman Brothers High-Yield Bond Index as of December 31, 1987–2004. As shown, the heavy concentration by market value is typically in the B class, which contains almost half of all value. There was a strong increase in the BB category that grew from 17 percent in 1987 to over 48 percent in 1995, and a subsequent range of 35–45 percent.

Ownership of High-Yield Bonds   The major owners of high-yield bonds have been mutual funds, insurance companies, and pension funds. As of the end of 2004, over 100 mutual funds were either exclusively directed to invest in high-yield bonds or included such bonds in their portfolio. Notably, there has been a shift of ownership away from insurance companies and savings and loans toward mutual funds. This shift occurred during the late 1980s when regulators "encouraged" the insurance companies and S&Ls to reduce or eliminate high-yield bonds from their portfolios.

---

[21]Almost everyone would acknowledge that the development of the high-yield debt market has had a positive impact on the capital-raising ability of the economy. For an analysis of this impact, see Perry and Taggart (1988). Updates on its characteristics are contained in Fridson (1994), Altman (1992), and Reilly and Wright (2001b).

Exhibit 17.6 | **High-Yield Bonds—New-Issue Volume: 1984–2004**

| Year | PUBLIC | | 144A | | TOTAL | | |
	Number of Issues	Principal Amount ($ Millions)	Number of Issues	Principal Amount ($ Millions)	Number of Issues	Principal Amount ($ Millions)	Average Issue Size ($ Millions)
1984	131	15,238.9			131	15,238.9	116.33
1985	175	15,684.8			175	15,684.8	89.63
1986	226	33,261.8			226	33,261.8	147.18
1987	190	30,522.2			190	30,522.2	160.64
1988	160	31,095.2			160	31,095.2	194.34
1989	130	28,753.2			130	28,753.2	221.18
1990	10	1,397.0			10	1,397.0	139.70
1991	48	9,967.0			48	9,967.0	207.65
1992	245	39,755.2	29	$ 3,810.8	274	43,566.0	159.00
1993	341	57,163.7	95	15,096.8	436	72,260.5	165.74
1994	191	34,598.8	81	7,733.5	272	42,332.3	155.63
1995	152	30,139.1	94	14,242.0	246	44,381.1	180.41
1996	142	30,739.4	217	35,172.9	359	65,912.3	183.60
1997	103	19,822.0	576	98,885.0	679	118,707.0	174.83
1998	116	29,844.0	604	111,044.7	720	140,888.7	195.68
1999	60	16,520.0	357	83,157.0	417	99,677.0	239.00
2000	32	10,621.1	149	39,593.6	181	50,214.7	277.40
2001	42	14,385.6	267	69,109.6	309	83,495.2	270.20
2002	27	6,551.0	224	54,516.1	251	61,067.1	243.30
2003	51	14,223.3	464	126,892.2	515	141,115.5	274.01
2004	52	13,473.9	577	147,374.9	629	160,848.8	255.72

Note: Includes nonconvertible, corporate debt rated below investment grade by Moody's or Standard & Poor's. Excludes mortgage- and asset-backed issues, as well as non-144a private placements.

Source: Merrill Lynch & Co.; Securities Data Company.

The purpose of this discussion has been to introduce you to high-yield bonds because of the growth in size and importance of this segment of the market for individual and institutional investors. We revisit this topic in Chapter 19 on bond portfolio management, where we review the historical rates of return and alternative risk factors, including the default experience for these bonds. As discussed by Altman (1990), Fabozzi (1990b), and Fridson (1989), all of this must be considered by potential investors in these securities.

Japanese Corporate Bond Market The corporate bond market in Japan is made up of two components: (1) bonds issued by industrial firms or utilities and (2) bonds issued by banks to finance loans to corporations. As noted in connection with Exhibit 17.2, the pure corporate bond sector has declined in relative size over time to about 11 percent of the total.

Japanese corporate bonds are regulated by the *Kisaikai,* a council composed of 22 bond-related banks and seven major securities companies. It operates under the authority of the Ministry of Finance (MOF) and the Bank of Japan (BOJ) to determine bond-issuing procedures,

Exhibit 17.7	**High Yield Index Composition by Credit Quality: 1994–2004 (Percentage of Market Value)**

Year	BB	B	CCC/Unrated
1994	42.61	48.00	9.38
1995	48.32	44.60	7.08
1996	45.67	47.36	6.97
1997	38.19	51.07	10.74
1998	35.28	52.04	12.68
1999	33.83	55.82	10.34
2000	36.63	53.94	9.43
2001	46.04	42.35	11.61
2002	41.20	39.70	19.20
2003	35.20	46.40	18.40
2004	39.30	45.10	15.60

Source: Lehman Brothers, *Global Family of Indices.* (New York: Lehman Brothers, Annual).

including specifying the coupons on corporate bonds in relation to coupons on long-term government bonds in order to prevent any competition with the government bond market.

Because of numerous bankruptcies during the 1930s depression, the government mandated that all corporate debt be secured. This requirement was abolished in 1988. The issuance of unsecured debt led to the birth of bond-rating agencies, which were not needed with completely secured debt. Currently, there are five major bond-rating agencies.

The Ministry of Finance specifies minimum issuing requirements and controls the issuance system that specifies who can issue bonds and when they can be issued. In addition, lead underwriting managers are predetermined in accordance with a lead manager rotating system that ensures balance among the major securities firms in Japan.

Bank Bonds   The substantial issuance of bank bonds is because of the banking system in Japan, which is segmented into the following components:

- Commercial banks (13 big-city banks and 64 regional banks)
- Long-term credit banks (3)
- Mutual loan and savings banks (6)
- Specialized financial institutions

During the post–World War II reconstruction, several banks were permitted to obtain funding by issuing medium- and long-term debentures at rates above yields on government bonds. These funds were used to make mortgage loans to firms in the industrial sector to rebuild plants and equipment. Currently, these financial institutions sell five-year coupon debentures and one-year discount debentures directly to individual and institutional investors. The long-term credit banks are not allowed to take deposits and thus depend on the debentures to obtain funds. These bonds are traded in the OTC market.

Pound Sterling Corporate Bond Market   Corporate bonds in the United Kingdom, denominated in pound sterling, are available in three forms: debentures, unsecured loans, and convertible bonds. The value of securities in each class are about equal. The maturity structure of the corporate bond market is fairly wide and the coupon structure of corporate bonds also is broad with high-coupon bonds in the 10 to 14 percent range. In contrast, convertible bonds have the low coupons. Almost all U.K. corporate bonds are callable term bonds.

U.K. corporate bonds are issued through both public offerings and private placements. Subsequently, primary dealers have begun trading corporate bonds directly with each other. All corporate bonds are issued in registered form.

Eurozone Corporate Bond Market   Corporate bonds in the Eurozone are divided between pure corporate bonds which includes industrial and utility firms (about 15 percent) and securitized/collaterlized bonds that include indirect corporate borrowing (about 12 percent).

International Bonds

Each country's international bond market has two components. The first, *foreign bonds,* are issues sold primarily in one country and currency by a borrower of a different nationality. An example would be U.S. dollar–denominated bonds sold in the United States by a Japanese firm. (These are referred to as *Yankee bonds.*) Second are *Eurobonds,* which are bonds underwritten by international bond syndicates and sold in several national markets. An example would be Eurodollar bonds that are securities denominated in U.S. dollars, underwritten by an international syndicate, and sold to non-U.S. investors outside the United States. The relative size of these two markets (foreign bonds versus Eurobonds) varies by country.

United States   The Eurodollar bond market has been much larger than the Yankee bond market (about $635 billion versus $220 billion). However, because the Eurodollar bond market is heavily affected by changes in the value of the U.S. dollar, it has experienced slower growth during periods when the dollar was weak. Such periods have created a desire for diversification by investors.

Yankee bonds are issued by foreign firms who register with the SEC and borrow U.S. dollars, using issues underwritten by a U.S. syndicate for delivery in the United States. These bonds are traded in the United States and pay interest semiannually. Over 60 percent of Yankee bonds are issued by Canadian corporations and typically have shorter maturities and longer call protection than U.S. domestic issues. These features increase their appeal.

The Eurodollar bond market is dominated by foreign investors, and the center of trading is in London. Eurodollar bonds pay interest annually. The Eurodollar bond market currently comprises almost 40 percent of the total Eurobond market.

Japan   Before 1985, the Japanese yen international bond market was dominated (over 90 percent) by foreign bonds (Samurai bonds) with the balance in Euroyen bonds. After the issuance requirements for Euroyen bonds were liberalized in 1985, the ratio of issuance swung heavily in favor of Euroyen bonds.

Samurai bonds are yen-denominated bonds sold by non-Japanese issuers and mainly sold in Japan. The market is fairly small and has limited liquidity. The market has experienced very little growth in terms of yen but substantial growth in U.S. dollar terms because of changes in the exchange rate.

Euroyen bonds are yen-denominated bonds sold in markets outside Japan by international syndicates. This market has grown substantially because of the liberal issue requirements. Its appeal over time is determined by the strength or weakness of the yen relative to other currencies.

United Kingdom   Pound sterling foreign bonds, referred to as *bulldog bonds,* are sterling-denominated bonds issued by non-English firms and sold in London. Eurosterling bonds are sold in markets outside London by international syndicates.

Similar to other countries, the U.K. international bond market has become dominated by the Eurosterling bonds. As of 2001, the ratio of Eurobonds versus foreign bonds (bulldogs) had grown to 3.4:1. The procedure for issuing and trading Eurosterling bonds is similar to that of other Eurobonds.

Eurozone   The growth of Eurobonds issued by nonresidents was impressive in both 2004 and 2003. This growth confirmed the popularity of the Euro markets among foreign issuers including issuers domiciled in the United States that accounted for over 7 percent of the market.

OBTAINING INFORMATION ON BOND PRICES

Historically, the price information available to bond investors has been substantially different from price information available to stock investors. Specifically, stock investors can receive up-to-the-minute transaction prices on all NYSE, AMEX, and Nasdaq National stocks as well as daily closing prices for most other Nasdaq stocks. In contrast, most bond trading has been done on the over-the-counter (OTC) market, and there was limited reporting of transactions, with the exception of the very liquid government bond market. Fortunately, this environment in the bond market changed dramatically during 2004 and 2005. As described by Lucchetti and Soloman (2004) and subsequently by Rappaport (2004b), the National Association of Securities Dealers (NASD), through its Trade Reporting and Compliance Engine (TRACE), began releasing more timely pricing data for a broad group of corporate bonds. Specifically, as of October 2004, NASD expanded the number of corporate bonds for which it reports pricing information, from 4,500 bonds within 45 minutes of the transaction to 17,000 bonds within 30 minutes of the transaction. The existence of more bond issues than stock issues is possible because companies can have more than one bond issue, but typically only one stock issue. As of February 2005 the NASD began reporting transactions on all 23,000 corporate bond issues. Finally, in July 2005 the goal was to reduce the reporting interval to within 15 minutes of the transaction. Clearly, the price transparency in the corporate bond market has changed dramatically and the transaction cost savings for bond investors has been dramatic—a conservative estimate was $1 billion a year.

In addition to better pricing data, as discussed by Rappaport (2004a), the overall bond market (and especially the corporate bond market) has benefitted from the introduction of electronic bond trading through Thomson Trade Web and Market Axess, the two leading trading platforms. Prior to late 2004 there had been electronic trading in government agency and mortgage backed securities, but it was not until late 2004 that the volume of trading and the size of corporate bond trading was notable and provided further transparency for this market. Observers contend that the next frontiers will be electronic trading in high-yield bonds, emerging market debt, and interest rate derivatives.

Given this background, the following discussion considers how investors read and interpret the rapidly expanding bond price information in newspapers and quote sheets.

Interpreting Bond Quotes

Essentially, all bonds are quoted on the basis of either yield or price. Price quotes are always interpreted as a *percentage of par.* For example, a quote of 98½ is interpreted not as $98.50 but 98½ percent of par. The dollar price is derived from the quote, given the par value. If the par value is $5,000 on a municipal bond, then the price of an issue quoted at 98½ would be $4,925. Actually, the market follows three systems of bond pricing: one system for corporates, another for governments (both Treasury and agency obligations), and a third for municipals.

Corporate Bond Quotes   Exhibit 17.8 is a listing of corporate bond quotes for the 40 most active fixed-coupon corporate bonds that appeared in *The Wall Street Journal* on May 26, 2005. The data pertain to trading activity on May 25, 2005. Several quotes have been designated for illustrative purposes.

The first issue designated is a Ford Motor Company (trading symbol *F*) issue that is representative of most corporate prices. This is a 7.450 percent coupon, which means that the annual coupon payment for this $1,000 par value bond is $74.50, or $37.25 every six months. The bond matures on July 16, 2031, which is a little more than 26 years from the end of May 2005. The last transaction price for a bond trade on May 25 was 80.625 of par or $806.25,

---

Exhibit 17.8 | **Sample Corporate Bond Quotations**

Corporate Bonds

Wednesday, May 25, 2005

Forty most active fixed-coupon corporate bonds

COMPANY (TICKER)	COUPON	MATURITY	LAST PRICE	LAST YIELD	*EST SPREAD	UST†	EST $ VOL (000's)
① → Ford Motor Co (F)	7.450	Jul 16, 2031	80.625	9.461	503	30	213,645
General Motors Acceptance (GM)	8.000	Nov 01, 2031	81.938	9.945	551	30	200,470
General Motors Acceptance (GM)	6.875	Sep 15, 2011	85.750	9.975	589	5	173,260
General Motors Acceptance (GM)	6.875	Aug 28, 2012	84.000	10.032	596	10	172,837
General Motors Acceptance (GM)	6.750	Dec 01, 2014	83.750	9.371	529	10	167,759
Pulte Homes (PHM)	5.200	Feb 15, 2015	97.743	5.500	142	10	120,400
DaimlerChrysler North America Holding (DCX)	6.500	Nov 15, 2013	105.073	5.734	165	10	104,275
Ford Motor Credit (F)	7.375	Oct 28, 2009	94.750	8.835	503	5	102,665
General Motors (GM)	8.375	Jul 15, 2033	84.000	10.096	567	30	99,734
General Motors Acceptance (GM)	7.750	Jan 19, 2010	92.500	9.797	600	5	99,590
UFJ Finance Aruba AEC (UFJ)	6.750	Jul 15, 2013	110.238	5.188	110	10	95,400
Comcast Cable Communications Holdings Inc (CMCSA)	8.375	Mar 15, 2013	122.185	4.911	84	10	92,306
Comcast Holdings Corp (CMCSA)	5.300	Jan 15, 2014	102.250	4.975	89	10	91,757
Comcast Holdings Corp (CMCSA)	6.500	Jan 15, 2015	111.081	5.032	96	10	89,900
Viacom (VIA)	5.625	May 01, 2007	102.076	4.480	88	2	87,116
Morgan Stanley (MWD)	5.300	Mar 01, 2013	102.235	4.948	86	10	85,991
General Motors Acceptance (GM)	5.625	May 15, 2009	88.813	9.049	524	5	85,612
② → General Motors Acceptance (GM)	7.250	Mar 02, 2011	86.760	10.357	656	5	83,929
JPMorgan Chase and Co (JPM)	4.750	Mar 01, 2015	99.476	4.817	80	10	77,355
Sprint Capital (FON)	8.750	Mar 15, 2032	136.598	5.989	158	30	76,077
American General Finance (AIG)	4.875	May 15, 2010	100.629	4.730	93	5	73,828
Washington Mutual Bank, FA (WM)	5.125	Jan 15, 2015	101.148	4.972	92	10	73,560
Lehman Brothers Holdings (LEH)	4.250	Jan 27, 2010	99.215	4.437	63	5	72,345
American General Finance (AIG)	5.375	Oct 01, 2012	102.716	4.928	86	10	72,000
General Motors Acceptance (GM)	6.125	Sep 15, 2006	99.500	6.526	292	2	70,558
JPMorgan Chase and Co (JPM)	5.125	Sep 15, 2014	101.277	4.951	87	10	70,245
International Business Machines (IBM)	5.875	Nov 29, 2032	108.121	5.310	88	30	62,362
Textron Financial Corp (TXT)	5.875	Jun 01, 2007	103.319	4.123	55	2	62,171
Ford Motor Credit (F)	7.000	Oct 01, 2013	90.250	8.664	458	10	61,303
Alcan (AL)	5.200	Jan 15, 2014	101.262	5.017	95	10	61,074
DaimlerChrysler North America Holding (DCX)	7.300	Jan 15, 2012	109.192	5.617	153	10	60,189
Goodrich Corp (GR)	7.625	Dec 15, 2012	116.542	4.968	90	10	59,800
International Lease Finance (AIG)	5.000	Apr 15, 2010	101.091	4.745	98	5	58,995
CIT Group Inc (CIT)	4.125	Nov 03, 2009	98.489	4.505	70	5	58,620
③ → Citigroup (C)	5.500	Aug 09, 2006	101.913	3.833	23	2	53,308
Ford Motor Credit (F)	6.500	Jan 25, 2007	100.000	6.493	289	2	52,307
Tyco International Group SA (TYC)	6.000	Nov 15, 2013	107.674	4.881	81	10	50,593
Wachovia (WB)	4.375	Jun 01, 2010	100.128	4.346	56	5	50,175
Bank of America (BAC)	5.250	Feb 01, 2007	102.190	3.877	27	2	49,794
Constellation Energy Group Inc (CEG)	6.350	Apr 01, 2007	103.638	4.265	67	2	49,764
Wells Fargo (WFC)	4.200	Jan 15, 2010	99.446	4.332	52	5	48,623

Volume represents total volume for each issue; price/yield data are for trades of $1 million and greater. * Estimated spreads, in basis points (100 basis points is one percentage point), over the 2, 3, 5, 10 or 30-year hot run Treasury note/bond. 2-year: 3.625 04/07; 3-year: 3.750 05/08; 5-year: 3.875 05/10; 10-year: 4.125 05/15; 30-year: 5.375 02/31. †Comparable U.S. Treasury issue.

Source: MarketAxess Corporate BondTicker

---

which implies a yield to maturity (YTM) for this bond (to be explained in detail in Chapter 18) of 9.461 percent. The estimated spread in basis points (100 basis points is one percentage point) indicates how the YTM for this bond compares to the prevailing yield to maturity for a Treasury note or bond of equal maturity. The Treasury issues are limited to the following maturities: 2, 3, 5, 10, and 30 years, and they use the latest issue at that maturity (that is referred to as "on the run") as listed. Because the Treasury has not issued a 30-year bond since February 2001, they use a security that now has a maturity of less than 26 years (this is ideal for the Ford issue, because it also matures in 2031). As shown, the computed spread for the Ford bond is 503 basis points (5.03 percent), which implies that at this time, the 30-year Treasury bond (a 5.375 coupon bond that matures in February 2031) is yielding about 4.43 percent. (9.461 − 5.03). As can be seen from the other bonds in the exhibit, this fairly large spread exists because both Ford and General Motors bonds were recently downgraded by the rating agencies to Baa- or Bb+, which border on high-yield status. Finally, this is the most active corporate bond on this day (May 25, 2005)—it had trading volume of over $213 million. Heavy trading volume is not unusual for Ford and has increased even more during this period due to the change in credit standing (as shown, General Motors bonds have also been very active).

The second issue designated is the General Motors Acceptance Corporation (GMAC) bonds for the financing subsidiary of General Motors (GM). These bonds, which are due to mature in about 5 years and 9 months, are compared to a 5-year Treasury security due to mature in May 2010. The spread of 656 points is the largest in the exhibit and is caused by the recent downgrade to a high-yield Bb rating. The yield of 10.357 percent compares to a 5-year Treasury security yield of about 3.80 percent, prompting trading of almost $84 million.

The third issue is the Citigroup 5.50 percent bond due in August 2006 (about 14 months' maturity), which has the smallest spread of only 23 basis points relative to a 2-year Treasury security of 3.60 percent. This can be explained mainly by its Aaa bond rating and its short maturity. These examples indicate that prices imply yields to maturity that are driven by the required spreads to Treasury securities, and show there is substantial trading in these corporate bonds.

All fixed-income obligations, with the exception of preferred stock, are traded on an *accrued interest basis*. The prices pertain to the value of all *future* cash flows from the bond and exclude interest that has accrued to the holder since the last interest payment date. The actual price of the bond will exceed the quote listed because accrued interest must be added. Assume a bond with a 7⅛ percent coupon. If two months have elapsed since interest was paid, the current holder of the bond is entitled to two-sixths (one-third) of the bond's semiannual interest payment that will be paid in four months. More specifically, the 7⅛ percent coupon provides semiannual interest income of $35.625. The investor who held the obligation for two months beyond the last interest payment date is entitled to one-third of that $35.625 in the form of accrued interest. Therefore, whatever the current price of the bond, an accrued interest value of $11.87 will be added. If a bond is trading "flat," interest is not being paid and accrued interest would not be added.

Treasury and Agency Bond Quotes   Exhibit 17.9 illustrates the quote system for Treasury and agency issues. These quotes resemble those used for OTC securities because they contain both bid and ask prices. For U.S. Treasury bond quotes, a small "n" behind the maturity date indicates that the obligation is a Treasury *note*. A small "i" indicates it is an inflation-indexed issue.

All other obligations in this section are Treasury bonds. The security identification is different because it is not necessary to list the issuer. Instead, the usual listing indicates the coupon, the month and year of maturity, and information on a call feature of the obligation. Call features have not been relevent for several years since the Treasury has not issued a bond with a call option since 1985 and previously outstanding callable issues have matured. The bid-ask figures provided are stated as a percentage of par. The yield figure provided is yield to

Exhibit 17.9 | **Sample Quotes for Treasury Bonds, Notes, and Bills**

Treasury Bonds, Notes and Bills   May 26, 2005

Explanatory Notes

Representative Over-the-Counter quotation based on transactions of $1 million or more. Treasury bond, note and bill quotes are as of mid-afternoon. Colons in bid-and-asked quotes represent 32nds; 101:01 means 101 1/32. Net changes in 32nds. n-Treasury note. i-Inflation-Indexed issue. Treasury bill quotes in hundredths, quoted on terms of a rate of discount. Days to maturity calculated from settlement date. All yields are to maturity and based on the asked quote. Latest 13-week and 26-week bills are boldfaced. For bonds callable prior to maturity, yields are computed to the earliest call date for issues quoted above par and to the maturity date for issues below par. *When issued.

Source: eSpeed/Cantor Fitzgerald

U.S. Treasury strips as of 3 p.m. Eastern time, also based on transactions of $1 million or more. Colons in bid and asked quotes represent 32nds; 99:01 means .99 1/32. Net changes in 32nds. Yields calculated on the asked quotation. ci-stripped coupon interest. bp-Treasury bond, stripped principal. np-Treasury note, stripped principal. For bonds callable prior to maturity, yields are computed to the earliest call date for issues quoted above par and to the maturity date for issues below par.

Source: Bear, Stearns & Co. via Street Software Technology Inc.

Government Bonds & Notes

RATE	MATURITY MO/YR	BID	ASKED	CHG	ASK YLD
1.250	May 05n	100:00	100:00	...	1.24
1.125	Jun 05n	99:27	99:28	...	2.45
1.500	Jul 05n	99:24	99:25	-1	2.71
6.500	Aug 05n	100:24	100:25	-1	2.82
10.750	Aug 05	101:23	101:24	-1	2.70
2.000	Aug 05n	99:24	99:25	...	2.83
1.625	Sep 05n	99:16	99:17	-1	2.95
1.625	Oct 05n	99:11	99:12	-1	3.07
5.750	Nov 05n	101:05	101:06	...	3.13
5.875	Nov 05n	101:07	101:08	...	3.12
1.875	Nov 05n	99:11	99:12	1	3.12
1.875	Dec 05n	99:05	99:06	-1	3.24
1.875	Jan 06n	99:01	99:02	...	3.26
5.625	Feb 06n	101:23	101:24	-1	3.12
9.375	Feb 06	104:18	104:19	-1	2.88
1.625	Feb 06n	98:23	98:24	...	3.30
1.500	Mar 06n	98:14	98:15	...	3.33
2.250	Apr 06n	98:29	98:30	-1	3.41
2.000	May 06n	98:21	98:22	...	3.39
4.625	May 06n	101:04	101:05	-1	3.38
6.875	May 06n	103:07	103:08	-2	3.41
2.500	May 06n	99:02	99:03	-1	3.40
2.750	Jun 06n	99:08	99:09	...	3.42
7.000	Jul 06n	103:27	103:28	-2	3.47
2.750	Jul 06n	99:05	99:06	-1	3.46
2.375	Aug 06n	98:21	98:22	-1	3.48
2.375	Aug 06n	98:19	98:20	-1	3.48
2.500	Sep 06n	98:20	98:21	-1	3.52
6.500	Oct 06n	104:00	104:00	-1	3.51
2.500	Oct 06n	98:17	98:18	-1	3.53
2.625	Nov 06n	98:21	98:22	-1	3.54
3.500	Nov 06n	99:30	99:31	-2	3.51
2.875	Nov 06n	99:00	99:00	-2	3.55
3.000	Dec 06n	99:02	99:03	-2	3.58

RATE	MATURITY MO/YR	BID	ASKED	CHG	ASK YLD
4.375	Aug 12n	103:17	103:18	-1	3.81
4.000	Nov 12n	100:29	100:30	-4	3.85
10.375	Nov 12	115:26	115:27	...	3.61
3.875	Feb 13n	99:20	99:21	-4	3.92
3.625	May 13n	98:00	98:00	-1	3.92
1.875	Jul 13i	102:11	102:12	-5	1.56
4.250	Aug 13n	101:22	101:23	-1	4.00
12.000	Aug 13	125:02	125:03	-6	3.66
4.250	Nov 13n	101:18	101:19	-2	4.02
2.000	Jan 14i	103:02	103:03	-7	1.61
4.000	Feb 14n	99:22	99:23	-2	4.04
4.750	May 14n	105:02	105:03	-2	4.06
4.250	May 14n	134:22	134:23	-4	3.75
2.000	Jul 14i	103:01	103:02	-7	1.64
4.250	Aug 14n	101:08	101:09	-2	4.08
12.500	Aug 14	133:23	133:24	-5	3.77
11.750	Nov 14	132:18	132:19	4	3.76
4.250	Nov 14n	101:06	101:07	-2	4.09
1.625	Jan 15i	99:20	99:21	-8	1.66
4.000	Feb 15n	99:05	99:06	-2	4.10
11.250	Feb 15	156:26	156:27	-3	4.10
4.125	May 15n	100:12	100:13	-2	4.07
10.625	Aug 15	153:22	153:23	-4	4.13
9.875	Nov 15	148:04	148:05	-3	4.15
9.250	Feb 16	143:16	143:17	-3	4.17
7.250	May 16	126:18	126:19	-3	4.20
7.500	Nov 16	129:16	129:17	-3	4.22
8.750	May 17	141:28	141:29	-3	4.25
8.875	Aug 17	143:19	143:20	-4	4.26
9.125	May 18	147:23	147:24	-3	4.29
9.000	Nov 18	147:13	147:14	-4	4.32
8.875	Feb 19	146:18	146:19	-4	4.33
8.125	Aug 19	139:19	139:20	-3	4.36
8.500	Feb 20	144:14	144:15	-2	4.37
8.750	May 20	147:20	147:21	-3	4.38
8.750	Aug 20	148:04	148:05	-4	4.38

U.S. Treasury Strips

MATURITY	TYPE	BID	ASKED	CHG	ASK YLD
Jul 05	ci	99:21	99:22	...	2.30
Aug 05	ci	99:13	99:14	...	2.63
Aug 05	bp	99:13	99:14	...	2.61
Aug 05	np	99:13	99:13	...	2.68
Oct 05	ci	98:28	98:29	...	2.89
Nov 05	ci	98:20	98:21	1	2.93
Nov 05	np	98:18	98:19	...	3.05
Nov 05	np	98:18	98:19	1	3.07
Jan 06	ci	98:06	98:07	...	2.86
Feb 06	ci	97:24	97:25	...	3.15
Feb 06	bp	97:29	97:30	...	2.92
Feb 06	np	97:24	97:25	...	3.15
Apr 06	ci	97:06	97:06	-1	3.23
May 06	ci	96:29	96:29	-1	3.27
May 06	np	96:25	96:26	-1	3.37
May 06	np	96:26	96:26	-1	3.36
Jul 06	ci	96:19	96:19	-1	3.06
Aug 06	ci	96:00	96:01	-1	3.35
Aug 06	np	95:28	95:29	-1	3.46
Oct 06	ci	95:12	95:12	-1	3.44
Nov 06	ci	95:02	95:02	-1	3.47
Nov 06	np	94:31	95:00	-1	3.53
Nov 06	np	94:31	95:00	-1	3.54
Feb 07	ci	94:05	94:06	-1	3.52
Feb 07	np	94:03	94:04	-1	3.55
May 07	ci	93:07	93:08	-1	3.58
May 07	np	93:06	93:07	-1	3.61
May 07	np	93:05	93:06	-1	3.62
Aug 07	ci	92:11	92:12	-2	3.60
Aug 07	np	92:10	92:10	-2	3.63
Aug 07	np	92:09	92:10	-2	3.63
Nov 07	ci	91:17	91:17	-2	3.61
Nov 07	np	91:14	91:15	-2	3.65
Feb 08	ci	90:21	90:22	-2	3.63
Feb 08	np	90:19	90:20	-2	3.65
Feb 08	np	90:18	90:19	-2	3.67
May 08	ci	89:25	89:25	-2	3.66
May 08	np	89:21	89:22	-2	3.70
Aug 08	ci	88:30	88:31	-2	3.66
Aug 08	np	88:26	88:26	-2	3.71
May 08	np	89:22	89:22	-2	3.70
Nov 08	ci	88:00	88:00	-3	3.72
Nov 08	np	87:29	87:30	-4	3.74
Nov 08	np	87:29	87:29	-4	3.75
Feb 09	ci	87:10	87:10	-2	3.68
Feb 09	np	87:02	87:03	-2	3.75
May 09	ci	86:13	86:13	-2	3.71
May 09	np	86:11	86:12	-1	3.73
May 09	np	86:07	86:08	-2	3.77

Treasury Bills

MATURITY	DAYS TO MAT	BID	ASKED	CHG	ASK YLD
Jun 02 05	6	2.33	2.32	-0.14	2.35
Jun 09 05	13	2.55	2.54	-0.08	2.58
Jun 16 05	20	2.68	2.67	0.02	2.71
Jun 23 05	27	2.73	2.72	-0.01	2.76
Jun 30 05	34	2.66	2.65	0.03	2.69
Jul 07 05	41	2.68	2.67	0.01	2.72
Jul 14 05	48	2.69	2.68	0.03	2.73
Jul 21 05	55	2.71	2.70	0.06	2.75
Jul 28 05	62	2.75	2.74	0.05	2.79
Aug 04 05	69	2.79	2.78	0.02	2.83
Aug 11 05	76	2.81	2.80	0.01	2.86
Aug 18 05	83	2.85	2.84	0.01	2.90
Aug 25 05	90	2.87	2.86	-0.01	2.92
Sep 01 05	97	2.91	2.90	...	2.96
Sep 08 05	104	2.93	2.92	...	2.99
Sep 15 05	111	2.94	2.93	...	3.00
Sep 22 05	118	2.95	2.94	-0.01	3.01
Sep 29 05	125	2.95	2.94	0.01	3.01
Oct 06 05	132	2.95	2.94	...	3.01
Oct 13 05	139	2.97	2.96	...	3.04
Oct 20 05	146	2.97	2.96	...	3.04
Oct 27 05	153	2.95	2.94	...	3.02
Nov 03 05	160	2.99	2.98	0.01	3.06
Nov 10 05	167	2.96	2.95	-0.01	3.03
Nov 17 05	174	3.02	3.01	-0.02	3.10
Nov 25 05	182	3.06	3.05	-0.01	3.14

Inflation-Indexed Treasury Securities

RATE	MAT	BID/ASKED	CHG	*YLD	ACCR PRIN
3.375	01/07	104-05/06	-4	0.796	1214
3.625	01/08	106-21/22	-5	1.048	1191
3.875	01/09	109-20/21	-6	1.157	1173
4.250	01/10	113-11/12	-4	1.271	1143
0.875	04/10	97-27/28	-4	1.325	1016
3.500	01/11	111-17/18	-5	1.362	1105
3.375	01/12	112-09/10	-6	1.424	1083
3.000	07/12	110-12/13	-11	1.459	1070
1.875	07/13	102-11/12	-5	1.563	1048
2.000	01/14	103-02/03	-7	1.615	1039
2.000	07/14	103-01/02	-7	1.638	1021
1.625	01/15	99-20/21	-8	1.664	1008
2.375	01/25	108-28/29	-3	1.832	1021
3.625	04/28	133-09/10	-33	1.836	1189
3.875	04/29	139-10/11	-37	1.834	1170
3.375	04/32	134-19/20	-41	1.754	1084

*Yield to maturity on accrued principal.

maturity, or *promised* yield based on the asking price. This system is used for Treasuries, agencies, and municipals.

Quote 1 is a 5.75 percent obligation, due in November 2005, that demonstrates the basic difference in the price system of government bonds (i.e., Treasuries and agencies). The bid quote is 101:05, and the ask is 101:06. Governments are traded in 32nds of a point (rather than 8ths), and the figures to the right of the colons indicate the number of 32nds in the fractional bid or ask. In this case, the bid price is actually 101.15625 percent of par. These quotes also are notable in terms of the bid-ask spread, which typically is one or two 32nds, or about half the size of the spread for most stocks. This small spread reflects the outstanding liquidity and low transaction costs for Treasury securities.

The third column contains quotes for U.S. Treasury securities that have been stripped. Specifically, the typical bond promises a series of coupon payments and its principal at maturity.

A stripped security is created by dividing into separate units each coupon payment and principal payment, which are treated like a zero coupon bond that matures on that date. The security labeled ② was originally a coupon that was to be paid in August 2008. The asking yield (3.66) is referred to as the spot rate for this maturity (spot rate will be discussed in Chapter 18). The coupon interest payment with no principal is designated as *ci* (stripped coupon interest), while the other strip for August 2008 containing only the principal payment is designated "np" (Treasury note, stripped principal).

The securities listed in the Treasury strip and Treasury bill section only report dates and days to maturity and no coupons. This is because these are pure discount securities, that is, the return is the difference between the price you pay and par at maturity.[22]

The final section contains Treasury Inflation Protection Securities (TIPS) discussed earlier. Notice the accrued principal in the last column that reflects the inflation since the bond was issued. The bond designated ③ was the original bond issued in January 1997, so it has the highest accrued principal value of 1,214, and its yield to maturity is computed using this as the principal amount to be paid at maturity.

Municipal Bond Quotes   Exhibit 17.10 contains municipal bond quotes from *The Blue List of Current Municipal Offerings*. These are ordered according to states and then alphabetically within states. Each issue gives the amount of bonds being offered (in thousands of dollars), the name of the security, the purpose or description of the issue, the coupon rate, the maturity (which includes month, day, and year), the yield or price, and the dealer offering the bonds. Bond quote 1 is for $200,000 of Indiana State Office Building bonds. The letters MBIA indicate that the bonds are guaranteed by the Municipal Bond Insurance Association (MBIA). These are zero (0.000) coupon bonds due July 1, 2010. In this instance, the yield to maturity is given (5.60 percent). To determine the price, compute the discount value or look up in a yield book the price of a zero coupon bond, due in 2010 to yield 5.60 percent. The dealer offering the bonds is Bearster. A list in the back of the publication gives the name and phone number of the firm offering the bond.

The second bond is for $115,000 of Indiana State Toll Road bonds with a 9 percent coupon. These bonds have an M/S/F (mandatory sinking fund) that becomes effective in 2011, although the bond matures in 2015. The letters ETM mean that the sinking fund is put into escrow till maturity. The market yield on these bonds is 6.30 percent, which means the bond would be selling at a premium.

Bond quote 3 refers to $10,000 of Indianapolis, Indiana, Airport Authority revenue bonds that are backed by a contract with US Air. Although the bonds mature in 2009, they were callable beginning in 1997 (C97) at 102 of par. The coupon is 7.50 percent and, in this case, the price of the bond is listed (100), which means its market yield also is 7.50 percent. Such bonds are called *dollar bonds*.

The "+" in the far left column indicates a new item since the prior issue of *The Blue List*. A "#" in the column prior to the yield to maturity or the price indicates that the price or yield has changed since the last issue. It is always necessary to call the dealer to determine the current yield/price because these quotes are at least one day old when they are published.

---

[22]For a discussion of calculating yields, see Fielitz (1983).

Exhibit 17.10 | **Quotes for Municipals**

INDIANA

No. of Bonds Offered	Municipal Issuer	Special Characteristics	Coupon	Maturity	Price/ YTM	Broker
45	INDIANA HEALTH FAC FING AUTH	P/R @ 102	7.750	08/15/20C00	5.25	EQUITSEC
200	INDIANA PORT COMMN PORT REV		6.750	07/01/10	993/4	NOYESDAV
200	INDIANA ST OFFICE BLDG COMMN	MBIA	0.000	07/01/10	5.60	BEARSTER ◄─①
335	INDIANA ST RECREATIONAL DEV		6.050	07/01/14	6.45	SMITHBCH
115	INDIANA ST TOLL RD COMMN TOLL	M/S/F 11	9.000	01/01/15ETM	6.30	DRIZOS ◄─②
95	INDIANA ST TOLL RD COMMN TOLL		9.000	01/01/15ETM	6.30	EMMET
1000	INDIANA ST TOLL RD COMMN TOLL	N/C S/F 11	9.000	01/01/15ETM	6.00	WILLIAMA
100	FORT WAYNE IND HOSP AUTH HOSP	P/R @ 102	9.125	07/01/15C95	3.80	GABRIELE
10	INDIANAPOLIS IND ARPT AUTH REV (CA @ 102.01)	US AIR	7.500	07/01/09C97	100	HSH ◄─③
15	INDIANAPOLIS IND ARPT AUTH REV	US AIR	7.500	07/01/19	8.25	STERLING
60	INDIANAPOLIS IND LOC PUB IMPT		0.000	08/01/07N/C	8.10	SAPNY
25	INDIANAPOLIS IND LOC PUB IMPT		6.750	02/01/20	100	COUGHLIN
300	MICHIGAN CITY IND SEW WKS REV		5.200	08/01/07	5.70	NOYESDAV
	Thursday May 28, 1994				PAGE 15.A	

Source: *The Blue List of Current Municipal Offerings,* May 28, 1994, 15A. The Blue List Division of Standard & Poor's, New York. Reprinted with permission.

The Internet

Investments Online

This chapter discusses some of the basics of bonds—terminology, ratings, and the differences between corporate and municipal bonds. Bonds are much simpler to evaluate than stocks, since they are debt, not ownership claims, and they (usually) have a fixed time to maturity and known cash flows to the investor (barring default). But bonds are an important part of many individual and institutional portfolios, and here's some helpful Web sites for bond information:

http://bondheads.com This site links to news about bonds and interest rates, including reports from the Federal Reserve Banks and economic news. It also includes links to current pricing and interest rates and commentary on the fixed-income market.

http://www.investinginbonds.com/ A good Web site to learn about bonds and bond investing. It reports pricing information for government, corporate, mortgage-and-asset-backed securities as well as municipal bonds. It offers news and commentary links and a section of education information from bond basics to items for the knowledgeable bond investor.

Three bond ratings firms with interesting Web sites are Fitch's Investor's Service LP (**http://www.fitchinv.com**), Moody's Investor Service (**http://www.moodys.com**), and **http://www.standardandpoors.com/ratings.** These sites feature ratings, research, products and services. In addition to featuring bond ratings, Moody's site also offers country sovereign risk ratings. Standard & Poor's site offers selected research reports, ratings, and their rating criteria.

http://www.bradynet.com is a good information source for emerging markets' fixed income securities. This site features bond prices, indexes as well as analysis and research.

http://www.publicdebt.treas.gov This Web site contains information about U.S. government securities and how to invest in them.

SUMMARY

- We considered the basic features of bonds: interest, principal, and maturity. Certain key relationships affect price behavior. Price is essentially a function of coupon, maturity, and prevailing market interest rates. Bond price volatility depends on coupon and maturity. As will be demonstrated in Chapter 18, bonds with longer maturities and/or lower coupons respond most vigorously to a given change in market rates.

- Each bond has unique intrinsic characteristics and can be differentiated by type of issue and indenture provisions. Major benefits to bond investors include high returns for nominal risk, the potential for capital gains, certain tax advantages, and possibly additional returns from active trading of bonds. Aggressive bond investors must consider market liquidity, investment risks, and interest rate behavior. We considered high-yield (junk) bonds because of the growth in size and status of this segment of the bond market.

- The global bond market includes numerous countries. The non-U.S. markets have experienced strong relative growth, whereas the U.S. market has been stable and constitutes about half the world bond market. The four major bond markets (the United States, Japan, Euroland, and the United Kingdom) have a different makeup in terms of the proportion of governments, agencies, municipals, corporates, and international issues. The various market sectors also are unique in terms of liquidity, yield spreads, tax implications, and operating features.

- To gauge default risk, most bond investors rely on agency ratings. For additional information on the bond market, prevailing economic conditions, and intrinsic bond features, individual and institutional investors rely on a host of readily available publications. Extensive up-to-date quotes are generally available on Treasury bonds and notes. In contrast, trading and price information for corporates has been relatively difficult to find, but this has changed dramatically during 2004–2005. Unfortunately, the information on municipals is still very limited.

- The world bond market is large and is continuing to grow due to government deficits around the world and the need for capital by corporations. It is also very diverse in terms of country alternatives and issuers within countries. This chapter provides the fundamentals that will allow us to consider the valuation of individual bonds in Chapter 18 and the alternative bond portfolio techniques in Chapter 19.

SUGGESTED READINGS

Barnhill, Theodore M., William F. Maxwell, and Mark R. Shenkman, eds. *High-Yield Bonds.* New York: McGraw-Hill, 1999.

European Bond Commission. *European Bond Markets.* Chicago: Probus Publishing, 1989.

Fabozzi, Frank J., ed. *Advances and Innovations in the Bond and Mortgage Markets.* Chicago: Probus Publishing, 1989.

Fabozzi, Frank J., ed. *The Handbook of Fixed-Income Securities,* 7th ed. New York: McGraw-Hill, 2005.

Norton, Joseph, and Paul Spellman, eds. *Asset Securitization.* Cambridge, MA: Basil Blackwell, Inc., 1991.

Sundaresan, Suresh. *Fixed-Income Markets and Their Derivatives,* 2nd ed. Cincinnati: South-Western, 2002.

Van Horne, James C. *Financial Market Rates and Flows,* 6th ed. Englewood Cliffs, NJ: Prentice Hall, 2001.

Wilson, Richard S., and Frank J. Fabozzi. *The New Corporate Bond Market.* Chicago: Probus Publishing, 1990.

Yago, Glenn. *Junk Bonds.* New York: Oxford University Press, 1991.

QUESTIONS

1. Explain the difference between calling a bond and a bond refunding.
2. Identify the three most important determinants of the price of a bond. Describe the effect of each.
3. Given a change in the level of interest rates, discuss how two major factors will influence the relative change in price for individual bonds.
4. Briefly describe two indenture provisions that can affect the maturity of a bond.
5. Explain the differences in taxation of income from municipal bonds, from U.S. Treasury bonds, and from corporate bonds.
6. For several institutional participants in the bond market, explain what type of bond each is likely to purchase and why.
7. Why should investors be aware of the trading volume for bonds in their portfolio?
8. What is the purpose of bond ratings?
9. Based on the data in Exhibit 17.1, which is the fastest-growing bond market in the world? Which markets are losing market share?
10. Based on the data in Exhibit 17.2, discuss the makeup of the Japanese bond market and how and why it differs from the U.S. market.
11. Discuss the positives and negatives of investing in a government agency issue rather than a straight Treasury bond.
12. Discuss the difference between a foreign bond (e.g., a Samurai) and a Eurobond (e.g., a Euroyen issue).

13. *CFA Examination Level I*
    List *three* differences between Eurodollar and Yankee bonds.

PROBLEMS

1. An investor in the 28 percent tax bracket is trying to decide which of two bonds to purchase. One is a corporate bond carrying an 8 percent coupon and selling at par. The other is a municipal bond with a 5½ percent coupon, and it, too, sells at par. Assuming all other relevant factors are equal, which bond should the investor select?
2. What would be the initial offering price for the following bonds (assume semiannual compounding):
   a. A 15-year zero coupon bond with a yield to maturity (YTM) of 12 percent.
   b. A 20-year zero coupon bond with a YTM of 10 percent.

3. An 8.4 percent coupon bond issued by the state of Indiana sells for $1,000. What coupon rate on a corporate bond selling at its $1,000 par value would produce the same after-tax return to the investor as the municipal bond if the investor is in
   a. the 15 percent marginal tax bracket?
   b. the 25 percent marginal tax bracket?
   c. the 35 percent marginal tax bracket?

4. The Shamrock Corporation has just issued a $1,000 par value zero coupon bond with an 8 percent yield to maturity, due to mature 15 years from today (assume semiannual compounding).
   a. What is the market price of the bond?
   b. If interest rates remain constant, what will be the price of the bond in three years?
   c. If interest rates rise to 10 percent, what will be the price of the bond in three years?

5. Complete the information requested for each of the following $1,000 face value, zero coupon bonds, assuming semiannual compounding.

Bond	Maturity (Years)	Yield (Percent)	Price ($)
A	20	12	?
B	?	8	601
C	9	?	350

Chapter 18

The Analysis and Valuation of Bonds

After you read this chapter, you should be able to answer the following questions:

- How do you determine the value of a bond based on the present value formula?
- What are the alternative bond yields that are important to investors?
- How do you compute the following yields on bonds: current yield, yield to maturity, yield to call, and compound realized (horizon) yield?
- What are spot rates and forward rates and how do you calculate these rates from a yield to maturity curve?
- What are the spot rate yield curve and the forward rate curve?
- How and why do you use the spot rate curve to determine the value of a bond?
- What are the alternative theories that attempt to explain the shape of the term structure of interest rates?
- What factors affect the level of bond yields at a point in time?
- What economic forces cause changes in bond yields over time?
- When yields change, what characteristics of a bond cause differential percentage price changes for individual bonds?
- What is meant by the duration of a bond, how do you compute it, and what factors affect it?
- What is modified duration and what is the relationship between a bond's modified duration and its price volatility?
- What is the convexity for a bond, how do you compute it, and what factors affect it?
- Under what conditions is it necessary to consider both modified duration and convexity when estimating a bond's price volatility?
- What happens to the duration and convexity of bonds that have embedded call options?
- What are effective duration and effective convexity and when are they useful?
- What is empirical duration and how is it used with common stocks and other assets?
- What are the static yield spread and the option-adjusted spread?

In this chapter, we apply the valuation principles that were introduced in Chapter 11 to the valuation of bonds. This chapter is concerned with how one goes about finding the value of bonds using the traditional single yield to maturity rate and using multiple spot rates. We will also come to understand the several measures of yields for bonds. It is important to understand why these bond values and yields change over time. To do this, we begin with a review of value estimation for bonds using the present value model introduced in Chapter 11. This background on valuation allows us to understand and compute the expected rates of return on bonds.

After mastering the measurement of bond yields, we consider what factors influence the level of bond yields and what economic forces cause changes in yields over time. This is followed by a consideration of the alternative shapes of the yield curve and the alternative theories that explain changes in its shape. We discuss the effects of various characteristics and indenture provisions that affect the required returns and, therefore, the value of specific bond issues. This includes such factors as time to maturity, coupon, callability, and sinking funds.

We return to the consideration of bond value and acknowledge that, when yields change, all bond prices do not change in the same way. An understanding of the factors that affect the price changes for bonds has become more important because the price volatility of bonds has increased substantially. Before 1950, the yields on bonds were fairly low and both yields and prices were stable. In this environment, bonds were considered a very safe investment and most investors in bonds intended to hold them to maturity. During the last several decades, however, the level of interest rates has increased substantially because of inflation, and interest rates have also become more volatile because of changes in the rate of inflation and monetary policy. As a result, bond prices and rates of return on bonds have been much more volatile and the rates of return on bond investments have increased. Although this increase in interest rate volatility has affected all bonds, the impact is more significant on bonds with embedded options, such as call features.

THE FUNDAMENTALS OF BOND VALUATION

The value of bonds can be described in terms of dollar values or the rates of return they promise under some set of assumptions. In this section, we describe both the present value model, which computes a specific value for the bond using a single discount value, and the yield model, which computes the promised rate of return based on the bond's current price.

The Present Value Model

In our introduction to valuation theory in Chapter 11, we saw that the value of a bond (or any asset) equals the present value of its expected cash flows. The cash flows from a bond are the periodic interest payments to the bondholder and the repayment of principal at the maturity of the bond. Therefore, the value of a bond is the present value of the semiannual interest payments plus the present value of the principal payment. Notably, the standard technique is to use a single interest rate discount factor, which is the required rate of return on the bond. We can express this in the following present value formula that assumes semiannual compounding.[1]

18.1
$$P_m = \sum_{t=1}^{2n} \frac{C_i/2}{(1 + i/2)^t} + \frac{P_p}{(1 + i/2)^{2n}}$$

where:

P_m = the current market price of the bond
n = the number of years to maturity

---

[1]Almost all U.S. bonds pay interest semiannually, so it is appropriate to use semiannual compounding wherein you cut the annual coupon rate in half and double the number of periods. To be consistent, you should also use semiannual compounding when discounting the principal payment of a coupon bond or even a zero coupon bond. All our present value calculations assume semiannual compounding.

C_i = the annual coupon payment for Bond i
i = the prevailing yield to maturity for this bond issue
P_p = the par value of the bond

The value computed indicates what an investor would be willing to pay for this bond to realize a rate of return that takes into account expectations regarding the *RFR,* the expected rate of inflation, and the risk of the bond. The standard valuation technique assumes holding the bond to the maturity of the obligation. In this case, the number of periods would be the number of years to the maturity of the bond (referred to as its *term to maturity*). In such a case, the cash flows would include all the periodic interest payments and the payment of the bond's par value at the maturity of the bond.

We can demonstrate this formula using an 8 percent coupon bond that matures in 20 years with a par value of $1,000. This calculation implies that an investor who holds this bond to maturity will receive $40 every 6 months (one half of the $80 coupon) for 20 years (40 periods) and $1,000 at the maturity of the bond in 20 years. If we assume a prevailing yield to maturity for this bond of 10 percent (the market's required rate of return on the bond), the value for the bond using Equation 18.1 would be:

$$P_m = \sum_{t=1}^{40} \frac{80/2}{(1 + .10/2)^t} + \frac{\$1,000}{(1 + .10/2)^{40}}$$

We know that the first term is the present value of an annuity of $40 every 6 months for 40 periods at 5 percent, while the second term is the present value of $1,000 to be received in 40 periods at 5 percent. This can be summarized as follows:

Present value of interest payments		
$40 × 17.1591	=	$686.36
Present value of principal payment		
$1,000 × 0.1420	=	142.00
Total value of bond at 10%		$828.36

As expected, the bond will be priced at a discount to its par value because the market's required rate of return of 10 percent is greater than the bond's coupon rate, that is $828.36 or 82.836 percent of par.

Alternatively, if the market's required rate was 6 percent, the value would be computed the same way except we would compute the present value of the annuity at 3 percent for 40 periods and the present value of the principal at 3 percent for 40 periods as follows:

Present value of interest payments		
$40 × 23.1148	=	$ 924.59
Present value of principal payment		
$1,000 × 0.3066	=	306.60
Total value of bond at 6%		$1,231.19

Because the bond's discount rate is lower than its coupon, the bond would sell at a premium above par value—that is, $1,231.19 or 123.119 of par.

The Price-Yield Curve   When you know the basic characteristics of a bond in terms of its coupon, maturity, and par value, the only factor that determines its value (price) is the market discount rate—its required rate of return. As has been shown, as we increase the required rate, the price declines. It is possible to demonstrate the specific relationship between the price of a bond and its yield by computing the bond's price at a range of yields as shown in Exhibit 18.1.

A graph of this relationship between the required return (yield) on the bond and its price is referred to as the price-yield curve, as shown in Exhibit 18.2. Besides demonstrating that price moves inverse to yield, it shows three other important points:

1. When the yield is below the coupon rate, the bond will be priced at a **premium** to its par value.
2. When the yield is above the coupon rate, the bond will be priced at a **discount** to its par value.

Exhibit 18.1	Price-Yield Relationship for a 20-Year, 8 Percent Coupon Bond ($1,000 Par Value)

Required Yield	Price of Bond
2	$1,985.09
4	1,547.12
6	1,231.19
8	1,000.00
10	828.36
12	699.05
14	600.07
16	522.98

Exhibit 18.2	The Price-Yield Curve for a 20-Year, 8 Percent Coupon Bond

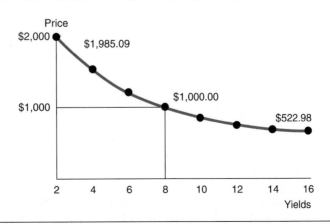

3. The price-yield relationship is not a straight line; rather, it is *convex*. As yields decline, the price increases at an increasing rate; and, as the yield increases, the price declines at a declining rate. This concept of a convex price-yield curve is referred to as *convexity* and will be discussed further in a later section.

The Yield Model

Instead of determining the value of a bond in dollar terms, investors often price bonds in terms of **yields**—the promised rates of return on bonds under certain assumptions. Thus far, we have used cash flows and our required rate of return to compute an estimated value for the bond. To compute an expected yield, we use the current market price (P_m) and the expected cash flows to *compute the expected yield on the bond.* We can express this approach using the same present value model. The difference is that in Equation 18.1, it was assumed that we knew the appropriate discount rate (the required rate of return), and we computed the estimated value (price) of the bond. In this case, we still use Equation 18.1, but it is assumed that we know the price of the bond and we compute the discount rate (yield) that will give us the current market price (P_m).

$$P_m = \sum_{t=1}^{2n} \frac{C_i/2}{(1 + i/2)^t} + \frac{P_p}{(1 + i/2)^{2n}}$$

where the variables are the same as previously, except

i = the discount rate that will discount the expected cash flows to equal the current market price of the bond

This i value gives the expected ("promised") yield of the bond under various assumptions to be noted, assuming you pay the price P_m. In the next section, we will discuss several types of bond yields that arise from the assumptions of the valuation model.

Approaching the investment decision stating the bond's value as a yield figure rather than a dollar amount, you consider the relationship of the computed bond yield to your required rate of return on this bond. If the computed promised bond yield is equal to or greater than your required rate of return, you should buy the bond; if the computed promised yield is less than your required rate of return, you should not buy the bond.

These approaches to pricing bonds and making investment decisions are similar to the two alternative approaches by which firms make investment decisions. We referred to one approach, the **net present value (NPV)** method, in Chapter 11. With the NPV approach, you compute the present value of the net cash flows from the proposed investment at your cost of capital and subtract the present value cost of the investment to get the net present value (NPV) of the project. If this NPV is positive, you consider accepting the investment; if it is negative, you reject it. This is basically the way we compared the value of an investment to its market price.

The second approach is to compute the **internal rate of return (IRR)** on a proposed investment project. The IRR is the discount rate that equates the present value of cash outflows for an investment with the present value of its cash inflows. You compare this discount rate, or IRR (which is also the estimated rate of return on the project), to your cost of capital, and accept any investment proposal with an IRR equal to or greater than your cost of capital. We do the same thing when we price bonds on the basis of yield. If the estimated (promised) yield on the bond (yield to maturity, yield to call, or horizon yield) is equal to or exceeds your required rate of return on the bond, you should invest in it; if the estimated yield is less than your required rate of return on the bond, you should not invest in it.

COMPUTING BOND YIELDS

Bond investors traditionally have used five yield measures for the following purposes:

Yield Measure	Purpose
Nominal yield	Measures the coupon rate.
Current yield	Measures the current income rate.
Promised yield to maturity	Measures the estimated rate of return for bond held to maturity.
Promised yield to call	Measures the estimated rate of return for bond held to first call date.
Realized (horizon) yield	Measures the estimated rate of return for a bond likely to be sold prior to maturity. It considers specific reinvestment assumptions and an estimated sales price. It also can measure the actual rate of return on a bond during some past period of time.

Nominal and current yields are mainly descriptive and contribute little to investment decision making. The last three yields are all derived from the present value model as described previously.

To measure an estimated realized yield (also referred to as the horizon yield or total return), a bond investor must estimate a bond's future selling price. Following our presentation of bond yields, we present the procedure for finding these prices. We conclude the valuation segment with a demonstration of valuing bonds using spot rates, which is becoming more prevalent.

Nominal Yield

Nominal yield is the coupon rate of a particular issue. A bond with an 8 percent coupon has an 8 percent nominal yield. This provides a convenient way of describing the coupon characteristics of an issue.

Current Yield

Current yield is to bonds what dividend yield is to stocks. It is computed as

18.2 $$CY = C_i / P_m$$

where:

CY = the current yield on a bond
C_i = the annual coupon payment of Bond i
P_m = the current market price of the bond

Because this yield measures the current income from the bond as a percentage of its price, it is important to income-oriented investors who want current cash flow from their investment portfolios. An example of such an investor would be a retired person who lives on this investment income. Current yield has little use for investors who are interested in total return because it excludes the important capital gain or loss component.

Promised Yield to Maturity

Promised yield to maturity is the most widely used bond yield figure because it indicates the fully compounded rate of return promised to an investor who buys the bond at prevailing prices, *if two assumptions hold true.* Specifically, the *promised* yield to maturity will be equal to the investor's *realized* yield *if* these assumptions are met. The first assumption is that the investor holds the bond to maturity. This assumption gives this value its shortened name, *yield to maturity* (YTM). The second assumption is implicit in the present value method of computation. Referring to Equation 18.1, recall that it related the current market price of the bond to the present value of all cash flows as follows:

$$P_m = \sum_{t=1}^{2n} \frac{C_i/2}{(1 + i/2)^t} + \frac{P_p}{(1 + i/2)^{2n}}$$

To compute the YTM for a bond, we solve for the rate i that will equate the current price (P_m) to all cash flows from the bond to maturity. As noted, this resembles the computation of the internal rate of return (IRR) on an investment project. Because it is a present value–based computation, it implies a reinvestment rate assumption because it discounts the cash flows. That is, the equation assumes that *all interim cash flows (interest payments) are reinvested at the computed YTM.* This is referred to as a *promised* YTM because the bond will provide this computed YTM *only if* you meet its conditions:

1. You hold the bond to maturity.
2. You reinvest all the interim cash flows at the computed YTM rate.

If a bond promises an 8 percent YTM, you must reinvest coupon income at 8 percent to realize that promised return. If you spend (do not reinvest) the coupon payments or if you cannot find opportunities to reinvest these coupon payments at rates as high as its promised YTM, then the actual realized yield you earn will be less than the promised yield to maturity. As will be demonstrated in the section on realized return, if you can reinvest cash flows at rates above the YTM, your realized (horizon) return will be greater than the promised YTM. The income earned on this reinvestment of the interim interest payments is referred to as **interest-on-interest,** and is discussed in detail in Homer and Leibowitz (1972, Chapter 1).

The impact of the reinvestment assumption (i.e., the interest-on-interest earnings) on the actual return from a bond varies directly with the bond's coupon and maturity. A higher coupon and/or a longer term to maturity will increase the loss in value from failure to reinvest the coupon cash flow at the YTM. Put another way, a higher coupon or a longer maturity makes the reinvestment assumption more important—i.e., greater reinvestment risk.

Exhibit 18.3 illustrates the impact of interest-on-interest for an 8 percent, 25-year bond bought at par to yield 8 percent. If you invested $1,000 today at 8 percent for 25 years and reinvested all the coupon payments at 8 percent, you would have approximately $7,100 at the end of 25 years. We will refer to this money that you have at the end of your investment horizon as your **ending-wealth value.** To prove that you would have an ending-wealth value of $7,100, look up the compound interest factor for 8 percent for 25 years (6.8493) or 4 percent for 50 periods (which assumes semiannual compounding and is 7.1073). In the case of U.S. bonds, the semiannual compounding is the appropriate procedure because almost all U.S. bonds pay interest every six months.

Exhibit 18.3 shows that this $7,100 is made up of $1,000 principal return, $2,000 of coupon payments over the 25 years ($80 a year for 25 years), and $4,100 in interest earned on the semiannual coupon payments reinvested at 4 percent semiannually. If you never reinvested any of the coupon payments, you would have an ending-wealth value of only $3,000. This ending-wealth value of $3,000 derived from the beginning investment of $1,000 gives you an

Exhibit 18.3	**The Effect of Interest-on-Interest on Total Realized Return**

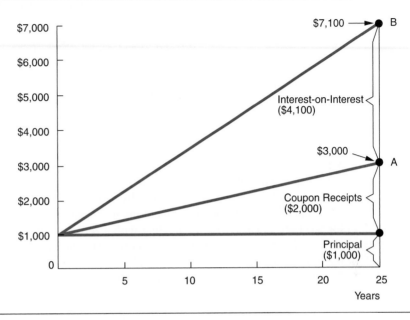

Promised yield at time of purchase: 8.00%
Realized yield over the 25-year investment horizon with no coupon reinvestment (A): 4.50%
Realized yield over the 25-year horizon with coupons reinvested at 8% (B): 8.00%

actual (realized) yield to maturity of only 4.5 percent. That is, the rate that will discount $3,000 back to $1,000 in 25 years is 4.5 percent. Reinvesting the coupon payments at some rate between 0 and 8 percent would cause your ending-wealth position to be above $3,000 and below $7,100; therefore, your actual realized rate of return would be somewhere between 4.5 percent and 8 percent. Alternatively, if you managed to reinvest the coupon payments at rates consistently above 8 percent, your ending-wealth position would be above $7,100, and your realized (horizon) rate of return would be above 8 percent.

Interestingly, during periods of very high interest rates, you often hear investors talk about locking in high yields. Many of these people are subject to **yield illusion** because they do not realize that attaining the high *promised* yield requires that they reinvest all the coupon payments at the very high *promised* yields. For example, if you buy a 20-year bond with a promised yield to maturity of 15 percent, you will actually realize the promised 15 percent yield *only* if you are able to reinvest all the coupon payments at 15 percent over the next 20 years.

Computing the Promised Yield to Maturity   The promised yield to maturity can be computed by using the present value model with semiannual compounding. The present value model gives the investor an accurate result and is the technique used by investment professionals.

The present value model equation—Equation 18.1—shows the promised yield valuation model:

$$P_m = \sum_{t=1}^{2n} \frac{C_i/2}{(1 + i/2)^t} + \frac{P_p}{(1 + i/2)^{2n}}$$

All variables are as described previously. This model is somewhat complex because the solution requires iteration. As noted, the present value equation is a variation of the internal rate of return (IRR) calculation where we want to find the discount rate, *i*, that will equate the present value of the cash flows to the market price of the bond (P_m). Using the prior example of an 8 percent, 20-year bond, priced at $900, the equation gives us a semiannual promised yield to maturity of 4.545 percent, which implies an annual promised YTM of 9.09 percent.[2]

$$900 = 40 \sum_{t=1}^{40} \left(\frac{1}{(1.04545)^t} \right) + 1000 \left(\frac{1}{(1.04545)^{40}} \right)$$

$$= 40(18.2574) + 1,000(0.1702)$$

$$= 900$$

The values for $1/(1 + i)$ were taken from the present value interest factor tables in the appendix at the back of the book using interpolation.

YTM for a Zero Coupon Bond   In several instances, we have discussed the existence of zero coupon bonds that only have the one cash inflow at maturity. This single cash flow means that the calculation of YTM is substantially easier as shown by the following example.

Assume a zero coupon bond maturing in 10 years with a maturity value of $1,000 selling for $311.80. Because you are dealing with a zero coupon bond, there is only the one cash flow from the principal payment at maturity. Therefore, you simply need to determine what the discount rate is that will discount $1,000 to equal the current market price of $311.80 in 20 periods (10 years of semiannual payments). The equation is as follows:

$$\$311.80 = \frac{\$1,000}{(1 + i/2)^{20}}$$

You will see that $i = 6$ percent, which implies an annual rate of 12 percent. For future reference, this yield also is referred to as the 10-year spot rate, which is the discount rate for a single cash flow to be received in 10 years.

Promised Yield to Call

Although investors use promised YTM to value most bonds, they must estimate the return on certain callable bonds with a different measure—the **promised yield to call (YTC)**. Whenever a bond with a call feature is selling for a price above par (that is, at a premium) equal to or greater than its call price, a bond investor should consider valuing the bond in terms of YTC rather than YTM. This is because the marketplace uses the lowest, most conservative yield measure in pricing a bond. As discussed in Homer and Leibowitz (1972, Chapter 4), when bonds are trading at or above a specified **crossover price**, which is approximately the bond's call price plus a small premium that increases with time to call, the yield to call will provide the lowest yield measure. The crossover price is important because at this price the YTM and the YTC are equal—this is the *crossover yield*. When the bond rises to this price above par, the computed YTM becomes low enough that it would be profitable for the issuer to call the bond and finance the call by selling a new bond at this prevailing market interest rate.[3] Therefore, the YTC measures the promised rate of return the investor will receive from holding this bond until it is retired at the first available call

---

[2]You will recall from your corporate finance course that you start with one rate (e.g., 9 percent or 4.5 percent semi-annual) and compute the value of the stream. In this example, the value would exceed $900, so you would select a higher rate until you had a present value for the stream of cash flows of less than $900. Given the discount rates above and below the true rate, you would do further calculations or interpolate between the two rates to arrive at the correct discount rate that would give you a value of $900.

[3]An extensive literature on the refunding of bond issues includes studies by Boyce and Kalotay (1979), Harris (1980), Kalotay (1982a), and Finnerty (1983).

date, that is, at the end of the deferred call period. Note that if an issue has multiple call dates at different prices (the call price will decline for later call dates), it will be necessary to compute which of these scenarios provides the *lowest* yield—this is referred to as computing **yield to worst**. Investors must consider computing the YTC for their bonds after a period when numerous high-yielding, high-coupon bonds have been issued. Following such a period, interest rates will decline, bond prices will rise, and the high-coupon bonds will subsequently have a high probability of being called—that is, their yields will fall below the crossover yield.

Computing Promised Yield to Call   Again, the present value method assumes that you hold the bond until the first call date and that you reinvest all coupon payments at the YTC rate.

Yield to call is calculated using a variation of Equation 18.1. To compute the YTC by the present value method, we would adjust the semiannual present value equation to give

18.3
$$P_m = \sum_{t=1}^{2nc} \frac{C_i/2}{(1 + i/2)^t} + \frac{P_c}{(1 + i/2)^{2nc}}$$

where:

P_m = the current market price of the bond
C_i = the annual coupon payment of Bond i
nc = the number of years to first call date
P_c = the call price of the bond

Following the present value method, we solve for i, which typically requires several computations or interpolations to get the exact yield. As before, this is a promised yield that requires the two assumptions noted earlier.

Realized (Horizon) Yield

The final measure of bond yield, **realized yield** or **horizon yield** (i.e., the actual return over a horizon period) measures the expected rate of return of a bond that you expect to sell prior to its maturity. In terms of the equation, the investor has a holding period *(hp)* or investment horizon that is less than *n*. Realized (horizon) yield can be used to estimate rates of return attainable from various trading strategies. Although it is a very useful measure, it requires several additional estimates not required by the other yield measures. The investor must estimate the expected future selling price of the bond at the end of the holding period. This measure also requires a specific estimate of the reinvestment rate for the coupon flows prior to the liquidation of the bond. This technique also can be used by investors to measure their actual yields after selling bonds.

Computing Realized (Horizon) Yield   The realized yields over a horizon holding period are variations on the promised yield equations. The substitution of P_f (future selling price) and *hp* into the present value model (Equation 18.1) provides the following realized yield model:

18.4
$$P_m = \sum_{t=1}^{2hp} \frac{C_i/2}{(1 + i/2)^t} + \frac{P_f}{(1 + i/2)^{2hp}}$$

Again, this present value model requires you to solve for the i that equates the expected cash flows from coupon payments and the estimated selling price to the current market price.

You will note from the present value realized yield formula in Equation 18.4 that the coupon flows are implicitly discounted at the computed realized (horizon) yield. In many cases, this is an inappropriate assumption because available market rates might be very different from the computed realized (horizon) yield. Therefore, to derive a realistic estimate of the estimated realized yield, you also need to *estimate your expected reinvestment rate during the investment horizon.* We will demonstrate this in a subsequent subsection.

Therefore, to complete your understanding of computing estimated realized yield for alternative investment strategies, the next section considers the calculation of future bond prices. This is followed by a section on calculating a realized (horizon) return with different reinvestment rates.

CALCULATING FUTURE BOND PRICES

Dollar bond prices need to be calculated in two instances: (1) when computing realized (horizon) yield, you must determine the future selling price (P_f) of a bond if it is to be sold before maturity or first call, and (2) when issues are quoted on a promised yield basis, as with municipals. You can easily convert a yield-based quote to a dollar price by using Equation 18.1, which does not require iteration. (You need only solve for P_m.) The coupon (C_i) is given, as is par value (P_p) and the promised YTM, which is used as the discount rate.

Consider a 10 percent, 25-year bond with a promised YTM of 12 percent. You would compute the price of this issue as

$$P_m = 100/2 \sum_{t=1}^{50} \frac{1}{\left(1 + \dfrac{0.120}{2}\right)^t} + 1,000 \ \frac{1}{\left(1 + \dfrac{0.120}{2}\right)^{50}}$$

$$= 50(15.7619) + 1,000(0.0543)$$

$$= \$842.40$$

In this instance, we are determining the prevailing market price of the bond based on the current market YTM. These market yields indicate the consensus of all investors regarding the value of this bond. An investor with a required rate of return on this bond that differs from the market YTM would estimate a different value for the bond.

In contrast to the current market price, you will need to compute a future price (P_f) when estimating the expected realized (horizon) yield performance of alternative bonds. Investors or portfolio managers who consistently trade bonds for capital gains need to compute expected realized (horizon) yield rather than promised yield. They would compute P_f through the following variation of the realized yield equation:

18.5
$$P_f = \sum_{t=1}^{2n-2hp} \frac{C_i/2}{(1 + i/2)^t} + \frac{P_p}{(1 + i/2)^{2n-2hp}}$$

where:

P_f = the future selling price of the bond
P_p = the par value of the bond
n = the number of years to maturity
h_p = the holding period of the bond (in years)
C_i = the annual coupon payment of Bond i
i = the expected market YTM at the end of the holding period

This equation is a version of the present value model that is used to calculate the expected price of the bond at the end of the holding period *(hp)*. The term $2n - 2hp$ equals the bond's remaining term to maturity at the end of the investor's holding period, that is, the number of six-month periods remaining after the bond is sold. Therefore, the determination of P_f is based on four variables: two that are known and two that must be estimated by the investor.

Specifically, the coupon (C_i) and the par value (P_p) are given. The investor must forecast the length of the holding period and, therefore, the number of years remaining to maturity at the time the bond is sold ($n - hp$). The investor also must forecast the expected market YTM at the time of sale (i). With this information, you can calculate the future price of the bond. The real difficulty (and the potential source of error) in estimating P_f lies in predicting hp and i.

Assume you bought the 10 percent, 25-year bond just discussed at $842, giving it a promised YTM of 12 percent. Based on an analysis of the economy and the capital market, you expect this bond's market YTM to decline to 8 percent in five years. Therefore, you want to compute its future price (P_f) at the end of Year 5 to estimate your expected rate of return, assuming you are correct in your assessment of the decline in overall market interest rates. As noted, you estimate the holding period (5 years), which implies a remaining life of 20 years, and the estimated future market YTM of 8 percent. Using Equation 18.5 gives a future price:

$$P_f = 50 \sum_{t=1}^{40} \frac{1}{(1.04)^t} + 1{,}000 \frac{1}{(1.04)^{40}}$$
$$= 50(19.7928) + 1{,}000(0.2083)$$
$$= 989.64 + 208.30$$
$$= \$1{,}197.94$$

Subsequently, we will use this estimate of the selling price in our calculation of the realized (horizon) yield on this investment.

Realized (Horizon) Yield with Differential Reinvestment Rates

The realized yield equation—Equation 18.4—is the standard present value formula with the changes in holding period and ending price. As such, it includes the implicit reinvestment rate assumption that all cash flows are reinvested at the computed i rate. There may be instances where such an implicit assumption is not appropriate, given your expectations for future interest rates. Assume that current market interest rates are very high and you invest in a long-term bond (e.g., a 20-year, 14 percent coupon) to take advantage of an expected decline in rates from 14 percent to 10 percent over a 2-year period. Computing the future price (equal to $1,330.95) and using the realized yield equation to estimate the realized (horizon) yield, we will get the following fairly high realized rate of return:

$$P_m = \$1{,}000$$
$$hp = 2 \text{ Years}$$
$$P_f = \sum_{t=1}^{36} 70/(1 + 0.05)^t + \$1{,}000/(1.05)^{36}$$
$$= \$1{,}158.30 + \$172.65$$
$$= \$1{,}330.95$$
$$\$1{,}000 = \sum_{t=1}^{4} \frac{70}{(1 + i/2)^t} + \frac{1{,}330.95}{(1 + i/2)^4}$$
$$i = 27.5\%$$

As noted, this calculation assumes that all cash flows are reinvested at the computed i (27.5 percent). However, it is unlikely that during a period when market rates are going from 14 percent to 10 percent, you could reinvest the coupon at 27.5 percent. It is more appropriate and realistic to *explicitly estimate the reinvestment rates* and calculate the realized yields based on your *ending-wealth position*. This procedure is more precise and realistic, and it is easier because it does not require iteration.

The basic technique calculates the value of all cash flows at the end of the holding period, which is the investor's ending-wealth value. We compare this ending-wealth value to our *beginning-wealth value* to determine the *compound rate of return that equalizes these two values.* Adding to our prior example, assume we have the following cash flows:

$$P_m = \$1,000$$
$$i = \text{interest payments of \$70 in 6, 12, 18, and 24 months}$$
$$P_f = \$1,330.95 \text{ (the ending market value of the bond)}$$

The ending value of the four interest payments is determined by our assumptions regarding specific reinvestment rates. Assume each payment is reinvested at a different declining rate that holds for its time period (that is, the first three interest payments are reinvested at progressively lower rates and the fourth interest payment is received at the end of the holding period).

$$
\begin{aligned}
i_1 \text{ at 13\% for 18 months} &= \$70 \times (1 + 0.065)^3 = \$\ 84.55 \\
i_2 \text{ at 12\% for 12 months} &= \$70 \times (1 + 0.06)^2 = \ \ \ 78.65 \\
i_3 \text{ at 11\% for\ \ 6 months} &= \$70 \times (1 + 0.055) = \ \ \ 73.85 \\
i_4 \text{ not reinvested} \ \ \ \ \ \ \ \ \ &= \$70 \times (1.0) \ \ \ \ \ \ \ \ \ = \ \ \ \underline{70.00} \\
\text{Future value of interest payments} &= \$307.05
\end{aligned}
$$

Therefore, our total ending-wealth value is

$$\$1,330.95 + \$307.05 = \$1,638.00$$

The compound realized (horizon) rate of return is calculated by comparing our ending-wealth value ($1,638) to our beginning-wealth value ($1,000) and determining what interest rate would equalize these two values over a two-year holding period. To find this, compute the ratio of ending wealth to beginning wealth (1.638). Find this ratio in a compound value table for four periods (assuming semiannual compounding). Table C.3 at the end of the book indicates that the realized rate is somewhere between 12 percent (1.5735) and 14 percent (1.6890). Interpolation gives an estimated semiannual rate of 13.16 percent, which indicates an annual rate of 26.32 percent. Using a calculator or computer, it is equal to $(1.638)^{1/4} - 1$. This compares to an estimate of 27.5 percent when we assume an implicit reinvestment rate of 27.5 percent.

This realized (horizon) yield computation specifically states the expected reinvestment rates as contrasted to assuming the reinvestment rate is equal to the computed realized yield. The actual assumption regarding the reinvestment rate can be very important.

The steps to calculate an expected realized (horizon) yield can be summarized as follows:

1. Calculate the future value at the horizon date of all coupon payments reinvested at estimated rates.
2. Calculate the expected sales price of the bond at your expected horizon date based on your estimate of the required yield to maturity at the horizon date.
3. Sum the values in Steps 1 and 2 to arrive at the total ending-wealth value.
4. Calculate the ratio of the ending-wealth value to the beginning value (the purchase price of the bond). Given this ratio and the time horizon, compute the compound rate of interest that will grow to this ratio over this time horizon.

$$\left[\frac{\text{Ending-wealth value}}{\text{Beginning value}} \right]^{\frac{1}{2n}} - 1$$

5. If all calculations assume semiannual compounding, double the interest rate derived from Step 4.

Price and Yield Determination on Noninterest Dates

So far, we have assumed that the investor buys (or sells) a bond precisely on the date that interest is due, so the measures are accurate only when the issues are traded on coupon payment dates.

However, when the semiannual model is used, and when more accuracy is necessary, another version of the price and yield model must be used for transactions on noninterest payment dates. Fortunately, the basic models need be extended only one more step because the value of an issue that trades X years, Y months, and so many days from maturity is found by extrapolating the bond value (price or yield) for the month before and the month after the day of transaction. Thus, the valuation process involves full months to maturity rather than years or semiannual periods.[4]

Accrued Interest Having computed a value for the bond at a noninterest payment date, it is also necessary to consider the notion of *accrued interest*. Because the interest payment on a bond, which is paid every six months, is a contractual promise by the issuer, the bond investor has the right to receive a portion of the semiannual interest payment if he/she held the bond for some part of the six-month period. For example, assume an 8 percent, $1,000 par value bond that pays $40 every six months. If you sold the bond two months after the prior interest payment, you have held it for one-third of the six-month period and would have the right to one-third of the $40 ($13.33). This is referred to as the accrued interest on the bond. Therefore, when you sell the bond, there is a calculation of the bond's remaining value until maturity, that is, its price. What you receive is this price *plus* the accrued interest ($13.33).

Yield Adjustments for Tax-Exempt Bonds

Municipal bonds, Treasury issues, and many agency obligations possess one common characteristic: Their interest income is partially or fully tax-exempt. This tax-exempt status affects the valuation of taxable versus nontaxable bonds. Although you could adjust each present value equation for the tax effects, it is not necessary for our purposes. We can envision the approximate impact of such an adjustment, however, by computing the fully taxable equivalent yield, which is one of the most often cited measures of performance for municipal bonds.

The **fully taxable equivalent yield (FTEY)** adjusts the promised yield computation for the bond's tax-exempt status. To compute the FTEY, we determine the promised yield on a tax-exempt bond using one of the yield formulas and then adjust the computed yield to reflect the rate of return that must be earned on a fully taxable issue. It is measured as

18.6
$$FTEY = \frac{i}{1 - T}$$

where:

i = the promised yield on the tax-exempt bond
T = the amount and type of tax exemption (i.e., the investor's marginal tax rate)

---

[4]For a detailed discussion of these calculations, see "Bond Pricing and Return Measures" (Fabozzi, 2005, Chapter 4).

For example, if the promised yield on the tax-exempt bond is 6 percent and the investor's marginal tax rate is 30 percent, the taxable equivalent yield would be

$$\text{FTEY} = \frac{0.06}{1 - 0.30} = \frac{0.06}{0.70} = 0.0857$$
$$= 8.57\%$$

The FTEY equation has some limitations. It is applicable only to par bonds or current coupon obligations, such as new issues, because the measure considers only interest income, ignoring capital gains, which are not tax-exempt. Therefore, we cannot use it for issues trading at a significant variation from par value (premium or discount).

Bond Yield Books

Bond value tables, commonly known as *bond books* or *yield books,* can eliminate most of the calculations for bond valuation. A bond yield table is like a present value interest factor table in that it provides a matrix of bond prices for a stated coupon rate, various terms to maturity (on the horizontal axis), and promised yields (on the vertical axis). Such a table allows you to determine either the promised yield or the price of a bond.

As might be expected, access to sophisticated calculators or computers has substantially reduced the need for and use of yield books. In addition, to truly understand alternative yield measures, you must master the present value model and its variations that generate values for promised YTM, promised YTC, realized (horizon) yield, and bond prices.

BOND VALUATION USING SPOT RATES

Thus far, we have used the valuation model, which assumes that we discount all cash flows by one common yield, reflecting the overall required rate of return for the bond. Similarly, we compute the yield on the bond (YTM, YTC, horizon yield) as the single interest rate that would discount all the flows from the bond to equal the current market price of the bond. It was noted in the YTM calculations that this was a promised yield that depended on two assumptions: holding the bond to maturity and reinvesting all cash flows at the computed YTM (the IRR assumption). Notably, this second assumption often is very unrealistic because it requires a flat, constant yield curve. We know that it is extremely rare for the yield curve to be flat, much less remain constant for any period of time. The yield curve typically is upward sloping for several reasons, which we discuss in a later section. Investors at any point in time require *a different rate of return for flows at different times.* For example, if investors are buying alternative zero coupon bonds (promising a single cash flow at maturity), they will almost always require different rates of return if they are offered a bond that matures in 2 years, 5 years, or 10 years.

As mentioned earlier, the rates used to discount a cash flow at a certain point are called spot rates. It is possible to demonstrate the desire for different rates by examining the rates on government discount notes with different maturities (i.e., spot rates) as of late May 2005, as shown in Exhibit 18.4. These rates indicate that investors require 3.60 percent for the cash flow in 2 years, 3.78 percent for the cash flow in 5 years, and 4.25 percent for the cash flow in 10 years. These differences in required rates for alternative maturities are relatively small compared to much larger differentials during 2003–2004. The difference in yield between the 1-year bond (3.28 percent) and the 30-year bond (4.43 percent), referred to as the *maturity spread*, was only 115 basis points in mid-2005, which is a small maturity spread historically.

Because of differences in spot rates across maturities, bond analysts and bond portfolio managers recognize that it is inappropriate to discount all the flows for a bond at one single rate

Exhibit 18.4	Yields on U.S. Treasury Strips with Alternative Maturities

Maturity	Yield
1 Year	3.28
2 Years	3.60
3 Years	3.67
4 Years	3.76
5 Years	3.78
6 Years	3.83
7 Years	3.97
8 Years	4.09
9 Years	4.10
10 Years	4.25
12 Years	4.28
14 Years	4.36
16 Years	4.41
18 Years	4.46
20 Years	4.48
25 Years	4.48
30 Years	4.43*

*This is the yield for last 30-year bond issued in February 2001; it is a 26-year bond, but used as a proxy for the 30-year bond.
Source: Data from *The Wall Street Journal,* 31 May 2005.

where the rate used is often based on the yield to maturity for a government bond with a single maturity. For example, when asked about the value of a particular 20-year bond rated AA, a bond trader typically will respond that the bond should trade a certain number of basis points higher than comparable maturity Treasury bonds (e.g., plus 70 basis points). This means that if 20-year Treasury bonds are currently yielding 4.48 percent, this AA-rated bond should trade at about a 5.18 percent yield. Notably, this rate would determine the price for the bond with no consideration given to the specific cash flows of this security (i.e., high or low coupon). Therefore, there is a growing awareness that the valuation formula should be specified such that *all cash flows should be discounted at spot rates consistent with the timing of the flows* as follows:

18.7
$$P_m = \sum_{t=1}^{2n} \frac{C_t}{(1 + i_t/2)^t}$$

where:

P_m = the market price for the bond
C_t = the cash flow at Time t
n = the number of years
i_t = the spot rate for Treasury securities at Maturity t

Note that this valuation model requires a different discount rate for each flow so it is not possible to use the annuity concept. Also, the principal payment at the end of the year n is no different from the interest coupon flow at year n.

Exhibit 18.5	Demonstration of Different Valuation of Alternative Five-Year Maturity Bonds with Unique Cash Flows, Discounted Using the Spot Rate Curve

| | | | CASH FLOWS | | | | | |
| | | | BOND A | | BOND B | | BOND C | |
Maturity (Years)	Spot Rate	Discount Factor	$	PV	$	PV	$	PV
0.5	5.00	0.9756	60	$ 58.536	30	$ 29.268	—	—
1.0	5.20	0.9499	60	56.994	30	28.497	—	—
1.5	5.50	0.9218	60	55.308	30	27.654	—	—
2.0	5.70	0.8937	60	53.622	30	26.811	—	—
2.5	5.80	0.8668	60	52.008	30	26.004	—	—
3.0	5.90	0.8399	60	50.394	30	25.197	—	—
3.5	6.10	0.8103	60	48.618	30	24.309	—	—
4.0	6.30	0.7803	60	46.818	30	23.409	—	—
4.5	6.40	0.7532	60	45.192	30	22.596	—	—
5.0	6.50	0.7270	1,060	770.620	1,030	748.810	1,000	727.00
Total present value				$1,238.110		$982.555		$727.00

　　To demonstrate the effect of this procedure, consider the following hypothetical spot rate curve for the next five years (in Exhibit 18.5) and three example bonds with equal maturities of five years, but with very different cash flows.

　　Beyond the differences in value because of the differences in cash flows and the rising spot rate curve, a significant comparison is the value that would be derived using a single discount rate based on the five-year maturity of all three bonds. If we assume two alternative yields to maturity of 6 percent and 6.5 percent for five-year bonds, the values for the three bonds are:

	6%		6.5%	
Bond A	$ 60 × 8.5302	= $ 511.81	$ 60 × 8.4254	= $ 505.52
	$1,000 × 0.7441	= 744.10	$1,000 × 0.7270	= 727.00
	Total Value	= $1,255.91		= $1,232.52
Bond B	$ 30 × 8.5302	= $ 255.90	$ 30 × 8.4254	= $ 252.76
	$1,000 × 0.7441	= 744.10	$1,000 × 0.7270	= 727.00
	Total Value	= $1,000.00		= $ 979.76
Bond C	$1,000 × 0.7441	= $ 744.10	$1,000 × 0.7270	= $ 727.00
	Total Value	= $ 744.10		= $ 727.00

　　Because there is a rising spot-yield curve, we know the YTM would be somewhere between these two values. The point is, under these conditions valuing the bonds with a single high rate tends to generate a value that is lower than that derived from the spot rate curve. This implies that a single-rate valuation technique would typically misvalue these bonds relative to the more appropriate technique that considers each flow as a single bond discounted by its own spot rate.

WHAT DETERMINES INTEREST RATES?

Now that we have learned to calculate various yields on bonds and to determine the value of bonds using yields and spot rates, the question arises as to what causes differences and changes in yields over time. Market interest rates cause these effects because the interest rates reported in the media are simply the prevailing YTMs for the bonds being discussed. For example, when you hear that the interest rate on long-term government bonds declined from 5.80 percent to 5.70 percent, this means that the price of this particular bond increased such that the computed YTM at the former price was 5.80 percent, but the computed YTM at the new, higher price is 5.70 percent. Yields and interest rates are the same. They are different terms for the same concept.

We have discussed the inverse relationship between bond prices and interest rates. When interest rates decline, the prices of bonds increase; when interest rates rise, there is a decline in bond prices. It is natural to ask which of these is the driving force—bond prices or bond interest rates? It is a simultaneous change, and you can envision either factor causing it. Most practitioners probably envision the changes in interest rates as causes because they constantly use interest rates to describe changes. They use interest rates because they are comparable across bonds, whereas the price of a bond depends not only on the interest rate but also on the bond's specific characteristics, including its coupon and maturity. The point is, as demonstrated in Exhibit 18.1 and Exhibit 18.2, when you change the interest rate (yield) on a bond, you simultaneously change its price in the opposite direction. Later in the chapter we will discuss the specific price-yield relationship for individual bonds and demonstrate that this price-yield relationship differs among bonds based on their particular coupon and maturity.

Understanding interest rates and what makes them change is necessary for an investor who hopes to maximize returns from investing in bonds. Therefore, in this section we review our prior discussion of the following topics: what causes overall market interest rates to rise and fall, why alternative bonds have different interest rates, and why the difference in rates (i.e., the yield spread) between alternative bonds changes over time. To accomplish this, we begin with a general discussion of what influences interest rates and then consider the **term structure of interest rates** (shown by yield curves), which relates the interest rates on a set of comparable bonds to their terms to maturity. The term structure is important because it implies a set of spot rates that can be used in the valuation of bonds. In addition, the term structure reflects what investors expect to happen to interest rates in the future and it dictates their current risk attitude. In this section, we specifically consider the calculation of spot rates and forward rates from the reported yield curve. Finally, we turn to the concept of *yield spreads,* which measure the differences in yields between alternative bonds. We describe various yield spreads and explore changes in them over time.

Forecasting Interest Rates

As discussed, the ability to forecast interest rates and changes in these rates is critical to successful bond investing. Later, we consider the major determinants of interest rates, but for now you should keep in mind that interest rates *are the price for loanable funds.* Like any price, they are determined by the supply and demand for these funds. On the one side, investors are willing to provide funds (the supply) at prices based on their required rates of return for a particular borrower. On the other side, borrowers need funds (the demand) to support budget deficits (government), to invest in capital projects (corporations), or to acquire durable goods (cars, appliances) or homes (individuals).

Although lenders and borrowers have some fundamental factors that determine supply and demand curves, the prices for these funds (interest rates) also are affected for short periods by events that shift the curves. Examples include major government bond issues that affect

| Exhibit 18.6 | Yields of International Long-Term Government Bonds: Quarterly 2002–2005 |

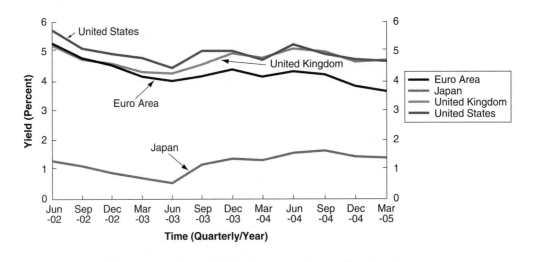

Source: *International Economic Trends* (May 2005), Research Department, Federal Reserve Bank of St. Louis.

demand for funds, or significant changes in Federal Reserve monetary policy that affect the supply of money.

Our treatment of interest rate forecasting recognizes that you must be aware of the basic determinants of interest rates and monitor these factors. We also recognize that detailed forecasting of interest rates is a very complex task that is best left to professional economists. Therefore, our goal as bond investors and bond portfolio managers is to monitor current and expected interest rate behavior. We should attempt to continuously assess the major factors that affect interest rate behavior but also rely on others—such as economic consulting firms, banks, or investment banking firms—for detailed insights on such topics as the real *RFR* and the expected rate of inflation.[5] This is precisely the way most bond portfolio managers operate.

Fundamental Determinants of Interest Rates

As shown in Exhibit 18.6, average interest rates (yields) for long-term (10-year) U.S. government bonds during the period from June 2002 to March 2005, went from about 5.90 percent to less than 5.00 percent. These results were midway between those of the United Kingdom and the Euro Area. U.K. bonds went from about 5.30 percent to less than 5.00 percent, while the rate on Japanese government bonds increased overall from about 1.20 percent to 1.50 percent. As a bond investor, you should understand *why* these differences exist and *why* interest rates changed.

As you know from your knowledge of bond pricing, bond prices increased dramatically during periods when market interest rates dropped, and some bond investors experienced very attractive returns. In contrast, some investors experienced substantial losses during periods

---

[5]Sources of information on the bond market and interest rate forecasts would include Merrill Lynch's *Fixed Income Weekly* and *World Bond Market Monitor;* Goldman Sach's *Financial Market Perspectives* and *The Pocket Chartroom;* and the Federal Reserve Bank of St. Louis, *Monetary Trends.*

when interest rates increased. A casual analysis of this chart, which covers about four years, indicates the need for monitoring interest rates. Essentially, the factors causing interest rates (i) to rise or fall are described by the following model:

18.8
$$i = RFR + I + RP$$

where:

RFR = the real risk-free rate of interest
I = the expected rate of inflation
RP = the risk premium

The relationship shown in this equation should be familiar from our presentations in Chapter 1 and Chapter 11. It is a simple but complete statement of interest rate behavior. The more difficult task is estimating the *future* behavior of such variables as real growth, expected inflation, and economic uncertainty. In this regard, interest rates, like stock prices, are extremely difficult to forecast with any degree of accuracy, as discussed by Fabozzi in "The Structure of Interest Rates" (2005, Chapter 6). Alternatively, we can visualize the source of changes in interest rates in terms of the economic conditions and issue characteristics that determine the rate of return on a bond:

18.9
$$i = f(\text{Economic Forces} + \text{Issue Characteristics})$$
$$= (RFR + I) + RP$$

This rearranged version of the previous equation helps isolate the factors that determine interest rates; as discussed in Van Horne (2001).

Effect of Economic Factors The real risk-free rate of interest (RFR) is the economic cost of money, that is, the opportunity cost necessary to compensate individuals for forgoing consumption. It is determined by the real growth rate of the economy with short-run effects due to ease or tightness in the capital market.

The expected rate of inflation is the other economic influence on interest rates. We add the expected level of inflation (I) to the real risk-free rate (RFR) to specify the nominal RFR, which is a market rate like the current rate on government T-bills. Given the stability of the real RFR, it is clear that the wide swings in nominal risk-free interest rates during the years covered by Exhibit 18.6 occurred because of expected inflation. Besides the unique country and exchange rate risk that we discuss in the section on risk premiums, differences in the rates of inflation between countries have a major impact on their level of interest rates.

To sum up, one way to estimate the nominal RFR is to begin with the real growth rate of the economy, adjust for short-run ease or tightness in the capital market, and then adjust this real rate of interest for the expected rate of inflation.

Another approach to estimating the nominal rate or changes in the rate is the macroeconomic view, where the supply and demand for loanable funds are the fundamental economic determinants of i. As the supply of loanable funds increases, the level of interest rates declines, other things being equal. Several factors influence the supply of funds. Government monetary policies imposed by the Federal Reserve have a significant impact on the supply of money. The savings patterns of U.S. and non-U.S. investors also affect the supply of funds. Non-U.S. investors have become a stronger influence on the U.S. supply of loanable funds during recent years, as shown by the significant purchases of U.S. securities by non-U.S. investors. It is widely acknowledged that this foreign supply of funds to the U.S. bond market has been very beneficial to the United States because it has helped reduce interest rates and the cost of capital.

Interest rates increase when the demand for loanable funds increases. The demand for loanable funds is affected by the capital and operating needs of the U.S. government, federal agencies, state and local governments, corporations, institutions, and individuals. Federal budget deficits increase the Treasury's demand for loanable funds. Likewise, the level of consumer demand for funds to buy houses, autos, and appliances affects rates, as does corporate demand for funds to pursue investment opportunities. The total of all groups determines the aggregate demand and supply of loanable funds and the level of the nominal *RFR*.

The Impact of Bond Characteristics   The interest rate of a specific bond issue is influenced not only by all the factors that affect the nominal *RFR* but also by the unique issue characteristics of the bond. These issue characteristics influence the bond's risk premium (*RP*). The economic forces that determine the nominal *RFR* affect all securities, whereas issue characteristics are unique to individual securities, market sectors, or countries. Thus, the differences in the yields of corporate and Treasury bonds are caused not by economic forces but, rather, by different issue characteristics that cause differences in the risk premiums.

Bond investors separate the risk premium into four components:

1. The quality of the issue as determined by its risk of default relative to other bonds
2. The term to maturity of the issue, which can affect price volatility
3. Indenture provisions, including collateral, call features, and sinking-fund provisions
4. Foreign bond risk, including exchange rate risk and country risk

Of the four factors, quality and maturity have the greatest impact on the risk premium for domestic bonds, while exchange rate risk and country risk are important components of risk for non-U.S. bonds.

The credit quality of a bond reflects the ability of the issuer to service outstanding debt obligations. This information is largely captured in the ratings issued by the bond rating firms. As a result, bonds with different ratings have different yields. For example, AAA-rated obligations possess lower risk of default than BBB obligations, so they can provide lower yield.

Notably, the risk premium differences between bonds of different quality levels change dramatically over time, depending on prevailing economic conditions. When the economy experiences a recession or a period of economic uncertainty, the desire for quality increases, and investors bid up prices of higher-rated bonds, which reduces their yields. This difference in yield is referred to as the *quality spread*. It also has been suggested by Dialynas and Edington (1992) that this yield spread is influenced by the volatility of interest rates. This variability in the risk premium over time was demonstrated and discussed in Chapter 1 and Chapter 11. The U.S. market experienced dramatic demonstrations of short-run risk premium explosions in August 1998 in response to Russia defaulting on its debt and following the terrorist attacks on September 11, 2001.

Term to maturity also influences the risk premium because it affects the price volatility of the bond. In the section on the term structure of interest rates, we will discuss the typical positive relationship between the term to maturity of a bond issue and its interest rate.

As discussed in Chapter 17, indenture provisions indicate the collateral pledged for a bond, its callability, and its sinking-fund provisions. Collateral gives protection to the investor if the issuer defaults on the bond because the investor has a specific claim on some assets in case of liquidation.

Call features indicate when an issuer can buy back the bond prior to its maturity. A bond is called by an issuer when interest rates have declined, so it is not to the advantage of the investor who must reinvest the proceeds at a lower interest rate. Obviously, an investor will charge the issuer for including the call option, and the cost of the option (which is a higher yield) will increase with the level of interest rates. Therefore, more protection against having the bond called reduces the risk premium. The significance (value) of call protection increases during periods of high interest rates. As noted by Marshall and Yawitz (1980) and Stanhouse and Stock (1999), when you buy a bond with a high coupon, you want protection from having it called away when rates decline.

As discussed by Kalotay (1981, 1982b), a sinking fund reduces the investor's risk and causes a lower yield for several reasons. First, a sinking fund reduces default risk because it requires the issuer to reduce the outstanding issue systematically. Second, purchases of the bond by the issuer to satisfy sinking-fund requirements provide price support for the bond because of the added demand. These purchases by the issuer also contribute to a more liquid secondary market for the bond because of the increased trading. Finally, sinking-fund provisions require that the issuer retire a bond before its stated maturity, which causes a reduction in the issue's average maturity. The decline in average maturity tends to reduce the risk premium of the bond much as a shorter maturity would reduce yield.

We know that foreign currency exchange rates change over time and that this increases the risk of global investing. The variability of exchange rates vary among countries because the trade balances and rates of inflation differ. Volatile trade balances, and inflation rates make exchange rates more volatile, which adds to the uncertainty of future exchange rates and increases the exchange rate risk premium.

In addition to changes in exchange rates, investors also are concerned with the political and economic stability of a country. If investors are unsure about the political environment or the economic system in a country, they will increase the required risk premium to reflect this country risk.

The Term Structure of Interest Rates

The term structure of interest rates (or the *yield curve,* as it is more popularly known) is a static function that relates the term to maturity to the yield to maturity for a sample of bonds at *a given point in time.*[6] Thus, it represents a cross section of yields for a category of bonds that are comparable in all respects but maturity. Specifically, the quality of the issues should be constant, and ideally you should have issues with similar coupons and call features within a single industry category. You can construct different yield curves for Treasuries, government agencies, prime-grade municipals, AAA utilities, and so on. The accuracy of the yield curve will depend on the comparability of the bonds in the sample.

As an example, Exhibit 18.7 shows yield curves for a sample of U.S. Treasury obligations. It is based on the yield to maturity information for a set of comparable Treasury issues from a publication such as the *Federal Reserve Bulletin* or *The Wall Street Journal.* These promised yields were plotted on the graph, and a yield curve was drawn that represents the general configuration of rates. These data represent yield curves at four different points in time to demonstrate the changes in yield levels and in the shape of the yield curve over time.

All yield curves, of course, do not have the same shape as those in Exhibit 18.7. Although individual yield curves are static, their behavior over time is quite fluid. As shown, the yield curve flattened dramatically from April 2004 to April 2005 mainly due to increases in short-term rates by the Federal Reserve. The further flattening in 2005 was due to small declines in long rates. Also, the shape of the yield curve can undergo dramatic alterations, following one of the four patterns shown in Exhibit 18.8. The rising yield curve is the most common and tends to prevail when interest rates are at low or modest levels. The declining yield curve tends to occur when rates are relatively high. The flat yield curve rarely exists for any period of time. The humped yield curve

---

[6]For a discussion of the theory and empirical evidence, see Sundaresan (2002).

Exhibit 18.7 | **Yields on U.S. Treasury Securities with Alternative Maturities at Different Times**

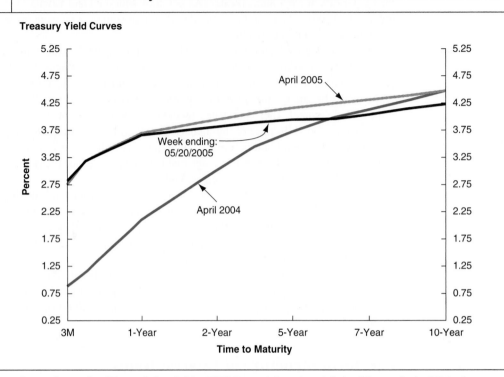

Source: *International Economic Trends* (May 2005), Research Department, Federal Reserve Bank of St. Louis.

prevails when extremely high rates are expected to decline to more normal levels. Note that the slope of the yield curve tends to level off after 15 years.

Why does the term structure assume different shapes? Three major theories attempt to explain this: the expectations hypothesis, the liquidity preference hypothesis, and the segmented market hypothesis.

Before we discuss these three alternative hypotheses, we must first discuss two previously noted rates that not only are an integral part of the term structure but also are important in the valuation of bonds. The next two subsections will deal with the specification and computation of *spot rates* and *forward rates*. Earlier, we discussed and used spot rates to value bonds with the idea that any coupon bond can be viewed as a collection of zero coupon securities.

Creating the Theoretical Spot Rate Curve[7]   Earlier in the chapter, we discussed the notion that the yield on a zero coupon bond for a given maturity is the spot rate for the maturity. Specifically, the **spot rate** is defined as the discount rate for a cash flow at a specific maturity. At that time, we used the rates on a series of zero coupon government bonds created by stripping coupon government bonds.

In this case, we will construct a theoretical spot rate curve from the observable yield curve that is based on the existing yields of Treasury bills and the most recent Treasury coupon securities (referred to as *on-the-run* Treasury issues). One might expect the

---

[7]This discussion of the theoretical spot rate curve and the subsequent presentation on calculating forward rates draw heavily from "The Structure of Interest Rates" by Fabozzi (2005, Chapter 6).

Exhibit 18.8	Types of Yield Curves

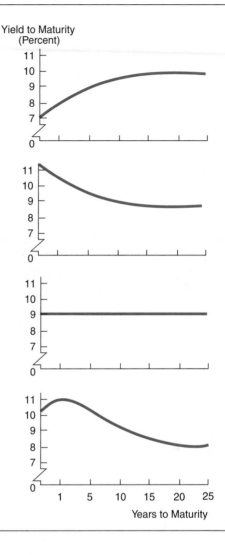

A rising yield curve is formed when the yields on short-term issues are low and rise consistently with longer maturities and flatten out at the extremes.

A declining yield curve is formed when the yields on short-term issues are high and yields on subsequently longer maturities decline consistently.

A flat yield curve has approximately equal yields on short-term and long-term issues.

A humped yield curve is formed when yields on intermediate-term issues are above those on short-term issues and the rates on long-term issues decline to levels below those for the short term and then level out.

theoretical spot rate curve and the spot rate curve derived from the stripped zero coupon bonds used earlier to be the same. The fact is, while they are close, they will not be exactly the same because the stripped zero coupon bonds will not be as liquid as the on-the-run issues. In addition, there are instances where institutions will have a strong desire for a particular spot maturity and this preference will distort the term structure relationship. Therefore, while it is possible to use the stripped zero coupon curve for a general indication, if you are going to use the spot rates for significant valuation, you would want to use the theoretical spot rate curve.

The process of creating a theoretical spot rate curve from coupon securities is called *bootstrapping* wherein it is assumed that the value of the Treasury coupon security should be equal to the value of the package of zero coupon securities that duplicates the coupon bond's cash flow. Exhibit 18.9 lists the maturity and YTM for six hypothetical Treasury bonds that will be used to calculate the initial spot rates.

Exhibit 18.9	Maturity and Yield to Maturity for Hypothetical Treasury Securities

Maturity (Years)	Coupon Rate	Price	Yield to Maturity
0.50	0.0000	96.15	0.0800
1.00	0.0000	92.19	0.0830
1.50	0.0850	99.45	0.0890
2.00	0.0900	99.64	0.0920
2.50	0.1100	103.49	0.0940
3.00	0.0950	99.49	0.0970

Sources: Federal Reserve Bulletin; Mergent Bond Record.

Consider the six-month Treasury bill in Exhibit 18.9. As discussed earlier, a Treasury bill is a zero coupon instrument so its annualized yield of 8 percent is equal to the spot rate. Similarly, for the one-year Treasury bill, the cited yield of 8.3 percent is equal to the one-year spot rate. Given these two spot rates, we can compute the spot rate for a theoretical 1.5-year zero coupon Treasury. The price for this 1.5-year security should equal the present value of three cash flows from an actual 1.5-year coupon Treasury, where the yield used for discounting a specific coupon payment is the spot rate corresponding to the cash flow.

Using $100 as par, the *cash flow* for the 1.5-year, 8.50 percent coupon Treasury is as follows:

0.5 years	$0.085 \times \$100 \times 0.5$	=	\$ 4.25
1.0 years	$0.085 \times \$100 \times 0.5$	=	\$ 4.25
1.5 years	$0.085 \times \$100 \times 0.5 + \$100$	=	\$104.25

The present value of the cash flows discounted at the appropriate spot rates is then

$$\frac{4.25}{(1 + z_1)^1} + \frac{4.25}{(1 + z_2)^2} + \frac{104.25}{(1 + z_3)^3}$$

where:

z_1 = ½ the annualized six-month theoretical spot rate
z_2 = ½ the one-year theoretical spot rate
z_3 = ½ the 1.5-year theoretical spot rate

Because the six-month spot rate and one-year spot rate are 8.0 percent and 8.3 percent, respectively, we know that

$$z_1 = 0.04 \quad and \quad z_2 = 0.0415$$

We can compute the present value of the 1.5-year coupon Treasury security as

$$\frac{4.25}{(1.0400)^1} + \frac{4.25}{(1.0415)^2} + \frac{104.25}{(1 + z_3)^3}$$

Because the price of the 1.5-year coupon Treasury security (from Exhibit 18.9) is $99.45, the following relationship must hold:

$$99.45 = \frac{4.25}{(1.0400)^1} + \frac{4.25}{(1.0415)^2} + \frac{104.25}{(1 + z_3)^3}$$

We can solve for the theoretical 1.5-year spot rate as follows:

$$99.45 = 4.08654 + 3.91805 + \frac{104.25}{(1 + z_3)^3}$$

$$91.44541 = \frac{104.25}{(1 + z_3)^3}$$

$$\frac{104.25}{91.44541} = (1 + z_3)^3$$

$$(1 + z_3)^3 = 1.140024$$

$$z_3 = 0.04465$$

Doubling this yield, we obtain the bond-equivalent yield of 0.0893 or 8.93 percent, which is the theoretical 1.5-year spot rate. That rate is the rate that the market would apply to a 1.5-year zero coupon Treasury, if such a security existed.

Given the theoretical 1.5-year spot rate, we can obtain the theoretical 2-year spot rate. The cash flow for the 2-year, 9.0 percent coupon Treasury security in Exhibit 18.9 is

0.5 years	0.090 × $100 × 0.5	=	$ 4.50
1.0 years	0.090 × $100 × 0.5	=	$ 4.50
1.5 years	0.090 × $100 × 0.5	=	$ 4.50
2.0 years	0.090 × $100 × 0.5 + 100	=	$104.50

The present value of the cash flow is then

$$\frac{4.50}{(1 + z_1)^1} + \frac{4.50}{(1 + z_2)^2} + \frac{4.50}{(1 + z_3)^3} + \frac{104.50}{(1 + z_4)^4}$$

where:

z_4 = ½ the two-year theoretical spot rate

Because the 6-month, 1-year, and 1.5-year spot rates are 8 percent, 8.3 percent, and 8.93 percent, respectively, then

$$z_1 = 0.04 \qquad z_2 = 0.0415 \qquad and \qquad z_3 = 0.04465$$

Therefore, the present value of the two-year coupon Treasury security is

$$\frac{4.50}{(1.0400)^1} + \frac{4.50}{(1.0415)^2} + \frac{4.50}{(1.04465)^3} + \frac{104.50}{(1 + z_4)^4}$$

Because the price of the two-year, 9.0 percent coupon Treasury security is $99.64, the following relationship must hold:

$$99.64 = \frac{4.50}{(1.0400)^1} + \frac{4.50}{(1.0415)^2} + \frac{4.50}{(1.04465)^3} + \frac{104.50}{(1 + z_4)^4}$$

Exhibit 18.10 | **Theoretical Spot Rates**

Maturity (Years)	Yield to Maturity	Theoretical Spot Rate
0.50	0.0800	0.08000
1.00	0.0830	0.08300
1.50	0.0890	0.08930
2.00	0.0920	0.09247
2.50	0.0940	0.09468
3.00	0.0970	0.09787

We can solve for the theoretical two-year spot rate as follows:

$$99.64 = 4.32692 + 4.14853 + 3.94730 + \frac{104,50}{(1 + z_4)^4}$$

$$87.21725 = \frac{104.50}{(1 + z_4)^4}$$

$$(1 + z_4)^4 = 1.198158$$

$$z_4 = 0.046235$$

Doubling this yield, we obtain the theoretical two-year spot rate bond-equivalent yield of 9.247 percent.

One can follow this approach sequentially to derive the theoretical 2.5-year spot rate from the calculated values of z_1, z_2, z_3, z_4 (the 6-month, 1-year, 1.5-year, and 2-year spot rates), and the price and the coupon of the bond with a maturity of 2.5 years. Subsequently, one could derive the theoretical spot rate for three years. The spot rates thus obtained are shown in Exhibit 18.10. They represent the term structure of spot interest rates for maturities up to three years, based on the prevailing bond price quotations.

As shown, with a rising YTM curve, the theoretical spot rate will increase at a faster rate such that the difference increases with maturity (i.e., the theoretical spot rate curve will be above a positively sloped YTM curve).

CALCULATING FORWARD RATES FROM THE SPOT RATE CURVE

Now that we have derived the theoretical spot rate curve, it is possible to determine what this curve implies regarding the market's expectation of *future* short-term rates, which are referred to as *forward rates*. The following illustrates the process of extrapolating this information about expected future interest rates.

Consider an investor who has a one-year investment horizon and is faced with the following two alternatives:

Alternative 1: Buy a one-year Treasury bill.
Alternative 2: Buy a six-month Treasury bill and, when it matures in six months, buy another six-month Treasury bill.

The investor will be indifferent between the two alternatives *if* they produce the same return for the one-year investment horizon. The investor knows the spot rate on the six-month Treasury bill and the one-year Treasury bill. However, she does not know what yield will be available on a six-month Treasury bill six months from now. The yield on a six-month Treasury bill six months from now is called a **forward rate**. Given the spot rate for the six-month Treasury bill and the one-year bill, we can determine the forward rate on a six-month Treasury bill *that will make the investor indifferent between the two alternatives.*

At this point, however, we need to digress briefly and recall several present value and investment relationships. First, if you invested in a one-year Treasury bill, you would receive $100 at the end of one year. The price of the one-year Treasury bill would be

$$\frac{100}{(1 + z_2)^2}$$

where:

z_2 = ½ the bond-equivalent yield of the theoretical one-year spot rate

Second, suppose you purchased a six-month Treasury bill for $X. At the end of six months, the value of this investment would be

$$\$X(1 + z_1)$$

where:

z_1 = ½ the bond-equivalent yield of the theoretical six-month spot rate

Let $_{t+0.5}r_{0.5}$ represent one-half the forward rate (expressed as a bond-equivalent yield) on a six-month Treasury bill (0.5) available six months from now ($t + 0.5$). If the investor were to renew her investment by purchasing that bill at that time, then the future dollars available at the end of the year from the $X investment would be

$$X(1 + z_1)(1 + {}_{t+0.5}r_{0.5}) = 100$$

Third, it is easy to use that formula to find out how many dollars the investor must invest in order to get $100 one year from now. This can be found as follows:

$$X(1 + z_1)(1 + {}_{t+0.5}r_{0.5}) = 100$$

which gives us

$$X = \frac{100}{(1 + z_1)(1 + {}_{t+0.5}r_{0.5})}$$

We are now prepared to return to the investor's choices and analyze what that situation says about forward rates. The investor will be indifferent between the two alternatives confronting her if she makes the same dollar investment and receives $100 from both alternatives at the end of one year. That is, the investor will be indifferent if

$$\frac{100}{(1 + z_2)^2} = \frac{100}{(1 + z_1)(1 + {}_{t+0.5}r_{0.5})}$$

Solving for ${}_{t+0.5}r_{0.5}$ we get

$$_{t+0.5}r_{0.5} = \frac{(1 + z_2)^2}{(1 + z_1)} - 1$$

Doubling r gives the bond-equivalent yield for the six-month forward rate six months from now.

We can illustrate the use of this formula with the theoretical spot rates shown in Exhibit 18.10. From that table, we know that

Six-month bill spot rate = 0.080 so $z_1 = 0.0400$
One-year bill spot rate = 0.083 so $z_2 = 0.0415$

Substituting into the formula, we have

$$_{t+0.5}r_{0.5} = \frac{(1.0415)^2}{(1.0400)} - 1$$
$$= 0.043$$

Therefore, the forward rate six months from now $(t + 0.5)$ on a six-month Treasury security, quoted annually, is 8.6 percent (0.043×2). Let us confirm our results. The price of a one-year Treasury bill with $100 maturity is

$$\frac{100}{(1.0415)^2} = 92.19$$

If $92.19 is invested for six months at the six-month spot rate of 8 percent, the amount at the end of six months would be

$$92.19(1.0400) = 95.8776$$

If $95.8776 is reinvested for another six months in a six-month Treasury bill offering 4.3 percent for six months (8.6 percent annually), the amount at the end of one year would be

$$95.8776(1.043) = 100$$

Both alternatives will have the same $100 payoff if the six-month Treasury bill yield six months from now is 4.3 percent (8.6 percent on a bond-equivalent basis). This means that, if an investor is guaranteed a 4.3 percent yield on a six-month Treasury bill six months from now, she will be indifferent between the two alternatives.

We used the theoretical spot rates to compute the forward rate. The resulting forward rate is called the *implied forward rate*.

It is possible to use the yield curve to calculate the implied forward rate for any time in the future for any investment horizon. This would include six-month or one-year forward rates for each year in the future. The one-year forward rates would be designated as follows:

$_{t+1}r_1$ = the 1-year forward rate, 1 year from now $(t+1)$
$_{t+2}r_1$ = the 1-year forward rate, 2 years from now $(t+2)$
$_{t+3}r_1$ = the 1-year forward rate, 3 years from now $(t+3)$

Given the calculations, it is clear that with a rising spot rate curve, the forward rate curve would be above the spot rate curve. From Exhibit 18.10, we have the following one-year spot rates, which imply the following one-year forward rates:

Maturity (Years)	Spot Rates	One–Year Forward Rates
1.0	0.08300	
2.0	0.09247	0.1020
3.0	0.09787	0.1087

Therefore:

$$_{t+1}r_1 = \frac{(1.09247)^2}{(1.08300)} - 1 = \frac{1.19349}{1.08300} - 1 = 0.1020$$

$$_{t+2}r_1 = \frac{(1.09787)^3}{(1.00247)^2} - 1 = \frac{1.32328}{1.19349} - 1 = 0.1087$$

Specifically, the one-year forward rate that is expected one year from now $(_{t+1}r_1)$ is 10.20 percent, while the one-year forward rate that is expected two years from now $(_{t+2}r_1)$ is 10.87 percent.

TERM-STRUCTURE THEORIES

Expectations Hypothesis

According to the expectations hypothesis, the shape of the yield curve results from the interest rate expectations of market participants. More specifically, it holds that *any long-term interest rate simply represents the geometric mean of current and future one-year interest rates expected to prevail over the maturity of the issue.* In essence, the term structure involves a series of intermediate and long-term interest rates, each of which is a reflection of the geometric average of current and expected one-year interest rates. Under such conditions, the equilibrium long-term rate is the rate the long-term bond investor would expect to earn through successive investments in short-term bonds over the term to maturity of the long-term bond.

Generally, this relationship can be formalized as follows:

18.10 $$(1 + {}_tR_n) = [(1 + {}_tR_1)(1 + {}_{t+1}r_1) \cdots (1 + {}_{t+n-1}r_1)]^{1/N}$$

where:

R_n = the actual long-term rate
N = the term to maturity (in years) of long issue
R = the current 1-year rate
$_{t+i}r_1$ = the expected 1-year yield during some future period, $t + i$ (these future 1-year rates are referred to as *forward rates*)

Given the relationship set forth in this equation, the formula for computing the one-period forward rate beginning at time $t + n$ and implied in the term structure at time t is

18.11
$$1 + {}_{t+n}r_{1t} = \frac{(1 + {}_tR_{1t})(1 + {}_{t+1}r_{1t})(1 + {}_{t+2}r_{1t}) \cdots (1 + {}_{t+n}r_{1t})(1 + {}_{t+n}r_{1t})}{(1 + {}_tR_{1t})(1 + {}_{t+1}r_{1t}) \cdots (1 + {}_{t+n-1}r_{1t})}$$

$$= \frac{(1 + {}_tR_{n+1})^{n+1}}{(1 + {}_tR_n)^n}$$

$${}_{t+n}r_{1t} = \frac{(1 + {}_tR_{n+1})^{n+1}}{(1 + {}_tR_n)^n} - 1$$

where ${}_{t+n}r_{1t}$ is the one-year forward rate prevailing at $t + n$, using the term structure at time t.

Assume that the five-year spot rate is 10 percent (${}_tR_5 = 0.10$) and the four-year spot rate is 9 percent (${}_tR_4 = 0.09$). The forward one-year rate four years from now implied by these spot rates can be calculated as follows:

$${}_{t+4}r_{1t} = \frac{(1 + {}_tR_5)^5}{(1 + {}_tR_4)^4} - 1$$

$$= \frac{(1 + 0.10)^5}{(1 + 0.09)^4} - 1$$

$$= \frac{1.6105}{1.4116} - 1$$

$$= 1.1409 - 1 = 0.1409 = 14.09\%$$

The term structure at time t implies that the one-year spot rate four years from now (during Year 5) will be 14.09 percent. This concept and formula can be used to derive future rates for multiple years. Thus, the two-year spot rate that will prevail three years from now (which is a forward rate) could be calculated using the three-year spot rate and the five-year spot rate. The general formula for computing the j-period forward rate beginning at time $t + n$ as of time t is

18.12
$${}_{t+n}r_{jt} = \sqrt[j]{\frac{(1 + {}_tR_{n+j})^{n+j}}{(1 + {}_tR_n)^n}} - 1$$

As a practical approximation of Equation 18.10, it is possible to use the *arithmetic* average of one-year rates to generate long-term yields.

The expectations theory can explain any shape of yield curve. Expectations for rising short-term rates in the future cause a rising yield curve; expectations for falling short-term rates in the future will cause long-term rates to lie below current short-term rates, and the yield curve will decline. Similar explanations account for flat and humped yield curves.

Consider the following explanation by the expectations hypothesis of the shape of the term structure of interest rates using arithmetic averages:

${}_tR_1 = 5\frac{1}{2}$ percent the 1-year rate of interest prevailing now (Period t)

${}_{t+1}r_1 = 6$ percent the 1-year rate of interest expected to prevail next year (Period $t + 1$)

${}_{t+2}r_1 = 7\frac{1}{2}$ percent the 1-year rate of interest expected to prevail 2 years from now (Period $t + 2$)

${}_{t+3}r_1 = 8\frac{1}{2}$ percent the 1-year rate of interest expected to prevail 3 years from now (Period $t + 3$)

Using these values and the known rate on a one-year bond, we compute rates on two-, three-, or four-year bonds (designated R_2, R_3, and R_4) as follows:

$_tR_1 = 5\frac{1}{2}$ percent
$_tR_2 = (0.055 + 0.06)/2 = 5.75$ percent
$_tR_3 = (0.055 + 0.06 + 0.075)/3 = 6.33$ percent
$_tR_4 = (0.055 + 0.06 + 0.075 + 0.085)/4 = 6.88$ percent

In this illustration (which uses the arithmetic average as an approximation of the geometric mean), the yield curve is upward sloping because, at present, investors expect future short-term rates to be above current short-term rates. This is not the formal method for constructing the yield curve. Rather, the yield curve is constructed on the basis of the prevailing promised yields for bonds with different maturities.

The expectations hypothesis attempts to explain *why* the yield curve is upward sloping, downward sloping, humped, or flat by explaining the expectations implicit in yield curves with different shapes. The evidence is fairly substantial and convincing that the expectations hypothesis is a workable explanation of the term structure. Because of the supporting evidence, its relative simplicity, and the intuitive appeal of the theory, the expectations hypothesis of the term structure of interest rates is rather widely accepted.

Consistent Investor Actions Besides the theory and empirical support, it is also possible to present a scenario wherein investor actions will cause the yield curve postulated by the theory. The expectations hypothesis predicts a declining yield curve when interest rates are expected to fall in the future rather than rise. In a case of expected falling rates, long-term bonds would be considered attractive investments because investors would want to lock in prevailing higher yields (which are not expected to be as high in the future) or they would want to capture the increase in bond prices (as capital gains) that will accompany a decline in rates. By the same reasoning, investors will avoid short-term bonds or sell them and reinvest the funds in long-term bonds that will experience larger price increases if rates decline. The point is, investor expectations will reinforce the declining shape of the yield curve as they bid up the prices of long-maturity bonds (forcing yields to decline) and short-term bond issues are avoided or sold (so prices decline and yields rise). At the same time, there is confirming action by suppliers of bonds. Specifically, government or corporate issuers will avoid selling long bonds at the current high rates, waiting until the rates decline. In the meantime, they will issue short-term bonds, if needed, while waiting for lower rates. Therefore, in the long-term market, you will have an increase in demand and a decline in the supply and vice versa in the short-term market. These shifts between long- and short-term maturities will continue until equilibrium occurs or expectations change.

Liquidity Preference Hypothesis

The theory of liquidity preference holds that long-term securities should provide higher returns than short-term obligations because investors are willing to sacrifice some yields to invest in short-maturity obligations to avoid the higher price volatility of long-maturity bonds. Another way to interpret the liquidity preference hypothesis is to say that lenders prefer short-term loans, and, to induce them to lend long term, it is necessary to offer higher yields.

The liquidity preference (also called term premium) theory contends that uncertainty and volatility cause investors to favor short-term issues over bonds with longer maturities because short-term bonds are less volatile and can easily be converted into predictable amounts of cash should unforeseen events occur. This theory argues that the yield curve should generally slope upward and that any other shape should be viewed as a temporary aberration.

This theory can be considered an extension of the expectations hypothesis because the formal liquidity preference position contends that the liquidity premium inherent in the yields for longer maturity bonds should be added to the *expected* future rate in arriving at long-term yields. Specifically, the liquidity premium *(L)* compensates the investor in long-term bonds for the added volatility inherent in long-term bonds compared to short-maturity securities. Because the liquidity premium *(L)* is provided to compensate the long-term investor, it is simply a variation of Equation 18.10 as follows:

$$(1 + {}_tR_N) = [(1 + {}_tR_1)(1 + {}_{t+1}r_1 + L_2) \cdots (1 + {}_{t+N-1}r_1 + L_N)]^{1/N}$$

In this specification, the *L*s are not the same but would be expected to increase with maturity because the price volatility increases with maturity. The liquidity preference theory has been found to possess some strong empirical support by Kessel (1965), Cagan (1969), and McCulloch (1975).

To see how the liquidity preference theory predicts future yields and how it compares with the pure expectations hypothesis, let us predict future long-term rates from a single set of one-year rates: 6 percent, 7.5 percent, and 8.5 percent. The liquidity preference theory suggests that investors add increasing liquidity premiums to successive rates to derive actual market rates. As an example, they might arrive at rates of 6.3 percent, 7.9 percent, and 9.0 percent.

As a matter of historical fact, the yield curve shows an upward bias, which implies that some combination of the expectations theory and the liquidity preference theory will more accurately explain the shape of the yield curve than either of them alone. Specifically, actual long-term rates consistently tend to be above what is envisioned from the price expectations hypothesis. This tendency implies the existence of a liquidity premium.

Segmented Market Hypothesis

Despite meager empirical support, a third theory for the shape of the yield curve is the segmented market hypothesis, which enjoys wide acceptance among market practitioners. Also known as the *preferred habitat,* the *institutional theory,* or the *hedging pressure theory,* it asserts that different institutional investors have different maturity needs that lead them to confine their security selections to specific maturity segments. That is, investors supposedly focus on short-, intermediate-, or long-term securities. This theory contends that the shape of the yield curve ultimately is a function of these investment policies of major financial institutions.

As noted in Chapter 17, financial institutions tend to structure their investment policies in line with such factors as their tax liabilities, the types and maturity structure of their liabilities, and the level of earnings demanded by depositors. For example, because commercial banks are subject to normal corporate tax rates and their liabilities are generally short- to intermediate-term time and demand deposits, they consistently invest in short- to intermediate-term municipal bonds.

The segmented market theory contends that the business environment, along with legal and regulatory limitations, tends to direct each type of financial institution to allocate its resources to particular types of bonds with specific maturity characteristics. In its strongest form, the segmented market theory holds that the maturity preferences of investors and borrowers are so strong that investors never purchase securities outside their preferred maturity range to take advantage of yield differentials. As a result, the short- and long-maturity portions of the bond market are effectively segmented, and yields for a segment depend on the supply and demand *within* that maturity segment.

Trading Implications of the Term Structure

Information on maturity yields can help you formulate yield expectations by simply observing the shape of the yield curve. If the yield curve is declining sharply, historical evidence suggests that interest rates will probably decline. Expectations theorists would suggest that you need to examine only the prevailing yield curve to predict the direction of interest rates in the future.

Based on these theories, bond investors use the prevailing yield curve to predict the shapes of future yield curves. Using this prediction and knowledge of current interest rates, investors can determine expected yield volatility by maturity sector. As suggested by Hourdouvelis (1988), the maturity segments that are expected to experience the greatest yield changes give the investor the largest potential price change opportunities.

Yield Spreads

Another technique that helps bond investors make profitable trades is the analysis of *yield spreads*—the differences in promised yields between bond issues or segments of the market at any point in time. Such differences are specific to the particular issues or segments of the bond market. Thus yield spreads further shape the rates determined by the basic economic forces (*RFR + I*).

There are four major yield spreads:

1. Different *segments* of the bond market may have different yields. For example, pure government bonds will have lower yields than government agency bonds, and government bonds have much lower yields than corporate bonds.
2. Bonds in different *sectors* of the same market segment may have different yields. For example, prime-grade municipal bonds will have lower yields than good-grade municipal bonds; you will find spreads between AA utilities and BBB utilities, or between AAA industrial bonds and AAA public utility bonds.
3. Different *coupons* or *seasoning* within a given market segment or sector may cause yield spreads. Examples include current coupon government bonds versus deep-discount governments or recently issued AA industrials versus seasoned AA industrials.
4. Different *maturities* within a given market segment or sector also cause differences in yields. You will see yield spreads between short-term agency issues and long-term agency issues, or between 3-year prime municipals and 25-year prime municipals.

The differences among these bonds cause yield spreads that may be either positive or negative. More important, *the magnitude or the direction of a spread can change over time.* These changes in size or direction of yield spreads offer profit opportunities. We say that the spread narrows whenever the differences in yield become smaller; it widens as the differences increase. Exhibit 18.11 contains data on a variety of past yield spreads that have changed over time.

As a bond investor, you should evaluate yield spread changes because these changes influence bond price behavior and comparative return performance. You should attempt to identify (1) any normal yield spread that is expected to become abnormally wide or narrow in response to an anticipated swing in market interest rates, or (2) an abnormally wide or narrow yield spread that is expected to become normal.

Economic and market analyses will help you develop expectations regarding the potential for yield spreads to change. Taking advantage of these changes requires a knowledge of historical spreads, an ability to *predict* future total market changes, and an understanding of why and when specific spreads will change.[8]

---

[8]An article that identifies four determinants of relative market spreads and suggests scenarios when they will change is Dialynas and Edington (1992).

| Exhibit 18.11 | Selected Mean Yield Spreads (Reported in Basis Points) |

Comparisons	1998	1999	2000	2001	2002	2003
1. Long governments–short governments	67	111	12	215	343	371
2. Long Aaa corporates–long governments	65	69	125	116	111	95
3. Long Aaa corporates–long Aaa municipals	146	152	180	177	178	164
4. Long Baa municipals–long Aaa municipals	17	24	54	62	51	71
5. Utilities–industrials	−10	−16	−12	19	106	18
6. Industrials–financials	31	39	44	85	44	60
7. Long CCC corporates–long BB corporates	601	871	1205	1587	1445	859

Note: Yield spreads are equal to the yield on the first bond minus the yield on the second bond—for example, the yield on long governments minus the yield on short governments.

Sources: Federal Reserve Bulletin, Mergent Bond Record.

WHAT DETERMINES THE PRICE VOLATILITY FOR BONDS?

In this chapter, we have learned about alternative bond yields, how to calculate them, what determines bond yields (interest rates), and what causes them to change. Now that we understand why yields change, we can logically ask, What is the effect of these yield changes on the prices and rates of return for different bonds? We have discussed the inverse relationship between changes in yields and the price of bonds, so we can now discuss *the specific factors that affect the amount of price change for a yield change* in different bonds. This can also be referred to as the *interest rate sensitivity* of a bond. This section lists the specific factors that affect bond price changes for a given change in interest rates (i.e., the interest rate sensitivity of a bond) and demonstrates the effect for different bonds.

A given change in interest rates can cause vastly different percentage price changes for alternative bonds, which implies different interest rate sensitivity. This section will help you understand what causes these differences in interest rate sensitivity. To maximize your rate of return from an expected decline in interest rates, for example, you need to know which bonds will benefit the most from the yield change. This section helps you make this bond selection decision.

Throughout this section, we talk about bond price changes or bond price volatility interchangeably. **Bond price volatility** is measured as the percentage change in the price of the bond, computed as follows:

$$\frac{\text{EPB}}{\text{BPB}} - 1$$

where:

EPB = the ending price of the bond
BPB = the beginning price of the bond

A bond with high price volatility or high interest rate sensitivity is one that experiences a relatively large percentage price change for a given change in yields.

Exhibit 18.12 | **Effect of Maturity on Bond Price Volatility**

Term to Maturity	PRESENT VALUE OF AN 8 PERCENT BOND ($1,000 PAR VALUE)							
	1 Year		10 Years		20 Years		30 Years	
Discount rate (YTM)	7%	10%	7%	10%	7%	10%	7%	10%
Present value of interest	$ 75	$ 73	$ 569	$498	$ 858	$686	$1,005	$757
Present value of principal	934	907	505	377	257	142	132	54
Total value of bond	$1,009	$980	$1,074	$875	$1,115	$828	$1,137	$811
Percentage change in total value	−2.9		−18.5		−25.7		−28.7	

Bond price volatility is influenced by more than yield behavior alone. Malkiel (1962) used the bond valuation model to demonstrate that the market price of a bond is a function of four factors: (1) its par value, (2) its coupon, (3) the number of years to its maturity, and (4) the prevailing market interest rate. Malkiel's mathematical proofs showed the following relationships between yield (interest rate) changes and bond price behavior:

1. Bond prices move inversely to bond yields (interest rates).
2. For a given change in yields (interest rates), longer-maturity bonds post larger price changes; thus, bond price volatility is *directly* related to term to maturity.
3. Bond price volatility increases at a diminishing rate as term to maturity increases.
4. Bond price movements resulting from equal absolute increases or decreases in yield are *not* symmetrical. A decrease in yield raises bond prices by more than an increase in yield of the same amount lowers prices.
5. Higher coupon issues show smaller percentage price fluctuation for a given change in yield; thus, bond price volatility is *inversely* related to coupon.

Homer and Leibowitz (1972) showed that the absolute level of market yields also affects bond price volatility. As the level of prevailing yields rises, the price volatility of bonds increases, *assuming a constant percentage change in market yields.* It is important to note that if you assume a constant percentage change in yield, the basis-point change will be greater when rates are high. For example, a 25 percent change in interest rates when rates are at 4 percent will be 100 basis points; the same 25 percent change when rates are at 8 percent will be a 200 basis-point change. In the discussion of bond duration, we will see that this difference in basis point change is important.

Exhibits 18.12, 18.13, and 18.14 demonstrate these relationships assuming semiannual compounding. Exhibit 18.12 demonstrates the effect of maturity on price volatility. In all four maturity classes, we assume a bond with an 8 percent coupon and assume that the discount rate (YTM) changes from 7 percent to 10 percent. The only difference among the four cases is the maturities of the bonds. The demonstration involves computing the value of each bond at a 7 percent yield and at a 10 percent yield and noting the percentage change in price. As shown, this constant change in yield caused the price of the one-year bond to decline by only 2.9 percent; the 30-year bond declined by almost 29 percent. Clearly, the longer-maturity bond experienced the greater price volatility.

Also, price volatility increased at a decreasing rate with maturity. When maturity doubled from 10 years to 20 years, the percent change in price increased by less than 50 percent (from 18.5 percent to 25.7 percent). A much smaller change occurred when going from 20 years to 30 years. Therefore, Exhibit 18.12 demonstrates the first three of our price-yield relationships:

| Exhibit 18.13 | **Effect of Coupon on Bond Price Volatility** |

	PRESENT VALUE OF 20-YEAR BOND ($1,000 PAR VALUE)							
	0 Percent Coupon		3 Percent Coupon		8 Percent Coupon		12 Percent Coupon	
Discount rate (YTM)	7%	10%	7%	10%	7%	10%	7%	10%
Present value of interest	$ 0	$ 0	$322	$257	$ 858	$686	$1,287	$ 1030
Present value of principal	257	142	257	142	257	142	257	142
Total value of bond	$257	$142	$579	$399	$1,115	$828	$1,544	$1,172
Percentage change in total value	−44.7		−31.1		−25.7		−24.1	

| Exhibit 18.14 | **Effect of Yield Level on Bond Price Volatility** |

	PRESENT VALUE OF 20-YEAR, 4 PERCENT BOND ($1,000 PAR VALUE)							
	(1)		(2)		(3)		(4)	
	Low Yields		Intermediate Yields		High Yields		100 Basis-Point Change at High Yields	
Discount rate (YTM)	3%	4%	6%	8%	9%	12%	9%	10%
Present value of interest	$ 602	$ 547	$ 462	$396	$370	$301	$370	$343
Present value of principal	562	453	307	208	175	97	175	142
Total value of bond	$1,164	$1,000	$ 769	$604	$545	$398	$545	$485
Percentage change in total value	−14.1		−21.5		−27.0		−11.0	

(1) bond price is inversely related to yields, (2) bond price volatility is positively related to term to maturity, and (3) bond price volatility increases at a decreasing rate with maturity.

It also is possible to demonstrate the fourth relationship with this exhibit. Using the 20-year bond for demonstration purposes, if you computed the percentage change in price related to an *increase* in rates (e.g., from 7 percent to 10 percent), you would get the answer reported—a 25.7 percent decrease. In contrast, if you computed the effect on price of a *decrease* in yields from 10 percent to 7 percent, you would get a 34.7 percent increase in price (from $828 to $1,115). This demonstrates that prices change more in response to a decrease in rates (from 10 percent to 7 percent) than to a comparable increase in rates (from 7 percent to 10 percent).

Exhibit 18.13 demonstrates the coupon effect. In this set of examples, all the bonds have equal maturity (20 years) and experience the same change in YTM (from 7 percent to 10 percent). The exhibit shows the *inverse* relationship between coupon rate and price volatility: The smallest coupon bond (the zero) experienced the largest percentage price change (almost 45 percent) versus a 24 percent change for the 12 percent coupon bond.

Exhibit 18.14 demonstrates the yield level effect. In these examples, all the bonds have the same 20-year maturity and the same 4 percent coupon. In the first three cases, the YTM changed by a constant 33.3 percent (i.e., from 3 percent to 4 percent, from 6 percent to 8 percent, and from 9 percent to 12 percent). Note that the first change is 100 basis points, the second is 200 basis points, and the third is 300 basis points. The results in the first three columns confirm the statement that when rates change by a *constant percentage,* the change in the bond price is larger when the rates are at a higher level.

The fourth column shows that if you assume a *constant basis-point change in yields,* you get the opposite results. Specifically, a 100 basis-point change in yields from 3 percent to 4 percent provides a price change of 14.1 percent, while the same 100 basis-point change from 9 percent to 10 percent results in a price change of only 11 percent. Therefore, the yield level effect can differ, depending on whether the yield change is specified as a constant percentage change or a constant basis-point change.

Thus, the price volatility of a bond for a given change in yield (i.e., its interest rate sensitivity) is affected by the bond's coupon, its term to maturity, the level of yields (depending on what kind of change in yield), and the direction of the yield change. However, although both the level and direction of change in yields affect price volatility, they cannot be used for trading strategies. When yields change, the two variables that have a dramatic effect on a bond's interest rate sensitivity are coupon and maturity.

Trading Strategies

Knowing that coupon and maturity are the major variables that influence a bond's interest rate sensitivity, we can develop some strategies for maximizing rates of return when interest rates change. Specifically, if you expect a major *decline* in interest rates, you know that bond prices will increase, so you want a portfolio of bonds with the *maximum interest rate sensitivity* so that you will enjoy maximum price changes (capital gains) from the change in interest rates. In this situation, the previous discussion regarding the effect of maturity and coupon indicates that you should attempt to build a portfolio of long-maturity bonds with low coupons (ideally a long-term zero coupon bond). A portfolio of such bonds should experience the maximum price appreciation for a given decline in market interest rates.

In contrast, if you expect an *increase* in market interest rates, you know that bond prices will decline, and you want a portfolio with *minimum interest rate sensitivity* to minimize the capital losses caused by the increase in rates. Therefore, you would want to change your portfolio to short-maturity bonds with high coupons. This combination should provide minimal price volatility for a change in market interest rates.

Duration Measures

Because the price volatility (interest rate sensitivity) of a bond varies inversely with its coupon and directly with its term to maturity, it is necessary to determine the best combination of these two variables to achieve your objective. This effort would benefit from a composite measure that considered both coupon and maturity.

A composite measure of the interest rate sensitivity of a bond is referred to as **duration**. This concept and its development as a tool in bond analysis and portfolio management have existed for almost 70 years. Notably, several specifications of duration have been derived over the past 20 years. First, **Macaulay duration**, developed almost 70 years ago by Frederick Macaulay (1938), is a measure of the time flow of cash from a bond. A modified version of Macaulay duration can be used under certain conditions to indicate the price volatility of a bond in response to interest rate changes. Second, **modified duration** is derived by making a small adjustment (modification) to the Macaulay duration value. As already noted, under certain restrictive conditions (most important, there are no embedded options), modified duration can provide an approximation to the interest rate sensitivity of a bond (or any financial asset). Third, **effective duration** is a direct measure of the interest rate sensitivity of a bond (or any financial instrument) in cases where it is possible to estimate price changes following an interest rate change for an asset using a valuation model. Finally, **empirical duration** measures directly the percentage price change of an asset for an actual change in interest rates. This measure can be used as an estimate for an asset when there is no exact valuation model available. Because of the development of many new financial instruments, which have very unique cash flows *that change with interest rates,* effective duration and empirical duration have become widely used because of their flexibility and ability to provide a useful measure of interest rate sensitivity—the primary goal of duration. Therefore, in this section, we discuss and demonstrate these four duration measures, including their limitations.

Macaulay Duration   Macaulay showed that the duration of a bond was a more appropriate measure of time characteristics than the term to maturity of the bond because duration considers both the repayment of capital at maturity and the size and timing of coupon payments prior to final maturity. Using annual compounding, duration (D) is

18.13

$$D = \frac{\sum_{t=1}^{n} \dfrac{C_t(t)}{(1 + i)^t}}{\sum_{t=1}^{n} \dfrac{C_t}{(1 + i)^t}}$$

where:

t = the time period in which the coupon or principal payment occurs
C_t = the interest or principal payment that occurs in period t
i = the yield to maturity on the bond

The denominator in this equation is the price of a bond as determined by the present value model. The numerator is the present value of all cash flows *weighted according to the time to cash receipt.* The following example, which demonstrates the specific computations for two bonds, shows the procedure and highlights some of the properties of Macaulay duration. Consider the following two sample bonds:

	Bond A	Bond B
Face value	$1,000	$1,000
Maturity	10 years	10 years
Coupon	4%	8%

Assuming annual interest payments and an 8 percent yield to maturity on the bonds, duration is computed as shown in Exhibit 18.15.[9] If duration is computed by discounting flows using the yield to maturity of the bond, it is called *Macaulay duration.*

Characteristics of Macaulay Duration   This example illustrates several characteristics of Macaulay duration. First, the Macaulay duration of a bond with coupon payments always will be less than its term to maturity because duration gives weight to these interim interest payments.

Second, there is *an inverse relationship between coupon and duration.* A bond with a larger coupon will have a shorter duration because more of the total cash flows come earlier in

[9]We assume annual interest payments to reduce the space requirements and computations. In practice you would assume semiannual payments that would cause a slightly shorter duration since you receive half the payments earlier.

Exhibit 18.15	Computation of Macaulay Duration (Assuming 8 Percent Market Yield)

BOND A

(1) Year	(2) Cash Flow	(3) PV at 8%	(4) PV of Flow	(5) PV as % of Price	(6) (1) × (5)
1	$ 40	0.9259	$ 37.04	0.0506	0.0506
2	40	0.8573	34.29	0.0469	0.0938
3	40	0.7938	31.75	0.0434	0.1302
4	40	0.7350	29.40	0.0402	0.1608
5	40	0.6806	27.22	0.0372	0.1860
6	40	0.6302	25.21	0.0345	0.2070
7	40	0.5835	23.34	0.0319	0.2233
8	40	0.5403	21.61	0.0295	0.2360
9	40	0.5002	20.01	0.0274	0.2466
10	1,040	0.4632	481.73	0.6585	6.5850
Sum			$731.58	1.0000	8.1193

Duration = 8.12 Years

BOND B

(1) Year	(2) Cash Flow	(3) PV at 8%	(4) PV of Flow	(5) PV as % of Price	(6) (1) × (5)
1	$ 80	0.9259	$ 74.07	0.0741	0.0741
2	80	0.8573	68.59	0.0686	0.1372
3	80	0.7938	63.50	0.0635	0.1906
4	80	0.7350	58.80	0.0588	0.1906
5	80	0.6806	54.44	0.0544	0.2720
6	80	0.6302	50.42	0.0504	0.3024
7	80	0.5835	46.68	0.0467	0.3269
8	80	0.5403	43.22	0.0432	0.3456
9	80	0.5002	40.02	0.0400	0.3600
10	1,080	0.4632	500.26	0.5003	5.0030
Sum			$1,000.00	1.0000	7.2470

Duration = 7.25 Years

the form of interest payments. As shown in Exhibit 18.15, the 8 percent coupon bond has a shorter duration than the 4 percent coupon bond.

A zero coupon bond or a pure discount bond, such as a Treasury bill, will have *duration equal to its term to maturity.* In Exhibit 18.15, if you assume a single payment at maturity, duration will equal term to maturity because the only cash flow comes in the final (maturity) year—that is, you receive 100 percent of cash flows in year n.

Third, there is *generally a positive relationship between term to maturity and Macaulay duration,* but duration increases at a decreasing rate with maturity. Therefore, a bond with longer term to maturity almost always will have a higher duration. The relationship is not direct because as maturity increases the present value of the principal declines in value.

Exhibit 18.16 | **Duration versus Maturity**

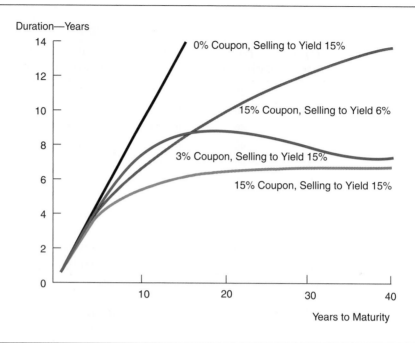

As shown in Exhibit 18.16, the shape of the duration-maturity curve depends on the coupon and the yield to maturity. The curve for a zero coupon bond is a straight line, indicating that duration equals term to maturity. In contrast, the curve for a low-coupon bond selling at a deep discount (due to a high YTM) will turn down at long maturities, which means that under these conditions, the longer-maturity bond will have lower duration because the discounted value of the principal payment becomes insignificant, which shifts the weight to the early interest payments, causing a decline in Macaulay duration.

Fourth, all else the same, there is an *inverse relationship between YTM and duration*. A higher yield to maturity of a bond reduces its duration. As an example, in Exhibit 18.15, if the yield to maturity had been 12 percent rather than 8 percent, the duration for the 4 percent bond would have gone from 8.12 to 7.75, and the duration of the 8 percent bond would have gone from 7.25 to 6.80.[10] The combined effect of the inverse relationships between duration and both coupon and yield can be seen with the curve for the 15 percent coupon and yield bond where the duration tops out at about six years. The real-world example of such a bond would be a high-yield bond.

Finally, sinking funds and call provisions can have a dramatic effect on a bond's duration. They can change the total cash flows for a bond and, therefore, significantly change its duration. Between these two factors, the characteristic that causes the greatest uncertainty is the call feature—it is difficult to estimate when the call option will be exercised since it is a function of changes in interest rates. We consider this further when we discuss the effect of embedded options on the duration and convexity of a bond.

---

[10]These properties are discussed and demonstrated in Reilly and Sidhu (1980) and Fabozzi, Buetow, and Johnson (2005).

A summary of Macaulay duration characteristics is as follows:

- The duration of a zero coupon bond will equal its term to maturity.
- The duration of a coupon bond always will be less than its term to maturity.
- There is an *inverse* relationship between coupon and duration.
- There is generally a *positive* relationship between term to maturity and duration. Note that the duration of a coupon bond increases at a decreasing rate with maturity and the shape of the duration/maturity curve will depend on the coupon and YTM of the bond. Also, the duration of a deep discount bond will decline at very long maturities (over 20 years).
- There is an *inverse* relationship between yield to maturity and duration.
- Sinking funds and call provisions can cause a dramatic change in the duration of a bond. The effect of embedded options is discussed in a subsequent section.

Modified Duration and Bond Price Volatility

An adjusted measure of duration called *modified duration* can be used to approximate the interest rate sensitivity of an option-free (straight) bond. Modified duration equals Macaulay duration (computed in Exhibit 18.15) divided by 1 plus the current yield to maturity divided by the number of payments in a year. As an example, a bond with a Macaulay duration of 10 years, a yield to maturity *(i)* of 8 percent, and semiannual payments would have a modified duration of

$$D_{mod} = 10 / \left(1 + \frac{0.08}{2}\right)$$
$$= 10/(1.04) = 9.62$$

It has been shown, both theoretically and empirically by Hopewell and Kaufman (1973), that price movements of option-free bonds *will vary proportionally* with modified duration for *small changes in yields*.[11] Specifically, as shown in the following equation, an estimate of the percentage change in bond price equals the change in yield times modified duration:

18.14
$$\frac{\Delta P}{P} \times 100 = -D_{mod} \times \Delta i$$

where:

ΔP = the change in price for the bond
P = the beginning price for the bond
$-D_{mod}$ = the modified duration of the bond
Δi = the yield change in basis points divided by 100. For example, if interest rates go from 8.00 to 8.50 percent, $\Delta i = 50/100 = 0.50$.

Consider a bond with Macaulay $D = 8$ years and $i = 0.10$. Assume that you expect the bond's YTM to decline by 75 basis points (e.g., from 10 percent to 9.25 percent). The first step is to compute the bond's modified duration as follows:

$$D_{mod} = 8 / \left(1 + \frac{0.10}{2}\right)$$
$$= 8/(1.05) = 7.62$$

---

[11]The importance of the specification "for small changes in yields" will become clear when we discuss convexity in the next section. Because modified duration is an approximate measure of interest rate sensitivity, the "years" label is not appropriate.

Exhibit 18.17 | **Bond Duration in Years for Bond Yielding 6 Percent under Different Terms**

Years to Maturity	COUPON RATES			
	0.02	0.04	0.06	0.08
1	0.995	0.990	0.985	0.981
2	4.756	4.558	4.393	4.254
10	8.891	8.169	7.662	7.286
20	14.981	12.980	11.904	11.232
50	19.452	17.129	16.273	15.829
100	17.567	17.232	17.120	17.064
∞	17.167	17.167	17.167	17.167

Source: L. Fisher and R. L. Weil, "Coping with the Risk of Interest Rate Fluctuations: Returns to Bondholders from Naive and Final Strategies," *Journal of Business* 44, no. 4 (October 1971): University of Chicago Press. Reprinted by permission of the University of Chicago Press.

The estimated percentage change in the price of the bond using Equation 18.14 is:

$$\% \Delta P = -(7.62) \times \frac{-75}{100}$$
$$= (-7.62) \times (-0.75)$$
$$= 5.72$$

This indicates that the bond price should increase by approximately 5.72 percent in response to the 75 basis-point decline in YTM. If the price of the bond before the decline in interest rates was $900, the price after the decline in interest rates should be approximately $900 × 1.0572 = $951.48.

The modified duration is always a negative value for a noncallable bond because of the inverse relationship between yield changes and bond price changes. Also, remember that this formulation provides an *estimate* or *approximation* of the percent change in the price of the bond. The following section on convexity shows that this formula that uses only modified duration provides an exact estimate of the percentage price change only for very small changes in yields of option-free securities.

Trading Strategies Using Modified Duration We know that the longest duration security provides the maximum price variation. Exhibit 18.17 demonstrates that numerous ways exist to achieve a given level of duration. The following discussion indicates that an active bond investor who wants to adjust his/her portfolio for anticipated interest rate changes can use this measure of interest rate sensitivity to structure a portfolio to take advantage of changes in market yields.

If you expect a *decline* in interest rates, you should *increase* the average modified duration of your bond portfolio to experience maximum price volatility. If you expect an *increase* in interest rates, you should *reduce* the average modified duration of your portfolio to minimize your price decline. Note that the modified duration of your portfolio is the market-value-weighted average of the modified durations of the individual bonds in the portfolio.

Bond Convexity

Modified duration allows us to estimate bond price changes for a change in interest rates. However, the equation we used to make this calculation (Equation 18.14) is accurate only for

Exhibit 18.18	Price-Yield Relationships for Alternative Bonds

A. 12 PERCENT, 20 YEAR		B. 12 PERCENT, 3 YEAR		C. ZERO COUPON, 30 YEAR	
Yield	Price	Yield	Price	Yield	Price
1.0%	$2,989.47	1.0%	$1,324.30	1.0%	$741.37
2.0	2,641.73	2.0	1,289.77	2.0	550.45
3.0	2,346.21	3.0	1,256.37	3.0	409.30
4.0	2,094.22	4.0	1,224.06	4.0	304.78
5.0	1,878.60	5.0	1,192.78	5.0	227.28
6.0	1,693.44	6.0	1,162.52	6.0	169.73
7.0	1,533.88	7.0	1,133.21	7.0	126.93
8.0	1,395.86	8.0	1,104.84	8.0	95.06
9.0	1,276.02	9.0	1,077.37	9.0	71.29
10.0	1,171.59	10.0	1,050.76	10.0	53.54
11.0	1,080.23	11.0	1,024.98	11.0	40.26
12.0	1,000.00	12.0	1,000.00	12.0	30.31

very small changes in market yields. We will see that the accuracy of the estimate of the price change deteriorates with larger changes in yields because the modified duration calculation is a *linear* approximation of a bond price change that follows a *curvilinear* (convex) function. To understand the effect of this **convexity**, we must consider the price-yield relationship for alternative bonds.[12]

The Price-Yield Relationship for Bonds Because the price of a bond is the present value of its cash flows at a particular discount rate, if you are given the coupon, maturity, and a yield for a bond, you can calculate its price at a point in time. The price-yield curve provides a set of prices for a specific maturity/coupon bond at a point in time using a range of yields to maturity (discount rates). As an example, Exhibit 18.18 lists the computed prices for a 12 percent, 20-year bond assuming yields from 1 percent to 12 percent. The exhibit shows that if you discount the flows from this bond at a yield of 1 percent, you would get a price of $2,989.47; discounting these same flows at 10 percent gives a price of $1,171.59. The graph of these prices relative to the yields that produced them (Exhibit 18.19) indicates that the price-yield relationship for this bond is not a straight line but a curvilinear relationship. That is, it is convex.

Two points are important about the price-yield relationship:

1. This relationship can be applied to a single bond, a portfolio of bonds, or any stream of future cash flows.
2. The convex price-yield relationship will differ among bonds or other cash flow streams, depending on the nature of the cash flow stream, that is, its coupon and maturity. For example, the price-yield relationship for a high-coupon, short-term security will be almost a straight line because the price does not change as much for a change in yields (e.g., the 12 percent, three-year bond in Exhibit 18.18). In contrast, the price-yield relationship for a low-coupon, long-term bond will curve radically (i.e., be very convex), as shown by the

---

[12]For a further discussion of this topic, see Dunetz and Mahoney (1988) and Fabozzi, Buetow, and Johnson (2005).

Exhibit 18.19 | **Price-Yield Relationship and Modified Duration at 4 Percent Yield**

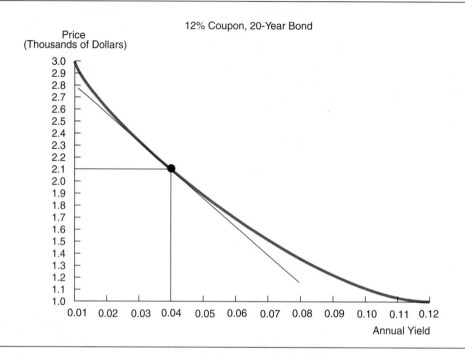

zero coupon, 30-year bond in Exhibit 18.18. These differences in convexity are shown graphically in Exhibit 18.20. The curved nature of the price-yield relationship is referred to as the bond's *convexity.*

The Desirability of Convexity   As shown by the graph in Exhibit 18.20, because of the convexity of the price-yield relationship (especially the long-term, zero coupon bond) as yield increases, the rate at which the price of the bond declines becomes slower. Similarly, when yields decline, the rate at which the price of the bond increases becomes faster. Therefore, convexity is considered a desirable trait. Specifically, if you have two bonds with equal duration but one has greater convexity, you would want the bond with greater convexity because it would have better price performance whether yields rise (the bond price declines less) or yields fall (the bond price increases more).

Given this price-yield curve, modified duration is the percentage change in price for a nominal change in yield as follows:[13]

18.15
$$D_{mod} = \frac{\dfrac{dP}{di}}{P}$$

Notice that the *dP/di* line is tangent to the price-yield curve *at a given yield* as shown in Exhibit 18.21. For *small* changes in yields (i.e., from y^* to either y_1 or y_2), this tangent straight line gives a good estimate of the actual price changes. In contrast, for larger changes in yields

---

[13]In mathematical terms, modified duration is the first differential of this price-yield relationship with respect to yield.

Exhibit 18.20 | **Price-Yield Curves for Alternative Bonds**

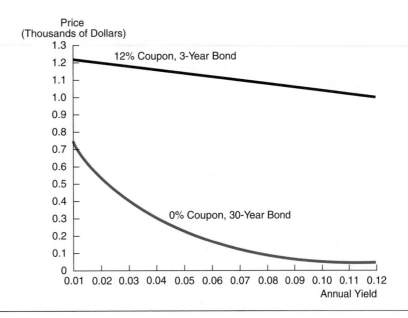

Exhibit 18.21 | **Price Approximation Using Modified Duration**

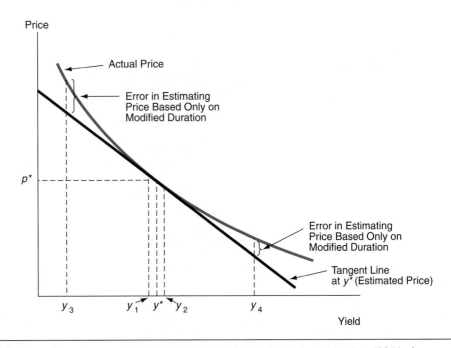

(i.e., from y^* to either y_3 or y_4), the straight line will estimate the new price of the bond at less than the actual price shown by the price-yield curve. This misestimate arises because the modified-duration line is a linear estimate of a curvilinear relationship. Specifically, the estimate using only modified duration will *underestimate* the actual price *increase* caused by a yield decline and *overestimate* the actual price *decline* caused by an increase in yields. This graph, which demonstrates the convexity effect, also shows that price changes are *not* symmetric when yields increase or decrease. As shown, when rates decline, there is a larger price error than when rates increase because, due to convexity, when yields decline prices rise at an *increasing* rate, while prices decline at a *decreasing* rate when yields rise.

Determinants of Convexity   Convexity is a measure of the curvature of the price-yield relationship. In turn, because modified duration is the slope of the curve at a given yield, convexity indicates changes in duration. Mathematically, convexity is the second derivative of price with respect to yield (d^2P/di^2) divided by price. Specifically, convexity is the percentage change in dP/di for a given change in yield:

18.16
$$\text{Convexity} = \frac{\dfrac{d^2P}{di^2}}{P}$$

Convexity is a measure of how much a bond's price-yield curve deviates from the linear approximation of that curve. As indicated by Exhibit 18.19 and Exhibit 18.21 for *noncallable* bonds, convexity always is a positive number, implying that the price-yield curve lies above the modified-duration (tangent) line. Exhibit 18.20 illustrates the price-yield relationship for two bonds with very different coupons and maturities. (The yields and prices are contained in Exhibit 18.18.)

These graphs demonstrate the following relationship between these factors and the convexity of a bond:

- There is an *inverse* relationship between coupon and convexity (yield and maturity constant)—that is, lower coupon, higher convexity.
- There is a *direct* relationship between maturity and convexity (yield and coupon constant)—that is, longer maturity, higher convexity.
- There is an *inverse* relationship between yield and convexity (coupon and maturity constant). This means that the price-yield curve is more convex at its lower-yield (upper left) segment.

Therefore, a short-term, high-coupon bond, such as the 12 percent coupon, three-year bond in Exhibit 18.20, has very low convexity—it is almost a straight line. In contrast, the zero-coupon, 30-year bond has high convexity.

Notably, the determinants of duration and convexity for option-free bonds are very similar. Specifically, the three factors are the same—maturity, coupon, and yield—and the direction of impact is the same—that is, maturity is positively related to both duration and convexity and both coupon and yield are inverse. Therefore, high-duration bonds have high convexity.

The Modified-Duration–Convexity Effects   In summary, the change in a bond's price resulting from a change in yield can be attributed to two sources: the bond's modified duration and its convexity. The relative effect of these two factors on the price change will depend on the characteristics of the bond (i.e., its convexity) and the size of the yield change. For example, if you are estimating the price change for a 300 basis-point change in yield for a zero coupon, 30-year bond, the convexity effect would be fairly large because this bond would have high convexity, and a 300 basis-point change in yield is relatively large. In contrast, if you are dealing with only a 10 basis-point change in yields, the convexity effect would be minimal because it is a small change in yield. Similarly, the convexity effect would likewise be small even if you assume a larger yield change if you are dealing with a bond with small convexity (i.e., a high-coupon, short-maturity bond) because the price-yield curve for such a bond is almost a straight line.

In conclusion, modified duration can help you derive an *approximate* percentage bond price change for a given change in interest rates, but you must remember that it is only a good estimate when you are considering small yield changes. The point is, you must also consider the convexity effect on price change when you are dealing with large yield changes and/or when the securities or cash flows have high convexity.

Computation of Convexity Again, the formula for computing the convexity of a stream of cash flows looks fairly complex, but it can be broken down into manageable steps. You will recall from our convexity equation (18.16) that

$$\text{Convexity} = \frac{d^2P/di^2}{P}$$

In turn,

18.17
$$\frac{d^2P}{di^2} = \frac{1}{(1+i)^2}\left[\sum_{t=1}^{n}\frac{CF_t}{(1+i)}(t^2+t)\right]$$

Exhibit 18.22 contains the computations related to this calculation for a three-year bond with a 12 percent coupon and 9 percent YTM assuming annual flows.

Exhibit 18.22 | **Computation of Convexity**

$$\text{Convexity} = \frac{d^2P/di^2}{\text{PV of Cash Flows}} = \frac{d^2P/di^2}{\text{Price}}$$

$$\frac{d^2P}{di^2} = \frac{1}{(1+i)^2}\left[\sum_{t=1}^{n}(t^2+t)\frac{CF_t}{(1+i)^t}\right]$$

$$\text{Convexity} = \frac{d^2P/di^2}{\text{Price}}$$

Example: 3-Year Bond, 12% Coupon, 9% YTM

(1) Year	(2) CFt	(3) PV @ 9%	(4) PV CF	(5) t^2+t	(4)×(5)
1	120	0.9174	$ 110.09	2	$ 220.18
2	120	0.8417	101.00	6	606.00
3	120	0.7722	92.66	12	1,111.92
3	1,000	0.7722	772.20	12	9,266.40
			Price = $1,075.95		$11,204.50

$$\frac{1}{(1+i)^2} = \frac{1}{(1.09)^2} = \frac{1}{1.19} = 0.84$$

$$\$11,204.50 \times 0.84 = \$9,411.78$$

$$\text{Convexity} = \frac{9,411.78}{1,075.95} = 8.75$$

The convexity for this bond is very low because it has a short maturity, high coupon, and high yield. Note that the *convexity of a security will vary along the price-yield curve.* You will get a different convexity at a 3 percent yield than at a 12 percent yield. In terms of the computation, the maturity and coupon will be the same, but you will use a different discount rate that reflects where you are on the curve. This is similar to the earlier observation that *you will get a different modified duration at different points on the price-yield curve* because the slope varies along the curve. You also can see this mathematically because, depending on where you are on the curve, you will be using a different market yield, and the Macaulay and modified durations are inverse to the discount rate.[14]

To compute the price change attributable to the convexity effect after you know the bond's convexity, use this equation:

18.18   Price change due to convexity = ½ × price × convexity × (Δ in yield)^2

Exhibit 18.23 shows the change in bond price considering the duration effect and the convexity effect for an 18-year bond with a 12 percent coupon and 9 percent YTM. For demonstration purposes, we assumed a decline of 100 and 300 basis points (BP) in rates (i.e., 9 percent to 8 percent and 9 percent to 6 percent).

With the 300 BP change, if you considered only the modified-duration effect, you would have *estimated* that the bond went from 126.50 to 158.30 (a 25.14 percent increase), when, in fact, the actual price is closer to 164.41, which is about a *30 percent increase.*

Duration and Convexity for Callable Bonds

The discussion and presentation thus far regarding Macaulay and modified durations and convexity have been concerned with option-free bonds. A callable bond is different because it provides the issuer with an option to call the bond under certain conditions and pay it off with funds from a new issue sold at a lower yield. Observers refer to this as a bond with an *embedded option.* We noted earlier that the duration of a bond can be seriously affected by an embedded call option if interest rates decline substantially below a bond's coupon rate. In such a case, the issuer will likely call the bond, which will dramatically change the maturity and the duration of the bond. For example, assume a firm issues a 30-year bond with a 9 percent coupon with a deferred call provision whereby the bond can be called in six years at 109 percent of par. If the bond is issued at par, its original *duration to maturity* will be about 11 years. A year later, if rates decline to about 7 percent, its duration to maturity will still be over *10 years* because duration is inversely related to yield and yields have declined. Notably, at a yield of 7 percent, this bond will probably trade at *yield to call* because at a 7 percent yield the firm will likely exercise its option and call the bond in five years. Notably, the bond's *duration to first call* would be about *four years.* Clearly, there is a significant difference between duration to maturity (over 10 years) and duration to first call (about 4 years).

To understand the impact of the call feature on the duration and convexity of a bond, it is important to consider what determines the price of a callable bond. A callable bond is a combination of a noncallable bond plus a *call option* that was *sold to the issuer,* which allows the issuer to call the bond under the conditions discussed earlier. Because the call option is owned by the issuer, it has negative value for the investor in the bond. Thus the bondholder's position is

18.19   Long a callable bond = Long a noncallable bond + A short position in a call option

---

[14]Exhibit 18A.1 in the appendix to this chapter is a table that combines the computation of Macaulay and modified duration and convexity using semiannual cash flows.

Exhibit 18.23	Analysis of Bond Price Change Considering Duration and Convexity

Example: 18-Year Bond, 12% Coupon, 9% YTM
Price: 126.50
Modified Duration: 8.38 (D^*)
Convexity: 107.70
Estimate of Price Change Using Duration:
  Percent Δ Price = D^* (Δ in YLD/100)
Estimate of Price Change from Convexity:
  Price Change = $\frac{1}{2} \times$ Price $\times$ Convexity $\times$ (Δ in YLD)^2

A. Change in Yield: −100 BP

  Duration Change: $-8.38 \times \left(\dfrac{-100}{100} \right) = +8.38\%$

  $+8.38\% \times 126.50 = +10.60$

  Convexity Change: $\dfrac{1}{2} \times (126.50) \times 107.70 \times (0.01)^2$

  $= 63.25 \times 107.70 \times 0.0001$

  $= 6{,}812.03 \times 0.0001 = 0.68$

  Combined Effect: 126.50

  $\underline{+\ 10.60\,(\text{Duration})}$

  137.10

  $\underline{+\ 0.68\,(\text{Convexity})}$

  137.78

B. Change in Yield: −300 BP

  Duration Change: $-8.38 \times \left(\dfrac{-300}{100} \right) = +25.14\%$

  $126.50 \times 1.2514 = 158.30 (+31.80)$

  Convexity Effect: $\dfrac{1}{2} \times (126.50) \times 107.70 \times (0.03)^2$

  $6{,}812.03 \times 0.0009 = 6.11$

  Combined Effect: 126.50

  $\underline{+\ 31.80\ (\text{Duration})}$

  158.30

  $\underline{+\ 6.11\,(\text{Convexity})}$

  164.41

Therefore, the value (price) of a callable bond is equal to

18.20   Callable bond price = Noncallable bond price − call option price

Given this valuation, anything that increases the value of the call option will reduce the value of the callable bond.[15] The point is, when interest rates decline, the right-hand side of this equation experiences a conflict between the value of the noncallable bond that increases in value, and the

[15]For a further discussion of the effect of these embedded options, see Fabozzi, Buetow, and Johnson (2005) and Fabozzi, Kalotay, and Williams (2005). Also see Winkelmann (1989).

value of the call option that also increases but this has a negative effect on the bond price. Notably, if the value of the call option increases faster than the value of the noncallable bond, the overall value of the callable bond will *decline* when interest rates decline and this is referred to as *negative duration*—that is, in contrast to the usual inverse relationship between yield changes and bond price changes, in this case yield changes and price changes both decline.

Option-Adjusted Duration[16]   Given these two extreme values of (1) duration to maturity and (2) duration to first call, the investment community derives a duration estimate that is referred to as an option-adjusted or call-adjusted duration based on *the probability that the issuing firm will exercise its call option* for the bond when the bond becomes freely callable. This option-adjusted duration will be somewhere between these two extreme values. Specifically, when interest rates are substantially above the coupon rate, the probability of the bond being called is very small (i.e., the call option has very little value) and the option-adjusted duration will approach the duration to maturity. In contrast, if interest rates decline to levels substantially below the coupon rate, the probability of the bond being called at the first opportunity is very high (i.e., the call option is very valuable and will probably be exercised) and the option-adjusted duration will approach the duration to first call. In summary, the bond's option-adjusted duration will be somewhere between these two extremes with the exact option-adjusted duration depending on the level of interest rates relative to the bond's coupon rate.

The option-adjusted duration can also be envisioned or computed based on the duration of the two components, as follows:

18.21   Option-adjusted duration = Duration of the noncallable bond − duration of the call option

If one conceives of duration as interest rate sensitivity, we know that at high interest rates a change in yield will have little if any impact on the value of the option. Thus the duration (i.e., interest rate sensitivity) of the option would be close to zero and the option-adjusted duration would equal that of a noncallable bond. In contrast, when yields decline below the coupon yield, the call option will be very interest rate sensitive since the option will experience a large increase in value at low yields. Thus, the duration (i.e., the interest rate sensitivity) of the option will be fairly high and have a large impact on the callable bond's option-adjusted duration—it will drive the duration of the callable bond toward the duration to first call. In fact, it is possible to conceive of an option that is very leveraged such that it is extremely interest rate sensitive (i.e., has a very large duration that exceeds the duration of the noncallable bond) resulting in a *negative option-adjusted duration*. An example is a mortgage-backed security that might *decline* in price when there is a *decline* in interest rates.

Convexity of Callable Bonds   Exhibit 18.24 shows what happens to the price of a callable bond versus the value of a noncallable bond when interest rates increase or decline. Starting from yield y^* (which is close to the par value yield), if interest *rates increase*, the value of the call option declines because, at market interest rates that are substantially above the coupon rate, it is unlikely the issuer will want to call the issue. Therefore, the call option has very little value and the price of the callable bond will be similar to the price of a noncallable bond. In contrast, when interest rates *decline below* y^*, there is an increase in the probability that the issuer will want to use the call option—that is, the value of the call option increases. As a result, the value of the callable bond will deviate from the value of the noncallable bond—that

---

[16]The discussion in this subsection will consider the option-adjusted duration on a conceptual and intuitive basis. For a detailed mathematical treatment, see Dunetz and Mahoney (1988).

| Exhibit 18.24 | **Noncallable and Callable Bond Price-Yield Relationship** |

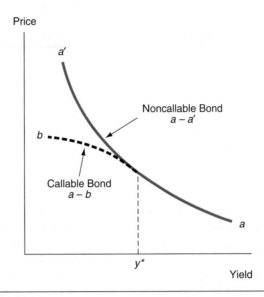

Source: Frank J. Fabozzi, Gerald W. Buetow, and Robert R. Johnson, "Measuring Interest Rate Risk" in the *Handbook of Fixed-Income Securities,* 7th ed., (New York: McGraw-Hill, 2005). Reproduced with permission from The McGraw-Hill companies.

is, the price of the callable bond will initially not increase as fast as the noncallable bond price and eventually will not increase at all. This is what is shown in curve $a-b$.

In the case of the noncallable bond, we indicated that it had *positive convexity* because as yields declined, the price of the bond increased at a *faster* rate. With the callable bond, when rates decline, the price increases at a *slower* rate and eventually does not change at all. This pattern of price-yield change for a callable bond when yields decline is referred to as *negative convexity.*

Needless to say, this price pattern (negative convexity) is one of the risks of a callable bond versus a noncallable bond when interest rates decline.

Limitations of Macaulay and Modified Duration

It is important to understand Macaulay and modified duration because of the perspective they provide regarding factors that affect the volatility and interest rate sensitivity of bonds. However, it also is important for bond analysts and portfolio managers to recognize the serious limitations of these measures in the real world. The major limitations are as follows.

First, as noted in the discussion of convexity, the percent change estimates using modified duration are good only for small-yield changes. This was demonstrated in Exhibit 18.21. As a result, two bonds with equal duration may experience different price changes for large-yield changes—depending on *differences in the convexity* of the bonds.

Second, it is difficult to determine the interest rate sensitivity of a portfolio of bonds when there is a change in interest rates and the yield curve experiences a *nonparallel shift.* It was noted earlier that the duration of a portfolio is the weighted average of the durations of the bonds in the portfolio. Everything works well as long as all yields change by the same amount—that is, there is a parallel shift of the yield curve. However, when yields change, the yield curve *seldom* experiences a parallel shift. Assuming a nonparallel shift, which yield do you use to describe the change—the short-, intermediate-, or long-maturity yield? Two portfolios that begin the period with the same duration can have different ending durations and perform very differently, depending on how the yield curve changed (i.e., did it steepen or flatten?) and the composition of the portfolio (i.e., relative to its duration, was it a bullet or a barbell?). Consider the following simple example for two portfolios that have a duration of 4.50 years:

Bond	Coupon	Maturity (Years)	Yield	Modified Duration	Weights
Portfolio A					
A	7.00	4	7.00	2.70	0.555
B	9.00	20	9.00	6.75	0.445
Portfolio B					
C	8.00	10	8.00	4.50	1.000

As shown, the modified durations are equal at the initiation of the portfolio. Assume a non-parallel change in yields where the *yield curve steepens*. Specifically, 4-year yields decline to 6 percent, 10-year yields do not change, and 20-year yields rise to 10 percent. Portfolio B would experience a very small change in value because of stability in yield for 10-year bonds. In contrast, the price for 4-year bonds will experience a small increase (because of small duration) and the value of 20-year bonds will experience a large decline. Overall, the value of Portfolio A will decline because of the weight of Bond B in the portfolio and its large decline in value due to its large modified duration. Obviously, if the yield curve had flattened or inverted, the barbell port-folio would have benefited from the change. This differential performance because of the change in the shape of the yield curve (i.e., it did not experience a parallel shift) is referred to as *yield curve risk,* which cannot be captured by the traditional duration-convexity presentation.

The third limitation of Macaulay and modified durations involves our initial calculation. We assumed that cash flows from the bond *were not affected by yield changes*—that is, we assumed option-free bonds. Later, we saw the effect on the computed duration and convexity when we considered the effect of an embedded call option in Exhibit 18.24. Specifically, we saw that the option-adjusted duration would be some value between the duration to maturity and duration to first call and the specific value would depend on the current market yield relative to the bond's coupon. Further, we saw that when interest rates declined with an embedded call option, the convexity of the bond went from some positive value to *negative* convexity because the price of the callable bond increased at a slower rate or it did not change when the yields declined (i.e., there is *price compression*).

Because of these limitations, practitioners have developed a way to approximate the dura-tion of a bond or any security that can be impacted by a change in interest rates. This is referred to as *effective duration,* which is discussed in the following section.

Effective Duration[17]   As noted previously, the purpose of duration is to indicate the price change of an asset to a change in yield—that is, it is *a measure of the interest rate sensitivity of an asset.* Because modified duration is based on Macaulay duration, it can provide a reason-able approximation of the interest rate sensitivity of a bond that experiences a small-yield change and one that is option free—if yield changes do not change the cash flows for the bond. Unfortunately, the Macaulay and modified-duration measures cannot be used (1) for large-yield changes; (2) for assets with embedded options; or (3) for assets that are affected by vari-ables other than interest rates, such as common stocks or real estate.

---

[17]This section benefited substantially from the thorough presentation in Fabozzi, Buetow, and Johnson (2005).

To overcome these limitations, practitioners use *effective duration,* a direct measure of the interest rate sensitivity of a bond or any asset where it is possible to use a pricing model to estimate the market prices surrounding a change in interest rates. As we will demonstrate, using this measure it is possible to derive negative durations (which is not mathematically possible with Macaulay) or durations that are longer than the maturity of the asset (likewise not possible with Macaulay). Specifically, effective duration measures the interest rate sensitivity of a bond taking into consideration that the cash flows of the bond can change when yields change due to the existence of embedded options (e.g., call or put options). It is also possible to calculate the effective duration for an option-free bond, in which case the computed duration value will be equal to what would be derived for small-yield changes using modified duration.

Notably, to implement the effective duration formula, it is necessary to use an interest rate model and a corresponding pricing model that will provide price estimates for the asset when interest rates and cash flows change. The formulas for calculating effective duration and effective convexity are:

18.22 $$\text{Effective Duration } (D_{Eff}) = \frac{(P_-) - (P_+)}{2PS}$$

18.23 $$\text{Effective Convexity } (C_{Eff}) = \frac{(P_-) - (P_+) - 2P}{PS^2}$$

where

P_- = the estimated price of the asset after a downward shift in interest rates
P_+ = the estimated price of the asset after an upward shift in interest rates
P = the current price of the asset (before any interest rate shifts)
S = the assumed shift in the term structure

The formulas are implemented by assuming small changes in yield (10 basis points) both down and up and using a pricing model to estimate the expected market prices (both P_- and P_+) at the new yields. Everything else in the formulas is given. Consider the following bond that we will initially assume is option free:

Par value	$1,000
Coupon	6%
Maturity	8 years
Initial YTM	6%
Initial price (P)	100

Given this initial scenario, we assume a change in yields of 10 basis points. The prices for the bond at yields to maturity of 5.90 percent (P_-) and 6.10 percent (P_+) are:

$$0.0590 \, (P_-) = 100.42760054$$
$$0.0610 \, (P_+) = 99.57457612$$
$$(P_-) - (P_+) = \overline{0.85302442}$$
$$2PS = (2)(100)(0.001) = 0.20$$
$$D_{Eff} = \frac{0.85302442}{0.20} = 4.265122$$

Because this is a noncallable bond (option free), we know that this effective duration equals the modified duration we would derive based upon the Macaulay duration of 4.39.

$$D_{mod} \frac{4.39}{\left(1 + \dfrac{0.06}{2}\right)} = \frac{4.39}{1.03} = 4.262$$

The difference is due to the rounding of the Macaulay duration.

The bond's effective convexity would equal

$$C_{Eff} = \frac{(P_-) + (P_+) - 2P}{PS^2}$$

$$= \frac{100.42760054 + 99.57457612 - 200}{(100)(0.001)^2}$$

$$= \frac{200.00217666 - 200}{0.0001}$$

$$= \frac{0.00217666}{0.0001} = 21.766$$

We know from our earlier discussion that, at a lower yield, the duration would be higher. Specifically, if we assumed a YTM of 4 percent, the effective and modified durations would be about 4.34 compared to about 4.26 at 6 percent.

Let us now assume that the bond is callable at 106 of par after 3 years. Using the Black, Derman, and Toy (1990) no-arbitrage binomial model to estimate prices for this bond beginning at a yield of 4 percent, we derive the following prices:

$$0.0390\ (P_-) = 108.55626094$$
$$0.0410\ (P_+) = 107.92318176$$
$$0.04\ (P) = 108.24082177$$

$$D_{Eff} = \frac{108.55626094 - 107.92318176}{(2)(108.24082177)(0.001)}$$
$$= 2.92$$

As expected, because of the embedded call option that would have increased in value with a decline in yields, this duration value (2.92) would be lower than the duration for the option-free bond discussed earlier (4.34). In contrast, the effective durations for callable bonds at higher yields (e.g., 8 percent) would be equal to the durations for option-free bonds because the value of the option approaches zero.

The effective convexity of this callable bond at 4 percent would be

$$C_{Eff} = \frac{108.55626094 + 107.92318176 - [2(108.24082177)]}{(108.24082177)(0.001)^2}$$
$$= -20.33$$

As discussed, this is an example of negative convexity because the price increase is limited because of the increasing value of the call option. For comparison purposes, the convexity of the option-free bond at 4 percent is 23.76, which is, as expected, slightly higher than its convexity of 21.77 at 6 percent (recall that both duration and convexity are inversely related to yield).

Putable Bonds   Although it is not feasible to discuss in detail the properties of bonds with put options (putable bonds), it is possible to envision the effects if one considers the basic value of a putable bond as follows:

18.24   Value of putable bond = Value of nonputable bond + value of the put option

In this instance, the investor owns the option that allows him/her to sell the bond back to the issuer at a stated price. This option has a positive impact on the value of the bond and this option *increases* in value when interest rates *increase.* Therefore, when rates increase, the price of the bond does not decline as much as an option-free bond, but when rates decline, its price pattern is similar to that of an option-free bond because the value of the put option approaches zero.

A visual presentation of the effect of the call option on the price-yield curve was contained in Exhibit 18.24. Alternatively, Exhibit 18.25 and Exhibit 18.26 contain the effective duration-yield curves and the effective convexity–yield curves, which show the significant impact of embedded options on the effective duration and convexity of fixed-income securities.

Effective Duration Greater than Maturity   Because effective duration is simply interest rate sensitivity, it is possible to have an asset that is highly levered such that its interest rate sensitivity exceeds its maturity. For example, there are five-year, collateralized mortgage obligations (CMOs) that are highly levered and their prices will change by 15 percent to 20 percent when interest rates change by 100 basis points. Using the formula discussed (Equation 18.22), you would compute an effective duration of 15 or 20 for this five-year maturity security.

Negative Effective Duration   We know from the formula for Macaulay duration that it is not possible to compute a negative duration. Further, in the calculation for price volatility where we use modified duration, we use $-D^*$ to reflect the negative relationship between price changes and interest rate changes for *option-free bonds*. At the same time, we know that when we leave the world of option-free bonds and consider bonds with embedded options, it is possible to envision cases where bond prices move in the same direction as yields, which implies negative duration. A prime example would be mortgage-backed securities where a significant decline in interest rates will cause a substantial increase in refinancing prepayments by homeowners, which will reduce the value of these bonds to holders. Therefore, you would see a decline in interest rates and a decline in the price of these mortgage-backed bonds, which implies *negative duration.* Another way to explain a price decline with lower interest rates is the value formula (Equation 18.20)—that is, with lower interest rates, the value of the call option increases in value by more than the increase in value of the noncallable bond, which causes a decline in the value of the callable bond.

Empirical Duration[18]   In the preceding discussion of effective duration, the point was made that these computations required the use of an interest rate model and a bond pricing model that considered cash flow changes when yields changed and generated market price estimates that were inputs into the effective duration and effective convexity formulas. The question arises regarding what happens when you want to estimate interest rate sensitivity for an asset class where it is not possible to generate well-specified market price estimates in response to yield changes. The classic example would be common stocks where there is an impact on price when interest rates change, but the interest rate effect can be overpowered by the growth rate effect that is likewise unknown. The other obvious example would be bonds with exotic embedded options (including mortgage-backed bonds) where prices can change based upon the value of the exotic option that is difficult to price. In order to derive some estimate of

---

[18]The discussion in this section considered the analysis in Hayre and Chang (1997).

Exhibit 18.25 | Effective Duration–Yield Curves

A. Effective Duration–Yield Curve for 8-Year, 6% Option-Free Bond

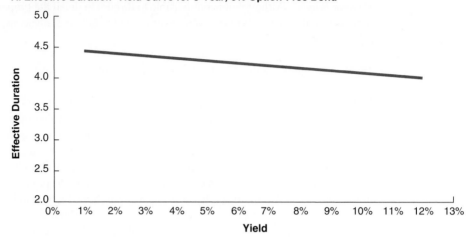

B. Effective Duration–Yield Curve for 8-Year, 6% Callable Bond after 3 Years

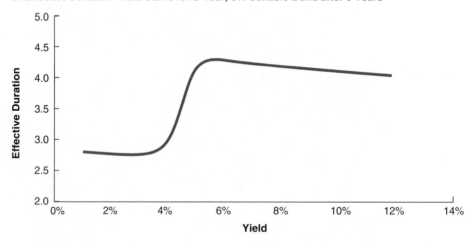

C. Effective Duration–Yield Curve for 8-Year, 6% Putable Bond after 3 Years

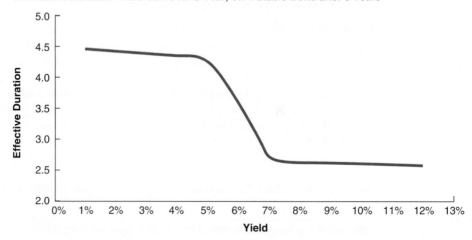

Exhibit 18.26 | **Effective Convexity—Yield Curves**

A. Effective Convexity–Yield Curve for 8-Year, 6% Option-Free Bond

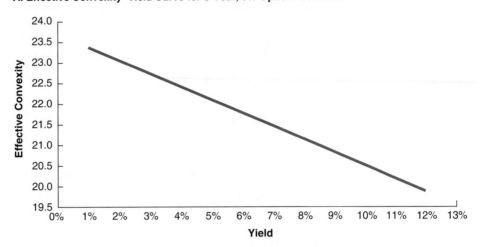

B. Effective Convexity–Yield Curve for 8-Year, 6% Callable Bond after 3 Years

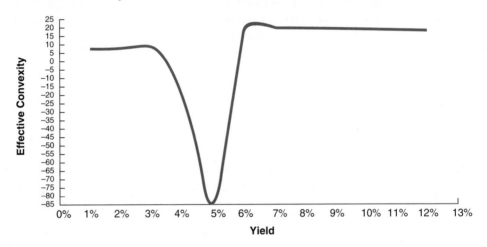

C. Effective Convexity–Yield Curve for 8-Year, 6% Putable Bond after 3 Years

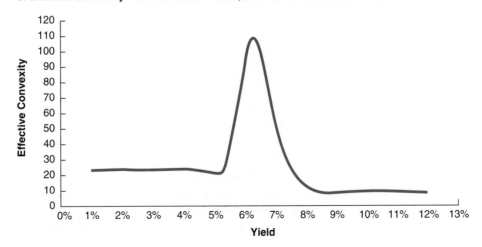

interest rate sensitivity under such circumstances, analysts and portfolio managers employ empirical duration, which is the actual percentage price change for an asset in response to a change in yield during a specified historical time period. The concept is best described by recalling the formula in Equation 18.14 used to determine the percentage price change for a bond using modified duration as follows:

$$\%\Delta Price = -D_{mod} \times (\Delta i)$$

where:

D_{mod} = the modified Macaulay duration
Δi = the change in interest rates in basis points divided by 100

The typical assumption is that we know D_{mod} and Δi and can solve for the approximate percentage price change. Alternatively, given this relationship, we can solve for D_{mod} as follows:

18.25
$$-D_{mod} = \frac{\%\Delta Price}{\Delta i}$$

When we solve for it this way, it is no longer D_{mod} (modified duration), but D_{emp}—empirical duration. Given this formulation, if you observe a change in interest rates (Δi) and the change in the price of an asset during the same time period, you can solve for the empirical duration of the asset. Consider the following simple example:

- Interest rates decline by 200 BP.
- The price of a bond increases by 10 percent.

$$D_{emp} = -\frac{10}{-200/100} = -\frac{10}{-2}$$

Therefore, the change in price coincident with a change in interest rates indicates that this bond has an empirical duration (D_{emp}) of 5. This is a direct measure of the bond's interest rate sensitivity. You should think of it as *the approximate percentage change in price for a 100-basis-point change in interest rates.*

While this simple example indicates the concept of empirical duration, the technique that is generally suggested for estimating empirical duration is to employ the following regression model:

18.26
$$\frac{\Delta P}{P} = \alpha + D^{**}\Delta Y + u$$

where:

$\dfrac{\Delta P}{P}$ = percentage change in price

α = constant term
D^{**} = an estimate of D_{emp} (empirical duration)
ΔY = change in yield in basis points
u = random error term

The time interval for the data and the time period considered can vary based upon the asset and purpose of the analysis. When working with bonds, some analysts employ daily data for short time periods (months), while investigators using the concept for stocks or real estate (to be discussed) have employed weekly and monthly data for longer time periods (quarters or years).

Empirical Duration for Common Stock If one considers the Macaulay duration of common stock, it is possible to envision a fairly high number because you are dealing with a perpetuity, and some growth stocks pay low dividends for many years. The values derived by Reilly and Sidhu (1980) using various assumptions of price and growth, ranged from 10 years to 20 years. In contrast, using empirical duration, one gets very different results.

Because we are dealing with the interest rate sensitivity of an asset, it is possible to compute an empirical duration for common stock that is much lower than what is implied by Macaulay duration and it is more variable. Observing a change in interest rates and the accompanying percentage change in stock prices would indicate the interest rate sensitivity of stocks. Leibowitz (1987) conducted such an analysis and derived a rolling, one-year effective duration for the S&P 500 that ranged *from about zero to almost seven*. When measuring the interest rate sensitivity of common stocks over time, you would expect changes because, as demonstrated by Reilly, Wright, and Chan (2000), the correlation between stock and bond returns varies substantially over time. In addition, you might anticipate significant differences in the effective duration for alternative stocks. For example, you would expect a large difference in the interest rate sensitivity (empirical duration) of a banking or utility stock (which is very interest rate sensitive) compared to the empirical duration of a small-cap or technology stock where its value is based more on changes in its specific growth expectations than interest rates. These differences are documented in Reilly, Wright, and Johnson (2005).

YIELD SPREADS WITH EMBEDDED OPTIONS

Earlier in the chapter, we discussed the analysis of yield spread as a technique to enhance bond investments or bond trades. At this point, it is necessary to revisit the concept of yield spreads, keeping in mind the term structure of interest rates but, more important, with an awareness of the significant impact that interest rate volatility has on the value of embedded options in bonds. In this revisitation, we will consider two spreads: (1) **static yield spreads** that consider the total term structure and (2) **option-adjusted spreads** that consider changes in the term structure and alternative estimates of the volatility of interest rates.

Static Yield Spreads

You will recall that the traditional yield spread compares the yields between two bonds with similar coupons and equal maturities as follows:

8%—20-Year AA Corporate Bond	8.20%
8%—20-Year Treasury Bond	7.10%
Yield Spread	1.10%
	110 bp

There are three problems with this "traditional" yield spread:

- The two yields do not consider the prevailing term structures of interest rates but only consider the yield spread at the one point on the curve (at 20 years).
- The analysis does not consider the fact that the corporate bond could have an embedded option (put or call), whereby expected interest rate volatility may alter the cash flow for this bond.

Exhibit 18.27	Calculation of the Price of a Five-Year, 8 Percent Coupon Bond Using Treasury Spot Rates

Period	Cash Flow	Treasury Spot Rate	Present Value
1	$ 40	6.20	$ 38.80
2	40	6.30	37.60
3	40	6.40	36.40
4	40	6.50	35.20
5	40	6.60	34.00
6	40	6.70	32.84
7	40	6.80	31.64
8	40	6.90	30.48
9	40	7.00	29.36
10	1040	7.10	734.24
		Theoretical price	$1,040.56

- While not true in this example, it is possible that investors would compare two bonds with equal maturities but different coupon cash flow (e.g., a zero coupon bond versus a coupon bond).

The first concern (neglect of the term structure) suggests the consideration of the *static spread*. It is contended that the proper way to compare non-Treasury bonds of the same maturity but with different coupon rates is to compare them to a portfolio of Treasury securities that have the same cash flow. The way to do this, if there is not an existing Treasury bond with the specified flows, is to discount the corporate bond's cash flow as if the flows were risk free. Specifically, discount them using the prevailing Treasury spot rates for the life of the corporate bond. Consider the following example:

Corporate bond—8%, five-year bond

If we discount this bond's flows using the hypothetical Treasury spot rate curve contained in Exhibit 18.27, the price would be $1,040.56, which is what this bond would sell at if it were a Treasury bond. In fact, the bond is priced at $1,006.70. The *static spread* (also called the *zero volatility spread*) is the spread that will make the present value of the cash flows from the corporate bond when discounted at the Treasury spot rate plus the static spread, equal to the corporate bond's market price. To put it another way, how much of a static spread across all points on the Treasury spot rate curve is required to generate the current market price for this bond? Adding 70 basis points to every spot rate generates a price above $1,006.70, which indicates that we need to consider a larger spread. As shown in Exhibit 18.28, using a spread of 80 basis points generates a price of $1,006.70, which equals the current price of the corporate bond, which indicates that there is a static (zero volatility) spread for the bond of 80 basis points or 0.80 percent.

Option-Adjusted Spread

As noted, the traditional spread was a problem because it did not consider the full-term structure or the impact of interest rate volatility. The term structure problem was addressed by estimating the static (zero volatility) spread.

Exhibit 18.28 | **Calculation of the Static Spread for a Five-Year, 8 Percent Coupon Corporate Bond**

Period	Cash Flow	Treasury Spot Rate	80 BP Spread Spot Rate	Present Value
1	$ 40	6.20	7.00	$ 38.64
2	40	6.30	7.10	37.30
3	40	6.40	7.20	35.98
4	40	6.50	7.30	34.66
5	40	6.60	7.40	33.36
6	40	6.70	7.50	32.07
7	40	6.80	7.60	30.81
8	40	6.90	7.70	29.57
9	40	7.00	7.80	28.35
10	1040	7.10	7.90	705.95
			Present Value	$1,006.70

The interest rate volatility factor is considered by the option-adjusted spread (OAS) analysis. Why is interest rate volatility a problem? The point is, as discussed earlier in the chapter, if a bond has an embedded call option, this option can affect the bond's expected cash flow. The likelihood of the call being exercised will depend on future interest rates, the remaining maturity of the bond, the call price, and other costs of a call and new issue.

The goal of the OAS is similar to the static spread except that the technique allows for a *change in the term structure* over time based on some estimates of interest rate volatility.

The concept of OAS is best understood by a presentation of the steps involved in estimating the OAS for a specific bond as follows:

1. Based upon the prevailing Treasury yield curve, estimate the term structure of interest rates (i.e., the prevailing Treasury spot rate curve) and the implied short-term forward rates derived from the spot rates.
2. Select a probability distribution for short-term Treasury spot rates. This should be based on the current term structure and the historical behavior of interest rates. The significant estimate is the volatility of interest rates (i.e., the standard deviation of yields)—that is, how much will the forward rates change each period?
3. Using the probability distribution specified in Step 2 and Monte Carlo simulation, it is possible to randomly generate a large number of interest rate paths (e.g., 1,000).
4. For bonds with embedded options (such as callable bonds), develop rules for determining when the option will be exercised. For example, given the coupon, maturity, and call option, at what interest rate will the issue be called?
5. For each interest rate path generated in Step 3, determine the cash flows from the bond, given (a) the information about the bond (i.e., its call provision) and (b) the rules established in Step 4 for calling the bond.
6. For an assumed spread relative to the Treasury term structure of spot rates along a path, calculate a present value for all paths created in Step 3.
7. Calculate the *average* present value for all the interest rate paths.
8. Compare the average present value calculated in Step 7 to the market price of the bond. If they are equal, the assumed spread used in Step 6 is the option-adjusted spread. If they are not, try another spread and repeat Steps 6, 7, and 8.

The computed option-adjusted spread (OAS) is the average spread over the Treasury spot rate curve based on the potential paths that can be realized in the future for interest rates. The reason it is referred to as "option adjusted" is because the potential paths of cash flow are adjusted to reflect the effect of the options embedded in the bonds.

The following are some technical issues that an analyst should be aware of when attempting to estimate the OAS and also factors that can cause differences in an estimate of the OAS for a bond by alternative dealers.

- It is necessary to have a large number of paths for the simulation.
- The estimate of the probability distribution, which includes your expected interest rate volatility, is crucial. Notably, if alternative firms differ in this estimate of expected interest rate volatility, it can cause differences in the OAS estimate.
- It is necessary to determine the relationship between short-term rates and refinancing rates. Specifically, how much more does the firm have to pay above the short-term forward rate (i.e., the refinancing rate is a long-term rate)? Empirically, what is this relationship?
- A call rule must be specified. This depends upon the coupon rate for the bond and other costs. It has been assumed to be almost 300 BP below the coupon rate (e.g., 5.0 percent with at least three years to maturity).

As noted, different assumptions regarding these technical issues can cause different estimates of the OAS by alternative dealers. The critical estimate is the expected interest rate volatility and this can vary between dealers; and, also, individual dealers can change their estimates over time.

The Internet   Investments Online

Bond valuation focuses on bond mathematics, the term structure, and bond features that add to the yield (such as callability) or lead to lower yields (such as putability). Bonds are normally easier to evaluate than stocks, given their stated life, cash flows, and discount rates, which can be read from the term structure. Nonetheless, bond pricing can become quite complicated if the bond has complex options or attributes. It is not surprising that bond market commentary typically focuses on interest rate trends and factors that can favorably or unfavorably affect credit quality.

http://www.bonds-online.com Perhaps the best source for bond market information on the Internet. It includes prices, yields, and market commentary for Treasuries, corporates, munis, and U.S. savings bonds. It contains several links to sites of interest to bond investors.

http://www.bondmarkets.com The Bond Market Association Web page contains market information, products of interest to bond traders, links, and research.

http://www.bondcalc.com This site discusses a software pricing system for fixed income securities. It includes a description of basic and sophisticated bond analyses.

http://www.pimco.com Pimco is a leader fixed-income portfolio management firm. Its chair, Bill Gross, is regularly featured in a variety of media sharing his well-respected views on the bond market and interest rate trends. The site provides information on bond sectors and offers primers on bond-investing topics and market commentary.

SUMMARY

- The value of a bond equals the present value of all future cash flows accruing to the investor. Cash flows for the conservative bond investor include periodic interest payments and principal return; cash flows for the aggressive investor include periodic interest payments and the capital gain or loss when the bond is sold prior to its maturity. Bond investors can maximize their portfolio rates of return by accurately estimating the level of interest rates and, more importantly, by estimating changes in interest rates, yield spreads, and credit quality. Similarly, they must compare coupon rates, maturities, and call features of alternative bonds.

- There are five bond yield measures: nominal yield, current yield, promised yield to maturity, promised yield to call, and realized (horizon) yield. The promised YTM and promised YTC equations include the interest-on-interest (or coupon reinvestment) assumption. For the realized (horizon) yield computation, the investor estimates the reinvestment rate and the future selling price for the bond. The fundamental determinants of interest rates are a real risk-free rate, the expected rate of inflation, and a risk premium.

- The yield curve (or the term structure of interest rates) shows the relationship between the yields on a set of comparable bonds and the term to maturity. Based upon this yield curve, it is possible to derive a theoretical spot rate curve. In turn, these spot rates can be used to value bonds using an individual spot rate for each cash flow. This valuation approach is becoming more useful in a world where bonds have very different cash flows. In addition, these spot rates imply investor expectations about future rates referred to as forward rates. Yield curves exhibit four basic patterns. Three theories attempt to explain the shape of the yield curve: the expectations hypothesis, the liquidity preference (term premium) hypothesis, and the segmented market (preferred habitat) hypothesis.

- It is important to understand what causes changes in interest rates and how these changes in rates affect the prices of bonds. Differences in bond price volatility are mainly a function of differences in yield, coupon, and term to maturity. There are four duration measures that have been used as measures of bond price volatility or interest rate sensitivity. The Macaulay duration measure incorporates coupon, maturity, and yield in one measure. In turn, modified duration (which is directly related to Macaulay dura-

tion) provides an estimate of the response of bond prices to changes in interest rates under certain assumptions. Because modified duration provides a straight-line estimate of the curvilinear price-yield function, you must consider modified duration together with the convexity of a bond for large changes in yields and/or when dealing with securities that have high convexity. Notably, an embedded call option feature on a bond can have a significant impact on its duration (the call feature can shorten it dramatically) and on its convexity (the call feature can change the convexity from a positive value to a negative value). Following a discussion of some of the limitations of Macaulay and modified durations as measures of interest rate sensitivity, effective duration is introduced as a direct measure of interest rate sensitivity—that is, it is the estimated percentage change in price for a 100-basis-point change in interest rates and allows for repricing due to changes in cash flow caused by changes in interest rates. Notably, with effective duration, it is necessary to have a valid bond pricing model and it is possible to have durations longer than maturity as well as negative duration.

- Finally, there are instances when it is very difficult to estimate the price when there is a change in interest rates as required for effective duration—such as with some mortgage-backed securities, common stock, and real estate. In these instances, analysts consider estimating empirical duration, which is based on the analysis of historical data on price changes that accompany interest rate changes. While it is possible to derive such estimates for a range of assets, it is important to remember that the duration values derived can vary dramatically and are notoriously unstable.

- We concluded the chapter with a revisitation to yield spreads for bonds with embedded options. To take account of the spread across the total term structure of interest rates, we described and demonstrated the static spread. In order to consider the impact of interest rate volatility on the embedded options, we discussed and described the steps to estimate the option-adjusted spread (OAS) for these bonds.

Given the background in bond valuation and the factors that influence bond value and bond return volatility, we are ready to consider how to build a bond portfolio that is consistent with our goals and objectives. Bond portfolio analysis is the topic of Chapter 19.

SUGGESTED READINGS

Fabozzi, Frank J. *Fixed-Income Mathematics*. Chicago: Probus, 1988.

Fabozzi, Frank J. *Bond Markets, Analysis and Strategies*, 5th ed. Upper Saddle River, NJ: 2004.

Fabozzi, Frank J. *Fixed-Income Analysis for the Chartered Financial Analyst Program,* 2nd ed. PA: New Hope, PA: Frank J. Fabozzi Associates, 2004.

Fama, Eugene F. "Forward Rates as Predictors of Future Spot Rates." *Journal of Financial Economics* 3, no. 4 (October 1976).

Tuckman, Bruce. *Fixed-Income Securities,* 2nd ed. New York: John Wiley & Sons, 2002.

QUESTIONS

1. Why does the present value equation appear to be more useful for the bond investor than for the common stock investor?

2. What are the important assumptions made when you calculate the promised yield to maturity? What are the assumptions when calculating promised YTC?

3. a. Define the variables included in the following model:

$$i = (RFR, I, RP)$$

   b. Assume that the firm whose bonds you are considering is not expected to break even this year. Discuss which factor will be affected by this information.

4. We discussed three alternative hypotheses to explain the term structure of interest rates. Briefly discuss the three hypotheses and indicate which one you think best explains the alternative shapes of a yield curve.

5. *CFA Examination Level I*

   a. Explain what is meant by the *structure of interest rates*. Explain the theoretical basis of an upward-sloping yield curve. [8 minutes]

   b. Explain the economic circumstances under which you would expect to see the inverted yield curve prevail. [7 minutes]

   c. Define "real" rate of interest. [2 minutes]

   d. Discuss the characteristics of the market for U.S. Treasury securities. Compare it to the market for AAA corporate bonds. Discuss the opportunities that may exist in bond markets that are less than efficient. [8 minutes]

   e. Over the past several years, fairly wide yield spreads between AAA corporates and Treasuries have occasionally prevailed. Discuss the possible reasons for this. [5 minutes]

6. *CFA Examination Level III*

   As the portfolio manager for a large pension fund, you are offered the following bonds:

	Coupon	Maturity	Price	Call Price	Yield to Maturity
Edgar Corp. (new issue)	14.00%	2012	$101.3/4	$114	13.75%
Edgar Corp. (new issue)	6.00	2012	48.1/8	103	13.60
Edgar Corp. (2000 issue)	6.00	2012	48.7/8	103	13.40

   Assuming that you expect a decline in interest rates over the next three years, identify and justify which of these bonds you would select. [10 minutes]

7. You expect interest rates to decline over the next six months.

   a. Given your interest rate outlook, state what kinds of bonds you want in your portfolio in terms of duration and explain your reasoning for this choice.

   b. You must make a choice between the following three sets of noncallable bonds. For each set, select the bond that would be best for your portfolio given your interest rate outlook and the consequent strategy set forth in Part a. In each case briefly discuss why you selected the bond.

		Maturity	Coupon	Yield to Maturity
Set 1:	Bond A	15 years	10%	10%
	Bond B	15 years	6%	8%
Set 2:	Bond C	15 years	6%	10%
	Bond D	10 years	8%	10%
Set 3:	Bond E	12 years	12%	12%
	Bond F	15 years	12%	8%

8. At the present time, you expect a decline in interest rates and must choose between two portfolios of bonds with the following characteristics:

	Portfolio A	Portfolio B
Average maturity	10.5 years	10.0 years
Average YTM	7%	10%
Modified duration	5.7 years	4.9 years
Modified convexity	125.18	40.30
Call features	Noncallable	Deferred call features that range from 1 to 3 years

Select one of the portfolios and discuss three factors that would justify your selection.

9. The Chartered Finance Corporation has issued a bond with the following characteristics:

> Maturity—25 years
> Coupon—9%
> Yield to maturity—9%
> Callable—after 3 years @ 109
> Duration to maturity—8.2 years
> Duration to first call—2.1 years

   a. Discuss the concept of call-adjusted duration and indicate the approximate value (range) for it at the present time.

   b. Assuming interest rates increase substantially (i.e., to 13 percent), discuss what will happen to the call-adjusted duration and the reason for the change.

   c. Assuming interest rates decline substantially (i.e., they decline to 4 percent), discuss what will happen to the bond's call-adjusted duration and the reason for the change.

   d. Discuss the concept of negative convexity as it relates to this bond.

10. *CFA Examination Level I*

Duration may be calculated by *two* widely used methods. Identify these *two* methods, and briefly discuss the primary differences between them. [5 minutes]

11. *CFA Examination Level II*

Option-adjusted duration and *effective duration* are alternative measures used by analysts to evaluate fixed-income securities with embedded options.

Briefly describe *each* measure and how to apply *each* to the evaluation of fixed-income securities with embedded options. [8 minutes]

12. *CFA Examination Level II*

As a portfolio manager, during a discussion with a client, you explain that historical return and risk premia of the type presented in the following table are frequently used in forming estimates of future returns for various types of financial assets. Although such historical data are helpful in forecasting returns, most users know that history is an imperfect guide to the future. Thus, they recognize that there are reasons why these data should be adjusted if they are to be employed in the forecasting process.

U.S. HISTORICAL RETURN AND RISK PREMIA (1926–1994)

	Per Year
Inflation rate	3.0%
Real interest rate on Treasury bills	0.5%
Maturity premium of long Treasury bonds over Treasury bills	0.8%
Default premium of long corporate bonds over long Treasury bonds	0.6%
Risk premium on stock over long Treasury bonds	5.6%
Return on Treasury bills	3.5%
Return on long corporate bonds	4.9%
Return on large-capitalization stocks	9.9%

---

   a. As shown in the table, the historical real interest rate for Treasury bills was 0.5 percent per year and the maturity premium on Treasury bonds over Treasury bills was 0.8 percent. Briefly describe and justify *one* adjustment to *each* of these two data items that should be made before they can be used to form expectations about future real interest rates and Treasury bond maturity premia. [6 minutes]
   b. You recognize that even adjusted historical economic and capital markets data may be of limited use when estimating future returns. Independent of your Part a response, briefly describe *three* key circumstances that should be considered when forming expectations about future returns. [8 minutes]

 13. *CFA Examination Level I*

A portfolio manager at Superior Trust Company is structuring a fixed-income portfolio to meet the objectives of a client. This client plans on retiring in 15 years and wants a substantial lump sum at that time. The client has specified the use of AAA-rated securities.

The portfolio manager compares coupon U.S. Treasuries with zero coupon stripped U.S. Treasuries and observes a significant yield advantage for the stripped bonds.

Maturity	Coupon U.S. Treasuries	Zero Coupon Stripped U.S. Treasuries
3 year	5.50%	5.80%
5 year	6.00%	6.60%
7 year	6.75%	7.25%
10 year	7.25%	7.60%
15 year	7.40%	8.80%
30 year	7.75%	7.75%

Briefly discuss *two* reasons why zero coupon stripped U.S. Treasuries could yield more than coupon U.S. Treasuries with the same final maturity. [5 minutes]

 14. *CFA Examination Level II*
   a. In terms of option theory, explain the impact on the offering yield of adding a call feature to a proposed bond issue. [5 minutes]
   b. Explain the impact on *both* bond duration and convexity of adding a call feature to a proposed bond issue. [10 minutes]

Assume that a portfolio of corporate bonds is managed to maintain targets for modified duration and convexity.

    c. Explain how the portfolio could include *both* callable and noncallable bonds while maintaining the targets. [5 minutes]

    d. Describe *one* advantage and *one* disadvantage of including callable bonds in this portfolio.

15. *CFA Examination Level II*

Beth Goetz, CFA, has decided to add some asset-backed securities (ABS) to her fixed-income portfolio. She has narrowed the choice to an automobile ABS and a fixed-rate home equity loan (second mortgage) ABS.

Automobile ABS are available at a pricing spread of 75 basis points over comparable-maturity Treasuries, with a zero volatility spread of 67 basis points. Home equity loan ABS are available at a pricing spread of 85 basis points over comparable-maturity Treasuries, with an option-adjusted spread of 60 basis points.

    a. Explain why pricing spread is not an appropriate measure of yield advantage for ABS. [3 minutes]

    b. Describe the concepts of

        (1) Zero volatility spread

        (2) Option-adjusted spread [8 minutes]

    c. Explain why option-adjusted spread is the appropriate measure of yield for a second mortgage ABS. [4 minutes]

16. *CFA Examination Level II*

The asset-backed securities (ABS) market has grown in the past few years partly as a result of credit enhancements to ABS.

    a. Describe a "letter of credit" and the risk to the investor associated with relying exclusively on this type of credit enhancement. [6 minutes]

    b. Describe "early amortization" and the risk to the investor associated with relying exclusively on this type of credit enhancement. [6 minutes]

17. *CFA Examination Level II*

Rachel Morgan owns a newly issued U.S. government agency fixed-rate pass-through mortgage-backed security (MBS) and wants to evaluate the sensitivity of its principal cash flow to the following interest rate scenario:

- Interest rates instantaneously decline by 250 basis points for all maturities, remain there for one year, and then,
- Interest rates instantaneously increase 350 basis points for all maturities and remain there for the next year.

Currently, the MBS is priced close to par and the yield curve is "flat." Morgan does not expect the shape of the yield curve to change during her interest rate scenario.

    a. (1) State whether, in the interest rate scenario described, the MBS principal cash flows

        • Increase or decrease in the first year

        • Increase or decrease in the second year

        (2) Discuss the reason why principal cash flows change. [6 minutes]

Morgan also wants to evaluate the price sensitivity of her MBS to changes in interest rates. She knows that modified duration and effective duration are two possible measures she could use to evaluate price sensitivity.

    b. Select *and* justify with *one* reason which duration measure Morgan should use to evaluate the price sensitivity of her MBS. [6 minutes]

Morgan also owns a newly issued U.S. government agency collateralized mortgage obligation interest-only (IO) security.

    c. State whether the IO security price increases or decreases in the first year of the interest rate scenario described. Justify your response. [6 minutes]

18. *CFA Examination Level III*

One common goal among fixed-income portfolio managers is to earn high incremental returns on corporate bonds versus government bonds of comparable durations. The approach of some corporate bond portfolio managers is to find and purchase those corporate bonds having the largest initial spreads over comparable-duration government bonds. John Ames, HFS's fixed-income manager, believes that a more rigorous approach is required if incremental returns are to be maximized.

The following table presents data relating to one set of corporate/government spread relationships present in the market at a given date:

CURRENT AND EXPECTED SPREADS AND DURATIONS OF HIGH-GRADE CORPORATE BONDS (ONE-YEAR HORIZON)

Bond Rating	Initial Spread Over Governments	Expected Horizon Spread	Initial Duration	Expected Duration One Year from Now
Aaa	31 BP	31 BP	4 years	3.1 years
Aa	40 BP	50 BP	4 years	3.1 years

a. Recommend purchase of *either* Aaa *or* Aa bonds for a one-year investment horizon given a goal of maximizing incremental returns. Show your calculations. (Base your decision *only* on the information presented in the preceding table.) [6 minutes]

Ames chooses not to rely *solely* on initial spread relationships. His analytical framework considers a full range of other key variables likely to impact realized incremental returns, including

- call provisions, and
- potential changes in interest rates.

b. Describe *two* variables, *in addition to those identified,* that Ames should include in his analysis *and* explain how *each* of these *two* variables could cause realized incremental returns to differ from those indicated by initial spread relationships. [10 minutes]

19. *CFA Examination Level II*

    On May 30, 1999, Janice Kerr is considering purchasing one of the following newly issued 10-year AAA corporate bonds shown in the following exhibit. Kerr notes that the yield curve is currently flat and assumes that the yield curve shifts in an instantaneous and parallel manner.

BOND CHARACTERISTICS

Description	Coupon	Price	Callable	Call Price
Sentinel due May 30, 2009	6.00%	100.00	Noncallable	Not applicable
Colina due May 30, 2009	6.20%	100.00	Currently callable	102.00

a. Contrast the effect on the price of *both* bonds if yields decline more than 100 basis points. (No calculation is required). [6 minutes]

b. State and explain under which *two* interest rate forecasts Kerr would prefer the Colina bond over the Sentinel bond. [6 minutes]

c. State the directional price change, if any, assuming interest rate volatility increases, for *each* of the following: [6 minutes]
   (1) The Sentinel bond
   (2) The Colina bond

PROBLEMS

1. Four years ago, your firm issued $1,000 par, 25-year bonds, with a 7 percent coupon rate and a 10 percent call premium.
   a. If these bonds are now called, what is the *approximate* yield to call for the investors who originally purchased them?
   b. If these bonds are now called, what is the *actual* yield to call for the investors who originally purchased them at par?

    c. If the current interest rate is 5 percent and the bonds were not callable, at what price would each bond sell?

2. Assume that you purchased an 8 percent, 20-year, $1,000 par, semiannual payment bond priced at $1,012.50 when it has 12 years remaining until maturity. Compute:
    a. Its promised yield to maturity
    b. Its yield to call if the bond is callable in three years with an 8 percent premium.

3. Calculate the duration of an 8 percent, $1,000 par bond that matures in three years if the bond's YTM is 10 percent and interest is paid semiannually.
    a. Calculate this bond's modified duration.
    b. Assuming the bond's YTM goes from 10 percent to 9.5 percent, calculate an estimate of the price change.

4. Two years ago, you acquired a 10-year zero coupon, $1,000 par value bond at a 12 percent YTM. Recently you sold this bond at an 8 percent YTM. Using semiannual compounding, compute the annualized horizon return for this investment.

5. A bond for the Chelle Corporation has the following characteristics:

> Maturity—12 years
> Coupon—10%
> Yield to maturity—9.50%
> Macaulay duration—5.7 years
> Convexity—48
> Noncallable

    a. Calculate the approximate price change for this bond using only its duration assuming its yield to maturity increased by 150 basis points. Discuss the impact of the calculation, including the convexity effect.
    b. Calculate the approximate price change for this bond (using only its duration) if its yield to maturity declined by 300 basis points. Discuss (without calculations) what would happen to your estimate of the price change if this was a callable bond.

6. *CFA Examination Level I*
The following table shows selected data on a German government bond (payable in Deutschemarks) and a U.S. government bond. Identify the components of return and calculate the total return in U.S. dollars for both of these bonds for the year 1991. Show the calculations for *each* component. (Ignore interest on interest in view of the short time period.) [8 minutes]

		MARKET YIELD		Modified	EXCHANGE RATE (DM/$U.S.)	
	Coupon	1/1/91	1/1/92	Duration	1/1/91	1/1/92
German government bond	8.50%	8.50%	8.00%	7.0	1.55	1.50
U.S. government bond	8.00%	8.00%	6.75%	6.5	—	—

7. *CFA Examination Level I*
Philip Morris has issued bonds that pay semiannually with the following characteristics:

Coupon	Yield to Maturity	Maturity	Macaulay Duration
8%	8%	15 years	10 years

a. Calculate modified duration using the preceding information. [5 minutes]
b. Explain why modified duration is a better measure than maturity when calculating the bond's sensitivity to changes in interest rates. [5 minutes]
c. Identify the direction of change in modified duration if
   (1) the coupon of the bond were 4 percent, not 8 percent.
   (2) the maturity of the bond were 7 years, not 15 years. [5 minutes]
d. Define convexity and explain how modified duration *and* convexity are used to approximate the bond's percentage change in price, given a change in interest rates. [5 minutes]

8. *CFA Examination Level I*
   You are a U.S. investor considering purchase of one of the following securities. Assume that the currency risk of the German government bond will be hedged, and the six-month discount on Deutschemark forward contracts is –0.75 percent versus the U.S. dollar.

Bond	Maturity	Coupon	Price
U.S. government	June 1, 2003	6.50%	100.00
German government	June 1, 2003	7.50%	100.00

Calculate the expected price change required in the German government bond that would result in the two bonds having equal total returns in U.S. dollars over a six-month horizon. [8 minutes]

9. *CFA Examination Level II*
   a. Using the information in the following table, calculate the projected price change for Bond B if the yield to maturity for this bond falls by 75 basis points. [7 minutes]
   b. Describe the shortcoming of analyzing Bond A strictly to call or to maturity. Explain an approach to remedy this shortcoming. [6 minutes]

MONTICELLO CORPORATION BOND INFORMATION

	Bond A (Callable)	Bond B (Noncallable)
Maturity	2012	2012
Coupon	11.50%	7.25%
Current price	125.75	100.00
Yield to maturity	7.70%	7.25%
Modified duration to maturity	6.20	6.80
Convexity to maturity	0.50	0.60
Call date	2006	—
Call price	105	—
Yield to call	5.10%	—
Modified duration to call	3.10	—
Convexity to call	0.10	—

10. *CFA Examination Level II*
    U.S. Treasuries represent a significant holding in Monticello's pension portfolio. You decide to analyze the yield curve for U.S. Treasury Notes.
    a. Using the data in the following table, calculate the five-year spot and forward rates assuming annual compounding. Show calculations. [8 minutes]

U.S. TREASURY NOTE YIELD CURVE DATA

Years to Maturity	Par Coupon Yield to Maturity	Calculated Spot Rates	Calculated Forward Rates
1	5.00	5.00	5.00
2	5.20	5.21	5.42
3	6.00	6.05	7.75
4	7.00	7.16	10.56
5	7.00	❐	❐

b. Define and describe *each* of the following *three* concepts:
   - Yield to maturity
   - Spot rate
   - Forward rate

   Explain how these *three* concepts are related. [9 minutes]

You are considering the purchase of a zero coupon U.S. Treasury Note with four years to maturity.

c. Based on the preceding yield curve analysis, calculate *both* the expected yield to maturity and the price for the security. Show calculations. [8 minutes]

 11. *CFA Examination Level II*

The following table shows yields to maturity on U.S. Treasury securities as of January 1, 1993:

Term to Maturity	Yield to Maturity
1 year	3.50%
2 years	4.50%
3 years	5.00%
4 years	5.50%
5 years	6.00%
10 years	6.60%

a. Based on the data in the table, calculate the implied forward one-year rate of interest at January 1, 1996. [5 minutes]

b. Describe the conditions under which the calculated forward rate would be an unbiased estimate of the one-year spot rate of interest at January 1, 1996. [5 minutes]

Assume that one year earlier, at January 1, 1992, the prevailing term structure for U.S. Treasury securities was such that the implied forward one-year rate of interest at January 1, 1996, was significantly higher than the corresponding rate implied by the term structure at January 1, 1993.

c. On the basis of the pure expectations theory of the term structure, briefly discuss two factors that could account for such a decline in the implied forward rate. [8 minutes]

Multiple scenario forecasting frequently makes use of information from the term structure of interest rates.

d. Briefly describe how the information conveyed by this observed decrease in the implied forward rate for 1996 could be used in making a multiple scenario forecast. [5 minutes]

12. *CFA Examination Level I*

Bonds of Zello Corporation with a par value of $1,000 sell for $960, mature in five years, and have a 7 percent annual coupon rate paid semiannually.

a. Calculate the
   (1) current yield;
   (2) yield to maturity (to the nearest whole percent, i.e., 3 percent, 4 percent, 5 percent, etc.); *and*

Table 1 | Bond Characteristics

	Bond A	Bond B
Coupons	Annual	Annual
Maturity	3 years	3 years
Coupon rate	10%	6%
Yield to maturity	10.65%	10.75%
Price	98.40	88.34

Table 2 | Spot Interest Rates

Term	Spot Rates (Zero Coupon)
1 year	5%
2 year	8%
3 year	11%

    (3) horizon yield (also called realized or total return) for an investor with a three-year holding period and a reinvestment rate of 6 percent over the period. At the end of three years, the 7 percent coupon bonds with two years remaining will sell to yield 7 percent.
Show your work. [9 minutes]
  b. Cite *one* major shortcoming for *each* of the following fixed-income yield measures:
    (1) current yield;
    (2) yield to maturity; *and*
    (3) horizon yield (also called realized or total return). [6 minutes]

13. *CFA Examination Level II*
Table 1 shows the characteristics of two annual pay bonds from the same issuer with the same priority in the event of default, and Table 2 displays spot interest rates. Neither bond's price is consistent with the spot rates.
    Using the information in Tables 1 and 2, recommend *either* Bond A *or* Bond B for purchase. Justify your choice. [10 minutes]

14. *CFA Examination Level II*
You ran a regression of the yield of KC Company's 10-year bond on the 10-year U.S. Treasury benchmark's yield using month-end data for the past year. You found the following result:

$$\text{Yield}_{KC} = 0.54 + 1.22\,\text{Yield}_{Treasury}$$

where Yield_{KC} is the yield on the KC bond and $\text{Yield}_{Treasury}$ is the yield on the U.S. Treasury bond.
    The modified duration on the 10-year U.S. Treasury is 7.0 years, and modified duration on the KC bond is 6.93 years.
  a. Calculate the percentage change in the price of the 10-year U.S. Treasury, assuming a 50-basis-point change in the yield on the 10-year U.S. Treasury. [3 minutes]
  b. Calculate the percentage change in the price of the KC bond, using the regression equation, assuming a 50-basis-point change in the yield on the 10-year U.S. Treasury. [6 minutes]

15. *CFA Examination Level II*
Patrick Wall is considering the purchase of one of the two bonds described in the following table. Wall realizes his decision will depend primarily on effective duration, and he believes that interest rates will decline by 50 basis points at all maturities over the next six months.

BOND DESCRIPTIONS		
Characteristic	CIC	PTR
Market price	101.75	101.75
Maturity date	June 1, 2008	June 1, 2008
Call date	Noncallable	June 1, 2003
Annual coupon	6.25%	7.35%
Interest payment	Semiannual	Semiannual
Effective duration	7.35	5.40
Yield to maturity	6.02%	7.10%
Credit rating	A	A

a. Calculate the percentage price change forecasted by effective duration for *both* the CIC and PTR bonds if interest rates decline by 50 basis points over the next six months. Show your work. [6 minutes]

b. Calculate the six-month horizon return (in percent) for *each* bond, if the actual CIC bond price equals 105.55 and the actual PTR bond price equals 104.15 at the end of six months. Assume you purchased the bonds to settle on June 1, 1998. Show your work. [6 minutes]

Wall is surprised by the fact that although interest rates fell by 50 basis points, the actual price change for the CIC bond was greater than the price change forecasted by effective duration, whereas the actual price change for the PTR bond was less than the price change forecasted by effective duration.

c. Explain why the actual price change would be greater for the CIC bond and the actual price change would be less for the PTR bond. [6 minutes]

 16. *CFA Examination Level II*

a. Discuss how *each* of the following theories for the term structure of interest rates could explain an upward slope of the yield curve:
   (1) Pure expectations (unbiased)
   (2) Uncertainty and term premiums (liquidity preference)
   (3) Market segmentation [9 minutes]

The following are the current coupon yields to maturity and spot rates of interest for six U.S. Treasury securities. Assume all securities pay interest annually.

YIELDS TO MATURITY AND SPOT RATES OF INTEREST		
Term to Maturity	Current Coupon Yield to Maturity	Spot Rate of Interest
1-year Treasury	5.25%	5.25%
2-year Treasury	5.75	5.79
3-year Treasury	6.15	6.19
5-year Treasury	6.45	6.51
10-year Treasury	6.95	7.10
30-year Treasury	7.25	7.67

b. Compute, under the pure expectations theory, the two-year implied forward rate three years from now, given the information provided in the preceding table. State the assumption underlying the calculation of the implied forward rate. [6 minutes]

APPENDIX
Chapter 18

Exhibit 18A.1	Calculation of Duration and Convexity for an 8 Percent Five-Year Bond Selling to Yield 6 Percent

Period	Cash Flow	Discount Factor	PV	PV × t	PV × t × (t + 1)
1	40.00	0.9709	38.83	38.83	77.67
2	40.00	0.9426	37.70	75.41	226.22
3	40.00	0.9151	36.61	109.82	439.27
4	40.00	0.8885	35.54	142.16	710.79
5	40.00	0.8626	34.50	172.52	1,035.13
6	40.00	0.8375	33.50	201.00	1,406.97
7	40.00	0.8131	32.52	227.67	1,821.32
8	40.00	0.7894	31.58	252.61	2,273.50
9	40.00	0.7664	30.66	275.91	2,759.10
10	1,040.00	0.7441	773.86	7,738.58	85,124.34
		Total	1,085.30	9,234.50	95,874.32

$$\text{Macaulay Duration} = \frac{9{,}234.50}{2 \times 1{,}085.30} = 4.25$$

$$\text{Modified Duration} = \frac{4.25}{1.03} = 4.13$$

$$\text{Convexity} = \frac{95{,}874.32}{(1.03)^2 \times 2^2 \times 1{,}085.30} = 20.82$$

Chapter 19

Bond Portfolio Management Strategies

After you read this chapter, you should be able to answer the following questions:

- What are the five major bond portfolio management strategies available?
- What are the two passive bond portfolio management strategies available?
- What are the five active bond portfolio management strategies available?
- What is meant by core-plus bond management and what are some plus strategies?
- What is meant by matched-funding techniques and what are the four specific strategies?
- What are the contingent procedure strategies that are referred to as structured active management strategies?
- What are the implications of capital market theory for bond portfolio managers?
- What is the evidence on the efficient market hypothesis as it relates to bond markets?
- What are the implications of efficient market studies for bond portfolio managers?

In this chapter, we shift attention from bond valuation and analysis to the equally important bond portfolio management strategies. Initially, we discuss the five alternative bond portfolio management strategies: passive management, active management, core-plus bond management, matched-funding techniques, and structured active management. Next, we consider the implications of capital market theory and market efficiency on bond portfolio management.

ALTERNATIVE BOND PORTFOLIO STRATEGIES

Bond portfolio management strategies can be divided into five groups:[1]

1. Passive portfolio strategies
   a. Buy and hold
   b. Indexing

---

[1]This breakdown benefited from the discussion in Leibowitz (1986a).

2. Active management strategies
   a. Interest rate anticipation
   b. Valuation analysis
   c. Credit analysis
   d. Yield spread analysis
   e. Bond swaps
3. Core-plus management strategy
4. Matched-funding techniques
   a. Dedicated portfolio, exact cash match
   b. Dedicated portfolio, optimal cash match and reinvestment
   c. Classical ("pure") immunization
   d. Horizon matching
5. Contingent procedures (structured active management)
   a. Contingent immunization
   b. Other contingent procedures

We discuss each of these alternatives because they are all viable for certain portfolios with different needs and risk profiles. Prior to the 1960s, only the first two groups were available, and most bond portfolios were managed on the basis of buy and hold. The early 1970s saw growing interest in alternative active bond portfolio management strategies, while the late 1970s and early 1980s were characterized by record-breaking inflation and interest rates as well as extremely volatile yields and rates of return in bond markets. This led to the introduction of many new financial instruments in response to the increase in return volatility. Since the mid-1980s, matched-funding techniques or contingent portfolio management techniques have been developed to meet the emerging needs of institutional clients.

Passive Management Strategies

Two specific passive portfolio management strategies exist. First is a **buy-and-hold strategy** in which a manager selects a portfolio of bonds based on the objectives and constraints of the client with the intent of holding these bonds to maturity. In the second passive strategy— **indexing**—the objective is to construct a portfolio of bonds that will equal the performance of a specified bond index, such as the Lehman Brothers Corporate/Government Bond Index.

Buy-and-Hold Strategy   The simplest portfolio management strategy is to buy and hold. Obviously not unique to bond investors, it involves finding issues with desired quality, coupon levels, term to maturity, and important indenture provisions, such as call features. Buy-and-hold investors do not consider active trading to achieve attractive returns but, rather, look for vehicles whose maturities (or duration) approximate their stipulated investment horizon to reduce price and reinvestment risk. Many successful bond investors and institutional portfolio managers follow a modified buy-and-hold strategy wherein an investment is made in an issue with the intention of holding it until the end of the investment horizon. However, they still actively look for opportunities to trade into more desirable positions.[2]

Whether the investor follows a strict or modified buy-and-hold approach, the key ingredient is finding investment vehicles that possess attractive maturity and yield features. The strategy does not restrict the investor to accept whatever the market has to offer, nor does it imply that selectivity is unimportant. Attractive high-yielding issues with desirable features and quality standards are actively sought. For example, these investors recognize that agency issues

---

[2]Obviously, if the strategy becomes too modified, it becomes one of the active strategies.

generally provide incremental returns relative to Treasuries with a little sacrifice in quality, that utilities provide higher returns than comparable rated industrials, and that various call features affect the risk and realized yield of an issue. Thus, successful buy-and-hold investors use their knowledge of markets and issue characteristics to seek out attractive realized yields. Aggressive buy-and-hold investors also incorporate timing considerations by using their knowledge of market rates, yield spreads, and expectations.

Indexing Strategy   As discussed in the chapter on efficient capital markets, numerous empirical studies have demonstrated that the majority of money managers have not been able to match the risk–return performance of common stock or bond indexes. As a result, many clients have opted to index some part of their bond portfolios, which means that the portfolio manager builds a portfolio that will match the performance of a selected bond market index, such as a Lehman Brothers Index, Merrill Lynch Index, or Salomon Brothers Index. In such a case, the portfolio manager is judged not on the basis of risk and return compared to an index but by how closely the portfolio *tracks* the designated index. Specifically, the analysis of performance involves examining the **tracking error**, which equals the difference between the rate of return for the portfolio and the rate of return for the bond market index. For example, if the portfolio experienced an annual rate of return of 8.2 percent during a period when the index had a rate of return of 8.3 percent, the tracking error would be minus 10 basis points (8.20 – 8.30 = –0.10).

When initiating an indexing strategy, the selection of the appropriate market index is very important because it directly determines the client's risk–return results. As such, it is necessary to be very familiar with all the characteristics of the index.[3] For bond indexes, it also is important to be aware of how the aggregate bond market and the indexes change over time.[4] Reilly, Kao, and Wright (1992) demonstrated that the market has experienced significant changes in composition, maturity, and duration since 1975. After the appropriate bond index is selected, several techniques are available to accomplish the actual tracking.[5]

Active Management Strategies[6]

Five active management strategies are available, including interest rate anticipation, which involves economic forecasting, as well as valuation analysis and credit analysis, which require detailed bond and company analysis. Alternatively, yield spread analysis and bond swaps, which require economic and market analysis, are also available.

Interest Rate Anticipation   **Interest rate anticipation** is perhaps the riskiest active management strategy because it involves relying on uncertain forecasts of future interest rates. The idea is to preserve capital when an increase in interest rates is anticipated and achieve attractive capital gains when interest rates are expected to decline. Such objectives usually are attained by altering the maturity (duration) structure of the portfolio (i.e., reducing portfolio duration when interest rates are expected to increase and increasing the portfolio duration when a decline in yields is anticipated). Thus, the risk in such portfolio restructuring is largely

---

[3]Two articles that discuss how the characteristics of indexes affect their performance in difference interest rate environments are Dialynas (2001) and Volpert (2001). For an analysis of a new comprehensive Treasury bond index, see Reilly and Wright (1997).

[4]An article that describes the major bond market indexes, discusses the risk–return characteristics, and analyzes the relationships between them, is Reilly and Wright (2005). A similar study for high-yield indexes is Reilly and Wright (1994).

[5]For a detailed discussion of the alternative tracking techniques available, see Mossavar-Rahmani (1991) and Fabozzi (2004, Chapter 20).

[6]For further discussion on this topic, see Fong (2005), Vock (1996), and Malvey (2005). For a set of readings, see Squires (1997a) and Churchill (1994).

a function of these duration (maturity) alterations. When maturities are shortened to preserve capital, substantial income could be sacrificed and the opportunity for capital gains could be lost if interest rates decline rather than rise. Similarly, the portfolio shifts prompted by anticipation of a decline in rates are very risky. Specifically, if we assume that we are at a peak in interest rates, it is likely that the yield curve is downward sloping, which means that bond coupons will decline with maturity. Therefore, the investor is sacrificing current income by shifting from high-coupon short bonds to longer-duration bonds. At the same time, the portfolio is purposely exposed to greater price volatility that could work against the portfolio if an unexpected increase in yields occurs. Note that the portfolio adjustments prompted by anticipation of an increase in rates involve less risk of an absolute capital loss. When you reduce the maturity, the worst that can happen is that interest income is reduced and/or capital gains are forgone (opportunity cost).

Once future (expected) interest rates have been determined, the procedure relies largely on technical matters. Assume that you expect an increase in interest rates and want to preserve your capital by reducing the duration of your portfolio. A popular choice would be high-yielding, short-term obligations, such as Treasury bills. Although your primary concern is to preserve capital, you would nevertheless look for the best return possible given the maturity constraint. Liquidity also is important because, after interest rates increase, yields may experience a period of stability before they decline, and you would want to shift positions quickly to benefit from the higher income and/or capital gains.

One way to shorten maturities is to use a *cushion bond*—a high-yielding, long-term obligation that carries a coupon substantially above the current market rate and that, due to its current call feature and call price, has a market price lower than what it should be given current market yields. As a result, its yield is higher than normal. An example would be a 10-year bond with a 12 percent coupon, currently callable at 110. If current market rates are 8 percent, this bond (if it were noncallable) would have a price of about 127; because of its call price, however, it will stay close to 110, and its yield will be about 10 percent rather than 8 percent. Bond portfolio managers look for cushion bonds when they expect a modest increase in rates because such issues provide attractive current income *and* protection against capital loss. Because these bonds are trading at an abnormally high yield, market rates would have to rise to that abnormal level before their price would react.

The portfolio manager who anticipates higher interest rates, therefore, has two simple strategies available: shorten the duration of the portfolio and/or look for an attractive cushion bond as described by Homer and Leibowitz (2004, Chapter 5). In either case, you would want very liquid issues.

A totally different posture is assumed by investors who anticipate a decline in interest rates. The significant risk involved in restructuring a portfolio to take advantage of a decline in interest rates is balanced by the potential for substantial capital gains and holding period returns. When you expect lower interest rates, you will recall that you should increase the duration of the portfolio because the longer the duration, the greater the positive price volatility. Also, liquidity is important because you want to be able to close out the position quickly when the drop in rates has been completed.

Notably, because interest rate sensitivity is critical, it is important to recall that the higher the quality of an obligation, the more sensitive it is to interest rate changes. Therefore, high-grade securities should be used, such as Treasuries, agencies, or corporates rated AAA through BAA. Finally, you want to concentrate on noncallable issues or those with strong call protection because of the substantial call risk discussed in Chapter 18 in connection with the analysis of duration and convexity.

Valuation Analysis   With valuation analysis, the portfolio manager attempts to select bonds based on their intrinsic value, which is determined based on their characteristics and the average value of these characteristics in the marketplace. As an example, a bond's rating will dictate a certain spread relative to comparable Treasury bonds: long maturity might be worth an added 60 basis points relative to short maturity (i.e., the maturity spread); a given deferred call feature might require a higher or lower yield; a specified sinking fund would likewise mean higher or lower required yields. Given all the characteristics of the bond and the normal cost of the characteristics in terms of yield, you would determine the bond's required yield and, therefore, its implied intrinsic value. After you have done this for a number of bonds, you would compare these derived bond values to the prevailing market prices to determine which bonds are undervalued or overvalued. Based on your confidence in the characteristic costs, you would buy the undervalued issues and ignore or sell the overvalued issues.

Success in valuation analysis is based on understanding the characteristics that are important in valuation and being able to accurately *estimate* the yield cost of these characteristics with the understanding that these yield costs change over time.

Credit Analysis   A **credit analysis** strategy involves detailed analysis of the bond issuer to determine expected changes in its default risk. This involves attempting to project changes in the credit ratings assigned to bonds by the three rating agencies discussed in Chapter 17.[7] These rating changes are affected by internal changes in the entity (e.g., changes in important financial ratios) and by changes in the external environment (i.e., changes in the firm's industry and the economy). During periods of strong economic expansion, even financially weak firms may survive and prosper. In contrast, during severe economic contractions, normally strong firms may find it very difficult to meet financial obligations. Therefore, historically there has been a strong cyclical pattern to rating changes: typically, downgradings increase during economic contractions and decline during economic expansions.

To use credit analysis as a portfolio management strategy, it is necessary to project rating changes prior to the announcement by the rating agencies. As the subsequent discussion on bond market efficiency notes, the market adjusts rather quickly to bond rating changes—especially downgradings. Therefore, you want to acquire bond issues expected to experience upgradings and sell or avoid those bond issues expected to be downgraded.

Credit Analysis of High-Yield (Junk) Bonds   One of the most obvious opportunities for credit analysis is the analysis of high-yield (junk) bonds. As demonstrated by several studies, the yield differential between junk bonds that are rated below BBB and Treasury securities ranges from about 200 basis points to almost 1,000 basis points. Notably, these yield differentials vary substantially over time as shown by a time-series plot in Exhibit 19.1. Specifically, the average yield spread ranged from a low of less than 300 basis points in 1985 and 1997 to a high of over 950 basis points during early 1991 and late 2002.

Although the spreads have changed, a study by Wigmore (1990) indicated that the average credit quality of high-yield bonds also changed over time as indicated by interest coverage changes over the business cycle. Also, the credit quality of bonds *within* rating categories changed over the business cycle as demonstrated by Reilly and Gentry (2004).

These changes in credit quality will make credit analysis of high-yield bonds more important, but also more difficult. This means that bond analysts–portfolio managers need to engage in detailed credit analysis to select bonds that will survive. Given the spread in promised yields, if a portfolio manager can—through rigorous credit analysis—avoid bonds with a high probability of default or downgrade, high-yield bonds will provide substantial rates of return for the investor.[8]

---

[7]For a discussion of changes in the aggregate financial risk of U.S. corporations and the opportunities this has created, see Reilly and Gentry (2004). For a presentation on credit analysis that emphasizes changes in credit ratings, see Fabozzi (2005a, Chapter 32). For a set of readings on global credit analysis, see Squires (1998b).
[8]For a discussion regarding the analysis of high-risk bonds, see Fabozzi (2005a, Chapter 32) and Vine (2001).

Exhibit 19.1	Yield Spread History, Merrill Lynch High-Yield Master Index versus 10-Year Treasury: Monthly, 1985–First Quarter, 2005

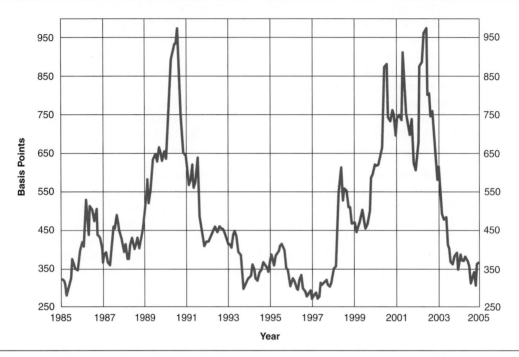

Source: M. Christopher Garman and Oleg Melentyev, Analysts, Merrill Lynch, "U.S. High Yield Market Update–1Q 2005," p. 25. Reprinted by permission. Copyright © 2005 Merrill Lynch, Pierce, Fenner & Smith Incorporated.

In summary, substantial rates of return can be derived by investing in high-yield bonds if you do the credit analysis required to avoid defaults, which occur with these bonds at substantially higher rates than the overall bond market as shown by Altman (1989); Asquith, Mullins, and Wolff (1989); and Altman (1992).

Exhibit 19.2 lists the results for a study that considers the full spectrum of bonds. It shows substantial differences in cumulative default rates for bonds with different ratings for the periods 5 and 10 years after issue. Over 10 years—the holding period that is widely discussed—the default rate for BBB investment-grade bonds is only 4.66 percent, but the default rate increases to over 17 percent for BB-rated, to almost 33 percent for B-rated bonds, and to over 52 percent for CCC-rated bonds.

These default rates do not mean that investors should avoid high-yield bonds, but they do indicate that extensive credit analysis is a critical component for success within this sector.

Investing in Defaulted Debt   Beyond high-yield bonds that have high credit risk and high default rates, a new set of investment opportunities has evolved—investing in defaulted debt. While this sector requires an understanding of legal procedures surrounding bankruptcy as well as economic analysis, as noted by Altman (1993a), the returns have generally been consistent with the risk, as demonstrated by Altman (1993b); Altman and Simon (2001); Ward and Griepentrog (1993); and Reilly, Wright, and Altman (1998).

Credit Analysis Models   The credit analysis of high-yield bonds can use a statistical model or basic fundamental analysis that recognizes some of the unique characteristics of these

Exhibit 19.2	Average Cumulative Default Rates for Corporate Bonds: 1978–2001

Ratings	YEARS SINCE ISSUE		
	5	10	15
AAA	0.10%	0.52%	0.52%
AA	0.26	0.83	1.31
A	0.57	1.58	2.32
BBB	2.16	4.66	6.64
BB	10.59	17.40	19.52
B	25.06	32.61	35.76
CCC	46.87	52.22	54.38

Source: *Rating Performance 2002* (New York: Standard & Poor's, February 2002): 8. Reprinted with permission.

bonds. Altman-Nammacher (1987) suggest that a modified *Z-score model* used to predict bankruptcy can also be used to predict default for these high-yield bonds or as a gauge of changes in credit quality. The Z-score model combines traditional financial measures with a multivariate technique known as *multiple discriminant analysis* to derive a set of weights for the specified variables. The result is an overall credit score (zeta score) for each firm. The model is of the form

$$\text{Zeta} = a_0 + a_1 X_1 + a_2 X_2 + a_3 X_3 + \cdots + a_n X_n$$

where:

Zeta = the overall credit score
$X_1 \ldots X_n$ = the explanatory variables (ratios and market measures)
$a_0 \ldots a_n$ = the weightings or coefficients

The final model used in this analysis included the following seven financial measures:

X_1 = profitability: earnings before interest and taxes (EBIT)/total assets (TA)
X_2 = stability of profitability measure: the standard error of estimate of EBIT/TA (normalized for 10 years)
X_3 = debt service capabilities (interest coverage): EBIT/interest charges
X_4 = cumulative profitability: retained earnings/total assets
X_5 = liquidity: current assets/current liabilities
X_6 = capitalization levels: market value of equity/total capital (five-year average)
X_7 = size: total tangible assets (normalized)

The weightings, or coefficients, for the variables were not reported. Studies by Jonsson and Fridson (1996); Helwege and Kleiman (1997); and Fridson, Garman, and Wu (1997) examined the aggregate default rate for high-yield bonds.

In contrast to using a model that provides a composite credit score, most analysts simply adapt their basic corporate bond analysis techniques *to the unique needs of high-yield bonds,* which have characteristics of common stock as shown by Reilly and Wright (1994, 2001). Fabozzi (2005a, Chapter 32), claims that the analysis of high-yield bonds is the same as with any bond except that the following areas of analysis should be expanded.

1. What is the firm's *competitive position* in terms of cost and pricing? This can be critical to a small firm.
2. What is the firm's *cash flow* relative to cash requirements for interest, research, growth, and periods of economic decline? Also, what is the firm's *borrowing capacity* that can serve as a safety net and provide flexibility?
3. What is the *liquidity value of the firm's assets?* Are these assets available for liquidation (are there any claims against them)? In many cases, asset sales are a critical part of the strategy for a leveraged buyout.
4. How good is the *total management team?* Is the management team committed to and capable of operating in the high-risk environment of this firm?
5. What is the firm's *financial leverage* on an absolute basis and on a market-adjusted basis (using market value of equity and debt)?

Hynes (1987) suggests that the following areas require additional analysis as part of the process of evaluating cash flows when analyzing a leveraged buyout (which typically involves the issuance of high-yield debt).

- Inherent business risk
- Earnings growth potential
- Asset redevelopment potential
- Refinancing capability

In addition to the potentially higher financial risks, presentations in Sondhi (1995) and Squires (1998b) point out several factors that can also impact business risk. An increase in business risk may exist if the firm sells off some operations that have favorable risk characteristics with the remaining operations—that is, business risk would increase if the firm sells a division or a company that has low correlation of earnings with other units of the firm. Further, a change in management operating philosophy could have a negative impact on operating earnings. The managements of leveraged buyout (LBO) firms are known for making optimistic growth estimates related to sales and earnings, so the analyst should evaluate these estimates very critically. Asset divestiture plans often are a major element of an LBO because they provide necessary capital that is used to reduce the substantial debt taken on as part of the buyout. Therefore, it is important to examine the liquidity of the assets, their estimated selling values, and the timing of these programs. You must ascertain whether the estimated sales prices for the assets are reasonable and whether the timing is realistic. In contrast, if the divestiture program is successful wherein the prices received are above normal expectations and the assets are sold ahead of schedule, this can be grounds for upgrading the debt. Finally, it is necessary to constantly monitor the firm's refinancing flexibility. Specifically, what refinancing will be necessary, what does the schedule look like, and will the capital suppliers be receptive to the refinancing?

The substantial increase in high-yield bonds issued and outstanding has been matched by an increase in research on credit analysis. The credit analysis of these bonds is similar to that of investment-grade bonds with an emphasis on the following factors: (1) *the use of cash flows* compared to debt obligations under very conservative assumptions; (2) the detailed analysis of *potential asset sales,* including a conservative estimate of sales prices, the asset's true liquidity, the availability of the assets, and a consideration of the timing of the sales; and (3) the recognition that high-yield bonds have many characteristics of common stock, which means that many equity analysis techniques are appropriate. An in-depth analysis of high-yield bonds is critical because of the number of issues, the wide diversity of quality within the high-yield bond universe, and the growing complexity of high-yield bond issues.

High-Yield Bond Research Because of the growth of high-yield bonds, several investment houses have developed specialized high-yield groups that examine high-yield bond issues and monitor high-yield bond spreads.

Merrill Lynch's weekly publication, *This Week in High Yield,* discusses current events in the high-yield market. This includes weekly yields and yield spreads for the various sectors of the market and news highlights for specific companies and issues.

High-Yield Market Update, a Salomon Brothers Smith Barney monthly publication, presents monthly and cumulative long-term returns for its high-yield indexes (long-term and intermediate-term corporates, long-term utilities), as well as spreads between rating categories relative to appropriate Treasuries. The publication also features commentary on timely topics within the high-yield market.

The high-yield research group at First Boston publishes *Monthly Market Review,* which contains an extensive performance review of the HY (high-yield) bond market that examines returns by sectors and industries as well as considering yield spreads and changing volatility for these bonds. First Boston also publishes an annual *High Yield Handbook,* which reviews annual events and considers every aspect of risk, return, and correlation of high-yield bonds with other asset classes. There also is a very helpful listing of new issues, retirements, and defaults.

Lehman Brothers publishes a weekly review, *High-Yield Portfolio Advisor,* which analyzes the performance of the firm's high-yield bond indexes and has detailed comments on news events that affect prominent industries in the high-yield market. The firm also publishes a monthly *High-Yield Bond Market Report* that briefly discusses the returns and new issues for the month, contains extensive data on returns for all components of the HY market (BB, B, CCC, CC-D, nonrated, default), and contains descriptive statistics regarding bonds in the composite index and various subindexes, such as average coupon, maturity, duration to worst, modified adjusted duration, price, and yield.

In addition, several bond-rating firms conduct research on these industries and firms. Standard & Poor's publication, *Speculative Grade Debt Credit Review,* discusses the credit analysis of high-yield bonds. The publication also includes a review of several major industries and specific comments on outstanding issues.

Yield Spread Analysis As discussed in Chapter 18, spread analysis assumes normal relationships exist between the yields for bonds in alternative sectors (e.g., the spread between high-grade versus low-grade industrial or between industrial versus utility bonds). Therefore, a bond portfolio manager would monitor these relationships and, when an abnormal relationship occurs, execute various sector swaps. The crucial factor is developing the background to know the normal yield relationship and to evaluate the liquidity necessary to buy or sell the required issues quickly enough to take advantage of the temporary yield abnormality.

A paper by Dialynas and Edington (1992) considers several specific factors that affect the aggregate spread. It is acknowledged that the generally accepted explanation of changes in the yield spread is that it is related to the economic environment. Specifically, the spread widens during periods of economic uncertainty and recession because investors require larger risk premiums (i.e., larger spreads). In contrast, the spread will decline during periods of economic confidence and expansion. Although not denying the existence of such a relationship, the authors contend that a more encompassing factor is the impact of interest rate (yield) volatility. They contend that yield volatility will affect the spread via three effects: (1) yield volatility and the behavior of embedded options, (2) yield volatility and transactional liquidity, and (3) the effect of yield volatility on the business cycle.

Recall that the value of callable bonds is equal to the value of a noncallable bond minus the value of the call option. Obviously, if the value of the option goes up, the value of the callable bond will decline and its yield will increase. When yield volatility increases, the value of the call option increases, which causes a decline in the price of the callable bond and a rise in the bond's yield and its yield spread relative to Treasury bonds. Similarly, an increase in yield volatility will raise the uncertainty facing bond dealers and cause them to increase their bid-ask spreads that reflect the transactional liquidity for these bonds. This liquidity will have a bigger effect on nongovernment bonds, so their yield spread relative to Treasury bonds will increase. Finally, interest rate volatility causes uncertainty for business executives and consumers regarding their cost of funds. This typically will precede an economic decline that will, in turn, lead to an increase in the yield spread. It is demonstrated that it is possible to have a change in yield spread for reasons other than economic uncertainty. If there is a period of greater yield volatility that is not a period of economic uncertainty, the yield spread will increase due to the embedded option effect and the transactional liquidity effect. This analysis implies that when examining yield spreads, you should pay particular attention to interest rate (yield) volatility.

Bond Swaps   **Bond swaps** involve liquidating a current position and simultaneously buying a different issue in its place with similar attributes but having a chance for improved return. Swaps can be executed to increase current yield, to increase yield to maturity, to take advantage of shifts in interest rates or the realignment of yield spreads, to improve the quality of a portfolio, or for tax purposes. Some swaps are highly sophisticated and require a computer for calculation. However, most are fairly simple transactions with obvious goals and risk. They go by such names as *profit takeouts, substitution swaps, intermarket spread swaps,* or *tax swaps.* Although many of these swaps involve low risk (such as the pure yield pickup swap), others entail substantial risk (the rate anticipation swap). Regardless of the risk involved, all swaps have one basic purpose: portfolio improvement.

Most swaps involve several different types of risk. One obvious risk is that the market will move against you while the swap is outstanding. Interest rates may move up over the holding period and cause you to incur a loss. Alternatively, yield spreads may fail to respond as anticipated. Possibly the new bond may not be a true substitute and so, even if your expectations and interest rate formulations are correct, the swap may be unsatisfactory because the wrong issue was selected. Finally, if the work-out time is longer than anticipated, the realized yield might be less than expected. As noted by Homer and Leibowitz (2004) and Fabozzi, Mann, and Choudhry (2005, Chapter 55), you must be willing to accept such risks to improve your portfolio. The following subsections consider three of the more popular bond swaps.

Pure Yield Pickup Swap   The pure yield pickup involves swapping out of a low-coupon bond into a comparable higher-coupon bond to realize an automatic and instantaneous increase in current yield and yield to maturity. Your risks are (1) that the market will move against you and (2) that the new issue may not be a viable swap candidate. Also, because you are moving to a higher-coupon obligation, there could be greater call risk.

An example of a pure yield pickup swap would be an investor who currently holds a 30-year, Aa-rated 10 percent issue that is trading at an 11.50 percent yield. Assume that a comparable 30-year, Aa-rated obligation bearing a 12 percent coupon priced to yield 12 percent becomes available. The investor would report (and realize) some book loss if the original issue was bought at par but is able to improve current yield and yield to maturity simultaneously if the new obligation is held to maturity as shown in Exhibit 19.3.

The investor need not predict rate changes, and the swap is not based on any imbalance in yield spread. The object simply is to seek higher yields. Quality and maturity stay the same as do all other factors *except coupon.* The major risk is that future reinvestment rates may not be as high as expected, and, therefore, the total terminal value of the investment (capital recovery, coupon receipts, and interest-on-interest) may not be as high as expected or comparable to the original obligation. This reinvestment risk can be evaluated by analyzing the results with a number of reinvestment rates to determine the minimum reinvestment rate that would make the swap viable.

Exhibit 19.3	A Pure Yield Pickup Swap

Pure yield pickup swap: A bond swap involving a switch—from a low-coupon bond to a higher-coupon bond of similar quality and maturity—in order to pick up higher current yield and a better yield to maturity.

Example: Currently hold: 30-year, 10.0% coupon priced at 874.12 to yield 11.5%
Swap candidate: 30-year, Aa 12% coupon priced at $1,000 to yield 12.0%

	Current Bond	Candidate Bond
Dollar investment	$874.12	$1,000.00[a]
Coupon	100.00	120.00
i on one coupon (12.0% for 6 months)	3.000	3.600
Principal value at year end	874.66	1,000.00
Total accrued	977.66	1,123.60
Realized compound yield	11.514%	12.0%

Value of swap: 48.6 basis points in one year (assuming a 12.0% reinvestment rate).

The rewards for a pure yield pickup swap are automatic and instantaneous in that both a higher-coupon yield and a higher yield to maturity are realized from the swap. Other advantages include:

1. No specific work-out period needed because the investor is assumed to hold the new bond to maturity
2. No need for interest rate speculation
3. No need to analyze prices for overvaluation or undervaluation

A major disadvantage of the pure yield pickup swap is the book loss involved in the swap. In this example, if the current bond were bought at par, the book loss would be $125.88 ($1,000 – 874.12). Other risks involved in the pure yield pickup swap include:

1. Increased risk of call in the event interest rates decline
2. Reinvestment risk is greater with higher-coupon bonds.

[a]Obviously, the investor can invest $874.12—the amount obtained from the sale of the bond currently held—and still obtain a realized compound yield of 12.0%.

Swap evaluation procedure is patterned after a technique suggested by Sidney Homer and Martin L. Leibowitz.

Source: Adapted from the book *Inside the Yield Book* by Sidney Homer and Martin L. Leibowitz, Ph.D. (Englewood Cliffs, NJ: Prentice Hall, 1972).

Substitution Swap　The substitution swap generally is short term and relies heavily on interest rate expectations. Therefore, it is subject to considerably more risk than the pure yield pickup swaps. The procedure assumes a short-term imbalance in yield spreads between issues that are perfect substitutes. The imbalance in yield spread is expected to be corrected in the near future. For example, the investor might hold a 30-year, 12 percent issue that is yielding 12 percent and be offered a comparable 30-year, 12 percent bond that is yielding 12.20 percent. Because the issue offered will trade at a price less than $1,000 for every issue sold, the investor can buy more than one of the offered obligations.

You would expect the yield spread imbalance to be corrected by having the yield on the offering bond decline to the level of your current issue. Thus, you would realize capital gains by switching out of your current position into the higher-yielding obligation. This swap is described in Exhibit 19.4.

Exhibit 19.4	A Substitution Swap

Substitution swap: A swap executed to take advantage of temporary market anomalies in yield spreads between issues that are equivalent with respect to coupon, quality, and maturity.

Example: Currently hold: 30-year, Aa 12.0% coupon priced at $1,000 to yield 12.0%
          Swap candidate: 30-year, Aa 12% coupon priced at $984.08 to yield 12.2%
          Assumed work-out period: 1 year
          Reinvested at 12.0%

	Current Bond	Candidate Bond
Dollar investment	$1,000.00	$ 984.08
Coupon	120.00	120.00
i on one coupon (12.0% for 6 months)	3.60	3.60
Principal value at year end (12.0% YTM)	1,000.00	1,000.00
Total accrued	1,123.60	1,123.60
Total gain	123.60	139.52
Gain per invested dollar	0.1236	0.1418
Realized compound yield	12.00%	13.71%
Value of swap: 171 basis points in one year		

The rewards for the substitution swap are additional basis-point pickups for YTM, additional realized compound yield, and capital gains that accrue when the anomaly in yield corrects itself. In the substitution swap, any basis-point pickup (171 points in this example) will be realized only during the work-out period. Thus, in our example, to obtain the 171 basis-point increase in realized compound yield, you must swap an average of once a year and pick up an average of 20 basis points in yield to maturity on each swap.

Potential risks associated with the substitution swap include:

1. A yield spread thought to be temporary may, in fact, be permanent, thus reducing capital gains advantages.
2. The market rate may change adversely.

Swap evaluation procedure is patterned after a technique suggested by Sidney Homer and Martin L. Leibowitz.

Source: Adapted from the book *Inside the Yield Book* by Sidney Homer and Martin L. Leibowitz, Ph.D. (Englewood Cliffs, NJ: Prentice Hall, 1972).

Although a modest increase in current income occurs as the yield imbalance is corrected, attractive capital gains are possible, causing a differential in *realized yield.* The work-out time will have an important effect on the differential realized return. Even if the yield is not corrected until maturity, 30 years later, you will still experience a small increase in realized yield (about 10 basis points). In contrast, if the correction takes place in one year, the differential realized return is much greater, as shown in Exhibit 19.4.

After the correction has occurred, you would have additional capital for a subsequent swap or other investment. Several risks are involved in this swap. In addition to the pressure of the work-out time, market interest rates could move against you, the yield spread may not be temporary, and the issue may not be a viable swap candidate (i.e., the spread may be due to the issue's lower quality).

Tax Swap   The tax swap is popular with individual investors because it is a relatively simple procedure that involves no interest rate projections and few risks. Investors enter into tax swaps due to tax laws and realized capital gains in their portfolios. Assume you acquired $100,000 worth of corporate bonds and after two years sold the securities for $150,000, implying a capital gain of $50,000. One way to eliminate the tax liability of that capital gain is to sell an issue that has a comparable long-term capital loss. If you had a long-term investment of $100,000 with a current market value of $50,000, you could execute a tax swap to establish the $50,000 capital loss. By offsetting this capital loss and the comparable capital gain, you would reduce your income taxes.

Municipal bonds are considered particularly attractive tax swap candidates because you can increase your tax-free income and use the capital loss (subject to normal federal and state taxation) to reduce capital gains tax liability. To continue our illustration, assume you own $100,000 worth of New York City, 20-year, 7 percent bonds that you bought at par, but they have a current market value of $50,000. Given this tax loss, you need a comparable bond swap candidate. Suppose you find a 20-year New York City bond with a 7.1 percent coupon and a market value of 50. By selling your New York 7s and instantaneously reinvesting in the New York 7.1s, you would eliminate the capital gains tax from the corporate bond transaction. In effect, you have $50,000 of tax-free capital gains, and you have increased your current tax-free yield. The money saved by avoiding the tax liability can then be used to increase the portfolio's yield, as shown in Exhibit 19.5.

An important caveat is that *you cannot swap identical issues* (such as selling the New York 7s to establish a loss and then buying back the same New York 7s). If it is not a different issue,

Exhibit 19.5	A Tax Swap

Tax swap: A swap undertaken when you wish to offset capital gains in other securities through the sale of a bond currently held and selling at a discount from the price paid at purchase. By swapping into a bond with as nearly identical features as possible, you can use the capital loss on the sale of the bond for tax purposes and still maintain your current position in the market.

Example: Currently hold: $100,000 worth of corporate bonds with current market value of $150,000 *and* $100,000 in NY, 20-year, 7% bonds with current market value of $50,000
Swap candidate: $50,000 in NY, 20-year, 7.1% bonds

A. Corporate bonds sold and long-term capital gains profit established	$50,000	
Capital gains tax liability (assume you have 20% capital gains tax rate) ($50,000 × 0.20)		$10,000
B. NY 7s sold and long-term capital *loss* established	$50,000	
Reduction in capital gains tax liability ($50,000 × 0.20)		($10,000)
Net capital gains tax liability		0
Tax *savings* realized		$10,000
C. Complete tax swap by buying NY 7.1s from proceeds of NY 7s Sale (therefore, amount invested remains largely the *same*)[a]		
Annual tax-free interest income—NY 7s	$ 7,000	
Annual tax-free interest income—NY 7.1s	$ 7,100	
Net *increase* in *annual* tax-free interest income	$ 100	

[a]NY 7.1s will result in substantial capital gains when liquidated at maturity (because they were bought at deep discounts) and, therefore, will be subject to future capital gains tax liability. The swap is designed to use the capital loss resulting from the swap to offset capital gains from other investments. At the same time, your funds remain in a security almost identical to your previous holding while you receive a slight increase in both current income and YTM. Because the tax swap involved no projections in terms of work-out period, interest rate changes, etc., the risks involved are minimal. Your major concern should be to avoid potential wash sales.

the IRS considers the transaction a *wash sale* and does not allow the loss. It is easier to avoid wash sales in the bond market than it is in the stock market because every bond issue, even with identical coupons and maturities, is considered distinct. Likewise, it is easier to find comparable bond issues with only modest differences in coupon, maturity, and quality. Tax swaps are common at year end as investors establish capital losses because the capital loss must occur in the same taxable year as the capital gain. This procedure differs from other bond swap transactions because it exists due to tax statutes rather than temporary market anomalies.

Ending Point on Swaps   Beyond these specific swap suggestions, it is important to be aware of the specific analysis involved in the decision. This includes detailed analysis of all cash flows involved from coupon payments and reinvestment of cash flows in order to arrive at an estimate of the *realized compound yield* from both the current bond and the candidate bond. The point is, this same analysis can and should be used to decide between an investment in two or more alternative bonds that are not being swapped. It is the analysis process that is important.

A Global Fixed-Income Investment Strategy

An active management strategy that considers one or several of the techniques discussed thus far should apply these techniques to a global portfolio. The optimum global fixed-income asset allocation must consider three interrelated factors: (1) the local economy in each country that includes the effect of domestic and international demand, (2) the impact of this total demand and domestic monetary policy on inflation and interest rates, and (3) the effect of the economy, inflation, and interest rates on the exchange rates among countries.[9] Based on the evaluation of these factors, a portfolio manager must decide on the relative weight for each country. In addition, one might consider an allocation within each country among government, municipal, and corporate bonds. In the examples that follow, most portfolio recommendations concentrate on the country allocation and do not become more specific except in the case of the United States.

Exhibit 19.6 is from the March 31, 2005, *Quarterly Investment Strategy* by UBS Global Asset Management, a global institutional asset manager. The table's "Benchmark" column indicates what the asset allocation would be if UBS had no opinion regarding the expected bond market performance in the alternative countries. In most cases, the normal allocation is based on the country's relative market value. Specifically, the normal allocation is 20.1 percent for the United States, 29.0 percent for Japan, and the remaining 50.9 percent for the other countries, including 40.0 percent for the combined EMU countries. Clearly, UBS *does* have an opinion regarding these countries (as shown in its implied *market strategy*, which equals the benchmark percentage plus or minus the over/underweight percentage). For example, it has overweighted the EMU block of countries bond markets with a market strategy allocation of 42.9 percent (versus the benchmark allocation of 40.0 percent) and underweighted the UK bond market with a market strategy allocation of only 3 percent (versus the benchmark of 5 percent) Another country overweighted was Australia, while several are underweighted, including Denmark, Norway, Poland, and Switzerland. In addition, UBS does a specific currency allocation between countries, which would likewise be based on the normal policy weight unless the firm had an opinion on currencies. Again, UBS has an opinion: it heavily underweighted the U.K. pound and overweighted the currencies of Japan and Singapore.

---

[9]For a detailed discussion of the benefits of international bond investing as well as what is involved in the analysis, see Steward (2005), Munves (2005), Malvey (2005), and Steward, Lynch, and Fabozzi (2005a). Also see Churchill (1994), Squires (1996; 1997a, b; 2000a), and Jost (2002).

In making your own allocations based on these specific expectations, you would look for U.S. securities in which yields were expected to decline relative to Treasury securities and for bond markets in foreign countries that likewise had bullish interest rate expectations. Finally, you would look for countries in which the currency was expected to be strong relative to the United States.

Exhibit 19.6	UBS Global Bond Portfolio Strategy

Market Allocation as of March 31, 2005

	GLOBAL		GLOBAL (EX-US)	
	Benchmark	Over/Under Weight	Benchmark	Over/Under Weight
North America	22.0%	−0.3%	2.4%	0.0%
Canada	1.9	0.0	2.4	0.0
US	20.1	−0.3	0.0	0.0
EMU	40.0	2.9	50.1	3.5
Other Europe (Ex-UK)	3.3	−2.4	4.2	−3.1
Denmark	0.8	−0.8	1.0	−1.0
Norway	0.2	−0.2	0.3	−0.3
Poland	0.6	−0.6	0.7	−0.7
Sweden	0.9	0.0	1.1	0.0
Switzerland	0.8	−0.8	1.0	−1.0
UK	5.0	−2.0	6.2	−2.2
Japan	29.0	0.0	36.3	0.0
Australia	0.3	2.0	0.4	2.0
Singapore	0.2	−0.2	0.3	−0.3
	100.0%		100.0%	

	EUROPE (EMU)	
	Benchmark	Over/Under Weight
Austria	3.6%	6.7%
Belgium	7.0	−3.3
Finland	1.5	5.6
France	20.7	1.2
Germany	23.0	18.2
Greece	4.6	−4.6
Ireland	1.0	−1.0
Italy	22.7	−11.5
Netherlands	5.6	−0.8
Portugal	1.8	−1.9
Spain	8.5	−8.5
	100.0%	

(continued)

| Exhibit 19.6 | **UBS Global Bond Portfolio Strategy (continued)** |

Currency Allocation

	GLOBAL		GLOBAL (EX-US)	
	Benchmark	Over/Under Weight	Benchmark	Over/Under Weight
North America	22.0%	0.0%	2.4%	0.0%
Canada	1.9	0.0	2.4	0.0
US	20.1	0.0	0.0	0.0
EMU	40.0	0.0	50.1	0.0
Other Europe (Ex-UK)	3.3	0.0	4.2	0.0
Denmark	0.8	0.0	1.0	0.0
Norway	0.2	0.0	0.3	0.0
Poland	0.6	0.0	0.7	0.0
Sweden	0.9	0.0	1.1	0.0
Switzerland	0.8	0.0	1.0	0.0
UK	5.0	−4.0	6.2	−4.0
Japan	29.0	2.0	36.3	2.0
Australia	0.3	0.0	0.4	0.0
Singapore	0.2	2.0	0.3	2.0
	100.0%		100.0%	

Totals may not add to 100% due to rounding.

Source: UBS Global Asset Management, *Quarterly Investment Strategy*, March 31, 2005 (Chicago, IL: UBS Global Asset Management).

In summary, assuming you want to actively manage a bond portfolio, this example shows an approach to the asset allocation decision on a global scale. Similar to our discussion on equity securities, global bond allocation requires substantially more research because you must evaluate each country—individually and relative to every other country. Finally, your global fixed-income recommendation also must consider exchange rate changes—that is, you must also make a currency decision for each country.

Core-Plus Bond Portfolio Management

Beyond a pure passive policy or one of the several active portfolio management styles, there has been an increase in a combination approach referred to as **core-plus bond-portfolio management**. The idea is to have a significant (core) part of the portfolio (e.g., 70 percent to 75 percent) managed passively in a widely recognized sector such as the U.S. Aggregate Sector or the U.S. Government/Corporate sector. The difference between these two sectors is that the aggregate includes the rapidly growing mortgage-backed and asset-backed sectors. It is suggested that this core of the portfolio be managed passively because these segments of the bond market are quite efficient so that it is not worth the time and cost to attempt to derive excess returns within these sectors. The rest of the portfolio would be managed actively in one or several additional "plus" sectors, where it is felt that there is a higher probability of achieving positive abnormal rates of return because of potential inefficiencies. The major areas suggested for the plus of the portfolio include high-yield bonds (HY bonds), foreign bonds, and emerging-market debt. These are considered good candidates for active management because they generally experience above-average rates of return; but, while they have *high total risk* as measured by their standard deviation of returns, they have relatively *low systematic risk* relative to a total bond market portfolio—i.e, they have low correlations with other fixed-income sectors. An example would be HY bonds that have *very high* standard deviations but are correlated only about 0.30 with investment-grade bonds and/or other large bond benchmarks so they have *very low* systematic risk.[10]

Matched-Funding Techniques[11]

As discussed previously, because of an increase in interest rate volatility and the needs of many institutional investors, there has been a growth in the use of matched-funding techniques ranging from pure cash-matched dedicated portfolios to portfolios involved in contingent immunization.

Dedicated Portfolios   **Dedication** refers to bond portfolio management techniques that are used to service a prescribed set of liabilities. The idea is that a pension fund has a set of future liabilities, and those responsible for administering these liabilities want a money manager to construct a portfolio of assets with cash flows that will match this liability stream. Such a "dedicated" portfolio can be created in several ways. We will discuss two alternatives.

A **pure cash-matched dedicated portfolio** is the most conservative strategy. Specifically, the objective of pure cash matching is to develop a portfolio of bonds that will provide a stream of payments from coupons, sinking funds, and maturing principal payments that will exactly match the specified liability schedules. An example of typical liability stream for a retired-lives component of a pension system is shown in Exhibit 19.7.

Exhibit 19.7	A Prescribed Schedule of Liabilities

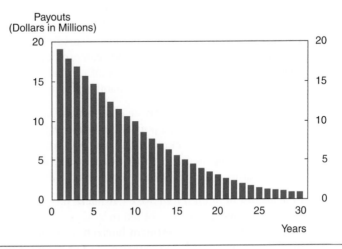

---

[10]Two recent conferences by the Association for Investment Management and Research (now the CFA Institute), considered this concept and discuss potential areas for active management. See *Global Bond Management II: The Search for Alpha* (2000) and *Core-Plus Bond Management* (2001).

[11]An overview of these alternative strategies is contained in Leibowitz (1986a) and by Fabozzi (2005a, Chapter 48).

The goal is to build a portfolio that will generate sufficient funds in advance of each scheduled payment to ensure that the payment will be met. One alternative is to find a number of zero coupon Treasury securities that will exactly cash match each liability. Such an exact cash match portfolio is referred to as a *total passive* portfolio because it is designed so that any prior receipts would not be reinvested (i.e., it assumes a zero reinvestment rate).

Dedication with reinvestment is the same as the pure cash-matched technique except it is assumed that the bonds and other cash flows do not have to exactly match the liability stream. Specifically, any inflows that precede liability claims can be reinvested at some reasonably conservative rate. This assumption allows the portfolio manager to consider a substantially wider set of bonds that may have higher return characteristics. In addition, the assumption of reinvestment within each period and between periods also will generate a higher return for the asset portfolio. As a result, the net cost of the portfolio will be lower, with almost equal safety, assuming the reinvestment rate assumption is conservative. An example would be to assume a reinvestment rate of 4 percent in an environment where market interest rates are currently ranging from 5 percent to 8 percent.

Potential problems exist with both of these approaches to a dedicated portfolio. For example, when selecting potential bonds for these portfolios, it is critical to be aware of call/prepayment possibilities (refundings, calls, sinking funds) with specific bonds or mortgage-backed securities. These prepayment possibilities become very important following periods of historically high rates. A prime example was the period 1982 to 1986, when interest rates went from over 18 percent to under 8 percent. Because of this substantial change in rates, many dedicated portfolios constructed without adequate concern for complete call protection were negatively affected when numerous bonds were called that were not expected to be called under normal conditions. For example, bonds selling at deep discounts (which typically provide implicit call protection), when rates were 16 percent to 18 percent, went to par and above when rates declined to under 10 percent. It is not surprising that they were called. Obviously, the reinvestment of these proceeds at the lower rates caused many dedicated portfolios to be underfunded. Therefore, it is necessary to find bonds with complete call protection or to consider deep discount bonds under conservative interest rate conditions.

Although quality also is a legitimate concern, it is probably not necessary to invest only in Treasury bonds if the portfolio manager diversifies across industries and sectors. A diversified portfolio of AA or A industrial bonds can provide a current and total annual return of 40 to 60 basis points above Treasuries. This differential over a 30-year period can have a significant impact on the net cost of funding a liability stream.

Immunization Strategies   Instead of using a passive strategy, an active strategy, or a dedicated portfolio technique, a portfolio manager (after client consultation) may decide that the optimal strategy is to immunize the portfolio from interest rate changes. The *immunization techniques* attempt to derive a specified rate of return (generally quite close to the current market rate) during a given investment horizon regardless of what happens to market interest rates.

Components of Interest Rate Risk   A major problem encountered in bond portfolio management is deriving a given rate of return to satisfy an ending-wealth requirement at a future specific date—that is, the **investment horizon**. If the term structure of interest rates were flat and market rates never changed between the time of purchase and the horizon date when funds were required, you could acquire a bond with a term to maturity equal to the desired investment horizon, and the ending wealth from the bond would equal the promised wealth position implied by the promised yield to maturity. Specifically, the ending-wealth position would be the beginning wealth times the compound value of a dollar at the promised yield to maturity. For example, assume you acquire a 10-year, $1 million bond with an 8 percent coupon at its par value (8 percent Y_m). If conditions were as specified (there was a flat yield curve and there were no changes in the curve), your wealth position at the end of your 10-year investment horizon (assuming semiannual compounding) would be

$$\$1,000,000 \times (1.04)^{20} = \$1,000,000 \times 2.1911 = \$2,191,100$$

You can get the same answer by taking the $40,000 interest payment every six months and compounding it semiannually to the end of the period at 4 percent and adding the $1,000,000 principal at maturity. Unfortunately, in the real world, the term structure of interest rates typically is not flat and the level of interest rates is constantly changing. Consequently, the bond portfolio manager faces **interest rate risk** between the time of investment and the future target date. Interest rate risk is the uncertainty regarding the ending-wealth value of the portfolio due to changes in market interest rates between the time of purchase and the investor's horizon date. Notably, interest rate risk involves two component risks: **price risk** and **coupon reinvestment risk**.

The price risk occurs because if interest rates change before the horizon date and the bond is sold before maturity, the realized market price for the bond will differ from the *expected* price, assuming there had been no change in rates. If rates increased after the time of purchase, the realized price for the bond in the secondary market would be below expectations, whereas if rates declined, the realized price for the bond would be above expectations. Because you do not know whether interest rates will increase or decrease, you are uncertain about the bond's future price.

The coupon reinvestment risk arises because the yield to maturity computation implicitly assumes that all coupon cash flows will be reinvested at the promised yield to maturity.[12] If, after the purchase of the bond, interest rates decline, the coupon cash flows will be reinvested at rates below the promised Y_m, and the ending wealth will be below expectations. In contrast, if interest rates increase, the coupon cash flows will be reinvested at rates above expectations, and the ending wealth will be above expectations. Again, because you are uncertain about future rates, you are uncertain about these reinvestment rates.

Classical Immunization and Interest Rate Risk   The price risk and the coupon reinvestment risk caused by a change in interest rates have opposite effects on the ending-wealth position. An increase in interest rates will cause an ending price below expectations, but the reinvestment rate for interim cash flows will be above expectations. A decline in market interest rates will cause the reverse situation. Clearly, a bond portfolio manager with a specific target date (investment horizon) will attempt to eliminate these two components of interest rate risk. The process intended to eliminate interest rate risk is referred to as **immunization** and was discussed by Redington (1952). It has been specified in detail by Fisher and Weil (1971) as follows:

> A portfolio of investments in bonds is *immunized* for a holding period if its value at the end of the holding period, regardless of the course of interest rates during the holding period, must be at least as large as it would have been had the interest-rate function been constant throughout the holding period.
>
> If the realized return on an investment in bonds is sure to be at least as large as the appropriately computed yield to the horizon, then that investment is immunized [p. 411].

Fisher and Weil found a significant difference between the *promised* yields and the *realized* returns on bonds for the period 1925 to 1968, indicating the importance of immunizing a bond

---

[12] This point was discussed in detail in Chapter 18 and in Homer and Leibowitz (2004).

portfolio. They showed that it is possible to immunize a bond portfolio if you can assume that any change in interest rates will be the same for all maturities—that is, if forward interest rates change, all rates will change by the same amount (there is a parallel shift of the yield curve). Given this assumption, Fisher and Weil proved that *a portfolio of bonds is immunized from interest rate risk if the modified duration of the portfolio is always equal to the desired investment horizon.* For example, if the investment horizon of a bond portfolio is eight years, the *modified duration* of the bond portfolio should equal eight years to immunize the portfolio. To attain a given modified duration, the weighted average modified duration (with weights equal to the proportion of value) is set at the desired length following an interest payment, and all subsequent cash flows are invested in securities *to keep the portfolio modified duration equal to the remaining investment horizon.*

Fisher and Weil showed that price risk and reinvestment rate risk are affected in opposite directions by a change in market rates and that modified duration is the time period when these two risks are of equal magnitude but opposite in direction. This is also discussed by Bierwag and Kaufman (1977) and Bierwag (1977).

Application of the Immunization Principle   Fisher and Weil (1971) simulated the effects of applying the immunization concept (a duration-matched strategy) compared to a naive portfolio strategy where the portfolio's maturity was equal to the investment horizon. They compared the ending-wealth ratio for the duration-matched and for the naive strategy portfolios to a wealth ratio that assumed no change in the interest rate structure. In a perfectly immunized portfolio, the actual ending wealth should equal the expected ending wealth implied by the promised yield, so these comparisons should indicate which portfolio strategy does a superior job of immunization. The duration-matched strategy results were consistently closer to the promised yield results; however, the results were not perfect. The duration portfolio was not perfectly immunized because the basic assumption did not always hold; that is, when interest rates changed, all interest rates did not change by the same amount.

Bierwag and Kaufman (1977) pointed out several specifications of the duration measure. The duration measure developed by Macaulay (1938) discussed in Chapter 18, discounts all flows by the prevailing yield to maturity on the bond being measured. Alternatively, Fisher and Weil (1971) defined duration using future one-period interest rates (forward rates) to discount the future flows. Depending on the shape of the yield curve, the two definitions could give different answers. If the yield curve is flat, the two definitions will compute equal durations. Bierwag and Kaufman (1977) computed alternative measures of duration and found that, except at high coupons and long maturities, the duration values of the alternative definitions were similar, and the Macaulay duration measure is preferable because it is a function of the yield to maturity of the bond. This means you do not need a forecast of one-period forward rates over the maturity of the bond.

Example of Classical Immunization   Exhibit 19.8 shows the effect of attempting to immunize a portfolio by matching the investment horizon and the duration of a bond portfolio using a single bond. The portfolio manager's investment horizon is eight years, and the current yield to maturity for eight-year bonds is 8 percent. Therefore, if we assumed no change in yields, the ending-wealth ratio for an investor should be 1.8509 (1.08^8) with annual compounding.[13] As noted, this also should be the ending-wealth ratio for a completely immunized portfolio.

The example considers two portfolio strategies: (1) the maturity strategy, where the portfolio manager would acquire a bond with a term to maturity of eight years, and (2) the duration strategy, where the portfolio manager sets the duration of the portfolio at eight years.

---

[13] We use annual compounding to compute the ending-wealth ratio because the example uses annual observations.

Exhibit 19.8	An Example of the Effect of a Change in Market Rates on a Bond (Portfolio) that Uses the Maturity Strategy versus the Duration Strategy

	RESULTS WITH MATURITY STRATEGY			RESULTS WITH DURATION STRATEGY		
Year	Cash Flow	Reinvestment Rate	End Value	Cash Flow	Reinvestment Rate	End Value
1	$ 80	.08	$ 80.00	$ 80	.08	$ 80.00
2	80	.08	166.40	80	.08	166.40
3	80	.08	259.71	80	.08	259.71
4	80	.08	360.49	80	.08	360.49
5	80	.06	462.12	80	.06	462.12
6	80	.06	596.85	80	.06	596.85
7	80	.06	684.04	80	.06	684.04
8	$1,080	.06	$1,805.08	$1,120.64[a]	.06	$1,845.72

Expected wealth ratio = 1.8509 or $1,850.90

[a]The bond could be sold at its market value of $1,040.64, which is the value for an 8 percent bond with two years to maturity priced to yield 6 percent. This market value plus the $80 coupon payment equals $1,120.64.

For the **maturity strategy**, the portfolio manager acquires an eight-year, 8 percent bond; for the **duration strategy**, the manager acquires a 10-year, 8 percent bond that has approximately an eight-year duration (8.12 years), assuming an 8 percent Y_m. We assume a single shock to the interest rate structure at the end of Year 4, when rates go from 8 percent to 6 percent and stay there through Year 8.

As shown, due to the interest rate change, the ending-wealth ratio for the maturity strategy bond is *below* the desired wealth ratio because of the shortfall in the reinvestment cash flow after Year 4 when the interim coupon cash flow was reinvested at 6 percent rather than 8 percent. Note that *the maturity strategy eliminated the price risk* because the bond matured at the end of Year 8. Alternatively, the duration strategy portfolio likewise suffered a shortfall in reinvestment cash flow because of the change in market rates. In contrast to the maturity strategy, this reinvestment shortfall was partially offset by an *increase* in the ending value for the bond because of the decline in market rates. This second bond is sold at the end of Year 8 at 104.06 of par because it is an 8 percent coupon bond with two years to maturity selling to yield 6 percent. Because of this partial offset due to the price increase, the duration strategy had an ending-wealth value (1,845.72) that was much closer to the expected wealth value (1,850.90) than the maturity strategy (1,805.08). The point is, the reinvestment rate shortfall was almost completely offset by the positive price effect in the duration strategy.

If market interest rates had increased during this period, the maturity strategy portfolio would have experienced an *excess* of reinvestment income compared to the expected cash flow and the ending-wealth ratio for this strategy would have been above expectations. In contrast, in the duration portfolio, the excess cash flow from reinvestment under this assumption would have been partially offset by a *decline* in the ending price for the bond (i.e., it would have sold at a small discount to par value). Although the ending-wealth ratio for the duration strategy would have been lower than the maturity strategy in this example, it would have been closer to the expected-wealth ratio. Although the maturity strategy would have provided a higher than expected ending value for this scenario, the whole purpose of immunization is to *eliminate uncertainty* due to interest rate changes by having the realized-wealth position equal the expected-wealth position. As shown, this is what is accomplished with the duration-matched strategy.

Another View of Immunization   The prior example assumed that both bonds were acquired and held to the end of the investment horizon. An alternative way to envision what is expected to happen with an immunized portfolio is to concentrate on the specific growth path from the beginning-wealth position to the ending-wealth position and examine what happens when interest rates change.

Assume that the initial-wealth position is $1 million, your investment horizon is 10 years, and the coupon and current YTM are 8 percent. We know from an earlier computation that this implies that the expected ending-wealth value is $2,191,100 (with semiannual compounding). Exhibit 19.9A shows the compound growth rate path from $1 million to the expected ending value at $2,191,100. In Exhibit 19.9B, it is assumed that at the end of Year 2, interest rates increase 200 basis points from 8 percent to 10 percent. We know that with no prior rate changes, at the end of Year 2 the value of the portfolio would have grown at an 8 percent compound rate to $1,169,900 [$1.04^4 = 1.1699$]. Given the rate change, we know there will be two changes for this portfolio: (1) the price (value of the portfolio) will decline to reflect the higher interest rate; and (2) the reinvestment rate, which is the growth rate, will increase to 10 percent. An important question is, How much will the portfolio value decline? The answer depends on the modified duration of the portfolio when rates change. Fisher and Weil (1971) showed that *if the modified duration is equal to the remaining horizon, the price change will be such that at the new reinvestment (growth) rate (10 percent), the new portfolio value will grow to the expected-wealth position.* You can approximate the change in portfolio value using the modified duration and the change in market rates. (Recall that this will not give an exact estimate because of the convexity of the portfolio.) The approximate change in price is 16 percent based on a modified duration of eight years and a 200-basis-point change. This would imply an approximate estimated portfolio value of $982,716 ($1,169,900 $\times$ 0.84). In fact, the actual value would be $1,003,743. (Recall that the estimated value based on using modified duration always is below the value implied by the price-yield curve.) If this new actual portfolio value grows at 10 percent a year for eight years, the projected ending-wealth value will be

$$\$1,003,743 \times 2.1829 \text{ (5\% for 16 periods)} = \$2,191,070$$

The difference between the expected value and projected value is due to rounding. This example shows that the price decline is almost exactly offset by the higher reinvestment rate—assuming that the modified duration of the portfolio at the time of the rate change was equal to the remaining investment horizon.

What happens if the portfolio is not properly matched? If the modified duration is greater than the remaining horizon, the price change will be greater. Thus, if interest rates increase, the value of the portfolio after the rate change will be less than $1,003,743. In this case, even if the new value of the portfolio grew at 10 percent a year, it would not reach the expected ending-wealth value. This scenario is shown in Exhibit 19.9C, where it is assumed that the value of the portfolio with a modified duration greater than eight declined to $950,000. If this new portfolio value grew at 10 percent a year for the remaining eight years, its ending value would be

$$\$950,000 \times 2.1829 \text{ (5\% for 16 periods)} = \$2,073,755$$

Therefore, the shortfall of $118,000 between the expected-wealth value and the realized-wealth value is because the portfolio was not properly duration matched (immunized) when interest rates changed.

Exhibit 19.9 | **The Growth Path to the Expected Ending-Wealth Value and the Effect of Immunization**

A. Constant 8 Percent Growth Rate

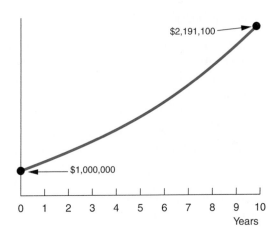

B. Effect of Interest Rate Increase after Two Years with Duration Equal to Investment Horizon

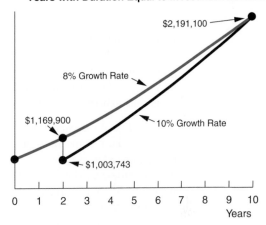

C. Effect of Interest Rate Increase with Duration Greater Than Investment Horizon

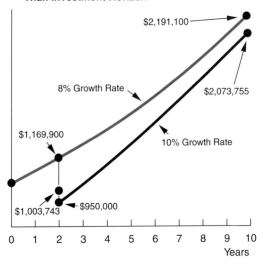

D. Effect of Interest Rate Decline with Duration Greater Than Investment Horizon

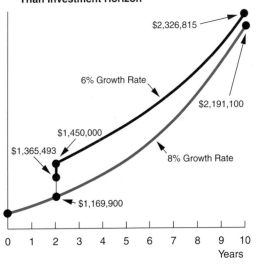

Alternatively, if we assume that interest rates had declined and again the modified duration had been longer than eight years, the portfolio value would have increased such that the new portfolio value would have been greater than the required value. Exhibit 19.9D shows what can happen if the portfolio is not properly matched and interest rates decline by 200 basis points to 6 percent. First, if we assume that the portfolio *is* properly matched, the value of the portfolio will increase to $1,365,493. If this new portfolio value grows at 6 percent for eight years, its ending value will be

$$\$1,365,493 \times 1.6047 \ (3\% \text{ for } 16 \text{ periods}) = \$2,191,207$$

Again, this projected ending-wealth value deviates slightly from the expected ending-wealth value ($2,191,100) due to rounding. Alternatively, if the modified duration had been above eight years, the new portfolio value would have been greater than the required current value of $1,365,493. Assume that because the duration of the portfolio exceeded the remaining horizon, the portfolio value increased to $1,450,000. If so, the ending value would be

$$\$1,450,000 \times 1.6047 \ (3\% \text{ for 16 periods}) = \$2,326,815$$

In this example, the projected ending-wealth value would have been greater than the expected-wealth value because you were mismatched and interest rates went in the right direction. When you are not duration matched, you are speculating on interest rate changes, and the result can be very good or very bad. The purpose of immunization is to avoid these uncertainties and to ensure the expected ending-wealth value ($2,191,100), regardless of interest rate changes.

Application of Classical Immunization   Once you understand the reasoning behind immunization (i.e., it is meant to offset the components of interest rate risk) and the general principle (you need to match modified duration and the investment horizon), you might conclude that this strategy is fairly simple to apply. You might even consider it a passive strategy; simply match modified duration and the investment horizon, and you can ignore the portfolio until the end of the horizon period. The following discussion will show that *immunization is neither a simple nor a passive strategy.*

Except for the case of a zero coupon bond, *an immunized portfolio requires frequent rebalancing* because the modified duration of the portfolio always should be equal to the remaining time horizon. The zero coupon bond is unique because it is a pure discount bond. As such, because there is no cash flow, there is *no reinvestment risk* because the discounting assumes that the value of the bond will grow at the discount rate. For example, if you discount a future value at 10 percent, the present value factor assumes that the value will grow at a compound rate of 10 percent to maturity. Also, there is *no price risk* if you set the duration at your time horizon, because you will receive the face value of the bond at maturity. Also, recall that the duration of a zero coupon bond always is equal to its term to maturity. In summary, if you immunize by matching your horizon with a zero coupon bond of equal duration, you do not have to rebalance.

In contrast, if you immunize a portfolio using coupon bonds, several characteristics of duration make it impossible to set a duration equal to the remaining horizon at the initiation of the portfolio and ignore it thereafter. First, *duration declines more slowly than term to maturity, assuming no change in market interest rates.* For example, assume you have a security with a computed duration of five years at a 10 percent market yield. A year later, if you compute the duration of the security at 10 percent, you will find that it has a duration of approximately 4.2 years; that is, although the term to maturity has declined by a year, the duration has declined by only 0.8 year. This means that, assuming no change in market rates, the portfolio manager must rebalance the portfolio to reduce its duration to four years. Typically, this is not difficult because cash flows from the portfolio can be invested in short-term T-bills if necessary.

Second, *duration changes with a change in market interest rates.* In Chapter 18, we discussed the inverse relationship between market rates and duration—with higher market rates, there will be lower duration and vice versa. Therefore, a portfolio that has the appropriate modified duration at a point in time can have its duration changed immediately if market rates change. If this occurs, a portfolio manager will have to rebalance the portfolio if the deviation from the required duration becomes too large.

Third, you will recall from our initial discussion of immunization that one of the assumptions is that when market rates change, they will change by the same amount and in the same direction (i.e., there will be a parallel shift of the yield curve). Clearly, if this does not happen, it will affect the performance of a portfolio of diffuse bonds. For example, assume you own a

Exhibit 19.10	The Concept of Horizon Matching

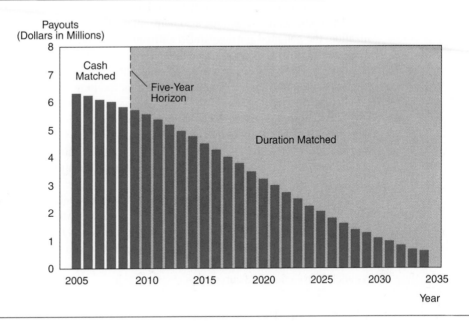

Source: "Horizon Matching: A New Generalized Approach for Developing Minimum Cost Dedicated Portfolios."
Copyright 1983 Salomon Brothers Inc. This chart was prepared for Salomon Brothers Inc. by Martin Leibowitz, a
former Managing Director; Thomas E. Klaffky, Managing Director; Steven Mandel, a former Managing Director;
and Alfred Weinberger, a former Director. Although the information in this chart has been obtained from sources
that Salomon Brothers Inc. believed to be reliable, SSB does not guarantee their accuracy, and such information
may be incomplete or condensed. All figures included in this chart constitute SSB's judgment as of the original
publication date. Reprinted with permission from SalomonSmithBarney.

portfolio of long- and short-term bonds with a weighted average 6-year duration (e.g., 2-year
duration bonds and 10-year duration bonds). Assume the term structure curve changes such
that short-term rates decline and long-term rates *rise* (there is an increase in the slope of the
yield curve). In such a case, you would experience a major price decline in the long-term bonds
but would be penalized on reinvestment, assuming you generally reinvest the cash flow in
short-term securities. This potential problem (caused by a change in the shape of the yield
curve) suggests that you should attempt to bunch your portfolio selections close to the desired
duration (i.e., use a bullet approach). For example, an eight-year duration portfolio should be
made up of seven- to nine-year duration securities to avoid this yield curve reshaping problem.

Finally, there always can be a problem acquiring the bonds you select as optimum for your
portfolio. For instance, can you buy long-duration bonds at the price you consider acceptable?
In summary, it is important to recognize that classical immunization, except for the case where
you can use all zero coupon bonds, is *not a passive strategy* because it is subject to all of these
potential problems, as discussed by Fabozzi (2005a, Chapter 47).

Horizon Matching   Horizon matching is a combination of two of the techniques discussed:
cash-matching dedication and immunization. As shown in Exhibit 19.10, the liability stream
is divided into two segments. In the first segment, the portfolio is constructed to provide a
cash match for the liabilities during this horizon period (e.g., the first five years). The second segment is the remaining liability stream following the end of the horizon period—in the example, it
is the 25 years after the horizon period. During this second time period, the liabilities are covered

by a duration-matched strategy based on immunization principles. As a result, Leibowitz (1986b) contends that the client receives the certainty of cash matching during the early years and the cost saving and flexibility of duration-matched flows thereafter.

The combination technique also helps alleviate one of the problems with classical immunization: the potential for nonparallel shifts in the yield curve. Most of the problems related to non-parallel shifts are concentrated in the short end of the yield curve because this is where the most severe curve reshaping occurs. Because the short end is taken care of by the cash matching, these are not of concern and we know that the long end of the yield curve tends toward parallel shifts.

An important decision when using horizon matching is the length of the horizon period. The trade-off when making this decision is between the safety and certainty of cash matching and the lower cost and flexibility of duration-based immunization. The portfolio manager should provide to the client a set of horizon alternatives and the costs and benefits of each of them and allow the client to make the decision.

As part of their discussion on horizon matching, Leibowitz, Klaffky, Mandel, and Weinberger (1983) point out that it also is possible to consider *rolling out* the cash-matched segment over time. Specifically, after the first year the portfolio manager would restructure the portfolio to provide a cash match during the original Year 6, which means that you would still have a five-year horizon. The ability and cost of rolling out depends on movements in interest rates (ideally, you would want parallel shifts in the yield curve).

Contingent Procedures

Contingent procedures are a form of structured active management. The procedure we discuss here is contingent immunization, which entails allowing the portfolio manager some opportunity to actively manage the portfolio with a structure that constrains the portfolio manager if he or she is unsuccessful.

Contingent Immunization   Subsequent to the development and application of classical immunization, Leibowitz and Weinberger (1982, 1983) developed a portfolio strategy called *contingent immunization.* Basically, it allows a bond portfolio manager to pursue the highest returns available through active strategies, while relying on classical bond immunization techniques to ensure a given minimal return over the investment horizon—that is, it allows active portfolio management with a safety net provided by classical immunization.

To understand contingent immunization, it is necessary to recall our discussion of classical immunization. Remember that when the portfolio duration is equal to the investment horizon, a change in interest rates will cause a change in the dollar value of the portfolio such that when the new asset value is compounded at the new market interest rate, it will equal the expected (desired) ending wealth value. This required change in value occurs *only* when the modified duration of the portfolio is equal to the remaining time horizon, which is why the modified duration of the portfolio must be maintained at the horizon value.

Consider the following example of this process. Assume that your desired ending-wealth value is $206.3 million. Given a specific ending value and the number of years to your horizon value, it is possible to determine how much you must invest today to attain that ending value if you assume a rate of return on the portfolio. Obviously, this is just the reverse of the price compounding exercise—that is, you compute the present value of the ending value at the expected yield for the horizon period.[14] In this case, we assume a 5-year horizon and a 15 percent

---

[14]Note that the article on this topic was written in 1982, when interest rates were at historically high levels of about 14–16 percent, which explains the high example rates. The concepts would be the same with lower rates.

return, which means we compute the present value of $206.3 million at 15 percent for 5 years or 7.5 percent for 10 periods assuming semiannual compounding. The present value factor of 0.48473 times the $206.3 million ending value equals $100 million—that is, this is the required initial investment under these assumptions to attain the desired ending value. Assuming the five-year horizon, we can do it for other interest rates as follows:

Percent	Present Value Factor[a]	Required Investment ($ Mil.)	Percent	Present Value Factor[a]	Required Investment ($ Mil.)
10	0.6139	$126.65	16	0.4632	$95.56
12	0.5584	115.20	18	0.4224	87.14
14	0.5083	104.86	20	0.3855	79.53
15	0.48473	100.00			

[a]Present value for 10 periods (5 years) at one-half the annual percent.

Exhibit 19.11 reflects these calculations—that is, the dark line indicates the required initial amount that must be invested at every yield level to attain $206.3 million in five years. Clearly, at lower yields you need a larger initial investment (e.g., $126 million at 10 percent), and it declines with higher yields (e.g., it is less than $80 million at 20 percent). The dotted line in Exhibit 19.11 indicates that the price sensitivity of a portfolio with a modified duration of five years will have almost exactly the price sensitivity required.

Exhibit 19.11	**Classical Immunization**

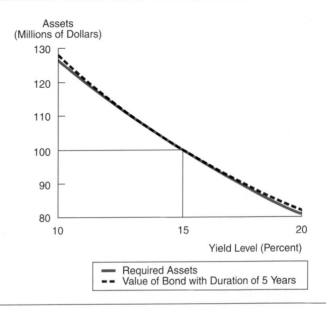

Exhibit 19.12 | **Price Behavior Required for Floor Return**

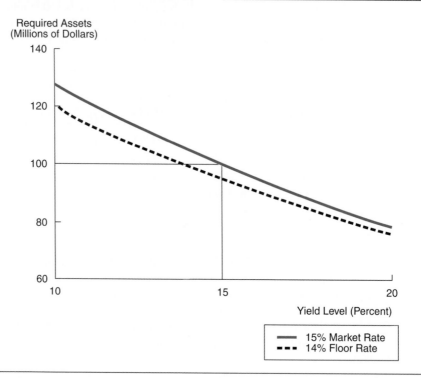

Contingent immunization requires that the client be willing to accept a potential return below the current market return, referred to as a *cushion spread*—the difference between the current market return and some floor rate. This cushion spread in required yield provides flexibility for the portfolio manager to engage in active portfolio strategies. For example, if current market rates are 15 percent, the client might be willing to accept a floor rate of 14 percent. If we assume the client initiated the fund with $100 million, the acceptance of this lower rate will mean that the portfolio manager does not have the same ending-asset requirements. Specifically, at 14 percent the required ending-wealth value would be $196.72 million (7 percent for 10 periods) compared to the $206.3 million at 15 percent. Because of this lower floor rate (and lower ending-wealth value), it is possible to experience some declines in the value of the portfolio while attempting to do better than the market through active management strategies.

Exhibit 19.12 shows the value of assets that are required at the beginning assuming a 14 percent required return and the implied ending-wealth value of $196.72 million. Notably, assuming current market rates of 15 percent, the required value of assets at the beginning would be $95.56 million, which is the present value of $196.72 million at 15 percent for 5 years. The difference between the client's initial fund of $100 million and the required assets of $95.56 million is the dollar cushion available to the portfolio manager. As noted, this dollar cushion arises because the client has agreed to a lower investment rate and, therefore, a lower ending-wealth value.

Exhibit 19.13 | **Safety Margin for a Portfolio of 30-Year Bonds**

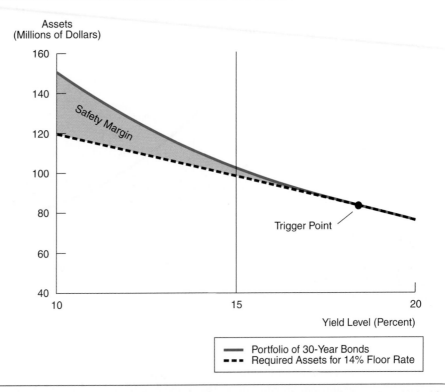

At this point, the portfolio manager can engage in various active portfolio management strategies to increase the ending-wealth value of the portfolio above that required at 14 percent. As an example, assume that the portfolio manager believes that market rates will decline. Under such conditions, the portfolio manager might consider acquiring a 30-year bond that has a modified duration greater than the investment horizon of 5 years and, therefore, has greater price sensitivity to changes in market rates. Hence, if rates decline as expected, the value of the long-duration portfolio will experience a rapid increase above the initial value. In contrast, if rates increase, the value of the portfolio will decline rapidly. In this case, depending on how high rates go, the value of the portfolio could decline to a value below that needed to reach the desired ending-wealth value of $196.72 million.

Exhibit 19.13 shows what happens to the value of this portfolio if we assume an instantaneous change in interest rates when the fund is established. Specifically, if rates decline from 15 percent, the portfolio of long-duration, 30-year bonds would experience a large increase in value and develop a *safety margin*—a portfolio value above the required value. In contrast, if rates increase, the value of the portfolio will decline until it reaches the asset value required at 14 percent. When the value of the portfolio reaches this point of minimum return (referred to as a *trigger point*), it is necessary to stop active portfolio management and use classical immunization with the remaining assets to ensure that you attain the desired ending-wealth value (i.e., $196.72 million).

Exhibit 19.14 | The Potential Return Concept

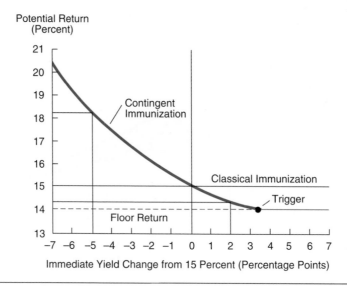

Potential Return   The concept of *potential return* is helpful in understanding the objective of contingent immunization. This is the return the portfolio would achieve over the entire investment horizon if, at any point, the assets in hand were immunized at the prevailing market rate. Exhibit 19.14 contains the various potential rates of return based on dollar asset values shown in Exhibit 19.13. If the portfolio were immediately immunized when market rates were 15 percent, it would naturally earn the 15 percent market rate; that is, its potential return would be 15 percent. Alternatively, if yields declined instantaneously to 10 percent, the portfolio's asset value would increase to $147 million (see Exhibit 19.13). If this $147 million portfolio were immunized at the market rate of 10 percent over the remaining five-year period, the portfolio would compound at 10 percent to a total value of $239.45 million ($147 million × 1.6289, which is the compound growth factor for 5 percent and 10 periods). This ending value of $239.45 million represents an 18.25 percent realized (horizon) rate of return on the original $100 million portfolio. Consequently, as shown in Exhibit 19.14, if rates decline by 5 percent, the potential return for this portfolio at this point in time is 18.25 percent.

In contrast, if interest rates increase, the value of the portfolio will decline substantially and the potential return will decline. For example, if market rates rise to 17 percent (i.e., a yield change of 2 percent), the asset value of the 30-year bond portfolio will decline to $88 million (see Exhibit 19.13). If this portfolio of $88 million were immunized for the remaining five years at the prevailing market rate of 17 percent, the ending value would be $199 million. This ending value implies a potential return of 14.32 percent for the total period.

As Exhibit 19.13 shows, if interest rates rose to 18.50 percent, the 30-year bonds would decline to a value of $81.16 million (the trigger point) and the portfolio would have to be immunized. At this point, if the remaining assets of $81.16 million were immunized at this current market rate of 18.50 percent, the value of the portfolio would grow to $196.73 million ($81.16 × 2.424, which is the compound value factor for 9.25 percent for 10 periods). This

Exhibit 19.15	**Contingent Immunization Floor Portfolio over Time**

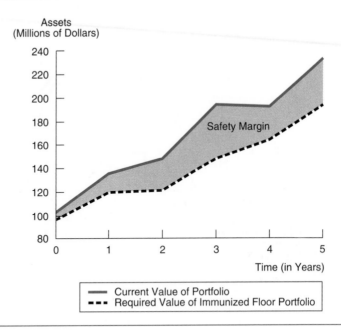

ending value implies that the potential return for the portfolio would be exactly 14 percent as shown in Exhibit 19.14. Regardless of what happens to subsequent market rates, the portfolio has been immunized at the floor rate of 14 percent. That is a major characteristic of the contingent immunized portfolio; if there is proper monitoring we will show in the following subsection that you will always know your trigger point where you must immunize and can be assured of receiving a return no less than the minimum rate of return specified.

Monitoring the Immunized Portfolio   Clearly, a crucial factor in managing a contingent immunized portfolio is monitoring it to ensure that if the asset value falls to the trigger point, it will be detected and the appropriate action taken to ensure that the portfolio is immunized at the floor-level rate. This can be done using a chart as in Exhibit 19.15. The top line is the current market value of the portfolio over time. The bottom line is the required value of the immunized floor portfolio. Specifically, the bottom line is *the required value of the portfolio* if we were to immunize at *today's rates* to attain the necessary ending-wealth value. This required minimum value for the portfolio is calculated by *computing the present value of the promised ending-wealth value at the prevailing market rate.*

   To demonstrate how this floor portfolio would be constructed, consider our example where we derived a promised ending-wealth value in five years of $196.72 million based on an initial investment of $100 million and an acceptable floor rate of 14 percent. If one year after the initiation of the portfolio, market rates were 10 percent, you would need a minimum portfolio value of approximately $133.14 million to get to $196.72 million in four years. To compute this minimum required value, you multiply the $196.72 million (promised ending-wealth value) times the present value factor for 5 percent for eight periods, assuming semiannual

| Exhibit 19.16 | **Comparison of Return Distributions** |

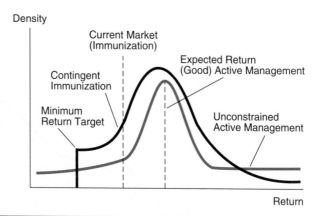

compounding (.6768). The logic is that $133.14 million ($196.72 × .6768) invested (immunized) at 10 percent for four years will equal $196.72 million.

If the active manager had predicted correctly that market rates would decline and had structured a long-duration portfolio under these conditions, the *actual* value of the portfolio would be much higher than this *minimum required* value, and there would be a safety margin. A year later (after Year 2), you would determine the assets needed at the rate prevailing at that point in time. Assuming interest rates had increased to 12 percent, you could determine that you would need a floor portfolio of about $138.69 million. Specifically, this is the present value of the $196.72 million for three years at 12 percent, assuming semiannual compounding (0.7050). Again, you would expect the actual value of the portfolio to be greater than this required floor portfolio, so you still have a safety margin. If you ever reached the point where the actual value of the portfolio was equal to the required floor value, you would stop the active management and immunize what was left *at the current market rate* to ensure that the ending value of the portfolio would be $196.72 million.

In summary, the contingent immunization strategy encompasses the opportunity for a bond portfolio manager to engage in various active portfolio strategies if the client is willing to accept a floor return (and ending-wealth value) that is below what is currently available. The graph in Exhibit 19.16 describes the trade-offs involved in contingent immunization. Specifically, by allowing for a slightly lower minimum target rate, the client is making it possible to experience a much higher potential return from active management by the portfolio manager.

IMPLICATIONS OF CAPITAL MARKET THEORY AND THE EMH ON BOND PORTFOLIO MANAGEMENT

The high level of interest rates that has prevailed during recent decades has provided increasingly attractive returns to bond investors, and the wide swings in interest rates that have accompanied these high market yields have provided numerous capital gains opportunities for bond portfolio managers. As a result, the average compound rates of return on bonds during

Exhibit 19.17 | **Mean Annual Rates of Return and Risk Measures for Lehman Brothers Bond Indexes, S&P 500 Stock Index, and the Citigroup 3-Month T-Bill: 1980–2003**

	Geometric Mean (%)	Arithmetic Mean (%)	Standard Deviation	Coefficient of Variation
Lehman Brothers Aggregate Bond	9.79	10.00	6.81	0.68
Lehman Brothers Government Bond	9.56	9.74	6.33	0.65
Lehman Brothers Corporate Bond	10.36	10.66	8.25	0.77
Lehman Brothers Hi-Yield Bond	9.90	10.21	8.25	0.81
Merrill Lynch World Govt. Bond	9.02	9.26	7.21	0.78
Merrill Lynch World (X-U.S.) Bond	9.92	10.49	11.30	1.08
S&P 500 Stock	13.64	15.03	17.87	1.19
Citigroup U.S. 3-month T-Bill	6.45	6.46	0.94	0.15

Source: Prepared by the authors using data from Lehman Brothers, Standard & Poor's Inc., and Citigroup.

the 1980s were the highest of any 10-year period in this century, and this performance continued into the 1990s. Specifically, the results contained in Exhibit 19.17 indicate that the annual returns on the aggregate of high-grade bonds during the period 1980–2003 were equal to a geometric mean return of 9.79 percent, which was clearly impressive even compared to the average returns on common stocks of 13.64 percent. Notably, while common stocks had a higher return than aggregate bonds, they also experienced higher risk as measured by standard deviation of returns—17.87 percent for stocks versus only 6.81 percent for bonds. This lower risk was confirmed by Reilly and Wright (2004) using beta relative to a composite index—the stock beta was 1.35 versus a beta for bonds of 0.24. These results indicate that there are some wonderful opportunities available in bonds. An important consideration for portfolio managers, therefore, is the proper role of fixed-income securities when considering the implications of portfolio theory, capital market theory, and research related to efficient capital markets.

Bonds and Total Portfolio Theory

The performance of bonds has improved even more than indicated by returns alone because bonds offer substantial diversification benefits. In an efficient market, neither stocks nor bonds should dominate a portfolio, but some combination of them should provide a superior risk-adjusted return compared to either one taken alone (assuming low correlation between stocks and bonds). Reilly and Wright (2004) showed that, due to the low correlation between bonds and equities (about 0.27), the combination of stocks and bonds in a portfolio vastly improved the return per unit of risk.

Bonds and Capital Market Theory

Capital market theory contends that there should be an upward-sloping market line, meaning that greater return should be accompanied by greater risk. Compared to other market vehicles, fixed-income securities were traditionally viewed as low risk and their rates of return were typically modest until the late 1970s. At that time, the inflation rate and bond yields increased. Also, Van Horne (2001) showed that during periods of high economic uncertainty,

Exhibit 19.18	Total Risk–Return Comparison for Alternative Capital Market Assets: 1980–2001

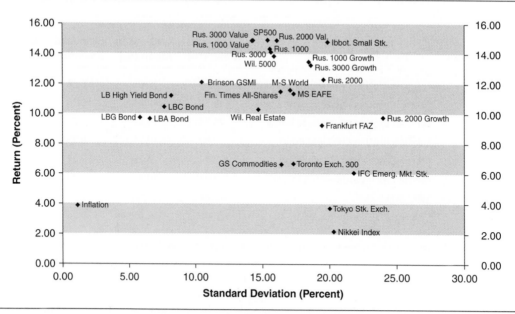

Source: Frank K. Reilly and David J. Wright, "An Analysis of Risk-Adjusted Performance of Global Market Assets," *Journal of Portfolio Management* 30, no. 3 (Spring 2004): 63–77.

such as the recessions of 1981–1982, 1990–1991, and 2001–2002, the risk premiums on bonds increased substantially because the risk of default for low-rated obligations increased. As demonstrated earlier in Exhibit 19.1, the risk premium on high-yield bonds has fluctuated dramatically over time.

Capital market theory also relates the risk–return behavior of fixed-income securities to other financial assets. Because fixed-income securities are considered to be relatively conservative investments, we would expect them to be on the lower end of the capital market line. A study by Reilly and Wright (2004) examined the comparative risk–return characteristics of 36 classes of long-term securities. Exhibit 19.18 shows the basic findings of the study and confirms the a priori expectations. Specifically, government and high-grade corporate bonds were at the low end of the risk spectrum, and it progressed to high-quality common stocks, small-cap stocks, foreign stocks, and, finally, emerging-market stocks.

Bond Price Behavior in a CAPM Framework

The capital asset pricing model (CAPM) is expected to provide a framework for explaining realized security returns as a function of nondiversifiable market risk. Bond returns should be linked directly to risk of default and interest rate risk. Although interest rate risk for investment-quality bonds should be nondiversifiable, some evidence exists that default risk also is largely nondiversifiable because default experience is closely related to the business cycle as demonstrated by Lucas and Lonski (1992); Helwege and Kleiman (1997); Fridson, Garman, and Wu (1997); and Zhon (2001). Therefore, because the major bond risks are largely nondiversifiable, this implies that we should be able to define bond returns in the context of the CAPM. Still, few studies have attempted it because of data-collection problems.

Evidence that high-grade bond risk is almost all systematic risk is found in the Reilly-Wright (2005) paper, which shows that the returns among these investment-grade bonds, regardless of sector (government, corporate, mortgages) or ratings, were correlated 0.90 to 0.99. This systematic interest rate risk has an overpowering effect on price performance and largely negates the effects of differential default risk, which is reflected in comparative agency ratings. Notably, the overpowering effect of systematic interest rate risk does *not* prevail when one considers high-yield (junk) bonds. As shown by Reilly and Wright (1999) the correlation between high-yield bonds and investment-grade bonds is *lower* than the strong correlation between high-yield bonds and common stock, which is because both high-yield bonds and common stocks have substantial unsystematic risk.

Weinstein (1981) computed betas for bonds using several market series and related the betas to term to maturity, coupon, and bond ratings. The results were affected by the market indexes used. No significant relationship existed between the betas and bond ratings for the top four classes of ratings, but there was a weak relationship using the top six ratings. The author postulated that the risk of default becomes significant only for low ratings, which is consistent with default rates in Exhibit 19.2.

In a subsequent study, Weinstein (1983) computed bond betas and examined their stability over time. He found that a bond's beta was related to firm characteristics (e.g., debt-equity ratios, and the variance of rate of return on assets) and to bond characteristics (coupon, term to maturity).

Thus, evidence on the usefulness of the CAPM for the bond market is mixed. Specifically, there are problems regarding the appropriate market index to use, the systematic risk measure is unstable, and the risk–return relationship using beta did not hold for the higher-quality bonds. Finally, there was a relationship between the systematic risk measure and some characteristics of the firm.

Bond Market Efficiency

Two versions of the efficient market hypothesis (EMH) are examined in the context of fixed-income securities: the weak and the semistrong theories. The weak-form hypothesis contends that security price movements are independent events so historical price information is useless in predicting future price behavior. Studies of weak-form efficiency have examined the ability of investors to forecast interest rates, because if you can forecast interest rates you can forecast bond price behavior. Also, interest rate expectations are important for bond portfolio management.

Bomberger and Frazer (1981), McNees (1981), and Throop (1981) reached the same conclusion: interest rate behavior cannot be consistently and accurately forecast! In all cases, the most naive model, or no forecast at all, provided the best measure of future interest rate behavior. Clearly, if it is not possible to forecast interest rates, then bond prices cannot be forecast using historical prices, all of which support the weak-form EMH.

The semistrong EMH asserts that current prices fully reflect all public knowledge and that efforts to act on public information are largely unproductive. Several studies have examined the informational value of bond rating changes. Katz (1974) examined monthly changes in bond yields surrounding ratings changes and found a significant impact of the change. Weinstein (1977) examined monthly bond returns surrounding the announcement of rating changes and found an effect during the interval from 18 months to 7 months before the announcement but no effect during the period from 6 months before the announcement to 6 months after the announcement.

In contrast, studies by Pinches and Singleton (1978), Griffin and Sanvicente (1982), and Holthausen and Leftwich (1986) examined the impact of bond rating changes on stock prices and returns. The results indicated a small impact on stocks and a differential impact, depending on whether it was an upgrade or a downgrade.

The Internet — Investments Online

Fixed-income management analytics and software are typically proprietary. The sites listed below offer some additional information about the techniques discussed in the text and will give you insight into the use of various analytical and portfolio management techniques.

http://www.cmsbondedge.com The home page of CMS BondEdge allows users to move to sites featuring CMS's various products. CMS sells fixed-income analytical software to institutional investment managers. Research papers on fixed income security analysis are offered free of charge to users who fill out an online form. BondEdge is a product offering "what-if" simulations, volatility appraisals, and other analytics to fixed-income portfolio managers.

http://www.ryanalm.com Ryan ALM, Inc. specialized in asset/liability management issues

such as those involving pension funds. Ronald J. Ryan developed a number of bond market indexes prior to starting his own firms. The Ryan ALM Web site offers links to the firm's newsletter and research on a variety of pension funding issues.

Brokerage houses offer fixed-income portfolio information and strategies with an orientation to the individual investor. See, for example,

**http://www.smithbarney.com/research/
fixed_income.html**
**http://www.smithbarney.com/
products_services/fixed_income/**
**http://www.bergencapital.com/research/
files/LadderedPortfolio.html**
http://www.askmerrill.ml.com/investments/
http://www.mlim.ml.com/usa/ (Merrill Lynch Investment Managers)

SUMMARY

- During the past decade, there has been a significant increase in the number and range of bond portfolio management strategies available. Bond portfolio management strategies include the relatively straightforward buy-and-hold and bond indexing strategies, several alternative active portfolio strategies, dedicated cash matching, classical immunization, horizon matching, and contingent immunization.

- Although you should understand the alternatives available and how to implement them, you also should recognize that the choice of a specific strategy is based on the needs and desires of the client. In turn, the success of any strategy will depend on the background and talents of the portfolio manager.

- The risk–return performance of bonds as a unique asset class has been consistent with expectations. In addition,

their inclusion has generally enhanced overall portfolio performance because of their low covariance with other financial assets. The application of CAPM concepts to bonds has been mixed because it has been difficult to derive acceptable measures of systematic risk, and the risk measures derived have been unstable.

- Studies in the bond market have supported the theory of weak-form efficiency. The evidence for semistrong efficiency has been mixed. The results that indicate a lack of efficiency could be due to the relatively inactive secondary markets for most corporate bonds, which causes pricing and adjustment problems compared to the active markets for equities. This may change in the future because of more transparency in this market, as discussed in Chapter 17.

SUGGESTED READINGS

Altman, Edward I., ed. *The High-Yield Debt Market.* Homewood, IL: Dow Jones–Irwin, 1990.

Barnhill, Theodore M., William F. Maxwell, and Mark R. Shenkman, eds. *High-Yield Bonds.* New York: McGraw-Hill, 1999.

Bierwag, G. O., George G. Kaufman, and Alden Toevs, eds. *Innovations in Bond Portfolio Management: Duration Analysis and Immunization.* Greenwich, CT: JAI Press, 1983.

Dattatreya, Ravi E., and Frank J. Fabozzi. *Active Total Return Management of Fixed-Income Portfolios,* rev. ed. Burr Ridge, IL: Irwin Professional, 1995.

Fabozzi, Frank J., ed. *Fixed-Income Readings for the Chartered Financial Analysts Program,* 2nd ed. New Hope, PA: Frank J. Fabozzi Associates, 2004.

Fridson, Martin. *High-Yield Bonds: Assessing Risk and Identifying Value in Speculative Grade Securities.* Chicago: Probus, 1989.

Global Bond Management II: The Search for Alpha. Charlottesville, VA: AIMR, 2000.

Howe, Jane Tripp. *Junk Bonds: Analysis and Portfolio Strategies.* Chicago: Probus, 1988.

Leibowitz, Martin L., William S. Krasker, and Ardavan Nozari. "Spread Duration: A New Tool for Bond Portfolio Management." *Journal of Portfolio Management* 16, no. 3 (Spring 1990).

Rosenberg, Michael R. *Currency Forecasting.* Burr Ridge, IL: Irwin Professional, 1996.

Ryan, Ronald J., ed. *Yield Curve Dynamics.* Chicago: Glen Lake Publishing Co. Ltd., 1997.

Wilson, Richard S., and Frank J. Fabozzi. *The New Corporate Bond Market.* Chicago: Probus, 1990.

QUESTIONS

1. What is meant by an indexing portfolio strategy and why is it used?
2. Briefly define the following bond swaps: pure yield pickup swap, substitution swap, and tax swap.
3. Briefly describe three active bond portfolio management strategies.
4. Discuss two variables you would examine very carefully if you were analyzing a high-yield bond, and indicate why they are important.
5. How would you explain to a casual observer why high-yield bond returns are more correlated to common stock returns than to investment-grade bond returns?
6. What are the advantages and difficulties of a cash-matched dedicated portfolio?
7. Describe the two components of interest rate risk.
8. What is meant by bond portfolio immunization?
9. If the yield curve were flat and did not change, how would you immunize your portfolio?
10. You begin with an investment horizon of four years and a portfolio with a duration of four years with a market interest rate of 10 percent. A year later, what is your investment horizon? Assuming no change in interest rates, what is the duration of your portfolio relative to your investment horizon? What does this imply about your ability to immunize your portfolio?
11. It has been contended that a zero coupon bond is the ideal financial instrument to use for immunizing a portfolio. Discuss the reasoning for this statement.
12. During a conference with a client, the subject of classical immunization is introduced. The client questions the fee charged for developing and managing an immunized portfolio. The client believes it is basically a passive investment strategy, so the management fee should be substantially lower. What would you tell the client to show that it is not a passive policy?
13. With contingent immunization, what do you give up and what do you gain?

14. *CFA Examination Level III*
    The ability to *immunize* a bond portfolio is very desirable for bond portfolio managers in some instances.
    a. Discuss the components of interest rate risk. Assuming a change in interest rates over time, explain the two risks faced by the holder of a bond.
    b. Define immunization and discuss why a bond manager would immunize a portfolio.
    c. Explain why a duration-matching strategy is a superior technique to a maturity-matching strategy for the minimization of interest rate risk.
    d. Explain in specific terms how you would use a zero coupon bond to immunize a bond portfolio. Discuss why a zero coupon bond is an ideal instrument in this regard.
    e. Explain how *contingent immunization,* another bond portfolio management technique, differs from *classical immunization.* Discuss why a bond portfolio manager would engage in contingent immunization. [35 minutes]

15. *CFA Examination Level III*

    During the past several years, there has been substantial growth in the dollar amount of portfolios managed using *immunization* and *dedication* techniques. Assume a client wants to know the basic differences between (1) classical immunization, (2) contingent immunization, (3) cash-matched dedication, and (4) duration-matched dedication.

    a. Briefly describe each of these four techniques.

    b. Briefly discuss the ongoing investment action you would have to carry out if managing an *immunized portfolio.*

    c. Briefly discuss three of the major considerations involved with creating a *cash-matched dedicated* portfolio.

    d. Describe two parameters that should be specified when using *contingent immunization.*

    e. Select one of the four alternative techniques that you believe requires the least degree of active management and justify your selection. [20 minutes]

16. *CFA Examination Level III*

    After you have constructed a structured fixed-income portfolio (i.e., one that is dedicated, indexed, or immunized), it may be possible over time to improve on the initial optimal portfolio while continuing to meet the primary goal. Discuss three conditions that would be considered favorable for a restructuring—assuming no change in objectives for the investor—and cite an example of each condition. [10 minutes]

17. *CFA Examination Level III*

    The use of bond index funds has grown dramatically in recent years.

    a. Discuss the reasons you would expect it to be easier or more difficult to construct a bond market index than a stock market index.

    b. It is contended that the *operational process* of managing a corporate bond index fund is more difficult than managing an equity index fund. Discuss three examples that support this contention. [15 minutes]

18. *CFA Examination Level I*

    Robert Devlin and Neil Parish are portfolio managers at the Broward Investment Group. At their regular Monday strategy meeting, the topic of adding international bonds to one of their portfolios came up. The portfolio, an ERISA-qualified pension account for a U.S. client, was currently 90 percent invested in U.S. Treasury bonds and 10 percent invested in 10-year Canadian government bonds.

    Devlin suggested buying a position in 10-year German government bonds, while Parish argued for a position in 10-year Australian government bonds.

    a. Briefly discuss the *three* major issues that Devlin and Parish should address in their analysis of the return prospects for German and Australian bonds relative to those of U.S. bonds. [6 minutes] Having made no changes to the original portfolio, Devlin and Parish hold a subsequent strategy meeting and decide to add positions in the government bonds of Japan, the United Kingdom, France, Germany, and Australia.

    b. Identify and discuss *two* reasons for adding a broader mix of international bonds to the pension portfolio. [9 minutes]

19. *CFA Examination Level III*

    The investment committee of the money management firm of Gentry, Inc., has typically been very conservative and has avoided investing in high-yield (junk) bonds, although they have had major positions in investment-grade corporate bonds. Recently, Pete Squire, a member of the committee, suggested that they should review their policy regarding junk bonds because they currently constitute over 25 percent of the total corporate bond market.

    As part of this policy review, you are asked to respond to the following questions:

    a. Briefly discuss the liquidity *and* pricing characteristics of junk bonds relative to *each* of the following types of fixed-income securities:
       • Treasuries
       • High-grade corporate bonds
       • Corporate loans
       • Private placements

    Briefly discuss the implications of these differences for Gentry's bond portfolio managers. The committee has learned that the correlation of rates of return between Treasuries and high-grade corporate bonds is approximately 0.98, while the correlation between Treasury/high-grade corporate bonds and junk bonds is approximately 0.45.

    b. Briefly explain the reason for this difference in correlations, and briefly discuss its implications for bond portfolios.

The committee has also heard that durations at the times of issue for junk bonds are typically much shorter than for newly issued high-grade corporate bonds.

    c. Briefly explain the reason for this difference in duration, and briefly discuss its implication for the volatility of high-yield bond portfolios. [15 minutes]

 20. *CFA Examination Level II*

Greg Kemp, CFA, Chief Investment Officer of Anchor Advisors, has received the following recommendation from his bond management group.

"We believe the current environment has focused excessive pessimism on high-grade corporate bonds. Fears of 'event risk' and weakness in the junk bond market have widened yield spreads to attractive levels.

    "It is recommended that our employee benefit bond accounts reduce their current U.S. Treasury weightings from 75 percent to 25 percent, with this money to be invested in callable Single-A and AA utility bonds with coupon rates between 9 percent and 11 percent. The durations of the bonds purchased will be equal to those sold."

Kemp accepts the idea that yield spreads are wider than normal between U.S. Treasury bonds and corporate issues. Interest rates on long-term U.S. Treasury issues are currently 9 percent. He expects a significant (more than 100 basis points) drop in interest rates.

    a. Kemp has some concerns about the volatility implications of the proposed trade in light of his understanding of the concepts of duration, convexity, and option-adjusted spreads. Given his interest rate expectations, identify and explain *two* key questions that Kemp should raise about the proposed trade. [10 minutes]

    b. Recommend *two* modifications to the proposed trade that would address Kemp's concerns mentioned in Part a. [5 minutes]

 21. *CFA Examination Level II*

Bond analysis often requires more than traditional credit ratio analysis. Discuss *each* of the following *three* considerations as they relate to evaluating a specific fixed-income security:

(a) Competition within the industry

(b) Liquidation value of net assets

(c) Management [6 minutes]

    22. *CFA Examinaton Level III*

A consultant suggests that the weighted-average portfolio duration calculation for a global bond portfolio is the same as for a domestic bond portfolio.

    a. State whether the use of portfolio duration in international bond portfolio management is more limiting than in domestic bond portfolio management. Support your conclusion with *two* reasons. [8 minutes]

The consultant recognizes that currency, duration, and investing outside the benchmark are possible sources of excess return in global bond management. He is also curious about additional methods of adding value through global bond management.

    b. List and discuss *two* additional potential sources of excess return. [6 minutes]

PROBLEMS

    1. You have a portfolio with a market value of $50 million and a Macaulay duration of seven years (assuming a market interest rate of 10 percent). If interest rates increase to 12 percent, what would be the estimated value of your portfolio using modified duration? Show all your computations.

    2. Answer the following questions assuming that at the initiation of an investment account, the market value of your portfolio is $200 million, and you immunize the portfolio at 12 percent for six years. During the first year, interest rates are constant at 12 percent.

   a. What is the market value of the portfolio at the end of Year 1?

   b. Immediately after the end of the year, interest rates *decline* to 10 percent. Estimate the new value of the portfolio, assuming you did the required rebalancing (use only modified duration).

3. Compute the Macaulay duration under the following conditions:

   a. A bond with a five-year term to maturity, a 12 percent coupon (annual payments), and a market yield of 10 percent.

   b. A bond with a four-year term to maturity, a 12 percent coupon (annual payments), and a market yield of 10 percent.

   c. Compare your answers to Parts a and b, and discuss the implications of this for classical immunization.

4. Compute the Macaulay duration under the following conditions:

   a. A bond with a four-year term to maturity, a 10 percent coupon (annual payments), and a market yield of 8 percent.

   b. A bond with a four-year term to maturity, a 10 percent coupon (annual payments), and a market yield of 12 percent.

   c. Compare your answers to Parts a and b. Assuming it was an immediate shift in yields, discuss the implications of this for classical immunization.

5. A major requirement in running a contingent immunization portfolio policy is monitoring the relationship between the current market value of the portfolio and the required value of the floor portfolio. In this regard, assume a $300 million portfolio with a horizon of five years. The available market rate at the initiation of the portfolio is 14 percent, but the client is willing to accept 12 percent as a floor rate to allow you to use active management strategies. The current market values and current market rates at the end of Years 1, 2, and 3 are as follows:

End of Year	Market Value ($ Mil)	Market Yield	Required Floor Portfolio	Safety Margin (Deficiency)
1	340.00	0.12		
2	375.00	0.10		
3	360.20	0.14		

   a. What is the required ending-wealth value for this portfolio?

   b. What is the value of the required floor portfolio at the end of Years 1, 2, and 3?

   c. Compute the safety margin or deficiency at the end of Years 1, 2, and 3.

6. Evaluate the following pure-yield pickup swap: You currently hold a 20-year, Aa-rated, 9.0 percent coupon bond priced to yield 11.0 percent. As a swap candidate, you are considering a 20-year, Aa-rated, 11 percent coupon bond priced to yield 11.5 percent. (Assume reinvestment at 11.5 percent.)

	Current Bond	Candidate Bond
Dollar investment	_____	_____
Coupon	_____	_____
i on one coupon	_____	_____
Principal value at year end	_____	_____
Total accrued	_____	_____
Realized compound yield	_____	_____
Value of swap: _____ basis points in one year		

7. Evaluate the following substitution swap: You currently hold a 25-year, 9.0 percent coupon bond priced to yield 10.5 percent. As a swap candidate, you are considering a 25-year, Aa-rated, 9.0 percent coupon bond priced to yield 10.75 percent. (Assume a one-year work-out period and reinvestment at 10.5 percent.)

	Current Bond	Candidate Bond
Dollar investment	_____	_____
Coupon	_____	_____
i on one coupon	_____	_____
Principal value at year end	_____	_____
Total accrued	_____	_____
Realized compound yield	_____	_____
Value of swap: _____ basis points in one year		

8. *CFA Examination Level III*
   Reinvestment risk is a major factor for bond managers to consider when determining the most appropriate or optimal strategy for a fixed-income portfolio. Briefly describe each of the following bond portfolio management strategies, and explain how each deals with reinvestment risk:
   a. Active management
   b. Classical immunization
   c. Dedicated portfolio
   d. Contingent immunization [20 minutes]

9. *CFA Examination Level III*
   A major requirement in managing a fixed-income portfolio using a contingent immunization policy is monitoring the relationship between the current market value of the portfolio and the required value of the floor portfolio. This difference is defined as the *margin of error*. In this regard, assume a $300 million portfolio with a time horizon of five years. The available market rate at the initiation of the portfolio is 12 percent, but the client is willing to accept 10 percent as a floor rate to allow use of active management strategies. The current market values and current market rates at the end of Years 1, 2, and 3 are as follows:

End of Year	Market Value ($ Mil)	Market Yield	Required Floor Portfolio ($ Mil)	Margin of Error ($ Mil)
1	$340.9	10%		
2	405.5	8		
3	395.2	12		

Table 1
Present Value Table (use tables in appendix in the back of book)
Table 2
Compound Value Table (use tables in appendix in the back of book)

Assuming semiannual compounding:
a. Calculate the required ending-wealth value for this portfolio.
b. Calculate the value of the required floor portfolios at the end of Years 1, 2, and 3.
c. Compute the margin of error at the end of Years 1, 2, and 3.
d. Indicate the action that a portfolio manager utilizing a *contingent immunization* policy would take if the margin of error at the end of any year had been zero or negative.

10. *CFA Examination Level II*
    PowerTool is the largest U.S. manufacturer of industrial hand tools. Its sales force is strong, but clients have complained that marketing is weak. The industrial tool business is mature, with little or no future expected growth.

    PowerTool has acquired Fenton Manufacturing, a small, innovative company whose sales are entirely in the retail tool market. The retail tool market is expected to grow at a 5 percent annual rate.

    Fenton recently developed a patented line of rechargeable home power tools that displayed strong potential in test markets. Fenton expects this line to generate 50 percent of its sales within

Table 1 | Financial Ratios and Debt Ratings: June 1, 1996

Company	Total Debt to Total Capital	Pretax Interest Coverage	Operating Cash Flow to Total Debt	Debt Rating
PowerTool	30%	6.2 times	50%	A+
Fenton	72	2.1 times	8	Not rated
Combined	42	5.4 times	40	To be determined

five years but lacks a sales force to market this product line. Jerry Fenton, the company's founder, recently retired.

PowerTool management is highly respected and the company has experienced little management turnover. However, the Chief Executive Officer has announced her retirement after 18 years of service and will be replaced by the current Chief Operating Officer.

You are a private investor with a large investment in PowerTool bonds and wish to determine the effect of the acquisition of Fenton on PowerTool's bonds.

Table 1 presents financial ratios and debt ratings of PowerTool and Fenton prior to the merger and pro forma ratios of the combined company following the acquisition.

a. Explain how *each* of the following *three* ratios should be used to evaluate a firm's financial risk:
    (1) Total debt to total capital
    (2) Pretax interest coverage
    (3) Operating cash flow to total debt [9 minutes]

PowerTool has issued debt with the following covenants, which continue in force after its acquisition of Fenton.

Dividend Test Covenant

PowerTool may not pay any cash dividend or repurchase shares if such payment would result in a total debt-to-capital ratio in excess of 50 percent.

Put Option Covenant

If PowerTool's debt rating falls below A, bondholders have the right to redeem the bonds at a price of 105 plus accrued interest within 60 days following the change in rating.

b. Discuss the impact of *each* of the *two* debt covenants as just described on PowerTool's financial flexibility following its acquisition of Fenton:
    (1) Dividend Test covenant
    (2) Put Option Covenant [8 minutes]

Use only the information provided in the introduction in answering the following question.

c. Discuss, *from the PowerTool bondholders' point of view, two* advantages and *two* disadvantages to PowerTool of the acquisition of Fenton, with regard to the following product lines:
    • Industrial tool business
    • Retail tool business [12 minutes]
        PowerTool debt has not yet been re-rated following the acquisition of Fenton. PowerTool bonds are currently trading at a price comparable to A-rated bonds.
    Table 2 displays financial ratios used to determine bond ratings.

d. Recommend whether you should *hold* or *sell* the PowerTool bonds. Support your recommendations with *four* reasons drawn from the Introduction, Tables 1 and 2, and your answers to Parts a through c. [13 minutes]

11. *CFA Examination Level II*

Mike Smith, CFA, an analyst with Blue River Investments, is considering buying a Montrose Cable Company Corporate bond. He has collected the following balance sheet and income statement information for Montrose as shown in Exhibit 1. He has also calculated the three ratios shown in

Table 2	**Bond Rating Criteria: June 1, 1996**

Debt Rating	Total Debt to Total Capital	Pretax Interest Coverage	Operating Cash Flow to Total Debt
AA	26%	8.8 times	75%
A	37	4.6 times	44
BBB	48	2.5 times	29

Exhibit 1	**Montrose Cable Company: Year Ended March 31, 1999 (US$ Thousand)**

Balance Sheet

Current assets	$ 4,735
Fixed assets	43,225
Total assets	$47,960
Current liabilities	$ 4,500
Long-term debt	10,000
Total liabilities	$14,500
Shareholder's equity	33,460
Total liabilities and shareholder's equity	$47,960

Income Statement

Revenue	$18,500
Operating and administrative expenses	14,050
Operating income	$ 4,450
Depreciation and amortization	1,675
Interest expense	942
Income before income taxes	$ 1,833
Taxes	641
Net income	$ 1,192

Exhibit 2, which indicate that the bond is currently rated "A" according to the firm's internal bond-rating criteria shown in Exhibit 4.

Smith has decided to consider some off-balance-sheet items in his credit analysis, as shown in Exhibit 3. Specifically, Smith wishes to evaluate the impact of each of the off-balance-sheet items on each of the ratios found in Exhibit 2.

a. Calculate the combined effect of the *three* off-balance-sheet items in Exhibit 3 on *each* of the following *three* financial ratios shown in Exhibit 2. [9 minutes]

   (1) EBITDA/interest expense.

   (2) Long-term debt/equity.

   (3) Current assets/current liabilities.

The bond is currently trading at a credit premium of 55 basis points. Using the internal bond-rating criteria in Exhibit 4, Smith wants to evaluate whether or not the credit yield premium incorporates the effect of the off-balance-sheet items.

b. State and justify whether or not the current credit yield premium compensates Smith for the credit risk of the bond based on the internal bond-rating criteria found in Exhibit 4. [6 minutes]

Exhibit 2	Selected Ratios and Credit Yield Premium Data for Montrose

EBITDA/interest expense	4.72
Long-term debt/equity	0.30
Current assets/current liabilities	1.05
Credit yield premium over U.S. Treasuries	55 basis points

Exhibit 3	Montrose Off-Balance-Sheet Items

- Montrose has guaranteed the long-term debt (principal only) of an unconsolidated affiliate. This obligation has a present value of $995,000.
- Montrose has sold $500,000 of accounts receivable with recourse at a yield of 8 percent.
- Montrose is a lessee in a new noncancelable operating leasing agreement to finance transmission equipment. The discounted present value of the lease payments is $6,144,000 using an interest rate of 10 percent. The annual payment will be $1,000,000.

Exhibit 4	Blue River Investments: Internal Bond-Rating Criteria and Credit Yield Premium Data

Bond Rating	Interest Coverage (EBITDA/ Interest Expense)	Leverage (Long-Term Debt/Equity)	Current Ratio (Current Assets/ Current Liabilities)	Credit Yield Premium over U.S. Treasuries (in Basis Points)
AA	5.00 to 6.00	0.25 to 0.30	1.15 to 1.25	30 BPs
A	4.00 to 5.00	0.30 to 0.40	1.00 to 1.15	50 BPs
BBB	3.00 to 4.00	0.40 to 0.50	0.90 to 1.00	100 BPs
BB	2.00 to 3.00	0.50 to 0.60	0.75 to 0.90	125 BPs

Part 6

Derivative Security Analysis

In recent years, it has been difficult to read the financial press without encountering at least a passing reference to an economic scandal attributed to trading in derivative securities. Procter and Gamble's ill-fated swap transactions and the equity index futures trades that brought down Barings Bank give the casual reader the impression that derivatives are highly volatile instruments used only by those investors interested in placing speculative "bets." Of course, nothing could be further from the truth. Although it is true that the companies in these examples either miscalculated or misunderstood the nature of their investment positions, the vast majority of derivative transactions are used by individuals and institutions seeking to reduce the risk exposures generated by their other business ventures.

Derivatives, in their many forms, have become a vital part of modern security markets, trailing only stocks and bonds in terms of importance. Unlike stocks and bonds, however, their widespread use is a relatively recent phenomenon; and misconceptions still exist about how derivatives work and the proper way for investors to trade them. The chapters in this section address this concern by providing the investor with a framework for understanding how derivatives are valued and used in practice. Chapter 20 begins this process by detailing the mechanics of the two basic forms of derivative contract—*forwards* and *options*. After providing an initial description of these instruments and the markets in which they trade, we present the fundamental principles that determine their prices. The chapter concludes with several specific examples of how investors use derivatives to adjust the risk-return characteristics of their stock and bond portfolios.

Chapter 21 analyzes forward and futures contracts—the most prevalent form of derivative instrument. The similarities and differences between forward and futures contracts are described, with particular emphasis on the creation of (and subsequent adjustments to) margin accounts and the concept of basis risk. In addition, the calculation of the optimal hedge ratio and the arbitrage-free approach to determining the contract delivery price are discussed. The chapter concludes with an examination of the features of forward and futures contracts that are designed to offset financial (as opposed to commodity) risk exposures, including interest rate, equity, and currency price movements. Applications and investment strategies involving each of these contract types illustrate this discussion.

In Chapter 22, the focus turns to option contracting. The discussion begins with a consideration of how option markets are organized and how both puts and calls—the two basic types of option

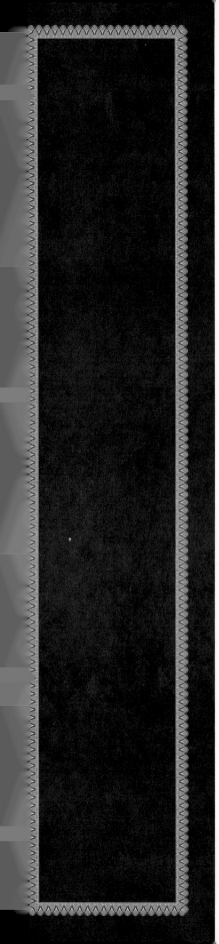

contracts—are quoted and traded. Several different option-based investment and hedging strategies are described as well as how these contracts can be used in conjunction with other securities to create customized payoff distributions. The chapter also includes a formal treatment of how option contracts are valued in an efficient market. Starting with the simple two-state option pricing model, which contains the essence of the basic valuation argument, the discussion progresses to include state-of-the-art approaches such as the binomial and the Black-Scholes models. In this development, special attention is paid to the role that price volatility plays in the valuation process.

Chapter 23, the last chapter of this section, considers four additional classes of derivative products. First, the rapidly developing market for swap, cap, and floor agreements is examined. After describing how these instruments are related to typical forward and option contracts, the discussion concentrates on the many ways in which investors and corporate risk managers use these products in practice. In particular, applications involving two different exposures—interest rates and equity prices—are developed. Second, the fundamentals of warrants and convertible securities are described. The emphasis of this discussion is on the option-like features of these instruments and how they alter the risk-return dynamics of traditional debt and equity products. Third, we examine the market for structured notes—instruments that can be viewed as "straight" bond issues into which derivatives have been embedded. Finally, the chapter concludes with a brief discussion of how understanding *real options* can help investors value certain types of complex investments that have embedded derivative-like features, such as oil fields or gold mines.

Chapter 20

An Introduction to Derivative Markets and Securities

After you read this chapter, you should be able to answer the following questions:

- What distinguishes a derivative security, such as a forward, futures, or option contract, from more fundamental securities, such as stocks and bonds?
- What are the important characteristics of forward, futures, and option contracts, and in what sense can they be interpreted as insurance policies?
- How are the markets for derivative securities organized and how do they differ from other security markets?
- What terminology is used to describe transactions that involve forward, futures, and option contracts?
- How are prices for derivative securities quoted and how should this information be interpreted?
- What are the similarities and differences between forward and futures contracts?
- What do the payoff diagrams look like for investments in forward and futures contracts?
- What do the payoff diagrams look like for investments in put and call option contracts?
- How are forward contracts, put options, and call options related to one another?
- How can derivatives be used in conjunction with stock and Treasury bills to replicate the payoffs to other securities and create arbitrage opportunities for an investor?
- How can derivative contracts be used to restructure cash flow patterns and modify the risks in existing investment portfolios?

So far, we have seen several ways in which individuals and institutions can design their investments to take advantage of future market conditions. We have also seen how investors can control the volatility associated with their stock and bond positions—at least in part—by forming well-diversified portfolios of securities around a common investment theme, thereby reducing or eliminating the unsystematic component of a security's risk.

In this chapter, we begin our formal investigation of the role played by **derivative securities** in modern investment portfolios. A derivative instrument is one for which the ultimate payoff to the investor depends directly on the value of another security or commodity. Earlier in the text, we briefly described two basic types of derivatives: (1) forward and futures contracts and (2) option contracts. A call option, for example, gives its owner the right to purchase an underlying security, such as a stock or a bond, at a fixed price within a certain amount of time. Naturally, this right to purchase would most certainly be exercised only if the value of the underlying asset at the call's expiration date was greater than the contractual purchase price. In this manner, the option's ultimate value can be said to depend on—and thus derive from—that of the other (underlying) asset. Similarly, a forward contract to sell a specific bond for a fixed price at a future date will see its value to the investor rise or fall with decreases or increases in the market price of the underlying bond.

The growth of the markets in which derivative securities are created and exchanged has been nothing short of phenomenal. The last few decades have seen the emergence of forward, futures, and option contracts to trade such fundamental products as agricultural commodities, energy, precious metals, currencies, common stock, and bonds. There are even derivatives to trade hypothetical underlying assets (e.g., options and futures contracts on the Standard & Poor's stock indexes) as well as combination derivatives, such as option contracts that allow the investor to decide at a later date to enter into a futures contract involving another security or commodity. Interest rate swaps, which will be shown in Chapter 23 to be forward contracts on a short-term borrowing or lending rate, are a good example of the prodigious growth of these markets. Starting with the first swap in 1981, the volume of swap market activity had grown in size to well over 100 trillion dollars by the year 2003. Although this sort of rapid expansion is not typical of all new derivative products, these instruments represent one of the true legacies of the financial markets in the latter part of the 20th century.

As we will see, derivative securities can be used by investors in the same way and for the same reasons as the underlying assets; an investor believing that a certain common stock will increase in value will likely benefit from either a purchase of the stock directly or through the acquisition of an option to purchase that stock at a predetermined price. The exact returns will not be equal for these two alternatives, but both will benefit from an upward movement in the stock's price. Ultimately, however, the real key to understanding how and why derivatives are used in practice lies in their ability to modify the risk and expected return characteristics of existing investment portfolios. That is, options and futures allow investors to **hedge** (or even increase) the risk of a collection of stocks in ways that go far beyond the diversification results presented in the preceding chapters. In addition, we will see that derivative securities also allow for the convenient duplication of cash flow patterns that already exist in other forms, thereby creating the possibility of **arbitrage** if two otherwise identical series of cash flows do not carry the same current price.

The balance of this chapter describes the fundamental nature and uses of forward, futures, and option contracts on common stock and bonds. (Subsequent chapters deal with more advanced forms of these products and valuation issues.) In the next section, we describe the basic terminology associated with the forward, futures, and option markets while the second section explains the similarities and differences in the payoff structures created by each of these instruments. The third section is devoted to developing the formal relationship between forwards and options, the result of which will be a series of conditions collectively known as **put-call parity**. In the final section, we briefly introduce three of the more popular ways in which derivatives have been used in managing stock and bond portfolios, with a particular emphasis on how derivatives can adjust risk to better suit the needs of the investor.

OVERVIEW OF DERIVATIVE MARKETS

As with any financial product, derivative transactions have a specific terminology that must be understood in order to use these instruments effectively. Unlike many other securities, however, the language used to describe forward, futures, and option contracts is often a confusing

Exhibit 20.1	**Basic Types of Derivative Positions**

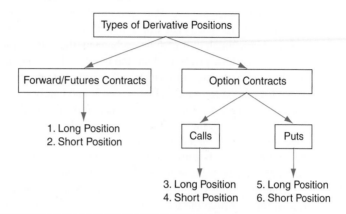

blend of jargon drawn from the equity, debt, and insurance markets with some unique expressions thrown in for good measure. Thus, we begin by summarizing the most important aspects of these products and the markets in which they trade.

Before we examine the relevant details of each contract, it is useful to first consider the basic types of positions that an investor can hold in these markets. Exhibit 20.1 illustrates the possibilities. The chart reinforces the point made earlier that, at the broadest level, there are only two kinds of derivatives available: (1) forward and futures contracts, and (2) option contracts. Further, as we will explain shortly, while there need be only one forward contract for any particular maturity date and underlying asset, there must be two types of options—calls and puts—in order to offer investors a full range of choices. Finally, for each of these three general derivative arrangements (i.e., the forward contract, the call option, and the put option), an investor can enter into a transaction as either the long position (i.e., the buyer) or the short position (i.e., the seller). This leads to the six possible basic positions enumerated in the display.

It is important to recognize that every derivative arrangement that an investor might hold in his or her portfolio can be viewed in terms of one of these six positions, or as a combination of these positions. For instance, later in the chapter, we consider how an equity investor can use derivatives to protect himself or herself against general declines in the stock market. Two such strategies involve (1) shorting an equity index forward contract, and (2) buying an equity index "collar" agreement. In terms of Exhibit 20.1, we will see that the forward-based strategy represents Position 2, while the collar strategy involves a combination of the purchase of a put option (Position 5) and the sale of a call option (Position 4).

The Language and Structure of Forward and Futures Markets

To most investors, the **forward contract** is the most basic derivative product available. Generally, a forward contract gives its holder both the *right and the full obligation* to conduct a transaction involving another security or commodity—the underlying asset—at a predetermined future date and at a predetermined price. The future date on which the transaction is to be consummated is called the contract's *maturity* (or expiration) *date,* while the predetermined price at which the trade takes place is the forward **contract price**. Notice there must always be two parties (sometimes called **counterparties**) to a forward transaction: the eventual buyer (or **long position**), who pays the contract price and receives the underlying security, and the eventual seller (or **short position**), who delivers the security for the fixed price.

Forward and Spot Markets   Forward contracts are not securities in the traditional sense; they are more appropriately viewed as *trade agreements* negotiated directly between two parties for a transaction that is scheduled to take place in the future. Suppose, for example, that two investors agree at Date 0 (the present) to transfer a bond from one party to the other at the future Date T. To specify the full terms of this agreement, the two parties must agree on which bond and how much of it is to be exchanged, the date and location at which this exchange will take place, and the price at which the bond will be bought and sold. Consequently, the terms that must be considered in forming a forward contract are the same as those that would be necessary for a bond transaction that settled immediately (i.e., a *spot market* transaction) but with two exceptions. First, the settlement date agreed to in the contract is purposefully set to be in the future. Second, the contract price—which we will represent as $F_{0,T}$, meaning a forward price set at Date 0 for a contract that matures at Date T—is usually different from the prevailing spot price (S_0) because of the different time frames involved. Typically, $F_{0,T}$ is chosen so that neither party needs to make an upfront payment to the other.

One important way in which spot and forward market transactions are similar is the conditions under which the long and short positions will profit. To illustrate this idea, suppose that at Date T, the long position in a bond forward contract is obligated to pay \$1,000 ($= F_{0,T}$) for a bond that is worth $S_T = \$1,050$ (i.e., the spot price at Date T). Since $F_{0,T} < S_T$, this will result in a profitable settlement for the long position in the contract since he will be able to acquire the bond for \$50 less than its current market value. On the other hand, the short position must deliver the bond at Date T and will lose \$50 on her forward position; she would have profited if S_T had been below the contract price of \$1,000. Thus, just as if the bond had been purchased at Date 0, the long position benefits when bond prices rise, at least relative to the contract price $F_{0,T}$. Conversely, the short position to the forward contract will gain from falling bond prices, just as if she had short sold the bond at Date 0. Even though the timing of the trade's settlement has shifted, "buy low, sell high" is still the way to make a profit in the forward market.

Forward and Futures Markets   Forward contracts are negotiated in the over-the-counter market. This means that forward contracts are agreements between two private parties—one of which is often a derivatives intermediary, such as a bank—rather than traded through a formal security or commodity exchange. One advantage of this private arrangement is that the terms of the contract are completely flexible; they can be whatever any two mutually consenting counterparties agree to. Another desirable feature to many counterparties is that these arrangements may not require *collateral;* instead, the long and short positions sometimes trust each other to honor their respective commitments at Date T. This lack of collateral means that forward contracts involve *credit* (or *default*) *risk,* which is one reason why banks are often market makers in these instruments.

One disadvantage of a forward contract is that it is quite often *illiquid,* meaning that it might be difficult or costly for a counterparty to exit the contract before it matures. Illiquidity is really a by-product of the contract's flexibility because the more specifically tailored an agreement is to the needs of a particular individual, the less marketable it will be to someone else. **Futures contracts** solve this problem by standardizing the terms of the agreement (e.g., expiration date, identity and amount of the underlying asset) to the extent that it can be exchange traded. In contrast to the forward market, both parties in a futures contract trade through a centralized market, called a *futures exchange.* Although the standardization of contracts reduces the ability of the ultimate end users to select the most desirable terms, it does create contract *homogeneity,* whereby the counterparties can always *unwind* a previous commitment prior to expiration by simply trading their existing position back to the exchange at the prevailing market price.

Exhibit 20.2	Popular Futures Contracts and Exchanges

Underlying Asset	Exchange
A. Physical Commodities	
Corn, soybeans, soybean meal, soybean oil, wheat	Chicago Board of Trade
Cattle—feeder, cattle—live, hogs, pork bellies Lumber	Chicago Mercantile Exchange
Dairy	
Cocoa, coffee, sugar—world, sugar—domestic	New York Board of Trade
Copper, gold, silver, platinum	New York Commodity Exchange
Crude oil, heating oil, gasoline, natural gas	New York Mercantile Exchange
B. Financial Securities	
Yen, Euro, Canadian dollar, Swiss franc,	International Monetary Market
British pound, Mexican peso, Australian dollar,	(Chicago Mercantile Exchange)
Treasury bills, Eurodollar (LIBOR), S&P 500	
Index, Nikkei 225 Index, Russell 2000 Index	
Treasury bonds, Treasury notes, Municipal bond index, federal funds	Chicago Board of Trade
Dow Jones Industrials Average	
Euro LIBOR, British gilt, German Euro government bond, Japanese government bond, FT-SE 100 Index	Euronext.liffe

The *futures price* is analogous to the forward contract price and, at any time during the life of a contract, is set at a level such that a brand-new long or short position would not have to pay a premium to enter the agreement. However, the futures exchange will require both counterparties to post collateral, or *margin,* to protect itself against the possibility of default. (A futures exchange is not a credit-granting institution.) These margin accounts are held by the exchange's *clearinghouse* and are *marked to market* (i.e., adjusted for contract price movements) on a daily basis to ensure that both end users always maintain sufficient collateral to guarantee their eventual participation. A list of some of the more popular futures contracts, along with the markets where they trade, is shown in Exhibit 20.2. Although generally quite diverse, all of these underlying assets have two things in common: *volatile price movements* and *strong interest* from both buyers and sellers.

Interpreting Futures Price Quotations: An Example

To illustrate how futures prices are typically quoted in financial markets, consider Exhibit 20.3, which lists spot and futures prices for contracts on the Standard & Poor's 500 index as of March 9, 2005. Recall from Chapter 5 that the S&P 500 is a value-weighted index of the relative value of a broad collection of industrial, financial, utility, and transportation companies representative of the entire United States stock market. At the close of trading on this particular day the index level stood at 1,207.01, which can be considered as the spot price of one

Exhibit 20.3	Standard & Poor's 500 Index Futures Contract Price Quotations

Session:**PIT**   **Contract   Table**
S&P 500 FUTURE   Delayed monitoring enabled
Exchange Web Page   Pricing Date: **3/ 9/05**
Chicago Mercantile Exchange   Delayed prices   --LATEST AVAILABLE---   **2**
Grey date = options trading   724325 170674 **Previous**

		Last	**1**Change	Time	High **2**	Low	OpenInt	TotVol	Close
1)	SPX spot	1207.01	-12.42	15:59	1219.43	1206.66	0	0	1219.43
2)	SPH5 Mar05	1207.00s	-13.60	Close	1220.00	1206.50	456034	107407	1220.60
3)	SPM5 Jun05	1211.40s	-13.70	Close	1224.50	1211.40	255048	63112	1225.10
4)	SPU5 Sep05	1216.70s	-13.70	Close			6539	150	1230.40
5)	SPZ5 Dec05	1222.50s	-13.70	Close			4947	5	1236.20
6)	SPH6 Mar06	1228.50s	-13.70	Close			1685	0	1242.20
7)	SPM6 Jun06	1235.50s	-13.70	Close			60	0	1249.20
8)	SPU6 Sep06	1242.50s	-13.70	Close			12	0	1256.20
9)	SPZ6 Dec06	1250.50s	-13.70	Close			0	0	1264.20

"share" of the S&P index (i.e., S_0).[1] Exhibit 20.3 also gives futures contract prices for eight different expiration dates falling in the months of March, June, September, and December for the years 2005 and 2006.

Focusing on a specific example, consider the futures contract that expires in June 2005. The closing (or last) contract price is listed as 1,211.40 (i.e., $F_{0,T}$). This means that an investor taking a long position in this contract would be committing in March to buy a certain number of shares in the S&P 500 index—250 shares in the case of this contract—at a price of $1,211.40 per share on the expiration date in June. Conversely, the short position in this contract would be committing to sell 250 S&P shares under the same conditions. It should once again be noted that, except for the margin posted with the futures exchange (i.e., the Chicago Mercantile Exchange for this contract), no money changes hands between the long and short positions at the origination of the contract in March.

Exhibit 20.4 summarizes the net profit for this contract from the long position's point of view, assuming a hypothetical set of S&P index levels on the June expiration date (i.e., S_T). The most important thing to note about the display is that the payoff to the long position is positive when the S&P index level rises (relative to the contract price of 1,211.40), while a loss is incurred when the S&P index falls. For instance, if the expiration date level of the index is 1,240.00, the long position will receive a profit of $28.60 per share ($= 1,240 - 1,211.4$). In that case, the profit is owed to the fact that the contract allows the investor to buy stock that is worth 1,240.00 for the predetermined price of only 1,211.40. On the other hand, if the June index level turns out to be 1,200, the futures contract still obligates the investor to purchase stock for the contract price, thus resulting in a loss of $11.40. This reinforces the fact that, as the buyer, the long position benefits when stock prices rise and suffers when prices fall, just as

---

[1] In reality, actually purchasing the portfolio of 500 stocks comprising the S&P index would cost considerably more than $1,207.01. However, as the eventual profit or loss from a stock index futures contract is simply determined by the difference between the futures contract price and the spot price prevailing at contract expiration, this interpretation is nevertheless valid. The trading mechanics of these contracts will be described in greater detail in Chapter 21.

Exhibit 20.4	Net Profit at Expiration from a Long Position in an S&P 500 Futures Contract

June S&P 500 Index Level	Futures Payoff at Expiration		Initial Futures Premium	Net Profit
1,140.00	(1,140 − 1,211.40)	= −71.40	0.00	−71.40
1,160.00	(1,160 − 1,211.40)	= −51.40	0.00	−51.40
1,180.00	(1,180 − 1,211.40)	= −31.40	0.00	−31.40
1,200.00	(1,200 − 1,211.40)	= −11.40	0.00	−11.40
1,211.40	(1,211.40 − 1,211.40)	= 0.00	0.00	0.00
1,220.00	(1,220 − 1,211.40)	= 8.60	0.00	8.60
1,240.00	(1,240 − 1,211.40)	= 28.60	0.00	28.60
1,260.00	(1,260 − 1,211.40)	= 48.60	0.00	48.60
1,280.00	(1,280 − 1,211.40)	= 68.60	0.00	68.60

would be the case for an investor purchasing stock directly in the spot market. Of course, the short position to the contract, as the seller, would have payoffs exactly the opposite of those shown in Exhibit 20.4.

The data displayed in Exhibit 20.3 contain other information useful to investors as well. First, recognize that the spot and all of the futures contract prices listed finished lower than they had been the day before; this can be seen from the negative entries in the "Change" column in comparison with the "Last" and "Previous Close" prices. This suggests that, although they depend on other factors as well, the futures contract prices are strongly linked to the prevailing level of the underlying spot index. Second, notice that the contract prices increase the farther into the future the expiration date occurs. That is, although all nine closing prices listed (i.e., the spot and the eight futures contracts) were set on the same day and correspond to the same S&P index share, the cost of that share gets increasingly more expensive, the further forward in time the delivery date is set. We will see later that this relationship is common for some securities but not for others. Finally, the display also lists the *open interest* and *trading volume* for each contract. Open interest is the number of outstanding contracts while trading volume is the number of those contracts that changed hands that day. Thus, it appears in this case that the nearest-term contracts (i.e., March and June 2005) are the most abundant and that about 24 percent (= 170,674 ÷ 724,325) of the total number of S&P contracts in existence were traded on March 9, 2005.

The Language and Structure of Option Markets

An **option contract** gives its holder the right—but not the obligation—to conduct a transaction involving an underlying security or commodity at a predetermined future date and at a predetermined price. Unlike the forward contract, the option gives the long position the right to decide whether or not the trade will eventually take place. On the other hand, the seller (or *writer*) of the option must perform on his side of the agreement if the buyer chooses to exercise the option. Thus, the obligation in the option market is inherently one-sided; buyers can do as they please, but sellers are obligated to the buyers under the terms of the agreement. As a consequence, two different types of options are needed to cover all potential transactions: a **call option**—the right to buy the underlying security—and a **put option**—the right to sell that same asset.

Option Contract Terms   There are two prices that are important in evaluating an option position. The **exercise**, or striking, **price** is the price the call buyer will pay to—or the put buyer will receive from—the option seller if the option is exercised. The exercise price (represented here as X) is to an option what the contract price (i.e., $F_{0,T}$) is to a forward agreement. The second price of interest is the price that the option buyer must pay to the seller at Date 0 to acquire the contract itself. To avoid confusion, this second price is typically referred to as the **option premium**. A basic difference between options and forwards is that an option requires this up-front premium payment from buyer to seller while the forward ordinarily does not. This is because the forward contract allowed both the long and short positions to "win" at Date T (depending on where S_T settled, relative to $F_{0,T}$), but the option agreement will only be exercised in the buyer's favor; hence the seller must be compensated at Date 0, or she would never agree to the deal. Notice also that although a premium payment will be required for both puts and calls, it is quite likely that these two prices will differ. In the analysis that follows, we will define the Date 0 premium to acquire an option expiring at Date T as $C_{0,T}$ for a call and $P_{0,T}$ for a put. For example, in lieu of a long position in a bond forward contract, the investor in an earlier example could have paid \$20 ($= C_{0,T}$) at Date 0 for a call option that would have given him the right to buy the bond for \$1,000 ($=X$) at Date T, but would not require him to do so if $S_T < \$1,000$.

Options can be designed to provide a choice of when the contract can be exercised. **European options** can only be exercised at maturity (Date T), while **American options** can be executed any time up to expiration. For a European-style call option, the buyer will only exercise when the expiration date market value of the underlying asset that could be purchased is greater than the exercise price. On the other hand, a European-style put option will only be rationally exercised when the Date T price of the asset that could be sold is lower than X. (The decision to exercise an American-style contract is more complex and will be considered in a later chapter.)

Option Valuation Basics   Given these parameters, the Date 0 premium for an option can be divided into two components: **intrinsic value** and **time premium**. Intrinsic value represents the value that the buyer could extract from the option if she exercised it immediately. For a call, this is the greater of either zero or the difference between the price of the underlying asset and the exercise price (i.e., max $[0, S_0 - X]$). For a put, intrinsic value would be max $[0, X - S_0]$ as X would now represent the proceeds generated from the asset's sale. An option with positive intrinsic value is said to be **in the money**, while one with zero intrinsic value is **out of the money**. For the special case where $S_0 = X$, the option is **at the money**. The time premium component is then simply the difference between the whole option premium and the intrinsic component: ($C_{0,T}$ − max $[0, S_0 - X]$) for a call and ($P_{0,T}$ − max $[0, X - S_0]$) for a put. The buyer is willing to pay this amount in excess of the option's immediate exercise value because of her ability to complete the transaction at a price of X that will remain in force until Date T. Thus, the time premium is connected to the likelihood that the underlying asset's price will move in the anticipated direction by the contract's maturity.

Although a more complete discussion of valuing option premiums will be deferred until Chapter 22, several basic relationships can be seen now. First, because the buyer of a call option is never obligated to exercise, the contract should always at least be worth its intrinsic value. (The situation for put option prices or when the underlying asset pays a dividend can be more complicated and will be discussed later.) In any event, neither a call nor a put option can be worth less than zero. Second, for call options having the same maturity and based on the same underlying asset, the lower the exercise price, the higher will be the contract's intrinsic value and, hence, the greater its overall premium. Conversely, put options with higher exercise prices are more valuable than those with lower striking prices for the same reason. Third,

Exhibit 20.5 | **Popular Option Contracts and Exchanges**

Underlying Asset	Exchange
A. Financial Securities	
Individual Equities	Chicago Board Options
S&P 100, Dow Jones Industrial Average	Exchange
Yen, Euro, Canadian dollar, Swiss franc, British pound, Australian dollar	Philadelphia Stock Exchange
Equity Sector Index	
B. Futures Options	
Cattle—feeder, cattle—live, hogs	Chicago Mercantile Exchange
Yen, Euro, Canadian dollar, Swiss franc, British pound	International Monetary Market (Chicago Mercantile Exchange)
Eurodollar (LIBOR), 2-year Eurodollar S&P 500 Index	
Corn, soybeans, soybean meal, soybean oil, wheat	Chicago Board of Trade
Treasury bonds, Treasury notes	
Dow Jones Industrials Average	
British gilt, GermanEuro Government Bonds	Euronext.liffe
EuroLIBOR	
Wheat, Sugar	
Crude oil, heating oil, gasoline, natural gas	New York Mercantile Exchange
Copper, gold, silver	New York Commodity Exchange

increasing the amount of time until any option expires will increase the contract's time premium because it allows the price of the underlying security more opportunity to move in the direction anticipated by the investor (i.e., up for a call option, down for a put option). Finally, because they provide investors with more choices about exercising the agreement, American-style options are at least as valuable as otherwise comparable European-style contracts.

Option Trading Markets   Like forwards and futures, options trade both in over-the-counter markets and on exchanges. When exchange-traded, just the seller of the contract is required to post a margin account because he is the only one obligated to perform on the contract at a later date. Also, options can be based on a wide variety of underlying securities, including futures contracts or other options. Exhibit 20.5 lists the underlying assets and exchanges where a number of the most popular option contracts trade.

Interpreting Option Price Quotations: An Example

Exhibit 20.6 shows data for a variety of call and put options on the S&P 500 index as of March 9, 2005. All of the contracts listed expire in June 2005, making them comparable to the S&P 500 futures contracts considered above. However, unlike the futures contracts, for which there was a single contract price for a given expiration month, Exhibit 20.6 indicates

Exhibit 20.6 | **Standard & Poor's 500 Index Option Contract Price Quotations**

```
                    Option Monitor:  S&P 500 INDEX
Center    ███1207.01 Number of Strikes  18 -or- ███% from Center    Exchange C
                                                                    (Composite  )
```

Ticker	Strike	Bid	Ask	Last	Volume	Ticker	Strike	Bid	Ask	Last	Volume
SPX 18 JUN 05	(Contract Size: 100)					SPX 18 JUN 05	(Contract Size: 100)				
1) SPQ+FO	1075	138.10	140.10	152.50 y		19) SPQ+RO	1075	3.60	4.40	2.90 y	
2) SPT+FT	1100	115.00	117.00	135.00 y		20) SPT+RT	1100	5.10	6.30	5.30	1579
3) SPT+FE	1125	92.70	94.70	100.00	10	21) SPT+RE	1125	7.60	8.80	8.00	1002
4) SPT+FH	1140	79.80	81.80			22) SPT+RH	1140	9.60	10.80	6.80 y	
5) SPT+FJ	1150	71.60	73.60	77.50	6	23) SPT+RJ	1150	11.10	12.70	11.80	1666
6) SPT+FO	1175	52.30	54.30	53.00	118	24) SPT+RO	1175	16.50	18.10	17.00	219
7) SZP+FT	1200	35.40	37.40	39.00	431	25) SZP+RT	1200	25.00	26.00	25.30	791
8) SZP+FE	1225	21.80	23.80	24.00	6	26) SZP+RE	1225	35.50	37.50	32.30	35
9) SZP+FG	1235	17.60	19.20			27) SZP+RG	1235	41.00	43.00		
10) SZP+FI	1245	13.80	15.40	20.00 y		28) SZP+RI	1245	47.20	49.20		
11) SZP+FJ	1250	13.00	13.80	13.50	166	29) SZP+RJ	1250	50.40	52.40	51.00	31
12) SZP+FO	1275	6.50	7.20	7.00	561	30) SZP+RO	1275	68.90	70.90	69.00	3
13) SXY+FT	1300	2.80	3.60	3.70	812	31) SXY+RT	1300	90.10	92.10	87.20	1
14) SXY+FE	1325	1.25	1.75	2.50 y		32) SXY+RE	1325	113.20	115.20	97.00 y	
15) SXY+FJ	1350	.45	.95	.75	87	33) SXY+RJ	1350	137.20	139.20	134.50	7
16) SXY+FH	1375	.20	.70	.50 y		34) SXY+RH	1375	161.60	163.60		
17) SXZ+FT	1400	.05	.55	.25 y		35) SXZ+RT	1400	186.30	188.30	165.00 y	
18) SXZ+FE	1425		.50	.90 y		36) SXZ+RE	1425	211.10	213.10		

that there are several June 2005 options with different exercise prices. In fact, the display lists bid and ask premium quotes for both puts and calls, with striking prices ranging from 1,075 to 1,425.[2] Consistent with our earlier observation, calls become more valuable (e.g., higher ask premiums) as the exercise price declines, with the opposite holding true for put options.

Consider the fortunes of two different investors, one of whom purchases a June S&P call struck at 1,200 (i.e., X) and the other who buys a June 1,200 put. At the origination of the transaction in March, these investors will pay their sellers the ask prices of $37.40 (i.e., $C_{0,T}$) and $26.00 (i.e., $P_{0,T}$), respectively. In return, the investor holding the call option has the right, but not the obligation, to buy one S&P share for $1,200 at the expiration date in June. Since the current (i.e., spot) price of the index is 1,207.01, this call option is in the money. Thus, the total put premium of $37.40 can be divided into an intrinsic value component of $7.01 (= 1,207.01 − 1,200) and a time premium of $30.39 (= 37.40 − 7.01). Similarly, the investor holding the put option has the right, but not the obligation, to sell one S&P share for $1,200 at the expiration date in June. The put is out of the money, however, as this exercise price is lower than the current index level. Thus, the put option has no intrinsic value, so that the $26.00 ask price is a time premium.

---

[2]Recall that an investor buys a security from a dealer—in this case, the options exchange—at the ask price, and sells securities to the dealer at the bid price. The difference in these prices, which is the *bid-ask spread*, represents part of the compensation to the exchange for making a market in these contracts.

The expiration date net payoffs to these long option positions are listed in Exhibit 20.7 for a variety of possible S&P index levels. Looking first at the call option payoffs in Panel A, notice that the investor will only exercise the contract to buy a share of the S&P index when the June S&P level is above 1,200; at index levels at or below 1,200, the option expires worthless and the investor will simply lose his initial investment. Recognize, though, that while the call is in the money at index levels above 1,200, the investor will not realize a net profit until the June index level rises above 1,237.40, an amount equal to the exercise price plus the call premium (i.e., $X + C_{0,T}$). For the put option payoffs shown in Panel B, the holder will exercise the contract at June index levels below the exercise price, using the contract to sell for $1,200 an S&P share that is worth less than that. However, the display also documents that the put investor will not realize a positive net profit until the index level falls below 1,174 (i.e., $X - P_{0,T}$). For June S&P values above $1,200, the put option expires out of the money.

Exhibit 20.7	Net Profit at Expiration from Long Positions in S&P 500 Call and Put Option Contracts

A. Long Call with Exercise Price of 1,200

June S&P 500 Index Level	Call Payoff at Expiration	Initial Call Premium	Net Profit
1,140.00	0.00	−37.40	−37.40
1,160.00	0.00	−37.40	−37.40
1,180.00	0.00	−37.40	−37.40
1,200.00	0.00	−37.40	−37.40
1,220.00	(1,220 − 1,200) = 20.00	−37.40	−17.40
1,237.40	(1,237.40 − 1,200) = 37.40	−37.40	0.00
1,240.00	(1,240 − 1,200) = 40.00	−37.40	2.60
1,260.00	(1,260 − 1,200) = 60.00	−37.40	22.60
1,280.00	(1,280 − 1,200) = 80.00	−37.40	42.60

B. Long Put with Exercise Price of 1,200

June S&P 500 Index Level	Put Payoff at Expiration	Initial Put Premium	Net Profit
1,140.00	(1,200 − 1,140) = 60.00	$−26.00	34.00
1,160.00	(1,200 − 1,160) = 40.00	$−26.00	14.00
1,174.00	(1,200 − 1,174) = 26.00	$−26.00	0.00
1,180.00	(1,200 − 1,180) = 20.00	$−26.00	−6.00
1,200.00	0.00	$−26.00	−26.00
1,220.00	0.00	$−26.00	−26.00
1,240.00	0.00	$−26.00	−26.00
1,260.00	0.00	$−26.00	−26.00
1,280.00	0.00	$−26.00	−26.00

INVESTING WITH DERIVATIVE SECURITIES

Although the preceding section highlighted many of the differences between forward and option agreements, the two types of derivatives are quite similar in terms of the benefits they produce for investors. The ultimate difference between forwards and options lies in the way the investor must pay to acquire those benefits. This concept, along with an examination of the basic payoff structures that exist in these markets, is described in the following sections.

The Basic Nature of Derivative Investing

Consider an investor—call him Investor 1—who has decided to purchase a share of stock in SAS Corporation six months from now, a time frame that coincides with an anticipated receipt of funds. We will assume that both SAS stock forward contracts and call options are available with the market prices of $F_{0,T}$ and $C_{0,T}$ (where $T = 0.50$ year) and that the exercise price of the call option, X, is equal to $F_{0,T}$. Thus, if the investor wants to secure the price now at which the stock purchase will eventually take place, he has two alternatives: a long position in the forward or the purchase of the call option. Exhibit 20.8 compares the Date 0 and Date T cash flow exchanges for both possibilities.

The clear difference between these strategies at the time of origination is that the forward position requires no payment or receipt by either party to the transaction whereas the investor

Exhibit 20.8	**Exchanges for Long Forward and Long Call Transactions**

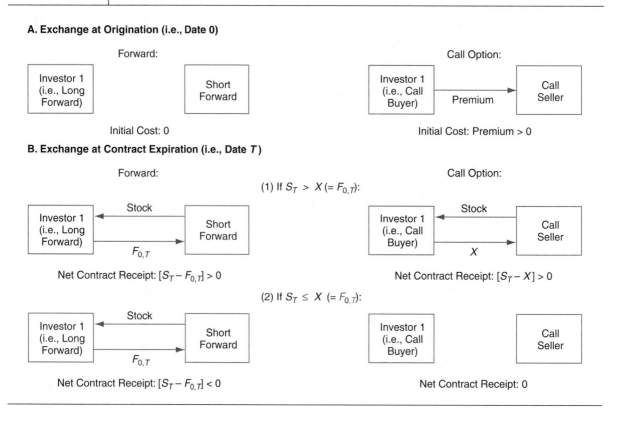

A. Exchange at Origination (i.e., Date 0)

Forward:

Investor 1 (i.e., Long Forward) — Short Forward

Initial Cost: 0

Call Option:

Investor 1 (i.e., Call Buyer) — Premium → Call Seller

Initial Cost: Premium > 0

B. Exchange at Contract Expiration (i.e., Date T)

(1) If $S_T > X (= F_{0,T})$:

Forward:

Investor 1 (i.e., Long Forward) ← Stock — Short Forward ; $F_{0,T}$

Net Contract Receipt: $[S_T - F_{0,T}] > 0$

Call Option:

Investor 1 (i.e., Call Buyer) ← Stock — Call Seller ; X

Net Contract Receipt: $[S_T - X] > 0$

(2) If $S_T \leq X (= F_{0,T})$:

Forward:

Investor 1 (i.e., Long Forward) ← Stock — Short Forward ; $F_{0,T}$

Net Contract Receipt: $[S_T - F_{0,T}] < 0$

Call Option:

Investor 1 (i.e., Call Buyer) — Call Seller

Net Contract Receipt: 0

(i.e., the call buyer) must pay a cash premium to the seller of the option. As noted earlier, this front-end option payment releases the investor from the obligation to purchase SAS stock at Date T if the terms of the contract turn out to be unfavorable (i.e., $S_T < X$). This is shown in Panel B of Exhibit 20.8. When the expiration date price of SAS stock exceeds the exercise price, the investor will exercise the call and purchase the share of stock. Notice however, that this leads to exactly the same exchange as did the long forward contract. It is only when the stock price falls below X (and $F_{0,T}$) on Date T that there is a difference between the two positions; under this condition, the right provided by the option *not* to purchase SAS stock is valuable since the investor will be required to execute his forward contract at a loss. In this sense, the call option can be viewed as the good half of the long forward position because it allows for the future acquisition of SAS stock at a fixed price but doesn't require the transaction to take place.

This is the critical distinction between forward and option contracts. Both the long forward and the long call positions have been structured to provide the investor with exactly the same amount of "insurance" against the price of SAS stock rising over the next six months. That is, both contracts provide a payoff of $[S_T - X] = [S_T - F_{0,T}]$ whenever S_T exceeds X, which reduces the effective purchase price for the stock back to X. The difference in contract design can then be viewed in terms of how the investor is required to pay for that price insurance. With a forward contract, no money is paid up front, but the investor will have to make a payment at the expiration date, even if the stock price falls below $F_{0,T}$. Conversely, the call option will never require a future settlement payment, but the investor will have to pay the premium at origination. Thus, for the same Date T benefit, the investor's decision between these two "insurance policies" comes down to choosing the certainty of a present premium payment (i.e., long call) versus the possibility of a future payment (i.e., long forward) that could potentially be much larger.

To see this distinction more clearly, suppose that Investor 1 plans to buy SAS stock in six months when some of the bonds in his portfolio mature. He is concerned that share values could rise substantially between now and the time he receives his investment funds, and so to hedge that risk he considers two insurance strategies to lock in the eventual purchase price: (1) pay nothing now to take the long position in a six-month SAS stock forward contract with a contract price of $F_{0,T} = \$45$, or (2) pay a premium of $C_{0,T} = \$3.24$ for a six-month, European-style call option with an exercise price of $X = \$45$. Assuming that at the time of his decision the price of SAS stock is $S_0 = \$40$, the call option is out of the money, meaning that its intrinsic value is zero and the entire \$3.24 is time premium. As mentioned earlier, an obvious difference between these two strategies is that the option entails a front-end expense while the forward position does not. The other difference occurs at the expiration date, depending on whether the SAS stock price is above or below \$45. If, for instance, $S_T = \$51$, both the long forward position and the call option will be worth \$6 (i.e., $51 - 45$) to the investor, reducing his net purchase price for SAS shares to \$45 ($= 51 - 6$). That is, when the stock settled above \$45 (i.e., the common value for $F_{0,T}$ and X), both the long forward and long call positions provided the same protection against rising prices. On the other hand, if $S_T = \$40.75$, the forward contract would have required that the investor pay \$4.25 ($= 40.75 - 45$) to his counterparty, which would have once again raised the net cost of his shares to \$45. With the call option, however, he could have let the contract expire without exercising it and purchased his SAS shares in the market for only \$40.75. Thus, in exchange for the option's front-end expense of \$3.24, the investor retains the possibility of paying less than \$45 for his eventual stock purchase.

The connection between forward contracts and put options can be made in a similar fashion. Suppose a different investor—call her Investor 2—has decided to liquidate a share of SAS stock from her portfolio in six months' time. Rather than risk a falling stock price over that period, she could arrange now to sell the share at that future date for a predetermined fixed

Exhibit 20.9	**Exchanges for Short Forward and Long Put Transactions**

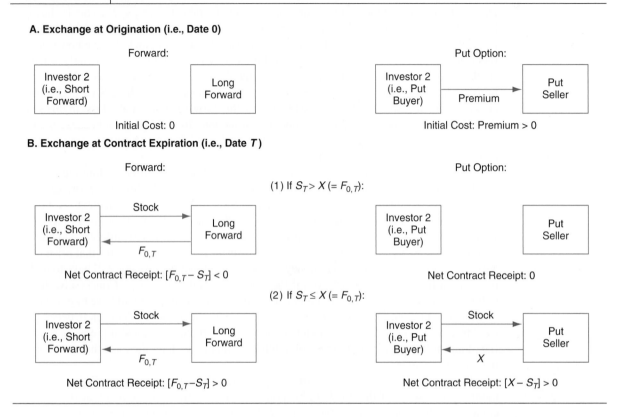

A. Exchange at Origination (i.e., Date 0)

Forward:

Put Option:

Initial Cost: 0

Initial Cost: Premium > 0

B. Exchange at Contract Expiration (i.e., Date T)

Forward:

Put Option:

(1) If $S_T > X (= F_{0,T})$:

Net Contract Receipt: $[F_{0,T} - S_T] < 0$

Net Contract Receipt: 0

(2) If $S_T \leq X (= F_{0,T})$:

Net Contract Receipt: $[F_{0,T} - S_T] > 0$

Net Contract Receipt: $[X - S_T] > 0$

price in one of two ways: a short forward position or the purchase of a put option. Exhibit 20.9 illustrates the exchanges for these alternatives. Once again, for the same insurance against SAS stock price declines, the choice comes down to the certainty of paying the put option premium versus the possibility of making a potentially larger payment with the forward contract by having to sell her stock for $X (= F_{0,T})$ when that value is considerably less than the stock's Date T market price. Importantly, notice once again that the put option allows the investor to walk away from her obligation under the short forward position to sell her stock on the expiration date under disadvantageous conditions. Thus, in exchange for a front-end premium payment, the put option enables the investor to acquire the "good half" of the short position in a forward contract.

Basic Payoff Diagrams for Forward Contracts

Exhibit 20.8 and Exhibit 20.9 show that the respective expiration date payoffs for long and short positions in a forward contract are $[S_T - F_{0,T}]$ and $[F_{0,T} - S_T]$ and that these values could be either positive or negative depending on the spot price prevailing at Date T. These terminal payoffs are plotted against the possible expiration date values of the underlying security price in Exhibit 20.10. There are two interesting items in this display.

First, the payoffs to both long and short positions in the forward contract are *symmetric*, or two-sided, around the contract price. This, of course, is a direct result of the terms of the

Exhibit 20.10 | **Expiration Date Payoffs to Long and Short Forward Positions**

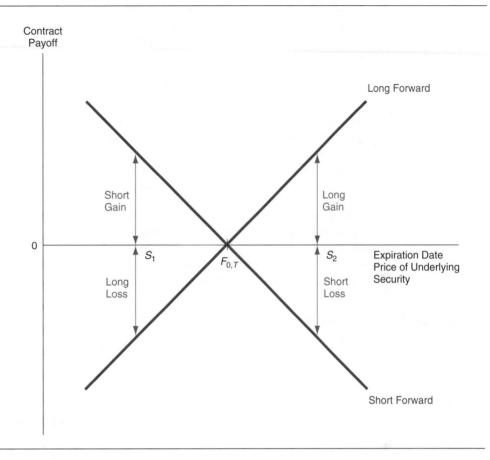

contract that fully obligate each party to complete the agreed-upon transaction—even at a financial loss. For instance, in the last example, the investor holding a long position in a SAS stock forward contract with a contract price of $45 lost $4.25 when the Date T price of SAS stock was $40.75 but gained $6 when $S_T = \$51$.

Second, the Date T payoffs to the short and long positions are mirror images of each other; in market jargon, forward contracts are *zero-sum games* because the long position gains must be paid by the short position and vice versa. This illustration shows that when the Date T spot price is lower than the contract price (i.e., S_1), the short position will receive the net payoff of $[F_{0,T} - S_1]$ from the long position while the settlement is reversed at S_2, where the security price is above $F_{0,T}$. Thus, forward markets reinforce the fundamental financial tenet that long positions benefit from rising prices while short positions benefit from falling prices. Finally, notice that these gains and losses can be quite large. In fact, the short forward position has the potential for unlimited loss while the long forward position has the potential for unlimited gain since there is no theoretical limit on how high the price for the underlying security can rise. Conversely, the loss potential for the long position (and the gain potential for the short position) is limited because the price of the underlying security cannot fall below zero.

Basic Payoff Diagrams for Call and Put Options

Exhibits 20.8 and 20.9 also show that options differ from forward contracts in two fundamental ways. Most directly, the expense of purchasing either a put or a call represents a sunk cost to the investor, reducing the upside return relative to the comparable forward position. In exchange for this initial fee, the investor receives expiration date payoffs that are decidedly *asymmetric,* or one-sided. Exhibit 20.11 shows the net effect these differences have on the terminal payoffs to both long and short positions in call options, while Exhibit 20.12 provides a similar illustration for put option traders. This analysis assumes that both options are European-style, and so they actually reach expiration without having been exercised prematurely.

For call option positions, notice again that the buyer of the contract still benefits whenever the terminal security price (i.e., S_T) exceeds the contract purchase (i.e., exercise) price of X. However, given that the holder had to pay an initial premium of $C_{0,T}$, the position doesn't generate a positive payoff until S_T is greater than X by the amount of the premium paid. Put another way, although the call option is in the money (and hence will be exercised) when $S_T > X$, it will not produce a capital gain for the buyer until $S_T > (X + C_{0,T})$.[3] (Recall that this result was shown for the S&P 500 index option example in Exhibit 20.7.) When $X < S_T < (X + C_{0,T})$, the option is exercised at a loss, but this loss will be less than the full cost of the option, which is what the long position would incur if the call were not exercised. In fact, when $S_T < X$, the option is out of the money and the buyer who makes the rational decision to let the contract expire will lose $C_{0,T}$.

Exhibit 20.11	**Expiration Date Payoffs to Long and Short Call Positions**

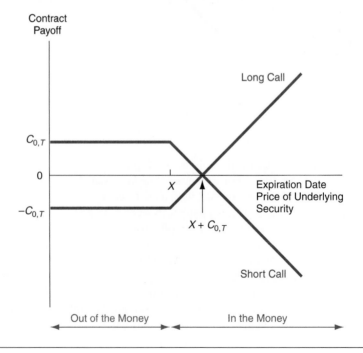

---

[3]The expiration date payoffs shown in Exhibits 20.11 and 20.12 are somewhat inaccurate in that they show the net of the Date T value of the option and its initial cost, which was paid at Date 0. Thus, although this is an accurate way of portraying capital gains and losses from an accounting standpoint, it ignores the value differential in the timing of the two payments.

Exhibit 20.12	**Expiration Date Payoffs to Long and Short Put Positions**

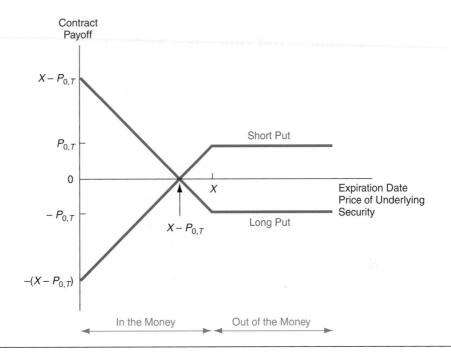

Notice, then, that the buyer of the call option has unlimited gain potential as the security price could rise indefinitely with losses limited to the option premium no matter how far prices fall. On the other hand, the short position benefits from a terminal price for the underlying asset beneath X but only to the extent that he gets to keep the full amount of the option premium. When $S_T > X$, the seller of the call has unlimited liability. Like forward contracts, the call option is a zero-sum game between the long and short positions.

For the put option positions shown in Exhibit 20.12, the buyer benefits whenever $X > S_T$ and receives a positive payoff when the Date T price of the underlying security falls below the contractual selling price, less the cost of the option. In this case, the put buyer's maximum capital gain is limited to $X - P_{0,T}$ as the underlying security itself is limited to a minimum price of zero; the best the put holder can hope for is to force the seller of the contract to buy worthless stock for X at the expiration date. On the other hand, as with the call option, the owner of an out-of-the-money put can only lose his initial investment of $P_{0,T}$, which will occur when $S_T > X$. Not surprisingly, the profit and loss opportunities for the put seller are exactly opposite of those for the put buyer. The contract seller will gain when $S_T > (X - P_{0,T})$, but this gain is limited to the amount of the option premium. A short position in a put also has limited loss potential; but, at a maximum of $X - P_{0,T}$, this can still be a large amount.

In summary, when they are held as investments, options are *directional views* on movements in the price of the underlying security. Call buyers and put sellers count on S_T to rise (or remain) above X, while put buyers and call sellers hope for S_T to fall (or remain) below the exercise price at the expiration date. However, the exact payoffs to each of these positions vary greatly for any given terminal security value. Importantly, option buyers—whether a put or a call—always have limited liability since they do not have to exercise an out-of-the-money position. This limited liability feature for option holders also means that the gain potential for the seller is limited as the two positions are mirror images of each other. For adverse price movements, though, option sellers face large potential losses, with the liability of the call writer being theoretically infinite just as if she had sold short the underlying security.

Option Payoff Diagrams: An Example

Although there will only be one value of $F_{0,T}$ that allows the present value of a forward contract to be zero (i.e., does not require an initial payment from either the long or the short position), we have seen that option contracts can be designed with several different values for the exercise price. It is interesting, therefore, to consider how the choice of the exercise price affects the instrument's expiration date payoff. Extending the last example, suppose that a share of SAS stock currently sells for $40 and six different SAS options—three calls and three puts—are available to investors. The options all expire on the same date in the future and have exercise prices of either $35, $40, or $45. Current market prices for these contracts, which are assumed to be European-style, are shown in Exhibit 20.13, where they are broken down into their intrinsic value and time premium components.

Given that S_0 = $40, call 1 (with X = 35) and Put 3 (with X = 45) are both $5 in the money, which leaves $3.07 and $1.47, respectively, of their value in the form of time premium. Call 3 and Put 1 are both currently $5 out of the money and so their market prices are purely time premium; someone buying either of these two contracts anticipates that stock prices will move in the desired direction by at least the option price *plus* $5. Notice that neither of the two at-the-money options, Call 2 and Put 2, have any intrinsic value, but they still sell in the market for different prices. Specifically, the call with X = $40 is more valuable than the comparable put option. As we will see shortly, this occurs because of **put-call parity**, which is the formal relationship that must exist between put and call options in efficient capital markets. (In fact, for options on a stock that does not pay a dividend, this situation should always hold. However, the value of an at-the-money put can exceed that of an at-the-money call if the underlying security is a stock, a bond, or currency that does pay a cash flow.) Finally, the last column of Exhibit 20.13 shows that the time premium is largest for the at-the-money options because, at this point, the greatest amount of uncertainty exists as to whether the option will be in or out of the money (and hence valuable) at expiration.

It is instructive to compare the expiration date payoff diagrams for options on the same security with varying exercise prices but similar in every other respect. This is done for both call and put options in Exhibit 20.14. For simplicity, only the payoffs for the long positions in these contracts are shown. The call option payoffs portrayed in Panel A of the exhibit indicate that,

Exhibit 20.13	**Hypothetical Stock and Option Prices**				
	Instrument	Exercise Price	Market Price	Intrinsic Value	Time Premium
	SAS Stock	—	$40.00	—	—
	Call: 1	$35.00	8.07	$5.00	$3.07
	2	40.00	5.24	0.00	5.24
	3	45.00	3.24	0.00	3.24
	Put: 1	35.00	1.70	0.00	1.70
	2	40.00	3.67	0.00	3.67
	3	45.00	6.47	5.00	1.47

Exhibit 20.14 | **Terminal Payoffs to Options with Different Exercise Prices**

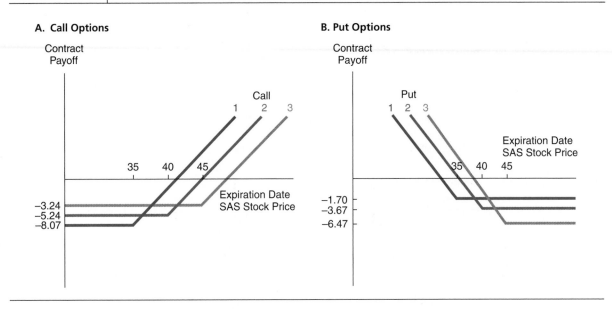

A. Call Options

Contract Payoff

Call
1 2 3

35 40 45

Expiration Date
SAS Stock Price

−3.24
−5.24
−8.07

B. Put Options

Contract Payoff

Put
1 2 3

Expiration Date
SAS Stock Price

35 40 45

−1.70
−3.67
−6.47

although it is the most expensive, the deepest in-the-money contract (Call 1) becomes profitable the quickest, requiring only that S_T rise to $43.07 (= 35 + 8.07). Call 3, on the other hand, is the least expensive to purchase but requires the greatest movement in the price of the underlying stock—to $48.24 in this example—before it provides a positive payoff to the investor. The put options illustrated in Panel B tell the same story, with Put 1 (the out-of-the-money contract) costing the least but needing the largest price decline to be profitable at expiration. In general, by varying the exercise price on a series of options with otherwise identical contract terms, an investor can create just as many different risk-reward trade-offs for herself. This is one of several ways in which derivatives can be used to modify investment risk and to customize a desired payoff structure.

Options and Leverage   As a final extension of this example, let us compare the returns to an investment in either a put or a call option with an investment (or short sale) in a share of the underlying SAS stock. To focus on the important issues, we will limit the analysis to Call 2 and Put 2, the two at-the-money contracts. Exhibit 20.15 summarizes the holding period returns for various positions assuming three different expiration date stock prices: $30, $40, and $50. Two different comparisons are made: (1) long stock versus long call and (2) short stock versus long put. In calculating the returns to the stock positions, we have measured the change in value of the SAS share as a percentage of the initial price of $40. For the option positions, the terminal payoffs of max [0, S_T − 40] for the call and max [0, 40 − S_T] for the put are listed relative to the contract's purchase price.

The most important thing to realize about these calculations is that both put and call options magnify the possible positive and negative returns of investing in the underlying security. In the case of the long call option position, for an initial cost of $5.24, the investor can retain the right to access the price appreciation of a share of SAS stock without spending $40 to own the share outright. This degree of financial *leverage* manifests itself in a 100 percent loss when the stock price falls by a quarter of that amount and a 91 percent gain when SAS shares increase in value from $40 to $50. Notably, if the stock price remains at $40, the owner

Exhibit 20.15 | **Stock and Option Investment Returns**

A. Long Stock versus Long Call

Terminal Stock Price	Long Stock	Long Call
30	$\dfrac{30}{40} - 1 = -25.0\%$	$\dfrac{0}{5.24} - 1 = -100.0\%$
40	$\dfrac{40}{40} - 1 = 0.0\%$	$\dfrac{0}{5.24} - 1 = -100.0\%$
50	$\dfrac{50}{40} - 1 = 25.0\%$	$\dfrac{10}{5.24} - 1 = 90.8\%$

B. Short Stock versus Long Put

Terminal Stock Price	Short Stock	Long Put
30	$1 - \dfrac{30}{40} = 25.0\%$	$\dfrac{10}{3.67} - 1 = 172.5\%$
40	$1 - \dfrac{40}{40} = 0.0\%$	$\dfrac{0}{3.67} - 1 = -100.0\%$
50	$1 - \dfrac{50}{40} = -25.0\%$	$\dfrac{0}{3.67} - 1 = -100.0\%$

of the share would not have lost anything while the call holder would have lost his entire investment, which was pure time premium at origination for the at-the-money contract. This suggests that in addition to anticipating the *direction* of the subsequent underlying stock price movement, the option investor also is taking a view on the *timing* of that movement. If the price of SAS stock had stayed at $40 through Date *T* and then rose to $50 on the following day, the stockholder would have experienced a 25 percent gain, while the buyer of the call option would have seen the instrument expire worthless.

THE RELATIONSHIP BETWEEN FORWARD AND OPTION CONTRACTS

The preceding discussion highlighted the fact that positions in forward and option contracts can lead to similar investment payoffs if the price of the underlying security moves in the anticipated direction. As we saw, the difference in the payoffs to these derivatives came when the security's price changed adversely. This similarity in payoff structures suggests that there is a tractable set of relationships between these instruments. In fact, we will see that the values of five different securities can be linked: a risk-free bond, an underlying asset, a forward contract for the future purchase or sale of that asset, a call option, and a put option. These relationships, known as put-call parity, specify how the put and call premiums should be set relative to one another. Further, these conditions can be expressed in terms of the connection between these two option types and either the spot or forward market price for the underlying asset. They depend on the assumption that financial markets are free from arbitrage opportunities, meaning that securities (or portfolios of securities) offering identical payoffs with identical risks must sell for the same current price. As such, put-call parity represents an important first step in understanding how derivatives are valued in an efficient capital market.[4]

Put-Call-Spot Parity

Suppose that at Date 0 (the present) an investor forms the following portfolio involving three securities related to Company WYZ:

- Long in a share of WYZ common stock at a purchase price of S_0.
- Long in a put option to deliver one share of WYZ stock at an exercise price of X on the Expiration Date T. This put could be purchased for the price of $P_{0,T}$,
- Short in a call option allowing the purchase of one share of WYZ stock at an exercise price of X on the Expiration Date T. This call could be sold for the price $C_{0,T}$.

In this example, both of the WYZ options are European-style and have the same expiration date and exercise price. However, the specific values of the expiration date and exercise price do not affect the conclusion of the analysis that follows. Further, we will assume initially that WYZ stock does not pay a dividend during the life of the options.

With these definitions, notice in Panel A of Exhibit 20.16 that the Date 0 investment necessary to acquire this portfolio is $(S_0 + P_{0,T} - C_{0,T})$, which is the cost of the long positions in the stock and the put option less the proceeds generated by the sale of the call option.[5] A more interesting thing to consider is the value that this portfolio will have at the expiration date of the two options. Given that the stock's value at Date T (i.e., S_T) is unknown when the investment is made at Period 0, two general outcomes are possible: (1) $S_T \leq X$ and (2) $S_T > X$. Panel B of Exhibit 20.16 shows the value of each position as well as the net value of the whole portfolio at Date T.

Exhibit 20.16	Put-Call-Spot Parity

A. Net Portfolio Investment at Initiation (Date 0)

Portfolio	
Long 1 WYZ stock	S_0
Long 1 put option	$P_{0,T}$
Short 1 call option	$-C_{0,T}$
Net investment:	$S_0 + P_{0,T} - C_{0,T}$

B. Portfolio Value at Option Expiration (Date T)

Portfolio	(1) If $S_T \leq X$:	(2) If $S_T > X$:
Long 1 WYZ stock	S_T	S_T
Long 1 put option	$(X - S_T)$	0
Short 1 call option	0	$-(S_T - X)$
Net position:	X	X

---

[4]The development of the relationships linking put and call option prices is commonly attributed to Stoll (1969). Others have embellished Stoll's findings in many interesting ways; those subsequent studies include Merton (1973a), Kamara and Miller (1995), and Bharadwaj and Wiggins (2001).

[5]In the "arithmetic" of engineering financial portfolios, a plus (+) sign can be interpreted as a long position, and a minus (–) sign represents a short position. Thus the portfolio investment represented by $(S_0 + P_{0,T} - C_{0,T})$ can also be expressed as (long stock) + (long put) + (short call). Smith (1989a) explains this approach in more detail.

Notice that whenever the Date T value of WYZ stock is less than the exercise price common to the put and call options, it is best for the investor to exercise the long position in the put and sell the WYZ share for X instead of its lower market value. Under the same condition, it will not be rational for the holder of the call to pay X for a share that is worth less. Therefore, the call will expire out of the money. On the other hand, when S_T exceeds X, the holder of the call will exercise the option to purchase WYZ stock for X from the investor while the put would be out of the money. In either case, the net expiration date value of the position is X because the combination of options contained in the portfolio guarantees that the investor will sell the share of WYZ stock at Date T for the fixed price X. That is, at stock prices lower than X, the investor will choose to sell the share at a profit, although he will be forced to sell at a loss when WYZ trades on the market at a price higher than X. The investor has, in effect, a guaranteed contract to sell the share of stock when the long put and short call positions are held jointly.

The consequence of this result is that when the investor commits $(S_0 + P_{0,T} - C_{0,T})$ to acquire the position at Date 0, he knows that it will be worth X at Date T. Thus, this particular portfolio has a comparable payoff structure to a U.S. Treasury bill, another risk-free, zero coupon security that can be designed to have a face value of X and a maturity date T. In an arbitrage-free capital market, this means that the Date 0 value of the portfolio must be equal to that of the T-bill, which is just the face value X discounted to the present using the risk-free rate. This "no arbitrage" condition can be formalized as follows:

20.1
$$S_0 + P_{0,T} - C_{0,T} = \frac{X}{(1 + RFR)^T}$$

where:

RFR = the annualized risk-free rate
T = the time to maturity (expressed in years)

Defining $[X (1 + RFR)^{-T}]$ as the present value of a T-bill, this equation can be expressed in financial arithmetic terms as:

$$(\text{Long Stock}) + (\text{Long Put}) + (\text{Short Call}) = (\text{Long T-Bill})$$

In either form, this condition—known as the *put-call-spot* parity condition—indicates the efficient market linkages between prices for stock, T-bills, put options, and call options.

Put-Call Parity: An Example

As an example of how put-call parity might be used, suppose that WYZ stock is currently valued at $53 and that call and put options on WYZ stock with an exercise price of $50 sell for $6.74 and $2.51, respectively. Assuming that both options can only be exercised in exactly six months, Equation 20.1 suggests that we can "make" a synthetic T-bill by purchasing the stock, purchasing the put, and selling the call for a net price of $48.77 (= $53.00 + 2.51 - 6.74$). At the options' expiration date, this portfolio would have a terminal value of $50. Thus, the risk-free rate implied by this investment can be established by solving the following equation for RFR:

$$48.77 = 50 (1 + RFR)^{-0.5}$$

or

$$RFR = [(50 \div 48.77)^2 - 1] = 5.11\%$$

The practical application of this finding is that if the rate of return on an actual six-month T-bill with a face value of $50 is not 5.11 percent, then an investor could exploit the difference. Suppose, for instance, that the actual T-bill rate is 6.25 percent and that there are no restrictions against using the proceeds from the short sale of any security. In such a situation, an investor wanting a risk-free investment would clearly choose the actual T-bill to lock in the higher return, while someone seeking a loan might attempt to secure a 5.11 percent borrowing rate by short-selling the synthetic T-bill. With an arithmetic rearrangement of the parity condition in the previous equation, such an artificial short position can be obtained as

(Short Stock) + (Short Put) + (Long Call) = (Short T-Bill)

With no transaction costs, a financial arbitrage could be constructed by combining a long position in the actual T-bill with a short sale of the synthetic portfolio. Given that the current value of the actual T-bill is $48.51 [= $50 $(1.0625)^{-0.5}$], this set of transactions would generate the cash flows shown in Exhibit 20.17 and produce a $0.26 profit per each T-bill pair created. However, as the arbitrage trade did not require the investor to bear any risk (i.e., both the Date 0 and Date T values of the net position were known at inception) nor commit any capital, there is nothing in this example to prevent the investor from expanding the size of the trade to increasingly larger levels. Unfortunately, as additional transactions take place, the price discrepancy will disappear. In this case, the purchase of the actual T-bill and sale of the synthetic (short stock, short put, and long call) will continue until rates are equalized. This is how the markets remain efficient through arbitrage trading.

Another way of seeing this trade is

$$C_{0,T} - P_{0,T} = S_0 - X(1 + RFR)^{-T}$$

Exhibit 20.17	**A Put-Call Parity Arbitrage Example**

A. Net Initial Investment (Date 0)

Transaction

1. Long actual T-bill at 6.25%	−48.51
2. Short synthetic T-bill at 5.11%:	
Short WYZ stock	53.00
Short put option	2.51
Long call option	−6.74
Net receipt:	0.26

B. Position Value at Option Expiration (Date T)

Transaction	(1) If $S_T \leq 50$:	(2) If $S_T > 50$:
1. Long actual T-bill at 6.25%	50	50
2. Short synthetic T-bill at 5.11%:		
Short WYZ stock	$-S_T$	$-S_T$
Short put option	$-(50 - S_T)$	0
Long call option	0	$(S_T - 50)$
Net position:	0	0

That is, the "no arbitrage" difference between the call and put prices should equal the difference between the stock price and the present value of the joint exercise price. The market-determined risk-free rate of 6.25 percent implies that the correct difference between the two derivatives should be $4.49 (= 53 − 48.51), which is $0.26 greater than the $4.23 (= 6.74 − 2.51) actual difference. This discrepancy suggests that if you assume the actual T-bill is priced correctly, the call price is undervalued relative to the put option. Not surprisingly, then, notice that the arbitrage transaction requires the purchase of the call option while shorting the put option.

Creating Synthetic Securities Using Put-Call Parity

The preceding example demonstrates that a risk-free portfolio could be created by combining three risky securities: stock, a put option, and a call option. The parity condition developed in the example can be expressed in other useful ways as well. In particular, one of the four assets represented in the first equation is always *redundant* because it can be defined in terms of the others. Three additional ways of manipulating this result are:

20.2
$$P_{0,T} = \frac{X}{(1 + RFR)^T} - S_0 + C_{0,T}$$

20.3
$$C_{0,T} = S_0 + P_{0,T} - \frac{X}{(1 + RFR)^T}$$

20.4
$$S_0 = \frac{X}{(1 + RFR)^T} - P_{0,T} + C_{0,T}$$

Equation 20.2 and Equation 20.3 indicate, respectively, that (1) the payoffs to a long position in a put option can be replicated by a portfolio consisting of a long position in a T-bill, a short stock position, and the purchase of a call option; and (2) a synthetic call option can be mimicked by a portfolio that is long in the stock and the put option and short in the T-bill. Equation 20.4 indicates that the payoff to the stock itself can be expressed by its derivative securities and the T-bill.

These results are useful in two ways. First, if there are not markets in either put or call options, the relationships summarized by these equations indicate how investors can create the desired, but unavailable, pattern of cash flows through the appropriate "packaging" of the other three interrelated assets. Suppose, for example, that a put option on WYZ stock did not exist but a call option does. Exhibit 20.18 shows the Date 0 and Date T cash flows associated with the portfolio replicating the terminal payoff. Combining both panels of the display, an initial investment of $[X (1 + RFR)_{-T} - S_0 + C_{0,T}]$ leads to a final cash flow that is no less than zero and as large as $X - S_T$ whenever $X > S_T$. Expressed in a more traditional manner, the expiration date payoff to the synthetic put is max $[0, X - S_T]$.

Another way the alternative expressions for the put-call parity model (summarized by Equations 20.2–20.4) are used in practice is the identification of arbitrage opportunities. Even when a particular derivative instrument trades actively in the market, if its cash flows and risks can be duplicated, this leads to the possibility that the price of the actual instrument and the net cost of the replicating portfolio will differ. Using the numbers from the previous example, the Date T distribution of max $[0, 50 - S_T]$ could be acquired through the synthetic strategy at a cost of $2.25 (= 48.51 − 53 + 6.74) or through the purchase of the actual put for $2.51.

This is the same $0.26 price differential we saw earlier when designing an arbitrage transaction involving the actual and synthetic T-bill. The put option arbitrage would be to short the

Exhibit 20.18	Replicating a Put Option

A. Net Portfolio Investment at Initiation (Date 0)

Portfolio

Long 1 T-bill	$X(1 + RFR)^{-T}$
Short 1 WYZ stock	$-S_0$
Long 1 call option	$C_{0,T}$
Net investment:	$X(1 + RFR)^{-T} - S_0 + C_{0,T}$

B. Portfolio Value at Option Expiration (Date *T*)

Portfolio	(1) If $S_T \leq X$:	(2) If $S_T > X$:
Long 1 T-bill	X	X
Short 1 WYZ stock	$-S_T$	$-S_T$
Long 1 call option	0	$(S_T - X)$
Net position:	$X - S_T$	0

actual put while buying the replicating portfolio (i.e., long T-bill, short stock, and long call), which is the same set of transactions we used in the T-bill arbitrage. This result underscores the important point that the put-call parity model only allows us to make *relative*—rather than absolute—statements about security values. Although we can change our perspective in identifying the misvalued instrument (e.g., T-bill versus put option), the real source of the market inefficiency came from examining the *difference* between the put and call prices in relation to the stock and T-bill prices. Consequently, all four securities need to be included in the arbitrage trade.

Adjusting Put-Call-Spot Parity for Dividends

A second extension of the put-call-spot parity model involves the payment of dividends to the shareholders of WYZ stock. Suppose for simplicity that in the basic portfolio listed in Exhibit 20.16, WYZ stock pays a dividend of D_T immediately prior to the expiration of the options at Date *T*. Assume further that the amount of this distribution is known when the investment is initiated, a condition that is almost certainly met for values of $T \leq 0.25$ year because U.S.-based companies typically pay quarterly dividends. The result of these modifications is that the terminal value of the long stock position will be $(S_T + D_T)$. On the other hand, the terminal payoffs to the put and call options remain max $[0, X - S_T]$ and max $[0, S_T - X]$, respectively, as the holders of the two derivative contracts will not participate directly in the payment of dividends to the stockholder.[6] Thus, the net Date *T* value of the portfolio acquired originally for $(S_0 + P_{0,T} - C_{0,T})$ is $(X + D_T)$.

With the critical assumption that the dividend payment is known at Date 0, the portfolio long in WYZ stock, long in the put, and short in the call once again can be viewed as equivalent

---

[6]The fact that the expiration date payoff to a call option on both a dividend- and nondividend-paying stock can be expressed as max $[0, S_T - X]$ does not mean that the two will generate the same dollar amount of cash flow. This is because the stock's value will be reduced by the payment of the dividend in the former case but not in the latter. Thus, with the lower terminal payout, the call on the dividend-paying stock will be less valuable than an otherwise comparable contract on a nondividend-paying equity. We will explore this topic more fully in Chapter 22.

to a T-bill, now having a face value of $(X + D_T)$. This allows Equation 20.1 to be adapted as follows:

$$S_0 + P_{0,T} - C_{0,T} = \frac{X + D_T}{(1 + RFR)^T} = \frac{X}{(1 + RFR)^T} + \frac{D_T}{(1 + RFR)^T}$$

which can be interpreted as:

(Long Stock) + (Long Put) + (Short Call) = (Long T-Bill) + (Long Present Value of Dividends)

Alternatively, it is often more useful to rearrange this equation as follows:

$$\left\{ S_0 - \frac{D_T}{(1 + RFR)^T} \right\} + P_{0,T} - C_{0,T} = \frac{X}{(1 + RFR)^T}$$

In this form, the equation can be compared directly with the no-dividend put-call-spot parity result and shows that the current stock price must be *adjusted downward* by the present value of the dividend. With an initial stock price of $53 and an annualized risk-free rate on a six-month T-bill of 6.25 percent, a $1 dividend paid just before the expiration of a call and a put option with an exercise price of $50 would result in a theoretical price differential of:

$$C_{0.05} - P_{0.05} = \left\{ 53 - \frac{1}{(1 + 0.0625)^{0.5}} \right\} - \frac{50}{(1 + 0.0625)^{0.5}} = \$3.52$$

This value differs from the parity differential for options on the nondividend-paying stock, which was shown earlier to be $4.49. Thus, the payment of the dividend has reduced the price of the call relative to the put by $0.97, which is the discounted amount of the $1 cash distribution.

Put-Call-Forward Parity

At this point in our analysis of the structural relationships between derivative instruments and their underlying securities, we have not explicitly included forward or futures contracts. Suppose that instead of buying the stock in the spot market at Date 0, we took a long position in a forward contract allowing us to purchase one share of WYZ stock at Date T. The price of this acquisition, $F_{0,T}$, would be established by the forward agreement at Date 0. As before, we will assume that this transaction is supplemented by the purchase of a put option and the sale of a call option, each having the same exercise price and expiration date. Exhibit 20.19 summarizes both the initial and terminal cash flows to this position.

Panel B of the exhibit reveals that this is once again a risk-free portfolio. There are, however, two important differences in its cash flow patterns. First, the net initial investment of $(P_{0,T} - C_{0,T})$ is substantially smaller than when the stock was purchased in the spot market. Second, the riskless terminal payoff of $(X - F_{0,T})$ also is smaller than before as the stock now must be purchased at Date T rather than at Date 0. This intuition leads directly to the *put-call-forward* parity condition:

20.5
$$P_{0,T} - C_{0,T} = \frac{X - F_{0,T}}{(1 + RFR)^T} = \frac{X}{(1 + RFR)^T} - \frac{F_{0,T}}{(1 + RFR)^T}$$

which says that for markets to be free from arbitrage, the difference between put and call prices must equal the discounted difference between the common exercise price and the contract price

Exhibit 20.19 | **Put-Call-Forward Parity**

A. Net Portfolio Investment at Initiation (Date 0)

Portfolio	
Long 1 forward contract	0
Long 1 put option	$P_{0,T}$
Short 1 call option	$-C_{0,T}$
Net investment:	$P_{0,T} - C_{0,T}$

B. Portfolio Value at Option Expiration (Date T)

Portfolio	(1) If $S_T \leq X$:	(2) If $S_T > X$:
Long 1 forward contract	$(S_T - F_{0,T})$	$(S_T - F_{0,T})$
Long 1 put option	$(X - S_T)$	0
Short 1 call option	0	$-(S_T - X)$
Net position:	$(X - F_{0,T})$	$(X - F_{0,T})$

of the forward agreement. Just as $F_{0,T}$ did not appear in the spot market version of the parity condition, the current stock price does not appear in Equation 20.5.

This result implies that the only time that put and call prices should be equal to one another in an efficient market is when $X = F_{0,T}$. That is, although the put-call parity result holds for any common exercise price, there is only one value of X for which there would be no net cost to the option combination and that is the prevailing forward price. Recall, for example, that when WYZ stock did not pay a dividend, the theoretical difference between $C_{0,0.5}$ and $P_{0,0.5}$ was $4.49 (= 53 − 48.51). This meant that an investor long in the call and short in the put with a joint $50 exercise price would have what amounted to a forward contract to buy WYZ stock in six months at a price of $50.[7] However, she would have to pay $4.49 for this arrangement, suggesting that $50 is a below-market forward price. How much below the prevailing forward contract price is $50? By the future value of $4.49, invested at the prevailing risk-free rate of 6.25 percent. Thus, the no-arbitrage forward price under these circumstances should be $54.63 $[= 50 + 4.49 (1 + 0.0625)^{0.5}]$.

Another way to see this result comes from combining the put-call-forward parity condition with the put-call-spot condition. Specifically, inserting the expression for $(P_{0,T} - C_{0,T})$ from the put-call-forward parity condition into the put-call-spot condition leaves

$$S_0 + \left\{ \frac{X}{(1 + RFR)^T} - \frac{F_{0,T}}{(1 + RFR)^T} \right\} = \frac{X}{(1 + RFR)^T}$$

[7]This interpretation follows by noting that the long call position will be exercised when $S_T \leq 50$ and the short put will be exercised against the investor when $S_T \leq 50$. Therefore, the investor's net option position produces an identical result to holding a long position in a forward contract with a contract price of $50. Generalizing this result, any time we have a call and a put option on the same underlying stock with a common exercise price and expiration date, the following is true: (long call at X) + (short put at X) = (long forward at X). Similarly, shorting the call and buying the put produces a synthetic short forward position.

which simplifies to

$$S_0 = \frac{F_{0,T}}{(1 + RFR)^T}$$

This equation indicates that, in the absence of dividend payments, the spot price for the share of stock should simply be the discounted value of purchasing the same security in the forward market. Equivalently, this equation can be rewritten so that $F_{0,T} = S_0 (1 + RFR)^T$. In the preceding example, this means that the market-clearing (i.e., no net initial cost) contract price for a WYZ stock forward agreement should be $F_{0,0.5} = (53)(1 + 0.0625)^{0.5} = \$54.63$. Finally, in the case where dividends are paid, the equation for the put-call-forward parity condition can be inserted into the dividend-adjusted spot parity condition to produce the more general relationship between spot and forward prices:

$$\left\{ S_0 - \frac{D_T}{(1 + RFR)^T} \right\} = \frac{F_{0,T}}{(1 + RFR)^T}$$

Thus, if a \$1 dividend were paid on WYZ stock just prior to the maturity of the contract in six months, the forward price would be adjusted down to $F_{0,0.5} = (53)(1 + 0.0625)^{0.5} - 1 = \$53.63$ to account for the cash distribution that would benefit the actual shareholders but not the derivative holder.

AN INTRODUCTION TO THE USE OF DERIVATIVES IN PORTFOLIO MANAGEMENT

Beyond the unique risk-reward profiles they offer as stand-alone investments, derivatives also are used widely in investment management to restructure the fundamental nature of an existing portfolio of assets. Typically, the intent of this sort of restructuring is to modify the portfolio's risk. In this section, we review three prominent derivative applications in the management of equity positions: shorting forward contracts, purchasing **protective puts**, and purchasing **equity collars**.

Restructuring Asset Portfolios with Forward Contracts

Suppose the manager of a small corporate pension fund currently has all of her investable funds committed to a well-diversified portfolio of equity securities designed to reflect the movements of a broad indicator of the stock market's performance, such as Standard & Poor's 500 index. Implicit in this investment approach is the manager's belief that she cannot add value by trying to select superior individual securities. She does, however, feel that it is possible to take advantage of perceived trends at a macroeconomic level by switching her funds between her current equity holding and any of several other portfolios mimicking different asset classes (e.g., fixed-income, cash equivalents), depending on her forecast of future events. Switching a portfolio's composition in an attempt to time general market movements instead of company-specific trends is known as *tactical asset allocation.*

The stock market has increased steadily over the past several months, and the pension fund has a present market value of \$100 million. At this time, though, the manager has become concerned about the possibility that inflationary pressures will dampen corporate earnings and drive stock prices down. Although it is unclear now whether this concern will be realized, she feels confident that the uncertainty will be resolved in the coming quarter. Accordingly, she would like to shift her allocation from 100 percent equity to 100 percent T-bills for the next three months. There are two ways she can make this change. The most direct method would be to sell her stock portfolio and buy $100 million (less the transaction costs) of 90-day T-bills. When the T-bills mature in three months, she could then repurchase her original equity holdings.

The second approach would be to maintain her current stock holdings but convert them into a synthetic risk-free position with a three-month forward contract specifying $100 million of the stock index as the underlying asset. As we will see later, the primary benefit of this approach is that it is often more cost-effective and quicker to implement. This is a classic example of a *hedge position,* wherein the price risk of the underlying asset is offset (rather than eliminated) by a supplementary derivative transaction. The following table captures the dynamics of this hedge at a basic level.

Economic Event	Actual Stock Exposure	Desired Forward Exposure
Stock prices fall	Loss	Gain
Stock prices rise	Gain	Loss

To neutralize the risk of falling stock prices, the fund manager will need to adopt a forward position that benefits from that potential movement. Said differently, the manager requires a hedge position with payoffs that are *negatively correlated* with those of the existing exposure. As we saw in Exhibit 20.10, this requires committing to the short side of the contract. This hedging argument is identical to the point we made in the portfolio formation analysis of Chapter 7 that it is always possible to combine two perfectly negatively correlated assets to create a risk-free position.

The primary benefit of converting the pension fund's asset allocation using this approach is that it is far more cost-effective than the physical transformations demanded by the first solution. For instance, Exhibit 20.20 shows that when all of the costs of transaction are considered

Exhibit 20.20 | **Comparative Stock and Stock Futures Trading Costs**

Cost Factor	United States (S&P 500)	Japan (NIKKEI 225)	United Kingdom (FT-SE 100)	France (CAC 40)	Germany (DAX)	Hong Kong (Hang Seng)
A. Stocks						
Commissions	0.12%	0.20%	0.20%	0.25%	0.25%	0.50%
Market impact	0.30	0.70	0.70	0.50	0.50	0.50
Taxes	0.00	0.21	0.50	0.00	0.00	0.34
Total	0.42%	1.11%	1.40%	0.75%	0.75%	1.34%
B. Futures						
Commissions	0.01%	0.05%	0.02%	0.03%	0.02%	0.05%
Market impact	0.05	0.10	0.10	0.10	0.10	0.10
Taxes	0.00	0.00	0.00	0.00	0.00	0.00
Total	0.06%	0.15%	0.12%	0.13%	0.12%	0.15%

(e.g., trading commissions, market impact, taxes), the average expense of actually rebalancing a U.S. equity portfolio is about 42 basis points of the position's value, while the same trade with an equity forward contract would cost just 6 basis points. Trading expenses in other countries, though different in absolute level, reflect this same general trend.

This synthetic restructuring is best understood through the effect that it has had on the systematic risk—or beta—of the portfolio. By its original construction, we will assume that the original stock holding had a beta of one, matching the volatility of a proxy for the market portfolio. The combination of being long $100 million of stock and short a forward covering $100 million of a stock index converts the systematic portion of the portfolio into a synthetic T-bill, which by definition has a beta of zero. Once the contract matures in three months, however, the position will revert to its original risk profile. This is illustrated in Exhibit 20.21. More generally, the short forward position can be designed to allow for intermediate combinations of stock and T-bills as well. To see this, let w_s be the stock allocation so that $(1 - w_s)$ is the allocation to the risk-free asset created synthetically. The net beta for the converted portfolio is simply a weighted average of the systematic risks of its equity and T-bill portions or

20.6
$$\beta_P = (w_S)\,\beta_S + (1 - w_S)\,\beta_{RFR}$$

Thus, if the manager had wished to change the original allocation from 100 percent stock to a "60–40" mix of stock and T-bills, she would have shorted only $40 million of the index forward to leave her with an unhedged equity position totaling $60 million (i.e., $w_s = 0.60$ and $(1 - w_s) = 0.40$). By Equation 20.6, this in turn would leave her with an adjusted portfolio beta of $[(0.6)\,(1) + (0.4)\,(0)] = 0.6$.

Protecting Portfolio Value with Put Options

Although the manager's concern in the previous example was to protect her stock portfolio against possible share price declines over the next three months, by shorting the stock index

---

Exhibit 20.21 | **Altering the Systematic Risk of a Stock Portfolio Synthetically**

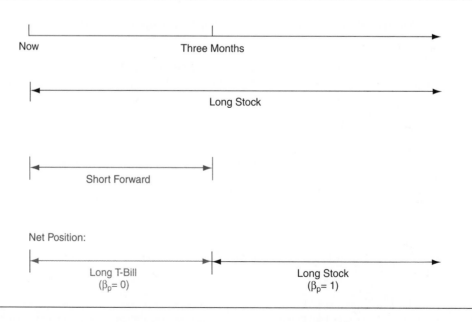

forward contract, she has effectively committed to "selling" her equity position—even if stock prices rise. That is, by using a derivative with a symmetric payoff structure to hedge her risk, the manager also has surrendered the upside potential of her original holding. Recognizing this, suppose instead that she attempted to design a hedge position correlated to her stock portfolio as shown in the following table.

Economic Event	Actual Stock Exposure	Desired Forward Exposure
Stock prices fall	Loss	Gain
Stock prices rise	Gain	*No loss*

In seeking an asymmetric hedge, this manager wants a derivative contract that allows her to sell stock when prices fall but keep her shares when prices rise. As we have seen, she must purchase a put option to obtain this exposure.

The purchase of a put option to hedge the downside risk of an underlying security holding is called a *protective put* position and is the most straightforward example of a more general set of derivative-based strategies known as *portfolio insurance*.[8] To see this insurance interpretation, suppose that in lieu of the short forward position, the manager purchased a three-month, at-the-money put option on her $100 million stock portfolio. Under the prevailing market conditions, let us also assume that this put cost the manager an up-front premium of $1.324 million. The value of the protective put position (net of the initial cost of the hedge) is calculated in Exhibit 20.22 for several different expiration date prices for the underlying stock portfolio. In particular, notice that with the exercise price set equal to the current portfolio value of $100 million, the put contract exactly offsets any expiration date share price decline while allowing the position to increase in value as stock prices

Exhibit 20.22 | **Expiration Date Value of a Protective Put Position**

Potential Portfolio Value	Value of Put Option	Cost of Put Option	Net Protective Put Position
60	(100 − 60) = 40	−1.324	(60 + 40) − 1.324 = 98.676
70	(100 − 70) = 30	−1.324	(70 + 30) − 1.324 = 98.676
80	(100 − 80) = 20	−1.324	(80 + 20) − 1.324 = 98.676
90	(100 − 90) = 10	−1.324	(90 + 10) − 1.324 = 98.676
100	0	−1.324	(100 + 0) − 1.324 = 98.676
110	0	−1.324	(110 + 0) − 1.324 = 108.676
120	0	−1.324	(120 + 0) − 1.324 = 118.676
130	0	−1.324	(130 + 0) − 1.324 = 128.676
140	0	−1.324	(140 + 0) − 1.324 = 138.676

[8]The concept and use of portfolio insurance has received a great deal of scrutiny in the research literature. See, for example, the studies by Rubinstein (1985), Kritzman (1986), and Bookstaber and Langsam (2000).

increase. Thus, the put provides the manager with insurance against falling prices with no *deductible.*[9]

An intriguing aspect of the terminal value of the combined stock and put option portfolio shown in the last column of Exhibit 20.22 is that it resembles the payoff diagram of the long call option position illustrated earlier in Exhibit 20.11. A different way of seeing this is shown in Exhibit 20.23, which indicates that being long in the stock and long in the put generates the same net payoff as an at-the-money long call option holding "elevated" by $100 million. Given the put-call-spot parity results of the previous section, however, this should come as no surprise. Indeed, the no-arbitrage equation (Equation 20.1) can be rewritten:

$$S_0 + P_{0,T} = C_{0,T} + \frac{X}{(1 + RFR)^T}$$

This expression says that the protective put method of providing portfolio insurance generates an equivalent expiration date payoff as a long position in a call option with the same characteristics as the put and a long position in a T-bill with a face value equal to the options' common exercise price. It is this final term that provides the elevation to the call payoff diagram in Exhibit 20.23. Thus, the manager has two ways of providing price insurance for her current stock holding: (1) continue to hold her shares and purchase a put option, or (2) sell her shares and buy both a T-bill and a call option. Her choice between them will undoubtedly come down to specific logistic considerations, such as relative option prices and transaction costs.[10]

Exhibit 20.23 | **Terminal Payoff to an Insured Stock Position**

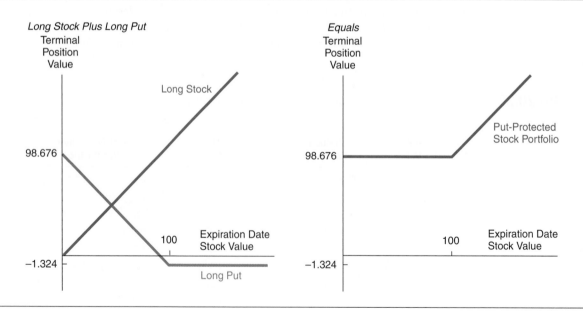

---

[9]In general, the deductible portion of the portfolio insurance contract can be defined as $[S_0 - X]$. For instance, with an exercise price of only 95, the manager would not receive compensation from the hedge until the portfolio value fell below $95 million; she would effectively be self-insuring the first $5 million of losses. Naturally, the larger this deductible amount, the lower the cost of the put option.

[10]Many authors have studied the effect that adding options to an underlying security position has on the risk of the combined portfolio. In particular, see Merton, Scholes, and Gladstein (1978); Bookstaber and Claske (1981); and Nederlof (1993).

An Alternative Way to Pay for a Protective Put

In the previous two examples, we saw how a pension manager could (1) use a short position in a forward contract to convert her $100 million stock portfolio to a risk-free position with no upfront expense, or (2) protect against adverse stock price movements while retaining the upside gain potential by purchasing a put option with an up-front expense of $1.324 million. There is also a third alternative, which fits between paying nothing for a hedge but surrendering future stock gains for the next three months (i.e., the short forward position) and keeping those potential gains in exchange for a considerable initial payment (i.e., the protective put position).

Specifically, suppose that the manager makes two simultaneous decisions that differ from those considered previously. First, she decides to purchase a three-month, out-of-the-money protective put option with an exercise price of $97 million and a commensurately lower initial cost of $0.560 million. (Notice that in purchasing an out-of-the-money contract, the manager is creating a $3 million deductible compared to her current portfolio value.) Second, she decides not to pay cash for the put option; instead, she sells back to the option dealer something worth an equivalent amount of money. In particular, suppose she sells back to the dealer a call option with a three-month expiration and an exercise price of $108 million that also carries an initial premium of $0.560 million. The simultaneous purchase of an out-of-the-money put and sale of an out-of-the-money call on the same underlying asset and with the same expiration date and market price is a strategy known as a **collar agreement**.

Exhibit 20.24 shows the expiration date outcomes of the manager's equity collar-protected portfolio for several different terminal stock portfolio values, while Exhibit 20.25 illustrates these outcomes graphically. There are two important things to notice from these displays. The first is that, like the forward contract hedge, there is no initial out-of-pocket expense associated with this derivative combination. Instead, the manager effectively pays for her desired portfolio insurance by surrendering an equivalent amount of the portfolio's future upside potential. That is, in exchange for being "made whole" for any stock decline below $97 million, she agrees to give up any stock price appreciation beyond $108 million. The second thing to notice is that, like the protective put in the last example (and unlike the

---

Exhibit 20.24 | **Expiration Date Value of an Equity Collar-Protected Portfolio**

Potential Portfolio Value	Net Option Expense	Value of Put Option	Value of Call Option	Net Collar-Protected Position
60	(0.56 − 0.56) = 0	(97 − 60) = 37	0	60 + 37 = 97
70	(0.56 − 0.56) = 0	(97 − 70) = 27	0	70 + 27 = 97
80	(0.56 − 0.56) = 0	(97 − 80) = 17	0	80 + 17 = 97
90	(0.56 − 0.56) = 0	(97 − 90) = 7	0	90 + 7 = 97
97	(0.56 − 0.56) = 0	0	0	97 + 0 = 97
100	(0.56 − 0.56) = 0	0	0	100 + 0 = 100
108	(0.56 − 0.56) = 0	0	0	108 − 0 = 108
110	(0.56 − 0.56) = 0	0	(108 − 110) = − 2	110 − 2 = 108
120	(0.56 − 0.56) = 0	0	(108 − 120) = −12	120 − 12 = 108
130	(0.56 − 0.56) = 0	0	(108 − 130) = −22	130 − 22 = 108
140	(0.56 − 0.56) = 0	0	(108 − 140) = −32	140 − 32 = 108

short forward position), she does retain some of the benefit of a rising stock market. As noted, however, this upside gain potential stops at the exercise price of the call option. As best indicated in Exhibit 20.25, the manager has placed a collar around her portfolio for the next three months—its net value will not fall below $97 million and will not rise above $108 million. At any terminal value for the stock portfolio between these extreme levels, both of the options expire out of the money and no contract settlement payment will be required of either the manager or the dealer.

Exhibit 20.25 | Terminal Payoff of a Collar-Protected Portfolio

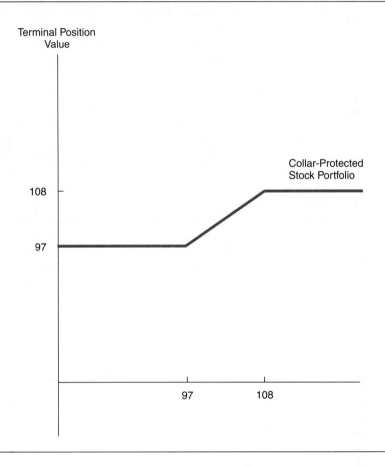

The Internet | Investments Online

A good way to learn more about the basics of futures and options is to visit some derivative-related Web sites. Interesting futures and options exchange sites include:

http://www.cboe.com The Web site of the Chicago Board Options Exchange. It presents an overview of the exchange and options on equities, indexes, and LEAPS and FLEX options. Market data, including quotes, are available. The site offers educational materials for beginners and discussions of investment strategies. By inputting some data, users can compute the theoretical value of an option using the site's options calculator.

http://www.cbot.com The home page of the Chicago Board of Trade, the world's largest futures exchange, includes an overview of the board, a dictionary of trading jargon, as well as price quotes and charts. The site offers government agriculture reports (many commodities are traded on the CBOT) with news about the weather (weather affects commodity yields).

http://www.cme.com The Chicago Mercantile Exchange's Web site features similar information as the other exchanges: news, price quotes, information on product, and educational resources. The Merc's site offers Web-based lessons on derivative strategies, and even offers an "Introduction to Hand Signals" used by floor traders.

http://www.onechicago.com Onechicago is a joint venture between the three Chicago-based options and futures exchanges: the CBOE, CBOT, and CME. It is designed for the trading of single-stock index futures, narrow-based indices and ETFs. Each narrow-based index typically includes three to nine companies in a specific sector.

http://www.euronext.com Euronext is a combined stock, bond, and derivatives exchange in Europe. The derivatives arm of the exchange (Euronext.Liffe, where Liffe stands for the London International Financial Futures and Options Exchange) can be reached by links on this hope page. Euronext.Liffe is Europe's premier derivatives exchange. The site's pages include information on money market, bond, equity, index, and commodity trading.

http://www.schaeffersresearch.com The Web site of options' guru Bernie Schaeffer. It advertises option-trading resources, but it also has several valuable (and free) educational resources. The site reviews option basics and option-trading strategies (from simple to complex). It offers users a daily options-market commentary, a market forecast, and free option quotes. This site is useful for those who want to get a flavor for how traders and investors use options.

http://www.eurexus.com The home page of the U.S. branch of Europe-based Eurex, an electronic derivatives trading market that offers 23-hour-a-day global trading of Treasury futures.

http://www.iseoptions.com The International Securities Exchange is an all-electronic options exchange. It facilitates trading in equity options and equity index options. The site offers pricing information, option calculators, education, and a description of its primary market maker and competitive market maker structure.

SUMMARY

- As their popularity in financial markets has increased over the past few decades, derivative securities have become an indispensable part of the investment manager's toolkit. Although forward, futures, and option contracts play important roles as stand-alone investments, the real advantage of derivatives is their ability to modify the risk–return characteristics of a collection of existing securities in a cost-effective manner. This use of forwards and options to restructure a portfolio synthetically has two dimensions. First, we saw that it is possible to combine derivatives with the underlying position in a way that replicates the cash flow patterns of another traded instrument. Second, derivatives can also be used with the original portfolio to create a payoff structure that is otherwise unavailable to the investor.

- At a fundamental level, forward and option contracts can be viewed as insurance policies that an investor can hold against adverse price movements in his underlying position. As forwards and options can be structured to provide exactly the same degree of "coverage," the basic difference between these contracts lies in how the investor must pay for the desired insurance. Forwards, with symmetrical terminal payoffs, typically do not require any initial payment but do obligate the investor to the possibility of an unfavorable transaction at a future date. Conversely, with options, which provide asymmetrical terminal payoffs, the investor must pay an up-front premium but then has no further obligation to his counterparty.

- Given these similarities, it is not surprising that there are well-defined relationships that must exist in an efficient capital market between the prices of forward and option contracts. In particular, the put-call parity conditions delineated the linkages between five different securities: the underlying asset (e.g., stock), T-bills, forward contracts, call options, and put options. An important consequence of these relationships is that one of these securities is always redundant because its cash flow patterns can be replicated by the remaining instruments. This realization leads to another important use for derivatives: arbitrage investing. Through their ability to help create synthetic replicas of existing securities, derivatives provide investors with the possibility of riskless excess returns when the synthetic and actual instruments sell for different prices.

- Although this chapter provides a broad overview of the dynamics of these important financial contracts, there are several issues related to the use and management of derivative securities that remain to be addressed. Chief among these are ways in which individual positions in forwards, futures, and options are valued and the adjustments that investors need to make when designing derivatives on an underlying asset other than common stock. These topics will be considered in subsequent chapters. For now, though, it is important to appreciate these instruments for their ability to assist investors in repackaging the risks and cash flows of their portfolios.

SUGGESTED READINGS

Brown, Keith C., ed. *Derivative Strategies for Managing Portfolio Risk.* Charlottesville, VA: AIMR, 1993.

Burns, Terrence E., ed. *Derivatives in Portfolio Management.* Charlottesville, VA: AIMR, 1998.

Chance, Don M. *An Introduction to Derivatives and Risk Management,* 6th ed. Mason, OH: Thomson South-Western, 2004.

Klemkosky, Robert C., and Bruce G. Resnick. "Put-Call Parity and Market Efficiency." *Journal of Finance* 34, no. 5 (December 1979).

Moriarty, Eugene, Susan Phillips, and Paula Tosini. "A Comparison of Options and Futures in the Management of Portfolio Risk." *Financial Analysts Journal* 37, no. 1 (January–February 1981).

QUESTIONS

1. Explain why the difference between put and call prices depends on whether or not the underlying security pays a dividend during the life of the contracts.

2. When comparing futures and forward contracts, it has been said that futures are more liquid but forwards are more flexible. Explain what this statement means and comment on how differences in contract liquidity and design flexibility might influence an investor's preference in choosing one instrument over the other.

3. Compare and contrast the gain and loss potential for investors holding the following positions: long forward, short forward, long call, short call, long put, and short put. Indicate what the terms *symmetric* and *asymmetric* mean in this context.

4. *CFA Examination Level III*

   The Franklin Medical Research Foundation is to be established with a gift from Mr. John Franklin in memory of his deceased wife. The foundation's grant-making and investment policy issues have been finalized. Receipt of the expected $45 million Franklin cash gift will not occur for 90 days, yet the committee believes current stock and bond prices are unusually attractive and wishes to take advantage of this perceived opportunity.

   a. Briefly describe two strategies that utilize derivative financial instruments and could be implemented to take advantage of the committee's market expectations.

   b. Evaluate whether or not it is appropriate for the foundation to undertake a derivatives-based hedge to bridge the expected 90-day time gap, considering both positive and negative factors.

5. *CFA Examination Level II*

Robert Chen, CFA, is reviewing the characteristics of derivative securities and their use in portfolios. Chen is considering the addition of either a short position in stock index futures or a long position in stock index options to an existing well-diversified portfolio of equity securities. Contrast the way in which each of these two alternatives would affect the risk and return of the resulting combined portfolios.

6. Explain how call and put options can represent a leveraged way of investing in the stock market and also enable investors to hedge their risk completely. Specifically, under what circumstances will the addition of an option increase the risk of an existing portfolio and under what circumstances will it decrease portfolio risk?

7. It has been said that, from an investor's perspective, a long position in a call option represents the "good half" of a long position in a forward contract. Explain what is meant by this statement. Also, describe what the "bad half" of the long forward position would have to be for this statement to be true.

8. Discuss the difficulties that having options in a security portfolio create for the measurement of portfolio risk. Specifically, explain why standard deviation is a deficient statistic for capturing the essence of risk in a put-protected portfolio. How could the standard deviation statistic be modified to account for this concern?

9. If the current price of a nondividend-paying stock is $32 and a one-year futures contract on that stock has a contract price of $35, explain how an investor could create an "off-market" long position in a forward contract at an exercise price of $25. Would this synthetic contract require a cash payment from either the long or short position? If so, explain which party would have to make the payment and how that payment should be calculated.

PROBLEMS

1. The common stock of Sophia Enterprises serves as the underlying asset for the following derivative securities: (1) forward contracts, (2) European-style call options, and (3) European-style put options.

   a. Assuming that all Sophia derivatives expire at the same date in the future, complete a table similar to the following for each of the following contract positions:

   (1) A long position in a forward with a contract price of $50

   (2) A long position in a call option with an exercise price of $50 and a front-end premium expense of $5.20

Expiration Date Sophia Stock Price	Expiration Date Derivative Payoff	Initial Derivative Premium	Net Profit
25	_____	_____	_____
30	_____	_____	_____
35	_____	_____	_____
40	_____	_____	_____
45	_____	_____	_____
50	_____	_____	_____
55	_____	_____	_____
60	_____	_____	_____
65	_____	_____	_____
70	_____	_____	_____
75	_____	_____	_____

(3) A short position in a call option with an exercise price of $50 and a front-end premium receipt of $5.20

In calculating net profit, ignore the time differential between the initial derivative expense or receipt and the terminal payoff.

b. Graph the net profit for each of the three derivative positions, using net profit on the vertical axis and Sophia's expiration date stock price on the horizontal axis. Label the breakeven (i.e., zero profit) point(s) on each graph.

c. Briefly describe the belief about the expiration date price of Sophia stock that an investor using each of these three positions implicitly holds.

2. Refer once again to the derivative securities using Sophia common stock as an underyling asset discussed in Problem 1.

    a. Assuming that all Sophia derivatives expire at the same date in the future, complete a table similar to the following for each of the following contract positions:

        (1) A short position in a forward with a contract price of $50

        (2) A long position in a put option with an exercise price of $50 and a front-end premium expense of $3.23

        (3) A short position in a put option with an exercise price of $50 and a front-end premium receipt of $3.23

Expiration Date Sophia Stock Price	Expiration Date Derivative Payoff	Initial Derivative Premium	Net Profit
25	_____	_____	_____
30	_____	_____	_____
35	_____	_____	_____
40	_____	_____	_____
45	_____	_____	_____
50	_____	_____	_____
55	_____	_____	_____
60	_____	_____	_____
65	_____	_____	_____
70	_____	_____	_____
75	_____	_____	_____

In calculating net profit, ignore the time differential between the initial derivative expense or receipt and the terminal payoff.

b. Graph the net profit for each of the three derivative positions, using net profit on the vertical axis and Sophia's expiration date stock price on the horizontal axis. Label the breakeven (i.e., zero profit) point(s) on each graph.

c. Briefly describe the belief about the expiration date price of Sophia stock that an investor using each of these three positions implicitly holds.

3. Suppose that an investor holds a share of Sophia common stock, currently valued at $50. She is concerned that over the next few months the value of her holding might decline and she would like to hedge that risk by supplementing her holding with one of three different derivative positions, all of which expire at the same point in the future:

    (1) A short position in a forward with a contract price of $50

    (2) A long position in a put option with an exercise price of $50 and a front-end premium expense of $3.23

    (3) A short position in a call option with an exercise price of $50 and a front-end premium receipt of $5.20

    a. Using a table similar to the following, calculate the expiration date value of the investor's com-

Expiration Date Sophia Stock Value	Expiration Date Derivative Payoff	Initial Derivative Premium	Combined Terminal Position Value
25	_____	_____	_____
30	_____	_____	_____
35	_____	_____	_____
40	_____	_____	_____
45	_____	_____	_____
50	_____	_____	_____
55	_____	_____	_____
60	_____	_____	_____
65	_____	_____	_____
70	_____	_____	_____
75	_____	_____	_____

bined (i.e., stock and derivative) position. In calculating net portfolio value, ignore the time differential between the initial derivative expense or receipt and the terminal payoff.

b. For each of the three hedge portfolios, graph the expiration date value of her combined position on the vertical axis, with potential expiration date share prices of Sophia stock on the horizontal axis.

c. Assuming that the options are priced fairly, use the concept of put-call parity to calculate the zero-value contract price (i.e., $F_{0,T}$) for a forward agreement on Sophia stock. Explain why this value differs from the $50 contract price used in Part a and Part b.

4. You strongly believe that the price of Breener Inc. stock will rise substantially from its current level of $137, and you are considering buying shares in the company. You currently have $13,700 to invest. As an alternative to purchasing the stock itself, you are also considering buying call options on Breener stock that expire in three months and have an exercise price of $140. These call options cost $10 each.

a. Compare and contrast the size of the potential payoff and the risk involved in each of these alternatives.

b. Calculate the three-month rate of return on both strategies assuming that at the option expiration date Breener's stock price has (1) increased to $155 or (2) decreased to $135.

c. At what stock price level will the person who sells you the Breener call option break even? Can you determine the maximum loss that the call option seller may suffer, assuming that he does not already own Breener stock?

5. The common stock of Company XYZ is currently trading at a price of $42. Both a put and a call option are available for XYZ stock, each having an exercise price of $40 and an expiration date in exactly six months. The current market prices for the put and call are $1.45 and $3.90, respectively. The risk-free holding period return for the next six months is 4 percent, which corresponds to an 8 percent annual rate.

a. For each possible stock price in the following sequence, calculate the expiration date payoffs (net of the initial purchase price) for the following positions: (1) buy one XYZ call option, and (2) short one XYZ call option:

20, 25, 30, 35, 40, 45, 50, 55, 60

Draw a graph of these payoff relationships, using net profit on the vertical axis and potential expiration date stock price on the horizontal axis. Be sure to specify the prices at which these respective positions will break even (i.e., produce a net profit of zero).

b. Using the same potential stock prices as in Part a, calculate the expiration date payoffs (net of the initial purchase price) for the following positions: (1) buy one XYZ put option, and (2) short one XYZ put option. Draw a graph of these payoff relationships, labeling the prices at which these investments will break even.

c. Determine whether the $2.45 difference in the market prices between the call and put options is consistent with the put-call parity relationship for European-style contracts.

6. Consider Commodity Z, which has both exchange-traded futures and option contracts associated with it. As you look in today's paper, you find the following put and call prices for options that expire exactly six months from now:

Exercise Price	Put Price	Call Price
40	$0.59	$8.73
45	1.93	—
50	—	2.47

a. Assuming that the futures price of a six-month contract on Commodity Z is $48, what must be the price of a put with an exercise price of $50 in order to avoid arbitrage across markets? Similarly, calculate the "no arbitrage" price of a call with an exercise price of $45. In both calculations, assume that the yield curve is flat and the annual risk-free rate is 6 percent.

b. What is the "no arbitrage" price differential that should exist between the put and call options having an exercise price of $40? Is this differential satisfied by current market prices? If not, demonstrate an arbitrage trade to take advantage of the mispricing.

7. *CFA Examination Level III*

Industrial Products Corp. (IPC), a publicly held company, is considering going private. It is extremely important to IPC's management that the pension fund's present surplus level be preserved pending completion of buyout financing. For the next three months (until September 1, 1990), management's goal is to sustain no loss of value in the pension fund portfolio. Today (June 1, 1990), this value is $300 million. Of this total, $150 million is invested in equities in the form of an S&P 500 Index fund, producing an annual dividend yield of 4 percent; the balance is invested in a single U.S. government bond issue, having a coupon of 8 percent and a maturity of 6/01/2005. Since the "no-loss strategy" has only a three-month time horizon, management does not wish to sell any of the present security holdings.

Assume that sufficient cash is available to satisfy margin requirements, transaction costs, and so on, and that the following market conditions exist as of June 1, 1990:

- The S&P 500 Index is at the 350 level, with a yield of 4.0 percent.
- The U.S. government 8.0 percent bonds due 6/1/2005 are selling at 100.
- U.S. Treasury bills due on 9/1/90 are priced to yield 1.5 percent for the three-month period (i.e., 6 percent annually).

Available investment instruments are the following:

Contract	Expiration	Current Contract Price	Strike Price	Contract Size
S&P 500 Index future	9/1/90	$355.00	—	$175,000
Future on U.S. government 8% bonds due 6/1/2005	9/1/90	101.00	—	100,000
S&P 500 call option	9/1/90	8.00	350	35,000
S&P 500 put option	9/1/90	7.00	350	35,000
U.S. government 8% due 6/1/2005 call option	9/1/90	2.50	100	100,000
U.S. government 8% due 6/1/2005 put option	9/1/90	4.50	100	100,000

a. Assume that the management wishes to protect the portfolio against any losses (ignoring the costs of purchasing options or futures contracts) but wishes also to participate in any stock or bond market advances over the next three months. Using the preceding instruments, design two strategies to accomplish this goal, and calculate the number of contracts needed to implement each strategy.

b. Using the put-call parity relationship and the fair value formula for futures (both follow), recommend which one of the two strategies designed in Part a should be implemented. Justify your choice.

Put Price   = Call Price Minus Security Price Plus Present Value of (Exercise Price Plus Income on the Underlying Security)

Futures Price = Underlying Security Price Plus (Treasury Bill Income Minus Income on the Underlying Security)

8. As an option trader, you are constantly looking for opportunities to make an arbitrage transaction (i.e., a trade in which you do not need to commit your own capital or take any risk but can still make a profit). Suppose you observe the following prices for options on DRKC Co. stock: $3.18 for a call with an exercise price of $60, and $3.38 for a put with an exercise price of $60. Both options expire in exactly six months, and the price of a six-month T-bill is $97.00 (for face value of $100).

a. Using the put-call-spot parity condition, demonstrate graphically how you could synthetically recreate the payoff structure of a share of DRKC stock in six months using a combination of puts, calls, and T-bills transacted today.

b. Given the current market prices for the two options and the T-bill, calculate the no-arbitrage price of a share of DRKC stock.

c. If the actual market price of DRKC stock is $60, demonstrate the arbitrage transaction you could create to take advantage of the discrepancy. Be specific as to the positions you would need to take in each security and the dollar amount of your profit.

9. You are currently managing a stock portfolio worth $55 million and you are concerned that, over the next four months, equity values will be flat and may even fall. Consequently, you are considering two different strategies for hedging against possible stock declines: (1) buying a protective put, and (2) selling a *covered call* (i.e., selling a call option based on the same underlying stock position you hold). An over-the-counter derivatives dealer has expressed interest in your business and has quoted the following bid and offer prices (in millions) for at-the-money call and put options that expire in four months and match the characteristics of your portfolio:

	Bid	Ask
Call	$2.553	$2.573
Put	1.297	1.317

a. For each of the following expiration date values for the unhedged equity position, calculate the terminal values for a protective put strategy.

35, 40, 45, 50, 55, 60, 65, 70, 75

b. Draw a graph of the protective put payoff structure in Part a and demonstrate how this position could have been constructed by using call options and T-bills, assuming a risk-free rate of 7 percent.

c. For each of these same expiration date stock values, calculate the terminal values for a covered call strategy.

d. Draw a graph of the covered call payoff structure in Part c and demonstrate how this position could have been constructed by using put options and T-bills, again assuming a risk-free rate of 7 percent.

10. *CFA Examination Level III*

A stock currently sells for $77.50. Call options on the stock have an exercise price of $75 and sell for $7.75, and put options have an exercise price of $75 and sell for $4. These options will expire in three months. The three-month U.S. Treasury bill annualized yield is 5 percent. There are no transaction costs and no restrictions against using the proceeds from the short sale of any security.

a. A synthetic Treasury bill can be constructed by investing in a combination of the securities identified.

  (1) Identify the three transactions needed to construct a synthetic Treasury bill.

  (2) Calculate the synthetic Treasury bill's annualized yield.

b. An arbitrage strategy can be constructed with 75 actual and 100 synthetic Treasury bills, producing a face amount of $750,000.

  (1) State the arbitrage strategy.

  (2) Calculate the immediate incoming net cash flow.

c. Determine the net cash flow of the arbitrage strategy at the six-month expiration date if the stock price at expiration is $80. (Ignore any cash flows stemming from the original arbitrage profit.)

Chapter 21

Forward and Futures Contracts

After you read this chapter, you should be able to answer the following questions:

- What are the differences in the way forward and futures contracts are structured and traded?
- How are the margin accounts on a futures contract adjusted for daily changes in market conditions?
- How can an investor use forward and futures contracts to hedge an existing risk exposure?
- What is a hedge ratio and how should it be calculated?
- What economic functions do the forward and futures markets serve?
- How are forward and futures contracts valued after origination?
- What is the relationship between futures contract prices and the current and expected spot price for the underlying commodity or security?
- How can an investor use forward and futures contracts to speculate on a particular view about changing market conditions?
- How do agricultural futures contracts differ from those based on financial instruments, such as stock indexes, bonds, and currencies?
- How can forward and futures contracts be designed to hedge interest rate risk?
- How are implied forward rates and actual forward rates related?
- What is stock index arbitrage and how is it related to program trading?
- How can forward and futures contracts be designed to hedge foreign exchange rate risk?
- What is interest rate parity and how would you construct a covered interest arbitrage transaction?

As we saw in Chapter 20, forward and futures contracts are the most straightforward form of *derivative instrument* because they allow an investor to lock in the purchase or sales price of a transaction that will not be completed until a later date. Having laid the foundation for why these contracts exist and how they are used, in this chapter we continue our discussion along several lines. First, we take a closer look at the contract terms and trading mechanics of forwards and futures. In particular, we examine the important differences that exist between the two markets and describe the process by which futures contracts are **marked to market** on a daily basis. Further, we discuss how these contracts are used to hedge the price risk inherent in an existing or anticipated position and how **hedge ratios** are computed.

Second, we consider how forward and futures contracts are priced in an efficient capital market. Given that these instruments are not really securities in the same sense that stocks and bonds are, the notion of traditional security valuation is not quite appropriate in this market. Instead, valuation involves specifying the proper relationship between the forward contract price and the spot price for the underlying position. In general, we develop the "no arbitrage" result that the forward contract price should be equal to the spot price plus the cumulative costs of transporting the underlying security or commodity from the present to the future delivery date. These carrying costs can be either positive or negative; therefore, the correct forward contract price can be either higher or lower than the spot price.

Finally, we demonstrate several applications and strategies in which an investor can use forward and futures contracts. This demonstration concentrates on a class of contracts—*financial forwards and futures*—that are particularly useful to investors. The underlying securities in financial futures include stock indexes, Treasury bonds, bank deposits, and foreign currencies. The use of these financial futures will be illustrated in a series of applications designed to demonstrate the connections between cash and futures markets.

AN OVERVIEW OF FORWARD AND FUTURES TRADING

Forward contracts are agreements negotiated directly between two parties in the OTC (i.e., nonexchange-traded) markets. A typical participant in a forward contract is a commercial or investment bank that, serving the role of the market maker, is contacted directly by the customer (although customers can form an agreement directly with one another). Forward contracts are individually designed agreements and can be tailored to the specific needs of the ultimate end user. Futures contracting, on the other hand, is somewhat more complicated. An investor wishing either to buy or to sell in the futures market gives his order to a broker (a *futures commission merchant*), who then passes it to a trader on the floor of an exchange (the *trading pit*). After a trade has been agreed on, details of the deal are passed to the **exchange clearinghouse**, which catalogs the transaction. The ultimate end users in a futures contract never deal with each other directly. Rather, they always transact with the clearinghouse, which is also responsible for overseeing the delivery process, settling daily gains and losses, and guaranteeing the overall transaction. Exhibit 21.1 highlights the differences in how these contracts are created.[1]

As an example, let us consider the traditional agricultural commodity futures that have been traded for more than 130 years beginning with the creation of the Chicago Board of Trade (CBT), the world's oldest and largest derivatives exchange. Futures contracts based on a wide array of commodities and securities have been created and now trade on almost 100 exchanges worldwide. Exhibit 21.2 lists the leading futures exchanges in the United States and the world, ranked by relative trading volume. Notice that two of the top three and three of the top seven exchanges in the world are located in the United States. Additionally, Exhibit 21.3 shows price and trade activity data for a representative sample of commodity futures contracts; financial futures will be described in detail later in the chapter. Each of these commodity contracts is standardized in terms of the amount and type of the commodity involved and the available dates on which it can be delivered. As we will see, this standardization can lead to an important source of risk that may not exist in forward contracts.

---

[1]For a more detailed discussion of the futures trading process, see Clarke (1992); some of this discussion is based on his book.

Exhibit 21.1	Forward and Futures Trading Mechanics

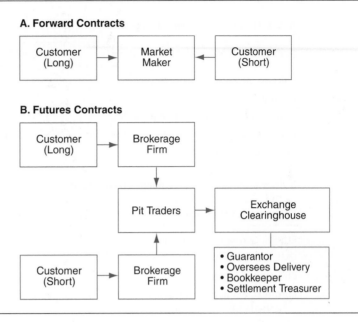

A. Forward Contracts

Customer (Long) → Market Maker ← Customer (Short)

B. Futures Contracts

Customer (Long) → Brokerage Firm

Pit Traders → Exchange Clearinghouse

Customer (Short) → Brokerage Firm

- Guarantor
- Oversees Delivery
- Bookkeeper
- Settlement Treasurer

Futures Contract Mechanics

To interpret the display in Exhibit 21.3, consider the gold futures contract traded on the Commodity Exchange (COMEX), a division of the New York Mercantile Exchange (NYM). Each contract calls for the long position to buy, and the short position to sell, 100 troy ounces of gold in the appointed months. With commodity futures, it usually is the case that delivery can take place any time during the month at the discretion of the short position. Contracts are available with settlement dates every other month for the next 16 months. An investor committing on this particular date to a long position in the June 2005 contract is obligated to buy 100 ounces of gold three months later for the contract price of $427.40 per ounce. The volume statistics show that almost 130,000 gold contracts changed hands on the last reported trading day. Open interest—the total number of outstanding contracts of any maturity—was 293,388, down 6,143 contracts from the previous day.[2]

Another important difference between forward and futures contracts is how the two types of agreements account for the possibility that a counterparty will fail to honor its obligation. Forward contracts may not require either counterparty to post collateral, in which case each is exposed to the potential default of the other during the entire life of the contract. In contrast, the futures exchange requires each customer to post an *initial* **margin account** in the form of cash or government securities when the contract is originated. (The futures exchange, as a well-capitalized corporation, does not post collateral to protect customers from its potential default.) This margin account is then adjusted, or marked to market, at the end of each trading

---

[2] New contracts are created when a new customer comes to the exchange at a time when no existing contract holder wishes to liquidate his position. On the other hand, if an existing customer wants to close out her short position and there is not a new customer to take her place, the contract price will be raised until an existing long position is enticed to sell back his agreement, thereby canceling the contract and reducing open interest by one.

| Exhibit 21.2 | Leading Futures Exchanges Ranked by Relative Trading Volume |

A. U.S. Futures Exchanges (2003 Data)

Exchange Name and Abbreviation	% of Trading Volume
Chicago Mercantile Exchange, CME	52.5%
Chicago Board of Trade, CBT	32.6%
New York Mercantile Exchange, NYM	12.7%
New York Board of Trade, NYBT	1.9%
Kansas City Board of Trade, KC	0.3%

B. International Futures Exchanges (2003 Data)

Exchange and Country	% of Trading Volume
EUREX, Germany & Switzerland	26.5%
CME, United States	22.0%
CBT, United States	13.7%
Euronext, Belgium, France, Netherlands, United Kingdom	10.9%
NYMEX, United States	5.3%
BM&F, Brazil	4.7%
Mexican Derivatives Exchange, Mexico	4.2%
Tokyo Commodity Exchange, Japan	3.7%
London Metal Exchange, United Kingdom	2.8%
Dalian Commodity Exchange, China	2.4%
Korea Stock Exchange, Korea	2.1%
Sydney Futures Exchange, Australia	1.7%

Source: Futures Industry Association. Reprinted with permission.

day according to that day's price movements. All outstanding contract positions are adjusted to the **settlement price**, which is set by the exchange after trading ends to reflect the midpoint of the closing price range.

The marked-to-market process effectively credits or debits each customer's margin account for daily trading gains or losses as if the customer had closed out her position, even though the contract remains open. For example, Exhibit 21.3 indicates that the settlement price of the June 2005 gold contract decreased by $0.50 per ounce from the previous trading day. This price increase benefits the holder of a short position by $50 (= 0.50 per ounce × 100 ounces). Specifically, if she had entered into the contract yesterday, she would have a commitment to sell gold for $427.90, which she could now buy for $427.40. Accordingly, her margin account will be increased by $50. Conversely, any party who is long June gold futures will have his margin account reduced by $50 per contract. To ensure that the exchange always has enough protection, collateral accounts are not allowed to fall below a predetermined *maintenance level*, typically about 75 percent of the initial level. If this $50 adjustment reduced the long position's account beneath the maintenance margin, he would receive a **margin call** and be required to restore the account to its full initial level or face involuntary liquidation.

Exhibit 21.3 | Commodity Futures Quotations

	OPEN	HIGH	LOW	SETTLE	CHG	LIFETIME HIGH	LIFETIME LOW	OPEN INT
Corn (CBT)-5,000 bu; cents per bu.								
May	210.75	210.75	209.25	210.50	−.25	344.00	201.75	298,767
July	218.50	218.75	217.00	218.50	−.25	342.00	209.00	161,782
Sept	225.00	225.00	223.75	224.75	−.75	299.00	216.75	35,913
Dec	234.50	234.50	232.75	233.75	−.50	288.50	226.00	137,037
Mr06	240.50	240.50	239.25	239.75	−.75	269.25	234.00	13,603
July	245.50	246.50	245.50	246.25	−.75	279.00	242.50	4,155
Dec	247.00	247.00	246.00	246.50	−.50	269.00	242.00	6,297
Est vol 64,495; vol Wed 122,302; open int 661,002, −15,577.								
Oats (CBT)-5,000 bu; cents per bu.								
May	157.00	159.00	157.00	158.25	1.25	184.00	145.50	5,530
July	152.00	152.25	151.50	151.50	.50	189.50	146.00	1,381
Dec	147.25	148.25	147.25	148.25	.50	166.00	144.75	207
Est vol 682; vol Wed 1,199; open int 7,205, +42.								
Soybeans (CBT)-5,000 bu; cents per bu.								
May	623.25	632.50	617.00	628.75	5.50	775.00	501.00	160,146
July	627.00	637.00	621.00	634.00	6.00	773.00	506.00	79,750
Aug	625.00	634.00	621.00	630.50	5.25	712.00	509.00	7,501
Sept	608.25	617.50	608.25	614.50	4.50	668.00	512.00	3,795
Nov	602.50	607.00	595.25	604.00	1.50	650.50	519.50	45,503
Ja06	600.50	607.00	600.50	606.00	2.50	651.00	526.00	3,171
Est vol 59,176; vol Wed 90,104; open int 302,497, −1,759.								
Wheat (CBT)-5,000 bu; cents per bu.								
May	336.50	340.50	333.25	338.50	1.75	430.00	295.00	140,473
July	345.75	348.50	341.75	347.00	1.25	400.00	302.25	57,223
Sept	350.00	354.00	349.00	353.00	2.50	380.00	308.25	4,968
Dec	358.50	362.00	355.50	360.50	1.75	406.00	315.00	24,798
Mr06	360.00	366.50	359.75	365.00	1.00	393.00	324.50	2,130
May	358.00	360.00	358.00	360.00	3.00	384.00	327.00	93
Est vol 18,387; vol Wed 45,334; open int 230,075, +2,820.								
Cotton (NYBOT)-50,000 lbs.; cents per lb.								
May	50.00	50.00	50.00	51.59	1.01	73.25	41.71	75,488
July	51.60	53.90	51.60	53.05	.96	72.00	42.60	25,708
Oct	53.90	55.30	53.90	54.95	.75	67.00	45.00	1,586
Dec	54.85	56.80	54.80	55.95	.78	68.50	46.25	11,082
Mr06	57.30	57.30	57.30	57.95	.80	69.00	48.30	2,002
July	59.60	59.60	59.60	59.50	.80	61.50	50.40	482
Est vol 9,674; vol Wed 10,265; open int 117,051, −718.								
Orange Juice (NYBOT)-15,000 lbs.; cents per lb.								
May	97.70	97.90	95.00	95.80	−.90	101.85	67.00	22,442
July	98.40	98.50	96.00	96.80	−.90	102.90	69.50	6,068
Sept	97.75	97.75	97.25	97.55	−.65	103.50	71.50	1,570
Nov	99.00	99.15	97.95	98.30	−.50	103.50	75.75	1,623
Est vol 2,639; vol Wed 2,266; open int 31,801, −150.								

	OPEN	HIGH	LOW	SETTLE	CHG	LIFETIME HIGH	LIFETIME LOW	OPEN INT
Copper-High (CMX)-25,000 lbs.; cents per lb.								
Mar	144.70	147.00	144.70	145.95	1.25	152.00	74.40	872
Apr	144.90	146.90	144.70	145.90	1.00	152.00	109.10	4,258
May	145.10	146.70	144.20	145.35	.90	152.10	104.20	69,178
June	145.50	146.70	144.50	144.95	.95	161.30	108.50	2,322
July	143.65	145.70	143.50	144.55	1.00	150.10	90.00	16,355
Aug	143.10	143.10	143.10	143.20	1.00	147.10	84.80	1,253
Sept	141.60	142.70	141.60	141.85	1.00	146.00	104.50	10,281
Oct	140.00	140.00	140.00	140.30	.95	142.50	106.50	1,004
Nov	138.20	138.20	138.20	138.80	.95	141.60	106.00	757
Dec	137.20	137.85	136.50	137.25	.90	141.30	99.00	7,848
Mr06	134.80	134.80	134.80	136.70	.90	136.70	98.00	510
Est vol 12,000; vol Wed 28,705; open int 115,347, −5,170.								
Gold (CMX)-100 troy oz.; $ per troy oz.								
Mar	425.60	426.50	424.30	424.70	−.50	436.00	411.90	0
Apr	425.60	426.50	424.30	424.80	−.60	460.50	380.00	117,559
June	428.50	429.10	426.80	427.40	−.50	490.00	302.00	114,242
Aug	430.00	431.30	429.60	430.00	−.50	461.10	379.00	10,049
Oct	433.60	434.40	433.10	432.90	−.50	465.80	401.50	5,243
Dec	435.70	437.50	435.50	435.80	−.50	471.00	298.40	20,391
Ja06	447.00	447.00	445.10	445.50	−.50	476.50	312.00	8,441
Ju07	468.00	468.00	468.00	466.80	−.50	471.20	367.00	2,790
Est vol 75,000; vol Wed 128,461; open int 293,388, −6,143.								
Platinum (NYM)-50 troy oz.; $ per troy oz.								
Apr	855.00	864.00	855.00	862.50	6.50	889.00	804.00	5,524
Est vol 3,293; vol Wed 2,896; open int 8,273, −438.								
Silver (CMX)-5,000 troy oz.; cents per troy oz.								
Mar	695.00	695.00	695.00	693.0	−4.4	828.00	485.00	539
May	697.5	702.0	691.5	693.8	−4.7	831.0	489.0	64,695
July	702.5	706.5	700.5	696.0	−4.7	836.0	436.0	10,838
Sept	700.0	706.0	700.0	702.7	−4.7	540.0	436.0	2,324
Dec	715.0	715.0	707.0	708.8	−4.7	831.0	436.0	14,637
Dc06	740.0	740.0	732.0	731.7	−4.7	840.0	469.0	4,874
Est vol 14,000; vol Wed 21,027; open int 102,837, −491.								
Crude Oil, Light Sweet (NYM)-1,000 bbls.; $ per bbl.								
May	54.12	54.90	53.41	54.84	1.03	58.16	23.75	260,009
June	54.90	55.75	54.30	55.65	.91	58.60	22.40	115,287
July	55.70	56.20	55.00	56.11	.79	58.80	23.60	50,428
Aug	56.10	56.30	55.35	56.35	.67	58.57	24.30	33,616
Sept	56.07	56.50	55.55	56.40	.54	58.50	24.00	29,295
Oct	56.04	56.22	55.66	56.32	.46	58.32	24.00	23,214
Nov	55.90	56.30	55.30	56.15	.39	58.10	26.00	17,785
Dec	55.55	56.13	55.55	55.75	.33	57.87	17.00	66,095
Ja06	55.55	55.55	55.10	55.75	.30	57.50	25.25	16,664
Feb	55.10	55.10	55.10	55.53	.27	57.20	25.85	8,648
Mr06	55.20	56.20	55.13	55.13	.21	56.65	27.10	7,715
Apr	54.33	54.80	54.33	54.79	.15	56.10	23.75	24,284
July	54.80	54.80	54.60	54.61	.12	55.75	30.05	4,087
Dec	53.55	53.92	53.30	53.58	−.03	54.90	19.10	46,718
Ju07	52.60	52.60	52.50	52.70	−.09	53.55	31.15	9,911
Dec	51.70	52.32	51.70	51.86	−.15	52.90	19.50	31,659
Dc08	50.40	51.00	50.40	50.49	−.27	51.35	19.75	26,185
Dc09	49.65	50.23	49.65	49.72	−.34	50.40	22.50	15,726
Dc10	49.80	49.80	49.15	49.22	−.34	50.00	27.15	15,690
Dc11	49.56	50.00	49.56	48.97	−.34	49.77	36.10	4,629
Est vol 204,372; vol Wed 333,982; open int 844,260, −1,587.								
Natural Gas (NYM)-10,000 MMBtu.; $ per MMBtu.								
Apr	7.160	7.180	6.970	7.062	−.076	7.750	3.400	28,754
May	7.285	7.298	7.070	7.184	−.071	7.520	3.500	79,174
June	7.390	7.394	7.210	7.292	−.068	7.580	3.530	29,204
July	7.475	7.476	7.280	7.379	−.061	7.650	3.560	34,567
Aug	7.530	7.530	7.340	7.436	−.053	7.680	3.230	24,968
Sept	7.530	7.556	7.400	7.451	−.051	7.700	3.570	23,989
Oct	7.556	7.560	7.415	7.480	−.051	7.720	3.540	42,513
Nov	7.896	7.896	7.760	7.819	−.054	8.055	3.790	15,236
Dec	8.226	8.226	8.070	8.147	−.053	8.365	3.960	27,872
Ja06	8.406	8.436	8.300	8.363	−.052	8.639	4.020	19,977
Feb	8.410	8.410	8.280	8.343	−.052	8.570	3.850	13,924
Mar	8.246	8.250	8.160	8.193	−.047	8.410	3.780	20,735
Apr	7.070	7.080	6.970	7.023	−.047	7.210	3.790	13,098
May	6.925	6.925	6.850	6.878	−.047	7.040	3.570	10,408
June	6.950	6.950	6.903	6.903	−.047	7.110	3.600	5,145
July	6.960	6.960	6.920	6.933	−.047	7.110	3.580	7,077
Aug	6.980	6.980	6.980	6.963	−.042	7.110	3.666	6,187
Sept	6.970	6.970	6.880	6.939	−.039	7.110	3.671	4,009
Oct	7.000	7.000	6.980	6.961	−.039	7.130	3.732	6,841
Dec	7.570	7.570	7.570	7.568	−.022	7.690	4.110	5,722
Mr07	7.560	7.560	7.560	7.583	−.007	7.610	4.760	4,478
June	6.370	6.380	6.370	6.446	−.007	6.480	4.000	894
Dec	7.000	7.000	7.000	7.054	.010	6.810	4.660	2,168
Est vol 88,719; vol Wed 69,006; open int 476,132, −1,476.								

Source: From *The Wall Street Journal*, March 25, 2005. Copyright 2005 by DOW JONES & CO INC. Reproduced with permission of DOW JONES & CO INC in the format Other Book via Copyright Clearance Center.

Comparing Forward and Futures Contracts

To summarize, the main trade-off between forward and futures contracts is *design flexibility* versus *credit and liquidity risks*, as highlighted by the following comparison.

	Futures	Forwards
Design flexibility:	Standardized	Can be customized
Credit risk:	Clearinghouse risk	Counterparty risk
Liquidity risk:	Depends on trading	Negotiated exit

These differences represent extremes; some forward contracts, particularly in foreign exchange, are quite standard and liquid while some futures contracts now allow for greater flexibility in the terms of the agreement. Also, forwards require less managerial oversight and intervention—especially on a daily basis—because of the lump-sum settlement at delivery (i.e., no margin accounts or marked-to-market settlement), a feature that is often important to unsophisticated or infrequent users of these products.

HEDGING WITH FORWARDS AND FUTURES

Hedging and the Basis

The goal of a *hedge* transaction is to create a position that, once added to an investor's portfolio, will offset the price risk of another, more fundamental holding. The word "offset" is used here rather than "eliminate" because the hedge transaction attempts to neutralize an exposure that remains on the balance sheet. In Chapter 20, we expressed this concept with the following chart, which assumes that the underlying exposure results from a long commodity position:

Economic Event	Actual Commodity Exposure	Desired Hedge Exposure
Commodity prices fall	Loss	Gain
Commodity prices rise	Gain	Loss

In this case, a short position in a forward contract based on the same commodity would provide the desired negative price correlation. By virtue of holding a short forward position against the long position in the commodity, the investor has entered into a **short hedge**. A **long hedge**, on the other hand, is created by supplementing a short commodity holding with a long forward position.

The basic premise behind either a short or a long hedge is that as the price of the underlying commodity changes, so too will the price of a forward contract based on that commodity. Further, the implicit hope of the hedger is that the spot and forward prices change in a predictable way relative to one another. For instance, the short hedger in the preceding example is hoping that if commodity prices fall and reduce the value of her underlying asset, the forward contract price also will fall by the same amount to create an offsetting gain on the derivative. Thus, a critical feature that affects the quality of a hedge transaction is the way in which the spot and forward prices change over time.

Defining the Basis   To understand better the relationship between spot and forward price movements, it is useful to develop the concept of the **basis**. At any Date t, the basis is the spot price minus the forward price for a contract maturing at Date T:

21.1
$$B_{t,T} = S_t - F_{t,T}$$

where:

S_t = the Date t spot price
$F_{t,T}$ = the Date t forward price for a contract maturing at Date T

Potentially, a different level of the basis may exist on each trading Date t. Two facts always are true, however. First, the *initial basis* at Date 0 ($B_{0,T}$) always will be known since both the current spot and forward contract prices can be observed. Second, the *maturity basis* at Date T ($B_{T,T}$) always is zero whenever the commodity underlying the forward contract matches the asset held exactly. For this to occur, the forward price must *converge* to the spot price as the contract expires ($F_{T,T} = S_T$).

Consider again the investor who hedged her long position in a commodity by agreeing to sell it at Date T through a short position in a forward contract. The value of the combined position is ($F_{0,T} - S_0$). If the investor decides to liquidate her entire position (including the hedge) prior to maturity, she will not be able to deliver the commodity to satisfy her forward obligation as originally intended. Instead, the investor will have to (1) sell her commodity position on the open market for S_t, and (2) buy back her short forward position for the new contract price of $F_{t,T}$.[3] The profit from the short hedge liquidated at Date t is

21.2
$$B_{t,T} - B_{0,T} = (S_t - F_{t,T}) - (S_0 - F_{0,T})$$

The term $B_{t,T}$ often is called the *cover basis* because that is when the forward contract is closed out, or covered.

Understanding Basis Risk

Equation 21.2 highlights an important fact about hedging. Once the hedge position is formed, the investor no longer is exposed to the absolute price movement of the underlying asset alone. Instead, she is exposed to **basis risk** because the terminal value of her combined position is defined as the cover basis minus the initial basis. Notice, however, that only the cover basis is unknown at Date 0, and so her real exposure is to the **correlation** between future changes in the spot and forward contract prices. If these movements are highly correlated, the basis risk will be quite small. In fact, it is usually possible to design a forward contract based on a specific underlying asset and deliverable on exactly the desired future date. This sort of customized design reduces basis risk to zero, since $F_{T,T} = S_T$. Conversely, basis risk is a possibility when contract terms are standardized and is most likely to occur in the futures market where standardization is the norm.

To illustrate the concept of basis risk, suppose the investor wishes in March to hedge a long position of 100,000 pounds of cotton she is planning to sell in June. Exhibit 21.3 shows that cotton futures contracts do exist, but with delivery months in either May or July. With each contract requiring the delivery of 50,000 pounds of cotton, she decides to short two of the July contracts, specifically intending to liquidate her position a month early. Suppose that on the date she initiates her short hedge, the spot cotton price was $0.4834 per pound and the July

---

[3]The mechanics of liquidating a forward or futures contract prior to maturity are described in the next section.

futures contract price was \$0.5305 per pound. This means that her initial basis was −4.71 cents, which she hopes will move toward zero in a smooth and predictable manner. Suppose, in fact, that when she closes out her combined position in June, cotton prices have declined so that $S_t = \$0.4660$ and $F_{t,T} = \$0.4753$, leaving a cover basis of −0.93 cent. This means the basis has increased in value, or *strengthened,* which is to the short hedger's advantage. The net June selling price for her cotton is \$0.5212 per pound, which is equal to the spot price of \$0.4660 plus the net futures profit of $\$0.0552 = (0.5305 - 0.4753)$. Notice that this is lower than the original futures price but considerably higher than the June spot price. Thus, the short hedger has benefited by exchanging pure price risk for basis risk.

Although it is difficult to generalize, substantial indirect evidence exists that minimizing basis risk is the primary goal of most hedgers. For example, Brown and Smith (1995a) noted that the phenomenal growth of OTC products to manage interest rate risk—despite the existence of exchange-traded contracts—is a response to the desire to create customized solutions. Further, a survey by Jesswein, Kwok, and Folks (1995) showed that corporate risk managers preferred to hedge their firms' foreign exchange exposure with forward contracts rather than with futures by a ratio of about five to one.

Calculating the Optimal Hedge Ratio

In the preceding example, the decision to short two cotton futures contracts was a simple one because the investor held exactly twice as much of the same commodity as was covered by a single contract. In most cases, calculating the appropriate hedge ratio, or the number of futures contracts per unit of the spot asset, is not that straightforward. The approach suggested by both Johnson (1960) and Stein (1961) is to choose the number of contracts that minimizes the variance of net profit from a hedged commodity position. The determination of the required number of contracts can be established as follows.

Consider the position of a short hedger who is long one unit of a particular commodity and short N forward contracts on that commodity. Rewriting Equation 21.2 for the profit from a short hedge and allowing for a variable number of contracts, the net profit (Π_t) of this position at Date t can be written

$$\Pi_t = (S_t - S_0) - (F_{t,T} - F_{0,T})\,(N) = (\Delta S) - (\Delta F)(N)$$

The variance of this value is then given as

$$\sigma_\Pi^2 = \sigma_{\Delta S}^2 + (N^2)\sigma_{\Delta F}^2 - 2(N)\mathrm{COV}_{\Delta S,\Delta F}$$

where:

COV = the covariance of changes in the spot and forward prices

Minimizing this expression and solving for N leaves

21.3
$$N^* = \frac{\mathrm{COV}_{\Delta S,\Delta F}}{\sigma_{\Delta F}^2} = \left(\frac{\sigma_{\Delta S}}{\sigma_{\Delta F}}\right)\rho$$

where:

ρ = the correlation coefficient between the spot and forward price changes[4]

---

[4] Given data for spot and forward prices, σ_Π^2 in the variance equation is a function of just one variable, N. Thus differentiating this equation with respect to N leaves $[d\sigma_\Pi^2/dN] = 2(N)\sigma_{\Delta F}^2 - 2\mathrm{COV}_{\Delta S,\Delta F}$, which can be set equal to zero and solved for N^*. It is easily confirmed that the second derivative of this function is positive and so N^* is a minimizing value.

The optimal hedge ratio (N^*) can be interpreted as the ratio of the spot and forward price standard deviations multiplied by the correlation coefficient between the two series. Recalling from Chapter 1 that standard deviation is a measure of a position's *total* risk, this means that the optimal number of contracts is determined by the ratio of total volatilities deflated by ρ to account for the *systematic* relationship between the spot and forward prices. (It is, in fact, directly comparable to the beta coefficient of a common stock.) An important implication of this is that the best contract to use in hedging an underlying spot position is the one that has the highest value of ρ. What if, for instance, a clothing manufacturer wanted to hedge the eventual purchase of a large quantity of wool, a commodity for which no exchange-traded futures contract exists? The expression for N^* suggests that it may be possible to form an effective **cross hedge** if prices for a contract based on a related commodity (e.g., cotton) are highly correlated with wool prices. In fact, the expected basis risk of such a cross hedge can be measured as $(1 - \rho^2)$. Finally, note that the value for N^* also can be calculated as the slope coefficient of a regression using ΔS and ΔF as the dependent and independent variables, respectively.[5] In the regression context, ρ^2 is called the coefficient of determination or, more commonly, R^2. Some examples of these calculations are presented in subsequent sections.

FORWARD AND FUTURES CONTRACTS: BASIC VALUATION CONCEPTS

Forward and futures contracts are not securities but, rather, *trade agreements* that enable both buyers and sellers of an underlying commodity or security to lock in the eventual price of their transaction. As such, they typically require no front-end payment from either the long or short position to motivate the other's participation and, consequently, the contract's initial market value usually is zero. Once the terms of the agreement are set, however, any change in market conditions will likely increase the value of the contract to one of the participants. For example, an obligation made in November to purchase soybeans in March for $6.20 per bushel is surely quite valuable in January if soybean prices in the spot market are already $6.50 and no additional harvest is anticipated in the next two months. A description of the valuation of these agreements, which is different for futures and forward contracts, follows.

Valuing Forwards and Futures

Suppose that at Date 0 you had contracted in the forward market to buy Q ounces of gold at Date T for $F_{0,T}$. At Date t, prior to the maturity Date T, you decide that this long position is no longer necessary for your portfolio and you want to get rid of the future price risk it entails. Accordingly, you want to **unwind** your original obligation. One way to do this is to take a short position in a Date t forward contract designed to offset the terms of the first. That is, at Date t you would agree to sell Q ounces of gold at Date T for the price of $F_{t,T}$. This is shown in Panel A of Exhibit 21.4. Notice that because you now have contracts to buy and sell Q ounces of gold, you have no exposure to gold price movements between Dates t and T. The profit or loss on this pair of forward contracts is $(Q)[F_{t,T} - F_{0,T}]$, or the difference between the selling and purchase prices multiplied by the quantity involved. However, this amount would not be received (if $F_{t,T} > F_{0,T}$) or paid until Date T, meaning that the value of the original long forward

---

[5]Some have questioned whether regression-based hedge ratios are stable enough to be useful in practice. Recent researchers, however, have concluded that they are stationary; see Ferguson and Leistikow (1998).

Exhibit 21.4 | **Unwind Values for Forward and Futures Contracts**

Date 0	Date t	Date T
(Origination)	(Unwind)	(Maturity)

A. Forward Contract

- Long Forward ($F_{0,T}$)   • Short Forward ($F_{t,T}$)
  - Contract Unwind Value: $V_{t,T} = (Q) [F_{t,T} - F_{0,T}] \div (1 + i)^{(T - t)}$

B. Futures Contract

- Long Futures ($F^*_{0,T}$)   • Short Futures ($F^*_{t,T}$)
  - Contract Unwind Value: $V^*_{t,T} = (Q) [F^*_{t,T} - F^*_{0,T}]$

---

position when it is sold on Date t (i.e., its unwind value) would be the *present value* of (Q) $[F_{t,T} - F_{0,T}]$, or

21.4
$$V_{t,T} = (Q) [F_{t,T} - F_{0,T}] \div (1 + i)^{(T-t)}$$

where:

i = the appropriate annualized discount rate

Equation 21.4 expresses the Date t value of a long forward contract maturing at Date t. Notice two things about this amount. First, $V_{t,T}$ can be either positive or negative depending on whether $F_{t,T}$ is greater or less than the original contract price, $F_{0,T}$. This means that any forward contract carries the potential for symmetric payoffs to both participants. Second, the value of the short side of the same contract is just $(Q) [F_{0,T} - F_{t,T}] \div (1 + i)^{(T - t)}$, reinforcing the fact that forward contracts are *zero-sum games* since whatever the long position gains, the short position loses, and vice versa. For example, if you had originally agreed to a long position in a six-month gold forward at $F_{0, 0.5} = \$400$, and after three months the new forward contract price is $F_{0.25, 0.5} = \$415$, the value of your position would be $\$1,464.68$ [$= (100) (415 - 400) \div (1.1)^{0.25}$], assuming a 10 percent discount rate. Conversely, the value of the original short position would then have to be $-\$1,464.68$. Finally, notice that as Date t approaches Date T, the value of the contract simply becomes $(Q)(F_{T,T} - F_{0,T})$.

Valuing a futures contract is conceptually similar to valuing a forward contract with one important difference. As we saw earlier, futures contracts are marked to market on a daily basis, and this settlement amount was not discounted to account for the temporal difference between Dates t and T. That is, the Date t value of the futures contract is simply the undiscounted difference between the futures prices at the origination and unwind (or cover) dates, multiplied by the contract quantity, as shown in Panel B of Exhibit 21.4. Thus, the forward contract valuation equation can be adapted for futures as

21.5
$$V^*_{t,T} = (Q)(F^*_{t,T} - F^*_{0,T})$$

where:

$*$ = the possibility that forward and futures prices for the same commodity at the same point in time might be different

Cox, Ingersoll, and Ross (1981) showed that $F^*_{0,T}$ and $F_{0,T}$ would be equal if short-term interest rates (i in Equation 21.4) are known but need not be the same under other circumstances.

Typically, for commodities and securities that support both forward and futures markets, differences between $F^*_{0,T}$ and $F_{0,T}$ exist but are relatively small. For instance, Cornell and Reinganum (1981) established few economically meaningful differences between forward and futures prices in the foreign exchange market, while Park and Chen (1985) found that certain agricultural and precious metal futures prices were significantly higher than the analogous forward prices. More recently, Grinblatt and Jegadeesh (1996) documented that the historical differences in prices for Eurodollar forward and futures contracts are due to a mispricing of the latter, although this mispricing has been eliminated over time. Finally, note once again that $V^*_{t,T}$ can be either positive or negative depending on how contract prices have changed since inception.

The Relationship between Spot and Forward Prices

In many respects, the relationship between the spot and forward prices at any moment in time is a more challenging question than how the contract is valued. We can understand the intuition for this relationship with an example: You have agreed at Date 0 to deliver 5,000 bushels of corn to your counterparty at Date T. What is a fair price ($F_{0,T}$) to charge? Recognizing that the contract price can be anything that two parties agree to, one way to look at this question is to consider how much it will cost you to fulfill your obligation. If you wait until Date T to purchase the corn on the spot market, you have a *speculative* position, since your purchase price (S_T) will be unknown when you commit to a selling price.

Alternatively, suppose you buy the corn now for the current cash price of S_0 per bushel and store it until you have to deliver it at Date T. Under this scheme, the forward contract price you would be willing to commit to would have to be high enough to cover (1) the present cost of the corn and (2) the cost of storing the corn until contract maturity. In general, these storage costs, denoted here as $SC_{0,T}$, can involve several things, including commissions paid for the physical warehousing of the commodity ($PC_{0,T}$) and the cost of financing the initial purchase of the underlying asset ($i_{0,T}$) but less any cash flows received ($D_{0,T}$) by owning the asset between Dates 0 and T. Thus, in the absence of arbitrage opportunities, the forward contract price should be equal to the current spot price plus the **cost of carry** necessary to transport the asset to the future delivery date:

21.6
$$F_{0,T} = S_0 + SC_{0,T} = S_0 + (PC_{0,T} + i_{0,T} - D_{0,T})$$

Notice that even if the funds needed to purchase the commodity at Date 0 are not borrowed, $i_{0,T}$ accounts for the opportunity cost of committing one's own financial capital to the transaction.

This cost of carry model is useful in practice because it applies in a wide variety of cases. For some commodities, such as corn or cattle, physical storage is possible but the costs are enormous. Also, neither of these assets pays periodic cash flows in the traditional sense of the term. In such situations, it is quite likely that $F_{0,T} > S_0$ and the market is said to be in **contango**. On the other hand, common stock is costless to store but often pays a dividend. The presence of this cash flow sometimes makes it possible for the basis to be positive (i.e., $F_{0,T} < S_0$), meaning that $SC_{0,T}$ can be negative. There is another reason why $SC_{0,T}$ might be less than zero. For certain storable commodities that do not pay a dividend, $F_{0,T} < S_0$ can occur when there is effectively a premium placed on currently owning the commodity. This premium, called a **convenience yield**, results from a small supply of the commodity at Date 0 relative to what is expected at Date T after, say, a crop harvest. (Oats are a commodity that sometimes satisfies this condition, as indicated in Exhibit 21.3.) Although it is extremely difficult to quantify, the convenience yield can be viewed as a potential negative storage cost component that works in a manner similar to $D_{0,T}$. A futures market in which $F_{0,T} < S_0$ is said to be **backwardated**.

An immediate implication of Equation 22.6 is that there should be a direct relationship between contemporaneous forward and spot prices; indeed, this positive correlation is the objective of any well-designed hedging strategy. A related question involves the relationship between $F_{0,T}$ and the spot price expected to prevail at the time the contract matures (i.e., $E(S_T)$). There are three possibilities. First, the *pure expectations* hypothesis holds that, on average, $F_{0,T} = E(S_T)$, so that futures prices serve as unbiased forecasts of future spot prices. When this is true, futures prices serve an important *price discovery* function for participants in the applicable market. Conversely, $F_{0,T}$ could be less than $E(S_T)$, a situation that Keynes (1930) and Hicks (1939) argued would arise whenever short hedgers outnumber long hedgers. In that case, a risk premium in the form of a lower contract price would be necessary to attract a sufficient number of long speculators. For reasons that are not entirely clear, this situation is termed *normal backwardation*. Finally, a *normal contango* market occurs when the opposite is true, specifically, when $F_{0,T} > E(S_T)$.

The existence of a risk premium in the futures market is hotly debated. Kamara (1984) surveyed the early literature on the subject and found the evidence from the commodity markets to be mixed. He concluded that although the normal backwardation hypothesis was supported, futures markets are mainly driven by risk-averse hedgers who have been able to acquire "cheap" insurance. Krehbiel and Collier (1996) examined the price behavior in the Eurodollar and Treasury bill futures markets and found evidence consistent with the existence of risk premia that were necessary to balance net hedging and net speculative positions. Finally, Brooks (1997) documented that the risk premia priced into Eurodollar futures contracts have a substantial impact on other financial securities as well. Specifically, he showed that prices for interest rate swaps—which can be viewed as portfolios of Eurodollar contracts—are biased upward, causing borrowers who use swaps to convert their variable-rate loans into synthetic fixed-rate debt to make higher payments, on average, than if they had not hedged.

FINANCIAL FORWARDS AND FUTURES: APPLICATIONS AND STRATEGIES

Originally, forward and futures markets were organized largely around trading agricultural commodities, such as corn and wheat. Although markets for these products remain strong, the most significant recent developments in this area have involved the use of financial securities as the asset underlying the contract. In fact, Exhibit 21.5 shows that the top three most heavily traded derivative contracts in the United States are based on financial securities. In this section, we take a detailed look at three different types of financial forwards and futures: interest rate, equity index, and foreign exchange.

Interest Rate Forwards and Futures

Interest rate forwards and futures were among the first derivatives to specify a financial security as the underlying asset. The earliest versions of these contracts were designed to lock in the forward price of a particular fixed-coupon bond, which in turn locks in its yield. As we will see in Chapter 23, this market has progressed to where such contracts as *forward rate agreements* and *interest rate swaps* now fix the desired interest rate directly without reference to any specific underlying security. To understand the nuances of the most popular exchange-traded instruments, it is useful to separate them according to whether they involve long- or short-term rates.

Exhibit 21.5 | **Leading U.S. Derivative Contract Categories Ranked by Trading Volume**

Underlying Asset of Contract	2003 Volume (mil)	2002 Volume (mil)
Individual equities	791.64	679.70
Interest rate	678.30	579.21
Equity indexes	420.55	327.72
Energy products	112.40	115.93
Agricultural commodities	107.86	97.70
Foreign currency	36.10	26.07
Precious metals	21.76	14.91
Nonprecious metals	3.25	2.92
Other	0.66	0.73

Source: Futures Industry Association. Reprinted with permission.

Exhibit 21.6 | **Treasury Bond and Note Futures Quotations**

Treasury Bonds (CBT)-$100,000; pts 32nds of 100%

June	110-03	110-14	109-31	110-05	7	116-21	100-00	660,369
Sept	109-23	110-00	109-23	109-23	7	116-11	108-15	29,769

Est vol 171,183; vol Wed 412,716; open int 742,730, +1,967.

Treasury Notes (CBT)-$100,000; pts 32nds of 100%

June	08-145	08-205	08-115	08-145	3.0	112-16	07-265	1,987,361
Sept	08-065	108-08	08-035	08-035	3.5	112-14	07-185	41,605

Est vol 530,546; vol Wed 1,343,262; open int 2,147,245, +28,558.

5 Yr. Treasury Notes (CBT)-$100,000; pts 32nds of 100%

June	106-18	106-22	106-16	06-175	1.0	110-06	106-04	1,232,864
Sept	06-045	06-045	06-005	106-01	1.0	108-20	105-26	96,541

Est vol 301,998; vol Wed 663,512; open int 1,344,282, +21,327.

2 Yr. Treasury Notes (CBT)-$200,000; pts 32nds of 100%

Mar	03-232	03-232	03-232	03-227	-.2	05-022	103-21	20,738
June	103-10	103-11	03-082	103-09	-.5	04-087	03-052	309,329

Est vol 41,717; vol Wed 90,411; open int 330,067, +543.

Source: From *The Wall Street Journal*, March 25, 2005. Copyright 2005 by DOW JONES & CO INC. Reproduced with permission of DOW JONES & CO INC in the format Other Book via Copyright Clearance Center.

Long-Term Interest Rate Futures

Treasury Bond and Note Contract Mechanics   The U.S. Treasury bond and note contracts at the Chicago Board of Trade (CBT) are among the most popular of all the financial futures contracts. A smaller T-bond contract—one-half the delivery amount—is also available at the CBT. Delivery dates for both note and bond futures fall in March, June, September, and December. Exhibit 21.6 shows a representative set of quotes for these contracts.

Both the T-bond and the longer-term T-note contracts traded at the CBT call for the delivery of $100,000 face value of the respective instruments. For the T-bond contract, any Treasury bond that has at least 15 years to the nearest call date or to maturity (if noncallable) can be used for delivery. Bonds with maturities ranging from 6.5 to 10 years and 4.25 to 5.25 years can be used to satisfy the 10-year and 5-year T-note contracts, respectively. Delivery can take place on any day during the month of maturity, with the last trading day of the contract falling seven business days prior to the end of the month.

Mechanically, the quotation process for T-bond and T-note contracts work the same way. For example, the settlement price of 110–05, for the June 2005 T-bond contract on the CBT represents $110\frac{5}{32}$ percent of the face amount, or $110,156.25. The contract price went up by 7 ticks from the previous day's settlement, meaning that the long side had its margin account increased by $\frac{7}{32}$ percent of $100,000—or $218.75—where each $\frac{1}{32}$ movement in the bond's price equals $31.25 (i.e., $1,000 \div 32$).

Although T-bond and T-note futures contracts are called interest rate futures, what the long and short positions actually agree to is the price of the underlying bond. Once that price is set, however, the yield will be locked in. When a yield is quoted, it is for reference only and typically assumes a coupon rate of 6 percent and 20 years to maturity. For the June 2005 bond contract, the settlement yield would be 5.1786 percent, which can be established by solving for the internal rate of return in the following bond math problem

$$\$1,101.5625 = \sum_{t=1}^{40} \frac{\$30}{(1 + i/2)^t} + \frac{\$1,000}{(1 + i/2)^{40}}$$

This pricing formula takes into account the fact that Treasury bonds pay semiannual interest. So, a 20-year, 6 percent bond makes 40 coupon payments of 3 percent each. Thus, the long position in this contract has effectively agreed in March to buy a 20-year T-bond in June priced to yield 5.18 percent. If, in June, the actual yield on the 20-year bond is below 5.18 percent (i.e., the bond's price is greater than $110,156.25), the long position will have made a wise decision. Thus, the long position in this contract gains as prices rise and rates decrease and loses as increasing rates lead to lower bond prices.

Because the bond and note futures contracts allow so many different instruments to qualify for delivery, the seller would naturally choose to deliver the least expensive bond if no adjustments were made for varying coupon rates and maturity dates. To account for this, the CBT uses **conversion factors** to correct for the differences in the deliverable bonds. The conversion factor is based on the price of a given bond if its yield is 6 percent at the time of delivery and the face value is $1. For example, the March 2005 conversion factor for the 8 percent T-bond maturing in November 2021 would be 1.2077, calculated as

$$1.2077 = \sum_{t=1}^{33} \frac{0.04}{(1 + 0.03)^t} + \frac{1}{(1 + 0.03)^{33}}$$

The actual delivery price, or invoice price, for that Treasury bond would be the quoted futures price, $110,156.25, times the conversion factor, 1.2077, for a total of $133,035.70 (plus accrued interest). The buyer must pay more than 110,156.25 because the seller is delivering more valuable bonds, since their coupon rate exceeds 6 percent.

The conversion factors used by the CBT are technically correct only when the Treasury yield curve is flat at 6 percent. Therefore, there usually will be a *cheapest to deliver* bond that maximizes the difference between the invoice price (the amount received by the short) and the cash market price (the amount paid by the short to acquire the delivery bond). Market participants always know which bond is the cheapest to deliver. Therefore, the T-bond futures contract trades as if this particular security were the actual underlying delivery bond. In fact, the cheapest to deliver security usually is the T-bond with the longest duration when yields are above 6 percent, and the one with the shortest duration for yields less than 6 percent.

A Duration-Based Approach to Hedging In Chapter 18, we stressed that the main benefit of calculating the duration statistic was its ability to link interest rate changes to bond price changes by the formula

$$\left(\frac{\Delta P}{P}\right) \approx -D\left(\frac{\Delta(1+i/n)}{(1+i/n)}\right)$$

We also saw that a more convenient way to write this expression is:

$$\left(\frac{\Delta P}{P}\right) \approx -\left(\frac{D}{(1+i/n)}\right)\Delta(1+i/n) = -D_{\text{mod}}\Delta(i/n)$$

where:

D_{mod} = the bond's modified duration, combining the Macaulay duration and its periodic yield into a single measure

Earlier in this chapter, we noted that the objective of hedging was to select a hedge ratio (N) such that $\Delta S - \Delta F(N) = 0$, where S is the current spot price of the underlying asset and F is the current futures contract price. Rewriting this leaves

$$N^* = \frac{\Delta S}{\Delta F}$$

Using the modified duration relationship, this optimal hedge ratio can now be expanded as follows:

$$N^* = \frac{\Delta S}{\Delta F} = \frac{\left(\frac{\Delta S}{S}\right)}{\left(\frac{\Delta F}{F}\right)} \times \frac{S}{F} = \frac{-D_{\text{mod}\,S} \times \Delta(i_S/n)}{-D_{\text{mod}\,F} \times \Delta(i_F/n)} \times \frac{S}{F}$$

or

21.7
$$N^* = \frac{D_{\text{mod}\,S}}{D_{\text{mod}\,F}} \times \beta_i \times \frac{S}{F}$$

where:

β_i = the "yield beta"

The yield beta is also called the ratio of changes in the yields applicable to the two instruments where n is the number of payment periods per year (e.g., $n = 2$ for semiannual coupon bonds).

As a general example of the duration-based approach to setting hedge ratios, consider the following fixed-income securities, each making annual payments (i.e., $n = 1$):

Instrument	Coupon	Maturity	Yield
A	8%	10 years	10%
B	10%	15 years	8%

How much of Instrument B is necessary to hedge A? This question can be answered in three steps. First, using the method shown in Chapter 18 (and summarized in Appendix 21A), the duration statistics for each position are:

$$D_A = 7.0439 \text{ so } D_{modA} = (7.0439) \div (1.10) = 6.4036 \text{ years}$$
$$D_B = 8.8569 \text{ so } D_{modB} = (8.8569) \div (1.08) = 8.2009 \text{ years}$$

Second, we will assume that yield beta is unity (i.e., $\beta_i = 1$). In general, this is calculated by observing historical yield curve movements across the 10- and 15-year maturities. Finally, current prices are easily confirmed to be 87.71 for Security A and 17.12 for Security B assuming par value of 100. Thus, the duration-based hedge ratio is

$$N^* = \left(\frac{6.4036}{8.2009}\right)(1)\left(\frac{87.71}{117.12}\right) = 0.5847$$

or 0.5847 unit of B short for every one unit of A held long.

Treasury Futures Applications

Hedging a Future Funding Commitment   In late July, the treasurer of a U.S.-based company begins to arrange the details of an anticipated 15-year, $100 million funding. He feels that the company will be ready to launch its new debt issue in mid- to late September but is concerned that, between July and September, interest rates may rise, thereby increasing the company's funding cost. Consequently, he decides to hedge this exposure in the T-bond futures market. In this case, he will need to take a *short* position in the futures market, which will appreciate in value if interest rates increase, thereby offsetting the higher payments that will be required on the underlying debt.

The treasurer feels that if the bond issue was placed today, the credit standing of the firm would lead to a funding cost of 8.25 percent for the 15-year period. He knows that a September T-bond futures contract is trading at a price of 83–16 to yield 7.62 percent. He is also aware that bond yields beyond 10 years to maturity tend to move in a parallel fashion to one another so he is comfortable that a yield beta of one is appropriate. Further, the treasurer is aware that T-bond futures cannot hedge for changes in the firm's risk premium over the risk-free rate; he will have to live with this source of basis risk.

If he plans to launch his new issue at par value, how many T-bond futures contracts would he need to short today? Assuming semiannual coupons for both the Treasury and corporate issues, their durations can be calculated using the closed-form equation shown in Appendix 21A:

$$D_{corp} = \frac{1.04125}{0.04125} - \frac{1.04125 + [30(0.04125 - 0.04125)]}{0.04125[(1.04125)^{30} - 1] + 0.04125} = 17.74 \text{ periods}$$

and

$$D_{trsy} = \frac{1.0381}{0.0381} - \frac{1.0381 + [40(0.03 - 0.0381)]}{0.03[(1.0381)^{40} - 1] + 0.0381} = 22.22 \text{ periods}$$

These statistics are denominated in half years so that the hedge ratio will be expressed in the same terms used to price the bonds. With these statistics, we can calculate the modified durations as follows: $D_{modC} = 17.04 \ (= 17.74 \div 1.04125)$ and $D_{modT} = 21.40 \ (= 22.22 \div$

1.0381). Finally, since each T-bond futures contract is standardized to a denomination of $100,000, the treasurer can calculate the optimal number of contracts to short as

$$(\text{Number of Contracts}) = \frac{(17.04)}{(21.40)} \times (1.0) \times \frac{(\$100,000,000)}{(\$83,500)} = 953.6, \text{ or } 954 \text{ Contracts}$$

A T-Bond/T-Note (NOB) Futures Spread   Frequently, speculators in the bond market will have a clear view on a change in the overall shape of the yield curve but be less certain as to the actual direction in future rate movements. Suppose, for instance, you think the yield curve—which is currently upward sloping across all maturities—will flatten, but you're not sure in which of several ways this might occur:

* Short-term rates rise and long-term rates fall.
* Short- and long-term rates both rise, but short-term rates rise by more.
* Short- and long-term rates both fall, but short-term rates fall by less.

Clearly, taking a long or short position in a single futures contract linked to a single point on the yield curve is too risky, given your view; you could be right about the shape shift but guess wrong about direction. One way to mitigate this unwanted risk while investing (based on your view) is to go both long and short in contracts representing different points on the yield curve. This is known as the Treasury "Notes over Bond" **spread** (or "NOB" spread) strategy.

Suppose in mid-February you observe the following price quotes (along with their implied yields to maturity) for T-bond and T-note futures contracts maturing in June:

Contract	Settle Price	Implied Yield
20-yr, 6% T-bond	103–02	5.74%
10-yr, 6% T-note	104–02	5.47%

Notice that your expectation of a flattening yield curve is identical to the view that the 27 basis point yield gap (= 0.0574 − 0.0547) between the longer- and shorter-term contracts will shrink. If you also feel this will occur by mid-June, the appropriate strategy would be:

* Go long in one Treasury bond futures.
* Go short in one Treasury note futures.

The net profit from this joint position when you close out the two contracts is calculated as the sum of the profits on the short T-note position and the long T-bond contract, or

$$\left[\frac{104.0625 - \text{June T-Note Price}}{100} + \frac{\text{June T-Bond Price} - 103.0625}{100} \right](\$100,000)$$

To see how this combined position would pay off if your view is correct, consider two scenarios in which the yield curve flattens to where there is no difference between 10- and 20-year rates by the time you close your positions in June:

1. *Rates increase to 6.00 percent by June.*
   In this case, both futures contracts will sell at par and so your net profit will be

$$\text{Net Profit} = [0.040625 - 0.030625](\$100,000) = \$1,000$$

Notice that this same calculation can be done on a "price tick" basis:

$$\text{Net Profit} = \{[(104\text{--}02) - (103\text{--}02)] - [(100\text{--}00) - (100\text{--}00)]\}(\$31.25)$$
$$= (32 \text{ Ticks})(\$31.25) = \$1,000$$

which is equivalent to the change in the number of ticks in the NOB spread multiplied by the dollar value of a tick (i.e., $31.25).

2. *Rates decrease to 5.00 percent by June.*
   Except when both bonds trade at par, it is generally not the case that two bonds with different maturities—but the same coupon and same yield—will trade at the same price. In this scenario, the settlement prices on the two futures contracts will be

$$P_{\text{T-note}} = \sum_{t=1}^{20} \frac{\$3}{(1 + 0.025)^t} + \frac{\$100}{(1 + 0.025)^{20}} = \$107.79 \approx 107\text{--}25$$

and

$$P_{\text{T-bond}} = \sum_{t=1}^{40} \frac{\$3}{(1 + 0.025)^t} + \frac{\$100}{(1 + 0.025)^{40}} = \$112.55 \approx 112\text{--}18$$

so that net profit from the NOB spread will be

$$\text{Net Profit} = \{[(104\text{--}02) - (103\text{--}02)] - [(107\text{--}25) - (112\text{--}18)]\} (\$31.25)$$
$$= (32+153) (\$31.25) = \$5,781.25$$

Interpreting this outcome differently, you made $9,500.00 on your long position in the T-bond contract ($= [(112\text{--}18) - (103\text{--}02)](31.25)$), but you lost $3,718.75 on your short T-note position ($= [(104\text{--}02) - (107\text{--}25)](31.25)$) for a net gain of $5,781.25.

These results show that the futures spread allows speculators to separate their views on yield curve shape from an explicit forecast of a change in the curve's position. When using this strategy, however, the investor must be careful to recognize that, because the duration of the T-bond is greater than that of the T-note, the former will be more sensitive to a given rate change.

Short-Term Interest Rate Futures

Short-term interest rate futures have become the most rapidly expanding segment of the exchange-traded market. Currently, investors can hedge their exposures to several different money market rates (e.g., T-bill, LIBOR, Banker's Acceptance, Federal Funds) denominated in a multitude of currencies (e.g., U.S. dollar, Japanese yen, Euro). In the following analysis, we concentrate on one of these contracts: Eurodollar futures.

Eurodollar Contract Mechanics The Eurodollar contract traded at the International Monetary Market (IMM) on the Chicago Mercantile Exchange (CME, or "Merc") has become enormously successful since it was launched in the early 1980s. Delivery dates occur monthly for a brief period before following the March, June, September, December cycle (the so-called IMM dates) and now extend 10 years into the future. The final trading and settlement date is the second London business day before the third Wednesday of the delivery month. A representative set of quotes is shown in Exhibit 21.7. Also traded on the London International Financial Futures and

Exhibt 21.7 | **Eurodollar (LIBOR) Futures Quotations**

Eurodollar (CME)-$1,000,000; pts of 100%

Apr	96.78	96.78	96.77	96.78	...	3.22	...	54,673
May	96.62	96.62	96.61	96.61	...	3.39	...	13,471
June	96.45	96.47	96.45	96.46	...	3.54	...	1,501,793
Sept	95.98	96.00	95.97	95.97	...	4.03	...	1,429,148
Dec	95.69	95.72	95.68	95.68	-.01	4.32	.01	1,168,141
Mr06	95.53	95.55	95.52	95.52	...	4.48	...	835,386
June	95.41	95.44	95.39	95.40	...	4.60	...	608,254
Sept	95.31	95.34	95.29	95.30	-.01	4.70	.01	449,259
Dec	95.23	95.26	95.22	95.23	...	4.77	...	396,062
Mr07	95.19	95.23	95.18	95.19	...	4.81	...	257,667
June	95.15	95.18	95.13	95.15	.01	4.85	-.01	208,239
Sept	95.10	95.13	95.08	95.10	.01	4.90	-.01	158,584
Dec	95.04	95.09	95.03	95.05	.01	4.95	-.01	139,453
Mr08	95.03	95.04	95.01	95.01	.01	4.99	-.01	128,616
June	94.99	95.01	94.98	94.97	.02	5.03	-.02	119,628
Sept	94.93	94.97	94.93	94.93	.02	5.07	-.02	110,039
Dec	94.90	94.91	94.88	94.87	.02	5.13	-.02	96,064
Mr09	94.86	94.88	94.84	94.84	.02	5.16	-.02	84,157
June	94.83	94.84	94.79	94.80	.02	5.20	-.02	75,979
Sept	94.79	94.79	94.74	94.75	.02	5.25	-.02	63,257
Dec	94.73	94.74	94.70	94.70	.02	5.30	-.02	44,151
Mr10	94.70	94.71	94.67	94.67	.02	5.33	-.02	19,978
June	94.65	94.68	94.64	94.64	.02	5.36	-.02	12,631
Sept	94.61	94.63	94.60	94.60	.03	5.40	-.03	9,805
Dec	94.56	94.58	94.55	94.55	.03	5.45	-.03	9,312
Mr11	94.51	94.55	94.51	94.52	.03	5.48	-.03	8,239
June	94.49	94.52	94.49	94.48	.03	5.52	-.03	5,149
Sept	94.45	94.48	94.44	94.44	.03	5.56	-.03	2,790
Dec	94.40	94.43	94.40	94.39	.03	5.61	-.03	2,178
Mr12	94.38	94.41	94.37	94.37	.03	5.63	-.03	1,142
June	94.34	94.35	94.33	94.33	.03	5.67	-.03	782

Est vol 981,928; vol Wed 2,703,080; open int 8,021,014, −52,712.

Options Exchange (LIFFE) on the Euronext system (although not shown here) are similar contracts for hedging Euro-IBOR (i.e., the Euro currency), Eurosterling, Euroyen, and Euroswiss rates.

Hypothetically, the Eurodollar contract requires the long position to make a $1,000,000, 90-day bank deposit with the short position at the maturity date. Unlike the Treasury bond and note futures just described, however, this contract requires all outstanding obligations to be settled in cash. This provision is necessary because the contract nominally requires the long position to make, and the short position to receive, a 90-day Euro-time deposit. However, that is something that the short position can't legally do unless it is a financial institution chartered for such business. The underlying interest rate is the 3-month (i.e., 90-day) LIBOR that is quoted on a 360-day bank add-on basis. As we will see, arbitrage trading should drive the sequence of Eurodollar (or LIBOR) futures rates to equal the forward rates implied by the yield curve for interbank lending in the cash market. That is, in an efficient market, the futures rates should be close to the comparable implied forward rates.

In Exhibit 21.7, the quoted contract price for the September 2006 contract is 95.30, which is not an actual purchase price but merely an index calculated as 100 minus the settlement yield of 4.70 (percent). Eurodollar futures use this settlement price index because it conveniently preserves the inverse relation between price and yield. Thus, a long position in this contract can still be thought to "win" when prices rise—and the short position wins with falling prices—even though it is the opposite movement in the underlying interest rate that matters.

The minimum price change, or "tick," for this contract is one basis point and equals a $25 change in the value of the contract. Therefore, the *basis point value* of the contract is

$25 (= \$1,000,000 \times 0.0001 \times 90/360)$. Thus, the one-tick (-0.01) decline in the price of the September 2006 contract means that LIBOR increased by one basis point from the prior day's settlement. This would benefit a person who acquired a short position at the close of the prior day, inasmuch as he would have a locked-in borrowing cost for the 90-day period from September to December 2006 that is now one basis point lower than the market level. In fact, all sellers of this contract gained $25 per contract (i.e., $25 per tick times one tick) in their margin accounts.

Finally, notice that Eurodollar open interest is spread over the various delivery dates to a greater extent than for the T-bond contract (shown in Exhibit 21.6). In fact, the Eurodollar contract is the deepest financial futures contract available with, as noted, maturities going out 10 years. This makes it possible to hedge a LIBOR-based exposure a decade into the future. Brown and Smith (1988) interpreted these trading patterns as suggesting that T-bond futures are used in the market more as a speculative trading contract and that Eurodollar futures are used more frequently as a buy-and-hold hedging instrument.

Short-Term Interest Rate Future Applications

Creating a Synthetic Fixed-Rate Funding with a Eurodollar Strip   Suppose that on March 15 a senior loan officer for a large regional bank is considering an investment scheme for lending $2,000,000 in temporary cash balances to a large-cap manufacturing firm. The plan would last for one year and have the payment rate reset on a quarterly basis at LIBOR. At the planning stage, the LIBOR yield curve appears as follows:

90-day LIBOR	5.00%
180-day LIBOR	5.10
270-day LIBOR	5.20
360-day LIBOR	5.30

Given the debt market convention that the funding rates on floating-rate deal structures always are determined in advance and paid in arrears, she knows that her loan receipt for the first three months would be based on the prevailing 5.00 percent rate and be receivable in 90 days. Her concern is what her receipts might be in the subsequent three quarters, and, specifically, she is worried that they may fall to an unacceptable level. Accordingly, she considers using the Eurodollar futures market to hedge her exposure.

As a prelude to checking futures contract price quotes, she calculates the forward rates implied by the current yield curve. Using the money-market implied forward rate formula shown in Appendix 21B, these computations generate:

$$_{180}IFR_{90} = \left[\frac{(0.051)(180) - (0.050)(90)}{(180 - 90)} \right] \left[\frac{1}{1 + \left(\frac{(90)(0.050)}{360} \right)} \right] = 5.14\%$$

$$_{270}IFR_{180} = \left[\frac{(0.052)(270) - (0.051)(180)}{(270 - 180)} \right] \left[\frac{1}{1 + \left(\frac{(180)(0.051)}{360} \right)} \right] = 5.27\%$$

$$_{360}IFR_{270} = \left[\frac{(0.053)(360) - (0.052)(270)}{(360 - 270)} \right] \left[\frac{1}{1 + \left(\frac{(270)(0.052)}{360} \right)} \right] = 5.39\%$$

She checks with her trading desk for quotes on the relevant Eurodollar futures contracts and receives the following information:

Contract Expiration	Settlement Price
June	94.86
September	94.73
December	94.61

The futures settlement prices indicate LIBOR contract rates that are identical to the implied forward rates, suggesting there is no arbitrage potential between the cash and futures markets on this date.

To lock in her receipts for the $2,000,000 loan, the banker would go long a *strip* of Eurodollar futures contracts. That is, she takes long positions in two June contracts, two September contracts, and two December contracts. (Recall that the long position in a Eurodollar contract gains when the price index rises with a falling LIBOR; this is the protection she is seeking.) With these positions, her quarterly interest receipts will be fixed at the following levels:

$$\text{June Receipt} = (\$2,000,000)\left[\frac{(0.0500)(90)}{360}\right] = \$25,000$$

$$\text{September Receipt} = (\$2,000,000)\left[\frac{(0.0514)(90)}{360}\right] = \$25,700$$

$$\text{December Receipt} = (\$2,000,000)\left[\frac{(0.0527)(90)}{360}\right] = \$26,350$$

$$\text{March (Next Year) Receipt} = (\$2,000,000)\left[\frac{(0.0539)(90)}{360}\right] = \$26,950$$

Although these cash inflows are fixed in advance, they clearly differ in amount from quarter to quarter. To get a better indication of her overall return, the banker asks herself the following question: What quarterly annuity payment does this sequence of receipts imply? This amount can be calculated as the solution to:

$$\frac{\$25,000}{\left[1 + \frac{(0.050)(90)}{360}\right]} + \frac{\$25,700}{\left[1 + \frac{(0.051)(180)}{360}\right]} + \frac{\$26,350}{\left[1 + \frac{(0.052)(270)}{360}\right]} + \frac{\$26,950}{\left[1 + \frac{(0.053)(360)}{360}\right]}$$

$$= \frac{\text{Annuity}}{\left[1 + \frac{(0.050)(90)}{360}\right]} + \frac{\text{Annuity}}{\left[1 + \frac{(0.051)(180)}{360}\right]} + \frac{\text{Annuity}}{\left[1 + \frac{(0.052)(270)}{360}\right]} + \frac{\text{Annuity}}{\left[1 + \frac{(0.053)(360)}{360}\right]}$$

Solving this formula for annuity gives a value of $25,989.38, where the discount rates are from the prevailing cash market LIBOR curve. Finally, notice that this annuity payment, when expressed on a full 360-day percentage basis, is

$$\left[\frac{\$25,989.38}{\$2,000,000}\right]\left[\frac{360}{90}\right] = 5.198\%$$

which is a time-weighted average of the 90-day spot LIBOR and the series of three implied forward rates.

Creating a TED Spread One of the features that makes the Eurodollar futures contract such a popular hedging vehicle is the rate it is based on—three-month LIBOR. This rate can be thought of as equivalent to the three-month T-bill yield *plus* a risk premium (i.e., credit spread). Sometimes, bond traders will have a view on future movements in this credit spread; for example, a trader might believe the current difference between the LIBOR and T-bill yield is too narrow and that it will soon widen. The problem with trying to play this view with a short position in the Eurodollar contract alone, however, is even if the trader is right about the spread, the general level of interest rates could still decline by more than enough to offset any spread gains.

The solution to this dilemma is to isolate the credit spread component in LIBOR through a strategy known as the *TED* (Treasury/EuroDollar) *spread.* The TED spread is created by taking simultaneous, but opposite, positions in both a Eurodollar and T-bill futures contract having the same maturity. In the parlance of the market, we have the following definitions.

Long TED Spread = (Long T-Bill Futures) + (Short Eurodollar Futures)
Short TED Spread = (Short T-Bill Futures) + (Long Eurodollar Futures)

Notice that a long position in a TED spread will gain when the credit spread increases; the short TED spread benefits from a narrowing of the credit spread. Exhibit 21.8 shows how volatile the three-month TED spread has been over time.

Exhibit 21.8	**TED Spread for Three-Month Contracts**

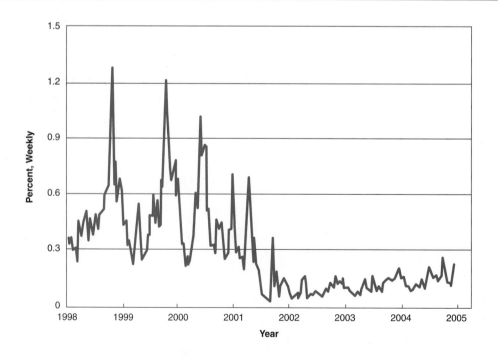

Source: Federal Reserve Bank of Cleveland. *Economic Trends*, July 2005, p. 8.

To see how an investor can profit from this volatility, consider the following example. Suppose that in early August you observe the following prices in the Eurodollar and T-bill futures markets:

	T-Bill	Eurodollar	Spread
September contracts	95.24	94.80	44 BP
December contracts	94.68	94.11	57 BP
March contracts	94.42	93.86	56 BP

Recall that the difference between the T-bill and Eurodollar price indexes is the spread built into the Eurodollar contract for a particular maturity.

If you believe the economy will remain sluggish for an extended period of time and that credit spreads currently are too narrow in the short-term contract, you would want to take a long TED spread position (i.e., short the Eurodollar futures and buy the T-bill contract). After you establish this position using the September contracts, the Federal Reserve Board tightens rates again so that by mid-September the following prices prevail when you unwind the strategy:

New September T-bill contract	94.55
New September Eurodollar contract	93.95
New spread	0.60

This new spread is more closely aligned with the December and March contracts. The profit on your transaction is calculated as

$$(\text{New TED Spread}) - (\text{Original TED Spread})$$

or

$$(\$94.55 - 93.95) - (\$95.24 - 94.80) = 16 \text{ Basis Points}$$

With each contract standardized so that a basis point is worth \$25, the profit per contract pair from this trade would be $(16 \times \$25) = \$400$. Another way to see this profit is that you made an 85-basis-point profit on the short position in the Eurodollar contract $(= \$94.80 - 93.95)$ but lost 69 basis points on the long T-bill contract $(=\$94.55 - 95.24)$. However, if both rates had declined, you still would have made money if the T-bill yield had fallen by more than LIBOR.

Stock Index Futures

Another important form of financial futures contracting specifies an equity index as the underlying asset. In this section, we consider the basics of stock index futures trading and discuss two applications for these instruments, including a popular form of computer-assisted trading known as stock index arbitrage.

Stock Index Futures Contract Fundamentals   Like interest rate futures, stock index futures were originally intended to provide a hedge against movements in an underlying financial asset. We have just seen that some interest rate futures can be settled with either a cash or physical transfer. As detailed in Chapter 5 and the introductory example in Chapter 20, however, the underlying financial asset for a stock index futures contract is a hypothetical creation that does not exist in practice and therefore cannot be delivered to settle a contract. Thus, stock index futures can only be settled in cash, similar to the Eurodollar (i.e., LIBOR) contract.

Stock index futures are intended to provide general hedges against stock market movements and can be applied to either whole (i.e., diversified) portfolios or individual stocks. Hedging an individual stock with an index futures contract is done in an attempt to isolate the unsystematic portion of that security's risk. Additionally, stock index futures often are used to convert entire stock portfolios into synthetic riskless positions to exploit an apparent mispricing between stock in the cash and futures markets. This strategy, commonly called **stock index arbitrage**, is the most prominent example of a wider class of computer-assisted trading schemes known as *program trading*.

Exhibit 21.9 lists quotes for futures contracts on several U.S. and foreign stock indexes, including the Dow Jones Industrial Average, the Standard and Poor's 500, the Standard and Poor's Midcap 400, the Russell 2000, the Nikkei 225 (Japan), the CAC 40 (France), the DAX 30 (Germany), and the FT-SE 100 (England). For instance, an investor planning in March to buy stock in June can hedge against his eventual purchase price increasing due to rising market prices by entering the long position of the June 2005 S&P 500 contract. With a settlement price of 1,175.50 for this contract (shown in the display as "117550"), he has obligated himself to the theoretical purchase of 250 shares of the S&P 500 on the third Friday of June for $293,875 (= 1,175.50 × 250). The minimum contract price movement is 0.10 points, which equals $25. Thus, if the actual level of the S&P index on the contract settlement date turned out to be 1,177.70, the long position would gain $550, or $25 times 22 ticks (i.e., (1,177.70 − 1,175.50) ÷ 0.10), thereby reducing the net purchase price for his desired equity investment.

Stock Index Futures Valuation and Index Arbitrage   Earlier, we established that the key to understanding the pricing of futures contracts is the concept of arbitrage. To see how this works for index contracts, suppose that at Date 0 an investor (1) purchases a portfolio of stock representing the underlying stock index for S_0, and (2) goes short a stock index future (with an expiration date of T) for $F_{0,T}$. Assume further that in order to avoid making any investment at Date 0, the funds for the long position are borrowed at the risk-free rate of RFR. On unwinding this position at Date t, the net profit (Π) is given by

$$\Pi = (F_{0,T} - F_{t,T}) + (S_t - S_0 - S_0 RFR_t + S_0 d_t) = (F_{0,T} - F_{t,T}) + [S_t - S_0(1 + RFR_t - d_t)]$$

where:

d_t = the dividend yield accruing to the stocks comprising the index between Dates 0 and t

In other words, the profit you make on this short hedge in stock index futures will consist of two components: the net difference in the futures position and the net difference in the underlying index position (after adding borrowing costs and subtracting dividends received from the initial purchase).

Now assume the long position in the stock portfolio is held until the expiration of the futures contract (i.e., Date $t = T$). The advantage of doing this is that the cash settlement feature of the stock index futures contract ensures that the futures price and index level will converge. That is, at Date T, we will have $F_{T,T} = S_T$, which means that the short hedge profit (Π) equation can be written

$$\Pi = [F_{0,T} - S_0 - S_0(RFR_t - d_T)]$$

As before, $RFR_t - d_T$ is called the net cost of carry and represents the difference between the borrowing cost paid and the dividend received.

Exhibit 21.9 | Stock Index Futures Quotations

DJ Industrial Average (CBT)-$10 x index
June   10478   10540   10450   10468   -2   11012   9868   38,914
Est vol 2,859; vol Wed 7,655; open int 38,941, +453.
Idx prl: Hi 10518.63; Lo 10442.87; Close 10442.87, -13.15.

Mini DJ Industrial Average (CBT)-$5 x index
June   10478   10542   10461   10468   -2   10995   10392   31,043
Vol Thu 75,470; open int 31,055, +197.

DJ-AIG Commodity Index (CBT)-$100 x index
Apr   ...   535.0   ...   1.3   556.6   482.8   207
Est vol 0; vol Wed 261; open int 433, +57.
Idx prl: Hi 158.973; Lo 157.480; Close 158.645, +.488.

S&P 500 Index (CME)-$250 x index
June   117480 118420 117450 117550   90 123410   95750 653,975
Sept   118080   90 123920   98970   9,186
Est vol 30,188; vol Wed 42,172; open int 669,954, -2,569.
Idx prl: Hi 1180.11; Lo 1171.42; Close 1171.42, -1.11.

Mini S&P 500 (CME)-$50 x index
June   117475 118425 117450 117550 100 123425 116450 859,285
Vol Thu 865,877; open int 859,706, +15,943.

S&P Midcap 400 (CME)-$500 x index
June   657.50 662.75 657.00 657.20   2.00 686.00 549.25 11,721
Est vol 238; vol Wed 1,120; open int 11,722, +17.
Idx prl: Hi 659.74; Lo 654.15; Close 655.24, +1.08.

Nasdaq 100 (CME)-$100 x index
June   147900 149500 147800 148000 100 164400 140350 55,154
Est vol 5,480; vol Wed 14,245; open int 55,158, +1,470.
Idx prl: Hi 1485.96; Lo 1469.94; Close 1469.94, -1.83.

Mini Nasdaq 100 (CME)-$20 x index
June   1479.0 1495.0 1478.0 1480.0   1.0 1652.0 1463.5 274,415
Vol Thu 309,763; open int 274,420, +5,847.

GSCI (CME)-$250 x nearby index
Apr   374.00 375.60 369.70 374.50   3.30 388.50 318.50 18,998
Est vol 176; vol Wed 460; open int 19,006, -128.
Idx prl: Hi 375.74; Lo 370.07; Close 375.11, +3.23.

TRAKRS Long-Short Tech (CME)-$1 x index
July   37.55   37.72   37.55   37.72   .03   45.25   19.76 116,235
Est vol 200; vol Wed 1; open int 116,235, -1.
Idx prl: Hi 37.71; Lo 37.45; Close 37.57, +.12.

Russell 2000 (CME)-$500 x index
June   616.90 621.25 615.50 616.25   3.00 655.25 517.25 29,440
Est vol 1,020; vol Wed 1,491; open int 29,440, +616.
Idx prl: Hi 619.65; Lo 612.06; Close 615.27, +3.21.

Russell 1000 (NYBOT)-$500 x index
June   634.15 636.90 633.70 633.00   .75 660.80 631.75 77,416
Est vol 993; vol Wed 700; open int 77,416, -116.
Idx prl: Hi 635.42; Lo 630.95; Close 630.95, -.34.

NYSE Composite Index (NYBOT)-$50 x index
June 7143.00 7175.00 7143.00 7145.00   6.00 7420.00 7135.00   774
Est vol 229; vol Wed 953; open int 774, +147.
Idx prl: Hi 7169.76; Lo 7127.18; Close 7128.80, +1.62.

U.S. Dollar Index (NYBOT)-$1,000 x index
June   83.97   84.16   83.74   84.11   .10   90.80   80.67   15,847
Sept   84.00   84.00   84.00   84.02   .10   88.65   80.74   2,561
Est vol 2,750; vol Wed 6,910; open int 18,428, -1,632.
Idx prl: Hi 84.22; Lo 83.74; Close 84.13, +.13.

Nikkei Stock Average (CME)-$5 x index
June   11670. 11770. 11670. 11735.   50   11980. 10665. 33,918
Est vol 6,527; vol Wed 6,191; open int 33,926, +1,136.
Index: Hi 11819.37; Lo 11706.27; Close 11745.97, +6.85.

Share Price Index (SFE)-AUD 25 x index
June   4175.0 4196.0 4143.0 4167.0   -8.0   4290.0 3407.0 171,949
Sept   4187.0 4205.0 4154.0 4177.0   -8.0   4297.0 3398.0   3,453
Dec   4219.0 4219.0 4219.0 4199.0   -7.0   4303.0 3531.0   3,520
Est vol 19,746; vol Wed 23,474; open int 181,155, -3,038.
Index: Hi 4169.5; Lo 4123.8; Close 4136.5, -34.3.

CAC-40 Stock Index (MATIF)-€10 x index
Apr   4034.0 4085.5 4034.0 4080.5   40.5   4117.5 3913.0 377,665
May   4005.5 4037.0 4005.5 4051.5   41.0   4049.0 3983.5   15,930
June   3963.0 4008.0 3961.5 4003.0   40.0   4039.5 3911.0   66,196
Est vol 55,319; vol Wed 73,560; open int 474,909, +17,842.
Index: Hi 4080.90; Lo 4036.30; Close 4078.31, +45.90.

Xetra DAX (EUREX)-€25 x index
June   4344.0 4382.5 4337.0 4375.5   23.5   4461.0 3890.0 184,769
Sept   4372.0 4404.5 4362.0 4400.0   23.5   4484.0 4231.0   4,965
Vol Thu 102,509; open int 189,840, -1,257.
Index: Hi 4347.72; Lo 4315.73; Close 4343.60, +26.40.

FTSE 100 Index (LIFFE)-£10 x index
June   4928.5 4951.0 4919.5 4941.0   9.0   5073.0 4338.5 473,548
Sept   4951.0 4951.0 4951.0 4957.5   9.0   5064.0 4755.0   20,008
Dec   4982.0 4984.0 4982.0 4989.0   9.5   5119.5 4828.5   9,441
Vol Thu 46,483; open int 503,222, +1,974.
Index: Hi 4933.70; Lo 4904.50; Close 4922.50, +12.10.

DJ Euro STOXX 50 Index (EUREX)-€10 x index
June   2994.0 3031.0 2990.0 3026.0   28.0   3076.0 2701.0 1,331,494
Sept   2998.0 3028.0 2998.0 3026.0   28.0   3100.0 2877.0   94,951
Vol Thu 388,286; open int 1,438,167, +18,186.
Index: Hi 3063.61; Lo 3037.20; Close 3060.67, +23.82.

DJ STOXX 50 Index (EUREX)-€10 x index
June   2829.0 2855.0 2825.0 2854.0   33.0   2897.0 2740.0 32,720
Vol Thu 735; open int 32,794, +330.
Index: Hi 2872.03; Lo 2851.17; Close 2867.44, +13.00.

If the dividend yield is known at Date 0, this position is riskless and requires no initial investment. Thus, buying and selling among arbitrageurs trading in both the stock and futures markets should ensure that $\Pi = 0$. Thus, the futures price set at Date 0 will be

21.8
$$F_{0,T} = S_0 + S_0(RFR_t - d_T)$$

As in the cost of carry model discussed earlier, the futures price could be set below the spot level of the index (i.e., a backwardated market) if $(RFR_t - d_T) < 0$. That is, the index futures contract will be priced lower than the current level of the stock price whenever the dividends received by holding stock exceed the borrowing cost.

To see how this parity relationship helps establish the appropriate level of the stock index futures price, assume that one share of the S&P 500 index can be purchased for $1,250.00 and that the dividend yield and risk-free rate over the holding period are 1.5 percent and 2.5 percent, respectively. Under these conditions, the contract price on a six-month S&P 500 futures should be

$$F_{0,0.5} = 1,250 + 1,250(0.025 - 0.015) = 1,262.50$$

Now suppose that you construct a short hedge position by (1) purchasing the index at 1,250.00 and (2) shorting the futures at 1,262.50. If the position is held to expiration, your profit at various expiration date levels of the S&P will be as shown in Exhibit 21.10. Notice that your net profit remains constant no matter the level of the index at the expiration date. More importantly, this net profit can be expressed as

$$(31.25) \div (1,250) = 2.5 \text{ percent}$$

which is the assumed cost of borrowing.

Implementing an Index Arbitrage Strategy   What if the parity condition between the stock index and the stock index futures price does not hold? Could you design a portfolio to take advantage of the situation? Specifically, suppose that in the preceding example the actual contract price on a six-month S&P 500 futures was 1,265.50 (i.e., $F_{0,T} > S_0 + S_0(RFR_t - d_T)$). You could then implement the following arbitrage transaction: (1) short the stock index future at a price of 1,265.50; (2) borrow money at 2.5 percent to purchase the stock index at 1,250.00; and (3) hold the position until maturity, collecting 18.75 in dividends and then selling the stock to repay your loan. Your net profit at maturity would be

$$1,265.50 - 1,250 - 1,250 (0.025 - 0.015) = \$3.00$$

Exhibit 21.10 | **Stock Index Futures Valuation Example**

	S&P AT EXPIRATION IS:				
	1,220	1,240	1,260	1,280	1,300
Net futures profit	42.50	22.50	2.50	(17.50)	(37.50)
Net index profit	(30.00)	(10.00)	10.00	30.00	50.00
Dividend	18.75	18.75	18.75	18.75	18.75
Net profit	31.25	31.25	31.25	31.25	31.25

However, since this strategy was riskless (i.e., the sales price of the stock and the dividends were known in advance) and none of your own capital was used, it is an arbitrage profit.

This is *stock index arbitrage,* which is possible whenever the index futures price is set at a level sufficiently different from the theoretical value for $F_{0,T}$ to account for trading costs. For example, if the actual level of $F_{0,T} < S_0 + S_0(RFR_t - d_T)$, the previous strategy could be reversed: (1) buy the stock index future at a price of $F_{0,T}$, (2) lend money at RFR_t and short the stock index at S_0, and (3) cover the position at the expiration date of the futures contract. Indeed, index arbitrage is a very popular form of trading. Exhibit 21.11 reports that about 11.5 percent

Exhibit 21.11	Program Trading and Stock Index Arbitrage

Program Trading

NEW YORK—Program trading in the week ended March 18 accounted for 71.4%, or an average of 1309.9 million shares daily, of New York Stock Exchange volume. Brokerage firms executed an additional 817.6 million daily shares of program trading away from the NYSE, with 4.4% of the overall total on foreign markets. Program trading is the simultaneous purchase or sale of at least 15 different stocks with a total value of $1 million or more.

Of the program total on the NYSE, 11.4% involved stock-index arbitrage. In this strategy, traders dart between stocks and stock-index options and futures to capture fleeting price differences. Less than 0.1% involved derivative product-related strategies. Index arbitrage can be executed only in a stabilizing manner when the Dow Jones Industrial Average moves 210 points or more from its previous day's close.

Some 50.2% of program trading was executed by firms for their clients, while 38.6% was done for their own accounts, or principal trading. An additional 11.2% was designated as customer facilitation, in which firms use principal positions to facilitate customer trades.

Of the five most-active firms overall for the week, **Credit Suisse Group**'s Credit Suisse First Boston and **UBS AG**'s UBS Securities executed most of their program trading as principal for their own accounts. **Goldman Sachs Group** Inc., **Deutsche Bank**'s Deutsche Bank Securities and **Morgan Stanley** executed most of their program trading activity for customers, as agent.

NYSE PROGRAM TRADING
Volume in millions of shares for the week ended March 18, 2005

TOP 15 FIRMS	INDEX ARBITRAGE	DERIVATIVE-RELATED*	OTHER STRATEGIES	TOTAL
Goldman Sachs	6.6	.....	921.4	928.0
Deutsche Bank Securities	194.5	.....	556.8	751.3
Credit Suisse First Boston	189.0	.....	529.7	718.7
UBS Securities, LLC.	.....	.....	682.5	682.5
Morgan Stanley	6.4	0.1	602.1	608.6
Lehman Brothers, Inc.	2.2	.....	475.9	478.1
Citigroup Global Markets	.....	.....	402.9	402.9
Banc of America Sec.	.....	.....	355.6	355.6
Merrill Lynch	.....	.....	307.6	307.6
RBC Capital Markets	175.0	.....	74.9	249.9
Bear Stearns	4.6	.....	186.5	191.1
CIBC World Markets	41.2	.....	84.6	125.8
SG Americas Sec.	61.1	.....	45.2	106.3
Interactive Brokers LLC	.....	.....	82.3	82.3
Nomura Sec. Int.	39.5	.....	39.2	78.7
OVERALL TOTAL	744.6	1.0	5804.2	6549.8

*Other derivative-related strategies besides index arbitrage

Source: New York Stock Exchange

Exhibit 21.12 | Actual and Theoretical Stock Index Futures Prices

Panel A. Mispricing in Stock Index Futures Throughout the World

1) Americas	Cash	Future	Theo. Future	Fair Value	Spread Basis	Percent Misprice
4 SPM5vsSPX	1174.28	1177.40	1177.68	3.40	3.12	-.024%
5 YUM5vsNYA	7131.52	7140.00	7136.98	5.46	8.48	+.042%
6 DJM5vsINDU	10485.65	10504.00	10504.95	19.30	18.35	-.009%
7 MDM5vsMID	655.66	659.50	658.52	2.86	3.84	+.149%
8 NDM5vsNDX	1472.71	1481.00	1481.83	9.12	8.29	-.056%
9 PTM5vsSPTSX60	524.79	524.60	525.58	.79	-.19	-.187%
2) Europe						
10 Q M5vsE100	2348.43	2325.00	2326.91	-21.52	-23.43	-.082%
11 Z M5vsUKX	4922.50	4941.00	4942.85	20.35	18.50	-.037%
12 CFJ5vsCAC	4078.31	4080.50	4082.82	4.51	2.19	-.057%
13 GXM5vsDAX	4343.60	4375.50	4364.36	20.76	31.90	+.255%
14 SMM5vsSMI	5935.45	5873.00	5864.14	-71.31	-62.45	+.151%
15 EOJ5vsAEX	371.62	370.70	370.39	-1.23	-.92	+.082%
3) Asia/Pacific						
16 NKM5vsNKY	11792.30	11810.00	11792.27	-.03	17.70	+.150%
17 NIJ5vsNKY	11792.30	11800.00	11792.33	.03	7.70	+.065%
18 TPM5vsTPX	1194.04	1192.50	1193.98	-.06	-1.54	-.124%
19 XPM5vsAS51	4136.50	4163.00	4163.23	26.73	26.50	-.006%

Panel B. Calculating the June 2005 S&P 500 Futures Contract Price

S&P 500 INDEX	Cash	Future	Theo. Future	Fair Value	Spread (Basis)	Upper Bound	Lower Bound
1) SPM5vsSPX	1174.28	1177.40	1177.68	3.40	3.12	4.57	2.24
Risk Free:	3.09%	Expire:	6/17/05	Dividend:	4.99	Dvd Yld:	1.84%
Implied Rate:	2.99%	Days:	83	Percent of Gross Dividend:	100.0%		

of all computer-assisted program trading used this strategy. Further program trading accounted for about 70 percent of trading volume on the New York Stock Exchange, an amount that is higher than normal because it occurred around a contract expiration date (i.e., the so-called *triple witching day*).

One important side effect of this sort of trading activity is that stock index futures prices tend to stay close to the theoretical levels generated by the preceding valuation equation. This is because the arbitrage prescription for a futures settlement price that is too low (too high) is to go long (short) in the contract, which, when done in sufficient volume, adjusts the price in the proper direction. Panel A of Exhibit 21.12 compares the actual and theoretical levels of the nearest-term future contract for several stock indexes throughout the world, including the S&P 500 (SPX), Dow Jones Industrial (INDU), and the Nikkei 225 (NKY). Notice that the pricing errors on this particular day never exceeded 3/10 of 1 percent for any contract and was much lower than that in most markets. Panel B of Exhibit 21.12 details the calculation of the theoretical level of the June 2005 S&P 500 futures price. The display shows that the actual contract price (1,177.40) was virtually identical to its theoretical value (1,177.68), which can be computed as the spot price (1,174.28) plus the net cost of carry [1,174.28 × (0.0309 − 0.0184) × (83/365)]. These values support the notion that the market for stock index futures is an efficient one.

The empirical evidence tends to support this view, particularly after transaction costs and other trading realities are considered. Cornell (1985), for instance, found that stock index futures prices tracked their model values more closely as the market matured, although Keim and Smirlock (1989) detected some temporal (i.e., day-of-the-week, January) pricing patterns. In response to the allegation that index arbitrage caused the worldwide stock market crash of October 1987, Roll (1988) documented that countries with the greatest level of program trading activity experienced less pronounced price declines. This finding is consistent with the notion that index arbitrage reduces volatility by stabilizing cash and futures prices.

A Stock Index Futures Application

Isolating the Unsystematic Risk of an Individual Stock   In Chapter 20, we demonstrated how stock index futures could alter the systematic risk of an otherwise well-diversified portfolio. When the holding is an individual stock, this process can isolate the unique attributes of the company. Recall from Chapter 1 that:

$$\text{Total Stock Risk} = \text{Systematic Risk} + \text{Unsystematic Risk}$$

with the systematic component representing about 25–40 percent of the total risk for the typical firm. Thus, using stock index futures to adjust the stock's beta to zero effectively isolates the unsystematic portion of risk.

To see how this might work, suppose that in mid-August you own 75,000 shares of Pharmco Inc., a multinational pharmaceutical firm. The current price of Pharmco stock is $46.75, and you calculate the company's beta at 0.99. You like the stock as an investment because of the quality of its management and some other unique attributes of the firm, but you are concerned that over the next few months the aggregate stock market might undergo a sizable correction that could more than offset any firm-specific gains.

To protect yourself, you decide to sell December S&P 500 futures contracts, which are currently trading at a settlement price of 271.10. At this price, we have seen that the implied dollar value of a single contract is $317,775. The current value of your Pharmco stock is $3,506,250. Since the stock's beta can be defined as $\rho\,[\sigma_{\Delta S} \div \sigma_{\Delta F}]$ the optional hedge ratio formula developed earlier can be adapted to provide the appropriate hedge ratio:

$$N^* = \left[\frac{\text{Market Value of Spot Position}}{\text{Value Implied by Futures Contract}}\right]\beta$$

$$= [(\$3{,}506{,}250) \div (\$317{,}775)](0.99) = 10.92$$

so you decide to short 11 contracts.

Now suppose that by mid-December when your futures position expires, the S&P 500 index settles at a level of 1,251.10 while the price of Pharmco stock has increased to $47.50. Although you have made a modest profit on your common stock holding (i.e., $56,250, or 1.60 percent), you will also benefit from a trading profit on the futures position of $55,000 (= (11) [1,271.10 − 1,251.10](250)). As a result, your total return is $111,250, which, expressed as a percentage of your original investment of $3,506,250 is equivalent to an unsystematic appreciation in Pharmco's stock of 3.17 percent. Notice in this case that the difference between this amount and the gross increase of 1.60 percent in Pharmco stock is equal to the 1.57 percent ($= [1,251.1 \div 1,271.1] - 1$) that the stock index future position fell.

Currency Forwards and Futures

Whether in the spot or forward markets, foreign exchange (FX) transactions often involve a confusing blend of unique terminology and market conventions. Although these conventions are easily assimilated, they represent an initial barrier to understanding how FX deals work. Thus, we begin our analysis of currency derivatives with a brief overview of some of the fundamental features of these products.

The Mechanics of Currency Transactions The market for foreign currency is no different than any other market, in that buyer and seller negotiate for the exchange of a certain amount of a predetermined commodity at a fixed cash price. The challenge in FX transactions is that the "commodity" involved is someone else's currency. This means that the transaction can be viewed in two ways. For example, suppose that Company A agrees to pay 100 U.S. dollars to Company B in exchange for 67 British pounds. In this case, is Company A buying sterling (GBP) or selling dollars (USD)?[6] Similarly, is Company B selling pounds or buying dollars? The answer is that both are correct, depending on one's point of view.

Because of this dual interpretation, the price for all FX transactions also can be quoted in two ways. Assuming that Company A is a U.S.-based firm, it would probably think of the transaction as the purchase of 67 pounds at a cost of 100 dollars, which would yield the price of USD 1.4925/GBP ($= 100/67$). This method of quoting FX prices is called the *direct,* or *American,* convention. Notice that under this convention, the pound (i.e., the foreign currency from the U.S. firm's perspective) is treated as the commodity, and its price per unit is expressed in terms of dollars. On the other hand, if Company B is a British corporation, its managers would likely think of prices in terms of the amount of sterling they have to pay to acquire dollars. Here, that amount translates into a price of GBP 0.67/USD. Treating the dollar as the commodity yields the *indirect,* or *European,* quotation method. Of course, the direct and indirect quotes are just *reciprocals* of one another, as they describe the same transaction from two different perspectives.

Exhibit 21.13 shows a representative set of FX quotes. Four prices are listed beside each currency. The first two columns report the current and previous days' dollar price, respectively, for trading one unit of that currency (i.e., direct quotes). For instance, the prevailing price of a Norwegian krone on that date was USD 0.1577, which was 0.07 cent lower than the day before. The last two columns express these same prices in indirect terms (e.g., NOK 6.3412/USD $= 1 \div$ USD 0.1577/NOK). Thus, the terms of a spot FX transaction can be structured to meet the particular needs of the counterparties involved.

Another important aspect of the FX markets highlighted by this display is that although many currencies trade in the spot market, relatively few also quote prices for forward transactions. In this list, only the British, Canadian, Japanese, and Swiss currencies have forward contracts. These contracts, which are negotiated in the over-the-counter market with a currency dealer (such as a multinational bank), carry maturities one, three, and six months into the future. For example, an investor wishing to buy Swiss francs would pay USD 0.8324 per franc if the transaction were completed immediately, 0.8339 if the transaction were negotiated now but consummated in 30 days, and USD 0.8373 or USD 0.8432 for exchanges completed in 90 or 180 days, respectively.

---

[6]Currency traders often use three-letter abbreviations to denote a particular currency. Some of the more common abbreviations include USD (U.S. dollars), CAD (Canadian dollars), GBP (British pounds), JPY (Japanese yen), CHF (Swiss franc), and EUR (the Euro currency). For a more complete listing, see Gastineau and Kritzman (2001).

Exhibit 21.13 | Spot and Forward Currency Quotations

Exchange Rates March 24, 2005

The foreign exchange mid-range rates below apply to trading among banks in amounts of $1 million and more, as quoted at 4 p.m. Eastern time by Reuters and other sources. Retail transactions provide fewer units of foreign currency per dollar.

Country	U.S. $ EQUIVALENT		CURRENCY PER U.S. $	
	Thu	Wed	Thu	Wed
Argentina (Peso)-y	.3432	.3432	2.9138	2.9138
Australia (Dollar)	.7717	.7711	1.2958	1.2968
Bahrain (Dinar)	2.6525	2.6525	.3770	.3770
Brazil (Real)	.3650	.3640	2.7397	2.7473
Canada (Dollar)	.8225	.8221	1.2158	1.2164
1-month forward	.8227	.8223	1.2155	1.2161
3-months forward	.8233	.8229	1.2146	1.2152
6-months forward	.8246	.8242	1.2127	1.2133
Chile (Peso)	.001699	.001697	588.58	589.28
China (Renminbi)	.1208	.1208	8.2765	8.2765
Colombia (Peso)	.0004190	.0004190	2386.63	2386.63
Czech. Rep. (Koruna)				
Commercial rate	.04295	.04301	23.283	23.250
Denmark (Krone)	.1737	.1742	5.7571	5.7405
Ecuador (US Dollar)	1.0000	1.0000	1.0000	1.0000
Egypt (Pound)-y	.1723	.1724	5.8048	5.8001
Hong Kong (Dollar)	.1282	.1282	7.8003	7.8003
Hungary (Forint)	.005221	.005236	191.53	190.99
India (Rupee)	.02289	.02287	43.687	43.725
Indonesia (Rupiah)	.0001062	.0001062	9416	9416
Israel (Shekel)	.2297	.2302	4.3535	4.3440

Country	U.S. $ EQUIVALENT		CURRENCY PER U.S. $	
	Thu	Wed	Thu	Wed
Japan (Yen)	.009406	.009426	106.32	106.09
1-month forward	.009427	.009448	106.08	105.84
3-months forward	.009478	.009500	105.51	105.26
6-months forward	.009563	.009585	104.57	104.33
Jordan (Dinar)	1.4114	1.4114	.7085	.7085
Kuwait (Dinar)	3.4247	3.4245	.2920	.2920
Lebanon (Pound)	.0006605	.0006605	1514.00	1514.00
Malaysia (Ringgit)-b	.2632	.2632	3.7994	3.7994
Malta (Lira)	3.0023	3.0082	.3331	.3324
Mexico (Peso)				
Floating rate	.0887	.0886	11.2740	11.2841
New Zealand (Dollar)	.7124	.7182	1.4037	1.3924
Norway (Krone)	.1577	.1584	6.3412	6.3131
Pakistan (Rupee)	.01684	.01683	59.382	59.418
Peru (new Sol)	.3067	.3067	3.2605	3.2605
Philippines (Peso)	.01844	.01845	54.230	54.201
Poland (Zloty)	.3137	.3135	3.1878	3.1898
Russia (Ruble)-a	.03614	.03611	27.670	27.693
Saudi Arabia (Riyal)	.2667	.2667	3.7495	3.7495
Singapore (Dollar)	.6083	.6080	1.6439	1.6447
Slovak Rep. (Koruna)	.03314	.03310	30.175	30.212
South Africa (Rand)	.1605	.1609	6.2305	6.2150
South Korea (Won)	.0009867	.0009877	1013.48	1012.45
Sweden (Krona)	.1419	.1423	7.0472	7.0274
Switzerland (Franc)	.8324	.8350	1.2013	1.1976
1-month forward	.8339	.8366	1.1992	1.1953
3-months forward	.8373	.8400	1.1943	1.1905
6-months forward	.8432	.8460	1.1860	1.1820
Taiwan (Dollar)	.03179	.03188	31.456	31.368
Thailand (Baht)	.02571	.02583	38.895	38.715
Turkey (New Lira)-d	.7313	.7329	1.3675	1.3645
U.K. (Pound)	1.8696	1.8678	.5349	.5354
1-month forward	1.8666	1.8646	.5357	.5363
3-months forward	1.8610	1.8592	.5373	.5379
6-months forward	1.8547	1.8529	.5392	.5397
United Arab (Dirham)	.2723	.2723	3.6724	3.6724
Uruguay (Peso)				
Financial	.03950	.03950	25.317	25.317
Venezuela (Bolivar)	.000466	.000466	2145.92	2145.92
SDR	1.5111	1.5165	.6618	.6594
Euro	1.2940	1.2976	.7728	.7707

Special Drawing Rights (SDR) are based on exchange rates for the U.S., British, and Japanese currencies. Source: International Monetary Fund.

a-Russian Central Bank rate. b-Government rate. d-Rebased as of Jan. 1, 2005. y-Floating rate.

Source: From *The Wall Street Journal*, March 25, 2005. Copyright 2005 by DOW JONES & CO INC. Reproduced with permission of DOW JONES & CO INC in the format Other Book via Copyright Clearance Center.

In the situation where it costs increasingly more dollars to buy the same franc the farther out in the future it is delivered, the dollar is said to be trading at a **forward discount** to the franc. Conversely, the franc is at a **forward premium** to the dollar. Notice that this relationship depends on the currencies being compared. In this set of quotes, the U.S. dollar is trading at a forward discount to the Swiss franc, Canadian dollar, and the Japanese yen, while it is at a forward premium to the British pound. It should come as no surprise by now that the relationship between the spot and forward FX rates is not a random one. In fact, we will see shortly that whether a particular currency trades at a discount or a premium to another depends on the relative level of the investment rates in the two countries.

Exhibit 21.14 lists quotes for a sample of exchange-traded currency futures contracts. These specific instruments are traded at the International Monetary Market at the CME. Each contract involving U.S. dollars follows the convention that the U.S. dollar is the native monetary unit and the foreign currency is the commodity, meaning that all prices are quoted using the direct method. Also, notice that these contracts are standardized to deliver a set number of units of the foreign currency on a specific date in the future. For instance, the June

Exhibit 21.14 | **Currency Futures Quotations**

	OPEN	HIGH	LOW	SETTLE	CHG	LIFETIME HIGH	LIFETIME LOW	OPEN INT

Japanese Yen (CME)-¥12,500,000; $ per ¥

| June | .9502 | .9515 | .9444 | .9469 | −.0027 | .9930 | .9040 | 107,891 |
| Sept | .9555 | .9563 | .9544 | .9559 | −.0027 | 1.0000 | .9544 | 473 |

Est vol 29,471; vol Wed 45,537; open int 108,448, −417.

Canadian Dollar (CME)-CAD 100,000; $ per CAD

June	.8233	.8257	.8206	.8223	−.0011	.8495	.7150	81,095
Sept	.8254	.8254	.8226	.8238	−.0011	.8490	.7160	1,814
Dec	na	.8270	.8263	.8253	−.0011	.8515	.7480	819

Est vol 16,438; vol Wed 29,741; open int 83,772, −6,072.

British Pound (CME)-£62,500; $ per £

| June | 1.8620 | 1.8667 | 1.8601 | 1.8627 | .0030 | 1.9350 | 1.7150 | 67,152 |
| Sept | 1.8529 | 1.8590 | 1.8529 | 1.8561 | .0030 | 1.9150 | 1.7600 | 650 |

Est vol 15,450; vol Wed 31,971; open int 67,815, −3,954.

Swiss Franc (CME)-CHF 125,000; $ per CHF

| June | .8405 | .8433 | .8350 | .8377 | −.0019 | .8920 | .7880 | 38,680 |
| Dec | ... | ... | ... | .8502 | −.0019 | .8922 | .8520 | 125 |

Est vol 21,296; vol Wed 31,456; open int 38,901, +623.

Australian Dollar (CME)-AUD 100,000; $ per AUD

June	.7680	.7696	.7659	.7670	.0006	.7933	.6670	90,625
Sept	...	...	...	.7621	.0006	.7855	.6600	869
Dec	.7565	.7565	.7565	.7584	.0006	.7835	.6664	146

Est vol 12,696; vol Wed 38,793; open int 91,645, −14,201.

Mexican Peso (CME)-MXN 500,000; $ per MXN

| June | .08740 | .08755 | .08717 | .08732 | 00007 | .08970 | .08160 | 61,521 |
| Sept | ... | ... | ... | .08585 | 00007 | .08790 | .08150 | 452 |

Est vol 3,399; vol Wed 16,810; open int 62,383, −3,401.

Euro/US Dollar (CME)-€125,000; $ per €

June	1.3016	1.3058	1.2959	1.2980	−.0024	1.3699	1.1750	117,626
Sept	1.3075	1.3096	1.2969	1.3025	−.0024	1.3711	1.1750	2,174
Dec	1.3080	1.3102	1.3074	1.3076	−.0024	1.3740	1.2068	1,148

Est vol 119,878; vol Wed 146,686; open int 121,008, +5,937.

Euro/US Dollar (NYBOT)-€200,000; $ per €

| June | 1.3010 | 1.3036 | 1.3003 | 1.2983 | −.0023 | 1.3444 | 1.2864 | 456 |

Est vol 180; vol Wed 313; open int 456, +23.

Euro/Japanese Yen (NYBOT)-€100,000; ¥ per €

| June | 137.07 | 137.76 | 137.07 | 137.06 | .10 | 139.62 | 136.75 | 18,858 |

Est vol 779; vol Wed 1,240; open int 18,858, +24.

Euro/British Pound (NYBOT)-€100,000; £ per €

| June | .6974 | .6974 | .6965 | .6971 | −.0023 | .7038 | .6920 | 4,917 |

Est vol 73; vol Wed 457; open int 4,919, +228.

Source: From *The Wall Street Journal*, March 25, 2005. Copyright 2005 by DOW JONES & CO INC. Reproduced with permission of DOW JONES & CO INC in the format Other Book via Copyright Clearance Center.

Mexican peso contract negotiated on that date required the long position to purchase—and the short position to deliver—500,000 pesos at the price of USD 0.08732 per peso. By convention, all currency futures on the IMM mature on the third Wednesday of the stated delivery month and can be settled with a wire transfer of the foreign currency. Notice that the dollar traded at a substantial forward premium to the peso at this point in time.

Interest Rate Parity and Covered Interest Arbitrage   A key concept in FX risk management is **interest rate parity**, a condition that specifies the no-arbitrage relationship between spot and forward FX rates (as priced into the futures contracts) and the level of interest rates in each currency. This connection is best seen through an example. Suppose that an institutional investor has USD 100,000 to invest for one year and is considering two different riskless alternatives. The first strategy entails the purchase of a U.S. Treasury bill. Assume that under current market conditions, the effective U.S. dollar risk-free interest rate is 4.50 percent per annum for a one-year maturity, so that a direct T-bill investment would return USD 104,500 at the end of the 12 months.

For the second strategy, suppose that the investor also can sell the USD 100,000 in the spot market at the current exchange rate of CAD 1.70/USD (or, equivalently, USD 0.5882/CAD) to obtain a total of 170,000 Canadian dollars. We assume that that amount can then be invested in a Canadian risk-free security at an annualized rate of 7.00 percent, returning CAD 181,900 at the end of the year. Of course, to make this return comparable to the USD-denominated proceeds from the first strategy, the Canadian dollars will have to be converted back into U.S. currency. If this translation is negotiated at the end of the investment, however, the investor will be subjected to foreign exchange risk in that he will not know at Date 0 what the CAD/USD exchange rate will be at Date T. Thus, to make the second strategy riskless, the investor must enter into a forward contract to exchange CAD back into USD at the end of the year. The question then is, What would the exchange rate priced into a one-year forward contract have to be at Date 0 to leave the investor indifferent between these two strategies?

These investments are depicted in Exhibit 21.15. The essence of the arbitrage argument is that the one-year forward FX rate must be such that USD 104,500 equals CAD 181,900. Otherwise, an arbitrage opportunity would exist, or at least a dominating investment choice. Therefore, the forward contract rate consistent with interest rate parity is CAD 1.7407/USD (= 181,900 ÷ 104,500) on an indirect basis, or USD 0.5745/CAD quoted directly. Notice that this is a breakeven value in the sense that it allows the 4.50 percent investment return in the United States to be equal to the 7.00 percent available in Canada when the two are converted to the same currency. That is, the Canadian return must be deflated by 250 basis points to leave the investor indifferent between the two strategies. This reduction occurs because, to invest in the CAD-denominated security, the investor buys Canadian dollars at a price of USD 0.5882/CAD but must sell them back in the forward market at the lower price of USD 0.5745/CAD. Thus, the loss on the round-trip currency translation required in the second strategy adjusts its net return down to the 4.50 percent available on the direct U.S. dollar investment.[7]

If the actual one-year forward contract FX rate were higher than this breakeven level—say, for instance, CAD 1.77/USD—the currency translation loss would be greater than 250 basis points, leaving the USD-based strategy the more profitable choice. Given that there is now a difference between the returns to two otherwise comparable riskless investments, arbitrage is possible. In this case, an arbitrageur could enter the following transactions:

1. Borrow CAD 170,000 at 7.00 percent; agree to repay CAD 181,900 in one year.
2. Sell the foreign currency on the spot market at CAD 1.70/USD; receive USD 100,000.
3. Invest the USD 100,000 at 4.50 percent; receive USD 104,500 in one year.

Exhibit 21.15 | **Interest Rate Parity**

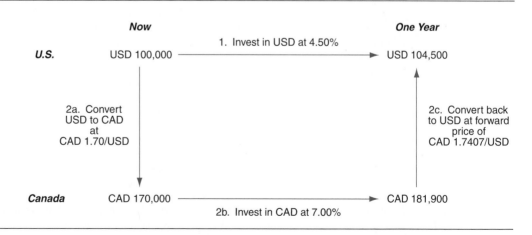

[7]Under these conditions, the actual currency loss is calculated as 0.5745/0.5882 − 1 = −2.33 percent. This, in turn, means the USD-denominated return to the second strategy is (1 + 0.07) × (1 − 0.0233) − 1 = 4.50 percent.

4. Sell USD 104,500 forward at CAD 1.77/USD; agree to receive CAD 184,965.
5. Repay the CAD loan; collect net profit of CAD 3,065.

If, on the other hand, the actual one-year forward rate were lower than breakeven—for instance, CAD 1.71/USD—the arbitrageur would implement the opposite trade:

1. Borrow USD 100,000 at 4.50 percent; agree to repay USD 104,500 in one year.
2. Sell the U.S. dollars on the spot market at CAD 1.70/USD; receive CAD 170,000.
3. Invest the CAD 170,000 at 7.00 percent; receive CAD 181,900 in one year.
4. Buy USD 104,500 forward at CAD 1.71/USD; agree to pay CAD 178,695.
5. Repay the U.S. dollar loan; collect net profit of CAD 3,205.

These strategies are known as **covered interest arbitrage** because the arbitrageur will always hold the security denominated in the currency that is the least expensive to deliver in the forward market. In this sense, the arbitrage position is hedged, or covered, against adverse foreign exchange movements while receiving the largest amount of net interest income. In practice, traders involved in covered interest arbitrage strategies utilize bank rates (e.g., LIBOR) for borrowing and lending, which injects a slight amount of credit risk into the scheme. After surveying the empirical evidence, Solnik (2004) has concluded that the ability to take these arbitrage positions keeps interest rate parity a viable description of the way spot and forward prices are set for the world's major currencies.

With exchange rates quoted on an *indirect basis* (i.e., foreign currency [FC] per U.S. dollar), the general formula for the forward rate implied by interest rate parity is

$$\text{Forward} = \text{Spot} \times \left(\frac{1 + (\text{Foreign Interest Rate})\left(\frac{T}{365}\right)}{1 + (\text{U.S. Interest Rate})\left(\frac{T}{365}\right)} \right)$$

where:

T = the number of days from the joint settlement of the futures and cash positions until they mature

In the last example, $T = 365$ so that CAD 1.7407/USD = CAD 1.70/USD $\times$ (1.07/1.045). This formula also assumes that the rates in question are quoted on a 365-day basis. If U.S. money market rates such as LIBOR are used, then the equation should be adjusted to a 360-day year.

Letting S_0 and $F_{0,T}$ once again denote the current spot and forward prices for an instrument that matures at Date T, the preceding expression can be rewritten as

21.9
$$\frac{F_{0,T}}{S_0} = \left(\frac{1 + (RFR_{FC})\left(\frac{T}{365}\right)}{1 + (RFR_{USD})\left(\frac{T}{365}\right)} \right)$$

where:

RFR_{USD} = the annualized risk-free rate in the United States
RFR_{FC} = the annualized risk-free rate in the foreign market

Equation 21.9 defines the relationship between four different prices, all of which are determined at Date 0: spot foreign exchange rate, forward foreign exchange rate, U.S. investment rate, and foreign investment rate. Importantly, notice that, if the markets are aligned properly, $F_{0,T}$ will be greater than S_0 whenever RFR_{FC} is greater than RFR_{USD}, with the opposite holding when $RFR_{FC} <$ RFR_{USD}. With indirect currency quotes, $F_{0,T} > S_0$ implies that the foreign currency is at a forward discount to the dollar. In other words, the country with the *lowest* investment rate should see its currency trade at a forward premium. The intuition behind this is that to keep investment capital from flowing to the country with the highest returns, the currency translation must adjust accordingly. Thus, the high-interest country will suffer from a weaker forward value for its currency.[8]

A Currency Futures Application

Calculating Implied World Investment Rates   Suppose that you are the cash manager for a multinational company and you have $1,000,000 in short-term balances that you can invest in sovereign-issued paper for the next four months. On Thursday, March 24, 2005, you obtain the following quotes for both spot and futures exchange rates for several currencies:

Currency	Spot (USD/FC)	September 2005 Futures (USD/FC)
Australian dollar	0.7717	0.7621
Japanese yen	0.009406	0.009559
Swiss franc	0.8324	0.8432
Canadian dollar	0.8225	0.8238
British pound	1.8696	1.8561
Mexican peso	0.08870	0.08585

If you enter into any of these transactions, they will settle on Monday, March 28 (i.e., two business days later). The futures contracts mature on Wednesday, September 21, 2005, which leaves a 177-day investment window from settlement to maturity.

You also observe that a U.S. Treasury bill maturing at virtually the same time (i.e., September 22) pays a bond equivalent (i.e., 365-day) yield of 3.14 percent. Before checking the actual quotes for foreign-currency-denominated government paper from these other countries, you first calculate the investment rates implied by the interest rate parity relationship. Specifically, for the six countries listed, you compute:

$$\text{Implied Rate} = \left[\left(\frac{\text{Spot}}{\text{Futures}}\right)\left(1 + (\text{U.S. Interest Rate})\left(\frac{177}{365}\right)\right) - 1\right]\left(\frac{365}{177}\right)$$

which is just the parity relationship rearranged to use direct currency quotes and to isolate the foreign interest rate. Notice that the direct parity formulation is the correct one to use because of the convention prevailing in the U.S. currency futures market. For British sterling, this calculation yields an implied 177-day annualized investment rate of:

$$\left[\left(\frac{1.8696}{1.8561}\right)\left(1 + (0.0314)\left(\frac{177}{365}\right)\right) - 1\right]\left(\frac{365}{177}\right) = 4.66\%$$

This means that with the current spot and futures prices for exchanging dollars and pounds, you would be indifferent between receiving a four-month investment rate of 3.14 percent in the United States or 4.66 percent in England.

---

[8]When using direct quotes (i.e., USD/FC), the interest rate parity condition must be adjusted by taking the reciprocal of the ratio on the left-hand side: $[S_0 \div F_{0,T}] = [(1 + RFR_{FC} (T \div 365)) \div (1 + RFR_{USD} (T \div 365))]$. In the example given, with the direct quotes for the spot and forward being USD 0.5882/CAD (= 1/1.70) and USD 0.5745/CAD, respectively, we have $S_0 = $ USD 0.5882/CAD = USD 0.5745/CAD $\times$ (1.07/1.045).

Summarizing this calculation for all of the countries leaves:

Country	Implied 177-Day Rate
Australia	5.78%
Japan	−0.21
Switzerland	0.46
Canada	2.81
Great Britain	4.66
Mexico	10.09

You can now compare these figures to the actual investment rates in each of the countries to determine if a futures-based synthetic foreign bond strategy is warranted. If, for example, the actual British six-month gilt rate were 5.00 percent, you could exceed the 3.14 percent dollar-denominated T-bill return by (1) exchanging your dollars for pounds in the spot market at USD 1.8696/GBP, (2) investing for 177 days in the sterling-based security at 5.00 percent, and (3) translating your proceeds back into dollars at maturity using the futures rate of USD 1.8561/GBP.

Finally, notice that the countries with implied rates higher than 3.14 percent (i.e., Australia, Great Britain, and Mexico) are those whose currencies sold at a forward discount to the U.S. dollar over this 177-day window. Conversely, Japan, Switzerland, and Canada had currencies at a forward premium to the dollar and thus had implied investment rates less than 3.14 percent. One caution necessary in interpreting these yields properly is that it is imperative that the futures and spot FX quotes were obtained simultaneously and pertain to the same investment denomination. In this example, these conditions were more than likely violated to some extent. [This, in fact, is the likely explanation for Japan's implied investment rate being negative (i.e., −0.21%), although Japan's actual short-term government rates were virtually zero at this time.]

The Internet — Investments Online

Some sites that focus on the use of these derivative products include:

http://www.nfa.futures.org The home page of the National Futures Association is an industry group whose purpose is to maintain the integrity of the marketplace. It features investor education links, training information, and regulatory issues.

http://www.futuresmag.com *Futures Magazine's* Web site features "hot market" analysis, technical analysis, and links to data and information about derivatives markets. It also provides free access to new, timely columns from industry experts, a Frequently Asked Questions section, a glossary of terms, and links to several articles that have apeared in *Futures Magazine.*

http://www.futuresbasics.com The Web site of Great Pacific Trading Company, which is a full service commodity brokerage offering services to beginning and advanced traders. Users can find links to good educational information concerning various aspects of futures trading, as well as access to economic reports about commodities.

http://tfc-charts.w2d.com The Web site of TFC Commodity Charts, a free source of daily commodity futures and financial market information. TFC tracks many commodities and financial indicators, making information available in both chart and quote form. Users are able to create their own personalized chart menu to gain quick access to the charts in which they are most interested. The site also includes futures discussion groups and many other educational materials.

SUMMARY

- There is no question that forward and futures contracts have become an important feature of the modern investment landscape. As the most fundamental type of derivative instruments available, they greatly increase the alternatives that investors have to create and manage their portfolios and establish new trading opportunities. In this chapter, we discuss how these contracts work and the ways they are used in practice. As different mechanisms for accomplishing the same goals, forwards and futures differ primarily in the areas of design flexibility and collateralization. Specifically, forward agreements generally are more flexible but carry more credit risk, while the process of marking margin accounts to market on a daily basis makes futures contracts more secure (to the exchange, at least) even as the standardization of contract terms makes them less adaptable to the end user.

- We also show that hedging is key to understanding forward-based contracting and that the basis is the most important concept in understanding hedging. In particular, the basis, which is defined as the difference between spot and forward prices at any point in time, contains the essence of a short hedge position so that the hedger effectively trades the price risk of the underlying asset for the basis risk inherent in the spot-forward combination. This notion also leads to the calculation of an optimal hedge ratio, which specifies the appropriate number of contracts by minimizing the amount of basis (i.e., correlation) risk in the combined position.

- Although forward and futures contracts are not securities, their contract settlement prices still must follow certain regularities for these markets to remain efficient. For example, the cost of carry model suggests that in order to avoid arbitrage, the forward price should be equal to the spot price plus the cost of transporting the underlying asset to the future delivery date. These carrying costs can include commissions for physical storage, an opportunity cost for the net amount of invested capital, and a premium for the convenience of consuming the asset now. When forward prices are set in this manner, the market value of a new contract should be zero, although this value can become either positive or negative as the contract matures under changing market conditions.

- Finally, we illustrate these concepts with detailed examinations of three types of financial futures contracts: interest rate, equity index, and foreign exchange. In addition to describing the dynamics of each of these markets, we discuss different applications, including those involving hedging, speculation, and arbitrage. These applications produce some useful adaptations of the basic concepts, such as duration, and beta-based hedge ratios for interest rate and stock index futures as well as the currency futures version of the cost of carry model known as interest rate parity. Although no such list of applications could ever be complete, they should provide an understanding of why these instruments have become so important in financial markets.

SUGGESTED READINGS

McDonald, Robert L. *Derivatives Markets.* Boston, MA: Pearson Education, 2003.

Siegel, Daniel, and Diane F. Siegel. *Futures Markets.* Hinsdale, IL: Dryden Press, 1990.

Smithson, Charles W., and Clifford W. Smith, Jr. *Managing Financial Risk,* 3rd ed. New York: McGraw-Hill, 1998.

Stulz, Reve M. *Risk Management and Derivatives.* Mason, OH: South-Western Publishing, 2003.

Telser, Lester G. "Futures Trading and the Storage of Cotton and Wheat." *Journal of Political Economy* 66 (June 1958).

Working, Holbrook. "Economic Functions of Futures Markets." In *Selected Writings of Holbrook Working.* Chicago: Chicago Board of Trade, 1977.

QUESTIONS

1. We have futures contracts on Treasury bonds, but we do not have futures contracts on individual corporate bonds. We have cattle and hog futures but no chicken futures. Explain why the market has developed in this manner. What do you think are the most important characteristics for the success of a new futures contract concept?

2. "Hedgers trade price risk for basis risk." What is meant by this statement? In particular, explain the concept of the basis in a hedge transaction and how forward and futures contracts can be selected to minimize risk.

3. Suppose you are a derivatives trader specializing in creating customized commodity forward contracts for clients and then hedging your position with exchange-traded futures contracts. Your latest position is an agreement to deliver 100,000 gallons of unleaded gasoline to a client in three months.
   a. Explain how you can hedge your position using gasoline futures contracts.
   b. In calculating your hedge ratio, how must you account for the different valuation procedures used for forward and futures contracts? That is, what difference does it make that forward contracts are valued on a discounted basis while futures contracts are marked to market without discounting?
   c. If the only available gasoline futures contracts call for the delivery of 42,000 gallons and mature in either two or four months, describe the nature of the basis risk involved in your hedge.

4. A multinational corporation is about to embark on a major financial restructuring program. One critical stage will be the issuance of seven-year Eurobonds sometime within the next month. The CFO is concerned with recent instability in capital markets and with the particular event that market yields rise prior to issuance, forcing the corporation to pay a higher coupon rate on the bonds. It is decided to hedge that risk by selling 10-year Treasury note futures contracts. Notice that this is a classic cross hedge wherein 10-year Treasury notes are used to manage the risk of 7-year Eurobonds.

   Describe the nature of the basis risk in the hedge. In particular what specific events with respect to the shape of the Treasury yield curve and the Eurobond spread over Treasuries could render the hedge ineffective? In other words, under what circumstances would the hedge fail and make the corporation worse off?

5. *CFA Examination Level II*
   Mike Lane will have $5 million to invest in five-year U.S. Treasury bonds three months from now. Lane believes interest rates will fall during the next three months and wants to take advantage of prevailing interest rates by hedging against a decline in interest rates. Lane has sufficient bonds to pay the costs of entering into and maintaining a futures position.
   a. Describe what action Lane should take using five-year U.S. Treasury note futures contracts to protect against declining interest rates.
   Assume three months have gone by and, despite Lane's expectations, five-year cash and forward market interest rates have increased by 100 basis points compared with the five-year forward market interest rates of three months ago.
   b. Discuss the effect of higher interest rates on the value of the futures position that Lane entered into in Part a.
   c. Discuss how the return from Lane's hedged position differs from the return he could now earn if he had not hedged in Part a.

6. You own an equally weighted portfolio of 50 different stocks worth about $5,000,000. The stocks are from several different industries, and the portfolio is reasonably well diversified. Which do you think would provide you with the best overall hedge: a single position in an index futures or 50 different positions in futures contracts on the individual stocks? What are the most important factors to consider in making this decision.

7. *CFA Examination Level II*
   Four factors affect the value of a futures contract on a stock index. Three of these factors are: the current price of the stock index, the time remaining until the contract maturity (delivery) date, and the dividends on the stock index. Identify the fourth factor and explain how and why changes in this factor affect the value of the futures contract.

8. It is often stated that a stock index arbitrage trade is easier to implement when the stock index futures contract price is above its theoretical level than when it is below that value. What institutional realities might make this statement true? Describe the steps involved in forming the arbitrage transaction in both circumstances. To the extent that the statement is valid, what does it suggest about the ability of the stock index futures market to remain efficient?

9. *CFA Examination Level III*
   The World Ecosystem Consortium (WEC) pension trust holds $100 million in long-term U.S. Treasury bonds. To reduce interest rate risk, you, as an independent advisor to the WEC, suggest that the trust diversify by investing $30 million in German government bonds (bunds) for six months. You

point out that a fixed-currency futures hedge (shorting a fixed number of contracts) could be used by WEC's pension trust to protect the $30 million in bunds against exchange rate losses over the six months.

Explain how a fixed-currency futures hedge could be constructed for the WEC trust by shorting currency futures contracts to protect against exchange rate losses. Describe one characteristic of this hedge that WEC's investment committee might deem undesirable.

10. Explain why the currency of Country A, whose interest rates are twice as great as those in Country B, must trade at a forward discount. If there were no difference between the spot and forward exchange rates in this interest rate environment, what arbitrage trade could be constructed to take advantage of the situation?

PROBLEMS

1. It is March 9, and you have just entered into a short position in a soybean meal futures contract. The contract expires on July 9 and calls for the delivery of 100 tons of soybean meal. Further, because this is a futures position, it requires the posting of a $3,000 initial margin and a $1,500 maintenance margin; for simplicity, however, assume that the account is marked to market on a monthly basis. Assume the following represent the contract delivery prices (in dollars per ton) that prevail on each settlement date:

March 9 (initiation)	$173.00
April 9	179.75
May 9	189.00
June 9	182.50
July 9 (delivery)	174.25

a. Calculate the equity value of your margin account on each settlement date, including any additional equity required to meet a margin call. Also compute the amount of cash that will be returned to you on July 9, and the gain or loss on your position, expressed as a percentage of your initial margin commitment.

b. Assuming that the underlying soybean meal investment pays no dividend and requires a storage cost of 1.5 percent (of current value), calculate the current (i.e., March 9) spot price for a ton of soybean meal and the implied May 9 price for the same ton. In your calculations, assume that an annual risk-free rate of 8 percent prevails over the entire contract life.

c. Now suppose that on March 9 you also entered into a long forward contract for the purchase of 100 tons of soybean meal on July 9. Assume further that the July forward and futures contract prices always are identical to one another at any point in time. Calculate the cash amount of your gain or loss if you unwind both positions in their respective markets on May 9 and June 9, taking into account the prevailing settlement conditions in the two markets.

2. You are a coffee dealer anticipating the purchase of 82,000 pounds of coffee in three months. You are concerned that the price of coffee will rise, so you take a long position in coffee futures. Each contract covers 37,500 pounds, and so, rounding to the nearest contract, you decide to go long in two contracts. The futures price at the time you initiate your hedge is 55.95 cents per pound. Three months later, the actual spot price of coffee turns out to be 58.56 cents per pound and the futures price is 59.20 cents per pound.

a. Determine the effective price at which you purchased your coffee. How do you account for the difference in amounts for the spot and hedge positions?

b. Describe the nature of the basis risk in this long hedge.

 3. *CFA Examination Level III*

June Klein, CFA, manages a $100 million (market value) U.S. government bond portfolio for an institution. She anticipates a small parallel shift in the yield curve and wants to fully hedge the portfolio against any such change.

PORTFOLIO AND TREASURY BOND FUTURES CONTRACT CHARACTERISTICS

Security	Modified Duration	Basis Point Value	Conversion Factor for Cheapest to Deliver Bond	Portfolio Value/Future Contract Price
Portfolio	10 years	$100,000	Not Applicable	$100,000,000
U.S. Treasury bond futures contract	8 years	$75.32	1	94–05

a. Discuss two reasons for using futures rather than selling bonds to hedge a bond portfolio. No calculations required.
b. Formulate Klein's hedging strategy using only the futures contract shown. Calculate the number of futures contracts to implement the strategy. Show all calculations.
c. Determine how each of the following would change in value if interest rates increase by 10 basis points as anticipated. Show all calculations.
   (1) The original portfolio
   (2) The Treasury bond futures position
   (3) The newly hedged portfolio
d. State three reasons why Klein's hedging strategy might not fully protect the portfolio against interest rate risk.
e. Describe a zero-duration hedging strategy using only the government bond portfolio and options on U.S. Treasury bond futures contracts. No calculations required.

4. A bond speculator currently has positions in two separate corporate bond portfolios: a long holding in Portfolio 1 and a short holding in Portfolio 2. All the bonds have the same credit quality. Other relevant information on these positions includes:

Portfolio	Bond	Market Value (Mil.)	Coupon Rate	Compounding Frequency	Maturity	Yield to Maturity
1	A	$6.0	0%	Annual	3 yrs	7.31%
	B	4.0	0	Annual	14 yrs	7.31
2	C	11.5	4.6	Annual	9 yrs	7.31

Treasury bond futures (based on $100,000 face value of 20-year T-bonds having an 8 percent semi-annual coupon) with a maturity exactly six months from now are currently priced at 109–24 with a corresponding yield to maturity of 7.081 percent. The "yield betas" between the futures contract and Bonds A, B, and C are 1.13, 1.03, and 1.01, respectively. Finally, the modified duration for the T-bond underlying the futures contract is 10.355 years.

a. Calculate the modified duration (expressed in years) for each of the two bond portfolios. What will be the *approximate* percentage change in the value of each if all yields increase by 60 basis points on an annual basis?
b. Without performing the calculations, explain which of the portfolios will *actually* have its value impacted to the greatest extent (in absolute terms) by the shift yields. (Hint: This explanation requires knowledge of the concept of *bond convexity.*)
c. Assuming the bond speculator wants to hedge her *net* bond position, what is the optimal number of futures contracts that must be bought or sold? Start by calculating the optimal hedge ratio between the futures contract and the two bond portfolios separately and then combine them.

5. *CFA Examination Level II*
Susan Baker is an investor who seeks to find arbitrage pricing discrepancies in the marketplace over the next six months. She has noted the following data:

Instrument	Spot Price	Futures Price for Contract Expiring In Six Months	Income from Treasury Note for Six Months	Finance Charge for Six Months
U.S. Treasury note deliverable on the futures contract	$101	$100 (invoice price)	$4.50	$2.50

List the components of the arbitrage transaction and calculate the arbitrage profits, if any, that are available to exploit a possible pricing discrepancy. Show your calculations.

6. As a relationship officer for a money-center commercial bank, one of your corporate accounts has just approached you about a one-year loan for $1,000,000. The customer would pay a quarterly interest expense based on the prevailing level of LIBOR at the beginning of each three-month period. As is the bank's convention on all such loans, the amount of the interest payment would then be paid at the end of the quarterly cycle when the new rate for the next cycle is determined. You observe the following LIBOR yield curve in the cash market.

90-day LIBOR	4.60%
180-day LIBOR	4.75
270-day LIBOR	5.00
360-day LIBOR	5.30

a. If 90-day LIBOR rises to the levels "predicted" by the implied forward rates, what will the dollar level of the bank's interest receipt be at the end of each quarter during the one-year loan period?
b. If the bank wanted to hedge its exposure to failing LIBOR on this loan commitment, describe the sequence of transactions in the futures markets it could undertake.
c. Assuming the yields inferred from the Eurodollar futures contract prices for the next three settlement periods are equal to the implied forward rates, calculate the annuity value that would leave the bank indifferent between making the floating-rate loan and hedging it in the futures market, and making a one-year fixed-rate loan. Express this annuity value in both dollar and annual (360-day) percentage terms.

7. Suppose that one day in early April, you observe the following prices on futures contracts maturing in June: 93.35 for Eurodollar and 94.07 for T-bill. These prices imply three-month LIBOR and T-bill settlement yields of 6.65 percent and 5.93, respectively. You think that over the next quarter the general level of interest rates will rise while the credit spread built into LIBOR will narrow. Demonstrate how you can use a TED (Treasury/Eurodollar) spread, which is a simultaneous long (short) position in a Eurodollar contract and short (long) position in the T-bill contract, to create a position that will benefit from these views.

8. An investment bank engages in stock index arbitrage for its own and customer accounts. On a particular day, the S&P index at the New York Stock Exchange is 602.25 when the futures contract for delivery in 90 days is 614.75. If the annualized 90-day interest rate is 8.00 percent and the (annualized) dividend yield is 3 percent, would program trading involving stock index arbitrage possibly take place? If so, describe the transactions that should be undertaken and calculate the profit that would be made per each "share" of the S&P 500 index used in the trade.

9. *CFA Examination Level III*

Alex Andrew, who manages a $95 million large-capitalization U.S. equity portfolio, currently forecasts that equity markets will decline soon. Andrew prefers to avoid the transaction costs of making sales but wants to hedge $15 million of the portfolio's current value using S&P 500 futures.

Because Andrew realizes that his portfolio will not track the S&P 500 index exactly, he performs a regression analysis on his actual portfolio returns versus the S&P futures returns over the past year. The regression analysis indicates a risk-minimizing beta of 0.88 with an R^2 of 0.92.

Futures Contract Data	
S&P 500 futures price	1,000
S&P 500 index	999
S&P 500 index multiplier	250

a. Calculate the number of futures contracts required to hedge $15 million of Andrew's portfolio, using the data shown. State whether the hedge is long or short. Show all calculations.

b. Identify two alternative methods (other than selling securities from the portfolio or using futures) that replicate the feature strategy in Part a. Contract each of these methods with the futures strategy.

10. The treasurer of a middle market, import-export company has approached you for advice on how to best invest some of the firm's short-term cash balances. The company, which has been a client of the bank that employs you for a few years, has $250,000 that it is able to commit for a one-year holding period. The treasurer is currently considering two alternatives: (1) invest all the funds in a one-year U.S. Treasury bill offering a bond equivalent yield of 4.25 percent, and (2) invest all the funds in a Swiss government security over the same horizon, locking in the spot and forward currency exchanges in the FX market. A quick call to the bank's FX desk gives you the following two-way currency exchange quotes.

	Swiss Francs per U.S. Dollar	U.S. Dollar per Swiss Franc
Spot	1.5035	0.6651
1-year CHF futures	—	0.6586

a. Calculate the one-year bond equivalent yield for the Swiss government security that would support the interest rate parity condition

b. Assuming the actual yield on a one-year Swiss government bond is 5.50 percent, which strategy would leave the treasurer with the greatest return after one year?

c. Describe the transactions that an arbitrageur could use to take advantage of this apparent mispricing and calculate what the profit would be for a $250,000 transaction.

11. *CFA Examination Level II*

Donna Doni, CFA, wants to explore potential inefficiencies in the futures market. The TOBEC stock index has a spot value of 185.00 now. TOBEC futures contracts are settled in cash, and underlying contract values are determined by multiplying $100 times the index value. The current annual risk-free interest rate is 6.0 percent.

a. Calculate the theoretical price of the futures contract expiring six months from now, using the cost-of-carry model. Show your calculations.

The total (round-trip) transaction cost for trading a futures contract is $15.00.

b. Calculate the lower bound for the price of the futures contract expiring six months from now. Show your calculations.

APPENDIX
Chapter 21

A. A Closed-Form Equation for Calculating Duration

To calculate the duration statistic, it helps to think of a bond that pays a fixed coupon for a finite maturity as being just a portfolio of zero coupon cash flows. Duration is then the weighted average of the payment (i.e., maturity) dates of those zero coupon cash flows. What the duration statistic essentially does is convert a bond with any given coupon and maturity into what it would look like if it had been a zero coupon bond. Thus, a bond's duration is its *zero coupon equivalent maturity*.

To see how this calculation works, consider a nonamortizing, five-year bond with a face value of $1,000 making annual coupon payments of $120 (i.e., 12 percent). Assuming a current yield to maturity of 10 percent, this bond will trade at a premium and its weighted average payment date (i.e., duration) is 4.074 years, as shown in Exhibit 21A.1. Interpreting the coupon bond as a portfolio of zero coupon cash flows, the duration of 4.0740 years is the weighted average maturity of that portfolio, where the weights are the respective shares of market value (e.g., the one-year zero coupon cash flow is 10.14 percent of the value of the portfolio, the five-year zero 64.64 percent).

This five-year coupon bond with a duration of 4.0740 years is equivalent in terms of price risk to a zero coupon bond having a maturity of 4.0740 years. As we saw in Chapter 18, this suggests that when the interest rate increases by 1 percent above its original level (i.e., $[\Delta (1 + i) \div (1 + i)] = 0.01$), then the price of this bond will decline by about 4.074 percent).

The Macaulay duration can be calculated with the following formula:

21.A1

$$D = \frac{1 + \dfrac{Y}{n}}{\dfrac{Y}{n}} - \frac{1 + \dfrac{Y}{n} + \left[(n \times T)\left(\dfrac{C}{F} - \dfrac{Y}{n}\right)\right]}{\dfrac{C}{F}\left[\left(1 + \dfrac{Y}{n}\right)^{n \times T} - 1\right] + \dfrac{Y}{n}}$$

where:

C = the periodic coupon payment
F = the face value at maturity
T = the number of years until maturity
n = the payments per year
Y = the yield to maturity

Note that the duration statistic in Equation 21A.1 is calculated on the basis of the underlying periodic cash flows even though it is often annualized when reporting the statistic by dividing it by n.

In the preceding numerical example, $Y = 0.10$, $n = 1$, $T = 5$, $C/F = 0.12$, and $Y/n = 0.10$. The bond's duration can therefore be solved as:

$$D = \frac{1 + 0.10}{0.10} - \frac{1 + 0.10 + 5(0.12 - 0.10)}{(0.12)[(1 + 0.10)^5 - 1] + 0.10} = 4.0740$$

As a second example of this formula, what is the duration of a 30-year Treasury bond with a 7⅝ percent coupon and a stated yield to maturity of 7.72 percent? Here you need to recall that T-bonds pay semiannual

Exhibit 21A.1 | **A Duration Calculation**

Year	Cash Flow	PV at 10%	PV ÷ Price	Year × (PV ÷ Price)
1	$120	$ 109.09	0.1014	0.1014
2	120	99.17	0.0922	0.1844
3	120	90.16	0.0838	0.2514
4	120	81.96	0.0762	0.3047
5	$1,120	695.43	0.6464	3.2321
		Price = $1,075.82		Duration = 4.0740 years

interest and so the appropriate definitions of the variables are: $C/F = 0.38125$, $T = 30$, $n = 2$, and $Y/n = 0.0386$. Therefore:

$$D = \frac{1 + 0.0386}{0.0386} - \frac{1 + 0.0386 + 60(0.038125 + 0.0386)}{(0.038125)[(1 + 0.0386)^{60} - 1] + 0.0386} = 24.18 \text{ periods}$$

or 12.09 years. Although the method summarized by Exhibit 22A.1 always will work for any nonamortizing bond, the closed-form expression is considerably quicker when a large number of coupon payments are involved.

B. Calculating Money Market Implied Forward Rates

Implied forward rates are an essential factor in understanding how short-term interest rate futures contracts are priced. In our discussion of the expectations hypothesis of yield curve in Chapter 18, we saw that implied forward rates represented the sequence of future short-term rates that were built into the yield to maturity of a longer-term security. However, implied forward rates can have another interpretation. Consider an investor who is deciding between the following strategies for making a two-year investment: (1) buy a single two-year, zero coupon bond yielding 6 percent per annum; or (2) buy a one-year, zero coupon bond with a 5 percent yield and replace it at maturity with another one-year instrument. An implied forward rate is the answer to the following question: At what rate must the investor be able to reinvest the interim proceeds from the second strategy to exactly equal the total return from the first investment? In other words, the implied forward rate is a *breakeven* reinvestment rate. In the notation of Chapter 18, we want to solve for $_2r_1$ in the following equation:

$$(1 + 0.06)^2 = (1 + 0.05)(1 + {_2r_1})$$

or $_2r_1 = [(1 + 0.06)^2 \div (1 + 0.05)] - 1 = 7$ percent. An alternative interpretation is that investing for two years with a return of 6 percent per year is exactly the same as investing for one year at 5 percent, with the principal and interest then reinvested for a second year at 7 percent.

Implied forward money market rates can be interpreted in the same way as bond yields, but they must be calculated differently because of differences in the quotation methods for the various rates. For example, we have seen that LIBOR is a bank *add-on yield* (AY) that is used to figure out how much money, F, an investor will have at maturity in T days given an initial investment of P (i.e., interest is "added on"):

$$F = P + \left[P \times AY \times \frac{T}{360}\right] = P\left[1 \times AY \times \frac{T}{360}\right]$$

With this expression, a 60-day investment of $50,000 in a bank deposit paying LIBOR equal to 5.30 percent would be worth $50,441.67 at maturity. Notice that LIBOR is based on a presumed 360-day year, the standard U.S. money market practice.

With these quotation conventions, Smith (1989) has shown that the implied forward rate between two money market instruments quoted on an add-on basis (e.g., LIBOR) can be calculated as

21B.1 $$_BAY_A = \left[\frac{(B \times AY_B) - (A \times AY_A)}{B - A}\right]\left[\frac{1}{1 + \left(\frac{A \times AY_A}{360}\right)}\right]$$

where AY_A and AY_B are add-on yields for A and B days from settlement to maturity, with $B > A$. The implied forward rate ($_BAY_A$) also is on an add-on basis and has maturity of $(B - A)$ days. That is, $_BAY_A$ corresponds to the time period between Date A and Date B.

As an example of these calculations, consider the following short-term yield curves for LIBOR:

Maturity	LIBOR
30 days	4.15%
60 days	4.25
90 days	4.35

What is the implied forward LIBOR between Days 60 and 90? Using $AY_A = 0.0425$, $AY_B = 0.0435$, $A = 60$ days, and $B = 90$ days for LIBOR, we have:

$$_{90}AY_{60} = \left[\frac{(90 \times 0.0435) - (60 \times 0.0425)}{90 - 60} \right] \left[\frac{1}{1 + \left(\dfrac{60 \times 0.0425}{360} \right)} \right] = 4.52\%$$

That is, investing in a 60-day bank deposit at 4.25 percent and then a 30-day deposit at 4.52 percent would have the same total return (or cost of funds) as the 90-day deposit at 4.35 percent. This can be confirmed by examining the cash flows on the transactions. For example, the total return on a $100,000, 60-day deposit at 4.25 percent would be $100,708. This amount reinvested in a 30-day deposit at 4.52 percent would provide a total of $101,087, equaling the payoff on a $100,000, 90-day deposit at 4.35 percent.

Chapter 22

Option Contracts

After you read this chapter, you should be able to answer the following questions:

- How are options traded on exchanges and in OTC markets?
- How are options for stock, stock indexes, foreign currency, and futures contracts quoted in the financial press?
- How can investors use option contracts to hedge an existing risk exposure?
- What are the three steps in establishing the fundamental no-arbitrage value of an option contract?
- What is the binomial (or two-state) option pricing model, and in what way is it an extension of the basic valuation approach?
- What is the Black-Scholes option pricing model, and how does it extend the binomial valuation approach?
- What is the relationship between the Black-Scholes and put-call parity valuation models?
- How does the payment of a dividend by the underlying asset impact the value of an option?
- How can models for valuing stock options be adapted to other underlying assets such as stock indexes, foreign currency, and futures contracts?
- How do American- and European-style options differ from one another?
- What is implied volatility, and what is its role in the contract valuation process?
- How do investors use options with the underlying security or in combination with one another to create payoff structures tailored to a particular need or view of future market conditions?
- What differentiates a spread from a straddle, a strangle, or a range forward?

Broken down to the most basic level, only two kinds of derivative contracts exist: forwards, which fix the price or rate of an underlying asset; and options, which allow holders to decide at a later date whether such a fixing is in their best interest. With our initial examination of forward and futures contracts now complete, this chapter turns our attention to issues concerning the trading and valuation of option contracts. We will develop the discussion in four parts. First, we consider more closely the contract terms and trading mechanics for both call and put options. Options trade on exchanges as well as in the OTC dealer markets and can be based on a wide array of securities and commodities. To focus this discussion, we concentrate on options that have financial instruments as underlying securities, including options on individual stocks, stock indexes, foreign currency, and futures contracts. A formal discussion of options on interest rates is highlighted in the next chapter.

The second topic we explore is how option contracts are valued in an efficient capital market. We show that, at least intuitively, this can be viewed as a simple, three-step process: (1) creating a riskless hedge portfolio combining options with the underlying security, (2) invoking a no-arbitrage assumption about the rate of return that such a portfolio should earn, and (3) solving for the option value consistent with the first two steps. We show that several of the most widely used valuation models, including the **binomial** and **Black-Scholes** models, are consistent with this approach. In this analysis, it is important to keep in mind that we will be *valuing* options and not *pricing* them. Indeed, prices are established through the actions of buyers and sellers; investors and analysts use valuation models to estimate what those prices should be.

Third, we consider several extensions and advanced topics in option valuation. In particular, we show how the Black-Scholes model for call options on stock can be adapted to value put options, as well as the other financial assets commonly used as underlying assets. We describe how the payment of dividends affects an option's value and how the model can be adjusted accordingly. We discuss the practical differences between the European and American styles of contracting, and we also examine price or return volatility—the role it plays in the valuation process and the ways an investor can estimate it in practice.

Finally, several option-based investment and hedging strategies are examined. After describing protective put and covered call strategies, we demonstrate how options can be used in combination with one another to create risk-reward trade-offs that do not otherwise exist in financial markets. In this sense, options can be used as building blocks to help investors design customized payoff schemes. We consider three broad classes of option combination strategies: **straddles**, which involve the purchase and sale of both puts and calls; **spreads**, in which the investor simultaneously buys one call (or put) while selling another; and **range forwards** (or collars), which require the purchase of a call and the concurrent sale of a put, or vice versa.

AN OVERVIEW OF OPTION MARKETS AND CONTRACTS

In Chapter 21, we discussed the primary difference between forward and futures contracts: futures are standardized and trade on exchanges, while forward contracts have negotiable terms and therefore must be arranged in the OTC market. With the development of organized option exchanges during the past several decades, option contracts offer investors similar trading alternatives. The most important features of how these contracts are traded and quoted in the financial press are highlighted in the following sections.

Option Market Conventions

Option contracts have been traded for centuries in the form of separate agreements or embedded in other securities. Malkiel (2004), for example, tells the story of how call options were used to speculate on flower prices during the tulip bulb frenzy in 17th-century Holland. Then, and for most of the time until now, options were arranged and executed in private transactions. Collectively, these private transactions represent the OTC market for options. Like forward contracts, OTC option agreements can be structured around any terms or underlying asset to which two parties can agree. This has been a particularly useful mechanism when the underlying asset is too illiquid to support a widely traded contract. Also, credit risk is a paramount concern in this market because OTC agreements typically are not collateralized. This credit risk is one-sided with an option agreement because the buyer worries about the seller's ability to honor his obligations, but the seller has received everything he will get up front and is not concerned about the buyer's creditworthiness.

As in all security markets, OTC options ultimately are created in response to the needs and desires of the corporations and individual investors who use these products. Financial institutions, such as money-center banks and investment banks, serve as market makers by facilitating the arrangement and execution of these deals. Over the years, various trade associations of broker-dealers in OTC options have emerged (and, in some cases, faded), including the Put and Call Brokers and Dealers Association, which helped arrange private stock option transactions, and the International Swap and Derivatives Association, which monitors the activities of market makers for interest rate and foreign exchange derivatives. These trade groups create a common set of standards and language to govern industry transactions.

In April 1973, the Chicago Board of Trade changed the dynamics of option trading when it opened the Chicago Board Options Exchange (CBOE). Specializing in stock and stock index options, the CBOE has introduced two important aspects of market uniformity. Foremost, contracts offered by the CBOE are standardized in terms of the underlying common stock, the number of shares covered, the delivery dates, and the range of available exercise prices. This standardization, which increases the possibility of basis risk, was meant to help develop a secondary market for the contracts. The rapid increase in trading volume on the CBOE and other options exchanges suggests that this feature is desirable compared to OTC contracts that must often be held to maturity due to a lack of liquidity.

The centralization of the trading function also necessitated the creation of the **Options Clearing Corporation (OCC)**, which acts as the guarantor of each CBOE-traded contract. Therefore, end users in option transactions ultimately bear the credit risk of the OCC. For this reason, even though the OCC is independent of the exchange, it demands that the option seller post margin to guarantee future performance. Again, the option buyer will not have a margin account because a future obligation to the seller is nonexistent. Finally, this central market structure makes monitoring, regulation, and price reporting much easier than in the decentralized OTC markets.

Price Quotations for Exchange-Traded Options

Equity Options Options on the common stock of individual companies have traded on the CBOE since 1973. Several other markets, including the American (AMEX), Philadelphia (PHLX), and Pacific (PSE) Stock Exchanges, began trading their own contracts shortly afterward. The CBOE remains the largest exchange in terms of option market volume with a market share of just under 40 percent, with the AMEX second at around 25 percent. Options on each of these exchanges are traded similarly, with a typical contract for 100 shares of stock. Because exchange-traded contracts are not issued by the company whose common stock is the underlying asset, they require secondary transactions in the equity if exercised.[1]

Panel A of Exhibit 22.1 displays price and volume statistics for a sample of the most actively traded equity options on March 25, 2005. Notice that several of the companies repre-

---

[1]Call options issued directly by the firm whose common stock is the underlying asset are called *warrants*. We discuss the use and valuation of these contracts in Chapter 23.

Exhibit 22.1	Stock Option Quotations

Panel A. Most Active Individual Stock Options

Name		Last	Chng	vol	Name		Last	Chng	vol
1)LU Jan07 C5	VEU+AA	.20	+.05	358679	15)F May05 C12½	F+EU	.10	unch	10830
2)MSFT May05 C22½	MSQ+EX	2.05	+.05	45459	16)SNDK Oct05 C32½	SWQ+JZ	2.95	+.15	10814
3)TASR Apr05 C15	QUR+DC	.60	+.45	24735	17)PFE Apr05 C25	PFE+DE	1.50	+.10	10788
4)S Apr05 C50	S+DJ	.05	-6.65	23607	18)F Jan06 C12½	WFO+AU	.80	+.20	10659
5)GM Jan07 P10	UGN+MB	.85	-.25	21457	19)HD Aug05 C37½	HD+HU	2.60	+.35	10246
6)LEXR Apr05 C7½	EQG+DU	.70	+.65	20188	20)ORCL Apr05 P12	ORQ+PN	.20	unch	10183
7)LEXR Apr05 C5	EQG+DA	1.75	+1.50	19364	21)GM Jan06 P15	WGN+MC	.70	-.20	9780
8)XLE Jun05 P40	XLE+RN	1.30	-.05	16015	22)ELN Apr05 C10	ELN+DB	.10	unch	9131
9)TASR Apr05 C12½	QUR+DU	1.85	+1.30	15223	23)XLF Jan06 P27	WFS+MA	1.05	-.10	9021
10)SMH Apr05 P32½	SMH+PZ	.65	-.07	14601	24)DAL Jan06 P2½	WDA+MZ	.70	-.05	8785
11)YHOO Apr05 C32½	YHQ+DZ	.55	+.05	14009	25)IWM May05 C129	DIW+EY	1.25	+.15	8783
12)YHOO Apr05 C35	YHQ+DG	.15	+.05	13905	26)GE Apr05 C35	GE+DG	1.05	+.15	8454
13)AIG May05 P55	AIG+QK	2.35	+.30	13092	27)GM Jan07 P20	WGN+MD	2.90	-.60	8327
14)PFE Apr05 C27½	PFE+DY	.25	+.10	11830	28)TASR Jun05 P10	QUR+RB	1.05	-.05	8278

Panel B. Stock Options for Microsoft (MSFT)

Underlying:	Last	Volume	1-Day Chg	Open	High	Low	Yest.	2-Day Ch
MSFT US	24.28	79041968	+.10	24.24	24.47	24.1998	24.18	+.29

Option	Symbol	Last	Chng	Vol	Option	Symbol	Last	Chng	Vol
1)May05 22.5 Calls	EX	2.05	+.05	45459	17)Oct05 17.5 Calls	JW	7.00	unch	540
2)Jul05 25 Calls	GJ	.80	+.05	6769	18)Oct05 27.5 Calls	JY	.33	+.03	440
3)Apr05 24.5 Calls	DR	.30	unch	6514	19)Jul05 22.5 Puts	SX	.40	unch	430
4)Jul05 25 Puts	SJ	1.35	-.05	5273	20)Jan07 27 Calls	AS	1.70	+.05	416
5)Apr05 24.5 Puts	PR	.45	-.10	2992	21)May05 22.5 Puts	QX	.15	-.10	389
6)May05 25 Calls	EJ	.40	-.05	1816	22)May05 27.5 Calls	EY	.05	unch	317
7)Jul05 22.5 Calls	GX	2.35	+.05	1402	23)Jul05 27.5 Calls	GY	.10	-.05	301
8)May05 25 Puts	QJ	1.05	-.10	1282	24)Apr05 22 Calls	DQ	2.40	+.15	292
9)Jan06 27 Calls	AS	.70	+.05	1213	25)Jan07 27 Puts	MS	3.40	unch	249
10)Apr05 25 Calls	DJ	.15	-.05	1094	26)Jan06 19.5 Puts	MP	.20	-.05	239
11)Jan06 30 Calls	AK	.20	unch	1005	27)Oct05 25 Puts	VJ	1.50	-.10	199
12)Apr05 27 Calls	DS	.05	unch	850	28)Jan06 22 Puts	MQ	.65	unch	192
13)Jul05 17.5 Calls	GW	6.90	+.10	831	29)Jan06 27 Puts	MS	3.00	unch	162
14)Jan06 29.5 Calls	AT	.25	+.05	797	30)Oct05 25 Calls	JJ	1.15	unch	153
15)Apr05 25 Puts	PJ	.75	-.10	632	31)Jan07 24.5 Calls	AR	2.85	unch	130
16)Jan06 24.5 Calls	AR	1.70	+.05	545	32)Jan06 24.5 Puts	MR	1.40	-.15	120

sented on this list—for example, Microsoft (MSFT), Sears (S), General Motors (GM), Yahoo! (YHOO), Pfizer (PFE)—would also rank among the most widely traded stocks. To interpret this exhibit, suppose that an investor wanted to buy an option on Microsoft Computer common stock, a quote for which is highlighted on the chart. The entry indicates that on this day the Microsoft call option with an exercise price of 22.5 and an expiration date in May 2005 was the second most widely traded position, with an exchange volume of almost 45,500 contracts.

By convention, stock options expire on the Saturday following the third Friday of the designated month. Panel B of Exhibit 22.1 provides more details for this contract, as well as many of the other MSFT options that were available to investors in March 2005.

To consider the dynamics of a specific option transaction in more detail, assume that on March 25, 2005, the investor did indeed buy the MSFT May 2005 22.5 call. Based on the last reported price, his contract would cost a total of $205.00, calculated as the stated per-share price of 2.05 multiplied by 100 shares. In exchange for that payment, the holder of this American-style call would then be able to exercise the option in mid-May—or any time before then—by paying $2,250 (= 22.50 × 100) and would receive 100 Microsoft shares from the option seller, who is obligated to make that exchange at the buyer's request. That request will only be rational if the mid-May price of MSFT is greater than $22.50. If that price closes below $22.50, the investor will simply let the call expire without acting on the option; that is her right as the derivative buyer. Finally, notice that with the prevailing Microsoft share price being $24.28 (which is shown on the second line in Panel B), the investor could immediately recover $1.78 of the $2.05 she paid for the contract. Her time premium of $0.27 (= 2.05 − 1.78) preserves her right to buy MSFT stock at a price of $22.50 for the next three months, even if the market value of those shares moves higher.[2]

Consider another investor who sells the May 22.5 Microsoft put, the details of which are also highlighted in Panel B of Exhibit 22.1. In return for an upfront receipt of $15.00 (= 0.15 × 100), he now must stand ready to buy 100 shares of stock in mid-May for $2,250 if the option holder chooses to exercise his option to sell. The stock price will, of course, have to fall from its current level before this can occur. The investor in this case has sold an out-of-the-money contract and hopes that it will stay out of the money through expiration, letting the passing of time decay the time premium to zero. As we saw earlier, the front-end premium is all that sellers of put or call options ever receive, and they hope to retain as much of it possible. Like the long position in the call, the short put position benefits from an increase in MSFT share prices.

Finally, notice that most of the options listed in both panels of Exhibit 22.1 expire within a few months of the quotation date. In fact, the expiration dates available for these exchange-traded contracts are the two nearest term months (April and May for Microsoft) and up to three additional months from a quarterly cycle beginning in either January, February, or March. In the case of Microsoft options, July 2005, October 2005, and January 2006 (which is part of the quarterly cycle beginning in January) are the additional months most frequently listed. Exhibit 22.2 gives quotations for Long-term Equity Anticipation Securities (LEAPS), as they appeared in *The Wall Street Journal*. Despite their more grandiose name, LEAPS are simply regular call and put options with longer expiration dates. Like the contracts just described, LEAPS are also traded on the CBOE and have comparable terms.

One advantage of LEAPS in the present context is that they allow us to see the effect that time to expiration has on the value of an option. For instance, consider the pricing data for two of the LEAPS contracts available for Citigroup, which are shaded in Exhibit 22.2. On this date, the share price of Citigroup was $44.52. Two call options having an exercise price of 50 are listed: one expiring in January 2006 and the other expiring in January 2007. Since the prevailing stock price (i.e., $44.52) is lower than the $50 exercise price, both contracts are currently out of the money. However, the shorter term contract sells for only $1.00 while the one expiring a year later

---

[2]Recall from Chapter 20 that a call option's value can be divided into two components: the *intrinsic value*, which is the greater of either zero or the stock price minus the striking price, and the *time premium*. In this example, the Microsoft call is said to be *in the money* because it has positive intrinsic value, whereas an option with no intrinsic value is *out of the money*.

Exhibit 22.2 | Long-Term Equity Anticipation Securities (LEAPS) Quotations

LEAPS-LONG TERM OPTIONS

OPTION/STRIKE		EXP	-CALL- VOL	LAST	-PUT- VOL	LAST	OPTION/STRIKE		EXP	-CALL- VOL	LAST	-PUT- VOL	LAST	OPTION/STRIKE		EXP	-CALL- VOL	LAST	-PUT- VOL	LAST
AMR	2.50	Jan 06	20	7.40	4850	0.15	ElecArt	60	Jan 06	2219	5.10	10	8.50	Nasd100Tr	37	Jan 06	1510	2.80	2161	2.45
AberFitch	25	Jan 06	...	...	2000	0.15	55.17	65	Jan 06	2474	3.60	32	12	Nasd100 o	39.63	Jan 06	2090	1.65	2618	3.92
Altria	70	Jan 06	2561	2.85	15	9.30	Exxon	65	Jan 06	2575	2.45	4	7.70	NikeB	60	Jan 06	13	24.90	2000	0.45
Amazon	35	Jan 06	73	4.50	2005	5.40	59.00	75	Jan 06	4306	0.65	...	...	Pfizer	27.50	Jan 06	7453	1.85	117	2.75
AmExpr	50	Jan 06	1023	4.80	2055	3.60	FstData	30	Jan 06	3051	11.10	150	0.55	26.17	30	Jan 07	1763	2.05	14	5
50.28	55	Jan 06	5020	2.70	...	...	39.88	35	Jan 06	3279	7.10	31	1.40	ProctGam	45	Jan 06	16	9	5150	0.65
AmIntGp	50	Jan 06	15	10.20	2562	2.35	FordM	12.50	Jan 06	10659	0.80	248	1.95	Qualcom	27.50	Jan 06	...	...	3546	1.15
55.61	70	Jan 06	2059	1.10	1013	14.10	11.29	15	Jan 06	5257	0.20	30	3.80	RylCarb	30	Jan 06	...	...	2500	0.50
AppleC	37.50	Jan 07	1850	13.60	...	...	FredMac	60	Jan 06	...	...	1773	4.10	SPDR	125	Dec 06	1500	7.30	3126	10.80
AthroGen	10	Jan 06	...	...	2000	1.50	GenElec	30	Jan 06	231	6.80	2630	0.40	SP Fncl	27	Jan 06	...	...	10021	1.05
13.92	25	Jan 07	2000	4.70	...	...	GenMotr	7.50	Jan 07	...	...	6201	0.55	Starbucks	35	Jan 06	...	...	2000	0.45
Avon	37.50	Jan 06	...	...	2006	1.60	GenMotrs	10	Jan 06	...	...	8124	0.30	WA Mutl	30	Jan 07	102	10	2220	1.40
BostSci	35	Jan 06	2015	1.65	16	6.70	GenMotr	10	Jan 07	...	...	21457	0.85	WillmsCos	17.50	Jan 06	2500	2.95	10	1.30
Bowater	40	Jan 07	1875	5.40	...	...	GenMotrs	15	Jan 06	...	...	9780	0.70							
BrMySq	25	Jan 06	3016	1.75	2	1.75	GenMotr	20	Jan 07	26	11.50	8327	2.90	**Volume & Open Interest**						
Calpine	2.50	Jan 06	180	0.90	5292	0.50	GenMotrs	25	Jan 06	262	6.20	2356	2.35	**Summaries**						
2.90	2.50	Jan 07	4586	1.30	20	0.85	29.30	30	Jan 06	2126	3.30	1769	4.30	**BOSTON**						
CircCity	10	Jan 06	3	5.70	2500	0.05	GenMotr	30	Jan 07	5843	5	506	6.40	Call Vol:			16,835	Open Int:		0
Citigrp	42.50	Jan 06	819	4.30	1724	2.20	IAC InterA	30	Jan 06	2104	0.55	35	8.80	Put Vol:			12,130	Open Int:		0
44.52	50	Jan 06	7300	1	151	6.40	21.09	40	Jan 06	2920	0.10	...	...	**CHICAGO BOARD**						
44.52	50	Jan 07	3166	2.65	51	7.57	iShRs2000	121	Jan 07	...	...	1900	10.60	Call Vol:			135,299	Open Int:		8,328,565
CompAsc	25	Jan 06	2700	4.20	...	...	IBM	95	Jan 06	39	4.30	2010	6.10	Put Vol:			32,184	Open Int:		7,357,669
DJIA Diam	104	Jan 07	2510	10.30	2503	6.50	IntGame	35	Jan 06	59	0.65	4012	8.60	**INTL SECURITIES**						
Dell Inc	40	Jan 06	91	2.75	2505	3.10	Morgan	35	Jan 06	165	2.40	2728	2.65	Call Vol:			104,343	Open Int:		28,313,257
DeltaAir	2.50	Jan 06	74	1.80	8785	0.70	KindMorg	50	Jan 06	...	...	2000	0.35	Put Vol:			75,445	Open Int:		26,862,244
eBay	20	Jan 06	...	...	4002	0.40	LexarMed	5	Jan 06	2354	2.85	293	1.20	**PACIFIC**						
35.50	27.50	Jan 06	2	10.40	5150	1.45	Lucent	5	Jan 06	3079	0.05	95	2.20	Call Vol:			38,985	Open Int:		30,487,063
35.50	37.50	Jan 06	53	4.50	6344	5.30	2.76	5	Jan 07	339751	0.20	22	2.20	Put Vol:			51,476	Open Int:		28,232,241
35.50	50	Jan 06	7333	1.30	42	14.90	Lyondell	35	Jan 06	6152	1.85	...	...	**TOTAL**						
35.50	52.50	Jan 06	15	1.15	2000	16.50	MBIA	50	Jan 06	...	...	2160	3.10	Call Vol:			295,462			
Elan	10	Jan 06	1723	1.65	40	4.20	MicronTc	10	Jan 06	131	1.65	2503	1.10	Put Vol:			171,235			

sells for $2.65. Of course, since these two contracts had the same exercise price, this difference in their market values is purely because of additional time premium. This time to expiration effect will be examined in greater detail shortly.

Stock Index Options   As we saw in Chapter 20, options on stock indexes, such as Standard and Poor's 100 or 500, are patterned closely after equity options. However, they differ in one important way: index options can only be settled in cash. This is because of the underlying index, which is a hypothetical portfolio that would be quite costly to duplicate in practice. First traded on the CBOE in 1983, index options are popular with investors for the same reason as stock index futures: they provide a relatively inexpensive and convenient way to take an investment or hedging position in a broad-based indicator of market performance. Index puts are particularly useful in portfolio insurance applications, such as the protective put strategy described earlier and again at the end of this chapter.

Prices for several of the more widely traded contracts are listed in Exhibit 22.3. They are interpreted in the same way as equity option prices, with each contract demanding the transfer of 100 "shares" of the underlying index. For example, the April S&P 500 index call and put

Exhibit 22.3 | Stock Index Option Quotations

INDEX OPTIONS TRADING

Underlying Indexes

	HIGH	LOW	CLOSE	NET CHG	FROM 12/31	% CHG
DJ Indus (DJX)	105.19	104.43	104.43	-0.13	-3.40	-3.2
DJ Trans (DTX)	376.42	373.33	374.47	1.24	-5.34	-1.4
DJ Util (DUX)	354.76	348.90	353.97	5.27	19.02	5.7
S&P 100 (OEX)	562.25	557.71	557.71	-1.16	-17.58	-3.1
S&P 500 (SPX)	1180.11	1171.42	1171.42	-1.11	-40.50	-3.3
CB-Tech (TXX)	581.78	574.92	576.18	1.26	-36.41	-5.9
CB-Mexico (MEX)	102.23	101.08	101.84	0.76	-2.45	-2.3
M5 Multintl (NFT)	656.71	651.50	651.50	-1.32	-8.70	-1.3
GSTI Comp (GTC)	173.46	171.72	171.72	-0.07	-18.14	-9.6
Nasdaq 100 (NDX)	1485.96	1469.94	1469.94	-1.83	-151.18	-9.3
NYSE (NYA)	7169.76	7127.18	7128.80	1.62	-121.26	-1.7
Russell 2000 (RUT)	619.65	612.06	615.27	3.21	-36.30	-5.6
Lps S&P 100 (OEX)	112.45	111.54	111.54	-0.23	-3.52	-3.1
Lps S&P 500 (SPX)	118.01	117.14	117.14	-0.11	-4.05	-3.3
Volatility (VIX)	13.88	12.97	13.42	-0.64	0.13	1.0
S&P Midcap (MID)	659.74	654.15	655.24	1.08	-8.07	-1.2
Major Mkt (XMI)	1142.10	1131.54	1131.54	-9.66	-8.75	-0.8
Eurotop 100 (AEUR)	235.09	234.07	234.84	1.47	8.32	3.7
HK Fltg (HKO)	268.04	268.04	268.04	-0.19	-14.83	-5.2
IW Internet (IIX)	146.22	144.45	144.45	-0.56	-29.29	-16.9
AM-Mexico (MXY)	120.77	118.41	120.21	1.80	-6.04	-4.8
Institut'l-A.M. (XII)	583.44	578.55	578.55	-1.50	-21.78	-3.6
Japan (JPN)			124.09	-0.03	3.61	3.0
MS Cyclical (CYC)	754.98	748.84	749.81	-0.86	-34.29	-4.4
MS Consumr (CMR)	576.58	573.92	573.92	-0.94	-16.87	-2.9
MS Hi Tech (MSH)	457.81	452.44	453.40	0.96	-54.27	-10.7
MS Internet (MOX)	13.00	12.84	12.84	-0.04	-2.00	-13.5
Pharmaceutical (DRG)	317.45	314.27	315.00	0.46	-1.62	-0.5
Biotech (BTK)	509.63	502.28	506.31	3.50	-37.94	-7.0
Gold/Silver (XAU)	94.50	92.88	92.97	-0.95	-6.38	-6.4
Utility Index (UTY)	387.79	382.85	386.71	4.82	13.10	3.5
Value Line (VAY)	1740.47	1724.95	1729.92	4.97	-64.27	-3.6
Bank (BKX)	96.46	95.30	95.30	-0.35	-8.81	-8.5
Semicond (SOXX)	420.34	415.18	415.88	1.02	-17.43	-4.0
Street.com (DOT)	184.64	182.43	182.44	-0.74	-25.87	-12.4
Oil Service (OSX)	136.82	134.66	135.40	0.79	11.46	9.2
PSE Tech (PSE)	733.46	726.41	727.73	1.44	-51.33	-6.6

CHICAGO

DJ INDUS AVG(DJX)

STRIKE		VOL	LAST	NET CHG	OPEN INT
Jun	100 p	7	3.80	-0.20	1,641
Apr	100 p	28	0.15	...	7,129
May	100 c	10	5.90	-4.00	20
May	100 p	30	0.55	-0.20	4,012
Jun	100 p	23	1.10	-0.05	17,687
Apr	101 p	40	0.20	-0.05	972
May	101 p	135	0.70	0.30	101
Apr	102 c	20	3.40	0.20	516
Apr	102 p	520	0.40	...	1,261
May	102 p	712	1.10	0.75	143
Jun	102 c	20	4.70	-0.40	19
Jun	102 p	803	1.55	-0.15	2,575
Apr	103 p	95	0.70	0.05	1,009
May	103 p	25	1.20	0.05	435
Apr	104 c	75	1.50	-0.20	1,420
Apr	104 p	94	0.85	-0.05	2,871
May	104 c	27	2.45	-0.10	640
May	104 p	2	1.70	...	3,883
Jun	104 c	12	3.10	...	11,496
Jun	104 p	78	2.25	0.05	15,237
Apr	105 c	602	0.95	-0.15	10,248
Apr	105 p	259	1.30	...	6,317
May	105 c	354	1.70	-0.30	140
May	105 p	1,256	2.25	0.55	1,327
Apr	106 c	437	0.50	-0.20	6,383
Apr	106 p	833	1.90	-0.10	9,254
May	106 c	109	1.40	-0.75	1,659
May	106 p	77	2.75	0.10	1,662
Apr	107 c	506	0.25	-0.15	6,743
Apr	107 p	39	2.60	...	4,813
May	107 c	61	0.95	-0.10	4,774
May	107 p	578	3.30	0.10	4,782
Apr	108 c	873	0.15	-0.05	18,661
Apr	108 p	158	3.50	-0.10	6,705
May	108 c	129	0.60	-0.80	4,094
May	108 p	5	3.60	0.20	2,104
Jun	108 c	20	1.25	-0.05	34,240
Jun	108 p	45	4.40	0.70	22,896
Apr	109 c	25	0.05	-0.15	3,514
Apr	109 p	34	4.10	-0.10	1,888
May	109 c	20	0.50	...	459
May	109 p	10	4.50	0.40	174
Apr	110 c	30	0.05	...	5,248
Apr	110 p	5	5	0.50	876
May	110 c	400	0.25	-0.05	4,316
Jun	110 c	252	0.60	-0.35	3,315
Apr	111 p	20	5.90	0.60	62
May	112 c	40	0.10	-0.05	3,878
Jun	112 c	120	0.30	-0.05	13,654
Jun	112 p	6	7.50	1.10	231
Jun	114 c	50	0.15	-0.10	455

Call Vol.........5,436 Open Int..290,135
Put Vol......... 5,976 Open Int..261,529

DJ TRANP AVG(DTX)

STRIKE		VOL	LAST	NET CHG	OPEN INT
Apr	370 p	1	3.10	-4.20	1

Call Vol................0 Open Int..........12
Put Vol.............. 1 Open Int.........793

NASDAQ-100(NDX)

STRIKE		VOL	LAST	NET CHG	OPEN INT
Jun	1200 c	1	283	...	...
Apr	1300 p	715	0.30	-0.45	9,969
May	1300 p	133	3.10	-0.10	5,340
Apr	1325 p	315	0.60	-0.30	9,937
May	1325 p	67	4.40	-1.60	1,711
Apr	1350 p	734	0.90	-0.60	52,307
May	1350 p	5	6.90	-1.90	1,458
Apr	1360 p	50	0.95	-0.65	16,442
Apr	1375 p	403	1.80	-0.45	52,342
May	1375 p	73	10.10	-1.00	1,594
Apr	1390 p	10	2.20	-0.50	16,816
Apr	1400 p	698	3.40	-1.00	10,567
May	1400 p	656	14.50	0.70	4,085
Jun	1400 c	1	105	-104.00	7
Jun	1400 p	3	21.30	-1.60	1,674
Apr	1425 p	269	7	-0.60	6,914
May	1425 p	115	19.80	-1.70	1,637
Apr	1450 c	15	40.30	-2.20	284
Apr	1450 p	554	13.10	-0.80	3,507
May	1450 p	11	27.70	-5.10	1,397
Apr	1475 c	130	20.40	-6.10	730
Apr	1475 p	17	22	-0.10	3,596
May	1475 c	500	45	...	504
May	1475 p	506	37.60	1.10	1,441
Jun	1475 c	4	59	1.10	136
Jun	1475 p	3	49	2.00	1,960
Apr	1500 c	57	10.50	-1.40	2,422
Apr	1500 p	81	37.50	4.20	4,744
May	1500 c	2	33	2.00	816
Jun	1500 c	35	47.50	2.50	4,315
Jun	1500 p	35	56	-3.00	5,013
Apr	1525 c	292	4.40	-1.30	3,455
Apr	1525 p	69	56.30	5.30	1,119
May	1525 c	40	19.30	-3.40	978
Apr	1550 c	75	1.95	-0.65	4,007
May	1550 c	25	11.60	-2.90	2,403
Apr	1575 c	21	0.85	-0.50	4,279
May	1575 c	1	8.30	0.50	2,653
Jun	1575 c	24	15.50	-3.60	1,156
Apr	1600 c	457	0.30	-0.40	5,767
May	1600 c	35	4	-0.90	2,350
May	1600 p	2	122.40	11.40	30
Jun	1600 c	5	11	-2.60	1,095
Apr	1625 c	75	0.25	-0.15	10,885
May	1625 c	1	2.50	...	1,426
Apr	1650 c	45	0.20	-0.05	13,908
Apr	1675 c	8	0.10	-0.15	7,302

Call Vol.......... 1,990 Open Int. 125,074
Put Vol.......... 4,281 Open Int. 281,332

RUSSELL 2000(RUT)

STRIKE		VOL	LAST	NET CHG	OPEN INT
Apr	580 p	38	1.90	-1.10	1,167
Apr	590 p	10	3.20	0.90	482
Apr	600 p	8	5.20	-1.30	1,624
Apr	610 p	4	7.90	-1.40	2,178
Apr	620 c	101	8	0.60	73
Apr	620 p	38	11	-1.00	1,745
May	620 c	1	17.20	...	...
May	620 p	2	17.60	-0.40	451
Jun	620 p	10	23.30	-0.60	362
Apr	630 c	1	4.80	0.10	738
Apr	630 p	400	18.50	-1.90	2,799
May	630 c	1	11.40	-5.40	744
May	640 c	1	8.30	-3.20	207
Apr	650 c	1	0.65	-0.95	253
May	650 c	2	4.90	-3.40	53
May	690 c	50	0.90	-0.65	154

Call Vol. .... 430 Open Int. .. 18,379
Put Vol............. 671 Open Int. .. 30,295

S & P 100(OEX)

STRIKE		VOL	LAST	NET CHG	OPEN INT
Apr	440 p	500	0.05	...	3,200
Apr	460 p	50	0.10	0.05	2,741
Jun	460 p	2	0.65	0.25	1,089
Jun	480 p	400	1.20	0.20	613
Apr	500 p	2,482	0.20	-0.05	15,476
Apr	510 p	64	0.30	...	2,015
May	510 p	200	1.30	0.25	136
Apr	515 p	60	0.30	-0.10	1,976
Apr	520 p	955	0.30	-0.20	16,015
Jun	520 p	10	3.40	-0.40	10,005
Apr	525 p	81	0.50	-0.15	5,230
Apr	530 p	34	0.60	-0.30	7,921
May	530 p	120	2.65	-0.75	2,637
Apr	535 p	191	0.90	-0.10	7,967
Apr	540 p	1,179	1.30	-0.15	13,880
May	540 p	25	4.40	-0.60	1,916
Jun	540 c	8	27.80	-5.30	1,207
Jun	540 p	10	6.40	0.50	6,798
Apr	545 c	2	16	-13.00	12
Apr	545 p	1,524	1.85	-0.35	10,415
Apr	550 c	18	14.10	1.10	65
Apr	550 p	290	2.70	-0.60	9,547
May	550 p	50	7.50	0.70	372
Jun	550 c	30	23.50	...	...
Jun	550 p	340	9.40	-1.00	1,369
Apr	555 c	74	8.20	-1.00	360
Apr	555 p	1,589	4.20	-0.60	4,867
Apr	560 c	4,845	5.40	-0.60	8,022
Apr	560 p	5,050	6.40	-0.50	14,097
May	560 c	127	12	1.00	481
May	560 p	27	11.50	1.30	5,169
Jun	560 c	76	14	-0.50	12,309
Jun	560 p	60	14	-0.20	16,181
Jul	560 c	10	16.50	-1.60	210
Jul	560 p	2	14.80	1.80	120
Apr	565 c	1,920	3.20	-0.50	5,005
Apr	565 p	274	9.40	-0.40	5,812
Apr	570 c	3,304	1.70	-0.40	13,615
Apr	570 p	248	12.20	...	4,366
May	570 c	213	7	...	1,388
Jun	570 c	73	9.40	-0.90	542
Jun	570 p	10	18.30	3.50	3,341
Apr	575 c	828	0.95	-0.15	9,930
Apr	575 p	52	17.80	-0.10	3,572
Apr	580 c	452	0.45	-0.20	15,720
Apr	580 p	255	21.50	-1.00	2,999
May	580 c	2	3	-0.20	2,903
Jun	580 c	12	6	-0.50	5,616
Apr	585 c	1,041	0.20	-0.20	5,417
Apr	590 c	1,351	0.15	-0.10	9,676
May	590 c	9	1.50	...	2,451
Apr	595 c	211	0.10	-0.05	7,386
May	595 c	243	0.80	-0.25	72
Apr	600 c	40	0.05	-0.05	5,790
Apr	605 c	20	0.05	...	3,836

Call Vol....... 19,468 Open Int. 150,690
Put Vol........ 29,087 Open Int. 250,295

S & P 500(SPX)

STRIKE		VOL	LAST	NET CHG	OPEN INT
Jun	750 p	60	0.40	0.25	18,753
Jun	875 p	450	0.40	-0.95	2,622
Jun	900 p	10,200	0.50	-0.30	102,856
Jun	925 p	400	0.75	-0.20	5,511
Jun	950 p	150	1.10	-0.30	30,344
Apr	975 p	5,100	0.20	...	3,434
Jun	975 p	395	1.75	-0.20	12,860
Jun	995 p	1	2.40	-0.10	10,754
Apr	1000 p	16,355	0.30	...	14,900
May	1000 p	370	0.95	...	...
Jun	1005 p	300	2.30	-0.20	17,241
May	1025 c	40	154.50	-3.80	125
May	1025 p	1,000	1.40	-0.45	8,756
Jun	1025 p	10	2.95	-0.55	24,937
Apr	1050 p	453	0.45	-0.10	22,691
May	1050 c	39	131.70	-9.10	255
May	1050 p	26	2.35	-0.25	9,839
Jun	1050 p	122	4.60	-0.40	60,540
Apr	1060 p	800	0.45	-0.40	4,190
Apr	1075 p	1,932	0.60	-0.05	57,069
May	1075 p	210	3	-1.00	9,615
Jun	1075 p	2,410	6	-1.00	37,510
Apr	1100 p	4,467	1	-0.50	...
May	1100 p	279	5.20	-0.80	23,191
Jun	1100 c	103	89	-13.80	14,986
Jun	1100 p	5,092	9.30	-0.90	67,639
Apr	1110 c	20	65	...	...
Apr	1110 p	3,548	1.30	-0.60	35,707
Apr	1115 p	10	1.30	-0.80	8,585
Apr	1120 c	2	61.70	-31.90	147
Apr	1120 p	984	1.80	-0.50	15,540
Apr	1125 p	1,063	2.25	-0.50	41,775
May	1125 p	1,092	8.30	-0.70	14,115
Jun	1125 c	51	67.10	1.60	19,620
Jun	1125 p	5,319	11.90	-1.60	50,305
Apr	1130 p	593	2.60	-0.60	4,487
Apr	1135 c	1	48	-6.00	136
Apr	1135 p	597	2.90	-0.80	3,525
Jun	1140 c	1	55.20	...	66
Apr	1145 p	135	4.30	-0.40	670
Apr	1150 c	283	28	-1.00	4,716
Apr	1150 p	2,823	5.50	-0.90	51,203
May	1150 c	8	39.50	0.50	143
May	1150 p	276	12.50	-1.50	23,634
Jun	1150 c	31	45	-2.30	14,304
Jun	1150 p	909	19	-1.20	49,794
Apr	1160 c	8	24.10	1.10	229
Apr	1160 p	6,546	7.60	-1.60	19,231
Apr	1170 c	226	14.50	-2.50	3,056
Apr	1170 p	4,882	12	-1.00	18,480
Apr	1175 c	1,131	12	-0.70	14,909
Apr	1175 p	5,751	14	-0.10	42,586
May	1175 c	132	22	-3.00	4,677
May	1175 p	874	22.50	-0.30	14,241
Jun	1175 c	7,693	29	-1.00	23,506
Jun	1175 p	8,690	30	-1.00	43,688
Apr	1180 c	750	9.50	-0.50	5,471
Apr	1180 p	182	16.50	-0.80	17,963
Apr	1190 c	1,897	6	-0.60	13,541
Apr	1190 p	3,604	22	-2.00	16,183
May	1190 c	2	15.50	...	100
Jun	1190 c	344	25	2.00	10,801
Jun	1190 p	110	32	-1.00	11,678
Apr	1195 c	2,609	4.70	-0.90	2,684
Apr	1195 p	152	21.50	-2.50	3,144
Jun	1195 c	13	20	-4.00	13,031
Apr	1200 c	5,427	3	-0.80	36,648
Apr	1200 p	883	30	-1.50	41,568
May	1200 c	1,341	10.90	-1.10	12,743
May	1200 p	127	36.60	-1.10	8,757
Jun	1200 c	220	19.90	1.70	58,745
Jun	1200 p	65	39.50	-2.10	51,556
Apr	1205 c	796	2.40	-0.50	860
Jun	1205 c	400	16.10	-1.20	4,299
Apr	1210 c	195	1.75	-0.70	12,212
Apr	1210 p	52	38.10	-1.70	5,567
Jun	1210 c	236	13.50	-1.60	8,104
Apr	1215 c	1,292	1.30	-0.30	3,166
Apr	1215 p	80	42	-2.20	270
Apr	1220 c	454	0.85	-0.55	...
Apr	1220 p	105	42	-3.00	3,058
Apr	1225 c	1,427	0.60	-0.30	34,121
Apr	1225 p	63	50	1.00	6,133
May	1225 c	799	4.50	-1.00	...
May	1225 p	1	50	-4.00	3,572
Jun	1225 c	2,410	10	-0.50	19,401
Apr	1230 c	49	0.55	-0.15	5,615
Apr	1235 c	20	0.40	-0.10	834
May	1235 c	102	3.50	-0.50	2,989
Apr	1240 c	586	0.50	...	10,897
Apr	1245 c	5,077	0.15	-0.20	835
May	1245 c	40	2.40	-0.60	1,642
Apr	1250 c	475	0.20	-0.10	37,698
May	1250 c	85	1.50	-0.60	10,468
Jun	1250 c	9	4.80	-0.40	42,893
Jun	1250 p	1	75	-3.00	12,152
Apr	1255 c	100	0.20	-0.15	1,536
Apr	1275 p	170	98	13.20	1,008
May	1275 c	10	0.45	-0.45	4,850
Jun	1275 c	5,265	2	-0.50	24,865
Apr	1280 c	5	0.15	-0.10	1,071
Apr	1300 c	5	0.05	-0.10	7,281
May	1300 c	18	0.45	...	843
Jun	1300 c	251	1	-0.15	34,436
Jun	1300 p	45	123.50	-3.50	4,968

Call Vol......... 54,578 Open Int.1,194,548
Put Vol....... 144,244 Open Int.2,554,360

AMERICAN

JAPAN INDEX(JPN)

STRIKE		VOL	LAST	NET CHG	OPEN INT
Apr	125 c	10	1.30	-0.60	7
Apr	125 p	20	1.95	0.30	52

Call Vol.............. 20 Open Int..... 3,906
Put Vol............... 40 Open Int..... 5,774

MAJOR MARKET(XMI)

STRIKE		VOL	LAST	NET CHG	OPEN INT
Apr	1125 p	3	8	6.00	16
Apr	1150 c	1	4.40	...	14
Apr	1175 c	1	2.25	0.70	24

Call Vol................ 2 Open Int... 24,130
Put Vol................. 3 Open Int... 24,079

Source: From *The Wall Street Journal,* March 25, 2005. Copyright 2005 by DOW JONES & CO INC. Reproduced with permission of DOW JONES & CO INC in the format Other Book via Copyright Clearance Center.

contracts with an exercise price of 1,170—which is close to the prevailing index level on March 25, 2005—could be purchased for $1,450 (= 14.50 × 100) and $1,200 (= 12 × 100), respectively. On the expiration date, which will be the third Friday of the month, the holder of the call would exercise the contract to buy $117,000 worth of the index if the prevailing S&P 500 level is greater than 1,170, with the put being exercised at index levels less than 1,170.

Foreign Currency Options   Foreign currency options are structurally parallel to the currency futures contracts discussed in Chapter 21. That is, each contract allows for the sale or purchase of a set amount of foreign (i.e., non-U.S. dollar) currency at a fixed exchange (FX) rate. A currency call option is like the long position in the currency futures since it permits the contract holder to buy the currency at a later date. (Of course, unlike futures, options do not require that this exchange be made.) A currency put is therefore the option analog to being short in the futures market. These contracts exist for several major currencies, including the Euro, Australian dollars, Japanese yen, Canadian dollars, British pounds, and Swiss francs. The majority of currency options trading, which began in 1982, occurs on the PHLX. Exhibit 22.4 shows quotes from a sample of the available CAD contracts, along with the spot foreign exchange rates for the same trading day.

Like the FX futures market, all the prices are quoted from the perspective of U.S.-based investors. Consider, for example, an investor who lives in New York and holds Canadian-dollar-denominated provincial government bonds in her portfolio. It is March, and when the bonds come due in one month, she will need to convert the proceeds back into U.S. dollars, which exposes her to a possible weakening in the Canadian currency. Accordingly, she buys the April put on the Canadian dollar with an exercise price of USD 0.825/CAD for a total price of USD 470.00 (= 50,000 × 0.0094). This option would allow the holder to sell CAD 50,000 in April for a total price of USD 41,250 (= 50,000 × 0.825). Obviously, our investor will only exercise the contract if the spot USD/CAD price prevailing in April is less than 0.825 (i.e., if the Canadian dollar weakened relative to the U.S. currency). Finally, because the spot rate is USD 0.82085/CAD, this option is in the money—that is, the contract price of 0.0094 consists of 0.00415 (= 0.825 − 0.82085) of intrinsic value and 0.00525 of time premium.

Options on Futures Contracts   Although they have existed for decades in the OTC markets, options on futures contracts have only been exchange-traded since 1982. Also known as futures options, they give the holder the right, but not the obligation, to enter into a futures contract on an underlying security or commodity at a later date and at a predetermined price. Purchasing a call on a futures contract allows for the acquisition of a long position in the futures market, while exercising a put would create a short futures position. On the other hand, the seller of the call would be obligated to enter into the short side of the futures contract if the option holder decided to exercise the contract, while the seller of the put might be forced into a long futures position. Exhibit 22.5 lists quotations for options based on a wide variety of underlying assets, including agricultural, metal, and energy commodities; Treasury bonds and notes; foreign currencies; and stock indexes. Consistent with the trading patterns for the futures contracts we examined earlier, futures options on financial assets represent the largest part of the market.

To understand how these contracts work, consider a commodity futures option. The May call option on copper with an exercise price of $1.50 per pound would cost the buyer $0.0320 per pound of copper covered by the futures position. As each copper futures contract on the Commodity Exchange (CMX) requires the transfer of 25,000 pounds of the metal, the total purchase price for this futures call is $800 (= 25,000 × 0.032). Also, because the May copper futures price on this day was $1.4535, this contract was out of the money so that its per-ounce price of 3.20 cents was purely a time premium.

Exhibit 22.4 | **Foreign Currency Option Quotations**

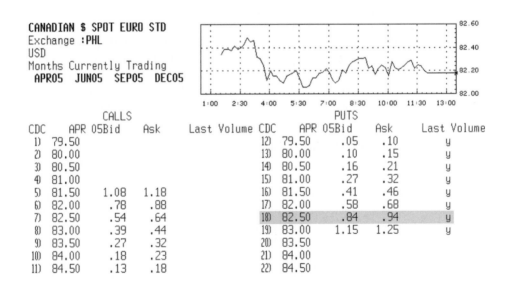

KEY CROSS CURRENCY RATES

	USD	EUR	JPY	GBP	CHF	CAD	AUD	NZD	HKD	NOK	SEK
SEK	7.0435	9.1263	6.6214	13.175	5.8701	5.7817	5.4376	5.0252	.90305	1.1120	....
NOK	6.3340	8.2070	5.9544	11.848	5.2788	5.1993	4.8898	4.5190	.81208	....	.89927
HKD	7.7997	10.106	7.3323	14.589	6.5003	6.4024	6.0214	5.5647	....	1.2314	1.1074
NZD	1.4016	1.8161	1.3176	2.6218	1.1681	1.1505	1.0821	....	.17970	.22129	.19900
AUD	1.2953	1.6784	1.2177	2.4229	1.0795	1.0633	....	.92416	.16608	.20451	.18391
CAD	1.2183	1.5785	1.1452	2.2787	1.0153	....	.94049	.86916	.15619	.19234	.17296
CHF	1.1999	1.5547	1.1280	2.2444	....	.98494	.92632	.85607	.15384	.18944	.17036
GBP	.53462	.69270	.50258	....	.44555	.43884	.41272	.38142	.06854	.08440	.07590
JPY	106.38	137.83	....	198.97	88.653	87.318	82.122	75.893	13.638	16.794	15.103
EUR	.77178	....	.72553	1.4436	.64321	.63352	.59582	.55063	.09895	.12185	.10957
USD	....	1.2957	.94007	1.8705	.83340	.82085	.77200	.71345	.12821	.15788	.14197

(×100)

CANADIAN $ SPOT EURO STD
Exchange :PHL
USD
Months Currently Trading
APR05 JUN05 SEP05 DEC05

	CALLS						PUTS			
CDC	APR 05Bid	Ask	Last Volume		CDC		APR 05Bid	Ask	Last Volume	
1) 79.50					12) 79.50		.05	.10	y	
2) 80.00					13) 80.00		.10	.15	y	
3) 80.50					14) 80.50		.16	.21	y	
4) 81.00					15) 81.00		.27	.32	y	
5) 81.50	1.08	1.18			16) 81.50		.41	.46	y	
6) 82.00	.78	.88			17) 82.00		.58	.68	y	
7) 82.50	.54	.64			18) 82.50		.84	.94	y	
8) 83.00	.39	.44			19) 83.00		1.15	1.25	y	
9) 83.50	.27	.32			20) 83.50					
10) 84.00	.18	.23			21) 84.00					
11) 84.50	.13	.18			22) 84.50					

As with any call position, the holder will only exercise at the expiration date if the prevailing price of the underlying asset exceeds the exercise price; she will let it expire worthless otherwise. This payoff structure might fit the need of an electronic appliance manufacturer exposed to higher copper prices as a factor of production or a speculator bullish on copper prices. In this example, suppose that on the expiration date of the option, the contract price of the May copper futures has risen to $1.53. At this point, the holder will exercise her option and

Exhibit 22.5 | **Futures Option Quotations**

FUTURES OPTIONS PRICES

Source: From *The Wall Street Journal*, March 25, 2005. Copyright 2005 by DOW JONES & CO INC. Reproduced with permission of DOW JONES & CO INC in the format Other Book via Copyright Clearance Center.

assume a long position in May futures with a contract price of $1.50 per pound, which will require posting a margin account. Her new position will immediately be marked to market, however, and $750 [= (1.53 − 1.50) × 25,000] will be added to her margin account. Alternatively, she may decide to unwind her below-market futures contract immediately and take the $750 in cash.

The primary attraction of this derivative is the leverage that it provides to an investor. In this example, the call buyer has been able to control 25,000 pounds of copper for two months for an investment of $800. Had she purchased the copper, it would have cost her $36,337.50 (= 25,000 × 1.4535), assuming that the spot and futures prices were the same on this date. Further, even if it only required a 5 percent margin, a long position in the copper futures contract would necessitate a cash outlay of $1,816.88. Since leverage is the driving force behind this market, in most cases the option is designed to expire at virtually the same time as the underlying futures contract. This indicates that actually acquiring a futures position is not a primary concern of the option users.

THE FUNDAMENTALS OF OPTION VALUATION

Although we know that options can be used by investors to anticipate future levels of security prices, the key to understanding how they are valued comes from recognizing that they also are risk reduction tools. Specifically, in this section we show that an option's theoretical value depends on combining it with its underlying security to create a *synthetic risk-free portfolio*. That is, it always is theoretically possible to use the option as a perfect *hedge* against fluctuations in the value of the asset on which it is based.

Recall that this was essentially the same approach we used in Chapter 20 to establish the put-call parity relationships. The primary differences between put-call parity and what follows are twofold. First, the hedge portfolio implied by the put-call parity transaction did not require special calibration; it simply consisted of one stock long, one put long, and one call short—a mixture that required no adjustment prior to the expiration date. However, hedging an underlying asset position's risk with a single option position—whether it is a put or a call—often involves using multiple contracts and frequent changes in the requisite number to maintain the riskless portfolio. Second, the put-call parity paradigm did not demand a forecast of the underlying asset's future price level whereas the following analysis will. Indeed, we will see that *forecasting the volatility of future asset prices* is the most important input the investor must provide in determining option values.

The Basic Approach

While the mathematics associated with option valuation can be complex, the fundamental intuition behind the process is straightforward and can be illustrated quite simply. Suppose you have just purchased a share of stock in WYZ Corp. for $50. The stock is not expected to pay a dividend during the time you plan to hold it, and you have forecast that in one year the stock price will either rise to $65 or fall to $40. This can be summarized as follows:

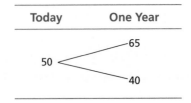

Suppose further that you can either buy or sell a call option on WYZ stock with an exercise price of $52.50. If this is a European-style contract that expires in exactly one year, it will have the following possible expiration date values:

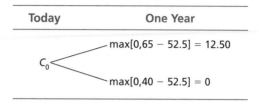

Today	One Year

$$\text{max}[0,65 - 52.5] = 12.50$$

$$C_0$$

$$\text{max}[0,40 - 52.5] = 0$$

Although you do not know what the call option is worth today, you know what it is worth at expiration, given your forecast of future WYZ stock prices. The dilemma is establishing what the option should sell for today (i.e., C_0).

This question can be answered in three steps. First, design a hedge portfolio consisting of one share of WYZ stock held long and some number of call options (i.e., h), so that the combined position will be riskless. The number of call options needed can be established by ensuring that the portfolio has the same value at expiration no matter which of the two forecasted stock values occurs, or

$$65 + (h)(12.50) = 40 + (h)(0)$$

leaving

$$h = \frac{(65 - 40)}{(0 - 12.5)} = -2.00$$

There are both *direction* and *magnitude* dimensions to this number. That is, the negative sign indicates that, in order to create the necessary negative correlation between two assets that are naturally positively correlated, call options must be *sold* to hedge a long stock position. Further, given that the range of possible expiration date option outcomes (i.e., $12.5 - 0$) is only half as large as the range for WYZ stock (i.e., $65 - 40$), twice as many options must be sold as there is stock in the hedge portfolio. The value h is known as the *hedge ratio*.[3] Thus, the risk-free hedge portfolio can be created by purchasing one share of stock and selling two call options.

The second step in the option valuation process assumes capital markets that are free from arbitrage. Specifically, suppose no arbitrage possibilities exist in these markets so that all riskless investments are priced to earn the risk-free rate over the time until expiration. That is, the hedge portfolio costing $[50 - (2)(C_0)]$ today would grow to the certain value of $40 by the following formula:

$$[50 - (2.00)(C_0)](1 + RFR)^T = 40$$

where:

RFR = the annualized risk-free rate
T = the time to expiration (i.e., one year)

Two unknown values exist in this formula: C_0 and RFR. Finding a suitable estimate for RFR seldom is a problem because the investor can use as a proxy the yield to maturity

---

[3]In some valuation models (e.g., Black-Scholes), the hedge ratio is expressed as the option's potential volatility divided by that of the stock. In this example, that would be $(0 - 12.5) \div (65 - 40) = -0.5$, meaning that the option is half as volatile in dollar terms as the share of stock. Of course, this alternative calculation is just the reciprocal of the value of $h = -2.00$.

on a U.S. Treasury security of appropriate length. For example, if the one-year T-bill yield is 8 percent, the formula for C_0 can be solved as follows:

$$C_0 = \frac{50 - 40/1.08}{2.00} = -\$6.48$$

This bit of algebraic manipulation is the third and final step in establishing the call's fair market value. That is, $6.48 represents the fundamental value of a one-year call option on WYZ stock, given both the prevailing market prices for two other securities (i.e., stock and T-bills) and the investor's forecast of future share values. Of course, since the security prices are observable, the investor's forecast of future share values becomes the critical element in determining if this present value is a reasonable estimate. Finally, since the call option is currently out of the money, this amount is purely a time premium.

Improving Forecast Accuracy

Because it is unrealistic to assume only two possible outcomes for future WYZ share prices, the quality of the preceding valuation is highly suspect. To improve the accuracy of this process, the expiration date forecast of stock prices can be expanded to allow for numerous possibilities. To see the consequences of this expansion in the simplest terms possible, consider a revised forecast that includes only one additional potential price falling between the previous extreme values:

Although the three-step riskless hedge approach to calculating C_0 is still conceptually valid, the exact methodology must be modified because it is now impossible to calculate a hedge ratio that simultaneously accounts for all three Date T possibilities. That is, there will be several different hedge ratios defined by each distinct pair of future share prices, which, in turn, means that it is impossible for the preceding valuation process to consider all three possible stock outcomes at once.

Creating a Stock Price Tree   The solution to this problem involves dividing the time to expiration into as many *subintervals* as necessary so that at any point in time the subsequent price can only move up or down. In this example, only one additional subinterval is needed. Exhibit 22.6 shows how the WYZ stock price forecast might be embellished in this manner. This illustration, which is sometimes called a *stock price tree,* indicates that before the current stock price can reach, say, $65 in one year, it must first move up to $57.01 in Subperiod S1 before moving up a second time to its final value of $65. Similarly, the lower extreme of $40 can only be reached by two consecutive "down" price changes. On the other hand, there are two different paths to the terminal outcome in the middle: (i) one "up" followed by one "down" or (ii) a down movement followed by an up movement both reach $50.99.

Once the investor fills in all the details in this price tree, the call option's value can be solved by working backward on each pair of possible outcomes from the future. If, for

Exhibit 22.6	**Forecasted Stock Price Tree (Three Terminal Outcomes)**

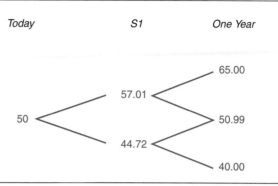

instance, one up movement left the price of WYZ stock at $57.01, a price change over the remaining subperiod could be characterized as:

S1	One Year
57.01	65.00
	50.99

The change in the value of the call option from this uppermost state of Subinterval S1 (i.e., C_{11}) can then be shown as

S1	One Year
C_{11}	12.50
	0.00

With $X = 52.50$, the call option will be in the money at expiration only if WYZ stock moves up in price again. This suggests a hedge ratio of:

$$h = \frac{(65.00 - 50.99)}{(0.00 - 12.50)} = -1.12$$

meaning that the riskless hedge portfolio at this point would contain one share of stock long and 1.12 calls short. The intermediate option value is then found by solving:

$$[57.01 - (1.12)(C_{11})](1.08)^{0.5} = [65 - (1.12)(12.50)] = 50.99$$

or

$$C_{11} = \frac{57.01 - 50.99/1.0392}{1.12} = \$7.09$$

Here the factor 1.0392 [= $(1.08)^{0.5}$] is roughly one-half the annual risk-free rate (plus one) since the original holding period was divided into two subintervals of equal length (i.e., six months each).

Valuing in Other Subintervals Having established the value for C_{11}, the value for the option corresponding to an S1 share price of $44.72 (i.e., C_{12}) can be established by the same three-step procedure with the stock and option price trees truncated as follows:

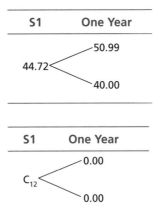

S1	One Year
44.72	50.99
	40.00

and

S1	One Year
C_{12}	0.00
	0.00

Notice that in this case the call option is certain to be out of the money at the expiration date one subinterval hence. That is, given this forecast of potential stock prices, if the WYZ stock falls in value to $44.72 after one subperiod, even a subsequent recovery to $50.99 (i.e., an up move in the second subperiod) would leave the share price below the $52.50 exercise price of the call option. Thus, it is clear that C_{12} must be $0.00; any security that is certain to be worthless in the future must also be worthless today. Further, it should also be noted that the concept of forming a riskless hedge portfolio under such circumstances is meaningless.

These intermediate calculations have little meaning to the investor who only cares about the current value of the option. They are, however, a necessary evil as C_0 cannot be established before determining C_{11} and C_{12}. With these values in hand, the relevant part of the stock price tree is

Today	S1
50.00	57.01
	44.72

with the corresponding call option tree being given by

Today	S1
C_0	7.09
	0.00

| Exhibit 22.7 | **Tree of Calculated Option Values (Three Terminal Outcomes)** |

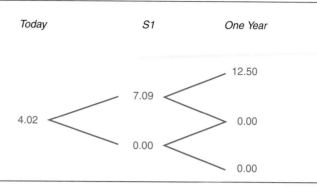

Once again applying the three-step valuation process, the initial (i.e., Date 0) hedge ratio is

$$h = \frac{(57.01 - 44.72)}{(0.00 - 7.09)} = -1.73$$

so that the riskless hedge portfolio at inception would short 1.73 calls for every share held long. The current option value is then found by solving

$$[50.00 - (1.73)(C_0)](1.08)^{0.5} = [44.72 - (1.73)(0.00)] = 44.72$$

or

$$C_{11} = \frac{50.00 - 44.72/1.0392}{1.73} = \$4.02$$

These initial, intermediate, and terminal option values are summarized in Exhibit 22.7.

Two interesting things resulted from this expansion from two to three possible stock price outcomes. First, notice that the addition of a third potential terminal stock price had the effect of reducing the Date 0 option value from $6.48 to $4.02. Although this reduction was a consequence of choosing a third stock price (i.e., $50.99) that caused the option to be out of the money—selecting a value closer to $65.00 would have increased C_0—it does underscore once again that the option valuation process critically depends on the investor's stock price forecast. Second, notice also that the hedge ratio changes with stock price changes prior to the expiration date. That is, the composition of the riskless hedge portfolio must be rebalanced after each share price movement. For example, from the initial position of being short 1.73 calls against one share held long, an upward movement in WYZ stock from $50.00 to $57.01 would require buying back 0.61 (= 1.73 − 1.12) options. Thus, replicating a risk-free position with stock and call options is a *dynamic* process, a point to which we will return shortly.

Expanding the Stock Price Tree This valuation process can become even more precise as more terminal share price outcomes are included in the forecast. Of course, as this happens, the number of pairwise calculations and the number of necessary subperiods will also increase. Consequently, although the three-step valuation method is quite flexible, there is a trade-off between realism and the volume of required calculations. To see how even seemingly minor expansions of the stock price forecast can dramatically increase the computational burden, consider the implications of including four potential expiration date stock prices:

Today	One Year
50	65.00
	55.29
	47.03
	40.00

Valuing the option in this case will require the creation of two subintervals (S1 and S2) and five intermediate stock price forecasts. These are illustrated in Exhibit 22.8.

In order to compute C_0, the investor must now work recursively backward through calculations for the five intermediate option values: C_{21}, C_{22}, and C_{23} in Subperiod S2 and C_{11} and C_{12} in Subperiod 1. Of course, each of these calculations applies the same three-step riskless hedge process outlined earlier, appropriately modified for the new length of a subperiod (i.e., one-third of a year instead of six months). If, for instance, two consecutive up movements took the price of WYZ stock from $50.00 to $54.57 to $59.56, a price change over the remaining subperiod could be characterized as

S2	One Year
59.56	65.00
	55.29

The change in the value of the call option from this uppermost state of Subinterval S2 (i.e., C_{21}) can then be shown as

S2	One Year
C_{21}	12.50
	2.79

Exhibit 22.8 | **Forecasted Stock Price Tree (Four Terminal Outcomes)**

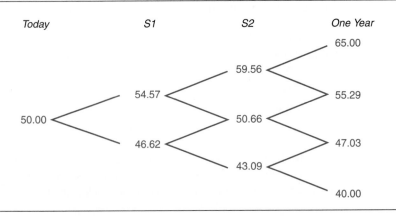

Given its exercise price of $52.50, the call option would be certain to be in the money for both expiration date stock values. This suggests a hedge ratio of

$$h = \frac{65.00 - 55.29}{2.79 - 12.50} = -1.00$$

meaning that the riskless hedge portfolio at this point would contain one share of stock long and one call short. As we have seen, C_{21} can then be found by solving

$$[59.56 - (1.00)(C_{21})](1.08)^{0.33} = [65 - (1.00)(12.50)] = 52.50$$

or

$$C_{21} = \frac{59.56 - 52.50/1.026}{1.00} = \$8.39$$

Notice that the discount factor of 1.026 $(= (1.08)^{0.33})$ is now based on roughly one-third of the annual risk-free rate since the one-year option expiration period was adjusted to accommodate three subintervals of equal length. Solving for the remaining values in turn leaves the option value tree shown in Exhibit 22.9. Notice once again that the net effect of these particular forecast improvements has been to change the current value of the derivative to $3.60.

The Binomial Option Pricing Model

A crucial element of this basic approach to option valuation is that future changes in the underlying asset's price always can be simplified to one of two possibilities: an up movement or a down movement. As shown by Rendleman and Bartter (1979) and Cox, Ross, and Rubinstein (1979), this analytical development is part of a more general valuation methodology known as the *two-state option pricing model*. One difficulty with the preceding examples, however, is that they required the investor to specify cash amounts for each of the future potential stock prices in all the subperiods demanded by the forecast. This can be a rather daunting task, because as the number of terminal outcomes is allowed to grow larger with the time to expiration of the contract.

Forecasting Price Changes   To simplify this forecasting process, suppose an investor focuses her estimates on how stock prices change from one subperiod to the next, rather than

Exhibit 22.9	Tree of Calculated Option Values (Four Terminal Outcomes)

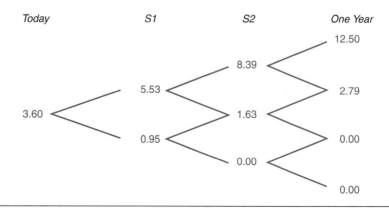

| Exhibit 22.10 | **Binomial Model Forecast Trees** |

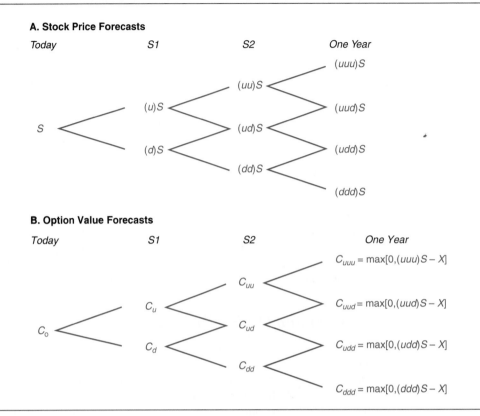

A. Stock Price Forecasts

Today   S1   S2   One Year

S → $(u)S$, $(d)S$ → $(uu)S$, $(ud)S$, $(dd)S$ → $(uuu)S$, $(uud)S$, $(udd)S$, $(ddd)S$

B. Option Value Forecasts

Today   S1   S2   One Year

C_0 → C_u, C_d → C_{uu}, C_{ud}, C_{dd} →

$C_{uuu} = \max[0, (uuu)S - X]$

$C_{uud} = \max[0, (uud)S - X]$

$C_{udd} = \max[0, (udd)S - X]$

$C_{ddd} = \max[0, (ddd)S - X]$

on the dollar levels. That is, beginning with today's known price for a stock, for the next subperiod she forecasts: (1) one plus the percentage change associated with an up *(u)* movement, and (2) one plus the percentage change associated with a down *(d)* movement. Further, to limit the number of required forecasts, suppose she also assumes that the same values for *u* and *d* apply to every up and down price change in all subsequent subperiods. With these assumptions, the investor need only forecast three things: *u, d,* and *N*—the total number of subperiods.

Exhibit 22.10 shows the effect that these modifications—which represent the essence of the **binomial option pricing model**—have on the forecasted stock price and option value trees. Consistent with the four-outcome version of the preceding example, this illustration allows for three subperiods (i.e., $N = 3$). The upper panel of the display shows that after an up and a down movement during the first two subperiods, the initial stock price of *S* will have changed to $(ud)S$. Of course, the values $(ud)S$ and $(du)S$ are equal, meaning that the forecast does not depend on whether the stock price begins its journey by rising or falling. As before, once *u, d,* and *N* are determined, the expiration date payoffs to the option (i.e., C_{uuu}, C_{uud}, C_{udd}, and C_{ddd}) are established.

As before, the initial value for the call, C_0, can be solved by working backward through the tree and solving for each of the remaining intermediate option values. However, another distinct advantage of the binomial model relative to the basic three-step approach is that these intermediate values are much easier to compute. In fact, in the *j*th state in any subperiod, the value of the option can be calculated by

22.1
$$C_j = \frac{(p)C_{ju} + (1-p)C_{jd}}{r}$$

where

$$p = \frac{r-d}{u-d}$$

and

r = one plus the risk-free rate over the subperiod

If p is interpreted as the probability of an up movement in the security's price, which would then mean that $(1-p)$ is the probability of a down move, then the formula for C_j has an intuitively appealing interpretation. That is, the option's value at any point in time can be viewed as its expected value one subperiod hence discounted back to the current time. Further, although p was not an explicit part of the investor's forecast, it is nevertheless generated by the model. In this sense, p is referred to as the *implied probability* of an upward price movement. To ensure that this interpretation holds, the binomial model requires that $d < r < u$, a condition that is quite reasonable in practice.

Generalizing the Model Equation 22.1 can be extended to a more useful format by recognizing that the value for C_j it generates is one of the inputs for valuing the option in the preceding subperiod. Thus, the formula for an option in Subperiod t can be inserted into the right-hand side of the formula for Subperiod $t - 1$. Carrying this logic all the way back to Date 0, the binomial option valuation model becomes

22.2
$$C_0 = \left\{ \sum_{j=0}^{N} \frac{N!}{(N-j)!j!} p^j (1-p)^{N-j} \max\left[0, (u^j d^{N-j})S - X\right] \right\} \div r^N$$

where

$$N! = [(N)(N-1)(N-2)\ldots(2)(1)]$$

To interpret Equation 22.2, the ratio $[N! \div (N-j)!j!]$ is the "combinatorial" way of stating how many distinct paths lead to a particular terminal outcome, $p^j(1-p)^{N-j}$ is the probability of getting to that outcome, and $\max[0, (u^j d^{N-j})S - X]$ is the payoff associated with that outcome. Letting m be the smallest integer number of up moves guaranteeing that the option will be in the money at expiration (i.e., $u^m d^{N-m})S > X$), this formula can be reduced further to

22.3
$$C_0 = \left\{ \sum_{j=m}^{N} \frac{N!}{(N-j)!j!} p^j (1-p)^{N-j} \left[(u^j d^{N-j})S - X\right] \right\} \div r^N$$

As an example of how this model works, assume the investor has gathered contract terms and price data and has made her forecasts as follows: $S = 50.00$, $X = 52.50$, T = one year, RFR = 8 percent (through expiration), $u = 1.09139$, $d = 0.92832$, and $N = 3$. By these forecasts, the investor has divided the one-year life of the option into three subperiods and estimated up and down moves during any subperiod as slightly greater than 9 and 7 percent, respectively. Also, the values for r and p implied by these forecasts are 1.026 [= $(1.08)^{0.33}$] and 0.599 [= $(1.026 - 0.92832) \div (1.09139 - 0.92832)$]. By Equation 22.3, which ignores the two terminal option outcomes in the full binomial formula that are equal to zero, the value of a one-year European-style call option with an exercise price of $52.50 is

$$C_0 = \frac{(3)(0.599)^2(0.401)(2.79) + (1)(0.599)^3(12.50)}{(1.026)^3} = \$3.60$$

It is not surprising that this is the same value the three-step approach produced in the previous example because the forecasted stock price tree in Exhibit 22.8 was generated with these same values of u and d (e.g., $(uu)S = (1.09139)^2(50) = \$59.56$). We also can confirm that the tree of forecasted option values illustrated in Exhibit 22.9 may be replicated through repeatedly calculating the "State j" equation.[4] Finally, with this notation, the hedge ratio for any state j becomes

$$h_j = \frac{(u - d)S_j}{(C_{jd} - C_{ju})}$$

Thus, a share of stock held long could be hedged initially by shorting 1.78 call options $[= (1.09139 - 0.92832)(50) \div (0.95 - 5.53)]$, a position that would be rebalanced to 1.32 calls after one subperiod if the first price change was positive.

The Black-Scholes Valuation Model

The binomial model is a *discrete* method for valuing options because it allows security price changes to occur in distinct upward or downward movements. It also can be assumed that prices change *continuously* throughout time. This was the approach taken by Black and Scholes (1973) in developing their celebrated equation for valuing European-style options.[5] This is not a more realistic assumption because it presumes that security prices change when markets are closed (e.g., at night, on weekends). The advantage of the Black-Scholes approach—identical in spirit to the basic three-step, riskless hedge method outlined earlier—is that it leads to a relatively simple, closed-form equation that is capable of valuing options accurately under a wide array of circumstances.

Specifically, the Black-Scholes model assumes that stock price movements can be described by a statistical process known as *geometric Brownian motion*. Ultimately, this process is summarized by a volatility factor, σ, which is analogous to the investor's stock price forecasts in the previous models. Formally, the stock price process assumed by Black and Scholes is

$$\frac{\Delta S}{S} = \mu[\Delta T] + \sigma\epsilon[\Delta T]^{1/2}$$

That is, a stock's return ($\Delta S/S$) from the present through any future Period T has both an expected component ($\mu[\Delta T]$) and a "noise" component ($\sigma\epsilon[\Delta T]^{1/2}$), where μ is the mean return and ϵ is the standard normally distributed random error term.[6]

Assuming the continuously compounded risk-free rate and the stock's variance (i.e., (σ^2) remain constant until the expiration date T, Black and Scholes used the riskless hedge intuition to derive the following formula for valuing a call option on a nondividend-paying stock:

22.4 $$C_0 = SN(d_1) - X(e^{-(RFR)T})N(d_2)$$

where $e^{-(RFR)T}$ is the discount function for continuously compounded variables,

$$d_1 = [(\ln(S/X) + (RFR + 0.5\sigma^2)[T])] \div (\sigma[T]^{1/2})$$

and

$$d_2 = d_1 - \sigma[T]^{1/2}$$

---

[4]For example, $C_{uu} = [(0.599)(12.50) + (0.401)(2.79)] \div (1.026) = \$8.39$.
[5]For an interesting related discussion of this model, see Black (1989b).
[6]For a detailed analysis of the mathematics underlying the Black-Scholes model, see Hull (2002).

with ln(·) being the natural logarithm function. The variable $N(d)$ represents the cumulative probability of observing a value drawn from the standard normal distribution (i.e., one with a mean of zero and a standard deviation of one) equal to or less than d. As the standard normal distribution is symmetric around zero, a value of $d = 0$ would lead to $N(d) = 0.5000$; positive values of d would then have cumulative probabilities greater than 50 percent, with negative values of d leading to cumulative probabilities of less than one-half.

Values for $N(d)$ can be established in two ways. First, an investor can use a table of calculated values for the standard normal distribution, such as the one shown in Appendix D at the end of the book. For example, if the value of d_1 is 0.65, $N(d_1)$ could be established by finding the entry corresponding to the 0.6 row and the 0.05 column, or 0.7422. This means that 74.22 percent of the observations in the standard normal distribution have a value of 0.65 or less. Notice also that if d_1 had been -0.65, the value of $N(-d_1) = 1 - N(d_1) = 1 - 0.7422 = 0.2578$, which must be the case since the distribution is symmetric.

A second approach to calculating cumulative normal probabilities is approximating them with the following formula:

$$N(d) \approx \begin{cases} 0.5e^{-(d^2)/2 - 281/(83 - 351/d)} & \text{if } d < 0 \\ 1 - 0.5e^{-(d^2)/2 - 281/(83 + 351/d)} & \text{if } d \geq 0 \end{cases}$$

For example, with $d = 0.65$, we have an approximate probability of

$$N(0.65) \approx 1 - 0.5e^{-(0.65^2)/2 - 281/(83 + 351/0.65)} = 0.7422$$

This matches the actual value to the fourth decimal place and will likely lead to reasonable valuations.[7]

Properties of the Model   The **Black-Scholes valuation model** has several attractive features. A joint examination of the expressions for C, d_1, and d_2 reveals that the option's value is a function of five variables:

1. Current security price
2. Exercise price
3. Time to expiration
4. Risk-free rate
5. Security price volatility

Functionally, the Black-Scholes model holds that $C = f(S, X, T, RFR, \sigma)$. The first and fourth factors are observable market prices, and the second and third variables are defined by the contract itself. Thus, the only variable an investor must provide in the Black-Scholes framework is the volatility factor. As noted earlier, the estimate of σ embeds the investor's forecast of future stock prices.

The value of the call option will rise with increases in each of the five factors *except* the exercise price. Exhibit 22.11 summarizes these relationships. Specifically, the middle column of the exhibit shows what will happen to the value of the call when one of the five factors increases. The intuition behind the first three of these relationships is straightforward. In particular, an increase in the underlying asset's price (i.e., S) will increase the call's intrinsic value; a larger exercise price (i.e., X) will reduce the intrinsic value. Also, the longer the option has

---

[7]For more on this approximation method, as well as how it can be written into a program usable on a hand-held financial calculator, see Carr (1988).

Exhibit 22.11	**Factors Affecting Black-Scholes Option Values**

	WILL CAUSE AN INCREASE/DECREASE IN:	
An Increase In:	**Call Value**	**Put Value**
Security price (*S*)	Increase	Decrease
Exercise price (*X*)	Decrease	Increase
Time to expiration (*T*)	Increase	Increase or decrease
Risk-free rate (*RFR*)	Increase	Decrease
Security volatility (σ)	Increase	Increase

until it expires, the more valuable the time premium component. This is because a greater opportunity exists for the contract to finish in the money. On the other hand, the relationships between *C, RFR,* and σ are less obvious. An increase in *RFR* will increase the call's value because this reduces the present value of *X,* an expense that the call holder must pay at expiration to exercise the contract. Similarly, when the volatility of the underlying asset's price increases, the call becomes more valuable since this increases the probability that the option will be deeper in the money at expiration.[8]

Another useful facet of the Black-Scholes model is that the hedge ratio at any moment is simply $N(d_1)$, the partial derivative of the call's value with respect to the stock price (i.e., $\delta C/\delta S$). Under this interpretation, $N(d_1)$ is the change in the option's value given a one dollar change in the underlying security's price. For this reason, $N(d_1)$ often is called the option's **delta**, and it indicates the number of stock shares that can be hedged by a single call—the exact reciprocal of the previous interpretation of the hedge ratio, *h.* Finally, although the Black-Scholes model was developed several years before the binomial framework, the former can be viewed as an extension of the latter. Specifically, as the number of subperiods (i.e., *N*) is allowed to approach infinity, the up or down price movements begin to occur on a continuous basis. If the values of *u* and *d* are then set equal to $e^{\sigma[\Delta T]^{1/2}}$ and $e^{-\sigma[\Delta T]^{1/2}}$, respectively, the binomial model collapses to become the Black-Scholes formula.

An Example   As an example of Black-Scholes valuation, consider the following values for the five input variables: $S = 40$, $X = 40$, $T =$ one year, $RFR = 9$ percent, and σ = 0.30. To calculate the fundamental value of a European-style call option under these conditions, which again will be purely time premium, first calculate:

$$d_1 = (\ln(40/40) + (0.09 + 0.5(0.3)^2)[1]) \div (0.3[1]^{1/2}) = 0.45$$

and

$$d_2 = 0.45 - 0.3[1]^{1/2} = 0.15$$

so that

$$N(d_1) = 1 - 0.5e^{-(0.45^2)/2 - 281/(83 + 351/0.45)} = 0.6736$$

---

[8]In more technical terms, these relationships can be summarized as $\delta C/\delta S > 0$, $\delta C/\delta RFR > 0$, $\delta C/\delta T > 0$, $\delta C/\delta \sigma > 0$, and $\delta C/\delta X < 0$.

Exhibit 22.12	**Example of Black-Scholes Valuation**

Stock Price ($)	Call Value ($)	Hedge Ratio
25	0.44	0.1321
30	1.51	0.3054
35	3.53	0.5020
40	6.49	0.6736
45	10.19	0.8003
50	14.42	0.8837
55	18.98	0.9347

Note: Assumes $X = 40$, $T = 1$ year, $RFR = 9\%$, and $\sigma = 0.30$.

and

$$N(d_2) = 1 - 0.5e^{-(0.15^2)/2 - 281/(83 + 351/0.15)} = 0.5596.$$

Thus,

$$C_0 = (40)(0.6736) - 40(e^{-.09})(0.5596) = \$6.49.$$

$N(d_1)$ says that the call option will change in value by about 67 cents for every dollar of a change in the underlying asset, which, in turn, suggests a hedge ratio of one-and-a-half calls short for every stock share held long. Exhibit 22.12 shows how both the option's value and $N(d_1)$ change as the security's value changes—with the other factors held constant. Notably, the hedge ratios range in value from 0 to 1, and increase as stock prices increase. Therefore, the deeper in the money the option is, the closer its price movements will come to duplicating those of the stock itself. The relationship between stock prices and call option prices for this example is shown in Exhibit 22.13. The delta, or hedge ratio, associated with a given stock price is simply the slope of a line tangent to the call option price curve.

Estimating Volatility

Just as the growth rate of dividends (i.e., g) was a crucial element in establishing the fundamental value of common stock using the dividend discount model, option valuation depends critically on an accurate forecast of the underlying asset's future price level. Of course, in the Black-Scholes framework, this means selecting the proper σ. From the description of the geometric Brownian motion process, it should be clear that σ is equivalent to the standard deviation of returns to the underlying asset. This value can be estimated in two ways. First, it can be calculated in the traditional manner using historical returns. Specifically, calculate the Day t *price relative* as $R_t = \ln(P_t \div P_{t-1})$. If a series of price relatives are then calculated for a sequence of N days in the recent past, the mean and standard deviation of this series can be calculated as

$$\overline{R} = \left(\frac{1}{N}\right)\sum_{t=1}^{N} R_t \text{ and } \sigma^2 = \left(\frac{1}{N-1}\right)\sum_{t=1}^{N}(R_t - \overline{R})^2$$

Exhibit 22.13 | **Black-Scholes Values**

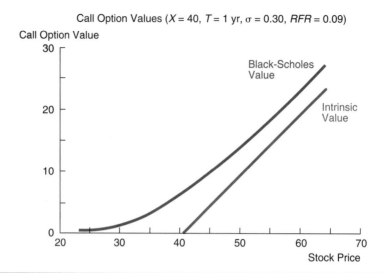

Call Option Values ($X = 40$, $T = 1$ yr, $\sigma = 0.30$, $RFR = 0.09$)

The factor σ is expressed in terms of daily price movements. To annualize this value, σ can be multiplied by the square root of the number of trading days in the year (usually assumed to be 250), which then becomes the estimate of volatility employed in the Black-Scholes formula. The advantage of historical volatility is that it is easy to compute and requires no prior assumption about stock market efficiency; its disadvantage is its presumption that stock price behavior in the future will continue as it has in the past, a sometimes dubious assumption in a rapidly changing world, as shown by Ineichen (2000). Exhibit 22.14 lists 30-day historical volatilities for a representative sample of optionable stocks during November 2004.

An alternative to relying on historical price movements is a second volatility estimation approach that involves the Black-Scholes equation. Recall that if we know all five input factors— S, X, T, RFR, and σ—we can solve for the value of the call option. However, because σ is the only unobservable input, and if we know the current price of the option (call it C^*) and the four other variables, we can calculate the level of σ that forces the Black-Scholes value to equal C^*. That is, the volatility implied by current market prices is established by finding σ^* such that $C^* = f(S, X, T, RFR, \sigma^*)$. Accordingly, the value σ^* is known as the **implied volatility**. No simple closed-form solution exists for performing this calculation; it must be done by trial and error.

Implied volatility is advantageous because it calculates the same volatility forecast investors use to set option prices. The disadvantage of implied volatility is its presumption that markets are efficient in that the option price set in the market corresponds directly to that generated by the Black-Scholes equation. Beckers (1981) has shown that implied volatilities do a better job than historical volatilities of predicting future stock price movements; however, Figlewski (1989b) and Mayhew (1995) caution that σ^* can be "noisy" because it picks up not only the true level of volatility but also any misestimate inherent in the valuation process.

As an example of this calculation, Brown, Harlow, and Tinic (1989) estimated the volatilities implied by the S&P 500 index call option contract for the 121-day period surrounding the stock market crash in October 1987. These calculations are reproduced in Exhibit 22.15. In this display, the time variable is denominated relative to "Black Monday" (i.e., Day 0), which occurred on October 19, 1987. To see how much market risk changed with the crash, the

Exhibit 22.14	Historical Volatility Estimates

Company	Ticker	30-Day Volatility Estimate (%)
Amazon.com	AMZN	32.66
Applied Materials	AMAT	27.98
Bank of America	BAC	12.44
Cendant	CD	18.95
Cisco Systems	CSCO	32.82
Citigroup	C	14.87
Coca-Cola	KO	9.16
Dell Computer	DELL	31.97
Duke Energy	DUK	20.97
eBay	EBAY	25.81
General Electric	GE	14.27
Halliburton	HAL	28.23
Intel	INTC	26.23
Merck	MRK	34.18
Oracle	ORCL	20.91
Pfizer	PFE	22.00
Philip Morris	MO	36.96
Tivo	TIVO	69.25
Wal-Mart	WMT	23.22
Xerox	XRX	26.10

Source: Chicago Board Options Exchange, March 24, 2005. Provided as a courtesy by Chicago Board Options Exchange, Incorporated.

Exhibit 22.15	Implied Volatilities and the Stock Market Crash of 1987

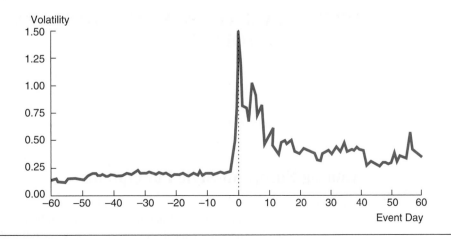

average implied volatility measure for the period Day −60 to Day −5 (i.e., the period beginning approximately two and a half months before the crash) was 18.9 percent. The comparable statistic for the period from Day +5 to Day +60 was 43.3 percent. Moreover, on Black Monday itself, the implied volatility rose to 145 percent, more than seven and a half times its precrash level!

Problems with Black-Scholes Valuation

The Black-Scholes option valuation model is popular with investors for at least two reasons: It is computationally convenient, and it produces reasonable values under a wide variety of conditions. There are, however, circumstances in which the model is less than desirable. The implied volatilities just described have also been useful in determining whether the fundamental values produced by Equation 22.4 match the traded prices for option contracts. In one of the earliest empirical tests of the Black-Scholes equation, MacBeth and Merville (1979) showed for a sample of six stocks that implied volatilities tended to be overly large when the associated call options were in the money and too small for out-of-the-money contracts. Assuming that at-the-money options are priced fairly by the market, this suggested that in-the-money options were priced higher by investors than their Black-Scholes values, with the opposite being true for the out-of-the-money contracts. Thus, for the authors' sample of stocks, the Black-Scholes model overvalued out-of-the-money call options and undervalued in-the-money contracts. Interestingly, in two different studies, Rubinstein (1985b, 1994) found evidence that both supported and contradicted these results.

In general, any violation of the assumptions upon which the Black-Scholes model is based could lead to a misvaluation of the option contract. For instance, it was already noted that stock prices do not change continuously, meaning that stocks that are less actively traded might have options that are priced differently in the market than those stocks that trade frequently. Indeed, Figlewski (1989a) has noted how such market imperfections as brokerage fees, bid-ask spreads, and inflexible position sizes can create arbitrageable differences between option values and prices. He cautioned that Black-Scholes values are best viewed as approximations, best suited for comparing prices of different contracts. Further, Black (1989a) has noted that other conditions of the model are almost certain to be violated in practice, such as the assumption that the risk-free rate and volatility level remain constant until the expiration date. He discusses how some of these problems can be exploited by investors.

OPTION VALUATION: EXTENSIONS AND ADVANCED TOPICS

The preceding discussion has concentrated on the valuation of European-style call options having a nondividend-paying stock as the underlying asset. Many other conditions and underlying assets exist for which options need to be valued. This section explores several extensions of the basic approach as well as other important topics relevant to the valuation process.

Valuing European-Style Put Options

The put-call-spot parity model of Chapter 20 held that, in an efficient market, the value of a European-style put on a nondividend-paying security should be equivalent to a portfolio short in the security while long in both a call option and a Treasury bill having a face value equal to the common exercise price X. Converting the discounting process for the T-bill to be a continuous function, this relationship can be expressed

$$P_0 = C_0 + X(e^{-(RFT)T}) - S$$

This formula implies that if we know the prices of the security, the call option, and the T-bill, we can solve for the value of the put option. Alternatively, if the Black-Scholes value for C is inserted into this expression, we have

$$P_0 = [SN(d_1) - X(e^{-(RFR)T})N(d_2)] + X(e^{-(RFR)T}) - S$$

which can be manipulated to equal

22.5 $$P_0 = X(e^{-(RFR)T})N(-d_2) - SN(-d_1)$$

where all the notation is the same as before. Equation 22.5 is the Black-Scholes put option valuation model.

The comparative statics of put option valuation were shown in the final column of Exhibit 22.11. In particular, the value of the put will increase with higher levels of X but decline with an increase in S because of the effect these movements have on the contract's intrinsic value. Like the call option, the put's value benefits from an increase in σ since this increases the likelihood that the contract will finish deep in the money. Also, an increase in the risk-free rate reduces the present value of X, which hurts the holder of the put who receives the striking price if the contract is exercised. Finally, the sign of $\delta P/\delta T$ could be either positive or negative depending on the trade-off between the longer time over which the security price could move in the desired direction and the reduced present value of the exercise price received by the seller at expiration.

In the preceding example of a Black-Scholes call option valuation, we had the following inputs: $S = 40$, $X = 40$, $T =$ one year, $RFR = 9$ percent, and $\sigma = 0.30$. With these assumptions, d_1 and d_2 still are 0.45 and 0.15, respectively, but now we need to compute $N(-0.45) = 1 - 0.6736 = 0.3264$ and $N(-0.15) = 1 - 0.5596 = 0.4404$. Thus:

$$P_0 = 40(e^{-.09})(0.4404) - 40(0.3264) = \$3.04$$

Finally, the hedge ratio for the put option in this model is $[N(d_1) - 1]$, which in this case is -0.3264 and indicates that the put option's value will *decrease* by approximately 33 cents for every dollar *increase* in S.

Valuing Options on Dividend-Bearing Securities

We learned earlier that the put-call parity relationship required an adjustment when the underlying asset common to both the put and call options paid a dividend. This adjustment is needed because the payment of the dividend reduces the asset's market value, converting the investor's return from capital appreciation to cash flow. Thus, other than the tax implications of this conversion, the underlying asset's owner should not lose any overall net worth over the payment of the dividend. On the other hand, the problem for the prospective call option owner is that he will not receive the dividend; therefore, the reduction in the present value of the stock will reduce the value of his derivative contract. Being rational, he will reduce the price he is willing to pay for the call option on the dividend-bearing security. Consequently, dividends become a sixth factor in the option valuation process.

The original Black-Scholes valuation model can be modified to incorporate dividend payments in two ways. The most straightforward and most accurate approach is reducing the current share price by the present value of the dividends paid during the option's life and then using this amount in place of the actual stock price, that is, replace S in the model with $S' = S - PV$ (dividends). For example, for the case of the one-year, at-the-money call option with an exercise price of \$40 that we saw earlier, assume that a dividend payment of \$1 is made in six months, with another \$1 paid just prior to expiration. Recalling that the continuously compounded risk-free rate and volatility factors were 9 percent and 30 percent, respectively, we would then have

$$S' = 40 - (1)e^{-(0.09)(0.5)} - (1)e^{-(0.09)(1.0)} = 38.13$$

When inserted into the formulas for d_1 and d_2, this S' would generate values of 0.29 and -0.01, respectively.

With these inputs, the Black-Scholes valuation then becomes

$$C_0 = (38.13)N(0.29) - (40)e^{-0.09}N(-0.01) = (38.13)(0.6141) - (36.56)(0.4960) = \$5.28$$

This amount can be compared to the \$6.49 contract value for an otherwise identical call on a nondividend-paying share that we estimated earlier. In particular, the reduction in option value (i.e., \$1.21) is not as great as the present value of the dividends (i.e., \$1.87). This is due to the possibility that the option would have expired out of the money even without the dividend payment, meaning that the dividend-induced stock price reduction will not always affect the contract's terminal payoff. Also, the hedge ratio in the formula is reduced from its original level of 0.6736 to 0.6141.

The second approach to adjusting the option valuation process for dividend payments involves modifying the model itself rather than the stock price input. This requires expressing the dividend in *yield* form, defined as the annual payment divided by the current stock price, and assuming that this yield is paid continuously. Merton (1973) first showed that the Black-Scholes model can be rewritten as

$$C_0 = (e^{-(D)T})SN(d_1) - X(e^{-(RFR)T})N(d_2)$$

with

$$d_1 = [\ln((e^{-(D)T})S/X) + (RFR + 0.5\sigma^2)[T]] \div (\sigma[T]^{1/2})$$

and

$$d_2 = d_1 - \sigma[T]^{1/2}$$

where:

D = the annualized dividend yield

The yield appears as a "discount" factor to the current stock value in two places in these equations. If we set $S' = (e^{-(D)T})S$, this second dividend adjustment is seen as just a continuous version of the first.

Extending the original example, we now have six factors to include: $S = 40$, $X = 40$, T = one year, RFR = 9 percent, σ = 30 percent, and $D = (2/40) = 5$ percent. Plugging these into the model, we get values of 0.28 for d_1 and -0.02 for d_2 so that

$$C_0 = (e^{-0.05})(40)N(0.28) - (e^{-0.09})(40)N(-0.02)$$
$$= (38.05)(0.6103) - (36.56)(0.4920) = \$5.23$$

This amount differs from the first adjustment process amount because the assumption of a continuous dividend stream does not match the reality of how these payments are made. However, by modifying the model's structure instead of the input level, this approach is often much more convenient.

Valuing American-Style Options

The preceding valuation discussion assumed European-style options. If the contract had been American-style—that is, its exercise is not limited to the expiration date—how would the valuation process change? The uncertainty over the possibility of early exercise makes the derivation of an exact closed-form analog to the Black-Scholes equation an elusive goal. Instead Roll (1977b), Geske (1979), and Whaley (1981) have designed elaborate approximation procedures for estimating the value of American-style calls, which have proven quite useful in practice. Further, Johnson (1983) and Barone-Adesi and Whaley (1986), among others, have taken different approaches to address the issue of American put valuation.

A formal summary of these models is beyond the scope of this discussion; however, we can consider several fundamental properties. Most important is that an American put or call has to be at least as valuable as its European-style counterpart because, by definition, the American option gives the holder more choices than the simpler contract. In other words, the American contract holder can exercise at the same time as the European option owner (i.e., at expiration) as well as any point prior to that terminal date. Since we have seen that an option's value ultimately derives from the choice to exercise the agreement or not, a better set of terms for that decision means a more valuable contract. Letting C_a and C_e represent the values of American and European calls, this relationship can be expressed as

$$S \geq C_a(S,T,X) \geq C_e(S,T,X) \geq \max[0, S - Xe^{-(RFR)T}] \geq \max[0, S - X] \geq 0$$

This expression says that (1) the American call is at least as valuable as the European contract, (2) neither call can be more valuable than the underlying stock, and (3) both contracts are at least as valuable as their intrinsic values, expressed on both a nominal and discounted basis. For puts, a similar boundary condition would be

$$X \geq P_a(S,T,X) \geq P_e(S,T,X) \geq \max[0, Xe^{-(RFR)T} - S] \geq 0$$

For a stock that does not pay dividends, C_a and C_e will be equal to one another. At any point prior to expiration, the preceding relationship shows that $C_a(S,T,X) - \max[0, S - X] > 0$, and $\max[0, S - X]$ is the value the investor would extract from the option's exercise. Therefore, without the depression in the stock's price caused by the dividend payment, an investor wishing to liquidate his American call position would sell it rather than exercise it so as not to surrender the contract's time premium. Thus, in the absence of dividends to consider during the life of the option, the American call offers choices that the investor neither wants nor will be willing to pay for. This result implies that the Black-Scholes model for C_e can be used to value C_a as well.[9]

When the stock pays dividends, however, this situation changes. Suppose an investor holds an American call option on a stock just prior to its ex-dividend date. On the ex-date—call it Date t—the value of the stock will decline by about the dividend amount, leaving $S_t = S_{t-1} -$ (dividend)$_t$ assuming no other new information impacted the share's value from the previous day. The value of the option will decline accordingly, from $C(S_{t-1})$ to $C(S_t)$. Of course, selling

[9]For a complete development of these boundary conditions, see Chance (2003).

| Exhibit 22.16 | **Comparing American and European Put Values** |

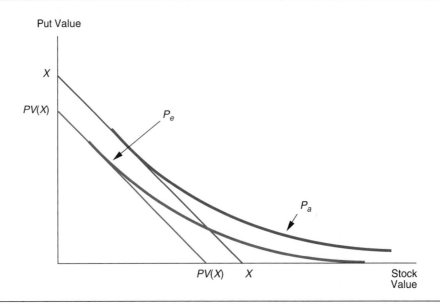

the contract on the day prior to the ex-date will not be possible since rational buyers will know what will happen the following day. Therefore, the investor must decide on Date $t - 1$ whether he should exercise his contract and receive only the intrinsic value of $\max[0, S_{t-1} - X]$. This will be the proper choice if the loss of the option's time premium is less than $C(S_{t-1}) - C(S_t)$, which will likely occur when the option is close to maturity (and, hence, the time premium is low) and the stock's dividend is large. Because the American option allows the investor the possibility of preserving value when the European contract cannot, we must have $C_a > C_e$ for almost all cases.

Deciding to exercise a put prior to maturity does not depend on the presence of dividends. Indeed, dividend payments increase a put's value because they reduce the underlying common stock's value without an offset in the exercise price. Instead, the relevant issue is the limited liability of the stock itself. For example, suppose an investor holds an American put on a nearly bankrupt company. The contract, which is struck at $50, has three more months before it expires, and the stock is currently selling for $1. In this case, the option holder would evaluate the trade-off between exercising the contract today to capture the $49 intrinsic value or waiting three months and hoping the stock becomes worthless. That is, she must decide whether she would rather have $49 now or the present value of the possibility of receiving $50. Depending on the discount rate and the estimated recovery probability, it is quite likely that she will exercise now.

On the other hand, the European put does not offer the investor this choice. Further, since the stock's expected return is positive, an efficient capital market would predict that the price of the nondividend-paying stock will be higher in three months, thereby reducing the expiration date value of the contract below $49. Consequently, without the ability to exercise the put prior to expiration, the European put sometimes can be worth less than its intrinsic value—unadjusted for the time value of money—which always is a lower bound for the American contract. Thus, P_e can be either greater or less than $\max[0, X - S]$, with the latter situation most likely to occur at extremely low values of S and large values of T. The preceding boundary condition shows that P_e must only be greater than the discounted version of the intrinsic value formula, or $\max[0, Xe^{-(RFR)T} - S]$. These relationships are illustrated in Exhibit 22.16.

Other Extensions of the Black-Scholes Model

The dividend-adjusted Black-Scholes model is also quite useful in valuing options for underlying assets other than common stock. Three of the more important applications along these lines follow.

Stock Index Options   As we have discussed, stock index options are fundamentally no different than regular stock options. That is, it is reasonable to assume that the index levels follow geometric Brownian motion just as the stock itself does. The primary difference is that, as a hypothetical creation, the stock index cannot be delivered to settle the contract and so it must be settled in cash. Beyond that, because it is a well-diversified portfolio, the volatility of the stock index's price usually is quite a bit lower than the typical stock. Finally, the applicable dividend yield can be assumed to be the average annualized yield on the index during the option's life, which is likely to be known to investors at least one calendar quarter into the future.

Suppose the Standard and Poor's 100 currently is at a level of 601.40 and a call option on the index with an exercise price of 600 is being offered at a price of $17.75. An investor wants to determine whether the fair value of this contract is above or below the market price. The option is set to expire in exactly 61 days, which translates to 0.1671 ($= 61/365$) year. The dividend yield on the S&P 100 is 2.00 percent, and the annualized yield on a 61-day Treasury bill is 5.70 percent. The investor forecasts the index's volatility to be 18 percent, and establishes that

$$d_1 = [\ln(601.40 e^{-(0.02)0.1671}/600) + (0.057 + 0.5(0.18)^2)[0.1671]] \div (0.18[0.1671]^{1/2}) = 0.1525$$

and

$$d_2 = 0.1525 - 0.18[0.1671]^{1/2} = 0.0789$$

Using the cumulative normal probability approximation function, this leads to $N(d_1) = 0.5607$ and $N(d_2) = 0.5315$. Thus, she estimates the call's value to be

$$C_0 = (599.39)(0.5607) - (600)(e^{-(0.057)0.1671})(0.5315) = \$20.20$$

Since this is higher than the market price of the option (i.e., $17.75), the contract appears undervalued. This is not necessarily an arbitrage opportunity, however, as the investor's valuation was based on two assumptions that may not match the consensus view of other market participants: (1) the Black-Scholes framework is appropriate, and (2) the index's volatility is 18 percent and not something lower. This, of course, is always the challenge confronting investors in an uncertain world.

Foreign Currency Options   Recall that prices for exchange-traded currency options are quoted in U.S. cents per unit of foreign currency, reflecting that a call option is the right to buy a fixed amount of foreign currency with U.S. dollars. Let RFR_f and RFR_d be the risk-free rates in the foreign and U.S. domestic markets, respectively. Further, let σ be the volatility of the exchange rate between the United States and the foreign country, denominated in USD per unit of FC. Garman and Kohlhagen (1983) showed that the Black-Scholes model for European-style calls and puts under these conditions can be written as[10]

$$C_0 = (e^{-(RFR_f)T})SN(d_1) - X(e^{-(RFR_d)T})N(-d_2)$$

$$P_0 = X(e^{-(REF_d)T})N(d_2) - (e^{-(RFR_f)T})SN(-d_1)$$

---

[10]See also Biger and Hull (1983) and Choi and Mascozzi (2001).

where:

$$d_1 = [\ln(e^{-(RFR_f)T})S/X + (RFR_d + 0.5\sigma^2)[T]] \div (\sigma[T]^{1/2})$$
$$d_2 = d_1 - \sigma[T]^{1/2}$$
$$S = \text{the spot exchange rate quoted on a direct (i.e., USD/FC) basis}$$

Again, this formula is equivalent to the dividend-adjusted Black-Scholes model for stock options when RFR_f is interpreted as the "dividend yield" on the foreign currency. As an example of valuing FX options, suppose the spot exchange rate between the U.S. dollar and the British pound is USD 1.50/GBP, and the risk-free rates in the United States and England are 4.5 percent and 9 percent, respectively. With these market conditions, interest rate parity holds that the dollar should trade at a forward premium relative to the pound. To the extent that forward FX rates "predict" future spot rates, this suggests that the dollar price of sterling will fall. Thus, an at-the-money put option should be more valuable to an investor than an at-the-money sterling call. To see if this is the case, consider the valuation of six-month contracts where $S = 1.50$, $X = 1.50$, $RFR_d = 4.5$ percent, $RFR_f = 9$ percent, $\sigma = 13$ percent, and $T = 0.5$. With these inputs, $S' = S(e^{-(.09)0.5}) = 1.434$ so that

$$d_1 = [\ln(1.434/1.50) + (0.045 + 0.5(0.13)^2)[0.5]] \div (0.13[0.5]^{1/2}) = -0.20$$

and

$$d_2 = -0.20 - 0.13[0.5]^{1/2} = -0.29$$

Therefore, the option values are

$$C_0 = (1.434)(0.4207) - (1.50)(e^{-(0.045)0.5})(0.3859) = \$0.037$$

and

$$P_0 = (1.50)(e^{-(0.045)0.5})(0.6141) - (1.434)(0.5793) = \$0.070$$

as expected.

Futures Options   In the preceding chapter, we showed that in the absence of physical storage costs or dividends, the futures contract price (F) should simply be the spot price (S) of the underlying asset carried forward to date T at the risk-free rate. With continuous yields, this can be written as $F = Se^{(RFR)T}$. Black (1976) showed that substituting F for S in the Black-Scholes formula for call options leaves

$$C_0 = [e^{-(RFR)T}F]N(d_1) - (e^{-(RFR)T})XN(d_2)$$
$$= (e^{-(RFR)T})[FN(d_1) - XN(d_2)]$$

where:

$$d_1 = (\ln(F/X) + 0.5\sigma^2[T]^{1/2})$$
$$d_2 = d_1 - \sigma[T]^{1/2}$$

In the expressions for d_1 and d_2, the risk-free rate factor drops out because a risk-free hedge portfolio with futures and call options requires no initial investment since futures contracts require no front-end payment. Also, here σ represents the futures price volatility, which normally is assumed to be equal to the underlying asset volatility. Put options on futures contracts can then be valued like the call options already described.

OPTION TRADING STRATEGIES

The introductory analysis in Chapter 20 highlighted two ways in which investors use options. First, we saw that the asymmetrical payoff structures they possess as stand-alone positions allowed investors to isolate the benefits of an anticipated change in the value of an underlying security while limiting the downside risk of an adverse price movement. Options are a leveraged alternative to making a direct investment in the asset on which the contract is based. Second, we also saw that put options could be used in conjunction with an existing portfolio to limit the portfolio's loss potential. After revisiting this protective put application in the context of individual stock holdings, in this section we will consider a **covered call** option strategy as another method for modifying the risk or enhancing the return of an existing equity position. Specifically, we will see that selling a call option while holding the underlying security can generate income for the investor in an otherwise static market environment.

This section also emphasizes a third way in which options are used: in *combination* with one another to create customized payoff distributions that do not exist in more fundamental securities, like stocks or bonds. The equity collar example that concluded Chapter 20 is a good example of this type of option strategy. In designing such combinations, the investor usually attempts to exploit a very specific view about future economic conditions. For example, he may feel that a particular company's stock returns will be extraordinarily volatile but have no clear impression about the price movement direction. On the other hand, he may feel that another company's shares will trade within a very narrow range around their current price during the next few months. In developing all these strategies, we will return to the hypothetical example of SAS Corporation, which has exchange-traded common stock as well as call and put options. Current prices for SAS stock and six different derivatives, all of which expire at the same time, are reproduced in Exhibit 22.17.

Protective Put Options

Although we have seen that the protective put strategy is most often used to provide insurance for price declines in entire portfolios, Brown and Statman (1987) have noted that the technique can also be employed with individual equity positions. To see how this "insured stock" concept works, consider an investor who holds SAS stock in her portfolio but is concerned that an unexpected downturn in the company's product sales may lead to a decline in the value of her

Exhibit 22.17 | **Hypothetical SAS Corporation Stock and Option Prices**

Instrument		Exercise Price ($)	Market Price ($)	Intrinsic Value ($)	Time Premium ($)
Stock:		—	40.00	—	—
Call:	#1	35.00	8.07	5.00	3.07
	#2	40.00	5.24	0.00	5.24
	#3	45.00	3.24	0.00	3.24
Put:	#1	35.00	1.70	0.00	1.70
	#2	40.00	3.67	0.00	3.67
	#3	45.00	6.47	5.00	1.47

Exhibit 22.18 | **Expiration Date Value of a Protective Put Position**

Potential SAS Stock Value	Value of Put Option	Cost of Put Option	Net Protective Put Position
20	(40 − 20) = 20	−3.67	(20 + 20) − 3.67 = 36.33
25	(40 − 25) = 15	−3.67	(25 + 15) − 3.67 = 36.33
30	(40 − 30) = 10	−3.67	(30 + 10) − 3.67 = 36.33
35	(40 − 35) = 5	−3.67	(35 + 5) − 3.67 = 36.33
40	0	−3.67	(40 + 0) − 3.67 = 36.33
45	0	−3.67	(45 + 0) − 3.67 = 41.33
50	0	−3.67	(50 + 0) − 3.67 = 46.33
55	0	−3.67	(55 + 0) − 3.67 = 51.33
60	0	−3.67	(60 + 0) − 3.67 = 56.33

position in the coming months. To hedge against this firm-specific exposure, she decides to purchase an at-the-money put option on SAS shares. From Exhibit 22.17, this would mean that she would spend $3.67 to buy put #2 with an exercise price of $40. If at expiration the price of SAS had declined below $40, the put option would pay her the difference.

The effect of this acquisition is shown in Exhibit 22.18, which lists the expiration date value of the combined protective put position for a range of possible SAS prices. As noted earlier, the primary benefit of the insured stock strategy is that it creates a combined pay-off equivalent to holding a call option on SAS stock. That is, the protective put holding preserves the investor's upside potential from rising share prices but limits her losses when share prices fall. In this case, the at-the-money put insures her against any losses beyond the $3.67 initial put premium. This is the same outcome the investor would have if instead of the put-protected SAS shares, she had held an at-the-money SAS call option and a T-bill; the risk-free security provides the safety and the call option provides the potential for price appreciation. Recall from the put-call parity model of Chapter 20 that this result was shown as

$$S_0 + P_{0,T} = C_{0,T} + PV(X)$$

which can be rewritten as follows:

$$(\text{Long Stock}) + (\text{Long Put}) = (\text{Long Call}) + (\text{Long T-bill})$$

To extend the insurance interpretation of the protective put, Exhibit 22.19 shows the expiration date payoffs (net of the initial $40 purchase price for the investor's SAS shares) for using each of three put options available to her. To interpret this display, if SAS shares are priced at $40 on the expiration date, for Protective Put #2 (i.e., the at-the-money contract), the investor's combined position will be worth $36.33, giving her a net loss of $3.67. The main thing about this illustration is the trade-off it shows between the risk and reward potential of the various positions. Put #1 has the smallest front-end expense, but its $35 exercise price forces the investor to bear the first $5 of SAS stock price declines; this $5 "deductible" leads to the largest potential loss of three positions at $6.70 (= 1.70 + 5.00). However, for this degree of self-insuring on the part of

| **Terminal Net Payoffs to Three Protective Put Positions**

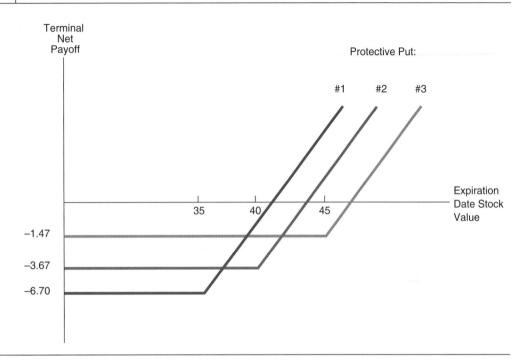

the investor, Protective Put #1 has, at $41.70 (= 35.00 + 6.70), the smallest breakeven price. Conversely, Put #3, with an exercise price above the current share value, does not break even until SAS prices reach $46.47 but has a maximum possible loss of only $1.47 and therefore provides the best downside protection.

Covered Call Options

Another popular way in which derivatives are used to alter the payoff structure of an equity position involves the sale of call options. When investors sell call options based on an under-lying position they own, they are said to be *writing* covered calls. Usually, the purpose of this strategy is to generate additional income for a stock holding that is not expected to change in value much over the near term. By selling a call in such a situation, an investor receives the premium from the option contract to bolster an otherwise small (or negative) return. As Yates and Kopprasch (1980) explain, however, the danger is that the value of the stock position rises above the exercise price by the end of the contract's life causing the shares to be called away at the lower price.

For example, suppose now that our investor believes that over the next few months the value of her SAS stock will neither rise nor fall by an appreciable amount. Accordingly, she decides not to insure her position against losses but, instead, to increase the cash flow of the investment by selling an at-the-money call option (Call #2). In exchange for granting the contract buyer the right to purchase her stock for $40 at the expiration date, she receives an immediate payment of $5.24. Using the same potential stock prices as before, the expiration date values for the covered call position are listed in Exhibit 22.20. The construction of the terminal payoff diagram—once again net of the current SAS share price—is depicted in Exhibit 22.21 (which is comparable to Exhibit 20.23 in Chapter 20 for a protective put option position).

| Exhibit 22.20 | Expiration Date Value of a Covered Call Position |

Potential SAS Stock Value	Value of Call Option	Proceeds from Call Option	Net Covered Call Position
20	0	5.24	(20 − 0) + 5.24 = 25.24
25	0	5.24	(25 − 0) + 5.24 = 30.24
30	0	5.24	(30 − 0) + 5.24 = 35.24
35	0	5.24	(35 − 0) + 5.24 = 40.24
40	0	5.24	(40 − 0) + 5.24 = 45.24
45	−(45 − 40) = −5	5.24	(45 − 5) + 5.24 = 45.24
50	−(50 − 40) = −10	5.24	(50 − 10) + 5.24 = 45.24
55	−(55 − 40) = −15	5.24	(55 − 15) + 5.24 = 45.24
60	−(60 − 40) = −20	5.24	(60 − 20) + 5.24 = 45.24

| Exhibit 22.21 | Terminal Net Payoff to a Covered Call Position |

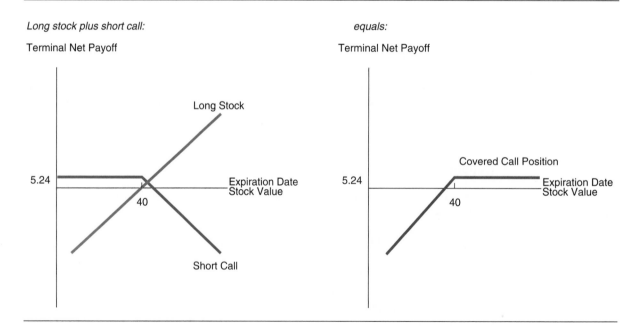

Both the numbers and the pictures from these displays indicate that the expiration date payoff to the covered call position is comparable in form to that of a short position in a put option. Once again, this can be seen directly by adjusting the put-call parity condition as follows:

$$(\text{Long Stock}) + (\text{Short Call}) = (\text{Long T-bill}) + (\text{Short Put})$$

Notice in Exhibit 22.21 that there are two dimensions to the price risk inherent in this strategy. First, if by the option expiration date, SAS stock has risen above $40, the investor will be forced to sell her shares for less than they are actually worth. However, this will represent a lost opportunity only at prices above $45.24, an amount equal to the exercise price plus the initial call premium. Second, if SAS stock experiences a decline in value, her potential loss is not hedged beyond the $5.24 in premium income that she received for selling the call; after prices fall beyond $31.09 (= 40 − 5.24 − 3.67), she would have been better off purchasing the at-the-money protective put option. Thus, to be profitable, the covered call strategy requires that the investor guess correctly that share values will remain in a reasonably narrow band around their present levels.

Straddles, Strips, and Straps

A *straddle* is the simultaneous purchase (or sale) of a call and a put option with the same underlying asset, exercise price, and expiration date. More precisely, a long straddle requires the purchase of the put and the call, while a short straddle sells both contracts. The long straddle takes positions in both a call and a put, giving the investor a combination that will appreciate in value whether stock prices rise or fall in the future. Buying two options increases the initial cost; that is, to profit from this investment, stock price movements must be more pronounced than if the investor had predicted changes in a single direction. In this sense, a straddle is a *volatility* play; the buyer expects stock prices to move strongly one way or the other, while the seller hopes for lower-than-normal volatility.

To illustrate this combination, suppose an investor who does not hold SAS stock purchases a put and a call, each with an exercise price of $40. The cost of this purchase will be the combined prices of Call #2 and Put #2, or $8.91 (= 5.24 + 3.67). Recalling that the terminal values of the options are max[0, S_T − 40] and max[0, 40 − S_T], respectively, the expiration date payoffs to the straddle position (net of the initial cost, unadjusted for the time value differential) are shown in Exhibit 22.22. These are illustrated in Exhibit 22.23, which also depicts the payoff to the seller of the straddle. The breakeven points on this graph occur at $31.09 (= 40 − 8.91) and $48.91 (= 40 + 8.91).

Not surprisingly, the expiration date values to the long and short positions are mirror images of each other; if the individual options themselves are zero-sum games, so too must be any combination of contracts. In particular, the buyer of the straddle is hoping for a dramatic event—such as a company-specific technological breakthrough or the impending judgment in

Exhibit 22.22 | **Expiration Date Payoffs to a Long Straddle Position**

SAS Stock Price at Expiration	Value of Calls	Value of Puts	Cost of Options	Net Profit
20.00	0.00	20.00	−8.91	11.09
25.00	0.00	15.00	−8.91	6.09
30.00	0.00	10.00	−8.91	1.09
35.00	0.00	5.00	−8.91	−3.91
40.00	0.00	0.00	−8.91	−8.91
45.00	5.00	0.00	−8.91	−3.09
50.00	10.00	0.00	−8.91	1.09
55.00	15.00	0.00	−8.91	6.09
60.00	20.00	0.00	−8.91	11.09

Exhibit 22.23	The Straddle Illustrated

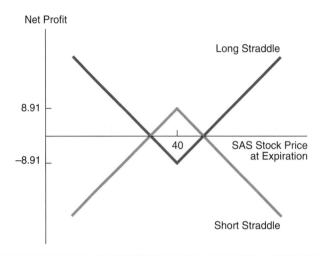

a major lawsuit—that will either increase or decrease the stock price from its present $40 by at least $8.91. Conversely, the best result for the straddle seller is for SAS stock to continue to trade at its current price through the expiration date (i.e., no volatility at all) so that both options expire worthless. The seller's position is particularly interesting because it demonstrates that it is possible to make money in the stock market even when prices do not change.

The long straddle position assumes implicitly that the investor has no intuition about the likely direction of future stock price movements. A slight modification of this format is overweighting either the put or call position to emphasize a directional belief while maintaining a contract that would profit from a price movement the other way. A long *strap* position is the purchase of two calls and one put with the same exercise price, suggesting an investor who thinks stock prices are more likely to increase. An investor with a more bearish view could create a long *strip* position by purchasing two puts and only one call. The terminal payoffs to both of these combinations are listed in Exhibit 22.24, which again assumes the use of the two at-the-money SAS contracts.

Panel A of the exhibit shows that for the higher up-front payment of $14.15 [= (2 × 5.24) + 3.67], the strap will accelerate the payoff in a rising market relative to the straddle. The settlement payment when SAS stock finishes above $40 on the expiration date is twice as great because the strap has doubled the investor's number of calls. The gross payoff when the price falls below $40 remains the same; however, the net amount received is considerably lower because the extra contract the investor purchased would then be out of the money. The net terminal value of the strip position tells a similar story, only with the acceleration of the profit generated by falling stock prices. The strap is more expensive than the strip under these conditions because SAS is a nondividend-paying common stock that is expected to increase in price to provide the investor with a positive expected return.

Strangles

One final variation on the straddle theme is an option combination known as a *strangle*. Like the straddle, a strangle is the simultaneous purchase or sale of a call and a put on the same underlying

| Exhibit 22.24 | Expiration Date Payoffs to Long Strap and Long Strip Positions |

A. Strap Position (Two Calls and One Put)

SAS Stock Price at Expiration	Value of Calls	Value of Puts	Cost of Options	Net Profit
20.00	0.00	20.00	−14.15	5.85
25.00	0.00	15.00	−14.15	0.85
30.00	0.00	10.00	−14.15	−4.15
35.00	0.00	5.00	−14.15	−9.15
40.00	0.00	0.00	−14.15	−14.15
45.00	10.00	0.00	−14.15	−4.15
50.00	20.00	0.00	−14.15	5.85
55.00	30.00	0.00	−14.15	15.85
60.00	40.00	0.00	−14.15	25.85

B. Strip Position (Two Puts and One Call)

SAS Stock Price at Expiration	Value of Calls	Value of Puts	Cost of Options	Net Profit
20.00	0.00	40.00	−12.58	27.42
25.00	0.00	30.00	−12.58	17.42
30.00	0.00	20.00	−12.58	7.42
35.00	0.00	10.00	−12.58	−2.58
40.00	0.00	0.00	−12.58	−12.58
45.00	5.00	0.00	−12.58	−7.58
50.00	10.00	0.00	−12.58	−2.58
55.00	15.00	0.00	−12.58	2.42
60.00	20.00	0.00	−12.58	7.42

security with the same expiration date. Unlike the straddle, however, the options used in the strangle do not have the same exercise price; instead, they are selected so that both are out of the money. By buying two out-of-the-money contracts, the investor reduces the original straddle position's initial cost. Offsetting this reduced cost, though, is that stock prices will have to change in either direction by a greater amount before the strangle becomes profitable. Thus, the strangle can be viewed as having a more modest risk-reward structure than the straddle.

As an example, suppose the investor purchased Call #3 and Put #1 for a combined price of $4.94 (= 3.24 + 1.70). If the price of SAS stock remained between the put exercise price of $35 and the call exercise price of $45, both contracts would expire worthless and the investor would lose his entire initial investment. Accordingly, prices would have to decline to $30.06 (= 35 − 4.94) or increase to $49.94 (= 45 + 4.94) before the investor would break even on the position. Exhibit 22.25 shows that these breakeven points for the strangle are outside those for the straddle described earlier. Thus, among the set of "volatility bets," the strangle costs less to implement than the straddle but requires greater movement in the underlying security's price before it generates a positive return. Finally, by varying the exercise prices on the two

| Exhibit 22.25 | Comparing the Long Strangle and Long Straddle Positions |

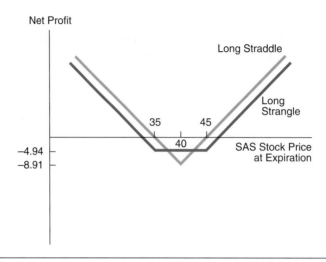

options—which is possible in the OTC market—the investor can create a strangle position that offers the exact trade-off between initial cost and future expected profit that he desires.

Chooser Options

The straddle is a special case of a wider class of option contracts sometimes called *chooser* options. With a chooser option, the investor selects an exercise price and expiration date but doesn't have to decide if the option should be a put or a call until after the contract is purchased. That is, the straddle is just a chooser option for which the decision can be deferred until the expiration date. Rubinstein (1992) has shown that the value of a chooser option will depend on when the investor has to make the put or call choice.

At one extreme, if the decision has to be made immediately, the buyer will select the option most likely to be in the money at expiration. In the previous example, with $X = 40$, we have seen that this will be the call. Thus, a chooser option in this case is worth $5.24. At the other extreme, a chooser option that allows the holder to defer the decision until expiration is, as already noted, equivalent to holding both a put and a call for the entire time to expiration. Consequently, the straddle price of $8.91 is the upper bound of the chooser option value struck at $40. The usual design for the chooser contract requires the holder to make a choice after the initial purchase but before expiration, which would create a position worth somewhere between $5.24 and $8.91.

Spreads

As described by Black (1975), option spreads are the purchase of one contract and the sale of another, where the options are alike in all respects except for one distinguishing characteristic. For example, in a *money* spread, the investor would sell an out-of-the-money call and purchase an in-the-money call on the same stock and expiration date. Alternatively, a *calendar* (or time) spread requires the purchase and sale of two calls—or two puts—with the same exercise price but different expiration dates. Option spreads are often used when one contract is perceived to be misvalued relative to the other. For instance, if an investor determines that a call option with an exercise price of X_1 and an expiration date T is selling at too high a price in the market, he can short it, thereby speculating on an eventual correction. However, if a broad-based increase in the stock market occurs before this contract-specific correction, he stands to lose a great deal because the short call position has unlimited liability. Thus, when he sells the first option, he can hedge some or all of the risk by buying a call with an exercise price of X_2 expiring at T.

Returning to the data for SAS options, suppose the investor purchases the in-the-money call (Call #1) and sells the contract that is out of the money (Call #3). In this case, the option he buys is more valuable than the one he sells, leading to a net cash outlay of $4.83 (= 8.07 − 3.24). At the common expiration date, three price ranges should be considered. If SAS stock settles below $35, both options will expire worthless and the investor will lose all of his initial investment. With an SAS price above $45, both contracts will be exercised, meaning that the investor must sell at $45 the share he bought for $35, leaving a $10 gross profit. Finally, if SAS prices fall between the two exercise prices, the investor's option will be in the money while the contract he sold will not. This situation is summarized by the net payoff calculations shown in Exhibit 22.26.

This combination is sometimes called a *bull* money spread because it will be profitable when stock prices rise. Specifically, with the initial cost of $4.83, the investor's breakeven point occurs when the stock price rises to $39.83 (= 35 + 4.83). His benefit stops increasing if SAS shares reach $45, since this is where the short position in Call #3 becomes a liability. Exhibit 22.27 contrasts this situation with the outright purchase of the in-the-money call. This contract would cost $8.07 initially, leading to the higher breakeven price of $43.07. It would not have a constraint on the upside profit potential, however, so once a share price of $48.24 is reached [= 45 + (8.07 − 4.83)], it would become the preferable alternative. Thus, in exchange for a lower initial purchase price, the bull spread investor is giving up the benefits of rising SAS prices after some point—a strategy that makes sense only if he expects the share price to settle within a fairly narrow range.

The profit for a *bear* money spread (the purchase of Call #3 and the sale of Call #1) is the opposite of that for the bull money spread. That is, buying a bear spread is equivalent to selling a bull spread. Consequently, a long bear spread position might be used by an investor who believed stock prices might decline but did not want to be short in the stock. Notice that a spread transaction also can be created using put options. For instance, suppose a new investor

| Exhibit 22.26 | **Expiration Date Payoffs to a Bull Money Spread Position** |

SAS Stock Price at Expiration	Value of Call #1	Value of Call #3	Cost of Options	Net Profit
20.00	0.00	0.00	−4.83	−4.83
25.00	0.00	0.00	−4.83	−4.83
30.00	0.00	0.00	−4.83	−4.83
35.00	0.00	0.00	−4.83	−4.83
40.00	5.00	0.00	−4.83	0.17
45.00	10.00	0.00	−4.83	5.17
50.00	15.00	−5.00	−4.83	5.17
55.00	20.00	−10.00	−4.83	5.17
60.00	25.00	−15.00	−4.83	5.17

Exhibit 22.27	**Comparing the Bull Money Spread and Long Call Positions**

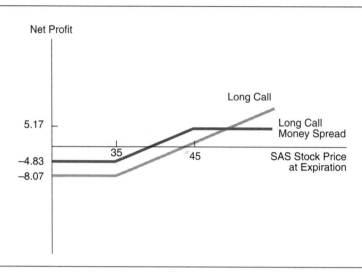

Exhibit 22.28	**A Bear Money Spread with Put Options**

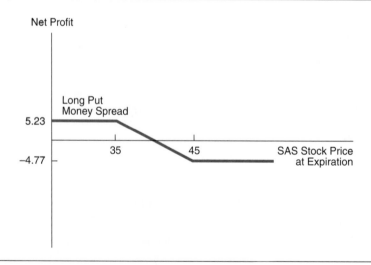

undertakes the simultaneous purchase of Put #3 and sale of Put #1. Her net cost to acquire the position would be $4.77 (= 6.47 − 1.70), which would then generate the terminal payoffs displayed in Exhibit 22.28. If SAS stock settled at $45 or higher, both puts would be worthless and the investor would lose all of her initial investment. If the expiration date share price was $35 or less, both options would be in the money, leaving the investor with a net position of $5.23 (= 45 − 35 − 4.77). Thus, this is the put option version of a bear money spread.

A final extension of this concept is the *butterfly* spread. Suppose an investor designed the following portfolio of SAS options: long one Call #1, short two Calls #2, and long one Call #3. This position is equivalent to holding

- a bull money spread (i.e., buy Call #1 and sell Call #2), *and*
- a bear money spread (i.e., buy Call #3 and sell Call #2).

Exhibit 22.29	Expiration Date Payoffs to a Butterfly Spread

SAS Stock Price at Expiration	Value Bull Spread	Value Bear Spread	Cost of Options	Net Profit
20.00	0.00	0.00	−0.83	−0.83
25.00	0.00	0.00	−0.83	−0.83
30.00	0.00	0.00	−0.83	−0.83
35.00	0.00	0.00	−0.83	−0.83
40.00	5.00	0.00	−0.83	4.17
45.00	5.00	−5.00	−0.83	−0.83
50.00	5.00	−5.00	−0.83	−0.83
55.00	5.00	−5.00	−0.83	−0.83
60.00	5.00	−5.00	−0.83	−0.83

Exhibit 22.30	Comparing the Butterfly Spread and Short Straddle Positions

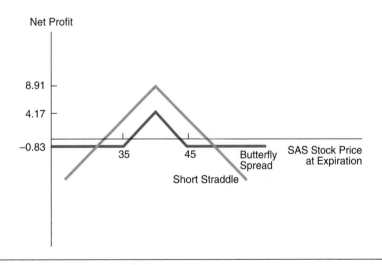

The net purchase price for these transactions is $0.83 [= (8.07 − 5.24) + (3.24 − 5.24)]. The expiration date payoffs are listed in Exhibit 22.29 and show that the value of the position peaks at a stock price of $40 and that the investor can lose, at most, her initial investment. The breakeven stock prices are $35.83 and $44.17. This form of the butterfly spread is equivalent to a hedged version of a short straddle position. That is, in exchange for receiving a smaller potential payoff (i.e., $4.17 vs. $8.91) from a view on low volatility, the investor has limited her losses if SAS's stock price is more explosive than she expected. This trade-off is shown in Exhibit 22.30.

Range Forwards

In Chapter 20, we discussed an *equity collar* as a way that an investor could protect her stock portfolio from adverse movements while allowing for some upside gain potential. We saw that

| Exhibit 22.31 | **Hypothetical CHF Derivative Prices and Terms** |

Derivative	Contract/Exercise Price (USD/CHF)	Expiration	CHF Amount	Price (USD/CHF)
Forward:	0.67	3 months	1,000,000	—
Calls:	0.64	3 months	1,000,000	0.034
	0.67	3 months	1,000,000	0.015
	0.70	3 months	1,000,000	0.004
Puts:	0.64	3 months	1,000,000	0.004
	0.67	3 months	1,000,000	0.015
	0.70	3 months	1,000,000	0.034

although the equity collar had some of the same attributes as a forward contract (e.g., no up-front premium expense), it was actually a combination of two options—the purchase of an out-of-the money put and sale of an out-of-the-money call in this case. Equity collars are an example of a wider class of option combinations known as **range** (or flexible) **forwards**, and they are used widely to manage the risk of underlying assets other than equity as well.

To see how range forward positions might be used in a different context, suppose that the treasurer of a U.S. multinational corporation knows today that he will have a bill for imported goods that must be paid in three months. This bill, denominated in Swiss francs and requiring payment of CHF 1,000,000, presents a challenge for a dollar-based company, which must buy the francs it needs rather than generate them in the natural flow of business. As shown in Chapter 21, this is a classic opportunity to use derivatives to hedge the firm's FX exposure.[11]

After contacting a number of dealers in the OTC market, the treasurer establishes prices and terms for several CHF forward and option contracts. These are listed in Exhibit 22.31, which states prices on a direct (i.e., USD/CHF) basis. The treasurer could lock in a three-month forward rate of USD 0.67/CHF without cost in two ways. First, he could commit to a long position in the CHF forward with a contract amount of CHF 1,000,000. Second, he could buy the CHF call option struck at USD 0.67/CHF and pay for it by selling the CHF put at the same exercise rate. As shown in Chapter 20, the put-call parity model indicates that buying a call and selling a put with the same exercise rate are equivalent to a long forward position. Further, this second strategy would generate a zero-cost forward (i.e., $C_0 = P_0$) only when the common exercise rate is set equal to the prevailing forward rate.

As a third alternative, what if the treasurer (1) bought the 0.70 call for USD $0.004 per franc and (2) sold the 0.64 put for the same price? Once again, this would be a costless combination of options; however, since the two options do not have a common exercise price, this combination is not equivalent to the actual forward—it is a range forward. At the expiration date, one of three things will happen: (1) if the spot FX rate is greater than USD 0.70/CHF, the treasurer will exercise his call and buy francs at that level; (2) if the spot FX rate is less than USD 0.64/CHF, the dealer to whom the treasurer sold the put will force him to buy francs for USD 0.64 per franc, and (3) if the spot FX rate is between these extremes, both options will finish out of the money and the treasurer will buy the required currency at the regular market price. This payoff scheme is contrasted with the regular contract in Exhibit 22.32.

[11]For a good discussion of currency risk management strategies such as the range forward position, see Clarke and Kritzman (1996).

| **Exhibit 22.32** | **Comparing Long Positions in Regular and Range Forwards** |

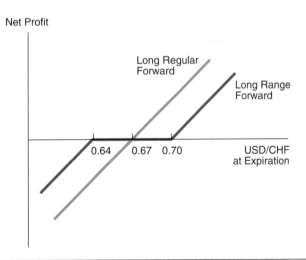

If the treasurer takes a long position in the regular forward contract, he will buy his francs at USD 0.67/CHF, whether or not the prevailing exchange rate in three months is above or below this level. Thus, although he is protected against a weakening dollar, he cannot benefit if the domestic currency strengthens. With a long position in the range forward, though, in exchange for worse FX insurance—namely, a maximum purchase USD 0.70/CHF—he could pay as little as USD 0.64/CHF if the dollar gets stronger. Finally, many zero-cost range forwards could be created; for any desired out-of-the money call option, there will be an out-of-the- money put at some exercise price that has the same premium. In fact, the actual forward contract can be viewed as a zero-cost range forward for which the put and the call options are both struck at USD 0.67/CHF.

The Internet   *Investments Online*

SUMMARY

- Along with forwards and futures, options represent another basic form of derivative contracting. Like the forward positions to which they are linked, puts and calls are used as either stand-alone investments or as supplements to an existing collection of assets. In the latter application, they provide investors with a convenient and inexpensive way to restructure the risk-reward trade-off in a portfolio. The flexibility of this form of contracting permits investors to create unique payoff structures by combining different options in various ways. Option straddles, for instance, allow the holder to take advantage of a view on the underlying asset's volatility while remaining neutral about the direction of future price movements. Forward contracts can be viewed as a specifically chosen pair of options; and these contracts are special cases of option combinations known as range forwards (or collars).

- We consider how option contracts are valued in an efficient market. Although the mathematics of some valuation models can be formidable, the intuition behind the process is not. Each of three models we discuss—the two-state, the binomial, and the Black-Scholes—is based on the same three-step evolution. The first step is combining options with the underlying asset in order to create a riskless position. Invariably, this synthetic risk-free portfolio requires the sale (purchase) of multiple calls (puts) to offset to the full cash exposure of a single share of stock held long. This hedge ratio changes with movements in the underlying asset's price and the passage of time; therefore, the riskless hedge portfolio needs to be rebalanced frequently. Once it is formed, however, the option's value can be established by assuming that the hedge portfolio should earn the risk-free rate (i.e., the no-arbitrage condition) and solving for the option value that makes this assumption true.

- The Black-Scholes model is extremely flexible. Although originally created for European-style call options on non-dividend-bearing stock, this model extends easily to valuing put options and options on dividend-paying stocks. The payment of dividends decreases the value of an otherwise identical call option but not by the amount of the dividend itself. We also discuss how volatility, the only user-provided variable in the valuation model, is either estimated directly from a historical series of asset prices or implied from option prices themselves.

- We discuss the process for valuing American-style puts and calls and how this differs from the valuation of their European counterparts. Further, we explain how the Black-Scholes model could be adapted to value options on other underlying assets, such as stock indexes, foreign currency, or commodity futures contracts.

SUGGESTED READINGS

Briys, Eric, Mondher Bellalah, Huu Minh Mai, and Francois De Varenne. *Options, Futures, and Exotic Derivatives.* New York: Wiley, 1998.

Chance, Don M. *Analysis of Derivatives for the CFA Program.* Charlottesville, VA: AIMR, 2003.

Cox, John C., and Mark Rubinstein. *Option Markets.* Englewood Cliffs, NJ: Prentice Hall, 1985.

Dubofsky, David A., and Thomas W. Miller. *Derivatives: Valuation and Risk Management.* New York: Oxford University Press, 2003.

Jarrow, Robert, and Stuart Turnbull. *Derivative Securities,* 2nd ed. Cincinnati, OH: Thomson Learning, 2000.

QUESTIONS

1. Straddles have been described as "volatility plays." Explain what this means for both long and short straddle positions. Given the fact that volatility is a primary factor in how options are priced, under what conditions might an investor who believes that markets are efficient ever want to create a straddle?

2. Put-call-forward parity and range forward positions both involve the purchase of a call option and the sale of a put option (or vice versa) on the same underlying asset. Describe the relationship between these two trading strategies. Is one a special case of the other?

3. *CFA Examination Level II*
   Michelle Industries issued a Swiss-franc denominated five-year discount note for CHF 200 million.

The proceeds were converted to U.S. dollars to purchase capital equipment in the United States. The company wants to hedge this currency exposure and is considering the following alternatives:

(a) At-the-money Swiss franc call options

(b) Swiss franc forwards

(c) Swiss franc futures

Contrast the essential characteristics of each of these three derivative instruments. Evaluate the suitability of each in relation to Michelle's hedging objective, including both advantages and disadvantages.

4. *CFA Examination Level III*

Six factors affect the value of call options on stocks. Three of these factors are: the current price of the stock, the time remaining until the option expires, and the dividend on the stock. Identify the other three factors and explain how and why changes in each of these three factors affect the value of call options.

5. "Although options are risky investments, they are valued by virtue of their ability to convert the underlying asset into a synthetic risk-free security." Explain what this statement means, being sure to describe the basic three-step process for valuing option contracts.

6. In valuing currency options with the Black-Scholes model, we saw that the risk-free rate on the foreign currency was equivalent to the dividend yield when an individual stock or stock index was the underlying asset. Discuss the appropriateness of this analogy. What sort of transaction involving foreign currency would be required to make this parallel exact?

7. Describe the condition under which it would be rational to exercise both an American-style put and call stock option before the expiration date. In both cases, comment specifically on the role that dividends play.

8. Explain why a change in the time to expiration (i.e., T) can have either a positive or negative impact on the value of a European-style put option. In this explanation, it will be useful to contrast the put's reaction with that of a European-style call, for which an increase in T has an unambiguously positive effect.

9. Currency option traders often speak of "buying low volatility (or 'vol') and selling high vol" rather than buying or selling the option itself. What does this mean exactly? From this perspective, what is the real underlying asset: volatility or foreign currency?

10. It has been shown empirically that stock volatility decreases as a stock's price increases. Comment on how this phenomenon would tend to bias the call and put option values generated by the Black-Scholes model, which assumes that volatility remains constant.

11. On October 19, 1987, the stock market (as measured by the Dow Jones Industrial Average) lost almost one-quarter of its value in a single day. Nevertheless, some traders made a profit buying call options on the stock index and then liquidating their positions before the market closed. Explain how this is possible, assuming that it was not a case of the traders taking advantage of spurious upward ticks in stock prices.

PROBLEMS

1. *CFA Examination Level III*

You are considering the sale of a call option with an exercise price of $100 and one year to expiration. The underlying stock pays no dividends, its current price is $100, and you believe it will either increase to $120 or decrease to $80. The risk-free rate of interest is 10 percent.

a. Describe the specific steps involved in applying the binomial option pricing model to calculate the option's value.

b. Compare the binomial option pricing model to the Black-Scholes option pricing model.

2. *CFA Examination Level II*

Joel Franklin is a portfolio manager responsible for derivatives. Franklin observes an American-style option and a European-style option with the same strike price, expiration, and underlying stock. Franklin believes that the European-style option will have a higher premium than the American-style option.

a. Critique Franklin's belief that the European-style option will have a higher premium. Franklin is asked to value a one-year European-style call option for Abaco Ltd. Common stock, which last traded at $43.00. He has collected the following information:

Closing stock price	$43.00
Call and put option exercise price	$45.00
One-year put option price	$ 4.00
One-year Treasury bill rate	5.50%
Time to expiration	One year

b. Calculate, using put-call parity and the information provided, the European-style call option value.
c. State the effect, if any, of each of the following three variables on the value of a call option: (1) an increase in short-term interest rate, (2) an increase in stock price volatility, and (3) a decrease in time to option expiration.

3. Assuming that a one-year call option with an exercise price of $38 is available for the stock of the DEW Corp., consider the following price tree for DEW stock over the next year:

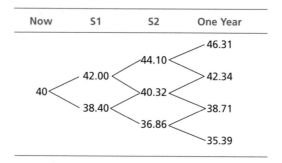

a. If the sequence of stock prices that DEW stock follows over the year is $40.00, $42.00, $40.32, and $38.71, describe the composition of the initial riskless portfolio of stock and options you would form and all the subsequent adjustments you would have to make to keep this portfolio riskless. Assume the one-year risk-free rate is 6 percent.
b. Given the initial DEW price of $40, what are the probabilities of observing each of the four terminal stock prices in one year? (Hint: In arriving at your answer, it will be useful to consider (1) the number of different ways that a particular terminal price could be achieved and (2) the probability of an up or down movement.)
c. Use the binomial option model to calculate the present value of this call option.
d. Calculate the value of a one-year put option on DEW stock having an exercise price of $38; be sure your answer is consistent with the correct response to Part c.

4. Following is a two-period price tree for a share of stock in SAB Corp.:

Now	S1	One Period
		36.30
	33.00	
30		29.70
	27.00	
		24.30

Using the binomial model, calculate the current fair value of a regular call option on SAB stock with the following characteristics: $X = 28$, $RFR = 5$ percent (per subperiod). You should also indicate the composition of the implied riskless hedge portfolio at the valuation date.

5. Consider the following questions on the pricing of options on the stock of ARB Inc.:

   a. A share of ARB stock sells for $75 and has a standard deviation of returns equal to 20 percent per year. The current risk-free rate is 9 percent and the stock pays two dividends: (1) a $2 dividend just prior to the option's expiration day, which is 91 days from now (i.e., exactly one quarter of a year); and (2) a $2 dividend 182 days from now (i.e., exactly one-half year). Calculate the Black-Scholes value for a European-style call option with an exercise price of $70.

   b. What would be the price of a 91-day European-style put option on ARB stock having the same exercise price?

   c. Calculate the change in the call option's value that would occur if ARB's management suddenly decided to suspend dividend payments and this action had no effect on the price of the company's stock.

   d. Briefly describe (without calculations) how your answer in Part a would differ under the following separate circumstances: (1) the volatility of ARB stock increases to 30 percent, and (2) the risk-free rate decreases to 8 percent.

6. Consider the following data relevant to valuing a European-style call option on a nondividend-paying stock: $X = 40$, $RFR = 9$ percent, $T =$ six months (i.e., 0.5), and $\sigma = 0.25$.

   a. Compute the Black-Scholes option and hedge ratio values for the series of hypothetical current stock price levels shown in Exhibit 23.12.

   b. Explain why the values in Part a differ from those shown in Exhibit 23.12.

   c. For $S = 40$, calculate the Black-Scholes value for a European-style put option. How much of this value represents time premium?

7. Suppose the current value of the Standard and Poor's 500 index is 653.50 and the dividend yield on the index is 2.8 percent. Also, the yield curve is flat at a continuously compounded rate of 5.5 percent.

   a. If you estimate the volatility factor for the index to be 16 percent, calculate the value of an index call option with an exercise price of 670 and an expiration date in exactly three months.

   b. If the actual market price of this option is $17.40, calculate its implied volatility coefficient.

   c. Besides volatility estimation error, explain why your valuation and the option's traded price might differ from one another.

8. Consider the following price data for TanCo stock in two different subperiods:

   Subperiod A: 168.375; 162.875; 162.5; 161.625; 160.75; 157.75; 157.25; 157.75; 161.125; 162.5; 157.5; 156.625; 157.875; 155.375; 150.5; 155.75; 154.25; 155.875; 156; 152.75; 150.5; 150.75
   Subperiod B: 122.5; 124.5; 121.875; 120.625; 119.5; 118.125; 117.75; 119.25; 122.25; 121.625; 120; 117.75; 118.375; 115.625; 117.75; 117.5; 118.5; 117.625; 114.625; 110.75

   a. For each subperiod, calculate the annualized historical measure of stock volatility that could be used in pricing an option for TanCo. In your calculations, you may assume that there are 250 trading days in a year.

   b. Suppose now that you decide to gather additional data for each subperiod. Specifically, you obtain information for a call option with a current price of $12.25 and the following characteristics: $X = 115$; $S = 120.625$; time to expiration $= 62$ days; $RFR = 7.42$ percent; and dividend yield $= 3.65$ percent. Here the risk-free rate and dividend yields are stated on an annual basis. Use the volatility measure from Subperiod B and the Black-Scholes model to obtain the "fair value" for this call option. Based on your calculations, is the option currently priced as it should be? Explain.

9. In March, a derivatives dealer offers you the following quotes for June British pound option contracts (expressed in U.S. dollars per GBP):

| | | MARKET PRICE OF CONTRACT | |
Contract	Strike Price	Bid	Offer
Call	USD 1.40	0.0642	0.0647
Put		0.0255	0.0260
Call	USD 1.44	0.0417	0.0422
Put		0.0422	0.0427
Call	USD 1.48	0.0255	0.0260
Put		0.0642	0.0647

a. Assuming each of these contracts specifies the delivery of GBP 31,250 and expires in exactly three months, complete a table similar to the following (expressed in dollars) for a portfolio consisting of the following positions:
   (1) Long one 1.44 call
   (2) Short one 1.48 call
   (3) Long one 1.40 put
   (4) Short one 1.44 put

June USD/GBP	Net Initial Cost	Call 1.44 Profit	Call 1.48 Profit	Put 1.40 Profit	Put 1.44 Profit	Net Profit
1.36	—	—	—	—	—	—
1.40	—	—	—	—	—	—
1.44	—	—	—	—	—	—
1.48	—	—	—	—	—	—
1.52	—	—	—	—	—	—

b. Graph the total net profit (i.e., cumulative profit less net initial cost, ignoring time value considerations) relationship using the June USD/GBP rate on the horizontal axis (be sure to label the breakeven point(s)). Also, comment briefly on the nature of the currency speculation represented by this portfolio.

c. If in exactly one month (i.e., in April) the spot USD/GBP rate falls to 1.385 and the effective annual risk-free rates in the United States and England are 5 percent and 7 percent, respectively, calculate the equilibrium price differential that should exist between a long 1.44 call and a short 1.44 put position. (Hint: Consider what sort of forward contract this option combination is equivalent to and treat the British interest rate as a dividend yield.)

10. *CFA Examination Level II*

Linda Morgan is evaluating option strategies that will allow her to profit from large moves in a stock's price, either up or down. She believes that a combination of a long put and a long call option with the same expiration and exercise price (straddle) would meet her objective.

Price information on APEX stock and options follows. (Assume it is June 1999.)

APEX Stock and Option Current Market Prices
APEX stock: $50
Call option with an exercise price of $50 expiring December 1999: $4
Put option with an exercise price of $50 expiring December 1999: $3
No transactions costs or taxes exist

a. Draw a net-profit-and-loss diagram at expiration for the straddle, using the preceding information. Calculate and label the following on a graph:

   • Maximum loss
   • The breakeven points of the position

Morgan is considering a lower-cost strategy that would allow her to profit from large changes in the stock's price.

APEX Stock and Option Current Market Prices
APEX stock: $50
Call option with an exercise price of $55 expiring December 1999: $2.50
Put option with an exercise price of $45 expiring December 1999: $2.00
No transactions costs or taxes exist

b. Draw a net-profit-and-loss diagram at expiration for the alternative option strategy, using this additional information. Calculate and label the following on a graph:

- Maximum loss
- The breakeven points of the position.

11. In mid-May, there are two outstanding call option contracts available on the stock of ARB Co.:

Call #	Exercise Price	Expiration Date	Market Price
1	$50	August 19	$8.40
2	60	August 19	3.34

a. Assuming that you form a portfolio consisting of *one* Call #1 held long and *two* Calls #2 held short, complete the following table showing your intermediate steps. In calculating net profit, be sure to include the net initial cost of the options.

Price of ARB Stock at Expiration ($)	Profit on Call #1 Position	Profit on Call #2 Position	Net Profit on Total Position
40	—	—	—
45	—	—	—
50	—	—	—
55	—	—	—
60	—	—	—
65	—	—	—
70	—	—	—
75	—	—	—

b. Graph the net profit relationship in Part a, using stock price on the horizontal axis. What is (are) the breakeven stock price(s)? What is the point of maximum profit?

c. Under what market conditions will this strategy (which is known as a *call ratio spread*) generally make sense? Does the holder of this position have limited or unlimited liability?

12. In developing the butterfly spread position, we showed that it could be broken down into two call option money spreads. Using the price data for SAS stock options from Exhibit 22.17, demonstrate how a butterfly payoff structure similar to that shown in Exhibit 22.30 could be created using put options. Be specific as to the contract positions involved in the trade and show the expiration date net payoffs for the combined transaction.

13. *CFA Examination Level II*

Donna Donie, CFA, has a client who believes the common stock price of TRT Materials (currently $58 per share) could move substantially in either direction in reaction to an expected court decision involving the company. The client currently owns no TRT shares but asks Donie for advice about implementing a strangle strategy to capitalize on the possible stock price movement. Donie gathers the TRT option pricing data shown in the following table:

TRT MATERIALS OPTION PRICING DATA (USD)		
Characteristic	Call Option	Put Option
Price	5	4
Strike Price	60	55
Time to Expiration	90 days from now	90 days from now

a. Recommend whether Donie should choose a long strangle strategy or a short strangle strategy to achieve the client's objective. Justify your recommendation with *one* reason.

b. Indicate, at expiration for the appropriate strangle strategy in Part a, the:
   - Maximum possible loss per share
   - Maximum possible gain per share
   - Breakeven stock price(s)

   Note: Your responses should ignore taxes and transaction costs.

   The delta of the call option is 0.625 and TRT common stock does not pay any dividents.

c. Calculate the appropriate change in price for the call option if TRT's stock price immediately increases to $59.

Chapter 23

Swap Contracts, Convertible Securities, and Other Embedded Derivatives

After you read this chapter, you should be able to answer the following questions:

- What are forward rate agreements and how can they be used to reduce the interest rate exposure of a borrower or an investor?
- What are interest rate swaps and how can they transform the cash flows of a fixed or floating rate security?
- How does the swap market operate and how are swap contracts quoted and priced?
- How can swaps be interpreted as a pair of capital market transactions and how does this aid in the swap valuation process?
- What are interest rate caps and floors and how are they related to interest rate swaps?
- How can the swap contracting concept be adapted to manage equity price risk?
- How do the derivatives in convertible securities and warrant issues differ from traditional exchange-traded products?
- What are the similarities and differences between convertible preferred stock and convertible bonds?
- What are structured notes and what factors make their existence possible?
- How can securities with embedded derivatives reduce the funding cost of a corporate borrower?
- What are real options and how can an investor use them to value company flexibility?

Although derivatives only come in two basic "flavors"—forwards and options—the preceding chapters have shown that they can be used in a virtually unlimited number of situations by simply changing the contract terms or the nature of the underlying asset. In this chapter, we discuss several more ways in which these instruments can be modified to the specific needs of a particular end user. Invariably, these modifications involve combining derivatives with other assets or liabilities to create the most highly valued cash flow pattern. We look at two general approaches to forming these combinations: "packages" of derivatives, such as **interest rate swaps**, caps, and floors; and derivatives that have been "embedded" in more fundamental assets, such as equity or debt issues.

To begin, we consider the market for OTC interest rate agreements—one of the fastest-growing segments of the derivatives industry in the past 25 years. In this examination, we once again focus on the differences between forward-based and option-based agreements while exploring the connection between the two. We then extend our discussion of swap contracting to include agreements based on equity price movements. Next, we provide an overview of the myriad ways in which forwards and options are incorporated into other financial instruments. This includes an analysis of convertible securities, warrants, and **structured notes**. These innovations allow investors to acquire any of four different exposures—interest rate, currency, equity, or commodity price risk—in a creative and cost-effective manner. We conclude with a discussion of how investors can value the options embedded in real assets.

OTC INTEREST RATE AGREEMENTS

In addition to futures and options contracts, an extremely active OTC market exists for products designed to manage an investor's or an issuer's interest rate risk. In describing strategies involving these instruments, it is useful to classify them as either forward-based or option-based contracts.[1]

Forward-Based Interest Rate Contracts

Forward Rate Agreements   The **forward rate agreement (FRA)** is the most basic of the OTC interest rate contracts. In an FRA, two parties agree today to a future exchange of cash flows based on two different interest rates. One of the cash flows is tied to a yield that is fixed at the deal's origination (the fixed rate); the other is determined at some later date (the floating rate). On the contract's settlement date, the difference between the two interest rates is multiplied by the FRA's **notional principal** (the scale of the transaction) and prorated to the length of the holding period. As the London Interbank Offer Rate (LIBOR) is frequently used as the floating rate index, FRAs are the OTC equivalent of the Eurodollar futures contracts traded at the Chicago Mercantile Exchange with two important exceptions: (1) FRAs typically require no collateral account, and (2) they are not marked to market on a daily basis.

An FRA's settlement date and maturity are defined by its name: a 3×6 FRA allows the investor to lock in three-month LIBOR, three months forward; a 12×18 FRA locks in six-month LIBOR, one year forward, and so forth. FRA market makers quote a bid-offer spread on a rate basis. For example, suppose the FRA rates for three-month LIBOR shown in Exhibit 23.1 prevail in the market at Date 0, with current three-month LIBOR assumed to be 4.50 percent. This means that on a 3×6 FRA, the market maker is prepared to pay a fixed rate of 4.81 percent for receipt of three-month LIBOR and to receive a fixed rate of 4.85 percent for payment of LIBOR. In either case, there will be no payment until LIBOR is revealed in Month 3. Settlement can then be made in arrears at Month 6 or in advance at Month 3. If in arrears, the settlement flow will be adjusted to the actual number of days in the holding period and calculated by the following formula:

23.1 $$[\text{LIBOR} - \text{Fixed Rate}] \times [\text{Notional Principal}] \times \left[\frac{\text{Number of Days}}{360} \right]$$

---

[1] Some of the discussion in this section is based on the tutorial by Brown and Smith (1995).

Exhibit 23.1	Indicative Bid-Offer Quotes on Three-Month Forward Rate Agreements

Period	Bid (%)	Offer (%)
3 × 6	4.81	4.85
6 × 9	5.20	5.24
9 × 12	5.64	5.68
12 × 15	6.37	6.41
15 × 18	6.78	6.82
18 × 21	7.10	7.14
21 × 24	7.36	7.40

Exhibit 23.2	A Matched Pair of 3 × 6 FRA Transactions

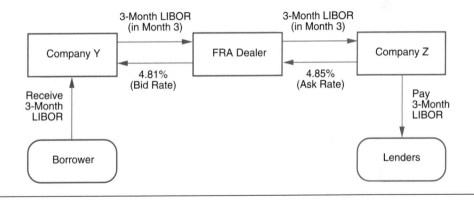

recalling that, in the U.S. market, LIBOR is based on a 360-day year. The advance settlement amount is calculated as the present value of the in-arrears amount, using the prorated level of the realized LIBOR as the discount rate. Notice that this settlement occurs on a net basis—that is, only a single check for the rate differential will be written.

To see how an FRA might be used, suppose that Company Z decides to borrow financial capital for a six-month period, in two three-month installments. Because of the "set in advance, pay in arrears" convention for interest rate determination used in most debt markets, the firm finds itself exposed to rising interest rates over the next three months because the level of its second interest payment will not be established until the end of that period. (The amount of Company Z's first three-month payment would be known at origination.) To solve this problem, the firm can acquire a 3 × 6 FRA whereby it pays the dealer's quoted fixed rate of 4.85 percent in exchange for receiving three-month LIBOR at the settlement date. This is illustrated on the right-hand side of Exhibit 23.2, which depicts both the borrowing and derivative transactions.

Once the dealer has committed to the FRA with Company Z, two things occur. First, Company Z no longer is exposed to a rising funding cost because it now has a forward contract that obligates the dealer to "sell" it the LIBOR it needs in Month 3 at a "price" of 4.85 percent. Second, the dealer now is exposed to rising LIBOR because it will be obligated to make the net settlement payment if LIBOR exceeds 4.85 percent three months from now. That is, Company Z has effectively used the FRA to transfer its interest rate exposure to the dealer. Unless the dealer wishes to hold this position as a speculation that rates will subsequently fall, the exposure can be hedged by "buying" LIBOR from another counterparty for its bid rate of 4.81 percent. This alternative is shown on the left-hand side of Exhibit 23.2 as a second FRA with Company Y, which is assumed to be an investor in a variable-rate asset who is naturally concerned about falling rates.

Now suppose that three-month LIBOR is 5.00 percent on the rate-determination date in Month 3 and that the agreements with Companies Y and Z were negotiated to have a notional principal of $10 million. If its contract specified settlement in arrears at Month 6, Company Y would be obligated to pay the market maker $4,750, calculated as

$$[0.0500 - 0.0481] \times [10,000,000] \times \left[\frac{90}{360}\right]$$

aassuming there are 90 days between Months 3 and 6. If settled in advance, the Month 3 payment would be

$$4.750 \div \left(1 + \frac{90 \times 0.0500}{360}\right) = \$4,691.36$$

Similarly, the payment from the dealer to Company Z would be $3,750 [= (0.0500 − 0.0485) × 10,000,000 × (90/360)] in Month 6, or $3,703.70 if accelerated to Month 3. By matching the FRAs, the market maker is fully hedged from interest rate risk. Its spread of four basis points, which translates into $1,000, compensates for the costs (e.g., transaction costs, credit risk) of making a market in these contracts.

Finally, although the terms *"buy"* and *"sell"* are awkward, they are commonly used when describing FRA transactions. Since the FRA has an initial value of zero and therefore is neither an asset nor a liability, a counterparty doesn't really buy or sell anything. Instead, the parties to the transaction enter into a contract that may obtain a positive or a negative value—depending on the direction of future interest rate level changes. Nevertheless, this language is consistent with interpreting LIBOR as the commodity involved in the deal. In that case, the fixed rate is then the price paid or received in exchange for LIBOR, so that the payer of the fixed rate (Company Z) is said to be buying LIBOR, with the fixed-rate receiver (Company Y) selling LIBOR.

Interest Rate Swaps   Although FRAs are quite useful, they represent a one-time-only solution to an interest rate risk management problem since they have a single settlement date. In fact, both investors and borrowers are routinely exposed to interest rate movements at regular intervals over an extended period of time, such as for the buyer and seller of a **floating-rate note (FRN)** that resets its coupon rate twice annually for several years according to movements in six-month LIBOR.[2] In that case, several exposure dates would need to be hedged, which could be accomplished with a series of FRAs. For example, suppose that an investor holding a one-year FRN paying quarterly coupons of three-month LIBOR becomes concerned

---

[2]As we discussed briefly in Chapter 17, a floating (or variable) rate note is a debt instrument that is similar to a fixed-income bond in that it pays coupons at regular (e.g., semiannual) dates during its life. The difference is that the floating-rate note, or FRN, pays a coupon that is adjusted in a predetermined way with changes in some reference rate. For instance, a typical payment formula might be to reset the coupon every six months at LIBOR + 0.25 percent, meaning that the coupon amount would vary directly with LIBOR. Do not confuse the two acronyms FRA and FRN: The former is an over-the-counter forward contract; the latter is a bond.

Exhibit 23.3	Converting A Floating-Rate Note with a Series of FRAs

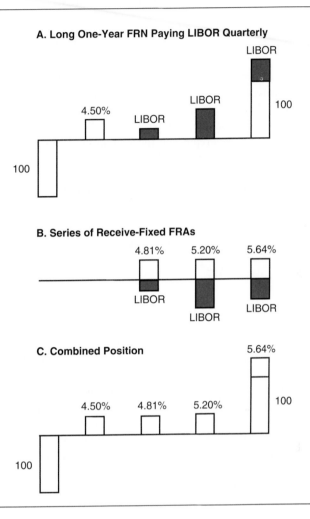

that rates may fall in the future, thereby depressing the level of her last three coupons. (Recall that by convention her first coupon, payable in three months, is based on current LIBOR, which was assumed to be 4.50 percent.) Accordingly, she offsets this exposure by agreeing to receive the fixed rate on three separate FRA contracts: the 3 × 6, the 6 × 9, and the 9 × 12. Given the bid rates quoted in Exhibit 23.1, these positions transform the cash flows on the floating-rate asset as shown in Exhibit 23.3.

This series of FRAs locks in the coupon levels, but they are at different fixed rates and require three separate contracts. This may be inconvenient to the investor, who might prefer a single contract that covers all the future coupon dates using the same fixed rate. This is exactly what an interest rate swap does. Specifically, the swap contract can be viewed as a prepackaged series of forward contracts to buy or sell LIBOR (i.e., FRAs) at the same fixed rate. Alternatively, an FRA can be viewed as a one-date interest rate swap. Of course, for the swap and FRA markets to remain efficient, the single fixed rate on the swap would have to be the appropriate average of 4.50 percent, 4.81 percent, 5.20 percent, and 5.64 percent. For simplicity, assume that each quarterly settlement period is exactly 0.25 year. This average can be approximated by solving for the internal rate of return on the hedged FRN:

$$100 = \frac{4.50 \times 0.25}{(1 + IRR)^1} + \frac{4.81 \times 0.25}{(1 + IRR)^2} + \frac{5.20 \times 0.25}{(1 + IRR)^3} + \frac{100 + [5.64 \times 0.25]}{(1 \times IRR)^4}$$

or $IRR = 1.258$ percent. Thus, 5.03 percent (1.258×4) would be the fixed rate on a one-year, receive-fixed swap consistent with the forward rate agreements listed in Exhibit 23.1. Notice that this IRR calculation is a very accurate approximation for the forward rate annuitization process we saw in Chapter 21. Specifically, a more general way to determine the swap fixed rate *(SFR)* that represents the appropriate average of this sequence of spot and forward LIBOR would be to solve the following equation:

$$\frac{(4.50)(0.25)(NP)}{\left[1 + \frac{i_{0.3}}{4}\right]^1} + \frac{(4.81)(0.25)(NP)}{\left[1 + \frac{i_{0.6}}{4}\right]^2} + \frac{(5.20)(0.25)(NP)}{\left[1 + \frac{i_{0.9}}{4}\right]^3} + \frac{(5.64)(0.25)(NP)}{\left[1 + \frac{i_{0.12}}{4}\right]^4}$$

$$= \frac{(SFR)(0.25)(NP)}{\left[1 + \frac{i_{0.3}}{4}\right]^1} + \frac{(SFR)(0.25)(NP)}{\left[1 + \frac{i_{0.6}}{4}\right]^2} + \frac{(SFR)(0.25)(NP)}{\left[1 + \frac{i_{0.9}}{4}\right]^3} + \frac{(SFR)(0.25)(NP)}{\left[1 + \frac{i_{0.12}}{4}\right]^4}$$

where NP is the swap's notional principal and $i_{0,t}$ is the spot discount rate for a cash flow received or paid at a date t months in the future. For a given interest rate term structure and contract notional principal, SFR is the only unknown element in this equation and can be solved for accordingly; see Bansal, Ellis, and Marshall (1993) and Brooks (1997).

Although interest rate swaps are priced off the LIBOR forward yield curve, they are quoted off the Treasury bond yield curve. That is, the fixed rate side of a U.S. dollar–based swap generally is broken down to two components for trading purposes: (1) the yield of a Treasury bond with a maturity comparable to that of the swap; and (2) a risk premium term known as the **swap spread**. Because the floating-rate side of the agreement typically is based on LIBOR "flat" (i.e., without any adjustment), the swap dealer can incorporate his bid-ask profit margin directly into this swap spread. Exhibit 23.4 lists a representative set of fixed-rate quotes for U.S. dollar swaps, both in absolute and swap spread terms. Each of the swaps represented in this exhibit assumes semiannual settlement dates with six-month LIBOR as the floating rate. For example, the swap dealer would be willing to pay the fixed rate of 4.079 percent on a five-year contract, a rate that is 38.13 basis points greater than the five-year T-bond yield. Notice that swaps with maturities as long as 30 years are quoted, although most contracts are transacted with maturities of 10 years or less.

With the fixed rate on the swap linked to a bond (i.e., 30/360 day count) yield and the floating rate as a money market (i.e., actual/360 day count in the U.S. market) yield, the swap settlement cash flows are calculated in a slightly different manner than for FRAs. Specifically, while the swap is still a net settlement contract, the Date t fixed- and floating-rate payments are determined separately as

$$(\text{Fixed-Rate Payment})_t = (\text{Swap Fixed Rate}) \times \left(\frac{\text{Number of "30/360" Days}}{360}\right) \times$$
$$(\text{Notional Principal})$$

and

$$(\text{Floating-Rate Payment})_t = (\text{Reference Rate})_{t-1} \times \left(\frac{\text{Number of Days}}{360}\right) \times (\text{Notional Principal})$$

Exhibit 23.4 | **Interest Rate Swap and Swap Spread Quotes**

Ticker	Bid	Ask	Mid	Chng	Ticker	Bid	Ask	Mid	Chng
US Semi 30/360					US SPREADS				
2) 2 YR	3.6260	3.6300	3.6280	+.0360	22) 2 YR	33.81	34.38	34.00	−.21
3) 3 YR	3.8040	3.8410	3.8225	+.0405	23) 3 YR	40.75	41.38	41.06	−.25
4) 4 YR	3.9690	3.9740	3.9715	+.0345	24) 4 YR	40.63	41.25	40.94	−.04
5) 5 YR	4.0790	4.1140	4.0965	+.0270	25) 5 YR	38.13	40.23	39.18	+.83
6) 6 YR	4.1880	4.2240	4.2060	+.0220	26) 6 YR	40.45	41.20	40.82	+.03
7) 7 YR	4.2810	4.3190	4.3000	+.0185	27) 7 YR	41.13	41.88	41.50	+.14
8) 8 YR	4.3700	4.4070	4.3885	+.0155	28) 8 YR	41.05	43.50	42.27	+.60
9) 9 YR	4.4430	4.4810	4.4625	+.0090	29) 9 YR	39.92	42.29	41.11	+.54
10) 10 YR	4.5140	4.5510	4.5325	+.0085	30) 10 YR	38.13	38.88	38.50	..
11) 15 YR	4.7870	4.8100	4.7985	+.0095	31) 15 YR	52.63	53.13	52.88	−.56
12) 20 YR	4.9110	4.9350	4.9230	+.0050	32) 20 YR	53.63	54.25	53.94	−.70
13) 30 YR	4.9700	5.0080	4.9890	..	33) 30 YR	38.13	40.59	39.36	+1.01

In these equations, the fixed rate never changes and the floating-rate reference rate (i.e., LIBOR) always is determined at the beginning of a given settlement period.

As an example of these calculations, assume that Counterparty A is an institutional investor who currently holds a three-year bond paying a semiannual coupon of 4.50 percent. He feels that interest rates are likely to rise in the near term and, although he does not want to sell this position, he is concerned about a reduction in the bond's value. Consequently, the investor decides to convert his investment into a synthetic floating-rate note whose coupons will rise with future LIBOR increases. Specifically, he accomplishes this by agreeing to pay the fixed rate on a three-year interest rate swap contract with Counterparty B (i.e., the swap dealer). The terms of this agreement would be summarized as follows:

- Origination date: January 30, 2005
- Maturity date: January 30, 2008
- Notional principal: $30 million
- Fixed-rate payer: Counterparty A (i.e., the investor)
- Swap fixed rate: 3.841 percent (semiannual, 30/360 bond basis)
- Fixed-rate receiver: Counterparty B (i.e., the swap dealer)
- Floating rate: Six-month LIBOR (money market basis)
- Settlement dates: January 30 and July 30 of each year
- LIBOR determination: Set in advance, paid in arrears

This "fixed-for-floating" transaction—the most basic form of a swap—is often called a *plain vanilla* agreement. Exhibit 23.5 illustrates the approximate effect (ignoring slight day count differentials) of combining the swap with the underlying bond position, while Exhibit 23.6 lists the precise settlement cash flows from the investor's perspective for a hypothetical time series of six-month LIBOR. In this display, the fixed-rate payer makes the net settlement payment when the day count-adjusted level of LIBOR is less than 3.841 percent; the fixed-rate receiver makes the settlement payment when LIBOR exceeds 3.841 percent.

Exhibit 23.5	Converting Cash Flows from a Fixed-Rate Bond Issue with a Swap Agreement

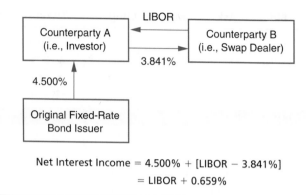

Net Interest Income = 4.500% + [LIBOR − 3.841%]

= LIBOR + 0.659%

Exhibit 23.6	Settlement Cash Flows for a Three-Year "Plain Vanilla" Interest Rate Swap (Fixed-Payer's Perspective)

Settlement Date	Number of Actual Days	Number of 30/360 Days	Current LIBOR	Fixed-Rate Payment	Floating-Rate Receipt	Net Payment (Receipt)
1/30/2005	—	—	3.30%	—	—	—
7/30/2005	181	180	3.60%	576,150	497,750	78,400
1/30/2006	184	180	4.15%	576,150	552,000	24,150
7/30/2006	181	180	4.30%	576,150	625,958	(49,808)
1/30/2007	184	180	3.90%	576,150	659,333	(83,183)
7/30/2007	181	180	3.65%	576,150	588,250	(12,100)
1/30/2008	184	180	3.85%	576,150	559,667	16,483

Plain vanilla swaps are generally used for the same reason as FRAs: namely, to restructure the cash flows of an interest-sensitive asset or liability. In this example, the investor has reduced the price sensitivity (i.e., duration) of his asset by converting the fixed-rate coupon into one that adjusts to shifting market conditions. We saw in Chapter 20 that making this change synthetically with derivatives—rather than through a physical rebalancing of the portfolio—is the more cost-effective method. Given A's original coupon rate of 4.5 percent, the net annualized cash flow he will receive after accounting for the swap position will be (again ignoring day count differentials):

Fixed-Rate Bond Coupon Receipt = 4.500%

Swap: (1) LIBOR Receipt = LIBOR

             (2) Fixed Payment = (3.841%)

Net Interest Income: = LIBOR + 0.659%

Exhibit 23.7	A Capital Market Interpretation of an Interest Rate Swap

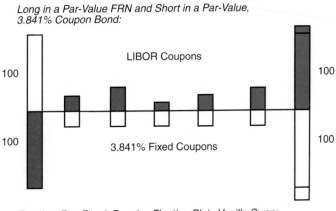

Long in a Par-Value FRN and Short in a Par-Value, 3.841% Coupon Bond:

Equals a Pay-Fixed, Receive-Floating Plain Vanilla Swap:

Thus, the net impact of combining the swap with the fixed-rate bond is to convert that security into a variable-rate asset paying a coupon of LIBOR plus 65.9 basis points.

There is another important way of viewing this swap transaction. With the swap agreement, Counterparty A is effectively paying the fixed-rate coupons he receives from his bond in exchange for receiving floating-rate coupons. That is, the pay-fixed swap position can be viewed as equivalent to holding a portfolio consisting of (1) a long position in a par-value FRN paying semiannual coupons of LIBOR, and (2) a short position in a par-value fixed-rate note paying semiannual coupons of 3.841 percent. This capital market interpretation is illustrated in Exhibit 23.7. Notice that by essentially buying and selling two different par-value instruments, no net principal amount exists at origination or maturity; this is what allows the swap's principal to be notional (i.e., not actually exchanged). Thus, all the swap agreement really does is transform the nature of the coupon payments.

The immediate consequence of this interpretation is that at any point in time the value of the pay-fixed swap position can be calculated as the present value of the floating-rate cash flows held as an asset minus the present value of the fixed-rate bond cash flow that is a liability, or

$$(PV \text{ of Pay-Fixed Swap}) = (PV \text{ of } FRN \text{ Paying LIBOR}) - (PV \text{ of Fixed-Rate Bond Paying } 3.841\%)$$

For example, suppose that one year after this swap was originated, yields have generally risen so that the fixed rate on a new two-year swap (i.e., the remaining time until the original maturity) is 4.841 percent. The value of this swap under these conditions can be established in two steps. First, on any settlement date, the FRN will be valued at par, since its coupon always is reset according to current market conditions. Second, the market value of a bond paying a coupon of only 3.841 percent will fall, which benefits Counterparty A to whom this is a liability. Thus, using the new swap rate as a discount factor, A's position in the agreement (which as a forward contract had no value at origination) is now worth

$$100 - \left[\sum_{t=1}^{4} \frac{(3.841/2)}{(1 + 0.04841/2)^t} + \frac{100}{(1 + 0.04841/2)^4} \right] = 1.8846$$

or 1.8846 percent of notional principal. Therefore, if Counterparty A chose to unwind his contract at this time, the dealer would be willing to pay as much as \$565,380 (= 0.018846 × \$30 million) and then find a new swap counterparty who would pay the now current fixed rate of 4.841 percent. The \$565,380 is considered to be the *marked-to-market value* of the swap. Given that interest rates have risen since inception, the original contract is now an asset to the fixed-rate payer (i.e., Counterparty A) and a liability to the fixed-rate receiver (i.e., the dealer).

An important characteristic of the swap agreement is that it becomes an *asset* to one participant and a *liability* to the other as soon as market conditions change after the terms of the contract are set. This means that swaps entail credit risk. To see why, consider what would happen to Counterparty A if, on a particular settlement date when LIBOR was 8 percent, the swap dealer was unable to make the net settlement payment. In that case, the investor would receive only the 4.5 percent coupon from his bond rather than the 8.659 percent (= LIBOR + 0.659 percent) coupon he expected from his synthetic FRN. The possibility that the swap counterparty either cannot or will not honor its obligation means that the synthetic floating-rate note carries *more* credit risk than the original fixed-rate bond. Further, notice that the swap dealer also will be concerned about the ability of Counterparty A to perform on the agreement when LIBOR is less than 3.841 percent. Thus, like any forward arrangement, the credit risk on a swap runs two ways.

What would it cost Counterparty A if, with exactly two years remaining on the contract described, the swap dealer suffered bankruptcy and defaulted on the remainder of the agreement? To retain his synthetic FRN, the investor would have to find a new swap dealer to replace the old contract. Unfortunately, with the change in market conditions, Counterparty A will now have to pay 4.841 percent to receive LIBOR over the next two years, implying an additional cost of 50 basis points (times 30 million) each settlement period. Thus, the economic consequence to A of the dealer's default can be measured as

$$\sum_{t=1}^{4} \frac{[(0.04841/2) - (0.03841/2)] \times (30,000,000)}{(1 + 0.04841/2)^t} = \$565,380$$

which, of course, is the same amount as the marked-to-market value of the swap. Thus, this figure represents the current potential default loss for the counterparty to whom the swap is an asset.[3]

Interest rate swaps have been in existence since 1981, and some empirical evidence exists on how they are priced in the marketplace. The available evidence includes Kim and Koppenhaver's (1993) investigation of commercial bank activity in the swap market; results from a study by Sun, Sundaresan, and Wang (1993), who examined the consistency of bid-ask quotes issued by two swap dealers with different credit grades; and findings by Brown, Harlow, and Smith (1994), as well as Minton (1997), who tested several theoretical relationships designed to explain the historical pattern of variation in the swap spread component. Although each of the studies examined a different aspect of the swap contracting process, the collective evidence they present is consistent

---

[3]For interesting discussions of credit risk in the swap market, see Sorensen and Bollier (1994) and Cossin and Pirotte (2000).

with the notion that this market works in an orderly and efficient manner. Further, the mechanics of swap pricing, which have matured over time, seem to be integrated with other affiliated securities, such as Treasury notes and bills and Eurodollar futures contracts.

Option-Based Interest Rate Contracts

In this section, we discuss two types of OTC interest rate option arrangements as well as their relationship with interest rate swaps: (1) caps and floors, the two most basic option-based products; and (2) collars, special combinations of caps and floors.

Caps and Floors   Interest rate cap and floor agreements are equivalent to portfolios of interest rate option contracts, with each contract corresponding to a different settlement period. A **cap agreement** is a series of cash settlement interest rate options, typically based on LIBOR. The seller of the cap, in return for the option premium that is usually paid at origination, is obliged to pay the difference between LIBOR and the exercise, or cap, rate (times the fraction of the year, times the notional principal) whenever that difference is positive. The seller of a **floor agreement** makes settlement payments only when LIBOR is below the floor rate. No payment is made if LIBOR is above the floor or below the cap rate. As with swaps and FRAs, settlement can be either in advance or in arrears. Payment in arrears is more common because these contracts usually are used to hedge exposure to floating-rate bank loans and notes, which typically settle in arrears.

From these descriptions, the Date t settlement payments on cap and floor agreements can be written as follows:

23.2   *Cap Settlement*: $\text{(Notional Principal)} \times \left(\dfrac{\text{Number of Days}}{360}\right) \times \max[\text{LIBOR}_{t-1} - X_c, 0]$

and

23.3   *Floor Settlement*: $\text{(Notional Principal)} \times \left(\dfrac{\text{Number of days}}{360}\right) \times \max[X_f - \text{LIBOR}_{t-1}, 0]$

where:

X_c = the cap exercise rate
X_f = the floor exercise rate

(Recall once again that a 360-day year is used because of the quotation convention for U.S. dollar LIBOR.) For example, consider a three-year, semiannual settlement, 8 percent cap on six-month LIBOR. The buyer of the cap pays the writer an up-front premium, quoted as a percentage of the notional principal. Assuming the cost is 120 basis points and the notional principal is $100 million, the cost of the cap is $1,200,000.[4] Suppose that settlement dates are on the 15th of May and November of each year and that LIBOR on one particular May 15th is 9.125 percent. The holder of the cap will receive settlement in arrears the following November in the amount of $575,000, calculated as (9.125 percent − 8 percent) × $100 million × (184/360).

---

[4]In practice, interest rate caps and floors are quoted by market makers on a volatility basis, for instance, 18.5 percent bid and 19.5 percent offered. That measure of volatility (stated as a standard deviation), plus the exercise rate, the current term structure of interest rates, and the time frame for the contract, are then entered into an option pricing model to obtain the actual amount of the premium. Hull (2002) has shown that this amount can be established by adapting Black's model for valuing futures options to price each separate option in the contract (i.e., "caplets" and "floorlets"), and then summing them across all settlement dates.

| Exhibit 23.8 | Payoff Diagrams for Buying and Writing an Interest Rate Cap and Floor |

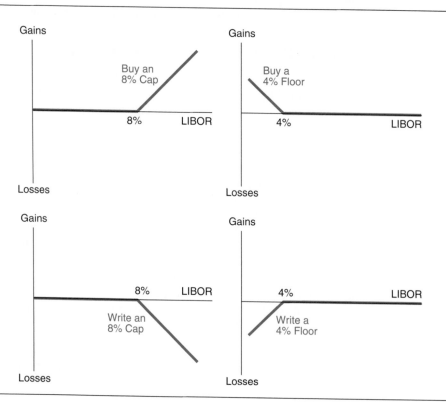

The payoff relationships for caps and floors can be illustrated using traditional, option-style diagrams. Exhibit 23.8 portrays an 8 percent cap and a 4 percent floor on LIBOR. Notice that the payoff diagram for the cap looks like a typical call option on a commodity and the floor takes the form of a put option. Indeed, following the convention where LIBOR is the commodity, caps are referred to as "calls on LIBOR," and floors as "puts on LIBOR." Alternatively, a cap agreement on LIBOR is a series of put options on an underlying Eurodollar time deposit. In effect, the owner of the option has the right, but not the obligation, to sell to the cap writer a time deposit having a coupon rate equal to the cap rate in the amount of the notional principal of the contract. The owner exercises that option if current LIBOR exceeds the cap rate, thus selling a relatively low coupon deposit at par value. The proceeds of that sale can then be used to buy a time deposit that earns the higher market rate. The gain on those hypothetical transactions is equivalent to the payoff on the cap agreement. Whether one interprets a cap as a call on LIBOR or a put on a time deposit (and, similarly, a floor as a put on LIBOR or a call on a time deposit) is purely a matter of semantic preference.

Collars   In Chapter 20, we saw that an equity collar arrangement consisted of a long position in an equity put option that was paid for with a short position in a call option on the same stock. Similarly, an **interest rate collar** is a combination of a cap and a floor, a long position in one and a short position in the other. To buy a 4 percent–8 percent collar on LIBOR is to buy an 8 percent cap and to write a 4 percent floor. The buyer will receive cash payments when LIBOR exceeds 8 percent, make payments when LIBOR is below 4 percent, and neither receive nor pay if LIBOR is between 4 percent and 8 percent. Often the motive for a firm to buy a collar is to reduce the initial cost of acquiring the protection from higher levels of LIBOR, as the up-front receipt from selling the floor can be used to offset the cost of buying the cap.

A special interest rate collar occurs when the initial premiums on the cap and the floor are equal and therefore offset each other. For instance, suppose that the premium on a three-year, 4 percent floor is 120 basis points, which matches the premium on the 8 percent cap. The combination is known as *zero-cost,* or zero-premium, collar. This is a useful concept because it is easy to show that an interest rate swap is just a special case of a zero-cost interest rate collar. To see this, consider again the 4 percent–8 percent zero-cost collar on LIBOR that was constructed from buying the 8 percent cap and selling the 4 percent floor. Now tighten the collar by lowering the cap rate to 7 percent. The up-front premium paid by the buyer must go up; an insurance policy providing protection whenever LIBOR exceeds 7 percent has to cost more than a policy that pays off only when LIBOR moves above 8 percent. Suppose that premium is 200 basis points (times the notional principal). To keep the collar at a zero initial cost, the written floor must then generate additional premium for the seller as well. This will require a higher floor rate because a contract in which the seller makes settlement payments whenever LIBOR is less than 5 percent certainly will be worth more than one with a floor rate of 4 percent. If we keep tightening the collar at some exercise rate common to both the cap and the floor, say 6 percent, the combination will be zero cost. That will be the pay-fixed swap fixed rate that prevails in the market. This is illustrated in Exhibit 23.9.

To summarize, buying a 6 percent cap and writing a 6 percent floor on LIBOR are equivalent in terms of settlement cash flows to an interest rate swap paying a fixed rate of 6 percent and receiving LIBOR. When LIBOR is above 6 percent, the net settlement receipt on the swap is the same as the receipt on the in-the-money cap that is owned. When LIBOR is below 6 percent, the net settlement payment on the swap is the same as the payment on the in-the-money floor that has been sold. Similarly, writing a cap and buying a floor at the same exercise rate are identical to a receive-fixed interest rate swap. Notice that a cap-floor combination at the same exercise rate always has the same payoffs as a swap contract. However, only when the combination also nets to a zero initial cost does that common rate match the prevailing swap fixed rate. This relationship is known as *cap-floor-swap parity* and is the swap market analog

Exhibit 23.9	An Illustration of Cap-Floor-Swap Parity

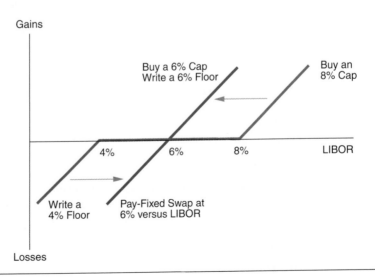

to the put-call-forward parity formula first discussed in Chapter 20 and extended to the range forward strategy in Chapter 22.

Along with the "portfolio of FRAs" and "pair of bonds" ways of viewing a swap contract, cap-floor-swap parity shows that a third interpretation exists: The swap can be viewed as a pair of option positions. This can be used to test the internal consistency of credit risk and valuation models for swaps. For example, because selling a cap and buying a floor at the same exercise rate can offer the same cash flows as a receive-fixed swap, the projected credit risk on the swap must be comparable to the credit risk on the floor agreement. (Note that a firm bears the counterparty's credit risk on purchased options and not on written options, because only with purchased options is the firm relying on the other party's future performance.) As Yaksick (1992) explains, this parity relationship also implies that variations of the option valuation models discussed in Chapter 22 can be used in the valuation of swap contracts.

A SWAP CONTRACTING EXTENSION

Although interest rate swaps are by far the most prevalent OTC rate contract, other extensions of this concept that are important for portfolio managers have been developed as well. All these variations preserve the essential feature of a swap contract by exchanging cash flows based on two different rates or prices. We will examine one such agreement in detail.

Equity Index-Linked Swaps

Similar in form to interest rate swaps, equity-index-linked swaps or **equity swaps** are equivalent to portfolios of forward contracts calling for the exchange of cash flows based on two different investment rates: (1) a variable-debt rate (e.g., three-month LIBOR) and (2) the return to an equity index (e.g., Standard and Poor's 500). The index-linked payment is based on either the total return (i.e., dividends plus capital gain or loss) or just the percentage index change for the settlement period plus a fixed spread adjustment, which is expressed in basis points and can be negative. The floating-rate payments typically are based on LIBOR flat. Like interest rate and currency swaps, equity swaps are traded in the OTC markets and can have maturities out to 10 years or beyond.

In addition to the S&P 500, equity swaps can be structured around foreign indexes, such as TOPIX (Japan), FT-SE 100 (Great Britain), DAX (Germany), CAC 40 (France), TSE 35 (Canada), and Hang Seng (Hong Kong). These agreements also can be designed so that the cash flows are denominated in the same currency or in two different currencies. The equity-index-based cash flow typically is denominated in the currency of the index's country of origination, but the swap can be designed so that this payment is automatically hedged into a different currency. Further, these agreements specify a notional principal that is not exchanged at origination but serves the purpose of converting percentage returns into cash flows. This notional principal can either be variable or fixed during the life of the agreement, but the same notional principal applies to both sides of the transaction.

The equity swap market has developed for several reasons. First, these agreements allow investors to take advantage of overall price movements in a specific country's stock market without having to purchase the equity securities directly.[5] This has the advantage of reducing

---

[5]For a more detailed analysis of the uses and development of this product, see Allen and Showers (1991) and Chance (2004).

on LIBOR, will have to be paid. Second, whenever $Index_{new}$ is less than $Index_{old}$, the company will make an equity-index-based payment to (i.e., "receive" a negative payment from) its counterparty. Thus, rather than netting one cash flow against the other, the company will pay both when the value of the equity index declines. (Examples of this situation are represented by the third and fifth payments in the exhibit.)

WARRANTS AND CONVERTIBLE SECURITIES

A popular investment strategy in recent years has involved the creation of security "packages" in which derivatives are combined with, or embedded into, more basic instruments, such as stock shares or bonds. In this section, we take a detailed look at two important variations on this theme: (1) bonds with warrants that give the investor the right to buy additional shares of the company's common stock; and (2) securities, such as debt or preferred stock, that the investor can convert into other securities.

Warrants

By its most commonly used definition, a **warrant** is an equity call option issued directly by the company whose stock serves as the underlying asset. The key feature that distinguishes it from an ordinary call option is that, if exercised, the company will create new shares of stock to give to the warrantholder. Thus, the exercise of a warrant will increase the total number of outstanding shares, which reduces the value of each individual share. Because of this dilutive effect, the warrant will not be as valuable as an otherwise comparable option contract. Indeed, the valuation of warrants is complicated by many factors, such as how and when the number of outstanding warrants will be exercised, what the company's current capital structure looks like, and what the company plans to do with the new capital it will receive if and when the warrant is exercised.

Galai and Schneller (1978) proposed a simple warrant valuation model in which a firm is presently financed with all equity and the warrants it issues are European-style. On its expiration date T, the warrant will be worth

$$W_T = \max\left[\frac{V_T + N_w X}{N + N_w} - X, 0\right]$$

where:

N = the current number of outstanding shares
N_W = the number of new shares created if the warrants are exercised
V_T = the value of the firm before the warrants are exercised
X = the exercise price

They show that this terminal value can be rewritten as

23.5
$$W_T = \left[\frac{1}{1 + (N_w/N)}\right]C_T$$

where:

C_T = the expiration date value of a regular call option with otherwise identical terms as the warrant

Consequently, at any point prior to expiration, the value of the warrant should be equal to the value of the call deflated (i.e., diluted) by the factor $[1 + (N_w/N)]^{-1}$.

Although warrants can be issued as stand-alone instruments, more frequently a company will attach them to a bond issue to lower its initial funding cost. Warrants created in this manner usually can be detached from the debt instrument by the buyer and traded separately. Suppose, for example, a firm with 1,000,000 shares of common stock outstanding at a current share price of $100 attempts to raise an additional $10 million by issuing a 10-year bond paying annual coupons. Given its current credit rating, assume further that the yield it would have to pay for a straight debt issue is 8.50 percent. The firm could lower this borrowing cost by attaching to the bond European-style equity warrants that mature in exactly one year and have an exercise price of $115 per share. Assuming the firm eventually hopes to raise an additional $5.75 million with these warrants, it will have to create new derivative contracts to cover 50,000 shares ($5.75 million ÷ $115).

Assuming that the one-year risk-free rate is 7 percent and the volatility of the firm's common stock is 25 percent, the Black-Scholes value for a one-year call option to buy one share at $X = \$115$ can be calculated as $7.09. By Equation 24.5, this means that the warrants are worth $6.75 (= 7.09 ÷ [1 + (50,000/1,000,000)]) per share. If each warrant allows for the purchase of one share and the face value of a single bond is $1,000, the firm will issue 10,000 bonds with five warrants attached to each. Assuming it pays an 8.50 percent coupon, the total proceeds it would generate from the sale of each bond with the warrants attached would be $1,033.75, or $1,000 for the bond and $33.75 (= 5 × $6.75) for the warrants. Thus, the firm can reduce its funding cost to 8.00 percent—the solution to the yield to maturity in the following bond calculation:

$$1033.75 = \sum_{t=1}^{10} \frac{85}{(1 + y)^t} + \frac{1000}{(1 + y)^{10}}$$

Packaging warrants with bonds to reduce debt expenses for the issuer and enhance return potential for the investor can be done in a variety of ways. In particular, a recent trend in financial markets is for a firm to attach to its bonds an option that is based on an underlying asset other than the company's own stock. To date, alternative structures have included foreign exchange and stock index transactions. For instance, Rogalski and Seward (1991) detail the development of the market for *foreign currency exchange warrants*, which give the holder the right, but not the obligation, to purchase a predetermined number of U.S. dollars for a price denominated in a foreign currency. Although called warrants, these contracts are closer in form to traditional call options on the dollar (or, equivalently, put options on the foreign currency) because they do not result in any direct change to the issuing firm's capital structure. That is, no dilutive valuation effect exists for these derivatives since there are no new shares of stock issued. Beyond that, these instruments generally can be settled only in cash but can be detached and traded separately from the original bond.[6]

Convertible Securities

A convertible security gives its owner the right, but not the obligation, to convert the existing investment into another form. Typically, the original security is either a bond or a share of

---

[6]For several additional discussions about how warrants are used in capital markets, see Francis, Toy, and Whittaker (1995) and Howe and Su (2001).

preferred stock, which can be exchanged into common stock according to a predetermined formula. From this description, it should be clear that a convertible security is a hybrid issue consisting of a regular bond or preferred stock holding and a call option that allows for the conversion. Similar to warrants, they have been popular with issuers because they generally lead to a lower initial borrowing cost and represent a future supply of equity capital. In fact, Pinches (1970) and McGuire (1991) have noted that these securities often are used in connection with mergers because they generate capital without immediately diluting the equity base of the acquiring firm. On the other hand, investors in convertibles gain the upside potential of common stock while actually holding a less-risky asset.

Convertible Preferred Stock

To see how convertible securities work, let us consider the dynamics of convertible preferred stock. As previously suggested, owning a share of convertible preferred is equivalent to holding a portfolio long in a normal share of preferred stock and long in a call option on the firm's common stock that can be exercised by surrendering the preferred stock. There generally is no waiting period before the conversion can be made, and the conversion privilege usually never expires. This means that the *minimum value of the convertible* issue must be:

$$\text{max[Preferred Stock Value, Conversion Value]}$$

where the **conversion value** is the value of the common stock into which the preferred issue can be exchanged.

Suppose that for a $1,000,000 investment, an institutional investor could purchase 25,000 shares of a convertible preferred issue with the following terms (per share):

- Current convertible share price: $40.00
- Annual convertible dividend: $ 3.00
- Convertible yield: 7.50% (= $3 ÷ $40)
- Regular preferred yield: 10.00%
- Current common stock price: $20.00
- Conversion ratio: 1.75

With these conditions, the share value of a regular preferred stock issue paying a $3 dividend would be $30.00 (= 3 ÷ 0.10), or the perpetual dividend amount divided by the prevailing regular yield. This means that the convertible issue sells at a 33 percent premium to the regular preferred. Also, given the **conversion ratio** of 1.75 shares of common to each share of preferred, the conversion value of the convertible issue is $35 (= 1.75 × 20). Thus, the minimum price of the convertible security would be $35, the greater of the regular preferred price and the conversion value. Since the market price of the convertible still is above this level, this implies a **conversion premium** of 14.29 percent [= (40 − 35) ÷ 35], meaning that the convertible currently is selling based on its option value.

The future value of the convertible issue will depend on two events: (1) interest rate movements, which directly affect the yield on the regular preferred stock component, and (2) changes in common stock prices, given the 1.75 conversion ratio. Consider the matrix of minimum values for various levels of these two variables shown in Exhibit 23.12. In this situation, the value of the convertible preferred stock will likely be driven by its conversion value when interest rates and common stock prices are high and by its preferred stock value when rates and share prices are low.

Exhibit 23.12	Minimum Convertible Preferred Stock Values as a Function of Regular Preferred Yields and Common Stock Prices

| | | COMMON STOCK PRICES | | |
		15	20	25
Yield	8%:	37.50	37.50	43.75
	10%:	30.00	35.00	43.75
	12%:	26.25	35.00	43.75

Convertible Bonds

Like convertible preferred stock, a convertible bond can be viewed as a prepackaged portfolio containing two distinct securities: a regular bond and an option to exchange the bond for a pre-specified number of shares of the issuing firm's common stock. Thus, a convertible bond represents a hybrid investment involving elements of both the debt and equity markets. From the investor's standpoint, there are both advantages and disadvantages to this packaging. Specifi-cally, although the buyer receives equity-like returns with a "guaranteed" terminal payoff equal to the bond's face value, he or she must also pay the option premium, which, as we will see shortly, is embedded in the price of the security. In fact, Lummer and Riepe (1993) have argued that the risk–return dynamics that convertible bonds offer to investors are sufficiently unique as to merit their own asset class. Conversely, the issuer of a convertible bond increases the com-pany's leverage while providing a potential source of equity financing in the future. Exhibit 23.13 shows a portion of a page from *Standard & Poor's Bond Guide* summarizing the perti-nent details of a sample of outstanding convertible bonds issued by U.S.-based companies.

As an example of how one such issue is structured and priced, consider the 4.75 percent coupon convertible notes issued by Amazon.com (AMZN), the Internet retailer whose stock trades in the over-the-counter market. The listing for this issue, which is scheduled to mature in February 2009, is shown on the 10th line from the bottom. After listing the issuer's name, the second and third columns indicate that this bond pays interest semiannually on February 1 and August 1 and has a default rating of B-. The bond issue has $1.1 billion outstanding and is convertible until maturity. At the time of this report (i.e., February 2005), the listed price of the note was 100.37 percent of par and the price of AMZN common stock was $43.22. Additional details of this security are shown in Exhibit 23.14, which was generated by Bloomberg.

As spelled out at the top of Exhibit 23.14—and approximated in the seventh column of Exhibit 23.13—each $1,000 face value of this bond can be converted into 12.816 shares of Amazon.com common stock. As in the convertible preferred example, this statistic is called the instrument's conversion ratio. At the listed share price of $43.22, an investor exercising her conversion option would have received only $553.91 (= $43.22 × 12.816) worth of stock, an amount considerably below the current market value of the bond. In fact, the **conversion par-ity price** (i.e., the common stock price at which immediate conversion would make sense) is equal to $78.32, which is the bond price of $1,003.70 divided by the conversion ratio of 12.816. (This is approximated at $78.29 in Exhibit 23.13, based on the rounded share conver-sion ratio of 12.82.) The prevailing market price of $43.22 is far below this parity level, mean-ing that the conversion option is currently out of the money. Of course, if the conversion parity price ever fell below the market price for the common stock, an astute investor could buy the bond and immediately exchange it into stock with a greater market value.

Exhibit 23.13 Convertible Bond Information Summary

Exchange / Issue, Rate, Interest Dates and Maturity	S&P Rating	Bond Form	Outstdg. Mil-$	Conv. Ex-pires	Shares per $1,000 Bond	Price per Share	Div. Income per Bond	2005 Price Range High	2005 Price Range Low	Curr Bid Sale(s) Ask(A)	Curr. Yield	Yield to Mat	Stock Value of Bond	Conv Parity	Stock Data Month End	Stock Data P/E Ratio	Yr. End	EPS 2003	EPS 2004	EPS Last 12 Mos
3M[1]Co[2](Sr-Zero)[3] ..... [4] 2032	AA	BE	[5]639	2032	[6]9.46	....	13.62	93.62	87.75	90.37	....	Flat	78.75	95.53	•84.36	21	Dc	v3.02	v3.75	[9]3.61
Aames Financial 5½s Ms15 2006	NR	R	114	2006	53.56	18.67	....	100.00	90.00	100.00	5.51	5.76	....	18.67	•10.49	13	Je	....	....	[9]0.89
AAR Corp[7](Sr)[8] ..... 2⅞s Fa 2024	BB–	BE	75.0	2024	[9]53.79	18.59	....	100.37	85.25	86.00	3.33	3.91	59.81	15.98	•11.65	55	My	vd0.39	v0.11	[8]0.24
Abgenix Inc[10] 3½s Ms15 2007	NR	BE	200	2007	36.26	27.58	....	99.87	91.62	98.12	3.56	4.43	31.80	27.06	8.78	d	Dc	vd2.23	Ed2.08	[9]d2.23
Acxiom[11]Corp[10] 3¾s Fa15 2009	BB–	BE	175	2009	54.79	18.25	8.77	148.75	116.00	127.37	3.00	0.02	124.26	23.24	23.08	31	Mr	v0.64	E0.85	[12]NA
Adaptec Inc[10] 3s Ms15 2007	B–	BE	250	2007	65.31	15.31	....	102.87	98.75	99.87	3.00	3.00	38.46	15.29	6.00	34	Mr	v0.54	E0.22	[9]0.12
ADC Telecommun[12](F/R[10]) Jd15 2013	NR	BE	200	2013	249.19	4.01	....	123.12	87.00	101.25	....	....	63.79	4.06	2.57	d	Oc	vd0.10	v0.02	0.02
ADC[10]Telecommunications 1s Jd15 2008	NR	BE	200	2008	249.19	4.01	....	120.50	84.25	98.25	1.02	1.51	63.79	3.94	2.57	d	Oc	vd0.10	v0.02	0.02
Adelphia Communications[13] ..... 6s §Fa15 2006	NR	BE	750	02-14-06	[14]18.02	55.49	....	70.00	15.50	16.00	....	Flat	0.63	8.87	0.37	d	Dc	vd3.31	....	....
Adelphia[15]Communications[13] ..... 3¼s §Mn 2021	NR	BE	500	2021	[14]22.85	43.75	....	64.00	15.50	16.00	....	Flat	0.79	7.00	0.37	d	Dc	vd3.31	....	....
• [16]ADT Operations(Zero) ..... [17] 2010	BBB–	R	[5]238	2010	[18]28.23	....	11.29	No Sale		196.37	....	Flat	101.62	69.56	•36.14	25	Sp	v□0.53	v1.35	1.35
Advanced Energy Indus[10] 5¼s mN15 2006	B–	BE	135	2006	20.19	49.53	....	102.50	96.25	96.37	5.43	7.12	14.03	47.73	7.15	57	Dc	vd1.37	E0.14	[9]0.24
Advanced Energy Indus[10] ..... 5s mS 2006	B–	BE	125	2006	33.53	29.83	....	114.37	96.75	96.37	5.17	6.86	23.30	28.74	7.15	57	Dc	vd1.37	E0.14	[9]0.24
Advanced[19]Micro[20]Dev[21](Sr) ..... 4¾s Fa 2022	B–	BE	500	2022	42.77	23.38	....	120.50	92.75	101.25	4.70	4.65	67.19	23.67	•15.80	88	Dc	vd0.79	v0.25	0.25
• AES Corp[10] 4½s fA15 2005	B–	BE	150	08-15-05	37.04	27.00	....	100.93	95.75	100.00	4.49	4.36	51.07	26.99	•14.05	17	Dc	v∆d0.74	E0.68	[9]d0.46
Affiliated[22]Managers[23](Sr-F/R[24]) ..... [25]QFeb25 2033	BBB–	BE	300	2033	[26]12.31	81.25	....	160.71	116.62	149.19	....	....	77.01	121.19	•63.41	33	Dc	....	v2.02	2.02
Affiliated[27]Managers[28](Sr-Zero) ..... [29] 2021	BBB–	BE	[5]251	2021	[6]11.62	....	....	119.12	94.25	114.00	....	Flat	72.69	98.10	•63.41	33	Dc	....	v2.02	2.02
Agere Systems[21] 6½s jD15 2009	B	BE	410	2009	302.34	3.31	....	163.50	99.25	106.87	6.10	4.97	42.62	3.53	•1.44	d	Sp	±vd0.20	±vd0.05	[12]NA
Agilent[30]Technologies[31](Sr)[21] ..... 3s jD 2021	BB	BE	1000	2021	31.04	32.22	....	123.75	97.87	100.37	3.00	2.99	67.07	32.33	•22.11	33	Oc	v□d3.78	v0.71	0.71
AirTran[32]Hldgs[21](Sr) ..... 7s jJ 2023	CCC	BE	125	2023	[9]89.93	11.12	....	175.00	125.25	108.62	6.58	6.40	73.47	12.07	•8.54	76	Dc	v1.21	v0.14	0.14
Akamai Technologies[13] ..... 5½s jJ 2007	NR	BE	300	2007	8.66	115.47	....	102.75	98.25	100.87	5.44	4.90	10.98	116.48	13.10	89	Dc	vd0.25	....	[9]0.14
Alexion Pharmaceuticals[33] 5¾s Ms15 2007	NR	BE	120	2007	9.40	106.425	....	101.00	91.50	100.75	5.70	5.28	23.15	107.18	24.74	d	Jl	vd4.64	vd3.43	[10]d3.12
Allergan[34]Inc(Sr-Zero)[35] ..... [36] 2022	A	BE	[5]642	2022	[26]11.41	....	4.11	107.87	87.75	93.37	....	Flat	87.06	81.83	•75.95	28	Dc	vd0.40	E2.74	[9]1.30
• Alpharma Inc[10] ..... 5¾s Ao 2005	CCC+	R	125	04-01-05	34.97	28.59	6.29	101.25	....	100.62	5.71	....	52.03	28.77	•15.05	24	Dc	±v0.32	E0.65	[9]0.13
Alpharma[37]Inc[38] ..... 3s Jd 2006	CCC+	BE	170	2006	[39]31.14	32.11	5.61	128.37	114.87	124.12	2.38	0.02	46.33	39.86	•15.05	24	Dc	±v0.32	E0.65	[9]0.13
• [40]ALZA Corp[41](Zero) ..... [42] 2014	AAA	R	[5]781	2014	[43]25.45	....	29.01	No Sale		164.62	....	Flat	164.45	64.68	•64.70	22	Dc	v2.40	v2.84	2.84
[44]ALZA Corp[45](Zero)[41] ..... [46] 2020	AAA	BE	[5]1090	2020	[43]13.75	....	15.68	87.62	70.25	88.87	....	Flat	88.85	64.63	•64.70	22	Dc	v2.40	v2.84	2.84
Amazon.com ..... 4¾s Fa 2009	B–	BE	1100	2009	12.82	78.03	....	102.12	98.12	100.37	4.72	4.57	54.12	78.29	43.22	41	Dc	v0.08	E0.96	[9]0.75
Amdocs Ltd[47](Sr)[48] ..... 2s Jd 2008	NR	BE	0.39	2008	[49]10.86	92.09	....	100.62	99.25	99.62	2.01	2.13	31.93	91.73	•29.75	24	Sp	v0.77	v1.10	[12]NA
Amer Greetings[10] 7s jJ15 2006	BB+	BE	175	2006	[50]71.95	13.90	17.27	207.87	147.50	180.75	3.95	0.02	169.80	25.12	•24.14	15	Fb	v1.40	E1.80	[8]1.41
Amer Intl Group[51](Sr) 0½s Mn15 2007	AAA	BE	210	2007	Exch for cash[52]			98.25	94.00	94.00	0.53	3.87	....	....	•66.29	15	Dc	....	E4.30	[9]4.15
Amer Tower Corp(Sr-Disc) 2¼s aO15 2009	CCC	BE	[5]260	2009	[53]29.38	24.00	....	84.62	79.12	79.75	2.82	7.18	53.55	27.14	•18.12	d	Dc	vd1.46	Ed0.45	[9]d0.93
Amer Tower Corp[54](Sr)[55] 2¼s aO15 2009	CCC	BE	[5]260	2009	[53]29.38	24.00	....	84.62	79.12	79.75	2.82	7.18	53.55	27.14	•18.12	d	Dc	vd1.46	Ed0.45	[9]d0.93
Amer Tower[56]Corp(Sr)[10] 5s Fa15 2010	CCC	BE	450	2010	[53]19.42	51.50	....	100.50	95.25	99.87	4.99	4.97	35.40	51.42	•18.12	d	Dc	vd1.46	Ed0.45	[9]d0.93
Amer[57]Finl[58]Group[59](Sr) ..... [60]Jd2 2033	BBB	BE	511	2033	[61]11.50	....	5.75	43.50	40.12	41.62	....	....	34.44	36.19	•30.79	5	Dc	....	....	[9]6.30
AmeriCredit[62]Corp[10](Sr) 1¾s mN15 2023	B	BE	200	2023	[26]53.53	18.68	....	143.12	108.87	142.87	1.25	0.02	127.45	26.69	•24.55	13	Je	....	....	[12]NA
AmerUs[63]Group[64] 2s Ms6 2032	BBB	BE	185	2032	[6]26.60	....	10.64	133.00	106.87	131.12	1.53	0.72	116.21	49.29	•44.57	10	Dc	....	E4.05	[9]4.13

Uniform Footnote Explanations—See Page 1. Other: [1] Contingent int pay fr 11-22-07 based on secur price. [2] (HRO)On 11-21-05(07,12,17,22&27)at $860.87 & accr OID.
[3] (HRO)On Chge of Ctrl at $860.87 & accr OID to 11-21-07. [4] Due 11-21-32. [5] Incl disc. [6] Not conv unless min com price met or called for red. [7] (HRO)On 2-1-10(14&19) at 100.
[8] (HRO)For Designated Event at 100. [9] Co may pay cash val of stk. [10] (HRO)On Chge of Ctrl at 100. [11] (HRO)On 2-15-07 at 100. [12] Int adj semi-anly(6 Mo LIBOR & 0.375%).
[13] (HRO)On Fundamental Chge at 100. [14] Into Adelphia Communications'A'com. [15] (HRO)On 5-1-05(07,11&16)at 100. [16] Gtd by & data of Tyco Int'l. [17] Due 7-6-10. [18] Conv into Tyco Int'l.
[19] On 8-1-08(11&16)int will be reset to 5-yr Treas Notes&0.43%. [20] (HRO)On 2-1-09(12&17)at 100. [21] (HRO)For Fundamental Chge at 100. [22] Int adj qtrly(3 Mo LIBOR less 0.50%).
[23] (HRO)On 2-25-08(13,18,23&28)at 100. [24] (HRO)On Chge of Ctrl at 100 to 2-25-08. [25] Contingent int pay fr 2-26-08 based on secur price. [26] Not cv unless min com price met or called for red.
[27] (HRO)On var dates to 2016 at $904.95&accr OID. [28] (HRO)On Chge of Ctrl at $904.95&accr OID to 5-7-06. [29] Due 5-7-21. [30] On 6-1-06(11&16)int will be reset to 5-yr Treas Notes less 1.3%.
[31] (HRO)On 12-1-06(11&16)at 100. [32] (HRO)On 7-1-10(13&18)at 100. [33] (HRO)For Repurch Event at 105. [34] (HRO)On 11-6-07(12&17)at $779.41&accr OID.
[35] (HRO)For Fundamental Chge at $779.41 & accr OID to 11-5-07. [36] Due 11-6-22. [37] (HRO)On Chge of Ctrl at curr red price. [38] At maturity,Co to pay 134.104% times princ amt. [39] Into Cl A.
[40] (HRO)On 7-14-09 at $771.74. [41] Gtd by & data of Johnson & Johnson. [42] Due 7-14-14. [43] Into Johnson & Johnson com. [44] (HRO)On Chge of Ctrl at $551.26 & accr OID.
[45] (HRO)On 7-28-08(& 13)at $551.26 & accr OID. [46] Due 7-28-20. [47] (HRO)On 6-1-06 at 100. [48] HRO)On Chge of Ctrl at 100. [49] Into Amdocs Ord. [50] Into Amer Greetings'A'com. [51] Issued in min denom $100T.
[52] Into cash equiv of 10.76 com shrs. [53] Conv into Cl'A'com. [54] (HRO)On 10-22-03 at 100(Accr Val). [55] (HRO)On Chge of Ctrl at 100(Accr Val). [56] (HRO)On 2-20-07 at 100.
[57] Int at 1.4861% paid in cash to 6-2-08,then zero cpn. [58] (HRO)On Chge of Ctrl at $371.53 & accr OID to 6-2-08. [59] (HRO)On 6-2-08(13,18,23&28)at $371.53 & accr OID.
[60] Contingent int pay fr 6-3-08 based on secur price. [61] Co may pay cash val of stk:Not cv unless min com price met or called for red. [62] (HRO)On 11-15-08 at 100.25(11-15-13&18 at 100).
[63] Co pays contingent int:At mat will pay 127% of prin amt. [64] (HRO)On Chge of Ctrl at 100(Accreted Val).

Source: *Standard & Poor's Bond Guide*, February 2005, p. 215.

Exhibit 23.14	**Details of Amazon.com's Convertible Bond Issue**

```
AMAZON.COM INC   AMZN 4 ¾ 02/09
CONV TO       12.8160 SHRS(PER   1000.0)AMZN  (NASD)
CONVERTIBLE UNTIL  2/ 1/ 9              ISSUER INFORMATION
 SECURITY INFORMATION       SERIES: 144A  NAME   AMAZON.COM INC
CPN FREQ      SEMI-AN                     TYPE   INDUSTRIAL
CPN TYPE      FIXED           IDENTIFICATION #'s    REDEMPTION INFO
MTY/REFUND TYP CONV/CALL      CUSIP    023135AD8  MATURITY DT   2/ 1/09
CALC TYP ( 49)CONVERTIBLE     MLNUM  AAE07        REFUNDING DT
DAY COUNT( 5) 30/360                             NEXT CALL DT   5/ 9/05
MARKET ISS    PRIV PLACEMENT  COMMON   009681582 WORKOUT DT     2/ 1/09
COUNTRY/CURR  US /USD                            RISK FACTOR    3.4449
COLLATERAL TYP SUB DEBENTURES     ISSUANCE INFO
AGGR AMT ISS      1,250,000(M)*  ANNOUNCE DT   1/29/99      RATINGS
AGGR AMT OUT        899,759(M)*  1ST SETTLE DT  2/ 3/99  MOODY   B3
MIN PC/INC    1,000/    1,000   1ST CPN DT     8/ 1/99  S & P   B-
PAR AMT          1,000.00       INT ACCRUE DT  2/ 3/99  COMP    B-
LEADMGR/UWRTR MSDW              PRICE @ ISSUE  100
EXCHANGE      TRACE
NOTES  NO PROSPECTUS, *AGGREGATE AMT FOR ALL FORMS
PROV CALL. PRX/SHR=$78.0275. CV PREM=27%. IF CALL BEF 2/6/02 ISSR WILL PAY ADDL
$212.60 LESS INT PD. 144A-FOR REG'D SEE CUSIP:#023135AF3. SHORT 1ST. POISON PUT.
```

As indicated in the "Security Information" and "Redemption Information" boxes of Exhibit 23.14, this AMZN convertible bond is also callable by the issuer, which is typical of these instruments. Of course, a firm will never call a bond selling for less than its call price (which is the case with the AMZN note since it is currently callable at a price of 101.90 percent of par). In fact, firms often wait until the bond is selling for significantly more than its call price before calling it.[7] If the company calls the bond under these conditions, investors will have an incentive to convert the bond into the stock that is worth more than they would receive from the call price; this situation is referred to as *forcing conversion*. Two other factors also increase the investors' incentive to convert their bonds. First, some instruments have conversion prices that step up over time according to a predetermined schedule. Since a stepped-up conversion price leads to a lower number of shares received, it becomes more likely that investors will exercise their option just before the conversion price increases. Second, a firm can help to encourage conversion by increasing the dividends on the stock, thereby making the income generated by the shares more attractive relative to the income from the bond.

Another important characteristic when evaluating convertible bonds is the **payback** or *breakeven time*, which measures how long the higher interest income from the convertible bond (compared to the dividend income from the common stock) must persist to make up for the difference between the price of the bond and its conversion value (i.e., the conversion premium). The calculation is as follows:

$$\text{Payback} = \frac{\text{Bond Price} - \text{Conversion Value}}{\text{Bond Income} - \text{Income from Equal Investment in Common Stock}}$$

[7]In an empirical study of this issue, Ingersoll (1977) showed that almost all of the convertible securities studied were called later than the theoretically optimal time. This topic was also investigated by Asquith and Mullins (1991).

For instance, the annual coupon yield payment on the Amazon.com convertible bond is $47.50, while the firm's dividend yield is zero. Thus, assuming that you sold the bond for $1003.70 and used the proceeds to purchase 23.223 shares ($=1,003.70/43.22$) of AMZN stock, the payback period would be

$$\frac{1,003.70 - 553.91}{47.50 - 0.00} = 9.47 \text{ years}$$

This implies a point in the future considerably past when the bond matures (i.e., 4.00 years), suggesting that investors are unlikely to make back the conversion premium with the incremental cash flow from the bond alone.

It is also possible to calculate the combined value of the investor's conversion option and issuer's call feature that are embedded in the note. In the Amazon.com example, with a market price of $1,003.70, the convertible's yield-to-maturity can be calculated as the solution to

$$\$1,003.70 = \sum_{t=1}^{8} \frac{23.75}{(1 + y/2)^t} + \frac{1,000}{(1 + y/2)^8}$$

or $y = 4.6$ percent (reported as 4.57 percent in the 14th column of Exhibit 23.13. This computation assumes 8 semiannual coupon payments of $23.75 ($= 47.50 \div 2$). Since the yield on an Amazon.com debt issue with no embedded options and the same (B-) credit rating and maturity was 7.0 percent, the present value of a straight fixed-income security with the same cash flows would be

$$\$922.67 = \sum_{t=1}^{8} \frac{23.75}{(1 + 0.035)^t} + \frac{1,000}{(1 + 0.035)^8}$$

This means that the net value of the combined options is $81.03, or $1,003.70 minus $922.67. Using the Black-Scholes valuation model, it is easily confirmed that a four-year call option to buy *one* share of Amazon.com stock—which does not pay a dividend—at an exercise price of $78.32 (i.e., the conversion parity value) is equal to $8.64.[8] Thus, the value of the investor's conversion option—which allows for the acquisition of 12.816 shares—must be $110.73 ($= 12.816 \times 8.64$). This means that the value of the issuer's call feature under these conditions must be $29.70 ($= 110.73 - 81.03$).

Exhibit 23.15 illustrates the value of a convertible bond in a more general way. The horizontal axis plots the value of the firm, which establishes an upper bound for the value of a convertible since it cannot sell for more than the firm's assets. Thus, there is a firm value line that bisects the plane and the value of the convertible must be below that line. Note that the line for the bond value is relatively flat for a wide range of firm values because higher firm values do not increase the value of the bond since bondholders receive only their promised payments. In contrast, at fairly low firm values, the value of the bond drops off as bankruptcy becomes more likely. Conversion value rises directly with the value of the firm. The exhibit shows that for low firm values, the bond value will be the minimum value of the convertible, whereas the convertible's price will be driven by its conversion potential for high firm values. Finally, the line for the value of the convertible shows that

---

[8]This calculation assumes the following input values: $S = 43.22$, $X = 78.32$, $T = 4$, $RFR = 0.04$, $\sigma = 0.43$, and $D = 0.00$.

Exhibit 23.15 | **Illustrating the Value of a Convertible Bond**

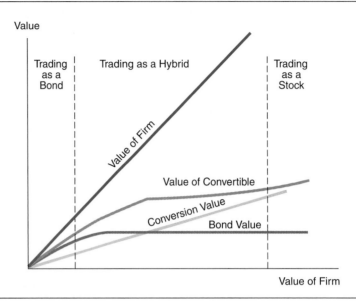

when the firm value is low, the convertible will act more like a bond, trading for only a slight premium over the bond value (as is the case with the Amazon.com note discussed earlier). Alternatively, when firm values are high, the convertible will act more like a stock, selling for only a slight premium over the conversion value. In the fairly wide middle range, the convertible will trade as the hybrid security that acts somewhat like a bond and somewhat like a stock.

OTHER EMBEDDED DERIVATIVES

For many years, the nature of borrowing and lending in securitized capital markets remained quite stable, with companies typically issuing bonds at par value and paying either a fixed or floating rate of interest in the same currency in which the money was borrowed. With few exceptions, the choice of maturity or coupon structure was driven by the economic situation faced by the borrower, rather than the investor. Over the past decade, however, this scenario has greatly changed with the development of the *structured note* market. Generally speaking, structured notes are debt issues that have their principal or coupon payments linked to some other underlying variable. Examples include bonds whose coupons are tied to the appreciation of an equity index, such as the S&P 500, or a zero coupon bond with a principal amount tied to the appreciation of an oil price index.

Crabbe and Argilagos (1994) and Das (2001) have pointed out several common features that distinguish structured notes from regular fixed-income securities, two of which are important for our discussion. First, structured notes are designed for and targeted to a specific investor with a very particular need. That is, these are not generic instruments but products tailored to address an investor's special constraints, which often are themselves created by tax, regulatory, or institutional policy restrictions. Second, after structuring the financing to meet the investor's needs, the issuer typically will hedge that unique exposure with swaps or exchange-traded derivatives. Inasmuch as the structured note most likely required an embedded derivative to create the desired payoff structure for the investor, this unwinding of the derivative position by the issuer generates an additional source of profit opportunity for the bond underwriter.

The growth of this market has been quite rapid. From its ostensible origin in the mid-1980s, by 2003 about $100 billion of these notes were issued annually. Equally impressive is the wide variety of economic risks that have been embedded and the maze of new acronyms that has accompanied these innovations (e.g., FLAG, LYON, SPEL, STEER, PERCS, and ICON). We will take a detailed look at four such structures representative of the major exposures an investor might desire: currency, equity, commodity, and interest rates.

Dual Currency Bonds

A dual currency bond is a debt instrument that has coupons denominated in a different currency than its principal amount. They have been popular funding instruments, particularly in the Euromarkets, for more than a decade and have been designed to include virtually all the world's major currencies. These bonds can be viewed as a combination of two simpler financial instruments: (1) a single-currency fixed-coupon bond, and (2) a forward contract to exchange the bond's principal into a predetermined amount of a foreign currency. They often are sold to investors who are willing to take a view over the longer term in the foreign exchange markets. By having the currency forward attached to the bond, fixed-income portfolio managers who might otherwise be restricted from trading in FX have the potential to enhance their performance if their beliefs about future market conditions prove correct.

To demonstrate a structure typical of these products, consider a five-year bond paying an annual coupon of 9 percent in U.S. dollars and redemption amount of JPY 110,000. The initial price of the bond is USD 1,020, relative to a par value of USD 1,000. Assuming further that a regular five-year, dollar-denominated bond of comparable risk yielding 9 percent could have been issued at par, this means that the forward contract portion of the dual currency instrument is off market because it carries a present value of USD 20. Exhibit 23.16 shows the cash flows for this structure from the investor's point of view. It also demonstrates how it can be assembled from its more basic component parts.

| Exhibit 23.16 | Cash Flows for a Dual Currency Bond from the Investor's Perspective |

	YEAR					
	0	1	2	3	4	5
Transaction						
1. Long 9% USD bond	−USD 1,000	+ USD 90	+ USD 90	+ USD 90	+ USD 90	+ USD 1,090
2. Long yen forward (pay USD, receive JPY)	−USD 20	—	—	—	—	+JPY 110,000 and −USD 1,000
3. Long dual currency bond (Transaction 1 + Transaction 2)	−USD 1,020	− USD 90	+ USD 90	+ USD 90	+ USD 90	+ JPY 110,000 and +USD 90

Notice that the embedded forward contract allows the bondholder to exchange the USD 1,000 for JPY 110,000, generating an implied *nominal* exchange rate of JPY 110/USD (or, equivalently, USD 0.0091/JPY). However, given that the investor has to pay an additional USD 20 today for this future transaction, this is not the *effective* exchange rate that the investor faces. Indeed, the fact that the investor is willing to pay the additional USD 20 suggests that JPY 110/USD is a favorable price to purchase yen forward. The effective exchange rate built into this transaction can be established by dividing JPY 110,000 by the sum of USD 1,000 and the future value (in Year 5) of USD 20. Calculating this latter amount as 30.77 [= 20 × (1.09)^5], the effective exchange rate becomes JPY 106.72/USD [= 110,000 ÷ (1,000 + 30.77)].

There are at least two reasons why this dual currency bond might trade at a premium over a single-currency 9 percent coupon bond of comparable creditworthiness. First, it is possible that the five-year forward exchange rate between yen and dollars is JPY 106.72/USD, meaning that at USD 1,020, the bond is priced properly. The more likely possibility, though, is that the five-year forward rate actually is JPY 110/USD and that investors are paying up for a desirable FX exposure that they cannot acquire in any other way. If this is true, the issuer—who is effectively short the regular dollar bond and short in the yen forward—can unwind its derivative position at a profit, thereby reducing its funding cost below 9 percent. That is, the issuer's commitment to sell JPY 110,000 to the investor in Year 5 can be offset by a long position in a separate yen forward (which, once again, is usually done with the bond's underwriter as the counterparty) at the market forward exchange rate of JPY 110/JSD. Thus, the issuer's net borrowing cost can be calculated by solving for the yield as follows:

$$1,020 = \sum_{t=1}^{5} \frac{90}{(1 + y)^t} + \frac{1,000}{(1 + y)^5}$$

or y = 8.49 percent. This 51-basis-point differential from the plain vanilla borrowing rate of 9 percent represents the issuer's compensation for creating an investment vehicle that is tailored to the needs of the investor.

Equity-Index Linked Notes

In July of 2002, Bank of America Corporation raised capital by issuing a class of unsecured senior debt securities called S&P 500 Return Linked Notes. These particular instruments are an example of a wider class of structured notes known as variable principal redemption (VPR) securities because the amount of the bond's principal that is refunded to the investor at maturity is not fixed but instead depends on the returns to an equity index. These particular VPR bonds mature on July 2, 2007, and—as their name implies—have their redemption amount tied to movements in the S&P 500 index between the origination and maturity dates. Other VPR notes that have traded in the market in recent years have tied the principal redemption to a wide variety of global stock indexes, including the Dow Jones Industrial Average, the Russell 1000, the FT-SE 100, and the Nikkei 225.

Bank of America designed this VPR note so that it would pay no coupons prior to maturity. Further, at maturity the bondholder receives the original issue price (stated here as 100 percent of minimum face value) plus a "supplemental redemption amount," the value of which depends on the level at which the S&P 500 index settles relative to a predetermined initial level. Given that this supplemental amount cannot be less than zero, the total payout to the investor at maturity can be written:

$$100 + \max\left[0, \left\{100 \times \left(\frac{\text{Final SPX Value} - \text{Initial SPX Value}}{\text{Initial SPX Value}}\right) \times 1.22\right\}\right]$$

where the initial S&P 500 (i.e., SPX) index value was specified as 973.53. The factor 1.22 indicates that the investor actually receives 122% of the return to the SPX over the five-year period, provided that return is positive.

From the preceding description, recognize that the VPR structure combines a five-year, zero-coupon bond with a SPX index call option, both of which were issued by Bank of America. Thus, the structured note investor essentially owns a "portfolio" that is (1) long in a bond and (2) long in an index call option position. This particular security might have been designed for those investors who wanted to participate in the equity market but, for regulatory or taxation reasons, were not permitted to do so directly. For example, the manager of a fixed-income mutual fund might be able to enhance her return performance by purchasing this bond and then hoping for an appreciating stock market. Notice that the use of the call option in this design makes it fairly easy for Bank of America to market to its institutional customers in that it is a no-lose proposition; the worst-case scenario for the investor is that she simply gets her money back without interest in five years. (Of course, the customer does carry the bank's credit risk for this period.) Thus, unlike the dual currency bond where the investor could either gain or lose from changing exchange rates, at origination this VPR issue had no downside exposure to stock price declines.

The call option embedded in this structure is actually a partial position. To see this, we can rewrite the option portion of the note's redemption value as:

$$\max\left[0, \left\{100 \times 1.22 \times \left(\frac{\text{Final SPX} - 973.53}{973.53}\right)\right\}\right]$$
$$= \max\left[0, \left\{\left(\frac{122}{973.53}\right)(\text{Final SPX} - 973.53)\right\}\right]$$

or

$$(0.1253)\{\max[0, (\text{Final SPX} - 973.53)]\}$$

Thus, given that a regular index option would have a terminal payoff of $\max[0, \text{Final SPX} - X]$, where X is the exercise price, the derivative in the VPR represents 12.53 percent of this amount. The terminal payoffs to the VPR embedded option are shown in Exhibit 23.17, along with those to a regular index call option for several potential July 2007 levels of the S&P 500 index. Notice that although both the VPR and regular options become in the money at the same point (i.e., 973.53), only the latter produces a dollar-for-dollar payoff with increasing values of the index beyond this level. The payoff to the call feature in the structured note still rises for any S&P 500 level above 973.53, but gains only $0.1253 for every one point gained by the index.

Exhibit 23.18 provides a different way to visualize the VPR investment structure. In particular, notice that for the initial (i.e., July 2002) payment of $100, the investor has purchased the equivalent of a five-year zero-coupon bond maturing in July 2007 plus a partial call option on the index on the S&P 500 index. Thus, the $100 initial payment can be split into the value of the zero-coupon bond—which is simply $100 discounted to the present at Bank of America's five-year bond yield—and the remainder, which must be the value of the embedded SPX call option at the origination date. This way of viewing the instrument also makes valuing the VPR at any point in its life a more transparent process. That is, it must always be the case that the value of the entire structure is just the value of the bond portion plus the value of the option component; any price synergy for the packaging will be a market-driven phenomenon.

To see how this might work, consider that on January 3, 2005, the closing level for the S&P 500 was 1,202.08. Further, the semiannually compounded yield of a zero-coupon (i.e., "stripped") Treasury bond on this date was 3.17 percent, while a Bank of America bond maturing at about the

| Exhibit 23.17 | **Terminal Payoffs to VPR Embedded Call Option and Regular Index Call Option** ($X = 973.53$) |

Final SPX Value	Regular Index Call	VPR Call
875	0.00	0.00
900	0.00	0.00
925	0.00	0.00
950	0.00	0.00
975	1.47	0.18
1000	26.47	3.32
1025	51.47	6.45
1050	76.47	9.58
1075	101.47	12.72
1100	126.47	15.85
1125	151.47	18.98
1150	176.47	22.12
1175	201.47	25.25
1200	226.47	28.38
1225	251.47	31.51
1250	276.47	34.65
1275	301.47	37.78
1300	326.47	40.91
1325	351.47	44.05
1350	376.47	47.18
1375	401.47	50.31
1400	426.47	53.45

same time as the VPR issue carried a yield of 3.65 percent. (This 48-basis-point credit spread was appropriate for Bank of America's credit rating of Aa2 and AA by Moody's and Standard & Poor's, respectively.) Given the remaining time to maturity (i.e., two years and six months, or five half-years), the bond portion of the VPR issue should be worth:

$$\text{VPR Bond Value} = \frac{100}{\left(1 + \dfrac{.0365}{2}\right)^5} = \$91.354.$$

As we saw in Chapter 22, the value of a regular call option on a stock index can be calculated with the dividend yield-adjusted version of the Black-Scholes model. To perform this computation, three additional inputs are needed. First, the S&P 500 dividend yield on January 3, 2005, was 1.80 percent. Second, the continuously compounded equivalent of the quoted risk-free rate is 3.15 percent.[9] Finally, the volatility of SPX index returns over the time to VPR issue's maturity is assumed to be 15.54 percent, a level approximated from the prevailing implied volatilities for traded index options on that date.

| Exhibit 23.18 | Illustrating the VPR Transaction |

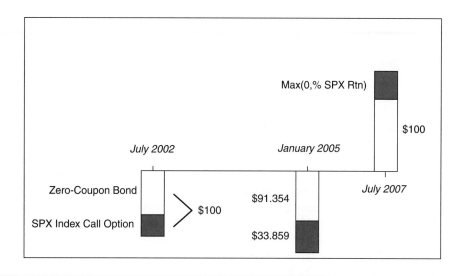

The value of an index call option with an exercise price of 973.53 can now be generated by the Black-Scholes formula using the following inputs: $S = 1{,}202.08$, $X = 973.53$, $T = 2.50$, $RFR = 0.0315$, $D = 0.018$, and $\sigma = 0.1554$. Under these conditions we have:

$$d_1 = [ln\,(1202.08e^{-(.018)2.50}/973.53) + (.0315 + 0.5(.1554)^2)(2.50)] \div (.1554\,[2.50]^{1/2}) = 1.1185$$

and

$$d_2 = 1.1185 - .1554\,[2.50]^{1/2} = 0.8728$$

so that $N(d_1) = 0.8682$ and $N(d_2) = 0.8086$. Thus the index call's Black-Scholes value is:

$$C_0 = (1202.08)\,(e^{-(.018)2.50})\,(0.8682) - (973.53)\,(e^{-(.0315)2.50})\,(0.8086) = 270.221$$

The value of the embedded VPR call is then established by multiplying 270.221 by 0.1253, which leaves a value of $33.859. Therefore, as shown in Exhibit 23.18, on this particular date the VPR issue was valued at $125.213 (= 91.354 + 33.859). Finally, notice that since the January 3, 2005, index value (i.e., 1,202.08) was already substantially greater than the initial (i.e., exercise) level, the VPR call feature is deep in the money and the value of the embedded option can be further broken down into $28.637 [= (.1253) (1202.08 − 973.53)] of intrinsic value and $5.222 (= 33.859 − 28.637) of time premium.

---

[9]This value can be established by solving for r in the following equation:
$$e^r = (1 + (.0317/2))^2$$
or
$$r = ln\,[(1 + (.0317/2))^2] = 0.0315$$

Commodity-Linked Bull and Bear Bonds

Besides linking their payoffs to currency or equity indexes, fixed-income securities can be designed to give an investor exposure to commodity price movements as well. The commodities involved in these structures are seldom exchanged but instead represented in the form of "cash settlement only" derivatives. Thus, virtually no theoretical limit exists to the number of different underlying assets that can be embedded into a bond issue. However, recall that innovation in the structured note market is dictated by investor demands, which to date have tended to concentrate on either oil or precious metals. As in the previous examples, the primary attractions to the investor of gaining the desired exposure through the purchase of structured notes are their convenience and their ability to avoid restrictions on taking commodity positions directly.

A particularly interesting form of the commodity-linked bond is the so-called bull-and-bear note. This structure gets its name from a bond that is issued in two portions: a bull tranche, whose principal redemption amount increases directly with the price of the designated commodity; and a bear tranche, whose principal refunding declines with increasing commodity prices. One of the first issues of this kind occurred in October 1986 when the Kingdom of Denmark raised $120 million in two separate $60 million tranches, each having a different payoff structure depending on the movement of an index of gold prices.[10] Both of these gold-linked note tranches had a seven-year maturity, paid an annual coupon of 3 percent, and were issued at a price of 100.125 percent of par value. The principal redemptions for each $1,000 of face value for the two tranches were:

Bull Redemption: $1,000 × [1.158 × (Index at Redemption ÷ Initial Index)]

and

Bear Redemption: $1,000 × {2.78 − [1.158 × (Index at Redemption ÷ Initial Index)]}

Finally, for both tranches, maximum and minimum redemption levels of $2,280 and $500, respectively, were set.

Exhibit 23.19 shows the redemption amount that the Kingdom of Denmark is obligated to pay on each tranche for a series of gold index levels relative to the initial level, which was set at 426.50. The final column of this display shows what the average redemption value is when the two tranches are considered together. Notice that this average amount does not vary—that is, *the issuer has no net exposure to gold price movements.* Unlike the dual currency bond example considered earlier, which required the issuer to adopt an additional derivative position to offset the instrument's inherent FX exposure, the virtue of this two-tranche approach is that the commodity exposure is neutralized internally. That is, the Kingdom of Denmark is effectively both long and short gold in equal amounts across the bear and bull segments, respectively. An immediate consequence of this is that they have a fixed funding cost for the full $120 million issue, calculated by solving:

$$1,001.25 = \sum_{t=1}^{7} \frac{30}{(1+y)^t} + \frac{1,390}{(1+y)^7}$$

---

[10]Additional details of this bull-and-bear structure are explained in Walmsley (1998), who also provides descriptions of an exhaustive set of such deals. It is recommended reading for anyone wishing to learn more about the development of these innovative products.

Exhibit 23.19	Redemption Values for the Bull-and-Bear Gold-Linked Note (in U.S. Dollars)

Terminal Gold Index	Bull Tranche	Bear Tranche	Average
100	500	2,280	1,390
150	500	2,280	1,390
200	543	2,237	1,390
250	679	2,101	1,390
300	815	1,965	1,390
350	950	1,830	1,390
400	1,086	1,694	1,390
450	1,222	1,558	1,390
500	1,358	1,422	1,390
550	1,493	1,287	1,390
600	1,629	1,151	1,390
650	1,765	1,015	1,390
700	1,901	879	1,390
750	2,036	744	1,390
800	2,172	608	1,390
850	2,280	500	1,390
900	2,280	500	1,390

or $y = 7.42$ percent. At the time this deal was launched, a regular seven-year, par-value debt issue would have required a yield of about 8 percent, a fact that underscores the Kingdom of Denmark's incentive to create this structure in the first place.

The attraction for the investors, of course, is the ability to purchase a fixed-income security that also allows for participation in gold price movements. In exchange for accepting a lower-than-market coupon, buyers of the bull (bear) tranche will receive a redemption value that exceeds their purchase price if the gold index increases (declines). Exhibit 23.20, which shows the redemption values for the two tranches in a graphical form, suggests that the commodity derivatives embedded in this transaction are not simple forward or option positions. Rather, the minimum and maximum principal payoffs effectively convert the gold exposure into a call option money spread—a bull spread for the bull tranche, a bear for the bear—as described in Chapter 22. The investors, who undoubtedly will be different people for the two positions, pay for this spread position through a reduction in their average yield to maturity relative to the regular bond.

Swap-Linked Notes

As we have seen, interest rate swaps are efficient mechanisms for transforming the cash flows of existing debt issues. They also are quite useful in the new-issue market when the desired rate exposures of the borrower and lender do not coincide naturally. Imagine, for example, that Company LMN wishes to raise $50 million by issuing a fixed-rate note with semiannual coupon payments over a three-year period. Having launched a similar issue in the capital

| Exhibit 23.20 | **Redemption Values for the Bull-And-Bear Gold-Linked Note** |

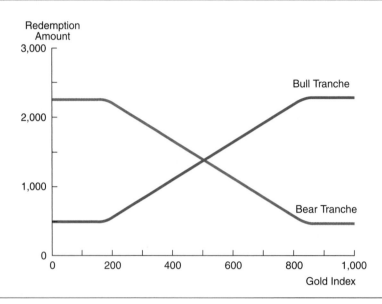

markets recently, however, LMN finds that little appetite exists for another one of its fixed-rate notes. On the other hand, a large institutional investor is willing to accept LMN's credit risk on a privately placed loan, providing that the deal can be structured to its satisfaction. In particular, the fund manager for this investment company thinks that interest rates are going to decline substantially over the next few years and wants to design the loan contract to take advantage of that possibility. Accordingly, she wants the semiannual coupon on the note to move inversely with the level of some variable interest rate index, such as LIBOR. This sort of arrangement is known as a *reverse floating-rate* contract; the coupon rate changes as the general level of interest rates moves but in the opposite direction.

Suppose the specific structure that LMN and the investor agree on resets the coupon on a semiannual basis at a level equal to 12 percent minus LIBOR. Thus, if six-month LIBOR on a particular settlement date is 7.5 percent, the coupon payment will be 4.5 percent ($\times$ .5 $\times$ $50,000,000). Conversely, a LIBOR of only 3.75 percent would generate a coupon of 8.25 percent. In this way, the investor gains the desired benefit from falling rates and does so in a convenient form that entails less credit risk than if it had transformed a regular bond issue with a derivative on its own. In addition, the reverse floater will actually benefit more from a rate decline than would a fixed-rate note of identical maturity. Specifically, while the price of a fixed-rate bond paying constant coupons will appreciate when yields fall, the reverse floater will increase the investor's periodic cash flow as well.

Unfortunately, although this design satisfies the investor's requirements, it does not do the same for the issuer. This discrepancy can be easily remedied, though, by combining Company LMN's debt position with a swap in which it receives the fixed rate and pays LIBOR. This is illustrated in Exhibit 23.21, assuming a three-year fixed swap rate of 6.5 percent against six-month LIBOR. One helpful way to see how a swap must be written to fix the coupon on this reverse rate structure is to notice that paying a coupon of 12 percent minus LIBOR is equivalent to paying a coupon of 12 percent and receiving one of LIBOR. Thus, to neutralize LMN's floating-rate exposure, it must pay out LIBOR on the swap.

Exhibit 23.21 | **Converting a Reserve Floating-Rate Note with a Swap**

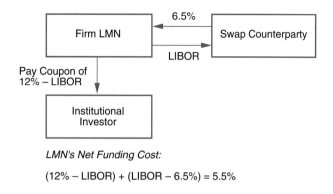

LMN's Net Funding Cost:

(12% − LIBOR) + (LIBOR − 6.5%) = 5.5%

Exhibit 23.21 also shows that the net synthetic fixed-rate funding cost to Company LMN is 5.5 percent (assuming the swap fixed rate has been converted to an actual/360 basis). This will only be true, however, whenever LIBOR does not exceed 12 percent. If LIBOR is greater than 12 percent, the benefit from paying lower coupons to the investor will stop—the coupon rate can never go negative—but LMN will continue having to make the higher net settlement payment on the swap, which raises the effective borrowing cost above 5.5 percent. Consequently, because there is an implicit cap on LIBOR built into the reverse floating-rate loan, Company LMN will need to offset this by purchasing an actual cap agreement with an exercise rate of 12 percent and a notional principal of $50 million. This option will not be expensive because it is quite far out of the money but it will not be free, which means the net funding cost will be somewhat greater than 5.5 percent.

Earlier in the chapter, we saw that an interest rate swap can be interpreted as a pair of capital market transactions. In this particular case, a "receive 6.5 percent fixed, pay LIBOR" swap can be viewed as a portfolio long in a fixed-rate note paying 6.5 percent and short in a LIBOR-based floating-rate note. Recalling that "+" represents a long position and "−" represents a short position, the synthetic fixed-rate issue from Company LMN's perspective can be written as follows:

$$
\begin{aligned}
-\text{(Synthetic Fixed Rate Bond at 5.5\%)} = {}& -\text{(Reverse Floater at 12\% } - \text{LIBOR)} \\
& + \text{(Receive 6.5\%, Pay LIBOR Swap)} \\
& + \text{(Cap at 12\% Exercise Rate)} \\
= {}& -\text{(Reverse Floater at 12\% } - \text{LIBOR)} \\
& - \text{(FRN at LIBOR)} + \text{(Fixed Rate Bond at 6.5\%)} \\
& + \text{(Cap at 12\% Exercise Rate)}
\end{aligned}
$$

As in the previous examples, this sort of structured solution would only make sense to the issuer if it could ultimately obtain funding cost that was lower than a direct fixed-rate loan. The biggest reason for this is that while a direct fixed-rate loan would carry no credit risk for Company LMN, the structured loan would because of the swap and cap positions. Thus, the swap-based borrowing is never as good as a direct approach and, therefore, requires a lower cost to entice the issuer.

As a final extension of this concept, consider what would have happened if the institutional investor decided to take an even more aggressive view of falling interest rates and

Exhibit 23.22 | **Converting a Leveraged Reserve Floater with Two Swaps**

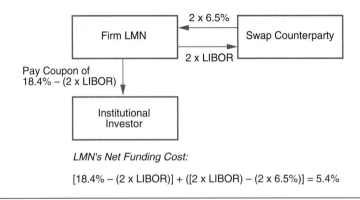

LMN's Net Funding Cost:

[18.4% − (2 x LIBOR)] + ([2 x LIBOR] − (2 x 6.5%)] = 5.4%

requested that the coupon reset the formula to 18.4 percent minus ($2 \times$ LIBOR). Such a design is called a *leveraged* reverse floating-rate note, with the leverage coming from the fact that the coupon increases twice as fast as the decline in yields. Exhibit 23.22 indicates that to convert this to a fixed-rate issue, Company LMN would have to enter into two $50 million receive-fixed swaps (or, more practically, one contract with a notional principal of $100 million). As before, to fix its funding cost completely, it also would have to purchase two $50 million cap agreements with a cap rate of 9.2 percent (= 18.4 percent ÷ 2). This converted position, which would have a net funding cost of 5.4 percent before factoring in the cost of the caps, can be represented as

$$
\begin{aligned}
-\text{(Synthetic Fixed-Rate Bond at 5.4\%)} = {}& -\text{(Reverse Floater at 18.4\%} - 2 \times \text{LIBOR)} \\
& + \text{(2 Receive 6.5\%, Pay LIBOR Swaps)} \\
& + \text{(2 Caps at 9.2\% Exercise Rate)} \\
= {}& -\text{(Reverse Floater at 18.4\%} - 2 \times \text{LIBOR)} \\
& -\text{(2 FRNs at LIBOR)} + \text{(2 Fixed-Rate Bonds at 6.5\%)} \\
& + \text{(2 Caps at 9.2\% Exercise Rate)}
\end{aligned}
$$

As Brown and Smith (1995) explain, although the net coupon on this swapped leveraged structure is lower than on the swapped unleveraged reverse floater, the cost of the required options will be more than twice as expensive since two contracts must be purchased at a lower cap rate.

VALUING FLEXIBILITY: AN INTRODUCTION TO REAL OPTIONS

Recently, energy companies have begun to open gas-fired power plants that generate electricity at an expense 50 percent to 70 percent greater than those of other, more cost-effective plants. Coy (1999) notes that these new, "inefficient" plants are intended to operate only when the price of electricity is high enough to justify the cost. The energy firms hope to make a profit on the new plants because power prices have become increasingly volatile and the new plants—although they cost more to run—are much less costly to fire up and shut down on short notice than traditional plants. Although these "peaking" plants are also cheaper to build, their main attraction lies in their *flexibility:* they allow energy companies to supply more electricity when prices are high and to cease production almost immediately when electricity prices have dropped.

How should investors value companies that possess this sort of operational flexibility? Conventional net present value calculations ignore the benefits of flexibility and may therefore undervalue projects that allow companies to react rapidly to changing circumstances. For example, the fact that these new power plants are expected to run only part of the year is easily incorporated into a standard value calculation. However, predicting the future cash flows based on factors like expected running time, expected electricity prices, or expected production costs will fail to capture the most valuable feature of these plants: namely, that they will only be generating electricity when the price of a megawatt-hour of electricity exceeds the cost of producing it. This is in contrast to conventional plants that produce electricity more cheaply overall but are sometimes forced to sell below-cost power because shutting down and then restarting the facility would be prohibitively expensive.

As we have seen earlier, options give their holders the right, but not the obligation, to trade an asset at a predetermined exercise price by a prespecified future date. So far, the derivative contracts we have discussed are exchanged in financial markets and the asset underlying the derivative contract is often another financial instrument (such as a share of common stock, a government bond, or a futures contract). However, options are also embedded in real assets owned by firms; these are known as **real options**. A pharmaceutical company, for instance, owns valuable options in the form of its collection of drug patents. The firm has the right, but not the obligation, to develop marketable drugs based on its patents and will do so if the value of those drugs (in terms of discounted present value) exceeds the cost of development and regulatory approval. In the language of derivative contracting, these costs can be considered as the strike price for the development option. For the energy example, the peaking plant in effect gives the firm the right but not the obligation to buy Y megawatt-hours of electricity at an exercise price X, where Y is the total capacity of the plant and X is the generating cost per megawatt-hour.

Although real options have existed ever since humans first walked the earth—for instance, storing food and other necessities gave people a valuable option, allowing them to consume more (or less) than the amount produced in a given time period—a number of recent changes have made understanding them more important than ever. These factors include (1) the *pace of technological innovation,* which has made a company's long-term planning more difficult to assess for managers and investors alike; (2) *deregulation and privatization,* which have created new incentives for firms to analyze and use real options in order to gain a competitive advantage; and (3) *advances in derivatives pricing theory* and *decreases in the computing costs,* making it easier to interpret and value real options, which are often quite complex in practice.

Company Valuation with Real Options

To highlight the advantages of the real options derivative-based approach over traditional company valuation methods, we present the case of the fictional GoldFlex Corporation.[11] One of GoldFlex's assets is a lease on a gold mine, which expires in exactly one year from now (i.e, Year 1). GoldFlex geologists estimate that the mine—which is currently idle—holds 100,000 Troy ounces of gold and that extraction costs are $260/ounce. The current (i.e, Year 0) spot

---

[11]This example follows a greatly simplified approach based on the valuation method first introduced by Brennan and Schwartz (1985).

price of an ounce of gold is $264.40, while the Year 1 forward contract price equals $268.40. For simplicity, we will assume that all the gold is extracted at the end of the year. To be able to mine gold in a year, the company must spend $1,000,000 today to restore the mining facilities to working order. Suppose further that the spot price of gold in one year will be either $290 or $240 and that the one-year risk-free rate is 5 percent. How should an investor establish the value of GoldFlex's mining lease?

To see the issues, first recognize that GoldFlex could sell all of its gold at the current forward price. Since the resulting sales proceeds a year from now would then be known, assuming that extraction costs and the quantity of gold are known with certainty, the appropriate discount rate is the one-year T-bill (i.e., risk-free) yield. Thus, the value of the mine calculated using a traditional net present value approach would be

$$NPV = \{[(268.40 - 260) \times 100,000] \div 1.05\} - 1,000,000 = -\$200,000$$

Of course, this calculation suggests that the lease has no value because opening the mine would be a money-losing project. However, the traditional approach ignores the value of flexibility: if gold prices decline in the future, management can shut down production and leave the gold in the ground. Once we consider the possibility of shutting down, the cash flows from the mine can be viewed in a different and more realistic manner.

The main premise behind the derivatives-based approach to valuing a real asset with embedded timing options (such as the mine) is that it is possible for an investor to assemble a portfolio of financial securities that will have the same pattern of future cash flows with the same level of risk. Specifically, such an investor could value the potential future cash flows by creating a hypothetical portfolio consisting of risk-free, one-year T-bills and gold forward contracts that would exactly mimic the mining operation. This *replicating portfolio* will have the same possible cash flows as the gold mine, so its value in an efficient capital market should also be the same. For example, we can use the two-state framework from Chapter 22 to view the valuation question as follows:

TODAY (YEAR 0)	IN ONE YEAR (YEAR 1)	
	Gold Price	Cash Flow
	$290	$3,000,000
Spend $1 Million to Reopen Mine?		[=(290 − 260) × 100,000]
	$240	$0 (No Production)

How many forward contracts are necessary to build a security position that duplicates these cash flows? Notice that the other asset involved in this process is risk free, so all the variation in the cash flows of the replicating portfolio must come from the payoff to the forward contract. With the assumed Year 1 gold price forecasts, a long position in a one-year gold forward contract will leave the investor with either a profit of $21.60 (= 290 − 268.40) or a loss of −$28.40 (= 240 − 268.40) per ounce. The difference between these two payoffs equals $50 [= $21.6 − (−$28.4)], while the difference between the two possible cash flows from the mine is $3,000,000. Therefore, the number of forward contracts necessary to form a replicating portfolio (where each contract stipulates the delivery of one ounce of gold) *is*

$$(3,000,000) \div (50) = 60,000$$

Exhibit 23.23	Creating a "Real Options" Replicating Portfolio

Step 1: Design a portfolio containing F forward contracts and T invested in a risk-free security that has the same future payoffs as the mine:

"Up" State (Gold Price = $290): $[F \times (290 - 268.4)] + [(1.05) \times (T)] = \$3,000,000$

"Down" State (Gold Price = $240): $[F \times (240 - 268.4)] + [(1.05) \times (T)] = \$0$

Step 2: Solve for F and T simultaneously:

a. Rewrite the "down" state cash flow equation:

$$T = F \times [(-28.4) \div (-1.05)] = F \times [(28.4) \div (1.05)]$$

b. Insert the "down" state T value into the "up" state cash flow equation:

$$[F \times (21.6)] + [(1.05) \times F \times [(28.4) \div (1.05)]] = 50 \times F = 3,000,000$$

c. Solve for F:

$$F = (3,000,000) \div 50 = 60,000$$

d. Solve for T from 2(a):

$$T = (60,000) \times [(28.4) \div (1.05)] = \$1,622,857$$

(*Note:* This is the "real options" value of the mine lease cash flows, before netting out the initial reopening expense.)

Step 3: Confirm the equality of replicating portfolio and mine future cash flows:

"Up" State: $[(60,000) \times (21.6)] + (1.05)(1,622,857) = \$3,000,000$

"Down" State: $[(60,000) \times (-28.4)] + (1.05)(1,622,857) = 0$

To find the amount of the T-bill investment needed in the replicating portfolio, notice that if the price of gold drops to $240 in one year, the holder of 60,000 forward contracts will lose $1,704,000 (= 28.4 × 60,000), while the cash flow from the mine would be zero. The payoff from the risk-free investment must make up for the difference, so the amount that must be invested in one-year T-bills to form a "synthetic mine" is

$$1,704,000 \div 1.05 = \$1,622,857$$

Exhibit 23.23 summarizes the process of creating this replicating portfolio.

Given that this portfolio of securities has, by design, the same future cash flows as the mine with the same level of volatility, in an efficient capital market the replicating portfolio and the mine should have the same present value. This can be expressed as

(Value of Gold Forward Position) + (Value of T-bill Position) = (Value of Mine Lease)

Since we saw in Chapter 21 that the present value of an "at-market" forward contract is zero, the replicating portfolio (and therefore the lease on the mine) is worth $1,622,857, which is greater than the $1,000,000 required to restore the facilities. Investors using traditional discounted cash flow analysis will consider the lease worthless and ignore an important asset when valuing GoldFlex. Also, recognize that increased volatility in future gold prices will have no effect on the traditional valuation estimate, while it would increase the value of the lease when using the real options methodology since greater uncertainty generally leads to higher option values.

Of course, in practice, real options are much more complex than this example. For instance, gold production typically takes place steadily during the year, so the analysis may require either a continuous-time (e.g., Black-Scholes) option valuation model or an expansion of the prior binomial tree approach to include a large number of subintervals. Note also that extraction costs and the exact amount of the gold deposits are rarely known with certainty. The problem of having uncertain extraction costs can be solved by realizing that the lease on the mine in effect becomes an *exchange option,* a problem that was first considered by Margrabe (1978). In this context, the leaseholder effectively has an option to exchange the gold in the mine for the extraction costs (e.g., the cost of the required equipment, material and manpower).[12]

The **Internet**   *Investments Online*

Otherwise straightforward financial instruments (e.g., bonds) can become quite complex when they have swap agreements attached or when they contain embedded options, such as convertible and call features or warrants. Several Web sites can help students and investors learn more about these advanced applications of derivatives:

http://www.isda.org The Web site of the International Swaps and Derivatives Association, which is the leading trade organization representing over-the-counter derivative market makers. Among other things, ISDA is committed to advancing the understanding and treatment of derivatives and risk management from public policy and regulatory capital perspectives. Their Web site contains a wealth of information about the nature and use of swap contracts.

http://www.numa.com This is the Web site of Numa Financial Systems. It provides access to a substantial amount of educational and strategic information concerning derivative securities. Of particular note is the availability of financial calculators for computing the value of options, multiple options, warrants, and convertible bonds.

http://www.goldmansachs.com A page on the Goldman Sachs Web site that features research papers on quantitative strategies by Goldman analysts, many of which involve derivative applications.

http://www.calamos.com Calamos Investments specializes in research, investment, and management of convertible securities. It offers a variety of mutual funds, as well. News, analysis, and market updates are available here.

http://www.dir.co.jp/InfoManage/datarsc. html The site of the Daiwa Convertible Bond Index (DCBI) includes data and information on how the index is constructed.

http://www.optionscentral.com The Options Clearing Corporation is the issuer and guarantor of all exchange-traded options contracts in the United States. Its home page allows users to download free software. It features a strategies for options trading and has a number of resource links to exchanges that trade options.

http://www.amex.com A link on the Web site of the American Stock Exchange contains details of several structured products, such as the VPR equity-index-linked notes.

---

[12]We would like to thank Professor Andras Marosi for his contributions to this section.

SUMMARY

- The genius of modern financial markets is that they continuously provide new products and strategies to meet the constantly changing needs of anyone willing to pay the required price. In this chapter, we explore several ways in which derivatives can aid in that development process. In particular, we see that innovation sometimes takes the form of creating a new set of instruments, such as interest rate swaps, while at other times it involves packaging existing securities in a creative way. Structured notes, which combine bonds with a derivative position based on a different sort of underlying asset, are a good example of this latter approach. It is important to keep in mind that the ultimate purpose of this financial engineering is to help borrowers and lenders manage one of four types of potential exposures: interest rate, currency, equity, or commodity price risk.

- We began our discussion with an examination of the market for OTC interest rate agreements. Although forward rate agreements are the most basic product in this category, interest rate swaps are the most popular. Swap contracts can be interpreted in three unique ways: as a series of FRAs, as a portfolio of bond positions, or as a zero-cost collar, which consists of a pair of cap and floor agreements. We then extended the plain vanilla swap concept to include contracts designed to handle other exposures, such as currency and equity swaps. Since all of these agreements are traded off of the organized exchanges, they are extremely flexible in the terms available—the primary appeal to investors and issuers.

- We conclude with an analysis of several ways in which derivatives can be embedded into other securities to create customized payoff distributions. Because these hybrid structures often are designed to the specific needs of a particular investor, the investor must "pay up" for the customization. Warrants, which are call options on common stock issued directly by the company itself, can be attached to a debt issue to offer investors the upside potential of equity with the safety of a bond. Further, bonds and preferred stock issues can be set up to allow for conversion into common stock at the investor's option. In both cases, the issuing firm will likely end up with a lower front-end funding cost because of the options it has implicitly sold. Finally, a class of instruments known as structured notes carries this concept even further by embedding into bonds derivatives that often are based on exposures that may not appear on the issuer's balance sheet. These instruments epitomize how much value derivatives can add when they are used properly, and are indicative of the ways in which investors are likely to see them appear in the market for years to come. Finally, we discuss how the derivative features embedded in physical assets (i.e., real options) can be used by investors to value companies.

SUGGESTED READINGS

Buetow, Gerald W., Jr., and Frank J. Fabozzi. *Valuation of Interest Rate Swaps and Swaptions.* New York: John Wiley, 2000.

Chance, Don M., and Pamela P. Peterson. *Real Options and Investment Valuation.* Charlottesville, VA: Research Foundation of AIMR, 2002.

Eckl, S., J. N. Robinson, and D. C. Thomas. *Financial Engineering: A Handbook of Derivative Products.* Cambridge, MA: Basil Blackwell, 1991.

Finnerty, John D. "An Overview of Corporate Securities Innovation." *Journal of Applied Corporate Finance* 4, no. 4 (Winter 1992).

Kat, Harry M. *Structured Equity Derivatives; The Definitive Guide to Exotic Options and Structured Notes.* London: Wiley, 2001.

QUESTIONS

1. *CFA Examination Level III*
   Several Investment Committee members for the pension fund you work for have asked about interest rate swap agreements and how they are used in the management of domestic fixed-income portfolios.

    a. Define an interest rate swap and briefly describe the obligation of each party involved.

    b. Cite and explain two examples of how interest rate swaps could be used by a fixed-income portfolio manager to control risk or improve return.

2. Explain how an interest rate swap can be viewed as either a series of forward rate agreements, a pair of bond transactions, or a pair of option agreements. To make your description more precise, take the point of view of the fixed-rate receiver in the swap.

3. "When the yield curve is upward sloping, the fixed rate on a multiyear swap must be higher than the current level of LIBOR. With a downward-sloping yield curve, the opposite will occur." Explain what is meant by this statement and why it must be true.

4. Three years ago, you entered into a five-year interest rate swap agreement by agreeing to pay a fixed rate of 7 percent in exchange for six-month LIBOR. If your counterparty were to default today when the fixed rate on a new two-year swap is 6.5 percent, would you experience an economic loss? Explain.

5. *CFA Examination Level III*

The manager of Bontemps International (BI) defined-benefit pension plan's fixed-income portfolio has shown exceptional security selection skills and has produced returns consistently above those on BI's fixed-income benchmark portfolio. The Board wants to allocate more money to this manager to enhance further the fund's alpha. This action would increase the proportion allocated to fixed income and decrease the proportion in equities. However, the Board wants to keep the present fixed-income/equity proportions unchanged.

    a. Identify two distinct strategies using derivative financial instruments that the Board could use to increase the fund's allocation to the fixed-income manager without changing the present fixed-income/equity proportions. Briefly explain how each of these two strategies would work. (Note: Make sure that equity swaps are one of the two strategies that you choose.)

    b. Briefly discuss one advantage and one disadvantage of each of the strategies you identified in Part a. Present your discussion in terms of the effect(s) of these advantages and disadvantages on the portfolio's

        (1) risk characteristics and

        (2) return characteristics.

6. *CFA Examination Level III*

The Board of Bontemps International (BI) will substantially increase the company's defined-benefit pension fund's allocation to international equities in the future. However, the board wants to retain the ability to reduce temporarily this exposure without making the necessary transactions in the cash markets. You develop a way to meet the board's condition:

> BI enters into a swap arrangement with Bank A for a given notional amount and agrees to pay the EAFE (Europe, Australia, and Far East) Index return (in U.S. dollars) in exchange for receiving the LIBOR interest rate plus 0.2 percent (20 basis points).

> On the same notional amount, BI arranges another swap with Bank B under which BI receives the return on the S&P 500 Index (in U.S. dollars) in exchange for paying the interest rate on the U.S. Treasury bill plus 0.1 percent (10 basis points).

> Both swaps would be for a one-year term.

From BI's perspective, identify and briefly describe

(a) the major risk that this transaction would eliminate,

(b) the major risk that this transaction would not eliminate (i.e., retain), and

(c) three risks that this transaction would create.

7. *CFA Examination Level III*

A pension plan is currently underfunded by about $400 million. This situation will be resolved soon when the plan sponsor issues a $400 million private placement two-year floater bond that will be placed into the plan under a stipulation that it will be held to maturity. This bond will carry an interest rate of 50 basis points (or 0.5 percent) above the rate of U.S. Treasury bills.

    The actual, as well as desired, asset allocation is 50 percent bonds and 50 percent domestic equities. When the bond is added, the portfolio will become significantly overweighted in fixed-income instruments. In addition, the overall duration will be decreased for the next two years. When the bond matures, the proceeds can be used to buy equities and liquid bonds with longer maturities. One Board member has suggested that futures or swaps could be used to keep the portfolio allocation in line with the desired asset allocation during the two-year period before the floater's maturity.

   a. Describe the transactions needed to restore the desired 50 percent/50 percent portfolio allocation using each of the following two derivative instruments: (1) futures, and (2) swaps.

   b. Discuss one advantage and one disadvantage of using futures instead of swaps to implement this strategy.

8. We have seen that equity warrants are not as valuable as an otherwise identical call option on the stock of the same company. Explain why this must be the case. Also, what is the incentive for a firm to issue a warrant rather than issuing stock directly?

9. Bonds and preferred stock that are convertible into common stock are said to provide investors with both upside potential and downside protection. Explain how one security can possess both attributes. What implications do these features have for the way a convertible security is priced?

10. *CFA Examination Level II*

Martin Bowman is preparing a report distinguishing traditional debt securities from structured note securities.

   a. Discuss how the following structured note securities differ from a traditional debt security with respect to coupon and principal payments:

     (1) Equity-index-linked notes

     (2) Commodity-linked bear bond

Bowman is also analyzing a dual currency bond (USD/CHF) as a possible addition to his bond portfolio. Bowman is a USD-based investor and believes the CHF will appreciate against the USD over the life of the bond.

   b. (1) Describe the principal and coupon components of a dual currency bond.

     (2) State one reason why a dual currency bond might trade at a premium over an otherwise identical single currency bond.

     (3) Discuss whether there is an impact on a dual currency bond's interest payments and principal payments if the CHF appreciates against the USD over the life of the bond.

PROBLEMS

1. With the interest rate swap quotations shown in Exhibit 23.4, calculate the swap cash flows from the point of view of the fixed-rate receiver on a two-year swap with a notional principal of $22.5 million. You may assume the relevant part of the settlement date pattern and the realized LIBOR path shown in Exhibit 23.6 for the three-year agreement. Also, calculate the fixed-rate payment on a 30/360-day count and the floating-rate payments on an actual/360-day basis.

2. *CFA Examination Level II*

To protect the value of the Star Hospital Pension Plan's bond portfolio against the rising interest rates that she expects, Sandra Kapple enters into a one-year pay fixed, receive floating U.S. LIBOR interest rate swap, as described in the following table.

U.S. LIBOR Interest Rate Swap Terms	
1-year Fixed Rate (annualized)	1.5%
90-day U.S. LIBOR Rate [$L_0(90)$] (annualized)	1.1%
Notional Principal	$1
Day Count Convention	90/360

Note: $L_i(m)$ is the m-day LIBOR on Day *i*.

Sixty days have passed since initiation of the swap, and interest rates have changed. Kapple is concerned that the value of her swap has also changed. The U.S. LIBOR term structure and present value factors of interest rates are described in this table:

U.S. LIBOR TERM STRUCTURE AND PRESENT VALUE FACTORS (60 DAYS AFTER SWAP INITIATION)	
U.S. LIBOR Term Structure (annualized)	Present Value Factors
$L_{60}(30)$ = 1.25 percent	0.9990
$L_{60}(120)$ = 1.50 percent	0.9950
$L_{60}(210)$ = 1.75 percent	0.9899
$L_{60}(300)$ = 2.00 percent	0.9836

Note: $L_i(m)$ is the m-day LIBOR on Day i

Calculate the dollar market value of the interest rate swap entered into by Kapple, at 60 days after the initiation of the swap and using a $1 notional principal. Show your calculations.

Note: Your calculations should be rounded to 4 decimal places.

3. The treasurer of a British brewery is planning to enter a plain vanilla, three-year, quarterly settlement interest rate swap to pay a fixed rate of 8 percent and to receive three-month sterling LIBOR. But first he decides to check various cap-floor combinations to see if any might be preferable. A market maker in British pound sterling OTC options presents the treasurer with the following price list for three-year, quarterly settlement caps and floors:

	INTEREST RATE CAPS		INTEREST RATE FLOORS	
Strike Rate	Buy	Sell	Buy	Sell
7%	582 GBP	597 GBP	320 GBP	335 GBP
8%	398	413	401	416
9%	205	220	502	517

The prices are in basis points, which when multiplied by the notional principal give the actual purchase or sale price in pounds sterling. These quotes are from the perspective of the market maker, not the firm. That is, the treasurer could buy a 9 percent cap from the market maker for 220 BP, or sell one for 205 BP. The strike rates are quoted on a 365-day basis, as is sterling LIBOR.

In financial analysis of this sort, the treasurer assumes that the three-year cost of funds on fully amortizing debt would be about 8.20 percent (for quarterly payments). Should another structure be considered in lieu of the plain vanilla swap?

 4. *CFA Examination Level II*

Takeda Development Corporation has issued a $100 million floating rate note (FRN) that will mature in three years. The FRN has quarterly coupons equal to three-month LIBOR, payable in arrears and due on the first business day of each quarter. Anne Yelland, Takeda Development's Treasurer, wants to hedge against an increase in three-month LIBOR during the remaining term to maturity of the FRN. To implement the hedge, she realizes she can use either of two alternatives: An interest rate cap or a package of over-the-counter (OTC) call options on interest rates.

a. State whether, to correctly implement the hedge using *each* of the two alternatives, Yelland should:
   i. buy or sell an interest rate cap
   ii. buy or sell a package of over-the-counter (OTC) call options on interest rates

   Discuss *one* requirement that *both* alternatives must meet for Yelland's hedge to be effective.

Yelland decides to implement the hedge using an interest rate cap with the following characteristics:

- The reference rate on the interest rate cap is three-month LIBOR.
- The cap rate (strike rate) is 5.50 percent.

- The length of the agreement is for the remaining three-year life of the FRN.
- The notional principal of the cap is $100 million.
- There is quarterly settlement of the cap, payable in arrears.

The following table shows the three-month annualized LIBOR observed on the first business day of each quarter during the first year of the cap.

THREE-MONTH ANNUALIZED LIBOR BEGINNING OF EACH QUARTER	
Quarter	Three-month Annualized LIBOR
1	4.50%
2	6.50%
3	7.50%
4	7.00%

    b. Compute the payoff (in dollars) to the interest rate cap at the beginning of *each* of the following two quarters:
      (1) Quarter 2
      (2) Quarter 3

5. On December 2, the manager of a tactical asset allocation fund that is currently invested entirely in floating-rate debt securities decides to shift a portion of her portfolio to equities. To effect this change, she has chosen to enter into the "receive equity index" side of a one-year equity swap based on movements in the S&P 500 index plus a spread of 10 basis points. The swap is to have quarterly settlement payments with the floating-rate side of the agreement pegged to three-month LIBOR denominated in U.S. dollars. At the origination of the swap, the value of the S&P 500 index was 463.11 and three-month LIBOR was 3.50 percent. The notional principal of the swap is set for the life of the agreement at $50 million, which matches the amount of debt holdings in the fund that she would like to convert to equity.

    a. Calculate the net cash receipt or payment—from the fund manager's perspective—on each future settlement date, assuming the value for the S&P 500 index (with all dividends reinvested) and LIBOR are as follows:

Settlement Date	Number of Days	S&P Level	LIBOR Level
December 2 (initial year)	—	463.11	3.50%
March 2 (following year)	90	477.51	3.25
June 2	92	464.74	3.75
September 2	92	480.86	4.00
December 2	91	482.59	—

    b. Explain why the fund manager might want the notional principal on this swap to vary over time and what the most logical pattern for this variation would be.

6. A Spanish pension fund is considering buying a five-year floating-rate note named "El Oso Grande." El Oso Grande would have a coupon reset formula of three times six-month (Spanish peseta) LIBOR minus 24 percent, subject to a minimum coupon rate of 0 percent if peseta LIBOR were to fall below 8 percent. Currently, six-month peseta LIBOR is 11.20 percent, so the initial coupon would be based on a rate of 9.60 percent. The five-year, semiannual payment, 100 million peseta floating-rate note can be bought at par value. The pension fund intends to use derivative instruments to convert El Oso Grande into a synthetic fixed-rate asset. Quotes for five-year, semiannual settlement interest rate swaps, caps, and floors on six-month Spanish peseta LIBOR are obtained from a Madrid commercial bank specializing in derivative products.

    Interest Rate Swaps: The pension fund can pay a fixed rate of 13.50 percent and receive six-month peseta LIBOR, or the fund can receive a fixed rate of 13.35 percent and pay six-month peseta LIBOR.

Interest Rate Caps:

Strike Rate	The Fund Buys the Cap	The Fund Writes the Cap
24%	125 BP	90 BP

Interest Rate Floors:

Strike Rate	The Fund Buys the Floor	The Fund Writes the Floor
8%	175 BP	140 BP

(Recall that the premiums on the caps and floors are quoted as a percentage of the notional principal.)

a. Indicate the specific combination of transactions that provides a synthetic fixed-rate asset to the pension fund.

b. Calculate the "all-in," fixed rate of return. Assume that Spanish peseta LIBOR, the coupon rate on El Oso Grande, the swap fixed rate, and the strike rate on the caps and floors are all stated on a semiannual bond basis.

7. You are considering the purchase of a convertible bond issued by Bildon Enterprises, a non-investment-grade medical service firm. The issue has seven years to maturity and pays a semiannual coupon rate of 7.625 percent (i.e., 3.8125 percent per period). The issue is callable by the company at par and can be converted into 48.852 shares of Bildon common stock. The bond currently sells for $965 (relative to par value of $1,000), and Bildon stock trades at $12.125 a share.

a. Calculate the current conversion value for the bond. Is the conversion option embedded in this bond in the money or out of the money? Explain.

b. Calculate the conversion parity price for Bildon stock that would make conversion of the bond profitable.

c. Bildon does not currently pay its shareholders a dividend, having suspended these distributions six months ago. What is the payback (i.e., break-even time) for this convertible security and how should it be interpreted?

d. Calculate the convertible's current yield to maturity. If a "straight" Bildon fixed-income issue with the same cash flows would yield 9.25 percent, calculate the net value of the combined options (i.e., the issuer's call and the investor's conversion) embedded in the bond.

 8. *CFA Examination Level II*

Rajiv Singh, a bond analyst, is analyzing a convertible bond. The characteristics of the bond and the underlying common stock follow.

CONVERTIBLE BOND AND UNDERLYING STOCK CHARACTERISTICS

Convertible Bond Characteristics	
Par Value	$1,000
Annual coupon rate (annual pay)	6.5%
Conversion ratio	22
Market price	105% of par value
Straight value	99% of par share
Underlying Stock Characteristics	
Current market price	$40 per share
Annual cash dividend	$1.20 per share

a. Compute the bond's

(1) Conversion value

(2) Market conversion price

(3) Premium payback period

   b. Determine whether the value of a callable convertible bond will increase, decrease, or remain unchanged in response to each of the following changes, and justify each of your responses with one reason:

     (1) An increase in stock price volatility

     (2) An increase in interest rate volatility

9. On May 26, 1991, Svensk Exportkredit (SEK), the Swedish export credit corporation, issued a Bull Indexed Silver Opportunity Note (BISON). Consider an extended version of this BISON issue that has the following terms:

Maturity:	May 26, 1993
Coupon:	6.50%, paid annually in arrears
Face value	USD 30 million
Purchase price	100,125% of par value

Additionally, this BISON includes a redemption feature that, for each USD 1,000 of face value held at maturity, repays the investor's principal according to the following formula:

$$\text{USD } 1,000 + [(\text{Spot Silver Price per Ounce} - \text{USD } 4.46) \times (\text{USD } 224.21525)]$$

   a. Demonstrate that, from SEK's perspective, the BISON represents a combination of a straight debt issue priced at a small premium and a derivative contract. Be explicit as to the type of derivative contract and the underlying asset on which it is based. What implicit speculative position are the investors who buy these bonds taking?

   b. Calculate the yield to maturity for an investor holding USD 10,000 in face value of these BISON if the May 1993 spot price for silver is (1) USD 4.96 per ounce, or (2) USD 3.96 per ounce.

   c. In May 1991 (i.e., when the BISON were used), the prevailing delivery price on a two-year silver futures contract was USD 4.35 per ounce. If SEK wanted to hedge its BISON-related exposure to silver prices with an offsetting futures position at this price, what type of position would need to be entered? Ignoring margin accounts and underwriting fees, calculate SEK's average annualized borrowing cost of funds for the resulting synthetic straight bond.

10. In July 1986, Guinness Finance B.V. placed a three-year, $100 million Eurobond issue known as *Stock Performance Exchange Linked* (SPEL) bonds. The concept of the SPEL is that the bond has its principal redemption amount tied to the level of the NYSE composite index at maturity (i.e., NY_3) by the following formula:

$$\text{Variable Redemption Amount} = \max \{100,100 \times (1 + [(NY_3 - 166) \div 166])\}$$

Notice that the investor is guaranteed redemption at par as a minimum. The bond also pays an annual coupon of 3 percent, which is 0.5 percent below the average annual dividend yield of shares on the NYSE. At the time the SPEL was launched, the NYSE composite index stood at 134.

   a. Demonstrate that the SPEL is a combination of a regular debt issue and an equity option by analyzing the pattern of annual cash flows generated by the issue. In your work, assume a par value of 100.

   b. The SPEL bonds were issued at a price of 100.625. Assuming that Guinness would ordinarily have to pay a borrowing cost of 7.65 percent on a three-year "straight" bond (i.e., one with no attached options), calculate the implicit dollar price of the equity index option embedded in this issue. How much of this amount represents intrinsic value and how much is time premium?

11. A firm has 100,000 shares of stock outstanding priced at $35 per share. The firm has no debt and does not pay a dividend. To raise more capital, it plans to issue 10,000 warrants, each allowing for the purchase of one share of stock at a price of $50. The warrants are European-style and expire in five years. The standard deviation of the firm's common stock is 34 percent and the continuously compounded, five-year risk-free rate is 5.2 percent.

   a. Estimate the fair value of the warrants, first using the relevant information to calculate the Black-Scholes value of an analogous call option.

  b. Determine the stock price at expiration, assuming the warrants are exercised if the value of the firm is at least $5,200,000.

  c. Using the information in Parts a and b about initial and terminal warrant and stock prices, discuss the relative merits of these two ways of making an equity investment in the firm.

12. You are an investor trying to value a gold mining company's lease on a gold mine that is currently not operating. It would cost $1,000,000 for the company to reopen the mine, and it is expected to produce 100,000 ounces of gold at the end of next year. The forward contract price on a one-year gold forward contract is $268.40/ounce and the current one-year risk-free rate is 5 percent. Extraction costs are estimated to be $260/ounce.

  a. Assuming the per-ounce gold price in the spot market one year from now is forecasted to be either $300 or $230, calculate (1) the composition of a portfolio of T-bills and gold forward contracts that would replicate the cash flows from the mine and (2) the "real options" value of the mine lease.

  b. Assuming the per-ounce gold price in the spot market one year from now is forecasted to be either $280 or $250, calculate (1) the composition of a portfolio of T-bills and gold forward contracts that would replicate the cash flows from the mine, and (2) the real options value of the mine lease.

  c. What do your answers in Parts a and b tell you about the effect that the volatility of future gold prices has on the current value of the mine lease?

Part 7

Specification and Evaluation of Asset Management

This final section of the book contains two chapters: the first deals with professional asset management, and the second is concerned with the evaluation of portfolio performance. The discussions of both of these topics are designed to address the needs of individual and institutional investors alike; both individual and institutional investors periodically need the services of a professional money manager and both types of investors also need to be aware of how one evaluates the performance of a portfolio.

Because many investors employ professional asset managers to manage their assets, Chapter 24 is an important wrap-up to their asset allocation and portfolio construction process. After a broad overview of the different ways that professional asset management firms can be organized, the chapter describes how the asset management industry has changed over time and how professional managers are compensated for their expertise. Particular emphasis is paid to the role of *investment companies* (also more commonly called mutual funds), which manage the majority of assets held by individual investors. The discussion includes a description of the major forms of investment companies and the general types of funds available, such as money market, growth, aggressive growth, income, balanced, and bond funds. It is argued that almost any investment objective can be met by investing in one or several investment companies. The chapter also provides a detailed examination of *hedge funds,* which is one of the fastest growing segments of the money management industry.

We conclude Chapter 24 with a discussion of ethical and regulatory issues that arise when hiring a professional asset manager. We argue that most of these issues arise from the classical *principal-agent problem* that defines many economic relationships. After first examining the myriad regulations that govern the behavior of professional portfolio managers, we then describe the set of standards that the industry has adopted voluntarily in an effort to foster an atmosphere of trust and responsibility. The chapter ends with several examples of ethical conflicts that can arise when investors employ professional money managers. Two issues that are of special concern are designing compensation contracts to provide managers with the proper incentives to act in the investor's best interest and the proper use of trading commission fees.

We conclude the book with Chapter 25, which deals with the evaluation of portfolio performance. Perhaps the most important concept to understand from this discussion is that any meaningful evaluation of an investment manager's performance must consider

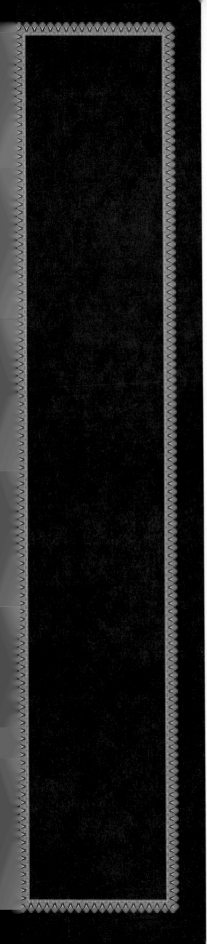

both the return and the riskiness of the portfolio. Thus, after a discussion of what is required of a portfolio manager, we review in detail the major *risk-adjusted* portfolio performance models including a recent performance attribution model that, in turn, is capable of evaluating a global portfolio that necessarily includes the effect of currency allocation. We also consider how the alternative models relate to each other. This is followed by a demonstration of their use with a sample of mutual funds.

As always, it is important to understand potential problems with a technique or model. Therefore, we discuss *holdings-based* measures, which evaluate a manager's performance by examining the contents of the portfolio rather than relying on a statistical model to measure expected returns (e.g., CAPM). We also consider potential problems with the traditional performance measures including a review of Roll's benchmark problem and its effect on these performance models. It is demonstrated that this benchmark problem has become more significant with the growth of global investing. Also, because the factors that determine success in bonds differ from what is important in equities, we review alternative models used to evaluate the performance of bond portfolio managers. The chapter finishes with a consideration of how investment performance results should be presented so as to be consistent with industry practice.

Chapter 24

Professional Asset Management

After you read this chapter, you should be able to answer the following questions:

- What are the different ways that professional asset management firms can be organized?
- How has the structure of the asset management industry changed over time?
- How are managers at investment advisory firms compensated?
- Who manages the investment company portfolio and how are its managers compensated?
- How do you compute the net asset value (NAV) for investment companies?
- What is the difference between closed-end and open-end investment companies?
- What is the difference between the NAV and the market price for a closed-end fund?
- What are load fees, 12b-1 fees, and management fees and how do they influence investment company performance?
- What are the two major means of fund distribution and what has been the trend for each approach?
- Given the breakdown of all funds by investment objectives, which groups have experienced relative growth or decline?
- What are hedge funds and how do they differ from traditional professionally managed investment products?
- What investment strategies do hedge funds follow and what has been the performance of those fund types over time?
- What legal and ethical standards exist to protect investors who employ professional asset managers?
- What are the ethical dilemmas involved in the professional asset management industry?
- What functions should investors expect professional asset managers to perform for them?

So far, we have discussed how to analyze the aggregate market, alternative industries, and individual companies as well as their stocks and bonds in order to build a portfolio that is consistent with your investment objectives. Part 6 centered on alternative investment vehicles, such as options, warrants, convertibles, and futures, that provide additional risk-return possibilities beyond those available from a straight stock-bond portfolio. This chapter introduces another possibility: entrusting your money to a professional portfolio manager. As we will see, using a professional money manager can entail establishing a private account with an investment advisor or purchasing shares of an established security portfolio managed by an investment company. In either form, professionally managed investments often represent a substantial portion of an individual's total holdings.

The efficient market studies we have seen indicated that few individual investors outperform the aggregate market averages. This makes using professional asset managers a potentially appealing alternative for several reasons, including the additional services they provide. For example, it is often the case that an investment company offers an investor a cost-effective way to choose among a wide variety of diversified portfolios spanning the risk–return spectrum. Further, hedge funds offer investors the opportunity to obtain risk and return combinations that might otherwise be unavailable. However, these relationships also create potential conflicts between the goals of the investor and the goals of the manager; we will consider some ethical implications of the investor-manager contract as well.

The initial sections of this chapter explain the various ways in which asset management firms are typically organized and charge for their services. Following that overview, we will explore three different types of professional asset management firms: private management firms, investment (i.e., fund) companies, and hedge funds. In this discussion, we will pay particular attention to the contrast between investment companies, which are the most prevalent way in which individual investors employ professional investment counsel, and hedge funds, which is the most rapidly growing segment of the industry. With both of these organizational forms, we consider how investors can select managers based on the investment objective of the managed portfolio, as well as the types of assets normally held in the funds. We then conclude with a description of the legal and regulatory environment that governs professional investors.

THE ASSET MANAGEMENT INDUSTRY: STRUCTURE AND EVOLUTION

At the most basic level, there are two ways in which professional asset management firms are organized. In arguably the most straightforward structure, individuals as well as institutional investors, such as the sponsors of pension and endowment funds, make contracts directly with a **management and advisory firm** for its services. These services can range from providing standard banking transactions (savings accounts, personal loans) to advising clients on structuring their own portfolios to actually managing the investment funds themselves. Although banking and financial advice were once the main services these firms offered, the last several decades have seen a dramatic shift toward the *assets under management* (AUM) approach. In that arrangement, the management firm becomes the custodian of the investor's capital, usually with full discretion as to how those funds are invested. An important feature of this structure is that each client of the management firm has a *separate account*. That is, even if investors select the firm because of its expertise in a particular niche—say, selecting small-capitalization growth stocks—the assets of each client will be accounted for separately regardless of whether the firm employs a single "model" portfolio. This situation is illustrated in Panel A of Exhibit 24.1.

A second general approach to asset management involves the *commingling* of investment capital from several clients. An **investment company** invests a pool of funds belonging to many individuals in a single portfolio of securities. In exchange for this commitment of capital, the investment company issues to each investor new shares representing his or her proportional ownership of the mutually held securities portfolio, which is commonly known as a *fund*. For example, suppose an investment company sells 10 million shares to the public at $10 a share, thereby raising $100 million. If the fund's purpose is to emphasize blue-chip common stocks, the manager would invest the proceeds of the fund share sale ($100 million less any brokerage fees) in the stock of such companies as Merck, IBM, Xerox, and General Electric. Each investor who bought shares of the investment company would then own the appropriate

| Exhibit 24.1 | Operating Structures of Asset Management Companies |

A. Private Management Firms

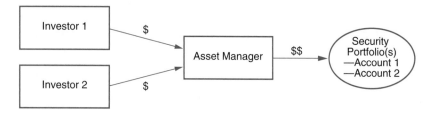

B. Investment (Fund) Companies

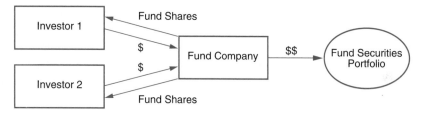

percentage of the overall fund, rather than any portion of the shares in the portfolio themselves. Panel B of Exhibit 24.1 shows how this structure might work.

There are important differences between these two organizational forms. Private management and advisory firms typically develop a personal relationship with their clients, getting to know the specific investment objectives and constraints of each. The collection of assets held in the various separate accounts can then be tailored to these special needs, even if a general blueprint portfolio is used for all clients. Of course, special attention comes at a cost, and for this reason private management firms are used mainly by investors with substantial levels of capital, such as pension fund sponsors and high net worth individuals. Conversely, a mutual fund offered by an investment company is formed as a general solution to an investment problem and then marketed to investors who might fit that profile. Not surprisingly, the primary clients who seek professional asset management through investment companies are individual investors with relatively small pools of capital. In fact, the Investment Company Institute (a nonprofit industry trade association) reported that in 2003, 77 percent of mutual fund shares were held by households, with only 11 percent being held by business organizations.[1]

It is not unusual for professional asset management firms to combine these two structures by offering private advisory services as well as publicly traded funds. For instance, consider T. Rowe Price Associates, a multi-asset, independent advisory firm located in Baltimore, Maryland. Founded in 1937, T. Rowe Price has seen its business grow to the point where it managed over $235 billion by the end of 2004, compared with less than $54 billion AUM just ten years earlier. The majority of this capital is invested in the firm's various public mutual fund portfolios, but T. Rowe Price also has several hundred private clients, including corporate retirement funds, public funds and unions, foundations and endowments, and individual investors.[2]

[1]See Chapter 6 of *2004 Mutual Fund Fact Book* (Washington, DC: Investment Company Institute).
[2]This, and much more, information is available from T. Rowe Price's public home page at http://www.troweprice.com.

The AUM growth that T. Rowe Price has experienced during the past few years has been typical for the entire industry. Exhibit 24.2 charts the top 50 asset management companies as of the end of 1994 and 2004. A striking feature of these lists is the rapid increase in the number of large asset management firms, defined as those organizations with AUM of more

Exhibit 24.2	Assets Under Management (AUM) for Leading Firms

	DECEMBER 31, 2004		DECEMBER 31, 1994	
Rank	Firm	AUM ($MM)	Firm	AUM ($MM)
1	Barclays Global Investors	1,362,000	Fidelity Management & Research	314,543
2	State Street Global Advisors	1,354,329	Bankers Trust Company	186,797
3	Fidelity Investments	1,105,700	Merrill Lynch Asset Management Group	163,822
4	The Vanguard Group	848,881	Capital Group	162,634
5	JPMorgan Asset Management	791,185	Wells Fargo/BMZ	158,392
6	Capital Research & Management Company	703,636	State Street Global Advisors	140,413
7	AllianceBemstein Institutional Investment Mgmt	538,764	Alliance Capital Management	121,290
8	Citigroup Asset Management	513,688	Franklin/Templeton Group	114,100
9	Merrill Lynch Investment Managers	496,171	JP Morgan Investment Management	111,983
10	UBS Global Asset Management	482,916	American Express Financial/IDS	102,128
11	AIG Global Investment Group	475,855	Putnam Investments	95,182
12	Wellington Management	469,884	INVESCO	94,066
13	Pacific Investment Management Co. (PIMCO)	445,721	Scudder Stevens & Clark	91,253
14	Morgan Stanley Investment Management Inc.	425,257	The Northern Trust Company	82,353
15	Goldman Sachs Asset Management	421,656	Wellington Management Company	81,970
16	MetLife Inc.	365,300	The Vanguard Group	81,743
17	SG Asset Management	363,428	Citibank Global Asset Management	73,999
18	TIAA-CREF	345,011	Pacific Investment Management Company (PIMCO)	72,175
19	BlackRock, Inc.	341,760	Smith Barney Capital	69,114
20	Credit Suisse Asset Management, LLC	341,719	Kemper Financial Services	62,748
21	American Express Retirement Services	328,003	Dreyfus Corp.	62,055
22	Northern Trust Global Investment Services	323,241	New England Investment Cos.	56,609
23	Deutsche Asset Management	303,962	PNC Asset Management Group	56,422
24	AXA Investment Managers Paris	303,791	T. Rowe Price Associates	53,705

(continued)

| Exhibit 24.2 | Assets Under Management (AUM) for Leading Firms (continued) |

	DECEMBER 31, 2004		DECEMBER 31, 1994	
Rank	Firm	AUM ($MM)	Firm	AUM ($MM)
25	Evergreen Investment Management Company, LLC	247,658	Dean Witter InterCapital	51,197
26	BNP Paribas Asset Management, Inc.	244,509	Federated Investors	50,743
27	T. Rowe Price	235,190	Van Kampen American Capital	46,699
28	HSBC Asset Management (Americas) Inc.	222,000	John Nuveen Co.	46,497
29	Putnam Investments	213,331	Chase Manhattan Corp.	44,839
30	Prudential Investment Management, Inc.	207,646	Bank of New York	42,599
31	Standish Mellon Asset Management Company LLC	204,813	TCW Group	41,981
32	Banc of America Capital Management, LLC	200,866	SunTrust Banks	41,811
33	INVESCO	199,871	Chemical Bank Portfolio Group	41,725
34	Western Asset Management Co.	197,837	Bank of America Investment Mgmt Services	41,328
35	Federated Investors Inc.	178,862	NationsBank	40,771
36	GE Asset Management Incorporated	178,475	Union Bank of Switzerland	38,685
37	OppenheimerFunds, Inc.	177,712	GE Investments	38,230
38	MFC Global Investment Management	176,879	Goldman Sachs Asset Management	37,400
39	Morley Fund Management Trading	168,672	Brinson Partners	36,540
40	ING Investment Management Americas	167,029	Boatmen's Trust Co.	36,420
41	Franklin / Franklin Templeton Institutional	165,702	Morgan Stanley Asset Management	35,678
42	Capital Guardian Trust Company	162,136	National Bank of Detroit	35,590
43	Columbia Management Group, Inc.	160,309	Mitchell Hutchins Asset Management	34,394
44	Banc One Investment Advisors	150,512	Harris Bankcorp.	33,827
45	Templeton / Franklin Templeton Institutional	146,816	Massachusetts Financial Services	33,432
46	MFS Investment Management	146,393	U.S. Trust Company of New York	33,032
47	Dodge & Cox	142,904	Mellon Capital Management	31,910
48	Scottish Widows Investment Partnership	140,045	Banc One Investment Corp.	31,537
49	Principal Global Investors	137,761	HSBC Asset Management	30,488
50	AIM Investments	137,600	Fiduciary Trust Co. Int'l	29,903

Source: *Nelson's Directory of Investment Management* and Goldman, Sachs.

than $100 billion. In 1994, there were only 10 such firms; by 2004, there were 64, including all 50 listed on the left side of Exhibit 24.2. Much of this asset growth can be explained by the strong performance of the U.S. equity market during this period, but another important contributing factor was the consolidation trend that marked the industry. Typical of this phenomenon was the merger of the asset management groups Union Bank of Switzerland and Brinson Partners (ranked 36th and 39th on the 1994 list, respectively) to become UBS Global Asset Management (ranked 10th on the 2004 list). This consolidation trend is likely to continue, because the competition among existing asset management firms for the flow of new investment capital is expected to increase significantly.[3]

PRIVATE MANAGEMENT AND ADVISORY FIRMS

Despite the notable movement toward larger management companies that offer a broader range of services and products, the majority of private management and advisory firms are still much smaller and more narrowly focused on a particular niche of the market. To examine one fairly typical organization in greater detail, we will consider Prudent Capital Management (PCM),[4] a growth-oriented equity and fixed-income manager located in Southern California. PCM utilizes a "bottom-up" security selection process, with its portfolio managers looking for companies that have exceptional profitability, market share, return on equity, and earnings growth. PCM's clients include both institutional investors and high net worth individuals (with between $2 million and $5 million in assets) in both separate and commingled accounts. The firm offers management of both taxed and nontaxed products. Exhibit 24.3 shows the myriad investment products that PCM offers, along with the minimum investment accepted in each.

Like the industry as a whole, PCM saw the assets under its management increase steadily over the past several years. Panel A of Exhibit 24.4 reports that over a recent five-year period, the firm's AUM grew by almost 80 percent, from $11.8 billion to $21.2 billion. During the same period, the median separate account size jumped from $24.8 million to over $39 million. This account size suggests that PCM's clients tend to be institutional investors, and the client profile summarized in Panel B of Exhibit 24.4 shows this to be true. Indeed, the company offers services to more than 350 clients, but the majority of these are—and the vast majority of the assets come from—institutional investors. Perhaps because of the minimum investment restrictions, relatively few of the clients are individual investors and the assets they represent are slightly less than 3 percent ($535 \div 21{,}165$) of PCM's business.

Panel C of Exhibit 24.4 shows fee schedules representative of both the equity and fixed-income management services that PCM offers. Typical of the entire industry, these fees are not flat amounts but are expressed as percentages of invested capital on an annual basis. Further, they are also graduated on a declining scale so that the more capital an investor commits to the firm, the lower his or her average cost would be. For example, an individual with $15 million would pay annual fees of $137,500 ($10{,}000{,}000 \times 0.01 + 5{,}000{,}000 \times 0.0075$), or 0.92 percent of total invested capital. On the other hand, the fee paid by a pension fund

---

[3]A good economic analysis of the professional asset management business can be found in Hurley, et al. (1995), Brinson (1998), and Bernstein (2003).

[4]Prudent Capital Management is a pseudonym for a real firm whose name has been changed by request. However, all of the subsequent information reported is real.

Exhibit 24.3	**Representative Private Management Firm Investment Products**

	Large-Cap	Mid-Cap	Small-Cap
Equity:	$5 million	$5 million	
	$2 million	$5 million	$10 million
	Commingled fund (Delaware Business Trust)	Commingled fund (Delaware Business Trust)	Commingled fund (closed)
	$2 million for sponsored program affiliates	$2 million for sponsored program affiliates	
Balanced:	$5 million		
	$2 million for sponsored program affiliates		
Concentrated:	$5 million		
	$2 million for sponsored program affiliates		
Tax-Sensitive Management:	$5 million		
	Equity, balanced, fixed		
	$2 million for sponsored program affiliates		
Concentrated Tax-Sensitive Management:	$5 million		
	$2 million for sponsored program affiliates		
Active Fixed Income:	$5 million		
	Separately managed		
	$2 million for sponsored program affiliates		

with $115 million under management would be $650,000 (10,000,000 × 0.01 + 10,000,000 × 0.0075 + 95,000,000 × 0.005), or 0.57 percent. Of course, one advantage to the investor of having the fee schedule tied directly to AUM is that, as the management firm performs better for the client, its fees will increase. This reward system helps to align the incentives of the investor and the manager.

Investment Strategy at a Private Money Management Firm

The schematic representation of a private money management firm shown in Panel A of Exhibit 24.1 indicated that each client's assets were held in a separate account. It was also noted, however, that the security portfolios formed for each client are likely to be guided by the firm's overall investment philosophy. Indeed, it is this investment philosophy—along with the returns it produces—that attracts clients to a particular money manager in the first place. Exhibit 24.5 reproduces the investment strategy and major holdings for two of PCM's model portfolios, one in equities and one in fixed-income securities.

| Exhibit 24.4 | Representative Private Management Firm: AUM, Clients, and Fees |

A. AUM

| Date | Assets Managed ($ Mil.) | No. of Institutional Clients | ACCOUNT SIZE | |
			Average ($ Mil.)	Median ($ Mil.)
Year 5	21,165.0	207	97.5	39.3
Year 4	18,441.0	206	85.1	34.9
Year 3	17,608.0	226	74.2	30.6
Year 2	17,808.0	233	72.3	30.4
Year 1	14,578.0	237	61.5	27.8
Year 0	11,833.0	230	51.4	24.8

B. Clients

	No. of Clients	Assets ($ Mil.)
Corporate retirement funds	126	7,937.0
Public funds	35	3,881.0
Unions (Taft-Hartley)	18	1,442.0
Foundations, endowments, associations	66	1,656.0
Commingled funds	4	1,682.0
General insurance accounts	N/A	N/A
Limited partnership	N/A	N/A
Mutual funds	18	3,411.0
Individuals: IRAs and other	75	535.0
Other	5	186.0
Taxable corporate	17	435.0

C. Fee Schedule

Large-Cap Growth Equity Accounts	Fixed-Income Accounts
• 1.00% on the first $10,000,000 • 0.75% on the next $10,000,000 • 0.50% above $20,000,000	• 0.375% on the first $25,000,000 • 0.30% over $25,000,000

Source: Data adapted from *Nelson's Directory of Investment Managers*.

Exhibit 24.5	**Investment Strategy at a Representative Private Management Firm**

A. Large-Cap Growth Equity Portfolio

Investment Approach:

Our focused, fundamental research process is primarily based on the ideas from our in-house analysts. Our analysts operate as specialists. They direct their expertise on specific industries and sectors covering seven key growth sectors: technology/components, technology/systems, telecom, healthcare, retail, consumer, and finance.

Our investment process seeks out companies that have at least one or more catalysts for growth. The catalysts may be identified as: new products, exploitation of demographic trends, proprietary products, gaining market share, and/or changing cost structure, in order to attain or maintain very strong earnings per share growth.

We search for companies that have: significant management ownership, well-thought-out management goals and growth plans supported by stringent controls, and a commitment to enhancing shareholder value. We also seek out companies with a proven track record (at least three to five years) of superior revenue and earnings growth, strong pretax margins, low levels of debt, exceptional profitability, market share, high return on equity, high reinvestment rates, and attractive valuations relative to their industry and the market in general.

Largest Holdings:

1. Microsoft
2. Nokia
3. Cisco Systems
4. MCI Worldcom
5. Lucent Technologies
6. Motorola
7. Sun Microsystems
8. EMC
9. Amgen
10. Solectron

Benchmark Used: Russell 1000 Growth index

B. Active Fixed Income

Investment Approach:

We believe that superior risk-adjusted returns can be achieved by capturing changes in relative value through active yield curve management, sector rotation and prudent security selection. We follow a disciplined process designed to add incremental value over long periods of time by taking advantage of relative value opportunities without accepting excessive interest rate risk. Our process is not dependent on forecasts of future interest rates or economic events. Rather our decisions are based on current conditions, analyzed in the context of historical relationships. Our performance record has been built employing this process. We expect that in the future market conditions will offer similar opportunities. While markets will change our process will not.

Largest Holdings:

1. A–Baa rated corporates (56.9%)
2. Treasury/agencies (33.6%)
3. Aaa–Aa rated corporates (9.5%)

Benchmark Used: Lehman Government/Corporate index

Source: Data adapted from *Nelson's Directory of Investment Managers.*

The investment approach expressed in Panel A of Exhibit 24.5 makes it clear that clients choosing to invest in PCM's large-cap growth stock product will have their money invested primarily in technology companies. While the specific stock allocations might vary from one client to another, the same fundamental orientation toward stock selection will be applied to all accounts. Similarly, a client choosing to invest in PCM's core fixed-income product will end up holding a portfolio of bonds split between government and investment-grade corporate names. Finally, notice that the stated investment process at PCM requires extensive interaction between the firm's portfolio managers and security analysts. At the time in question, PCM employed 11 equity portfolio managers, 10 equity analysts, 3 equity traders, and 6 additional manager/analysts.

ORGANIZATION AND MANAGEMENT OF INVESTMENT COMPANIES

As noted earlier, an investment company typically is a corporation that has as its major assets the portfolio of marketable securities referred to as a fund. The management of the portfolio of securities and most of the other administrative duties are handled by a separate **investment management company** hired by the board of directors of the investment company. This legal description oversimplifies the typical arrangement. The actual management usually begins with an investment advisory firm that starts an investment company and selects a board of directors for the fund. Subsequently, this board of directors hires the investment advisory firm as the fund's portfolio manager.

The contract between the investment company (the portfolio of securities) and the investment management company indicates the duties and compensation of the management company. The major duties of the investment management company include investment research, the management of the portfolio, and administrative duties, such as issuing securities and handling redemptions and dividends. The management fee is generally stated as a percentage of the total value of the fund and typically ranges from ¼ to ½ of 1 percent, with a sliding scale as the size of the fund increases.

To achieve economies of scale, many management companies start numerous funds with different characteristics. The variety of funds allows the management group to appeal to many investors with different risk-return preferences. In addition, it allows investors to switch among funds as economic or personal conditions change. This "family of funds" promotes flexibility and increases the total capital managed by the investment firm.

Valuing Investment Company Shares

When clients have their invested capital held in separate accounts, as is typical in a private management and advisory firm, the value of any given account can be calculated by simply totaling the market value of the securities held in the portfolio, less fees. When the securities are held jointly, as they are in an investment company, the appropriate way to value a client's investment is to multiply the number of shares in the fund he or she owns by the per-share value of the entire security fund. This per-share value is known as the **net asset value (NAV)** of the investment company. It equals the total market value of all the firm's assets divided by the total number of fund shares outstanding, or

$$\text{Fund NAV} = \frac{(\text{Total Market Value of Fund Portfolio}) - (\text{Fund Expenses})}{(\text{Total Fund Shares Outstanding})}$$

Notice that the NAV for an investment company is analogous to the share price of a corporation's common stock; like common stock, the NAV of the fund shares will increase as the value of the underlying assets (the fund security portfolio) increases.

In an earlier example, we saw that an investment company with a $100 million blue-chip stock portfolio and 10 million outstanding shares would have an NAV of $10. What would happen, however, if during a holding period the value of the stock portfolio increased to $112.5 million while the fund incurred $0.1 million in trading expenses and management fees? If no new shares were sold during the period, the net value of the total investment company is $112.4 million, which leaves a net asset value for each existing fund share of $11.24 ([112,500,000 − 100,000] ÷ 10,000,000). Thus, the NAV provides an immediate reflection of the investment company's market value net of operating expenses. Also, had the investment company made any capital gain or dividend distributions to its investors, these too would be reflected in the NAV calculation because they would reduce the value of the fund portfolio. For publicly traded funds, NAVs are calculated and reported on a daily basis.

Closed-End Versus Open-End Investment Companies

Investment companies begin like any other company—someone sells an issue of common stock to a group of investors. An investment company, however, uses the proceeds to purchase the securities of other publicly held companies rather than buildings and equipment. An open-end investment company (often referred to as a **mutual fund**) differs from a closed-end investment company (typically referred to as a *closed-end fund*) in the way each operates *after* the initial public offering.

A **closed-end investment company** operates like any other public firm. Its stock trades on the regular secondary market, and the market price of its shares is determined by supply and demand. The typical closed-end investment company offers no further shares and does not repurchase the shares on demand. Thus, if you want to buy or sell shares in a closed-end fund, you must make transactions in the public secondary market. The shares of many of these funds are listed on the NYSE or AMEX. No new investment dollars are available for the investment company unless it makes another public sale of securities. Similarly, no funds can be withdrawn unless the investment company decides to repurchase its stock, which is quite unusual.

The closed-end investment company's NAV is computed twice daily based on prevailing market prices for the portfolio securities. The *market price* of the investment company shares is determined by the relative supply and demand for the investment company stock in the public secondary market. When buying or selling shares of a closed-end fund, you pay or receive this market price plus or minus a regular trading commission. You should recognize that *the NAV and the market price of a closed-end fund are almost never the same!* Over the long run, the market price of these shares has historically been from 5 to 20 percent below the NAV (i.e., closed-end funds typically sell at a discount to NAV). Panel A of Exhibit 24.6 is a list of closed-end stock funds, including general equity funds; specialized equity funds; convertible securities, dual-purpose funds; and world equity funds as quoted in *The Wall Street Journal.* The display also contains a listing of closed-end bond funds, including loan participation funds, high-yield bond funds, world income funds, national municipal bond funds, and single state municipal bond funds. Exhibit 24.7 breaks down the number of closed-end funds by category and AUM and indicates that a total of more than 600 such portfolios traded on U.S. exchanges by early 2005.

At the time of the quotes in Exhibit 24.6, many of the funds were selling at discounts to their NAV. This typical relationship has prompted questions from investors: Why do these funds sell at a discount? Why do the discounts differ between funds? What are the returns available to investors from funds that sell at large discounts? This final question arises because an investor who acquires a portfolio at a price below market value (i.e., below NAV) expects an above-average dividend yield. Still, the total rate of return on the fund depends on what happens to the discount during the holding period. If the discount relative to the NAV declines, the investment should generate positive excess returns. If the discount increases, the investor will likely experience negative excess returns. The analysis of these discounts remains a major question of modern finance.[5]

---

[5]Studies over the years include research by Lee, Shleifer, and Thaler (1991); Barclay, Holderness, and Pontiff (1993); Malkiel (1995b); and Klibanoff, Lamont, and Wizman (1998). For a discussion of bond funds, see Richards, Fraser, and Groth (1982).

Exhibit 24.6 Closed-End Funds: Price Quotations and Index

A. Fund Price Quotations

CLOSED-END FUNDS

Tuesday, March 22, 2005

AMEX

STOCK	(SYM)	DIV	LAST	NET CHG
♣AbrdnAP IncFd	FAX	.42	6.46	−0.08
♣AbrdnAusEq	IAF	.77e	13.25	−0.28
♣AbrdnGlobIncFd	FCO	.72	13.97	0.05
♣BancroftFd	BCV	.70e	17.98	−0.14
Bexil	BXL		14.81	−0.09
♣BlkRkBIG Tr	BCT	.90a	15.71	...
♣BlkRkCA Tr	RAA	.85a	14	−0.10
♣BlkRkCA Tr2	BCL	.98	14	−0.06
♣BlkRkFL IQM Tr	RFA	.85a	14.54	−0.24
♣BlkRkMD Muni	BZM	.86	15.40	0.06
♣BlkRkMuniInco Tr2	BLE	1.01	14.08	−0.17
♣BlkRkNJ Tr	RNJ	.81	14.03	−0.16
♣BlkRkNJ Muni	BLJ	.94a	14.50	−0.10
♣BlkRkNY IQM Tr	RNY	.88	14	−0.12
♣BlkRkNY MI Tr2	BFY	.90m	13.98	−0.02
♣BlkRkPA Tr	BPS	.89	14.72	...
♣BlkRkVA Muni	BHV	.87	16.03	0.06
CIM HiYld	CIM	.37	4.09	−0.05
CastleFd	CVF	.68m	22.72	−0.24
♣CntlFdCan	CEF	.01g	5.50	−0.05
CntlSec	CET	1.32e	23.20	−0.05
♣CloughGlblFd	GLV n	.60e	22.35	0.19
♣ColCAInsMun	CCA	.84	13.51	0.07
♣ColInsMun	CFX	.89	13.56	−0.09
♣ColNYInsMun	CNM	.90	14.62	0.08
CornstnStrat	CLM	1.04	7.10	0.01
CornstnTtlRtn Fd	CRF	2.11	14.73	0.23
DE AZ Mun Fd	VAZ	.96a	15.41	0.01
DE CO InsFd	VCF	.96a	17.10	−0.02
DE MN Fd II	VMM	1.05	16.55	−0.05
DE MN Fd III	VYM	.96	15.90	−0.16
DE MN Fd	VMN	.84	15.68	...
DreyfMunInc	DMF	.56	8.93	−0.04
EtnVncCA MIT	CEV	.96	14.48	0.04
EtnVncFL MIT	FEV	.99	14.50	−0.36
EtnVncCA	EVM x	.88	13.49	−0.03
EtnVncCA II	EIA x	.95a	14.60	−0.12
EtnVncFL	EIF x	.93a	14.46	−0.40
EtnVncMA	MAB x	.95a	16.72	−0.20
EtnVncMI	MIW x	.95	16.10	−0.12
EtnVncMuni	EIM x	.94	13.83	−0.16
EtnVncMuni II	EIV x	1.00a	14.86	0.04
EtnVncNJ	EMJ x	.96a	15.55	0.17
EtnVncNY	ENX x	.86	13.67	−0.02
EtnVncNY II	NYH x	.96a	14.86	0.08
EtnVncOH	EIO x	.91	15.47	0.12
EtnVncPA	EIP x	.94a	15.52	−0.08
EtnVncLtdFd	EVV	1.61	18.01	−0.03
EtnVncMA MIT	MMV	.95	16.50	−0.10
EtnVncMI MIT	EMI	.94	16.59	0.06
EtnVncNJ MIT	EVJ	.96	14.50	−0.15
EtnVncNY MIT	EVY	1.04	15.43	−0.07
EtnVncOH MIT	EVO	1.00	16.35	−0.04
♣ElsworthFd	ECF	.30e	7.71	−0.10
Engex	EGX		10.50	−0.15
EqInc AT&T Fd	ATF	3.07f	77.50	−1.55
EvrgrnIncoFd	EAD	1.54m	13.97	−0.17
EvrgrnMgdFd	ERC	1.40	17.18	−0.08
EvrgrnUtilFd	ERH n	1.20	19.94	−0.25
FstTr4CrnrsFd	FCM	1.14	18.87	−0.02
FstTrVal100Fd	FVL	.66e	15.65	−0.05
FstTrVallbtsaFd	FVI n	.02p	20.32	−0.09
FstTrValDivFd	FVD	.38f	14.34	−0.17
Foxby	FXX		2.25	−0.01
FrkInTmpltnTr	FTF	1.19	14.58	0.05
GabelliUtilInco	GLU n	1.20	18.76	−0.10
♣GlblIncoFd	GIF	.28m	4.41	0.08
IndonesiaFd	IF	.10e	5.80	0.10
ING ClrnGlbRlEst	IGR	1.26a	13.96	−0.19
ING ClrnRlEst	IIA	.46	14.49	−0.21
IntmMuniFd	SBI	.61	9.06	−0.12
MA HlthEdu	MHE	.78	14.51	0.01
MN MuniInco	MXA	.94a	15.30	−0.05
MunivestFd	MVF	.67	9.13	−0.14
MuniyldAZ II	MZA	.92a	14.66	−0.01
NeubrgrBrmCA	NBW	.75	13.15	−0.09
NeubrgrBrmDivAdv	NDD n	1.20	18.67	−0.25
NeubrgrIncoOpp	NOX	1.27	13.82	−0.11
NeubrgrBrm	NBH	.80	13.29	−0.02
NeubrgrBrmNY	NBO	.78	13.04	0.13
NubrgrRlEstSec	NRO	1.20	13.28	−0.13
♣NuvAZ	NFZ	.92a	16.05	...
♣NuvAZ Fd2	NKR	.86a	14.70	−0.12
♣NuvAZ Fd3	NXE	.80	13.78	−0.03
♣NuvCA Fd2	NVX	.91	13.88	0.05
♣NuvCA Fd3	NZH	.86	13.44	−0.01
♣NuvCA Prm	NCU	.84m	13.26	−0.28
♣NuvCT	NFC	.86m	16.18	−0.11
♣NuvCT Fd2	NGK	.85m	16	−0.14
♣NuvCT Fd3	NGO	.78	14.61	0.10
♣NuvDivAdv2	NXZ	1.03	14.87	−0.16
♣NuvDivAdv 3	NZF	.97	13.91	−0.16
♣NuvGA	NZX	.88a	14.69	0.03
♣NuvGA Fd2	NKG	.74m	13.69	0.12
♣NuvCA InsDivAdv	NKL	.91a	14.50	−0.15
♣NuvCA Muni	NKX	.83m	14.04	−0.20
♣NuvInsDivAdv	NVG	.89m	13.88	−0.06
♣NuvFL Muni	NWF	.75m	13.25	−0.22
♣NuvMA Muni	NGX	.80m	15.69	0.09
♣NuvNY InsDivAdv	NKO	.86m	14.07	−0.32
♣NuvNY Muni	NRK	.76m	13.80	−0.11
♣NuvMuni	NEA	.82m	14	−0.03
♣NuvMD	NFM	.91m	15.82	−0.28
♣NuvMD Fd2	NZR	.88a	15.46	0.33
NuvMD Fd3	NWI	.75m	13.93	0.18
♣NuvMA	NMB	.89m	16.42	−0.08
♣NuvMI	NZW	.89	15.28	−0.18
♣NuvMO Prm	NOM	.88	16.76	0.13
♣NuvMuniIncoOpp	NMZ	1.07a	14.85	−0.05
♣NuvNJ	NXJ	.91m	14.90	−0.01
♣NuvNJ Fd2	NUJ	.92a	14.36	−0.10
♣NuvNY Fd2	NXK	.95a	14.67	−0.01
♣NuvNC Fd2	NNO	.86a	16.05	−0.05
♣NuvNC	NRB	.92a	16.55	−0.20
♣NuvNC Fd3	NII	.77m	14.29	−0.06
♣NuvOH	NXI	.94m	15.46	−0.17
♣NuvOH Fd3	NVJ	.88a	15.66	−0.13
♣NuvPA	NXM	.93m	15.50	−0.03
♣NuvPA Fd2	NVY	.85m	14.06	−0.04
♣NuveenRlEst	JRS	1.62	18.07	−0.56
♣NuvVA	NGB	.91m	17.85	0.26
♣NuvVA Fd2	NNB	.86m	15.86	−0.25
♣PachldrHi	PHF	.90	8.87	−0.21
PutnmCA Inv	PCA x	.70	13.42	0.07
RMR FIRE Fd	RFR n	.44e	20.18	...
RMR HospFd	RHR n	1.50	18.03	−0.38
RMR RlEstFd	RMR	1.20	13.15	−0.07
♣ReavesUtilFd	UTG	1.20	19.30	−0.42
S&P GlblEquty	BQY n	.75	13.83	−0.20
♣ScudderRE	SRQ	1.58	19.20	−0.32
♣ScudderRE II	SRO	1.26	14.62	−0.26
♣ThaiCapFd	TF	.04e	9.12	−0.22
♣VnKmAdvII	VKI	.96	13.95	−0.05
♣VnKmCA	VKC	.56a	9.32	−0.14
♣VnKmMAInc	VMV	.97a	16.54	0.06
♣VnKmOHInc	VOV	.86	15.46	−0.17
♣VnKmSelect	VKL	.78	12.27	−0.14
VestaurSec	VES	.86e	13.73	−0.03

NASDAQ

STOCK	(SYM)	DIV	LAST	NET CHG
♣HnckJ Fnl	JHFT	1.17e	15.57	−0.29
RoyceFocus	FUND	1.86e	9.91	...
S&P 500 Fd	PEFX	.05e	8.86	...

NYSE

STOCK	(SYM)	DIV	LAST	NET CHG
ACM OppFd	AOF	.51	7.68	−0.11
ACM IncFd	ACG	.72	8.12	0.03
ACM MgdDlr	ADF	.68	7.43	−0.16
ACM MgdInco	AMF	.23m	3.51	−0.01
ACM MuniSec	AMU	.70	10.35	−0.15
♣ASA	ASA	.40m	39.77	−0.69
♣AdamsExp	ADX	.90e	12.76	−0.09
♣AdvntClymrFd	AVK	2.06a	23.92	−0.02
AdvntClEnhGrth	LCM n		18.72	−0.08
♣AimSelREIF	RRE	1.24a	15.05	−0.37
AllncAll	AMO	1.40e	14.30	−0.09
AllianceCal	AKP	.96	14.05	−0.06
AllianceNa	AFB	1.00	14.14	−0.02
AllianceNY	AYN	.92	13.65	−0.13
AllncWrld	AWG	.83	11.81	−0.02
AllncWrld II	AWF	.89	11.72	−0.04
AllmrST	ALM	.54f	9.22	0.08
AmIncmFd	MRF	.57	8.12	−0.02
AmMuniInco	XAA	.94a	14.38	−0.17
AmSelPort	SLA	.84	12.17	−0.07
AmStrat	ASP	.78m	11.85	−0.10
! AmStratII	BSP	.96a	11.61	−0.20
AmStratIII	CSP	.96	11.54	−0.29
ApexMunFd	APX	.58	8.84	−0.04
♣AsiaPacFd	APB	.15e	14.95	−0.06
AsiaTigers	GRR		11.65	−0.10
! BlkRkGlblEngy Tr	BGR n	.38p	23.95	−0.60
♣BlkRkAdvTr	BAT	.60m	10.29	...
♣BlkRkTrmTr	BFC	.77a	16.05	−0.04
♣BlkRkInsCA Tr	BCK	.90a	14.15	−0.01
♣BlkRkCA MT Tr	BJZ	.74	13.90	...
♣BlkRkCA Muni	BZA	.96a	14.27	−0.03
♣BlkRkCA MI Tr	BFZ	.91	13.65	−0.09
♣BlkRkCB Tr	BHK	1.05a	13.17	−0.26
BlkRkDivAch Tr	BDV	.90	14.02	−0.17
♣BlkRkFL08 Tr	BRF	.75a	15.60	0.08
♣BlkRkFL Muni20	BFO	.81a	14.88	−0.17
♣BlkRkFL Muni	BIE	.93a	14.81	−0.09
♣BlkRkFL MI Tr	BBF	.90	14.34	−0.06
BlkrkFltRt InTr	BGT n	1.12	18.63	−0.03
♣BlkRkHiYld Tr	BHY	.82	9.60	0.05
♣BlkRkIncoOpp Tr	BNA	.84a	10.68	−0.13
♣BlkRkInco Tr	BKT	.61a	7.17	−0.05
♣BlkRkInsFL Tr	BAF	.90a	13.93	−0.14
♣BlkRk Tr	BYM	.94	13.96	−0.01
♣BlkRkMuni Tr	BMT	.58a	10.85	−0.05
! ♣BlkRkIM08 Tr	BRM	.80a	15.94	0.08
♣BlkRkInsNY Tr	BSE	.90	14.25	−0.05
♣BlkRkIQM Tr	BKN	.91	15.35	−0.08
♣BlkRkDurInco Tr	BLW	1.40m	18.48	0.02
♣BlkRkMT Tr	BPK	.78	14.84	−0.07
♣BlkRkMuni20	BKK	.94	14.96	−0.15
♣BlkRkMuniBd Tr	BBK	1.04	14.50	−0.04
♣BlkRkMuniInco Tr	BFK	.97	14.13	−0.23
♣BlkRkMTT Tr	BMN	.48a	10.20	−0.01
♣BlkRkNJ MI Tr	BNJ	.90	14.43	−0.14
♣BlkRkNY Tr	BLN	.75a	15.60	...
♣BlkRkNY MT Tr	BLH	.74	14.98	−0.17
♣BlkRkNY Muni	BQH	.93	13.99	−0.08
♣BlkRkNY MI Tr	BNY	.90	14.25	−0.10
♣BlkRkPfOppTr	BPP	2.00a	22.89	−0.06
♣BlkRkStrBd Tr	BHD	1.38m	13.90	−0.60
BlkRkStrDivAch	BDT n	.90	14.48	0.12
♣BlkRkStrMuni Tr	BSD	.96	14.22	−0.20
♣BlueChipVal	BLU	.56e	6.71	−0.04
BoulderGro	BIF	m	6.68	−0.07
BouldrTotR	BTF		17.80	0.03
BrazilEqty	BZL	.16e	9.70	−0.12
♣BrazilFd	BZF	1.04e	33.57	−1.50
♣CignaHiInco	HIS	.28	2.77	−0.02
CignaInv	IIS	.88	18.12	−0.13
CalamosConvHi	CHY	1.46	15	0.01
CalamosConvOp	CHI	1.80a	18.35	0.05
CalamosStratTot	CSQ n	.90	12.90	−0.20
CapIncoStratFd	CII n	.90e	17.36	−0.14
CntlEurRus Fd	CEE	.17e	29.71	−0.19
♣ChrtwlDvdInco	CWF	1.00	10.06	−0.10
ChileFd	CH	2.23e	14.40	...
ChinaFund	CHN s	3.57e	31.63	−0.14
! CitigrpInvLnFd	TLI	.69	13.57	−0.08
♣ChnStrAdvInco	RLF	1.80a	18.80	−0.37
♣ChnStrPrInco	RPF	1.80a	18.84	−0.33
♣ChnStrQuInco	RQI	1.68a	18	−0.30
♣ChnStrPfInco	RNP	2.34a	24.54	−0.24
ChnStrMjrs	DVM n	.30e	18.40	−0.30
♣ChnStrUtilFd	RTU	1.38	17.15	−0.52
♣ChnStrSelUtil	UTF n	1.20	19.21	−0.25
♣ChnStrTR	RFI	1.32a	18.25	−0.05
♣ColonlHiInco	CXE	.48	6.25	−0.14
♣ColonlIntmk	CMK	.65a	8.77	−0.10
♣ColonialIntr	CIF	.31	3.44	0.06
♣ColonlInvMun	CXH	.65	10.15	−0.01
♣ColonlMuni	CMU	.42	5.55	−0.14
CpHiYld III	CYE	.89	8.09	−0.14
CpHiYld	COY	.89	8.18	−0.09
CpHiYld V	HYV	1.61a	14.40	−0.09
CpHiYld VI	HYT	1.45a	13.45	−0.30
CrSuisInco	CIK	.42	4.37	0.02
CrSuisHighYld	DHY	.51	4.63	−0.13
DebtStratFd	DSU	.64	6.08	−0.05
! DfndStratFd	DSF n	.12p	16.22	−0.33
DE InpDivInco	DDF	.96	11.43	−0.06
DE InGlbDiv	DGF	.96	12.58	−0.24
! DiverIncStrat	DVF n	.12p	18.66	−0.49
DivCapRltyInco	DCA n		15.05	0.05
DNP SelInc	DNP	.78	10.70	0.22
♣DrmnClayDivInco	DCS	1.30	18.44	−0.10
DryfsHiYldFd	DHF	.48	4.38	−0.04
DreyfStMnBd	DSM	.61	8.31	−0.05
DreyfStrMuni	LEO	.55	8.20	−0.04
DTFTxFrInco	DTF	.96a	15.25	−0.25
DufPhlpsBnd	DUK	1.02	13.07	−0.25
! EtnVncEqtyInco II	EOS n	.14p	19.21	−0.36
EtnVncEqtyInco	EOI n	.41e	19.78	−0.31
EtnVncFltRte IncoTr	EFT nx	1.20f	19.12	0.03
EtnVnc MIT	EVN	1.19	15.80	−0.12
EtnVncSrFltRte	EFR x	1.21f	19.92	0.06
EtnVncSrInco	EVF	.46m	8.50	−0.06
EtnVncShrtDur	EVG n		20	...
EtnVncTxAdvGbl	ETG x	1.35	18.95	−0.45
EtnVncTxAdvOpp	ETO nx	1.29a	20.40	−0.48
EtnVncTxAdvDiv	EVT x	1.35	20.08	−0.42
♣1838BondFd	BDF	1.15m	18.27	−0.12
EmergMktTele	ETF		9.55	−0.02
♣Equus II	EQS	.57e	8.05	...
♣EuropeFd	EF	.77e	11.35	0.05
FedPrmrIntMuni	FPT	.78	13.17	0.09
FedPrmrMuni	FMN	1.01	14.46	0.06
♣FdcryClymrOppFd	FMO n	.31p	20.02	0.05
FstFnlFd	FF	5.10e	18.05	−0.22
FstIsrael	ISL		17	0.08
! FstTrAbrGlbOpp	FAM n	.26e	17.38	−0.98
FstTrFidAstFd	FFA n	.94e	19.80	−0.17
FstTr4CrnrsFd II	FCT n	1.11	18.70	−0.07
♣FlrtyClayPfdSec	FFC x	2.07a	22.31	−0.36
♣FlrtyPfd Income	PFD x	1.14a	15.80	−0.41
♣FlrtyPfdIncomOp	PFO x	.91a	12.13	−0.34
♣FlrtyClayTotRet	FLC x	1.95a	21.51	−0.35
FltngRteInco II	FRB n	1.15	18.99	−0.20
FltngRteIncoFd	FRA	1.15	19.25	−0.09
♣FtDearborn	FDI	.80a	14.53	−0.01
40/86StrInco	CFD	.93e	9.94	0.09
FrnklnMulti	FMI	.42	8.97	−0.10
FrnklnUnvlTr	FT	.42	5.99	−0.08
GabelliConv	GCV	.80	9.49	0.13
GabelliDivInco	GDV	1.20	17.59	−0.02
GabelliTr	GAB	.72a	8.90	0.01
GabelliMlti	GGT	.12e	10.20	−0.10
GabelliUtilTr	GUT	.72a	9.12	−0.05
♣GenAmInv	GAM	1.17e	30.80	−0.35
GermanyFd	GER	.06e	8.05	0.05
GlblHiInco	GHI	3.17e	17.29	−0.45
♣GtChina	GCH	.55e	16.16	0.04
♣H&Q Hlth	HQH	1.53e	16.50	0.10
♣H&Q LifeSci	HQL	1.35e	14.78	0.13
♣HnckJ BkOpp	BTO	1.10e	9.53	−0.18
♣HnckJ IncSec	JHS	1.12f	14.62	−0.36
♣HnckJ Invst	JHI	1.56m	21.30	−0.29
♣HnckJ PtGlb	PGD	.97	12.84	0.07
♣HnckJ PtPfd	PPF	.86a	12.46	−0.05
♣HnckJ PtPrem	PDF	.65a	9.03	−0.03
♣HnckJ PtPremII	PDT	.78a	11.50	−0.26
♣HnckJ PtSel	DIV	.90	12.93	−0.07
♣HnckJ PfdInco	HPI	1.86	21.80	−0.20
♣HnckJ PfdInco II	HPF	1.86	21.94	−0.03
♣HnckJ PfdInco III	HPS	1.91	21.20	−0.27
♣HnckJ TxAdv	HTD x	1.16	17.13	−0.18
HrtfrdIncoFd	HSF	.55	7.32	−0.15
HiIncoFd	HIO	.54	6.21	−0.09
HiYldFd	HYI	.48m	5.17	−0.07
HiYldPlsFd	HYP	.42	3.93	0.05
Hyperion05	HTO	.01m	9.69	−0.01
Hyperion	HSM	1.30	13.88	0.08
HyperionFd	HTR	.90	10.05	−0.06
IndiaFd	IFN	1.52e	26.25	−0.50
♣ING Prime	PPR	.46e	7.25	0.01
InsrdMuniFd	PIF	.66	12.66	−0.13
InvGrdMuni	PPM	.75a	13.18	...
JF China fd	JFC		12.81	0.06
♣JapanEquity	JEQ		6.35	−0.07
JapanSmlCap	JOF		11.55	−0.11
KoreaEqty	KEF		6.77	−0.08
♣KoreaFd	KF	.65e	26.93	−0.33
LatAmDiscv	LDF	.27e	18.39	−0.18
LatAmEq	LAQ	.46e	21.81	0.17
LazrdGlblFd	LGI n	1.25	19.50	−0.20
♣LibtyASE	USA	.87e	8.79	−0.14
♣LibtyASG	ASG	.61e	5.90	−0.07
♣LnclnNtlSec	LNV	.91	14.10	−0.09
! ♣LndnNtlInco	LND	1.05e	12	−0.23
MFS Charter	MCR	.52	8.54	...
MFS GvMkTr	MGF	.30	6.50	0.04
MFS Intermd	MIN	.36	6.36	0.01
MFS MultInco	MMT	.40	6.10	0.03
MFS MuniTr	MFM	.55	7.32	−0.20
MFS SpcVal	MFV	1.02e	11.92	−0.02
MacqFstTrGlbl	MFD n	1.32	21.21	0.25
♣MdsnClymrCvrd	MCN n	1.32f	15.20	0.02
MalaysaFd	MF	.06e	5.94	0.14
MgdHiInc	MHY	.52	6.13	−0.03
MgdHiYldPl	HYF	.63	5.26	−0.09
MgdMuni	MMU	.62	10.59	0.06
MassMuInv	MCI	1.84a	27.60	−0.40
MassMuPrt	MPV	.96a	12.25	−0.20
! ♣MBIA CapClymrFd	MZF	.67	12.41	−0.12
MexEqIncoFd	MXE		16.16	0.31
♣MexicoFd	MXF	.71e	22.10	0.28
♣MntgmrySt	MTS	1.23e	17.78	−0.06
MS CA QtyTr	IQC	.84	14.11	−0.04
MS EmMktFd	MSF	.09e	17.86	0.01
MS IM Sec	IMS	.63a	13.78	−0.09
MS IMB	IMB	.78a	13.43	−0.12
MS HiYld	MSY	.54a	6.18	−0.12
MS InsCa	ICS	.66a	14.07	0.12
MS CA InsTr	IIC	.72	13.33	...
MS GlblOpp	MGB	.63e	8.72	0.03
MS EmMktDebtFd	MSD	.72a	9.82	−0.01
MS IMT	IMT	.81	13.37	−0.05
MS MPI	PIA	.54a	8.81	0.01
MS QtyInv	IQT	.81a	13.38	−0.06
MS InSec	ICB	.98	15.32	−0.11
MS QtyInc	IQI	.81	13.35	−0.10
MS GvtIn	GVT	.42	8.72	...
MS EstEur	RNE	8.39e	28.65	0.35
MS QtySec	IQM	.84a	13.83	−0.11
MS NY Qty	IQN	.75a	13.33	−0.17
MS India	IIF	.09e	28.79	−0.36
MS IMInc	IIM	.81	13.56	−0.13
MS MIO	OIA	.51a	7.56	−0.01
MS MIOII	OIB	.48	7.64	−0.03
MS MIOIII	OIC	.51a	8.24	−0.01
MS Asia	APF	.11e	13.17	0.03
MuniIntrDur	MUI	.86a	13.54	−0.15
MuniNYIntrDur	MNE	.72	12.98	−0.08
MuniAssets	MUA	.83	12.37	−0.11
♣MuniAdvntg	MAF	.72a	12.81	−0.01
MuniHiInco	MHF	.47	7.13	−0.04
MunienFd	MEN	.73	10.65	−0.06
MuniHldgCA	MUC	.95	14.20	−0.15
MuniHldgFL	MFL	1.00	14.65	−0.13
MuniHldgFd	MHD	1.15	15.74	−0.07
MuniHldgFd II	MUH	1.04	14.40	−0.02
MuniHldgInsII	MUE	.88	12.90	−0.08
MuniHldgIns	MUS	.91	13.60	−0.12
MuniHldgNJ	MUJ	.95	14.31	−0.16
MuniHldgNYIns	MHN	.95	13.90	−0.20
MunivestFdII	MVT	1.10	15.11	−0.09
MuniyldCAFd	MYC	.91	13.84	...
MuniyldCAInFd	MCA	.88	13.50	−0.03
MuniyldFL Fd	MYF	.92	13.66	−0.09
MuniyldFL Ins	MFT	.90	14.43	−0.01
MuniyldFd	MYD	1.00	13.83	−0.08
MuniyldInsFd	MYI	.96a	14.13	−0.09
MuniyldMInsII	MYM	.90	13.45	−0.16
MuniyldMI Ins	MIY	.97	14.76	−0.03
MuniyldNJ Fd	MYJ	.94	14.17	−0.07
MuniyldNJ Ins	MJI	.94a	14.51	−0.09
MuniyldNYIns	MYN	.84	12.82	−0.10
MuniyldPAIns	MPA	.96	15.12	−0.03
MuniyldQlty	MQY	.97	14.31	−0.04
MuniyldQltyII	MQT	.86	12.32	−0.15
MVC Captl	MVC	.12e	9.21	−0.04
NFJ DivPremStrat	NFJ n		25	...
NeubergerInc	NRL	1.38	18.93	−0.18
NeubrgrBrmRlty	NRI	1.35a	16.36	−0.34
NewAmFd	HYB	.21a	2.08	0.01
NewGrmnyFd	GF	.28e	9.26	−0.02
NewIrelandFd	IRL	.03e	21.70	0.26
♣NichlsAplgFd	NCV	1.50a	14.82	...
♣NichlsAplgFd II	NCZ	1.39a	14.08	−0.05
♣NuvAZ Prm	NAZ	.82m	15.60	−0.01
♣NuvCA	NAC	.98a	14.59	−0.02
♣NuvCA Inv	NQC	.92m	14.37	...
♣NuvCA MuniMkt	NCO	.91m	14.50	−0.01
♣NuvCA Val	NCA	.46a	9.32	−0.13
♣NuvCA PP	NCP	.89m	14.20	−0.10
♣NuvCA Qual	NUC	.96m	14.66	−0.09
♣NuvCA Sel	NVC	.93m	14.33	−0.25
♣NuvCA TxF	NXC	.66a	13.64	0.26
♣NuvCT Prm	NTC	.85a	15.65	−0.28
♣NuvDivInco	JDD	1.23	14.31	−0.05
♣NuvDivAdv	NAD	.99m	14.19	−0.13
! NuvEqtyPrmInco	JPZ n	1.70	19.85	−0.21
! NuvEqtyPrmOpp	JSN n	.15p	19.55	−0.07
NuvFloatRteInc	JFR n	.91f	14.63	−0.05
NuvFloatRteOpp	JRO n	.91	14.12	−0.04
♣NuvFL Inv	NQF	.93m	15	−0.18
♣NuvFL Qual	NUF	.91m	14.49	−0.21
♣NuvInsCA	NPC	.89m	15.01	...
♣NuvInsCA 2	NCL	.88m	14.64	0.06
♣NuvInsFL	NFL	.92m	15.15	−0.09
♣NuvInsMuni	NIO	.94m	14.68	−0.21
♣NuvNY Prm	NNF	.89m	14.58	−0.13
♣NuvInsPrm2	NPX	.84m	13.26	−0.04
♣NuvInsQual	NQI	.98m	15.02	−0.20
♣NuvInvQual	NQM	.97m	14.50	−0.17
♣NuvMD Prm	NMY	.88m	15.75	−0.15
♣NuvMA Prm	NMT	.85m	14.88	−0.18
♣NuvMI Prm	NMP	.89m	14.89	...
♣NuvMI Qual	NUM	.91m	16	−0.18
♣NuvMuniAdv	NMA	1.00m	14.85	−0.20
♣NuvMuniInco	NMI	.53	9.82	−0.20
♣NuvMuniMkt	NMO	.91	13.55	−0.07
♣NuvValue	NUV	.47a	9.02	−0.07
♣NuvNJ Inv	NQJ	.92m	14.92	−0.05
♣NuvNJ Prm	NNJ	.90m	14.91	−0.30
♣NuvNY	NAN	.99	15.28	−0.10
♣NuvNY Inv	NQN	.98a	15.11	0.01
♣NuvNY Valu	NNY	.43a	9.17	−0.08
♣NuvNY PP	NNP	.98m	14.95	−0.05
♣NuvNY Qual	NUN	.88m	14.49	0.05
♣NuvNY Sel	NVN	.92m	14.69	−0.24
♣NuvNY TxF	NXN	.64a	13.48	−0.15
♣NuvNC Prm	NNC	.86m	16.69	0.29
♣NuvOH Qual	NUO	.97m	16.37	−0.18
♣NuvPA Inv	NQP	.86m	14.19	−0.45
♣NuvPA Inc2	NPY	.90m	15.19	−0.01
♣NuvPP	NPP	.94m	13.87	−0.24
♣NuvPfConvFd	JPC	1.15m	12.69	−0.13
♣NuvPfConvFd2	JQC	1.12m	12.56	−0.03
♣NuvPremIns	NIF	.94m	14.76	−0.11
♣NuvPremier	NPF	.89m	13.54	−0.07
♣NuvPremInco	NPI	.92m	13.88	−0.07
♣NuvPremInco2	NPM	.94m	13.60	−0.17
♣NuvPremInco4	NPT	.82m	11.89	−0.06
♣NuvQltyInco	NQU	.93m	13.74	−0.08
♣NuvQltyFd	JTP	1.16	12.85	−0.11
♣NuvQltyFd2	JPS	1.19m	13.20	−0.20
♣NuvQltyFd3	JHP	1.20a	13.60	−0.21
♣NuvSelMat	NIM	.47a	9.42	−0.06
♣NuvSelQlty	NQS	.96m	14.13	−0.17
♣NuvSelTxF	NXP	.68a	13.65	−0.09
♣NuvSelTxF2	NXQ	.66	13.02	0.01
♣NuvSelTxF3	NXR	.65a	12.75	−0.11
♣NuveenSrInc	NSL	.61f	9.18	−0.33
♣NuvTaxAdv	JTA	1.20	19.19	−0.17
♣NuvTX Qual	NTX	.92m	14.82	−0.43
♣NuvVA Prm	NPV	.88m	17.15	...
OppenMulti	OMS	.45	9.21	−0.09
PacAmShrs	PAI	.90a	14.09	−0.36
♣PeteRes	PEO	1.32e	29.54	−0.09
♣PIMCO CA	PCQ	.92	14.11	−0.12
♣PIMCO CAMuniII	PCK	.98a	14.24	−0.03
♣PIMCO CAMuniIII	PZC	.96a	14.10	−0.03
♣PIMCO Comrcl	PCM	1.13a	13.74	0.09
♣PIMCO CpInco	PCN	1.27a	14.20	−0.10
♣PIMCO OppFd	PTY	1.65	15.66	−0.12
♣PIMCO FltRteFd	PFL	1.28e	20.88	0.01
PIMCO FltRteStrat	PFN n	.38e	19.49	0.03
♣PIMCO HiInco	PHK	1.46a	13.80	−0.08
♣PIMCO Muni	PMF	.98a	14.41	−0.06
♣PIMCO MuniII	PML	1.01a	14.51	−0.10
♣PIMCO MuniIII	PMX	1.00a	14.30	−0.07
♣PIMCO NY	PNF	.90a	13.82	0.11
♣PIMCO NYMuniII	PNI	.98a	14.45	0.17
♣PIMCO NYMuniIII	PYN	.96a	14.35	0.07
♣PIMCO Stratg	RCS	.89a	11.66	0.10
PionrFloatRte	PHD n	.10p	18.93	−0.05
PionrHI Tr	PHT	1.65a	14.78	−0.05
PionrIntrst	MUO	.68m	11.05	−0.06
PionrHiIncAdv	MAV	1.13a	14.48	−0.03
PionrMuniHI Tr	MHI	1.08a	14.60	−0.01
PionrTxAdvBalTr	PBF	.82	12.86	−0.02
PfdCpIncoStrat	PSW	2.00	21.43	−0.18
PfdIncoStrat	PSY	2.00	21.14	−0.26
ProspctSt	PHY	.33	3.36	−0.01
ProspectSt	CNN	.56e	6	−0.16
PutnmHiInco	PCF x	.56	7.39	−0.04
PutnmHiMun	PYM x	.38a	6.54	−0.07
PutnmInvMun	PGM x	.60a	9.26	−0.08
PutnmMgdYld	PTM x	.59	7.80	−0.13
PutnmMgdMun	PMM x	.46	7.08	−0.06
PutnmMstIntm	PIM x	.42	6.35	−0.06
PutnmMunicBnd	PMG x	.78	12.01	−0.08
! PutnmMunOpp	PMO x	.77	11.50	−0.17
PutnmPrem	PPT x	.47	6.33	−0.06
PutnmTxF	PMH x	.56	11.80	−0.11
RMK StrtIncoFd	RSF	1.80	15.06	−0.14
REITFnd	RIT	1.31	16.31	−0.35
RMK HiIncoFd	RMH	1.80a	15.91	...
RycMcroCap	RMT	1.64e	14	0.06
RoyceValTr	RVT	1.94e	18.92	0.13
! S&P 500 GearedFd	GRE n	.09p	18.65	−0.09
! SlBrVarRte	GFY n	1.05	18.10	−0.09
SlBrWld	SBG	.88a	10.69	−0.18
SlBrCapInco	SCD	1.20	16.48	−0.19
SlBrEmergDebt	ESD	1.80	18.35	−0.04
SlBrEmergMktFlt	EFL	.88	12.85	−0.34
SlBrEmergMkt II	EDF	1.65	15.94	−0.18
SlBrEmergMktInco	EMD	1.65a	18.45	0.10
SlBrosFd	SBF	.14e	12.57	−0.15
SlBrGlHiInco	EHI	1.27a	13.09	−0.24
SlBrGlblIncoFd	GDF	1.24	14	−0.16
SlBrHIF II	HIX	1.14	10.80	−0.25
! SlBrHIF	HIF	.72	9.24	−0.01
! SlBrInflMgmt	IMF n	1.05a	17.80	−0.12
SlBrMuniPtnr	MNP	.84	13.20	−0.14
SlBrMuniPtnr II	MPT	.82	12.80	−0.06
SlBrWldInco	SBW	1.42a	17.20	−0.03
♣ScddrGKommFd	GCS n	.83p	14.94	−0.07
♣ScddrGlblFd	LBF	.56	7.26	−0.03
♣ScudderHigh	KHI	.64	6.87	0.02
♣ScudderGvt	KGT	.32	7.01	−0.03
♣ScudderMulti	KMM	.78	10.19	0.12
♣ScudderMuni	KTF	.81	11.52	−0.12
♣ScddrNwAsia	SAF	.02e	15.65	0.11
♣ScudderStratIn	KST	1.08	13.80	−0.10
♣ScudderStrat	KSM	.90	12.34	−0.33
♣SeligQual	SQF	.60	11.90	−0.01
♣SeligSel	SEL	.69	10.25	−0.09
SrHighInc	ARK	.56	5.61	0.02
♣SingaporeFd	SGF	.22e	9.19	0.02
SourceCap	SOR	4.00	71.60	0.35
SpainFd	SNF	.90e	11.81	0.06
StrtGlblInc	SGL	2.08e	12.85	−0.54
♣SwissHelvFd	SWZ	.93e	14.37	−0.13
♣TCW Fd	CVT	.40f	5.28	−0.09
♣TSW ClymrTxAdvFd	TYW n	.94	13.16	−0.20
TaiwanFd	TWN	.03e	12.70	−0.29
TaiGreatChina	TFC	.01e	4.90	−0.05
TempltnDrgn	TDF x	.66e	17.38	0.01
TemplMktFd	EMF	.25e	17.18	−0.74
TempIncoFd	TEI	1.00	13.51	−0.01
TemplGlob	GIM	.48a	8.85	−0.05
TempltnRusEEur fd	TRF	3.57e	39.88	0.43
ThaiFd	TTF	.12e	9.91	0.06
TransamInco	TAI	1.56	21.66	−0.09
♣TriContl	TY	.20f	17.57	−0.16
TurkishFd	TKF	.08e	15.61	0.25
♣VnKmAdvtg	VKA	.99	14.51	−0.08
♣VnKmAdvPA	VAP	.82	14.50	−0.22
♣VnKmBond	VBF	1.00m	16.95	−0.26
♣VnKmCAQua	VQC	1.03	15.75	−0.05
♣VnKmCAInc	VCV	.97a	15.02	−0.04
♣VnKmFLQua	VFM	.90	14.80	−0.08
♣VnKmHiInc	VIT	.36	3.63	−0.14
♣VnKmTrII	VLT	.44	4.45	−0.20
♣VnKmIncTr	VIN	.33	5.74	0.03
♣VnKmInv	VIG	.49	8.71	−0.01
♣VnKmMun	VMT	.60a	8.82	−0.07
♣VnKmOpp	VMO	1.00	14.49	−0.13
♣VnKmOpII	VOT	.89	12.99	−0.13
♣VnKmMunTr	VKQ	.94a	13.97	−0.20
♣VnKmNYQua	VNM	.86	14.11	−0.19
♣VnKmNYInc	VNV	.92a	14.55	0.03
♣VnKmOHQua	VOQ	.92a	15.70	−0.05
♣VnKmPA	VPQ	.86	14.70	−0.22
♣VnKmPAInc	VPV	.93	15.25	−0.10
♣VnKmSenInc	VVR	.48	8.36	−0.08
♣VnKmMuniTr	VKS	.82	12.41	−0.04
♣VnKmInsMun	VIM	.92	14.39	−0.15
♣VnKmNJ	VTJ	.98	15.84	−0.12
♣VnKmFL	VTF	.83	14.63	−0.07
♣VnKmInvGrd	VGM	.99	14.66	−0.01
♣VnKmNY	VTN	.98a	14.89	−0.07
♣VnKmInvPA	VTP	.89	14.60	−0.09
♣VnKmValMuni	VKV	.87	13.22	−0.10
WstAssetFd	WEA	1.13m	13.99	−0.33
♣WstAstClymrTreas	WIA	.79a	13.48	−0.03
♣WstAstClymrTreas2	WIW	.83	13.20	0.13
ZenixFd	ZIF	.32	3.32	−0.06
♣ZweigFd	ZF	.46e	5.46	−0.01
♣ZweigTotFd	ZTR	.55	5.12	−0.02

NASDAQ SMALL-CAP

STOCK	(SYM)	DIV	LAST	NET CHG
HerzfldCarib	CUBA		5.87	...

(continued)

Source: *The Wall Street Journal,* March 23, 2005. Copyright 2005 by DOW JONES & CO. INC. Reproduced with permission of DOW JONES & CO. INC in the format Textbook via Copyright Clearance Center; and *Investor's Guide to Closed-End Funds,* December 2004, Thomas Herzfeld Advisors, Inc., reprinted with permission.

| Exhibit 24.6 | Closed-End Funds: Price Quotations and Index (continued) |

B. Herzfeld Index: Discount/Premium to NAV

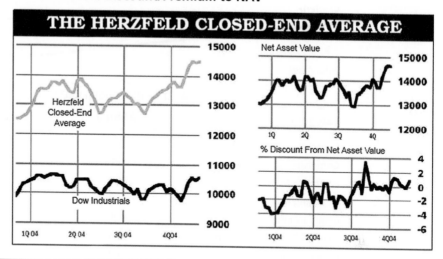

Source: *The Wall Street Journal,* March 23, 2005, Dow Jones & Co., Inc., reprinted with permission; and *Investor's Guide to Closed-End Funds,* December 2004, Thomas Herzfeld Advisors, Inc., reprinted with permission.

The interest in closed-end funds has led Thomas J. Herzfeld Advisors, a firm that specializes in closed-end funds, to create an index that tracks the market price performance of a sample of U.S. closed-end funds that invest principally in U.S. equities. The price-weighted series is based on fund market values rather than on NAVs. In addition to its market price index, Herzfeld also computes the average discount from NAV. The one lower right-hand graph in Panel B of Exhibit 24.6 indicates that the average discount from NAV changes over time and has a major impact on the market performance of the index. For example, during 2004, this value changed from a discount of four percent to a premium of about four percent. Despite this, the performance of the Herzfeld closed-end average at the end of this period was ahead of the DJIA.

Open-end investment companies, or mutual funds, continue to sell and repurchase shares after their initial public offerings. They stand ready to sell additional shares of the fund at the NAV, with or without sales charge, or to buy back (redeem) shares of the fund at the NAV, with or without redemption fees.

Open-end investment companies have enjoyed substantial growth since World War II, as shown by the figures in Exhibit 24.8. Clearly, open-end funds account for a substantial portion of invested assets, and they provide a very important service for more than 200 million accounts.

Load Versus No-Load Open-End Funds   One distinction of open-end funds is that some charge a sales fee for share sales. The offering price for a share of a *load fund* equals the NAV of the share plus a sales charge, which can be as large as 7.5 to 8.0 percent of the NAV. A fund with an 8 percent sales charge (load) would give an individual who invested $1,000 in the fund shares that are worth only $920. Such funds generally charge no redemption fee, which means the shares can be redeemed at their NAV. These funds typically are quoted with an NAV and an offering price. The NAV price is the redemption (bid) price, and the offering (ask) price equals the NAV divided by 1.0 minus the percent load. For example, if the NAV of a fund with

Exhibit 24.7	**Closed-End Funds: Categories and AUM**

Statistic	Value
Total number of closed-end funds (U.S. exchanges only):	662
Total Assets*:	$201,214.34

ASSETS BY CLASSIFICATION

Category	Abbrev	Funds	Assets
Corporate—High Yield	CHY	39	$12,314.17
Corporate—Investment Grade	CIG	5	1,167.43
Emerging Market Equity	EME	3	672.13
Emerging Market Income	EMI	8	2,251.93
Equity Income	EQI	58	28,074.69
General Bond—Investment Grade	BDI	12	4,159.62
General Mortgage	MTG	11	2,020.67
Global Equity	GLE	12	3,272.13
Global Income	GLI	32	11,397.95
Government Bond	GOV	6	3,863.92
Growth & Income	GCI	49	23,460.86
Growth—Domestic	GRD	35	10,906.15
Loan Participation	LPF	18	7,655.56
Multi-Sector Bond	MLT	8	3,559.22
Municipal—High Yield	MHY	7	1,834.34
Municipal—National	MNL	109	38,779.33
Municipal Single State	MSS	176	22,655.41
Non-U.S. Equity	FOR	44	10,150.91
Sector—Energy/Natural Res	ENR	8	2,858.60
Sector—Financial Services	FIN	6	1,820.79
Sector—Health/Biotechnology	HLT	5	3,002.16
Sector—Precious Metals	GPM	2	897.88
Sector—Utilities	UTL	9	4,438.50

*Assets are net assets, expressed in $millions, and exclude leveraged capital (preferred stock, debt, etc.).
Source: Closed-End Fund Association, April 22, 2005. Reprinted with permission.

an 8 percent load is $8.50 a share, the offering price would be $9.24 ($8.50/0.92). The 74-cent differential is really 8.7 percent of the NAV. The load percentage typically declines with the size of the order.

A **no-load fund** imposes no initial sales charge so it sells shares at their NAV. Some of these funds charge a small redemption fee of about one-half of 1 percent. In *The Wall Street Journal*, quotes for these no-load funds list bid prices as the NAV with the designation "NL" (no load) for the offering price—that is, the bid and offer are the same. The number of no-load funds has

Exhibit 24.8	Open-End Investment Companies: Number and Value of Assets: 1945–2003

Year	Number of Reporting Funds	Assets ($ Billions)	Year	Number of Reporting Funds	Assets ($ Billions)
1950	98	2.5	1991	2,583	850.7
1955	125	7.8	1992	2,960	1,096.3
1960	161	17.0	1993	3,614	1,504.6
1965	170	35.2	1994	4,362	1,544.3
1970	361	47.6	1995	4,728	2,058.3
1975	390	42.2	1996	5,260	2,624.0
1980	458	58.4	1997	5,671	3,409.3
1985	1,068	251.6	1998	6,288	4,173.5
1986	1,348	423.5	1999	6,746	5,233.2
1987	1,769	453.1	2000	7,116	5,119.4
1988	2,127	471.4	2001	7,292	4,689.6
1989	2,262	552.6	2002	7,255	4,118.4
1990	2,338	566.8	2003	7,153	5,362.4

Note: Does not include money market and short-term bond funds.
Source: Adapted from data in Investment Company Institute, *2004 Mutual Fund Fact Book*.

increased substantially in recent years. In fact, the Investment Company Institute noted that in 2003, the number of no-load equity funds exceeded the number of load funds for the first time.

Between the full-load fund and the pure no-load fund, several important variations exist. The first is the **low-load fund**, which imposes a front-end sales charge when the fund is bought, but it is typically in the 3 percent range rather than 7 to 8 percent. Generally, low-load funds are used for bond funds or equity funds offered by management companies that also offer no-load funds. For example, most Fidelity Management funds were no load prior to 1985, but several of their newer funds have carried a low load of 3 percent. Alternatively, some funds—previously charging full loads—have reduced their loads.

The second major innovation is the **12b-1 plan**, named after a 1980 SEC ruling. This plan permits funds to deduct as much as 0.75 percent of average net assets *per year* to cover distribution costs, such as advertising, brokers' commissions, and general marketing expenses. A large and growing number of no-load funds are adopting these plans, as are a few low-load funds. You can determine if a fund has a 12b-1 plan only by reading the prospectus or using an investment service that reports charges in substantial detail.

Finally, some funds have instituted **contingent, deferred sales loads** in which a sales fee is charged when the fund is sold if it is held for less than some time period, perhaps three or four years.

Fund Management Fees

In addition to selling charges (loads or 12b-1 charges), all investment firms charge annual **management fees** to compensate professional managers of the fund. Similar to the compensation structure for private management firms, such a fee typically is a percentage of the average net assets of the fund varying from about 0.25 to 1.00 percent. Most of these management fees are on sliding scales that decline with the size of the fund. For example, a fund with assets under $1 billion might charge 1 percent, funds with assets between $1 billion and $5 billion might charge 0.50 percent, and those over $5 billion would charge 0.25 percent.

These management fees are a major factor driving the creation of new funds. More assets under management generate more fees, but the costs of management do not increase at the same rate as the managed assets because substantial economies of scale exist in managing financial assets. Once the research staff and management structure have been established, the incremental costs do not rise in line with the assets under management. For example, the cost of managing $1 billion of assets is *not* twice the cost of managing $500 million. Finally, one consequence of the industry consolidation we discussed earlier is that mutual fund fees have been declining. For instance, the Investment Company Institute reported that between 1980 and 1998 total shareholder costs to equity fund investors decreased by 40 percent, from 2.25 to 1.35 percent of average fund AUM.

Investment Company Portfolio Objectives

In principle, a mutual fund can be created around any portfolio of assets. As a practical matter, however, mutual funds tend to exist for only the more liquid asset classes, such as stocks and bonds. Further, it is the nature of the assets held in the underlying portfolio that defines the investment objective for the mutual fund. There are four broad fund objective categories recognized by the Investment Company Institute: common stock funds, hybrid funds, bond funds, and money market funds. Each of these strategies is described briefly here, while Exhibit 24.9 provides a more detailed list of many of the more popular subcategories within these objective classes.

Common stock funds, as the category title suggests, invest almost exclusively in common stocks. Within that broad mission, however, substantial differences can be found, including funds that focus on specific industries (e.g., Chemical Fund, Oceanography Fund), collection of industries (e.g., Technology Fund), security characteristics (e.g., Growth Fund, Large-Cap Fund), or even geographic areas (e.g., Global Funds, Northeast Fund). With several thousand to choose from, any investor can almost certainly find an existing equity fund that matches his or her desired investment strategy. Thus, the important thing that an investor must do is to decide what that preferred strategy happens to be.

Balanced funds diversify outside the stock market by combining common stock with fixed-income securities, including government bonds, corporate bonds, convertible bonds, or preferred stock. The ratio of stocks to fixed-income securities will vary by fund, as stated in each fund's prospectus. **Flexible portfolio** (or *asset allocation*) **funds** seek high total returns by investing in a mix of stocks, bonds, and money-market securities.

Bond funds concentrate on various types of bonds to generate high current income with minimal risk. They are similar to common stock funds; however, their investment policies differ. Some funds concentrate on U.S. government or high-grade corporate bonds, others hold a mixture of investment-grade bonds, and some concentrate on high-yield (junk) bonds. Management strategies also can differ, ranging from buy and hold to extensive trading of the portfolio bonds.

In addition to government, mortgage, and corporate bond funds, a change in the tax law in 1976 caused the creation of numerous municipal bond funds. These funds provide investors with monthly interest payments that are exempt from federal income taxes, although some of the interest may be subject to state and local taxes. To avoid the state tax, some municipal bond funds concentrate on bonds from specific states, such as the New York Municipal Bond Fund, which allows New York residents to avoid most state taxes on the interest income.

Exhibit 24.9 | **Mutual Fund Objectives**

Equity Funds

Capital Appreciation Funds seek capital appreciation; dividends are not a primary consideration

- *Aggressive growth funds* invest primarily in common stocks of small, growth companies.
- *Growth funds* invest primarily in common stocks of well-established companies.
- *Sector funds* invest primarily in companies in related fields.

Total Return Funds seek a combination of current income and capital appreciation.

- *Growth and income funds* invest primarily in common stocks of established companies with the potential for growth and a consistent record of dividend payments.
- *Income equity funds* invest primarily in equity securities of companies with a consistent record of dividend payments. They seek income more than capital appreciation.

World Equity Funds invest primarily in stocks of foreign companies.

- *Emerging market funds* invest primarily in companies based in developing regions of the world.
- *Global equity funds* invest primarily in equity securities traded worldwide, including those of U.S. companies.
- *International equity funds* invest primarily in equity securities of companies located outside the United States.
- *Regional equity funds* invest in companies based in a specific part of the world.

Hybrid Funds

Hybrid Funds may invest in a mix of equities, fixed-income securities, and derivative instruments.

- *Asset allocation funds* invest in various asset classes including, but not limited to, equities, fixed-income securities, and money market instruments. They seek high total return by maintaining precise weightings in asset classes. Global asset allocation funds invest in a mix of equity and debt securities issued worldwide.
- *Balanced funds* invest in a mix of equity securities and bonds with the three-part objective of conserving principal, providing income, and achieving long-term growth of both principal and income. These funds maintain target percentages in asset classes.
- *Flexible portfolio funds* invest in common stocks, bonds, other debt securities, and money market securities to provide high total return. These funds may invest up to 100 percent in any

one type of security and may easily change weightings depending upon market conditions.

- *Income-mixed funds* invest in a variety of income-producing securities, including equities and fixed-income instruments. These funds seek a high level of current income without regard to capital appreciation.

Taxable Bond Funds

Corporate Bond Funds seek current income by investing in high-quality debt securities issued by U.S. corporations.

- *Corporate bond funds—general* invest two-thirds or more of their portfolios in U.S. corporate bonds with no explicit restrictions on average maturity.
- *Corporate bond funds—intermediate-term* invest two-thirds or more of their portfolios in U.S. corporate bonds with an average maturity of five to 10 years. These funds seek a high level of income with less price volatility than longer-term bond funds.
- *Corporate bond funds—short-term* invest two-thirds or more of their portfolios in U.S. corporate bonds with an average maturity of one to five years. These funds seek a high level of income with less price volatility than intermediate-term bond funds.

High-Yield Funds invest two-thirds or more of their portfolios in lower-rated U.S. corporate bonds (Baa or lower by Moody's and BBB or lower by Standard and Poor's rating service.)

World Bond Funds invest in debt securities offered by foreign companies and governments. They seek the highest level of current income available worldwide.

- *Global bond funds—general* invest in worldwide debt securities with no stated average maturity or an average maturity of five years or more. These funds may invest up to 25 percent of assets in companies located in the United States.
- *Global bond funds—short-term* invest in debt securities worldwide with an average maturity of one to five years. These funds may invest up to 25 percent of assets in companies located in the United States.
- *Other world bond funds,* such as international bond and emerging market debt funds, invest in foreign government and corporate debt instruments. Two-thirds of an international bond funds portfolio must be invested outside the United States. Emerging market debt funds invest primarily in debt from underdeveloped regions of the world.

Government Bond Funds invest in U.S. government bonds of varying maturities. They seek high current income.

- *Government bond funds—general* invest two-thirds or more of their portfolios in U.S. government securities of no stated average maturity. Securities utilized by investment managers may change with market conditions.
- *Government bond funds—intermediate-term* invest two-thirds or more of their portfolios in U.S. government securities with an average maturity of five to 10 years. Securities utilized by investment managers may change with market conditions.
- *Government bond funds—short-term* invest two-thirds or more of their portfolios in U.S. government securities with an average maturity of one to five years. Securities utilized by investment managers may change with market conditions.
- *Mortgage-backed* funds invest two-thirds or more of their portfolios in pooled mortgage-backed securities.

Strategic Income Funds invest in a combination of U.S. fixed-income securities to provide a high level of current income.

Tax-Free Bond Funds

State Municipal Bond Funds invest primarily in municipal bonds issued by a particular state. These funds seek high after-tax income for residents of individual states.

- *State municipal bond funds—general* invest primarily in single-state municipal bonds with an average maturity of greater than five years or no specific stated maturity. The income from these funds is largely exempt from federal as well as state income tax for residents of the state.
- *State municipal bond funds—short-term* invest primarily in single-state municipal bonds with an average maturity of one to five years. The income of these funds is largely exempt from federal as well as state income tax for residents of the state.

National Municipal Bond Funds invest primarily in the bonds of various municipal issuers in the United States. These funds seek high current income free from federal tax.

- *National municipal bond funds—general* invest primarily in municipal bonds with an average maturity of more than five years or no specific stated maturity.
- *National municipal bond funds—short-term* invest primarily in municipal bonds with an average maturity of one to five years.

Source: Adapted from data in Investment Company Institute, *2004 Mutual Fund Fact Book.*

Exhibit 24.10 | **Taxable Money Market Funds: 1975–2003**

	Number of Funds	Total Accounts Outstanding (Thousands)	Average Maturity (Days)	Total Net Assets ($ Billions)
1975	36	209	—	3.7
1980	96	4,746	24	74.4
1985	348	14,435	42	207.5
1990	506	21,578	41	414.7
1995	674	27,859	52	630.0
2000	703	45,480	51	1,607.2
2001	689	44,415	58	2,012.9
2002	679	42,726	53	1,997.2
2003	661	38,396	57	1,763.3

Note: Does not include money market and short-term bond funds.
Source: Adapted from data in Investment Company Institute, *2004 Mutual Fund Fact Book*.

Money market funds were initiated during 1973 when short-term interest rates were at record levels. These funds attempt to provide current income, safety of principal, and liquidity by investing in diversified portfolios of short-term securities, such as Treasury bills, banker certificates of deposit, bank acceptances, and commercial paper. They typically are no-load funds and impose no penalty for early withdrawal. Also, they generally allow holders to write checks against their account. Exhibit 24.10 documents the significant growth of these funds. Changes in their growth rate usually are associated with investor attitudes toward the stock market. When investors are bullish toward stocks, they withdraw funds from their money market accounts to invest; when they are uncertain, they shift from stocks to the money funds.

Breakdown by Fund Characteristics

Exhibit 24.11 groups funds by their method of sale and by investment objectives. The two major means of distribution are (1) by a sales force and (2) by direct purchase from the fund or direct marketing. Sales forces would include brokers, such as Merrill Lynch; commission-based financial planners; or dedicated sales forces, such as those of American Express Retirement Services. Almost all mutual funds acquired from these individuals charge sales fees (loads) from which salespeople are compensated.

Investors typically purchase shares of directly marketed funds through the mail, telephone, bankwire, or an office of the fund. These direct sales funds usually impose a low sales charge or none at all. In the past, because they had no sales fee, they had to be sold directly because a broker had no incentive to sell a no-load fund. This has changed recently because some brokerage firms, most notably Charles Schwab & Co., have developed agreements with specific no-load funds whereby they will sell these funds to their clients and collect a fee from the fund. As of March 2005, Schwab had a list of thousands of no-load funds that they would sell through their OneSource service. As seen in the most recent figures available in Exhibit 24.11, the division between these two major distribution channels is currently about 60 to 40 percent in favor of the sales force method, although there has been a steady shift toward direct institutional marketing. Given the investor preference for no-load funds and the increasing availability through firms like Charles Schwab, this trend toward direct marketed funds should continue.

Exhibit 24.11	**Total Net Assets by Fund Characteristics ($ Billions)**

	2002		1995	
	Dollars	**Percent**	**Dollars**	**Percent**
Total Net Assets	$4,119.6	100.0%	$2,067.3	100.0%
Method of Sale:				
Sales Force	—	62.0%	—	59.0%
Direct Institutional Marketing	—	25.0%	—	20.0%
Direct Retail Sales	—	13.0%	—	21.0%
Investment Objective:				
Aggressive Growth	436.1	10.6%	190.8	9.2%
Growth	784.3	19.0%	354.2	17.1%
Growth & income	860.5	20.9%	429.2	20.8%
World equity	358.4	8.7%	196.7	9.5%
Income equity	106.3	2.6%	93.3	4.5%
Flexible & Asset Allocation	88.8	2.2%	52.4	2.5%
Balanced	178.9	4.3%	81.3	3.9%
Income-mixed	59.6	1.4%	77.4	3.7%
Corporate bond	178.3	4.3%	31.7	1.5%
High-yield bond	100.3	2.4%	59.7	2.9%
World bond	21.1	0.5%	33.4	1.6%
Government bond	130.6	3.2%	87.9	4.3%
Govt. bond-mortgage-backed	107.4	2.6%	55.3	2.7%
Strategic income-bond	259.0	6.3%	66.1	3.2%
State municipal bond	154.6	3.8%	117.2	5.7%
National municipal bond	173.9	4.2%	135.8	6.6%
Other (e.g., Sector, Metals)	121.4	2.9%	4.7	0.2%

Source: Adapted from data in Investment Company Institue, *2004 Mutual Fund Fact Book.*

The breakdown by investment objective indicates the investment companies' response to a shift in investor emphasis. The growth of an alternative investment objective category reflects not only the overall growth of the industry but also the creation of new funds in response to the evolving demands of investors. For example, aggressive growth, growth, and growth and income funds have continued to grow and generally increased their percentages. Finally, the growing desire for international diversification is reflected in the ongoing popularity of world equity funds. This trend is discussed more thoroughly in the next section.

Global Investment Companies

As discussed throughout this text, serious thought should be given to global diversification of your investment portfolio. Funds that invest in non-U.S. securities are generally called *foreign funds.* More specific designations include either *international funds* or *global funds.*

International funds include only non-U.S. stocks from such countries as Germany, Japan, Singapore, and Korea. Global funds contain both U.S. and non-U.S. securities. Ideally, a global fund should invest in a large number of countries. Both international and global funds fall into familiar categories: money funds, long-term government and corporate bond funds, and equity funds. In turn, an international equity fund might limit its focus to a segment of the non-U.S. market, such as the European Fund or Pacific Basin Fund, or to a single country, such as Germany, Italy, Japan, or Korea. In the chapter on global investing, there was an extensive discussion about investing in emerging markets. Given the need to invest in a diversified portfolio of emerging markets, an emerging market mutual fund that contains a number of them is an ideal vehicle for this asset allocation.

Although most global or international funds are open-end funds (either load or no load), a significant number are closed-end funds, including most of the single country and the emerging-market funds. These funds have opted to be closed end so that they are not subject to major investor liquidations that require the sale of stocks in the portfolio on an illiquid foreign stock exchange. Because of the growth and popularity of foreign funds, most sources of information include separate sections on foreign stock or bond funds.

A final alternative that all investors—particularly those in the United States—should appreciate is the large number of non-U.S. investment companies that offer both domestic and global products in their local markets. In fact, the Investment Company Institute reported that of $13.96 trillion invested worldwide in open-end investment companies at the end of 2003, almost 47 percent of these assets were controlled by firms located outside the United States. In order, the largest concentrations of these AUM occurred in France, Luxembourg, Japan, Italy, Canada, Australia, and Germany. Further, of the 54,015 investment companies in operation during 2003, slightly more than 8,000 were domiciled in the United States. From these statistics, it is reasonable to assume that no single region of the world has a monopoly on investment management skill.

Mutual Fund Organization and Strategy: An Example

The Dreyfus Corporation, established in 1951 and headquartered in New York City, is one of the leading mutual fund companies in the United States, managing approximately $161 billion in more than 200 mutual fund portfolios nationwide as of March 2005.[6] The Dreyfus Appreciation Fund (DGAGX) is a one of several equity-oriented portfolios that the company offers to its institutional and retail investors. The Appreciation Fund, which follows a large-cap blend investment style, is different than many of the other funds in the Dreyfus family in that it is not managed in house by portfolio managers that it employs directly. Rather, DGAGX is managed by Fayez Sarofim, a Houston, Texas money manager who has run his own private management firm since 1958 and serves Dreyfus as a subinvestment advisor. A portion of Bloomberg's description of DGAGX is shown in Exhibit 24.12. In particular, notice that DGAGX has about $4.4 billion (Panel A) of assets under management and is a no-load fund that also does not charge a 12b-1 fee (Panel B). However, investors do pay an annual management fee of 0.55% of the portfolio's assets and the expense ratio, which accounts for the cost of actually running the fund, is 0.95% of AUM.

One of the reasons why Dreyfus chose to enter into this arrangement was to allow investors who would not otherwise have sufficient capital to gain access to a private manager with an outstanding long-term performance record. Fayez Sarofim's investment philosophy is

---

[6]Much of the information contained in this example is available from Dreyfus Corporation's Web site at http://www.dreyfus.com.

Exhibit 24.12 | **Description of Dreyfus Appreciation Fund (DGAGX)**

Panel A. Overview

DGAGX US   **DESCRIPTION**   Page   1/ 4
DREYFUS APPRECIATION FD INC   Objective - Blue Chip

Dreyfus Appreciation Fund, Inc. is an open-end fund incorporated in the USA. The Fund's objective is long-term capital growth consistent with the preservation of capital. Its secondary goal is current income. The Fund invests at least 80% of its net assets in the common stock of U.S. and foreign blue-chip companies of market capitalization of more than $5 billion.

Bloomberg Classification Data		Current / Operational Data		
Asset Class	Equity	1)GP NAV	$	38.24
Style	Blue Chip	Assets(mil) 3/31/05	$	4380.87
Market Cap Focus	Multi-cap	Inception Date		1/18/84
Geographic Focus	Global			

Performance/Percentile Ranking		
as of 4/22/05	Return	Rank in Obj.
3)TRA 1 Month	-.81	83
YTD	-1.14	91
1 Year	2.17	66
2004	5.57	35
5 Year	-1.16	84

1 Yr Performance vs. Benchmark Indices
DGAGX SPX
30APR04 30JUN 31AUG 29OCT 31DEC 28FEB05

{FPC<GO>} FOR FUND PERFORMANCE CHARTS AND {FSRC<GO>} FOR FUND SEARCH
Subadvisor: Fayez Sarofim & Co.

Panel B. Management & Fee Structure

DGAGX US   **DESCRIPTION**   Page   2/ 4
DREYFUS APPRECIATION FD INC   Fund Type - Open-End Fund

Contact Details	Fees & Expenses		
Fund Manager	Front Load		.000 %
11)FAYEZ S SAROFIM	Back Load		.000 %
	Early Withdraw		.000 %
Management Company	Current Mgmt Fee		.550 %
Dreyfus Corp/New York	Performance Fee		%
Address	Expense Ratio		.950 %
Dreyfus Funds	12b1 fee		.000 %
200 Park Avenue	Min Investment	$	2500
New York, NY 10166	Min Subsequent	$	100
USA	Min IRA	$	750

Distributions		- Semi-Anl	
Telephone 1-800-645-6561 Domestic	6)DVD		Income	Capital Gain
1-516-794-5452 Intl	YTD	$	.01	.00
Web Site	2004	$	.52	.00
7)www.dreyfus.com	2003	$	.41	.00
Transfer Agent	2002	$	.30	.02
Dreyfus Transfer Inc	2001	$	.31	.00
	2000	$	.29	3.22

Isin	US2619701079	Valor	N.A.
Cusip	261970107	Sicovam	N.A.
Sedol	2291244 US	WPK	N.A.

Pricing Source
  NASDAQ

somewhat unique among mutual fund managers, in that he preaches a patient approach to port-folio formation that seeks to keep turnover below 15 percent per annum. The firm describes its investment approach as follows:

> Our investment philosophy leads us to construct a portfolio comprised predominantly of large capitalization, US-based, multinational companies. These companies are global leaders in structurally attractive industries. They benefit from increasing global market share, ongoing product introduction or innovation, and productivity enhancements—three key drivers of long-term earnings growth. In addition, their financial strength allows them to make profitable investments at any point in the economic cycle. We believe these busi-nesses are most capable of generating superior growth in earnings, dividends, and cash flow over time, leading to greater capital appreciation. Investing in high quality compa-nies at reasonable prices also produces two additional advantages for our clients—low portfolio turnover and a higher likelihood of preservation of capital.[7]

One interesting concept implied in this statement of philosophy is that Fayez Sarofim can be considered a global portfolio manager, even though the majority of the stocks he selects are from companies domiciled in the United States. The equity holdings of DGAGX are designed to mimic the portfolios that Sarofim assembles for his own private clients, and thus follows the same philosophy. Panel A of Exhibit 24.13 shows the top 10 holdings of the fund as of December 2004. Not surprisingly, all of these stocks (e.g., Exxon Mobil, Intel, General Electric) fit the profile of being large companies with dominant global franchises. Also, the DGAGX port-folio has a lower level of systematic risk than the market, as indicated by its beta coefficient of 0.85. Finally, Panel B of the exhibit shows that DGAGX outperformed the Standard & Poor's 500 index (which is a relevant comparison for a large-cap blend fund manager) by almost 10 percent during the five-year period ending in March 2005, although both entities produced negative returns due to the pronounced bear market that existed in 2000 through 2002.

HEDGE FUNDS

One of the most significant developments in the professional asset management industry over the past 15 years has been the emergence of the global market for **hedge fund** investing. Exhibit 24.14 shows that the increase in both the number of hedge funds in existence as well as the assets under management those funds control has been nothing short of phenomenal. From about 1,000 funds at the start of the 1990s controlling less than $50 billion in assets, by 2004 there were almost 9,000 active funds controlling an estimated $975 billion in assets. This represents AUM expansion of about 20 percent per annum over the past several years.

Despite this recent surge in growth, hedge fund investing is not new. In fact, Lhabitant (2002) notes that use of the term "hedge fund" originated in 1949, when Alfred Winslow Jones tested his security selection skills by forming a portfolio that combined both long and short position in the equity market with the use of financial leverage to enhance returns. Jones did this using a general partnership structure that avoided Security and Exchange Commission restrictions and also included an incentive fee for superior performance. Despite the fact that the performance of this original hedge fund was indeed spectacular—it outperformed the best mutual fund of the era by almost 90 percent over a 10-year period—Jones's strategy was not widely imitated for several decades. However, as indicated in Exhibit 24.14, that situation has certainly changed.

---

[7]The complete statement of the Fayez Sarofim investment philosophy can be found on the firm's website (http://www.sarofim.com).

Exhibit 24.13 | DGAGX Portfolio Holdings and Performance

Panel A. Portfolio Composition

DGAGX US
DREYFUS APPRECIATION FD INC   Objective – Blue Chip

Asset Allocation as of 12/31/04	
Government	2.01%
Corporate	.00%
Mortgage	.00%
Preferred	.00%
Municipal	.00%
Equity	97.99%
Cash and Other	.00%

Sector/Geo Allocation	12/31/04
Oil&Gas	15.03
Diversified Finan Serv	12.84
Retail	8.40
Pharmaceuticals	8.11
Beverages	7.03
Cosmetics/Personal Care	6.32
U.S.	91.68
U.K.	4.18
Switzerland	2.64
France	.84
Netherlands	.65

Top 10 Holdings 12/31/04	Position	% Net
Exxon Mobil Corp	5332598	6.170
Altria Group Inc	4100000	5.655
General Electric Co	5600000	4.614
Intel Corp	7650000	4.039
Citigroup Inc	3600333	3.915
Pfizer Inc	5775000	3.505
Procter & Gamble Co	2800000	3.481
ChevronTexaco Corp	2600000	3.082
Johnson & Johnson	2150000	3.078
BP PLC	2300000	3.032
5)MHD		

Portfolio Statistics 12/31/04			
Top 10 Hldgs % Port	40.57	Avg P/E	16.81
Median Market Cap	125.41BLN	Avg P/C	15.68
Avg Wtd Mkt Cap	143.17BLN	Avg P/S	1.70
Avg Div Yield	2.46	Avg P/B	3.13
Sharpe Ratio	.43	Beta	.85

Panel B. Returns Compared to S&P 500 Index

	Securities	Crncy	Prc Appr	Total Ret	Difference	Annual Eq
	Range 3/31/00 – 3/31/05		Period Monthly		60 Mo. Period	
1	DGAGX US Equity	USD	-15.22 %	-5.20 %	9.64 %	-1.06 %
2	SPX Index	USD	-21.22 %	-14.84 %		-3.16 %
3						

(* = No dividends or coupons)

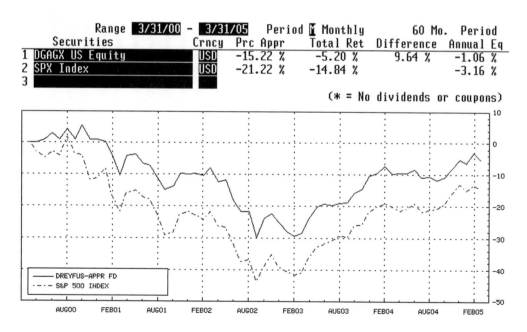

| Exhibit 24.14 | **Development of the Hedge Fund Industry** |

A. Estimated Number of Hedge Funds

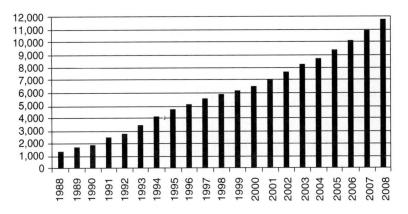

B. Estimated Hedge Fund Assets under Management ($ Billions)

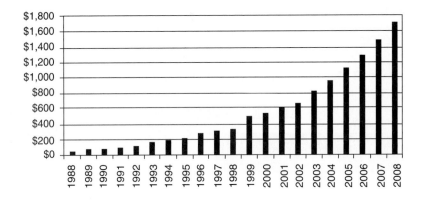

Note: Estimates for 2004–2008 are projections based on current data and may be revised in the future.
Source: © 2004 Van Hedge Fund Advisors International LLC.

As we saw earlier in the chapter, one of the reasons that investors consider hiring a professional asset manager is the belief that he or she will be able to deliver superior investment performance relative to simple indexed investments, such as an index mutual fund or an exchange-traded fund. In the parlance of the asset management industry, investors feel that professional managers can consistently add *alpha,* which is defined as the difference between a fund's actual and expected (e.g., CAPM) return. As Singer, Staub, and Terhaar (2002) point out, one of the reasons for the impressive recent development of the hedge fund market is the growing belief that hedge funds are better able to produce superior returns than traditional investment structures, such as mutual funds. This argument is summarized in Exhibit 24.15, which illustrates an excess returns form of the Security Market Line (SML) for several different asset classes. Notice that standard "long-only" positions in U.S. stocks and bonds plot virtually on the SML—indicating very little possibility for adding alpha—while the alternative asset classes (i.e., hedge funds, private equity) have substantially more potential in that area.

| Exhibit 24.15 | Security Market Line for Traditional and Alternative Asset Classes |

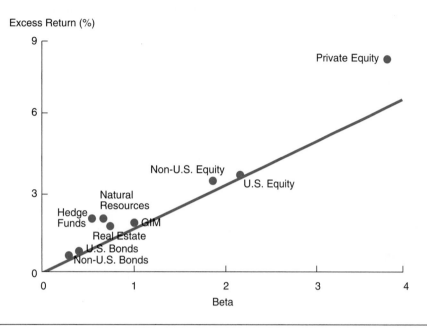

Note: GIM = Global Investment Market.

Source: Brian D. Singer, Renato Staub, and Kevin Terhaar, "Determining the Appropriate Allocation to Alternative Investments," *Hedge Fund Management* (Charlottesville, VA: CFA Institute, 2002), 10. Copyright © 2002 CFA Institute. Reproduced and republished from *Financial Management Journal* with permission from the CFA Institute. All Rights Reseved.

Characteristics of a Hedge Fund

Hedge fund investing can take place either through the creation of separate accounts for each investor or through the commingling of investor capital into a single pool of assets. Thus, a hedge fund structure can appear as either Panel A or Panel B in Exhibit 24.1. Most often, though, a hedge fund is structured as a commingled collection of assets (i.e., Panel B), with the important difference that it is usually formed as a limited partnership rather than as a mutual fund. There are several immediate consequences to creating a hedge fund as a partnership. Most notably, hedge fund investments are far less liquid than mutual fund (or even closed-end fund) shares; there are severe limitations on when and how often investment capital can be contributed to or removed from a partnership. On the other hand, as a private partnership, hedge funds are generally less restricted in how and where they can make investments, which is perhaps the biggest reason why investors believe that these vehicles have the ability to deliver abnormally large returns on a consistent basis.

Exhibit 24.16 highlights several important features related to the way hedge funds are structured. As just mentioned, notice that the average hedge fund only permits investors to enter or exit a few times a year (i.e., monthly and quarterly, respectively) compared to the daily ownership adjustments allowed by mutual funds. Also, most hedge funds allow managers to use leverage (71%), short sell (82%), and derivatives (69%). By contrast, Almazan et al. (2004) document that the vast majority of mutual fund managers cannot employ these investment tools. Notice further that it is typical for hedge fund managers to receive their compensation in two components:

Exhibit 24.16 | **Characteristics of Hedge Fund Investments, December 2003**

	Mean	Median	Mode
Fund Size	$83 million	$26.5 million	$20 million
Fund Age	6.8 years	6.2 years	8.0 years
Minimum Investment Required	$649,000	$250,000	$1,000,000
Number of Entry Dates per Year	22	12	12
Number of Exit Dates per Year	17	4	4
Management Fee	1.4%	1.0%	1.0%
Performance Allocation ("Fee")	17.2%	20.0%	20.0%

	YES
Fund has hurdle rate (of those with a performance allocation)	14%
Fund has high water mark	93%
Fund has audited financial statements or audited performance	95%
Manager has $500,000 of own money in fund	78%
Fund can handle "hot issues"	56%
Fund is diversified	44%
Fund can short sell	82%
Fund can use leverage	71%
Fund uses derivatives for hedging only, or none	69%

Level of turnover	Low (0–25%) = 17%	Medium (26–75%) = 26%	High (>75%) = 58%
Capitalization of underlying investments	Small ($1–$500m) = 12%	Medium ($500–$1,000m) = 4%	Large (>$1,000m) = 10% Mixed = 73%

Source : © 2004 Van Hedge Fund Advisors International LLC.

a regular management fee (e.g., 1 percent of AUM) and a performance allocation fee, which normally amounts to 20 percent of the fund's profits beyond a certain pre-specified return level (i.e., hurdle rate). In calculating this performance fee, it is typical for investors to require that any past losses be recouped before managers receive the additional payout; this arrangement is known as a *high water mark*. Finally, as a tangible signal to investors of belief in their abilities, most hedge fund managers put a substantial amount of their own capital into the fund.

Hedge Fund Strategies

Saying you are invested in a hedge fund is a little like saying you play a sport—it is a statement that conveys some information but could actually mean a great many different things. In fact, several investment strategies are often included under the hedge fund designation, and these vary greatly in the risk and expected return profiles they imply. Further, within a given strategic category, there can be as many interpretations of how the portfolio should be designed as there are fund managers. Nevertheless, some common features define the more popular hedge fund strategies, and we will now describe them.[8]

I. Equity-based Strategies

- *Long-short equity:* The original and perhaps the most basic form of hedge fund investing. Managers attempt to identify misvalued stocks and take long positions in the undervalued ones and short positions in the overvalued ones. Given that investors may participate in both the long and the short side of the market, one major advantage of the long-short strategy is the ability to generate "double alpha" (i.e., profit from price corrections for both undervalued and overvalued securities), unlike the long-only possibilities in the mutual fund industry.

- *Equity market neutral:* Like the long-short strategy, fund returns are generated by exploiting perceived pricing inefficiencies between securities. However, equity market neutral strategies also attempt to limit the overall volatility exposure of the fund by taking offsetting risk positions on the long and short side, an effort that might also involve adopting derivative positions. Absent leverage, these portfolios are expected to produce returns of 2 to 4 percent above the risk-free rate, which has led some investors to refer to them as *absolute return* strategies.

II. Arbitrage-based Strategies

- *Fixed-income arbitrage:* Fixed-income arbitrage returns are generated by taking advantage of bond pricing disparities caused by changing market events, investor preferences, or fluctuations in the fixed-income market. Because the valuation disparities between related instruments (e.g., coupon-bearing Treasury bonds and zero-coupon Treasury strips) are typically small, managers usually employ leverage to enhance their overall returns. The ability to generate alpha is driven largely by the manager's skill at building quantitative models, as well as structuring and managing fixed-income portfolios.

- *Convertible arbitrage:* Convertible arbitrage seeks to profit from disparities in the relationship between prices for convertible bonds and the underlying common stock. A typical position involves purchasing the convertible bond and short selling the underlying stock, thereby isolating the conversion option embedded in the bond. Returns are generated in several ways, including interest income on the convertible bonds, interest on the proceeds of related equity short sales, and the price appreciation of the convertible bonds as the instruments gradually assume the value of the equity into which they are exchangeable. Like the fixed-income arbitrage strategy just described, convertible arbitrage positions often utilize leverage to enhance returns.

- *Merger (risk) arbitrage:* Merger arbitrage returns are dependent upon the magnitude of the spread on merger transactions, which are directly related to the likelihood of the deal not being completed due to regulatory, financial, or company-specific reasons. As the probability of the merger improves, the spread narrows, generating profits for the position. Merger arbitrage investors essentially bet that their subjective assessment of whether the proposed deal will ultimately be completed is superior to that of the other investors in the market.

III. Opportunistic Strategies

- *High yield and distressed:* One advantage that bond investors enjoy relative to stock investors is that, if the issuer does not default, a bond's price will return to par at maturity. When companies are distressed, their securities can be purchased at deep discounts.

---

[8]The following list of hedge fund strategies, which draws from the discussion in Nicholas (1999), is intended to be representative rather than exhaustive. Alternative lists of strategies can be found at the following Web sites: http://www.hedgefund.com and http://www.thehfa.com.

If and when the turnaround materializes, security prices will approach their intrinsic value, generating profits for the distressed manager. *Emerging market* investing can be viewed as a global application of this strategy using sovereign securities instead of corporate instruments.

- *Global macro:* This broad class of strategies seeks to profit from changes in global economies, typically brought about by shifts in government policy that impact interest rates, in turn affecting currency, stock, and bond markets. Fund managers in this class typically use a "top-down" global approach to identifying opportunities and often participate in all major markets—equities, bonds, currencies, and commodities—though not always at the same time. The strategy uses leverage and derivatives to enhance returns, but also might hedge exposures on a situational basis.

- *Managed futures:* This strategy entails using long and short positions in a variety of futures contracts, both to take "directional" positions on certain economic or company specific events (e.g., changing conditions in stock or bond markets) and to exploit pricing discrepancies between various contracts. The assets underlying these futures positions may involve commodities, equities, interest rates, or foreign currencies. Because of the inherent nature of futures investing, these strategies frequently employ a substantial degree of financial leverage.

- *Special situations*: Special situation returns occur due to the outcomes of significant events that occur during the normal life cycle of a corporation. These strategies may involve investing in companies around the time of bankruptcies, financial restructurings or recapitalizations, spinoffs, or carveouts. Given the nature of the underlying reason for the investment, positions are usually directional and not fully hedged. Depending on the manager's specific strategy, *event-driven* returns are realized when the catalyst necessary to generate the position's intrinsic value (e.g., the spinoff of an operating division) takes place.

IV. Multiple Strategies

- *Fund of funds:* Although not formally a separate strategic category, this investment vehicle acts like a mutual fund of hedge funds, giving investors access to managers that might otherwise be unavailable to them. The primary benefit to the investor of a fund of funds position is that it is a convenient method for achieving a well-diversified allocation to the hedge fund investment space. A fund of funds can offer either a concentration in a particular strategy (e.g., long-short equity) and then diversify across different hedge fund managers—this is a *multiple manager* approach—or it can diversify across strategies, which is the *multiple strategy* approach. The primary disadvantage to the fund of funds investor is that there will be an extra layer of fees necessary to compensate the fund of funds manager; this additional fee can be as high as 3 percent of the assets under management.

Risk Arbitrage Investing: A Closer Look

A popular hedge fund strategy involves taking equity positions in companies that are the target of a merger or takeover attempt. As mentioned above, these risk arbitrage investments require managers to compare their own subjective judgment about the ultimate success of the proposed takeover with the success probability implied by the market price of the target firm's stock following the announcement of the prospective deal. If the manager thinks the takeover is more likely to occur than the market does, he or she will buy shares in the target firm. Conversely, the manager might short sell the target firm shares if he thinks the proposed deal is less likely to be completed.

To understand how a manager can establish the market's consensus forecast for the success of an announced takeover, consider the following hypothetical example. Suppose the

Exhibit 24.17	Implied Probabilities for Proposed Corporate Takeovers

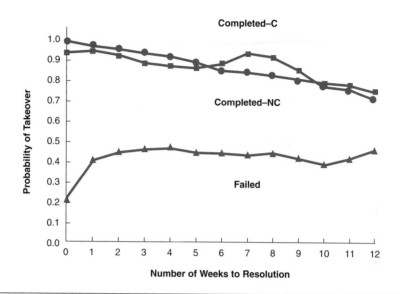

Source: Keith C. Brown and Michael V. Raymond, "Risk Arbitrage and the Prediction of Successful Corporate Takeovers," *Financial Management* 15, no. 3 (August 1986), 54–63.

shareholders of Company XYZ receive an unsolicited cash tender offer for $30 per share. At the time of the offer—which we will assume was a complete surprise—XYZ's shares traded for $20. Suppose further that shortly after the takeover announcement—which still must be approved by regulatory authorities—the price of XYZ's shares rises to $28. Brown and Raymond (1986) showed that a simple estimate of the market's *implied probability* that the takeover bid will ultimately be successful is $(28 - 20) \div (30 - 20)$, or 80 percent. In this situation, the risk arbitrage hedge fund manager must think the deal has better than a four-in-five chance of being completed in order to justify purchasing XYZ stock for $28 in the hope of selling at the tender offer price of $30; if the deal falls apart, the manager can assume that XYZ's shares will return to $20. Exhibit 24.17 compares the implied probabilities for a sample of proposed takeovers that were ultimately completed (both competing and noncompeting) to those for a sample of deals that failed. Notice that investors in the market are very good at discriminating between "good" and "bad" deals as far as three months prior to the final resolution.

To now see how this process might work in practice, Panel A of Exhibit 24.18 summarizes the relevant aspects of JP Morgan Chase (JPM) Bank's recent takeover of Hambrecht & Quist (HQ), a San Francisco–based investment bank specializing in transactions involving technology firms. In an effort to bolster their equity business, JPM made a tender offer of $50 per share for all of the outstanding shares of HQ, which at the time of the announcement were trading for $39.28. This represents a tender premium of $10.72, and capturing as much of this premium as possible is the goal of the risk arbitrage investor. However, Panel B indicates that within a day of the announcement, HQ shares were already trading for $48.69. This means that the market had already assessed the probability of this friendly takeover attempt to be 88 percent $[= (48.69 - 39.28) \div (50 - 39.28)]$. Thus, a hedge fund manager who did not already own HQ stock would have to be extremely confident that this deal would ultimately be completed to purchase shares at that point.

Exhibit 24.18 | **JP Morgan Chase's Takeover of Hambrecht & Quist**

Panel A. Tender Offer Details

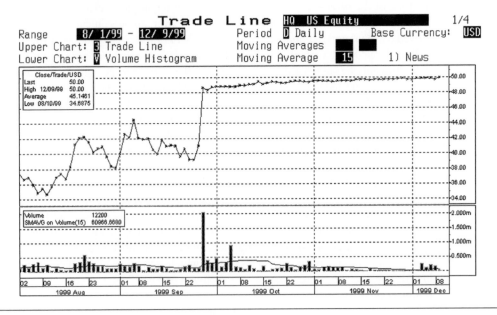

Panel B. HQ Share Price Movements

Exhibit 24.19 | **HFRI Index Risk–Return Comparison**

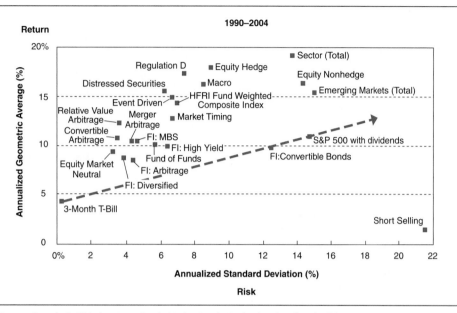

Source: Joseph G. Nicholas, *Investing in Hedge Funds: Revised and Updated Edition*
(New York: Bloomberg Press, 2005).

Hedge Fund Performance

Nicholas (2005) studied the performance of several of the strategies that defined the early hedge fund market. His findings are summarized in Exhibit 24.19, which plots a Capital Market Line (CML) comparing total risk and return characteristics over the period from 1990 to 2004. During this time, all of the indicated strategies plotted above the CML, demonstrating the ability of hedge fund managers to add a positive alpha to their investors over and above the returns that investments in traditional products such as Treasury bills or the S&P 500 equity index produced. Beyond that, there is also tremendous variation in the level of risk inherent in the myriad strategies. In particular, arbitrage-based strategies and those that take both long and short positions (e.g., equity market neutral) tend to exhibit far less volatility than those that adopt directional positions (e.g., macro and event-driven strategies). Clearly, not all hedge funds are the same when it comes to their risk and return profiles, a fact that participants in this market need to understand.

While these CML results are encouraging for potential hedge fund investors, it is important to keep in mind that they represent comparisons based on long-term averages over one specific time period. Investors should also be aware that the returns to these strategies show a high degree of variability on a year-to-year basis, in both an absolute and a relative sense. Exhibit 24.20, which lists the annual returns and rankings for nine different broad hedge fund categories, documents this *strategy rotation* effect. Some of the swings represented in the display can be dramatic. For example, convertible arbitrage (CA) was the best performing strategy in 1995, returning 6.1 percent to investors. However, it was the worst performing strategy during the previous year, posting a return of –2.5 percent. Similar patterns exist throughout the exhibit; for instance, distressed security (ED) investing dominated in 2003 and 2004, but actually lost money in 2002. Finally, notice that there are only 3 (of 11) years in which every strategy class earned positive returns.

| Exhibit 24.20 | Hedge Fund Strategy Risk-Adjusted Return Performance: 1994–2004 |

1994	1995	1996	1997	1998	1999	2000	2001	2002	2003	2004
MF 2.1%	CA 6.1%	FI 18.3%	CA 5.3%	MN 3.9%	MN 8.0%	MN 6.7%	CA 5.8%	GM 5.6%	ED 8.8%	ED 5.6%
RA 2.0%	FI 5.1%	CA 17.6%	ED 4.4%	MF 1.6%	CA 7.7%	CA 6.0%	ED 5.7%	MN 4.0%	EM 5.3%	MN 2.9%
EM 0.5%	ED 5.1%	MN 8.9%	FI 3.4%	LS 1.1%	FI 5.8%	FI 5.4%	GM 5.1%	FI 1.4%	MN 5.2%	GM 2.8%
ED 0.1%	RA 4.1%	RA 6.7%	MN 2.8%	RA 0.6%	ED 5.7%	RA 4.4%	MN 4.3%	MF 1.3%	GM 4.4%	FI 2.8%
FI 0.1%	LS 3.7%	ED 5.5%	RA 2.5%	ED -0.1%	LS 3.2%	GM 1.1%	FI 4.2%	EM 0.9%	LS 4.1%	LS 2.1%
GM -0.6%	MN 3.4%	EM 3.3%	GM 2.5%	GM -0.2%	RA 2.5%	ED 0.6%	RA 1.4%	CA 0.8%	FI 3.6%	EM 1.9%
MN -0.8%	GM 2.5%	LS 2.4%	LS 2.0%	CA -0.5%	EM 2.3%	MF 0.4%	EM 0.5%	ED -0.1%	CA 3.2%	RA 1.9%
LS -1.3%	MF -0.4%	GM 1.4%	EM 1.4%	FI -0.9%	GM 0.4%	LS 0.1%	MF 0.1%	LS -0.3%	RA 2.9%	CA 0.8%
CA -2.5%	EM -1.0%	MF 1.2%	MF 0.3%	EM -1.4%	MF -0.6%	EM -0.3%	LS -0.9%	RA -0.9%	MF 1.1%	MF 0.4%

Legend:
CA = Convertible Arbitrage
ED = Event Driven-Distressed
EM = Emerging Markets
FI = Fixed-Income Arbitrage
GM = Global Macroeconomic
LS = Long/Short Equity
MF = Managed Futures
MN = Equity Market Neutral
RA = Event Driven-Risk Arbitrage

Source: Data from a report to the Board of Trustees at Texas Teachers Retirement System by CSFB/Tremont Capital Management.

ETHICS AND REGULATION IN THE PROFESSIONAL ASSET MANAGEMENT INDUSTRY

The issue of ethical behavior arises any time one person is hired to perform a service for or look after the interests of another. Economists often refer to this potential conflict as the *principal-agent problem*, which can be summarized as follows: A principal (owner of the assets) hires an agent (manager) to manage her assets. She rightfully expects that the manager will make decisions that are in her best interest. However, although he is being paid to protect the owner's assets, the manager also has the incentive to take actions that may be in his best interest rather than the client's. For instance, the manager might misuse the owner's assets in both subtle ways (e.g., generating unnecessary expenses for first-class travel or office furnishings) and more blatant ways (e.g., expropriation of resources).

This sort of **agency conflict** occurs frequently in financial relationships. The stockholders of a corporation (i.e., principals) are the owners of the firm's assets, but they usually hire professional managers (i.e., agents) to run the company. Thus, the stockholders face the constant challenge of how they can keep the managers' incentives aligned with theirs. This topic is particularly important for the investment management business because the entire industry is based on handling someone else's money, meaning that agency issues are always present. In this section, we consider how the industry addresses these conflicts, both from a legal (i.e., regulatory) and ethical standpoint.

Regulation in the Asset Management Industry

As we have seen earlier in the chapter, professional portfolio managers are currently entrusted with the management of trillions of dollars. It is therefore not surprising that the investment industry is highly regulated to ensure a minimum level of acceptable practice. These regulations, which often involve a complex interaction between state and federal laws, are designed for the primary purpose of ensuring that portfolio managers act in the best interests of their investors. At their most basic level, these regulations are written to promote adequate disclosure of information related to the investment process and to provide various antifraud protections. Exhibit 24.21 describes the four principal securities laws that govern investment companies, including the Investment Company Act of 1940 (primary regulatory target: mutual funds), the Securities Act of 1933 (security issuers), the Securities Exchange Act of 1934 (security brokers), and the Investment Advisers Act of 1940 (advisers and private managers).

Notice that one of the main intentions of these regulations is to guarantee that investment companies keep accurate and detailed transaction records and that account information is re-

---

Exhibit 24.21	**Principal Securities Laws for the Asset Management Industry**

The Investment Company Act of 1940 regulates the structure and operations of mutual funds and other investment companies. Among other things, the 1940 Act requires mutual funds to maintain detailed books and records, safeguard their portfolio securities, and file semiannual reports with the U.S. Securities and Exchange Commission (SEC).

The Securities Act of 1933 requires federal registration of all public offerings of securities, including mutual fund shares. The 1933 Act also requires that all prospective investors receive a current prospectus describing the fund.

The Securities Exchange Act of 1934 regulates broker-dealers, including mutual fund principal underwriters and others who sell mutual fund shares, and requires them to register with the SEC. Among other things, the 1934 Act requires registered broker-dealers to maintain extensive books and records, segregate customer securities in adequate custodial accounts, and file detailed, annual financial reports with the SEC.

The Investment Advisers Act of 1940 requires federal registration of all investment advisers to mutual funds. The Advisers Act contains various antifraud provisions and requires fund advisers to meet recordkeeping, custodial, reporting, and other requirements.

Source: *2004 Mutual Fund Fact Book,* copyright © 2004 Investment Company Institute. Reprinted by permission of the Investment Company Institute (http://www.ici.org).

ported to investors in a fair and timely manner. As the Investment Company Institute notes, the U.S. Securities and Exchange Commission (SEC) is the main federal agency responsible for regulating professional asset management activities in the United States. In addition to monitoring compliance with existing statutes, the SEC performs the following functions:

- Maintains strict standards on the use of leverage so that funds do not take undue risk;
- Ensures that funds maintain effective governance systems;
- Requires understandable reporting and full disclosure to investors and works to eliminate fraud and abuse;
- Reviews required filings of investment companies; and
- Develops and revises rules to adapt regulations to new circumstances.

Other regulatory agencies that help to govern behavior in the investment industry include the U.S. Department of Labor (protection of pension plans, including 401(k) plans), NASDR (regulation of the securities industry under National Association for Securities Dealer rules), the U.S. Commodity and Futures Trading Commission (monitors futures and commodities trading activities), and the U.S. Internal Revenue Service (setting and enforcing of tax policies).

The main federal regulation governing the management of private pension funds is the Employee Retirement Income Security Act (ERISA), which was enacted in 1974 and primarily impacts the activities of private management companies as well as mutual funds. ERISA clearly states that pension funds are to be managed to the needs of the plan participants and their beneficiaries—as opposed to the corporation sponsoring the plan—and that managers should diversify plan assets so as to minimize the risk of large losses. As Del Guercio (1996) discusses, a key feature of ERISA is the *prudent man* statute, which outlines the level of fiduciary care that the manager must provide to the investor. Interestingly, this definition of the manager's required level of "care, skill, prudence, and diligence" was the first legal recognition of prudence involving the entire portfolio, rather than the individual securities on a case-by-case basis.

As we saw earlier, one of the appreciable advantages that the hedge fund industry enjoys is that it is relatively free from regulatory prohibitions that might otherwise impede the investment process. In fact, these funds tend to adopt a limited liability format (e.g., limited partnership, limited liability company) purposely to avoid having to register with the SEC. This freedom allows hedge fund managers to employ certain strategic tools (e.g., leverage, short selling) that are not available to traditional fund managers. A hedge fund qualifies for an exemption from the Investment Company Act if it has fewer than 100 investors, while hedge fund managers are exempt from the Investment Advisors Act if they manage less than $25 million in assets. Beyond this, the National Securities Markets Improvement Act of 1996 further increased the number of hedge funds and investors that are exempt from government regulation. On the other hand, if a quarter of a hedge fund's assets consist of retirement plan assets, the fund must comply with the restrictions set forth under ERISA.

Standards for Ethical Behavior

As Lhabitant (2002) points out, many developed economies like that in the United States are founded on the notion of financial market discipline. In such a system, government intervention is necessary to remedy situations when market forces fail to adequately protect investor interests. Unfortunately, we know that such failures do occur. Investors are well aware of the securities scandals of the 1980s that made Ivan Boesky and Michael Milken household names. Further, the market timing trading scandals that tainted the mutual fund industry in 2003 proved that lapses in ethical judgment could take place at the company level as well. Finally, the financial rescue of Long Term Capital Management that occurred in the 1990s created considerable interest in increasing governmental oversight of the hedge fund industry.

Transgressions of this nature attest to the fact that although regulations can punish those found in violation of the law, they cannot prevent all such abuses from occurring in the first place. Absolute prevention requires self-regulation on the part of the asset manager in the form of a strict set of personal ethical standards. Jennings (2000) has stressed that the desire of individuals and firms in the investment management business to maintain their reputation with clients is a major motivating factor in the practice of self-regulation. Avera (1994) has outlined four general principles that should form the cornerstone of the standards of conduct in the profession. First, managers must conduct themselves with integrity and act in an ethical manner in all dealings. Second, they should perform financial analysis in a professional and ethical manner. Third, managers should act with competence and strive to maintain and improve their competence. Finally, they should always use proper care and exercise independent professional judgment.[9]

The CFA (i.e., Chartered Financial Analysts) Institute—which was formerly known as the Association for Investment Management and Research (AIMR)—has developed for its worldwide membership of security analysts and money managers a rigorous *Code of Ethics* and *Standards of Professional Conduct* based on these principles. (These are available on-line at www.cfainstitute.org/standards/ethics/.) The *Code of Ethics* contains an expanded version of the four primary themes listed above and can be stated as follows:

Members of the CFA Institute shall

- Act with integrity, competence, dignity, and in an ethical manner when dealing with the public, clients, prospects, employers, employees, and fellow members.
- Practice and encourage others to practice in a professional and ethical manner that will reflect credit on members and their profession.
- Strive to maintain and improve their competence and the competence of others in the profession.
- Use reasonable care and exercise independent professional judgment.

The specific standards of practice suggested by these ethical mandates are summarized at the back of the book in Appendix B. These standards provide asset managers with precisely defined conduct and actions that are acceptable (or, more to the point, unacceptable) in daily practice. For example, the general principle that managers should use proper care becomes a specific requirement that they must be able to justify the suitability of any investment decision made on behalf of a particular client. The CFA Institute expects all of its members, which includes everyone holding the CFA designation, to uphold these standards on a voluntary basis. Violations deemed severe enough can result in the loss of a manager's charter.

To further promote ethical behavior in the asset management industry, the CFA Institute recently launched the Centre for Financial Market Integrity. The stated purpose of the Centre is "to be a leading voice on issues of fairness, efficiency, and investor protection in global capital markets and to promote high standards of ethics, integrity and professional excellence with the investment community."[10] The Centre's guiding principles—which stress the fact that investors should come first in all of the manager's activities, from investment decisions to financial reporting—are listed in Exhibit 24.22. In recognition of the unique place of trust that portfolio managers enjoy, one recent initiative that the Centre has undertaken on behalf

---

[9]For interesting discussions of the investing public's perception of ethics in the asset management industry, see Lummer (1994) and Ware (2000).

[10]A more complete description of the Centre's goals and activities can be found at http://www.cfainstitute.org/cfacentre.

Exhibit 24.22	**Guiding Principles for Ethical Behavior in the Asset Management Industry**

- Investors come first. The interests of the investing client must always take precedence over the interests of investment professionals and their employers.
- Investment professionals must act ethically and in accordance with the highest professional standards. They must:
  - act with integrity in all their dealings
  - maintain independence and objectivity
  - continuously strive to maintain and improve their professional knowledge and competence.
- Investors need complete, accurate, timely and transparent information from securities issuers.
- Financial statements should be reported from the perspective of the shareholder who bears the ultimate risk, and with the shareholder's best interests held paramount.
  - Financial statements should be fully transparent and report the fair values of all assets, liabilities, exchanges and transactions that could potentially impact the investor
  - All assets and liabilities should be included in the balance sheet, with no hidden assets, hidden debt or hidden obligations.
- Markets should move toward one set of global, high-quality standards for reporting financial information.
- Self-regulation is generally the preferred method for promoting fair and efficient markets. However, we recognize that some circumstances require additional regulation in order to ensure adequate investor protection.

Source: CFA Centre for Financial Market Integrity.

of the worldwide constituency of the CFA Institute has been the creation of a comprehensive *Asset Manager Code of Professional Conduct.* When it is fully developed and implemented, the *Asset Manager Code* will set forth minimum standards for providing asset management services to clients. It seeks to extend the voluntary standards of practice governing individual conduct to a set of rules that pertains to entire investment management firms. Although many firms already have such standards in place, others (including both traditional managers and hedge funds) do not, and this is the niche the new *Code* is designed to fill.

Examples of Ethical Conflicts

Many ethical breaches, such as plagiarizing research reports or falsifying performance statements, are unambiguously wrong. Other lapses, however, are not as clear-cut. We will conclude this section with a discussion of three examples of how possible conflicts between the manager and the investor can arise from accepted business practices.

Incentive Compensation Schemes   The first example is related to the way in which managers are compensated for their services. We saw earlier in the chapter that traditional asset management companies—both public and private—typically receive fees based on AUM. Further, hedge fund managers also receive a performance allocation fee that is tied directly to the portfolio's performance. The managers at these companies, in turn, are often compensated with a base salary and bonus that depends on the performance of their portfolios relative to those of their peers. Brown, Harlow, and Starks (1996) argued that this arrangement is analogous to a golf or tennis tournament where the players with the best relative performance at the end of the competition receive the largest payoffs. They documented that mutual fund managers with the worst relative performance midway through a compensation period were more likely to increase the risk of the portfolio in an effort to increase their final standing. Of course, altering fund risk to enhance their own compensation suggests that some managers may not always act in their clients' best interests.

Soft Dollar Arrangements   A second potential ethical dilemma for professional asset managers involves the use of **soft dollars**. Soft dollars are generated when a manager commits the investor to paying a brokerage commission that is higher than the simple cost of executing a security trade in exchange for the manager receiving additional bundled services from the broker. A typical example of this practice would be for a manager to route her equity trades through a nondiscount broker in order to receive security research reports that the brokerage firm produces. It may not be hard for the manager to justify how this additional research benefits the investor—who, of course, is ultimately paying for the service—but the story is quite different if, instead of research, the manager receives from the broker "perks," such as office equipment, secretarial services, or even payment for personal travel. Authors such as Blume (1993) have argued that this practice can result in a misallocation of resources or an expropriation of investor wealth by the manager, although Horan and Johnsen (2000) document that the use of soft dollars is actually a cost-effective way for investors to monitor a manager's behavior. In May 1998, the CFA Institute adopted a comprehensive set of voluntary standards designed to give its members guidance on the permissible uses of soft dollar arrangements.

Marketing Investment Management Services   A final example of an ethical dilemma that confronts professional asset management organizations is how and when to advertise their services. Conventional wisdom holds that it would be in the investors' best interests for any particular investment management company to build a steady awareness over time of its relative merits. However, in their consumer (i.e., investor) survey in the mutual fund market, Capon, Fitzsimons, and Prince (1996) documented that the main factor in the decision of which fund's shares to buy was the immediate past total return performance of the portfolio. Zweig (2000) observed that a consequence of this tendency has been the development of a situation in which mutual funds time their advertisements around relative peaks in their performance. Further, firms that run a family of funds can choose which portfolio or manager they want to promote on a situational basis, while still maintaining continuous brand awareness for the entire complex. Despite the usual disclaimers to the effect that "past performance is not an indication of future performance," the decision to always promote the "hot hand" is likely to be effective, but it is also likely to result in a misallocation of investor capital.

In summary, it is important for investors to recognize that potential ethical conflicts will exist any time they hire professional investment managers. Investors are protected by the series of regulations that oversee the security industry as well as the strict standards imposed by trade associations such as the CFA Institute. Of course, perhaps the best protection that investors have is the vast majority of the thousands of investment advisors and managers throughout the world who are unwilling to do anything that would jeopardize their personal and professional reputations.

WHAT DO YOU WANT FROM A PROFESSIONAL ASSET MANAGER?

What functions do you want your portfolio manager to perform for you? The list probably includes some or all of the following:

1. Help determine your investment objectives and constraints (e.g., return goals, risk tolerance) and develop a portfolio that is consistent with them.
2. Diversify your portfolio to eliminate unsystematic risk.
3. Maintain your portfolio diversification within your desired risk class while allowing flexi-

bility so that you can shift between alternative investment instruments as desired.

4. Attempt to achieve a risk-adjusted performance level that is superior to that of your relevant benchmark; some investors may be willing to sacrifice diversification for superior returns in limited segments of their portfolios.

5. Administer the account, keep records of costs and transactions, provide timely information for tax purposes, and reinvest dividends if desired.

6. Maintain ethical standards of behavior at all times.

Not all of the types of asset management organizations we have discussed in this chapter address each of these goals. For instance, mutual funds do not determine your risk preference for you, while hedge funds are seldom well diversified. However, once you determine your risk–return preferences, you can choose a mutual fund from a large and growing variety of alternatives designed to meet almost any investment goal. In general, these types of managers are consistent in meeting their stated goals for investment strategies, risk, and returns. Private asset management companies are oriented toward providing similar services (including investment policy development) for clients who have larger amounts of investable capital.

Diversifying your portfolio to eliminate unsystematic risk is one of the major benefits of both private management companies and mutual funds. In fact, many mutual funds provide *instant diversification,* which is especially beneficial to small investors who do not have the resources to form their own large-scale portfolios. Although diversification varies among funds, typically a large percentage of existing portfolios have a correlation with the market above 0.80. Therefore, most mutual funds provide excellent diversification, especially if they state this goal as an explicit objective.

The third function your portfolio manager might perform for you is to maintain the diversification of your portfolio within your desired risk class. It should not be too surprising that both types of traditional asset manager (i.e., private management companies and mutual funds) generally maintain the stability of their correlation with the market over time because few managers change the makeup of reasonably well-diversified portfolios very much. Strong evidence exists regarding the consistency of the risk class mandates for portfolios regardless of whether the overall performance is better or worse than average. On the other hand, hedge fund portfolios often vary significantly within the broad context of their designated strategy as managers attempt to add the maximum amount of alpha (i.e., the difference between actual and expected return).

Mutual funds have met the desire for flexibility to change investment instruments by creating numerous funds within a given management company. Typically, investment groups—such as T. Rowe Price, Vanguard, or Fidelity Investments—will allow you to shift between portfolios in their family of funds without a charge simply by calling the company. Therefore, you can shift between an aggressive stock fund, a money market fund, and a bond fund for much less than it would cost you in time and money to buy and sell numerous individual issues. By their nature, both private management companies and hedge funds tend to restrict an investor's ability to make these sorts of changes; accordingly, both of these management types are considered to be less liquid than mutual funds.

The fourth function of your portfolio manager is to provide risk-adjusted performance that is superior to your benchmark, which implies that it is superior to a naive buy-and-hold investment policy. The rapid development of the hedge fund industry over the past several years suggests two things in this regard. First, investors increasingly view hedge fund managers as being better suited to produce positive and consistent alphas than traditional managers. Second, it is becoming more and more difficult for many traditional asset managers to generate superior risk-adjusted returns because of the many constraints imposed on their investment process (e.g., short sale prohibitions, leverage restrictions).

The fifth function of a portfolio manager is account administration. All managers provide this service to some degree. However, private management companies are the most likely to see all (or substantially all) of a client's assets and so these firms are in the best position to administer the account most effectively. Conversely, most mutual funds also provide many valuable administrative services. For instance, they allow automatic reinvestment of dividends with no charge and supply annual statements of dividend income and capital gain distribution that can be used to prepare tax returns. Give their partnership format, hedge funds also provide investors with necessary tax information as well as periodic accounting of investment activity.

The final function that you should expect from your portfolio manager is ethical behavior that strictly follows the prevailing regulations and standards of conduct in the industry. For all investors, this is—and should be—a nonnegotiable requirement of any manager, regardless of the organizational form of the company. As we have seen, professional asset management is a fiduciary business, and those managers whose conduct violates the trust of those whose wealth they protect and grow will not last long. In extreme cases, they may even suffer legal consequences.

In summary, as an investor, you probably want your portfolio manager to perform a broad array of functions. Typically, however, no single manager is equipped to provide all of the services that you may require. Therefore, it is quite common these days for investors to form a "portfolio" of managers with different talents and capabilities (e.g., a hedge fund manager to provide superior risk-adjusted returns, an index mutual fund manager to provide diversification for the majority of your assets). Given what we know about the value of diversifying our financial capital across different asset classes and securities, it should come as no surprise that the same principle holds for portfolio management skills as well.

The Internet — Investments Online

As mutual funds have grown in popularity as a means to gain instant diversification and professional management, so have the number of Web sites devoted to some aspect of mutual fund investing. Any of the major fund companies (Fidelity, T. Rowe Price, Vanguard, Scudder, and so on) will have interesting Web sites to visit. Here are some others:

http://www.morningstar.com Morningstar is a leading provider of mutual fund information. The site features much information and many links of interest to mutual fund investors. Items on the Web site include news, analysis, and columns by several *Morningstar* writers, and an interview with a fund manager. Past articles are available in an archive. The site also features sections dealing with learning, planning, and researching about mutual funds. A mutual fund screen allows users to find funds from *Morningstar*'s database that meet certain investment category, return, rating, and volatility criteria.

http://www.lipperweb.com/ Lipper is a service which provides information, ratings, and research on mutual funds. This site provides research reports related to mutual funds. A companion site, **http://www.lipperleader.com/**, allows the user to use screens to find mutual funds which satisfy certain criteria.

http://www.brill.com The Mutual Funds Interactive Web site offers basic information about mutual fund investing, via charts, market commentary, and fund price quotes. It has a number of educational features, including a Q&A section, a manager profile, and discussions of various investment topics and of the different types of mutual funds.

http://www.mfea.com A good place to start if you want to learn more about mutual funds is this home page for the Mutual Fund Education Alliance. This site, called the Mutual Fund Investor's Center, offers a great deal of information. The Fund Center allows users to research, track, and customize their own fund portfolio from a list of over 1,000 funds. Investors can search by a specific fund's name or search for funds by their characteristics, including investment category, level of 12b-1 fee, expense ratio, and sales charge. Investors can also discover the three top-performing funds year-to-date in different investment categories and find the lowest-cost fund by investment category. The Education Center page deals with the basics of mutual fund investing, while the Planning

and Retirement Center page covers information and investment strategies for retirement, future education, and children. The site has links to a number of fund families.

http://www.investorguide.com/funds.html This page from the InvestorGuide Web site focuses on mutual fund investing and has links to a variety of mutual-fund-related sites. Topics include learning about mutual funds, getting performance data and ratings, screening mutual funds, and obtaining a mutual fund prospectus.

http://www.ici.org The Investment Company Institute is a mutual fund trade organization. Visitors to their home page can view issues of their annual publication, *Investment Company Fact Book*, learn mutual fund facts and figures, read ICI's newsletter, and get information about financial market and mutual fund regulation issues.

SUMMARY

- There are two primary types of professional asset management companies. Management and advisory firms hold the assets of individual and institutional investors in separate accounts, which allows for the possibility of managing each client's portfolio in a unique manner. Conversely, investment companies, such as closed- and open-end funds, are pools of assets that are managed collectively. Investors in these funds receive shares representing their proportional ownership in the underlying portfolio of stocks, bonds, or other securities. These fund shares can either be traded in the secondary market (closed-end) or sold directly back to the investment company (mutual fund) at the prevailing net asset value. A wide variety of funds are available, so you can find one to match almost any investment objective or combination of investment objectives.

- In recent years, the professional asset management industry has undergone considerable structural change. Two changes are particularly notable. First, among traditional "long-only" asset management firms, there has been a trend toward consolidating assets under management

(AUM) in large, multiproduct companies. This trend has had a beneficial effect for investors of reducing management fees, which are usually charged on a declining percentage of AUM. Investment companies also often charge fees for marketing their shares. These sales charges can take the form of front-end fees, annual 12b-1 fees, or back-end load fees. A substantial amount of publicly available information exists on mutual fund investment practices and performance, to help investors make decisions that are appropriate for their circumstances.

- A second trend that has marked the professional asset management industry in recent years has been the rapid development of hedge funds, both in the number of portfolios that exist and the amount of assets that they control. One of the main advantages that hedge funds enjoy over traditional investment companies is that hedge funds are generally less restricted in what strategies they can follow and investment techniques they can employ. An example of this is the use of both leverage and short selling to supplement main portfolio formation strategy. As a consequence of this additional level of flexibility, many investors have come to regard hedge funds as being in a unique position to produce superior risk-adjusted returns.

- Issues of ethical behavior arise any time one person is hired to perform a service for another. The professional asset management industry protects investors through a series of government regulations and voluntary standards of practice imposed by trade associations on their mem-

bers. The primary purpose of these regulations and standards is to ensure that managers deal with all investors fairly and equitably and that information about investment performance is accurately reported. Two areas of particular concern in the investment community involve manager compensation arrangements and the use of soft dollars.

SUGGESTED READINGS

Association for Investment Management and Research. *Standards of Practice Handbook,* 8th ed. Charlottesville, VA: AIMR, 1999.

Caccese, Michael S. "Ethics and the Financial Analyst." *Financial Analysts Journal* 53, no. 1 (January/February 1997).

CFA Institute. *Points of Inflection: New Directions for Portfolio Management.* Charlottesville, VA: 2004.

Lakonishok, Josef, Andrei Shleifer, and Robert W. Vishny. "The Structure and Performance of the Money Management Industry." In *Brookings Papers on Economic Activity.* Washington, DC: Brookings Institute, 1992.

Pozen, Robert C. *The Mutual Fund Business,* 2nd ed. Boston, MA: Houghton Mifflin, 2001.

QUESTIONS

1. What are the differences between a management and advisory firm and an investment company? Describe the approach toward portfolio management adopted by each organization.

2. It has been suggested that the professional asset management community is rapidly becoming dominated by a fairly small number of huge, multiproduct firms. Discuss whether the data presented in Exhibit 24.2 support that view.

3. Closed-end funds generally invest in securities and financial instruments that are relatively illiquid whereas most mutual funds invest in widely traded stocks and bonds. Explain the difference between closed-end and open-end funds and why this liquidity distinction matters.

4. What is the difference between a load fund and a no-load fund?

5. Should you care about how well a mutual fund is diversified? Why or why not?

6. As an investigator evaluating how well mutual fund managers select undervalued stocks or project market returns, discuss whether net or gross returns are more relevant.

7. You are told that Fund X experienced *above-average* performance over the past two years. Do you think it will continue over the next two years? Why or why not?

 8. *CFA Examination Level III*

Catherine Marco is a portfolio manager with Mouton Investments, Inc., a regional money management firm. She is considering investments in alternative assets and decides to research the following three questions about long-short strategies and hedge funds:

1. How can the alpha generated from a long-short strategy in one asset class be transported to another asset class?

2. What are the *three* major quantifiable sources of risk that a fund of hedge funds manager must consider in risk monitoring?

3. For a fund of hedge funds, how does risk-based leverage differ from accounting-based leverage?

a. Formulate *one* correct response to *each* of Marco's three questions.

Marco decides to explore various hedge fund investment strategies and reviews the following three strategy components:

1. Buy stocks after positive earnings surprise announcements, anticipating that the stock price will rise in the short term.
2. Establish appropriate long and short positions in stocks of companies that have announced a merger or acquisition or are rumored to be considering such a transaction.
3. Use neural networks to detect patterns in historical data.

b. Identify the hedge fund investment strategy that is best characterized by *each* of the three strategy components reviewed by Marco.

Following her research, Marco applies her findings to the situation of an individual client. This client currently holds only traditional equity and fixed income investments and is willing to consider investing in alternative assets to lower the risk of his portfolio. Marco forms the following five conclusions about investing in alternative assets for this client:

1. Investing in a fund of hedge funds is likely to increase the client's portfolio diversification and allow the client's portfolio to have exposure to a wide variety of hedge funds that may not otherwise be available to the client.
2. A lack of transparency and the fund manager's inability to add value through portfolio construction are both disadvantages of investing in a fund of hedge funds.
3. Because a directional hedge fund is expected to exhibit a lower dispersion of returns than a non-directional hedge fund, a directional hedge fund is a more appropriate investment for this client.
4. One appropriate hedge fund investment strategy for this client is a macro hedge fund, which is likely to provide increased returns with a relatively low standard deviation of returns.
5. Another approach that is consistent with the client's objectives is to use an equitized long-short strategy, which can be expected to neutralize market risk.

c. Judge whether *each* of Marco's five conclusions is correct or incorrect. If incorrect, give *one* reason why the conclusion is incorrect.

9. Most money managers have a portion of their compensation tied to the performance of the portfolios they manage. Explain how this arrangement can create an ethical dilemma for the manager.

10. What are soft dollar arrangements? Describe one potential way they can be used to transfer wealth from the investor to the manager.

PROBLEMS

1. Suppose ABC Mutual fund had no liabilities and owned only four stocks as follows:

Stock	Shares	Price	Market Value
W	1,000	$12	$12,000
X	1,200	15	18,000
Y	1,500	22	33,000
Z	800	16	12,800
			$75,800

The fund began by selling $50,000 of stock at $8.00 per share. What is its NAV?

2. Suppose you are considering investing $1,000 in a load fund that charges a fee of 8 percent, and you expect your investment to earn 15 percent over the next year. Alternatively, you could invest in a no-load fund with similar risk that charges a 1 percent redemption fee. You estimate that this no-load fund will earn 12 percent. Given your expectations, which is the better investment and by how much?

3. Consider the recent performance of the Closed Fund, a closed-end fund devoted to finding undervalued, thinly traded stocks:

Period	NAV	Premium/Discount
0	$10.00	0.0%
1	11.25	−5.0
2	9.85	+2.3
3	10.50	−3.2
4	12.30	−7.0

Here price premiums and discounts are indicated by pluses and minuses, respectively, and Period 0 represents Closed Fund's initiation date.
   a. Calculate the average return per period for an investor who bought 100 shares of the Closed Fund at the initiation and then sold her position at the end of Period 4.
   b. What was the average periodic growth rate in NAV over that same period?
   c. Calculate the periodic return for another investor who bought 100 shares of Closed Fund at the end of Period 1 and sold his position at the end of Period 2.
   d. What was the periodic growth rate in NAV between Periods 1 and 2?

4. CMD Asset Management has the following fee structure for clients in its equity fund:

1.00% of first $5 million invested
0.75% of next $5 million invested
0.60% of next $10 million invested
0.40% above $20 million

   a. Calculate the annual dollar fees paid by Client 1, which has $27 million under management, and Client 2, which has $97 million under management.
   b. Calculate the fees paid by both clients as a percentage of their assets under management.
   c. What is the economic rationale for a fee schedule that declines (in percentage terms) with increases in assets under management?

 5. *CFA Examination Level II*
   Describe a potential conflict of interest in each of the following four situations:
   a. An investment advisor whose compensation is based on commissions from client trades
   b. An investment manager's use of client brokerage ("soft dollars") to purchase research or other services
   c. A portfolio manager of a mutual fund who purchases, for the fund, a substantial amount of stock in a small-capitalization company whose warrants the manager owns
   d. A research analyst who accepts reimbursement for food, lodging, and air transportation expenses for a site visit from the company on which she is writing a research report

> *Note:* In formulating your answers, you should consider AIMR's *Code of Ethics and Standards of Professional Conduct.*

6. Suppose that at the start of the year, a no-load mutual fund has a net asset value of $27.15 per share. During the year, it pays its shareholders a capital gain and dividend distribution of $1.12 per share and finishes the year with an NAV of $30.34.
   a. What is the return to an investor who holds 257.876 shares of this fund in his (nontaxable) retirement account?
   b. What is the after-tax return for the same investor if these shares were held in an ordinary savings account? Assume that the investor is in the 30 percent tax bracket.
   c. If the investment company allowed the investor to automatically reinvest his cash distribution in additional fund shares, how many additional shares could the investor acquire? Assume that the

distribution occurred at year end and that the proceeds from the distribution can be reinvested at the year-end NAV.

7. The Focus Fund is a mutual fund that holds long-term positions in a small number of nondividend-paying stocks. Their holdings at the end of two recent years are as follows:

	YEAR 1		YEAR 2	
Stock	Shares	Price	Shares	Price
A	100,000	$45.25	100,000	$48.75
B	225,000	25.38	225,000	24.75
C	375,000	14.50	375,000	12.38
D	115,000	87.13	115,000	98.50
E	154,000	56.50	154,000	62.50
F	175,000	63.00	175,000	77.00
G	212,000	32.00	212,000	38.63
H	275,000	15.25	275,000	8.75
I	450,000	9.63	450,000	27.45
J	90,000	71.25	90,000	75.38
K	87,000	42.13	87,000	49.63
L	137,000	19.88	0	27.88
M	0	17.75	150,000	19.75
Cash		$3,542,000		$2,873,000
Expenses		$ 730,000		$ 830,000

At the end of both years, Focus Fund had 5,430,000 shares outstanding.

a. Calculate the net asset value for a share of the Focus Fund at the end of Year 1, being sure to include the cash position in the net total portfolio value.

b. Immediately after calculating its Year 1 NAV, Focus Fund sold its position in Stock L and purchased its position in Stock M (both transactions were done at Year 1 prices). Calculate the Year 2 NAV for Focus Fund and compute the growth rate in the fund share value on a percentage basis.

c. At the end of Year 2, how many fund shares of the Focus Fund could the manager redeem without having to liquidate her stock positions (i.e., using only the cash account)?

d. If immediately after calculating the Year 2 NAV, the manager received investor redemption requests for 500,000 shares, how many shares of each stock would she have to sell in order to maintain the same proportional ownership position in each stock? Assume that she liquidates the entire cash position before she sells any stock holdings.

8. Mutual funds can effectively charge sales fees in one of three ways: front-end load fees, 12b-1 (i.e., annual) fees, or deferred (i.e., back-end) load fees. Assume that the SAS Fund offers its investors the choice of the following sales fee arrangements: (1) a 3 percent front-end load, (2) a 0.50 percent annual deduction, or (3) a 2 percent back-end load, paid at the liquidation of the investor's position. Also, assume that SAS Fund averages NAV growth of 12 percent per year.

a. If you start with $100,000 in investment capital, calculate what an investment in SAS would be worth in three years under each of the proposed sales fee schemes. Which scheme would you choose?

b. If your investment horizon were 10 years, would your answer in Part a change? Demonstrate.

c. Explain the relationship between the timing of the sales charge and your investment horizon. In general, if you intend to hold your position for a long time, which fee arrangement would you prefer?

 9. *CFA Examination Level II*

Clark & Kerns (C&K), a U.S. pension fund manager for more than 20 years, plans to establish offices in a European and a Pacific Rim country in order to manage pension funds located in those countries and invested in their local stock markets. Tony Clark, CFA, managing partner, learns that

investment organizations and their affiliates in the European country perform three functions:
- consult with corporate pension sponsors on how the pension fund should be managed and by whom;
- manage their portfolios; and
- execute securities transactions as a broker for the funds.

Common practice in this country is to withhold disclosure of the ownership of business organizations. Clark believes that C&K must provide all three functions to compete effectively. He therefore decides to establish offices in Europe to offer all three services to prospective pension fund clients, through local organizations owned by C&K. The pension consulting organization will be Europension Group; the portfolio management firm will be C&K International; and the broker-dealer operation will be Alps Securities.

a. Briefly describe two AIMR Standards of Professional Conduct that apply to Clark, if C&K provides all three functions on a combined basis. Describe the specific duty Clark is required to perform to comply with these Standards.

Clark learns that a customary practice in the European country is to allocate at least 80 percent of pension fund assets to fixed-income securities.

b. Identify and briefly explain two AIMR Standards of Professional Conduct that apply to this situation. Clark observes that portfolio managers in the Pacific Rim country frequently use insider information in their investment decisions. Because the pension fund management industry is performance oriented, Clark decides to adopt local investment practices as the only way to attract and retain local corporate clients in that country.

c. Identify and briefly explain two AIMR Standards of Professional Conduct that apply to this situation.

10. *CFA Examination Level III*

Peter and Andrea Mueller have built up their $600,000 investment portfolio over many years through regular purchases of mutual funds holding only U.S. securities. Each purchase was based on personal research but without consideration of their other holdings. They would now like advice on their total portfolio, which follows:

	Type	Market Sector	Beta	Percent of Total
Andrea's company stock	Stock	Small-cap growth	1.40	35
Blue-chip growth fund	Stock	Large-cap growth	1.20	20
Super beta fund	Stock	Small-cap growth	1.60	10
Conservative fund	Stock	Large-cap value	1.05	2
Index fund	Stock	Large-cap index	1.00	3
No dividend fund	Stock	Large-cap growth	1.25	25
Long-term zero coupon fund	Bond	Government	—	5

Evaluate the Mueller's portfolio in terms of the following criteria:
a. Preference for "minimal volatility"
b. Equity diversification
c. Asset allocation (including cash flow needs)

Chapter 25

Evaluation of Portfolio Performance

After you read this chapter, you should be able to answer the following questions:

- What major requirements do clients expect from their portfolio managers?
- What can a portfolio manager do to attain superior performance?
- What is the peer group comparison method of evaluating an investor's performance?
- What is the Treynor portfolio performance measure?
- What is the Sharpe portfolio performance measure?
- What is the Jensen portfolio performance measure and how can it be adapted to include multifactor models of risk and expected return?
- What is the information ratio and how is it related to the other performance measures?
- When evaluating a sample of portfolios, how do you determine how well diversified they are?
- What is the Fama portfolio performance measure and what information does it provide beyond other measures?
- How can investment performance be measured by analyzing the security holdings of a portfolio?
- What is attribution analysis and how can it be used to distinguish between a portfolio manager's market timing and security selection skills?
- What is the benchmark error problem and what are the two factors that are affected when computing portfolio performance measures?
- What are customized benchmarks and what are the important characteristics that any benchmark should possess?
- How do bond portfolio performance measures differ from equity portfolio performance measures?
- What are time-weighted and dollar-weighted returns, and which should be reported under the CFA Institute's Performance Presentation Standards?

At some level, people are always interested in evaluating the performance of their investments. Having spent the time and incurred the expense to design an asset allocation strategy and select the specific set of securities to form their portfolios, investors—whether they are individuals, corporations, or financial institutions—must periodically determine whether this effort is worthwhile. Investors managing their own portfolios should evaluate their performance, as should those who pay one or several professional money managers to make these decisions for them. In the latter case, it is imperative to determine whether the realized investment performance justifies the additional costs of engaging professional management.

This chapter outlines the theory and practice of evaluating the performance of an investment portfolio. We begin this discussion by considering what an investor should require of his or her portfolio manager. Specifically, we pinpoint what to look for before we discuss techniques to evaluate portfolio managers. We also briefly discuss how investment performance was evaluated before portfolio theory and the asset pricing models were developed and examine an assessment technique—called a *peer group comparison*—still widely used today that does not require an explicit adjustment for the risk exposure of the portfolio.

While comparing a portfolio's historical returns to those produced by other managers or indexes can be instructive, such comparisons do not produce a complete picture of the portfolio's performance. Indeed, the central tenet of the modern approach to performance measurement is that it is impossible to make a thorough evaluation of an investment without explicitly controlling for the risk of the portfolio. Given the complexity and importance of the issues involved, it should not be surprising to learn that there is not a single universally accepted procedure for risk-adjusting portfolio returns. Nevertheless, there are several techniques that are commonly employed in practice and we will consider several of the most prominent of these in detail. As we will see, there are four portfolio performance evaluation techniques (referred to as *composite performance measures*) that comprise the basic "toolkit" for measuring risk-adjusted performance. Although some redundancy exists among the measures, each of them provides unique perspectives, so they are best viewed as complementary measures.

Following this discussion of the most prevalent tools, we also consider some additional techniques that measure different aspects of investment performance. Prominent in this development will be a consideration of how an investor can evaluate a manager's performance by looking at the underlying security holdings of the portfolio as well as an examination of attribution analysis, a measurement technique designed to establish the source of a portfolio manager's skill. We will also consider how measuring the performance of a bond portfolio differs from that of a collection of stocks.

The chapter concludes with a discussion of a number of factors to consider when applying these various measures. In particular, we examine the controversy surrounding the selection of the proper benchmark to use in the risk-adjustment process and discuss why this *benchmark problem* becomes larger when you begin investing globally. The characteristics of a good benchmark are also described. Finally, we examine industry standards for calculating returns and reporting portfolio performance to investors.

WHAT IS REQUIRED OF A PORTFOLIO MANAGER?

There are two major requirements of a portfolio manager's performance:

1. The ability to derive above-average returns for a given risk class
2. The ability to diversify the portfolio completely to eliminate all unsystematic risk, relative to the portfolio's benchmark

In terms of return, the first requirement is obvious, but the need to consider *risk* in this context was generally not apparent before the 1960s, when work in portfolio theory showed its significance. In modern theory, superior risk-adjusted returns can be derived through *either* superior timing or superior security selection.

An equity portfolio manager who can do a superior job of predicting the peaks or troughs of the equity market can adjust the portfolio's composition to anticipate market trends, holding a completely diversified portfolio of high-beta stocks through rising markets and favoring low-beta stocks and money market instruments during declining markets. Bigger gains in rising markets and smaller losses in declining markets give the portfolio manager above-average risk-adjusted returns.

A fixed-income portfolio manager with superior timing ability changes the portfolio's duration in anticipation of interest rate changes by increasing the duration of the portfolio in anticipation of failing interest rates and reducing the duration of the portfolio when rates are expected to rise. If properly executed, this bond portfolio management strategy likewise provides superior risk-adjusted returns.

As an alternative strategy, a portfolio manager and his or her analysts may try consistently to select undervalued stocks or bonds for a given risk class. Even without superior market timing, such a portfolio would likely experience above-average risk-adjusted returns.

The second factor to consider in evaluating a portfolio manager is the ability to diversify completely. As noted in Chapter 8, on average the market rewards investors only for bearing systematic (market) risk. Unsystematic risk is not considered when determining required returns because it can be eliminated in a diversified market portfolio. Because they can expect no reward for bearing this uncertainty, investors often want their portfolios completely diversified, which means they want the portfolio manager to eliminate most or all unsystematic risk. The level of diversification can be judged on the basis of the correlation between the portfolio returns and the returns for a market portfolio or some other benchmark index. A completely diversified portfolio is perfectly correlated with the fully diversified benchmark portfolio.

These two requirements of a portfolio manager are important because some portfolio evaluation techniques take into account one requirement but not the other. Other techniques implicitly consider both factors but do not differentiate between them.

EARLY PERFORMANCE MEASUREMENT TECHNIQUES

Portfolio Evaluation before 1960

At one time, investors evaluated portfolio performance almost entirely on the basis of the rate of return. They were aware of the concept of risk but did not know how to quantify or measure it, so they could not consider it explicitly. Developments in portfolio theory in the early 1960s showed investors how to quantify and measure risk in terms of the variability of returns. Still, because no single measure combined both return and risk, the two factors had to be considered separately, as researchers such as Friend, Blume, and Crockett (1970) had done in early studies. Specifically, the investigators grouped portfolios into similar risk classes based on a measure of risk (such as the variance of return) and then compared the rates of return for alternative portfolios directly within these risk classes.

This section describes in detail the four major composite equity portfolio performance measures that combine risk and return performance into a single value. We describe each measure and its intent and then demonstrate how to compute it and interpret the results. We also compare the measures and discuss how they differ and why they rank portfolios differently.

Peer Group Comparisons

Before examining measures of portfolio performance that adjust an investor's return for the level of investment risk, we first consider the concept of a **peer group comparison**. This method, which Kritzman (1990) describes as the most common manner of evaluating portfolio managers, collects the returns produced by a representative universe of investors over a specific period of time and displays them in a simple boxplot format. To aid the comparison, the universe is typically divided into percentiles, which indicate the relative ranking of a given investor. For instance, a portfolio manager who produced a one-year return of 12.4 percent would be in the 10th percentile if only 9 other portfolios in a universe of 100 produced a higher return. Although these comparisons can get quite detailed, it is common for the boxplot graphic to include the maximum and minimum returns, as well as the returns falling at the 25th, 50th (i.e., the median), and 75th percentiles.

Exhibit 25.1 shows the returns from periods of varying length for a representative investor—labeled here as "U.S. Equity with Cash"—relative to its peer universe of other U.S. domestic equity managers.[1] Also included in the comparison are the periodic returns to three indexes of the overall market: Standard and Poor's 500, Russell 1000, and Russell 3000. The display shows return quartiles for investment periods ranging from 5 to 10 years. In this example, the investor in question (indicated by the large dot) performed admirably, finishing above the median in each of the comparison periods. Indeed, the manager of this portfolio produced the largest 9-year return (16.5 percent), well above the median return of 13.0 percent. Notice, however, that although the investor's 10-year average return exceeds the 9-year level (16.6 percent), it falls below the fifth percentile, which, while still laudable, is no longer the best.

There are several potential problems with the peer group comparison method of evaluating an investor's performance. First, and foremost, the boxplots shown in Exhibit 25.1 do not make any explicit adjustment for the risk level of the portfolios in the universe. In fact, investment risk is only *implicitly* considered to the extent that all the portfolios in the universe have essentially the same level of volatility. This is not likely to be the case for any sizable peer group, particularly if the universe mixes portfolios with different investment styles. A second, related point is that it is almost impossible to form a truly comparable peer group that is large enough to make the percentile rankings valid and meaningful. Finally, by focusing on nothing more than relative returns, such a comparison loses sight of whether the investor in question—or any in the universe, for that matter—has accomplished his individual objectives and satisfied his investment constraints.

COMPOSITE PORTFOLIO PERFORMANCE MEASURES

Treynor Portfolio Performance Measure

Treynor (1965) developed the first **composite measure** of portfolio performance that included risk. He postulated two components of risk: (1) risk produced by general market fluctuations and (2) risk resulting from unique fluctuations in the portfolio securities. To identify risk due to market fluctuations, he introduced the *characteristic line,* which defines the relationship between the rates of return for a portfolio over time and the rates of return for an appropriate market portfolio, as we discussed in Chapter 8. He noted that the characteristic line's slope measures the *relative volatility* of the portfolio's returns in relation to returns for the aggregate market. As we also know from Chapter 8, this slope is the portfolio's beta coefficient. A higher slope (beta) characterizes a portfolio that is more sensitive to market returns and that has greater market risk.

---

[1]This example comes from Singer (1996) and was based on data from the Frank Russell Company.

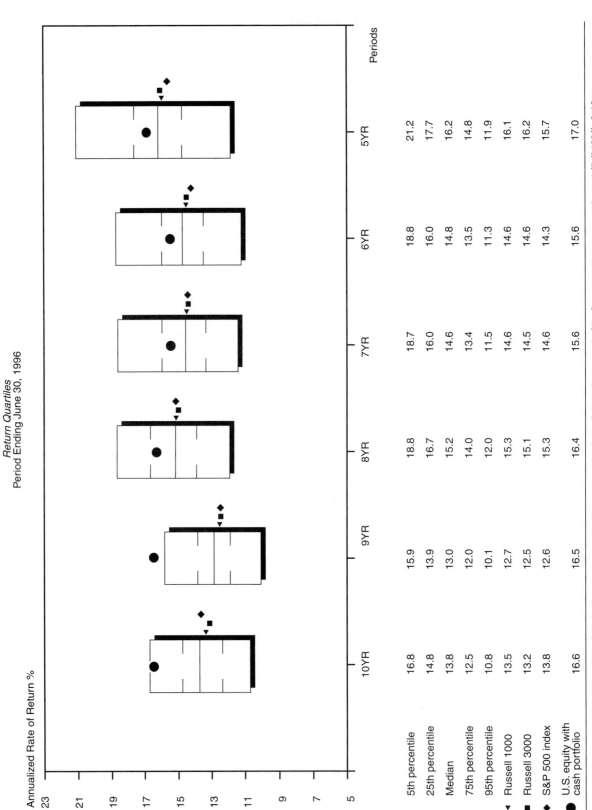

Exhibit 25.1 | **An Illustrative Peer Group Comparison**

Return Quartiles
Period Ending June 30, 1996

Annualized Rate of Return %

	10YR	9YR	8YR	7YR	6YR	5YR
5th percentile	16.8	15.9	18.8	18.7	18.8	21.2
25th percentile	14.8	13.9	16.7	16.0	16.0	17.7
Median	13.8	13.0	15.2	14.6	14.8	16.2
75th percentile	12.5	12.0	14.0	13.4	13.5	14.8
95th percentile	10.8	10.1	12.0	11.5	11.3	11.9
▼ Russell 1000	13.5	12.7	15.3	14.6	14.6	16.1
■ Russell 3000	13.2	12.5	15.1	14.5	14.6	16.2
◆ S&P 500 index	13.8	12.6	15.3	14.6	14.3	15.7
● U.S. equity with cash portfolio	16.6	16.5	16.4	15.6	15.6	17.0

Periods

Source: Brian Singer, "Valuation of Portfolio Performance: Aggregate Return and Risk Analysis," *The Journal of Performance Measurement* 1, no. 1 (Fall 1996): 6–16.

Deviations from the characteristic line indicate unique returns for the portfolio relative to the market. These differences arise from the returns on individual stocks in the portfolio. In a completely diversified portfolio, these unique returns for individual stocks should cancel out. As the correlation of the portfolio with the market increases, unique risk declines and diversification improves. Because Treynor was not concerned about this aspect of portfolio performance, he gave no further consideration to the diversification measure.

Treynor's Composite Performance Measure   Treynor was interested in a measure of performance that would apply to all investors—regardless of their risk preferences. Building on developments in capital market theory, he introduced a risk-free asset that could be combined with different portfolios to form a straight portfolio possibility line. He showed that rational, risk-averse investors would always prefer portfolio possibility lines with larger slopes because such high-slope lines would place investors on higher indifference curves. The slope of this portfolio possibility line (designated T) is equal to[2]

25.1
$$T = \frac{\overline{R}_i - \overline{RFR}}{\beta_i}$$

where:

$\overline{R}_i$ = the average rate of return for Portfolio i during a specified time period
$\overline{RFR}$ = the average rate of return on a risk-free investment during the same time period
β_i = the slope of the fund's characteristic line during that time period (this indicates the portfolio's relative volatility)

As noted, a larger T value indicates a larger slope and a better portfolio for all investors (regardless of their risk preferences). Because the numerator of this ratio $(\overline{R}_i - \overline{RFR})$ is the *risk premium* and the denominator is a measure of risk, the total expression indicates the portfolio's *risk premium return per unit of risk.* All risk-averse investors would prefer to maximize this value. Note that the risk variable beta measures systematic risk and tells us nothing about the diversification of the portfolio. It *implicitly assumes* a completely diversified portfolio, which means that systematic risk is the relevant risk measure.

Comparing a portfolio's T value to a similar measure for the market portfolio indicates whether the portfolio would plot above the SML. Calculate the T value for the aggregate market as follows:

$$T_M = \frac{\overline{R}_M - \overline{RFR}}{\beta_M}$$

In this expression, β_M equals 1.0 (the market's beta) and indicates the slope of the SML. Therefore, a portfolio with a higher T value than the market portfolio plots above the SML, indicating superior risk-adjusted performance.

Demonstration of Comparative Treynor Measures   To understand how to use and interpret this measure of performance, suppose that during the most recent 10-year period, the average annual total rate of return (including dividends) on an aggregate market portfolio, such as the S&P 500, was 14 percent ($\overline{R}_M = 0.14$) and the average nominal rate of return on government T-bills was 8 percent ($\overline{RFR} = 0.08$). Assume that, as administrator of a large pension fund that has been divided among three money managers during the past 10 years, you must decide whether to renew your investment management contracts with all three managers. To do this, you must measure how they have performed.

[2]The terms used in the formula differ from those used by Treynor but are consistent with our earlier discussion. Also, our discussion is concerned with general *portfolio* performance rather than being limited to mutual funds.

Assume you are given the following results:

Investment Manager	Average Annual Rate of Return	Beta
W	0.12	0.90
X	0.16	1.05
Y	0.18	1.20

You can compute T values for the market portfolio and for each of the individual portfolio managers as follows:

$$T_M = \frac{0.14 - 0.08}{1.00} = 0.060$$

$$T_W = \frac{0.12 - 0.08}{0.90} = 0.044$$

$$T_X = \frac{0.16 - 0.08}{1.05} = 0.076$$

$$T_Y = \frac{0.18 - 0.08}{1.20} = 0.083$$

These results indicate that Investment Manager W not only ranked the lowest of the three managers but did not perform as well as the aggregate market. In contrast, both X and Y beat the market portfolio, and Manager Y performed somewhat better than Manager X. In terms of the SML, both of their portfolios plotted above the line, as shown in Exhibit 25.2.

Exhibit 25.2	**Plot of Performance on SML (T Measure)**

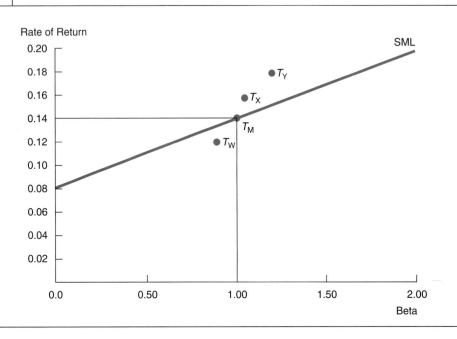

Very poor return performance or very good performance with very low risk may yield negative T values. An example of poor performance is a portfolio with both an average rate of return below the risk-free rate and a positive beta. For instance, in the preceding case, assume that a fourth portfolio manager, Z, had a portfolio beta of 0.50 but an average rate of return of only 0.07. The T value would be

$$T_Z = \frac{0.07 - 0.08}{0.50} = -0.02$$

Obviously, this performance would plot below the SML in Exhibit 25.2.

A portfolio with a *negative* beta and an average rate of return above the risk-free rate of return would likewise have a negative T value. In this case, however, it indicates exemplary performance. As an example, assume that Portfolio Manager G invested heavily in gold mining stocks during a period of great political and economic uncertainty. Because gold often has a negative correlation with most stocks, this portfolio's beta could be negative. Assume that our gold portfolio G had a beta of -0.20 and yet experienced an average rate of return of 10 percent. The T value for this portfolio would then be

$$T_G = \frac{0.10 - 0.08}{-0.20} = -0.100$$

Although the T value is -0.100, if you plotted these results on a graph, it would indicate a position substantially above the SML in Exhibit 25.2.

Because negative betas can yield T values that give confusing results, it is preferable either to plot the portfolio on an SML graph or to compute the expected return for this portfolio using the SML equation and then compare this expected return to the actual return. This comparison will reveal whether the actual return was above or below expectations. In the preceding example for Portfolio G, the expected return would be

$$
\begin{aligned}
E(R_G) &= RFR + \beta_i(R_M - RFR) \\
&= 0.08 + (-0.20)(0.06) \\
&= 0.08 - 0.012 \\
&= 0.068
\end{aligned}
$$

Comparing this expected (required) rate of return of 6.8 percent to the actual return of 10 percent shows that Portfolio Manager G has done a superior job.

Sharpe Portfolio Performance Measure

Sharpe (1966) likewise conceived of a composite measure to evaluate the performance of mutual funds.[3] The measure followed closely his earlier work on the capital asset pricing model (CAPM), dealing specifically with the capital market line (CML).

The **Sharpe measure** of portfolio performance (designated S) is stated as follows:

25.2
$$S_i = \frac{\overline{R_i} - \overline{RFR}}{\sigma_i}$$

where:

$\overline{R_i}$ = the average rate of return for Portfolio i during a specified time period
$\overline{RFR}$ = the average rate of return on risk-free assets during the same time period
σ_i = the standard deviation of the rate of return for Portfolio i during the time period

---

[3]For a more recent interpretation of this measure, also see Sharpe (1994) as well as Lo (2002).

This composite measure of portfolio performance clearly is similar to the Treynor measure; however, it seeks to measure the *total risk* of the portfolio by including the standard deviation of returns rather than considering only the systematic risk summarized by beta. Because the numerator is the portfolio's risk premium, this measure indicates the *risk premium return earned per unit of total risk.* In terms of capital market theory, this portfolio performance measure uses total risk to compare portfolios to the CML, whereas the Treynor measure examines portfolio performance in relation to the SML. Finally, notice that in practice the standard deviation can be calculated using either total portfolio returns or portfolio returns in excess of the risk-free rate.

Demonstration of Comparative Sharpe Measures   The following examples use the Sharpe measure of performance. Again, assume that $\overline{R}_M = 0.14$ and $\overline{RFR} = 0.08$. Suppose you are told that the standard deviation of the annual rate of return for the market portfolio over the past 10 years was 20 percent ($\sigma_M = 0.20$). Now you want to examine the performance of the following portfolios:

Portfolio	Average Annual Rate of Return	Standard Deviation of Return
D	0.13	0.18
E	0.17	0.22
F	0.16	0.23

The Sharpe measures for these portfolios are as follows:

$$S_M = \frac{0.14 - 0.08}{0.20} = 0.300$$

$$S_D = \frac{0.13 - 0.08}{0.18} = 0.278$$

$$S_E = \frac{0.17 - 0.08}{0.22} = 0.409$$

$$S_F = \frac{0.16 - 0.08}{0.23} = 0.348$$

The D portfolio had the lowest risk premium return per unit of total risk, failing even to perform as well as the aggregate market portfolio. In contrast, Portfolios E and F performed better than the aggregate market: Portfolio E did better than Portfolio F.

Given the market portfolio results during this period, it is possible to draw the CML. If we plot the results for Portfolios D, E, and F on this graph, as shown in Exhibit 25.3, we see that Portfolio D plots below the line, whereas the E and F portfolios are above the line, indicating superior risk-adjusted performance.

Treynor Versus Sharpe Measure   The Sharpe portfolio performance measure uses the standard deviation of returns as the measure of total risk, whereas the Treynor performance measure uses beta (systematic risk). The Sharpe measure, therefore, evaluates the portfolio manager on the basis of both rate of return performance and diversification.

For a completely diversified portfolio, one without any unsystematic risk, the two measures give identical rankings because the total variance of the completely diversified portfolio is its systematic variance. Alternatively, a poorly diversified portfolio could have a high ranking on the basis of the Treynor performance measure but a much lower ranking on the basis of

Exhibit 25.3	Plot of Performance on CML (*S* Measure)

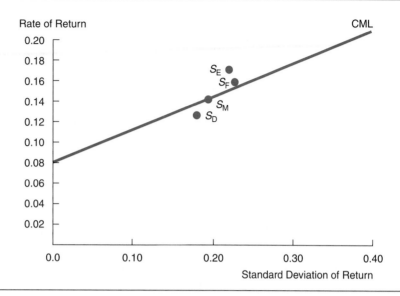

the Sharpe performance measure. Any difference in rank would come directly from a difference in diversification.

Therefore, these two performance measures provide complementary yet different information, and both measures should be used. If you are dealing with a group of well-diversified portfolios, as many mutual funds are, the two measures provide similar rankings.

A disadvantage of the Treynor and Sharpe measures is that they produce relative, but not absolute, rankings of portfolio performance. That is, the Sharpe measures for Portfolios E and F illustrated in Exhibit 25.3 show that both generated risk-adjusted returns above the market. Further, E's risk-adjusted performance measure is larger than F's. What we cannot say with certainty, however, is whether any of these differences are statistically significant.

Jensen Portfolio Performance Measure

The **Jensen measure** (Jensen, 1968) is similar to the measures already discussed because it is based on the capital asset pricing model (CAPM). All versions of the CAPM calculate the expected one-period return on any security or portfolio by the following expression:

25.3
$$E(R_j) = RFR + \beta_j[E(R_M) - RFR]$$

where:

$E(R_j)$ = the expected return on security or Portfolio j
RFR = the one-period risk-free interest rate
β_j = the systematic risk (beta) for security or Portfolio j
$E(R_M)$ = the expected return on the market portfolio of risky assets

The expected return and the risk-free return vary for different periods. Consequently, we are concerned with the time series of expected rates of return for Security or Portfolio j. Moreover, assuming the asset pricing model is empirically valid, you can express Equation 25.3 in terms of *realized* rates of return as follows:

$$R_{jt} = RFR_t + \beta_j[R_{mt} - RFR_t] + e_{jt}$$

This equation states that the realized rate of return on a security or portfolio during a given time period should be a linear function of the risk-free rate of return during the period, plus a risk premium that depends on the systematic risk of the security or portfolio during the period plus a random error term (e_{jt}).

Subtracting the risk-free return from both sides, we have

$$R_{jt} - RFR_t = \beta_j[R_{mt} - RFR_t] + e_{jt}$$

This shows that the risk premium earned on the *j*th portfolio is equal to β_j times a market risk premium plus a random error term. In this form, an intercept for the regression is not expected if all assets and portfolios were in equilibrium.

Alternatively, superior portfolio managers who forecast market turns or consistently select undervalued securities earn higher risk premiums than those implied by this model. Specifically, superior portfolio managers have consistently positive random error terms because the actual returns for their portfolios consistently exceed the expected returns implied by this model. To detect and measure this superior performance, you must allow for an intercept (a nonzero constant) that measures any positive or negative difference from the model. Consistent positive differences cause a positive intercept, whereas consistent negative differences (inferior performance) cause a negative intercept. With an intercept or nonzero constant, the earlier equation becomes

25.4 $$R_{jt} - RFR_t = \alpha_j + \beta_j[R_{mt} - RFR_t] + e_{jt}$$

In Equation 25.4, the α_j value indicates whether the portfolio manager is superior or inferior in market timing and/or stock selection. A superior manager has a significant positive α (or "alpha") value because of the consistent positive residuals. In contrast, an inferior manager's returns consistently fall short of expectations based on the CAPM model giving consistently negative residuals. In such a case, α is a significant negative value.

The performance of a portfolio manager with no forecasting ability but not clearly inferior equals that of a naive buy-and-hold policy. In the equation, because the rate of return on such a portfolio typically matches the returns you expect, the residual returns generally are randomly positive and negative. This gives a constant term that differs insignificantly from zero, indicating that the portfolio manager basically matched the market on a risk-adjusted basis.

Therefore, the α represents how much of the rate of return on the portfolio is attributable to the manager's ability to derive above-average returns adjusted for risk. Superior risk-adjusted returns indicate that the manager is good at either predicting market turns, or selecting undervalued issues for the portfolio, or both.

Applying the Jensen Measure   The Jensen measure of performance requires using a different *RFR* for each time interval during the sample period. For example, to examine the performance of a fund manager over a 10-year period using yearly intervals, you must examine the fund's annual returns less the return on risk-free assets for each year and relate this to the annual return on the market portfolio less the same risk-free rate. This contrasts with the Treynor and Sharpe composite measures, which examine the *average* returns for the total period for all variables (the portfolio, the market, and the risk-free asset).

Also, like the Treynor measure, the Jensen measure does not directly consider the portfolio manager's ability to diversify because it calculates risk premiums in terms of systematic risk. As noted earlier, to evaluate the performance of a group of well-diversified portfolios such as mutual funds, this is likely to be a reasonable assumption. Jensen's analysis of mutual fund performance showed that complete diversification was a fairly reasonable assumption for funds that are correlated with the market at rates above 0.90.

Jensen Measure and Multifactor Models   The Jensen composite measure of performance has several advantages over the Treynor and Sharpe measures. First, it is easier to interpret, in that an alpha value of 0.02 indicates that the manager generated a return of 2 percent per period more than what was expected given the portfolio's risk level. Second, because it is estimated from a regression equation, it is possible to make statements about the statistical significance of the manager's skill level, or the difference in skill levels between two different managers.

A third advantage of the Jensen performance measure is that it is flexible enough to allow for alternative models of risk and expected return than the CAPM. Specifically, risk-adjusted performance (i.e., a) can be computed relative to any of the multifactor models discussed in Chapter 9 as follows:

25.5
$$R_{jt} - RFR_t = \alpha_j + [b_{j1} F_{1t} + b_{j2}F_{2t} + \cdots + b_{jk}F_{kt}] + e_{jt}$$

where F_{kt} represents the Period t return to the kth common risk factor. Notice that the Sharpe measure, which focuses on total risk, ignores the specific form of the return-generating process altogether, while the Treynor measure requires a single measure of systematic risk.

The Information Ratio Performance Measure

Closely related to the statistics just presented is a fourth widely used performance measure: the **information ratio**. Also known as an *appraisal ratio,* this statistic measures a portfolio's average return in excess of that of a comparison or **benchmark portfolio** divided by the standard deviation of this excess return. Formally, the information ratio (*IR*) is calculated as:

25.6
$$IR_j = \frac{\overline{R}_j - \overline{R}_b}{\sigma_{ER}} = \frac{\overline{ER}_j}{\sigma_{ER}}$$

where:

   IR_j = the information ratio for Portfolio j
   $\overline{R}_j$ = the average return for Portfolio j during the specified time period
   $\overline{R}_b$ = the average return for the benchmark portfolio during the period
   σ_{ER} = the standard deviation of the excess return during the period

To interpret *IR,* notice that the mean excess return in the numerator represents the investor's ability to use her talent and information to generate a portfolio return that differs from that of the benchmark against which her performance is being measured (e.g., the Standard and Poor's 500 index). Conversely, the denominator measures the amount of residual (unsystematic) risk that the investor incurred in pursuit of those excess returns. As discussed in Chapter 16, the coefficient σ_{ER} is sometimes called the *tracking error* of the investor's portfolio and it is a "cost" of active management, in the sense that fluctuations in the periodic ER_j values represent random noise, beyond an investor's control, that could hurt performance. Thus, the *IR* can be viewed as a benefit-to-cost ratio that assesses the quality of the investor's information deflated by unsystematic risk generated by the investment process.

Goodwin (1998) has noted that the Sharpe ratio is a special case of the *IR* where the risk-free asset is the benchmark portfolio, despite the fact that this interpretation violates the spirit of a statistic that should have a value of zero for any passively managed portfolio. More importantly, he also showed that if excess portfolio returns are estimated with historical data using the same single-factor regression equation used to compute Jensen's alpha, the *IR* simplifies to

$$IR_j = \frac{\alpha_j}{\sigma_e}$$

where:

σ_e = the standard error of the regression[4]

Finally, he showed that one way an information ratio based on periodic returns measured *T* times per year could be annualized is as follows:

$$\text{Annualized } IR = \frac{(T)\alpha_j}{\sqrt{T}\sigma_e} = \sqrt{T}(IR)$$

For instance, an investor that generated a quarterly ratio of 0.25 would have an annualized *IR* of 0.50 = ($\sqrt{4} \times 0.25$).

Grinold and Kahn (2000) have argued that reasonable information ratio levels should range from 0.50 to 1.00, with an investor having an *IR* of 0.50 being good, and one with an *IR* of 1.00 being exceptional. These, however, appear to be unusually difficult hurdles to clear. Goodwin (1998) studied the performance of more than 200 professional equity and fixed-income portfolio managers with various investment styles over a 10-year period. He found that the *IR* of the median manager in each style group was positive but that the ratio never exceeded 0.50. Thus, although the average manager appears to add value to investors—α (and hence *IR*) is greater than zero—she doesn't qualify as "good." Further, no style group had more than 3 percent of its managers deliver an *IR* in excess of 1.00. Information ratio histograms summarizing this research are shown in Exhibit 25.4.

APPLICATION OF PORTFOLIO PERFORMANCE MEASURES

To apply these measures, we selected 30 open-end mutual funds from the nine investment style classes described in Chapter 16 and used monthly data for the five-year period from July 1999 to June 2004. The monthly rates of return for one of these funds (Vanguard Primecap Fund) and the S&P 500 are contained in Exhibit 25.5. The total rate of return for each month is computed as follows:

$$R_{it} = \frac{EP_{it} + Div_{it} + Cap.Dist._{it} - BP_{it}}{BP_{it}}$$

where

R_{it} = the total rate of return on Fund *i* during month *t*
EP_{it} = the ending price for Fund *i* during month *t*
Div_{it} = the dividend payments made by Fund *i* during month *t*
$Cap.Dist._{it}$ = the capital gain distributions made by Fund *i* during month *t*
BP_{it} = the beginning price for Fund *i* during month *t*

---

[4]The development of this form of the information ratio is credited to Treynor and Black (1973).

Exhibit 25.4	Information Ratios for Six Investment Styles: 1986:Q1 to 1995:Q4

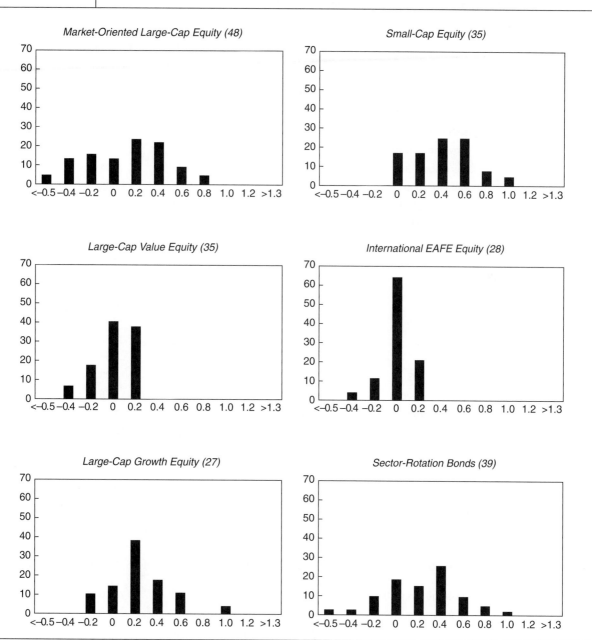

Note: Midpoints of ranges. Information ratios are on the x-axes; relative frequencies, in percentages, are on the y-axes.

Source: Copyright 1998, Association for Investment Management and Research. Reproduced and republished from "The Information Ratio" in the *Financial Analysts Journal*, July/August 1998, with permission from the CFA Institute. All Rights Reserved.

These return computations do not take into account any sales charges by the funds. Given the monthly results for the fund and the aggregate market (as represented by the S&P 500), you can compute the composite measures presented in Exhibit 25.5.

Exhibit 25.5 | **Example of Computing Portfolio Evaluation Measures Using Vanguard Primecap (VPMCX) Fund**

	R_{it}	R_{mt}	RFR_t	$R_{it}-RFR_t$	$R_{mt}-RFR_t$
July 1999	1.21	−3.03	0.39	0.82	−3.42
August 1999	1.12	−0.50	0.41	0.72	−0.91
September 1999	−2.25	−2.79	0.40	−2.66	−3.19
October 1999	6.24	6.49	0.42	5.82	6.07
November 1999	3.92	2.11	0.44	3.48	1.67
December 1999	8.60	6.34	0.45	8.16	5.89
January 2000	−1.03	−4.96	0.46	−1.49	−5.42
February 2000	15.38	−1.76	0.48	14.91	−2.24
March 2000	4.68	9.93	0.49	4.19	9.44
April 2000	−1.71	−3.24	0.49	−2.19	−3.72
May 2000	−4.78	−2.25	0.50	−5.28	−2.75
June 2000	3.97	2.67	0.49	3.48	2.18
:	:	:	:	:	:
:	:	:	:	:	:
:	:	:	:	:	:
July 2003	3.64	1.76	0.08	3.56	1.69
August 2003	4.46	1.95	0.08	4.38	1.87
September 2003	−1.88	−1.06	0.08	−1.96	−1.14
October 2003	7.63	5.66	0.08	7.55	5.58
November 2003	0.90	0.88	0.08	0.82	0.80
December 2003	3.05	5.24	0.08	2.97	5.17
January 2004	3.60	1.84	0.08	3.53	1.76
February 2004	2.46	1.39	0.08	2.38	1.31
March 2004	−0.92	−1.51	0.08	−1.00	−1.59
April 2004	−1.25	−1.57	0.08	−1.33	−1.65
May 2004	1.60	1.37	0.09	1.51	1.29
June 2004	3.09	1.94	0.11	2.98	1.84
Average (annual)	6.23	−0.53	3.03	3.20	−3.56
Standard deviation	20.67	16.83	0.59		
Beta	1.052				
S_i	0.155				
S_m	−0.211				
T_i	3.041				
T_m	−3.558				
Jensen alpha (1 factor)	0.578				
R^2_{im}	0.737				

The arithmetic average annual rate of return for Vanguard Primecap Fund was 6.23 percent versus −0.53 percent for the market, and the fund's beta was greater than 1.00 (1.052). Using the average annual rate of T-bills of 3.03 percent as the $\overline{RFR}$, the Treynor measure for the VPMCX (T_i) was substantially bigger than the comparable measure for the market (T_M) (3.041 vs. −3.558), primarily because the S&P index lost value over this five-year period. Likewise, the standard deviation of returns for the Vanguard Fund was greater than the market's (20.67 vs. 16.83), but the Sharpe measure for the fund (S_i) was still bigger than the measure for the market (S_M) (0.155 vs. −0.211).

Finally, a one-factor regression of the fund's annual risk premium ($R_{it} - RFR_t$) and the market's annual risk premium ($R_{Mt} - RFR_t$) indicated a positive intercept (constant) value of 0.578 but was not statistically significant. If this intercept value had been significant, Vanguard Primecap's risk-adjusted annual rate of return would have averaged about half a percent above the market on a reliable basis.

Total Sample Results The overall results in Exhibit 25.6 indicate that active fund managers performed much better than has been documented in earlier performance studies. A primary factor for this outcome was the abnormally poor performance of the index during the latter half of the sample period. Also, our sample was rather casually selected because we intended it for demonstration purposes only. The mean annual return for all the funds was considerably above the market return (8.04 vs. −0.53). Considering only the rate of return, 27 of the 30 funds outperformed the market.

The R^2 for a portfolio with the market can serve as a measure of diversification. The closer the R^2 is to 1.00, the more completely diversified the portfolio. The average R^2 for our sample was not very high at 0.584, and the range was quite large, from 0.325 to 0.981. This suggests that many of the funds were not well diversified. Of the 30 funds, 21 had R^2 values less than 0.70.

The two risk measures (standard deviation and beta) also show a wide degree of dispersion but generally are consistent with expectations. Specifically, 21 of the 30 funds had larger standard deviations than the market, and the mean standard deviation was larger (18.99 vs. 16.83). Only seven of the funds had a beta above 1.00; the average beta was 0.865.

Alternative measures ranked the performance of individual funds somewhat differently. (These rankings are listed in parentheses beside each measure.) Using the Treynor measure, only 4 out of 30 funds had a value worse than that of the market; also, only 4 funds had a Sharpe measure worse than that of the market. The Jensen measure using the Single-Index Market Model indicated that 26 of the 30 had positive intercepts, but just 11 of these were statistically significant. The mean values for the Sharpe and Treynor measures were considerably higher than the aggregate market figure. These results indicate that, on average, and without considering transaction costs, this sample of funds had essentially much better risk-adjusted results than the market during this time period.

You should analyze the individual funds and consider each of the components: rate of return, risk (both standard deviation and beta), and the R^2 as a measure of diversification. One might expect the best performance by funds with low diversification, because they apparently are attempting to beat the market by being unique in their selecting or timing. This seems to be true for some of the top-performing funds such as American Century Small Value Fund, whereas portfolios that produced returns more closely aligned with overall market, such as the Fidelity Magellan Fund, were among the worse performing funds. It appears that during this period it was better to *not* look like the market portfolio, although this is often not true.

Exhibit 25.7 reports information ratios for these 30 funds. To interpret the display, consider that the Strong Large Cap Growth Fund had a monthly *IR* value of 0.197, which was

Exhibit 25.6 | **Performance Measures for 30 Selected Mutual Funds**

Fund	Ticker	Style Class	Average Annual Rate of Return	Standard Deviation	Beta	R^2	Treynor	Sharpe	Jensen (1 Factor)
AllianceBerstein Growth	AGRYX	Large Growth	-3.67	21.21	1.142	0.819	-5.865 (29)	-0.316 (29)	-0.220 (29)
American Century Sm Val	ASVIX	Small Value	17.33	15.65	0.639	0.478	22.369 (3)	0.914 (3)	1.381[a] (3)
Buffalo Small Cap	BUFSX	Small Growth	22.98	24.93	0.929	0.397	21.479 (4)	0.800 (4)	1.939[a] (1)
Corbin Small Cap Value	CORBX	Small Value	6.42	28.06	1.017	0.373	3.334 (19)	0.121 (22)	0.584 (19)
Aim Constellation	CSTGX	Large Growth	0.93	24.51	1.216	0.701	-1.725 (25)	-0.086 (26)	0.186 (23)
Dreyfus Appreciation	DGAGX	Large Blend	-0.09	13.47	0.725	0.821	-4.299 (27)	-0.231 (27)	-0.045 (27)
Fidelity Magellan	FMAGX	Large Blend	-1.80	16.97	0.998	0.981	-4.835 (28)	-0.284 (28)	-0.106 (28)
Goldman Sachs Mid Value	GCMAX	Mid Value	11.46	15.09	0.580	0.420	14.540 (6)	0.558 (8)	0.874[a] (11)
Hotchkis & Wiley Lrg Val	HWLIX	Large Value	9.26	17.34	0.732	0.505	8.507 (13)	0.359 (13)	0.736 (13)
Janus Twenty	JAVLX	Large Growth	-4.52	23.10	1.127	0.675	-6.691 (30)	-0.327 (30)	-0.294 (30)
Kemper Dreman High Rtn	KDHBX	Large Value	5.96	18.14	0.702	0.428	4.176 (17)	0.162 (18)	0.452 (21)
Scudder Dynamic Growth	KSCAX	Mid Growth	-0.20	37.96	1.355	0.364	-2.379 (26)	-0.085 (25)	0.133 (26)
Lazard Mid Cap	LZMIX	Mid Blend	10.79	16.16	0.774	0.654	10.033 (10)	0.481 (9)	0.877[a] (10)
Morgan Stanley Small Value	MCVAX	Small Blend	4.42	4.34	0.794	0.438	1.756 (22)	0.321 (14)	0.627 (16)
Munder Mid Cap Select	MGOYX	Mid Growth	14.94	18.74	0.881	0.633	13.522 (8)	0.636 (7)	1.254[a] (4)
Numeric Investors Mid Cap	NIGVX	Mid Blend	7.01	17.53	0.874	0.705	4.555 (16)	0.227 (17)	0.591 (18)
Neuberger Berman Partners	NPRTX	Large Blend	1.64	17.95	0.977	0.840	-1.416 (24)	-0.077 (24)	0.174 (24)

(continued)

Exhibit 25.6 | **Performance Measures for 30 Selected Mutual Funds (continued)**

Fund	Ticker	Style Class	Average Annual Rate of Return	Standard Deviation	Beta	R^2	Treynor	Sharpe	Jensen (1 Factor)
Wells Fargo Small Cap Op	NVSOX	Small Growth	14.43	17.27	0.812	0.631	14.043 (7)	0.660 (6)	1.191[a] (6)
PIMCO OpCap Value	PDLIX	Large Value	13.05	21.14	0.955	0.582	10.502 (9)	0.474 (10)	1.119[a] (8)
One Group Small Growth	PGSGX	Small Growth	8.44	22.26	0.841	0.407	6.436 (14)	0.243 (15)	0.701 (14)
T. Rowe Price Small Value	PRSVX	Small Value	15.80	13.58	0.518	0.412	24.658 (2)	0.941 (2)	1.218[a] (5)
RS Partners	RSPFX	Small Blend	21.38	17.61	0.596	0.325	30.816 (1)	1.043 (1)	1.706[a] (2)
Royce Premier	RYPRX	Small Blend	14.43	15.41	0.701	0.588	16.264 (5)	0.740 (5)	1.158[a] (7)
Strong Large Growth	SLGIX	Large Growth	7.26	18.12	0.869	0.656	4.870 (15)	0.233 (16)	0.610 (17)
State Street Research Alpha	SSEBX	Mid Value	11.30	19.97	0.892	0.569	9.277 (11)	0.415 (12)	0.954 (9)
TCW Galileo	TGDVX	Large Value	5.44	16.90	0.841	0.702	2.875 (21)	0.143 (20)	0.451 (22)
Tweedy, Browne American	TWEBX	Mid Value	3.21	12.01	0.495	0.483	0.371 (23)	0.015 (23)	0.162 (25)
Van Kampen Mid Growth	VGRAX	Mid Growth	6.88	27.27	1.091	0.457	3.527 (18)	0.141 (21)	0.644 (15)
Vanguard Primecap	VPMCX	Large Blend	6.23	20.67	1.052	0.737	3.041 (20)	0.155 (19)	0.578 (20)
JPMorgan Mid Cap Equity	VSNGX	Mid Blend	10.44	16.42	0.837	0.740	8.858 (12)	0.451 (11)	0.866[a] (12)
Average Fund			8.04	18.99	0.865	0.584	7.087	0.294	0.683
S&P 500			-0.53	16.83	1.000	1.000	-3.558	-0.211	0.000
90-day T-bill rate			3.03	0.59					

[a]Significant at the 0.05 level.

Exhibit 25.7	Information Ratios for 30 Funds

Fund	Alpha	Standard Error	IR	Annualized IR	Rank
AllianceBerstein Growth	−0.220	2.64	−0.083	−0.288	(29)
American Century Sm Val	1.381	3.29	0.420	1.455	(1)
Buffalo Small Cap	1.939	5.63	0.344	1.192	(8)
Corbin Small Cap Value	0.584	6.48	0.090	0.312	(22)
Aim Constellation	0.186	3.90	0.048	0.165	(25)
Dreyfus Appreciation	−0.045	1.66	−0.027	−0.093	(27)
Fidelity Magellan	−0.106	0.69	−0.155	−0.537	(30)
Goldman Sachs Mid Value	0.874	3.35	0.261	0.904	(11)
Hotchkis & Wiley Lrg Val	0.736	3.57	0.206	0.715	(14)
Janus Twenty	−0.294	3.85	−0.076	−0.265	(28)
Kemper Dreman High Rtn	0.452	3.99	0.113	0.393	(20)
Scudder Dynamic Growth	0.133	8.82	0.015	0.052	(26)
Lazard Mid Cap	0.877	2.77	0.317	1.097	(9)
Morgan Stanley Small Value	0.627	4.43	0.142	0.491	(18)
Munder Mid Cap Select	1.254	3.30	0.380	1.315	(6)
Numeric Investors Mid Cap	0.591	2.78	0.213	0.737	(13)
Neuberger Berman Partners	0.174	2.10	0.083	0.288	(23)
Wells Fargo Small Cap Op	1.191	3.05	0.390	1.352	(5)
PIMCO OpCap Value	1.119	3.98	0.281	0.974	(10)
One Group Small Growth	0.701	5.00	0.140	0.485	(19)
T. Rowe Price Small Value	1.218	3.04	0.400	1.387	(4)
RS Partners	1.706	4.22	0.404	1.401	(2)
Royce Premier	1.158	2.89	0.401	1.389	(3)
Strong Large Growth	0.610	3.09	0.197	0.683	(15)
State Street Research Alpha	0.954	3.82	0.250	0.866	(12)
TCW Galileo	0.451	2.70	0.167	0.579	(17)
Tweedy, Browne American	0.162	2.52	0.064	0.223	(24)
Van Kampen Mid Growth	0.644	5.85	0.110	0.382	(21)
Vanguard Primecap	0.578	3.09	0.187	0.648	(16)
JPMorgan Mid Cap Equity	0.866	2.44	0.355	1.229	(7)
Mean	0.683	3.631	0.188	0.651	
Median	0.636	3.296	0.192	0.666	

calculated by dividing its alpha (0.610) by its regression standard error (3.09). This statistic is then annualized to 0.683 by multiplying the monthly *IR* by the square root of 12. Notice that 26 of the 30 funds had positive *IR* levels, which follows directly from the number of funds that had a positive value for Jensen's alpha measure. The mean annualized *IR* for the sample was 0.651, which exceeded the Grinold-Kahn standard of 0.500 for "good" performance. Thus, on average, even after accounting for tracking error costs, this collection of funds adds substantial value to its investors.

Potential Bias of One-Parameter Measures   Friend and Blume (1970) pointed out that, theoretically, the composite measures of performance should be independent of alternative measures of risk because they are *risk-adjusted* measures. An analysis of the relationship between the composite measures of performance and two measures of risk (standard deviation and beta) for 200 random portfolios from the NYSE indicated a significant *inverse* relationship (the risk-adjusted performance of low-risk portfolios was better than the comparable performance for high-risk portfolios).

Subsequently, Klemkosky (1973) examined the relationship between composite performance measures and risk measures using actual mutual fund data in contrast to the random portfolio data used by Friend and Blume. Beyond the preceding risk-adjusted performance measures, the author derived two statistics that computed the excess return above the risk-free rate relative to the semistandard deviation and relative to the mean absolute deviation as risk measures. The results indicated a *positive* bias—that is, a *positive* relationship between the composite performance measures and the risk involved. This was especially true for the Treynor and Jensen measures. The performance measures that used the mean absolute deviation and the semistandard deviation as risk proxies were less biased than the three standard performance measures. He concluded that although a bias might exist, one could not be certain of its direction. More recently, Leland (1999) has shown that alpha can be biased downward for those portfolios designed to limit downside risk.

Measuring Performance with Multiple Risk Factors   Equation 25.5 showed how the Jensen composite measure could be estimated relative to multifactor models of risk and expected return. Exhibit 25.8 shows the Jensen measures calculated for the 30 mutual funds compared to the Fama-French three-factor model discussed at length in Chapter 9.[5] The form of this estimation equation is

$$R_{jt} - RFR_t = \alpha_j + [b_{j1}(R_{mt} - RFR_t) + b_{j2}SMB_t + b_{j3}HML_t] + e_{jt}$$

where, in addition to the excess return on the market portfolio, two additional common risk factors are included: *SMB,* based on the return differential between portfolios of small-cap and large-cap stocks, and *HML,* based on the return differential between portfolios of stocks with high book-to-market ratios (i.e., "value" stocks) and low book-to-market ratios (i.e., growth stocks).

The performance results in Exhibits 25.6 and 25.7 show that the vast majority of the active mutual fund managers in the sample were able to outperform the market on a risk-adjusted basis over the July 1999–June 2004 period. However, it is possible that some of this superior performance was an illusion, because the S&P 500 index was not the appropriate benchmark for many of the portfolios. In fact, the style classifications for the 30 funds in Exhibit 25.6 show that only four portfolios followed the large-cap blend style, the category for which the S&P 500 index applies. Thus, the advantage of measuring a fund's alpha using Equation 25.5 is that it is designed to control for both market (i.e., R_m) and style (i.e., *SMB* and *HML*) risk influences.

Although not listed in Exhibit 25.8, the average annual returns (i.e., risk premia) for the *SMB* and *HML* factors were 0.08 percent and 0.52 percent, respectively. This indicates that in the stock market as a whole over the July 1999 to June 2004 investment period, small stocks outperformed large stocks (i.e., a positive mean *SMB* return) and value stocks outperformed

---

[5]See Fama and French (1993). Also, the data for this analysis came from Professor Kenneth French's Web site at http://mba.tuck.dartmouth.edu/pages/faculty/ken.french.

| Exhibit 25.8 | Performance Measures for 30 Funds Using a Three-Factor Model |

Fund	Style Class	FACTOR BETAS			Jensen Alpha (3-Factor)	Rank
		R_m-RFR	SMB	HML		
AGRYX	Large Growth	1.126	0.241	−0.071	−0.447	(29)
ASVIX	Small Value	0.629	0.423	0.377	0.723[a]	(4)
BUFSX	Small Growth	0.874	1.061	0.118	0.715	(6)
CORBX	Small Value	0.975	0.852	0.176	−0.441	(28)
CSTGX	Large Growth	1.181	0.398	−0.371	−0.061	(23)
DGAGX	Large Blend	0.739	−0.247	0.014	0.219	(19)
FMAGX	Large Blend	0.994	0.029	−0.064	−0.105	(25)
GCMAX	Mid Value	0.590	0.033	0.355	0.656	(7)
HWLIX	Large Value	0.751	−0.034	0.483	0.526	(13)
JAVLX	Large Growth	1.106	0.103	−0.437	−0.183	(27)
KDHBX	Large Value	0.723	−0.133	0.381	0.403	(14)
KSCAX	Mid Growth	1.270	1.093	−0.675	−0.719	(30)
LZMIX	Mid Blend	0.768	0.211	0.166	0.561	(9)
MCVAX	Small Blend	0.751	0.685	−0.125	−0.061	(24)
MGOYX	Mid Growth	0.861	0.245	−0.177	1.076[a]	(1)
NIGVX	Mid Blend	0.860	0.246	−0.008	0.325	(16)
NPRTX	Large Blend	0.975	0.194	0.243	−0.163	(26)
NVSOX	Small Growth	0.791	0.405	0.056	0.718[a]	(5)
PDLIX	Large Value	0.973	−0.026	0.476	0.903[a]	(3)
PGSGX	Small Growth	0.793	0.707	−0.230	0.043	(21)
PRSVX	Small Value	0.496	0.531	0.212	0.527	(12)
RSPFX	Small Blend	0.572	0.601	0.276	0.905	(2)
RYPRX	Small Blend	0.686	0.438	0.256	0.547	(10)
SLGIX	Large Growth	0.848	0.192	−0.271	0.539	(11)
SSEBX	Mid Value	0.891	0.305	0.449	0.389	(15)
TGDVX	Large Value	0.844	0.134	0.318	0.141	(20)
TWEBX	Mid Value	0.504	−0.004	0.255	0.036	(22)
VGRAX	Mid Growth	1.040	0.562	−0.575	0.323	(17)
VPMCX	Large Blend	1.028	0.367	−0.104	0.230	(18)
VSNGX	Mid Blend	0.821	0.252	−0.054	0.618[a]	(8)
	Mean	0.849	0.329	0.048	0.298	

[a]Significant at the 0.05 level.

growth stocks (i.e., a positive mean *HML* return). For this particular collection of 30 funds, the mean factor betas—0.849 for the market factor, 0.329 for the *SMB* factor, and 0.048 for the *HML* factor—indicate that the average fund has less systematic market risk than average and is oriented toward holding smaller and more value-oriented stocks.

Exhibit 25.9 | **Correlations between Alternative Portfolio Performance Measures**

	Treynor	Sharpe	Jensen (1-Factor)	Jensen (3-Factor)	Information Ratio
Treynor	—				
Sharpe	0.978	—			
Jensen (1-Factor)	0.967	0.970	—		
Jensen (3-Factor)	0.883	0.869	0.868	—	
Information Ratio	0.953	0.969	0.939	0.885	—

The Jensen alpha results for the three-factor model show some important differences with the comparable findings from the one-factor model reported in Exhibit 25.6. In particular, the mean value for alpha, while still positive, is now less than half as big as before (0.298 vs. 0.683). Also, 22 (rather than 26) of the funds had positive alpha values, but only 5 (rather than 11) of the funds with positive alphas had statistically significant outperformance. For instance, BUFSX, a small-cap growth fund, had a dramatic and significant alpha of 1.939 when its performance was measured relative to a large-cap blend index (i.e., S&P 500), but relative to a model that takes investment style into account, its alpha was reduced to 0.715. This highlights the fact that the one-factor and three-factor Jensen measures produce similar but distinct performance rankings and should therefore be considered as different from one another as the Sharpe and Treynor measures.

Relationship between Performance Measures Exhibit 25.9 contains the matrix of rank correlation coefficients between the Treynor, Sharpe, Jensen (both one-factor and three-factor), and Information Ratio measures. The striking feature of the display is that all of these statistics are positively correlated with one another, but not perfectly so. This suggests that, although the measures provide a generally consistent assessment of portfolio performance when taken as a whole, they remain distinct at an individual level. This reinforces our earlier point that it is best to consider these composites collectively and that the user must understand what each means.

PORTFOLIO PERFORMANCE EVALUATION: SOME EXTENSIONS

In this section, we will consider four extensions of the basic performance measurement "toolkit" that we have just developed: (1) an additional composite performance measure that takes the portfolio's diversification level into account; (2) techniques that focus on the portfolio's holdings rather than its returns; (3) attribution analysis, which attempts to establish why a portfolio manager's portfolio performed the way that it did; and (4) measuring market timing skills.

Components of Investment Performance

Following the work of Treynor, Sharpe, and Jensen, Fama (1972) suggested a somewhat finer breakdown of performance. The basic premise for Fama's technique is that *overall performance* of a portfolio, which is its return in excess of the risk-free rate, can be decomposed into measures of risk-taking and security selection skill. That is,

$$\text{Overall Performance} = \text{Excess Return} = \text{Portfolio Risk} + \text{Selectivity}$$

Notice that the *selectivity* component represents the portion of the portfolio's actual return beyond that available to an unmanaged portfolio with identical systematic risk. Thus, this selectivity measure is used to assess the manager's investment prowess.

Evaluating Selectivity   Formally, you can measure the return due to selectivity as follows:

$$\text{Selectivity} = R_a - R_x(\beta_a)$$

where:

R_a = the actual return on the portfolio being evaluated
$R_x(\beta_a)$ = the return on the combination of the riskless asset and the market portfolio M that has risk β_x equal to β_a, the risk of the portfolio being evaluated

As shown in Exhibit 25.10, selectivity measures the vertical distance between the actual return and the *ex post* market line and is quite similar to Treynor's measure.

As already noted, you can examine overall performance in terms of selectivity and the returns from assuming risk as follows:

25.7 $$\text{Overall Performance} = \text{Selectivity} + \text{Risk}$$
$$[R_a - RFR] = [R_a - R_x(\beta_a)] + [R_x(\beta_a) - RFR]$$

Exhibit 25.10 shows that overall performance is the total return above the risk-free return and includes the return that *should* have been received for accepting the portfolio risk (β_a).

Exhibit 25.10 | **An Illustration of the Performance Measures**

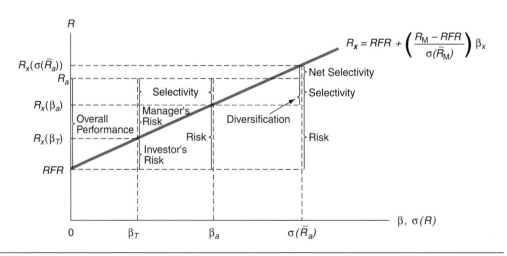

Source: Eugene F. Fama, "Components of Investment Performance," *Journal of Finance* 27, no. 3 (June 1972): 588. Reprinted with permission of Blackwell Publishing.

This expected return for accepting risk (β_a) is equal to $[R_x(\beta_a) - RFR]$. Any excess over this expected return is due to selectivity.

Evaluating Diversification The selectivity component in Equation 25.7 can also be broken down into two parts. If a portfolio manager attempts to select undervalued stocks and in the process gives up some diversification, it is possible to measure the added return necessary to justify this diversification decision. The portfolio's *gross selectivity* is made up of *net selectivity* plus *diversification* as follows:

$$\overbrace{R_a - R_x(\beta_a)}^{\text{Selectivity}} = \text{Net Selectivity} + \overbrace{[R_x(\sigma\,(R_a)) - R_x(\beta_a)]}^{\text{Diversification}}$$

or

25.8
$$\text{Net Selectivity} = R_a - R_x(\beta_a) - \overbrace{[R_x(\sigma\,(R_a)) - R_x(\beta_a)]}^{\text{Selectivity} - \text{Diversification}}$$
$$= R_a - R_x(\sigma\,(R_a))$$

where:

$R_x(\sigma\,(R_a)) =$ the return on the combination of the riskless asset and the market portfolio that has return dispersion equivalent to that of the portfolio being evaluated

Therefore, the diversification measure in Equation 25.8 indicates the *added return* required to justify any loss of diversification in the portfolio. The term emphasizes that diversification is the elimination of all unsystematic variability. If the portfolio is completely diversified so that total risk (σ) is equal to systematic risk (β), then the $R_x(\sigma\,(R_a))$ would be the same as $R_x(\beta_a)$, and the diversification term would equal zero.

Because the diversification measure always is nonnegative, net selectivity will always be equal to or less than gross selectivity. The two will be equal when the portfolio is completely diversified. If the investor is not concerned with the diversification of the portfolio, this particular breakdown will not be important, and only selectivity will be considered.[6]

Example of Fama Performance Measure Suppose that over a recent five-year investment period you observed that the average annual return on the market portfolio (e.g., S&P 500 index) and the risk-free security were 22.96 percent and 5.28 percent, respectively. Thus, an investment portfolio with a beta of 0.815 would be expected to deliver a return of 19.69 percent [= 5.28 + 0.815 (22.96 − 5.28)]. Suppose further, however, that this portfolio actually returned 19.67 percent per annum. The return for *selectivity* is the difference between the actual excess performance (19.67 − 5.28 = 14.39) and the required excess return for risk of 14.41 (= 19.69 − 5.28). Thus, this fund had an average annual return of −0.02 for selectivity, indicating the manager fell slightly short of matching expectations consistent with the actual risk level of the portfolio.

What if the manager in this example also did not fully diversify the portfolio? Assume, in fact, that the standard deviations on the market and the manager's portfolio were 14.95 percent and 13.41 percent, respectively. In this case, the ratio of total risk in the portfolio per unit of market total risk is 0.897 (= 13.41/14.95), but since the manager's beta (0.815) is less than this it appears that the portfolio contained elements of unsystematic risk. Recalling that beta is

---

[6]Modigliani and Modigliani (1997) present a performance measure (dubbed M²) that is a variation of both the Sharpe measure and Fama's $R_x[\sigma(R_a)]$ component.

defined as the total risk ratio multiplied by the correlation between the portfolio and the market [$0.815 = (13.41/14.95) \times r_{p,m}$], the manager's level of diversification is captured by an R^2 coefficient of 0.82. Thus, the selectivity measure of -0.02 understates the true performance shortfall.

To adjust the selectivity measure for the lack of complete diversification in the portfolio, notice that the fund's required return given its standard deviation is 21.14 [$= 5.28 + 0.897 (22.96 - 5.28)$]. The difference of 1.45 ($= 21.14 - 19.69$) between the required returns using total versus systematic risk is the added return required because of less-than-perfect diversification. This increment is subtracted from the selectivity measure to create the manager's *net selectivity* performance of -1.47 ($= -0.02 - 1.45$). This indicates that, after accounting for the added cost of incomplete diversification, this manager's performance would plot substantially below the market line in Exhibit 25.10.

Holdings-Based Performance Measurement

Although they differ in fundamentals ways, each of the conventional performance measures just discussed are similar in that they are based on the returns produced by the investment portfolios being compared. In general, there are two distinct advantages to assessing performance based on investment returns. First, whether calculated gross or net of management fees, returns are usually easy for the investor to observe on a frequent (e.g., daily) basis. Second, they also represent the bottom line that the investor actually takes away from the portfolio manager's investing prowess. On the other hand, *returns-based* measures of performance are indirect indications of the decision-making ability of a manager in that they do not allow investors to understand the underlying reasons why the portfolio produced the returns it did.

As an alternative to relying exclusively on returns-based measures, it is also possible to view investment performance in terms of which securities the manager buys or sells from the portfolio. By looking at how the portfolio's holdings change over time, the investor is able to not only asses how the portfolio fared relative to a particular index, but also establish precisely which stock or bond positions were responsible for creating that performance. Thus, when investors can observe how the contents of a professionally managed portfolio change over time, using a **holdings-based measure** can provide additional insights about the quality of their portfolio manager than would be possible using just the returns-based statistics. Two of the most popular holdings-based performance measures are described below.

Grinblatt-Titman (GT) Performance Measure   Grinblatt and Titman (1993) were among the first to assess the quality of the services provided by money managers by looking at adjustments they made to the contents of their portfolios. Assuming that the investor knows the exact investment proportions of each security position in the portfolio on two consecutive reporting dates (e.g., quarterly reports for mutual funds), the manager's security selection ability can be established by how he adjusted these weights. Specifically, for a particular reporting period t, their performance measure is:

25.9
$$GT_t = \sum_j (w_{jt} - w_{jt-1}) R_{jt}$$

where:

(w_{jt}, w_{jt-1}) = the portfolio weights for the jth security at the beginning of Period t and Period $t - 1$, respectively,

R_{jt} = the return to the jth security during Period t, which begins on Date $t - 1$ and ends on Date t.

Grinblatt and Titman then recommend that a series of GT_t for a manager can be averaged over several periods to create a better indication of the on-going quality of his decision-making ability.

$$\text{Average GT} = \frac{\sum_t GT_t}{T}$$

where T is the total number of investment periods used in the evaluation.

Exhibit 25.11 illustrates how the GT performance measure is calculated for two different portfolios: (1) a passive value-weighted index of all the stocks in the market, and (2) an active portfolio manager. For simplicity, the example assumes that the entire investable universe consists of five different stocks. Panel A shows the share prices for each security on six different dates relative to the current Date 0. Assuming that no dividends are paid, the returns to each stock position are also shown for the four full holding periods starting at Date 0 (e.g., Period 1 begins at Date 0 and ends at Date 1).

Panel B shows the total shares outstanding for each of the five stocks on Date −1, Date 0, Date 1, Date 2, and Date 3, which are the beginning dates for Period 0, Period 1, Period 2, Period 3, and Period 4, respectively. In this example, the shares outstanding for each security are assumed to be stable. Alongside the shares outstanding in Panel B are the corresponding index weights that would apply at the beginning of each investment period. For instance, the index weight shown for Stock A at the beginning of Period 2 (i.e., w_2) is 28.0 percent, which is calculated by multiplying the share price at Date 1 (i.e., $14) by the shares outstanding at Date 1 (i.e., 200) and then dividing that product by the total market value of all five stocks at Date 1 (i.e., [200 × 14] + ... + [200 × 10] = $10,000). Notice that as the share prices change over time, the value-based index weights for the five stocks will also change even though the number of shares outstanding do not.

Panel C provides similar shareholding and investment weight data for a hypothetical active portfolio manager whose performance is to be assessed using the GT measure. Of particular interest in this example is the fact that this manager has made two explicit adjustments to his portfolio holdings. First, on Date 0 (i.e., the beginning of Period 1), he has sold half of his share positions in Stocks B and C in order to buy 10 shares of Stock A. Second, on Date 2 (i.e., the beginning of Period 3), he sells the remainder of his Stock B holding to repurchase five shares of Stock C. As a consequence, the portfolio weights of this active manager change over time because of both explicit stock trades and implicit adjustments due to changing market prices.

The last panel of Exhibit 25.11 calculates the GT measure for both the stock index and the active manager. For the index, the average GT across the four investment periods is virtually zero (i.e., −0.03 percent = [0.00 − 0.57 + 0.18 + 0.29]/4). This should be the case for any passive buy-and-hold portfolio, assuming that the stock returns are not correlated from one period to the next. That is, while index weights will vary with stock prices (e.g., $w_2 - w_1 = 0.280 - 0.200 = 0.080$, for Stock A), the product of these weight changes with the subsequent stock returns should net out over time if there is no momentum effect present in the returns. This is consistent with Grinblatt and Titman's interpretation of the GT measure as the return to a zero-cost hedge portfolio that is long at the current investment weights and short at the previous weights.

In contrast, the GT measure for an active portfolio manager will likely not be zero. In this example, the manager's average GT value is 3.41 percent [= (15.00 − 0.71 − 0.97 + 0.34)/4], indicating that the manager added a substantial amount of value through his stock-picking prowess. To see this, notice that in Period 1, the decision to buy Stock A at Date 0, whose price subsequently rose, contributed 10.00 percent [= (0.250 − 0.000) × 40%] whereas the decisions to

Exhibit 25.11 | Holdings-Based Performance Measurement with the GT Method

A. Stock Market Data

| | SHARE PRICE ($): | | | | | | RETURN (%): | | | |
Stock	Date -1	Date 0	Date 1	Date 2	Date 3	Date 4	Period 1	Period 2	Period 3	Period 4
A	10	10	14	13	13	14	40.00	-7.14	0.00	7.69
B	10	10	8	8	8	6	-20.00	0.00	0.00	-25.00
C	10	10	8	8	7	6	-20.00	0.00	-12.50	-14.29
D	10	10	10	11	12	12	0.00	10.00	9.09	0.00
E	10	10	10	10	10	10	0.00	0.00	0.00	0.00

B. Value-Weighted Index Holding Data

| | SHARES OUTSTANDING ON: | | | | | INDEX WEIGHT (w_{jt}) AT BEGINNING OF: | | | | |
Stock	Date -1	Date 0	Date 1	Date 2	Date 3	Period 0	Period 1	Period 2	Period 3	Period 4
A	200	200	200	200	200	0.200	0.200	0.280	0.260	0.260
B	200	200	200	200	200	0.200	0.200	0.160	0.160	0.160
C	200	200	200	200	200	0.200	0.200	0.160	0.160	0.140
D	200	200	200	200	200	0.200	0.200	0.200	0.220	0.240
E	200	200	200	200	200	0.200	0.200	0.200	0.200	0.200

C. Active Manager Holding Data

| | SHARES HELD ON: | | | | | PORTFOLIO WEIGHT (w_{jt}) AT BEGINNING OF: | | | | |
Stock	Date -1	Date 0	Date 1	Date 2	Date 3	Period 0	Period 1	Period 2	Period 3	Period 4
A	0	10	10	10	10	0.000	0.250	0.333	0.310	0.310
B	10	5	5	0	0	0.250	0.125	0.095	0.000	0.000
C	10	5	5	10	10	0.250	0.125	0.095	0.190	0.167
D	10	10	10	10	10	0.250	0.250	0.238	0.262	0.286
E	10	10	10	10	10	0.250	0.250	0.238	0.238	0.238

(continued)

Exhibit 25.11 | Holdings-Based Performance Measurement with the GT Method (continued)

D. Calculation of GT Measure

INDEX:

Stock	$(w_1 - w_0) \times R_1$	$(w_2 - w_1) \times R_2$	$(w_3 - w_2) \times R_3$	$(w_4 - w_3) \times R_4$
A	0.00	−0.57	0.00	0.00
B	0.00	0.00	0.00	0.00
C	0.00	0.00	0.00	0.29
D	0.00	0.00	0.18	0.00
E	0.00	0.00	0.00	0.00
GT_t:	0.00%	−0.57%	0.18%	0.29%
Average GT:	−0.03%			

ACTIVE MANAGER:

Stock	$(w_1 - w_0) \times R_1$	$(w_2 - w_1) \times R_2$	$(w_3 - w_2) \times R_3$	$(w_4 - w_3) \times R_4$
A	10.00	−0.59	0.00	0.00
B	2.50	0.00	0.00	0.00
C	2.50	0.00	−1.19	0.34
D	0.00	−0.12	0.22	0.00
E	0.00	0.00	0.00	0.00
GT_t:	15.00%	−0.71%	−0.97%	0.34%
Average GT:	3.41%			

sell some of Stocks B and C contributed 2.50 percent each [= $(0.125 - 0.250) \times -20\%$] since both stocks declined in value during Period 1. On the other hand, the decision to repurchase Stock C on Date 2 subtracted 1.19 percent of value [= $(0.190 - 0.095) \times -12.5\%$] since the price of these shares fell from \$8 to \$7 during Period 3. Overall, though, the manager's portfolio adjustments had a net positive outcome for the investor.

One of the main advantages of the GT measure that this example demonstrates is that it is possible to create a very detailed analysis of how each decision the manager made contributed to his overall performance. Additionally, the GT statistic can be computed without reference to any specific benchmark, which was not the case for returns-based measures such as the Information Ratio. However, one shortcoming of the GT measure is that it fails to reward or penalize the manager for portfolio adjustments where the share price change actually occurs in a later period. For instance, the manager received no credit in Period 3 for the decision to sell Stock B because the subsequent share price decline from \$8 to \$6 did not occur until Period 4. Grinblatt and Titman recommend that this deficiency can be overcome by calculating portfolio weight adjustments over longer holding periods (e.g., annual vs. quarterly).

Characteristic Selectivity (CS) Performance Measure   One of the potential limitations of the GT measure is that it does not control directly for changes in either risk or investment style that result from a manager's decision to revise her portfolio holdings. For instance, if a manager sells a less risky stock in order to buy a more risky one, she should be rewarded with higher gross returns over time, but not necessarily higher risk-adjusted returns. Similarly, the GT measure does not distinguish between stocks that perform well because of security-specific factors and those that merely benefit from broader phenomena, such as price momentum effects. Daniel et al. (1997) developed an alternative holdings-based performance measure that compares the returns of each stock held in an actively managed portfolio to the return of a benchmark portfolio that has the same aggregate investment characteristics as the security in question. Specifically, their *characteristic selectivity* (CS) performance measure is given by:

25.10
$$CS_t = \sum_j w_{jt}(R_{jt} - R_{Bjt})$$

where, in addition to the earlier notation, R_{Bjt} is the Period t (i.e., from Date $t - 1$ to Date t) return to a passive portfolio whose investment characteristics are matched at the beginning of Period t with those of Stock j. Comparable to the GT measure, a series of periodic CS_t values for a particular portfolio can be averaged to indicate the manager's ability to pick specific stocks within the context of a larger investment style mandate:

$$\text{Average CS} = \frac{\sum_t CS_t}{T}$$

The CS measure credits the active manager whenever she holds a stock in the portfolio that outperforms a style-matched index investment and penalizes the manager when the opposite is true. The implicit assumption underlying this calculation is that, in lieu of hiring the active manager, investors could always purchase an indexed product (e.g., a mutual fund or exchange-traded fund) with equivalent investment characteristics. Thus, the true test of the active manager's skill is whether she can pick a sufficient number of specific stocks that outperform portfolios that investors could have formed for themselves.

The major obstacle to implementing the CS performance measure is identifying a broad enough set of benchmark portfolios to match the risk and style characteristics of every stock that an active manager might want to hold. Daniel et al. (1997) proposed forming 125 different

Exhibit 25.12	Comparison of GT, CS, and Jensen Performance Measures

Investment Period	Number of Funds	Gross Return (%)	GT Measure (%)	CS Measure (%)	1-Factor Jensen (%)	4-Factor Jensen (%)
1975–1979	214	21.33	2.06[a]	1.58[b]	2.78[b]	1.44
1980–1984	508	16.31	2.10[b]	0.79	0.62	0.98
1984–1989	786	20.07	1.79[b]	0.33	−0.80	0.83
1990–1994	1,973	10.26	1.86[b]	0.45	−0.16	−0.36
1975–1994	—	16.99	1.94[a]	0.79[b]	0.60	0.39

[a]Significant at the 0.01 level.
[b]Significant at the 0.05 level.

Source: Kent Daniel, Mark Grinblatt, Sheridan Titman, and Russ Wermers, "Measuring Mutual Fund Performance with Characteristic Benchmarks," *Journal of Finance* 52, no. 3 (July 1997). Reprinted with permission of Blackwell Publishing.

passive portfolios, based on three investment characteristics that past research has shown to be significant components of the systematic risk of a firm: (1) market capitalization (i.e., size), (2) book-to-market ratio, and (3) stock price momentum. At the beginning of each investment period, they created their benchmarks by taking every stock listed on the NYSE, AMEX, and Nasdaq exchanges and using a $5 \times 5 \times 5$ sorting procedure that categorized the securities into quintiles based first on size, then on book-to-market ratios, and finally on price momentum. The benchmark returns (i.e., R_{Bjt}) were then calculated as value-weighted averages of all of the stocks contained in that particular portfolio. Using this method, the appropriate characteristic-matched benchmark for any given stock position is simply the one that contains that stock.

Exhibit 25.12 summarizes the results of a performance evaluation Daniel et al. (1997) performed on almost 2,000 mutual funds with a diverse set of investment objectives using port-folio holdings and return data from 1975 to 1994. They compared four different measures of performance: (1) GT, (2) CS, (3) one-factor Jensen, and (4) four-factor Jensen.[7] The display shows the average annualized values of each performance measure over the entire investment period as well as over several subperiods. Perhaps the most interesting finding is that the GT measure, which captures the net benefit of the broad range of trading strategies employed by active fund managers, showed that the average fund added an average of 1.94 percent of value per year over the 20-year horizon. However, the CS measure—which is specifically designed to control for momentum, size, and value-versus-growth effects—shows that the benefit provided by just the manager's security selection skills accounted for less than half of this amount (i.e., 0.79 percent per year). Both of the returns-based Jensen performance measures were also positive, but they were statistically insignificant.

Performance Attribution Analysis

As noted earlier, portfolio managers can add value to their investors in either of two ways: selecting superior securities or demonstrating superior market timing skills by allocating funds to different asset classes or market segments. **Attribution analysis** attempts to distinguish which of these factors is the source of the portfolio's overall performance. Specifically,

---

[7]Recall from Chapter 9 that the four-factor characteristic-based model of Carhart (1997) supplements the three-factor model of Fama and French (1993) with a price momentum factor.

this method compares the total return to the manager's actual investment holdings to the return for a predetermined benchmark portfolio and decomposes the difference into an *allocation effect* and a *selection effect*. The most straightforward way to measure these two effects is as follows:

25.11
$$\text{Allocation Effect} = \Sigma_i[(w_{ai} - w_{pi}) \times (R_{pi} - R_p)]$$
$$\text{Selection Effect} = \Sigma_i[(w_{ai}) \times (R_{ai} - R_{pi})]$$

where:

w_{ai}, w_{pi} = the investment proportions given to the *i*th *market segment* (e.g., asset class, industry group) in the manager's actual portfolio and the benchmark portfolio, respectively

R_{ai}, R_{pi} = the investment return to the *i*th market segment in the manager's actual portfolio and the benchmark portfolio, respectively

R_p = the total return to the benchmark portfolio

With Equation 25.11, the allocation effect measures the manager's decision to over- or underweight a particular market segment (i.e., $[w_{ai} - w_{pi}]$) in terms of that segment's return performance relative to the overall return to the benchmark (i.e., $[R_{pi} - R_p]$). Good timing skill is therefore a matter of investing more money in those market segments that end up producing greater than average returns. The selection effect measures the manager's ability to form specific market segment portfolios that generate superior returns relative to the way in which the comparable market segment is defined in the benchmark portfolio (i.e., $[R_{ai} - R_{pi}]$), weighted by the manager's actual market segment investment proportions. When constructed in this manner, the manager's total value-added performance is the sum of the allocation and selection effects.[8]

An Example   Consider an investor whose top-down portfolio strategy consists of two dimensions. First, he decides on a broad allocation of his investment dollars across three asset classes: U.S. stocks, U.S. long-term bonds, and cash equivalents, such as U.S. Treasury bills or certificates of deposit. Once this judgment is made, the investor's second general decision is choosing which specific stocks, bonds, and cash instruments to buy. As a benchmark, he selects a hypothetical portfolio with a 60 percent allocation to the Standard and Poor's 500 index, a 30 percent investment in the Lehman Corporate Long Bond index, and a 10 percent allocation to three-month Treasury bills.

Suppose that at the start of the investment period, the investor believes equity values are somewhat inflated and is not optimistic about the near-term performance of the stock market. Compared to the benchmark, he therefore decides to underweight stocks and overweight bonds and cash in his actual portfolio. The investment proportions he chooses are 50 percent in equity, 38 percent in bonds, and 12 percent in cash. Further, instead of selecting a broad portfolio of equities, he decides to concentrate on the interest rate–sensitive sectors, such as utilities and financial companies, while deemphasizing the technology and consumer durables sectors. Finally, he resolves to buy shorter duration bonds of a higher credit quality than are contained in the benchmark bond index and to buy commercial paper rather than Treasury bills.

---

[8] Wainscott (1995) has argued that a better way to measure the selection effect is to multiply the market segment return differential by the benchmark for that segment, or $\Sigma_i[(w_{pi}) \times (R_{ai} - R_{pi})]$. A drawback of this approach, however, is that the allocation and selection effects no longer sum to the total value-added return. To balance the equation, he calculates an *interaction effect* as $\Sigma_i[(w_{ai} - w_{pi}) \times (R_{ai} - R_{pi})]$ to measure the residual performance.

Exhibit 25.13 | Asset Class Performance Attribution Analysis

	INVESTMENT WEIGHTS			RETURNS		
Asset Class	Actual	Benchmark	Excess	Actual	Benchmarck	Excess
Stock	0.50	0.60	−0.10	9.70%	8.60%	1.10%
Bonds	0.38	0.30	0.08	9.10	9.20	−0.10
Cash	0.12	0.10	0.02	5.60	5.40	0.20

In this example, the manager has made active investment decisions involving both the allocation of assets and the selection of individual securities. To determine if either (or both) of these decisions proved to be wise ones, at the end of the investment period he can calculate his overall and segment-specific performance. Exhibit 25.13 summarizes these hypothetical returns for the investor's actual and benchmark asset class portfolios as well as the investment weightings for each. The overall actual and benchmark returns can be computed as follows:

$$\text{Overall Actual Return} = (0.50 \times 0.097) + (0.38 \times 0.091) + (0.12 \times 0.056)$$
$$= 8.98\%$$

and

$$\text{Overall Benchmark Return} = (0.60 \times 0.086) + (0.30 \times 0.092) + (0.10 \times 0.054)$$
$$= 8.46\%$$

Thus, the manager beat the benchmark by 52 basis points ($= 0.0898 - 0.0846$) over this particular investment horizon.

The goal of attribution analysis is to isolate the reason for this value-added performance. The manager's allocation effect can be computed by multiplying the excess asset class weight by that class's relative investment performance:

$$[-0.10 \times (0.086 - 0.0846)] + [0.08 \times (0.092 - 0.0846)] + [0.02 \times (0.054 - 0.0846)] = -0.02\%$$

This shows that if the investor had made just his market timing decisions and not picked different securities than those represented in the benchmark, his performance would have lagged behind the target return by two basis points. This total allocation effect can be broken down further into an equity allocation return of −2 basis points [$= -0.10 \times (0.086 - 0.0846)$], a bond allocation return of 6 basis points [$= 0.08 \times (0.092 - 0.0846)$], and a cash allocation return of −6 basis points [$= 0.02 \times (0.054 - 0.0846)$]. Therefore, the decision to underweight stock and overweight cash (asset classes that generated returns above and below the benchmark, respectively) resulted in diminished performance that was more than enough to offset the benefit of emphasizing bonds.

Since the investor knows that he outperformed the benchmark overall, a negative allocation effect necessarily implies that he exhibited positive security selection skills. His selection effect can be computed as

$$[0.50 \times (0.097 - 0.086)] + [0.38 \times (0.091 - 0.092)] + [0.12 \times (0.056 - 0.054)] = 0.54\%$$

In this example, the investor formed superior stock and cash portfolios, although his bond selections did not perform quite as well as the Lehman Long Bond index. One important caveat in this analysis is that, because the returns are not risk-adjusted, it is possible that the asset class portfolios formed by the investor are riskier than their benchmark counterparts. If this is the case, which is almost certainly true for a cash portfolio that holds short-term corporate debt obligations instead of Treasury bills, the investor should expect a higher return that has nothing to do with his skill. Finally, notice that the investor's total incremental return of 52 basis points can be decomposed as

$$\text{Total Value Added} = \text{Allocation Effect} + \text{Selection Effect}$$
$$= -0.02\% + 0.54\% = 0.52\%$$

Using a procedure similar to the one just described, Brinson, Hood, and Beebower (1986) examined the return performance of a group of 91 large U.S. pension plans over the decade from 1974 to 1983. They established that the mean annual return for this sample was 9.01 percent, compared to 10.11 percent for their benchmark. Thus, they documented that active management cost the average plan 110 basis points of return per year. This "value subtracted" return increment consisted of a -77-basis-point allocation effect and a -33-basis-point selection effect. Further, they concluded that a plan's initial strategic asset allocation choice, rather than any of its active management decisions, was the primary determinant of portfolio performance. In a follow-up study, Brinson, Singer, and Beebower (1991) reached a similar conclusion for a different group of 82 pension plans over the 1977–1987 period. For this new sample, however, they showed that the total active return shortfall had fallen to -7 basis points, which was divided into an 18-basis-point selection effect and a -25-basis-point allocation effect.

Performance Attribution Extensions   Although the preceding example concentrated partly on an investor's ability to time broad asset class movements, the attribution methodology can be used to distinguish security selection skills from any of several other decisions that an investor might make. For instance, the manager of a broad-based, all-equity portfolio must decide what economic sectors (e.g., basic materials, consumer nondurables, transportation) to under- and overweight before she can choose her preferred companies in those sectors. In such cases, performance attribution analysis is still applicable, with a "sector rotation" effect replacing the market timing effect. To see how this might work, Exhibit 25.14 summarizes the performance of the growth-oriented stock portfolio managed by The MBA Investment Fund, L.L.C., a privately funded investment management company run by a group of graduate students at the University of Texas. During the time of this analysis, the managers were restricted to investing in U.S.-traded equities and ADRs only. Because the Fund's investment mandate was to beat the return on the Standard and Poor's 500, the managers had two basic decisions to make: which sectors to emphasize and which individual stocks to buy within those sectors.

Over the course of the year, the overall returns to the S&P 500 and the Fund were 29.63 percent and 29.54 percent, respectively. The second and third columns of Exhibit 25.14 document the actual and benchmark weights for the 10 economic sectors comprising the S&P 500 index, with the Fund's excess weightings (i.e., $[w_{ai} - w_{pi}]$) listed in the fourth column. The entries in the last column show the benchmark sector return relative to the overall S&P return (i.e., $[R_{pi} - R_p]$). Thus, the sector allocation effect can be calculated by summing the product of the entries in the last two columns:

$$(-0.0339 \times -0.1515) + (0.0703 \times -0.0331) + \cdots + (-0.0242 \times -0.1315) = -0.28\%$$

| Exhibit 25.14 | MBA Investment Fund Sector Performance Attribution Analysis |

	INVESTMENT WEIGHTS			EXCESS RETURNS
S&P 500 Sector	Actual	S&P 500	Excess	S&P Sector—Overall S&P
Basic materials	0.0331	0.0670	−0.0339	−15.15%
Capital equipment and technology	0.2544	0.1841	0.0703	−3.31
Consumer services	0.0208	0.0692	−0.0484	6.95
Consumer durables	0.0588	0.0353	0.0235	−21.34
Consumer nondurables	0.2752	0.2851	−0.0099	5.85
Energy	0.1170	0.0935	0.0235	−7.08
Financial	0.1619	0.1249	0.0370	7.15
Transportation	0.0199	0.0172	0.0027	−1.72
Utilities	0.0590	0.1000	−0.0410	1.91
Miscellaneous	0.0000	0.0242	−0.0242	−13.15

With an overall return difference of −9 basis points (= 0.2954 − 0.2963), this means that the Fund's managers generated a security selection effect of 19 basis points [= (−0.0009) − (−0.0028)]. Consequently, although the student managers virtually matched the strong performance of the entire stock market, it appears they were better at picking stocks than forecasting broader economic trends.

This general attribution analysis methodology has been extended to other specific asset classes as well. Kuberek (1995) showed that producing fixed-income attributions for bond portfolio managers is quite straightforward once the relevant decision variables have been specified. He noted that these decision variables might include allocations to different countries, foreign exchange effects, individual bond selections, and other risk factors, such as the portfolio's term structure positioning. Karnosky and Singer (1994) and Ankrim and Hensel (1994) have developed a comprehensive, unified framework for attributing performance in a global asset management context. In particular, they have added both active and hedged currency allocation returns to the single-currency attribution model of Brinson, Hood, and Beebower to allow for the intricacies of cross-border investing. In a comparison of the performance of one of their global investment portfolios relative to the MSCI World Equity Index during 1989, they demonstrated that the combined effect of the currency selection decision accounted for 563 basis points of the 7.66 percent return advantage that the portfolio enjoyed.

Measuring Market Timing Skills

As we saw in Chapter 16, tactical asset allocation (TAA) is a portfolio management strategy in which a manager attempts to produce active value-added returns solely through allocation decisions. Specifically, instead of trying to pick superior individual securities, TAA managers adjust their asset class exposures based on perceived changes in the relative valuations of those classes. A typical TAA fund shifts money between three asset classes—stocks, bonds, and cash equivalents—although many definitions of these categories (e.g., large cap versus small cap, value versus growth, long term versus short term) are used in practice. Of course, this means that the relevant performance measurement criterion for a TAA manager is how well he is able to time broad market movements. There are two reasons why attribution analysis is ill-suited for this task. First, by design, a TAA manager indexes his actual asset class investments and so the selection effect is not relevant. Second, a TAA approach to investing might entail dozens of changes to asset class weightings during an investment period, which could render meaningless an attribution effect computed on the average holdings. Because of these problems, many analysts consider a regression-based method for measuring timing skills to be a superior approach.

Weigel (1991) tested the market timing skills of a group of 17 U.S.-based managers using the TAA approach. His methodology was motivated by the pioneering work of Merton (1981) and Hendriksson and Merton (1981) and assumed that perfect market timing ability was equivalent to owning a lookback call option that pays at expiration the return to the best-performing asset class. That is, for any given Investment Period t, a manager with perfect market timing skills would have a return (R_{pt}) equal to

$$R_{pt} = RFR_t + \max[R_{st} - RFR_t, R_{bt} - RFR_t, 0]$$

where R_{st} and R_{bt} are the Period t returns to the stock and bond benchmark portfolios, respectively. Thus, controlling for stock and bond price movements in a manner comparable to Jensen's method, the following regression equation can be calculated:

$$(R_{pt} - RFR_t) = \alpha + \beta_b(R_{bt} - RFR_t) + \beta_s(R_{st} - RFR_t)$$
$$+ \gamma\{\max[R_{st} - RFR_t, R_{bt} - RFR_t, 0]\} + e_t$$

Weigel showed that the samplewide average value for γ, which measures the proportion of the perfect timing option that the TAA managers were able to capture, was 0.30. This value was statistically significant, meaning that this group of managers had reliable, although not perfect, market timing skills. He also demonstrated that the average alpha was -0.5 percent per quarter, indicating that these same managers had negative nonmarket timing skills (e.g., hedging strategies).

Many other studies have examined the market timing ability of portfolio managers who are not exclusively TAA practitioners. Several investigations, as typified by Kon (1983) and Chang and Lewellen (1984), concluded that mutual fund managers generally possess negative market timing skills. Coggin, Fabozzi, and Rahman (1993) carried this analysis further by looking at both the timing and selectivity skills of a group of U.S. equity pension fund managers. Using a regression-based model with monthly return data for an eight-year period, they demonstrated that their sample of managers possessed positive, but small, selection skills and negative timing skills. From these studies, it is reasonable to conclude that only those managers explicitly trying to time market movements have a chance of doing so.

FACTORS THAT AFFECT USE OF PERFORMANCE MEASURES

All the performance measures just described are only as good as their data inputs. You must be careful when computing the rates of return to take proper account of all inflows and outflows. More importantly, you should use judgment and be patient in the evaluation process. It is not possible to evaluate a portfolio manager on the basis of a quarter or even a year. Your evaluation should extend over several years and cover at least a full market cycle. This will allow you to determine whether the manager's performance differs during rising and declining markets as Ferson and Schadt (1996) demonstrate. Beyond these general cautions, several specific factors should be considered when using these measures.

Many of the equity portfolio performance measures we have discussed are derived from the CAPM and assume the existence of a market portfolio at the point of tangency on the Markowitz efficient frontier. Theoretically, the market portfolio is an efficient, completely diversified portfolio because it is on the efficient frontier. As we discussed in Chapter 8, this market portfolio must contain all risky assets in the economy, so that it will be completely diversified, and all components must be market-value weighted. The problem arises in finding a realistic proxy for this theoretical market portfolio. As noted previously, analysts typically use the Standard and Poor's 500 Index as the proxy for the market portfolio because it contains a fairly diversified portfolio of stocks, and the sample is market-value weighted. Unfortunately, it does not represent the true composition of the market portfolio. Specifically, it includes only common stocks and most of them are listed on the NYSE. Notably, it excludes many other risky assets that theoretically should be considered, such as numerous AMEX and OTC stocks, foreign stocks, foreign and domestic bonds, real estate, coins, precious metals, stamps, and antiques.

This lack of completeness was highlighted in several articles by Roll (1977a, 1978, 1980, 1981), who detailed the problem with the market proxy and pointed out its implications for measuring portfolio performance. Although a detailed discussion of Roll's critique will not be repeated here, we need to consider his major problem with the measurement of the market portfolio, which he refers to as a **benchmark error**. He showed that if the proxy for the market portfolio is not a truly efficient portfolio, then the SML using this proxy may not be the true SML—the true SML could have a higher slope. In such a case, a portfolio plotted above the SML and derived using a poor benchmark could actually plot below the SML that uses the true market portfolio.

Another problem is that the beta could differ from that computed using the true market portfolio. For example, if the true beta were larger than the beta computed using the proxy, the true position of the portfolio would shift to the right. In an empirical test, Brown and Brown (1987) documented a considerable amount of ranking reversal when the definition of the market portfolio was changed in a Jensen's alpha analysis of a sample of well-established mutual funds. Also, as we have seen earlier, Grinblatt and Titman (1993) attempted to avoid the conflict altogether by introducing a performance measurement process that did not require benchmarks while Daniel et al. (1997) developed benchmarks based on the characteristics of the stock held, such as firm size and book-to-market ratios. Terhaar (2001) shows how the benchmark error problem can also affect attribution analysis.

Demonstration of the Global Benchmark Problem

To illustrate the impact of the benchmark problem in an environment of global capital markets, consider what happens to the individual measures of risk when the world equity market is employed to estimate the beta coefficient from the SML. Exhibit 25.15 contains beta estimates for the 30 stocks in the Dow Jones Industrial Average (DJIA) using the S&P 500, which is the typical proxy for stocks of companies domiciled in the United States, and the Morgan Stanley Capital International (MSCI) World Stock Index, which is a market-value-weighted index that contains stocks from around the world. These findings were calculated using monthly returns from two different five-year periods: 1996–2000 and 2000–2005. For each stock in both time intervals, the percentage difference between the U.S. beta and the World beta is also shown, using the higher of the two risk estimates as the base.

There are two major differences in the various beta statistics. First, notice that for any particular stock, the beta estimates change a great deal over time. For example, Alcoa's U.S. and

Exhibit 25.15	Beta Estimates for Dow Jones Industrials Stock Using Domestic and World Stock Market Indices: 1996–2000 and 2000–2005

Stock	Ticker	1996–2000:			2000–2005:		
		Beta—US	Beta—World	% Difference	Beta—US	Beta—World	% Difference
Alcoa	AA	1.11	1.34	17.2%	1.70	1.76	3.4%
American Intl Group	AIG	1.11	1.10	0.9%	0.68	0.70	2.9%
American Express	AXP	1.20	1.28	6.3%	1.13	1.17	3.4%
Boeing	BA	0.57	0.49	14.0%	0.80	0.86	7.0%
Caterpillar	CAT	0.78	0.84	7.1%	1.04	1.10	5.5%
Citigroup	CAT	1.50	1.56	3.8%	1.31	1.26	3.8%
Du Pont	DD	0.77	0.84	8.3%	0.89	0.90	1.1%
Walt Disney	DIS	0.94	0.90	4.3%	1.17	1.20	2.5%
General Electric	GE	1.24	1.35	8.1%	0.91	0.87	4.4%
General Motors	GM	1.12	1.10	1.8%	1.30	1.29	0.8%
Home Depot	HD	0.95	1.28	25.8%	1.26	1.32	4.5%
Honeywell	HON	0.97	1.04	6.7%	1.45	1.43	1.4%
Hewlett-Packard	HPQ	1.47	1.73	15.0%	2.05	2.02	1.5%
Intl Business Machines	IBM	1.22	1.18	3.3%	1.63	1.55	4.9%
Intel	INTC	1.44	1.38	4.2%	2.36	2.25	4.7%
Johnson & Johnson	JNJ	0.65	0.54	16.9%	0.21	0.23	8.7%
JPMorgan	JPM	1.20	1.20	0.0%	1.79	1.82	1.6%
Coca-Cola	KO	0.68	0.69	1.4%	0.28	0.40	30.0%
McDonald's	MCD	0.74	0.77	3.9%	0.80	0.93	14.0%
3M Company	MMM	0.43	0.49	12.2%	0.57	0.61	6.6%
Altria Group	MO	0.32	0.16	50.0%	0.55	0.62	11.3%
Merck	MRK	0.57	0.37	35.1%	0.43	0.39	9.3%
Microsoft	MSFT	1.83	1.84	0.5%	1.36	1.27	6.6%
Pfizer	PFE	0.72	0.56	22.2%	0.43	0.44	2.3%
Procter & Gamble	PG	0.36	0.39	7.7%	0.03	0.01	66.7%
SBC Communications	SBC	0.66	0.57	13.6%	0.75	0.71	5.3%
United Technologies	UTX	1.30	1.54	15.6%	0.79	0.84	6.0%
Verizon	VZ	0.68	0.57	16.2%	0.89	0.84	5.6%
Wal-Mart Stores	WMT	0.88	1.17	24.8%	0.40	0.40	0.0%
ExxonMobil	XOM	0.38	0.40	5.0%	0.45	0.50	10.0%
	Mean:	0.93	0.96	11.7%	0.98	0.99	7.9%
	Median:	0.91	0.97	7.9%	0.89	0.89	4.8%

World betas during 1996–2000 were 1.11 and 1.34, respectively. However, during 2000–2005, both of these values increased substantially (to 1.70 and 1.76, respectively). Second, although the mean and median values for the U.S. and World beta estimates appear to be quite similar during both time periods, the "% Difference" columns show that there are some substantial differences in betas estimated for the same stock over the same time period when two different definitions of the benchmark portfolio are employed. For instance, the U.S. and World beta estimates for Johnson & Johnson differed by almost 17 percent in 1996–2000 and then by almost 9 percent in 2000–2005. Overall, the median size of this discrepancy decreased over time—from 7.9 percent to 4.8 percent—but this is still a sizable difference. It indicates that the specification of the proper benchmark remains a critical issue in the performance evaluation process.

Reilly and Akhtar (1995) examined the effect of the choice of a benchmark on global performance measurement. Their results are summarized in Exhibit 25.16, which plots the SMLs for six different indexes over three time horizons: 1983–1988, 1989–1994, and 1983–1994. Four country-specific benchmarks—the S&P 500 (United States), the Nikkei (Japan), the FT-All Shares (England), and the FAZ (Germany)—and two aggregate benchmarks—M-S World and Brinson GSMI—were used in the analysis. The results indicate that using alternative market proxies for different countries or alternative composite series will generate SMLs that differ substantially during a given time period and that these SMLs tend to be very unstable over time. For instance, the Nikkei SML goes from the largest risk premium during 1983–1988 to a negative risk premium during 1989–1994, which clearly is contrary to capital market theory. Notice, however, that this volatility would be masked by anyone looking at Japanese performance over the entire 1983–1994 period, during which the Nikkei SML assumed a more normal shape. Finally, the S&P 500 provided investors with the biggest performance hurdle over the whole sample period, which was mostly due to the high risk premiums in the United States during 1989–1994.

Implications of the Benchmark Problems

Several points are significant regarding this benchmark criticism. First, the benchmark problems noted by Roll, which are increased with global investing, do not negate the value of the CAPM as a *normative* model of equilibrium pricing; the theory is still viable. The problem is one of *measurement* when using the theory to evaluate portfolio performance.

You need to find a better proxy for the market portfolio or to adjust measured performance for benchmark errors. In fact, Roll (1981) and Grinold (1992) have made several suggestions to help overcome this problem. From Chapter 5, we know that new comprehensive stock market and bond market series are being developed that will be available as market portfolio proxies. Finally, the multiple markets index (MMI), developed by Brinson, Diermeier, and Schlarbaum (1986), is a major step toward a truly comprehensive world market portfolio.

Alternatively, you might consider giving greater weight to the Sharpe portfolio performance measure because it does not depend heavily on the market portfolio. Recall that this measure relates excess return to the *standard deviation* of return—that is, to total risk. Although this evaluation process generally uses a benchmark portfolio as an example of an unmanaged portfolio for comparison purposes, the risk measure for the portfolio being evaluated does not directly depend on a market portfolio. Also, recall that the portfolio rank from the Sharpe measure typically correlates highly with the ranks derived from alternative performance measures (see Exhibit 25.9).

Required Characteristics of Benchmarks

The benchmark problem just discussed was described as being related to finding a proxy for the theoretical market portfolio, especially given the trend toward global capital markets. Concurrent with this search for a global market portfolio, there has also been a search for appropriate **normal portfolios**, which are customized benchmarks that reflect the specific styles of alternative managers. Bailey, Richards, and Tierney (1990) and Richards (2001) consider this a critical need of pension plans and endowments who hire multiple managers with widely divergent styles. They point out that if a broad market index is used rather than a specific benchmark portfolio, it is implicitly assumed that the portfolio manager does not have an investment style, which is quite unrealistic. Also, it does not allow the plan sponsors to determine if the

Exhibit 25.16 | Security Market Lines for S&P 500, Nikkei, FT-All Shares, FAZ, M-S World, and Brinson GSMI Indexes

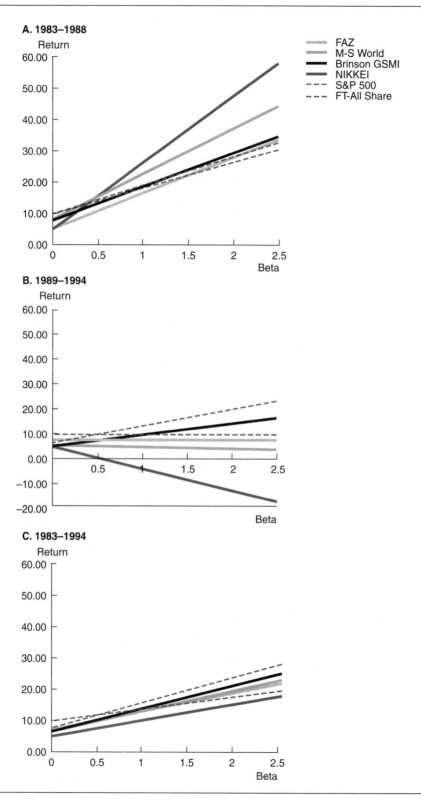

Source: Frank K. Reilly and Rashid A. Akhtar, "The Benchmark Error Problem with Global Capital Markets," *Journal of Portfolio Management* 22, no. 1 (Fall 1995): 33–52.

money manager is consistent with his or her stated investment style. The authors contend that any useful benchmark should have the following characteristics:

- *Unambiguous.* The names and weights of securities comprising the benchmark are clearly delineated.
- *Investable.* The option is available to forgo active management and simply hold the benchmark.
- *Measurable.* It is possible to calculate the return on the benchmark on a reasonably frequent basis.
- *Appropriate.* The benchmark is consistent with the manager's investment style or biases.
- *Reflective of current investment opinions.* The manager has current investment knowledge (be it positive, negative, or neutral) of the securities that make up the benchmark.
- *Specified in advance.* The benchmark is constructed prior to the start of an evaluation period.

If a benchmark does not possess all of these properties, it is considered flawed as an effective management tool. One example of a flawed benchmark is the use of the median manager from a broad universe of managers or even a limited universe of managers. This criticism is spelled out in detail by Bailey (1992), who argues that the manager universe is inadequate on almost every characteristic. Finally, Dialynas (2001) considers the special problems of creating benchmarks for fixed-income portfolios.

In summary, because of a growing desire to evaluate aggregate performance and identify what factors contribute to superior or inferior performance, benchmarks must be selected at two levels: (1) a *global* level that contains the broadest mix of risky assets available from around the world and (2) a fairly specific level consistent with the management style of an individual money manager (i.e., a customized benchmark).

EVALUATION OF BOND PORTFOLIO PERFORMANCE

As discussed, the analysis of risk-adjusted performance for equity portfolios began in the late 1960s following the development of portfolio theory and the CAPM. The common stock risk measures have been fairly simple—either total risk (the standard deviation of returns) or systematic risk (betas). No such development has simplified analysis for the bond market, where numerous and complex factors can influence portfolio returns. One reason for this lack of development of bond portfolio performance measures was that, prior to the 1970s, most bond portfolio managers followed buy-and-hold strategies, so their performance probably did not differ much. In this era, interest rates were relatively stable, so one could gain little from the active management of bond portfolios.

The environment in the bond market changed considerably in the late 1970s and especially in the 1980s, when interest rates increased dramatically and became more volatile. This created an incentive to trade bonds, and this trend toward more active management led to substantially more dispersed performance by bond portfolio managers. This dispersion in performance in turn created a demand for techniques that would help investors evaluate the performance of bond portfolio managers. Equally important for bond markets, was the historic decline in interest rates that began in the early 1990s and continued through 2004. This enhanced level of rate volatility brought with it a renewed interest in measuring the risk-adjusted performance of bond portfolios as well as attempts to explain the causes of that performance.

As it has developed over the past several years, performance measurement can also be divided into attempts to assess *how* portfolio managers performed relative to investor expectations and *why* the managers produced the performance they did. We now consider techniques that address both of these questions.[9]

Returns-Based Bond Performance Measurement

Early attempts to analyze fixed-income performance often involved peer group comparisons of the returns generated by a group of bond portfolio managers with comparable investment styles. For instance, Kritzman (1983) examined the ranking for 32 bond managers employed by AT&T. He divided a 10-year period into two 5-year periods, determined each manager's percentile ranking in each period, and correlated the rankings. The results revealed no relationship between levels of performance in the two periods. A further test also revealed no relationship between past and future performance, even when comparing performance levels of the best and worst performers. Based on these results, he concluded that it would be necessary to look at something besides past performance to determine superior bond portfolio managers.

As we saw with equity portfolio evaluation, peer group comparisons are potentially flawed because they do not account for investment risk directly. In principle, the Jensen's alpha approach described in previous sections can be employed to measure the performance of *any* asset portfolio. In practice, however, we have seen that the issue of how the risk factors are measured is a crucial one. When the assets in the portfolio change from stocks to bond, it is likely that a straightforward application of the conventional risk models will not produce the most meaningful results. Fama and French (1993) addressed this issue by expanding their three-factor equation to include two additional factors specifically related to how returns are generated for fixed-income securities:

25.12 $R_{jt} - RFR_t = \alpha_j + [b_{j1}(R_{mt} - RFR_t) + b_{j2}SMB_t + b_{j3}\text{HML}_t] + [b_{j4}TERM_t + b_{j4}DEF_t] + e_{jt}$

In Equation 25.12, the two additional risk factors are defined as follows: (1) *TERM* is the term premium built into the slope of the Treasury yield curve and is calculated as the difference between the long-term and short-term government bond yields, and (2) *DEF* is the default premium and is calculated by the credit spread between the long-term corporate and government bond yields.

Fama and French (1993) tested this expanded model by measuring the performance of seven different bond portfolios over the 342-month period from July 1963 to December 1991. The seven bond portfolios were formed with the following securities: 1- to 5-year Treasuries (1-5G) 6- 10-year Treasuries (6-10G), Aaa-rated corporates, Aa-rated corporates, A-rated corporates, Baa-rated corporates, and low-grade corporates rated below Baa (LG). Their findings are summarized in Exhibit 25.17.

Although both stock and bond risk factors were included in the model, the findings show that it is the two bond factors that provide the dominant explanation for how these bond portfolio returns varied over time. While all of the portfolios groups had significant positive exposures to *TERM* and *DEF*, only a few of the categories also had significant loadings on the stock market variables. Further, the reported alpha coefficients in the last row show are quite small and were insignificant for all of the corporate bond portfolios. Since these portfolios represent the performance of indexed fixed-income investments, these results are what you would expect. However, the same process can be used to assess the value added by active bond managers as well.

---

[9]A good overview of this area and a discussion of the historical development of the various performance measures are contained in Fong (2001).

Exhibit 25.17 | **Risk Factor and Jensen's Alpha Estimates for Seven Bond Portfolios: 1963–1991**

| | BOND PORTFOLIOS | | | | | | |
| | Government | | Corporate | | | | |
Risk Factor:	1-5FG	6-10G	Aaa	Aa	A	Baa	LG
$(R_m - RFR)$	−0.02[a]	−0.04[a]	−0.02[a]	0.00	0.00	0.02	0.18[a]
SMB	0.00	−0.02	−0.02[a]	−0.01[a]	0.00	0.05[a]	0.08[a]
HML	0.00	−0.02	−0.02[a]	−0.00	0.00	0.04[a]	0.12[a]
TERM	0.47[a]	0.75[a]	1.03[a]	0.99[a]	1.00[a]	0.99[a]	0.64[a]
DEF	0.27[a]	0.32[a]	0.97[a]	0.97[a]	1.02[a]	1.05[a]	0.80[a]
Portfolio Alpha:	0.09[a]	0.11[a]	−0.00	−0.00	−0.00	0.02	−0.07

[a]Significant at the 0.05 level.

Source: Eugene F. Fama and Kenneth R. French, "Common Risk Factors in the Returns on Stocks and Bonds," *Journal of Financial Economics* 33, no. 1 (January, 1993): 3–56.

Bond Performance Attribution

As with attribution analysis in the equity market, the critical questions are: (1) How did the performance levels of portfolio managers compare to the overall bond market? and (2) What factors lead to superior or inferior bond portfolio performance? In this section, we present one such attempt to develop bond portfolio performance evaluation systems that consider multiple-risk factors.

The Bond Market Line Wagner and Tito (1977) attempted to apply asset pricing techniques to the evaluation of bond performance. The main factor necessary for a proper bond performance attribution is the development of an appropriate index and for this a measure of risk is necessary, similar to the beta coefficient for equities. As we have seen in Chapter 18, a bond's duration statistic captures the net effect of the volatility inherent in the underlying coupon and maturity structure.

Using this as a measure of risk, the authors derived a bond market line much like the security market line used to evaluate equity performance. Duration simply replaces beta as the risk variable. The bond market line in Exhibit 25.18 is drawn from points defined by returns on Treasury bills to the Lehman Brothers Government–Corporate Bond Index rather than the S&P 500 index.[10] The Lehman Brothers Index gives the market's average annual rate of return during some common period, and the duration for the index is the value-weighted duration for the individual bonds in the index.

Given the bond market line, this technique divides the portfolio return that differs from the return on the Lehman Brothers Index into four components: (1) a **policy effect**, (2) a **rate anticipation effect**, (3) an **analysis effect**, and (4) a **trading effect**. When the latter three effects are combined, they are referred to as the **management effect**. These effects are portrayed in Exhibit 25.19.

The policy effect measures the difference in the expected return for a given portfolio because of a difference in policy regarding the duration of this portfolio compared to the

---

[10]We saw in Chapter 5 that it would be equally reasonable to use a comparable bond market index series from Merrill Lynch, Salomon Brothers, or the Ryan Index.

Exhibit 25.18	**Specification of Bond Market Line Using Lehman Brothers Bond Index**

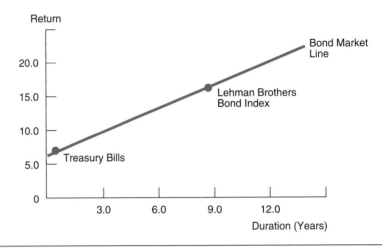

Source: Wayne H. Wagner and Dennis A. Tito, "Definitive New Measures of Bond Performance and Risk," *Pension World* (May 1977): 17–26.

Exhibit 25.19	**Graphic Display of Bond Portfolio Performance Breakdown**

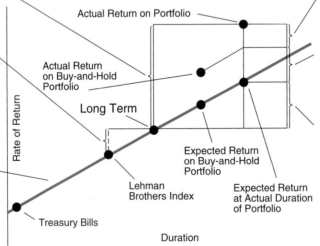

Management effect is the improvement in investment performance of a passive strategy through active bond management. It is the difference between total bond portfolio return and the expected return at the long-term average duration.

Trading effect is the result of the current quarter's trading, either through effective trade-desk operation or short-term selection abilities. It is the difference between total management effect and the effects attributable to analysis and interest rate anticipation.

Policy effect is the difference between long-term duration of a bond portfolio and the duration of a bond market index resulting from long-term investment policy. Measured as the return at the long-term average less the return on the Lehman Brothers Index.

Analysis effect, attributable to the selection of issues with better-than-average long-term prospects, is the difference between the actual return of the buy-and-hold portfolio at the beginning of the quarter and the expected return of that buy-and-hold portfolio.

Bond market line is a straight line drawn through the return/duration of Treasury bills and the return/duration of the Lehman Brothers Index.

Interest rate anticipation effect is attributable to changes in portfolio duration resulting from attempts to profit from and ability to predict bond market movements. It is the difference between the expected return at the actual portfolio duration and the expected return at the long-term duration.

Buy-and-hold portfolio is the composition of the portfolio at the beginning of the quarter. Used to differentiate between trading gains secured within a quarter and long-term analysis gains.

Duration is a measure of the average time to receipt of cash flows from an investment. It is a measure of the sensitivity of a bond's price to changes in interest rates.

Source: Wayne H. Wagner and Dennis A. Tito, "Definitive New Measures of Bond Performance and Risk," *Pension World* (May 1977): 17–26.

duration of the index.[11] The duration of a portfolio being evaluated that differs from the index duration indicates a basic policy decision regarding relative risk (measured by duration), and there should be a difference in expected return consistent with that risk policy decision. For example, assume the duration and return for the Lehman Brothers Index is 9.0 years and 8.25 percent, respectively. If your portfolio has a duration of 9.5 years, according to the prevailing bond market line, your return should be about 8.60 percent. In this example, the policy effect is 0.5 year and 0.35 percent (35 basis points). Specifically, the higher duration implies that your portfolio should have a higher average return of 0.35 percent (this positive relationship assumes the typical upward-sloping yield curve).

Given the expected return and duration for this long-term portfolio, all deviations from the index portfolio are attributable to the remaining management effect components. The interest rate anticipation effect attempts to measure the differential return from changing the duration during this period compared to the portfolio's long-term duration. For example, assume the duration for the long-term portfolio is 9.5 years, which implies an expected return of 8.60 percent, and that the prevailing duration for the portfolio being evaluated is 10.0 years, which implies an expected return of 9.00 percent using the bond market line. Therefore, the rate anticipation effect during this period is 0.40 percent (9.00 − 8.60).

The difference between this expected return based on the portfolio's duration and the actual return for the portfolio during this period is a combination of an analysis effect and a trading effect. The analysis effect is the differential return attributable to acquiring bonds that are temporarily mispriced relative to their risk level. To measure the analysis effect, compare the *expected* return for the portfolio held at the beginning of the period (using the bond market line) to the *actual* return of this same portfolio. If the actual return is greater than the expected return, it implies that the portfolio manager acquired some underpriced issues that became properly priced and thus provided excess returns during the period. For example, if the portfolio at the beginning of the period had a duration of 10 years, this might indicate that the portfolio's expected return was 9.00 percent for the period. In turn, if the actual return for this buy-and-hold portfolio was 9.40 percent, it would indicate an analysis effect of 40 basis points.

Finally, the trading effect occurs because of short-run changes in the portfolio during the period. It is measured as the residual after taking account of the analysis effect from the total excess return based on duration. For example, assume the total actual return is 10.50 percent with a duration of 10.0 years. The prevailing bond market line indicates an expected return of 9 percent for a portfolio with a 10-year duration. Thus, the combination of the analysis and trading effects is 1.50 percent (= 10.50 − 9.00). Previously, we determined that the analysis effect was 0.40 percent, so the trading effect must be 1.10 percent. In summary, for this portfolio manager, the actual return was 10.50 percent, compared to a return for the Lehman Brothers Index of 8.25 percent. This total excess of 2.25 percent would be divided as follows:

- 0.35 percent policy effect due to higher long-term duration
- 0.40 percent interest rate anticipation effect due to increasing the duration of the current portfolio above the long-term portfolio duration
- 0.40 percent analysis effect—the impact of superior selection of individual issues in the beginning portfolio
- 1.10 percent trading effect—the impact of trading the issues *during* the period

---

[11]Notably, the duration of the various bond market indexes has changed over time (i.e., the duration of the corporate bond series has declined, whereas the duration of the government bond series has increased slightly). For a presentation and discussion of this phenomenon, see Reilly and Wright (2001).

This technique breaks down the return based on the duration as a comprehensive risk measure. The only concern is that *it does not consider differences in the risk of default.* Specifically, the technique does not differentiate between an Aaa bond with a duration of eight years and a Baa bond with the same duration. This could clearly affect the performance. A portfolio manager who invested in Baa bonds, for example, could experience a very positive analysis effect simply because the bonds were lower quality than the average quality implicit in the Lehman Brothers Index. The only way to avoid this would be to construct differential market lines for alternative ratings or construct a benchmark line that matches the quality makeup of the portfolio being evaluated.

Layard-Liesching (2001) used the information ratio performance measure to assess the relative impact of each possible decision that a bond manager could make on the return to the overall portfolio. His analysis showed that while large-scale duration "bets" could certainly be taken, their payoffs were likely to be low once the high degree of tracking error they created was taken into account. On the other hand, he also argued that credit quality bets were more likely to be fruitful, particularly as the global movement to privatizing companies that were previously under governmental control continues to create new investment opportunities.[12]

REPORTING INVESTMENT PERFORMANCE

The performance measures described in this chapter represent the essential elements of how any investor's performance should be evaluated. However, before the various composite statistics can be calculated, a more fundamental question must be addressed: How should the returns upon which the performance measures are based be reported to the investor? We conclude our discussion by exploring two dimensions of this problem. First, we consider the issue of how returns should be computed for a portfolio that experiences infusions and withdrawals of cash during the investment period. Second, we will briefly summarize the **performance presentation standards (PPS)** created by the CFA Institute, an international organization of over 70,000 investment practitioners and educators in more than 100 countries.

Time-Weighted and Dollar-Weighted Returns

As we saw in Chapter 1, the holding period yield (HPY) for any investment position was determined by that position's market value at the end of the period divided by its initial value:

$$HPY = \frac{\text{Ending Value of Investment}}{\text{Beginning Value of Investment}} - 1$$

For any security or portfolio of securities, we also saw that there are two basic reasons why the ending and beginning values could differ: the receipt of cash payments (e.g., dividends) or a change in price (e.g., capital gains) during the period. Thus, for most investment positions, calculating returns during any given time frame is a reasonably straightforward matter.

For professional money managers and management companies, however, there is another reason why the beginning and ending value of a portfolio can differ, and it has nothing to do

---

[12]Other attribution models that decompose bond returns in somewhat different ways can be found in Dietz, Fogler, and Hardy (1980) and Fong, Pearson, and Vasicek (1983). For more detailed discussions of bond performance measurement, see Reilly and Sidhu (1980), Gudikunst and McCarthy (1992), and Kahle, Maxwell, and Xu (2005).

with the manager's investment prowess. Specifically, if the investor either withdraws or adds to her initial investment capital during the period, the ending value of the position will reflect these changes. Of course, it would be unfair to credit the manager with having produced high returns that were due to additional capital commitments. Similarly, it would be equally unfair to penalize him for reductions in the ending value of the investment that were caused by the investor removing funds from her account. Consequently, an evaluation of the manager's true performance must take these contributions and withdrawals into account.

To see the potential problem more clearly, consider two portfolio managers (A and B) who have exactly identical investment styles and stockpicking abilities. Indeed, we will assume further that over a two-period investment horizon, they produce exactly the same capital gains with the investment capital entrusted to them: 25 percent in Period 1, and 5 percent in Period 2. Further, suppose that each manager receives from his respective investor $500,000 to invest. The difference is that Manager A receives all of these funds immediately whereas Manager B's investor commits only $250,000 initially and the remaining $250,000 at the end of the first period.

The immediate effect of this investment timing discrepancy can be seen by calculating the terminal (Period 2) value of each portfolio:

$$\text{Portfolio A: } 500,000\,[(1 + 0.25)(1 + (0.05)] = \$656,250$$

and

$$\text{Portfolio B: } 250,000[(1 + 0.25)(1 + 0.05)] + 250,000(1 + 0.05) = \$590,625$$

Obviously, Manager B's portfolio is worth less than Manager A's, but this is a result of the way the investment funds were committed rather than of any real differences in the performance of the two managers. Accordingly, the managers' performance evaluation should not be affected by the investors' decisions concerning the timing of their capital commitments. In other words, Manager B should not be held accountable for the fact that Investor B did not have all of her funds invested during the high-return environment of the first period.

One common method of computing average returns that we have seen is to use a discounted cash flow approach to calculate an investment's internal rate of return. For the two managers in this example, these calculations generate the following returns:

$$\text{Manager A: } 500,000 = \frac{656,250}{(1 + r_{dA})^2}, \text{ or } r_{dA} = 14.56 \text{ percent}$$

and

$$\text{Manager B: } 250,000 = \frac{-250,000}{(a + r_{dB})^1} = \frac{590,625}{(1+r_{dB})^2}, \text{ or } r_{dB} = 11.63 \text{ percent}$$

These returns (r_{dA} and r_{dB}) are sometimes called *dollar-weighted* returns because they are the discount rates that set the present value of future cash flows (including future investment contributions and withdrawals) equal to the level of the initial investment. Unfortunately, in this case, dollar-weighted returns give an inaccurate impression of Manager B's ability; he did not actually perform 2.93 percent (= 0.1456 − 0.1163) worse than Manager A. Thus, while this internal rate of return method gives an accurate assessment of *Investor* B's return, it is a misleading measure of *Manager* B's talent.

A better way of evaluating a manager's performance would be to consider how well he did regardless of the size or timing of the investment funds involved. For both managers in this example, the *time-weighted* average return is simply the geometric average of (one plus) the periodic returns:

$$r_{tA} = r_{tB} = \sqrt[2]{(1 + 0.25)(1 + 0.05)} - 1 = 14.56\%$$

Notice that dollar-weighted and time-weighted returns are only the same when there are no interim investment contributions within the evaluation period. This was the case for Manager A. For Manager B, on the other hand, the dollar-weighted return understates the true (time-weighted) performance because of the way the investor deployed her funds. When there are contributions, Dietz and Kirschman (1990) have suggested a method for adjusting holding period yields:

$$\text{Adjusted HPY} = \frac{\text{Ending Value of Investment} - (1 - DW)(\text{Contribution})}{\text{Beginning Value of Investment} + (DW)(\text{Contribution})} - 1$$

where the contribution can be either positive (a new commitment) or negative (a withdrawal). This adjustment process alters the initial and terminal values of the portfolios by the weighted amount of the contribution made during the holding period. In this calculation, the day-weight (*DW*) factor represents the portion of the period that the contribution is actually held in the account. For example, if a contribution were placed in the portfolio halfway through a 30-day month, *DW* would be 0.5 [= (30 − 15)/30].

Performance Presentation Standards

The preceding example underscores the fact that there may not always be a single answer to a seemingly simple question. For instance, although Portfolio B had an internal rate of return of 11.63 percent, its manager generated an average return of 14.56 percent. Which should be reported to the investor? Although Security and Exchange Commission regulations guard against the publication of outright fraudulent claims, only recently has the investment community begun to demand the adoption of a more rigorous set of reporting guidelines. In an effort to fulfill the call for uniform, accurate, and consistent performance reporting, CFA Institute (formerly known as the Association for Investment Management and Research, or AIMR) has developed a comprehensive set of performance presentation standards (PPS). As the organization states its mission:

> The investment community's need for a common, accepted set of guidelines to promote fair representation and full disclosure in every firm's presentation of its performance results to clients and prospective clients has guided the development of the AIMR-PPS. The Standards are the manifestation of a set of guiding ethical principles and should be interpreted as *minimum* standards for presenting investment performance. The standards have been designed to meet the following four goals:
>
> - achieve greater uniformity and comparability among performance presentations;
> - improve the service offered to investment management clients;
> - enhance the professionalism of the industry;
> - bolster the notion of self-regulation.

The Standards set expectations and provide an industry yardstick for evaluating fairness and accuracy in investment performance presentation.[13]

A complete discussion of these standards can be found in *AIMR Performance Presentation Standards Handbook,* second edition (Charlottesville, VA: AIMR, 1997), as well as *Performance Reporting for Investment Managers* (Charlottesville, VA: AIMR, 1991).

Introduced in 1987, formally adopted in 1993, and modified in 1999, the AIMR-PPS have become accepted standards for practice within the investment management community. Further, in 1999, AIMR also adopted a companion set of *Global Investment Performance Standards,* which were intended to serve the following purpose:

> A global investment performance standard leads to readily accepted presentations of investment performance that (1) present performance results that are readily comparable among investment managers, without regard to geographic location, and (2) facilitate a dialogue between investment managers and their prospective clients about the critical issues of how the manager achieved performance results and future investment strategies. (p. 1)

Although a detailed analysis of these standards (which are revised frequently) is beyond our current scope, it is worth noting several of the fundamental principles on which they are based:

- Total return, including realized and unrealized gains plus income, must be used when calculating investment performance.
- Time-weighted rates of return must be used.
- Portfolios must be valued at least monthly, and periodic returns must be geometrically linked.
- If composite return performance is presented, this composite must contain all actual fee-paying accounts, including all terminated accounts for periods up through the last full reporting period the account was under management. Composite results may not link simulated or model portfolios with actual performance.
- Performance must be calculated after the deduction of trading expenses (e.g., broker commissions and SEC fees), if any.
- For taxable clients, taxes on income and realized capital gains must be recognized in the same period they were incurred and must be subtracted from results regardless of whether taxes are paid from assets outside the account.
- Annual returns for all years must be presented. Performance of less than one year must not be annualized. A 10-year performance record (or a record for the period since firm inception if less than 10 years) must be presented.
- Performance presentation must disclose whether performance results are calculated gross or net of investment management fees and what the firm's fee schedule is. Presentation should also disclose any use of leverage (including derivatives) and any material change in personnel responsible for investment management.

In addition to the preceding requirements, AIMR also encourages managers to disclose the volatility of the aggregate composite return and to identify benchmarks that parallel the risk or investment style the composite is expected to track. Exhibit 25.20 shows a sample performance presentation that is in compliance with the Standards.

---

[13]See http://www.cfainstitute.org/standards/pps.

Exhibit 25.20 | **A Sample Performance Presentation**

SAMPLE 1 INVESTMENT FIRM
BALANCED COMPOSITE
1 JANUARY 1995 THROUGH 31 DECEMBER 2004

Year	Gross-of-Fees Return (percent)	Net-of-Fees Return (percent)	Benchmark Return (percent)	Number of Portfolios	Internal Dispersion (percent)	Total Composite Assets (CAD Million)	Total Firm Assets (CAD Million)
1995	16.0	15.0	14.1	26	4.5	165	236
1996	2.2	1.3	1.8	32	2.0	235	346
1997	22.4	21.5	24.1	38	5.7	344	529
1998	7.1	6.2	6.0	45	2.8	445	695
1999	8.5	7.5	8.0	48	3.1	520	839
2000	−8.0	−8.9	−8.4	49	2.8	505	1014
2001	−5.9	−6.8	−6.2	52	2.9	499	995
2002	2.4	1.6	2.2	58	3.1	525	1125
2003	6.7	5.9	6.8	55	3.5	549	1225
2004	9.4	8.6	9.1	59	2.5	575	1290

Sample 1 Investment Firm has prepared and presented this report in compliance with the Global Investment Performance Standards (GIPS*).

Notes:

1. Sample 1 Investment Firm is a balanced portfolio investment manager that invests solely in Canadian securities. Sample 1 Investment Firm is defined as an independent investment management firm that is not affiliated with any parent organization. For the periods from 2000 through 2004, Sample 1 Investment Firm has been verified by Verification Services Inc. A copy of the verification report is available upon request. Additional information regarding the firm's policies and procedures for calculating and reporting performance results is available upon request.

2. The composite includes all nontaxable balanced portfolios with an asset allocation of 30% S&P TSX and 70% Scotia Canadian Bond Index Fund, which allow up to a 10% deviation in asset allocation.

3. The benchmark: 30% S&P TSX; 70% Scotia Canadian Bond Index Fund rebalanced monthly.

4. Valuations are computed and performance reported in Canadian dollars.

5. Gross-of-fees performance returns are presented before management and custodial fees but after all trading expenses. Returns are presented net of nonreclaimable withholding taxes. Net-of-fees performance returns are calculated by deducting the highest fee of 0.25% from the quarterly gross composite return. The management fee schedule is as follows: 1.00% on first CAD25M; 0.60% thereafter.

6. This composite was created in February 1995. A complete list and description of firm composites is available upon request.

7. For the periods 1995 and 1996, Sample 1 Investment Firm was not in compliance with the GIPS standards because portfolios were valued annually.

8. Internal dispersion is calculated using the equal-weighted standard deviation of all portfolios that were included in the composite for the entire year.

The Internet

Investments Online

Mutual fund performance is a matter of public knowledge, but performance for the vast variety of pension funds, endowments, insurance company portfolios, trust portfolios, and other private investment pools may not be public. Investors will have to use the tools discussed in this chapter to evaluate the performance of nonpublic portfolios. Many investor consultant and software firms have proprietary databases and products, and they try to sell their services to individual and institutional investors as a means of evaluating portfolio performance. Consultants who evaluate money managers for clients will not offer the proprietary results of that research for free on the Internet. Nonetheless, some sites are helpful in showing applications of the material covered in this chapter.

http://www.nelsons.com The Web site of the Nelson Investment Manager database calls itself the "World's Best Money Managers" page. Nelson has a database of over 1,500 investment managers. After registering at the site, users can specify investment categories and obtain ranking performance data in a variety of formats. The site offers links to industry analysis and news as well as to investment managers' home pages and to sites of institutional investment managers.

http://www.styleadvisor.com Zephyr Associates, Inc.'s Web site features information about StyleADVISOR. StyleADVISOR is a returns-based style and performance analysis software package. It uses Sharpe's techniques of performance analysis and attribution. Pages offer visitors the chance to learn about StyleADVISOR and to view sample reports. Visitors can view past newsletters, which give analysis and insights into portfolio performance attribution issues.

http://www.morningstar.com This site, mentioned in Chapter 24, allows users to obtain summary reports on funds. The reports offer information on returns, the *Morningstar* rating, graphs of fund performance versus a benchmark, and the sector weightings of a fund's investments. The report gives the fund's style, as well, using *Morningstar's* 3 × 3 style box.

http://www.cfainstitute.org First mentioned in Chapter 2, the CFA Institute's home page offers a link to information about the CFA Institute's Global Investment Performance Standards (GIPS®) and the AIMR Performance Presentation Standards (AIMR-PPS®). These are a set of ethical principles and guidelines to help ensure fair representation, full disclosure, and comparability in reported portfolio performance results. The site provides links to resources for training and for library information on the standards.

SUMMARY

- The first major goal of portfolio management is to derive rates of return that equal or exceed the returns on a naively selected portfolio with equal risk. The second goal is to attain complete diversification relative to a suitable benchmark. Several techniques have been derived to evaluate equity portfolios in terms of both risk and return (composite measures). The Treynor measure considers the excess returns earned per unit of systematic risk. The Sharpe measure indicates the excess return per unit of total risk. The Jensen and Information Ratio measures likewise evaluate performance in terms of the systematic risk involved and show how to determine whether the difference in risk-adjusted performance (good or bad) is statistically significant. Additional work in equity portfolio evaluation has been concerned with models that focus on

how a portfolio's security holdings change and those that indicate what components of the management process contributed to the results. A model by Fama divided the composite return into measures related to total risk, systematic risk, diversification, and selectivity, in addition to measuring overall performance. Finally, attribution analysis seeks to establish whether market timing or security selection skills (or both) are the source of a manager's performance.

- Roll challenged the validity of all techniques that assume a market portfolio that theoretically includes all risky assets when actual investigators use a proxy such as the S&P 500 that is limited to U.S. common stocks. This criticism does not invalidate the normative asset pricing model, only its application because of measurement problems related to the proxy for the market portfolio. It is demonstrated that the measurement problem is increased in an environment where global investing is the norm. The good news is that more comprehensive indexes are feasible and are constantly being developed.

- Although the techniques for evaluating equity portfolio performance have been in existence for almost 40 years, comparable techniques for examining bond portfolio performance were initiated more recently. Notably, while it is possible to adapt equity risk models for the evaluation of bond managers, it is often necessary to consider separately the several important decision variables related to bonds: the overall market factor, the impact of maturity-duration decisions, the influence of sector and quality factors, and the impact of individual bond selection.

- In conclusion, investors need to evaluate their own performance and the performance of hired managers. The various techniques we discuss provide theoretically justifiable measures that differ slightly. Although there is high rank correlation among the alternative measures, *all the measures should be used* because they provide different insights regarding the performance of managers. Finally, an evaluation of a portfolio manager should be done many times over different market environments before a final judgment is reached regarding the strengths and weaknesses of a manager.

SUGGESTED READINGS

DeFusco, Richard A., Dennis W. McLeavey, Jerald E. Pinto, and David E. Runkle. *Quantitative Methods for Investment Analysis.* Baltimore, MD: AIMR, 2001.

Feibel, Bruce J. *Investment Performance Measurement* Hoboken, NJ: Wiley, 2003.

Grinblatt, Mark, and Sheridan Titman. "Performance Evaluation." In *Handbook in Operations Research and Management Science,* ed. R. Jarrow et al. New York: Elsevier Science B.V., 1995.

Sharpe, William F. "Asset Allocation: Management Style and Performance Measurement." *Journal of Portfolio Management* 18, no. 2 (Winter 1992).

Sherrerd, Katrina F., ed. *Benchmarks and Attribution Analysis.* Charlottesville, VA: Association for Investment Management and Research, 2001.

QUESTIONS

1. Describe two major factors that a portfolio manager should consider before designing an investment strategy. What types of decisions can a manager make to achieve these goals?

2. Compare and contrast four prominent approaches to measuring investment performance on a risk-adjusted basis. In developing your answer, comment on the conditions under which each measure will be most useful.

3. The Sharpe and Treynor performance measures both calculate a portfolio's average excess return per unit of risk. Under what circumstances would it make sense to use both measures to compare the performance of a given set of portfolios? What additional information is provided by a comparison of the rankings achieved using the two measures?

4. Describe how the Jensen measure of performance is calculated. Under what conditions should it give a similar set of portfolio rankings as the Sharpe and Treynor measures? Is it possible to adjust the Jensen measure so that a portfolio's alpha value is measured relative to an empirical form of the arbitrage pricing theory rather than the capital asset pricing model? Explain.

5. The information ratio *(IR)* has been described as a benefit-cost ratio. Explain how the *IR* measures portfolio performance and whether this analogy is appropriate.

 6. *CFA Examination Level I*
   a. Explain why the asset allocation decision is the primary determinant of total portfolio performance over time.
   b. Describe three reasons why successful implementation of asset allocation decisions is even more difficult in practice than in theory.

7. Performance attribution analysis is an attempt to divide a manager's "active" residual return into an allocation effect and a selection effect. Explain how these two effects are measured and why their sum must equal the total value-added return for the manager. Is this analysis valid if the actual portfolio in question is riskier than the benchmark portfolio to which it is being compared?

8. *CFA Examination Level III*

During the annual review of Acme's pension plan, several trustees questioned Lucy Graham, a pension consultant, about various aspects of performance measurement and risk assessment. In particular, one trustee asked about the appropriateness of using each of the following benchmarks:
   - Market index
   - Benchmark normal portfolio
   - Median of the manager universe

   a. Explain *two* different weaknesses of using each of the three benchmarks to measure the performance of a portfolio.

   Another trustee asked how to distinguish among the following performance measures:
   - The Sharpe ratio
   - The Treynor measure
   - Jensen's alpha

   b. (1) Describe how *each* of the three performance measures is calculated.

   (2) State whether *each* measure assumes that the relevant risk is systematic, unsystematic, or total. Explain how each measure relates excess return and the relevant risk.

9. *CFA Examination Level III*

Richard Roll, in an article on using the capital asset pricing model (CAPM) to evaluate portfolio performance, indicated that it may not be possible to evaluate portfolio management ability if there is error in the benchmark used.

   a. In evaluating portfolio performance, describe the general procedure, with emphasis on the benchmark employed.

   b. Explain what Roll meant by the benchmark error and identify the specific problem with this benchmark.

   c. Draw a graph that shows how a portfolio that has been judged as superior relative to a "measured" security market line (SML) can be inferior relative to the "true" SML.

   d. Assume that you are informed that a given portfolio manager has been evaluated as superior when compared to the DJIA, the S&P 500, and the NYSE Composite Index. Explain whether this consensus would make you feel more comfortable regarding the portfolio manager's true ability.

   e. While conceding the possible problem with benchmark errors as set forth by Roll, some contend this does not mean the CAPM is incorrect, but only that there is a measurement problem when implementing the theory. Others contend that because of benchmark errors, the whole technique should be scrapped. Take and defend one of these positions.

10. It has been contended that the derivation of an appropriate model for evaluating the performance of a bond manager is more difficult than an equity portfolio evaluation model because more decisions are required. Discuss some of the specific decisions that need to be considered when evaluating the performance of a bond portfolio manager.

PROBLEMS

1. The following portfolios are being considered for investment. During the period under consideration, $RFR = 0.07$.

Portfolio	Return	Beta	σ_i
P	0.15	1.0	0.05
Q	0.20	1.5	0.10
R	0.10	0.6	0.03
S	0.17	1.1	0.06
Market	0.13	1.0	0.04

a. Compute the Sharpe measure for each portfolio and the market portfolio.
b. Compute the Treynor measure for each portfolio and the market portfolio.
c. Rank the portfolios using each measure, explaining the cause for any differences you find in the rankings.

2. *CFA Examination Level II*

An analyst wants to evaluate Portfolio X, consisting entirely of U.S. common stocks, using both the Treynor and Sharpe measures of portfolio performance. The following table provides the average annual rate of return for Portfolio X, the market portfolio (as measured by the Standard and Poor's 500 Index), and U.S. Treasury bills (T-bills) during the past eight years.

	Annual Average Rate of Return	Standard Deviation of Return	Beta
Portfolio X	10%	18%	0.60
S&P 500	12	13	1.00
T-bills	6	n/a	n/a

n/a = not applicable

a. Calculate both the Treynor measure and the Sharpe measure for both Portfolio X and the S&P 500. Briefly explain whether Portfolio X underperformed, equaled, or outperformed the S&P 500 on a risk-adjusted basis using both the Treynor measure and the Sharpe measure.
b. Based on the performance of Portfolio X relative to the S&P 500 calculated in Part a, briefly explain the reason for the conflicting results when using the Treynor measure versus the Sharpe measure.

3. You have been assigned the task of comparing the investment performance of five different pension fund managers. After gathering 60 months of excess returns (i.e., returns in excess of the monthly risk-free rate) on each fund as well as the monthly excess returns on the entire stock market, you perform the regressions of the form:

$$(R_{fund} - RFR)_t = \alpha + \beta (R_{mkt} - RFR)_t + e_t$$

You have prepared the following summary of the data, with the standard errors for each of the coefficients listed in parentheses.

Portfolio	REGRESSION DATA:			$(R_{FUND} - RFR)$:	
	α	β	R^2	Mean	σ
ABC	0.192	1.048	94.1%	1.022%	1.193%
	(0.11)	(0.10)			
DEF	−0.053	0.662	91.6	0.473	0.764
	(0.19)	(0.09)			
GHI	0.463	0.594	68.6	0.935	0.793
	(0.19)	(0.07)			
JKL	0.355	0.757	64.1	0.955	1.044
	(0.22)	(0.08)			
MNO	0.296	0.785	94.8	0.890	0.890
	(0.14)	(0.12)			

    a. Which fund had the highest degree of diversification over the sample period? How is diversification measured in this statistical framework?

    b. Rank these funds' performance according to the Sharpe, Treynor, and Jensen measures.

    c. Since you know that according to the CAPM the intercept of these regressions (i.e., alpha) should be zero, this coefficient can be used as a measure of the value added provided by the investment manager. Which funds have statistically outperformed and underperformed the market using a two-sided 95 percent confidence interval? (Note: The relevant *t*-statistic using 60 observations is 2.00.)

4. You have just gathered the following performance data for three different money managers, based on a regression of their excess returns relative to those for the S&P 500 index. Each manager's performance was measured over the same three-year period, but the return period for each was different.

Manager	Alpha	Beta	Std. Error of Regression	Return Period
A	0.058%	0.95	0.533%	Weekly
B	0.115	1.12	5.884	Biweekly
C	0.250	0.78	2.165	Monthly

    a. Calculate the information ratio for each manager, ignoring the difference in return reporting periods.

    b. Calculate the annualized information ratio for each manager.

    c. Rank the managers' performance according to your answers in Parts a and b. Which manager performed the best? Explain.

5. Consider the following historical performance data for two different portfolios, the Standard and Poor's 500, and the 90-day T-bill.

Investment Vehicle	Average Rate of Return	Standard Deviation	Beta	R^2
Fund 1	26.40%	20.67%	1.351	0.751
Fund 2	13.22	14.20	0.905	0.713
S&P 500	15.71	13.25		
90-day T-bill	6.20	0.50		

    a. Calculate the Fama overall performance measure for both funds.

    b. What is the return to risk for both funds?

    c. For both funds, compute the measures of (1) selectivity, (2) diversification, and (3) net selectivity.

    d. Explain the meaning of the net selectivity measure and how it helps you evaluate investor performance. Which fund had the best performance?

6. *CFA Examination Level III*

Your discussion with a client has turned to the measurement of investment performance, particularly with respect to international portfolios.

International Manager/Index	Total Return	Country/Security Return	Currency Return
PERFORMANCE AND ATTRIBUTION DATA: ANNUALIZED RETURNS FOR 5 YEARS ENDED 12/31/94			
Manager A	−6.0%	2.0%	−8.0%
Manager B	−2.0	−1.0	−1.0
EAFE Index	−5.0	0.2	−5.2

a. Assume that the data in the table for Manager A and Manager B accurately reflect their investment skills and that both managers actively manage currency exposure. Briefly describe one strength and one weakness for each manager.

b. Recommend and justify a strategy that would enable the Fund to take advantage of the strengths of each of the two managers while minimizing their weaknesses.

7. Consider the following performance data for two portfolio managers (A and B) and a common benchmark portfolio:

	BENCHMARK		MANAGER A		MANAGER B	
	Weight	Return	Weight	Return	Weight	Return
Stock	0.6	−5.0%	0.5	−4.0%	0.3	−5.0%
Bonds	0.3	−3.5	0.2	−2.5	0.4	−3.5
Cash	0.1	0.3	0.3	0.3	0.3	0.3

a. Calculate: (1) the overall return to the benchmark portfolio; (2) the overall return to Manager A's actual portfolio; and (3) the overall return to Manager B's actual portfolio. Briefly comment on whether these managers have under- or outperformed the benchmark fund.

b. Using attribution analysis, calculate (1) the *selection effect* for Manager A, and (3) the *allocation effect* for Manager B. Using these numbers in conjunction with your results from Part a, comment on whether these managers have added value through their selection skills, their allocation skills, or both.

 8. *CFA Examination Level III*

A U.S. pension plan hired two off-shore firms to manage the non-U.S. equity portion of its total portfolio. Each firm was free to own stocks in any country market included in Morgan Stanley/ Capital International's Europe, Australia, and Far East Index (EAFE) and free to use any form of dollar and/or nondollar cash or bonds as an equity substitute or reserve. After three years had elapsed, the records of the managers and the EAFE Index were as follows:

	Currency	Country Selection	Stock Selection	Cash/Bond Allocation	Total Return Recorded
SUMMARY: CONTRIBUTIONS TO RETURN					
Manager A	(9.0%)	19.7%	3.1%	0.6%	14.4%
Manager B	(7.4)	14.2	6.0	2.81	5.6
Composite of A & B	(8.2)	16.9	4.5	1.71	5.0
EAFE Index	(12.9)	19.9	—	—	7.0

You are a member of the plan sponsor's Pension Committee, which will soon meet with the plan's consultant to review manager performance. In preparation for this meeting, you go through the following analysis:

a. Briefly describe the strengths and weaknesses of each manager, relative to the EAFE Index data.

b. Briefly explain the meaning of the data in the "Currency" column.

9. *CFA Examination Level III*

To illustrate for the Investment Committee of the profit-sharing plan to which you are a consultant on some of the issues that arise in measuring performance, you have identified three U.S. fixed-income management firms whose investment approaches are representative of general practice. Each firm's approach follows.

Firm A: An enhanced index fund manager that seeks to add value by superior security selection while maintaining portfolio duration and sector weights equal to the overall bond market.

Firm B: An active duration manager investing only in the government and corporate bond sectors. The firm uses futures to manage portfolio duration.

Firm C: An active manager seeking to add value by correctly anticipating changes in the shape of the yield curve, while maintaining portfolio duration and sector weights roughly equal to the overall bond market.

You have provided the Committee with the following additional information about these firms, derived from a consultant's database.

ANNUALIZED TOTAL RETURN DATA (PAST FIVE YEARS)			
	Firm A	Firm B	Firm C
Reported Returns	9.2%	9.3%	9.0%

		INDEX SECTORS			
	Aggregate Index	Governments	Corporates	Government/ Corporate	Mortgages
Index Return	8.7%	9.0%	9.8%	9.5%	8.3%

	CONSULTANT'S MANAGER UNIVERSE		
	All Managers	Managers Using the Aggregate Index as Their Benchmark	Managers Using the Govt./Corp. Sector as Their Benchmark
Return 5th percentile	6.0%	7.7%	8.4%
25th percentile	7.1	8.1	8.9
50th percentile	8.0	8.6	9.4
75th percentile	8.6	9.1	9.9
95th percentile	9.3	13.1	13.9

a. Evaluate the performance of each of these three firms relative to its appropriate Index and to the manager universe. Use only the data from the descriptions and the preceding table, even though other information would be required for a more complete and accurate appraisal.

To provide additional guidance to the Committee, you decide to do an attribution analysis on the returns produced by Firm A and Firm C and have prepared the following table:

PERFORMANCE ATTRIBUTION ANALYSIS (PAST FIVE YEARS—ANNUALIZED TOTAL RETURNS)

	Total Return	=	Duration Decisions	+	Yield Curve Decisions	+	Sector Weighting Decisions	+	Security Selection Decisions & Residuals
RETURN ATTRIBUTED TO									
Firm A									
Total return	9.20%		8.00%		0.80%		0.00%		0.40%
Benchmark index return	8.70		7.00		0.50		0.70		0.50
Difference	0.50		1.00		0.30		−0.70		−0.10
Firm C									
Total return	9.00%		7.03%		0.80%		0.71%		0.46%
Benchmark index return	8.70		7.00		0.50		0.70		0.50
Difference	0.30		0.03		0.30		0.01		−0.04

b. Evaluate the performance of Firm A and of Firm C based on all the information previously provided and your interpretation of the data in this new table.

c. Based solely on the attribution analysis you performed in Part b, state which firm produced the better result and justify your conclusion.

10. For each of the last six quarters, Managers L and M have provided you with the total dollar value of the funds they manage, along with the quarterly contributions or withdrawals made by their clients. (*Note:* Contributions are indicated by positive numbers, withdrawals by negative numbers.)

| | **MANAGER L** | | **MANAGER M** | |
	Total Funds Under Management	Contributions/ Withdrawals	Total Funds Under Management	Contributions/ Withdrawals
Quarter				
Initial	$500,000	—	$700,000	—
1	527,000	12,000	692,000	−35,000
2	530,000	7,500	663,000	−35,000
3	555,000	13,500	621,000	−35,000
4	580,000	6,500	612,000	−35,000
5	625,000	10,000	625,000	−35,000

For each manager, calculate:

a. her dollar-weighted return;

b. her time-weighted return; and

c. estimates of her quarterly performance returns using the Dietz approximation method, assuming contributions/withdrawals are made exactly halfway through the quarter.

How to Become a CFA® Charterholder

As mentioned in the section on career opportunities, the professional designation of Chartered Financial Analyst (CFA) is becoming a significant requirement for a career in investment analysis and/or portfolio management. For that reason, this section presents the history and objectives of CFA Institute and general guidelines for acquiring the CFA designation. If you are interested in the program, you can write or email CFA Institute for more information.

The CFA examinations were first offered in 1963 by the Institute of Chartered Financial Analysts (ICFA), which was formed in 1959 to enhance the professionalism of those involved in various aspects of the investment decision-making process and to recognize those who achieve a high level of professionalism. The ICFA combined with the Financial Analysts Federation in 1990 to form the Association for Investment Management and Research, which became CFA Institute in early 2004.

The mission of CFA Institute is to lead the investment profession globally by setting the highest standards of ethics, education, and professional excellence. As applied to the CFA program, the focus of CFA Institute is:

- To develop and keep current a "body of knowledge" applicable to the investment decision-making process. The principal components of this knowledge are financial accounting, economics, both debt and equity securities analysis, portfolio management, ethical and professional standards, and quantitative techniques.
- To administer a study and examination program for eligible candidates, the primary objectives of which are to assist the candidate in mastering and applying the body of knowledge and to test the candidate's competency in the knowledge gained.
- To award the professional CFA designation to those candidates who have passed three examination levels (encompassing a total of 18 hours of testing over a minimum of two years), who meet stipulated standards of professional conduct, and who otherwise are eligible for membership in CFA Institute.
- CFA Institute also provides a useful and informative program of continuing education through seminars, publications, and other formats that enable members, candidates, and others in the investment constituency to be more aware of and to better utilize the changing and expanding body of knowledge.

- Importantly, CFA Institute also sponsors and enforces a Code of Ethics and Standards of Professional Conduct that apply to enrolled candidates and to all members.

To enter the CFA program an applicant must have a bachelor's degree (or the equivalent work experience). Students who confirm they are in their final year of a degree program may register and enroll for Level I of the CFA program. Student candidates can take the CFA Level I exam and receive results but will not be allowed to enroll for the Level II exam until confirmation of a degree has been provided. A candidate may sit for all three examinations without having had investment experience *per se* or having joined a member society or chapter of CFA Institute. However, after passing the three examination levels, the CFA Charter will not be awarded unless or until the candidate:

- has at least four years of acceptable work experience and
- has been accepted for regular membership in CFA Institute and has applied for regular membership in an affiliated society.

The curriculum of the CFA study program covers:

1. Ethical and Professional Standards
2. Quantitative Methods
3. Economics
4. Financial Statement Analysis
5. Corporate Finance
6. Analysis of Debt Investments
7. Analysis of Equity Investments
8. Analysis of Derivatives
9. Analysis of Alternative Investments
10. Portfolio Management

Members and candidates are typically employed in the investment field. From 1963 to September 2005, over 73,000 charters have been awarded. More than 100,000 individuals were enrolled in the 2005 CFA Candidate Program. If you are interested in learning more about the CFA Program, CFA Institute has a booklet that describes the program and includes an application form. The address is: CFA Institute, Attn: Information Central, PO Box 3668, Charlottesville, Virginia, 22903, USA. You may also find more information at the CFA Institute website, http://www.cfainstitute.org, or by requesting a booklet by email to info@cfainstitute.org.

Code of Ethics and Standards of Professional Conduct

Preamble

The CFA Institute Code of Ethics and Standards of Professional Conduct (Code and Standards) are fundamental to the values of CFA Institute and essential to achieving its mission to lead the investment profession globally by setting high standards of education, integrity, and professional excellence. High ethical standards are critical to maintaining the public's trust in financial markets and in the investment profession. Since their creation in the 1960s, the Code and Standards have promoted the integrity of CFA Institute members and served as a model for measuring the ethics of investment professionals globally, regardless of job function, cultural differences, or local laws and regulations. All CFA Institute members (including holders of the Chartered Financial Analyst® (CFA®) designation) and CFA candidates must abide by the Code and Standards and are encouraged to notify their employer of this responsibility. Violations may result in disciplinary sanctions by CFA Institute. Sanctions can include revocation of membership, candidacy in the CFA Program, and the right to use the CFA designation.

The Code of Ethics

Members of CFA Institute (including Chartered Financial Analyst® [CFA®] charterholders and candidates for the CFA designation ("Members and Candidates") must:

- Act with integrity, competence, diligence, respect, and in an ethical manner with the public, clients, prospective clients, employers, employees, colleagues in the investment profession, and other participants in the global capital markets.
- Place the integrity of the investment profession and the interests of clients above their own personal interests.
- Use reasonable care and exercise independent professional judgment when conducting investment analysis, making investment recommendations, taking investment actions, and engaging in other professional activities.
- Practice and encourage others to practice in a professional and ethical manner that will reflect credit on themselves and the profession.
- Promote the integrity of, and uphold the rules governing, capital markets.
- Maintain and improve their professional competence and strive to maintain and improve the competence of other investment professionals.

Standards of Professional Conduct

I. Professionalism

A. Knowledge of the Law. Members and Candidates must understand and comply with all applicable laws, rules, and regulations (including the CFA Institute Code of Ethics and Standards of Professional Conduct) of any government, regulatory organization, licensing agency, or professional association governing their professional activities. In the event of conflict, Members and Candidates must comply with the more strict law, rule, or regulation. Members and Candidates must not knowingly participate or assist in and must dissociate from any violation of such laws, rules, or regulations.

B. Independence and Objectivity. Members and Candidates must use reasonable care and judgment to achieve and maintain independence and objectivity in their professional activities. Members and Candidates must not offer, solicit, or accept any gift, benefit, compensation, or consideration that reasonably could be expected to compromise their own or another's independence and objectivity.

C. Misrepresentation. Members and Candidates must not knowingly make any misrepresentations relating to investment analysis, recommendations, actions, or other professional activities.

D. Misconduct. Members and Candidates must not engage in any professional conduct involving dishonesty, fraud, or deceit or commit any act that reflects adversely on their professional reputation, integrity, or competence.

II. Integrity of Capital Markets

A. Material Nonpublic Information. Members and Candidates who possess material nonpublic information that could affect the value of an investment must not act or cause others to act on the information.

B. Market Manipulation. Members and Candidates must not engage in practices that distort prices or artificially inflate trading volume with the intent to mislead market participants.

III. Duties to Clients

A. Loyalty, Prudence, and Care. Members and Candidates have a duty of loyalty to their clients and must act with reasonable care and exercise prudent judgment. Members and Candidates must act for the benefit of their clients and place their clients' interests before their employer's or their own interests. In relationships with clients, Members and Candidates must determine applicable fiduciary duty and must comply with such duty to persons and interests to whom it is owed.

B. Fair Dealing. Members and Candidates must deal fairly and objectively with all clients when providing investment analysis, making investment recommendations, taking investment action, or engaging in other professional activities.

C. Suitability.
  1. When Members and Candidates are in an advisory relationship with a client, they must:
     a. Make a reasonable inquiry into a client's or prospective clients' investment experience, risk and return objectives, and financial constraints

prior to making any investment recommendation or taking investment action and must reassess and update this information regularly.

   b. Determine that an investment is suitable to the client's financial situation and consistent with the client's written objectives, mandates, and constraints before making an investment recommendation or taking investment action.

   c. Judge the suitability of investments in the context of the client's total portfolio.

2. When Members and Candidates are responsible for managing a portfolio to a specific mandate, strategy, or style, they must only make investment recommendations or take investment actions that are consistent with the stated objectives and constraints of the portfolio.

D. Performance Presentation. When communicating investment performance information, Members or Candidates must make reasonable efforts to ensure that it is fair, accurate, and complete.

E. Preservation of Confidentiality. Members and Candidates must keep information about current, former, and prospective clients confidential unless:

1. The information concerns illegal activities on the part of the client or prospective client.
2. Disclosure is required by law.
3. The client or prospective client permits disclosure of the information.

IV. Duties to Employers

A. Loyalty. In matters related to their employment, Members and Candidates must act for the benefit of their employer and not deprive their employer of the advantage of their skills and abilities, divulge confidential information, or otherwise cause harm to their employer.

B. Additional Compensation Arrangements. Members and Candidates must not accept gifts, benefits, compensation, or consideration that competes with, or might reasonably be expected to create a conflict of interest with, their employer's interest unless they obtain written consent from all parties involved.

C. Responsibilities of Supervisors. Members and Candidates must make reasonable efforts to detect and prevent violations of applicable laws, rules, regulations, and the Code and Standards by anyone subject to their supervision or authority.

V. Investment Analysis, Recommendations, and Action

A. Diligence and Reasonable Basis. Members and Candidates must:

1. Exercise diligence, independence, and thoroughness in analyzing investments, making investment recommendations, and taking investment actions.
2. Have a reasonable and adequate basis, supported by appropriate research and investigation, for any investment analysis, recommendation, or action.

B. Communication with Clients and Prospective Clients. Members and Candidates must:

1. Disclose to clients and prospective clients the basic format and general principles of the investment processes used to analyze investments, select securities, and construct portfolios and must promptly disclose any changes that might materially affect those processes.
2. Use reasonable judgment in identifying which factors are important to their investment analyses, recommendations, or actions and include those factors in communications with clients and prospective clients.
3. Distinguish between fact and opinion in the presentation of investment analysis and recommendations.

C. Record Retention. Members and Candidates must develop and maintain appropriate records to support their investment analysis, recommendations, actions, and other investment-related communications with clients and prospective clients.

VI. Conflicts of Interest

A. Disclosure of Conflicts. Members and Candidates must make full and fair disclosure of all matters that could reasonably be expected to impair their independence and objectivity or interfere with respective duties to their clients, prospective clients, and employer. Members and Candidates must ensure that such disclosures are prominent, are delivered in plain language, and communicate the relevant information effectively.

B. Priority of Transactions. Investment transactions for clients and employers must have priority over investment transactions in which a Member or Candidate is the beneficial owner.

C. Referral Fees. Members and Candidates must disclose to their employer, clients, and prospective clients, as appropriate, any compensation, consideration, or benefit received from, or paid to, others for the recommendation of products or services.

VII. Responsibilities as a CFA Institute Member or CFA Candidate

A. Conduct as Members and Candidates in the CFA Program. Members and Candidates must not engage in any conduct that compromises the reputation or integrity of CFA Institute or the CFA designation or the integrity, validity, or security of the CFA examinations.

B. Reference to CFA Institute, the CFA designation, and the CFA Program. When referring to CFA Institute, CFA Institute membership, the CFA designation, or candidacy in the CFA Program, Members and Candidates must not misrepresent or exaggerate the meaning or implications of membership in CFA Institute, holding the CFA designation, or candidacy in the CFA Program.

Interest Tables

TABLE C.1 Present Value of $1: PVIF $= 1/(1 + k)^t$

Period	1%	2%	3%	4%	5%	6%	7%	8%	9%	10%	12%	14%	15%	16%	18%	20%	24%	28%	32%	36%
1	.9901	.9804	.9709	.9615	.9524	.9434	.9346	.9259	.9174	.9091	.8929	.8772	.8696	.8621	.8475	.8333	.8065	.7813	.7576	.7353
2	.9803	.9612	.9426	.9246	.9070	.8900	.8734	.8573	.8417	.8264	.7972	.7695	.7561	.7432	.7182	.6944	.6504	.6104	.5739	.5407
3	.9706	.9423	.9151	.8890	.8638	.8396	.8163	.7938	.7722	.7513	.7118	.6750	.6575	.6407	.6086	.5787	.5245	.4768	.4348	.3975
4	.9610	.9238	.8885	.8548	.8227	.7921	.7629	.7350	.7084	.6830	.6355	.5921	.5718	.5523	.5158	.4823	.4230	.3725	.3294	.2923
5	.9515	.9057	.8626	.8219	.7835	.7473	.7130	.6806	.6499	.6209	.5674	.5194	.4972	.4761	.4371	.4019	.3411	.2910	.2495	.2149
6	.9420	.8880	.8375	.7903	.7462	.7050	.6663	.6302	.5963	.5645	.5066	.4556	.4323	.4104	.3704	.3349	.2751	.2274	.1890	.1580
7	.9327	.8706	.8131	.7599	.7107	.6651	.6227	.5835	.5470	.5132	.4523	.3996	.3759	.3538	.3139	.2791	.2218	.1776	.1432	.1162
8	.9235	.8535	.7894	.7307	.6768	.6274	.5820	.5403	.5019	.4665	.4039	.3506	.3269	.3050	.2660	.2326	.1789	.1388	.1085	.0854
9	.9143	.8368	.7664	.7026	.6446	.5919	.5439	.5002	.4604	.4241	.3606	.3075	.2843	.2630	.2255	.1938	.1443	.1084	.0822	.0628
10	.9053	.8203	.7441	.6756	.6139	.5584	.5083	.4632	.4224	.3855	.3220	.2697	.2472	.2267	.1911	.1615	.1164	.0847	.0623	.0462
11	.8963	.8043	.7224	.6496	.5847	.5268	.4751	.4289	.3875	.3505	.2875	.2366	.2149	.1954	.1619	.1346	.0938	.0662	.0472	.0340
12	.8874	.7885	.7014	.6246	.5568	.4970	.4440	.3971	.3555	.3186	.2567	.2076	.1869	.1685	.1372	.1122	.0757	.0517	.0357	.0250
13	.8787	.7730	.6810	.6006	.5303	.4688	.4150	.3677	.3262	.2897	.2292	.1821	.1625	.1452	.1163	.0935	.0610	.0404	.0271	.0184
14	.8700	.7579	.6611	.5775	.5051	.4423	.3878	.3405	.2992	.2633	.2046	.1597	.1413	.1252	.0985	.0779	.0492	.0316	.0205	.0135
15	.8613	.7430	.6419	.5553	.4810	.4173	.3624	.3152	.2745	.2394	.1827	.1401	.1229	.1079	.0835	.0649	.0397	.0247	.0155	.0099
16	.8528	.7284	.6232	.5339	.4581	.3936	.3387	.2919	.2519	.2176	.1631	.1229	.1069	.0930	.0708	.0541	.0320	.0193	.0118	.0073
17	.8444	.7142	.6050	.5134	.4363	.3714	.3166	.2703	.2311	.1978	.1456	.1078	.0929	.0802	.0600	.0451	.0258	.0150	.0089	.0054
18	.8360	.7002	.5874	.4936	.4155	.3503	.2959	.2502	.2120	.1799	.1300	.0946	.0808	.0691	.0508	.0376	.0208	.0118	.0068	.0039
19	.8277	.6864	.5703	.4746	.3957	.3305	.2765	.2317	.1945	.1635	.1161	.0829	.0703	.0596	.0431	.0313	.0168	.0092	.0051	.0029
20	.8195	.6730	.5537	.4564	.3769	.3118	.2584	.2145	.1784	.1486	.1037	.0728	.0611	.0514	.0365	.0261	.0135	.0072	.0039	.0021
25	.7798	.6095	.4776	.3751	.2953	.2330	.1842	.1460	.1160	.0923	.0588	.0378	.0304	.0245	.0160	.0105	.0046	.0021	.0010	.0005
30	.7419	.5521	.4120	.3083	.2314	.1741	.1314	.0994	.0754	.0573	.0334	.0196	.0151	.0116	.0070	.0042	.0016	.0006	.0002	.0001
40	.6717	.4529	.3066	.2083	.1420	.0972	.0668	.0460	.0318	.0221	.0107	.0053	.0037	.0026	.0013	.0007	.0002	.0001	•	•
50	.6080	.3715	.2281	.1407	.0872	.0543	.0339	.0213	.0134	.0085	.0035	.0014	.0009	.0006	.0003	.0001	•	•	•	•
60	.5504	.3048	.1697	.0951	.0535	.0303	.0173	.0099	.0057	.0033	.0011	.0004	.0002	.0001	•	•	•	•	•	•

*The factor is zero to four decimal places.

TABLE C.2 Present Value of an Annuity of $1 Per Period for n Periods:

$$PVIFA = \sum_{t=1}^{n} \frac{1}{(1+k)^t} = \frac{1 - \frac{1}{(1+k)^n}}{k}$$

Number of Payments	1%	2%	3%	4%	5%	6%	7%	8%	9%	10%	12%	14%	15%	16%	18%	20%	24%	28%	32%
1	0.9901	0.9804	0.9709	0.9615	0.9524	0.9434	0.9346	0.9259	0.9174	0.9091	0.8929	0.8772	0.8696	0.8621	0.8475	0.8333	0.8065	0.7813	0.7576
2	1.9704	1.9416	1.9135	1.8861	1.8594	1.8334	1.8080	1.7833	1.7591	1.7355	1.6901	1.6467	1.6257	1.6052	1.5656	1.5278	1.4568	1.3916	1.3315
3	2.9410	2.8839	2.8286	2.7751	2.7232	2.6730	2.6243	2.5771	2.5313	2.4869	2.4018	2.3216	2.2832	2.2459	2.1743	2.1065	1.9813	1.8684	1.7663
4	3.9020	3.8077	3.7171	3.6299	3.5460	3.4651	3.3872	3.3121	3.2397	3.1699	3.0373	2.9137	2.8550	2.7982	2.6901	2.5887	2.4043	2.2410	2.0957
5	4.8534	4.7135	4.5797	4.4518	4.3295	4.2124	4.1002	3.9927	3.8897	3.7908	3.6048	3.4331	3.3522	3.2743	3.1272	2.9906	2.7454	2.5320	2.3452
6	5.7955	5.6014	5.4172	5.2421	5.0757	4.9173	4.7665	4.6229	4.4859	4.3553	4.1114	3.8887	3.7845	3.6847	3.4976	3.3255	3.0205	2.7594	2.5342
7	6.7282	6.4720	6.2303	6.0021	5.7864	5.5824	5.3893	5.2064	5.0330	4.8684	4.5638	4.2883	4.1604	4.0386	3.8115	3.6046	3.2423	2.9370	2.6775
8	7.6517	7.3255	7.0197	6.7327	6.4632	6.2098	5.9713	5.7466	5.5348	5.3349	4.9676	4.6389	4.4873	4.3436	4.0776	3.8372	3.4212	3.0758	2.7860
9	8.5660	8.1622	7.7861	7.4353	7.1078	6.8017	6.5152	6.2469	5.9952	5.7590	5.3282	4.9464	4.7716	4.6065	4.3030	4.0310	3.5655	3.1842	2.8681
10	9.4713	8.9826	8.5302	8.1109	7.7217	7.3601	7.0236	6.7101	6.4177	6.1446	5.6502	5.2161	5.0188	4.8332	4.4941	4.1925	3.6819	3.2689	2.9304
11	10.3676	9.7868	9.2526	8.7605	8.3064	7.8869	7.4987	7.1390	6.8052	6.4951	5.9377	5.4527	5.2337	5.0286	4.6560	4.3271	3.7757	3.3351	2.9776
12	11.2551	10.5753	9.9540	9.3851	8.8633	8.3838	7.9427	7.5361	7.1607	6.8137	6.1944	5.6603	5.4206	5.1971	4.7932	4.4392	3.8514	3.3868	3.0133
13	12.1337	11.3484	10.6350	9.9856	9.3936	8.8527	8.3577	7.9038	7.4869	7.1034	6.4235	5.8424	5.5831	5.3423	4.9095	4.5327	3.9124	3.4272	3.0404
14	13.0037	12.1062	11.2961	10.5631	9.8986	9.2950	8.7455	8.2442	7.7862	7.3667	6.6282	6.0021	5.7245	5.4675	5.0081	4.6106	3.9616	3.4587	3.0609
15	13.8651	12.8493	11.9379	11.1184	10.3797	9.7122	9.1079	8.5595	8.0607	7.6061	6.8109	6.1422	5.8474	5.5755	5.0916	4.6755	4.0013	3.4834	3.0764
16	14.7179	13.5777	12.5611	11.6523	10.8378	10.1059	9.4466	8.8514	8.3126	7.8237	6.9740	6.2651	5.9542	5.6685	5.1624	4.7296	4.0333	3.5026	3.0882
17	15.5623	14.2919	13.1661	12.1657	11.2741	10.4773	9.7632	9.1216	8.5436	8.0216	7.1196	6.3729	6.0472	5.7487	5.2223	4.7746	4.0591	3.5177	3.0971
18	16.3983	14.9920	13.7535	12.6593	11.6896	10.8276	10.0591	9.3719	8.7556	8.2014	7.2497	6.4674	6.1280	5.8178	5.2732	4.8122	4.0799	3.5294	3.1039
19	17.2260	15.6785	14.3238	13.1339	12.0853	11.1581	10.3356	9.6036	8.9501	8.3649	7.3658	6.5504	6.1982	5.8775	5.3162	4.8435	4.0967	3.5386	3.1090
20	18.0456	16.3514	14.8775	13.5903	12.4622	11.4699	10.5940	9.8181	9.1285	8.5136	7.4694	6.6231	6.2593	5.9288	5.3527	4.8696	4.1103	3.5458	3.1129
25	22.0232	19.5235	17.4131	15.6221	14.0939	12.7834	11.6536	10.6748	9.8226	9.0770	7.8431	6.8729	6.4641	6.0971	5.4669	4.9476	4.1474	3.5640	3.1220
30	25.8077	22.3965	19.6004	17.2920	15.3725	13.7648	12.4090	11.2578	10.2737	9.4269	8.0552	7.0027	6.5660	6.1772	5.5168	4.9789	4.1601	3.5693	3.1242
40	32.8347	27.3555	23.1148	19.7928	17.1591	15.0463	13.3317	11.9246	10.7574	9.7791	8.2438	7.1050	6.6418	6.2335	5.5482	4.9966	4.1659	3.5712	3.1250
50	39.1961	31.4236	25.7298	21.4822	18.2559	15.7619	13.8007	12.2335	10.9617	9.9148	8.3045	7.1327	6.6605	6.2463	5.5541	4.9995	4.1666	3.5714	3.1250
60	44.9550	34.7609	27.6756	22.6235	18.9293	16.1614	14.0392	12.3766	11.0480	9.9672	8.3240	7.1401	6.6651	6.2402	5.5553	4.9999	4.1667	3.5714	3.1250

TABLE C.3   Future Value of \$1 at the End of n Periods: $FVIF_{k,n} = (1 + k)^n$

Period	1%	2%	3%	4%	5%	6%	7%	8%	9%	10%	12%	14%	15%	16%	18%	20%	24%	28%	32%	36%
1	1.0100	1.0200	1.0300	1.0400	1.0500	1.0600	1.0700	1.0800	1.0900	1.1000	1.1200	1.1400	1.1500	1.1600	1.1800	1.2000	1.2400	1.2800	1.3200	1.3600
2	1.0201	1.0404	1.0609	1.0816	1.1025	1.1236	1.1449	1.1664	1.1881	1.2100	1.2544	1.2996	1.3225	1.3456	1.3924	1.4400	1.5376	1.6384	1.7424	1.8496
3	1.0303	1.0612	1.0927	1.1249	1.1576	1.1910	1.2250	1.2597	1.2950	1.3310	1.4049	1.4815	1.5209	1.5609	1.6430	1.7280	1.9066	2.0972	2.3000	2.5155
4	1.0406	1.0824	1.1255	1.1699	1.2155	1.2625	1.3108	1.3605	1.4116	1.4641	1.5735	1.6890	1.7490	1.8106	1.9388	2.0736	2.3642	2.6844	3.0360	3.4210
5	1.0510	1.1041	1.1593	1.2167	1.2763	1.3382	1.4026	1.4693	1.5386	1.6105	1.7623	1.9254	2.0114	2.1003	2.2878	2.4883	2.9316	3.4360	4.0075	4.6526
6	1.0615	1.1262	1.1941	1.2653	1.3401	1.4185	1.5007	1.5869	1.6771	1.7716	1.9738	2.1950	2.3131	2.4364	2.6996	2.9860	3.6352	4.3980	5.2899	6.3275
7	1.0721	1.1487	1.2299	1.3159	1.4071	1.5036	1.6058	1.7138	1.8280	1.9487	2.2107	2.5023	2.6600	2.8262	3.1855	3.5832	4.5077	5.6295	6.9826	8.6054
8	1.0829	1.1717	1.2668	1.3686	1.4775	1.5938	1.7182	1.8509	1.9926	2.1436	2.4760	2.8526	3.0590	3.2784	3.7589	4.2998	5.5895	7.2058	9.2170	11.703
9	1.0937	1.1951	1.3048	1.4233	1.5513	1.6895	1.8385	1.9990	2.1719	2.3579	2.7731	3.2519	3.5179	3.8030	4.4355	5.1598	6.9310	9.2234	12.166	15.916
10	1.1046	1.2190	1.3439	1.4802	1.6289	1.7908	1.9672	2.1589	2.3674	2.5937	3.1058	3.7072	4.0456	4.4114	5.2338	6.1917	8.5944	11.805	16.059	21.646
11	1.1157	1.2434	1.3842	1.5395	1.7103	1.8983	2.1049	2.3316	2.5804	2.8531	3.4785	4.2262	4.6524	5.1173	6.1759	7.4301	10.657	15.111	21.198	29.439
12	1.1268	1.2682	1.4258	1.6010	1.7959	2.0122	2.2522	2.5182	2.8127	3.1384	3.8960	4.8179	5.3502	5.9360	7.2876	8.9161	13.214	19.342	27.982	40.037
13	1.1381	1.2936	1.4685	1.6651	1.8856	2.1329	2.4098	2.7196	3.0658	3.4523	4.3635	5.4924	6.1528	6.8858	8.5994	10.699	16.386	24.758	36.937	54.451
14	1.1495	1.3195	1.5126	1.7317	1.9799	2.2609	2.5785	2.9372	3.3417	3.7975	4.8871	6.2613	7.0757	7.9875	10.147	12.839	20.319	31.691	48.756	74.053
15	1.1610	1.3459	1.5580	1.8009	2.0789	2.3966	2.7590	3.1722	3.6425	4.1772	5.4736	7.1379	8.1371	9.2655	11.973	15.407	25.195	40.564	64.358	100.71
16	1.1726	1.3728	1.6047	1.8730	2.1829	2.5404	2.9522	3.4259	3.9703	4.5950	6.1304	8.1372	9.3576	10.748	14.129	18.488	31.242	51.923	84.953	136.96
17	1.1843	1.4002	1.6528	1.9479	2.2920	2.6928	3.1588	3.7000	4.3276	5.0545	6.8660	9.2765	10.761	12.467	16.672	22.186	38.740	66.461	112.13	186.27
18	1.1961	1.4282	1.7024	2.0258	2.4066	2.8543	3.3799	3.9960	4.7171	5.5599	7.6900	10.575	12.375	14.462	19.673	26.623	48.038	85.070	148.02	253.33
19	1.2081	1.4568	1.7535	2.1068	2.5270	3.0256	3.6165	4.3157	5.1417	6.1159	8.6128	12.055	14.231	16.776	23.214	31.948	59.567	108.89	195.39	344.53
20	1.2202	1.4859	1.8061	2.1911	2.6533	3.2071	3.8697	4.6610	5.6044	6.7275	9.6463	13.743	16.366	19.460	27.393	38.337	73.864	139.37	257.91	468.57
21	1.2324	1.5157	1.8603	2.2788	2.7860	3.3996	4.1406	5.0338	6.1088	7.4002	10.803	15.667	18.821	22.574	32.323	46.005	91.591	178.40	340.44	637.26
22	1.2447	1.5460	1.9161	2.3699	2.9253	3.6035	4.4304	5.4365	6.6586	8.1403	12.100	17.861	21.644	26.186	38.142	55.206	113.57	228.35	449.39	866.67
23	1.2572	1.5769	1.9736	2.4647	3.0715	3.8197	4.7405	5.8715	7.2579	8.9543	13.552	20.361	24.891	30.376	45.007	66.247	140.83	292.30	593.19	1178.6
24	1.2697	1.6084	2.0328	2.5633	3.2251	4.0489	5.0724	6.3412	7.9111	9.8497	15.178	23.212	28.625	35.236	53.108	79.496	174.63	374.14	783.02	1602.9
25	1.2824	1.6406	2.0938	2.6658	3.3864	4.2919	5.4274	6.8485	8.6231	10.834	17.000	26.461	32.918	40.874	62.668	95.396	216.54	478.90	1033.5	2180.0
26	1.2953	1.6734	2.1566	2.7725	3.5557	4.5494	5.8074	7.3964	9.3992	11.918	19.040	30.166	37.856	47.414	73.948	114.47	268.51	612.99	1364.3	2964.9
27	1.3082	1.7069	2.2213	2.8834	3.7335	4.8223	6.2139	7.9881	10.245	13.110	21.324	34.389	43.535	55.000	87.259	137.37	332.95	784.63	1800.9	4032.2
28	1.3213	1.7410	2.2879	2.9987	3.9201	5.1117	6.6488	8.6271	11.167	14.421	23.883	39.204	50.065	63.800	102.96	164.84	412.86	1004.3	2377.2	5483.8
29	1.3345	1.7758	2.3566	3.1187	4.1161	5.4184	7.1143	9.3173	12.172	15.863	26.749	44.693	57.575	74.008	121.50	197.81	511.95	1285.5	3137.9	7458.0
30	1.3478	1.8114	2.4273	3.2434	4.3219	5.7435	7.6123	10.062	13.267	17.449	29.959	50.950	66.211	85.849	143.37	237.37	634.81	1645.5	4142.0	10143.
40	1.4889	2.2080	3.2620	4.8010	7.0400	10.285	14.974	21.724	31.409	45.259	93.050	188.88	267.86	378.72	750.37	1469.7	5455.9	19426.	66520.	•
50	1.6446	2.6916	4.3839	7.1067	11.467	18.420	29.457	46.901	74.357	117.39	289.00	700.23	1083.6	1670.7	3927.3	9100.4	46890.	•	•	•
60	1.8167	3.2810	5.8916	10.519	18.679	32.987	57.946	101.25	176.03	304.48	897.59	2595.9	4383.9	7370.1	20555.	56347.	•	•	•	•

*FVIFA > 99,999

TABLE C.4   Sum of an Annuity of $1 Per Period for *n* Periods:

$$FVIFA_{k,n} = \sum_{t=1}^{n}(1+k)^{t-1} = \frac{(1+k)^n - 1}{k}$$

Number of Periods	1%	2%	3%	4%	5%	6%	7%	8%	9%	10%	12%	14%	15%	16%	18%	20%	24%	28%	32%	36%
1	1.0000	1.0000	1.0000	1.0000	1.0000	1.0000	1.0000	1.0000	1.0000	1.0000	1.0000	1.0000	1.0000	1.0000	1.0000	1.0000	1.0000	1.0000	1.0000	1.0000
2	2.0100	2.0200	2.0300	2.0400	2.0500	2.0600	2.0700	2.0800	2.0900	2.1000	2.1200	2.1400	2.1500	2.1600	2.1800	2.2000	2.2400	2.2800	2.3200	2.3600
3	3.0301	3.0604	3.0909	3.1216	3.1525	3.1836	3.2149	3.2464	3.2781	3.3100	3.3744	3.4396	3.4725	3.5056	3.5724	3.6400	3.7776	3.9184	4.0624	4.2096
4	4.0604	4.1216	4.1836	4.2465	4.3101	4.3746	4.4399	4.5061	4.5731	4.6410	4.7793	4.9211	4.9934	5.0665	5.2154	5.3680	5.6842	6.0156	6.3624	6.7251
5	5.1010	5.2040	5.3091	5.4163	5.5256	5.6371	5.7507	5.8666	5.9847	6.1051	6.3528	6.6101	6.7424	6.8771	7.1542	7.4416	8.0484	8.6999	9.3983	10.146
6	6.1520	6.3081	6.4684	6.6330	6.8019	6.9753	7.1533	7.3359	7.5233	7.7156	8.1152	8.5355	8.7537	8.9775	9.4420	9.9299	10.980	12.135	13.405	14.798
7	7.2135	7.4343	7.6625	7.8983	8.1420	8.3938	8.6540	8.9228	9.2004	9.4872	10.089	10.730	11.066	11.413	12.141	12.915	14.615	16.533	18.695	21.126
8	8.2857	8.5830	8.8923	9.2142	9.5491	9.8975	10.259	10.636	11.028	11.435	12.299	13.232	13.726	14.240	15.327	16.499	19.122	22.163	25.678	29.731
9	9.3685	9.7546	10.159	10.582	11.026	11.491	11.978	12.487	13.021	13.579	14.775	16.085	16.785	17.518	19.085	20.798	24.712	29.369	34.895	41.435
10	10.462	10.949	11.463	12.006	12.577	13.180	13.816	14.486	15.192	15.937	17.548	19.337	20.303	21.321	23.521	25.958	31.643	38.592	47.061	57.351
11	11.566	12.168	12.807	13.486	14.206	14.971	15.783	16.645	17.560	18.531	20.654	23.044	24.349	25.732	28.755	32.150	40.237	50.398	63.121	78.998
12	12.682	13.412	14.192	15.025	15.917	16.869	17.888	18.977	20.140	21.384	24.133	27.270	29.001	30.850	34.931	39.580	50.894	65.510	84.320	108.43
13	13.809	14.680	15.617	16.626	17.713	18.882	20.140	21.495	22.953	24.522	28.029	32.088	34.351	36.786	42.218	48.496	64.109	84.852	112.30	148.47
14	14.947	15.973	17.086	18.291	19.598	21.015	22.550	24.214	26.019	27.975	32.392	37.581	40.504	43.672	50.818	59.195	80.496	109.61	149.23	202.92
15	16.096	17.293	18.598	20.023	21.578	23.276	25.129	27.152	29.360	31.772	37.279	43.842	47.580	51.659	60.965	72.035	100.81	141.30	197.99	276.97
16	17.257	18.639	20.156	21.824	23.657	25.672	27.888	30.324	33.003	35.949	42.753	50.980	55.717	60.925	72.939	87.442	126.01	181.86	262.35	377.69
17	18.430	20.012	21.761	23.697	25.840	28.212	30.840	33.750	36.973	40.544	48.883	59.117	65.075	71.673	87.068	105.93	157.25	233.79	347.30	514.66
18	19.614	21.412	23.414	25.645	28.132	30.905	33.999	37.450	41.301	45.599	55.749	68.394	75.836	84.140	103.74	128.11	195.99	300.25	459.44	700.93
19	20.810	22.840	25.116	27.671	30.539	33.760	37.379	41.446	46.018	51.159	63.439	78.969	88.211	98.603	123.41	154.74	244.03	385.32	607.47	954.27
20	22.019	24.297	26.870	29.778	33.066	36.785	40.995	45.762	51.160	57.275	72.052	91.024	102.44	115.37	146.62	186.68	303.60	494.21	802.86	1298.8
21	23.239	25.783	28.676	31.969	35.719	39.992	44.865	50.422	56.764	64.002	81.698	104.76	118.81	134.84	174.02	225.02	377.46	633.59	1060.7	1767.3
22	24.471	27.299	30.536	34.248	38.505	43.392	49.005	55.456	62.873	71.402	92.502	120.43	137.63	157.41	206.34	271.03	469.05	811.99	1401.2	2404.6
23	25.716	28.845	32.452	36.617	41.430	46.995	53.436	60.893	69.531	79.543	104.60	138.29	159.27	183.60	244.48	326.23	582.62	1040.3	1850.6	3271.3
24	26.973	30.421	34.426	39.082	44.502	50.815	58.176	66.764	76.789	88.497	118.15	158.65	184.16	213.97	289.49	392.48	723.46	1332.6	2443.8	4449.9
25	28.243	32.030	36.459	41.645	47.727	54.864	63.249	73.105	84.700	98.347	133.33	181.87	212.79	249.21	342.60	471.98	898.09	1706.8	3226.8	6052.9
26	29.525	33.670	38.553	44.311	51.113	59.156	68.676	79.954	93.323	109.18	150.33	208.33	245.71	290.08	405.27	567.37	1114.6	2185.7	4260.4	8233.0
27	30.820	35.344	40.709	47.084	54.669	63.705	74.483	87.350	102.72	121.09	169.37	238.49	283.56	337.50	479.22	681.85	1383.1	2798.7	5624.7	11197.9
28	32.129	37.051	42.930	49.967	58.402	68.528	80.697	95.338	112.96	134.20	190.69	272.88	327.10	392.50	566.48	819.22	1716.0	3583.3	7425.6	15230.2
29	33.450	38.792	45.218	52.966	62.322	73.639	87.346	103.96	124.13	148.63	214.58	312.09	377.16	456.30	669.44	984.06	2128.9	4587.6	9802.9	20714.1
30	34.784	40.568	47.575	56.084	66.438	79.058	94.460	113.28	136.30	164.49	241.33	356.78	434.74	530.31	790.94	1181.8	2640.9	5873.2	12940.	28172.2
40	48.886	60.402	75.401	95.025	120.79	154.76	199.63	259.05	337.88	442.59	767.09	1342.0	1779.0	2360.7	4163.2	7343.8	22728.	69377.	*	*
50	64.463	84.579	112.79	152.66	209.34	290.33	406.52	573.76	815.08	1163.9	2400.0	4994.5	7217.7	10435.	21813.	45497.	*	*	*	*
60	81.669	114.05	163.05	237.99	353.58	533.12	813.52	1253.2	1944.7	3034.8	7471.6	18535.	29219.	46057.	*	*	*	*	*	*

*FVIF > 99,999

Appendix D

Standard Normal Probabilities

z	0.00	0.01	0.02	0.03	0.04	0.05	0.06	0.07	0.08	0.09
0.0	.5000	.5040	.5080	.5120	.5160	.5199	.5239	.5279	.5219	.5359
0.1	.5398	.5438	.5478	.5517	.5557	.5596	.5636	.5675	.5714	.5753
0.2	.5793	.5832	.5871	.5910	.5948	.5987	.6026	.6064	.6103	.6141
0.3	.6179	.6217	.6255	.6293	.6331	.6368	.6406	.6443	.6480	.6517
0.4	.6554	.6591	.6628	.6664	.6700	.6736	.6772	.6808	.6844	.6879
0.5	.6915	.6950	.6985	.7019	.7054	.7088	.7123	.7157	.7190	.7224
0.6	.7257	.7291	.7324	.7357	.7389	.7422	.7454	.7486	.7517	.7549
0.7	.7580	.7611	.7642	.7673	.7704	.7734	.7764	.7794	.7823	.7852
0.8	.7881	.7910	.7939	.7967	.7995	.8023	.8051	.8078	.8106	.8133
0.9	.8159	.8186	.8212	.8238	.8264	.8289	.8315	.8340	.8365	.8389
1.0	.8413	.8438	.8461	.8485	.8508	.8531	.8554	.8577	.8599	.8621
1.1	.8643	.8665	.8686	.8708	.8729	.8749	.8770	.8790	.8810	.8830
1.2	.8849	.8860	.8888	.8907	.8925	.8943	.8962	.8980	.8997	.9015
1.3	.9032	.9049	.9066	.9082	.9099	.9115	.9131	.9147	.9162	.9177
1.4	.9192	.9207	.9222	.9236	.9251	.9265	.9279	.9292	.9306	.9319
1.5	.9332	.9345	.9357	.9370	.9382	.9394	.9406	.9418	.9429	.9441
1.6	.9452	.9463	.9474	.9484	.9495	.9505	.9515	.9525	.9535	.9545
1.7	.9554	.9564	.9573	.9582	.9591	.9599	.9608	.9616	.9625	.9633
1.8	.9641	.9649	.9656	.9664	.9671	.9678	.9686	.9693	.9699	.9706
1.9	.9713	.9719	.9726	.9732	.9738	.9744	.9750	.9756	.9761	.9767
2.0	.9772	.9778	.9783	.9788	.9793	.9798	.9803	.9808	.9812	.9817
2.1	.9821	.9826	.9830	.9834	.9838	.9842	.9846	.9850	.9854	.9857
2.2	.9861	.9864	.9868	.9871	.9875	.9878	.9881	.9884	.9887	.9890
2.3	.9893	.9896	.9898	.9901	.9904	.9906	.9909	.9911	.9913	.9916
2.4	.9918	.9920	.9922	.9925	.9927	.9929	.9931	.9932	.9934	.9936
2.5	.9938	.9940	.9941	.9943	.9945	.9946	.9948	.9949	.9951	.9952
2.6	.9953	.9955	.9956	.9957	.9959	.9960	.9961	.9962	.9963	.9964
2.7	.9965	.9966	.9967	.9968	.9969	.9970	.9971	.9972	.9973	.9974
2.8	.9974	.9975	.9976	.9977	.9977	.9978	.9979	.9979	.9980	.9981
2.9	.9981	.9982	.9982	.9983	.9984	.9984	.9985	.9985	.9986	.9986
3.0	.9987	.9987	.9987	.9988	.9988	.9989	.9989	.9989	.9990	.9990

Comprehensive References List

Aber, John. 1976. "Industry Effects and Multivariate Stock Price Behavior." *Journal of Financial and Quantitative Analysis* 11, no. 5 (November).

Albright, S. Christian. 1987. *Statistics for Business and Economics.* New York: Macmillan.

Alexander, Gordon J. 1980. "Applying the Market Model to Long-Term Corporate Bonds." *Journal of Financial and Quantitative Analysis* 15, no. 5 (December): 1063–1080.

Alford, A., R. Jones, and K. Winkelmann. 2003. "A Spectrum Approach to Active Risk Budgeting." *Journal of Portfolio Management* 30: 49–60.

Allen, Julie A., and Janet L. Showers. 1991. *Equity-Index-Linked Derivatives: A User's Guide.* New York: Salomon Brothers.

Almazan, Andres, Keith C. Brown, Murray Carlson, and David A. Chapman. 2004. "Why Constrain Your Mutual Fund Manager?" *Journal of Financial Economics* 73, no. 2 (August): 289–321.

Altman, Edward I. 1968. "Financial Ratios, Discriminant Analysis and the Prediction of Corporate Bankruptcy." *Journal of Finance* 23, no. 4 (September): 589–609.

Altman, Edward I. 1989. "Measuring Corporate Bond Mortality and Performance." *Journal of Finance* 44, no. 4 (September): 909–922.

Altman, Edward I., ed. 1990. *The High-Yield Debt Market.* Homewood, IL: Dow Jones–Irwin.

Altman, Edward I. 1992. "Revisiting the High-Yield Bond Market." *Financial Management* 21, no. 2 (Summer): 78–92.

Altman, Edward I. 1993a. *Corporate Financial Distress and Bankruptcy,* 2nd ed. New York: Wiley.

Altman, Edward I. 1993b. "Defaulted Bonds: Demand, Supply, and Performance, 1987–1992." *Financial Analysts Journal* 49, no. 3 (May–June): 55–60.

Altman, Edward I., Robert G. Haldeman, and P. Narayanan. 1997. "Zeta Analysis: A New Model to Identify Bankruptcy Risk of Corporations." *Journal of Banking and Finance* 1, no. 2 (June).

Altman, Edward I., and Scott A. Nammacher. 1987. *Investing in Junk Bonds.* New York: Wiley.

Altman, Edward I., and Babe E. Simon. 2001. "The Investment Performance of Defaulted Bonds for 2000 and 1987–2000." New York: New York University Salomon Center, February.

Amihad, Y., and H. Mendelson. 1987. "Trading Mechanisms and Stock Returns. An Empirical Investigation." *Journal of Finance* 42, no. 3 (July): 533–553.

Ammann, Manuel, and Heinz Zimmermann. 2001. "Tracking Error and Tactical Asset Allocation." *Financial Analysts Journal* 57, no. 2 (March/April): 32–43.

Anderson, Jenny. 2005. "Cheap Seats Provide View of Troubles at Exchange." *New York Times,* January 10, pp. C1, C8.

Ankrim, Ernest M., and Chris R. Hensel. 1994. "Multicurrency Performance Attribution." *Financial Analysts Journal* 50, no. 2 (March–April): 29–35.

Arbel, Avner, and Paul Strebel. 1983. "Pay Attention to Neglected Firms!" *Journal of Portfolio Management* 9, no. 2 (Winter): 37–42.

Ascarelli, Silvia, and Peter McKay. 2005. "European Exchanges Gobble Up Each Other." *Wall Street Journal,* January 20, pp. C1, C4.

Asquith, Paul, and David W. Mullins, Jr. 1991. "Convertible Debt: Corporate Call Policy and Voluntary Conversion." *Journal of Finance* 46, no. 4 (September): 1273–1289.

Asquith, Paul, David W. Mullins, Jr., and Eric D. Wolff. 1989. "Original-Issue High-Yield Bonds: Aging Analysis of Defaults, Exchanges, and Calls." *Journal of Finance* 44, no. 4 (September): 929–952.

Association for Investment Management and Research (AIMR). 1999. *Standards of Practice Handbook,* 8th ed. Charlottesville, VA: AIMR.

Atkinson, Thomas R. 1967. *Trends in Corporate Bond Quality.* New York: National Bureau of Economic Research.

Avera, William F. 1994. "Definition of Industry Ethics and Development of a Code." In *Good Ethics: The Essential Element of a Firm's Success,* ed. K. Baker. Charlottesville, VA: AIMR.

Aziz, A., and G. H. Lawson. 1989. "Cash Flow Reporting and Financial Distress Models: Testing of Hypothesis." *Financial Management* 18, no. 1 (Spring): 55–63.

Babcock, Guilford. 1970. "The Concept of Sustainable Growth." *Financial Analysts Journal* 26, no. 3 (May–June): 108–114.

Baesel, Jerome, George Shows, and Edward Thorp. 1982. "Can Joe Granville Time the Market?" *Journal of Portfolio Management* 8, no. 3 (Spring): 5–9.

Bailey, Jeffrey V. 1992. "Are Manager Universes Acceptable Performance Benchmarks?" *Journal of Portfolio Management* 18, no. 3 (Spring): 9–13.

Bailey, Jeffrey V., Thomas M. Richards, and David E. Tierney. 1990. "Benchmark Portfolios and the Manager/Plan Sponsor Relationship." In *Current Topics in Investment Management,* ed. Frank J. Fabozzi and T. Dessa Fabozzi. New York: Harper & Row.

Bailey, Warren, and Joseph Lim. 1992. "Evaluating the Diversification Benefits of the New Country Funds." *Journal of Portfolio Management* 18, no. 3 (Spring): 74–80.

Baker, H. Kent, ed. 1992. *Improving the Investment Decision Process—Better Use of Economic Inputs in Security Analysis and Portfolio Management.* Charlottesville, VA: AIMR.

Ball, Ray. 1995. "The Theory of Stock Market Efficiency: Accomplishments and Limitations." *Journal of Applied Corporate Finance* 8, no. 1 (Spring): 4–18.

Balog, James, ed. 1993. *The Health Care Industry.* Charlottesville, VA: AIMR.

Bansal, Vipul S., M. E. Ellis, and John F. Marshall. 1993. "The Pricing of Short-Dated and Forward Interest Rate Swaps." *Financial Analysts Journal* 49, no. 2 (March–April): 82–87.

Banz, R. W. 1981. "The Relationship between Return and Market Value of Common Stocks." *Journal of Financial Economics* 9, no. 1 (March): 3–18.

Barber, Brad, and Terrance Odean. "Online Investors: Do the Slow Die First?" *Review of Financial Studies* 15, no. 2 (2002): 455–489.

Barber, Brad, and Terrance Odean. 1999. "The Courage of Misguided Convictions: The Trading Behavior of Individual Investors." *Financial Analysts Journal* 55, no. 6 (November–December): 41–55.

Barber, Brad, and Terrance Odean. 2000. "Trading Is Hazardous to Your Wealth: The Common Stock Investment Performance of Individual Investors." *Journal of Finance* 55, no. 2 (April): 773–806.

Barber, Brad, and Terrance Odean. 2001. "Boys Will Be Boys: Gender, Overconfidence, and Common Stock Investment." *Quarterly Journal of Economics* 116, no. 1 (February): 261–292.

Barclay, Michael J., William G. Christie, Jeffrey H. Harris, Eugene Kandel, and Paul Schultz. 1999. "The Effects of Market Reform on the Trading Costs and Depth of Nasdaq Stocks." *Journal of Finance* 54, no. 1 (March): 1–66.

Barclay, Michael, Clifford Holderness, and Jeffrey Pontiff. 1993. "Private Benefits from Block Ownership and Discounts on Closed-End Funds." *Journal of Financial Economics* 33, no. 3 (June): 263–292.

Barnhill, Theodore M., Jr., William F. Maxwell, and Mark R. Shenkman, eds. 1999. *High-Yield Bonds.* New York: McGraw-Hill.

Barone-Adesi, Giovanni, and Robert E. Whaley. 1986. "The Valuation of American Call Options and the Expected Ex-Dividend Stock Price Declines." *Journal of Financial Economics* 17, no. 1 (September): 91–112.

Barry, Christopher B., and Stephen J. Brown. 1984. "Differential Information and the Small Firm Effect." *Journal of Financial Economics* 13, no. 2 (June): 283–294.

Baruch, Lev. 1989. "On the Usefulness of Earnings and Earnings Research: Lessons and Directions from Two Decades of Empirical Research." *Journal of Accounting Research* 27 (Supplement).

Basu, Senjoy. 1977. "Investment Performance of Common Stocks in Relation to Their Price-Earnings Ratios: A Test of the Efficient Market Hypothesis." *Journal of Finance* 32, no. 3 (June): 663–682.

Battalio, Robert H. 1997. "Third Market Broker-Dealers: Cost Competitors or Cream Skimmers?" *Journal of Finance* 52, no. 1 (March): 341–352.

Battalio, Robert, Jason Greene, and Robert Jennings. 1997. "How Do Competing Specialists and Preferencing Dealers Affect Market Quality?" *Review of Financial Studies* 10: 969–993.

Baumol, William J., and Burton Malkiel. 1993. "Redundant Regulation of Foreign Security Trading and U.S. Competitiveness." *Journal of Applied Corporate Finance* 5, no. 4 (Winter): 19–27.

Beard, Allison. 2001. "Short Selling Goes from Strength to Strength." *Financial Times,* March 16, p. 29.

Beard, Craig, and Richard Sias. 1997. "Is There a Neglected-Firm Effect?" *Financial Analysts Journal* 53, no. 5 (September–October): 19–23.

Beaver, William H. 1966. "Financial Ratios as Predictors of Failure." *Empirical Research in Accounting: Selected Studies,* supplement to vol. 4, *Journal of Accounting Research.*

Beaver, William H. 1968. "Market Prices, Financial Ratios, and the Prediction of Failure." *Journal of Accounting Research* 6, no. 2 (Autumn).

Beaver, William H. 1989. *Financial Reporting: An Accounting Revolution.* Englewood Cliffs, NJ: Prentice Hall.

Beaver, William H., Paul Kettler, and Myron Scholes. 1970. "The Association between Market-Determined and Accounting-Determined Risk Measures." *Accounting Review* 45, no. 4 (October): 654–672.

Beaver, William H., and Dale Morse. 1978. "What Determines Price-Earnings Ratios?" *Financial Analysts Journal* 34, no. 4 (July–August): 65–76.

Beckers, Stan. 1981. "Standard Deviations Implied in Option Prices as Predictors of Future Stock Price Variability." *Journal of Banking and Finance* 5, no. 3 (September): 363–381.

Beidleman, Carl R., ed. 1991. *Interest Rate Swaps.* Homewood, IL: Business One–Irwin.

Belfer, Nathan. 1988. "Economic Indicators and Their Significance." In *The Financial Analysts Handbook,* 2nd ed., ed. Sumner N. Levine. Homewood, IL: Dow Jones–Irwin.

Belkaoui, Ahmed. 1980. "Industrial Bond Ratings: A New Look." *Financial Management* 9, no. 3 (Fall): 44–52.

Benesh, Gary A., and Pamela P. Peterson. 1986. "On the Relation between Earning Changes, Analysts' Forecasts and Stock Price Fluctuations." *Financial Analysts Journal* 42, no. 6 (November/December): 29–39.

Benning, Carl J. 1997. "Prediction Skills of Real-World Market Timers." *The Journal of Portfolio Management* 23, no. 2 (Winter): 55–65.

Benveniste, L. M., A. J. Marcus, and W. J. Wilhelm. 1992. "What's Special about the Specialist?" *Journal of Financial Economics* 32, no. 1 (August): 61–86.

Berkman, Neil. 1977. "Institutional Investors and the Stock Market." *New England Economic Review* (November–December): 60–77.

Berkowitz, Stephen A., Louis D. Finney, and Dennis Logue. 1988. *The Investment Performance of Corporate Pension Plans.* New York: Quorum Books.

Bernard, Victor. 1989. "Capital Markets Research in Accounting during the 1980s: A Critical Review." In *The State of Accounting Research as We Enter the 1990s,* ed. Thomas J. Frecka. Urbana: University of Illinois Press.

Bernard, Victor L., and Jacob K. Thomas. 1989. "Post-Earnings–Announcements Drift: Delayed Price Response or Risk Premium?" *Journal of Accounting Research* 27 (Supplement).

Bernard, Victor L., and Jacob K. Thomas. 1990. "Evidence That Stock Prices Do Not Fully Reflect the Implications of Current Earnings for Future Earnings." *Journal of Accounting and Economics* (December): 305–341.

Bernstein, Leopold A., and John J. Wild. 1998. *Financial Statement Analysis: Theory, Application, and Interpretation,* 6th ed. Homewood, IL: Irwin/McGraw-Hill.

Bernstein, Peter L. 2003. "Points of Inflection: Investment Management Tomorrow." *Financial Analysts Journal* 59, no. 4 (July–August): 18–23.

Bernstein, Richard. 1995. *Style Investing: Unique Insight into Equity Management.* New York: Wiley.

Bhandari, Laxmi Chand. 1988. "Debt/Equity Ratio and Expected Common Stock Returns: Empirical Evidence." *Journal of Finance* 43, no. 2 (June): 507–528.

Bharadwaj, Anu, and James B. Wiggins. 2001. "Box Spread and Put-Call Parity Tests for the S&P 500 Index LEAPS Market." *Journal of Derivatives* 8, no. 4 (Summer): 62–71.

Bhatia, Sanjiv, ed. 1995a. *The Consumer Staples Industry: Proceedings of the AIMR Seminar "Industry Analysis: Consumer Staples," March 28–29, 1995, St. Louis, Missouri.* Charlottesville, VA: AIMR.

Bhatia, Sanjiv, ed. 1995b. *Managing Assets for Individual Investors.* Charlottesville, VA: AIMR.

Bhatia, Sanjiv, ed. 1996a. *Global Equity Investing: Proceedings of the AIMR Seminar "Exploring the Frontiers of Global Equity Investing," November 29–December 1, 1995, Singapore.* Charlottesville, VA: AIMR.

Bhatia, Sanjiv, ed. 1996b. *The Media Industry: Proceedings of the AIMR Seminar "The Media Industry," January 31–February 1, 1996, New York, New York.* Charlottesville, VA: AIMR.

Bierwag, G. O. 1977. "Immunization, Duration, and the Term Structure of Interest Rates." *Journal of Financial and Quantitative Analysis* 12, no. 5 (December): 725–742.

Bierwag, G. O., and George G. Kaufman. 1977. "Coping with the Risk of Interest Rate Fluctuations: A Note." *Journal of Business* 50, no. 3 (July): 364–370.

Bierwag, G. O., George G. Kaufman, and Alden Toevs, eds. 1983. *Innovations in Bond Portfolio Management: Duration Analysis and Immunization.* Greenwich, CT: JAI Press.

Biger, Nahum, and John Hull. 1983. "The Valuation of Currency Options." *Financial Management* 12, no. 1 (Spring): 24–28.

Billingsley, Randall S., ed. 1994. *The Telecommunications Industry: November 10–11, 1993, New York, New York.* Charlottesville, VA: AIMR.

Billingsley, Randall, ed. 1995. *Corporate Financial Decision Making and Equity Analysis: Proceedings of the AIMR Seminar "Equity Analysis: The Role of Corporate Financial Decision Making," January 18, 1995, Washington, DC.* Charlottesville, VA: AIMR.

Billingsley, Randall S., R. Lamy, M. Marr, and T. Thompson. 1985. "Split Ratings and Bond Reoffering Yields." *Financial Management* 14, no. 2 (Summer): 59–65.

Black, Fischer. 1972. "Capital Market Equilibrium with Restricted Borrowing." *Journal of Business* 45, no. 3 (July): 444–445.

Black, Fischer. 1975. "Fact and Fantasy in the Use of Options." *Financial Analysts Journal* 31, no. 4 (July–August): 36–41, 61–72.

Black, Fischer. 1976. "The Pricing of Commodity Contracts." *Journal of Financial Economics* 3, no. 1/2 (January–March): 167–179.

Black, Fischer. 1989a. "How to Use the Holes in Black-Scholes." *Journal of Applied Corporate Finance* 1, no. 4 (Winter): 67–73.

Black, Fischer. 1989b. "How We Came Up with the Option Formula." *Journal of Portfolio Management* 15, no. 2 (Winter): 4–8.

Black, Fischer, E. Derman, and Wo Toy. 1990. "A One-Factor Model of Interest Rates and Its Application to Treasury Bond Options." *Financial Analysts Journal* 46, no. 1 (January–February): 33–39.

Black, Fischer, Michael Jensen, and Myron Scholes. 1972. "The Capital Asset Pricing Model: Some Empirical Tests." In *Studies in the Theory of Capital Markets,* ed. Michael Jensen. New York: Praeger.

Black, Fischer, and Myron Scholes. 1973. "The Pricing of Options and Corporate Liabilities." *Journal of Political Economy* 81, no. 2 (May–June): 637–654.

Black, Fischer, and Myron Scholes. 1979. "The Effects of Dividend Yield and Dividend Policy on Common Stock Prices and Returns." *Journal of Financial Economics* 1, no. 1 (March): 1–22.

Blake, Christopher R., Edwin J. Elton, and Martin J. Gruber. 1993. "The Performance of Bond Mutual Funds." *Journal of Business* 66, no. 3 (July): 371–403.

Bleakley, Fred R. 1996. "Economy's Strength Is Seen Cooling in Second Half." *Wall Street Journal,* July 1, p. A2.

Blume, Lawrence, David Easley, and Maureen O'Hara. 1994. "Market Statistics and Technical Analysis: The Role of Volume." *Journal of Finance* 49, no. 1 (March): 153–181.

Blume, Marshall E. 1993. "Soft Dollars and the Brokerage Industry." *Financial Analysts Journal* 49, no. 2 (March–April): 36–44.

Blume, Marshall E., and Jeremy J. Siegel. 1992. "The Theory of Security Pricing and Market Structure." *Financial Markets, Institutions and Instruments* 1, no. 3. New York University Salomon Center.

Boland, Vincent. 2001. "Securing a Future." *Financial Times,* March 5.

Bomberger, William A., and W. J. Frazer. 1981. "Interest Rates, Uncertainty, and the Livingston Data." *Journal of Finance* 36, no. 3 (June): 661–675.

Bookstaber, Richard M., and Roger G. Clarke. 1981. "Options Can Alter Portfolio Return Distributions." *Journal of Portfolio Management* 7, no. 3 (Spring): 63–70.

Bookstaber, Richard M., and Joseph A. Langsam. 2000. "Portfolio Insurance Trading Rules." *Journal of Futures Markets* 20, no. 1 (January).

Born, Jeffery, James Moses, and Dennis Officer. 1988. "Changes in Dividend Policy and Subsequent Earnings." *Journal of Portfolio Management* 14, no. 4 (Summer): 56–62.

Boyce, W. M., and A. J. Kalotay. 1979. "Optimum Bond Calling and Refunding." *Interfaces* (November): 36–49.

Bradford, R. W. 1989. "How to Lose a Mint." *Barron's,* March 6, pp. 54, 55.

Branch, Ben. 1977. "A Tax Loss Trading Rule." *Journal of Business* 50, no. 2 (April): 198–207.

Branch, Ben, and Kyun Chun Chang. 1985. "Tax-Loss Trading—Is the Game Over or Have the Rules Changed?" *Financial Review* 20, no. 1 (February): 55–69.

Brealey, Richard A., and Stewart C. Myers. 2004. *Principles of Corporate Finance,* 8th ed. New York: McGraw-Hill.

Brennan, Michael. 1969. "Capital Market Equilibrium with Divergent Borrowing and Lending Rules." *Journal of Financial and Quantitative Analysis* 4, no. 1 (March): 4–14.

Brennan, Michael J., and Eduardo S. Schwartz. 1985. "Evaluating Natural Resource Investments." *Journal of Business* 58, no. 2 (April): 135–158.

Brennan, Michael J., and A. Subramanyam. 1996. "Market Microstructure and Asset Pricing on the Compensation for Illiquidity in Stock Returns." *Journal of Financial Economics* 41, no. 3 (July): 341–344.

Brigham, Eugene. 2004. *Fundamentals of Financial Management,* 10th ed. Mason, OH: South-Western.

Brigham, Eugene, and Louis C. Gapenski. 2003. *Financial Management: Theory and Practice,* 10th ed. Cincinnati, OH: South-Western.

Brinson, G. 1998. "Investment Management in the 21st Century." In *The Future of Investment Management.* Charlottesville, VA: AIMR.

Brinson, Gary P., Jeffrey J. Diermeier, and G. G. Schlarbaum. 1986. "A Composite Portfolio Benchmark for Pension Plans." *Financial Analysts Journal* 42, no. 2 (March–April): 15–24.

Brinson, Gary P., L. Randolph Hood, and Gilbert L. Beebower. 1986. "Determinants of Portfolio Performance." *Financial Analysts Journal* 42, no. 4 (July–August): 39–44.

Brinson, Gary P., Brian D. Singer, and Gilbert L. Beebower. 1991. "Determinants of Portfolio Performance II: An Update." *Financial Analysts Journal* 47, no. 3 (May–June): 40–48.

Briys, Eric, Mondher Bellalah, Huu Minh Mai, and Francois De Varenne. 1998. *Options, Futures, and Exotic Derivatives.* New York: Wiley.

Brooks, Robert. 1997. *Interest Rate Modeling and the Risk Premiums in Interest Rate Swaps.* Charlottesville, VA: Research Foundation of the Institute of Chartered Financial Analysts.

Brown, David P., and Robert H. Jennings. 1989. "On Technical Analysis." *Review of Financial Studies* 2, no. 4 (October).

Brown, Gregory. 1999. "Volatility, Sentiment, and Noise Traders." *Financial Analysts Journal* 55, no. 2 (March–April): 82–90.

Brown, Gregory. 2001. "Managing Foreign Exchange Risk with Derivatives." *Journal of Financial Economics* 60, nos. 2–3 (May/June): 401–448.

Brown, Keith C., ed. 1993. *Derivative Strategies for Managing Portfolio Risk.* Charlottesville, VA: AIMR.

Brown, Keith C., and Gregory D. Brown. 1987. "Does the Composition of the Market Portfolio Really Matter?" *Journal of Portfolio Management* 13, no. 2 (Winter): 26–32.

Brown, Keith C., and W.V. Harlow, 2004. "Staying the Course: Performance Persistence and the Role of Investment Style Consistency in Professional Asset Management," Working Paper.

Brown, Keith C., W. V. Harlow, and Donald J. Smith. 1994. "An Empirical Analysis of Interest Rate Swap Spreads." *Journal of Fixed Income* 3, no. 3 (March): 61–78.

Brown, Keith C., W. V. Harlow, and Laura T. Starks. 1996. "Of Tournaments and Temptations: An Analysis of Managerial Incentives in the Mutual Fund Industry." *Journal of Finance* 51, no. 1 (March): 85–110.

Brown, Keith C., W. V. Harlow, and Seha M. Tinic. 1989. "How Rational Investors Deal with Uncertainty (or, Reports of the Death of Efficient Market Theory Are Greatly Exaggerated)." *Journal of Applied Corporate Finance* 2, no. 3 (Fall): 45–58.

Brown, Keith C., and Michael V. Raymond. 1986. "Risk Arbitrage and the Prediction of Successful Corporate Takeovers." *Financial Management* 15, no. 3 (August), 54–63.

Brown, Keith C., and Donald J. Smith. 1988. "Recent Innovations in Interest Rate Risk Management and the Reintermediation of Commercial Banking." *Financial Management* 17, no. 4 (Winter): 45–58.

Brown, Keith C., and Donald J. Smith. 1995a. *Interest Rate and Currency Swaps: A Tutorial.* Charlottesville, VA: Research Foundation of Institute of Chartered Financial Analysts.

Brown, Keith C., and Donald J. Smith. 1995b. "Structured Swaps." In *Yearbook of Fixed Income Investing,* ed. J. Finnerty and M. Fridson. Burr Ridge, IL: Irwin Professional.

Brown, Keith C., and Meir Statman. 1987. "The Benefits of Insured Stocks for Corporate Cash Management." *Advances in Futures and Options Research* 2: 243–261.

Brown, Ken. 2000. "Fund Diversification Dies a Not Very Slow Death." *Wall Street Journal,* February 7, pp. R1, R5.

Brown, Stephen J., and William Goetzmann. 1995. "Performance Persistence." *Journal of Finance* 50, no. 3 (June): 679–698.

Brown, Stephen J., William Goetzmann, Roger G. Ibbottson, and Stephen A. Ross. 1992. "Survivorship Bias in Performance Studies." *Review of Financial Studies* 5, no. 4 (December).

Brown, Stephen J., and Mark I. Weinstein. 1983. "A New Approach to Testing Asset Pricing Models: The Bilinear Paradigm." *Journal of Finance* 38, no. 3 (June): 711–743.

Buetow, Gerald W., Jr., and Frank J. Fabozzi. 2000. *Valuation of Interest Rate Swaps and Swaptions.* New York: Wiley.

Burmeister, Edwin, and Marjorie B. McElroy. 1988. "Joint Estimation of Factor Sensitivities and Risk Premia for the Arbitrage Pricing Theory." *Journal of Finance* 43, no. 3 (July): 721–733.

Burmeister, Edwin, Richard Roll, and Stephen A. Ross. 1994. "A Practitioner's Guide to Arbitrage Pricing Theory." In *A Practitioner's Guide to Factor Models,* ed. John Peavy. Charlottesville, VA: Research Foundation of the Institute of Chartered Financial Analysts.

Burns, Terence E., ed. 1998. *Derivatives in Portfolio Management.* Charlottesville, VA: AIMR.

Burns, Terence E., ed. 1999. *Investment Counseling for Private Clients.* Charlottesville, VA: AIMR.

Bush, Janet. 1990. "Hoping for a New Broom at the NYSE." *Financial Times,* August 16, p.13.

Byrnes, Nanette, and David Henry. 2001. "Confused about Earnings?" *BusinessWeek,* November 26, pp. 77–84.

Byrnes, Nanette, Mike McNamee, Diane Brady, Louis Lavelle, and Christopher Palmeri. 2002. "Accounting in Crisis." *BusinessWeek,* January 28, pp. 44–48.

Caccese, Michael S. 1997. "Ethics and the Financial Analyst." *Financial Analysts Journal* 53, no. 1 (January/February): 9–14.

Cagan, Phillip. 1969. *Essays on Interest Rates.* New York: Columbia University Press for the National Bureau of Economic Research.

Campbell, John Y., and John Ammer. 1993. "What Moves the Stock and Bond Markets? A Variance Decomposition for Long-Term Asset Returns." *Journal of Finance* 48, no. 1 (March): 3–38.

Cantor, Richard, and Frank Packer. 1995. "The Credit Rating Industry." *Journal of Fixed Income* 5, no. 3 (December): 10–34.

Capaul, Carlo, Ian Rowley, and William F. Sharpe. 1993. "International Value and Growth Stock Returns." *Financial Analysts Journal* 49, no.1 (January/February): 27–36.

Capon, N., G. Fitzsimons, and R. Prince. 1996. "An Individual Level Analysis of the Mutual Fund Investment Decision." *Journal of Financial Services Research* 10: 59–82.

Carhart, Mark M. 1997. "On Persistence in Mutual Fund Performance." *Journal of Finance* 52, no. 1 (March): 57–82.

Carpenter, Michael D., and David E. Upton. 1981. "Trading Volume and Beta Stability." *Journal of Portfolio Management* 7, no. 2 (Winter): 60–64.

Carr, Peter. 1988. "A Calculator Program for Option Values and Implied Standard Deviations." *Journal of Financial Education* 17, no. 1 (Fall): 89–93.

Carter, Richard B., Frederick Dark, and Asah Singh. 1998. "Underwriter Reputation, Initial Returns, and the Long-Run Performance of IPO Stocks." *Journal of Finance* 53, no. 1 (February): 285–311.

Case, Carl, and Robert Shiller. 1987. "Price of Single Family Homes since 1970: New Indexes for Four Cities." Working Paper no. 2393. New York: National Bureau of Economic Research.

Casey, Cornelius, and Norman Bartczak. 1985. "Using Operating Cash Flow Data to Predict Financial Distress: Some Extensions." *Journal of Accounting Research* 23, no. 1 (Spring).

Cavaglia, Stefano, Christopher Brightman, and Michael Aked. 2000. "The Increasing Importance of Industry Factors." *Financial Analysts Journal* 56, no. 5 (September–October): 41–54.

CFA Institute. 2004. *Points of Inflection: New Directions for Portfolio Management.* Charlottesville, VA: CFA Institute.

CFA Institute. 2005. *Managing Investment Portfolios: A Dynamic Process,* 3rd ed. Charlottesville, VA: CFA Institute.

Chan, Louis, Narasimhan Jegadeesh, and Josef Lakonishok. 1999. "The Profitability of Momentum Strategies." *Financial Analysts Journal* 55, no. 6 (November/December): 80–90.

Chan, Louis, and Josef Lakonishok. 2004. "Value and Growth Investing: Review and Update." *Financial Analysts Journal* 60, no. 1 (January/February): 71–86.

Chan, Wesley. 2003. "Stock Price Reaction to News and No-News: Drift and Reversal after Headlines." *Journal of Financial Economics* 70, no. 2 (November): 223–260.

Chance, Don M. 2003a. *Analysis of Derivatives for the CFA Program.* Charlottesville, VA: AIMR.

Chance, Don M. 2003b. *Introduction to Derivatives and Risk Management,* 6th ed. Fort Worth, TX: South-Western.

Chance, Don M. 2004. "Equity Swaps and Equity Investing." *Journal of Alternative Investing* 7 (Summer): 75–97.

Chance, Don M., and Pamela P. Peterson. 2002. *Real Options and Investment Valuation.* Charlottesville, VA: Research Foundation of AIMR.

Chance, Don M., and Don Rich. 1998. "The Pricing of Equity Swaps and Swaptions." *Journal of Derivatives* 5, no. 2 (Summer): 19–31.

Chang, Eric C., and Wilbur G. Lewellen. 1984. "Market Timing and Mutual Fund Investment Performance." *Journal of Business* 57, no. 1 (January): 57–72.

Charron, Terry Sylvester. 1999. "Tax Efficient Investing for Tax-Deferred and Taxable Accounts." *Journal of Private Portfolio Management* 2, no. 2 (Fall): 31–37.

Chemmanur, Thomas, and An Yan. 2004. "A Theory of Corporate Spin-offs." *Journal of Financial Economics* 72, no. 2 (May): 259–290.

Chen, H. L., N. Jegadeesh, and R. Wermers. 2000. "An Examination of the Stockholdings and Trades of Mutual Fund Managers." *Journal of Financial and Quantitative Analysis* 35 (September): 343–368.

Chen, Nai-fu. 1983. "Some Empirical Tests of the Theory of Arbitrage Pricing." *Journal of Finance* 38, no. 5 (December): 1393–1414.

Chen, Nai-fu, Richard Roll, and Stephen A. Ross. 1986. "Economic Forces and the Stock Market." *Journal of Business* 59, no. 3 (April): 383–404.

Chen, Son-Nan. 1981. "Beta Nonstationarity, Portfolio Residual Risk, and Diversification." *Journal of Financial and Quantitative Analysis* 16, no. 1 (March): 95–111.

Cherney, Elena, and Thom Beal. 2000. "As NYSE Plans for Global Market, Nasdaq Gets Left Out in the Cold." *Wall Street Journal,* June 8, p. C1.

Chernoff, Joel. 1996. "OECD Eyes Pension Rules." *Pensions and Investments,* December 23, pp. 2, 34.

Cho, D. Chinhyung. 1984. "On Testing the Arbitrage Pricing Theory: Inter-Battery Factor Analysis." *Journal of Finance* 39, no. 5 (December): 1485–1502.

Cho, D. Chinhyung, Edwin J. Elton, and Martin J. Gruber. 1984. "On the Robustness of the Roll and Ross Arbitrage Pricing Theory." *Journal of Financial and Quantitative Analysis* 19, no. 1 (March): 1–10.

Choi, Frederick D. S., Carol Ann Frost, and Gary Meek. 2000. *International Accounting.* Englewood Cliffs, NJ: Prentice Hall.

Choi, Seungmook, and Michael D. Mascozzi. 2001. "A Numerical Approach to American Currency Option Valuation." *Journal of Derivatives* 9, no. 2 (Winter): 19–29.

Choie, Kenneth S. 1990. "A Simplified Approach to Bond Portfolio Management: DDS." *Journal of Portfolio Management* 16, no. 3 (Spring): 40–45.

Chote, Robert. 1998. "Indonesia Risks Further Unrest as Debt Talks Falter." *Financial Times,* May 11, p. 1.

Chowdhury, M., J. S. Howe, and J. C. Lin. 1993. "The Relation between Aggregate Insider Transactions and Stock Market Returns." *Journal of Financial and Quantitative Analysis* 28, no. 3 (September): 431–437.

Christie, William. 1990. "Dividend Yield and Expected Returns." *Journal of Financial Economics* 28, no. 1 (November–December): 95–125.

Christie, William, and Paul Schultz. 1994. "Why Do Nasdaq Market Makers Avoid Odd-Eighth Quotes?" *Journal of Finance* 49, no. 5 (December): 1813–1840.

Christopherson, Jon A., Wayne E. Ferson, and Debra A. Glassman. 1998. "Conditioning Manager Alphas on Economic Information: Another Look at the Persistence of Performance," *Review of Financial Studies* 11, no. 1 (Spring): 111–142.

Christopherson, Jon A., and C. Nola Williams. 1995. "Equity Style: What It Is and Why It Matters." In *The Handbook of Equity Style Management,* ed. T. Daniel Coggin and Frank J. Fabozzi. New Hope, PA: Frank J. Fabozzi Associates.

Churchhill, Dwight D., ed. 1994. *Fixed-Income Management: Techniques and Practices.* Charlottesville, VA: AIMR.

Clarke, Roger G. 1992. *Options and Futures: A Tutorial.* Charlottesville, VA: Research Foundation of the Institute of Chartered Financial Analysts.

Clarke, Roger G., and Mark P. Kritzman. 1996. *Currency Management: Concepts and Practices.* Charlottesville, VA: Research Foundation of the Institute of Chartered Financial Analysts.

Clark, Roger G., and Meir Statman. 1998. "Bullish or Bearish." *Financial Analysts Journal* 54, no. 3 (May–June): 63–72.

Claus, James, and Jacob Thomas. 2001. "Equity Premium as Low as 3 Percent? Evidence from Analysts Earnings Forecasts for Domestic and International Stock Markets." *Journal of Finance* 56, no. 5 (October): 1629–1666.

Clayman, Michelle. 1987. "In Search of Excellence: The Investor's Viewpoint." *Financial Analysts Journal* 43, no. 3 (May–June): 54–63.

Clements, Jonathan. 1997a. "Retirement Honing: How Much Should You Have Saved for a Comfortable Life?" *Wall Street Journal,* January 28, p. C1.

Clements, Jonathan. 1997b. "Squeezing the Right Amount from a Retirement Stash." *Wall Street Journal,* February 25, p. C1.

Clements, Jonathan. 1997c. "Jam Today or Jam Tomorrow? Roth IRA Will Show Many Investors It Pays to Wait." *Wall Street Journal,* September 16, p. C1.

Coggin, Daniel T., Frank J. Fabozzi, and Shafiqur Rahman. 1993. "The Investment Performance of U.S. Equity Pension Fund Managers: An Empirical Investigation." *Journal of Finance* 48, no. 3 (July): 1039–1055.

Cohen, Abby J. 1996. "Economic Forecasts and the Asset Allocation Decision." In *Economic Analysis for Investment Professionals.* Charlottesville, VA: AIMR, November.

Cohen, Abby J., and Gabrielle Napolitano, eds. 2001. *Investment Strategy Chartbook.* New York: Goldman Sachs.

Colby, Robert W., and Thomas A. Mayers. 1988. *The Encyclopedia of Technical Market Indicators.* Homewood, IL: Dow Jones–Irwin.

Connor, Gregory. 1995. "The Three Types of Factor Models: A Comparison of Their Explanatory Power." *Financial Analysts Journal* 51, no. 3 (May/June): 42–46.

Connor, Gregory, and Robert A. Korajczyk. 1993. "A Test for the Number of Factors in an Approximate Factor Model." *Journal of Finance* 48, no. 4 (September): 1263–1291.

Cooper, Richard V. L. 1974. "Efficient Capital Markets and the Quantity Theory of Money." *Journal of Finance* 29, no. 3 (June): 887–908.

Copeland, Tom, Tim Koller, and Jack Murrin. 2001. *Valuation: Measuring and Managing the Value of Companies,* 3rd ed. New York: Wiley.

Core-Plus Bond Management. 2001. Charlottesville, VA: AIMR.

Cornell, Bradford. 1985. "Taxes and the Pricing of Stock Index Futures: Empirical Results." *Journal of Futures Markets* 5, no. 1: 89–101.

Cornell, Bradford. 1993. *Corporate Valuation.* Burr Ridge, IL: Irwin Professional.

Cornell, Bradford, and Marc R. Reinganum. 1981. "Forward and Futures Prices: Evidence from Foreign Exchange Markets." *Journal of Finance* 36, no. 5 (December): 1035–1045.

Corrado, Charles J., and Thomas W. Miller, Jr. 1996. "Efficient Option-Implied Volatility Estimators." *Journal of Futures Markets* 16, no. 3 (June): 247–272.

Cossin, Didier, and Hugues Pirotte. 2000. *Advanced Credit Risk Analysis.* Hoboken, NJ: Wiley.

Cox, John C., Jonathan Ingersoll, and Stephen Ross. 1981. "The Relation between Forward Prices and Futures Prices," *Journal of Financial Economics* 9, no. 4 (December): 321–346.

Cox, John C., Stephen A. Ross, and Mark Rubinstein. 1979. "Option Pricing: A Simplified Approach." *Journal of Financial Economics* 7, no. 3 (September): 229–264.

Cox, John C., and Mark Rubinstein. 1985. *Option Markets.* Englewood Cliffs, NJ: Prentice Hall.

Coy, Peter. 1999. "Exploiting Uncertainty: The 'Real Options' Revolution in Decision Making." *BusinessWeek Online,* June 7.

Crabbe, Leland E., and Joseph D. Argilagos. 1994. "Anatomy of the Structured Note Market." *Journal of Applied Corporate Finance* 7, no. 3 (Fall): 85–98.

Craig, Susanne, and Kate Kelly. 2004. "NYSE Chief Has Balancing Act." *Wall Street Journal,* February 3, pp. C1, C4.

Cummisford, R., and Scott Lummer. 1996. "Controlling the Limitations of Style Analysis." *Journal of Financial Planning* 9, no. 5 (October): 70–76.

Damodaran, Aswath. 1994. *Damodaran on Valuation.* New York: Wiley.

Damodaran, Aswath. 1996. *Investment Valuation.* New York: Wiley.

Daniel, Kent, Mark Grinblatt, Sheridan Titman, and Russ Wermers. 1997. "Measuring Mutual Fund Performance with Characteristics-Based Portfolios." *Journal of Finance* 52, no. 3 (July): 1035–1058.

Danielson, M. G. 1998. "A Simple Valuation Model and Growth Expectations." *Financial Analysts Journal* 54, no. 3 (May–June): 50–57.

Das, Satyajit. 2001. *Structured Products and Hybrid Securities,* 2nd ed. Hoboken, NJ: Wiley.

Dattatreya, Ravi E., and Frank J. Fabozzi. 1995. *Active Total Return Management of Fixed-Income Portfolios,* rev. ed. Burr Ridge, IL: Irwin Professional.

Davidson, Lawrence S., and Richard T. Froyen. 1982. "Monetary Policy and Stock Returns: Are Stock Markets Efficient?" Federal Reserve Bank of St. Louis *Review* 64, no. 3 (March): 3–12.

DeBondt, Werner F. M., and Richard Thaler. 1985. "Does the Stock Market Overreact?" *Journal of Finance* 40, no. 3 (July): 793–805.

DeFusco, Richard A., Dennis W. McLeavey, Jerald E. Pinto, and David E. Runkle. 2004. *Quantitative Methods for Investment Analysis,* 2nd ed. Charlottesville, VA: CFA Institute.

Del Guercio, Diane, "The Distorting Effect of the Prudent-Man Laws on Institutional Equity Investments," *Journal of Financial Economics* 40, no. 1 (January 1996), 31–62

DeMark, Thomas R. 1999. *The New Science of Technical Analysis.* New York: Wiley.

Dennis, Patrick, Steven Perfect, Karl Snow, and Kenneth Wiles. 1995. "The Effects of Rebalancing on Size and Book-to-Market Ratio Portfolio Returns." *Financial Analysts Journal* 51, no. 3 (May–June): 47–57.

Der Hovanesian, Mara. 2004. "Put the Big Board on the Big Board." *BusinessWeek,* September 13, pp. 90–91.

Desai, H., and P. Jain. 1999. "Firm Performance and Focus: Long-Run Stock Market Performance Following Spin-offs." *Journal of Financial Economics* 54, no. 1 (February): 75–102.

Dhrymes, Phoebus J., Irwin Friend, Mustofa N. Gultekin, and N. Bulent Gultekin. 1985. "New Tests of the APT and Their Implications." *Journal of Finance* 40, no. 3 (July): 659–674.

Dhrymes, Phoebus J., Irwin Friend, and N. Bulent Gultekin. 1984. "A Critical Re-examination of the Empirical Evidence on the Arbitrage Pricing Theory." *Journal of Finance* 39, no. 2 (June): 323–346.

Dialynas, Chris P. 2001. "The Active Decisions in the Selection of Passive Management and Performance Bogeys." In *The Handbook of Fixed-Income Securities,* 6th ed., ed. Frank J. Fabozzi. New York: McGraw-Hill.

Dialynas, Chris P., and David H. Edington. 1992. "Bond Yield Spreads—A Postmodern View." *Journal of Portfolio Management* 19, no. 1 (Fall): 60–75.

Diermeier, Jeffrey J. 1990. "Capital Market Expectations: The Macro Factors." In *Managing Investment Portfolios: A Dynamic Process,* 2nd ed., eds. John L. Maginn and Donald L. Tuttle. Boston: Warren, Gorham, & Lamont.

Dietz, Peter O. , H. Russell Fogier, and Donald J. Hardy. 1980. "The Challenge of Analyzing Bond Portfolio Returns." *Journal of Portfolio Management* 6, no. 3 (Spring): 53–58.

Dietz, Peter O., and Jeannette R. Kirschman. 1990. "Evaluating Portfolio Performance." In *Managing Investment Portfolios,* 2nd ed., ed. J. Maginn and D. Tuttle. Boston: Warren, Gorham, & Lamont.

Dimson, E. 1979. "Risk Management When Shares Are Subject to Infrequent Trading." *Journal of Financial Economics* 7, no. 2 (June): 197–226.

Douglas, G. W. 1969. "Risk in the Equity Markets: An Empirical Appraisal of Market Efficiency." *Yale Economic Essays* 9, no. 1: 3–48.

Dow Jones Investor's Handbook. Princeton, NJ: Dow Jones Books (annual).

Dreman, David M. 1998. *Contrarian Investment Strategies: The Next Generation.* New York: Simon & Schuster.

Droms, William G., ed. 1991. *Initiating and Managing a Global Investment Program.* Charlottesville, VA: AIMR.

Dubofsky, David A., and Thomas W. Miller. 2003. *Derivatives: Valuation and Risk Management.* New York: Oxford University Press.

DuBois, Charles H. 1992. "Tactical Asset Allocation: A Review of Current Techniques." In *Active Asset Allocation,* ed. R. Arnott and F. Fabozzi. Chicago: Probus.

Dudley, William C., and Jan Hatzius. 2000. "The Goldman Sachs Financial Conditions Index: The Right Tool for a New Monetary Policy Regime." *Goldman Sachs Global Economics Paper,* no. 44 (June 8). New York: Goldman Sachs Global Research.

Dudley, William C., and Edward F. McKelvey. January 1997. "The Brave New Business Cycle: No Recession in Sight." *U.S. Economics Research,* Goldman Sachs.

Dumbolena, I. G., and J. M. Shulman. 1988. "A Primary Rule of Detecting Bankruptcy: Watch the Cash." *Financial Analysts Journal* 44, no. 5 (September–October): 74–78.

Dunetz, Mark L., and James M. Mahoney. 1988. "Using Duration and Convexity in the Analysis of Callable Bonds." *Financial Analysts Journal* 44, no. 3 (May–June): 53–73.

Durand, David. 1957. "Growth Stocks and the Petersburg Paradox." *Journal of Finance* 12, no. 3 (September): 348–363.

Dutta, Prajit, and Ananth Madhaven. 1997. "Competition and Collusion in Dealer Markets." *Journal of Finance* 52, no. 1 (March): 245–276.

Dwyer, Paula, A. Osterland, K. Capell, and S. Reier. 1998. "The 21st Century Stock Market." *BusinessWeek,* August 10, pp. 66–72.

Dybvig, Philip H., and Stephen A. Ross. 1985. "Yes, The APT Is Testable." *Journal of Finance* 40, no. 4 (September): 1173–1188.

Easley, David, Nicholas Kiefer, and Maureen O'Hara. 1996. "Cream-Skimming or Profit Sharing? The Curious Role of Purchased Order Flow." *Journal of Finance* 51, no. 3 (July): 811–833.

Economides, Nicholas, and Robert A. Schwartz. 1995. "Electronic Call Market Trading." *Journal of Portfolio Management* 21, no. 3 (Spring): 10–18.

Ederington, L. H. 1985. "Why Split Ratings Occur." *Financial Management* 14, no. 1 (Spring): 37–47.

Edwards, Franklin. 1993. "Listing of Foreign Securities on U.S. Exchanges." *Journal of Applied Corporate Finance* 5, no. 4 (Winter): 28–36.

Edwards, R. D., and John Magee, Jr. 1992. *Technical Analysis of Stock Trends,* 6th ed. Boston: New York Institute of Finance.

Eichholtz, A. 1996. "Does International Diversification Work Better for Real Estate than for Stocks and Bonds?" *Financial Analysts Journal* 52, no. 1 (January–February): 56–62.

Ellis, Charles D. 1985. *Investment Policy: How to Win the Loser's Game.* Homewood, IL: Dow Jones–Irwin.

Elton, Edwin J., and Martin J. Gruber, eds. 1990. *Japanese Capital Markets.* New York: Harper & Row.

Elton, Edwin J., Martin J. Gruber, and Christopher R. Blake. 1996. "The Persistence of Risk-Adjusted Mutual Fund Performance." *Journal of Business* 69, no. 2 (April): 133–157.

Elton, Edwin J., Martin J. Gruber, Stephen J. Brown, and William N. Goetzmann. 2003. *Modern Portfolio Theory and Investment Analysis,* 6th ed. New York: Wiley.

Elton, Edwin J., Martin J. Gruber, and Joel Rentzler. 1983. "A Single Examination of the Empirical Relationship between Dividend Yields and Deviations from the CAPM." *Journal of Banking and Finance* 7, no. 1 (March): 135–146.

Emmons, William R. 1997. "Indexed Bonds and Falling Inflation Expectations." Federal Reserve Bank of St. Louis *Monetary Trends* (September).

Emmons, William R. 1999. "What Can 'Buy-and-Hold' Stock Investors Expect?" Federal Reserve Bank of St. Louis *Monetary Trends* (June).

European Bond Commission. 1989. *European Bond Markets.* Chicago: Probus.

Evans, John, and Stephen Archer. 1968. "Diversification and the Reduction of Dispersion: An Empirical Analysis." *Journal of Finance* 23, no. 5 (December): 761–767.

Evans, Thomas G., Martin E. Taylor, and Oscar Holzmann. 1985. *International Accounting and Reporting.* New York: Macmillan.

Ewing, Terzah, and Silvia Ascarelli. 2000. "One World, How Many Stock Exchanges?" *Wall Street Journal,* May 15, p. C1.

Ezra, D. Don. 1998. "Strategic Asset Allocation and Total Portfolio Returns." In *Asset Allocation in a Changing World.* Charlottesville, VA: AIMR.

Fabozzi, Frank J. 1988. *Fixed-Income Mathematics.* Chicago: Probus.

Fabozzi, Frank J., ed. 1989. *Advances and Innovations in the Bond and Mortgage Markets.* Chicago: Probus.

Fabozzi, Frank J., ed. 1990a. *The Japanese Bond Markets.* Chicago: Probus.

Fabozzi, Frank J., ed. 1990b. *The New High-Yield Debt Market.* New York: Harper Business.

Fabozzi, Frank J. 2000. *Fixed-Income Analysis.* New Hope, PA: Frank J. Fabozzi Associates.

Fabozzi, Frank J. 2004. *Fixed-Income Analysis for the Chartered Financial Analysts Program,* 2nd ed. New Hope, PA: Frank J. Fabozzi Associates.

Fabozzi, Frank J., ed. 2004. *Fixed-Income Readings for the Chartered Financial Analysts Program,* 2nd ed. New Hope, PA: Frank J. Fabozzi Associates.

Fabozzi, Frank J. 2004. *Bond Markets, Analysis and Strategies,* 5th ed. Upper Saddle River, NJ: Pearson Prentice Hall.

Fabozzi, Frank J., Steven V. Mann, and Mourad Choudhry. "Interest Rate Swaps and Swaptions." In *The Handbook of Fixed-Income Securities,* 7th ed. New York: McGraw-Hill.

Fabozzi, Frank J., Gerald W. Buetow, and Robert R. Johnson. 2005. "Measuring Interest Rate Risk." In *The Handbook of Fixed-Income Securities,* 7th ed., ed. Frank J. Fabozzi. New York: McGraw-Hill.

Fabozzi, Frank J. 2005. "Bond Immunization: An Asset/Liability Optimization Strategy." In *The Handbook of Fixed-Income Securities,* 7th ed., ed. Frank J. Fabozzi. New York: McGraw-Hill.

Fabozzi, Frank J. 2005. "Dedicated Bond Portfolios." In *The Handbook of Fixed-Income Securities,* 7th ed., ed. Frank J. Fabozzi. New York: McGraw-Hill.

Fabozzi, Frank J., Andrew J. Kalotay, and George O. Williams. 2005. "Valuation of Bonds with Embedded Options." In *The Handbook of Fixed-Income Securities,* 7th ed., ed. Frank J. Fabozzi. New York: McGraw-Hill.

Fabozzi, Frank J., and Christopher K. Ma. 1988. "The Over-the-Counter Market and New York Stock Exchange Trading Halts." *Financial Review* 23, no. 4 (November): 427–437.

Fabozzi, Frank J., and Chuck Ramsey. 2005. "Mortgages and Overview of Mortgage-Backed Securities." In *The Handbook of Fixed-Income Securities,* 7th ed., ed. Frank J. Fabozzi. New York: McGraw-Hill.

Fabozzi, Frank J., Richard Wilson, and Richard Todd. 2005. "Corporate Bonds." In *The Handbook of Fixed-Income Securities,* 7th ed., ed. Frank J. Fabozzi. New York: McGraw-Hill.

Fairfield, Patricia. 1994. "P/E, P/B, and the Present Value of Future Dividends." *Financial Analysts Journal* 50, no. 4 (July–August): 23–31.

Fama, Eugene F. 1970. "Efficient Capital Markets: A Review of Theory and Empirical Work." *Journal of Finance* 25, no. 2 (May): 383–417.

Fama, Eugene F. 1972. "Components of Investment Performance." *Journal of Finance* 27, no. 3 (June): 551–567.

Fama, Eugene F. 1976. "Forward Rates as Predictors of Future Spot Rates." *Journal of Financial Economics* 3, no. 4 (October): 361–377.

Fama, Eugene F. 1981. "Stock Returns, Real Activity, Inflation, and Money." *American Economic Review* 71, no. 4 (September): 545–565.

Fama, Eugene F. 1991a. "Efficient Capital Markets: II." *Journal of Finance* 46, no. 5 (December): 1575–1617.

Fama, Eugene F. 1991b. "Stock Returns, Real Activity, Inflation and Money." *American Economic Review* 71, no. 2 (June): 545–565.

Fama, Eugene F., L. Fisher, M. Jensen, and R. Roll. 1969. "The Adjustment of Stock Prices to New Information." *International Economic Review* 10, no. 1 (February): 1–21.

Fama, Eugene F., and Kenneth French. 1989. "Business Conditions and Expected Returns on Stocks and Bonds." *Journal of Financial Economics* 25, no. 1 (November): 23–49.

Fama, Eugene F., and Kenneth French. 1992. "The Cross Section of Expected Stock Returns." *Journal of Finance* 47, no. 2 (June): 427–465.

Fama, Eugene F., and Kenneth R. French. 1993. "Common Risk Factors in the Returns on Stocks and Bonds." *Journal of Financial Economics* 33, no. 1 (January): 3–56.

Fama, Eugene F., and Kenneth French. 1995. "Size and Book-to-Market Factors in Earnings and Returns." *Journal of Finance* 50, no. 1 (March): 131–155.

Fama, Eugene F., and Kenneth French. 1996. "Multifactor Explanations of Asset Pricing Anomalies." *Journal of Finance* 51, no. 1 (March): 55–84.

Fama, Eugene F., and Kenneth R. French. 1998. "Value versus Growth: The International Evidence." *Journal of Finance* 53, no. 6 (December): 1975–1999.

Fama, Eugene F., and Merton H. Miller. 1972. *The Theory of Finance.* New York: Holt, Rinehart and Winston.

Farinella, Joseph A., Edward Graham, and Cynthia McDonald. 2001. "Does High Short Interest Lead Underperformance?" *Journal of Investing* 10, no. 2 (Summer).

Farrell, James L. 1985. "The Dividend Discount Model: A Primer." *Financial Analysts Journal* 41, no. 6 (November–December): 16–25.

Farrell, James L., Jr. 1997. *Portfolio Management Theory and Application,* 2nd ed. New York: McGraw-Hill.

Feibel, Bruce J. 2003. *Investment Performance Measurement.* Hoboken, NJ: Wiley.

Feldstein, Sylvan G. 2005. "Guidelines in the Credit Analysis of General Obligation and Revenue Municipal Bonds." In *The Handbook of Fixed-Income Securities,* 7th ed., ed. Frank J. Fabozzi. New York: McGraw-Hill.

Feldstein, Sylvan, Frank J. Fabozzi, and Patrick M. Kennedy. 2005. "Municipal Bonds." In *The Handbook of Fixed-Income Securities,* 7th ed., ed. Frank J. Fabozzi. New York: McGraw-Hill.

Ferguson, Robert, and Dean Leistikow. 1998. "Are Regression Approach Futures Hedge Ratios Stationary?" *Journal of Futures Markets* 18, no. 7 (October): 851–866.

Fernholz, Robert, Robert Garvy, and John Hannon. 1998. "Diversity-Weighted Indexing." *Journal of Portfolio Management* 24, no. 2 (Winter): 74–82.

Ferris, Stephen P., and Anil K. Makhija. 1987. "A Search for Common Stock Inflation Hedges." *Review of Business and Economic Research* 22, no. 2 (Spring): 27–36.

Ferson, Wayne E., and Rudi W. Schadt. 1996. "Measuring Fund Strategy and Performance in Changing Economic Conditions." *Journal of Finance* 52, no. 2 (June): 425–461.

Fielitz, Bruce D. 1983. "Calculating the Bond Equivalent Yield for T-Bills." *Journal of Portfolio Management* 9, no. 3 (Spring): 58–60.

Figlewski, Stephen. 1989a. "Options Arbitrage in Imperfect Markets." *Journal of Finance* 44, no. 5 (December): 1289–1311.

Figlewski, Stephen. 1989b. "What Does an Option Pricing Model Tell Us about Option Prices?" *Financial Analysts Journal* 45, no. 5 (September–October): 12–15.

Finkel, Sidney R., and Donald L. Tuttle. 1971. "Determinants of the Aggregate Profit Margin." *Journal of Finance* 26, no. 5 (December): 1067–1075.

Finnerty, John D. 1983. "Evaluating the Economics of Refunding High-Coupon Sinking-Fund Debt." *Financial Management* 12, no. 1 (Spring): 5–10.

Finnerty, John D. 1992. "An Overview of Corporate Securities Innovation." *Journal of Applied Corporate Finance* 4, no. 4 (Winter).

Finnerty, John D., and Dean Leistikow. 1993. "The Behavior of Equity and Debt Risk Premiums." *Journal of Portfolio Management* 19, no. 4 (Summer): 73–84.

Fisher, Irving. 1961. *The Theory of Interest.* New York: Augustus M. Kelley. (Orig. publ. Macmillan, 1930)

Fisher, Kenneth L. 1984. *SuperStocks.* Woodside, CA: Business Classics.

Fisher, Lawrence. 1959. "Determinants of Risk Premiums on Corporate Bonds." *Journal of Political Economy* 67, no. 3 (June): 217–237.

Fisher, Lawrence, and James H. Lorie. 1977. *A Half Century of Returns on Stocks and Bonds.* Chicago: University of Chicago Graduate School of Business.

Fisher, Lawrence, and Roman L. Weil. 1971. "Coping with the Risk of Interest-Rate Fluctuations: Returns to Bondholders from Naive and Optimal Strategies." *Journal of Business* 44, no. 4 (October): 408–431.

Fisher, Phillip A. 1984. *Common Stocks and Uncommon Profits.* Woodside, CA: PSR Publications. (Orig. publ. Harper, 1958)

Fogler, H. Russell. 1993. "A Modern Theory of Security Analysis." *Journal of Portfolio Management* 19, no. 3 (Spring): 6–14.

Fogler, H. Russell, ed. 1994. *Blending Quantitative and Traditional Equity Analysis: March 30–31, 1994, Boston, Massachusetts.* Charlottesville, VA: AIMR.

Fogler, H. Russell, ed. 2001. *Developments in Quantitative Investment Models.* Charlottesville, VA: AIMR.

Fong, Gifford, Charles Pearson, and Oldrich Vasicek. 1983. "Bond Performance: Analyzing Sources of Return." *Journal of Portfolio Management* 9, no. 3 (Spring): 46–50.

Fong, Gifford, Charles Pearson, Oldrich Vasicek, and Theresa Conroy. 1991. "Fixed-Income Portfolio Performance: Analyzing Sources of Returns." In *The Handbook of Fixed-Income Securities,* 3rd ed., ed. Frank J. Fabozzi. Homewood, IL: Business One–Irwin.

Fong, H. Gifford. 2001. "Bond Management: Past, Current, and Future." In *The Handbook of Fixed-Income Securities,* 6th ed., ed. Frank J. Fabozzi. New York: McGraw-Hill.

Fons, Jerome S. 1991. "An Approach to Forecasting Default Rates." New York: Moody's Investors Services, August.

Foster, F. D., and S. Viswanathan. 1993. "The Effects of Public Information and Competition on Trading Volume and Price Volatility." *Review of Financial Studies* 6, no. 1 (Spring): 23–56.

Francis, Jack Clark, William W. Toy, and J. Gregg Whittaker. 1995. *The Handbook of Equity Derivatives.* Chicago: Irwin Professional.

Frecka, Thomas J., and Cheng F. Lee. 1983. "Generalized Financial Ratio Adjustment Processes and Their Implications." *Journal of Accounting Research* 27, no. 1 (Spring).

Fridson, Martin. 1989. *High-Yield Bonds: Assessing Risk and Identifying Value in Speculative Grade Securities.* Chicago: Probus.

Fridson, Martin S. 1994. "The State of the High-Yield Bond Market: Overshooting or Return to Normalcy." *Journal of Applied Corporate Finance* 7, no. 1 (Spring): 85–97.

Fridson, Martin S. 2002. "This Year in High Yield—2001." Merrill Lynch *Extra Credit* (January–February).

Fridson, Martin S., M. Christopher Garman, and Sheng Wu. 1997. "Real Interest Rates and the Default Rate on High-Yield Bonds." *Journal of Fixed Income* 7, no. 2 (September): 29–34.

Friedman, Milton. 1969. *The Optimum Quantity of Money and Other Essays.* Chicago: Aldine.

Friedman, Milton, and Leonard J. Savage. 1948. "The Utility Analysis of Choices Involving Risk." *Journal of Political Economy* 56, no. 3 (August): 279–304.

Friedman, Milton, and Anna J. Schwartz. 1963. "Money and Business Cycles." *Review of Economics and Statistics* 45, no. 1, part 2, supplement (February): 32–78.

Friend, Irwin, and Marshall Blume. 1970. "Measurement of Portfolio Performance under Uncertainty." *American Economic Review* 60, no. 4 (September): 561–575.

Friend, Irwin, Marshall Blume, and Jean Crockett. 1970. *Mutual Funds and Other Institutional Investors.* New York: McGraw-Hill.

Fruhan, William E., Jr. 1979. *Financial Strategy.* Homewood, IL: Richard D. Irwin.

Gahlon, James M., and James A. Gentry. 1982. "On the Relationship between Systematic Risk and the Degrees of Operating and Financial Leverage." *Financial Management* 11, no. 2 (Summer): 15–23.

Galai, Dan, and Meir I. Schneller. 1978. "Pricing Warrants and the Value of the Firm." *Journal of Finance* 33, no. 5 (December): 1333–1342.

Gall, Carlotta. 1998. "Moscow Stock Market Falls by 11.8%." *Financial Times,* May 19, p. 1.

Garman, Mark B., and Steven W. Kohlhagen. 1983. "Foreign Currency Option Values." *Journal of International Money and Finance* 2, no. 3 (December): 231–237.

Gastineau, Gary. 1988. *The Options Manual,* 3rd ed. New York: McGraw-Hill.

Gastineau, Gary. 1993. "Using Swaps in Equity Portfolios." In *Derivative Strategies for Managing Portfolio Risk,* ed. K. Brown. Charlottesville, VA: AIMR.

Gastineau, Gary. 2001. "Exchange-Traded Funds: An Introduction." *Journal of Portfolio Management* 27, no. 3 (Spring): 88–96.

Gastineau, Gary L., and Sanjiv Bhatia, eds. 1995. *Risk Management.* Proceedings of a seminar by the Association for Investment Management and Research. Charlottesville, VA: AIMR.

Gastineau, Gary L., and Mark P. Kritzman. 2001. *Dictionary of Financial Risk Management,* 3rd ed. New York: Wiley.

Gentry, James A., Paul Newbold, and David T. Whitford. 1985a. "Classifying Bankrupt Firms with Funds Flow Components." *Journal of Accounting Research* 23, no. 1 (Spring).

Gentry, James A., Paul Newbold, and David T. Whitford. 1985b. "Predicting Bankruptcy: If Cash Flow's Not the Bottom Line, What Is?" *Financial Analysts Journal* 41, no. 5 (September–October): 47–56.

Gentry, James A., David T. Whitford, and Paul Newbold. 1988. "Predicting Industrial Bond Ratings with a Profit Model and Funds Flow Components." *Financial Review* 23, no. 3 (August): 269–286.

Geske, Robert. 1979. "A Note on an Analytical Valuation Formula for Unprotected American Call Options on Stocks with Known Dividends." *Journal of Financial Economics* 7, no. 4 (June): 375–380.

Geweke, John, and Guofu Zhou. 1996. "Measuring the Price of the Arbitrage Pricing Theory." *Review of Financial Studies* 9, no. 2 (Summer): 557–587.

Gibbons, Michael. 1982. "Multivariate Tests of Financial Models: A New Approach." *Journal of Financial Economics* 10, no. 1 (March): 3–28.

Glickstein, David A., and Rolf E. Wubbels. 1983. "Dow Theory Is Alive and Well." *Journal of Portfolio Management* 9, no. 3 (Spring): 28–32.

Global Bond Management II: The Search for Alpha. 2000. Charlottesville, VA: AIMR.

Global Investment Performance Standards. 1999. Charlottesville, VA: AIMR.

Goetzmann, William N., and Roger G. Ibbotson. 1990. "The Performance of Real Estate as an Asset Class." *Journal of Applied Corporate Finance* 3, no. 1 (Spring): 65–76.

Gombola, M. F., M. E. Haskins, J. E. Katz, and D. D. Williams. 1987. "Cash Flow in Bankruptcy Prediction." *Financial Management* 16, no. 4 (Winter): 55–65.

Goodman, D. A., and John W. Peavy, III. 1983. "Industry Relative Price-Earnings Ratios as Indicators of Investment Returns." *Financial Analysts Journal* 39, no. 2 (March–April): 60–66.

Goodwin, Thomas H. 1998. "The Information Ratio." *Financial Analysts Journal* 54, no. 4 (July–August): 34–43.

Gordon, Myron J. 1962. *The Investment, Financing, and Valuation of the Corporation.* Homewood, IL: Irwin.

Grabbe, J. Orlin. 1986. *International Financial Markets.* New York: Elsevier Science.

Gray, H. Peter. 1976. "Determinants of the Aggregate Profit Margin: A Comment." *Journal of Finance* 31, no. 1 (March): 163–165.

Greenberg, Herb. 2000. "Alphabet Dupe: Why EBITDA Falls Short." *Fortune* 10 (July): 240–241.

Griffin, Paul A., and Antonio Z. Sanvicente. 1982. "Common Stock Returns and Rating Changes: A Methodological Comparison." *Journal of Finance* 37, no. 1 (March): 103–119.

Grinblatt, Mark, and Narasimhan Jegadeesh. 1996. "Relative Pricing of Eurodollar Futures and Forward Contracts." *Journal of Finance* 51, no. 4 (September): 1499–1522.

Grinblatt, Mark, and Sheridan Titman. 1992. "The Persistence of Mutual Fund Performance." *Journal of Finance* 47, no. 5 (June): 1977–1984.

Grinblatt, Mark, and Sheridan Titman. 1993. "Performance Measurement without Benchmarks: An Examination of Mutual Fund Returns." *Journal of Business* 66, no. 1 (January): 47–68.

Grinblatt, Mark, and Sheridan Titman. 1995. "Performance Evaluation." In *Handbook in Operations Research and Management Science,* ed. R. Jarrow et al. New York: Elsevier Science B.V.

Grinold, Richard C. 1992. "Are Benchmark Portfolios Efficient?" *Journal of Performance Management* 19, no. 1 (Fall): 34–40.

Grinold, Richard C., and Ronald N. Kahn. 1994. "Multiple-Factor Models for Portfolio Risk." In *A Practitioner's Guide to Factor Models,* ed. John Peavy. Charlottesville, VA: Research Foundation of the Institute of Chartered Financial Analysts.

Grinold, Richard C., and Ronald N. Kahn. 2000. *Active Portfolio Management,* 2nd ed. New York: McGraw-Hill.

Grossman, Sanford J., and Merton H. Miller. 1988. "Liquidity and Market Structure." *Journal of Finance* 43, no. 3 (July): 617–633.

Grundy, Kevin, and Burton Malkiel. 1996. "Reports of Beta's Death Have Been Greatly Exaggerated." *Journal of Portfolio Management* 22, no. 3 (Spring): 36–44.

Gudikunst, Arthur, and Joseph McCarthy. 1992. "Determinants of Bond Mutual Fund Performance." *Journal of Fixed Income* 2, no. 1 (June): 95–101.

Guerico, Diane Del. 1996. "The Distorting Effect of the Prudent-Man Laws on Institutional Equity Investments." *Journal of Financial Economics* 40, no. 1 (January): 31–62.

Gultekin, Mustofa N., and N. Bulent Gultekin. 1987. "Stock Return Anomalies and the Tests of APT." *Journal of Finance* 42, no. 5 (December): 1213–1224.

Gumbel, Peter. 1995. "The Hard Sell: Getting Germans to Invest in Stocks." *Wall Street Journal,* August 4, p. A2.

Hackel, Kenneth S., and Joshua Livnat. 1996. *Cash Flow and Security Analysis,* 2nd ed. Burr Ridge, IL: Irwin Professional.

Hafer, R. W. 1985. "The Response of Stock Prices to Changes in Weekly Money and the Discount Rate." Federal Reserve Bank of St. Louis *Review* 64, no. 3 (March): 5–14.

Hagstrom, Robert G. 2001. *The Essential Buffett.* New York: Wiley.

Hamao, Yasushi. 1989. "Japanese Stocks, Bonds, Inflation, 1973–1987." *Journal of Portfolio Management* 16, no. 2 (Winter): 20–26.

Handa, Puneet, S. P. Kothari, and Charles Wasley. 1989. "The Relation between the Return Interval and Betas: Implications of the Size Effect." *Journal of Financial Economics* 23, no. 1 (June): 79–100.

Handa, Puneet, and Robert A. Schwartz. 1996. "How Best to Supply Liquidity to a Securities Market." *Journal of Portfolio Management* 22, no. 2 (Winter): 44–51.

Hanks, Sara. 1990. "SEC Ruling Creates a New Market." *Wall Street Journal,* May 16, p. A12.

Hardy, Eric S. 1995. "The Ground Floor." *Forbes,* August 14, p. 185.

Harrington, Diana R. 1987. *Modern Portfolio Theory, the Capital Asset Pricing Model, and Arbitrage Pricing Theory: A User's Guide,* 2nd ed. Englewood Cliffs, NJ: Prentice Hall.

Harris, Diane. 1984. "An Investment for Rent." *Money,* April, pp. 87–90.

Harris, Jeffrey, and Paul Schultz. 1998. "The Trading Profits of SOES Bandits." *Journal of Financial Economics* 50, no. 1 (October): 39–62.

Harris, Larry. 2003. *Trading and Exchanges.* New York: Oxford University Press.

Harris, R. S. 1980. "The Refunding of Discounted Debt: An Adjusted Present Value Analysis." *Financial Management* 9, no. 4 (Winter): 7–12.

Hasbrouck, Joel. 1993. "Assessing the Quality of a Security Market: A New Approach to Transaction-Cost Measurement." *Review of Financial Studies* 6, no. 1.

Hasbrouck, Joel. 1995. "One Security, Many Markets: Determining the Contribution to Price Discovery." *Journal of Finance* 50, no. 4 (September): 1175–1200.

Haugen, Robert A., and Nardin L. Baker. 1996. "Commonality in the Determinants of Expected Stock Returns." *Journal of Financial Economics* 41, no. 3 (July): 401–439.

Hawawini, Gabriel. 1983. "Why Beta Shifts as the Return Interval Changes." *Financial Analysts Journal* 39, no. 3 (May–June): 73–77.

Hawawini, Gabriel. 1984. *European Equity Markets: Price Behavior and Efficiency.* Monograph Series in Finance and Economics, monograph no. 1984-4/5. New York: Salomon Brothers Center for the Study of Financial Institutions, Graduate School of Business, New York University.

Hawthorne, Fran. 1986. "The Battle of the Bond Indexes." *Institutional Investor* 20, no. 4 (April).

Hayre, Lakhbir, and Hubert Chang. 1997. "Effective and Empirical Durations of Mortgage Securities." *Journal of Fixed Income* 6, no. 4 (March): 17–33.

Hayre, Lakhbir S., Cyrus Mohebbi, and Thomas A. Zimmerman. 2005. "Mortgage Pass-Throughs." In *The Handbook of Fixed-Income Securities,* 7th ed., ed. Frank J. Fabozzi. New York: McGraw-Hill.

Heckle, Kenneth S., and Joshua Livnat. 1996. *Cash Flow and Security Analysis,* 2nd ed. Burr Ridge, IL: Business One–Irwin.

Helfert, Erich A. 2000. *Techniques of Financial Analysis,* 10th ed. Burr Ridge, IL: Irwin McGraw-Hill.

Helwege, Jean, and Paul Kleiman. 1997. "Understanding Aggregate Default Rates of High-Yield Bonds." *Journal of Fixed Income* 7, no. 1 (June): 55–61.

Hendershott, Terrence, and Haim Mendelson. 2000. "Crossing Networks and Dealer Markets: Competition and Performance." *Journal of Finance* 55, no. 5 (October): 2071–2115.

Hendriksson, Roy D., and Robert C. Merton. 1981. "On Market Timing and Investment Performance: Statistical Procedures for Evaluating Forecasting Skills." *Journal of Business* 54, no. 4 (October): 513–534.

Henriques, Diana. 1989. "Don't Take Any Wooden Nickels." *Barron's,* June 19, pp. 16, 18, 20, 32.

Henry, David. 2001. "The Numbers Game." *BusinessWeek,* May 14, pp. 100–110.

Hickman, Kent, and Glenn Petry. 1990. "A Comparison of Stock Price Predictions Using Court Accepted Formulas, Dividend Discount, and P/E Models." *Financial Management* (Summer): 76–87.

Hickman, W. Braddock. 1958. *Corporate Bond Quality and Investor Experience.* Princeton, NJ: Princeton University Press.

Hicks, John. 1939. *Value and Capital.* Oxford, UK: Clarendon Press.

Higgins, Robert C. 2000. *Analysis for Financial Management,* 5th ed. Chicago: Richard D. Irwin.

Holt, Charles C. 1962. "The Influence of Growth Duration on Share Prices." *Journal of Finance* 7, no. 3 (September): 465–475.

Holthausen, Robert W., and Richard W. Leftwich. 1986. "The Effect of Bond Rating Changes on Common Stock Prices." *Journal of Financial Economics* 17, no. 1 (September): 57–89.

Homa, Kenneth, and Dwight Jaffee. 1971. "The Study of Money and Stock Prices." *Journal of Finance* 26, no. 5 (December): 1015–1066.

Homer, Sidney, and Martin L. Leibowitz. 2004. *Inside the Yield Book: The Book that Changed Bond Analysis.* New York: Bloomberg.

Hopewell, Michael H., and George Kaufman. 1973. "Bond Price Volatility and Term to Maturity: A Generalized Respecification." *American Economic Review* 63, no. 4 (September): 749–753.

Hopewell, Michael H., and Arthur L. Schwartz, Jr. 1978. "Temporary Trading Suspensions in Individual NYSE Securities." *Journal of Finance* 33, no. 5 (December): 1355–1373.

Hopkins, Peter J. B., and C. Hayes Miller. 2001. *Country, Sector, and Company Factors in Global Equity Portfolios.*

Charlottesville, VA: Research Foundation of AIMR.

Horan, Stephen M., and D. Bruce Johnsen. 2000. *The Welfare Effects of Soft Dollar Brokerage: Law and Economics.* Charlottesville, VA: Research Foundation of the Institute of Chartered Financial Analysts.

Horowitz, Jed, and Kate Kelly. 2005. "NASD Completes Its Sale of Amex to Member Group." *Wall Street Journal,* January 4, p. C3.

Hourdouvelis, Gikas A. 1988. "The Predictive Power of the Term Structure during Recent Monetary Regimes." *Journal of Finance* 43, no. 2 (June): 339–356.

Howe, Jane Tripp. 1988. *Junk Bonds: Analysis and Portfolio Strategies.* Chicago: Probus.

Howe, John S., and Tie Su. 2001. "Discretionary Reductions in Warrant Exercise Prices." *Journal of Financial Economics* 61, no. 2 (August): 227–252.

Hsueh, L. Paul, and David S. Kidwell. 1988. "Bond Ratings: Are Two Better Than One?" *Financial Management* 17, no. 1 (Spring): 46–53.

Huang, Roger, and Hans Stoll. 1996. "Dealer versus Auction Markets: A Paired Comparison of Execution Costs on Nasdaq and the NYSE." *Journal of Financial Economics* 41, no. 3 (July): 313–357.

Huberman, Gur, and Shmuel Kandel. 1990. "Market Efficiency and Value Line's Record." *Journal of Business* 63, no. 2 (April).

Hudson-Wilson, Susan, and Bernard L. Elbaum. 1995. "Diversification Benefits for Investors in Real Estate." *Journal of Portfolio Management* 21, no. 3 (Spring): 92–99.

Hull, John. 2002. *Options, Futures, and Other Derivatives,* 5th ed. Upper Saddle River, NJ: Prentice Hall.

Hurley, M., S. Meers, B. Bornstein, and N. Strumingher. 1995. *The Coming Evolution of the Investment Management Industry: Opportunities and Strategies.* New York: Goldman Sachs, October.

Hynes, Joseph. 1987. "Key Risk Factors for LBOs." *Speculative Grade Debt Credit Review.* New York: Standard & Poor's, June 15.

Ibbotson Associates. *Stocks, Bonds, Bills, and Inflation.* Chicago: Ibbotson Associates, annual.

Ibbotson, Roger G., and Gary P. Brinson. 1993. *Global Investing.* New York: McGraw-Hill.

Ibbotson, Roger G., and Paul D. Kaplan. 2000. "Does Asset Allocation Policy Explain 40, 90, or 100 Percent of Performance?" *Financial Analysts Journal* 56, no. 1 (January–February): 26–33.

Ibbotson, Roger G., Paul D. Kaplan, and James D. Peterson. 1997. "Estimates of Small-Stock Betas Are Much Too Low." *Journal of Portfolio Management* 23, no. 4 (Summer): 104–111.

Ibbotson, Roger G., Jody Sindelar, and Jay R. Ritter. 1988. "Initial Public Offerings." *Journal of Applied Corporate Finance* 1, no. 3 (Summer).

Ibbotson, Roger G., Jody L. Sindelar, and Jay R. Ritter. 1994. "The Market Problems with the Pricing of Initial Public Offerings." *Journal of Applied Corporate Finance* 7, no. 1 (Spring): 66–74.

Ibbotson, Roger G., and Rex A. Sinquefield. 1982. *Stocks, Bonds, Bills and Inflation: The Past and Future.* Charlottesville, VA: Financial Analysts Research Foundation.

Imhoff, Eugene, and G. Lobo. 1984. "Information Content of Analysts' Composite Forecast Revisions." *Journal of Accounting Research* 22, no. 3 (Autumn).

Implementing Global Equity Strategy: Spotlight on Asia. 1997. Charlottesville, VA: AIMR.

Ineichen, Alexander M. 2000. "Twentieth Century Volatility." *Journal of Portfolio Management* 27, no. 1 (Fall): 93–101.

Ingersoll, Jonathan E., Jr. 1977. "An Examination of Corporate Call Policies on Convertible Securities." *Journal of Finance* 32, no. 2 (May): 463–478.

Investing Worldwide. Annual conference (beginning 1990) sponsored by the Association for Investment Management and Research (AIMR), Charlottesville, VA.

Ip, Greg. 1998a. "Prices Soften for Exchange Seats." *Wall Street Journal,* May 27, pp. C1, C17.

Ip, Greg. 1998b. "What's Behind the Trailing Performance of the Dow Industrials vs. the S & P 500?" *Wall Street Journal,* August 20, pp. C1, C17.

Ip, Greg. 1999. "Instinet Expands Its Presence." *Wall Street Journal,* July 28, p. C1.

Ip, Greg. 2000. "Margin Debt Set a Record in January, Sparking Fresh Fears Over Speculation." *Wall Street Journal,* February 15, pp. C1, C2.

Ip, Greg. 2001a. "Big Board Specialists: A Profitable Anachronism." *Wall Street Journal,* March 12, p. A10.

Ip, Greg. 2001b. "If Big Board Specialists Are an Anachronism, They're a Profitable One." *Wall Street Journal,* March 12, pp. A1, A10.

Ip, Greg, and Randal Smith. 1999. "Big Board Members Face Off on the Issue of Automated Trading." *Wall Street Journal,* November 15, p. 1.

Iqbal, M. Zafar. 2002. *International Accounting: A Global Approach.* Cincinnati, OH: South-Western.

Ivkovic, A., and N. Jegadeesh. 2004. "The Timing and Value of Forecast and Recommendation Revisions." *Journal of Financial Economics* 73, no. 3 (September): 433–463.

Jaffe, Jeffrey F., Donald Keim, and Randolph Westerfield. 1989. "Earnings Yields, Market Values, Stock Returns." *Journal of Finance* 44, no. 1 (March): 135–148.

Jaffe, Jeffrey F., and Gershon Mandelker. 1976. "The 'Fisher Effect' for Risky Assets: An Empirical Analysis." *Journal of Finance* 31, no. 2 (May): 447–458.

Jaffee, Dwight M. 1975. "Cyclical Variations in the Risk Structure of Interest Rates." *Journal of Monetary Economics* 1, no. 2 (July): 309–325.

Jagannathan, Ravi, and Zhenyu Wang. 1996. "The Conditional CAPM and the Cross Section of Expected Returns." *Journal of Finance* 51, no. 1 (March): 3–53.

Jain, Prom C. 1988. "Response of Hourly Stock Prices and Trading Volume to Economic News." *Journal of Business* 61, no. 2 (April).

James, Christopher, and Robert Edmister. 1983. "The Relation between Common Stock Returns, Trading Activity, and Market Value." *Journal of Finance* 38, no. 4 (September): 1075–1086.

Jarrow, Robert, and Stuart Turnbull. 2000. *Derivative Securities,* 2nd ed. Cincinnati, OH: Thomson Learning.

Jegadeesh, Narasimhan. 1990. "Evidence of Predictable Behavior of Security Returns." *Journal of Finance* 45, no. 3 (July): 881–898.

Jegadeesh, Narasimhan, J. Kim, S. Krische, and C. M. Lee. 2004. "Analyzing the Analysts: When Do Recommendations Add Value?" *Journal of Finance* 59, no. 3 (June): 1083–1124.

Jennings, Marianne M. 2000. "Professional Responsibilities, Ethics, and the Law." In *Ethical Issues for Today's Firm.* Charlottesville, VA: AIMR.

Jennings, Robert. 1984. *Reaction of Financial Analysts to Corporate Management Earnings per Share Forecasts.* Monograph no. 20. New York: Financial Analysts Research Foundation.

Jensen, Gerald R., Jeffrey Mercer, and Robert R. Johnson. 1996. "Business Conditions, Monetary Policy, and Expected Security Returns." *Journal of Financial Economics* 40, no. 2 (February): 213–237.

Jensen, Gerald R., Robert R. Johnson, and Jeffrey M. Mercer. 1997. "New Evidence on Size and Price-to-Book Effects in Stock Returns." *Financial Analysts Journal* 53, no. 6 (November–December): 34–42.

Jensen, Gerald R., Robert R. Johnson, and Jeffrey M. Mercer. 1998. "The Inconsistency of Small Firm and Value Stock Premiums." *Journal of Portflio Management* 24, no. 2 (Winter): 27–36.

Jensen, Gerald R., Robert R. Johnson, and Jeffrey M. Mercer. 2000. *The Role of Monetary Policy in Investment Management.* Charlottesville, VA: Research Foundation of AIMR.

Jensen, Michael C. 1968. "The Performance of Mutual Funds in the Period 1945–1964." *Journal of Finance* 23, no. 2 (May): 389–416.

Jensen, Michael C., and Clifford W. Smith, Jr., eds. 1986. "Symposium on Investment Banking and the Capital Acquisition Process." *Journal of Financial Economics* 15, no. 1/2 (January–February): 3–29.

Jensen, Michael C., and Jerald B. Warner. 1988. "The Distribution of Power among Corporate Managers, Shareholders, and Directors." *Journal of Financial Economics* 20, no. 1–2 (January–March): 3–24.

Jesswein, Kurt, Chuck C. Y. Kwok, and William R. Folks. 1995. "What New Currency Risk Products Are Companies Using and Why?" *Journal of Applied Corporate Finance* 8, no. 3 (Fall): 103–114.

Jobson, J. D. 1982. "A Multivariate Linear Regression Test for the Arbitrage Pricing Theory." *Journal of Finance* 37, no. 4 (September): 1037–1042.

Johnson, H. E. 1983. "An Analytic Approximation for the American Put Price." *Journal of Financial and Quantitative Analysis* 18, no. 1 (March): 143–151.

Johnson, Leland L. 1960. "The Theory of Hedging and Speculation in Commodity Futures." *Review of Economic Studies* 27: 139–160.

Johnson, R. S., Lyle Fiore, and Richard Zuber. "The Investment Performance of Common Stocks in Relation to Their Price-Earnings Ratios: An Update of the Basu Study." *Financial Review* 24, no. 3 (August 1989): 499–505.

Jones, C. N., G. Kaul, and M. L. Lipson. 1994. "Information, Trading and Volatility." *Journal of Financial Economics* 36, no. 1 (August): 127–154.

Jones, C. P., R. J. Rendleman, Jr., and H. A. Latané. 1985. "Earnings Announcements: Pre- and Post-Responses." *Journal of Portfolio Management* 11, no. 3 (Spring): 28–32.

Jones, Thomas P. 1995. "The Economic Value-Added Approach to Corporate Investments." In *Corporate Financial Decision Making and Equity Analysis.* Charlottesville, VA: AIMR.

Jonsson, Jon G., and Martin S. Fridson. 1996. "Forecasting Default Rates on High-Yield Bonds." *Journal of Fixed Income* 6, no. 1 (June): 69–77.

Jorion, Philippe. 1991. "The Pricing of Exchange Rate Risk in the Stock Market." *Journal of Financial and Quantitative Analysis* 26, no. 3 (September): 363–376.

Jost, Kathryn Dixon, ed. 2001a. *Best Execution and Portfolio Performance.* Charlottesville, VA: AIMR.

Jost, Kathryn Dixon, ed. 2001b. *Evolution in Equity Markets: Focus on Asia.* Charlottesville, VA: AIMR.

Jost, Kathryn Dixon, ed. 2002. *Fixed-Income Management for the 21st Century.* Charlottesville, VA: AIMR.

Kahle, Kathleen M., William F. Maxwell, and Danielle Xu. 2005. "Measuring Abnormal Bond Returns." Working paper, University of Arizona, February.

Kalotay, A. J. 1981. "On the Management of Sinking Funds." *Financial Management* 10, no. 2 (Summer): 34–40.

Kalotay, A. J. 1982a. "On the Structure and Valuation of Debt Refundings." *Financial Management* 11, no. 1 (Spring): 41–42.

Kalotay, A. J. 1982b. "Sinking Funds and the Realized Cost of Debt." *Financial Management* 11, no. 1 (Spring): 43–54.

Kamara, Avraham. 1984. "The Behavior of Futures Prices: A Review of Theory and Evidence." *Financial Analysts Journal* 40, no. 4 (July–August): 68–75.

Kamara, Avraham, and Thomas W. Miller, Jr. 1995. "Daily and Intradaily Tests for European Put-Call Parity." *Journal of Financial and Quantitative Analysis* 30, no. 4 (December): 519–539.

Kaplan, Robert S., and Gabrial Urwitz. 1979. "Statistical Models of Bond Ratings: A Methodological Inquiry." *Journal of Business* 52, no. 2 (April).

Kaplan, S. N., and R. S. Ruback. 1995. "The Valuation of Cash Flow Forecasts: An Empirical Analysis." *Journal of Finance* 50, no. 4 (September): 1059–1093.

Karnosky, Denis S., and Brian D. Singer. 1994. *Global Asset Management and Performance Measurement.* Charlottesville, VA: Research Foundation of the Institute of Chartered Financial Analysts.

Kat, Harry M. 2001. *Structured Equity Derivatives: The Definitive Guide to Exotic Options and Structured Notes.* London: Wiley.

Katz, Steven. 1974. "The Price Adjustment Process of Bonds to Rating Reclassifications: A Test of Bond Market Efficiency." *Journal of Finance* 29, no. 2 (May): 551–559.

Kee, C. 1993. "Market Integration and Price Execution for NYSE-Listed Securities." *Journal of Finance* 48, no. 3 (June): 1009–1038.

Keim, Donald B. 1983. "Size-Related Anomalies and Stock Return Seasonality." *Journal of Financial Economics* 12, no. 1 (June): 13–32.

Keim, Donald B. 1986. "The CAPM and Equity Return Regularities." *Financial Analysts Journal* 42, no. 3 (May–June): 19–34.

Keim, Donald B., and Michael Smirlock. 1989. "Pricing Patterns in Stock Index Futures." In *The Handbook of Stock Index Futures and Options,* ed. F. Fabozzi and G. Kipnis. Homewood, IL: Dow Jones–Irwin.

Keim, Donald B., and Robert F. Stambaugh. 1986. "Predicting Returns in Stock and Bond Markets." *Journal of Financial Economics* 17, no. 2 (December): 357–390.

Kelly, Kate. 2004a. "A Little Scary: NYSE's Chief Seeks to Sell Electronic Trading to the Floor." *Wall Street Journal,* February 2, pp. C1, C6.

Kelly, Kate. 2004b. "NYSE's Automatic Transition." *Wall Street Journal,* June 22, pp. C1, C5.

Kelly, Kate, and Deborah Solomon. 2004. "NYSE May Receive 'Fast Market' Status, as SEC Forges Rules." *Wall Street Journal,* February 24, p. C3.

Keran, Michael W. 1971. "Expectations, Money, and the Stock Market." Federal Reserve Bank of St. Louis *Review* 53, no. 1 (January): 16–31.

Kessel, Reuben A. 1965. "The Cyclical Behavior of the Term Structure of Interest Rates." Occasional Paper 91. New York: National Bureau of Economic Research.

Keynes, John Maynard. 1930. *A Treatise on Money.* London: Macmillan.

Khorana, Ajay, Edward Nelling, and Jeffrey Trester. 1998. "The Emergence of Country Index Funds." *Journal of Portfolio Management* 24, no. 4 (Summer): 78–84.

Kidwell, D. S., E. H. Sorenson, and J. M. Wachowicz. 1987. "Estimating the Signaling Benefits of Debt Insurance: The Case of Municipal Bonds." *Journal of Financial and Quantitative Analysis* 22, no. 3 (September): 299–313.

Kim, Sung-Hwa, and Gary D. Koppenhaver. 1993. "An Empirical Analysis of Bank Interest Rate Swaps." *Journal of Financial Services Research* 7, no. 1 (January): 57–72.

Klemkosky, Robert C. 1973. "The Bias in Composite Performance Measures." *Journal of Financial and Quantitative Analysis* 8, no. 3 (June): 505–514.

Klemkosky, Robert C., and Bruce G. Resnick. 1979. "Put-Call Parity and Market Efficiency. *Journal of Finance* 34, no. 5 (December): 1141–1155.

Klibanoff, Peter, Owen Lamont, and Thierry A. Wizman. 1998. "Investor Reaction to Salient News in Closed-End Country Funds." *Journal of Finance* 53, no. 2 (April): 673–699.

Koenig, Evan, and Kenneth Emery. 1991. "Misleading Indicators? Using the Composite Leading Indicators to Predict Cyclical Turning Points." Federal Reserve Bank of Dallas *Economic Review* (July): 1–14.

Kon, Stanley J. 1983. "The Market-Timing Performance of Mutual Fund Managers." *Journal of Business* 56, no. 3 (July): 323–347.

Kostovetsky, Leonard. 2003. "Index Mutual Funds and Exchange-Traded Funds." *Journal of Portfolio Management* 29, no. 4 (Summer): 80–92.

Kothari, S. P., and Jay Shanken. 2004. "Asset Allocation with Inflation-Protected Bonds." *Financial Analysts Journal* 60, no. 1 (January/February): 54–70.

Kothari, S. P., Jay Shanken, and Richard G. Sloan. 1995. "Another Look at the Cross Section of Expected Stock Returns." *Journal of Finance* 50, no. 2 (March): 185–224.

Kramer, Charles. 1994. "Macroeconomic Seasonality and the January Effect." *Journal of Finance* 49, no. 5 (December): 1883–1891.

Kraus, Alan, and Robert Litzenberger. 1976. "Skewness Preference and the Valuation of Risky Assets." *Journal of Finance* 31, no. 4 (September): 1085–1094.

Krehbiel, Tim, and Roger Collier. 1996. "Normal Backwardation in Short-Term Interest Rate Markets." *Journal of Futures Markets* 16, no. 8 (December): 899–913.

Kritzman, Mark. 1983. "Can Bond Managers Perform Consistently?" *Journal of Portfolio Management* 9, no. 4 (Summer): 54–56.

Kritzman, Mark. 1986. "What's Wrong with Portfolio Insurance?" *Journal of Portfolio Management* 13, no. 1 (Fall): 13–17.

Kritzman, Mark P. 1990. "Quantitative Methods in Performance Measurement." In *Quantitative Methods for Financial Analysis,* 2nd ed., ed. S. Brown and M. P. Kritzman. Homewood, IL: Dow Jones–Irwin.

Kuberek, Robert C. 1995. "Attribution Analysis for Fixed Income." In *Performance Evaluation, Benchmarks, and Attribution Analysis,* ed. J. Squires. Charlottesville, VA: AIMR.

Kuhn, Susan E. 1996. "Real Estate: A Smart Alternative to Stocks." *Fortune,* May 27, p. 186.

Laderman, Jeffrey M. 1996. "The Stampede to Index Funds." *Business Week,* April 1, pp. 78–79.

Lakonishok, Josef, Andrei Shleifer, and Robert W. Vishny. 1992. "The Structure and Performance of the Money Management Industry." In *Brookings Papers on Economic Activity.* Washington, DC: Brookings Institute.

Largay, J. A., and C. P. Stickney. 1980. "Cash Flows Ratio Analysis and the W. T. Grant Company Bankruptcy." *Financial Analysts Journal* 36, no. 4 (July–August): 51–54.

Lascelles, David. 1989. "Calls to Bring Watchdogs into Line." *Financial Times,* August 14, p. 10.

Layard-Liesching, Ronald. 2001. "Exploiting Opportunities in Global Bond Markets." In *Core-Plus Bond Management,* ed. Katrina Sherrerd. Charlottesville, VA: AIMR.

Lee, C. F., Joseph Finnerty, and Edgar Norton. 2003. *Foundations of Financial Management,* 3rd ed. St. Paul, MN: West.

Lee, Charles. 2003. "Fusion Investing." In *Equity Valuation in a Global Context.* Charlottesville, VA: AIMR.

Lee, Charles, Andrei Shleifer, and Richard Thaler. 1991. "Investor Sentiment and the Closed- End Fund Puzzle." *Journal of Finance* 46, no. 1 (March): 76–110.

Lehman Bros., Inc. 2005. "Collateralized Mortgage Obligations." In *The Handbook of Fixed-Income Securities,* 7th ed., ed. Frank J. Fabozzi. New York: McGraw-Hill.

Lehmann, Bruce N., and David M. Modest. 1988. "The Empirical Foundations of the Arbitrage Pricing Theory." *Journal of Financial Economics* 21, no. 3 (September).

Leibowitz, Martin L. 1986a. "The Dedicated Bond Portfolio in Pension Funds—Part I: Motivations and Basics." *Financial Analysts Journal* 42, no. 1 (January–February): 68–75.

Leibowitz, Martin L. 1986b. "The Dedicated Bond Portfolio in Pension Funds—Part II: Immunization, Horizon Matching, and Contingent Procedures." *Financial Analysts Journal* 42, no. 2 (March–April): 47–57.

Leibowitz, Martin L. 1987. *New Perspectives on Asset Allocation.* Charlottesville, VA: Research Foundation of the Institute of Chartered Financial Analysts.

Leibowitz, Martin L. 1997. *Sales Driven Franchise Value.* Charlottesville, VA: Research Foundation of the Institute of Chartered Financial Analysts.

Leibowitz, Martin L., Thomas E. Klaffky, Steven Mandel, and Alfred Weinberger. 1983. *Horizon Matching: A New Generalized Approach for Developing Minimum-Cost Dedicated Portfolios.* New York: Salomon Brothers.

Leibowitz, Martin L., and Stanley Kogelman. 1990. "Inside the P/E Ratio: The Franchise Factor." *Financial Analysts Journal* 46, no. 6 (November–December): 17–35.

Leibowitz, Martin L., and Stanley Kogelman. 1994. *Franchise Value and the Price-Earnings Ratio.* Charlottesville, VA: Research Foundation of the Institute of Chartered Financial Analysts.

Leibowitz, Martin L., William S. Krasker, and Ardavan Nozari. 1990. "Spread Duration: A New Tool for Bond Portfolio Management." *Journal of Portfolio Management* 16, no. 3 (Spring): 46–53.

Leibowitz, Martin L., and Alfred Weinberger. 1982. "Contingent Immunization—Part I: Risk Control Procedures." *Financial Analysts Journal* 38, no. 6 (November–December): 17–32.

Leibowitz, Martin L., and Alfred Weinberger. 1983. "Contingent Immunization—Part II: Problem Areas." *Financial Analysts Journal* 39, no. 1 (January–February): 35–50.

Leland, Hayne E. 1999. "Beyond Mean-Variance: Performance Measurement in a Nonsymmetrical World." *Financial Analysts Journal* 55, no. 1 (January–February): 27–36.

Lessard, Donald R. 1988. "International Diversification." In *The Financial Analyst's Handbook,* 2nd ed., ed. Sumner N. Levine. Homewood, IL: Dow Jones–Irwin.

Lev, Baruch. 1989. "On the Usefulness of Earnings and Earning Research: Lessons and Directions from Two Decades of Empirical Research." *Journal of Accounting Research* (Supplement).

Lev, Baruch, and S. Ramu Thiagarajan. 1993. "Fundamental Information Analysis." *Journal of Accounting Research* 37, no. 2 (Fall).

Levine, Sumner N., ed. 1988a. "Bond Ratings." In *The Financial Analyst's Handbook,* 2nd ed. Homewood, IL: Dow Jones–Irwin.

Levine, Sumner N., ed.1988b. *The Financial Analyst's Handbook,* 2nd ed. Homewood, IL: Dow Jones–Irwin.

Levy, Robert A. 1966. "Conceptual Foundations of Technical Analysis." *Financial Analysts Journal* 22, no. 4 (July–August): 83.

Lhabitant, Francois-Serge. 2002. *Hedge Funds: Myths and Limits.* Hoboken, NJ: Wiley.

Lim, Kian-Guan. 1989. "A New Test of the Three-Moment Capital Asset Pricing Model." *Journal of Financial and Quantitative Analysis* 24, no. 2 (June): 205–216.

Lintner, John. 1965. "Security Prices, Risk and Maximal Gains from Diversification." *Journal of Finance* 20, no. 4 (December): 587–615.

Litzenberger, Robert, and K. Ramaswamy. 1979. "The Effect of Personal Taxes and Dividends on Capital Asset Prices: Theory and Empirical Evidence." *Journal of Financial Economics* 7, no. 2 (June): 163–196.

Liu, P., and W. T. Moore. 1987. "The Impact of Split Bond Ratings on Risk Premia." *The Financial Review* 22, no. 1 (February).

Livingston, Douglas G. 1993. *The Fixed-Income Almanac.* Chicago: Probus.

Livingston, Miles. 1977. "Industry Movements of Common Stocks." *Journal of Finance* 32, no. 2 (June): 861–874.

Lo, Andrew W. 2002. "The Statistics of Sharpe Ratios." *Financial Analysts Journal* 58, no. 4 (July–August): 36–52.

Lo, Andrew W., and A. Craig MacKinley. 1999. *A Non-Random Walk down Wall Street.* Princeton, NJ: Princeton University Press.

Lo, Andrew W., Harry Mamasky, and Jiang Wang. 2000. "Foundations of Technical Analysis: Computational Algorithms, Statistical Inference, and Empirical Implementation." *Journal of Finance* 55, no. 4 (August): 1705–1765.

Loomis, Carol J. 1996. "Short Sellers and the Seamy Side of Wall Street." *Fortune,* July 22, pp. 66–72.

Lorie, James. 1975. "Diversification: Old and New." *Journal of Portfolio Management* 1, no. 2 (Winter): 25–28.

Loughran, Timothy, and Jay Ritter. 1995. "The New Issues Puzzle." *Journal of Finance* 50, no. 1 (March): 23–51.

Lowenstein, Roger. 1995. *Buffett: The Making of an American Capitalist.* New York: Random House.

Lucas, Douglas J., and John G. Lonski. 1992. "Changes in Corporate Credit Quality 1970–1990." *Journal of Fixed Income* 1, no. 4 (March): 7–14.

Lucchetti, Aaron, and Deborah Solomon. 2004. "Better Data on Prices of Corporate Bonds Would Slash Costs." *Wall Street Journal,* September 30, p. C4.

Lummer, Scott L. 1994. "Public Perception of the Investment Industry: Trends and Counteractions." In *Good Ethics: The Essential Element of a Firm's Success,* ed. K. Baker. Charlottesville, VA: AIMR.

Lummer, Scott L., and Mark W. Riepe. 1993. "Convertible Bonds as an Asset Class: 1957–1992." *Journal of Fixed Income* 3, no. 2 (September): 47–56.

Lynch, Peter. 1989. *One Up on Wall Street.* New York: Simon & Schuster.

Lynch, Peter. 1993. *Beating the Street.* New York: Simon & Schuster.

Macaulay, Frederick R. 1938. *Some Theoretical Problems Suggested by the Movements of Interest Rates, Bond Yields, and Stock Prices in the United States since 1856.* New York: National Bureau of Economic Research.

MacBeth, James D., and Larry J. Merville. 1979. "An Empirical Examination of the Black-Scholes Call Option Pricing Model." *Journal of Finance* 34, no. 5 (December): 1173–1186.

Madhaven, Ananth. 1992. "Trading Mechanisms in Securities Markets." *Journal of Finance* 47, no. 2 (June): 607–641.

Madhaven, Ananth. 1995. "Consolidation, Fragmentation, and the Disclosure of Trading Information." *Review of Financial Studies* 8, no. 2 (June).

Madhaven, Ananth, and George Sofianos. 1998. "An Empirical Analysis of NYSE Specialist Trading." *Journal of Financial Economics* 48, no. 2 (May): 189–210.

Maginn, John L., and Donald L. Tuttle, eds. 1990. *Managing Investment Portfolios: A Dynamic Process,* 2nd ed. Sponsored by the Institute of Chartered Financial Analysts. Boston: Warren, Gorham, & Lamont.

Malkiel, Burton G. 1962. "Expectations, Bond Prices, and the Term Structure of Interest Rates." *Quarterly Journal of Economics* 76, no. 2 (May): 197–218.

Malkiel, Burton G. 1995. "The Structure of Closed-End Fund Discounts Revisited." *Journal of Portfolio Management* 21, no. 4 (Summer 1995): 32–38.

Malkiel, Burton G. 2004. *A Random Walk down Wall Street.* New York: Norton.

Malkiel, Burton G., and John G. Cragg. 1970. "Expectations and the Structure of Share Prices." *American Economic Review* 60, no. 4 (September): 601–617.

Malvey, Jack. 2005. "Global Credit Bond Portfolio Management." In *The Handbook of Fixed-Income Securities,* 7th ed., ed. Frank J. Fabozzi. New York: McGraw-Hill.

Mandelker, Gershon M., and S. Ghon Rhee. 1984. "The Impact of Degrees of Operating and Financial Leverage on the Systematic Risk of Common Stock." *Journal of Financial and Quantitative Analysis* 19, no. 1 (March).

Margrabe, William. 1978. "The Value of an Option to Exchange One Asset for Another." *Journal of Finance* 33, no. 1 (March): 177–186.

Markowitz, Harry. 1952. "Portfolio Selection." *Journal of Finance* 7, no. 1 (March): 77–91.

Markowitz, Harry. 1959. *Portfolio Selection—Efficient Diversification of Investments.* New York: Wiley.

Marshall, William, and Jess B. Yawitz. 1980. "Optimal Terms of the Call Provision on a Corporate Bond." *Journal of Financial Research* 3, no. 3 (Fall): 203–211.

Mayhew, Stewart. 1995. "Implied Volatility." *Financial Analysts Journal* 51, no. 4 (July–August): 8–20.

McConnell, John J., and Gary Sanger. 1989. "A Trading Strategy for New Listings on the NYSE." *Financial Analysts Journal* 40, no. 1 (January–February): 38–39.

McCulloch, J. Huston. 1975. "An Estimate of the Liquidity Premium." *Journal of Political Economy* 83, no. 1 (January–February): 95–119.

McCulloch, Robert, and Peter Rossi. 1990. "Posterior, Predictive, and Utility-Based Approaches to Testing the Arbitrage Pricing Theory." *Journal of Financial Economics* 28, nos. 1 and 2 (November–December): 7–38.

McDonald, Robert L. 2003. *Derivatives Markets.* Boston, MA: Pearson Education.

McElravey, John N. 2005. "Securities Backed by Credit Card Receivables." In *The Handbook of Fixed-Income Securities,* 7th ed., ed. Frank J. Fabozzi. New York: McGraw-Hill.

McGee, Suzanna. 1998. "'$2 Brokers' Worried about Notoriety from Charges of Illegal Trading Scheme." *Wall Street Journal,* March 5, pp. C1, C22.

McGuire, S. R. 1991. *The Handbook of Convertibles.* New York: Simon & Schuster.

McNees, Stephen K. 1981. "The Recent Record of Thirteen Forecasters." Federal Reserve Bank of Boston *New England Economic Review* (September–October): 3–10.

Merjos, Anne. 1990. "How's the Market Doing?" *Barron's,* August 20, 18–20, 27, 28.

Merton, Robert C. 1973a. "The Relationship between Put and Call Option Prices: Comment." *Journal of Finance* 28, no. 1 (March): 183–184.

Merton, Robert C. 1973b. "Theory of Rational Option Pricing." *Bell Journal of Economics and Management* 4, no. 1 (Spring): 141–183.

Merton, Robert C. 1981. "On Market Timing and Investment Performance: An Equilibrium Theory of Value for Market Forecasts." *Journal of Business* 54, no. 3 (July): 363–406.

Merton, Robert C., Myron S. Scholes, and Matthew L. Gladstein. 1978. "A Simulation of the Returns and Risk of Alternative Option Portfolio Investment Strategies." *Journal of Business* 51, no. 2 (April): 183–242.

Meyers, Stephen L. 1973. "A Reexamination of Market and Industry Factors in Stock Price Behavior." *Journal of Finance* 28, no. 3 (June): 695–705.

Meyers, Thomas A. 1989. *The Technical Analysis Course.* Chicago: Probus.

Miller, Janet T., ed. 2001. *Investment Counseling for Private Clients, III.* Charlottesville, VA: AIMR.

Miller, Merton H. 1991. *Financial Innovations and Market Volatility.* Cambridge, MA: Blackwell.

Miller, Merton H., and Franco Modigliani. 1961. "Dividend Policy, Growth, and the Valuation of Shares." *Journal of Business* 34, no. 4 (October): 411–433.

Miller, Merton H., and Myron Scholes. 1982. "Dividends and Taxes: Some Empirical Evidence." *Journal of Political Economy* 90, no. 4 (December): 1118–1141.

Miller, Robert E., and Frank K. Reilly. 1987. "Examination of Mispricing, Returns, and Uncertainty for Initial Public Offerings." *Financial Management* 16, no. 2 (January): 33–38.

Milligan, John W. 1990. "Two Cheers for 144A." *Institutional Investor* 24, no. 9 (July): 117–119.

Minton, Bernadette A. 1997. "An Empirical Examination of Basic Valuation Models for Plain Vanilla U.S. Interest Rate Swaps." *Journal of Financial Economics* 44, no. 2 (May): 251–277.

Mitchell, Roger S., ed. 2000. *Investment Counseling for Private Clients, II.* Charlottesville, VA: AIMR.

Modigliani, Franco, and Leah Modigliani. 1997. "Risk-Adjusted Performance." *Journal of Portfolio Management* 23, no. 2 (Winter): 45–54.

Moore, Geoffrey. 1983. "An Introduction to International Economic Indicators." *Business Cycles, Inflation, and Forecasting,* 2nd ed. Studies in Business Cycles, No. 24. New York: National Bureau of Economic Research.

Moore, Geoffrey, and John P. Cullity. 1988. "Security Markets and Business Cycles." In *The Financial Analyst's Handbook,* 2nd ed., ed. Sumner N. Levine. Homewood, IL: Dow Jones–Irwin.

Moriarty, Eugene, Susan Phillips, and Paula Tosini. 1981. "A Comparison of Options and Futures in the Management of Portfolio Risk." *Financial Analysts Journal* 37, no. 1 (January–February): 61–67.

Mossavar-Rahmani, Sharmin. 1988. "Customized Benchmarks in Structured Management." *Journal of Portfolio Management* 13, no. 4 (Summer): 65–68.

Mossavar-Rahmani, Sharmin. 1991. *Bond Index Funds.* Chicago: Probus.

Mossavar-Rahmani, Sharmin. 2001. "Indexing Fixed-Income Assets." In *The Handbook of Fixed-Income Securities,* 6th ed., ed. Frank J. Fabozzi. New York: McGraw-Hill.

Mossavar-Rahmani, Sharmin. 2005. "Indexing Fixed-Income Assets." In *The Handbook of Fixed-Income Securities,* 7th ed., ed. Frank J. Fabozzi. New York: McGraw-Hill.

Mossin, J. 1966. "Equilibrium in a Capital Asset Market." *Econometrica* 34, no. 4 (October): 768–783.

Mozina, Dave, ed. 2001. "Size and Structure of the World Bond Market: 2001." International Fixed Income Research, Merrill Lynch, April.

Mull, S. R., and L. A. Socnen. 1997. "U.S. REITs as an Asset Class in International Investment Portfolios." *Financial Analysts Journal* 53, no. 2 (March–April): 55–61.

Munves, David. 2005. "The Eurobond Market." In *The Handbook of Fixed-Income Securities,* 7th ed. ed. Frank J. Fabozzi. New York: McGraw-Hill.

Myer, C. F., and James Webb. 1993. "Return Properties of Equity REITs, Common Stocks, and Commercial Real Estate: A Comparison." *Journal of Real Estate Research* 8, no. 1: 87–106.

Nasdaq Fact Book. Washington, DC: National Association of Securities Dealers, published annually.

Neal, Robert. 1992. "A Comparison of Transaction Cost between Competitive Market Maker and Specialist Market Structures." *Journal of Business* 65, no. 3 (July).

Nederlof, Maarten L. 1993. "The Comparison of Strategies Using Derivatives." In *Derivative Strategies for Managing Portfolio Risk,* ed. K. Brown. Charlottesville, VA: AIMR.

"New Ways to Play the Indexing Game." 1988. *Institutional Investor* 22, no. 13 (November): 92–98.

Nicholas, Joseph G. 1999. *Investing in Hedge Funds: Strategies for the New Marketplace.* Princeton, NJ: Bloomberg Press.

Norton, Joseph, and Paul Spellman, eds. 1991. *Asset Securitization.* Cambridge, MA: Basil Blackwell.

NYSE Fact Book. New York: New York Stock Exchange, published annually.

O'Shaughnessy, James P. 1997. *What Works on Wall Street.* New York: McGraw-Hill.

Odean, Terrance. 1998. "Are Investors Reluctant to Realize Their Losses?" *Journal of Finance* 53, no. 5 (October): 1775–1798.

Odean, Terrance. 1999. "Do Investors Trade Too Much?" *American Economic Review* 89 (December): 1279–1298.

Officer, R. R. 1973. "The Variability of the Market Factor of the New York Stock Exchange." *Journal of Business* 46, no. 3 (July): 434–453.

Ohlson, J. A. 1980. "Financial Ratios and the Probabilistic Prediction of Bankruptcy." *Journal of Accounting Research* 18, no. 2 (Spring).

Olsen, Robert A. 1998. "Behavioral Finance and Its Implications for Stock-Price Volatility." *Financial Analysts Journal* 54, no. 2 (March/April): 10–18.

Ou, J., and S. Penman. 1989. "Financial Statement Analysis and the Prediction of Stock Returns." *Journal of Accounting and Economics,* no. 4 (November).

Pagano, M. 1989. "Trading Volume and Asset Liquidity." *Quarterly Journal of Economics* 104, no. 2.

Palepu, Krishna, Victor Bernard, and Paul Healy. 2004. *Business Analysis and Valuation.* Cincinnati, OH: South-Western.

Pardee, Scott E. 1987. "Internationalization of Financial Markets." Federal Reserve Bank of Kansas City *Economic Review* (February): 3–7.

Park, H. Y., and Andrew H. Chen. 1985. "Differences between Forward and Futures Prices: A Further Investigation of Marking to Market Effects." *Journal of Futures Markets* 5, no. 7 (February): 77–88.

Patelis, Alex D. 1997. "Stock Returns Predictability and the Role of Monetary Policy." *Journal of Finance* 52, no. 5 (December): 1951–1972.

Peavy, John. 1990. *Cases in Portfolio Management.* Charlottesville, VA: AIMR.

Peavy, John W., III, and David A. Goodman. 1983. "The Significance of P/Es for Portfolio Returns." *Journal of Portfolio Management* 9, no. 2 (Winter).

Penman, S. H. 1996. "The Articulation of Price-Earnings Ratios and Market-to-Book Ratios and the Evaluation of Growth." *Journal of Accounting Research* 34, no. 2 (Spring).

Performance Reporting for Investment Managers. 1991. Charlottesville, VA: AIMR.

Perry, Kevin J., and Robert A. Taggart, Jr. 1988. "The Growing Role of Junk Bonds in Corporate Finance." *Journal of Applied Corporate Finance* 1, no. 1 (Spring): 37–45.

Peters, Donald J. 1991. "Valuing a Growth Stock." *Journal of Portfolio Management* 17, no. 3 (Spring): 49–51.

Peterson, Pamela P., and David Peterson. 1996. "Company Performance Measures of Value Added." Charlottesville,

VA: Research Foundation of the Institute of Chartered Financial Analysis.

Petrie, Thomas A., ed. 1993. *The Oil and Gas Industries.* Proceedings from the fourth AIMR Industry seminar, November 12–13, 1992, in Houston, Texas. Charlottesville, VA: AIMR.

Pettengill, Glenn, Sridhar Dundaram, and Ike Matthur. 1995. "The Conditional Relation between Beta and Returns." *Journal of Financial and Quantitative Analysis* 30, no. 1 (March): 101–115.

Pettit, R. R., and P. C. Venkatesh. 1995. "Insider Trading and Long-Run Return Performance." *Financial Management* 24, no. 2 (Summer): 88–103.

Pierce, Douglas, and Vance Roley. 1985. "Stock Prices and Economic News." *Journal of Business* 59, no. 1 (Summer).

Pierce, Phyllis S., ed. *The Business One Irwin Investor's Handbook.* Burr Ridge, IL: Dow Jones Books, published annually.

Pinches, George E. 1970. "Financing with Convertible Preferred Stock, 1960–1967." *Journal of Finance* 25, no. 1 (March): 56–63.

Pinches, George E., and Clay Singleton. 1978. "The Adjustment of Stock Prices to Bond Rating Changes." *Journal of Finance* 33, no. 1 (March): 29–44.

Porter, Michael E. 1980a. *Competitive Strategy: Techniques for Analyzing Industries and Competitors.* New York: Free Press.

Porter, Michael E. 1980b. "Industry Structure and Competitive Strategy: Keys to Profitability." *Financial Analysts Journal* 36, no. 4 (July–August).

Porter, Michael E. 1985. *Competitive Advantage: Creating and Sustaining Superior Performance.* New York: Free Press.

Porter, Michael E. 1988. "How to Conduct an Industry Analysis." In *The Financial Analysts Handbook,* 2nd ed., ed. Sumner N. Levine. Homewood, IL: Dow Jones–Irwin.

Power, William. 1992. "Big Board, at Age 200, Scrambles to Protect Grip on Stock Market." *Wall Street Journal,* May 13, pp. A1, A8.

Power, William. 1993. "Short Sellers Set to Catch Tumbling Overhead Stocks." *Wall Street Journal,* December 28, pp. C1, C2.

Pozen, Robert C. 2001. *The Mutual Fund Business,* 2nd ed. Boston, MA: Houghton Mifflin.

Pring, Martin J. 1991. *Technical Analysis Explained,* 3rd ed. New York: McGraw-Hill.

Pruitt, Stephen, and Robert White. 1988. "The CRISMA Trading System: Who Says Technical Analysis Can't Beat the Market?" *Journal of Portfolio Management* 14, no. 3 (Spring): 55–58.

Quan, D. C., and S. Titman. 1997. "Commercial Real Estate Prices and Stock Market Returns: An International Analysis." *Financial Analysts Journal* 53, no. 3 (May–June): 21–34.

Rappaport, Liz. 2004a. "Electronic Platforms See Surge in Trading of Corporate Bonds." *Wall Street Journal,* November 3, p. C5.

Rappaport, Liz. 2004b. "Transparency Increases for Price Data." *Wall Street Journal,* October 6, p. C4.

Redington, F. M. 1952. "Review of the Principles of Life—Office Valuations." *Journal of the Institute of Actuaries* 78: 286–340.

Reichenstein, William, and Steven P. Rich. 1993. "The Market Risk Premium and Long-Term Stock Returns." *Journal of Portfolio Management* 19, no. 4 (Summer): 63–72.

Reilly, Frank K. 1975. "Companies and Common Stocks as Inflation Hedges." New York University, Center for the Study of Financial Institutions, *Bulletin* (April).

Reilly, Frank K. 1987. "Risk and Return on Art and Antiques: The Sotheby's Indexes." Paper presented at Eastern Finance Association Meeting, Baltimore, MD, May.

Reilly, Frank K., ed. 1990. *High-Yield Bonds: Analysis and Risk Assessment.* Charlottesville, VA: Institute of Chartered Financial Analysts.

Reilly, Frank K. 1991. "Using Cash Flows and Financial Ratios to Predict Bankruptcies." In *Analyzing Investment Opportunities in Distressed and Bankrupt Companies,* ed. Thomas A. Bowman. Charlottesville, VA: Institute of Chartered Financial Analysts.

Reilly, Frank K. 1997. "The Impact of Inflation on ROE, Growth, and Stock Prices." *Financial Services Review* 6, no. 1: 1–17.

Reilly, Frank K., and Rashid A. Akhtar. 1995. "The Benchmark Error Problem with Global Capital Markets." *Journal of Portfolio Management* 22, no. 1 (Fall): 33–52.

Reilly, Frank K., and James A. Gentry. 2004. "The Growing Importance of Credit Analysis." Working paper, University of Notre Dame.

Reilly, Frank K., Frank T. Griggs, and Wenchi Wong. 1983. "Determinants of the Aggregate Stock Market Earnings Multiple." *Journal of Portfolio Management* 10, no. 1 (Fall): 36–45.

Reilly, Frank K., and Michael D. Joehnk. 1976. "The Association between Market-Determined Risk Measures for Bonds and Bond Ratings." *Journal of Finance* 31, no. 5 (December): 1387–1403.

Reilly, Frank K., Wenchi Kao, and David J. Wright. 1992. "Alternative Bond Market Indexes." *Financial Analysts Journal* 48, no. 3 (May–June): 44–58.

Reilly, Frank K., and Dominic R. Marshall. 1999. "Using P/E/Growth Ratios to Select Stocks." Paper presented at Financial Management Association Meeting, Seattle, October.

Reilly, Frank K., and Rupinder Sidhu. 1980. "The Many Uses of Bond Duration." *Financial Analysts Journal* 36, no. 4 (July–August): 58–72.

Reilly, Frank K., and David J. Wright. 1984. "Block Trades and Aggregate Stock Price Volatility." *Financial Analysts Journal* 40, no. 2 (March–April): 54–60.

Reilly, Frank K., and David J. Wright. 1988. "A Comparison of Published Betas." *Journal of Portfolio Management* 14, no. 3 (Spring): 64–69.

Reilly, Frank K., and David J. Wright. 1994. "An Analysis of High-Yield Bond Benchmarks." *Journal of Fixed Income* 3, no. 4 (March): 6–25.

Reilly, Frank K., and David J. Wright. 1995. "Global Bond Markets: An Analysis of Alternative Benchmarks and Risk-Return Performance." Paper presented at Midwest Finance Association Meeting, Chicago, March.

Reilly, Frank K., and David J. Wright. 1997. "Introducing a Comprehensive U.S. Treasury Bond Market Benchmark." In *Yield Curve Dynamics,* ed. Ronald J. Ryan. Chicago: Glen Lake.

Reilly, Frank K., and David J. Wright. 1999. "An Analysis of High-Yield Bond Indices." In *High-Yield Bonds,* ed. Theodore M. Barnhill, Jr., William F. Maxwell, and Mark R. Shenkman. New York: McGraw-Hill.

Reilly, Frank K., and David J. Wright. 2001b. "Unique Risk-Return Characteristics of High-Yield Bonds." *Journal of Fixed Income* 11, no. 2 (September): 65–82.

Reilly, Frank K., and David J. Wright. 2002a. "Alternative Small-Cap Stock Benchmarks." *The Journal of Portfolio Management* 28, no. 3 (Spring): 82–95.

Reilly, Frank K., and David J. Wright. 2004. "Analysis of Risk-Adjusted Performance for Global Market Assets." *Journal of Portfolio Management* 30, no. 3 (Spring): 63–77.

Reilly, Frank K., and David J. Wright. 2005. "Bond Market Indexes." In *The Handbook of Fixed-Income Securities,* 7th ed., ed. Frank J. Fabozzi. New York: McGraw-Hill.

Reilly, Frank K., David J. Wright, and Edward I. Altman. 1998. "Including Defaulted Bonds in the Capital Markets Asset Spectrum." *Journal of Fixed Income* 8, no. 3 (December): 33–48.

Reilly, Frank K., David J. Wright, and Kam C. Chan. 2000. "Bond Market Volatility Compared to Stock Market Volatility." *Journal of Portfolio Management* 27, no. 1 (Fall): 82–92.

Reilly, Frank K., David J. Wright, and Robert R. Johnson. 2005. "An Analysis of the Interest Rate Sensitivity of Common Stocks." Paper presented at Financial Management Association European Meeting June 6, Siena, Italy.

Reilly, Frank K., and Thomas Zeller. 1974. "An Analysis of Relative Industry Price–Earnings Ratios." *Financial Review,* 17–33.

Reinganum, Marc R. 1981. "The Arbitrage Pricing Theory: Some Empirical Results." *Journal of Finance* 36, no. 2 (May): 313–321.

Reinganum, Marc R. 1983. "Portfolio Strategies Based on Market Capitalization." *Journal of Portfolio Management* 9, no. 2 (Winter).

Reinganum, Marc R. 1992. "A Revival of the Small-Firm Effect." *Journal of Portfolio Management* 18, no. 3 (Spring): 55–62.

Rendleman, Richard J., Jr., and Brit J. Bartter. 1979. "Two-State Option Pricing." *Journal of Finance* 34, no. 5 (December): 1093–1110.

Rendleman, Richard J., Jr., Charles P. Jones, and Henry A. Latané. 1982. "Empirical Anomalies Based on Unexpected Earnings and the Importance of Risk Adjustments." *Journal of Financial Economics* 10, no. 3 (November): 269–287.

Rhoads, Christopher. 2001. "Germany Is Poised for a Pension Overhaul." *Wall Street Journal,* May 10.

Richards, Malcolm, Donald Fraser, and John Groth. 1982. "The Attractions of Closed-End Bond Funds." *Journal of Portfolio Management* 8, no. 2 (Winter): 56–61.

Richards, Thomas M. 2001. "Alternatives in Broad Market Indexes." In *Benchmarks and Attribution Analysis,* ed. Katrina Sherrerd. Charlottesville, VA: AIMR.

Ritter, Jay R. 1991. "The Long-Run Performance of Initial Public Offerings." *Journal of Finance* 46, no. 1 (March): 3–27.

Roenfeldt, Rodney L., Gary L. Griepentrog, and Christopher C. Pflamm. 1978. "Further Evidence on the Stationarity of Beta Coefficients." *Journal of Financial and Quantitative Analysis* 13, no. 1 (March): 117–121.

Roever, W. Alexander, John McElravey, and Glenn Schultz. 2005. "Securities Backed by Automobile Loans." In *The Handbook of Fixed-Income Securities,* 7th ed., ed. Frank J. Fabozzi. New York: McGraw-Hill.

Rogalski, Richard J., and James K. Seward. 1991. "Corporate Issues of Foreign Currency Warrants." *Journal of Financial Economics* 30, no. 2 (December): 347–366.

Rogowski, Robert J., and Eric H. Sorensen. 1985. "Deregulation in Investment Banking: Shelf Registration, Structure and Performance." *Financial Management* 14, no. 1 (Spring): 5–15.

Roll, Richard. 1977a. "A Critique of the Asset Pricing Theory's Tests." *Journal of Financial Economics* 4, no. 4 (March): 129–176.

Roll, Richard. 1977b. "An Analytic Valuation Formula for Unprotected American Call Options on Stocks with Known Dividends." *Journal of Financial Economics* 5, no. 2 (November): 251–258.

Roll, Richard. 1978. "Ambiguity When Performance Is Measured by the Securities Market Line." *Journal of Finance* 33. no. 4 (September): 1051–1069.

Roll, Richard. 1980. "Performance Evaluation and Benchmark Error I." *Journal of Portfolio Management* 6, no. 4 (Summer): 5–12.

Roll, Richard. 1981. "Performance Evaluation and Benchmark Error II." *Journal of Portfolio Management* 7, no. 2 (Winter): 17–22.

Roll, Richard. 1988. "The International Crash of October 1987." *Financial Analysts Journal* 44, no. 5 (September–October): 19–35.

Roll, Richard. 2004. "Empirical TIPS." *Financial Analysts Journal* 60, no. 1 (January/February): 31–53.

Roll, Richard, and Stephen A. Ross. 1980. "An Empirical Investigation of the Arbitrage Pricing Theory." *Journal of Finance* 35, no. 5 (December): 1073–1103.

Roll, Richard, and Stephen A. Ross. 1984. "A Critical Re-examination of the Empirical Evidence on the Arbitrage Pricing Theory." *Journal of Finance* 39, no. 2 (June): 347–350.

Roll, Richard, and Stephen A. Ross. 1995. "The Arbitrage Pricing Theory Approach to Strategic Portfolio Planning." *Financial Analysts Journal* 51, no. 1 (January/February): 122–131.

Rosenberg, Barr. 1984. "Prediction of Common Stock Investment Risk." *Journal of Portfolio Management* 11, no. 1 (Fall): 44–53.

Rosenberg, Barr. 1985. "Prediction of Common Stock Betas." *Journal of Portfolio Management* 11, no. 2 (Winter): 5–14.

Rosenberg, Barr, Kenneth Reid, and Ronald Lanstein. 1985. "Persuasive Evidence of Market Inefficiency." *Journal of Portfolio Management* 11, no. 3 (Spring): 9–17.

Rosenberg, Michael R. 1996. *Currency Forecasting.* Burr Ridge, IL: Irwin.

Ross, Stephen. 1976. "The Arbitrage Theory of Capital Asset Pricing." *Journal of Economic Theory* 13, no. 2 (December): 341–360.

Ross, Stephen. 1977. "Return, Risk, and Arbitrage." In *Risk and Return in Finance,* ed. I. Friend and J. Bicksler, pp. 189–218. Cambridge, MA: Ballinger.

Ross, Stephen, and Randall Zisler. 1991. "Risk and Return in Real Estate." *Journal of Real Estate Financial Economics* 4, no. 2: 175–190.

Rozeff, M. S. 1974. "Money and Stock Prices: Market Efficiency and the Lag Effect of Monetary Policy." *Journal of Financial Economics* 1, no. 3 (September): 245–302.

Rozeff, Michael. 1984. "Dividend Yields Are Equity Risk Premiums." *Journal of Portfolio Management* 11, no. 1 (Fall): 68–75.

Rubinstein, Mark. 1985a. "Alternative Paths to Portfolio Insurance." *Financial Analysts Journal* 41, no. 4 (July–August): 42–52.

Rubinstein, Mark. 1985b. "Nonparametric Tests of Alternative Options Pricing Models Using All Reported Trades and Quotes on the 30 Most Active CBOE Options Classes from August 23, 1976, through August 31, 1978." *Journal of Finance* 40, no. 2 (June): 455–480.

Rubinstein, Mark. 1992. "Options for the Undecided." In *From Black-Scholes to Black Holes.* London: Risk Magazine, 1992.

Rubinstein, Mark. 1994. "Implied Binomial Trees." *Journal of Finance* 49, no. 3 (July): 771–818.

Rueschhoff, Norlin, and David Strupeck. 2000. "Equity Returns: Local GAAP versus US GAAP for Foreign Issuers from Developing Countries." *Journal of International Accounting* 33, no. 3 (Spring).

Ruffenach, Glenn. 2001. "Fewer Americans Save for Their Retirement." *Wall Street Journal,* May 10, p. A2.

Ryan, Ronald J., ed. 1997. *Yield Curve Dynamics.* Chicago: Glen Lake.

Salomon, Ezra. 1963. *The Theory of Financial Management.* New York: Columbia University Press.

Saudagaran, Shakrokh. 2001. *International Accounting: A User Perspective.* Cincinnati, OH: South-Western.

Schmid, Frank A. 1999. "Extracting Inflation Expectations from Bond Yields." Federal Reserve Bank of St. Louis *Monetary Trends* (April).

Schulz, Ellen R. 1996. "Workers Put Too Much in Their Employer's Stock." *Wall Street Journal,* September 13, pp. C1, C25.

Schwert, G. William. 1989. "Why Does Stock Market Volatility Change over Time?" *Journal of Finance* 44, no. 5 (December): 1115–1153.

Scott, J., M. Stumpp, and P. Xu. 1999. "Behavioral Bias Valuation and Active Management." *Financial Analysts Journal* 55, no. 4 (July–August): 49–57.

Sears, R. Stephen, and John Wei. 1988. "The Structure of Skewness Preferences in Asset Pricing Models with Higher Moments." *Financial Review* 23, no. 1 (February): 25–38.

Selling, Thomas, and Clyde P. Stickney. 1989. "The Effects of Business Environment and Strategy on a Firm's Rate of Return on Assets." *Financial Analysts Journal* 45, no.1 (January–February): 43–52.

Senchak, A. J., Jr., and John D. Martin. 1987. "The Relative Performance of the PSR and PER Investment Strategies." *Financial Analysts Journal* 43, no. 2 (March–April): 46–56.

Seyhun, H. Nejat. 1986. "Insider Profits, Costs of Trading, and Market Efficiency." *Journal of Financial Economics* 16, no. 2 (June): 189–212.

Shackalford, Aaron L., ed. 1997. *Economic Analysis for Investment Professionals.* Charlottesville, VA: AIMR.

Shakla, Ravi, and Charles Trzcinka. 1990. "Sequential Tests of the Arbitrage Pricing Theory: A Comparison of Principle Components and Maximum Likelihood Factors." *Journal of Finance* 45, no. 5 (December): 1542–1564.

Shanken, Jay. 1982. "The Arbitrage Pricing Theory: Is It Testable?" *Journal of Finance* 37, no. 5 (December): 1129–1140.

Shanken, Jay. 1985a. "Multi-Beta CAPM or Equilibrium APT? A Reply." *Journal of Finance* 40, no. 4 (September): 1189–1196.

Shanken, Jay. 1985b. "Multivariate Tests of the Zero Beta CAPM." *Journal of Financial Economics* 14, no. 3 (September): 327–348.

Sharpe, William F. 1964. "Capital Asset Prices: A Theory of Market Equilibrium under Conditions of Risk." *Journal of Finance* 19, no. 3 (September): 425–442.

Sharpe, William F. 1966. "Mutual Fund Performance." *Journal of Business* 39, no. 1, part 2 (January): 119–138.

Sharpe, William F. 1984. "Factor Models, CAPMs, and the APT." *Journal of Portfolio Management* 11, no. 1 (Fall): 21–25.

Sharpe, William F. 1987. "Integrated Asset Allocation." *Financial Analysts Journal* 43, no. 5 (September/October): 25–32.

Sharpe, William F. 1990. "Asset Allocation." In *Managing Investment Portfolios: A Dynamic Process,* 2nd ed., eds. John L. Maginn and Donald L. Tuttle. Boston: Warren, Gorham, & Lamont.

Sharpe, William F. 1992. "Asset Allocation: Management Style and Performance Measurement." *Journal of Portfolio Management* 18, no. 2 (Winter): 7–19.

Sharpe, William F. 1994. "The Sharpe Ratio." *Journal of Portfolio Management* 21, no. 1 (Fall): 49–59.

Sharpe, William F., and Guy M. Cooper. 1972a. "Risk-Return Classes of New York Stock Exchange Common Stocks." *Financial Analysts Journal* 28, no. 2 (March–April): 35–43.

Sharpe, William F., and Guy M. Cooper. 1972b. "Risk-Return Classes of New York Stock Exchange Common Stocks: 1931–1967." *Financial Analysts Journal* 28, no. 2 (March–April): 46–54.

Sharpe, William F., and Katrina Sherrerd, eds. 1989. *Quantifying the Market Risk Premium Phenomenon for Investment Decision Making: September 26–27, 1989, New York, New York.* Charlottesville, VA: AIMR.

Shasta, Theodore, ed. 1994. *The Automotive Industry: January 25–26, 1994, Chicago, Illinois.* Charlottesville, VA: AIMR.

Shaw, Alan R. 1988. "Market Timing and Technical Analysis." In *The Financial Analyst's Handbook,* 2nd ed., ed. Sumner N. Levine. Homewood, IL: Dow Jones–Irwin.

Shefrin, Hersh. 1999. *Beyond Greed and Fear: Understanding Behavioral Finance and the Psychology of Investing.* Boston: Harvard Business School Press.

Shefrin, Hersh. 2001. "Behavioral Corporate Finance." *Journal of Applied Corporate Finance* 14, no. 3 (Fall): 113–124.

Shefrin, Hersh, and Meir Statman. 1995a. "Behavioral Capital Asset Pricing Theory." *Journal of Financial and Quantitative Analysis* 30, no. 3 (September).

Shefrin, Hersh, and Meir Statman. 1995b. "Making Sense of Beta, Size, and Book-to-Market." *Journal of Portfolio Management* 21, no. 2 (Winter): 26–34.

Shen, Pu. 1998. "Features and Risks of Treasury Inflation Protection Securities." Federal Reserve Bank of Kansas City *Economic Review* (First Quarter): 23–38.

Sherrerd, Katrina F., ed. 1993. *Execution Techniques, True Trading Costs, and the Microstructure of Markets.* Charlottesville, VA: AIMR.

Sherrerd, Katrina F., ed. 2001. *Benchmarks and Attribution Analysis.* Charlottesville, VA: AIMR.

Shiller, Robert J. 1984. "Stock Prices and Social Dynamics." *Brookings Papers on Economic Activity,* 2:457–498. Washington, DC: Brookings Institute.

Shiller, Robert J., and John Campbell. 1988. "Stock Prices, Earnings, and Expected Dividends." *Journal of Finance* 43, no. 3 (July): 661–676.

Shiskin, Julius. 1963. "Business Cycle Indicators: The Known and the Unknown." *Review of the International Statistical Institute* 31, no. 3: 361–383.

Siegel, Daniel, and Diane F. Siegel. 1990. *Futures Markets.* Hinsdale, IL: Dryden.

Siegel, Jeremy J. 1991. "Does It Pay Stock Investors to Forecast the Business Cycle?" *Journal of Portfolio Management* 18, no. 1 (Fall): 27–34.

Siegel, Laurence B., and Paul D. Kaplan. 1990. "Stocks, Bonds, Bills, and Inflation around the World." In *Managing Institutional Assets,* ed. Frank J. Fabozzi. New York: Harper & Row.

Singer, Brian. 1996. "Valuation of Portfolio Performance: Aggregate Return and Risk Analysis." *Journal of Performance Measurement* 1, no. 1 (Fall): 6–16.

Singer, Brian D., Renato Staub, and Kevin Terhaar. 2002. "Determining the Appropriate Allocation to Alternative Investments." In *Hedge Fund Management*, Charlottesville, VA: AIMR.

Smith, Clifford W., Jr. 1986. "Investment Banking and the Capital Acquisition Process." *Journal of Financial Economics* 15, no. 1–2 (January–February): 3–29.

Smith, Donald J. 1989a. "The Arithmetic of Financial Engineering." *Journal of Applied Corporate Finance* 1, no. 4 (Winter): 49–58.

Smith, Donald J. 1989b. "The Calculation and Use of Money Market Implied Forward Rates." *Journal of Cash Management* 98, no. 5 (September/October): 46–49.

Smithson, Charles W., and Clifford W. Smith, Jr. 1998. *Managing Financial Risk,* 3rd ed. New York: McGraw-Hill.

Solnik, Bruno. 1993. *Predictable Time-Varying Components of International Asset Returns.* Charlottesville, VA: AIMR.

Solnik, Bruno, and Dennis McLeavey. 2004. *International Investments,* 5th ed. Reading, MA: Addison-Wesley.

Solomon, Deborah, and Kate Kelly. 2003. "Wide SEC Review May Revamp Structure of U.S. Stock markets." *Wall Street Journal,* September 19, pp. A1, A2.

Solt, Michael, and Meir Statman. 1989. "Good Companies, Bad Stocks." *Journal of Portfolio Management* 15, no. 4 (Summer): 39–44.

Sondhi, Ashwinpaul C., ed. 1995. *Credit Analysis of Nontraditional Debt Securities.* Charlottesville, VA: AIMR.

Sorensen, Eric H., and Thierry F. Bollier. 1994. "Pricing Interest Rate Swap Default Risk." *Financial Analysts Journal* 50, no. 3 (May–June): 23–33.

Sorensen, Eric H., Keith L. Miller, and Vele Samak. 1998. "Allocating between Active and Passive Management." *Financial Analysts Journal* 54, no. 4 (September/October): 18–31.

Spiro, Peter S. 1990. "The Impact of Interest Rate Changes on Stock Price Volatility." *Journal of Portfolio Management* 16, no. 2 (Winter): 63–68.

Sprinkel, Beryl W. 1971. *Money and Markets: A Monetarist View.* Homewood, IL: Irwin.

Squires, Jan R., ed. 1995. *Performance Evaluation, Benchmarks, and Attribution Analysis.* Charlottesville, VA: AIMR.

Squires, Jan R., ed. 1996. *Global Portfolio Management.* Charlottesville, VA: AIMR.

Squires, Jan R., ed. 1997a. *Global Bond Management.* Charlottesville, VA: AIMR.

Squires, Jan R., ed. 1997b. *Managing Currency Risk.* Charlottesville, VA: AIMR.

Squires, Jan R., ed. 1998a. *Asset Allocation in a Changing World.* Charlottesville, VA: AIMR.

Squires, Jan R., ed. 1998b. *Credit Analysis around the World.* Charlottesville, VA: AIMR.

Squires, Jan R., ed. 1998c. *Equity Research and Valuation Techniques.* Charlottesville, VA: AIMR.

Squires, Jan R., ed. 2000a. *Global Bond Management II: The Search for Alpha.* Charlottesville, VA: AIMR.

Squires, Jan R., ed. 2000b. *Practical Issues in Equity Analysis.* Charlottesville, VA: AIMR.

Stambaugh, Robert. 1982. "On the Exclusion of Assets from Tests of the Two-Parameter Model: A Sensitivity Analysis." *Journal of Financial Economics* 10, no. 4 (November): 237–268.

Standard and Poor's Corporation. 2000. *Corporate Ratings Criteria.* New York: Standard & Poor's.

Stanhouse, Bryan, and Duane Stock. 1999. "How Changes in Bond Call Features Affect Coupon Rates." *Journal of Applied Corporate Finance* 12, no. 1 (Spring): 92–99.

Starkman, Dean, and Patrick McGeehan. 1998. "Floor Brokers on Big Board Charged in Scheme." *Wall Street Journal,* February 26, pp. C1, C21.

Statman, Meir. 1981. "Betas Compared: Merrill Lynch vs. Value Line." *Journal of Portfolio Management* 7, no. 2 (Winter): 41–44.

Statman, Meir. 1987. "How Many Stocks Make a Diversified Portfolio?" *Journal of Financial and Quantitative Analysis* 22, no. 3 (September): 353–363.

Statman, Meir, and Neal L. Ushman. 1987. "Bonds versus Stocks: Another Look." *Journal of Portfolio Management* 13, no. 3 (Winter): 33–38.

Steidtmann, Carl E. 1993. "General Trends in Retailing." In *The Retail Industry—General Merchandisers and Discounters,* ed. Charles Ingene. Charlottesville, VA: AIMR, pp. 6–9.

Stein, Jerome L. 1961. "The Simultaneous Determination of Spot and Futures Prices." *American Economic Review* 51, no. 5 (December): 1012–1025.

Steward, Christopher. 2005. "International Bond Markets and Instruments." In *The Handbook of Fixed-Income Securities,* 7th ed., ed. Frank J. Fabozzi. New York: McGraw-Hill.

Steward, Christopher, J. Hank Lynch, and Frank J. Fabozzi. 2005. "International Bond Portfolio Management." In *The Handbook of Fixed-Income Securities,* 7th ed., ed. Frank J. Fabozzi. New York: McGraw-Hill.

Stewart, G. Bennett, III. 1991. *The Quest for Value.* New York: Harper Business.

Stewart, Samuel S. 1988. "Forecasting Corporate Earnings." In *The Financial Analyst's Handbook,* 2nd ed., ed. Sumner N. Levine. Homewood, IL: Dow Jones–Irwin.

Stickney, Clyde P., Paul Brown, and James Wahlen. 2004. *Financial Reporting and Statement Analysis,* 5th ed. Mason, OH: South-Western.

Stoll, Hans R. 1969. "The Relationship between Put and Call Option Prices." *Journal of Finance* 24, no. 5 (December): 801–824.

Stoll, Hans R. 1985. *The Stock Exchange Specialist System: An Economic Analysis.* Monograph Series in Financial Economics, monograph no. 1985-2. New York: New York University.

Stoll, Hans R. 1993. "Organization of the Stock Market: Competition or Fragmentation?" *Journal of Applied Corporate Finance* 5, no. 4 (Winter): 89–93.

Stoll, Hans R., and Robert E. Whaley. 1983. "Transaction Costs and the Small Firm Effect." *Journal of Financial Economics* 12 no. 1: 57–79.

Stoll, Hans R., and Robert E. Whaley. 1990. "Stock Market Structure and Volatility." *Review of Financial Studies* 3, no. 1.

Stulz, Rene M. 2003. *Risk Management and Derivatives.* Mason, OH: South-Western.

Sun, Tong-sheng, Suresh Sundaresan, and Ching Wang. 1993. "Interest Rate Swaps: An Empirical Investigation." *Journal of Financial Economics* 34, no. 1 (August): 77–99.

Sundaresan, Suresh. 2002. *Fixed-Income Markets and Their Derivatives,* 2nd ed. Cincinnati: South-Western.

Swales, George S., Jr., and Young Yoon. 1992. "Applying Artificial Neural Networks to Investment Analysis." *Financial Analysts Journal* 48, no. 4 (September/October): 78–80.

Sweeney, Richard J. 1988. "Some New Filter Rule Tests: Methods and Results." *Journal of Financial and Quantitative Analysis* 23, no. 3 (September): 285–300.

Telser, Lester G. 1958. "Futures Trading and the Storage of Cotton and Wheat." *Journal of Political Economy* 66 (June).

Terhaar, Kevin. 2001. "Return, Risk, and Performance Attribution." In *Benchmarks and Attribution Analysis,* ed. Katrina Sherrerd. Charlottesville, VA: AIMR.

Thoenes, Sander. 1998. "Economy Hit as Jakarta Is Paralysed." *Financial Times,* May 15, p. 17.

Thompson, Donald J., II. 1976. "Sources of Systematic Risk in Common Stocks." *Journal of Business* 49, no. 2 (April): 173–188.

Thorbecke, Willem. 1997. "On Stock Market Returns and Monetary Policy." *Journal of Finance* 52, no. 2 (June): 635–654.

Thornhill, John. 1998. "Russian Stocks Fall 10% over Lack of Support from IMF." *Financial Times,* June 2, p. 1.

Throop, Adrian W. 1981. "Interest Rate Forecasts and Market Efficiency." Federal Reserve Bank of San Francisco *Economic Review* (Spring): 29–43.

Tito, Dennis A., and Wayne H. Wagner. 1977. "Is Your Bond Manager Skillful?" *Pension World* (June): 10–16.

Tobin, James. 1958. "Liquidity Preference as Behavior Towards Risk." *Review of Economic Studies* 25, no. 2 (February): 65–85.

Tokyo Stock Exchange Fact Book. Tokyo: TSE, published annually.

Tole, Thomas. 1982. "You Can't Diversify without Diversifying." *Journal of Portfolio Management* 8, no. 2 (Winter): 5–11.

Torres, Craig. 1990. "Third Market Trading Crowds Stock Exchanges." *Wall Street Journal,* March 8, pp. C1, C9.

Treynor, Jack L. 1965. "How to Rate Management of Investment Funds." *Harvard Business Review* 43, no. 1 (January–February): 63–75.

Treynor, Jack L., and Fischer Black. 1973. "How to Use Security Analysis to Improve Security Selection." *Journal of Business* 46, no. 1 (January): 66–86.

Tuckman, Bruce. 1995. *Fixed-Income Securities.* New York: Wiley.

Tully, S. 1993. "The Real Key to Creating Wealth." *Fortune* (September).

van der Does, Rein W. 1988. "Investing in Foreign Securities." In *The Financial Analyst's Handbook,* 2nd ed., ed. Sumner N. Levine. Homewood, IL: Dow Jones–Irwin.

Van Horne, James C. 2001. *Financial Market Rates and Flows,* 6th ed. Englewood Cliffs, NJ: Prentice Hall.

Vine, Allen A. 2001. "High-Yield Analysis of Emerging Markets Debt." In *The Handbook of Fixed-Income Securities,* 6th ed., ed. Frank J. Fabozzi. New York: McGraw-Hill.

Viner, Aron. 1988. *Inside Japanese Financial Markets.* Homewood, IL: Dow Jones–Irwin.

Vock, Thomas. 1996. "Managing Global Fixed-Income Portfolios." In *Global Portfolio Management,* ed. Jan R. Squires. Charlottesville, VA: AIMR.

Volpert, Kenneth E. 2001. "Managing Indexed and Enhanced Indexed Bond Portfolios." In *The Handbook of Fixed-Income Securities,* 6th ed., ed. Frank J. Fabozzi. New York: McGraw-Hill.

Wagner, Wayne H., and Dennis A. Tito. 1977. "Definitive New Measures of Bond Performance and Risk." *Pension World* (May): 17–26.

Wahab, Mahmoud, and Amit Khandwala. 1993. "Why Not Diversify Internationally with ADRs?" *Journal of Portfolio Management* 19, no. 2 (Winter): 75–82.

Wainscott, Craig B. 1995. "Attribution Analysis for Equities." In *Performance Evaluation, Benchmarks, and Attribution Analysis,* ed. J. Squires. Charlottesville, VA: AIMR.

Walmsley, Julian. 1998. *The New Financial Instruments,* 2nd ed. New York: Wiley.

Walter, John R. 1989. "Monetary Aggregates: A User's Guide." Federal Reserve Bank of Richmond *Economic Review* (January/February): 53–61.

Ward, David J., and Gary L. Griepentrog. 1993. "Risk and Return in Defaulted Bonds." *Financial Analysts Journal* 49, no. 3 (May–June): 61–65.

Ware, James W. 2000. "Drawing the Line in a Gray Area." In *Ethical Issues for Today's Firm.* Charlottesville, VA: AIMR.

Waymire, G. 1984. "Additional Evidence on the Information Content of Management Earnings Forecasts." *Journal of Accounting Research* 22, no. 3 (Autumn).

Weigel, Eric J. 1991. "The Performance of Tactical Asset Allocation." *Financial Analysts Journal* 47, no. 5 (September–October): 63–70.

Weinstein, Mark I. 1977. "The Effect of a Rating Change Announcement on Bond Price." *Journal of Financial Economics* 5, no. 3 (December): 329–350.

Weinstein, Mark I. 1981. "The Systematic Risk of Corporate Bonds." *Journal of Financial and Quantitative Analysis* 16, no. 3 (September): 156–278.

Weinstein, Mark I. 1983. "Bond Systematic Risk and the Option Pricing Model." *Journal of Finance* 38, no. 5 (December): 1415–1429.

Weiss, Gary. 1996. "The Secret World of Short Sellers." *BusinessWeek,* August 5, pp. 62–68.

Wermers, Russ. 2000. "Mutual Fund Performance: An Empirical Decomposition into Stock-Picking Talent, Style, Transaction Costs, and Expenses." *Journal of Finance* 55, no. 4 (August): 1655–1695.

Whaley, Robert E. 1981. "On the Valuation of American Call Options on Stocks with Known Dividends." *Journal of Financial Economics* 9, no. 2 (June): 207–212.

White, Gerald I., Ashwinpaul C. Sondhi, and Dov Fried. 2001. *The Analysis and Use of Financial Statements,* 3rd ed. New York: Wiley.

White, James A. 1991. "The Index Boom: It's No Longer Just the S&P 500 Stock Index." *Wall Street Journal,* May 19, pp. C1, C3.

Widder, Pat. 1992. "Nasdaq Has Its Eyes Set on the Next 100 Years." *Chicago Tribune,* May 17, Section 7, pp. 1, 4.

Wigmore, Barrie A. 1990. "The Decline in Credit Quality of New Issue Junk Bonds." *Financial Analysts Journal* 46, no. 5 (September–October): 53–62.

Wilcox, Jarrod W. 1984."The P/B-ROE Valuation Model." *Financial Analysts Journal* 40, no. 1 (January–February): 58–66.

Williams, J. B. 1938. *The Theory of Investment Value.* Cambridge, MA: Harvard University Press.

Wilson, Richard S. 2001. "Domestic Floating-Rate and Adjustable-Rate Debt Securities." In *The Handbook of Fixed-Income Securities,* 6th ed., ed. Frank J. Fabozzi. New York: McGraw-Hill.

Wilson, Richard S., and Frank J. Fabozzi. 1990. *The New Corporate Bond Market.* Chicago: Probus.

Winkelmann, Kurt. 1989. "Uses and Abuses of Duration and Convexity." *Financial Analysts Journal* 45, no. 5 (September–October): 72–75.

Witschi, Daniel. 1998. "European Pension Funds: Turning More Aggressive?" In *Asset Allocation in a Changing World.* Charlottesville, VA: AIMR, pp. 72–84.

Womack, Kent L. 1996. "Do Brokerage Analysts' Recommendations Have Investment Value?" *Journal of Finance* 51, no. 1 (March): 137–167.

Wood, Arnold S., ed. 1995. *Behavioral Finance and Decision Theory in Investment Management.* Charlottesville, VA: AIMR.

Woolridge, Randall. 1995. "Do Stock Prices Reflect Fundamental Values?" *Journal of Applied Corporate Finance* 8, no. 1 (Spring): 64–69.

Working, Holbrook. 1977. "Economic Functions of Futures Markets." In *Selected Writings of Holbrook Working.* Chicago: Chicago Board of Trade.

Yago, Glenn. 1991. *Junk Bonds.* New York: Oxford University Press.

Yaksick, Rudy. 1992. "Swaps, Caps, and Floors: Some Parity and Price Identities." *Journal of Financial Engineering* 1, no. 1: 105–115.

Yates, Jr., James W., and Robert W. Kopprasch, Jr. 1980. "Writing Covered Call Options: Profits and Risks." *Journal of Portfolio Management* 7 (Fall).

Zhon, Chunsheng. 2001. "Credit Rating and Corporate Defaults." *Journal of Fixed Income* 11, no. 3 (December): 30–40.

Zweig, Martin E. 1986. *Winning on Wall Street.* New York: Warner Books.

Zweig, Martin E. 1987. *Understanding Technical Forecasting.* New York: Dow Jones.

Zweig, Martin E. 2000. "You Get the Clients You Deserve." In *Ethical Issues for Today's Firm.* Charlottesville, VA: AIMR.

Glossary

Abnormal rate of return The amount by which a security's actual return differs from its expected rate of return which is based on the market's rate of return and the security's relationship with the market.

Accumulation phase Phase in the investment life cycle during which individuals in the early-to-middle years of their working career attempt to accumulate assets to satisfy short-term needs and longer-term goals.

Actuarial rate of return The discount rate used to find the present value of a defined benefit pension plan's future obligations and thus determine the size of the firm's annual contribution to the plan.

Agency conflict An ethical problem that can arise any time one person (i.e., agent) is hired to perform a service or act in the interest of another (i.e., principal).

Alpha A term commonly used to describe a manager's abnormal rate of return, which is the difference between the return the portfolio actually produced and the expected return given its risk level.

Alternative trading system (ATS) A nontraditional, computerized trading system that competes with or supplements dealer markets and traditional stock exchanges. While they facilitate trading in shares, they do not provide listing services.

American Depository Receipts (ADRs) Certificates of ownership issued by a U.S. bank that represent indirect ownership of a certain number of shares of a specific foreign firm. Shares are held on deposit in a bank in the firm's home country.

American option An option contract that can be exercised at any time until its expiration date.

Analysis effect The difference in performance of a security portfolio from that of a chosen index due to acquisition of temporarily mispriced issues that then move to their correct prices.

Anomalies Security price relationships that appear to contradict a well-regarded hypothesis; in this case, the efficient market hypothesis.

Arbitrage A trading strategy designed to generate a guaranteed profit from a transaction that requires no capital commitment or risk bearing on the part of the trader. A simple example of an arbitrage trade would be the simultaneous purchase and sale of the same security in different markets at different prices.

Arbitrage pricing theory (APT) A theory that posits that the expected return to a financial asset can be described by its relationship with several common risk factors. The multifactor APT can be contrasted with the single-factor CAPM.

Arithmetic mean (AM) A measure of mean annual rates of return equal to the sum of annual holding period rates of return divided by the number of years.

Asset allocation The process of deciding how to distribute an investor's wealth among different asset classes for investment purposes.

Asset class Securities that have similar characteristics, attributes, and risk/return relationships.

Assets under management (AUM) The total market value of the assets managed by an investment firm.

At the money A special case of an option where the exercise price and the price of the underlying asset are identical.

Attribution analysis An assessment technique designed to establish whether a manager's performance relative to a benchmark resulted from market timing or security selection skills.

Autocorrelation test A test of the efficient market hypothesis that compares security price changes over time to check for predictable correlation patterns.

Average tax rate A person's total tax payment divided by his or her total income.

Backtest A method of testing a quantitative model in which computers are used to examine the composition and returns of portfolios based on historical data to determine if the selected strategy would have worked in the past.

Backwardated A situation in a futures market where the current contract price is less than the current spot price for the underlying asset.

Balance sheet A financial statement that shows what assets the firm controls at a fixed point in time and how it has financed these assets.

Balanced fund A mutual fund with, generally, a three-part investment objective: (1) to conserve the investor's principal, (2) to pay current income, and (3) to increase both principal and income. The fund aims to achieve this by owning a mixture of bonds, preferred stocks, and common stocks.

Basis The difference between the spot price of the underlying asset and the futures contract price at any point in time (e.g., the *initial* basis at the time of contract origination, the *cover* basis at the time of contract termination).

Basis of an asset For tax purposes, the cost of an asset.

Basis risk The residual exposure to the price volatility of an underlying asset that results from a cross hedge transaction.

Bearer bond An unregistered bond for which ownership is determined by possession. The holder receives interest payments by clipping coupons attached to the security and sending them to the issuer for payment.

Behavioral finance Involves the analysis of various psychological traits of individuals and how these traits affect how they act as investors, analysts, and portfolio managers.

Benchmark error Situation where an inappropriate or incorrect benchmark is used to compare and assess portfolio returns and management.

Benchmark portfolio A comparison standard of risk and assets included in the policy statement and similar to the investor's risk preference and investment needs, which can be used to evaluate the investment performance of the portfolio manager.

Beta A standardized measure of systematic risk based upon an asset's covariance with the market portfolio.

Binomial option pricing model A valuation equation that assumes the price of the underlying asset changes through a series of discrete upward or downward movements.

Black-Scholes option pricing model A valuation equation that assumes the price of the underlying asset changes continuously through the option's expiration date by a statistical process known as *geometric Brownian motion.*

Bond price volatility The percentage changes in bond prices over time.

Bond swap An active bond portfolio management strategy that exchanges one position for another to take advantage of some difference between them.

Business risk The variability of operating income arising from the characteristics of the firm's industry. Two sources of business risk are sales variability and operating leverage.

Buy-and-hold strategy A passive portfolio management strategy in which securities (bonds or stocks) are bought and held to maturity.

Call market A market in which trading for individual stocks only takes place at specified times. All the bids and asks available at the time are combined and the market administrators specify a single price that will possibly clear the market at that time.

Call option Option to buy an asset within a certain period at a specified price called the *exercise price.*

Call premium Amount above par that an issuer must pay to a bondholder for retiring the bond before its stated maturity.

Call provisions Specifies when and how a firm can issue a call for bonds outstanding prior to their maturity.

Cap agreement A contract that on each settlement date pays the holder the greater of the difference between the reference rate and the cap rate or zero; it is equivalent to a series of call options at the reference rate.

Capital appreciation A return objective in which the investor seeks to increase the portfolio value, primarily through capital gains, over time to meet a future need rather than dividend yield.

Capital asset pricing model (CAPM) A theory concerned with deriving the expected or required rates of return on risky assets based on the assets' systematic risk relative to a market portfolio.

Capital market instruments Fixed-income or equity investments that trade in the secondary market.

Capital market line (CML) The line from the intercept point that represents the risk-free rate tangent to the original efficient frontier; it becomes the new efficient frontier since investments on this line dominate all the portfolios on the original Markowitz efficient frontier.

Capital preservation A return objective in which the investor seeks to minimize the risk of loss; generally a goal of the risk-averse investor.

Certificates of deposit (CDs) Instruments issued by banks and S&Ls that require minimum deposits for specified terms and that pay higher rates of interest than deposit accounts.

Characteristic line Regression line that indicates the systematic risk (beta) of a risky asset.

Closed-end investment company An investment company that issues only a limited number of shares, which it does not redeem (buy back). Instead, shares of a closed-end fund are traded in securities markets at prices determined by supply and demand.

Coefficient of variation (CV) A measure of relative variability that indicates risk per unit of return. It is equal to: standard deviation divided by the mean value. When used in investments, it is equal to: standard deviation of returns divided by the expected rate of return.

Coincident indicators A set of economic variables whose values reach peaks and troughs at about the same time as the aggregate economy.

Collar agreement A hedging arrangement where an underlying asset is protected against decreases in value by the simultaneous purchase of a put option and sale of a call option.

Collateral trust bonds A mortgage bond wherein the assets backing the bond are financial assets like stocks and bonds.

Collateralized mortgage obligation (CMO) A debt security based on a pool of mortgage loans that provides a relatively predictable term by paying of tranches in specified order.

Commission brokers Employees of a member firm who buy or sell securities for the customers of the firm.

Common stock An equity investment that represents ownership of a firm, with full participation in its success or failure. The firm's directors must approve dividend payments.

Common-size statements The normalization of balance sheet and income statement items to allow for more meaningful comparison of different-size firms. Balance sheet items are divided by total assets; income statement items are divided by total sales.

Competitive bid An underwriting alternative wherein an issuing entity (governmental body or a corporation) specifies the type of security to be offered (bonds or stocks) and the general characteristics of the issue, and the issuer solicits bids from competing investment banking firms with the understanding that the issuer will accept the highest bid from the bankers.

Competitive environment The level of intensity of competition among firms in an industry, determined by an examination of five competitive forces.

Competitive strategy The search by a firm for a favorable competitive position within an industry within the known competitive environment.

Completely diversified portfolio A portfolio in which all unsystematic risk has been eliminated by diversification.

Completeness fund A specialized index used to form the basis of a passive portfolio whose purpose is to provide diversification to a client's total portfolio by excluding those segments in which the client's active managers invest.

Composite measure An investment performance statistic that considers both the return and risk associated with a portfolio (e.g., Sharpe measure, Treynor measure, Jensen measure).

Computer-Assisted Execution System (CAES) A service created by Nasdaq that automates order routing and execution for securities listed on domestic stock exchanges and involved on the Intermarket Trading System (ITS).

Consolidated Quotation Sytem (CQS) An electronic quotation service for issues listed on the NYSE, the AMEX, or regional exchanges and traded on the Nasdaq InterMarket.

Consolidation phase Phase in the investment life cycle during which individuals who are typically past the midpoint of their career have earnings that exceed expenses and invest them for future retirement or estate planning needs.

Construct the portfolio Given the strategy and economic outlook, what specific stocks and/or bonds will be put into the portfolio at the present time that are consistent with the client's policy statement.

Contango A situation in a futures market where the current contract price is greater than the current spot price for the underlying asset.

Contingent deferred sales load A mutual fund that imposes a sales charge when the investor sells or redeems shares. Also referred to as *rear-end loads* or *redemption charges*.

Continual monitoring The constant evaluation of the economic environment, the policy statement, and the portfolio to ensure that it is consistent with the policy statement. Also involves evaluating performance to determine if changes are required in the portfolio, the strategy, or the policy statement.

Continuous market A market where stocks are priced and traded continuously by an auction process or by dealers when the market is open.

Contract price The transaction price specified in a forward or futures contract.

Contrarian An investment strategy that attempts to buy (sell) securities on which the majority of other investors are bearish (bullish).

Convenience yield An adjustment made to the theoretical forward or futures contract delivery price to account for the preference that

consumers have for holding spot positions in the underlying asset.

Conversion factors The adjustments made to Treasury bond futures contract terms to allow for the delivery of an instrument other than the standardized underlying asset.

Conversion parity price The price at which common stock can be obtained by surrendering the convertible instrument at par value.

Conversion premium The excess of the market value of the convertible security over its equity value if immediately converted into common stock. Typically expressed as a percentage of the equity value.

Conversion ratio The number of shares of common stock for which a convertible security may be exchanged.

Conversion value The value of the convertible security if converted into common stock at the stock's current market price.

Convertible bonds A bond with the added feature that the bondholder has the option to turn the bond back to the firm in exchange for a specified number of common shares of the firm.

Convexity A measure of the degree to which a bond's price-yield curve departs from a straight line. This characteristic affects estimates of a bond's price volatility for a given change in yields.

Core-plus bond portfolio management This is a combination approach to bond portfolio management wherein a significant (core) part of the portfolio (e.g., 70–75 percent) of the portfolio is managed passively in a widely recognized sector of the bond market, such as an aggregate bond index or a U.S. Government/corporate sector. The rest of the portfolio would be actively managed in one or several "plus" sectors that are less efficient than the core component—for example, high-yield bonds, foreign bonds, or emerging market debt.

Correlation coefficient A standardized measure of the relationship between two variables that ranges from –1.00 to +1.00.

Cost of carry The net amount that would be required to store a commodity or security for future delivery, usually calculated as physical storage costs plus financial capital costs less dividends paid to the underlying asset.

Counterparty A participant to a derivative transaction.

Country risk Uncertainty due to the possibility of major political or economic change in the country where an investment is located. Also called *political risk.*

Coupon Indicates the interest payment on a debt security. It is the coupon rate times the par value that indicates the interest payments on a debt security.

Coupon reinvestment risk The component of interest rate risk due to the uncertainty of the rate at which coupon payments will be reinvested.

Covariance A measure of the degree to which two variables, such as rates of return for investment assets, move together over time relative to their individual mean returns.

Covered call A trading strategy in which a call option is sold as a supplement to a long position in an underlying asset or portfolio of assets.

Covered interest arbitrage A trading strategy involving borrowing money in one country and lending it to another designed to exploit price deviations from the interest rate parity model.

Credit analysis An active bond portfolio management strategy designed to identify bonds that are expected to experience changes in rating. This strategy is critical when investing in high-yield bonds.

Cross hedge A trading strategy in which the price volatility of a commodity or security position is hedged with a forward or futures contract based on a different underlying asset or different settlement terms.

Crossover price The price at which the yield to maturity equals the yield to call. Above this price, yield to call is the appropriate yield measure; below this price, yield to maturity is the appropriate yield measure.

Cross-sectional analysis An examination of a firm's performance in comparison to other firms in the industry with similar characteristics to the firm being studied.

Cross-sectional return studies Studies wherein investigators look for public information that can be used to predict the cross-sectional distribution of risk-adjusted returns—e.g., is there an inverse relationship between market-value size of a firm and future risk-adjusted rates of return for its stock?

Current income A return objective in which the investor seeks to generate income rather than capital gains; generally a goal of an investor who wants to supplement earnings with income to meet living expenses.

Current yield A bond's yield as measured by its current income (coupon) as a percentage of its market price.

Cyclical change An economic trend arising from the ups and downs of the business cycle.

Cyclical company A firm whose earnings rise and fall with general economic activity.

Cyclical stock A stock with a high beta; its gains typically exceed those of a rising market and its losses typically exceed those of a falling market.

Debentures Bonds that promise payments of interest and principal but pledge no specific assets. Holders have first claim on the issuer's income and unpledged assets. Also known as *unsecured bonds.*

Declining trend channel The range defined by security prices as they move progressively lower.

Dedication A portfolio management technique in which the portfolio's cash flows are used to retire a set of liabilities over time.

Dedication with reinvestment A dedication strategy in which portfolio cash flows may precede their corresponding liabilities. Such cash flows can be reinvested to earn a return until the date the liability is due to be paid.

Defensive company Firms whose future earnings are likely to withstand an economic downturn.

Defensive competitive strategy Positioning the firm so that its capabilities provide the best means to deflect the effect of the competitive forces in the industry.

Defensive stock A stock whose return is not expected to decline as much as that of the overall market during a bear market (a beta less than one).

Defined benefit pension plan A pension plan to which the company contributes a certain amount each year and promises to pay employees a specified income after they retire. The benefit size is based on factors such as workers' salary and time of employment.

Defined contribution pension plan A pension plan in which worker benefits are determined by the size of employees' contributions to the plan and the returns earned on the fund's investments.

Delta The change in the price of the option with respect to a one dollar change in the price of the underlying asset; this is the option's *hedge ratio,* or the number of units of the underlying asset that can be hedged by a single option contract.

Derivative security An instrument whose market value ultimately depends upon, or derives from, the value of a more fundamental investment vehicle called the underlying asset or security.

Diffusion index for stocks An indicator of the number of stocks rising during a specified period of time relative to the number of stocks declining and not changing price.

Discount A bond selling at a price below par value due to capital market conditions.

Dividend discount model (DDM) A technique for estimating the value of a stock issue as the present value of all future dividends.

Dollar-weighted return The discount rate that sets the present value of a future set of cash flows equal to the investment's current value; also known as the *internal rate of return*.

DuPont system A method of examining *ROE* by breaking it down into three component parts: (1) profit margin, (2) total asset turnover, and (3) financial leverage.

Duration A measure of the interest rate sensitivity of a bond's market price taking into consideration its coupon and term to maturity. The percent change in price for 100 basis point change in yield.

Duration strategy A portfolio management strategy employed to reduce the interest rate risk of a bond portfolio by matching the modified duration of the portfolio with its investment horizon. For example, if the investment horizon is 10 years, the portfolio manager would construct a portfolio that has a modified duration of 10 years. This strategy is referred to as *immunization of the portfolio*.

Earnings momentum A strategy in which portfolios are constructed of stocks of firms with rising earnings.

Earnings multiplier model A technique for estimating the value of a stock issue as a multiple of its future earnings per share.

Earnings surprise A company announcement of earnings that differ from analysts' prevailing expectations.

EBITDA Earnings before interest, taxes, depreciation, and amortization.

Economic value added (EVA) Internal management performance measure that compares net operating profit to total cost of capital. Indicates how profitable company projects are as a sign of management performance.

Effective duration Direct measure of the interest rate sensitivity of a bond (or any financial instrument) based upon price changes derived from a pricing model.

Efficient capital market A market in which security prices rapidly reflect all information about securities.

Efficient frontier The set of portfolios that has the maximum rate of return for every given level of risk, or the minimum risk for every potential rate of return.

Electronic Communication Network (ECN) A computerized trading system that matches buy and sell orders, usually for retail and small institutional trading. ECNs act for customers as a broker—they do not buy or sell from their own accounts.

Electronic Crossing System (ECS) An electronic trading system that matches large buy and sell orders.

Empirical duration Measures directly the interest rate sensitivity of an asset by examining the percentage price change for an asset in response to a change in yield during a specified period of time.

Ending-wealth value The total amount of money derived from investment in a bond until maturity, including principal, coupon payments, and income from reinvestment of coupon payments.

Equipment trust certificates Mortgage bonds that are secured by specific pieces of transportation equipment like boxcars and planes.

Equity collar An option-based hedging strategy that protects a stock position from price declines by purchasing a put option that is paid for by the sale of a call option.

Equity swap A swap transaction in which one cash flow is tied to the return to an equity portfolio position, often an index such as the Standard and Poor's 500, while the other is based on a floating-rate index.

Estimated rate of return The rate of return an investor anticipates earning from a specific investment over a particular future holding period.

Eurobonds Bonds denominated in a currency not native to the country in which they are issued.

European option An option contract that can only be exercised on its expiration date.

Event study Research that examines the reaction of a security's price to a specific company, world event, or news announcement.

Exchange clearinghouse The functional unit attached to a futures exchange that guarantees contract performance, oversees delivery, serves as a bookkeeper, and calculates settlement transactions.

Exchange rate risk Uncertainty due to the denomination of an investment in a currency other than that of the investor's own country.

Exchange-traded fund (ETF) A tradable depository receipt that gives investors a pro rata claim to the returns associated with a portfolio of securities (often designed to mimic an index, such as the Standard & Poor's 500) held in trust by a financial institution.

Exercise price The transaction price specified in an option contract; also known as the *strike price*.

Expected rate of return The return that analysts' calculations suggest a security should provide, based on the market's rate of return during the period and the security's relationship to the market.

Expiry The expiration date of a derivative security.

Extended DuPont System A method of exammining *ROE* by breaking it down into five component parts.

External efficiency A market in which prices adjust quickly to new information regarding supply or demand. Also referred to as *informational efficiency.*

Fiduciary A person who supervises or oversees the investment portfolio of a third party, such as in a trust account, and makes investment decisions in accordance with the owner's wishes.

Filter rule A trading rule that recommends security transactions when price changes exceed a previously determined percentage.

Financial risk The variability of future income arising from the firm's fixed financing costs, for example, interest payments. The effect of fixed financial costs is to magnify the effect of changes in operating profit on net income or earnings per share.

Fixed-income investments Loans with contractually mandated payment schedules from firms or governments to investors.

Flat trend channel The range defined by security prices as they maintain a relatively steady level.

Flexible portfolio fund Mutual fund that allows managers to shift assets between stocks, bonds, and cash according to changing market conditions; also known as *asset allocation* fund.

Floating-rate note (FRN) Short- to intermediate-term bonds with regularly scheduled coupon payments linked to a variable interest rate, most often LIBOR.

Floor agreement A contract that on each settlement date pays the holder the greater of the difference between the floor rate and the reference rate or zero; it is equivalent to a series of put options on the reference rate.

Floor brokers Independent members of an exchange who act as brokers for other members.

Forward contract An agreement between two counterparties that requires the exchange of a commodity or security at a fixed time in the future at a predetermined price.

Forward discount A situation where, from the perspective of the domestic country, the spot exchange rate is smaller than the forward exchange rate with a foreign country.

Forward premium A situation where, from the perspective of the domestic country, the spot exchange rate is larger than the forward exchange rate with a foreign country.

Forward rate A short-term yield for a future holding period implied by the spot rates of two securities with different maturities.

Forward rate agreement (FRA) A transaction in which two counterparties agree to a single exchange of cash flows based on a fixed and floating rate, respectively.

Franchise factor A firm's unique competitive advantage that makes it possible for a firm to earn excess returns (rates of return above a firm's cost of capital) on its capital projects. In turn, these excess returns and the franchise factor cause the firm's stock price to have a *P/E* ratio above its base *P/E* ratio that is equal to $1/k$.

Free cash flow to equity This cash flow measure equals cash flow from operations minus capital expenditures and debt payments.

Full replication A technique for constructing a passive index portfolio in which all securities in an index are purchased in proportion to their weights in the index.

Fully taxable equivalent yield (FTEY) A yield on a tax-exempt bond that adjusts for its tax benefits to allow comparisons with taxable bonds.

Futures contract An agreement that provides for the future exchange of a particular asset at a specified delivery date in exchange for a specified payment at the time of delivery.

General obligation bond (GO) A municipal issue serviced from and guaranteed by the issuer's full taxing authority.

Generally accepted accounting principles (GAAP) Accounting principles formulated by the Financial Accounting Standards Board and used to construct financial statements.

Geometric mean (GM) The *n*th root of the product of the annual holding period returns for *n* years minus 1.

Gifting phase Phase in the investment life cycle during which individuals use excess assets to financially assist relatives or friends, establish charitable trusts, or construct trusts to minimize estate taxes.

Growth company A company that consistently has the opportunities and ability to invest in projects that provide rates of return that exceed the firm's cost of capital. Because of these investment opportunities, it retains a high proportion of earnings, and its earnings grow faster than those of average firms.

Growth stock A stock issue that generates a higher rate of return than other stocks in the market with similar risk characteristics.

Hedge A trading strategy in which derivative securities are used to reduce or completely offset a counterparty's risk exposure to an underlying asset.

Hedge fund An investment vehicle designed to manage a private, unregistered portfolio of assets according to any of several strategies. The investment strategy often employs arbitrage trading and significant financial leverage (e.g., short selling, borrowing, derivatives) while the compensation arrangement for the manager typically specifies considerable profit participation.

Hedge ratio The number of derivative contracts that must be transacted to offset the price volatility of an underlying commodity or security position.

High-yield bond A bond rated below investment grade. Also referred to as *speculative-grade bonds* or *junk bonds.*

Holdings-base measure A performance measure based on how a manager changes the portfolio's security holdings over time, often in comparison to a benchmark portfolio.

Holding period return (HPR) The total return from an investment, including all sources of income, for a given period of time. A value of 1.0 indicates no gain or loss. Equal to ending wealth/beginning wealth.

Holding period yield (HPY) The total return from an investment for a given period of time stated as a percentage. Equal to HPR−1.

Immunization A bond portfolio management technique of matching modified duration to the investment horizon of the portfolio to eliminate interest rate risk.

Implied volatility The standard deviation of changes in the price of the underlying asset that can be inferred from an option's market price in relation to a specific valuation model.

In the money An option that has positive intrinsic value.

Incentive compensations A scheme for paying investment managers according to the performance of the portfolio, often based on the level of assets under management.

Income bonds Debentures that stipulate interest payments only if the issuer earns the income to make the payments by specified dates.

Income statement A financial statement that shows the flow of the firm's sales, expenses, and earnings over a period of time.

Indenture The legal agreement that lists the obligations of the issuer of a bond to the bondholder, including payment schedules, call provisions, and sinking funds.

Indexing A passive bond portfolio management strategy that seeks to match the composition, and therefore the performance, of a selected market index.

Industry life cycle analysis An analysis that focuses on the industry's stage of development.

Information An attribute of a good market that includes providing buyers and sellers with timely, accurate information on the volume and prices of past transactions and on all currently outstanding bids and offers.

Information ratio Statistic used to measure a portfolio's average return in excess of a comparison, benchmark portfolio divided by the standard deviation of this excess return.

Informationally efficient market A more technical term for an efficient capital market that emphasizes the role of information in setting the market price.

Initial public offering (IPO) A new issue by a firm that has no existing public market.

Interest rate anticipation An active bond portfolio management strategy designed to preserve capital or take advantage of capital gains opportunities by predicting interest rates and their effects on bond prices.

Interest rate collar The combination of a long position in a cap agreement and a short position in a floor agreement, or vice versa; it is equivalent to a series of range forward positions.

Interest rate parity The relationship that must exist in an efficient market between the spot and forward foreign exchange rates between two countries and the interest rates in those countries.

Interest rate risk The uncertainty of returns on an investment due to possible changes in interest rates over time.

Interest rate swap An agreement calling for the periodic exchange of cash flows, one based on an interest rate that remains fixed for the life of the contract and the other that is linked to a variable-rate index.

Interest-on-interest Bond income from reinvestment of coupon payments.

Intermarket Trading System (ITS) A computerized system that connects competing exchanges and dealers who trade stocks listed on an exchange. Its purpose is to help customers find the best market for these stocks at a point in time.

Internal liquidity (solvency) ratios Financial ratios that measure the ability of the firm to meet future short-term financial obligations.

Internal rate of return (IRR) The discount rate at which cash outflows of an investment equal cash inflows.

International domestic bonds Bonds issued by a foreign firm, denominated in the firm's native currency, and sold within its own country.

Intrinsic value The portion of a call option's total value equal to the greater of either zero or the difference between the current value of the underlying asset and the exercise price; for a put option, intrinsic value is the greater of either zero or the exercise price less the underlying asset price. For a stock, it is the value derived from fundamental analysis of the stock's expected returns or cash flows.

Investment The current commitment of dollars for a period of time in order to derive future payments that will compensate the investor for the time the funds are committed, the expected rate of inflation, and the uncertainty of future payments.

Investment company A firm that sells shares of the company and uses the proceeds to buy portfolios of stock, bonds, or other financial instruments.

Investment decision process Estimation of intrinsic value for comparison with market price to determine whether or not to invest.

Investment horizon The time period used for planning and forecasting purposes or the future time at which the investor requires the invested funds.

Investment management company A company separate from the investment company that manages the portfolio and performs administrative functions.

Investment strategy A decision by a portfolio manager regarding how he or she will manage the portfolio to meet the goals and objectives of the client. This will include either active or passive management and, if active, what style in terms of top-down or buttom-up or fundamental versus technical.

January effect A frequent empirical anomaly where risk-adjusted stock returns in the month of January are significantly larger than those occurring in any other month of the year.

Jensen measure An absolute measure of a portfolio's risk-adjusted performance, computed as the intercept in a regression equation where the excess returns to a manager's portfolio and the market index are, respectively, the dependent and independent variables.

Lagging indicators A set of economic variables whose values reach peaks and troughs after the aggregate economy.

Leading indicators A set of economic variables whose values reach peaks and troughs in advance of the aggregate economy.

Limit order An order that lasts for a specified time to buy or sell a security when and if it trades at a specified price.

Liquid Term used to describe an asset that can be quickly converted to cash at a price close to fair market value.

Liquidity The ability to buy or sell an asset quickly and at a reasonable price based on information.

Liquidity risk Uncertainty due to the ability to buy or sell an investment in the secondary market.

Long hedge A long position in a forward or futures contract used to offset the price volatility of a short position in the underlying asset.

Long position The buyer of a commodity or security or, for a forward contract, the counterparty who will be the eventual buyer of the underlying asset.

Long-term, high-priority goal A long-term financial investment goal of personal importance that typically includes achieving financial independence, such as being able to retire at a certain age.

Lower-priority goal A financial investment goal of lesser personal importance, such as taking a luxurious vacation or buying a car every few years.

Low-load fund A mutual fund that imposes a moderate front-end sales charge when the investor buys the fund, typically about 3 to 4 percent.

Macaulay duration A measure of the time flow of cash from a bond where cash flows are weighted by present values discounted by the yield to maturity.

Maintenance margin The required proportion that the investor's equity value must be to the total market value of the stock. If the proportion drops below this percent, the investor will receive a margin call.

Management and advisory firm A firm that provides a range of services from standard banking transactions (savings accounts, personal loans) to advising individual and institutional investors on structuring their portfolios and managing investment funds.

Management effect A combination of the interest rate anticipation effect, the analysis effect, and the trading effect.

Management fee The compensation an investment company pays to the investment management company for its services. The average annual fee is about 0.5 percent of fund assets.

Margin The percent of cost a buyer pays in cash for a security, borrowing the balance from the broker. This introduces leverage, which increases the risk of the transaction.

Margin account The collateral posted with the futures exchange clearinghouse by an outside counterparty to

insure its eventual performance; the *initial* margin is the deposit required at contract origination while the *maintenance* margin is the minimum collateral necessary at all times.

Margin call A request by an investor's broker for additional capital for a security bought on margin if the investor's equity value declines below the required maintenance margin.

Marginal tax rate The part of each additional dollar in income that is paid as tax.

Marked to market The settlement process used to adjust the margin account of a futures contract for daily changes in the price of the underlying asset.

Market The means through which buyers and sellers are brought together to aid in the transfer of goods and/or services.

Market order An order to buy or sell a security immediately at the best price available.

Market portfolio The portfolio that includes all risky assets with relative weights equal to their proportional market values.

Market risk premium The amount of return above the risk-free rate that investors expect from the market in general as compensation for systematic risk.

Market value added (MVA) External management performance measure to compare the market value of the company's debt and equity with the total capital invested in the firm.

Maturity strategy A portfolio management strategy employed to reduce the interest rate risk of a bond portfolio by matching the maturity of the portfolio with its investment horizon. For example, if the investment horizon is 10 years, the portfolio manager would construct a portfolio that will mature in 10 years.

Mean rates of return The average of an investment's returns over an extended period of time.

Modified duration A measure of Macaulay duration divided by one plus the bond's periodic yield used to approximate the bond's price volatility.

Money market The market for short-term debt securities with maturities of less than one year.

Money market fund A fund that invests in short-term securities sold in the money market. (Large companies, banks, and other institutions also invest their surplus cash in the money market for short periods of time.) In the entire investment spectrum, these are generally the safest, most stable securities available. They include Treasury bills, certificates of deposit of large banks, and commercial paper (short-term IOUs of large corporations).

Mortgage bonds Bonds that pledge specific assets such as buildings and equipment. The proceeds from the sale of these assets are used to pay off bondholders in case of bankruptcy.

Moving average The continually recalculating average of security prices for a period, often 200 days, to serve as an indication of the general trend of prices and also as a benchmark price.

Multifactor model An empirical version of the APT where the investor chooses the exact number and identity of the common risk factors used to describe an asset's risk-return relationship. Risk factors are often designated as *macroeconomic* variables (e.g., inflation, changes in gross domestic product) or *microeconomic* variables (e.g., security-specific characteristics like firm size or book-to-market ratios).

Mutual fund An investment company that pools money from shareholders and invests in a variety of securities, including stocks, bonds, and money market securities. A mutual fund ordinarily stands ready to buy back (redeem) its shares at their current net asset value, which depends on the market value of the fund's portfolio of securities at the time. Mutual funds generally continuously offer new shares to investors.

Nasdaq InterMarket A trading system that includes Nasdaq market makers and ECNs that quote and trade stocks listed on the NYSE and the AMEX. It involves dealers from the Nasdaq market and the Intermarket Trading System (ITS). In many ways, this has become what had been labeled the third market.

National Association of Securities Dealers Automated Quotation (Nasdaq) system An electronic system for providing bid-ask quotes on OTC securities.

Near-term, high-priority goal A short-term financial investment goal of personal importance, such as accumulating funds for making a house down payment or buying a car.

Negotiated sales An underwriting arrangement wherein the sale of a security issue by an issuing entity (governmental body or a corporation) is done using an investment banking firm that maintains an ongoing relationship with the issuer. The characteristics of the security issue are determined by the issuer in consultation with the investment banker.

Net asset value (NAV) per share The market value of an investment company's assets (securities, cash, and any accrued earnings) after deducting liabilities, divided by the number of shares outstanding.

Net present value (NPV) A measure of the excess cash flows expected from an investment proposal. It is equal to the present value of the cash *inflows* from an investment proposal, discounted at the required rate of return for the investment, minus the present value of the cash *outflows* required by the investment, also discounted at the investment's required rate of return. If the derived net present value is a positive value (i.e., there is an excess net present value), the investment should be acquired since it will provide a rate of return above its required returns.

New issue Common stocks or bonds offered by companies for public sale.

No-load fund A mutual fund that sells its shares at net asset value without adding sales charges.

Nominal yield A bond's yield as measured by its coupon rate.

Normal portfolio A specialized or customized benchmark constructed to evaluate a specific manager's investment style or philosophy.

Notes Intermediate-term debt securities with maturities longer than 1 year but less than 10 years.

Notional principal The principal value of a swap transaction, which is not exchanged but is used as a scale factor to translate interest rate differentials into cash settlement payments.

Objectives The investor's goals expressed in terms of risk and return and included in the policy statement.

Offensive competitive strategy A strategy whereby a firm attempts to use its strengths to affect the competitive forces in the industry and, in so doing, improves the firm's relative position in the industry.

Open-end investment company The more formal name for a mutual fund, which derives from the fact that it continuously offers new shares to investors and redeems them (buys them back) on demand.

Operating efficiency ratios Financial ratios intended to indicate how efficiently management is utilizing the firm's assets in terms of dollar sales generated per dollar of assets. Primary examples would be: total asset turnover, fixed asset turnover, or equity turnover.

Operating leverage The use of fixed-production costs in the firm's operating cost structure. The effect of fixed costs is to magnify the effect of a change in sales on operating profits.

Operating profitability ratios Financial ratios intended to indicate how profitable the firm is in terms of the percent of profit generated from sales. Alternative measures would include: operating profit (EBIT)/net sales; pretax profit (EBT)/net sales; and net profit/sales.

Optimal portfolio The portfolio on the efficient frontier that has the highest utility for a given investor. It lies at the point of tangency between the efficient frontier and the curve with the investor's highest possible utility.

Options Clearing Corporation (OCC) A company designed to guarantee, monitor margin accounts, and settle exchange-traded option transactions.

Option contract An agreement that grants the owner the right, but not the obligation, to make a future transaction in an underlying commodity or security at a fixed price and within a predetermined time in the future.

Option premium The initial price that the option buyer must pay to the option seller to acquire the contract.

Option-adjusted spread A type of yield spread that considers changes in the term structure and alternative estimates of the volatility of interest rates. It is spread after adjusting for embedded options.

OTC Electronic Bulletin Board (OTCBB) A regulated quotation service that displays real-time quotes, last-sale prices, and volume information for a specified set of over-the-counter (OTC) securities that are not traded on the formal Nasdaq market.

Out of the money An option that has no intrinsic value.

Overfunded plan A defined benefit pension plan in which the present value of the pension liabilities is less than market value of the plan's assets.

Overweighted A condition in which a portfolio, for whatever reason, includes more of a class of securities than the relative market value alone would justify.

Par value *See* Principal.

Payback The time required for the added income from the convertible

security relative to the stock to offset the conversion premium.

Peak The culmination of a bull market when prices stop rising and begin declining.

Peer group comparison A method of measuring portfolio performance by collecting the returns produced by a representative universe of investors over a specific period of time.

Performance presentation standards (PPS) A comprehensive set of reporting guidelines created by the Association for Investment Management and Research (AIMR) (now the CFA Institute), in an effort to fulfill the call for uniform, accurate, and consistent performance reporting.

Perpetuity An investment without any maturity date. It provides returns to its owner indefinitely.

Personal trust An amount of money set aside by a grantor and often managed by a third party, the trustee. Often constructed so one party receives income from the trust's investments and another party receives the residual value of the trust after the income beneficiaries' death.

Policy effect The difference in performance of a bond portfolio from that of a chosen index due to differences in duration, which result from a fund's investment policy.

Policy statement A statement in which the investor specifies investment goals, constraints, and risk preferences.

Portfolio A group of investments. Ideally, the investments should have different patterns of returns over time.

Preferred stock An equity investment that stipulates the dividend payment either as a coupon or a stated dollar amount. The firm's directors may withhold dividend payments.

Premium A bond selling at a price above par value due to capital market conditions.

Price continuity A feature of a liquid market in which there are small price changes from one transaction to the next due to the depth of the market.

Price momentum A portfolio strategy in which you acquire stocks that have enjoyed above-market stock price increases.

Price risk The component of interest rate risk due to the uncertainty of the market price of a bond caused by changes in market interest rates.

Price/earnings (P/E) ratio The number by which expected earnings per share is multiplied to estimate a stock's value; also called the *earnings multiplier.*

Price-weighted index An index calculated as an arithmetic mean of the current prices of the sampled securities.

Primary market The market in which newly issued securities are sold by their issuers, who receive the proceeds.

Principal (par value) The original value of the debt underlying a bond that is payable at maturity.

Private placement A new issue sold directly to a small group of investors, usually institutions.

Promised yield to call (YTC) A bond's yield if held until the first available call date, with reinvestment of all coupon payments at the yield-to-call rate.

Promised yield to maturity (YTM) The most widely used measure of a bond's yield that states the fully compounded rate of return on a bond bought at market price and held to maturity with reinvestment of all coupon payments at the yield to maturity rate.

Protective put A trading strategy in which a put option is purchased as a supplement to a long position in an underlying asset or portfolio of assets; the most straightforward form of *portfolio insurance.*

Public bond A long-term, fixed-obligation debt security in a convenient, affordable denomination for sale to individuals and financial institutions.

Pure cash-matched dedicated portfolio A conservative dedicated portfolio management technique aimed at developing a bond portfolio that will provide cash payments that exactly match the specified liability schedules.

Put options Options to sell a security (stock or bond) within a certain period at a specified price.

Put-call parity The relationship that must exist in an efficient market between the prices for put and call options having the same underlying asset, exercise price, and expiration date.

Quadratic optimization A technique that relies on historical correlations in order to construct a portfolio that seeks to minimize tracking error with an index.

Quality financial statements Financial statements that most knowledgeable observers (analysts, portfolio managers) would consider conservatively prepared in terms of sales, expenses, earnings, and asset valuations. The results reported would reflect reasonable estimates and indicate what truly happened during the period and the legitimate value of assets and liabilities on the balance sheet.

Range forward A trading strategy based on a variation of the put-call parity model where, for the same underlying asset but different exercise prices, a call option is purchased and a put option is sold (or vice versa).

Rate anticipation effect The difference in return because of changing the duration of the portfolio during a period as compared with the portfolio's long-term policy duration.

Real estate investment trusts (REITs) Investment funds that hold portfolios of real estate investments.

Real options Options embedded in a firm's real assets that give managers valuable decision-making flexibility, such as the right to either undertake or abandon an investment project.

Real risk-free rate (RRFR) The basic interest rate with no accommodation for inflation or uncertainty. The pure time value of money.

Realized capital gains Capital gains that result when an appreciated asset is sold; realized capital gains are taxable.

Realized yield The expected compounded yield on a bond that is sold before it matures assuming the reinvestment of all cash flows at an explicit rate. Also called *horizon yield* for the yield realized during an investment horizon period.

Refunding issue Bonds that provide funds to prematurely retire another bond issue. These bonds can be either a junior or senior issue.

Registered bond A bond for which ownership is registered with the issuer. The holder receives interest payments by check directly from the issuer.

Registered competitive market makers (RCMMs) Members of an exchange who are allowed to use their memberships to buy or sell for their own account within the specific trading obligations set down by the exchange.

Registered traders Members of the stock exchange who are allowed to use their memberships to buy and sell for their own account, which means they save commissions on their trading but they provide liquidity to the market, and they abide by exchange regulations on how they can trade.

Relative-strength (RS) ratio The ratio of a stock price or an industry index value to a market indicator series, indicating the stock's or the industry's performance relative to the overall market.

Required rate of return The return that compensates investors for their time, the expected rate of inflation, and the uncertainty of the return.

Resistance level A price at which a technician would expect a substantial increase in the supply of a stock to reverse a rising trend.

Return prediction studies Studies wherein investigations attempt to predict the time series of future rates of return using public information. An example would be predicting above-average returns for the stock market based on the aggregate dividend yield—e.g., high dividend yield indicates above average future market returns.

Revenue bond A bond that is serviced by the income generated from specific revenue-producing projects of the municipality such as toll roads or athletic stadiums.

Rising trend channel The range defined by security prices as they move progressively higher.

Risk The uncertainty that an investment will earn its expected rate of return.

Risk averse The assumption about investors that they will choose the least risky alternative, all else being equal.

Risk premium (RP) The increase over the nominal risk-free rate that investors demand as compensation for an investment's uncertainty.

Risk-free asset An asset with returns that exhibit zero variance.

Risky asset An asset with uncertain future returns.

Runs test A test of the weak-form efficient market hypothesis that checks for trends that persist longer in terms of positive or negative price changes than one would expect for a random series.

Sampling A technique for constructing a passive index portfolio in which the portfolio manager buys a representative sample of stocks that comprise the benchmark index.

Seasoned equity issues New equity shares offered by firms that already have stock outstanding.

Secondary market The market in which outstanding securities are bought and sold by owners other than the issuers. Purpose is to provide liquidity for investors.

Sector rotation strategy An active strategy that involves purchasing stocks in specific industries or stocks with specific characteristics (low *P/E*, growth, value) that are anticipated to rise in value more than the overall market.

Secured (senior) bond A bond backed by a legal claim on specified assets of the issuer.

Security market index An index created as a statistical measure of the performance of an entire market or segment of a market based on a sample of securities from the market or segment of a market.

Security market indicator series An index created as a statistical measure of the performance of an entire market or segment of a market based on a sample of securities from the market or segment of a market.

Security market line (SML) The line that reflects the combination of risk and return of alternative investments. In CAPM, risk is measured by systematic risk (beta).

SelectNet An order-routing and trade-execution system for institutional investors (brokers and dealers) that allows communication through the Nasdaq system rather than by phone.

Semistrong-form efficient market hypothesis The belief that security prices fully reflect all publicly available information, including information from security transactions and company, economic, and political news.

Separation theorem The proposition that the investment decision, which involves investing in the market portfolio on the capital market line, is separate from the financing decision, which targets a specific point on the CML based on the investor's risk preference.

Serial obligation bond A bond issue that has a series of maturity dates. Typical for municipal bonds.

Settlement price The price determined by the exchange clearinghouse with which futures contract margin accounts are marked to market.

Sharpe measure A relative measure of a portfolio's benefit-to-risk ratio, calculated as its average return in excess of the risk-free rate divided by the standard deviation of portfolio returns.

Short hedge A short position in a forward or futures contract used to offset the price volatility of a long position in the underlying asset.

Short position The seller of a commodity or security or, for a forward contract, the counterparty who will be the eventual seller of the underlying asset.

Short sale The sale of borrowed securities with the intention of repurchasing them later at a lower price and earning the difference.

Sinking fund Bond provision that requires the issuer to redeem some or all of the bond systematically over the term of the bond rather than in full at maturity.

Small-firm effect A frequent empirical anomaly where risk-adjusted stock returns for companies with low market capitalization (i.e., share price multiplied by number of outstanding shares) are significantly larger than those generated by high market capitalization (large cap) firms.

Small-Order Execution System (SOES) A quotation and execution system for retail (nonprofessional) investors who place orders with brokers who must honor their prevailing bid–ask for automatic excution up to 1,000 shares.

Soft dollars A form of compensation to a money manager generated when the manager commits the investor to paying higher brokerage fees in exchange for the manager receiving additional services (e.g., stock research) from the broker.

Specialist The major market maker on U.S. stock exchanges who acts as a broker or dealer to ensure the liquidity and smooth functions of the secondary stock market.

Speculative company A firm with a great degree of business and/or financial risk, with commensurate high earnings potential.

Speculative stock A stock that appears to be highly overpriced compared to its intrinsic valuation.

Spending phase Phase in the investment life cycle during which individuals' earning years end as they retire. They pay for expenses with income from social security and returns from prior investments and invest to protect against inflation.

Spot rate The required yield for a cash flow to be received at some specific date in the future—for example, the spot rate for a flow to be received in one year, for a cash flow in two years, and so on.

Spread A trading strategy where long and short positions in two call (or two put) option contracts having the same underlying asset but different exercise prices or expiration dates are combined to create a customized return distribution.

Standard deviation A measure of variability equal to the square root of the variance.

Statement of cash flows A financial statement that shows the effects on the firm's cash flow of income flows and changes in its balance sheet.

Static yield spread Yield spreads over the total term structure.

Stock index arbitrage A trading strategy involving a long position in a stock portfolio and a short position in a stock index futures contract (or vice versa) designed to exploit a mispricing in the futures contract relative to the underlying index.

Straddle A trading strategy requiring the simultaneous purchase of a call option and a put option having the same exercise price, underlying asset, and expiration date. Variations of this theme include *strips, straps, strangles,* and *chooser options.*

Strong-form efficient market hypothesis The belief that security prices fully reflect all information from both public and private sources.

Structural change Economic trend occurring when the economy is undergoing a major change in organization or in how it functions.

Structured note A bond with an embedded derivative designed to create a payoff distribution that satisfies the needs of a specific investor clientele.

Style analysis An attempt to explain the variability in the observed returns to a security portfolio in terms of the movements in the returns to a series of benchmark portfolios designed to capture the essence of a particular security characteristic such as size, value, and growth.

Style grid A graph used to classify and display the investment style that best defines the nature of a security portfolio.

Subordinate (junior) bonds Debentures that, in case of default, entitle holders to claims on the issuer's assets only after the claims of holders of senior debentures and mortgage bonds are satisfied.

Support level A price at which a technician would expect a substantial increase in price and volume for a stock to reverse a declining trend that was due to profit taking.

Sustainable growth rate A measure of how fast a firm can grow using internal equity and debt financing and a constant capital structure. Equal to retention rate × ROE.

Swap spread A measure of the risk premium for an interest rate swap, calculated as the difference between the agreement's fixed rate and the yield on a Treasury bond with the same maturity.

SWOT analysis An examination of a firm's Strengths, Weaknesses, Opportunities, and Threats. This analysis helps an analyst evaluate a firm's strategies to exploit its competitive advantages or defend against its weaknesses.

Systematic risk The variability of returns that is due to macroeconomic factors that affect all risky assets. Because it affects all risky assets, it cannot be eliminated by diversification.

Tactical asset allocation An investment strategy that adjusts the investor's mix of stocks and bonds by increasing the allocation to the asset class that is relatively undervalued.

Technical analysis Estimation of future security price movements based on past price and volume movements.

Term bond A bond that has a single maturity date.

Term structure of interest rates The relationship between term to maturity and yield to maturity for a sample of comparable bonds at a given time. Popularly known as the *yield curve*.

Term to maturity Specifies the date or the number of years before a bond matures or expires.

Third market Over-the-counter trading of securities listed on an exchange.

Tick The minimum price movement for the asset underlying a forward or futures contract; for Treasury bonds, one tick equals 1/32 of 1 percent of par value.

Time premium The difference between an option's total market value and its intrinsic value.

Time-series analysis An examination of a firm's performance data over a period of time.

Time-weighted return The geometric average of (one plus) the *holding period yields* to an investment portfolio.

Total return A return objective in which the investor wants to increase the portfolio value to meet a future need by both capital gains and current income reinvestment.

Tracking error The standard deviation of the difference in returns between an active investment portfolio and its benchmark portfolio; also called *tracking error volatility.*

Trading effect The difference in performance of a bond portfolio from that of a chosen index due to short-run changes in the composition of the portfolio.

Trading rule A formula for deciding on current transactions based on historical data.

Trading turnover The percentage of outstanding shares traded during a period of time.

Transaction cost The cost of executing a trade. Low costs characterize an operationally efficient market.

Treasury bill A negotiable U.S. government security with a maturity of less than one year that pays no periodic interest but yields the difference between its par value and its discounted purchase price.

Treasury bond A U.S. government security with a maturity of more than 10 years that pays interest periodically.

Treasury note A U.S. government security with maturities of 1 to 10 years that pays interest periodically.

Treynor measure A relative measure of a portfolio's performance calculated as its average return in excess of the risk-free rate divided by its beta coefficient.

Trough The culmination of a bear market at which prices stop declining and begin rising.

12b-1 plan A fee charged by some funds, named after the SEC rule that permits it. Such fees pay for distribution costs, such as advertising, or for brokers' commissions. The fund's prospectus details any 12b-1 charges that apply.

Underfunded plan A defined benefit pension plan in which the present value of the fund's liabilities to employees exceeds the value of the fund's assets.

Underweighted A condition in which a portfolio, for whatever reason, includes less of a class of securities than the relative market value alone would justify.

Unrealized capital gains Capital gains that reflect the price appreciation of currently held unsold assets.

Unsecured bonds Bonds that promise payments of interest and principal but pledge no specific assets. Holders have first claim on the issuer's income and unpledged assets. Also known as *debentures.*

Unsystematic risk Risk that is unique to an asset, derived from its particular characteristics. It can be eliminated in a diversified portfolio.

Unweighted index An indicator series affected equally by the performance of each security in the sample regardless of price or market value. Also referred to as an *equal-weighted series.*

Unwind The negotiated termination of a forward or futures position before contract maturity.

Valuation analysis An active bond portfolio management strategy designed to capitalize on expected price increases in temporarily undervalued issues.

Valuation process Part of the investment decision process in which you estimate the value of a security.

Value stocks Stocks that appear to be undervalued for reasons besides earnings growth potential. These stocks are usually identified based on high dividend yields, low *P/E* ratios, or low price-to-book ratios.

Value-weighted index An index calculated as the total market value of the securities in the sample. Market value is equal to the number of shares or bonds outstanding times the market price of the security.

Variable-rate note A debt security for which the interest rate changes to follow some specified short-term rate, for example, the T-bill rate; see *Floating rate note.*

Variable principal redemption (VPR) A class of debt securities whose principal redemption at maturity is not fixed but tied to changes in the value of another economic entity, such as a stock index or commodity price.

Variance A measure of variability equal to the sum of the squares of a return's deviation from the mean, divided by the total number of returns.

Warrant An instrument that allows the holder to purchase a specified number of shares of the firm's common stock from the firm at a specified price for a given period of time.

Weak-form efficient market hypothesis The belief that security prices fully reflect all security market information.

Yankee bonds Bonds sold in the United States and denominated in U.S. dollars but issued by a foreign firm or government.

Yield The promised rate of return on an investment under certain assumptions.

Yield illusion The erroneous expectation that a bond will provide its stated yield to maturity without recognizing the implicit reinvestment assumption related to coupon payments.

Yield spread The difference between the promised yields of alternative bond issues or market segments at a given time relative to yields on Treasury issues of equal maturity.

Yield to worst Given a bond with multiple potential maturity dates and prices due to embedded call options, the practice is to calculate a yield to maturity for each of the call dates and prices and select the lowest yield (the most conservative possible yield) as yield to worst.

Zero coupon bond A bond that pays its par value at maturity but no periodic interest payments. Its yield is determined by the difference between its par value and its discounted purchase price. Also called *original issue discount (OID) bonds.*

Index